CW00553291

Greenhill Books

A HISTORY
OF THE
PENINSULAR
WAR

A HISTORY OF
THE PENINSULAR WAR
by Sir Charles Oman

Volume I: 1807–1809
From the Treaty of Fontainebleau to the
Battle of Corunna

Volume II: January to September 1809
From the Battle of Corunna to the End of the Talavera
Campaign

Volume III: September 1809 to December 1810
Ocaña, Cadiz, Bussaco, Torres Vedras

Volume IV: December 1810 to December 1811
Masséna's Retreat, Fuentes de Oñoro, Albuera,
Tarragona

Volume V: October 1811 to August 1812
Valencia, Ciudad Rodrigo, Badajoz, Salamanca, Madrid

Volume VI: September 1, 1812 to August 5, 1813
The Siege of Burgos, The Retreat from Burgos, The
Campaign of Vittoria, The Battles of the Pyrenees

Volume VII: August 1813 to April 14, 1814
The Capture of St. Sebastian, Wellington's Invasion of
France, Battles of the Nivelle, The Nive, Orthez and
Toulouse

Volume VIII: The Biographical Dictionary of
British Officers Killed and Wounded,
1808–1814
by John A. Hall

A HISTORY
OF THE
PENINSULAR
WAR

Volume VIII
The Biographical Dictionary of
British Officers Killed and Wounded,
1808–1814

JOHN A. HALL

Greenhill Books, London
Stackpole Books, Pennsylvania

Greenhill Books

A History of the Peninsular War, Volume VIII:
The Biographical Dictionary of British Officers Killed and Wounded,
1808–1814
first published 1998 by Greenhill Books, Lionel Leventhal Limited,
Park House, 1 Russell Gardens, London NW11 9NN
and
Stackpole Books, 5067 Ritter Road, Mechanicsburg, PA 17055, USA

British Library Cataloguing in Publication Data
Hall, John Alexander
A history of the Peninsular War
Vol. 8: the biographical dictionary of British officers
killed and wounded, 1808–1814
1. Peninsular War, 1807–1814 – Casualties – Biography
2. War casualties – Great Britain
I. Title
940.2'7'09232

ISBN 1-85367-315-3

Library of Congress Cataloging-in-Publication Data available

Designed by David Gibbons, DAG Publications Ltd.
Printed and bound in Great Britain.

CONTENTS

INTRODUCTION

It has been my intention, in this new volume, to focus on some of the many individuals who fought through the campaigns so well portrayed by Sir Charles Oman and to build on the tremendous tradition of scholarship exemplified by his monumental *History of the Peninsular War*. In this volume can be found the biographical and career details of many who are mentioned in Oman's classic history. The Peninsular War was a pivotal event not only in the history of Europe and the development of the British Army, but also in terms of the impact on the lives of those who participated. From the initial campaigns of 1808, until the conclusion of a victorious peace in 1814, the British troops fighting in Portugal, Spain and the south of France demonstrated a resilience, fighting spirit, and determination in the face of extraordinary hardship and danger that still amazes almost two centuries later.

In the memorable phrase of Napier, the veterans of the Peninsular War 'had won nineteen pitched battles and innumerable combats; had made or sustained ten sieges, and taken four great fortresses; had twice expelled the French from Portugal, and once from Spain; had penetrated France, and killed, wounded, or captured two hundred thousand enemies, leaving of their own number forty thousand, whose bones whiten the plains and mountains of the Peninsula.'

Hundreds of books have been written about the Peninsular War, from general and sweeping histories, to the highly specialised studies of single battles or specific aspects of the armies involved. It is a period that continues to fascinate, and grips the popular imagination. Yet, ironically, the individuals who participated in those extraordinary events are largely forgotten. It is probably true to say that fictional characters, like Bernard Cornwell's heroic Sharpe, are now better known than the real men who fought the war. This is particularly sad, as in many cases the true stories of the Peninsular War are even more extraordinary than the fiction.

This national amnesia is not new and indeed was recognised by Peninsula veterans almost as soon as the war was over. William Napier, for example, who was himself a veteran of the campaigns in Portugal and Spain, chose to end his great history of the Peninsular War with the biting comment: 'Thus terminated the war, and with it all remembrances of the veteran's services.'

Unlike 'Waterloo Men', Peninsula veterans received no campaign medal for over thirty years, nor were they granted the two years' service bonus that was automatically awarded survivors of Waterloo. That more British soldiers had died in the Peninsula than were even present on the field at Waterloo was, it seems, not relevant. This comparative obscurity was foreseen by Jonathan Leach, a veteran of both the Peninsula and Waterloo: 'Ere many years elapse, if the names of Vimeira, Talavera, Salamanca, Vittoria, &c. &c. should be partially remembered, the actors in these scenes (with a very few exceptions) will be entirely forgotten.'

A handful of the individuals who took part in the Peninsula campaigns remain, of course, well-known, thanks primarily to published diaries and autobiographies, many of which are still in print and continue to find an appreciative audience. Thus, most serious students of the war are familiar with the likes of Leach, Simmons, Bell, Grattan, Blakeney, Gronow and Kincaid. Others are remembered thanks to the survival of their medals or portraits. A few more, particularly those of high rank, are to be found in a host of secondary sources. Who, for example, has not heard of Wellington, Picton, Moore, Beresford or Hill? But the overwhelming majority of the roughly ten thousand British officers who served in the Peninsula are indeed, just as Leach predicted, totally forgotten.

I first became interested in this project when attempting to research a British officer about whom I was hoping to publish an article. I soon came to realise that there was a significant gap in the available literature. Charles Dalton's remarkable *Waterloo Roll Call*, which is still the definitive reference book in its field, contains only sporadic information concerning Peninsula service, and then only for those officers who went on to serve at Waterloo. There was nothing, it soon became clear, comparable to Dalton for the Peninsular War. The hard-to-find *Royal Military Calendar* from 1820 offers extensive biographical information on hundreds of officers, but only those who were serving at the rank of major and above in 1820. Hart's *New Army List* of 1840 and later provides thumb-nail sketches of Peninsula service, but only for officers still serving at that date.

The casualty returns from the Peninsula are to be found in the *London Gazette* from 1808 to 1814, but access to a complete run is difficult, and locating each of the hundreds of published returns prohibitively time-consuming. The Military General Service Medal rolls edited by Foster and Mullen, by their nature, provide only the barest information about individual officers. Regimental histories are of uneven quality and detail, and while some provide accurate information about specific officers, most do not. Finally, of course, there are the virtually untapped manuscript holdings of the Public Record Office in London, but most of the material contained therein is not readily available in published form outside the PRO, requiring either a personal trip to Kew or the hiring of a professional researcher to locate relevant materials. What was needed, I concluded, was a Dalton-style reference book for the Peninsular War.

I became aware of the work of Lionel Challis as a result of the 1949 one-volume typescript index to his card index, a copy of which is in the PRO, and the article he published in that same year in the *Journal of the Society of Army Historical Research*. Challis devoted almost forty years of his life, from before the First World War to after the Second, to an undertaking of almost incomprehensible scope: a card index giving details of the service record of every British officer who served in the Peninsular War. This index, completed in 1948, contained detailed information of over ten thousand individuals, and was initially housed in a series of file cabinets in the Royal United Services Institution in

London. When the RUSI subsequently disposed of much of its collection, however, the Challis card index disappeared. The National Army Museum currently has several boxes of original Challis cards, though it remains unclear whether the entire set was moved there or whether the rest of the cards were dispersed elsewhere or destroyed. The nature of the surviving cards, which are hand-written and annotated in such a way as to make cross-checking of the information virtually impossible, suggest that it is improbable that they could ever be published. Nevertheless, the depth and scope of Challis's project are unlikely ever to be repeated, and it is to be hoped that the entire collection can be reunited and made available in some form at a suitable public archive such as the PRO. The Challis card index deserves to be treated as a national research treasure.

I have been writing this book for over seven years – somewhat longer than the Peninsular War itself actually lasted – and I quickly came to accept that a Challis- or Dalton-style book on the Peninsula was impractical, as it would not only take a lifetime to produce, but would be too long and unwieldy ever to publish. Dalton listed in his book every officer who served in a single large battle. But the Peninsular War consisted of a series of huge campaigns, sieges, pitched battles, and hundreds of skirmishes, spread over many years and involving at one time or another virtually every regiment and corps in the British Army. As many as ten thousand officers served at one point or another in Portugal, Spain or the south of France, and providing a biographical sketch of each of them, much as Challis had attempted, was simply not practical. The question became, therefore, how to define more narrowly the project in order for it both to offer new information not readily available elsewhere, while at the same time being both logically defined and achievable? A biographical dictionary of British officers killed and wounded in action, 1808–1814, seemed to meet these criteria, and it is for that reason that this book came into being.

This volume is not intended to be a complete listing of all of the British officers who served in the Peninsula. It is, rather, an attempt to establish a list of those officers who were recorded as having been killed or wounded in action with the enemy in Portugal, Spain, and the south of France. What actually constituted a wound is not necessarily clear, and was somewhat ambiguous even at the time. The casualty returns published in the *London Gazette*, which provided the majority of names appearing in this book, usually distinguished between 'severe' and 'slight' wounds, though there appears to have been considerable discretion available to regiments in the field as to what exactly these terms meant in practice. Some colonels were apparently reluctant to have returned as 'serious' anything short of amputation or wounds likely to prove fatal, while others were more liberal in their interpretation. The officers themselves, it seems, were often able to influence how a wound was recorded. For some it became a point of honour not to return their wounds, what George Bell referred to as a 'little point of modesty': 'Some slight wounds were never returned. We did not think it very warlike to notice every skelp one got when little

8

harm was done.' For Bell, 'the loss of a little claret or broken bone' was clearly not worth reporting. Even when dangerously wounded, some officers, out of personal motives, requested that they be either returned as 'slightly' wounded or not returned at all. Lt. Col. Inglis of the 57th, for example, was recorded as only 'slightly' wounded at Albuera, when he had been grievously injured by a grapeshot that had entered his left breast and lodged in his back, a wound so serious that it was expected to prove fatal.

Most usually, the motive for such under-reporting was to avoid causing undue fear among loved-ones and family at home. William Napier, for example, did not return his name among the list of wounded despite a wound in the hip that was not healed for six weeks, for fear of alarming his pregnant wife. Richard Hill noted in 1828: 'In reference to the letter of, dated War Office 10th Septr. 1828 ... wherein the grounds of the refusal of my claim to a year's full pay is stated as owing to the slightness of the wound received at the Battle of Toulouse on the 10th April 1814, I beg most respectfully to submit to the consideration of the Rt. Honble. the Secretary at War, it was for family reasons, and on account of the infirm state of health, of an only, aged, and respected parent at my own earnest request that my name was returned as only slightly wounded; for the correctness of this statement, I beg respectfully to refer to Surgeon Smyth late 45th Regt. Slightly as the wound has been represented it deprived me of all recollection for a considerable time, and of the use of my left arm for upwards of one month afterwards.'

It seems likely, therefore, that the published casualty returns under-recorded the actual number and nature of wounds, though the extent of this is difficult to assess. After certain battles, the volume of casualties seems to have resulted in only the most serious of wounds being officially recorded by certain regiments. As William Napier noted, describing his regiment, the 43rd, following the storming of Badajoz: 'Every officer and man has received two or three wounds each; those that are returned are amputations or body wounds.' It is not surprising to find, therefore, that many officers recorded more wounds in their 1829 Statement of Service than were noted in the contemporary casualty returns. This was not always the case, however, as in a few instances the Officers' Statement of Service actually record fewer wounds than noted in published returns. In most cases this probably resulted from the rather ambiguous wording of the 1829 Statement of Service for Retired Officers, which was different from that sent to serving officers, and which was read by some as asking only for details of wounds that later resulted in the payment of a pension.

The casualty returns published in the *London Gazette* were occasionally inaccurate. In some instances, officers were actually recorded as having been killed when in fact they had been wounded or captured. John Joyce, of the 60th Foot, for example, was inaccurately listed amongst those killed in the Pyrenees in July 1813. Although seriously wounded, he was still very much alive in 1818. Perhaps best known of such reports was the case of Capt. John Browne of the 4th Foot, who was fearfully wounded above the ear by a musket ball at Waterloo while leading his company, was left for dead on the field, and news of whose death was sent to his family in Ireland. To their great joy, however, in the midst of their grieving came news that he had survived as a result of trepanning.

Such errors are understandable when one considers the frequently chaotic circumstances surrounding attempts to ascertain casualties. All too often, wounded men could not be removed during the heat of battle, nor could they easily be checked on, but lay where they fell. As James Anton noted: 'It is not in one's power to give correct returns of the casualties on the night after an action; some are returned missing who have been killed; others returned killed who may have been severely wounded, and left behind, yet may recover; they fall on the field where our feet never again pass.' In the post-battle accounting it was often difficult to distinguish those killed from those wounded, unless a corpse or the surviving officer could be located. Despite every care, inaccurate returns undoubtedly occurred. This was even more likely to be the case when the French occupied the field at the end of the day, as in the well-known case of Charles Napier at Corunna.

In other instances, the published returns are ambiguous or even identify the wrong officer. Early in the war, the casualty returns rarely gave Christian names, which inevitably caused confusion in regiments which contained, for example, more than one man with the same surname. As a result, casualty returns began routinely to publish Christian names, though errors still occured. For example, John Plunkett, of the 50th, was recorded as being wounded at the Nive, when in fact it had been Patrick Plunkett. At times the spelling of names in the published casualty returns was both erratic and imaginative. The 'Ensign Domewer' recorded as having been wounded at the Nive, for example, was in fact Daniel Donovan of the 27th Foot, who was serving as a Lieutenant in the 14th Portuguese Line. Many such errors of transcription resulted, presumably, from attempts to read poorly written returns submitted by the regiments in the field, something with which I have infinite patience after years spent deciphering the frequently illegible attempts at penmanship displayed by some officers.

Identifying the correct individual from ambiguous or outright inaccurate references proved to be one of the most testing, and rewarding, aspects of research for this book. Common surnames (the Campbells in the Scottish regiments, for example) posed a particular problem. Nevertheless, in the overwhelming majority of cases I have been able to substantiate the correct (or most likely) identities of specific casualties. In the few cases where I have not felt comfortable drawing a conclusion, I have stated so in the text. Names of foreign officers serving in the British Army were prone to being butchered in both casualty returns and Army Lists, correct spellings ignored in favour of anglicised or phonetic approximations, and first and family names confused. For example, the 'Captain Laroche' who was recorded in the casualty returns as having been 'dangerously' wounded at Burgos on 18 Oct. 1812, was in fact La Roche de Starkenfels of the 1st Line Battn. K.G.L., who died of wounds on 31 Oct. of that year. At times it seems that for some British observers, the fact that foreigners had distinctly foreign names was something of an irritant, as though the individuals concerned were being purposefully difficult. This sentiment was wonderfully expressed in an 1845 review of Siborne's *History of the Waterloo Campaign*, published in the *United Service Journal*:

> Very few readers have a memory capable of retaining so many names; nor can their wish be very great to remember numerous names of men whom they never heard of before – names, too (many of them), of excessive length, and so rugged as to defy pronunciation by English lips. Capt. Siborne, different from us, seems to be fond of these long unspeakable names, all of which he takes care to give at full length... We hope that Capt. Siborne is preparing an abridgement of his work, which we are sure will be more useful than the massive original. In that case, nine out of ten of these hard names will, no doubt, be omitted.

I fear that my book would have been a profound disappointment to this particular reviewer, as I share Siborne's determination to include whenever possible all the 'long unspeakable names', however 'rugged' and 'excessive'! Nevertheless, I have maintained anglicised spellings if the original German or French names could not be confirmed, or if the officer himself commonly used such versions of his name in his Statement of Service or other documentation.

The British were not alone in altering names, however, and British officers serving in the Portuguese Army were likely to find their first names transformed into something more readily understood and pronounced by their troops. Thus Peter Fearon of the 31st, who was mortally wounded at Garris in 1814 in command of the 6th Caçadores, appears as 'Pedro' in the casualty returns, while William Gordon of the 10th Portuguese Line was recorded as 'Guilherme Gordon' when wounded at Nivelle.

Aside from using the published casualty returns, I have incorporated those officers who record wounds in their 1829 Statement of Service, the manuscripts for which are held in massive bound volumes in the Public Record Office. These Statements offer invaluable biographical and service information, and their inclusion in this book, by generous permission of the Controller of Her Majesty's Stationery Office, provides an enormous quantity of material not readily available previously. The Statements additionally served to cross-check the accuracy of the casualty returns.

Various other published and manuscript sources were also of use in assembling and cross-referencing the individual officers, ranging from published memoirs and autobiographies, to obituaries, regimental musters, registers of deceased officers, regimental monthly returns, musters and pension records.

In order to make the book less impersonal, I have selected anecdotes and descriptions from a few Peninsular memoirs, and some modern studies which are reasonably accessible for further research, in order to give a flavour of what may be ascertained from the many works available, but have deliberately limited the number in order to keep the text to an acceptable length.

It is appropriate that I make clear which officers do not appear in this book: basically, any officer who died or was injured for any reason other than in combat, *unless* he had previously been wounded. Thus, officers who died of disease, natural causes, exhaustion, suicide, murder or accident, are generally not included in the main part of the text. As a result you will not find Major-General Richard Stewart, who fell from a balcony in Lisbon; or G. Welch, of the Medical Staff, who died suddenly while eating breakfast; or Sir Thomas Styles of the 1st Foot Guards, who cut his own throat; or Lewis Lindener of the K.G.L., who drowned while bathing; or even Ensign Alexander Dickenson of the 42nd, who was 'wilfully murdered' by a soldier of his own regiment in Aldea de Serra. In contrast, the unfortunate Lt. W. Thomas Masterman, of the 34th Foot, who was killed when struck by lightning near Pampeluna, is incorporated, as he had previously been wounded in action at Badajoz. I have included, however, as an Appendix to the volume, a list of additional officers who died of disease, accident and other non-combat injuries. Though incomplete, it represents a significant improvement over anything previuosly available.

Undoubtedly this book will contain errors of both omission and commission, and it would be absurd for me to claim otherwise, but I have tried in good faith to be both accurate and conservative in my conclusions. Despite every effort on my part, however, I am sure that the names of some British officers who were killed or wounded will have escaped my notice, and I hope that any such errors will be brought to my attention. I beg the reader's indulgence for any faults, but in my defence will point out that the sheer scope of this project, combined with the nature of the primary and secondary sources available, ensure that a fault-free product is beyond a reasonable expectation. That said, I believe that this book provides a worthwhile step forward, and offers both the casual reader and the serious scholar a large quantity of new information not readily available elsewhere.

John A. Hall, 1998

ACKNOWLEDGEMENTS

First and foremost, I want to extend my warmest thanks to Philip Haythornthwaite, without whom this project would have got nowhere. From the very beginning he helped me to shape and direct my research and was selfless in reading and rereading draft after draft, year after year. In addition, Philip found and photocopied for me every casualty return published in the *London Gazette*, which proved to be the central foundation for the book. This, along with locating the obituaries in *The Gentleman's Magazine*, was a monumental commitment that took him months of hard work at a time when he was already busy with his own projects. His generosity of spirit, gentle good humour, professional vision and unflagging enthusiasm have kept me going when the undertaking appeared at times overwhelming. I am honoured to count him as one of my friends.

I would also like to thank the staff of the Public Record Office in Kew, who assisted me greatly during my numerous trips to London. The PRO is a remarkable archive, blessed with a gifted, professional and helpful staff. In particular I would like to thank Dr Keith Bartlett, who was of extraordinary assistance and without whom this book would be far weaker than it is. He went out of his way to locate relevant documents for me, he generously shared his considerable expertise as well as loaning me books and photocopies from his personal collection. My sincere and heartfelt thanks go out to him. William Spencer, also of the PRO, helped me fathom the intricacies of the naval documents, and researched and identified for me the Royal Navy casualties that appear in this book. Tim Padfield, Copyright Officer, PRO, enabled me to make use of the Crown Copyright materials.

My thanks also to the 'Coffee Break' group, particularly Judith Farrington, whose convivial good cheer and good conversation made Kew so pleasurable, and whose fine company I miss greatly. Gary and Chris Buckland, of Naval and Military Press, generously provided me with an early copy of the 1818 Pension Book that they have recently discovered and reprinted. Allowing me to use their book in this fashion was a generous act in the finest tradition of scholarly exchange. Thanks also for the assistance of Berthold Sander-Nagashima, Pete Jordan and Jeff Dunkin. Ken Trotman Books and Maggs Bros helped locate Army Lists. The Hewlett-Mellon Foundation provided funding for summer research, as did the Albion College Faculty Development Committee. I am especially grateful to Lionel Leventhal, Jonathan North and Kate Ryle at Greenhill, and to John Gilbert.

My particular thanks go to the trustees of Sir Charles Oman's estate, who gave permission for this book to be published as a supplementary volume to Oman's *History*. My thanks also to Di, who was so understanding and supportive throughout this process. Finally, I want to thank my parents, Gladys and Harry, for their love and encouragement.

MAJOR BATTLES AND ACTIONS OF THE PENINSULAR WAR

Capital letters denote battles for which bars were later awarded for the Military General Service Medal.

1808

17 Aug.	Battle of ROLEIA/ROLICA.
21 Aug.	Battle of VIMIERO.
21 Dec.	Action at SAHAGUN.
29 Dec.	Action at BENAVENTE.

1809

Jan.	Retreat to Corunna.
16 Jan.	Battle of CORUNNA.
10 May	Action at Albergaria Nova.
11 May	Action on the Heights of Grijon.
12 May	Action at Passage of the Douro.
27–28 July	Battle of TALAVERA.

1810

Defence of Cadiz, including:

22 Feb.–22 April	Defence of Fort Matagorda.
19 March	Action at Barba del Puerco.
11 July	Action at Alverca.
24 July	Action near Almeida (Coa).
28 Aug.	Action near Fraxedas.
25–26 Sept.	Action near Busaco.
27 Sept.	Battle of BUSACO.
8 Dec.	Action at Evora.

1811

5 March	Battle of BARROSA.
12 March	Action near Redinha.
15 March	Action at Foz de Aronce.
25 March	Action at Campo Mayor.
3 April	Action at Sabugal.
23 April	Action at Azava.
3–5 May	Battle of FUENTES DE ONORO.
16 May	Battle of ALBUERA.
25 Sept.	Action at El Bodon.
28 Oct.	Action at Arroyo dos Molinos.

Dec. 1811–Jan. 1812.	Defence of Tarifa.

1812

8–19 Jan.	Siege of CIUDAD RODRIGO:
8 Jan.	Capture of Francisco redoubt.
19 Jan.	Storming and capture of Ciudad Rodrigo.
16 March–6 April	Siege of BADAJOZ:
25 March	Capture of Fort Picurina.
6 April	Storming and capture, Badajoz.
19 May	Action at Almaraz, taking of Fort Napoleon.
18 July	Action at Canizal.
22 July	Battle of SALAMANCA.
23 July	Affair at La Serna/Garcia Hernandez.
24 July	Affair near Ribera.
11 Aug.	Action at Majalahonda.
27 Aug.	
20 Sept.–19 Oct.	Capture of Seville. Siege of Burgos:
19 Sept.	Capture of Fort St Michael.
22 Sept.	Assault on outer defences.
4 Oct.	Capture of exterior line of Burgos castle.
18 Oct.	Failed assault on inner defences.
22–29 Oct.	Retreat from Burgos, including:
23 Oct.	Action at El Bodon.
25 Oct.	Action at Villa Muriel.

1813

12–13 April	Action at Castalla.
2 June	Action at Morales.
June	Siege of Tarragona:
2-7 June	Taking of Fort St Phillippe.
21 June	Battle of VITTORIA.
24 June	Action at Villafranca.
25 June	Action at Tolosa.
17 July	Taking of the convent of

14

25 July – Aug.	San Bartolome. Battles of the PYRENEES, which consisted of:	31 Aug. 7–9 Oct.	Actions near Urdax, Salain, and Bridge. Crossing the Bidassoa/Heights of Vera.
25 July.	Battles at the passes at Maya and Roncesvalles.	10 Nov. 23 Nov.	Battle of the NIVELLE. Skirmish near Bayonne.
28 July.	Battle of Sorauren, near Pampelona.	9–13 Dec. 10 Dec.	Battles of the NIVE, near Bayonne, which included: Actions at Anglet and
30 July.	Second battle of Sorauren.	13 Dec.	Arcangues. Battle of St Pierre.
28 June– 31 Aug.	Siege of SAN SEBASTIAN:	**1814** 23 Feb.	Action at Agarve.
25 July.	First failed assault.	27 Feb.	Battle of ORTHES.
27 Aug.	Capture of the Island of Santa Clara.	2 March 20 March	Action at Aire. Action at Tarbes.
31 Aug.	Storming and capture, San Sebastian.	10 April 14 April	Battle of TOULOUSE. Sortie from Bayonne.

ABBREVIATIONS

AAG	Assistant Adjutant General	EOPS	Engaged on Particular Service
ADACG	Acting Deputy Assistant Commissary General	Gold Medal	Peninsular War Gold Medal or Cross
ADC	Aide-de-Camp	KGL	King's German Legion
Adjt.	Adjutant	KIA	Killed in Action
A/L	Army List	Lt.	Lieutenant
AQMG	Assistant Quarter Master General	Lt. Col.	Lieutenant Colonel
Bart. or Bt.	Baronet	MGS	Military General Service Medal
Bde. Maj.	Brigade Major: brigade staff officer	NGS	Naval General Service Medal
Bvt.	Brevet rank	PRO	Public Record Office, Kew
Capt.	Captain		
CB	Companion of the Order of the Bath	Qr. Mr.	Quarter Master
		QMG	Quarter Master General
Col.	Colonel	Sgt. Maj.	Sergeant Major
DACG	Deputy Assistant Commissary General	WIR	West India Regiment
DAG	Deputy Adjutant General	WO	War Office
DAQMG	Deputy Assistant Quarter Master General	The symbol + preceding an entry indicates that the officer concerned died in the Peninsula between 1808 and 1814.	
DOW	Died of Wounds		

NOTE TO ENTRIES

The main body of the text is arranged alphabetically by surname, with rank and regiment at time of wound or death given in bold letters. In case of multiple wounds at differing rank or in different regiments, each rank and regiment is given in chronological order. In the Regimental Index the officers are listed alphabetically under each regiment in which they were recorded as having become a casualty. Some officers, accordingly, will be found under more than one regiment. An Appendix lists those officers who died of disease, accident or misadventure in the Peninsula between 1808 and 1814.

I have followed the guidelines established by the British Records Association for English and foreign prefixes. English and American surnames are accordingly indexed by their prefixes (thus De La Warr, De Quincey, De Burgh will all come under 'D'). The justification for this treatment is that prefixes are integral parts of the name. For foreign names with prefixes the rule is slightly more complex. Articles, and compounds of articles and prepositions, precede the main part of the name (e.g. French names beginning with 'L', 'Le', 'La', 'Les', 'Du' and 'Des' are indexed under those words as with English names). But the name comes first and the prefix follows all forenames if the prefix is a preposition (names beginning with 'De', 'Da', 'Von' and 'Van' are indexed under the word following).

Again in accordance with British Records Association standards, names beginning 'M', 'Mc' and 'Mac' are arranged as though they all began 'Mac', the result being a sequence such as ...

McPartland, John
Macphail, John
McPhee, Alice
Macpherson, Thomas.

THE
BIOGRAPHICAL
DICTIONARY

A

ABELL, Francis, Lt., 83rd Foot: Ensign, 83rd Foot, 8 May 1805; Lt. 11 March 1808. Severely wounded, Talavera, 28 July 1809 [*London Gazette*].

+ACKLAND, Dudley, Major, 57th Foot: Major, 57th Foot, 13 Dec. 1810. Killed, Nivelle, 10 Nov. 1813 (1st Battn.) [*London Gazette*]. *Register of dead officers*: Return dated: Nov. 1813 [PRO: WO 25/2965].

ACKLAND, John, Lt./Capt., 9th Foot: *1829 Statement of Service for Retired Officers*: Aged 18 'on first Appointment to His Majesty's Service'. 'Ensign, 9th Regiment, 20th October 1806. Lieutenant, 9th Regiment, 7 June 1807. Captain, 9th Regiment, 26th June 1814. The Dates of each Commission as I have stated are as nearly correct as I can recollect.' [Actually: Ensign 24 Oct. 1806; Lt. 28 Aug. 1807; Capt. 26 Aug. 1813; Capt., Half Pay, 25 July 1816]. Half Pay 'on Reduction of the 2nd Battalion of the 9th Regiment of Foot at Chatham'. 'Exchanged to full pay 30 Foot 9 July 1829 and afterwards sold out.' 'From the length of time I have been allowed to remain on Half Pay, I do not now feel desirous to return to full with the chance of being sent on Foreign Service but humbly beg leave to submit that my Services in the Army as follow are as may entitle me to hope that some adequate situation may be granted. I was appointed an Ensign to the 9th Regt. of Foot in 1806 served under Sir Arthur Wellesley Campaign of 1808 in Portugal and in that severe and trying Campaign under Sir John Moore in Spain, that shortly after I served in the Expedition to Walcheron when my health was much impaired by the disastrous sickness which prevailed. That prior to my perfect recovery from this severe illness I again returned to the Peninsular under Lord Wellington where I remained Actively engaged until severely Wounded on the retreat from Burgos although I had been previously so at Salamanca. I was ordered to England for the recovery of my health from the wounds and on its being established I accompanied the 1st Battalion of the Regiment to America although not effective therein, on my return to Europe with the Regiment I was placed on Half Pay on the reduction of the 2nd Battn. and have since made frequent ineffectual attempts to get again actively employed and now being 13 years since my reduction and fearing that all hopes of again been placed on full pay were vanished, I married and have now a Family which would much retard that active life I spent in the Service and would again wish to do if not now encumbered.' *Where serving when wounded*: 'At the Battle of Salamanca and on the Retreat from Burgos 25th of October 1812.' *Details of pension*: One hundred pounds per annum, commencing 25 Oct. 1813. *Family*: Married in Dublin, 17 Jan. 1824. Two children by 1829. No employment. *Where generally resident during last five years*: 'Drogheda, Ireland.' [PRO: WO25/749 f11]. Slightly wounded, Salamanca, 22 July 1812 (1st Battn.) [*London Gazette*]. Severely wounded, during 'movements of the Army' (Retreat from Burgos: Villa Muriel], 25 Oct. 1812) [*London Gazette*]. Pension of one hundred pounds per annum, commencing 26 Oct. 1813, for 'loss of the use of a hand' at Burgos, 1812 [*1818 Pension Return*, pp. 6–7]. MGS.

ADAIR, Robert, Capt., 1st Foot Guards: Lt. and Capt., 1st Foot Guards, 26 Oct. 1809. Slightly wounded, Barossa, 5 March 1811 [*London Gazette*]. Wounded at Quatre Bras, and died of his wounds at Brussels, 23 June 1815.

ADAIR, Walter William, Capt., 88th Foot: Capt., 88th Foot, 30 June 1808. Severely wounded, Salamanca, 22 July 1812 (2nd Battn.) [*London Gazette*].

ADAM, Frederick, Lt. Col., 21st Foot: Lt. Col., Army, 28 Aug. 1804; Lt. Col., 21st Foot, 5 Jan. 1805. ADC to HRH the Prince Regent in 1811. Col., Army, 20 Feb. 1812. Mentioned in Murray's Castalla dispatch, 14 April 1813 [12 April: 'Colonel Adam, who commands the advance, claims the first place in this honourable list. I cannot sufficiently praise the judicious arrangements he made and the ability with which he executed his orders on the 12th instant... The enemy attacked this corps with from five to six thousand men, and for five hours (and then only in consequence of order) succeeded in possessing himself of the pass. This fact alone says more in favour of Colonel Adam, and in praise of those he commands, than any words of mine can express... Colonel Adam was wounded very early in the attack, but continued, and still continues in charge of his division... On the 13th ... a most gallant charge of the 2d 27th led by Colonel Adam and Lieutenant Colonel Reeves, decided the fate of the day.'] [*London Gazette*]. Slightly wounded, Castalla, 12 April 1813, while serving as 'D.A.G. commanding the advance' [*London Gazette*]. Severely wounded, 'not dangerously', Heights of Ordal, night of 12/13 Sept. 1813, while 'Commanding the Advance' [*London Gazette*]. Major-General 4 June 1814. Wounded, Waterloo. Temporary pension of three hundred pounds per annum, commencing 14 Sept. 1814, 'for wounds' received at Ordal, 1813 [*1818 Pension Return*,

pp. 6–7]. Letter from Capt. F. Arabin, Royal Artillery, to Major Williamson, dated Tarragona, 7 Sept. 1813 [describing the action at the Heights of Ordal, 12/13 Sept. 1813: 'Shortly after the action commenced Colonel Adam was severely wounded and obliged to quit the field.'] [*London Gazette*, 9 Oct. 1813]. *Dalton*, 6, 26 ['Bn. 1781... In 1813 obtained command of a brigade in the army, and was sent to the Pa., where there was a great lack of good commanders. Adam maintained his reputation, despite several reverses. When the French stormed and took Ordal, 12th Sept., 1813, he had his left arm broken and his left hand shattered. Made maj.-gen. in 1814. The rout of the Old Guard at Waterloo by General Adam's Brigade was the turning-point of the battle, and ensured victory... D. 17th Aug., 1853, very suddenly at Greenwich railway station. His widow d. 26th May, 1904.'] *Royal Military Calendar*, Vol. III, pp. 384–9 ['558. Major-General Sir Frederick Adam, KCB... [Ordal, 12 Sept. 1813:] 'Colonel Adam received two wounds, one which broke his left arm, and another which shattered his left hand, about one in the morning, and was forced to leave the field.']

+ADAMS, George Herbert, Capt., 66th Foot: Major, Army, 1 March 1794; Capt., 66th Foot, 27 June 1807. Severely wounded, as Bvt. Lt. Col., Talavera, 28 July 1809 [*London Gazette*]. Obituary, *The Gentleman's Magazine*, Oct. 1809, p. 987 ['Lately... In Spain, of a malignant fever, brought on by being removed too early from Talavera, Lieut.-col. G. H. Adams, of the 66th Foot. He was reported severely wounded in that ever-memorable battle.']

+ADAMS, John, Capt., 5th Foot: Capt., Army, 9 June 1804; Capt., 5th Foot, 7 March 1805. Killed, Vittoria, 21 June 1813 (1st Battn.) [*London*

Gazette]. *Register of dead officers*: Return dated: 25 June 1813 [PRO: WO 25/2965].

ADAMSON, Peter, Capt., 71st Foot; Major, 4th Caçadores: *1829 Statement of Service for Retired Officers*: Aged '15 years nearly ... on first Appointment to His Majesty's Service'. Lt., Tay Fencibles, Oct. 1794, 'Recruited men'; Ensign, 71st Foot, 1800, 'Recruited men from Tey Regt'; Lt., 71st Foot, 1801, 'Raised men'; Half-pay, 'By reduction at the Peace of 1802 as far as I can recall'; Lt., 71st Foot, 1803, 'at the commencement of Hostilities'; Capt., 3rd Garrison Battn., 1808 [Army List gives 21 April]; Capt., 71st Foot, 1808 [Army List gives 26 May]; Bvt. Major, 71st Foot, 1813 [Army List gives 26 Dec.]; Major, 'on Staff of Marshal Beresford', 1814; Half-pay, '1816 at general reduction' [Army List gives Half Pay, 1814, 'Late serving with the Portuguese Army']; Bvt. Lt. Col., 'in the Portuguese Service', 1817. 'Not having Documents with me I am not particularly sure of the dates.' *Where serving when wounded*: 'at Buenos Ayres. Fuentes de Honor'. No pension. *Title and nature of employment*: 'Justice of Peace Upper Canada. Colonel in the Portuguese Service, but no Emolument has been received, nor the amount determined.' *Where generally resident during last five years*: 'Toronto near York Upper Canada.' [PRO: WO25/749 f28]. Gold Medal (Salamanca), in command of 4th Caçadores. Served in Portuguese Army Dec. 1811 to April 1814 [*Challis, Portuguese Army*].

ADDISON, John, Lt., 6th Foot: Ensign, 6th Foot, 5 Jan. 1809. Lt., 6th Foot, 21 Nov. 1811. Severely wounded, Pyrenees, 2 Aug. 1813 (1st Battn.) [*London Gazette*]. MGS.

AGAR, Edward, Ensign/Lt., 47th Foot: Ensign, 47th Foot, 3 April 1811. Slightly wounded, storming of San Sebastian, 31 Aug. 1813 ('Lieutenant') (2nd Battn.) [*London Gazette*].

AGNEW, Matthew, Lt., 52nd Foot: Ensign, 52nd Foot, 11 April 1811. Lt., 52nd Foot, 9 July 1812. Slightly wounded, Nivelle, 10 Nov. 1813 (1st Battn.) [*London Gazette*].

AGNEW, Thomas Ramsden, Lt., 82nd Foot: Lt., 82nd Foot, 12 Oct. 1809. Severely wounded, Vittoria, 21 June 1813 (1st Battn.) [*London Gazette*]. Pension of one hundred pounds per annum, commencing 23 June 1814, for 'loss of a leg' at Vittoria, 1813 [*1818 Pension Return*, pp. 18–19]. MGS.

+AHLERS, George, Cornet, Duke of Brunswick Oels' Corps (Cavalry): Cornet, Duke of Brunswick Oels' Corps (Cavalry), 6 Dec. 1810. Severely wounded, 'since dead', Heights of Ordal, 12/13 Sept. 1813 ('Cornet Ahlers ... Brunswick Hussars') [*London Gazette*].

AICKEN, Francis, Capt., 5th Dragoon Guards: Capt., 5th Dragoon Guards, 24 Feb. 1803. Severely wounded, Salamanca, 22 July 1812 ('Aiken') [*London Gazette*].

AITCHISON, John, Ensign, 3rd Foot Guards: Ensign, 3rd Foot Guards, 25 Oct. 1805. Slightly wounded, Talavera, 28 July 1809 ('Atcheson') [*London Gazette*]. MGS. His letters and diary published as *An Ensign in the Peninsular War. Aitchison*, 12 ['On 15 May 1875 this obituary notice appeared in *The Times*. "We have to announce the death of General Sir John Aitchison G.C.B., Colonel of the Royal Scots Fusilier Guards, on Thursday night, at his residence in Devonshire Place, at the advanced age of 87 years. He entered the Army just 70 years since – namely, in October 1805. He served in 1807

at the siege and capture of Copenhagen, and the following year
embarked for the Peninsula. In 1809
he was present at the passage of
the Douro, capture of Oporto and
subsequent pursuit of Soult's Army
to Salamanca. At the battle of
Talavera he was wounded in the
arm while carrying the King's
Colour, which was also shot
through. Sir John also served in the
campaigns of 1810, 1812, 1813 and
1814, and was present at the battle
of Busaco and the retreat to the
lines of Torres Vedras; the battle of
Salamanca, the capture of Madrid,
the siege of Burgos and the retreat
from thence into Portugal; the affair
of Osma, the battle of Vittoria,
affair at Tolosa, the siege of San
Sebastian, the battles of the Nivelle
and Nive, passage of the Ardour,
investment of Bayonne, siege of the
citadel, and repulse of the sortie.
The veteran General had received
the war medal with six clasps. He
commanded the Scots Fusilier
Guards for upwards of four years till
promoted to Major General. Sir
John served in India from June 1845
to November 1851, as Major
General on the staff of the Madras
Presidency, in command of the
Mysore Division (including Coorg)
and of the province of Malabar and
Canara. In 1851 he was appointed
Colonel of the 72nd Highlanders,
and was transferred as Colonel to
the Scots Fusilier Guards in 1870. In
1859 he had been made a Knight
Commander of the Bath and
promoted to General in the
following year. In 1867 he received
the Grand Cross of the Order of the
Bath."], 53 ['Talavera de la Reyna,
29th July 1809... I received, while
carrying the colours, a contusion in
the right shoulder-blade from a
musket ball – but my wound is
slight. It is stiff at present'], 55
['Talavera de la Reyna, 31st July
1809... My wound has been very
slight and the stiffness has left my
arm and now only on the part
struck by the ball.'], 57 ['Belem,

14th September 1809... I am to
remain here till my shoulder is quite
well'].

**ALEXANDER, Henry, Ensign, 28th
Foot**: Ensign, 28th Foot, 13 June
1811. Slightly wounded, Vittoria, 21
June 1813 (1st Battn.) [*London
Gazette*]. Lt., 28th Foot, 26 Aug.
1813. 'Served Peninsula and South
of France 1812–14 – Vittoria
(wounded), Maya Pass, Pyrenees
28, 29, 30, 31 July 1813; Nivelle, St
Palais, Nive, Bayonne, Orthes,
Aure, Tarbes and Toulouse.' [*Hart's
1840 Army List*]. MGS.

**+ALGEO, J. H., Capt., 34th Foot;
Major/Lt.Col., 1st Caçadores**: Lt.,
34th Foot, 6 June 1798 ('Aldjoes');
Capt., 34th Foot, 23 May 1805.
Wounded, storming of Badajoz, 6
April 1812, while serving as a Major
in the 1st Caçadores [*London
Gazette*]. Mentioned in Wellington's
Badajoz dispatch, 7 April 1812 (in
command of 1st Caadores)
[*London Gazette*]. Killed, crossing
the Bidassoa, 7/9 Oct. 1813, while
serving as Lt. Col., 1st Caçadores
[*London Gazette*]. In Portuguese
Service April 1810 to Oct. 1813.
Gold Medal. *Challis, Portuguese
Army*, p. 52.

**ALLEN, James, Capt., 23rd Light
Dragoons**: Capt., Army, 2 Oct. 1800;
Capt., 23rd Light Dragoons, 3 Feb.
1804. Recorded as 'wounded and
missing', Talavera, 28 July 1809
[*London Gazette*].

**ALLEN, Thomas, Ensign, 1st Line
Battn., K.G.L**: Ensign, 1st Line
Battn. K.G.L., 1 Feb. 1809. Slightly
wounded, Talavera, 28 July 1809
[*London Gazette*]. Lt., 1st Line
Battn. K.G.L., 8 Sept. 1809. Served
in Peninsula 1809–14. Waterloo.
Beamish, vol. II, p. 572 [Died 'at
Springfield in England, Nov. 1833.'].

**ALLEY, William Henry, Lt., 4th
Foot**: Lt., 4th Foot, 23 Oct. 1804.
Severely wounded, storming of

ALLIX

Badajoz, 6 April 1812 ('Aley') [*London Gazette*]. Temporary pension of seventy pounds per annum, commencing 7 April 1813, 'for wounds' received at Badajos, 1812 [*1818 Pension Return*, pp. 4–5].

ALLIX, Charles, Lt. and Capt., 1st Foot Guards: *1829 Statement of Service for Retired Officers*: Aged seventeen on his first appointment in the Army. Ensign, 1st Foot Guards, 28 April 1804; Lt. and Capt., 1st Foot Guards, 13 Dec. 1810; Capt. and Lt. Col., 1st Foot Guards, 4 July 1815; Adjutant, 2nd Battn. 1st Foot Guards, 13 Dec. 1813 to 3 July 1815 [Army List gives 4 July]. 'Adjutant during Expedition to Walcheren... Grenadiers of the Foot Guards, 1809.' 'A.D.C. to Sir Henry Campbell in Portugal, March 1811 to Novr. 1812.' 'Brigade Major in Portugal in the 4th Divn, 1813.' 'My health and private affairs require a temporary retirement on Half Pay.' *Where serving when wounded*: 'Wounded at the Battle of Nivelle 10th Novr. 1813.' No Pension. Not married in 1829. No employment. *Where generally resident during last five years*: 'Serving with the Regiment until April 1827, since which in various parts of England.' [PRO: WO 25/749 f79]. Brother of William Allix, 95th Rifles. Born 24 April 1787. Brigade-Major to Maj.-Gen. Anson at Pyrenees and Nivelle. Severely wounded, Nivelle, 10 Nov. 1813, while serving as Brigade-Major [*London Gazette*]. Waterloo. MGS. Died, 24 April 1862. *Kincaid, Adventures*, pp. 140–1 [Following the Storming of Badajoz: 'On the morning of the 7th, when some of our officers were performing the last duties to their fallen comrades, one of them had collected the bodies of four of our young officers, who had been slain. He was in the act of digging a grave for them, when an officer of the guards [Charles Allix], arrived on the spot, from a distant division of the army, and demanded tidings of

his brother [William], who was at that moment lying a naked lifeless corpse, under his very eyes. The officer had the presence of mind to see that the corpse was not recognised, and, wishing to spare the other's feelings, told him that his brother was dangerously wounded, but that he would hear more of him by going out to the camp; and thither the other immediately bent his steps, with a seeming presentiment of the sad intelligence that awaited him.'] *Haythornthwaite, Die Hard*, p. 187 [Badajoz: 'Captain Charles Allix of the 1st Foot Guards went in search of his brother William, a lieutenant in the 95th. The officer in charge of burying the slain officers tried to spare Allix the ghastly sight of his dead brother, and sent him to the 95th's camp. There he learned the truth, and returned to the site of the slaughter where he encountered Harry Smith, who commented on Allix's downcast expression. Allix replied, "Do you not know my brother in the Rifles was killed last night?" "God help him and you!" said Smith. "No, for I and we all loved him." Allix burst into tears, pointed to a body, presented a pair of scissors to Smith and asked, "Go and cut off a lock of his hair for my mother. I came for the purpose, but I am not equal to doing it."], fn. 51 p. 191 ['Kincaid's account of Allix's arrival does not name him, and Smith calls him "Allen", but it is obvious that it was the Allix brothers who were involved.']. *Harry Smith*, p. 67.

+ALLIX, William, Lt., 95th Foot: Brother of Charles Allix, 1st Foot Guards. Lt., Army, 12 April 1810; 1st Lt., 95th Foot, 17 May 1810. Killed, storming of Badajoz, 6 April 1812 (3rd Battn.) [*London Gazette*]. Obituary, *The Gentleman's Magazine*, June 1812, p. 594 ['At the storming of Badajoz, by a musket-shot through the head, aged 23, Lieut. W. Allix, 95th Rifle regiment, third son of the late J. P. Allix, esq.

of Swaffham House, co. Cambridge.']. *Register of dead officers*: Date of return: 25 April 1812 [PRO: WO 25/2965]. *Simmons*, p. 232 [Killed]. *Kincaid, Adventures*, pp. 140–1, quoted above under Allix, Charles.

ALLMAN, Francis, Capt., 48th Foot: *1829 Statement of Service for Retired Officers*: Aged nineteen on his first appointment to the Army. Ensign, 2nd Foot, 5 Aug. 1799; Lt., 2nd Foot, 20 Aug. 1801; Lt., 48th Foot, 9 July 1803; Capt., 48th Foot, 1 June 1809 [Note: Army List gives 5 Jan. 1805]. Note added: 'Sold out in April 1829.' *Where serving when wounded*: 'Albuera in Spain.' *Details of pension*: 100 Pounds per annum commenced 17 May 1812. *Family*: Married in Gibraltar, 1 Oct. 1807. Eight children by 1829. No employment. *Where generally resident during last five years*: 'My papers Inwarded by the Lt. Genl. commanding N. S. Wales' [PRO: WO 25/749 f53]. Reported as 'Missing', Albuera, 16 May 1811 (2nd Battn.) [*London Gazette*]. Temporary pension of seventy pounds per annum, commencing 17 May 1812, 'for wounds' received at Albuera, 1811 [*1818 Pension Return*, pp. 12–13]. MGS.

ALSTONE, James, Ensign, 1st Foot: Ensign, 1st Foot, 14 May 1812. Recorded as 'Missing', 'at the Siege of St Sebastian', 7–27 July 1813 ('Ensign Alston') (3rd Battn.) [*London Gazette*]. Lt., 1st Foot, 21 Oct. 1813. Temporary pension of fifty pounds per annum, commencing 26 July 1814, 'for wounds' received at St Sebastian ('Alston') [*1818 Pension Return*, pp. 4–5]. Waterloo. Died 9 Nov. 1854.

ALTEN, Victor von, Major-General: Col. Commandant, 2nd Light Dragoons K.G.L., 19 Dec. 1804; Major-General, 25 July 1810. Severely wounded, 'not dangerously', Salamanca, 22 July 1812

[*London Gazette*]. Gold Medal. Waterloo. *Beamish*, vol. II, p. 552 [Died 'at Osnabruck, 23d Aug. 1820, a lieut.-general H.S.']. *Leach*, p. 274 [Salamanca, 22 July 1812: 'Just before dark the Light Division was ordered to advance, and attack the 1st French Division, commanded by General Foy, which had been in our front the whole day; but as they offered no serious resistance, and were already in the act of retrograding, nothing more than a sharp fire of light troops took place, in which our general, Baron Alten, was wounded, with some other officers and men.'], pp. 323–4 [24 June 1813: 'At this moment there was a strange mixed fight of the three arms, cavalry, infantry, and artillery, all scuffling and pounding their adversaries simultaneously. Never did the commandant of an advanced guard bring into play more quickly, and with better judgement and effect, the different description of troops under his command than Baron Alten, and, moreover, without the least confusion or delay. He was always with the most advanced party, whether it happened to be cavalry or infantry; and in his quiet, cool manner, did the business to admiration.'].

ALTENSTEIN, Henry von, Ensign, 60th Foot: Ensign, 60th Foot, 19 Jan. 1809 (' – Von Stein Altenstein'). Severely wounded, Talavera, 28 July 1809 (5th Battn.) [*London Gazette*]. Lt., 60th Foot, 28 Feb. 1810 ('Henry, Baron Altenstein'). Lt., Half-pay, West India Regiment, 9 Dec. 1824. MGS.

ALVES, John, Lt., 74th Foot: *1829 Statement of Service*: 'Born at Elgin N.B. [North Britain], 17th March 1788. Aged 19 Years & 8 Months on his first Entrance into the Army. Ensign, 74th Regt., 5th Novr. 1807. Lieut., 74th Regt., 25th Decr. 1810. Captain, Half Pay, Unattached, 13th March 1827. Captain, 65th Regt.,

9th April 1829.' *Battles, sieges and campaigns*: 'Served the whole of the Campaigns of 1810–11–12–13 & 14 in the 3rd Division of the Army with the 74th Reg. in the Peninsula ... at the Battle of Busaco 27th Septr. 1810. Various Affairs during the retreat of the French from Torris-Vedras viz. Pombal Redinha, Foz-de-Arronce, Guarda & Sabugal. Battle of Fuentes de Anor 5th May 1811. Elbaden 25th Septr. 1811. Aldea-de-Ponte 27 Sept. Siege of Badajoz in June 1811. Siege and Storm of Ciudad Rodrigo in Jany. 1812. Siege and Escalade of Badajoz 6th April 1812. Battle of Salamanca 22d July. Capture of Madrid 13th Augt. 1812. Battle of Vittoria 21st June 1813. Battles in the Pyrenees 27–28th & 30th July 1813. Battles of Neville & Nive Novr. 1813. Battle of Orthes 27th Feby. 1814. Affairs at Tarbes-Vic-de-Bijon &c &c. in March 1814. Battle of Toulouse 10th Apriil 1814. During the Campaigns of 1813 & 14 acted as Adjutant as also during part of the Campaign of 1812 the Adjutant being wounded.' *Wounds received in action*: 'Lost the total use of an Eye in consequence of inflammation at Capture of Badajoz. Recd. a Pension of L70 per Annum from December 1812 Permanent.' *Service abroad*: '24th Jany. 1810 to 25th July 1814, Peninsula & France. 13th May 1818 to 24th Augst. 1825, N. America.' [PRO: WO 25/797 f333]. Also, *1829 Statement of Service for Retired Officers* [PRO: WO 25/749 f80]. Pension of seventy pounds per annum, commencing 25 Dec. 1813, for 'loss of an eye' in Spain, 1812 [*1818 Pension Return*, pp. 18–19]. MGS.

ALY, William, Capt., 1st Light Dragoons K.G.L.: Capt., 1st Light Dragoons K.G.L., 15 June 1804. Slightly wounded while skirmishing, 9–14 Oct. 1810 [*London Gazette*]. Severely wounded, Salamanca, 18 July 1812 [*London Gazette*]. Capt., 2nd Hussars K.G.L., 26 Jan. 1814.

Served in Peninsula 1809–14. *Beamish*, vol. II, p. 553 ['slightly wounded, 9th Oct. 1810, at Quinta de Torre; severely wounded, 18th July, 1812, at Canizal... [Died] at Osnabruck, 26th March 1833, colonel Han. 6th dragoons, (lancers.)'].

+AMBROSE, William. Capt., 50th Foot: Capt., 50th Foot, 25 Sept. 1807. *Register of dead officers*: 1st Battn. Peninsula. Died of wounds, 25 July 1813. Date of return: Oct. 1813 [PRO: WO 25/2965].

ANDERSON, Alexander, Lt./Capt., 42nd Foot; Major, 11th Portuguese Line Regt: *1829 Statement of Service for Retired Officers*: Aged sixteen on his first appointment. Ensign, 92nd Foot, 9 Oct. 1799; Lt., 42nd Foot, 9 April 1801 [Army List gives: Lt., Army, 9 April 1801; Lt., 42nd Foot, 9 July 1803]; Capt., 42nd Foot, 9 Feb. 1809; Bvt. Major, 42nd Foot, 21 June 1813; Major, Portuguese Service, 25 Oct. 1814; Bvt. Lt. Col., Portuguese Service, 2 Nov. 1816; Major, 23rd Foot, 20 July 1826; Half-pay 29 Aug. 1826. *Where serving when wounded*: 'Corunna, Badajoz, Salamanca.' *Family*: Married in Kensington, 8 April 1817. Five children by 1829. *Where generally resident during last five years*: 'Scotland'. [PRO: WO 25/749 f103]. Wounded, 'in the Army lately in Spain' (1st Battn.) [*March 1809 Army List, 105*]. *Monthly Return*, 1st Battn., dated 25 Feb. 1809: 'Left wounded at Plymouth' [PRO: WO 17/152]. Slightly wounded, storming of Badajoz, 6 April 1812, while serving as a Major in the 11th Portuguese Line Regt. [*London Gazette*]. Mentioned in Wellington's Castrejon dispatch, 21 July 1802 ['In these affairs ... Lieutenant-Colonel Anderson, commanding the 11th, and Major de Azeredo, commanding the 23rd Portuguese regiment, distinguished themselves.'] [*London Gazette*]. Slightly wounded, Salamanca, 22 July 1812, as Lt. Col. in 11th Portuguese Line [*London Gazette*]. Gold Medal. Served in Portuguese Army from May 1810 to April 1814. Mentioned in dispatches for Badajoz, Orthes, Toulouse. *Challis, Portuguese Army*, p. 52.

ANDERSON, Alexander, Lt., 45th Foot: Lt., 45th Foot, 1 Dec. 1804. Slightly wounded, Busaco, 27 Sept. 1810 (1st Battn.) [*London Gazette*].

+ANDERSON, Charles, Capt., 94th Foot: Capt., 94th Foot, 26 Jan. 1804. Killed in the storming of Ciudad Rodrigo, 19 Jan. 1812 [*London Gazette*]. *Register of dead officers*: Return dated: 25 Jan. 1812 [PRO: WO 25/2965]. *Register of officers' effects*: Single. Effects totalled £171. 8s. 5d. [PRO: WO 25/2964].

ANDERSON, Francis, Lt., 23rd Light Dragoons: Lt., 23rd Light Dragoons, 1 Jan. 1798. Recorded as 'wounded and missing', Talavera, 28 July 1809 [*London Gazette*]. Capt., 14th Light Dragoons, 2 Aug. 1810. MGS.

+ANDERSON, Henry, Capt., 68th Foot: Capt., 68th Foot, 21 June 1810. Killed, Vittoria, 21 June 1813 [*London Gazette*]. *Register of officers' effects*: Single. Effects totalled £22. 11s. [PRO: WO 25/2964]. *Register of dead officers*: Date of return: 25 June 1813 [PRO: WO 25/2965]. Obituary, *The Gentleman's Magazine*, 1813 Supplement Part I, p. 664 ['At the memorable battle of Vittoria, in his 27th year, Captain Henry Anderson, 68th regt. son of Henry A. esq. of Bath. Among the many who have found an honourable grave beneath the plains of the Peninsula, few have fallen more sincerely lamented by their comrades than this gallant young officer, in whom real goodness of heart, inviolable integrity, and unalterable friendship, united to form a man deserving and receiving the

warmest esteem when living, the deepest regret when dead.'].

+ANDERSON, James, Lt., 71st Foot: Lt., 71st Foot, 6 Aug. 1812. Killed, Aire, 2 March 1814 (1st Battn.) [*London Gazette*]. *Register of officers' effects*: Killed in Action, 2 March 1814, Aire. Single. Effects totalled £7. 2s. 4d, 'Paid to liquidate his Debts.' [PRO: WO 25/2964]. *Register of dead officers*: Return dated: March 1814 [PRO: WO 25/2965].

+ANDERSON, John, Lt., 1st Foot: Lt., 1st Foot, 22 July 1809. Killed, 'at the Siege of St Sebastian,' 7-27 July 1813 (3rd Battn.) [*London Gazette*]. *Register of dead officers*: Killed in Action, St Sebastian, 25 July 1813. Return dated: Aug. 1813 [PRO: WO 25/2965].

ANDERSON, John, Lt., 28th Foot: *1829 Statement of Service*: Aged sixteen on his first appointment. Ensign, 42nd Foot, Feb. 1807; Lt., 28th Foot, 26 Oct. 1809; Half-pay, Capt., 28th Foot, Dec. 1814, 'By Reduction'; Capt., 1st Foot, June 1826; Half-pay, Major, unattached, Dec. 1826. 'Very desirous' of service. *Where serving when wounded*: 'Barossa'. No pension. *Family*: Married in Gordon Castle, Scotland, July 1817. No children in 1829. *Where generally resident during last five years*: 'In Aberdeen & Forfar Shire.' [PRO: WO 25/749 f102]. Severely wounded, Barossa, 5 March 1811 (1st Battn.) [*London Gazette*].

ANDERSON, John, Ensign, 38th Foot: Ensign, 38th Foot, 29 Nov. 1810. Severely wounded, Salamanca, 22 July 1812 (2nd Battn.) [*London Gazette*].

ANDERSON, Joseph, Lt., 24th Foot: *1829 Statement of Service*: 'Born Durness, Sutherlandshire, 1st July 1790. Aged fifteen on his first Entrance into the Army. Ensign, 78th Foot, 27th June 1805. Lieutenant, 24th Foot, 6th Octobr. 1808. Company, York Chass., 20th January 1814. Half Pay, 25th Decr. 1818, on reduction of the Regiment. Company, 50th Foot, 3 May 1821. Major, 50th Foot, 16th Feby. 1826.' *Battles, sieges and campaigns*: 'Was with the Expedition to Lower Calabria under Sir John Stuart in 1806, at the Battle of Maida on 4th July, subsequent operations, and at the Capture of the Fortress off Catrona on the East Coast of Italy on the 31st of the same month. With the Expedition to Egypt in 1807... at the Siege of Rozetta from 7th to 20th April, Retreat of 21 April & subsequent campaign till Sept. 1807, as Ensign in 78th Foot. With 24th Regiment in Portugal and Spain from April 1809 till January 1812, was present at the Battle of Talavera 27th and 28th July 1809, at Busaco on the 29th September 1810, Subsequent Retreat to the Lines of Torres Vedras, various affairs there; with the advance of Major General Sherbrooks Brigade in March 1811, at Esperille; at the Battles of Fuentes D'Onor 3, 4 and 5th May 1811, and otherwise with the 24th Regiment as Lieutenant in all the movements until obliged from ill Health to return to England in January 1812. Was at the Capture of Guadeloupe on the 9th and 10th August 1815 ... on the Staff of the Army as Major of Brigade but doing duty for the time with his Company in the York Chasseurs & as A.D. Camp to Major Genl. R. Douglass.' *Distinguished conduct*: 'Special Report of Services at Guadeloupe made to His late Royal Highness the Duke of York, through Lieut. Genl. Sir H. Taylor by Major Genl. R. Douglass on the 12th June 1826.' *Wounds received in action*: 'Slightly wounded at Talavera, but not returned. Received a Pension as Captain for the loss of Vision of the right Eye from Ophthalmia in Egypt in 1807. One years pay as Ensign, received for the same in 1818 & Pension finally granted as

Captain in 1821 or 1822, Permanently.' *Service abroad*: '23rd Sept. 1805 to 8th January 1808, Gibraltar, Sicily, Italy and Egypt. 9th April 1809 to 12th January 1812, Portugal and Spain. 22nd Octobr. 1814 to 31st March 1818, Barbadoes, St Vincents, Dominica, Guadeloupe and Jamaica. 26th Novr. 1822 to 2nd May 1825, Jamaica. Memdm. Certain as to the months but not positive as to the days of the months being here correctly recorded.' *Family*: Married Mary Campbell, 25 Nov. 1826, 'St Pancreas, London.' They had two children by 1830. [PRO: WO 25/794 f336]. MGS.

ANDERSON, Matthew, Lt., 52nd Foot: Lt., Army, 12 Oct. 1809; Lt., 52nd Foot, 19 July 1810. Severely wounded, Nivelle, 10 Nov. 1813 (1st Battn.) [*London Gazette*]. Waterloo. Pension of seventy pounds per annum, commencing 19 June 1816, for 'loss of leg' at Waterloo, 1815 [*1818 Pension Return*, pp. 14–15]. *Dalton*, pp. 169, 172 ['Retd. 1821'].

+ANDERSON, William, Lt., 91st Foot: Lt., 91st Foot, 25 Aug. 1807. *Register of dead officers*: 'Killed, France. Date of Decease: unknown.' Return dated: March 1814 [PRO: WO 25/2965].

ANDREWS, Alexander, Capt., 60th Foot: Lt., 60th Foot, 5 April 1796; Capt. 2 June 1803. Slightly wounded, Talavera, 28 July 1809 [*London Gazette*], 'Andrew'. Slightly wounded, Busaco, 27 July 1810 [*London Gazette*]. Major, 60th Foot, 17 Jan. 1811.

ANDREWS, Francis, Lt., 45th Foot: Ensign, 45th Foot, 13 Aug. 1807; Lt., 45th Foot, 1 June 1809. Severely wounded, siege of Badajoz, 26 March 1812 [*London Gazette*]. MGS.

ANDREWS, Matthias, Lt., 30th Foot: Lt., 30th Foot, 19 Sept. 1809. Slightly wounded, during 'movements of the Army' [Retreat from Burgos], 25 Oct. 1812 [*London Gazette*]. Wounded, Waterloo.

+**ANDREWS, Thomas, Capt., 74th Foot**: Capt., 35th Foot, 23 June 1808; Capt., 74th Foot, 11 March 1813. Recorded as 'Missing, severely wounded, since dead', Toulouse, 10 April 1814 (1st Battn.) *Register of officers' effects*: Killed in Action, 10 April 1814, Toulouse. Single. [PRO: WO 25/2964]. *Register of dead officers*: Return dated: April 1814 [PRO: WO 25/2965]. *Hurt*, p. 80.

+**ANGROVE, John, Lt., 43rd Foot**: Lt., 43rd Foot, 24 May 1810. Severely wounded, Nivelle, 10 Nov. 1813 (1st Battn.) [*London Gazette*]. *Return of dead officers*: Died of wounds, 14 Nov. 1813. Return dated: Nov. 1813 [PRO: WO 25/2965]. *Hurt*, p. 78 ['Lt. Geo. Angrove, D.O.W., Nivelle, Nov. 14'].

ANNESLEY, Marcus, Capt., 61st Foot: *1829 Statement of Service*: He recorded as 'unknown' both the place and date of birth, though indicates he was 'Eighteen years on his first Entrance into the Army.' 'Ensign, 67th Regt., 10th Jany. 1798. Lieutenant, 61st, 26 April 1798.' Half Pay, 25th June 1802, 'Reduction, retained supernumerary on Full Pay.' Reappointed, 'Lieutenant, 61st, 9th July 1803. Captain, 61st, 24th Decr. 1807. Major, 61st, 12th June 1823.' *Battles, sieges and campaigns*: 'Secret Expedition Febry. 1801, Sir Samuel Echmuty. Campaigns. Egypt 1801... Campaign Italy 1805... Battle of Maida 4th July 1806. Adjutant Grenadier Battalion. Siege Shilla Castle. Campaign Calabria 1806... Secret Expedition September 1807, Sir John Moore. Forts of Salamanca June 1812. Siege of Busaco September 1812. Battles. Salamanca 22nd July 1812. Pyrenees 28th July to 2nd August 1813. Nivelle 10th November 1813. Campaigns 1811, 1812, 1813 and 1814.' *Distinguished*

conduct: 'Siege of Burgos, Commanded the Party who carried the Ladders in the successful Storm on the 4th October 1813.' *Wounds received in action*: 'Wounded in the Ancle at Nivelle 10th November 1813, forcing the Lines. Grant one years Pay. Pension 100£ per year Permanently.' *Titles, honorary distinctions and medals*: 'Medal Salamanca Commanding the 61st Regt.' *Service abroad*: '12 Augt. 1798 to 24th June 1802, Cape of Good Hope, Egypt, Malta. 25th June 1802 to 8th July 1803, Italy, Sicily, Calabria. 9th July 1803 to 23rd Decr. 1807, Gibraltar. 24th Decr. 1807 to 24th May 1808, Gibraltar. 20th Augt. 1811 to 20th Febry. 1814, Peninsula. 12th March 1817 to 23rd Jany. 1820, Jamaica.' [PRO: WO 25/797 f3]. Severely wounded, Nivelle, 10 Nov. 1813 (1st Battn.) [*London Gazette*]. Gold Medal. Temporary pension of seventy pounds per annum, commencing 11 Nov. 1814, 'for a wound' received at St Pe, 1813 [*1818 Pension Return*, pp. 16–17].

+**ANSALDO, John, Lt., 1st Batt. 48th Foot**: Lt., Army, 5 Dec. 1805; Lt., 48th Foot, 22 Oct. 1807. Killed, Albuera, 16 May 1811 (1st Battn.) [*London Gazette*]. *Register of dead officers*: Return dated: 25 May 1811 [PRO: WO 25/2965].

ANSTRUTHER, Windham A., Ensign, Coldstream Guards: Ensign, Coldstream Guards, 5 July 1810. Severely wounded, Nivelle, 10 Nov. 1813 (1st Battn.) [*London Gazette*]. Temporary pension of fifty pounds per annum, commencing 11 Nov. 1814, 'for wounds' received at St Jean de Luz, 1813 [*1818 Pension Return*, pp. 2-3]. MGS.

ANTHONY, James, Lt., 40th Foot: *1829 Statement of Service for Retired Officers*: Aged eighteen on first appointment. Ensign, 40th Foot, 9 April 1809 [Army list gives 9 Feb. 1809]; Lt., 40th Foot, 'April

1811' [Army List gives 16 May 1811].
'HP 1819.' *Where serving when wounded*: '1st at Badajos 2 severely, 2nd at Tholouse, 3rd at Waterloo.' *Details of pension*: 70 Pounds per annum from 1815. Not married in 1829. *Where generally resident during last five years*: 'England, Ireland'. Title and nature of employment: 'None, unfortunately.' [PRO: WO 25/749 f111]. Severely wounded, storming of Badajoz, 6 April 1812 (1st Battn.) [*London Gazette*]. Severely wounded, Toulouse, 10 April 1814 (1st Battn.) [*London Gazette*]. Wounded at Waterloo. Waterloo Medal. Half-pay 18 Nov. 1819. Pension of seventy pounds per annum, commencing 11 April 1815, 'for wounds' received at Badajoz, Toulouse and Waterloo [*1818 Pension Return*, pp. 10–11].

ANWYLL, Robert, Capt., 4th Foot: Capt., 4th Foot, 14 Aug. 1804. Severely wounded, storming of Badajoz, 6 April 1812 ('Hanwell') [*London Gazette*]. Slightly wounded, the Nive, 9 Dec. 1813, while serving as Brigade Major ('Brevet Major Robert Anwyl') [*London Gazette*]. Gold Medal (St Sebastian), as Brigade Major, and became senior Officer of the Brigade.

APPUHN, George, Lt., 3rd Line Battn. K.G.L.: Lt., 3rd Line Battn. K.G.L., 27 Jan. 1806; Adjutant, 3rd Line Battn. K.G.L., 30 Oct. 1807. Severely wounded, Castalla, 12–13 April 1813 [*London Gazette*].

APPUHN, William Joachim Ernst, Lt., 3rd Line Battn. K.G.L.: *1829 Statement of Service for Retired Officers*: Aged seventeen and a half on his first appointment. Ensign, 3rd Line Battn. K.G.L., 8 Sept. 1806; Lt., 3rd Line Battn. K.G.L., 14 Nov. 1809. Placed on Half-pay by reduction of the Corps. *Where serving when wounded*: 'in Spain'. *Details of pension*: '£70 per annum.' Commenced '13th of April 1814 and

after a second examination of my severe wound, after having been called to England for that purpose, the Pension was again granted permanently since the 25th of December 1817.' *Family*: Married in Hamburg, 21 Jan. 1816. Eight children by 1829. *Where generally resident during last five years*: 'In the Town of Hanover.' [PRO: WO 25/749 f41]. Served in Peninsula 1812–13. *Beamish*, vol. II, p. 582 ['severely wounded, 12th April 1813, near Biar, in Spain... [Died] at Hanover, 4th July 1837.'].

+ARBUTHNOT, Hon. Duncan, Lt., 95th Foot: Ensign, 77th Foot, 25 Sept. 1806; Lt., Army, 18 Dec. 1806; 1st Lt., 95th Foot, 20 Aug. 1807. *Register of dead officers*: Date of return: 25 March 1811. 1st Battn. Killed in Action, 3 April 1811 [PRO: WO 25/2965]. *Register of officers' effects*: Single. Value of Effects 'Paid his Mother'. [PRO: WO 25/2964]. 5th son of John, 7th Viscount Arbuthnott [*Burke's Peerage*]. *Simmons*, pp. 162, 178 [Sabugal, 3 April 1811: 'One lieutenant of ours had his head dashed to pieces by a cannon shot – a very brave young soldier.'].

ARBUTHNOT, Thomas, Major, 5th West India Regt.: Major, 5th West India Regt., 7 April 1808; Bvt. Lt. Col., 24 May 1810. Severely wounded, 'in Action with the Enemy', 20 March 1814, while serving on the General Staff as AQMG [*London Gazette*].

ARCHDALL, Henry, Capt., 68th Foot: Lt., 68th Foot, 14 Nov. 1805. Capt., 68th Foot, 26 Aug. 1813. Slightly wounded, Nivelle, 10 Nov. 1813 ('Archdale') [*London Gazette*].

+ARCHER, Holt, Lt., 7th Foot: Lt., 7th Foot, 3 Nov. 1808. Killed, Albuera, 16 May 1811, (2nd Battn.) [*London Gazette*]. *Register of dead officers*: Date of return: 25 May 1811 [PRO: WO 25/2965].

+**ARDEN, Henry, Lt., 61st Foot**: Lt., 61st Foot, 13 May 1809. Severely wounded, 'since dead', Toulouse, 10 April 1814 (1st Battn.) [*London Gazette*]. *Register of officers' effects*: Died of wounds, 11 April 1814, Toulouse. Single. Effects totalled £32. 4s. 10d. [PRO: WO 25/2964]. *Register of dead officers*: Return dated: April 1814 [PRO: WO 25/2965]. *Hurt*, p. 79 ['D.O.W., Toulouse, Apl. 10.'"].

+**ARGENT, Matthew, Lt., 44th Foot**: Ensign, 44th Foot, 25 Aug. 1808; Lt. 8 Aug. 1811. Killed, storming of Badajoz, 6 April 1812 (2nd Battn.) [*London Gazette*]. *Register of dead officers*: Return dated: 25 April 1812 [PRO: WO 25/2965].

ARGUIMBAU, Lawrence, Lt./Capt., 1st Foot: *1829 Statement of Service for Retired Officers*: Aged seventeen on his first appointment. Ensign, 1st Foot, 1801; Lt., 1st Foot, 1803; Capt., 1st Foot, 9 March 1809; Bvt. Major, 42nd Foot, 11 Aug. 1814; Bvt. Lt. Col., 42nd Foot, 18 June 1815. *Where serving when wounded*: 'Storming of St Sebastian in Spain.' *Details of pension*: 250 Pounds from 28 July 1814 'as Major Commg. the Battn... £300 on obtaining Rank of Lt. Colonel 18th June 1815.' *Family*: Married in Mahon on the Island of Minorca, 21 Dec. 1817. Four children by 1829. *Where generally resident during last five years*: "Mahon, Island of Minorca." [PRO: WO 25/749 f134]. Mentioned in Graham's report to Wellington, concerning the storming of the convent of San Bartolomé, dated 18 July 1813 ['a reserve of three companies of the Royal Scots, under Captain Auguimbeau'] [*London Gazette*]. Severely wounded, 'left arm amputated', Siege of St Sebastian, 7 to 27 July 1813 ('Argimbeau') (3rd Battn.) [*London Gazette*]. Pension of three hundred pounds, commencing 26 July 1814, for 'loss of arm', St Sebastian, 1813, as 'Major Commanding' ('Arguimbeau') [*1818 Pension Return*, pp. 2–3]. Wounded, Waterloo. MGS. *Dalton*, pp. 116, 117 ['A protégé of H.R.H. the Duke of Kent, the Col.-in-Chf. of the regt. Attained the rank of Lt.-gen. and Col.-in-Chf. 80th Foot. D. 18th Aug., 1854, at Port Mahon.']. *Mullen*, p. 128 ['A/L gives bars Bus Sal Vitt SS, though as he lost an arm during the first unsuccessful assault on St Sebastian it is doubtful whether he was entitled. Robert Mullen, who succeeded to the command of the stormers upon the death of Maj Frazer did not receive this bar.']. 'Arguimbeau' in Army List.

ARMIT, John, Ensign, 27th Foot: Ensign, 27th Foot, 21 Jan. 1813. Severely wounded, Toulouse, 10 April 1814 ('Armett') (3rd Battn.) [*London Gazette*]. Lt., 27th Foot, 10 March 1814.

ARMSTRONG, Francis W., Ensign/Lt., 48th Foot: Ensign, 48th Foot, 1 Sept. 1808; Lt., 48th Foot, 21 June 1810. Slightly wounded, storming of Badajoz, 6 April 1812 [*London Gazette*]. Slightly wounded, Salamanca, 22 July 1812 [*London Gazette*]. MGS.

ARMSTRONG, Frederick, Capt., 4th Caçadores: Slightly wounded, the Nive, 13 Dec. 1813, while serving as Capt., 4th Caçadores [*London Gazette*]. Bvt. Lt. Col., E.O.P.S., 25 Oct. 1814, 'serving with the Portuguese Army'. Pension of two hundred and fifty pounds per annum, commencing 13 Dec. 1814, for 'loss of an arm', Navarre, 1813, while Capt., 4th Caçadores [*1818 Pension Return*, pp. 26–27]. *Challis, Portuguese Army*, p. 52.

ARMSTRONG, George, Capt., 50th Foot: Lt., 50th Foot, 20 June 1805; Capt., 50th Foot, 4 Feb. 1808. Wounded, 'in the Army lately in Spain' (1st Battn.) [*March 1809 Army List*, p. 105].

ARMSTRONG, John, Lt., 1st Foot: Lt., 1st Foot, 27 April 1809. Slightly wounded, Vittoria, 21 June 1813 (3rd Battn.) [*London Gazette*]. Slightly wounded, 'at the Siege of St Sebastian,' 7-27 July 1813 (3rd Battn.) [*London Gazette*]. Slightly wounded, storming of San Sebastian, 31 Aug. 1813 (3rd Battn.) [*London Gazette*]. Killed, Waterloo.

ARMSTRONG, John, Lt., 88th Foot: Lt., Army, 26 Sept. 1804; Lt., 88th Foot, 4 June 1807. Slightly wounded, siege of Ciudad Rodrigo, 16 Jan. 1812 [*London Gazette*]. MGS. NGS.

ARMSTRONG, Richard, Capt., 97th Foot; Lt. Col, 10th Caçadores: *1829 Statement of Service*: Born 24 Jan. 1782, Lincoln. Aged twelve years and one month on his first entrance into the Army. Ensign, Westmeath Militia, Feb. 1794; Ensign, 24th Foot, 23 June 1796; Lt., 5th Foot, 5 Nov. 1799; Half-pay, Oct. 1802; Lt., 11th Foot, May 1803; Capt., 9th Battn. of Reserve, 9 July 1803; Capt., 89th Foot, 2 Aug. 1804; Capt., 9th Royal Veterans' Battn., 10 April 1805; Capt., 97th Foot, 7 July 1808; 'Major to serve with Portuguese Army 30th May 1811'; Lt. Col., 'ditto', 26 Aug. 1813 'without purchase for Conduct in Action'; Half-pay 25 Dec. 1816 ['Reduced on half pay of Lieut. Colonel though still serving with the Portuguese Army by order of British Government. Being thus employed I calculate my service during this period as on full pay.']; Lt. Col., 1st Foot, 18 Oct. 1821; Lt. Col., 26th Foot, 24 Jan. 1829; 'Colonel in the Army in India 5 June 1829.' *Battles, sieges and campaigns*: 'Present at capture of Oporto 12th May 1809 as Captain 97th Foot, but Regt. not engaged. Battle of Burace 27th Sept. 1810 as Major Comg. 16th Portuguese Regt. Actions at Pombal & Redinha 11th & 12th March 1811 as Major of 16th Portuguese Regt. Defence of Alba de Tormes 10th Novr. 1812, Lieut. Colonel Comdt. 10th Battn. Caçadores. Battle of Vittoria 21st June 1813, Lt. Col. 10th Battn. Caçadores. Battle of Pyrenees 27th July 1813, Lt. Col. 10th Battn. Caçadores. Battle of Toulouse 8th April 1814, Lieut. Colonel Comg. 4th Portuguese Regt. Served Peninsula Campaigns of 1808, 1809, 1810, 1811, 1812, 1813, 1814. Besides General Actions I was present and engaged in great numbers of minor affairs, such as Santa Combadao, when Major Comg. 16th Portuguese Infantry with General Pack's Brigade in 1810. The defence of Calhariz Bridge on the Rio Maior in Novr. 1810, when Field Officer Comg. Pickets of General Packs Brigade, when I successfully resisted a strong reconnaissance of the French from Santorem for several hours & until supported. Received General Pack's unqualified thanks on the occasion. I entirely formed the 10th Battn. of Caçadores at Oporto in 1811 of which I was Lieut. Col. Comdt. In March 1812 I led them to the field and was employed to cover Badajos when stormed on 6th April 1812. I was in the advance with my Battn. at Salamanca when we pushed the French out in 1812. I was with my Battn. and constantly employed in all that Campaign and in retreat from Burgos. I was in 1813 in various small actions such as near Forequemada, at Villa Alba, Almandrelego & Los Alduides. I was subsequently Colonel of 4th Portuguese Infantry and lastly a Brigadier General and Commanded a Brigade in that service, where on all occasions I received the unqualified approbation of my services from Marshal General Lord Viscount Beresford until I retired from it in the year 1821. Served Burmese Campaign of 1825 & 1826 as Brigadier Major General Sir Archd. Campbell comg. in Chief. Stormed and carried various Stockades on 1st & 5th December 1825 near Prome in Birmah.' *Distinguished Conduct*: 'My name mentioned in dispatch of Battle of Busaco & gallant conduct of 16th Portuguese Regt. reported which I commanded as Major. Present with that corps as Major at Battle of Redinha in Gel. Packs Brigade and troops conduct highly approved. At Alba de Tormes I commanded 10th Battn. Caçadores in Sir Archd. Campbells Brigade. Defence and gallantry of troops set forth by Lieut. Genl. Sir John Hamilton. At Battle of Pyrenees my conduct as Lieut. Col. Comg. 10th Battn. Caçadores drew attention of Duke of Wellington and by His Graces recommendation I was promoted to Lieut. Colonel in the British Army. As Lieut. Colonel of the Royals and Brigadier in Birmah my name was mentioned in Dispatches for assaults of Stockades on 1st and 5th December 1825, and thanked by Governor Genl. of India in Orders, at the end of Burmese War.' *Wounds received in action*: 'Severely wounded through the Arm in Battle of the Pyrenees 27th July 1813 when Lieut. Colonel Comg. 10th Battn. Caçadores. Received a gratuity of One Years Pay but no pension.' *Titles, honorary distinctions and medals*: 'Medal & Two Clasps conferred on me by order of His Majesty, for Battles of Busaco, Vittoria & Pyrenees. Nominated a Companion of the Bath on first institution. Nominated a Knight of the Tower & Sword by His Majesty the King of Portugal in 1816, for distinguished and gallant services in the field during Peninsula War. Nominated a Knight Commander of same order by His Most Faithful Majesty in 1822 after I became a Brigadier General. Condecorated with Portuguese Cross for Battles of Busaco, Vittoria, Pyrenees. Condecorated with Portuguese Campaign Medal for having served six campaigns in the field with that Army. Received the honor of Knighthood from His Majesty King William the 4th on my return from India in consideration of my services.' *Service abroad*: 'Augt. 1796 to May 1800, Canada and Halifax. May 1801 to Septr. 1802, Gibraltar. Augt. 1808 to April 1821, Spain, France and Portugal. May 1822 to Feby. 1825, East Indies. Feby. 1825 to Septr. 1826, Burmese Territory. Septr. 1826 to 31 Decr. 1829, East Indies.' *Family*: Married Elizabeth Champion, 3 Nov. 1803, Edgbaston Church, near Birmingham. They had two daughters, though one died 17 April 1830. [PRO: WO 25/790 f6]. Severely wounded, Pyrenees, 25–28 July 1813, while serving as Lt. Col., 10th Caçadores [*London Gazette*]. In Portuguese Service June 1809 to Sept. 1813. Gold Medal. MGS. *Challis, Portuguese Army*, p. 52.

ARNOLD, Robert, Ensign, 4th Foot; Lt., 16th Light Dragoons: *1829 Statement of Service*: Born May 1795, Hulsteed, Kent. Ensign, 4th Foot, Sept. 1809 [Note: Army List gives 21 Nov. 1809]; Lt., 16th Light Dragoons, 13 May 1812; Half Pay Aug. 1814; Capt., 10th Light Dragoons, 9 July 1818; Major 14 April 1825; Lt. Col., Half Pay, 10th Lancers, 8 April 1826; Lt. Col., 16th Lancers, 22 June 1826. *Battles, sieges and campaigns*: 'Served in the Campaigns of 1811 – 12 – 13 & 14. Joined the 16th Lancers in India in February 1827.' *Wounds received in action*: 'Siege of Bardajos, Victoria, & Waterloo, on each of which occasions I received 1 years Pay.' Titles, honorary distinctions, and medals: 'Waterloo Medal.' *Service abroad*: '1809 to June 1814, Peninsula. 11 April 1815 to 15 Decr. 1818, France. Jany. 1827 to 31 Dec. 1829, East Indies.' [PRO: WO 25/784 f252]. Severely wounded, storming of Badajoz, 6 April 1812 [*London Gazette*]. Slightly wounded, Vittoria, 21 June 1813 [*London Gazette*].

+ARNOT, Lawrence, Capt., 56th Foot; Capt., 92nd Foot; Major, 12th Portuguese Line: Capt., 56th Foot,

25 Sept. 1808. Wounded, siege of Burgos, 5–10 Oct. 1812, while serving as Major, 12th Portuguese Line [*London Gazette*]. Severely wounded, Pyrenees, 25–28 July 1813, while serving as Major, 12th Portuguese Line [*London Gazette*]. *Register of officers' effects*: Died of wounds, 'date not known, Spain'. Single. Effects not valued. 2nd Batt. 92nd Foot. [PRO: WO 25/2964]. Obituary, *The Gentleman's Magazine*, Nov. 1813, p. 504 ['Of wounds received in the action of the 28th of July, Major Lawrence Arnot, 92d foot, youngest son of the late Hugo A. esq. of Balcormo.']. *Challis, Portuguese Army*, p. 52 ['Died of Wounds 13 Oct. '13'].

ASHE, Richard, Ensign, 71st Foot: *1829 Statement of Service*: Aged twenty on his first appointment. Ensign, 71st Foot, March 1813; Lt., 71st Foot, Jan. 1814. 'Placed on half pay by the reduction of the 2nd Batn 71st Regt.' *Where serving when wounded*: 'Was slightly wounded on the 13th of Decr. 1813 near Bayonne.' No pension. *Family*: Married in Christ Church in the city of Cork, July 1819. One child by 1829. *Where generally resident during last five years*: 'Coolehane, Macroom.' [PRO: WO 25/749 f191].

ASHWORTH, Charles, Lt.Col., E.O.P.S.; Brigadier-General, Portuguese Staff: Major, 6th West India Regt., 8 Aug. 1805; Lt. Col., E.O.P.S., 18 Jan. 1810, 'Spain and Portugal'. Mentioned in Wellington's Fuentes de Onoro dispatch, 8 May 1811 (commanding a Portuguese Brigade) [*London Gazette*, 26 May 1811]. Mentioned in Hill's Almaraz dispatch, 21 Aug. 1812 ['I cannot avoid to mention the steadiness and good discipline of the 6th Portuguese infantry, and two companies of the 60th Regiment, under Colonel Ashworth, which formed the reserve to this attack.'] [*London Gazette*]. Severely wounded, the Nive, 13 Dec. 1813, while

serving as Brigadier-General on Portuguese General Staff [*London Gazette*]. In Portuguese Service Aug. 1808 to Feb. 1814. Gold Cross. Not at Waterloo. No MGS. *Challis, Portuguese Army*, p. 52 ['Wd. Pyrenees']. *Webber*, pp. 110–11 [commanding a brigade of Portuguese Infantry], p. 162.

ATKIN, William, Lt., 2nd Light Battn. K.G.L.: *1829 Statement of Service*: [completed in Nov. 1841] 'Born in Co. Wexford, Ireland, in 1793. Aged 14 years on his first Entrance into the Army. Volunteer, 3d or Kings Drags., end of 1806. Ensign, 2nd Lt. Infantry K.G. Legion, end of 1809. Lieut., 2nd Lt. K.G. Legion, 2d July 1811. Half Pay, 1816, By reduction. Lieut., 3d R.V. Btn., Octr. 1822. Half Pay, June 1826, By reduction. Lieut., 77th Foot, 1827. Captn., Half Pay, Unattached, 31st Decr. 1830. Capt., 73rd Foot, July 1833. Capt., Half Pay, 81st Foot, Octbr. 1836. Capt., R.C.R.R., 28th July 1841.' *Battles, sieges and campaigns*: 'Flushing 1809. Olivensa 1811. Albuhera 1811. Ciudad Rodrigo 1812. Badajos 1812. Salamanca Forts 1812. Burgos 1812. Madrid 1812.' 'Covering retreat from Burgos when the two Light Infantry Battalions, Kings German Legion, repulsed a large body of French Cavalry.' 'Vittoria 1813. Vitta Abochuco 1813. Tolosa 1813. Pampeluna 25th 27th & 30th July 1813. St Sebastian 1813. Bayonne 1814. Pyrenees 1814. Nive & Nivelle 1814. Capture of Paris 1815... During the whole of the above served as a Subaltern.' 'Besides numerous affairs of minor importance.' *Wounds received in action*: 'At the Crossing of the Bidassoa 7th Octobr. 1813. And Siege of Bayonne 28th Feby. 1814.' *Service abroad*: '1806 to 1809, Flushing.' 'Decr. 1810 to Aug. 1814, Peninsula. Nov. 1814 to Jany. 1816, Netherlands & France.' '1827 to 1831, Jamaica. 28th Augt. 1841, Canada.' *Family*: Married Miss Ann Stewart, 17 Jan.

33

1816, Ostend. They had two children by 1841. [PRO: WO 25/800 f113; WO 25/800 f114]. Slightly wounded, Crossing the Bidassoa, 7/9 ct. 1813 (1st Light Battn.) [*London Gazette*]. MGS. *Beamish*, vol. II, p. 609 ['Atkins'].

+**ATKINS, Thomas, Lt., 45th Foot**: Lt., 8th Garrison Battn., 16 April 1807; Lt., 45th Foot, 15 March 1810. Killed, siege of Badajoz, 26 March 1812 [*London Gazette*].

ATKINSON, Abraham, Ensign/Lt., 74th Foot: *1829 Statement of Service*: Born in Ireland, September 1787. Aged twenty-two years three months on his first appointment to the Army. Ensign, 74th Foot, 21 Dec. 1809, 'from Down Militia'; Lt., 74th Foot, 28 April 1812; Half-pay, 10 Sept. 1830. *Battles, sieges and campaigns*: 'Served the whole of the Campaigns of 10–11–12–13 & 14 in the 3d Division of the Army with the 74th Regt. in the Peninsula... At the Battle of Busaco 27 Septr. 1810. Fuentes de Onor 5th May 1811. Badajos Siege and Storm of Ciudad Rodrigo in Jany. 1812. Salamanca 22 July 1812. Vittoria 21st June 1813. Pyrenees 27, 28 & 30 July 1813. Nivelle Nov. 1813. Orthes 27 February 1814. Tarbes in March 1814.' *Wounds received in action*: 'Was Wounded at Badajos and severely at Tarbes, received a Pension of £70 per annum, Permanent, as also One Year's Pay.' *Service abroad*: 'March 1810 to 25th July 1814, Peninsula & France. 13 May 1818 to 30 July 1828, N. America.' [PRO: WO 25/799 f250]. Slightly wounded, siege of Badajos, 19 March 1812 ('Lieutenant') [*London Gazette*]. Severely wounded, 'in Action with the Enemy', 20 March 1814 [*London Gazette*].

AUBIN, Philip, Lt., 57th Foot: *1829 Statement of Service*: 'Born St. Heliers, Jersey, 12th Feby. 1795. Aged 16 years and 2 days on his first Entrance into the Army.

Ensign, 57th Regt., 14 Feby. 1811. Lieutenant, 57th Regt., 29 April 1813. Half Pay, March 1817, by reduction of the Additional Lieutenant. Lieutenant, 57th Regt., May 1817. Adjutant, 57th Regt., 7 April 1825. Captain, 57th regt., 22 June 1826.' Note added: 'Major, 57th Regt., 12 April 31. retired on Full Pay 11th Feby. 1842.' *Battles, sieges and campaigns*: 'Berlingen 1812. Vittoria 21 June 1813. Arnegin 2 July 1813. Pass of Ronce Veaux 25 July 1813. Pyrenees 28th & 30th July 1813. Elissondo 31 July 1813. Neville 10 Novr. 1813. Cembo 12 Novr. 1813. Crossing the Nieve at Cembo 9 Decr. 1813. Near Bayonne 11 & 13 Decr. 1813. Hilette & Expelleta 14 Feby 1814. Ayres 15 March 1814. Conchez between Ayres and Tarles 18 March 1814. Besides several minor affairs.' *Distinguished Conduct*: 'Near Bayonne 11 & 13 Decr. 1813, commanded Lt. Company and received the thanks of Lt. Col. Cameron on the field.' *Wounds received in action*: 'Conchez between Ayres and Tarles 18 March 1814, Received a severe Wound through the left side being in Command of the Light Company received a Captains years pay being only a Lieut. at the time.' *Service abroad*: 'November 1811 to June 1814, Portugal, Spain & France. 1814 to 1815, Canada. 1815 to 1816, Flanders & France. Augt. 1816 to 1818, France. 1829, N.S. Wales.' Note added: '1 Jany. 1830 to 1 July 1831, N.S. Wales. 1 Aug. 1831 to 31 May 1840, India.' *Family*: Married Frances Pounden of Daphne, County Wexford, 8 May 1822, Ballinasloe. [PRO: WO 25/796 f84]. Severely wounded, 'in Action with the Enemy', 18 March 1814 (1st Battn.) [*London Gazette*]. MGS.

+**AVEMANN, Charles Christian Frederick von, Capt., 1st Line Battn. K.G.L.**: Capt., Army, 19 July 1804; Capt., 1st Line Battn. K.G.L., 24 April 1808. Killed, Pyrenees, 28

July 1813 ('Avenant') [*London Gazette*]. Served in the Peninsula 1808–13. *Register of dead officers*: Date of return: Aug. 1813 [PRO: WO 25/2965]. 'George de Avemann' in Army List. *Beamish*, p. 632 ['Killed in the battle of the Pyrenees, near Pamplona in Spain, 28th July 1813, whilst serving as brigade major in the 4th infantry division.'].

+AYLING, John, Lt., 40th Foot: Ensign, 40th Foot, 4 Dec. 1805; Lt., 40th Foot, 9 Feb. 1807. Killed, storming of Badajoz, 6 April 1812 (1st Battn.) [*London Gazette*]. *Register of dead officers*: Date of return: 25 April 1812 [PRO: WO 25/2965]. *Lawrence*, p. 114 [Storming of Badajoz: 'Lieutenant Elland [sic] was brought in by a man of the name of Charles Filer, who had seen him lying wounded at the breach with a ball in the thigh, and on his asking him to convey him from the breach, had raised him on his shoulders for that object. But during his march a cannon-ball had taken the officer's head clean off without Filer finding it out on account of the darkness of the night, and the clamour of cannon and musketry mingled with the cries of the wounded. Much it was to Filer's astonishment, then, when the surgeon asked him what he had brought in a headless trunk for; he declared that the lieutenant had a head on when he took him up.'].

AYSHFORD, Aaron Moore, Ensign., 5th Foot: *1829 Statement of Service for Retired Officers*: Aged twenty-one on his first appointment. 'I purchased an Ensignce in the 53rd Regt. of Foot in the year of 1800. Some months after I paid the difference for a Cornetcy in the 18th Lt. Drgns. and in the summer of 1803 I sold out of the 18th Dragoons... 25 July 1803, South Devon Militia full pay as Ensign and Surgeon's mate. 17 Aug. 1809, 5th Foot, Ensign full pay. April 1812, 12th Foot Lieut., full pay.' 'I have entirely forgotten the exact dates of my two first commissions... When I was gazetted to the Twelfth foot, I was in Spain sick and wounded. I believe I was promoted on the 14th or 17th of April 1812.' Placed on Half-pay as a result of 'ill health and unfit for service by a Wound in the leg'. *Where serving when wounded*: 'Cuidad Rodrigo'. *Details of pension*: seventy pounds, commencing 17 Jan. 1813. Family: Married in Culmstock, 29 Jan. 1801. No children by 1829. *Where generally resident during last five years*: 'Culmstock.' [PRO: WO 25/749 f232; WO 25/749 f233]. Severely wounded, siege of Ciudad Rodrigo, 16 Jan. 1812 (2nd Battn.) [*London Gazette*]. Temporary pension of seventy pounds, commencing 17 Jan. 1813, 'for wounds' received at Ciudad Rodrigo, 1812 [*1818 Pension Return*, pp. 4–5]. MGS.

B

BACE, William, Lt./Adjutant, 61st Foot: *1829 Statement of Service for Retired Officers*: Aged seventeen on his first appointment. Ensign and Adjutant, 61st Foot, 9 Feb. 1809; Lt. and Adjt., 61st Foot, 2 Oct. 1811; Half-pay, 3rd Foot, 19 Dec. 1816. *Why placed on half-pay*: 'Ill health, in consequence of severe Injuries sustained in the Service, viz. loss of sight of left eye in Portugal. Double hernia, proceeding fm. fatigue &c at the Battles of the Pyrenees; also severe bodily injury received at the Battle of Toulouse, (by the plunging of my horse when it met its death wound) which subsequently became cancer, when I underwent a most severe surgical operation, which was performed by Surgeon Peile, Inspector of Hospitals, Dublin.' *Where serving when wounded*: 'Portugal, loss of left Eye. Pyrenees, and Toulouse, as detailed in column explanatory of my having been placed on the Half-pay. Honoured with a Gold Medal from the King in commemoration of the Battle of Toulouse.' *Details of pension*: 'Seventy pounds for loss of eye, an additional seventy for subsequent injuries in the Pyrenees and at Toulouse, the first commencing 25 Dec. 1813, the latter on 25 Dec. 1816.' 'Am at present serving as a Depy. Ass. Qrmar. Genl in Dublin.' *Title and nature of civil employment*: 'One of the Captain Pensioners of the Royal Hospl. Kilmainham. If considered a civil situation, it has not any duty or Employment attached to it; is for maimed officers and soldiers.' *Family*: Married in Malta, 11 Oct. 1804. Seven children by 1829. *Where generally resident during last five years*: 'Fairview Gardens, Dublin.' [PRO: WO 25/750 f77]. Gold Medal. Pension for 'loss of an eye' in 1812 *1818 Pension Return*, pp. 16–17. MGS.

BACMEISTER, Christian, Lt., 4th Line Battn. K.G.L.: *1829 Statement of Service*: Aged eighteen on his first appointment in the Army. 'Serjant Cadet', 3rd Battn. K.G.L., April 1804; Ensign, 4th Battn. K.G.L., 21 Dec. 1804; Lt., 4th Battn. K.G.L., 10 Aug. 1807; Capt., 4th Battn. K.G.L., 'In the last quarter of the year 1818 or somewhat earlier.' 'As the Commission (whoever often asked for it) has never been delivered by the Agent, the date of the month cannot exactly be stated.' *Where serving when wounded*: 'Spain.' *Details of pension*: Seventy Pounds commencing '14th Sepr. 1814, and after further examination of the Medical Board, permanently granted in the year 1820.' *Family*: Married on 30 Sept. 1828. *Where generally resident during last five years*: 'Misberg near Hanover.' [PRO: WO 25/750 f12]. Initially recorded as severely wounded, Heights of Ordal, 12/13 Sept. 1813 ('Backmeister') 'Rifle Company 4th King's German Legion') [*London Gazette*, 9 Oct. 1813]. Subsequently recorded as severely wounded, 'since dead', in the revised casualty list ('Backmeister') [*London Gazette*, 23 Oct. 1813]. Obviously the report of his death was somewhat premature. Served in Peninsula 1812–14. *Beamish*, vol. II, p. 586 ['severely wounded, 13th Sept. 1813, at the pass of Ordal.'].

+BACMEISTER, John William Lucas, Capt., 5th Line Battn. K.G.L.: Capt., 5th Line Battn. K.G.L., 7 Nov. 1803. Severely wounded, 'right arm amputated', siege of Burgos, 18 Oct. 1812 ('Buckmeister') [*London Gazette*]. *Beamish*, p. 637 [Died '2d Nov. 1812, at Penaranda in Spain, of the wounds he received before the castle of Burgos, 18th Oct. 1812.']. 'Lucas Bacmeister' in Army List. *Mullen*, p. 592, incorrectly attrib-

utes an MGS to him. See Bacmeister, Julius.

BACMEISTER, Julius, Capt., 5th Line Battn. K.G.L.: *1829 Statement of Service for Retired Officers*: Aged thirty-one on his first appointment into the Army. Lt., 5th Line Battn. K.G.L., 10 Dec. 1805; Capt., 5th Line Battn. K.G.L., 26 Sept. 1811; Half-pay, 'from ill health', 25 July 1815. *Where serving when wounded*: 'In Spain.' *Details of pension*: 100 Pounds from 26 June 1814. *Family*: Married in Ratzeburg, Dukedom of Lauenburg, 25 May 1817. At least eight children by 1829. *Where generally resident during last five years*: 'City of Hanau, Electorate of Hessia.' [PRO: WO 25/750 f11]. Severely wounded, in an action near Tolosa, 25 June 1813 [*London Gazette*]. Served in Peninsula 1808–14. MGS. Note: *Mullen*, p. 592, confuses Julius and John William Lucas, indicating that the MGS was awarded to the latter ['Julius in Foster. Variously Lucas and Lewis in A/Ls.']. In fact, as Foster noted, the MGS roll names Julius. See PRO: WO 100/10 p. 30 ['143. Bacmeister, Julius. Major Hanr. Army. Capt. 5 Line Bn.']. *Beamish*, vol. II, p. 655 ['severely wounded, 25th June 1813, at Toloza; slightly wounded, 14th April 1814, before Bayonne.'].

BADCOCK, Lovell Benjamin, Lt., 14th Light Dragoons: Cornet, 14th Light Dragoons, 18 Dec. 1805; Lt., 14th Light Dragoons, 19 May 1808. Slightly wounded, Fuentes de Onoro, 5 May 1811 [*London Gazette*]. Capt., 14th Light Dragoons, 12 Dec. 1811. Not at Waterloo. No MGS. *Brotherton*, p. 42 [Fuentes de Onoro: 'Captain [sic] Badcock was sitting on his horse at the head of his squadron, when he took for Spaniards running away (a very usual occurrence) some cavalry rapidly approaching him in line... He was, however, not very agreeably surprised by being undeceived by a

cut across the face from the French officer (for the supposed Spaniards were French). Badcock, however, who was an excellent officer, contrived, notwithstanding his surprise, to drive the enemy back in gallant style, with the loss, however, of two of his teeth; but he never thought of his wound till he had completed his duty, and then even never left the field for one moment.']. *Cocks*, p. 76 [8 Sept. 1810: 'Lt Badcock, 14th Light Dragoons joined me.'], p. 77 [n10, quoting a letter written by Badcock to his father, Sept. 1810: 'I was three times nearly taken, once with four men cut off from the rest of the Party but succeeded in joining them again by leaping some fences... I had the misfortune to lose a stirrup which broke from the tree of the saddle whilst I was galloping with some French Chasseurs so close at my heels that one of them cut the Croup of the Man's horse next to mine.'], p. 78 [12 Sept. 1810: 'About eight I heard two shots in the plain and saw Lt Badcock returning and a column of the enemy following him... We had some sharp skirmishing in Guarda and I retreated; a squadron followed me as far as Macainhas. This was the best French cavalry I have seen, the men were Bavarians, well mounted and rather dashing fellows.'].

BAGENAL, John Doyle, Lt., 87th Foot: Lt., 87th Foot, 1 Dec. 1807. Severely wounded, Talavera, 27 July 1809 ('Bagnall') [*London Gazette*]. Pension of one hundred pounds per annum, commencing 25 Dec. 1811, for 'loss of an arm' at Talavera [*1818 Pension Return*, pp. 20–21].

BAGENALL, Robert Sedley, Volunteer, 87th Foot: Severely wounded, Nivelle, 10 Nov. 1813 ('Volunteer Robert Bagenall') (2nd Battn.) [*London Gazette*]. Ensign, 87th Foot, 18 Nov. 1813. Pension of fifty pounds per annum, commencing 11 Dec. 1814, 'for a wound' received at

St Pe, 1813 [*1818 Pension Return*, pp. 20–21]. MGS.

BAILEY, Henry, Ensign, 87th Foot: Ensign, 87th Foot, 8 Oct. 1812. Severely wounded, Nivelle, 10 Nov. 1813 (2nd Battn.) [*London Gazette*].

BAILLIE, Andrew, Lt., 30th Foot: Ensign, 30th Foot, 29 June 1809; Lt. 27 June 1811. Slightly wounded, storming of Badajoz, 6 April 1812 ('Bailie') (2nd Battn.) [*London Gazette*]. At Antwerp when Waterloo was fought. Half-pay, 3 July 1817. MGS.

+BAILLIE, Mackay Hugh, Lt., 43rd Foot: Ensign, 43rd Foot, 9 Nov. 1809; Lt., 43rd Foot, 18 July 1811. Severely wounded, storming of Badajoz, 6 April 1812 ('Bailie') (1st Battn.) [*London Gazette*]. Slightly wounded, during operations, 15–19 Nov. 1812 ('H. M. Bailie') [*London Gazette*]. Killed, in a skirmish near Bayonne involving advancement of outposts of the Light Division, 23 Nov. 1813 (1st Battn.) [*London Gazette*]. *Bruce*, p. 162 [Letter from William Napier to his wife, dated Arcangues, 24 Nov. 1813: 'We have had an affair yesterday which has caused me much mortification... Some young sanguine officers who are more vain than good, concluded that with three or four companies they could drive the whole French army before them; the result was that I lost 75 men – more than I did in the last action; poor Bailey, who you will remember dined twice with us, was killed... And I run much risk of being called the cause of the misfortune, as I know that generals are sometimes not very scrupulous in blaming others to save their own credit.'].

BAINBRIGGE, John Hankey, Lt., 20th Foot: *1829 Statement of Service for Retired Officers*: Aged '16 years and 8 months' on his first appointment. Ensign, 20th Foot, 24 March 1808; Lt., 20th Foot, 9 April 1809; Capt., 41st Foot, 9 Dec. 1813. *Where serving when wounded*: 'In the Peninsula, at the battle of the 28th July 1813, near Pampeluna.' *Details of pension*: '£100 p.a... I have no document by me to shew the date of the Grant but my left arm was amputated on the 12th August 1813 at Vittoria in Spain, and I understood that my pension of £70 p. annum was to commence one year after that period. Subsequent to the battle of Waterloo His Majesty was graciously pleased to augment it to £100 per annum.': 'Willing to serve if required, but not desirous, as he considers the nature of his wounds such as to render him unfit for active service.' *Family*: Married in St Pierre du Bois, Guernsey, 4 May 1819. He had four children by 1829. *Where generally resident during last five years*: 'In the Island of Guernsey.' [PRO: WO 25/750 f42]. Severely wounded, Pyrenees, 28 July 1813 [*London Gazette*]. Pension of one hundred pounds per annum, commencing 29 July 1814, for 'loss of arm' at 'Pampeluna', 1813 [*1818 Pension Return*, pp. 6–7]. MGS.

BAIRD, David, Lt.-General: Col., 54th Foot, 8 May 1801; Lt.-General, 30 Oct. 1805. Gold Medal. Pension of four hundred and fifty pounds per annum, commencing 25 Dec. 1811, for 'loss of an arm' at Corunna [*1818 Pension Return*, pp. 6–7]. *Blakeney*, p. 122 [Corunna, 16 Jan. 1809: 'At this period the battle raged in its utmost fury; and an active general movement was taking place from left of both lines, the enemy retiring, the British pressing forward; and now Sir David also was knocked down, receiving the wound for which he subsequently suffered the amputation of his arm.']. He had a long and distinguished service in India, leading the storm of Seringapatam (1799), led the force sent from India to Egypt (1801) and led the expedition to the Cape. His biographies include Haley, A., *Our Davey: General Sir David Baird* (Liverpool, 1989); Hook, T. E., *The Life of General Rt. Hon. Sir David Baird Bart.* (London, 1832); Wilken, W. H., *The Life of Sir David Baird* (London, 1912).

BAIRD, Patrick, Capt., 77th Foot: Ensign, 77th Foot, 22 Jan. 1801; Lt., 22 Sept. 1803; Capt., 77th Foot, 6 June 1811. Severely wounded, storming of Ciudad Rodrigo, 19 Jan. 1812 [*London Gazette*].

BAKER, George, Lt., 16th Light Dragoons: Cornet, 16th Light Dragoons, 6 July 1809; Lt., 16th Light Dragoons, 15 Aug. 1811. Slightly wounded, Salamanca, 18 July 1812 [*London Gazette*]. Recorded as 'Missing', during 'movements of the Army' [Retreat from Burgos], 23 Oct. 1812 [*London Gazette*]. Waterloo. MGS. Died 22 Dec. 1859.

+BAKER, James Harrison, Capt., 34th Foot: Capt., 34th Foot, 8 July 1806. Severely wounded, Toulouse, 10 April 1814 (2nd Battn.) [*London Gazette*]. *Register of dead officers*: Capt. Died of wounds, 11 April 1814. Return dated April 1814. [PRO: WO 25/2965]. *Hurt*, p. 77 ['Maj. Jas. H. Baker, D.O.W., Toulouse, Apl. 11.']. Obituary, *The Gentleman's Magazine*, June 1814, p. 624 ['April 10. Whilst gallantly leading his regiment into the intrenchments before Toulouse, in the late unfortunate action, Major James Harrison Baker, 34th foot, second son of Rev. Dr B. of Camston, Norfolk, brother of Rev. R. B. of Botley.'].

BAKEWELL, Robert, Ensign/Lt., 27th Foot: *1829 Statement of Service for Retired Officers*: Ensign, 27th Foot, 12 April 1810; Lt., 27th Foot, 22 Oct. 1812. 'In consequence of being incapacitated, I tendered my resignation, it was accepted by the Marquis of Hastings on the 27 of

Jany. 1813.' Ensign, full pay, 27th Foot, 17 Jan. 1815. Half-pay, 'by reduction of the Battn.', 24 May 1817. 'I am not desirous to pass thro' the ordeal of an Ensigncy a third time. But supposing that I should have been appointed, I would in that case endeavour to attend strictly to the letter of my instructions.' *Where serving when wounded*: 'Wounded in the Peninsula, but not pensioned.' *Family*: Not married and 'no legitimate' children. *Where generally resident during the last five years*: 'Castle Donington, Leicestershire.' [PRO: WO 25/750 f34].

BALDWIN, Anthony, Lt., 7th Foot: Lt., 7th Foot, 27 Aug. 1807; Capt., 7th Foot, 3 June 1813; Half-pay, 25 Feb. 1816. Wounded, storming of Badajoz, 6 April 1812 [*London Gazette*]. MGS. Died 18 Jan. 1851.

BALDWIN, Connell James, Lt., 83rd Foot: *1829 Statement of Service for Retired Officers*: Aged 'about 20 or 21, never knew exactly', on his first appointment to Army. Paymaster, 37th Foot, 'about 1805 or 1806'; Ensign, 37th Foot, 1807; Lt., 83rd Foot, 1808 [Army List gives 16 March 1808]; Capt., 50th Foot, 1820. *Where serving when wounded*: 'In the Peninsula & France viz. Talavera, Vittoria, Orthes.' *Details of pension*: 'Was £200 & reduced to £70 tho still suffering severely from the effects of the wounds a great hardship' commenced 'about 1814 or 15'. *Where generally resident during last five years*: 'Honduras, Jamaica, England, N & S America' [PRO: WO 25/150 f160]. Slightly wounded, Talavera, 28 July 1809 [*London Gazette*]. Severely wounded, Vittoria, 21 June 1813 (2nd Battn.) [*London Gazette*]. Severely wounded, Orthes, 27 Feb. 1814 ('J. Baldwin') (2nd Battn.) [*London Gazette*]. MGS. *Mullen*, p. 465 ['Later Canadian Militia']. Colville, 170 [Letter from John Keane to Sir

Charles Colville, 17 March 1814, concerning Orthes: 'Baldwin severely [wounded], right arm broken.'].

BALL, Robert, Ensign, 68th Foot: Ensign, 68th Foot, 14 May 1812. Severely wounded, Vittoria, 21 June 1813 (Ensign) (2nd Battn.) [*London Gazette*]. Lt., 68th Foot, 26 Aug, 1813.

BALL, Thomas Gerrard, Lt., 34th Foot: *1829 Statement of Service*: Born 24 Jan. 1791, Chester. Aged sixteen years seven months on his first appointment to the Army. Ensign, 34th Foot, 17 Sept. 1807; Lt., 34th Foot, 1 Dec. 1808; Capt., 34th Foot, 7 April 1814; Capt., 8th Foot, 24 Dec. 1817; Major, 34th Foot, 24 June 1824. *Battles, sieges and campaigns*: '27th Sept. 1810 – Busaco... 16th May 1811, Albuera... Octr. 1811, Arrozo de Molinas... 19th May 1812, Almaraz... 25th June 1813, Vittoria... 5th & 7th July 1813, Maya... May 1811, Siege of Badajoz... In the campaigns of 1809, 1810, 1811, 1812 & 1813 in the Peninsula.' *Wounds received in action*: '25th June 1813, Vittoria, wounded in the head. 7th July 1813, Maya, in the Pyrenees, wounded severely in the left leg – Received a years Pay.' *Service abroad*: 'June 1809 to Novr. 1813, Peninsula. Feby. 1818 to 24th Augt. 1824, Mediterranean.' *Family*: Married Elizabeth Massy, 14 Nov. 1829, Chester. No children by 1830. [PRO: WO 25/786 f159]. Slightly wounded, Vittoria, 21 June 1813 (2nd Battn.) [*London Gazette*]. Severely wounded, 'in Action with the Enemy', 4–8 July 1813 (2nd Battn.) [*London Gazette*]. MGS. *Bell, Rough Notes*, p. 74.

BALL, William Robert, Ensign, 68th Foot: *1829 Statement of Service for Retired Officers*: Aged eighteen on his first appointment. Ensign, 68th Foot, 14 May 1812; Lt., 68th Foot, 26 Aug. 1813. 'Not sure what time it was I exchanged in the 71st Regt. as my commission is at

the agent.' *Where serving when wounded*: 'At the Battle of Vittoria in Spain 21st June 1813.' Details of pension: 'Received a Pension for three years' commencing 21 June 1813. *Family*: Married in Sydney, Cape Breton, 5 Nov. 1820. One child in 1829. *Where generally resident during last five years*: 'Sydney, Cape Breton.' [PRO: WO 25/750 f64].

BALVAIRD, William, Capt./Major, 95th Foot: Lt., 78th Foot, 17 April 1804; Capt., Army, 16 May 1805; Capt., 95th Foot, 15 Aug. 1805. Severely wounded, storming of Badajoz, 6 April 1812 (1st Battn.) [*London Gazette*]. Bvt. Major, 22 Nov. 1813; Major, 95th Foot, 21 July 1814. Gold Medal. MGS. *Simmons*, pp. 204, 232 [wounded, Badajoz].

BARAILLER, Joseph, Lt., 71st Foot; Capt., 23rd Portuguese Line: Lt., 71st Foot, 7 Feb. 1808. In Portuguese Service June 1812 to April 1814. *Challis, Portuguese Army*, p. 52 ['Capt. 23 Line... Wd. Salamanca 22 July '12']. Wounded, Waterloo.

BARCKHAUSEN, Augustin, Ensign, 24th Foot; Lt., 6th Caçadores: Ensign, 24th Foot, 10 Dec. 1812. Served in Portuguese Service Feb. 1813 to April 1814. *Challis, Portuguese Army*, p. 52 ['Lt. 6 Caçad... Wd. Pyrenees, 30 July '13'].

+BARCLAY, Robert, Lt. Col., 52nd Foot: Lt. Col., 52nd Foot, 29 May 1806. Slightly wounded, Busaco, 27 Sept. 1810 [*London Gazette*]. Died, reportedly of wounds, May 1811. *Hay*, pp. 18–19 ['we arrived and reported ourselves at the headquarters of the 52nd Light Infantry, two evenings after the battle of Busaco ... several of the officers had been killed and wounded in the late engagements; amongst the latter was my father's old friend, Colonel Berkeley [sic], who, notwithstanding his own misfortune, had not forgotten me – a young lad, soon to come under his protection. He had, before his removal to the rear, left particular instructions ... to see that I was placed in the company of an officer who would look after a youngster... Poor Colonel Berkeley died of his wounds after his arrival in England.']. *Moorsom*, p. 101 [Retreat to Corunna: 'The present [1859] Major-General Diggle, quoting this time of distress, writes: "I should have fallen into the hands of the French, had not Colonel Barclay sent his horse to the rear for me, being unable from weakness to fetch up my lee-way." ']. *Simmons*, p. 115. *Leach*, pp. 154, 160.

BARCLAY, Robert, Capt., 71st Foot: Capt., Army, 6 Feb. 1806; Capt., 71st Foot, 13 March 1806. Severely wounded, the Nive, 13 Dec. 1813 (1st Battn.) [*London Gazette*].

BARING, George von, Capt., 1st Light Battn. K.G.L.: Capt., 1st Light Battn. K.G.L., 10 Nov. 1803. Slightly wounded, Albuera, 16 May 1811, while serving as ADC to General Alten [*London Gazette*]. Served in Peninsula 1808–14. Waterloo. MGS. *Beamish*, vol. II, p. 566.

+BARKER, John, Ensign, 48th Foot: Ensign, 48th Foot, 15 June 1811. Killed, storming of Badajoz, 6 April 1812 [*London Gazette*]. *Register of dead officers*: Return dated 25 April 1812 [PRO: WO 25/2965].

+BARKER, Thomas, Adjutant/Lt., 4th Foot: Adjutant, 4th Foot, 7 June 1805; Lt., 48th Foot, 27 July 1808. Killed, Vittoria, 21 June 1813, while serving as Adjutant (1st Battn.) [*London Gazette*].

+BARLOW, Frederick, Lt.Col., 61st Foot: Lt. Col., 61st Foot, 8 May 1806. Killed, Salamanca, 22 July 1812 (1st Battn.) [*London Gazette*]. *Register of officers' effects*: Married. Effects totalled £195. 9s. 5d. [PRO: WO 25/2964]. Return dated 25 July 1812 [PRO: WO 25/2965]. Obituary, *The Gentleman's Magazine*, Nov. 1812, 493 ['July 22. At the battle of Salamanca, Lieut.-col. Barlow. The Prince Regent, in addition to the usual pension, has settled 250£. per annum on his widow.'].

BARLOW, George Ulrick, Lt., 52nd Foot: Born 8 Oct. 1791. Lt., Army, 4 May 1809. Lt., 52nd Foot, 17 Aug. 1809. Severely wounded, storming of Badajoz, 6 April 1812 [*London Gazette*]. Severely wounded, Nivelle, 10 Nov. 1813 (1st Battn.) [*London Gazette*]. Capt., 52nd Foot, 30 Dec. 1813. Temporary pension of fifty pounds per annum, commencing 11 Nov. 1814, 'for a wound' received in the Pyrenees, 1813 [*1818 Pension Return*, pp. 14–15]. Waterloo. Capt., 4th Dragoons, 5 April 1821. Died in India, 1824.

BARNARD, Andrew Francis., Lt. Col., 95th Foot: Born at Fahan, County Donegal, in 1773. Lt. Col., Army, 28 Jan. 1808. Lt. Col., 95th Foot, 29 March 1810. Severely wounded, Barossa, 5 March 1811 (3rd Battn.) [*London Gazette*]. Mentioned in Graham's Barossa dispatch, 6 March 1811 ['Lieutenant-Colonel Barnard's flank battalion formed on the left... Lieutenant-Colonel Barnard (twice wounded) and the Officers of his flank battalion, executed the duty of skirmishing in advance with the enemy in a masterful manner'] [*London Gazette*, 25 March 1811]. Mentioned in Wellington's Ciudad Rodrigo dispatch, 20 Jan. 1812 ['I particularly request your Lordship's attention to the conduct of ... Lieutenant-Colonel Barnard of the 95th'] [*London Gazette*]. Mentioned in Wellington's Badajoz dispatch, 6 April 1812 ['In consequence of the absence, on account of sickness, of Major-General Vandeleur and Colonel Beckwith, Lieutenant-Colonel Barnard commanded the light division in the assault, and distinguished himself, not less by his personal gallantry in its execution.'] [*London Gazette*]. Severely wounded, Nivelle, 10 Nov. 1813 ('Lieutenant-Colonel Andrew F. Barnard, (Colonel)') (1st Battn.) [*London Gazette*]. Mentioned in Wellington's Nivelle dispatch ['I am concerned to add, that Colonel Barnard, of the 95th, has been severely, though I hope not, dangerously wounded'] [*London Gazette*, 25 Nov. 1813]. Aide-de-Camp to His Royal Highness the Prince Regent, *1814 Army List*. Gold Medal. Wounded, Waterloo. Was the commandant of the British division occupying Paris after the capitulation. He died as Lt.-Gov. of the Royal Hospital Chelsea, 17 Jan. 1855. Brett-James mentions a typescript copy of Barnard's Peninsular War letters, edited by Capt. M. C. Spurrier (1966), in the Ministry of Defence Library, London. *Simmons*, p. 192 ['Aug. 21st [1811]. Colonel Barnard joined the Division with four companies of the 3rd Battalion Rifles; these men had been with the army stationed in Cadiz. They were placed in Colonel Beckwith's Brigade.'], pp. 321–2 [wounded, Nivelle, 10 Nov. 1813: 'Colonel Barnard, towards the end of this day's fighting, received a musket-ball in his right breast, which made him tumble from his horse; he fell upon the hilt of his sword and bruised his side very much. I was near him when he fell, and put my hand into his bosom to feel where the ball entered. I found his lungs had been wounded, as blood in quantities and air issued from the wound; some blood was passing from his mouth also. He in a most collected manner said, "Do you think I am dying? Did you ever see a man so wounded recover?" I observed, "Your wound is a very bad one, but there have been instances of men recovering from such wounds, and your pulse does not indicate immediate dissolu-

tion." "Thank you," he exclaimed, "you give me hopes. If any man can recover, I know I shall." He was immediately bled very largely and taken by four men in a blanket to a farmhouse ... having a good constitution he speedily recovered.']. *Leach*, p. 262 ['During the siege and storming of Badajoz, the command of [the Light Division] had devolved on Lieutenant-Colonel Barnard, of the 95th Rifle Corps, who conducted it most ably and gallantly through all its arduous duties. If a thorough knowledge of their profession, calm, cool courage, great presence of mind in action, frank and gentlemanly manners, and the total absence of what may be termed teazing those under their command, are qualities to be appreciated, I do say ... that both Baron Alten and Colonel Barnard merited the high estimation in which they were held.'], p. 348 [Nivelle, 10 Nov. 1813: 'The commandant of our battalion, Colonel Barnard, was shot through the body whilst leading it against the entrenchments. His instant death was expected, the ball having entered his breast and lodged under the shoulder-blade. No man would have been more universally or deservedly regretted, had the ball proved fatal; and his recovery caused the most lively satisfaction and pleasure to all under his command.'], p. 391 [Waterloo: 'Sir Andrew Barnard received a wound early in the action, and the command of our battalion then devolved on Lieutenant-Colonel Cameron.']. *Harris*, p. 170. *Kincaid, Adventures*, pp. 115–16 [Trying to restore order amongst the troops following the Storming of Ciudad Rodrigo: 'the voice of Sir Thomas Picton, with the power of twenty trumpets, began to proclaim damnation to every body, while Colonel Barnard, Colonel Cameron, and some other active officers, were carrying it into effect with a strong hand; for, seizing the broken barrels of muskets, which were lying about in great abundance, they belaboured every fellow, most unmercifully, about the head who attempted either to load or fire, and finally succeeded in reducing them to order. In the midst of the scuffle, however, three of the houses in the square were set on fire; and the confusion was such that nothing could be done to save them; but, by the extraordinary exertions of Colonel Barnard, during the whole of the night, the flames were prevented from communicating to the adjoining buildings.'], pp. 130, 133 [Storming of Badajoz: 'I was near Colonel Barnard after midnight, when he received repeated messages, from Lord Wellington, to withdraw from the breach ... but ... it went against his gallant soul to order a retreat while yet a chance remained; but after heeding repeated attempts himself, he saw that it was hopeless.'], pp. 137, 215, 243, 252, 266 [Nivelle, 10 Nov. 1813: 'Towards the end of the action, Colonel Barnard was struck with a musket-ball, which carried him clean off his horse. The enemy, seeing that they had shot an officer of rank, very maliciously kept up a heavy firing on the spot, while we were carrying him under the brow of the hill. The ball having passed through the lungs, he was spitting blood, and, at the moment, had every appearance of being in a dying state; but, to our joy and surprise, he, that day month, rode up to the battalion, when it was in action, near Bayonne; and, I need not add, that he was received with three hearty cheers.'], pp. 315, 323, 325, 329, 337 [Wounded, Waterloo]. *Brett-James*, pp. 118, 147 ['Beckwith of the 95th Rifles assures his friend William Napier: "Our mode of life is exactly the same as when you left us. I ride about all the morning in pursuit of nothing. Barnard smokes segars [sic] until

the very atmosphere between the Coa and the Agueda is impregnated with the 'herbiforous herb' as Doctor Morgan says." ']. *Bruce*, p. 158 [Letter from William Napier to his wife, dated 'France, Camp 1 league in front of San Pe' following Nivelle: 'Barnard, for whom I had a great admiration, and whom I really loved, is also wounded in such a manner that I expect to hear of his death every moment.'].

+**BARNARD, Charles Levyns, Capt., 38th Foot**: Capt., Army, 20 Dec. 1806; Capt., 38th Foot, 18 June 1807. Severely wounded, storming of Badajoz, 6 April 1812 (2nd Battn.) [*London Gazette*]. Half pay, 1st Dragoon Guards, 1814; Capt., 2nd Dragoons, 2 Feb. 1815. Killed at Waterloo as Captain in the 2nd (or Royal North British) Regiment of Dragoons.

BARNES, Edward, Major-General: Lt. Col., Army, 1 Jan. 1800; Lt. Col., 46th Foot, 23 April 1807. Severely wounded, the Nive, 13 Dec. 1813 [*London Gazette*]. Slightly wounded, Aire, 2 March 1814 [*London Gazette*]. Gold Medal. Waterloo. Described as 'our fire eating adjutant-general' during the Waterloo campaign [*Dalton*, p. 29]. Born 1776. Died, London, 19 March 1838.

BARNES, James Stevenson, Lt. Col., 1st Foot: Lt. Col., Army, 6 Nov. 1806; Lt. Col., 1st Foot, 21 April 1808. Severely wounded, Salamanca, 22 July 1812 [*London Gazette*]. Gold Medal. Bvt. Col., 1st Foot, 4 June 1814.

BARNETT, John Henry, Capt., 40th Foot: Lt., 48th Foot, 28 Sept. 1804; Capt., 40th Foot, 13 June 1811. Severely wounded, Vittoria, 10 Nov. 1813 (1st Battn.) [*London Gazette*]. Slightly wounded, Toulouse, 10 April 1814 (1st Battn.) [*London Gazette*]. Wounded, Waterloo. *Lawrence*, p. 230 [Waterloo]. 'Burnett' in Army List.

BARNEY, George, 1st Lt., Royal Engineers: 1st Lt., Royal Engineers, 24 June 1809. Severely wounded, storming of San Sebastian, 31 Aug. 1813 [*London Gazette*].

BARRA, Joseph, Lt., 16th Light Dragoons: *1829 Statement of Service for Retired Officers*: Aged seventeen on his first Appointment in the Army. Cornet and Adjutant, 16th Light Dragoons, 27 Aug. 1807; Lt., 16th Light Dragoons, 4 Oct. 1808; Capt., 16th Light Dragoons, 27 July 1815. *Where serving when wounded*: 'Vittoria in Spain. One years pay as Lieut. granted in lieu of pension for wounds, 1814.' *Whether desirous of service*: 'Not particularly so while attached to the King's Regiment of Cheshire Yeomanry Cavalry as Adjutant unless it is the wish of his Majesty.' *Family*: Married in Blatchington, Sussex, 12 June 1804. No children in 1829. *Where generally resident during last five years*: 'Knitsford, County of Chester.' [PRO: WO 25/750 f165]. Slightly wounded, Vittoria, 21 June 1813 [*London Gazette*]. Waterloo. Died, 13 July 1839.

BARRETT, Edward, Lt., 15th Light Dragoons: Lt., 15th Light Dragoons, 28 June 1810. Severely wounded, 'in Action with the Enemy', 26 March 1814 [*London Gazette*]. Waterloo. Half-pay, 25 May 1816.

BARRETT, James, 2nd Lt., Royal Marines: *1829 Statement of Service*: Born in Minsterworth, Gloucestershire, 21 Aug. 1792. Aged eighteen on his 'first Entrance into the Army.' 2nd Lt., Royal Marines, Jan. 1810; Ensign, 24th Foot, 7 Nov. 1811; Lt., 12th Foot, 30 Oct. 1812; 'Reduced to Half Pay on the Reduction of the 2d Battalion in the year 1818'; Lt., 89th Foot, 3 July 1826; Capt., 86th Foot, 8 Feb. 1827; Major, 86th Foot, 31 Dec. 1830. *Battles, sieges and campaigns*: 'in Spain on Retreat from Burgos'. *Wounds received in action*: 'Shot through the left thigh at an attack upon Palomos in Catalonia on 12 Dec. 1810, for which he has received no pension.' [PRO: WO 25/802 f13]. Unfortunately Barrett failed to complete any more of the form. Note: when wounded he was serving in the Marines.

BARRINGTON, Charles, Lt., 7th Foot: Lt., 7th Foot, 9 April 1809. Slightly wounded in 'an Affair with the Enemy near Aldea de Ponte', 27 Sept. 1811 [*London Gazette*]. Severely wounded, storming of Badajoz, 6 April 1812 [*London Gazette*]. Capt., 60th Foot, 14 Aug. 1813.

BARRON, Peter Stone, Lt., 34th Foot: Lt., 34th Foot, 8 Sept. 1807. Severely wounded, Pyrenees, 25 July 1813 (2nd Battn.) [*London Gazette*].

BARRY, Francis M., Lt., 83rd Foot: Ensign, 83rd Foot, 22 Dec. 1808. Lt., 83rd Foot, 29 May 1811. Slightly wounded, storming of Badajoz, 6 April 1812 [*London Gazette*]. Slightly wounded, Nivelle, 10 Nov. 1813 (2nd Battn.) [*London Gazette*].

BARRY, Joseph, Lt., 87th Foot: Lt., 87th Foot, 30 Nov. 1807. Severely wounded, 'in Action with the Enemy', 24 Feb. 1814 (2nd Battn.) [*London Gazette*].

BARTLET, Spry, Ensign, 61st Foot: *1829 Statement of Service for Retired Officers*: Aged nineteen on his first appointment. Ensign, 61st Foot, 25 Oct. 1812; Lt., 61st Foot, 4 Nov. 1816; Half-pay, 89th Foot, 9 Jan. 1817. 'Incapable [of service] from wounds.' *Where serving when wounded*: 'Toulouse.' *Details of pension*: Fifty Pounds, commencing 11 April 1815. *Family*: Married in Salisbury, 31 July 1818. No children in 1829. *Where generally resident during last five years*: 'France & Jersey.' [PRO: WO 25/750 f37]. Severely wounded, Toulouse, 10

April 1814 ('Bartlett') (1st Battn.) [*London Gazette*]. *1818 Pension Return*, pp. 16–17.

BARTLETT, William Benjamin, Ensign, 57th Foot: Ensign, 57th Foot, 8 Aug. 1811. Severely wounded, the Nive, 13 Dec. 1813 (1st Battn.) [*London Gazette*].

BARTON, James Campbell, Lt., 87th Foot: *1829 Statement of Service for Retired Officers*: Aged seventeen on his first appointment. Ensign, 87th Foot, 6 Aug. 1807; Lt., 87th Foot, 18 Feb. 1808; Capt., 87th Foot, 8 Dec. 1814; Half-pay, by reduction of 2nd Battn., 25 March 1817. *Where serving when wounded*: 'Battle of Barrosa.' *Details of pension*: 100 Pounds commencing 25 June 'Incapable of active service having lost materially the use of my right leg by contraction of the thigh in consequence of wounds received in the Service.' *Family*: Married in Guernsey, 12 July 1815. No children in 1829. *Nature of civil employment*: 'Deputy Barrack Master at Malta.' *Where generally resident during last five years*: 'Guernsey & Malta.' [PRO: WO 25/750 f83]. Severely wounded, Barossa, 5 March 1811 (2nd Battn.) [*London Gazette*]. *1818 Pension Return*, pp. 20–21.

+BARTON, Richard, Lt., 36th Foot: Lt., 36th Foot, 1 March 1808. Killed, Salamanca, 22 July 1812 (1st Battn.) [*London Gazette*]. Return dated 25 July 1812 ('Burton') [PRO: WO 25/2965].

+BASSETT, John, Volunteer, 23rd Foot: Killed, Pyrenees, 28 July 1813 ('Barnett') (1st Battn.) [*London Gazette*]. *Challis, Index*, p. 93 ['John Bassett'].

BATEMAN, Robert, Capt., 5th Foot: *1829 Statement of Service*: 'Born in Calcutta, E.I. [East Indies], 24th August 1786. Ensign, 5th Foot, 4th March 1804. Lieutenant, 5th Foot, 3d July 1805.

Captain, 5th Foot, 5th March 1807. Half Pay, Nov. 1818, Ill health from Wound. Paymaster, 79th Regt., 25 April 1824. Capt. & Bt. Major, 77th Regt., 16th Feby. 1829.' Note added: 'Major, unattd., 13 Aug. 1830.' *Battles, sieges and campaigns*: 'Lieut. 5th Regt. Sailed with the Expedition under command of Lord Cathcart, was shipwrecked & made Prisoner... Sailed with the Expedition under comd. Genl. Crawford to Cape of Good Hope. St Helena. Monte Video. Was at the Siege of Buenos Ayres... Captain 5th Regt. Sailed with the Expedition under comd. Genl. Crawford to Portugal. Joined the Regiment at Salamanca, marched to Madrid, retreated and was at Vittoria. After the recovery of my Wound, joined the Regt. at Orthes. Embkd. at Bordeaux for N. America, was present at the Siege of Platsburgh. Returned to Europe & remained with the Army of occupation in France.' *Wounds received in action*: 'Battle of Vittoria 21st June 1813, received Pension, which ceased on the 24th June 1832, at the rate of £100 pr. annum.' *Service abroad*: '1805 to 1806, Holland. June 1806 to 1807, South America. 1809 to 1810, Portugal. 1811 to 1813, Spain. 1814 to 1818, North America, France. 1824 to 15 Feby. 1829, N. America.' *Family*: He married the same woman twice! He first married Roze Chospeid, 6 Dec. 1816, in France, in a Roman Catholic ceremony. Their first child, Clara, was born 6 Jan. 1817; their second, Harriet, was born in March 1818. The couple was remarried, 5 April 1818, in a Church of England ceremony in Dover. They had a further five children by 1830. [PRO: WO 25/800 f99]. Severely wounded, Vittoria, 21 June 1813 (1st Battn.) [*London Gazette*]. MGS.

BATEMAN, Samuel/Daniel, Ensign, 50th Foot: Ensign, 50th Foot, 16 Dec. 1812. Severely wounded, Pyrenees, 25 July 1813 (1st Battn.) [*London Gazette*]. Not at Waterloo. *Challis, Index*, p. 146 ['Samuel (or Daniel) Bateman'].

BATTERSBY, George, Capt., 23rd Light Dragoons: Lt., 23rd Light Dragoons, 18 May 1809; Capt., 23rd Light Dragoons, 2 Sept. 1813. Severely wounded, sortie from Bayonne, 10 April 1814, while serving as ADC to Major-General Howard [*London Gazette*]. Born 20 April 1788. Killed, Waterloo, as Capt., 1st Dragoon Guards.

BAXTER, George, Lt., 57th Foot: Ensign, 57th Foot, 9 July 1803; Lt., 57th Foot, 5 Oct. 1804. Slightly wounded, Albuera, 16 May 1811 [*London Gazette*].

BAXTER, William, Volunteer, 57th Foot: Severely wounded, the Nive, 13 Dec. 1813 ('Volunteer W. Baxter') (1st Battn.) [*London Gazette*]. Ensign, 57th Foot, 9 Feb. 1814.

BAYLEE, Edmund, Ensign, 58th Foot: Ensign, 58th Foot, 16 Nov. 1809. Slightly wounded, siege of Burgos, 16 Oct. 1812 ('Baylie') [*London Gazette*]. Severely wounded, Pyrenees, 2 Aug. 1813 ('Baylie') (2nd Battn.) [*London Gazette*].

BAYLEE, Henry Gough, Ensign, 87th Foot: *1829 Statement of Service for Retired Officers*: Aged '17 years 2 months' on his first appointment in the Army. Ensign, 87th Foot, 8 Oct. 1812; Lt., 87th Foot, 9 June 1814; Capt., 87th Foot, 10 May 1827; Half-pay 24 Aug. 1827, 'as 11th Captain on arrival from India.' 'Desirous of Service particularly in the 87th Regt.' *Where serving when wounded*: 'Wounded in Spain at the Battle of the Nivelle 10th Nov. 1813 and recd. one years pay as Ensign.' *Family*: Married in Limerick, 20 May 1828. *Where generally resident during last five years*: 'With 87th Regt. till its arrival in England. Limerick till May 1828.

Tenby till Ocbr. 1828. Ilfracoomb.' [PRO: WO 25/750 f161].

BAYLY, Henry, Lt., 51st Foot: Ensign, 51st Foot, 30 April 1807. Lt., 51st Foot, 6 May 1809. Severely wounded, 'in the Operations of the Army', 31 Aug. 1813 ('Bayley') [*London Gazette*]. One hundred pounds per annum pension, commencing 1 Sept. 1814, for 'loss of an arm' at Lazaca, 1813 [*1818 Pension Return*, pp. 14–15]. MGS. *Wheeler*, p. 143–4 [near Lezaca, 31 Aug. 1813: 'General English had ridden to the front to become better acquainted with the ground, when by some unforseen accident he became separated from his men and would have been made prisoner but for the little band who at a great disadvantage rescued him. Captain Frederick saw the danger his general was in, ordered his buglar to sound the charge, the sound was answered by three cheers, and off his company went accompanied by Lieutenant Bayly's Company and one company of the C. B. Regiment. In a moment they were mixed with the enemy and down the hill they went together, pel mel, into the wood. The General was rescued... Our loss was severe... Lieutenants Bayley [sic] (severely left arm amputated)'].

BAYNES, Henry, 2nd Capt., Royal Artillery: 2nd Capt., Royal Artillery, 1 Feb. 1808. Slightly wounded, Talavera, 28 July 1809 [*London Gazette*]. Gold Medal. Wounded, Waterloo, while serving as Brigade-Major. Died, Guernsey, 15 July 1844.

BAYNES, Thomas, Lt., 39th Foot: Lt., 39th Foot, 20 July 1809. Slightly wounded, Vittoria, 21 June 1813 ('Baines') (1st Battn.) [*London Gazette*]. ADC to Major-General Lambert at Waterloo. Died, Brussels, 27 May 1847.

BAXTER, William, Ensign, 53rd Foot: *1829 Statement of Service*:

Born 3 Dec. 1787, Shrewsbury. Aged twenty-three on his first entrance into the Army. Ensign, 53rd Foot, 9 May 1811; Lt. 10 June 1813; Half Pay, 22nd Foot, 1816; Lt., 30th Foot, May 1825. *Battles, sieges and campaigns*: 'Present with 53rd Regt. in the Campaigns of Portugal & Spain 1811 & 1812, and present at the Siege of the Forts & Battle of Salamanca... Served in the South of France in 1814.' *Wounds received in action*: 'July 22nd 1812 wounded slightly at Salamanca. No compensation claimed.' *Service abroad*: 'July 1811 to Jany. 1813, Portugal and Spain. Feby. 1814 to July 1814, France. June 1825 to June 1829, East Indies.' Not married in 1830. [PRO: WO 25/790 f346]. MGS.

BEAMISH, George, Lt., 31st Foot: Ensign, 31st Foot, 21 Feb. 1805; Lt. 13 March 1806. Severely wounded, Talavera, 27 July 1809 [*London Gazette*]. Severely wounded, Talavera, 28 July 1809 [*London Gazette*]. Temporary pension of seventy pounds per annum, commencing 20 Aug. 1817, for 'Injury sustained on service, 1816' [*1818 Pension Return*, pp. 8–9]. MGS.

+BEARD, George, Lt., 39th Foot: Lt., 39th Foot, 14 June 1809. Killed, Albuera, 16 May 1811 (2nd Battn.) [*London Gazette*]. *Register of dead officers*: Return dated 25 May 1811 [PRO: WO 25/2965]. *Register of officers' effects*: Single. [PRO: WO 25/2963]. *Haythornthwaite, Die Hard*, p. 153 [Albuera: 'Lieutenant George Beard of the 39th, in Abercrombie's brigade, was wounded in the wrist early in the action but declined his captain's advice to retire for treatment; remaining with his company, this "brave young officer" was killed by the bursting of a shell.' Quoting *The Gentleman's Magazine*, 1811, I, p. 679].

BEARDSLEY, Samuel Lt., 51st Foot: Lt., 51st Foot, 20 Aug. 1806.

Severely wounded, siege of Badajoz, 6–11 June 1811 [*London Gazette*]. Capt., 51st Foot, 16 Sept. 1813. Wounded, Waterloo. *Wheeler*, p. 65 [Wounded, Badajoz, 9 June 1811], p. 204 [Wounded, Waterloo].

+BEAUFOY, John Henry, Lt., 7th Foot: Lt., 7th Foot, 17 Dec. 1807. Killed, Talavera, 28 July 1809 [*London Gazette*].

BECK, Adolphus von der, Major, 1st Line Battn. K.G.L.; Lt. Col., 2nd Line Battn. K.G.L.: Major, 1st Line Battn. K.G.L., 2 July 1805. Slightly wounded, Fuentes de Onoro, 5 May 1811 [*London Gazette*]. Lt. Col., 1st Line Battn. K.G.L., 1 Jan. 1812; Lt. Col., 2nd Line Batt. K.G.L., 8 Sept. 1813. Slightly wounded, sortie from Bayonne, 14 April 1814 [*London Gazette*]. Gold Medal. *Beamish*, p. 653 ['Placed upon half-pay, 25th May 1815, at Celle, in Han.'].

BECKETT, Richard, Lt. and Capt., Coldstream Guards: Lt. and Capt., Coldstream Guards, 16 July 1801. Killed, Talavera, 28 July 1809, while serving as Brigade Major to the Brigade of Guards [*London Gazette*]. Obituary, *The Gentleman's Magazine*, Aug. 1809, p. 780 ['Captain Walker, of the 3d Dragon Guards [sic], and Captain Beckett, Brigade-Major in the Coldstream Guards, killed in the battle of Talavera, were both natives of Leeds. The former was the fourth son of William Walker, esq. of Killingbeck-hall, and the latter was one of the sons of John Beckett, esq. of Meanwood, an Alderman of Leeds.']. *Brotherton*, pp. 11–12 [Egypt, 1801: 'When part of the army moved to the west of Alexandria, we had to embark in flat-bottomed boats on a lake. Beckett (afterwards killed at Talavera), was a very tall man – six feet two or three, I think. We were shelled by the enemy, and one shell fell in the boat, took off the legs of two men, and sunk it. The lake was very shallow, so much so that Beckett stalked along, walking with his colour in his hand, with the water just up to his chin... Beckett, who was a delightful, good-natured fellow, stuck to me and assisted me all he could, but shot and shell fell thick around and many men suffered from them and were drowned... It is singular that Beckett met with nearly a similar adventure on the landing in Egypt, two months before, and then had to swim for it, with the colours in his hand.']. *Haythornthwaite, Armies of Wellington*, p. 238, [quoting from a manuscript account of the battle of Talavera by an unidentified sergeant of the 1/2nd Foot Guards: 'Lines of running fire half a mile in length were frequent & fatal to many a Soldier ... lying weltering in their gore with the devouring element approaching & death most horrid staring them in the face! Thus perished many & among the rest our Major of Brigade, one of the most gallant & at the same time useful Officers in his Majesty's service when in the act of rallying the Brigade after retiring in disorder, he was knocked off his horse & fell a victim to the flames before assistance could be given.'].

BECKWITH, Robert, 1st Lt., 95th Foot: 1st Lt., 95th Foot, 3 Jan. 1810. Wounded, during 'several Affairs with the French Army' (at Redinha), 12 March 1811 [*London Gazette*]. *Simmons*, pp. 76, 141 [wounded, Redinha, 12 March 1811].

BECKWITH, Thomas Sidney, Lt. Col., 95th Foot: Lt. Col., 95th Foot, 20 Jan. 1803. Mentioned in Wellington's dispatch for Barba del Puerco, 19 April 1810 [*London Gazette*]. Slightly wounded during 'several affairs with the French Army', 18 March–7 April 1811 [*London Gazette*]. Slightly wounded at Sabugal, 3 April 1811, though not included in the casualty

returns. Mentioned in Wellington's Barba del Puerco dispatch ['I am sorry to say that Lieutenant Mercer of the 95th, and three men were killed, and ten were wounded in this affair; which was highly creditable to Colonel Beckwith, and displayed the gallantry and discipline of the officers and troops under his command.'] [*London Gazette*]. Gold Medal. Born 1772, Major-General 4 June 1814, Lieutenant-General 1830, died in India 1831. K.C.B. Son of Major-General John Beckwith who had led the 20th in their celebrated charge at Minden. Joined the 95th (then the Experimental Corps of Riflemen) 1800 and was instrumental in formulating light infantry and rifle tactics. His brother was General Sir George Beckwith (1753–1823) and their nephew Major-General John Charles Beckwith (1789–1862) who lost a leg as AQMG at Waterloo, and who also served in the 95th in the Peninsula, as brigade-major in the Light Division. *Du Cane*, p. 752. *Simmons*, pp. 6, 27, 54–5, 63 [Barba del Puerco, 19 March 1810: 'Our gallant colonel received a musket ball through his cap.'] pp. 78, 82, 131, 135–6, 144, 160–2, [Sabugal, 3 April 1811: "wounded and his horse shot"], 165, 176–7, 192–3 [sick, returned to England, July/Aug. 1811]. *Leach*, pp. 109, 110–12 ['I have ever considered Lieutenant-Colonel Sidney Beckwith to have been better calculated to command of a regiment of light troops than most men who are to be found ... I must confess that the marching and counter-marching in a barrack-yard have but few charms for me. Colonel Beckwith was, indeed, the very reverse of such commanding-officers ... and I may safely say, that he held those matters very cheap when compared with other things of so much greater importance, which daily presented themselves. Far be it from me to insinuate that Colonel Beckwith did not feel the vast and imperious necessity of discipline, or that any iota of regimental detail was not performed to the letter; but he was always averse to tease and torment the old soldier with more than a certain quantum of drill.'], pp. 120-2 ['we frequently got up foot-races ... played matches at foot-ball, and rackets, ... and sometimes turned a pig loose, with his tail greased, when he was pursued by the soldiers... Our gallant commander, Colonel Beckwith, was ever the first to encourage those meetings, considering no doubt, and very justly, that to divert and to amuse his men, and to allow them every possible indulgence compatible with the discipline of the battalion, whilst an interval of quiet permitted it, was the surest way to make the soldiers follow him cheerfully through fire and water, when the day of trial came; for they well knew that he was the last man on earth who would give them unnecessary trouble, or, on the other hand, would spare either man or officer, when the good of the service demanded their utmost exertions.'], pp. 127, 129 [Barba del Puerco, 19 March 1810: 'Colonel Beckwith received a shot through his cap, whilst in the act of rolling a huge piece of rock down on the fugitives, by way of accelerating their retreat. Lord Wellington sent a handsome letter of thanks to Colonel Beckwith, expressive of his approbation of the conduct of the regiment.'], pp. 154, 160, 204, 206-8 [Sabugal: 'Colonel Beckwith's forehead was grazed by a bullet, and his horse was shot under him. That cool courage which can look calmly at danger, and adopt measures to meet it at the instant, under the most critical and appalling circumstances, Colonel Beckwith possessed in an eminent degree.'], pp. 219, 230 ['... Colonel Beckwith's absence in England, from ill health']. *Harris*, pp. 46, 163. *Kincaid, Adventures*, pp. 65, 68-9 [Sabugal, 3 April 1811: '... the

conduct of our gallant fellows, led on by Sir Sidney Beckwith, was so truly heroic, that, incredible as it may seem, we had the best of the fight throughout... Lord Wellington's despatch on this occasion did ample justice to Sir Sidney Beckwith and his brave brigade. Never were troops more judiciously or more gallantly led. Never was a leader more devotedly followed.'], pp. 141-2 [11 April 1812, near Ciudad Rodrigo: 'Sir Sidney Beckwith, one of the fathers of the rifles, was, at this time, obliged to proceed to England for the recovery of health, and did not again return to the Peninsula. In his departure, that army lost one of the ablest of its out-post generals. Few officers knew so well how to make the most of a small force. His courage, coupled with his thorough knowledge of the soldier's character, was of that cool intrepid kind, that would, at any time, convert a routed rabble into an orderly effective force. A better officer, probably, never led a brigade into the field!']. *Kincaid, Random Shots*, pp. 17, 51-2, 54-5 [Barba del Puerco, 19 March 1811: 'The colonel [Beckwith], while urging the fight, observed a Frenchman within a yard or two, taking deliberate aim at his head. Stooping suddenly down and picking up a stone, he immediately shyed it at him, calling him at the same time a "scoundrel, to get out of that". It so far distracted the fellow's attention that while the gallant Beckwith's cap was blown to atoms, the head remained untouched.'], pp. 102, 153, 164-9 [Sabugal, 3 April 1811: 'Beckwith was an actor of the immortal Nelson's principle – that if a commander is in doubt he never can do wrong in placing himself alongside the enemy... Beckwith himself was the life and soul of the fray ... and his calm, clear, commanding voice was distinctly heard amid the roar of battle, and cheerfully obeyed. He had but single companies to oppose to the enemy's battalions; but, strange as it may appear, I saw him twice lead successful charges with but two companies of the 43d, against an advancing mass of the enemy... Beckwith's manner of command on those occasions was nothing more than a familiar sort of conversation with the soldier ... seeing the necessity for immediate retreat, he called out, "Now, my lads, we'll just go back a little if you please." On hearing which every man began to run, when he shouted again, "No, no, I don't mean that – we are in no hurry – we'll just walk quietly back, and you can give them a shot as you go along." ... and regulating their movements by his, as he rode quietly back in the midst of them, conversing aloud in a cheerful encouraging manner... A musket-ball had, in the meantime, shaved his forehead, and the blood was streaming down his countenance, which added not a little to the exciting interest of his appearance. As soon as we had got a little way up the face of our hill, he called out, "Now, my men, this will do – let us shew them our teeth again!" This was obeyed as steadily as if the words halt, front, had been given on parade, and our line was instantly in battle array, while Beckwith, shaking his fist in the faces of the advancing foe, called out to them, "Now, you rascals, come on here if you dare!"... as soon as they came near enough, another dash by Beckwith, at the head of the 43d, gave them the coup de grace.'], p. 172 [Sabugal: 'Immediately after the action, we drew up behind an old cow-shed, which Lord Wellington occupied for a short time, while it poured torrents of rain. Sir William Erskine, with some of his horsemen, joined us there, and I heard him say to the commander-in-chief that he claimed no merit for the victory, as it belonged alone to Sidney Beckwith! I believe his lordship wanted no conjurer to tell him so, and did ample justice to the combatants, by stating in his dispatch that "this was one of the most glorious actions that British troops were ever engaged in." '].

BEDELL, Walter Death, 1st Lt., 95th Foot: *1829 Statement of Service for Retired Officers*: Aged twenty-eight on his first appointment in the Army. 'To the best of my recollection I received a Lieutcy. in the 3rd or Prince of Wales's Regt. Royal Lancashire Militia in 1803 & was promoted to 95th or Rifle Corps in 1807 and exchanged to Half Pay in 1815.' [Army List gives: 2nd Lt., 95th Foot, 19 March 1807; 1st Lt., 95th Foot, 11 Aug. 1808]. *Why placed on half-pay*: 'Without meaning it offensively I should say from unfair treatment and ill health &c &c.' 'My age and rank will not admit of active service.' *Where serving when wounded*: 'Storming of Ciudad Rodrigo.' *Family*: Married in London in 1799. He had three children by 1829. *Where generally resident during last five years*: 'Mistleg, Essex.' [PRO: WO 25/750 f224]. Severely wounded, storming of Ciudad Rodrigo, 19 Jan. 1813 (2nd Battn.) [*London Gazette*]. MGS. *Simmons*, p. 223 [wounded, Ciudad Rodrigo]. *Harris*, p. 181 ['Lieutenant Bardell'].

BEERE, Henry, Ensign, 30th Foot: Ensign, 30th Foot, 28 Feb. 1812. Slightly wounded, during 'movements of the Army' [Retreat from Burgos: Villa Muriel], 25 Oct. 1812 (2nd Battn.) [*London Gazette*]. Lt., 30th Foot, 7 Sept. 1814. Killed, Waterloo. Brother of Hercules Beere.

+BEERE, Hercules, Ensign, 61st Foot: Ensign, 61st Foot, 15 Aug. 1809. Severely wounded, Salamanca, 22 July 1812 [*London Gazette*]. *Register of officers' effects*: 'Killed in Action, 22 July 1812'. Single. 'Effects delivered to his Brother, Ensign Beere, 30th Foot.' 1st Battn. [PRO: WO 25/

2964]. *Register of dead officers*: 'Killed in action, 22 July'. Return dated 25 July 1812 [PRO: WO 25/2965].

BEHNE, Lewis, Lt., 2nd Light Battn. K.G.L.: *1829 Statement of Service for Retired Officers*: Aged '17 years 6 months' on his first appointment in the Army. Ensign, 2nd Light Battn. K.G.L., 5 Jan. 1810; Lt., 2nd Light Battn. K.G.L., 1 July 1811; Capt., 2nd Light Battn. K.G.L., 28 Aug. 1815; Major, Half-pay, 17 Oct. 1826. *Where serving when wounded*: 'With the Army in France near Bajonne and St Jean de Luz.' *Details of pension*: One hundred pounds commencing 3 July 817. Family: Married in 'Morse, Hannover', 12 Oct. 1818. He had one child by 1829. *Title and nature of civil employment*: 'Districts Commissary for the 2nd Battalion 4th Regiment of the Line Hanoverian Army, that is the Business to recruit and dismiss the Soldiers of the above named Battalion.' *Where generally resident during the last five years*: 'Wallersleben, Kingdom of Hannover.' [PRO: WO 25/750 f248]. Severely wounded, Nivelle, 10 Nov. 1813 [*London Gazette*]. Severely wounded, sortie from Bayonne, 14 April 1814 ('Lewis Behue') [*London Gazette*]. Served in Peninsula 1811–14. MGS. *Beamish*, vol. II, p. 567 ['severely wounded, 10th Nov. 1813, at Urugne; severely wounded, 14th April 1814, before Bayonne.'].

BEHRENS, Henry, Cornet, 1st Light Dragoons K.G.L.: Cornet, 1st Light Dragoons K.G.L., 25 July 1811. Slightly wounded 'during the advance from Fuente Guinaldo to Salamanca', 16–18 June 1812 ('Bohrens') [*London Gazette*]. Slightly wounded, Salamanca, 22 July 1812 ('Behrends') [*London Gazette*]. Lt., 1st Hussars K.G.L., 19 Nov. 1813. Served in Peninsula 1812–14. Waterloo. MGS. *Beamish*, vol. II, p. 550 ['Slightly wounded,

16th June, 1812, near Salamanca; slightly wounded, 22d July, 1812, at Salamanca.'].

+BELL, Alexander, Lt., 45th Foot: Ensign, 45th Foot, 26 Oct. 1809. Listed under 'Alterations while Printing' in 1812 Army List ['45F. Alexander Bell. Lieutenant. Hinde, res. 5 Dec. 1811']. Killed in the storming of Ciudad Rodrigo, 19 Jan. 1812 (1st Battn.) [*London Gazette*]. *Register of dead officers*: Return dated 25 Jan. 1812 [PRO: WO 25/2965]. Obituary, *The Gentleman's Magazine*, March 1812, p. 297 ['Jan. 19. In the breach of Ciudad Rodrigo, in his 20th year, Lieut. Alex. Bell, of the 45th regt. The glorious circumstances attending his fate, together with the recollection that he has fallen in the service of his country, leaving behind him an unsullied reputation as a gentleman and a soldier, are great alleviations to grief, and soften even the keen feelings of parental affliction in lamenting his irreparable loss.'].

BELL, John, Lt., 52nd Foot: Ensign, 52nd Foot, 15 Aug. 1805; Lt., 52nd Foot, 1 Oct. 1807. Wounded, Vimeiro, 21 Aug. 1808 [*London Gazette*]. Gold Medal. MGS.

BELL, Thomas, Capt., 48th Foot: *1829 Statement of Service*: 'Born Dunse, Berwickshire, 8 December 1782. Aged Seventeen on his first Entrance into the Army. Ensign, 48th Regt., 13th Novr. 1799. Lieutenant, 48th Regt., 1801. Captain, 48th Regt., 13th Septr. 1805 [Army List gives 12 Sept.]. [Major, Army, 26 Aug. 1813]. Major, 48th, March 1824. Lieut. Colonel, 48th, 20th Sepr. 1827.' *Battles, sieges and campaigns*: 'Blockade and Siege of Savallette Island of Malta... Duro 12th May 1809. Albuhera 16th May 1811. Aldea-de-Ponte 27th Septr. 1811. Siege of Rodrigo. Siege and Assault of Badajos. Battle of Salamanca. Pyrenees from 25th July to

31st July 1813. 10th October 10th Novr. 1813 Nivelle. 12th January near Bayonne. Battle of Orthes and Tolouse.' *Distinguished conduct*: 'Received the Rank of Major for Commanding 48th Regt. 28th July 1813.' *Wounds received in action*: 'Wounded at Albuhera & Badajos. One years pay received.' *Titles, honorary distinctions and medals*: 'Commander of the Military Order of the Bath and Four Medals Military Cross for Commanding 48th Regiment at Salamanca, Pyrenees, Nivelle and Orthes.' *Service abroad*: '1800 to 1803, Malta. 1803 to March 1805, England. 1805 to 1806, Gibraltar. 1806 to 1809, with the 2nd Battn. in Ireland. 1809 to 1814, Portugal, Spain, and France. 1814 to 1817, Ireland. 1817 to 1824, New South Wales & Van Diemans Land. 1824 to December 1829, Madras Presidency.' *Family*: Married Mary Caroline Bourne, in Hints, Staffordshire, on 19 Jan. 1806. They had six children between 1806 and 1820. [PRO: WO 25/794 f155]. Slightly wounded at Albuera, 16 May 1811 [*London Gazette*]. Slightly wounded, storming of Badajos, 6 April 1812 [*London Gazette*]. Gold Medal. MGS.

BELLEVILLE, Charles de, Major, 2nd Line Batt. K.G.L.: Major, 2nd Line Battn. K.G.L., 16 June 1804. Slightly wounded, Talavera, 28 July 1809 ('Bellaville') [*London Gazette*]. Lt. Col., 2nd Line Battn. K.G.L., 7 Dec. 1809. Gold Medal. 'Belville' in Army List. Served in Peninsula 1808–11. *Beamish*, vol. II, p. 607 [Died 'at Hameln 30th April, 1826.'].

BELLI, John Henry, Capt., 16th Light Dragoons: Capt., Army, 11 July 1805; Capt., 16th Light Dragoons, 29 Jan. 1807; Bvt. Major, 16th Light Dragoons, 7 May 1812. Reported 'missing', Fuentes de Onoro, 5 May 1811 [*London Gazette*]. Waterloo. Major, 16th Light Dragoons, 10 Oct. 1816; Lt. Col., Army, 21 Jan. 1819. Half-Pay,

unattached list, 1826. MGS. *Cocks*, p. 34 [July 1809: sent to hospital at Elvas], p. 64 [Villa de Puerco, 11 July 1810], pp. 103, 108 [Fuentes d'Onoro, 5 May 1811: 'Belli charged first. He was overpowered; a French officer cut him down and took him but was then killed himself.'], p. 110 ['I experienced mortification the day before, when Belli came up and took command of the squadron I had always had last year and I was removed to the command of another. This squadron under Belli's command was early and severely engaged while the one I commanded scarcely suffered at all and did not charge. Belli himself was cut down by a French officer and taken.'].

+BELLINGHAM, Henry T., Capt., 4th Foot: Capt., 4th Foot, 14 Feb. 1811. Killed, storming of Badajoz, 6 April 1812 (1st Battn.) [*London Gazette*]. Return dated 25 April 1812 [PRO: WO 25/2965].

BELSON, George John, 1st Lt., Royal Artillery: 1st Lt., Royal Artillery, 6 July 1805. Severely wounded, Salamanca, 18 July 1812 [*London Gazette*]. Served in A Troop R.H.A. MGS. *Webber*, p. 80 [2 Oct. 1812: 'Belson, who was wounded by a dragoon's sabre...'].

BELSTEAD, Henry, Lt., 85th Foot: Lt., 85th Foot, 9 June 1813. Slightly wounded, the Nive, 10 Dec. 1813 ('H. Belsted') (2nd Battn.) [*London Gazette*].

BELTON, Robert, Lt., 61st Foot: *1829 Statement of Service for Retired Officers*: Aged 'seventeen and half' on first appointment to the Army. Ensign, 61st Foot, 11 May 1807; Lt., 61st Foot, 9 May 1809 [Army List gives 11 May]; 'exchanged to half Pay 8th August 1816.' 'Desirous to Serve, being nearly at the top of the Lieutenants of the 61st Regt. when placed on Half Pay nothing but extreme ill health prevented my remaining on full pay. My health is now restored.' *Where serving when wounded*: 'Wounded severely by a Musket ball passing through the Wrist of my Right Arm in Action with the Enemy at St Pie in France on the 10th Novr. 1813. Which Wound remained open and small portions of bone coming from it for 14 years after.' 'Served during three Campaigns in the Peninsula in consequence of which my health suffered severely for some years afterwards.' *Family*: Married in 'Newry County-Down, Ireland' on 29 April 1815. He had five children by 1829. *Where generally resident during last five years*: 'Pea-Field near Mountrath, Queens County, Ireland.' [PRO: WO 25/750 f200]. Severely wounded, Nivelle, 10 Nov. 1813 (1st Battn.) [*London Gazette*].

BENCE, Henry Bence, Lt., 16th Light Dragoons: Lt., 16th Light Dragoons, 20 Oct. 1808. Slightly wounded, Talavera, 28 July 1809 [*London Gazette*]. Capt., 60th Foot, 15 Aug. 1811. MGS.

BENNET, Henry, Lt., 6th Foot: *1829 Statement of Service*: Born 20 Jan. 1789, Overton, Chester. Aged 15 years and 11 months on his first entrance into the Army. Ensign, 6th Foot, 22 Dec. 1804; Lt. 1 March 1807; Capt. 22 June 1820. *Battles, sieges and campaigns*: 'Roleia, 17 Aug. 1808. Vimiera, 21 August 1808... Corunna, 16 January 1809... Expedition to Walcheren, 1809... Vittoria, 21 June 1813. Pyrenees, July 25-26-27 and 28th 1813. Attack on the Heights of Echallar, 2nd Aug. 1813. Nivelle, 10th November 1813. Nive, December 9-10-11-12 & 13th 1813. Orthes, February 27th 1814... Affair near Fort Blaze on the River Garonne, April 1814... Siege of Fort Erie Upper Canada, October 1814.' *Wounds received in action*: 'Wounded in the Attack on the Heights of Echallar 2nd August 1813. Never Applied for any Grant

of Pay.' *Service abroad*: '12th March 1808 to 8th June 1808, Gibraltar;... 9th August 1808 to 18th January 1809, Portugal & Spain;... 9th August 1809 to 24th December 1809, Walcheren;... 15th November 1812 to 4th May 1814, Portugal, Spain & France;... 2nd July 1814 to 30th June 1815, Canada;... 10th August 1815 to 30th October 1818, Holland & France; 4th November 1821 to 1st December 1824, Cape of Good Hope;... 25th May 1828 to 31st December 1830, Poonah & Bombay.' Not married by 1829. [PRO: WO 25/786 f11].

BENNETT, Alexander Maxwell, Capt., 5th Foot: Capt., 5th Foot, 8 May 1809. Mentioned in Wellington's dispatch, 27 March 1812 [Storming of Fort Picurina, Badajoz, 26 March 1812: 'Major-General Kempt particularly mentions ... Captain Bennett, his Aide-de-Camp'] [*London Gazette*]. Severely wounded, storming of Badajoz, 6 April 1812, serving on the Staff as ADC to Major-General Kempt [*London Gazette*]. Bvt. Major, 5th Foot, 12 April 1814. Temporary pension of one hundred pounds per annum, commencing 7 April 1813, 'for wounds' received at Badajoz, 1812 [*1818 Pension Return*, pp. 4-5].

+BENNETT, Joseph, Lt., 28th Foot: Lt., 28th Foot, 29 March 1805. 'Dangerously wounded, since dead', Barossa, 5 March 1811 (1st Battn.) [*London Gazette*]. *Blakeney*, pp. 204-5 [Barossa: 'Poor Bennet [sic] was shot through the head whilst gallantly cheering on the men through an incessant shower of grape and musketry. On seeing him fall I darted to the spot and too plainly discovered the cause. It grieved me that I could not stop for an instant with my dearest friend and first companion of my youth... I could only cast a mournful look at Bennet, poor fellow. It may be that our friendship conduced to his fate.

A vacancy occurred in the light company a few days before the action, and I saw that Bennet would willingly fill it up; but it was an established rule, at least in the regiment, that a senior lieutenant could never be put over the head of a junior already serving in the light company. Perceiving that his delicacy prevented his asking, I prevailed upon Colonel Belsen to appoint him, although my senior. With the battalion two officers only were wounded... In the flank companies no officer escaped, and poor Bennet fell, to rise no more. But after all man must have a final place to rest, and the appropriate bed of a soldier is the battlefield; and it will be some consolation to his friends to know that never did a soldier fall more gallantly or on a day more glorious, and never was an officer more highly esteemed when living, nor, when he fell, more sincerely regretted by the whole of his brother officers. He was wounded about noon on the 5th; the brain continually oozed through the wound; yet strange to say he continued breathing until the morning of the 7th, when he calmly expired with a gentle sigh. A marble slab was subsequently erected in the chapel of the Government House at Gibraltar, to the memory of Bennet and Lieutenant Light of the Grenadiers, by their affectionate brother officers who unfeignedly regretted the early fall of the two gallant youths.'].
Haythornthwaite, Die Hard, p. 138 ['two of the wounded officers died of their injuries: Lieutenant John Light of the 28th's grenadiers, and Blakeney's friend Bennett, who never regained consciousness and died on the morning of 7 March.'].

BENNETT, L. H., Capt., 95th Foot: Capt., 95th Foot, 7 May 1805. *Blakeney*, pp. 67–8 [Retreat to Corunna, 4 Jan. 1809: 'I was aroused by my hearing my name, and recognised an old acquaintance, Captain Bennet, of the 95th. He rode slowly and was much bent over his saddle-bow, suffering severely from a wound received the previous evening at Calcabellos. He bore up stoutly, notwithstanding his sufferings, which were manifold. His mind was afflicted with thoughts of his family; he dreaded falling into the hands of the advancing foe, and the bodily pain which he was suffering may be imagined, as he had ridden upwards of five-and-twenty miles with a musket ball in his groin, during a freezing night through a country covered with snow. Poor Bennet! the only assistance which I could then afford was to give him a silk pocket-handkerchief, which I placed between his wounded side and the saddle; yet little as this assistance was, it added to his ease, which he more gratefully acknowledged than the trifling incident merited.'].

+BENNETT, Thomas, Ensign, 47th Foot: Killed, storming of San Sebastian, 31 Aug. 1813 (2nd Battn.) [*London Gazette*].

+BENNING, Conway, Capt., 66th Foot: Capt., 66th Foot, 8 Jan. 1807. Slightly wounded, passage of the Douro, 12 May 1809 ('Binning') (2nd Battn.) [*London Gazette*]. Killed, Albuera, 16 May 1811 (2nd Battn.) [*London Gazette*]. *Register of dead officers*: Return dated 25 May 1811 [PRO: WO 25/2965]. *Register of officers' effects*: Single. Effects totalled £55.1s.7d, 'To his Brother in law.' [PRO: WO 25/2964].

BENSON, George Thomas, Ensign, 3rd Foot: *1829 Statement of service*: Born 1791, Ardpatrick County, Louth, Ireland. Aged nineteen on first appointment to the Army. Ensign, 3rd Foot, 16 Dec. 1811; Lt. 25 Aug. 1813; Half Pay 17 July 1817; Lt., 11th Foot, 8 April 1825. *Battles, sieges and campaigns*: 'Vittoria, Nivelle, Nive, Pyrenees, Pamplona, Orthes, and Toulouse... Platsburg, in North America.' *Wounds received in action*: 'Slightly Wounded in the Arm at the Pyrenees. – At Platsburg in North America, severely Wounded in the Right Breast by a Rifle Ball. Received One Year's pay as Lieutenant.' *Service abroad*: 'July 1812 to June 1815, Spain & France. July 1815 to July 1816, North America. August 1816 to July 1817, Flanders & France.' *Family*: Married I. E. McGhee, 30 March 1818, Castletown, Isle of Man. One child by 1830. [PRO: WO 25/787 f32] MGS.

+BENT, James, Capt., 20th Foot: Capt., Army, 27 Aug. 1802; Capt., 20th Foot, 31 March 1803. Slightly wounded, Pyrenees, 25 July 1813 [*London Gazette*]. Major, 20th Foot, 23 Sept. 1813. Killed, Orthes, 27 Feb. 1813 [*London Gazette*].

BENTINCK, Charles Anthony Frederick, Ensign, Coldstream Guards: Born 4 March 1792. Ensign, Coldstream Guards, 16 Nov. 1808. Slightly wounded, Barossa, 5 March 1811 [*London Gazette*]. Adjutant, Coldstream Guards, 4 June 1812; Lt. and Capt., Coldstream Guards, 24 Sept. 1812. Waterloo. MGS. Half-pay, 25 April 1848. Lt. Gen. and Col.-in-Chf. 12th Foot in 1857. Died 28 Oct. 1864. *Royal Military Calendar*, vol. V, p. 324 ['Major Chas. Anthy. Ferdinand Bentinck']. 'Cha. Au. Fred. Bentinck' in Army List.

BENWELL, Thomas, Volunteer, 4th Foot: *1829 Statement of Service for Retired Officers*: Aged twenty-six on his first appointment to the Army. 'Volunteer to Portugal', 4th Foot, 1812; Ensign, 4th Foot, 21 Sept. 1813; Lt., 4th Foot, 17 March 1815; Half-pay, 4th Foot, 25 Feb. 1816, 'by Reduction on the Peace establishment.' 'Lt Benwell still feels the effects of his severe wound before New Orleans and he can not consider himself efficient for any great exertion and therefore he is not desirous of Service.' *Where*

serving when wounded*: 'Seige of St Sebastian, and before New Orleans twice.' *Details of pension*: Fifty Pounds per annum commencing in 1816. *Family*: Married in St Mary's Church, Lambeth, Surrey, 3 April 1820. He had two children by 1829. *Where generally resident during last five years*: 'Kennington Nr London.' [PRO: WO 25/750 f202]. Slightly wounded, storming of San Sebastian, 31 Aug. 1813 ('Volunteer Bennett') (1st Battn.) [*London Gazette*]. Temporary pension of fifty pounds per annum, 'for wounds' received in New Orleans, 1815, commencing 9 Jan. 1816 [*1818 Pension Return*, pp. 4–5]. Pension 'for wounds' received at New Orleans [*1818 Pension Return*, pp. 4–5]. MGS.

+BERESFORD, John, Lt., 88th Foot: Lt. 28 June 1810. Severely wounded, storming of Ciudad Rodrigo, 19 Jan. 1812 [*London Gazette*]. *Register of officers' effects*: Died of wounds, 28 Jan. 1812, Ciudad Rodrigo. Single. 'Balances supposed to have been paid to ... friends or lodged with the Agents.' [PRO: WO 25/2964]. *Register of dead officers*: Return dated 25 Feb. 1812 [PRO: WO 25/2965]. Mentioned in Wellington's Ciudad Rodrigo dispatch, 20 Jan. 1812 ['It is but justice also to the 3d division to report, that the men who performed the sap belonged to the 45th, 74th, and 88th Regiments, under the command of ... Lieutenant Beresford, of the 88th ... and they distinguished themselves not less in the storm of the place, than they had in the performance of their laborious duty during the siege.'] [*London Gazette*, 5 Feb. 1812].

BERESFORD, William Carr, Lt-General: Col., 88th Foot, 9 Feb. 1807; Major-General, Army, 25 April 1808. Marshal Commanding the Portuguese Army. Thanked by Parliament for his actions at Albuera. Major-General, 1 Jan.

1812. Wounded, 'severely, but not dangerously', Salamanca, 22 July 1812 [*London Gazette*]. Created Baron Beresford of Albuera, 3 May 1814. Gold Medal. MGS. *Challis, Portuguese Army*, p. 52. For biographical details, see *Royal Military Calendar*, vol. II, pp. 236–48.

BERGER, Augustus von, Major, 7th Line Battn. K.G.L.: Major, 7th Line Battn. 18 Jan. 1806. Slightly wounded, Talavera, 28 July 1809 [*London Gazette*]. Served in Peninsula 1808–9. Gold Medal. *Beamish*, vol. II, p. 651 ['Retired on an allowance of 5s. per day. 28th Sep. 1810, lieutenant-general, h.p. at Nienburg in Han.'].

+BERGMANN, George, Capt., 1st Light Dragoons/Hussars K.G.L.: Capt., 1st Light Dragoons K.G.L., 12 Dec. 1810. Severely wounded, El Bodon, 25 Sept. 1811 [*London Gazette*]. *Register of dead officers*: Died of wounds, 17 Oct. 1811. Return dated 25 Oct. 1811 [PRO: WO 25/2965]. Served in the Peninsula since 1809. *Beamish*, vol. II, p. 617.

+BERWICK, John, Capt., 44th Foot: Capt., 44th Foot, 16 Aug. 1805. Severely wounded, storming of Badajoz, 6 April 1812 (2nd Battn.) [*London Gazette*]. Killed, Salamanca, 22 July 1812 (2nd Battn.) [*London Gazette*]. *Register of dead officers*: Return dated 25 July 1812 [PRO: WO 25/2965].

BETHELL, J., Lt./Adjutant, 40th Foot: Adjutant, 40th Foot, 11 Sept. 1806; Lt., 40th Foot, 11 Feb. 1808. Severely wounded, Salamanca, 22 July 1812 ('Bethel') [*London Gazette*]. 'Date of Decease: 21 Oct. 1812'. Spain. Return dated 25 Nov. 1812. [PRO: WO 25/2965].

BEURMANN, Charles, Lt./Capt., 2nd Line Battn. K.G.L.: Lt., 2nd Line Battn. K.G.L., 12 Jan. 1806. Severely wounded, Talavera, 28 July 1809 ('Beuerman') [*London*

Gazette]. Capt., 2nd Line Battn. K.G.L., 18 Feb. 1813. Severely wounded, in an action near Tolosa, 25 June 1813 ('Beuerman') [*London Gazette*]. Variously 'Buerman', 'Beurmann' and 'Beuerman' in Army List. Served in Peninsula 1808–14. Waterloo. *Beamish*, vol. II, p. 576 [Died 'at Waltzen near Hoya, in Han. 26th Aug. 1817.'].

+BEVAN, Samuel, Capt., 92nd Foot: Lt., 92nd Foot, 9 July 1803. Wounded, Pyrenees, 25 July 1813 (Captain) (1st Battn.) [*London Gazette*]. Died of wounds, 21 Aug. 1813, Vittoria. Single. Effects totalled £19.12s.9d. [PRO: WO 25/2964]. Return dated Sept. 1813. [PRO: WO 25/2965].

BIERMON, Charles, Ensign, Duke of Brunswick Oels' Corps (Infantry): Ensign, Duke of Brunswick Corps (Infantry), 15 Oct. 1812. Severely wounded, Nivelle, 10 Nov. 1813 ('Ensign Charles Burman') [*London Gazette*]. Lt., Duke of Brunswick Oels' Corps, 11 Nov. 1813.

BIGGS, Thomas, Lt., 29th Foot: Lt., 29th Foot, 18 Jan. 1810. Severely wounded, Albuera, 16 May 1811 ('Brigg') [*London Gazette*].

+BIGNALL, Francis, Capt., 27th Foot: Lt., 27th Foot, 3 June 1805; Capt., 27th Foot, 14 Nov. 1811. Killed, Toulouse, 10 April 1814 (3rd Battn.) [*London Gazette*]. Mentioned in the 1830 Statement of Service of William Boyle ['At the Battle of Vitteria the evening of the 21 June 1813 Two Companies of the Regiment were ordered to the Front to act as light Infantry, when the Command devolved upon me in consequence of Captain Bignal [sic] not being able to proceed from Fatigue'] [*Public Records Office*: WO25–789–82].

BILLEB, Charles, Ensign, 2nd Line Battn. K.G.L.: Ensign, 2nd Line

Battn. K.G.L., 26 Aug. 1808 ('—Bilep'). Severely wounded, Talavera, 28 July 1809 ('Ensign Billeb') [*London Gazette*]. Lt., 2nd Line Battn. K.G.L., 17 March 1812. Served in Peninsula 1808–14. Waterloo. *Beamish*, vol. II, p. 577.

BINGHAM, George Ridout, Lt. Col., 53rd Foot: Lt. Col., 53rd Foot, 14 March 1805. Severely wounded, Salamanca, 22 July 1812 [*London Gazette*]. Mentioned in Wellington's Salamanca dispatch, 24 July 1812 [*London Gazette*]. Gold Medal. KCB.

+BIRCHALL, Hugh, Lt., 50th Foot: Lt., 50th Foot, 30 Dec. 1807. Killed, Pyrenees, 25 July 1813 (1st Battn.) [*London Gazette*]. 'Burchall' in *Challis, Index*, p. 146.

BIRD, Charles Elias, Lt., 5th Foot: Lt., Army, 3 Feb. 1805. Lt., 5th Foot, 18 July 1805. Slightly wounded, Vittoria, 21 June 1813 [*London Gazette*]. Severely wounded, Nivelle, 10 Nov. 1813 (1st Battn.) [*London Gazette*]. MGS.

BIRD, Henry, Capt., 5th Foot: Capt., 5th Foot, 10 Sept. 1802; Bvt. Major, 5th Foot, 1 Jan. 1805. Slightly wounded, Salamanca, 22 July 1812 ('Brevet Lieutenant-Colonel') (1st Battn.) [*London Gazette*].

+BIRMINGHAM, John, Major, 27th Foot: Major, 27th Foot, 30 April 1807. Wounded, 'since dead', during the repulse of a sortie from Badajoz, 10 May 1811 (3rd Battn.) [*London Gazette*]. Died of wounds, 11 May 1811. Return dated 25 May 1811 [PRO: WO 25/2965].

BIRMINGHAM, Robert, Lt., 29th Foot: Lt., Army, 28 July 1801; Lt., 29th Foot, 3 July 1802. Wounded, Rolica, 17 Aug. 1808 [*London Gazette*].

+BIRMINGHAM, Walter, Capt., 29th Foot: Lt. Col., 21st Portuguese Line: Lt., Army, 27 July 1801; Lt., 29th Foot, 2 July 1802. Recorded as 'missing', Rolica, 17 Aug. 1808 [*London Gazette*]. Capt., 29th Foot, 2 Sept. 1808. Killed, Toulouse, 10 April 1814, while serving as Lt. Col., 21st Portuguese Line [*London Gazette*]. Portuguese Service April 1810 to April 1814. Gold Medal. *Challis, Portuguese Army*, p. 52.

BISHOP, Peter, Capt., 40th Foot: Capt., 40th Foot, 12 March 1812. Severely wounded, Nivelle, 10 Nov. 1813 (1st Battn.) [*London Gazette*]. Waterloo.

+BLACHFORD, John, Lt,, 14th Light Dragoons: Cornet, 14th Light Dragoons, 4 Jan. 1809; Lt., 14th Light Dragoons, 14 Feb. 1810. Severely wounded, Coa, 24 July 1810 ('Blatchford') [*London Gazette*]. His death is recorded in 'Casualties since the last publication', *1815 Army List. Perrett*, p. 15 [quoting Brotherton: 'One of the officers under my immediate command, Cornet B–, was hit by a fragment of a shell in the posterior, and as he was rather a soft sort of fellow, I thought, at first, that he made too great a fuss about it, though he turned deadly pale. But he had good reason to complain, for the piece of shell had buried itself deep in his buttock, and caused his death.' No date given].

BLACHLEY, Henry, 1st Lt., Royal Artillery: 1st Lt., Royal Artillery, 18 Feb. 1805. Slightly wounded, sortie from Bayonne, 14 April 1814 ('Blackley ... Royal Horse Artillery') [*London Gazette*]. MGS ('Blatchley').

+BLACKALL, Andrew, Capt., 53rd Foot: Capt., 4th Ceylon Regt., 14 March 1810; Capt., 53rd Foot, 21 Nov. 1811. Severely wounded, Salamanca, 22 July 1812 [*London Gazette*]. *Register of dead officers*: Died, 'Peninsula, 28 Aug. 1812'. Return dated 25 Sept. 1812 [PRO:

WO 25/2965]. Obituary, *The Gentleman's Magazine*, Feb. 1813, p. 182 ['Lately... At Seville, of his wounds, Capt. Blackall of the 53d reg.'].

+BLACKWOOD, Robert, Lt., 52nd Foot: Lt., 52nd Foot, 20 July 1808. Severely wounded, storming of Badajoz, 6 April 1812 [*London Gazette*]. Capt., 69th Foot, 8 Nov. 1813. Killed, Waterloo. *Dalton*, pp. 175, 177 ['Bn. 13th July, 1788. Buried in the orchard at Hougomont.'].

BLAIR, Thomas Hunter, Capt., 91st Foot: *1829 Statement of Service*: Born in Edinburgh, 5 Oct. 1783. Aged eighteen on first appointment to the Army. Ensign, 72nd Foot, 24 July 1802; Half-pay, 13 Aug. 1804; Lt., 91st Foot, 14 Sept. 1804; Capt., 91st Foot, 28 March 1805; Bvt. Major, 91st Foot, 30 May 1811; Bvt. Lt. Col., 91st Foot, 18 June 1815; Major, 91st Foot, 8 Jan. 1818; Major, 87th Foot, 1 April 1819; Lt. Col., 87th Foot, 6 June 1825. *Battles, sieges and campaigns*: 'July 1808 apptd. by Duke of Wellington, Major of Brigade to B. Genl. Cataline Crawford, present at affair of Obidos 15th, Battle of Rolica 17th & Vimeira 21st of August. Again A.D.C. to Sir Hew Dalrymple when he commanded in Portugal. On Sir John Moore's succeeding to Command A.D.C. to late Earl of Hopetown. Present at Affair of Lugo 7th and Battle of Corunna 16th Jany. 1809. April 1809 returned to Portugal as Major of Brigade with Force under Lord Hill. Apptd. to M. Genl. Sir A. Cameron's Brigade, present at Capture of Oporto 12th and affair of Salamonde 16th May. Severely wounded at Talavera 27th and 28th July. Made prisoner in Hospital. End of war in 1814 got Brevet Rank of Major antedated to 30th of May 1811... End of 1815 ... embarked at Cork for New Orleans under M. Genl. Johnstone. Sailed and twice driven back by contrary winds. On peace with America transferred with same apptmt. to Flanders and joined Light Brigade under Major Genl. Sir Fred. Adam. Severely wounded at Waterloo... May 1819 accompanied Lt. Genl. Sir Charles Colville to Bombay as Military Secretary. Sept. 1825 resigned Staff – travelled overland to Calcutta to join Regt. ordered to Army in Ava under M. Genl. Sir Archd. Campbell. Apptd. Brigadier, Commanded Brigade at Capture of Melloon 18th Jany. 1826. At end of War charged with commd. of above 5000 Men of all Arms who retired by Land, and with the evacuation of line of operations 600 Miles deep. On reduction of Staff June 1826 assumed command of 87 Regt. and landed with it in England in June 1827. Have the honour to be the first commanding officer of Royal Irish Fusiliers, established for first time in British Army 10th July 1827.' *Wounds received in action*: 'Severely wounded at Talavera July 1809. Recd. 1 years Pay as Captain. Severely wounded at Waterloo June 1815. Recd. 1 years pay as Captain.' *Titles, honorary distinctions and medals*: 'Waterloo Medal'. *Service abroad*: '10 Sept. 1806 to 2 Feb. 1808, Gibraltar. July 1808 to 25 Jany. 1809, Peninsula. 5 April 1809 to 3 Aug. 1809, Peninsula. 11 Aug. 1809 to 5 July 1814, Peninsula 3 months, remainder in France as Prisoner of War. 23d March 1815 to 24 Nov. 1818, Flanders & France. 5 May 1819 to 23 June 1827, At Sea, East Indies, Ava.' *Family*: Married Eliza Norris, 13 July 1820, Bombay. They had no children by 1830. [PRO: WO 25/802 f76]. Severely wounded, Talavera, 28 July 1809, while serving as Brigade Major to General Cameron [*London Gazette*]. Waterloo. MGS.

+BLAKE, Andrew, Capt., 88th Foot: Lt., 88th Foot, 4 July 1794; Capt., 88th Foot, 25 June 1803. Killed, Talavera, 28 July 1809 [*London Gazette*].

+BLAKE, John, Lt., 16th Light Dragoons: Lt., 16th Light Dragoons, 26 Nov. 1806. Severely wounded, 'since dead', Fuentes de Onoro, 5 May 1811 [*London Gazette*]. Died of wounds, 7 May 1811. Return dated 25 May 1811 [PRO: WO 25/2965]. *Cocks*, p. 103 ['Lt Blake killed with six men'], p. 108 ['Belli charged first. He was overpowered; a French officer cut him down and took him, but was then killed himself. Lt. Blake was killed, Weyland run through the body'].

BLAKE, Robert, Lt., 3rd Foot: *1829 Statement of Service for Retired Officers*: Aged sixteen on his first appointment to the Army. Ensign, 3rd Foot, 30 April 1812; Lt., 3rd Foot, 23 Sept. 1813; Half-pay, Dec. 1816, 'Rendered incapable of Duty by my Wounds'; Lt., 9th Royal Veterans Battn., Jan. 1820. 'Incapable of service by the loss of my leg and other severe wounds.' *Where serving when wounded*: 'South of France.' *Details of pension*: '£70 increased to £100' commencing 25 Dec. 1814. *Where generally resident during last five years*: 'Sholisham, Norfolk.' [PRO: WO 25/750 f313]. Severely wounded, 'leg amputated', the Nive, 13 Dec. 1813 (1st Battn.) [*London Gazette*]. One hundred pounds per annum pension, for 'loss of a leg' at Bayonne, 1813, commencing 14 Dec. 1814 [*1818 Pension Return*, pp. 4–5]. MGS.

BLAKENEY, Edward, Major, 7th Foot: Major, 7th Foot, 24 March 1804; Lt. Col., Army, 25 April 1808. Severely wounded, Albuera, 16 May 1811 (2nd Battn.) [*London Gazette*]. Lt. Col., 7th Foot, 20 June 1811. Severely wounded, storming of Badajoz, 6 April 1812 (2nd Battn.) [*London Gazette*]. Mentioned in Wellington's Badajoz dispatch, 7 April 1812 ['I must likewise mention ... Lieutenant-Colonel Blakeney of the Royal Fusileers'] [*London Gazette*]. Gold Cross. K. C. B. MGS. Died, 1868. *Kincaid,*

Random Shots, p. 283 [Storming of Badajoz: 'The seventh Fusileers came gallantly on, headed by Major –, who, though a very little man, shouted with the lungs of a giant, for the way to be cleared, to "let the royal Fusileers advance!" Several of our officers assisted him in such a laudable undertaking; but in the mean time, a musket-ball found its way into some sensitive part, and sent the gallant major trundling heels over head among the loose stones, shouting to a less heroic tune – while his distinguished corps went determinedly on, but with no better success than those who had just preceeded them, for the thing was not to be done.'].

BLAKENEY, Robert, Lt., 28th Foot; Capt., 36th Foot: Lt., 28th Foot, 31 July 1805. Slightly wounded, Barossa, 5 March 1811 (1st Battn.) [*London Gazette*]. Capt., 36th Foot, 16 Jan. 1812. Severely wounded, Nivelle, 10 Nov. 1813 (1st Battn.) [*London Gazette*]. Temporary pension of one hundred pounds per annum, commencing 11 Nov. 1814, 'for a wound' received at Bayonne, 1813 [*1818 Pension Return*, pp. 10–11]. MGS. Died 1858. See Robert Blakeney, *A Boy in the Peninsular War; The Services, Adventures and Experiences of Robert Blakeney, Subaltern in the 28th Regiment. Blakeney*, pp. 190–1 [Wounded in the thigh, Barossa, March 1811], pp. 191–2 [Barossa: 'I now contrived to get eight or ten of the men together, principally 9th Grenadiers and 28th Light Infantry, to this little force I proposed charging a howitzer, which was pouring forth destruction immediately in our front... We now darted forward and were so fortunate as to capture the gun at the very moment when it was being reloaded. Two artillerymen were bayoneted; the others rode off on their mules. This was not a gun fallen into our hands – it was taken at the point of the bayonet; and however I may be criticised for saying it, I was the first person who placed a hand on the howitzer; and afterwards with some chalky earth I marked it "28th Regiment." '], p. 319 [Nivelle: 'I immediately placed my cap on the point of my sword and passing to the front of the colours gave the word, "Quick march. Charge!" We all rushed forward, excited by the old British cheer. But my personal advance was momentary; being struck by a shot which shattered both bones of my left leg, I came down.'], pp. 368–9 ['Thus the author of these Memoirs left the Army. He served at the seige and capture of Copenhagen; he was for twelve days in constant fight during Sir John Moore's retreat to Corunna, and at the end of this campaign he fought at the battle of Corunna in that division of the army who drove the whole of the enemy's cavalry off the field and turned his left wing; he was for more than twelve months at Tarifa continually engaged with the enemy's foraging detachments, and he was in both attacks on the strong post of Casa Vieja; he served in the ever memorable battle of Barossa in that flank battalion (to use the words of Lord Lynedoch) "which so greatly distinguished itself in the action"; he served in the action of Arroyo Molinos, and he was present at the siege and storming of Badajoz, where valour's self might stand appalled; he served through the Pyrenees as a volunteer, where more continued hard fighting occurred than elsewhere throughout the whole Peninsula campaigns, and finally fought in the great battle of the Nivelle, in which his leg was shattered. Innumerable skirmishes in which he was engaged and in which light companies are so frequently employed need not be mentioned. Of his conduct in these many actions the testimonials of commanding officers and colonels of regiments are a sufficient

witness. And yet after serving for a quarter of a century, with feelings harassed by neglect and petty vexations, he felt himself driven to retire, and that without the slightest badge or mark of military service save those indelibly imprinted by the searching weapons of the more considerate foe. Whether he has been dealt with as might be expected from a liberal, just and great nation is a question humbly submitted to his Sovereign and his country.']

BLAKISTON, John, Capt., East India Company Engineers: *1829 Statement of Service for Retired Officers*: Aged only nine on his first appointment in the Army. Ensign, 119th Foot, 29 March 1795; Half-pay, 71st Foot, 12 Nov. 1794; Lt., Full-pay, 87th Foot, 18 March 1813; Capt., 27th Foot, 30 Sept. 1813; Half-pay, 25 Feb. 1816, 'by reduction.' 'Captain Blakiston begs to remark that he entered the E. I. Company service in 1801, that he served in all the Wars in India till 1812, that he then gave up the service in consequence of ill health ... on his return to England ... he then served the last Campaigns under the Duke of Wellington in the Peninsula & South of France, that he served as an Engineer at the Siege of St Sebastian when he was wounded, that he was promoted to a Company in consequence and that he was reduced with the third Battalion of the 27th Regt.' 'Is desirous of Service in case of European War.' *Where serving when wounded*: 'St Sebastian.' No pension. *Family*: Married on 26 Sept. 1814. He had four children by 1829. *Where generally resident during last five years*: 'Lymington, Hants.' [PRO: WO 25/750 f338]. Slightly wounded, 'at the Siege of St Sebastian,' 7–27 July 1813 ('Engineers E. I. Comp. Service') [*London Gazette*]. Gold Medal. *Challis, Portuguese Army*, p. 52. Distinguished in India (as the engineer who blew down the gate at Vellore at the time of the mutiny there), and author of *Twelve Years' Military Adventure, in three Quarters of the Globe* (1829).

BLAQUIERE, John, Major, 83rd Foot: Major, 83rd Foot, 13 June 1811. Slightly wounded, Orthes, 27 Feb. 1813 (2nd Battn.) [*London Gazette*].

+BLASSIERE, Frederick Peter, Capt., 60th Foot: Capt., 60th Foot, 4 Dec. 1805. Severely wounded, 'in Action with the Enemy', 14 Feb. 1814 (5th Battn.) [*London Gazette*]. *Register of dead officers*: Died of wounds, 22 Feb. 1814. Return dated Feb. 1814. [PRO: WO 25/2965].

BLEMUR, Lt., Chasseurs Britanniques: Lt., Chasseurs Britanniques, 10 Sept. 1807. Slightly wounded, Fuentes de Onoro, 5 May 1811 ('Blemer') [*London Gazette*]. Slightly wounded, Pyrenees, 31 July 1813 ('Blemour') [*London Gazette*]. Slightly wounded, 'in the Operations of the Army', 31 Aug. 1813 ('Blemnr') [*London Gazette*].

BLOOD, John A., Volunteer, 59th Foot: *1829 Statement of Service*: Born at 'Grouse Lodge, Co. Clare', 27 Dec. 1797. Aged seventeen on first appointment to the Army. Volunteer, 59th Foot, 3 Nov. 1813; Ensign, 68th Foot, 3 March 1814; Lt., 7th Foot, 26 March 1825. *Battles, sieges and campaigns*: 'Nivelle 10th Novr. 1813. Biddar, 9th 10th & 11th Decr. 1813, volr.' *Wounds received in action*: 'Wounded in the right Leg at Nivelle 10th Novr. 1813.' *Service abroad*: '3d Novr. 1813 to 3d March 1814, Peninsula. 3d Mar. 1814 to 26th July 1814, Peninsula. 4th July 1818 to 16th July 1825, Canada. 14th Augt. 1829 to 15th Novr. 1829, Canada.' *Family*: Married Frederica Gamble, 5 July 1828, London. They had one child by 1830. [PRO: WO 25/798 f165]. Slightly wounded, Nivelle, 10 Nov. 1813 ('Volunteer

John A. Blood') (2nd Battn.) [*London Gazette*]. MGS.

BLOOD, Thomas, Ensign, 6th Foot: *1829 Statement of Service for Retired Officers*: Aged twenty on his first appointment in the Army. 'Born ... near Ennistymond, Co. Clare. I inlisted with a recruiting Party of the 43rd Lt. Regt. in Castlebar, Co. Mayo, in October, 1810. Joined the 2nd Battn. at Colchester, England, February 1811. Joined the 1st Bn. on the frontier of Portugal, in July 1811. Appointed full Corpal. February 1812, Sergeant in May following, Colour Sergeant in Augt. 1813. Appointed Ensign to the 6th Foot 18th Novr. 1813, and to Lieut. on the 8th Septr. 1814. Both appointments without Purchase, transferred to the 6th Royl. Vn. Battn. in May, 1816, appointed to the late 8th Royl. Vn. Battn. in decr. 1819, disbanded in March, 1821. Appointed to the late 7th Royl. Vn. Battn. in decem. 1821. Replaced on the retired list, owing to incapacity of serving from Wounds &c. May, 1824.' *Where serving when wounded*: 'France, Battle of Orthes, 27th February, 1814.' *Details of pension*: Seventy pounds per annum, commencing 28 Feb. 1815. *Family*: Married in Saint Ann's Church, Dublin, 4 Jan. 1819. No children by 1829. *Where generally resident during last five years*: 'Generally in Dublin and Cork.' [PRO: WO 25/750 f315]. Severely wounded, Orthes, 27 Feb. 1814 (1st Battn.) [*London Gazette*]. Temporary pension of £50 per annum, commencing 28 Feb. 1815, 'for wounds' received at Orthes, 1814 [*1818 Pension Return*, pp. 4–5]. MGS.

BLOOD, William, Ensign, 32nd Foot: Ensign, 32nd Foot, 6 Nov. 1811. Slightly wounded, Salamanca, 22 July 1812 [*London Gazette*].

+BLOOMFIELD, John C., 1st Lt., Royal Artillery: 1st Lt., Royal Artillery, 1 June 1806. *Register of*

dead officers: Killed, 'Messina, by a shot from the Enemy', 29 Oct. 1811. Return dated 25 Nov. 1811. [PRO: WO 25/2965].

+BLOXHAM, Robert, Lt., 83rd Foot: Lt., 83rd Foot, 16 Aug. 1810. Killed, Vittoria, 21 June 1813 ('Bloxam') (2nd Battn.) [*London Gazette*]. *Register of officers' effects*: Single. Effects totalled £11. 9s. 6d. [PRO: WO 25/2964]. *Register of dead officers*: Return dated 25 June 1813 [PRO: WO 25/2965].

+BLUMENBACH, Charles Edward, 1st Lt., K.G.L. Artillery: 1st Lt., K.G.L. Artillery, 9 Nov. 1807. Reported as 'Missing', Albuera, 16 May 1811 [*London Gazette*]. Killed, Toulouse, 10 April 1814 ('Edmund Blumenbach') [*London Gazette*]. Served in Peninsula from 1808. *Beamish*, vol. II, p. 612 ['Slightly wounded, 16th May 1811, at Albuera.'].

BLUMENHAGEN, Frederick Gottfried Ludewig, Ensign, 2nd Line Batt. K.G.L.: Ensign, 2nd Line Battn. K.G.L., 16 March 1809. Severely wounded, Talavera, 28 July 1809 [*London Gazette*]. Cornet, 1st Light Dragoons K.G.L., 26 Sept. 1811. Served in Peninsula 1809–14. Waterloo. *Beamish*, vol. II, p. 550 [Died 'at Hameln, in Han. 1st Jan. 1826'].

BLUNT, Francis Scawen, Ensign, 1st Foot Guards: Ensign, 1st Foot Guards, 26 Feb. 1807. Wounded, 'in the Army lately in Spain' (3rd Battn.) [*March 1809 Army List*, p. 105]. Fifty pounds per annum pension, 'for wounds' received at Corunna, 1809, commencing 25 Dec. 1811 [*1818 Pension Return*, pp. 2–3].

BOASE, John, Lt., 32nd Foot: *1829 Statement of Service for Retired Officers*: Aged twenty-three on first appointment to the Army. Ensign, 32nd Foot, 'Octr. or Novr. 1807'; Lt., 32nd Foot, June 1808 [Army List

gives 9 June]; Half-pay, 94th Foot, June 1817, 'On account of ill health occasioned by wounds.' *Whether desirous of service*: 'Desirous, but incapacitated for active duty, by the effects of wounds received in the Service.' *Where serving when wounded*: 'Salamanca, France, Quatre Bras.' *Details of pension*: Seventy pounds per annum, commencing 25 Dec. 1824. *Where generally resident during last five years*: 'Wadbridge, Cornwall.' [PRO: WO 25/751 f17]. Severely wounded, Salamanca, 22 July 1812 ('Bowes') [*London Gazette*]. Slightly wounded, Nivelle, 10 Nov. 1813 (1st Battn.) [*London Gazette*]. Waterloo. MGS.

+BOCK, Lewis von, Lt., 2nd Light Dragoons/Hussars K.G.L.: Lt., 2nd Light Dragoons, 1 Aug. 1810. Slightly wounded, Barossa, 5 March 1811 [*London Gazette*]. *Beamish*, vol. II, p. 618 ['Severely wounded, 5th March 1811, at Barossa; lost with his father, major-general [Eberhardt Otto George] von Bock, on board the Bellona transport, No. 342, on the 21st Jan. 1814 ... (on his way from Passages in Spain, to England, on the rocks of Tulbest near the coast of Pleubian, Arrondissement de Paimpol in France).'].

BODECKER, Rudolphus, Major, 1st Line Battn., K.G.L.: Major, 1st Line Battn. K.G.L., 7 July 1804. Severely wounded, Talavera, 28 July 1809 ('Bodeker') [*London Gazette*]. Gold Medal. Served in Peninsula 1808–14. *Beamish*, vol. II, p. 570 ['slightly wounded, 28th July, 1809, at Talavera... [Died] at Emden, 17th January, 1831, major general H. S. and col. commanding 10th regiment of infantry.'].

BOGGIE, Thomas, Ensign, 83rd Foot: Ensign, 83rd Foot, 17 March 1808. Severely wounded, Talavera, 28 July 1809 [*London Gazette*]. Lt., 83rd Foot, 16 Aug. 1809.

BOGLE, James, Capt., 94th Foot: *1829 Statement of Service*: Born in Glasgow, 23 Aug. 1778. Aged seventeen 'on his first Entrance into the Army.' Ensign, 94th Foot ('late Scotch Brigade'), 1 Sept. 1795. Lt., 94th Foot, 10 Feb. 1796. Capt. 94th Foot, 25 Dec. 1804. Half Pay, 25 Dec. 1818, 'By reduction of the late 94th Regt.' Capt., 94th Foot, 1 Dec. 1823. 'Note – In August 1813 I obtained for my Services in the Field a Majority by Brevet, and in July 1830 was included in the Brevet as Lieut. Colonel, on 3d August of the latter year I was placed on Half pay of Major Unattached.' *Battles, sieges and campaigns*: '28th February 1799 as Lieutenant while serving with detachment of my Regiment in La Sybelle Frigate, Capt. Cook, she engaged and Captured the French Frigate La Forte 52 guns in the Indian Sea. In 1803, while Lieut. with my Regt. as follows: At Ahmednagun 5 Sept., Lasselgum 7 Sept., Asserghun 21 Oct., [ ]aulna Augt., Argaum 29 Nov., Gavelghur 15 Dec. In 1804: At Chizligaum 20 Oct., Gulna Novr. As Captain with my Regt. In Spain & Portugal, 1811 – At Pombal 11 March, Redinia 12 March, At Fuentes d'Honore, 3d and 5th May 1811, as Captain with my Regt. At the Siege and Capture of Ciudad Rodrigo, 19 January 1812. At the Siege and Capture of Badajos, 6 April 1812, as Captain in Command of Regt. At the Battle of Salamanca, 22 July 1812, as Actg. Major. At the Battle of Vittoria, 21 June 1813, as Captain commg. Light Troops. At the Battles in the Pyrenees, 27, 28, and 29 July 1813, as Captain Commg. Light Troops. At the Battle of Nivelle, 10 Nov. 1813, as Bt. Major Commg. Light Troops. At the Battle of Orthes, 27 Feby. 1814, as Bt. Major Commg. Light Troops. In the Action at Vic Bigorre, 19 March 1814, as Bt. Major Commg. Light Troops. At the Battle of Toulouse, 10 April 1814, as Bt. Major Commg. Light Troops... In addition to the above I was frequently engaged in minor affairs and skirmishes. I was present at the Blockade of Cadiz and the Isle of Leon from March to September in 1810. During the years 1827, 1828 and 1829 I held the Command of the neutral ground at Gibraltar and had charge of the Cordon of health. In 1828 while an alarming fever prevailed eight Thousand of the Inhabitants were encamped and placed under my charge, and on leaving the Garrison in 1830 I received from General Sir George Don a letter of thanks and recommendation for my services.' *Distinguished conduct*: 'Frequently mentioned in Regimental and Brigade Orders for good conduct, though not in General Orders.' *Wounds received in action*: 'Slightly wounded at the taking of the La Forte Frigate by La Sybelle on 28th February 1799. Severely wounded at Redhinia in Portugal on 12th March 1811 while in Command of Light Troops. Received One years pay of my rank being that of Captain. No Pension.' *Titles, honorary distinctions and medals*: 'A Companion of the Order of the Bath, for General Services. A Medal for having commanded my Regiment at the Siege and Capture of Badajos in 1812. A Clasp for having Commanded a Division of Light troops at the Nivelle on 10 Nov. 1813.' *Service abroad*: '1795 to 1796, Gibraltar. 1796 to 1798, Cape of Good Hope. 1798 to 1808, in the East Indies and at Sea. 1809 to 1814, Peninsula. 1824 to 1830, Gibraltar.' *Family*: Married Margaret Maule Orr, 28 March 1815, in Edinburgh. They had nine children by 1834. [PRO: WO 25/803 f220; WO 25/803 f119].

BOGUE, John, Lt., 94th Foot: Lt., 94th Foot, 29 Sept. 1808. Severely wounded, during 'several Affairs with the French Army', 12 March 1811 ('Capt.') [*London Gazette*]. Slightly wounded, siege of Ciudad Rodrigo, 12 Jan. 1812 [*London*

Gazette]. Severely wounded, storming of Badajoz, 6 April 1812 [*London Gazette*]. Capt., 94th Foot, 17 Feb. 1814.

+BOLTON, Charles Edward, Ensign, 5th Foot: Ensign, 5th Foot, 2 Nov. 1809. Killed, Vittoria, 21 June 1813 (1st Battn.) [*London Gazette*]. Return dated 25 June 1812. [PRO: WO 25/2965].

+BOLTON, George, Ensign, 9th Foot: Ensign, 9th Foot, 22 Oct. 1812. Killed, the Nive, 10 Dec. 1813 ('Ensign George Bolton') (1st Battn.) [*London Gazette*]. Return dated Dec. 1813 [PRO: WO 25/2965].

+BOLTON, Robert Dawson, Capt., 18th Light Dragoons: Capt., 18th Light Dragoons, 4 March 1807. *Register of dead officers*: Died of wounds, 19 Dec. 1813. Return dated Dec. 1813. [PRO: WO 25/2965].

BOLTON, Samuel, Lt., 31st Foot: *1829 Statement of Service*: Born 1790, Sligo. Aged seventeen on his first Entrance into the Army. Ensign, 31st Foot, 6 Feb. 1807; Lt., 31st Foot, 6 April 1809; Adjutant, 31st Foot, 31 March 1813; Capt., 24 Dec. 1822. *Battles, sieges and campaigns*: 'Was present at the Battle of Talavera 27th and 28th July 1809. Busaco 27th September 1810. Albuhera 16th May 1811. Capture of General Gerands Division at Arouya-de-Molina 28th October 1811. Battle of Vittoria 21st June 1813. Pyrenees in July 1813. Nive 13th December 1813. Garris 15th Feb. 1814. Orthes 27th February 1814. Aire 2nd March 1814, and Toulouse 10th April 1814, as Adjutant of the 2nd Bn. 31st Foot from 31st March 1813 to 24th Oct. 1814, & as Lieutenant under the Command of the Duke of Wellington.' *Wounds received in action*: 'Slightly Wounded at the Battle of Albuhera on the 16th May 1811.' *Service abroad*: '1808 to 1814,

Peninsula. 1815 to 1818, Mediterranean. 1825 to 31st decr. 1829, Bengal.' *Family*: Married Elenor Raffington, 29 May 1819. They had four children by 1830. [PRO: WO 25/791 f7].

+BONE, Peter Joseph, Lt., 36th Foot: Lt., 36th Foot, 30 March 1809. Severely wounded, Toulouse, 10 April 1814 (1st Battn.) [*London Gazette*]. *Hurt*, p. 77 ['D.O.W.', Toulouse, Apl. 10.'].

BONTEIN, John Pitt, Lt., 11th Light Dragoons: Cornet, 11th Light Dragoons, 14 Feb. 1811; Lt., 11th Light Dragoons, 4 July 1811. Slightly wounded, Salamanca, 18 July 1812 [*London Gazette*]. Capt., 2nd Dragoons, 26 May 1814. Half-pay with the reduction of the regt. in 1814. MGS.

BOOKER, Gordon William Francis, 1st Lt./Capt., 23rd Foot: *1829 Statement of Service for Retired Officers*: 'Note – all my commissions were granted to me while I bore the name "Booker". I assumed the name of "Gregor" (By his Majesty's permission) in 1825.' Aged sixteen on first appointment to the Army. Ensign, 10th Foot, 23 May 1806; Lt., 23rd Foot, 14 May 1807; Capt., 23rd Foot, 17 June 1813. Half-pay, by reduction. Served eight and a half years on full-pay. *Where serving when wounded*: 'Spain. The pension was granted for wounds received at Albuera in 1811, and commenced in 1812.' *Details of pension*: Seventy pounds per annum, commencing 1812. *Family*: Married in St German's, Cornwall, 20 June 1814. Five children by 1829. *Where generally resident during last five years*: 'Trewarthwick ... Cornwall.' [PRO: WO 25/760 f170]. Severely wounded, Albuera, 16 May 1811 (1st Battn.) [*London Gazette*]. Slightly wounded, Pyrenees, 25 July 1813 (Captain) (1st Battn.) [*London Gazette*]. Pension of seventy pounds per annum, commencing 17 May 1812, 'for wounds' received at Albuera, 1811 [*1818 Pension Return*, pp. 6–7].

+**BOOTH, Charles, Lt., 52nd Foot**: Lt., 52nd Foot, 3 July 1805. Killed, storming of Badajoz, 6 April 1812 (2nd Battn.) [*London Gazette*]. Return dated 25 April 1812 [PRO: WO 25/2965].

BOOTH, George, Volunteer, 40th Foot: Severely wounded, Nivelle, 10 Nov. 1813 ('Volunteer') (1st Battn.) [*London Gazette*]. Ensign, 40th Foot, 6 Jan. 1814. Pension of fifty pounds per annum, commencing 11 Nov. 1814, 'for wounds' received in the Pyrenees, 1813 [*1818 Pension Return*]. MGS.

BOOTHBY, Charles, Capt., Royal Engineers: 1st Lt., Royal Engineers, 1 March 1805. Severely wounded, 'in the thigh', Talavera, 27 July 1809 ('Captain') [*London Gazette*]. Author of *A Prisoner of France. The Memoirs, Diary, and Correspondence of Charles Boothby, Captain, Royal Engineers, during his last Campaign* (1898), and *Under England's Flag from 1804 to 1809* (1900). *Rice Jones*, p. 8 ['Capt. Charles Boothby, a young Engineer officer of high promise, had the misfortune to lose his leg and his liberty at the Battle of Talavera, six months after landing, and remained a prisoner-of-war, in France, till July, 1810. His career as a soldier having thus been cut short, Boothby took Holy Orders, and was presented to the Crown living of Sutterton, in Lincolnshire, where he died in 1846.'], p. 11 ['Lisbon, April 5, 1809... On Sunday ... Lts ... Boothby ... arrived here from England'], pp. 19, 29, 37 ['Saturday, July 29th... We went to the Col.'s Quarters at Talavera and found poor Boothby with his leg badly wounded ever since the night of the 27th July; I went directly for Fitzpatrick, Surgeon to the Ordnance, and luckily found him; he said that amputation was the only chance of saving his life, and very soon after he performed the operation about 2½in. above the knee; from that time Boothby gradually got better.'], p. 38 ['Talavera, July 29, 1809... Capt. Boothby was wounded by a musquet ball in the calf of his leg and has been obliged to suffer amputation.'], pp. 42-3 ['Badajoz, September 12th, 1809... Out of less than 18,000 men which was our total that morning, 5300 were either killed, or wounded, or taken before the action ended, and we have been obliged to leave 2200 and odd behind at Talavera who of course have fallen into the enemy's hands (by the bye we have heard from Boothby of ours who lost his leg...)']. *Brett-James*, pp. 54, 68, 152, 263 ['Captain Charles Boothby, Royal Engineers, had one leg badly mangled by a musket ball at the battle of Talavera, and the staff surgeons decided to amputate. Boothby is candid in his account of the operation he underwent after the instruments had been laid out and a mattress placed on the table. "One of the surgeons came to me and exhorted me to summon my fortitude. I told him that he need not be afraid; and Fitzpatrick stopped him, saying that he could answer for me. They then took me to the table and laid me on the mattress. Mr Miller wished to place a handkerchief over my eyes; but I assured him that it was unnecessary – I would look another way. The tornequet [sic] being adjusted, I saw that the knife was in Fitzpatrick's hand; which being as I wished, I averted my head... 'Is it off?' said I, as I felt it separate. 'Yes,' said Fitzpatrick. 'Your sufferings are over.' 'Ah, no! You have yet to take up the arteries!' 'It will give you no pain,' he said, kindly; and that was true – at least, after what I had undergone, the pain seemed nothing. I was carried back to my bed, free from pain, but much exhausted. The surgeons complimented me upon my firmness, and I felt gratified that I had gone through what lay before me without flinching, or admitting a thought of cowardly despair." '].

BORCHERS, Daniel, Lt., 2nd Light Dragoons/Hussars K.G.L.: Lt., 2nd Light Dragoons, 23 Aug. 1811. Served in Peninsula 1811–13. *Beamish*, vol. II, p. 554 ['Slightly wounded, 23d June 1811, at Quinta de Gremezia.'].

BORGH, Anthony Philipp de, Lt., 60th Foot; Capt., 11th Portuguese Caçadores: *1829 Statement of Service for Retired Officers*: Aged thirty-six on first appointment to the Army. Ensign, 60th Foot, 7 March 1810; Lt., 60th Foot, 18 April 1811; Capt., 11th Portuguese Caçadores, Sept. 1811; Capt., 'in the Army', 6 June 1815, 'being appointed to serve with the Portuguese Troops'; Half-pay, unattached, 25 Dec. 1816, 'In common with all the other British officers then serving with the Portuguese Army.' *Where serving when wounded*: 'In France, on the third day of January 1814, near a small town called Hasparren (vicinity of Bayonne) while holding the Rank and discharging the Duties of Captain of a company in the 11th Battalion of Portuguese Caçadores.' *Details of pension*: One hundred pounds per annum, commencing 4 Jan. 1815. *Family*: Married in St Mary's Church, Lambeth, Surrey, 1 July 1824. No children by 1829. *Titles and nature of civil employment*: 'Not employed in any civil office under His Majesty's Government. Attached, by Permission, to the Portuguese Service, as Captain of Light Infantry.' *Annual salary*: 'Having received nothing (absolutely nothing) from Portugal since the month of January 1816, Capt. de B. is utterly ignorant what his Portuguese salary and emoluments would amount to, should they ever

be given to him.' *Where generally resident during last five years*: 'From the year 1815 to July 1821, in London. From the latter part of July 1821 till the present period, in Roxburghshire N.B. [Scotland]'. [PRO: WO 25/755 f177]. Letter, dated 22 Nov. 1828, enclosed with Statement of Service: '... my Military Services prior to my Appointment as Ensign in His Majesty's 60th Regiment of Foot ... after having served against Revolutionary France with the Prussian Armies, from the year 1792 to the beginning of the year 1795, the inglorious (half-forced) secession of Prussia ... caused me to come over to England in August 1796, strongly, warmly recommended to the Patronage and Protection of His Royal Highness the late Duke of York, who, within less than six weeks, appointed me Cornet in the Hussar Regiment of Baron ch. Hompesh [?] (then styled Prince of Wales's Hussars), which Regiment I joined in the island of St Domingo and served with, till, reduced to almost nothing, it returned to England to be disbanded, while I was left in the island in a dying state and not expected to recover. Is it necessary to state who the Persons were who had recommended me to His Royal Highness His late Duke of York? They were the Principal members of the Royal Family of Prussia; and Lord Elgin (the British Minister at the Prussian Court), and Capt. Anstruther of the Guards, who, if I mistake not, died a General officer, at or near Corunna...'. [PRO: WO 25/755 f177 encl.].

BORSTEL, Herrmann Christian Ludwig ('Lewis') von, Capt., 1st Line Battn. K.G.L.: *1829 Statement of Service for Retired Officers*: Aged twenty seven on first appointment to the Army. Born 16 Sept. 1776. Lt., 1st Line Battn. K.G.L., April 1804; Capt., 1st Line Battn. K.G.L., 17 Aug. 1809; Half-pay 25 Feb. 1816, by reduction. 'The date of the lieu-tenants Commission can not be stated, this Commission having been lost with His Majesty's Trans-port Augustus Caesar, wrecked upon the Dutch Coast in October 1807 on the return to England from the Expedition to Copenhagen'. *Where serving when wounded*: 'In the 1st Line Battalion King's German Legion in action with the Enemy near Bayonne on the 27th February 1814'. *Details of pension*: One hundred pounds, commencing 28 Feb. 1815. *Family*: Married in 'Buxtehude', 15 Jan. 1825. Two children by 1829. *Where generally resident during last five years*: 'Buxtehude in the Kingdom of Hanover'. Signed 'Lewis Borstel' [PRO: WO 25/776 f324]. 'Lewis de Borstell' in Army List. Served in Peninsula 1808–14. MGS. *Beamish*, vol. II, p. 571.

BOTELER, Richard, Capt., Royal Engineers: 2nd Capt., Royal Engineers, 24 June 1809. Severely wounded in the trenches before Badajoz, 8–15 May 1811 [*London Gazette*].

BOTHMER, Charles de, Lt., 5th Line Battn. K.G.L.: *1829 Statement of Service for Retired Officers*: Born in 'Schwarmsleet in the Kingdom of Hannover', 2 Aug. 1785. Ensign, 5th Line Battn. K.G.L., 27 Jan. 1806; Lt., 5th Line Battn. K.G.L., 1 Aug. 1809; Capt., 5th Line Battn. K.G.L., 27 June 1815; Half-pay, 24 April 1816, by reduction. *Where serving when wounded*: 'Light wounded, near Bayonne in France in the month of June 1814. Light wounded at Waterloo the 18th June 1815.' *Where generally resident during last five years*: 'at Ebstorf in the Kingdom of Hannover.' [PRO: WO 25/755 f143]. Letter from de Bothmer, dated Ebstorf, 23 Dec. 1828, enclosed with Statement of Service: 'I am not employed in any Military or Civil Office, my health is after the Campaign in the Peninsula, after

the Battel near Tollawera, near Terros Vedras 1811, Battel near Salamanca in Spain 1812, Battel near Vittoria 1813, the Battel in the Pyrenaen 1814, near Bayonne 1814, and the Battel bear Waterloo 1815, noth to be able for any Employ-ment, and I am obliget to be very attention.' [PRO: WO25/755 f143 encl].

+BOTHMER, Lewis, von, Lt., 1st Line Battn. K.G.L.: Lt., 1st Line Battn. K.G.L., 28 Jan. 1806. Killed, siege of Burgos, 19 Oct. 1812 [*London Gazette*]. *Register of dead officers*: 'Killed before Burgos', 18 Oct. 1812. Return dated 25 Oct. 1812 [PRO: WO 25/2965]. Recorded as having died '5 Feby. 1813. From Prisoner of War, Spain'. Return dated July 1813 [PRO: WO 25/2965]. Served in Peninsular 1808–12. *Beamish*, vol. II, p. 639 ['Died of his wounds 5th Jan. 1813, at Burgos in Spain, he being severely wounded in the assault of the castle of Burgos, and taken prisoner by the enemy on the 18th Oct. 1812.'].

BOURCHIER, Richard James, Ensign, 36th Foot: Ensign, 36th Foot, 11 Jan 1810. Severely wound-ed, Salamanca, 22 July 1812 ('Bouchier') [*London Gazette*]. MGS.

BOURKE, Charles Thomas, Ensign, 48th Foot: *1829 Statement of Service for Retired Officers*: Aged fifteen on his first appoint-ment in the Army. Ensign, 48th Foot, 14 June 1811; Lt., 100th Foot, 20 May 1813; exchanged to 48th Foot, Aug. 1813. 'Placed on Half Pay on the reduction of the 2nd Battn. 48th Regt. October 1814.' 'During the Waterloo Campaign, Acting Assist. Engineer to the British Army in the Netherlands, was stationed at Ypres, which situation he quitted on the opening of the Campaign & was present in the field of Waterloo during the latter part of the Engagement but being unattached to any corps did not receive the Waterloo Medal. Humbly submits the above to the consideration of the Right Honble. the Secretary at War.' 'Was present during the peninsula War at all the Actions in which his regt. was engaged from the time of his appointment to his exchange, viz. Ciudad Rodrigo, Badajoz (where he was wounded), Salamanca, Vittoria, Pamplona, Pyrenees &c.' *Where serving when wounded*: 'Received a severe bayonet wound at the storming of Badajoz on the 6th April 1812. For which he has no pension but received a gratificatin of a years pay as Ensign.' *Where generally resident during last five years*: 'Seor. 1823, Genoa. December 1823 to March 1824, Pisa. June, Sept., Decr. 1824 & March 1825, at Bologna. 1826 at Paris until Septr. 1823. Decr. to March 1828 at Nantes. June, Septr. & December 1828 at Nancy, France.' [PRO: WO 25/751 f22]. Slightly wounded, storming of Badajoz, 6 April 1812 [*London Gazette*]. MGS.

BOURNE, William Henry, Volunteer, 87th Foot: *1829 Statement of Service for Retired Officers*: Aged twenty on his first appointment in the Army. 'Served as volunteer with the 87th Regt. during the Campaign of 1813 and was appointed to an Ensigncy in the 82nd Regt. on the 6th of January 1814. Promoted to a Lieutenancy in the same Regt. on the 2nd May 1816. Placed on Half pay in the latter part of that year.' 'Having been reported unfit for service by a Medical board at Newport, Isle of Wight, I was placed on Half pay, and allowed to receive the difference in consequence of my excessive sufferings from my wound... The effects of my wound, I regret to say, continue to unfit me from any active pursuit; yet I shall be always ready and most willing to serve His Majesty to the best of my ability.' *Where serving when wounded*: 'At the battle of St Pe in the Pyrenees.' *Details of pension*: Seventy pounds per annum, commencing 'early in the year 1815.' *Family*: Married in 'St George's Church, Southwark, Surrey' on 11 July 1825. Two children by 1829. *Where generally resident during last five years*: 'London and Dunkerque.' [PRO: WO 25/751 f5]. Severely wounded, Nivelle, 10 Nov. 1813 ('Volunteer W. H. Bourne') (2nd Battn. 87th Foot) [*London Gazette*]. *1818 Pension Return*, pp. 20–21. MGS.

BOUSSINGAULT, Pierre F. Louis, Adjutant/Lt., Chasseurs Britanniques: Adjutant, Chasseurs Britanniques, 26 June 1806. Lt., Chasseurs Britanniques, 3 April 1810. Wounded, Pyrenees, 30 July 1813 ('Adjutant Bosingault') [*London Gazette*]. Slightly wounded, Nivelle, 10 Nov. 1813 ('Adjutant Boussingault') [*London Gazette*].

BOUVERIE, Henry Frederick, Lt. and Capt., Coldstream Guards: Lt. and Capt., Coldstream Guards, 19 Nov. 1800. Slightly wounded, Talavera, 28 July 1809, while serving as ADC to Sir Arthur Wellesley [*London Gazette*]. Capt. and Lt. Col., Coldstream Guards, 28 June 1810. Mentioned in Wellington's Vittoria dispatch, 22 June 1813 ['Lieutenant-General Sir Thomas Graham particularly reports his sense of the assistance he received from ... Lieutenant-Colonel Bouverie, of the Adjutant-General's Department'] [*London Gazette*]. Gold Medal. MGS.

BOWEN, Edward Cole, Capt., 40th Foot: Lt., Army, 21 July 1800; Lt., 40th Foot, 5 Sept. 1805; Capt. 7 Nov. 1811. Slightly wounded, storming of Badajoz, 6 April 1812 (1st Battn.) [*London Gazette*]. Severely wounded, Pyrenees, 26 July 1813 (1st Battn.) [*London Gazette*]. Waterloo.

BOWER, William, Lt., 50th Foot: Lt., 50th Foot, 6 Aug. 1807. Severely wounded, Vittoria, 21 June 1813 (1st Battn.) [*London Gazette*]. Capt., 50th Foot, 7 Oct. 1813. Slightly wounded, the Nive, 13 Dec. 1813 ('Captain W. Bowen') (1st Battn.) [*London Gazette*].

+BOWES, Barnard Foord, Major-General: Lt. Col., 6th Foot, 1 Dec. 1796; Major-General, 25 July 1810. Severely, 'but not dangerously', storming of Badajoz, 6 April 1812 [*London Gazette*]. Severely wounded, 'since dead', in the siege of the Forts of St Vincente, St Cayetano, and La Merced at Salamanca, 18–24 June 1812 [*London Gazette*]. *Register of dead officers*: 'Killed at Salamanca', 23 June 1812 [PRO: WO 25/2965]. Obituary, *The Gentleman's Magazine*, Oct. 1812, p. 404 ['Major-general Foord Bowes. From Gibraltar he volunteered his services originally in the cause of Spain, and at the battle of Vimiera he received the public thanks. When again second in command at Gibraltar, he petitioned for leave to act under Lord Wellington, to which the Commander-in-chief assented; and, leaving his family, he went to Spain. At the storming of Badajoz he was wounded in two places, shot through the thigh and bayoneted, and had his aide-de-camp, Capt. [James] Johnson [28th Foot], killed by his side. On recovering from his wounds, after a severe confinement, he again went forward; and, at the storming of Fort St Cayetano, where he headed his brigade (so eager was he that all should go right) he was amongst the first wounded. Taken from the field to have his wound dressed, he heard his men were repulsed; on which, instantly returning to cheer and push them forward, he was shot; and thus has fallen an officer, who, on every possible occasion, sought service, and was only too forward to distinguish himself.']. *Surtees*, p. 164 [Forts at Salamanca: 'An

attempt had been made to carry them by escalade, but it had failed; General Bowes, who led the attacking party, with several officers and men, having fallen in the attempt.'].

BOWLES, Charles Proby, Lt., 83rd Foot: Lt., 83rd Foot, 9 Nov. 1809. Severely wounded, storming of Badajoz, 6 April 1812 (2nd Battn.) [*London Gazette*]. Temporary pension of one hundred pounds per annum, commencing 7 April 1813, 'for wounds' received at Badajoz, 1812 [*1818 Pension Return*, pp. 18–19]. MGS.

BOWLES, John, Capt., 28th Foot: *1829 Statement of Service for Retired Officers*: Aged twenty-nine on his first appointment in the Army. Ensign, 40th Foot, 15 Aug. 1799, 'obtained by takeing the Quota of Volunteers from East Somerset Regt. of Militia'; Lt., 40th Foot, 7 March 1807; Half-pay 25 Aug. 1802; Lt., Full-pay, 28th Foot, 9 July 1803; Capt., 28th Foot, 20 July 1809; Half-pay, 42nd Foot, 25 April 1817. 'Placed on the H.P. as a Reduced Capt. of 42nd Regt. being permitted to exchange in consequence of severe wounds recd. in Action with the Enemy, receiving the Difference, as an especial favor of His late R. H. The Duke of York, on account of being incapable of performing active service, using crutches.' 'I have no hesitation to serve my King and Country to the extent of my ability, provided my humble efforts should be required.' *Where serving when wounded*: 'Near Vittoria in Spain. Les Quatre Bras in Belgium.' *Details of pension*: One hundred pounds for each wound: that for Quatre Bras commenced 17 June 1816, while that for Vittoria was 'supposed to commence Decr. 25th 1821, as the Notification was left at the Office of The Director Genl. of the Medical Department in London.' *Where generally resident during last five*

BOWLES

years: 'Episcopi W. Langport &
Weytown Cottage, W. Beaminster.'
[PRO: WO 25/751 f13]. Seriously
wounded, Vittoria, 21 June 1813
(1st Battn.) [*London Gazette*]. *1818
Pension Return*, pp. 8–9.

**+BOYD, George, Lt., 1st Line
Battn. K.G.L.**: Ensign, 1st Line
Battn. K.G.L., 29 May 1809; Lt., 1st
Light Battn. K.G.L., 18 March 1812.
Slightly wounded, in an action near
Tolosa, 25 June 1813 ('Lieutenant')
[*London Gazette*]. Killed, Nivelle,
10 Oct. 1813 ('1st Light Batt.')
[*London Gazette*]. Served in Penin-
sula 1809–13. *Beamish*, vol. II, p. 636
['1st line battalion ... slightly
wounded, 25th June 1813, at Toloza,
killed 10th Nov. 1813, in action near
Urugne, in France.'].

BOYD, Hygatt, Lt., 4th Foot: Lt.,
4th Foot, 16 Aug. 1810. Slightly
wounded, storming of Badajoz, 6
April 1812 [*London Gazette*].
Wounded, Waterloo. Half-pay 22
Aug. 1816. *Dalton*, p. 120.

BOYD, John, Lt., 82nd Foot: Lt.,
82nd Foot, 26 May 1807. Severely
wounded, Pyrenees, 30 July 1813
('Boyde') (1st Battn.) [*London
Gazette*]. Temporary pension of
seventy pounds per annum,
commencing 31 July 1814, 'for a
wound' received in the Pyrenees
[*1818 Pension Return*, pp. 18–19].
MGS.

+BOYD, Thomas, Ensign, 1st Foot:
Ensign, 1st Foot, 12 March 1812.
Killed, storming of San Sebastian,
31 Aug. 1813 [*London Gazette*].

**BOYLE, William, Ensign/Lt., 27th
Foot**: *1829 Statement of Service*:
Born 10 May 1784, Brakely, Tyrone.
Aged twenty-two on first appoint-
ment to the Army. Ensign, Royal
Tyrone Militia, 10 Jan. 1807; Ensign,
27th Foot, 22 July 1808; Lt. 6 Feb.
1812; Half Pay 25 Aug. 1817;
Paymaster, 21st Foot, 3 Nov. 1825.
'Obtained an Ensigncy into the

27th Regt. on getting 76 men to
volunteer to the line. Remained an
Ensign so long in consequence
of the Regiment having three
Battalions.' *Battles, sieges and
campaigns*: 'In the Campaign of
1810. Battle of Busaco 27th
September 1810, an Ensign carrying
the colours on the retreat at Torres
Vidras advance from thence after
Marshal Masséna – 15 November
1810 took up cantonments for the
winter... In the Campaign of 1811 in
pursuit of Marshal Masséna's Army,
and in the Affair of Joz-de-Aronse
15 March – 16th March the 4th Division was detached to the Alentigo –
25 March in the Affair near Campo-
mayor... Seige and Capture of Oliv-
erea 15 April... 8th My in the Seige
commenced against Fort St Christoval – 10th May the French made a
sortie – 11th May. Seige raised... In
the Campaign of 1812, at the
Assault and Capture of Badajos
from the 11th March to the 6th
April. At the Capture of the Retiro
12 Augt. 27th October commenced
the retreat to Portugal during this
campaign in the Seiges was
employed assisting the Engineers,
at other times in command of a
Company... In the Campaigns of
1813 and 1814. Battle of Vitteria 21
June. Battles in the Pyrenees from
25 July to 2nd August. Taking the
Heights of Vera 13 October Nivella
10th Novr. Nive from the 9th to 14th
October on the 27th February 1814
Toulause 10 April 1814. In the
Actions at and from Viteria in
Command of a Company.' *Distinguished conduct*: 'At the Battle of
Vitteria the evening of the 21 June
1813 Two Companies of the Regiment were ordered to the Front to
act as light Infantry, when the
Command devolved upon me in
consequence of Captain Bignal not
being able to proceed from Fatigue,
coming up with the French Stores
by great persuasion induced the
men to desist entering the
waggons, got them formed and
dispersed a Body of French Cavalry

that were approaching the stores. 1st August 1813 was ordered with Captain Butler and two Companies of the 3rd Battalion 27th Regiment to attack a Body of French Troops on a height adjoining the Village of Lesaka in the Pyrenees at the Commencement Captain Butler was severely wounded and Borne to the rear, as next in command I proceeded with the Two Companies and performed the duty required.' *Wounds received in action*: '10th May 1811. Had my cocked hat shot off my head, and slightly wounded in the right ear in an affair with the French before Fort Saint Christoval. 28th July 1813. Received a Wound in the right side of my face and had four Musket Balls through my Regimental Cap, in the Action of the Pyrenees on the Mountains near Pampeluna and to the Right of the village of Sourarer. Volunteered to go to the Seige of St Sebastian with the men ordered from the 4th Division. But General Loury Cole ordered the officers first for duty on that service. I never applied for nor received any remuneration of Pay, or Pension for Wounds.' *Service abroad*: '20 May 1809 to 1 July 1814, Portugal, Spain and France. 24 June 1815 to 22 March 1817, France. 14th Decr. 1825 to 28th Feb. 1827, St Vincent, Wst Indies.' *Family*: Married Letitia Harvey, 11 Oct. 1827, Cheltenham. No children by 1830. [PRO: WO 25/789 f82]. MGS.

BOYS, Edmond French, Lt., 45th Foot: *1829 Statement of Service*: Born in Dublin, 13 Jan. 1788. Aged twenty on first appointment to the Army. Ensign, 45th Foot, 17 Nov. 1808; Lt., 45th Foot, April 1810 [Army List gives 3 April]; Capt., 45th Foot, 8 June 1815; Major, 45th Foot, 3rd Feby. 1829. *Battles, sieges and campaigns*: 'At Sabugal 1811... Fuentes D'Onor 5th May 1811... Retreat of Massina... Orthes 27th February 1814... Toulouse 10th April 1814' *Wounds received in action*:

'Fuentes D'Onor. Toulouse. No grant of Pay.' *Service abroad*: '1809 to 1811, and 1813 to 1814, Peninsula. 1819 to 1825, Ceylon. 1825 to 1828, Burman Empire.' *Family*: Married Catharine Alicia Edwards, Dec. 1817, in Dublin. They had two sons, born in 1822 and 1825 in Ceylon and Madras respectively. Catharine Boys was dead by 1830. [PRO: WO 25/793 f318]. Severely wounded, Toulouse, 10 April 1814 (1st Battn.) [*London Gazette*]. MGS.

BRACKENBURY, William, Ensign/Lt., 61st Foot: *1829 Statement of Service for Retired Officers*: Aged eighteen on his first appointment in the Army. Ensign, 61st Foot, 15 March 1808; Lt., 61st Foot, 16 Aug. 1809; Half-pay, 101st Foot, 3 Oct. 1816, 'at my own request from ill health and the severity of my wounds.' 'Unable to serve in consequence of my wounds.' *Where serving when wounded*: 'At the Battle of Salamanca in Spain.' *Details of pension*: Seventy pounds per annum, commencing 23 July 1813, and an additional seventy pounds commencing 25 Dec. 1824. *Family*: Married in Newry, Ireland, 4 Oct. 1820. He had four children by 1829. *Where generally resident during last five years*: 'At Grimsby until Augt. 1828, since then at Bayswater.' [PRO: WO 25/751 f130]. Slightly wounded, Talavera, 28 July 1809 ('Brackenburg') [*London Gazette*]. Severely wounded, Salamanca, 22 July 1812 ('Brackenburg') [*London Gazette*]. *1818 Pension Return*, pp. 16–17.

+BRADBEY, Joseph, Capt., 28th Foot: Capt., Army, 20 May 1802; Capt., 28th Foot, 9 July 1803. Slightly wounded, Talavera, 28 July 1809, while serving with 1st Battn. Detachments ('Bradley') [*London Gazette*]. Slightly wounded, Barossa, 5 March 1811 [*London Gazette*]. Slightly wounded, Pyrenees, 25 July 1813 ('Bradley') (1st Battn.) [*London Gazette*]. Obituary, *The Gentleman's Magazine*, Nov. 1813, p. 504 ['At Vittoria, of wounds received in that battle (sic), Major Bradby, 28th reg. nephew of the late Admiral B.']. *Webber*, p. 115 [16 Nov. 1812: 'Another party of French Hussars charged Captain Bradley's [sic] Company of the 28th, but were obliged to wheel about, exposed to a volley which annoyed them a good deal.']. *Blakeney*, p. 109 [Retreat to Corunna: 'I beg to make a few remarks about the light company, 28th Regiment, during the retreat which ended at El-Burgo ... they must have suffered at least as many casualties as any company of the army; and finally, they marched, the last company of the whole army, through the village of El-Burgo under a heavy cannonade and a sharp fire of musketry... I could not say, so far as my memory serves, that a single individual of that company fell out of the ranks, or was left behind, in consequence of intolerable fatigue. The captain of the company (Bradby) was left behind, sick, at Lisbon; and the senior lieutenant (English) was sent in the sick-carts from Benevente to Corunna on December 27th, 1808, suffering from dysentery; but no man fell out on the march.'].

+BRADFORD, Keating James, Lt. and Capt., 3rd Foot Guards: Lt. and Capt., 3rd Foot Guards, 28 Aug. 1806. Killed, Rolica, 17 Aug. 1808, while serving on the General Staff as DAAG. [*London Gazette*]. Obituary, *The Gentleman's Magazine*, Sept. 1808 ['17... Capt. Bradford, of the Guards, gloriously fell this day, in the battle of Rolein, in Portugal. He was a son of T. Bradford, esq. of Ashdown park, Sussex.'].

BRADFORD, Thomas, Major-General: Lt. Col., 82nd Foot, 21 Dec. 1809; Bvt. Col., 82nd Foot, 25 July 1810; Major-General, 4 June 1813. Pension of three hundred and fifty

pounds per annum, commencing 15 April 1815, 'for a wound' received at Bayonne, 1814 [*1818 Pension Return*, pp. 24–25]. Not at Waterloo. *Royal Military Calendar*, vol. III, p. 295 ['This officer served in Spain and Portugal as Assistant Adjutant-General, till he received the brevet of Major-General, which removing him from his Staff situation, he was placed under the orders of Lord Beresford, and appointed to the command of a Portuguese Brigade. He was present at the battles of [Vimiera], Corunna, Salamanca, Vittoria and Nive, and the siege of St Sebastian'].

BRAHAM, Henry, Adjutant/Lt., 83rd Foot: Ensign, 83rd Foot, 27 March 1806; Adjutant, 27 March 1806; Lt., 83rd Foot, 13 March 1808. Slightly wounded, Talavera, 28 July 1809 ('Adjutant') [*London Gazette*].

+BRAMWELL, John, Lt., 43rd Foot: Lt., 43rd Foot, 28 Sept. 1809. Severely wounded, storming of Ciudad Rodrigo, 19 Jan. 1812 (1st Battn.) [*London Gazette*]. *Register of dead officers*: Died of wounds, 27 Jan. 1812. Return dated 25 Feb. 1812 [PRO: WO 25/2965]. *Bruce*, p. 78 [Letter of Lt. Col Charles Macleod to Major William Napier, La Encina, 21 Jan. 1812: 'All our own are likely to do well; Brummel [sic] is the only one there is any doubt about; his wound is near the femoral artery.'], p. 80 [Macleod to Napier, El Bodem, 4 Feb. 1812: 'Poor Brummel died of his wounds about a week ago.'].

BRANDER, James, Lt., 42nd Foot: Lt., 42nd Foot, 2 May 1811. Slightly wounded, Orthes, 27 Feb. 1814 (1st Battn.) [*London Gazette*]. Wounded, Waterloo. MGS. Died at Pitgavenny, 1854. *Anton*, pp. 88–9 [9 Dec. 1813: 'Towards the close of the day, the enemy retired upon a farmhouse situated on a commanding eminence, having some of the adjoining fields enclosed by low dry-stone walls and quickset hedges, behind which they appeared in considerable force, supported by some artillery. In dislodging these troops ... Lieutenant Brander was severely wounded.'].

+**BRANDERS, Lewis, Ensign, Brunswick Oels' Corps (Infantry)**: Ensign, Brunswick Oels' Corps, 14 Oct 13. Severely wounded, Orthes, 27 Feb. 1814 ('Brander') [*London Gazette*]. Died of wounds, 1 March 1814. Return dated March 1814 ('Brandis') [PRO: WO 25/2965]. 'Brandes' in *Challis, Index*, p. 274.

BRANDIS, Eberhard von, Ensign, 5th Line Battn. K.G.L.: *1829 Statement of Service for Retired Officers*: Aged sixteen on first appointment to the Army. Ensign, 5th Line Battn. K.G.L., 7 Sept. 1807; Lt., 5th Line Battn. K.G.L., 9 Oct. 1809 [Army List gives 18 Oct. 1809]; Capt., 5th Line Battn. K.G.L., 27 July 1815; Half-pay, 25 Feb. 1816, by reduction. *Where serving when wounded*: 'Wounded at Talavera la Reyne.' No pension. *Family*: Married in Celle, Hanover, 4 July 1817. Four children by 1829. *Where generally resident during last five years*: 'Celle, Kingdom of Hannover.' [PRO: WO 25/755 f142]. Slightly wounded, Talavera, 28 July 1809 ('Brandes') [*London Gazette*]. Served in Peninsula 1808–14. Waterloo. MGS. *Beamish*, vol. II, p. 591 ['slightly wounded, 28th July 1809, at Talavera; slightly wounded, 22d July 1812, at Salamanca.'].

BRANFILL, Champion Edward, Lt., 3rd Dragoons: Lt., 3rd Dragoons, 15 Nov. 1810. Slightly wounded, Salamanca, 18 July 1812 ('Bramfield') [*London Gazette*]. Capt., 3rd Dragoons, 21 Oct. 1813. 'On the English Half-Pay' following reduction of the regt. in 1814. *Bragge*, p. 124 ['St Jean de Luz, March 4th 1814 ... our remount has

landed and I and Capt. Branfill will in a few Days receive an order to join the Depot at Canterbury, which we purpose taking Advantage of the first fair Wind and tranquil Sea'], p. 133 ['Branfill, Champion Edward (1789–1844). Cornet 3rd Dr May 1810... Ret. 1816.'].

+**BRAUNS, John, Lt. Col., 2nd Line Battn. K.G.L.**: Lt. Col., 4th Line Battn. K.G.L., 6 Jan. 1805. Severely wounded, Talavera, 28 July 1809 ('Col. 2nd Line Batt KGL') [*London Gazette*]. *Beamish*, vol. II, p. 636 [Died '6th Oct. 1809, of the wounds he received in the battle of Talavera de la Reyna, 28th July 1809.']. Served in the Peninsula 1808–9.

+**BRAXEIN, Ernst de, Capt., Duke of Brunswick Oels' Corps (Infantry)**: Capt., Duke of Brunswick Oels' Corps (Infantry), 16 Aug. 1810. Slightly wounded, Pyrenees, 25 July 1813 [*London Gazette*]. Killed, Orthes, 27 Feb. 1813 [*London Gazette*]. *Hurt*, p. 61 ['Branxion, Edward de'].

BREM, Nicolas Philibert de, Capt., Chasseurs Brittanniques: *1829 Statement of Service for Retired Officers*: Aged twenty-eight on first appointment to the Army. Lt., Chasseurs Britanniques, 1 April 1801; Capt., Chasseurs Britanniques, 25 Nov. 1803; Bvt. Major, Chasseurs Britanniques, 4 June 1814. Half-pay, by reduction. *Where serving when wounded*: 'Severely wounded at the Battle 30th July near Pamplona, Spain, Lord Wellington's Army.' *Family*: Married Marie Barbe Justine Renauld, in St Arold, Dept. Moselle, France, 4 Sept. 1816. Three children by 1829. *Where generally resident during last five years*: 'St Arold, Dept. Moselle, France.' [PRO: WO 25/756 f12]. Severely wounded, Pyrenees, 30 July 1813 [*London Gazette*].

BRERETON, William, Lt., Royal Artillery: 1st Lt., Royal Artillery, 1

June 1806. Slightly wounded, Barossa, 5 March 1811 [*London Gazette*]. D Troop R.H.A. Wounded, Waterloo. *Dalton*, pp. 217, 219 ['Served as maj.-gen, and was second in command of the expedition under M.-Gen. D'Aguilar, who assaulted and took the forts of the Bocca Tigris in the Canton River. Served with the fleets off Sebastopol in Oct. 1854, and directed the rockets fired from the Britannia against the city and forts.']. MGS. Died, 27 July 1864. *Webber*, pp. 87, 89.

+**BRETT, Spencer P., 1st Lt., Royal Artillery**: 1st Lt., Royal Artillery, 21 Dec. 1803. Killed, 'at the Capture of the City of Seville by Assault,' 27 Aug. 1812 [*London Gazette*]. Mentioned in Skerrett's dispatch concerning the capture of Seville, 28 Aug. 1812 ['I have only to regret the loss of one officer, Lieutenant Brett, royal artillery, who was killed, gallantly fighting his gun, at the bridge. The intrepidity of this valuable officer was observed by the whole detachment.'] [*London Gazette*]. *Register of dead officers*: 'Arty. Seville. Killed in action, 27 Aug. 1812'. Return dated 25 Sept. 1812. [PRO: WO 25/2965].

BREUNIG, Anthony Francis de, Capt., 8th Caçadores: see De Breunig, A. F.

BREYMANN, Frederick Leopold, Capt., 2nd Line Battn. K.G.L.: Capt., 2nd Line Battn. K.G.L., 11 Nov. 1803. Slightly wounded, siege of Burgos, 20–26 Sept. 1812 ('Breyman') [*London Gazette*]. Served in Peninsula 1808–14. Waterloo. *Beamish*, vol. II, p. 602 ['slightly wounded, 28th July 1809, at Talavera; slightly wounded, 22d Sept. 18122, before Burgos... [Died] at Tesperhude near Lauenburg, Denmark, 24th Jan. 1821.'].

BRICE, Alexander Adair, 1st Lt., 23rd Foot: 2nd Lt., 23rd Foot, 8 Aug.

1811; 1st Lt. 21 May 1812. Slightly wounded, Pyrenees, 28 July 1813 (1st Battn.) [*London Gazette*]. Waterloo. MGS. See Isaac Watkins Harris.

BRICE, George Tito, Capt., 3rd Dragoon Guards: Capt., 3rd Dragoon Guards, 27 Dec. 1803. Severely wounded, Talavera, 28 July 1809 ('Bryce') [*London Gazette*]. Bvt. Major, 3rd Dragoon Guards, 27 May 1813. One hundred pounds pension, 'for wounds' received at Talavera, 1809, commencing 25 Dec. 1811 [*1818 Pension Return*, pp. 2–3]. MGS.

BRICKELL, James, Capt., 24th Foot: Capt., Army, 28 Sept. 1804; Capt., Royal Regt. of Malta, 5 Jan. 1805; Capt., 24th Foot, 4 June 1812. Slightly wounded, Pyrenees, 2 Aug. 1813, as Capt. 24th Foot (2nd Battn.) ('Brecknell') [*London Gazette*]. Severely wounded, Nivelle, 10 Nov. 1813 (2nd Battn.) [*London Gazette*]. Capt., Half-pay, 24th Foot, upon the reduction of the regt., 1814. MGS.

BRIDGEMAN, Hon. Orlando, Ensign, 1st Foot Guards: Ensign, 1st Foot Guards, 14 Feb. 1811. Slightly wounded, storming of San Sebastian, 31 Aug. 1813 (3rd Battn.) [*London Gazette*]. Wounded, Waterloo. Born 6 May 1794, third son of Orlando, 1st Earl of Bradford [*Burke's Peerage*]. Died, 1827.

+**BRIGHT, Henry, Capt., 87th Foot**: Capt., 87th Foot, 18 Aug. 1808. Killed, Toulouse, 10 April 1814 ('Captain Henry Bright (Major)') [*London Gazette*]. *Register of officers' effects*: Single. Effects totalled £203. 0s. 3d. [PRO: WO 25/2964].

BRINE, James, Capt., 39th Foot: Capt., 39th Foot, 3 March 1808. Severely wounded, Albuera, 16 May 1811 (3rd Battn.) [*London Gazette*]. Half-pay 21 May 1825. Pension of one hundred pounds per annum, commencing 17 May 1812, 'for wounds' received at Albuera [*1818 Pension Return*]. MGS.

BRINGHURST, John Dorset, Capt., 1st Dragoon Guards: Capt., Army, 18 July 1811; Capt., 1st Dragoon Guards, 24 Oct. 1811. Slightly wounded, Vittoria, 21 June 1813, while serving as ADC to Major-General Fane [*London Gazette*]. Bvt. Major, 12 April 1814. Killed, Waterloo.

BRISAC, George William Augustus, Lt., 30th Foot: Lt., 30th Foot, 26 June 1811. Slightly wounded, during 'movements of the Army'. [Retreat from Burgos: Villa Muriel], 25 Oct. 1812 [*London Gazette*].

BRISBANE, Thomas, Major-General: Lt. Col., 69th Foot, 4 April 1800; Col., Army, 25 July 1810. Major-General, 4 June 1813. Wounded, Toulouse, 10 April 1814 [*London Gazette*]. Gold Medal. MGS.

BROCK, James Loftus, Lt., 85th Foot: Lt., 85th Foot, 20 Sept. 1808. Wounded, 'dangerously', Fuentes de Onoro, 5 May 1811 [*London Gazette*]. Lt., 6th Foot, 25 Jan. 1813. Not at Waterloo. Half-pay, 6th Foot, 2 Oct. 1817. MGS.

BROCK, Saumarez, Capt., 43rd Foot: *1829 Statement of Service*: 'Born in Guernsey, 15th September 1787. Aged Sixteen on his first entrance into the Army. Ensign, 52nd Regt., 1803. Half Pay, 1803, from ill health. Ensign, 54th Regt., 1803. Lieutenant, 48th Regt., 14th April 1804. Captain, 48th Regt., 28th March 1805. Captain, 43rd Foot, [6 Aug.] 1807. Major, 43rd Regt., 12th Octr. 1815. Half Pay, 25th March 1817, by reduction of the 2nd Battn. 43rd Regt. Major, 55th Regt., 29th Augt. 1822. Lieut. Colonel, 55th Regt., 12th June 1830.' *Battles, sieges and campaigns*: 'Vimiera. Vittoria.

Nivelle. Nive. Toulouse. Peninsula. New Orleans. Surrender of Paris and many other partial Actions in which it was the good fortune of the 43rd Regt. to be engaged with the Enemy at Vira, Tarbes, Arcangues &c. &c. &c. &c.' *Wounds received in action*: 'On the 21st August 1808 at the Battle of Vimiera, Shot completely through the Ancle Bone. One years Pay. A Captains Pension permanent.' *Service abroad*: '19th Augt. 1808 to Novr. 1808, Portugal. June 1811 to Decr. 1811, Portugal. Novr. 1812 to July 1814, Spain and France. June 1815 to Jany. 1816, Netherlands and France. 29th May 1823 to 27th Feby. 1828, Africa. Decbr. 1814 to March 1815, America. Sept. 1830 to June 1831, Asia, and still remain there.' *Family*: Married Miss Catherine de Saumarez, 1 Feb. 1823, in Guernsey. They had no children by 1830. [PRO: WO 25/795 f318]. Wounded, Vimeiro, 21 Aug. 1808 [*London Gazette*]. Temporary pension of one hundred pounds per annum, commencing 25 Dec. 1811, 'for wounds' received at Vimeiro [*1818 Pension Return*, pp. 12–13]. MGS.

BROETZ, Peter, Lt., 60th Foot: Ensign, 60th Foot, 12 July 1810; Adjutant, 60th Foot, 14 March 1811; Lt., 60th Foot, 9 Oct. 1811. Severely wounded, storming of Badajoz, 6 April 1812 (5th Battn.) [*London Gazette*]. Lt., 13th Royal Veteran Battalion, 25 Jan. 1813. Seventy pounds per annum pension, commencing 7 April 1813, for 'loss of a leg' at Badajoz, 1812 [*1818 Pension Return*, pp. 14–15].

BROHIER, John Boyle, Lt., 59th Foot: *1829 Statement of Service for Retired Officers*: Aged eighteen on his first appointment in the Army. Ensign, 4th Garrison Battn., 21 Jan. 1809; Lt., 59th Foot, 3 June 1809; Half-pay, 15 March 1816, by reduction of 2nd Battn. 'altho' then a senior lieutenant in the first Battn.'; Lt., 61st Foot, 23 Oct. 1816; Half-pay, 25 Nov. 1818, 'By the reduction of the additional lieutenants.' 'I shall be happy to serve whenever my services are required, relying on the Gracious consideration of the Commander in Chief giving me that Rank I have lost by being placed upon half Pay contrary to my wishes.' *Where serving when wounded*: 'At the Battle of Bayone was severely wounded in the head, but did not apply for a Pension.' *Where generally resident during last five years*: 'London & Jersey.' [PRO: WO 25/751 f195]. Severely wounded, the Nive, 9 Dec. 1813 ('Broheir') (2nd Battn.) [*London Gazette*]. MGS.

BROKE, Horatio George, Capt., 58th Foot: Lt., 52nd Foot, 15 Feb. 1808; Capt., 58th Foot, 18 March 1813. Severely wounded, Orthes, 27 Feb. 1814, while serving as A.D.C. to Lt.-General Sir H. Clinton ('Brook') [*London Gazette*]. Bvt. Major, 58th Foot, 28 July 1814.

BROMBSON, Adolph Otto von, Lt., Duke of Brunswick Oels' Corps (Infantry): *1829 Statement of Service for Retired Officers*: Aged eighteen on first appointment to the Army. 'After having served as Non-Commissioned Officer for the space of 3 years & 16 days in the British Service I was promoted to an Ensigncy.' Ensign, Duke of Brunswick Oels' Corps (Infantry), 26 Aug. 1812; Lt., Duke of Brunswick Oels' Corps, 6 May 1813; Half-pay, 25 Dec. 1814, by reduction. *Where serving when wounded*: 'I received as officer four wounds while in the British Service in the Peninsula, and have received no Pension. At the Battle of Waterloo, in the Brunswick Service, I received a ball in the breast, which has not been extracted, and in consequence of my ill state of health, I applied in the year 1825 for permission to hold a civil employment.' *Family*: 'Married in Medingen near Lueneburg in the

Kingdom of Hannover', 11 Feb. 1817. Six children by 1829. 'I have no civil employment, but should I be inclined to hold one, I have the permission to do so from the Right Honorable the Secretary of War: dated the 28th of Decr. 1825.' *Where generally resident during last five years*: Brunswick. [PRO: WO 25/776 f355]. Slightly wounded, Pyrenees, 2 Aug. 1813 ('Broembsen') [*London Gazette*]. Severely wounded, Nivelle, 10 Nov. 1813 ('Otto Broembsen') [*London Gazette*]. Slightly wounded, Orthes, 27 Feb. 1814 ('Broeemben') [*London Gazette*]. MGS. 'Otto Broemsen' in *Challis, Index*, p. 274.

BROOK, Thomas, Lt., 51st Foot: Lt., 51st Foot, 18 May 1809. Slightly wounded, 'in the Operations of the Army', 31 Aug. 1813 [*London Gazette*]. Waterloo. Half-pay, 1825. Died, 21 Dec. 1845, at Askham Bryan, Yorkshire. *Wheeler*, p. 144 [Wounded, 'slightly', near Lezaca, 31 Aug. 1813.].

+BROOKE, George, Lt., 20th Foot: Lt., 20th Foot, 21 Feb. 1805. Killed, Vimeiro, 21 Aug. 1808 [*London Gazette*].

BROOKE, James, Lt., 29th Foot: Lt., 29th Foot, 6 Feb. 1808. Slightly wounded, Albuera, 16 May 1811 [*London Gazette*].

BROOKE, John, Lt., 48th Foot: Lt., 48th Foot, 25 June 1807. Severely wounded, storming of Badajoz, 6 April 1812 (1st Battn.) [*London Gazette*]. Seventy pounds per annum pension, commencing 8 April 1813, 'for wounds' received at Badajoz, 1812 [*1818 Pension Return*, pp. 12–13].

+BROOKE, W. H., Capt., 48th Foot: Capt., 48th Foot, 28 Feb. 1805. Killed, storming of Badajoz, 6 April 1812 (1st Battn.) [*London Gazette*]. Return dated 25 April 1812 [PRO: WO 25/2965].

BROOKE, William, Major, 48th Foot: Major, Army, 25 April 1808; Major, 48th Foot, 2 Nov. 1809. Reported as 'Missing', Albuera, 16 May 1811 (2nd Battn.) [*London Gazette*]. Severely wounded, 'not dangerously', storming of Badajoz, 6 April 1812, while serving on the Staff as Permanent AQMG [*London Gazette*]. Pension of three hundred pounds per annum, commencing 17 May 1812, 'for wounds' received at Albuera, while serving as 'Major Commanding' his regiment [*1818 Pension Return*, pp. 12–13]. On account of his tribulations after Albuera appears in 'A Prisoner of Albuera', in Oman, Sir Charles, *Studies in the Napoleonic Wars* (London, 1929). Not at Waterloo. *Haythornthwaite, Die Hard*, pp. 148–9 [Albuera: 'Major William Brooke of the 48th, captured after receiving a severe head wound, recorded that he was being escorted to the rear by two French infantryman, a lancer rode up, deliberately cut him down and tried to make his horse trample him. He was rescued by two more infantrymen and a dragoon who saw him safely to the rear of the French position; Brooke believed that the Poles were all drunk.']

BROOKES, Robert, Lt., 9th Foot: *1829 Statement of Service*: Born in Ross, Herefordshire, October 1795. Aged sixteen on first appointment to the Army. Ensign, 9th Foot, May 1811; Lt., 9th Foot, Aug. 1813; Half-pay, Jan. 1817, by Reduction; Lt., 9th Foot, Oct. 1817; Capt., Half-pay, unattached, 27 Aug. 1825; Capt., 69th Foot, 30 Aug. 1826. Note added: 'Major, 69th Foot, 3 May 1831. Lt. Col., Half Pay, Unattached, 27 April 1846. Lt. Col., 24th Regt., 28 April 1846. Killed in Action at Chillianwallah, 13 January 1849.' *Battles, sieges and campaigns*: 'Ensign 9th Foot. Badajos 6 Apl. 1812. Salamanca 22 July 1812. Burgos Sep. 1812. Palentia 25 Octr. 1812. Asma 18 June 1813. Vittoria 21 June 1813.

Lieut. 9th Foot. St Sebastian Actg. Engineer during the Siege in Augt. & Septr. 1813. Volunteer at the Storming of the Island of Santa Clara on the 26th Augst. 1813, under the Comd. of Captn. Cameron 9 Foot & Captn. Henderson Royal Engineers. Lieut. Comg. a Company 9th Foot at the Biddasoa on the 7th Octr. 1813. Nive 9, 10th & 11th Decr. 1813. Nivelle 16 Nov. 1813. Lieut. 9 Foot at Bayonne 14th April 1814... Commanded the Regt. at Chillianwallah.' *Distinguished conduct*: 'Noticed in Orders for Services Volunteered as Acting Engineer during the Siege of St Sebastian.' *Wounds received in action*: 'At Santa Clara near San Sebastian in August 1813. Storming the heights of the Biddasoa 7th Octr. 1813. Received One Years Pay as Captn. having Commanded the Light Company of my Regt. on that Day. Bayonne 10 Decr. 1813 received One Year's Pay as Lieutenant.' *Service abroad*: '7 July 1811 to June 1814, Peninsula. June 1814 to Aug. 1815, N. America. Aug. 1815 to Novr. 1818, France. 3 Feby. 1819 to Aug. 1821, W. Indies. Novr. 1824 to July 1826, W. Indies.' Note added: '23 Dec. 1831 to 30 May 1831, W. Indies. 10 Feb. 1839 to 23 Oct. 1840, N. America. 8 May 1846 to 8 March 1848, E. Indies. 9 Novr. 1848 to 13 Jany. 1849, E. Indies.' *Family*: Note added after his death: 'Left Widow.' [PRO: WO 25/798 f230]. Severely wounded, crossing the Bidassoa, 7/9 Oct. 1813 ('Brooks') (1st Battn.) [*London Gazette*]. Slightly wounded, the Nive, 10 Dec. 1813 (1st Battn.) [*London Gazette*]. MGS.

BROOMFIELD, Charles, Lt., 83rd Foot: Ensign, 83rd Foot, 13 April 1809; Lt., 83rd Foot, 12 Feb. 1812. Severely wounded, storming of Badajoz, 6 April 1812 ('Bloomfield') [*London Gazette*].

+BROOMFIELD, Joseph, Lt., 38th Foot: Lt., 38th Foot, 28 Aug 1807.

Killed, Salamanca, 22 July 1812 (1st Battn.) [*London Gazette*]. Return dated 25 July 1812 [PRO: WO 25/2965].

BROTHERTON, Thomas William, Major, 14th Light Dragoons: Born in 1785. With the Coldstream Guards in Egypt. Capt., Army, 17 July 1801; Capt., 14th Dragoons, 4 June 1807; Major 26 March 1812. Slightly wounded, Salamanca, 18 July 1812 [*London Gazette*]. Recorded as 'missing', the Nive, 12 Dec. 1813 [*London Gazette*]. Wounded and taken prisoner, Hasparren, 13 Dec. 1813. Lt. Col., Army, 19 May 1814. MGS. General Sir Thomas Brotherton, CB, died 21 Jan. 1868 in Esher, Surrey. Author of *A Hawk at War: The Peninsular Reminiscences of General Sir Thomas Brotherton, CB*. Perrett, p. 15 ['Captain Thomas Brotherton, a former Guards officer who had transferred to the Fourteenth in 1807, by which date he was already an experienced soldier. Brotherton had an eye for detail which made him a fine raconteur, and he was undoubtedly a good companion who could be relied upon to proffer his canteen, which he filled with 'strong wine', at suitable moments, as well as providing entertainment with his fiddle around the campfire. He tended to seek action rather than await its coming and complained little when injured, but was somewhat intolerant of those who might not share these views.']

BROWN, Andrew, Capt., 79th Foot: *1829 Statement of Service*: Born in Edinburgh, 6 Jan. 1766. Aged '29 years on his first Entrance into the Army.' Ensign and Adjt., 79th Foot, 24 June 1795. Lieut., 79th Foot, 8 Sept. 1795. Capt., 79th Foot, 17 Sept. 1803. Bt. Major 30 May 1811. Major, 79th Foot, 15 Oct. 1812. Bt. Lt. Col., 79th Foot, 26 Aug. 1813. Bt. Col., 79th Foot, 22 July 1830. *Battles, sieges and campaigns*: 'Present at the landing in Holland in the year 1799 and at the Battle of Bergen-op-Zoom on the 2nd of October under the Command of Sir Ralph Abercromby. Present at the landing in Egypt on the 8th March 1801... and at the Battles of the 13th and 21st March 1801. Present at the Siege and surrender of Alexandria and Cairo. With the Expedition to Copenhagen in 1807... and present at its surrender. Present with the Regiment during the whole of the Expedition to Sweden under Sir J. Moore. Served during the campaigns in Spain and Portugal in the Year 1809 under Sir J. Moore and at the Battle of Corunna 16th January 1809. With the Expedition to Flushing in August 1809 and present at the Siege and surrender of that place. Served with the Regiment through the whole of the Campaigns in Portugal, Spain & France from the year 1810 to 1814 ... and was present at the following General Actions and Sieges: Battle of Fuentes-de-honor on the 3d May & 5th May 1811. Battle of Salamanca on the 22d July 1812. The Siege of Burgos 1812. Battle of the Pyrenees in July 1813. Battle of the Nivelle on the 10th Novr. 1813. Battle of the Nive on the 9th Decr. 1813. Battle of Toulouse on the 10th April 1814. Battle of Quatre Bras on the 16th June 1815.' *Wounds received in action*: 'Received Two severe contusions at the Battle of Fuentes-de-honor on the 5th May 1811. No grant of Pay or Pension. Wounded at Burgos in the year 1812. No grant of Pay or Pension. Severely wounded at Quatre Bras on the 16th June 1815. Received One Years Pay and a Pension of £200 a year. Permanent.' *Titles, honorary distinctions and medals*: 'A Gold Medal for services in Egypt. The Ribbon and Badge of the Companion of the Most Honorable Military Order of the Bath. Medal for the Battle of Waterloo.' *Service abroad*: '26th Sept. 1795 to 10th Augt. 1796, West Indies. 27th Augt. 1799 to 1st Novr. 1799, Holland. 8th

March 1801 to 31st July 1802. Egypt. 26th July 1807 to October 1807, Denmark. 29th April 1808 to 1809, Spain & Portugal. 15th July 1809 to 8th Septr. 1809, Holland. 28th Decr. 1810 to 3d July 1814, Portugal, Spain & France. 7th May 1815 to 29th Octr. 1818, Netherlands & France. 1st Sept. 1825 to 31st Decr. 1829, Canada.' *Family*: Married his first wife, Ann Dixon, 26 Aug. 1794, St Mary's the Virgin in Dover. They had two children prior to her death. He then remarried, Mary Balfour, 10 Sept. 1803, in the Parish of Templemore, Londonderry. They had an additional two children by 1830. [PRO: WO 25/800 f230]. Waterloo.

BROWN, Charles, Lt., 50th Foot: *1829 Statement of Service for Retired Officers*: Aged nineteen on his first appointment to the Army. 'Volunteer from the Royal East Middx. Militia.' Ensign, 50th Foot, 'the Spring of 1810, I forget the precise day... I think the date of my first commission was the 10th May 1810' [Army List gives 8 March 1810]; 'Lieut. Novr. 13 1813' [Army List gives Lt., 50th Foot, 7 Oct. 1813]; Half-pay, 'at the reduction of the 2nd Battn. of the 50th foot, but for which I should have been placed on H.P. owing to the nature of my wound.' *Where serving when wounded*: 'St Palais in the South of France.' *Details of pension*: Seventy pounds commencing 18 Feb. 1815. 'Examined the last time in 1822, at which period his majesty was pleased to direct that my pension should be continued.' *Family*: Married in Egham, Surrey, 17 April 1828. *Title and nature of civil employment*: 'I hold a situation as Superintendant of the royal Park of Windsor. Am a private steward of his Majesty paid from the privy purse.' *Where generally resident during last five years*: 'Egham, Surrey.' [PRO: WO 25/751 f145]. Slightly wounded, the Nive, 13 Dec. 1813 (1st Battn.) [*London Gazette*]. Severely wounded, 'in

Action with the Enemy', 17 Feb. 1814 (1st Battn.) [*London Gazette*]. *1818 Pension Return*, pp. 14–15. MGS.

BROWN, Charles, Ensign, 79th Foot: *Statement of Service of Retired Officers*: Aged twenty on his first appointment to the Army. Ensign, 79th Foot, 2 Nov. 1809; Lt., 79th Foot, 9 May 1811; Half-pay, 25 June 1814, 'in consequence of a Memorial to that effect, from the loss of a leg at Fuentes d'onore.' *Where serving when wounded*: 'Fuentes d'onore.' *Details of pension*: Seventy pounds commencing 4 May 1812. *Where generally resident during last five years*: 'Paris, Corbeil Dept. of Seine et aise Marseilles, Bordeaux, Switzerland, Genoa, Florence, Naples, Switzerland, Nice, Naples, Strasburg, Bruxelles.' [PRO: WO 25/751 f257]. Severely wounded, Fuentes de Onoro, Evening 3 May 1811 [*London Gazette*]. *1818 Pension Return*, pp. 18–19.

BROWN, George, Lt., 43rd Foot: *1829 Statement of Service*: Born in Linkwood, near Elgin, 12 Aug. 1790. Aged fifteen 'on his first Entrance into the Army.' Ensign, 43rd Foot, 23 Jan. 1806, 'from Rl. Mil. College.' Lt., 43rd Foot, 18 Sept. 1806. Capt., 3rd Garrison Battn., 20 June 1811. Capt., 85th Foot, 2 July 1812. Major, 85th Foot, 26 May 1814. Bvt. Lt. Col., 85th Foot, 29 Sept. 1814. Lt. Col., Half Pay, unattached, 17 July 1823. Lt. Col., Rifle Brigade, 5 Feb. 1824. 'Asst. to the Qr. Mr. Genl. of the Forces, 11th May 1815 to June 1816.' *Battles, sieges and campaigns*: 'At the Siege & Capture of Copenhagen in 1807... At the Battle of Vimiera 21 Aug. 1808. At the Passage of the Douro & Capture of Oporto 11 May 1809, with the previous & subsequent actions. The Battle of Talavera 27 & 28 July 1809. The Action of the Light Div. at the Bridge of Almeida 24 July 1810. Battle of Busaco 27th

Sept. 1810. In the different actions during the Retreat of the French Army from Portugal. Action at Sabugal 3d April & Battle of Fuentes d'Onoro 5th May 1811. San Sebastian Septr. 1813. Neville 10 Novemr. 1813. Nive 9 Decr. 1813. Investment of Bayonne 1814... The Battle of Bladensburgh & Capture of Washington 24th August 1814.' *Distinguished conduct*: 'In Command of the advanced Guard at Bladensburgh, thanked in General Orders by Major Genl. Ross.' *Wounds received in action*: '1. Wounded severely through both Thighs at Talavera, on the 28 July 1809. 2. Slightly in the Head & very severely in the left Groin at Bladensburg, on the 24th August 1814. The ball is still lodged within the Pelvis. Received one years pay as Lieutenant and one years Pay as Major, in 1815. A temporary Pension of £200, from year to year, from 25 Decr. 1815 to 24th Decr. 1820, when it ceased. Pension received and made permanent from 25th Decr. 1826.' *Service abroad*: 'July 1807 to Nov. 1807, Denmark. Aug. 1808 to July 1811, Portugal. July 1813 to May 1814, Spain & France. June 1814 to May 1815, America. June 1821 to Aug. 1823, Malta, in 85 Regt. 13 Jany. 1826 to 31 Dec. 1829, Malta.' *Family*: Married Maria Macdonell, 7 June 1827, Florence. They had no children by 1830. [PRO: WO 25/804 f310]. Slightly wounded, Talavera, 28 July 1809, while serving with 1st Battn. of Detachments [*London Gazette*]. MGS. Died 27 Aug. 1865. Army List gives as 'Browne'. *Mullen*, p. 312 ['Commanded Light Division in the Crimea.'].

BROWN, Gustavus, Major, 60th Foot; Lt. Col., 9th Portuguese Caçadores: Major, Army, 25 July 1810; Major, 60th Foot, 3 Oct. 1811. In Portuguese Service April 1810 to Jan. 1814. Gold Medal. *Challis, Portuguese Army*, p. 52 ['Lt.-Col. 9 Caçad... Wd. Nive 13 Dec. '13'].

BROWN, Henry, Lt., 59th Foot: Lt., 59th Foot, 26 Oct. 1810. Slightly wounded at the storming of San Sebastian, 31 Aug. 1813 ('Browne') (2nd Battn.) [*London Gazette*]. Waterloo.

BROWN, John, Capt., 27th Foot; Major, Portuguese Staff: *1829 Statement of Service*: Born 1 Oct. 1777, Dulwich, Surrey. Aged seventeen on his first entrance into the Army. Cornet, 6th Dragoons, 27 May 1795; Lt. 17 May 1796; Capt. 1 June 1796; Capt., 34th Foot, 25 June 1807; Capt., 8th Garrison Battn., 10 Nov. 1807; Capt., 27th Foot, 17 Aug. 1808; Major, Portuguese Staff, 16 Feb. 1809; Lt. Col., Portuguese Staff, 14 March 1811; Lt. Col., 46th Foot, 13 Aug. 1812; Lt. Col., Greek Light Infantry, 25 Jan. 1813; Lt. Col., 21st Light Dragoons, 6 April 1815; Lt. Col., 13th Light Dragoons, 9 May 1820; Colonel, Army, 19 July 1821. *Battles, sieges and campaigns*: 'Expedition under the Command of Lt. General Whitlock to S. America latter end of 1807 & beginning of 1808, as Aid-De-Camp. Roleca & Vimero ... as Dy. A.A. General in 1808. Surprise of French at Rueda in Spain ... as DA A Genl. 1809. Retreat thro' Spain & Battle of Corunna ... as D A A Genl. 1810. 2 Campaigns in Portugal in 13th Regt. Port. Inf ... as Lt. Col. 1810 & 1811 – the remainder of latter year as Lt. Col. in 5th Port. Cavy. attached to a Spanish Division, under the command of Lt. General Mendizabel. Surprise of 200 French Cavalry under command of General Breche at Fuente-los-Cantos, as Lt. Col. same year. Retreat of the above Division to Badajos same year. Skirmish with French Cavalry in Retiring from Badajos to Elvas same year, as Colonel in 8th Portuguese Cavalry.' *Distinguished conduct*: 'In the surprise of French Cavalry at Fuente-los-Cantos, and Retreat to Badajos, noticed in Division Orders, by Order of Lt. General Mendizabel. In retiring from

Badajos to Elvas. In attempting to save a Spanish Brigade under the Command of Lt. General Don Carlos D'Hispanha – and for which conduct received that General's written thanks.' *Wounds received in action*: '5 Wounds in retiring from Badajos to Elvas 1811, No Pension received, but the usual allowance of 1 year's Pay.' *Titles, honorary distinctions and medals*: 'British Knight by Patent, – at the recommendation of His Grace The Duke of Wellington, and General Lord Beresford. Knight of the Tower & sword by the King of Portugal, for Services in His Army. Knight of Charles the 3d, by the King of Spain, for Services in Spain with the Spanish Army.' *Service abroad*: 'Latter end of 1807 to Beginning of 1808, South America. 1808 to Beginning of 1815, Spain & Portugal.' *Family*: Married Mrs Franks, 1 June 1801, Bath. They had no children by 1830. [PRO: WO 25/784 f56].

BROWNE, Arthur Piggott, Lt., 50th Foot: *1829 Statement of Service*: Born 10 Aug. 1793, Moynr, County Galway. Aged sixteen on his first entrance into the Army. Ensign, 50th Foot, 13 April 1809; Lt., 50th Foot, 13 Feb. 1812; Capt., 50th Foot, 18 April 1822; Half-pay, 26th Foot, 1824; Capt., 16th Foot, 19 May 1825. *Battles, sieges and campaigns*: 'Severe engagement with the Batteries of Cabstende in the Scheldt 1809... Capture of Flushing 1809... Affair at Sobal 14 Oct. 1810. Retreat of Massina, March 1811. Battle of Fuentes de Honore May 1811. Battle of Arroyo de Molinus Octr. 1811. Storming of Almaraz, May 1812. Affair at Byar Febr. 1813. Battle of Vittoria 21 June 1813. Skirmishing on Pyrenees 5th, 6th & 7th July 1813. Battle of Maya 25th July 1813. Battle of Pampluna 28 July 1813. De Casso 30 July 1813. Donna Maria 31 July 1813. Passage of Nivelle Nov. 1813. Nive 9 Decr. 1813. B. of Pierre, 13 Decr 1813. Battle of Garris Feb. 1814. St. Palais, 11 Feb.

1814.' *Distinguished conduct*: 'Complimented and thanked by the Hon. Sir W. Stewart, Commg. the Division on the 14th Feby. 1814 when leading the Light Company.' *Wounds received in action*: 'Wounded in the abdomen 14 February 1814 by a musket ball at St Palais. Received compensation Captain's year's Pay having been in Command of a Company at the time.' *Service abroad*: 'July 1809 to Jany. 1810, Walcheren; August 1810 to August 1814, Peninsula and France. Jany 1819 to May 1824, Jamaica. July 1828 to Decr. 1829, Bengal. 1 Jany 1830 to 3 Jany. 1835, Bengal.' *Family*: Married Maria Graham, 2 Jan. 1824, Dublin. They had four children by 1830. [PRO: WO 25/788 f16]. Slightly wounded, 'in Action with the Enemy', 14 Feb. 1814 ('Lieutenant Arthur Pigot, Brown') (1st Battn.) [*London Gazette*].

BROWNE, George, 1st Lt., 23rd Foot: *1829 Statement of Service for Retired Officers*: Aged seventeen on his first appointment in the Army. '2nd Lieut., Lieutenant, Captain.' [Army List gives 1st Lt., 23rd Foot, 17 June 1807]. '23rd Regiment Royal Welsh Fusilier, served in that corps & was present in the field of most of the great Battles fought by the Duke of Wellington... Succeeded to a Company by a Death vacancy in the Field... Reduced with the 2nd Battn. 23rd in Decr. 1814. Appointed to the 34th Regt. May 1815, reduced with the 2nd Battn. of that Corp 24th April 1817. Went to Canada & served four years and a half in the Department of the Military Secretary. Appointed April 1825 to the 37th Regt. & purchased an unattached Majority August 1826... Never placed on half pay from private motive or ill health, but always by circumstances over which I have no control... Most desirous of service. I resigned a good appointment in Canada to return to the regular line as my

BROWNE

profession & would most willingly join any Regiment of the Line, and in any part of the world.' *Where serving when wounded*: 'Pyrenees, but wounded in other engagements.' *Details of pension*: Seventy pounds commencing in 1814. *Family*: Married, Ireland, Feb. 1817. *Description of civil employment*: 'Sub Inspector of Police for the County of Kilkenny.' *Where generally resident during last five years*: 'In Canada. Regimental duty at Portsmouth. In Wales & in Ireland.' [PRO: WO 25/751 f170]. Severely wounded, storming of Badajoz, 6 April 1812 ('G. Brown') [*London Gazette*]. Slightly wounded, Pyrenees, 25 July 1813 ('G. Browne') (1st Battn.) [*London Gazette*]. *1818 Pension Return*, pp. 6-7 [Temporary pension of seventy pounds per annum, commencing 26 July 1814, 'for wounds' received at 'Roncevalles, 1813']. Later Lt. Col. MGS.

BROWNE, John, Lt., 4th Foot: *1829 Statement of Service*: Born in 1789. Aged fifteen 'on his first Entrance into the Army.' Ensign, 4th Foot, 21 Oct. 1804. Lt., 4th Foot, 28 Feb. 1805. Capt., Half Pay, 4th Foot, Aug. 1815, 'Reduction of 2nd Battn.' Capt., 92nd Foot, 12 Nov. 1818. Bvt. Major, 92nd Foot, 21 Jan. 1819. Major, Half Pay, unattached, 19 Nov. 1830. *Battles, sieges and campaigns*: '1810, Lieutenant at the Lines of Torres Vedras... 1811, Lieutenant in the affairs in the pursuit of Massena at Redinha &c. Fuentes de Honor and Siege of Badajoz... 1814, Lieutenant at the Capture of Ciudad Rodrigo [sic]... 1815 Lieutenant in the actions of Quatre Bras & Waterloo.' *Wounds received in action*: 'Wounded at the Seige of Badajos. Received one years pay and permanent pension of £70 per annum. Wounded at Waterloo, received one years pay and a permanent pension of £100 per annum.' *Titles, honorary distinctions and medals*: 'A Waterloo Medal.' *Service abroad*: 'May 1808

to Nov. 1812, In Sweden, Portugal and Spain. June 1815 to Sept. 1815, Netherlands. 4 June 1819 to April 1820, Jamaica. 25th April 1822 to 21st May 1827, Jamaica.' *Family*: Married Frances Jane Hawthorn, 2 Oct. 1823, 'Inverness Island of Jamaica.' They had four children by 1830. [PRO: WO 25/803 f80]. Severely wounded, storming of Badajoz, 6 April 1812 ('Brown') [*London Gazette*]. Seventy pounds per annum pension, commencing 7 April 1813, 'for wounds' received at Badajoz, 1812. A second pension of one hundred pounds, commencing 19 June 1816, 'for a wound' received at Waterloo, 1815. [*1818 Pension Return*, pp. 4-5]. Died 21 Nov. 1849. *Dalton*, p. 121 ['At Waterloo, whilst at the head of his company, Capt. Browne received a fearful wound from a bullet, just over the ear, and fell senseless. He was left on the field for dead and was reported killed. His family in Ireland went into mourning for him. However, he recovered by trepanning.'].

+BROWNE, Richard Robert, Capt., 88th Foot: Capt., 88th Foot, 5 Aug. 1804. Severely wounded, Talavera, 28 July 1809 [London Gazette]. Died, Portugal, 26 July 1810 [PRO: WO 25/2965].

BROWNE, Hon. Thomas, Lt., 40th Foot: Lt., 40th Foot, 14 July 1808. Wounded during the repulse of a sortie from Badajoz, 10 May 1811 ('Brown') [*London Gazette*]. Slightly wounded, Salamanca, 22 July 1812 ('Brown') [*London Gazette*]. MGS.

BROWNE, Thomas Henry, Capt., 23rd Foot: *1829 Statement of Service for Retired Officers*: Aged seventeen on his first appointment in the Army. 2nd Lt., 23rd Foot, Oct. 1806; 1st Lt., 23rd Foot, Sept. 1807 [Army List gives 18 Sept]; Capt., 23rd Foot, April 1813; Half-pay by reduction [n.d.]. *Where serving when wounded*: 'Martinique, 1809.

Vitoria, 1813.' *Family*: Married in Gosforth near Newcastle, 13 March 1827. No children by 1829. [PRO: WO 25/751 f189]. Slightly wounded, Vittoria, 21 June 1813, while serving as DAAG on General Staff ('Captain T. H. Brown') [*London Gazette*].

BROWNING, Thomas, Volunteer/ Ensign, 68th Foot: *1829 Statement of Service for Retired Officers*: Aged 21 on his first appointment to the Army. Ensign, 68th Foot, 26 Aug. 1813; Lt., 68th Foot, 16 Oct. 1816; Half-pay by reduction. *Where serving when wounded*: 'Was wounded twice, in the thigh severely, & arm slightly. Recd. 1st one at the battle of Pampluna or Piranees, the other at St Pie or Nivelle, France.' *Family*: Married in Waterford near Cork, 8 Jan. 1824. He had two children by 1829. *Where generally resident during last five years*: 'Partly at Cork, Passage West ... in the Co. Cork.' [PRO: WO 25/751 f259]. Slightly wounded, Pyrenees, 31 July 1813, while serving as a Volunteer in the 68th Foot [*London Gazette*]. Severely wounded, Nivelle, 10 Nov. 1813 [*London Gazette*]. Lt., 68th Foot, 17 Oct. 1816. MGS.

+BROWNLOW, William, Capt., 6th Foot: Capt., Army, 5 Feb. 1807. Capt., 6th Foot, 12 Feb. 1807. Killed, Pyrenees, 2 Aug. 1813 (1st Battn.) [*London Gazette*].

BROWNSON, William Henry, 1st Lt., 23rd Foot: 1st Lt., 23rd Foot, 18 June 1807. Severely wounded, storming of Badajoz, 6 April 1812 [*London Gazette*]. Capt., 23rd Foot, 13 Jan. 1814. Half pay upon reduction of the regiment in 1814.

BRUCE, Charles, Lt. Col., 39th Foot: *1829 Statement of Service*: Born in the East Indies, 24th March 1777. Aged fifteen on first appointment to the Army. Ensign, 52nd Foot, Feb. 1792; Lt., 99th Foot, Aug. 1793;

Capt., 105th Foot, April 1794; Capt., 39th Foot, Oct. 1795; Bvt. Major, 1803; Major, 39th Foot, 1805 [Army List gives 21 March]; Lt. Col., 39th Regt., [25] July 1810; Half-pay, 1816, by reduction; Bvt. Col., Aug. 1819; Lt. Col., 69th Foot, March 1820; Half-pay, April 1826, by reduction; Lt. Col., 6th Foot, April 1827; Lt. Col., 64th Foot, May 1828. *Battles, sieges and campaigns*: 'Capture of the South American Colonies of Demerara, Rerbice, Esequebo &c &c as Captain in 1796... In Sicily ... as Major in 1809. The 39th Regiment joined the Army in the Peninsula under the Command of the Duke of Wellington in 1810, and continued to serve with it till the conclusion of the War in 1814. Commanded the 39th Regt. as Lt. Colonel in the six following mentioned General Actions and besides in several other minor affairs during the operations of the 2nd Division of that Army under the Orders of Lord Hill. Victtoria 21st June 1813. Battles of the Pyrenees between the 28th July and 2d Augt. 1813. Nivelle 10th Novr. 1813. Nive 9th to 13th Decr. 1813. Orthes 21st Febr. 1814. Toulouse 10th April 1814. Embarked from Bordeaux for Canada and returned to France in 1815 and remained serving with the Army before Paris and of occupation till 1816. On the occasion of the attack of the Heights of Garris before St Pallais in France on the 15th February 1814.' *Wounds received in action*: 'Severely wounded at Garris near St Pallais in France on the 15th February 1814 and received a Gratuity of one Years Pay.' *Titles, honorary distinctions and medals*: 'Obtained the Decoration as Companion of the Most Honble. Military Order of the Bath, and Received Medals and a Cross for the Battles of the Pyrenees; Nive; Nivelle and Orthez.' *Service abroad*: 'October 1795 to Decr. 1803, West Indies. Decr. 1805 to April 1816, Malta, Sicily, Portugal, Spain, and France. North America and again in

BRUCE

France. March 1820 to April 1825, East Indies.' *Family*: Married 'Miss Chalotte Huber, the 2nd Daughter of the late James Huber Esqr. of Hutton Hall in the County of Essex,' 14 July 1818, at Hutton, Essex. They had three children by 1830. [PRO: WO 25/797 f240]. Severely wounded, 'in Action with the Enemy', 15 Feb. 1814 (1st Battn.) [*London Gazette*]. Mentioned in Wellington dispatch, dated 'St Jean de Luz', 20 Feb. 1814: 'On the 15th ... towards St Palais ... the 2d division ... should attack in front. Those troops made a most gallant attack upon the enemy's position, which was remarkably strong, but which was carried without very considerable loss ... the enemy ... made repeated attempts to regain the position, particularly in two attacks, which were most gallantly received and repulsed by the 39th regiment... The Major-General [Pringle], and Lieutenant-Colonel Bruce, of the 39th, were unfortunately wounded']. Gold Medal.

BRUCE, Edward John, Ensign, 60th Foot: Ensign, 60th Foot, 6 Feb. 1813. Severely wounded, Toulouse, 10 April 1814 ('John Bruce') (5th Battn.) [*London Gazette*].

BRUGH, Adam, Capt., 44th Foot: Capt., Army, 12 Feb. 1807; Capt., 44th Foot, 11 June 1807. Severely wounded, storming of Badajoz, 6 April 1812 (2nd Battn.) [*London Gazette*]. Wounded, Waterloo. Died 1825.

BRUNTON, Richard, Lt., 43rd Foot; Capt., 6th Caçadores; Capt., 60th Foot: *1829 Statement of Service*: Born London, 20 Dec. 1788. Aged '19 years and 10 months' on 'his first entrance into the Army.' Ensign, 43rd Foot, 10 Nov. 1808; Lt. 12 Dec. 1809; 'I was appointed to a Company in the 6th Caçadores in February 1811'; Capt., 60th Foot, 10 Nov. 1813; Half Pay 25 Dec. 1818; Capt., 13th Light Dragoons, 29 April

1819; Major 2 March 1826; Lt. Col. 31 Dec. 1830. *Battles, sieges and campaigns*: 'As Ensign 43rd, Campaign of 1809 in the Lt. Division... Lieut. 43rd Action at Bridge of the Coa nr. Almeida 24th July 1810... Capt. 6th Caçadores, Fuentes d'Onor, 3 & 5th May 1811... Capt. 6th Caçs., Arroyo de Molinos 28th October 1811... Capt. 6th Caçs., Almarez (castle of Miravete) 19 May 1812... Capt., 6th Caçs., Vittoria, 21 June 1813... Capt. 6th Caçs., Puerto de Maya, 7th July 1813... Capt. 6th Caçs., Pyrenees, 30 July 1813... Capt., 6th Caçs., Nivelle, 10 Nov. 1813... Capt. 6th Caçs., Nive, 9th Decem. 1813... Capt. 6th Caçs., St. Pierre d'Arrube nr. Bayonne, 13th Decr. 1813... Dep. Ass. QMasr. General 4th Division, Waterloo, 18 June 1815.' *Distinguished conduct*: 'My Conduct was never noticed in General Orders, but it frequently received the approbation of my Superior Officers and particularly of Lord Hill at the Puerto de Maya on the 7th July 1813, and of the Honble Sir William Stewart on the 25th at the same place. I was also on several occasions recommended by my commanding officer for promotion, which is proved by letters from Lord Hill, Lord Beresford, and Genl. Pinto (then commanding the 6th Caçadores) sent in with a memorial to H.R. Highness the Commander in Chief on the 16th of August 1818.' *Wounds received in action*: 'Slightly at the Battle of the Pyrenees on the 30th of July 1813. Severely at St Pierre d'Arrube near Bayonne on the 13th of December 1813. For the latter wound I received a grant of one years full Pay.' *Titles, honorary distinctions and medals*: 'The Portuguese Cross of Distinction for three Campaigns in that Service. The Waterloo Medal. A certificate of qualification for the General Staff of the Army from the Royal Military College, 11th December 1817.' *Service abroad*: '22 May 1809 to 6th Feby. 1814, Portugal, Spain, &

France. 25 April 1815 to 24 Feby. 1816, Netherlands & France. 1 March 1820 to 20 Feby. 1826, Madras. 2 March 1828 to 21 Dec. 1829, Madras.' *Family*: Married 'Mrs E. A. Wallace, widow of Major Wallace of the Madras Cavalry, and Daughter of the late Revd. I Thomas Archdeacon of Bath', 30 June 1829, St. Thomas's Mount, Madras. [PRO: WO 25/784 f60]. *Challis, Portuguese Army*, p. 52.

+BRYAN, George, Adjutant/Lt. and Capt., Coldstream Guards: Ensign, Coldstream Guards, 6 Dec. 1803; Adjutant, Coldstream Guards, 1 May 1805; Lt. and Capt., Coldstream Guards, 24 July 1807. Severely wounded, Talavera, 27 July 1809 [*London Gazette*]. Obituary, *The Gentleman's Magazine*, Nov. 1809, p. 1076 ['30 [Sept.]. At Talavera, Capt. Bryan, adjutant of the 1st Battalion of the Coldstream Regiment of Guards.'].

+BUCHANAN, James, Lt. and Capt., 3rd Foot Guards: Lt., Army, 6 June 1799; Lt. and Capt., 3rd Foot Guards, 7 Feb. 1800. Killed, Talavera, 28 July 1809 [*London Gazette*].

+BUCKERIDGE, John Charles, Ensign, Coldstream Guards: Ensign, Coldstream Guards, 29 March 1810. Killed, siege of Burgos, 5–10 Oct. 1812 [*London Gazette*]. 'Killed before Burgos', 7 Oct. 1812. Return dated 25 Oct. 1812. [PRO: WO 25/2965].

BUCKLEY, William, Captain, 1st Foot: Capt., 1st Foot, 11 Oct. 1810. Severely wounded, 'at the Siege of St Sebastian,' 7–27 July 1813 (3rd Battn.) [*London Gazette*]. Slightly wounded, sortie from Bayonne, 14 April 1814 (3rd Battn.) [*London Gazette*]. Killed at Quatre Bras.

BUDGEN, John Robert, 1st Lt., 95th Foot: *1829 Statement of Service for Retired Officers*: Aged sixteen on his first appointment to the Army. 2nd Lt., 95th Foot, 17 March 1808; 1st Lt., 95th Foot, April 1809 [Army List gives 4 May 1809]; Capt., 95th Foot, 15 June 1815; Half-pay, 'By reductin of the 3 Batt. Rifle Brigade in 1818.' *Where serving when wounded*: 'At Aranjues, Spain.' *Details of pension*: Seventy-five pounds, commencing 27 Oct. 1813. *Family*: Married in Cheltenham, 13 Jan. 1823. Two children by 1829. *Title and nature of civil employment*: 'Depty. Lieut. and Majestrate for the County of Surrey.' *Where generally resident during last five years*: 'Nutfield, Surrey.' [PRO: WO 25/751 f361]. Slightly wounded, Crossing the Bidassoa, 7/9 Oct. 1813 ('Budgeon') (2nd Battn.) [*London Gazette*]. Waterloo. MGS. Died, 1866. *Dalton*, p. 201 ['Born 1st Dec., 1791.'].

+BUIST, Richard, Lt./Adjutant, 20th Foot: Lt., 20th Foot, 20 March 1800; Adjutant 11 May 1809. Killed, Pyrenees, 25 July 1813 [*London Gazette*].

BULSTRODE, Augustus, Capt., 66th Foot: Capt., 66th Foot, 21 Dec. 1809. Severely wounded, the Nive, 13 Dec. 1813 (2nd Battn.) [*London Gazette*]. Two pensions, each of one hundred pounds per annum, commencing 14 Dec. 1814, 'for wounds' received at Bayonne, 1813 [*1818 Pension Return*, pp. 16–17].

+BUNBURY, Ralph, 1st Lt., 95th Foot: The first British officer killed in the Peninsular War. 1st Lt., 95th Foot, 14 Nov. 1805. Killed, Obidos, 15 Aug. 1808. *Simmons*, p. 1. *Leach*, p. 45 ['On the 15th of August, after a long march, a party of French cavalry and infantry were found near the town of Obidos, where there is a Moorish castle. Four companies of ours and of the 60th regiment instantly attacked and obliged them to retire. In the ardour of pursuit, our people pushed on a considerable distance from any support, and were met by a very superior body of the enemy, sent forward to support their advanced party. A sharp skirmish ensued, in which we lost some few killed, wounded and missing. The Honourable Captain Pakenham, of our regiment, was wounded, and Lieutenant Bunbury killed, the first British officer who fell in the Peninsular wars. He was much regretted by us all.']. *Harris*, p. 27 ['It was on the 15th of August when we first came up with the French, and their skirmishers immediately commenced operations by raining a shower of balls upon us as we advanced, which we returned without delay. The first man that was hit was Lieutenant Bunbury; he fell pierced through the head with a musket-ball, and died almost immediately.']. Note: a handwritten addition to the 1808 Army List in the Bodleian Library, Oxford, reads: 'brother to Capt. Benjn. Bunbury, Tipperary Militia.'

BUNBURY, Thomas, Lt., 91st Foot; Capt., 5th Caçadores: *1829 Statement of Service*: Born in Gibraltar, 19 May 1791. Aged sixteen on his first Entrance into the Army. Ensign, 90th Foot, 7 May 1807. Ensign, 3rd Foot, 13 Aug. 1807. Lt., 91st Foot, 17 Aug. 1809. Capt., 'attached to the Portuguese Service', 25 Oct. 1814. Half Pay, 25 Dec. 1816, 'By Reduction'. Captain, 80th Foot, 10 Oct. 1822. *Battles, sieges and campaigns*: '1. At Oporto 12 May 1809 with the Two companies of the 3rd Foot which frst crossed the Douro. 2. At Talavera 27th and 28th July 1809. Carried the Colours of the 3d Foot... 3... At Barrosa 5th Mar. 1811... having volunteered, as Captain, with a Detachment 20th Portuguese. 4. 1812 at Tarifa during the defence, being the Brigade Major under Col. Skerrett also in the same capacity with the Expedition to the Condada de Niebla under same officer which took Seville 1812. 5. At the defence

of the Bridge of Puento Laigo near Aranjuez as Brigade Major 1812... 6. At the Nivelle Captn. 5th Caçadores Portuguese Service 10th Novr. 1813. 7. At the Nive Capt. 5th Caçadores 9th Decr. 1813. 8. At the Investment and subsequent siege of Bayonne being Brevet Major 5th Caçadores. 9. At Toulouse 10 Apl. 1814. Major Commandg. 6th Caçadores.' *Distinguished conduct*: '1. Noticed in General Orders by Field Marshal Lord Beresford 1st May 1811. 2. Noticed in General Orders by Col. Skerrett after the repulse of the French before Tarifa. 3. In the Despatches of 23d Sep. 1812 on the taking of Seville. 4. In the Despatches of 3d Decr. 1812 when acting as Asst. Qr. Mr. General to Lt. Genl. Sir J. Hamilton's Division ... on the retreat from Burgos. 5. By Field Marshal Lord Beresford promoted on the field to the rank of Major in General Orders 23rd Decr. 1813 at the Battle of the Nive.' *Wounds received in action*: 'Ruptured during the Retreat from Burgos and received a Permanent Pension of £100 pr. ann. since 24 Decr. 1827. Severely wounded at the Battle of the Nive, received a gratuity of One Years Pay.' *Titles, honorary distinctions and medals*: 'Received from the Portuguese Government a Gold Medal for Five Campaigns in which he served in their Army.' Note added in pencil: 'And also from the late King of Portugal D. John the 6th a commission as Knight of the Military Order of the Tower & Sword dated 18 April 1824 for Military service but not having appeared in the London Gazette although duly notified by their Ambassador he does not conceive himself entitled to wear the Insignia.' *Service abroad*: '1808 to 1820, Peninsula. 1823 to 1827, Malta.' [PRO: WO 25/800 f314]. Mentioned in Skerrett's dispatch concerning the capture of Seville, 28 Aug. 1812 ['The exertions of ... Staff Officers, attached to the detachment, have been indefatigable.

Captain Bunbury, 20th Portuguese Regiment, Brigade-Major and Lieutenant Smith, Royal Engineers, were at this time detached on other service.'] [*London Gazette*]. Mentioned in Hamilton's dispatch of 11 Nov. 1812, concerning the Affair at Alba de Tormes, 10–11 Nov. 1812 ['and to Captain Bunbury, my Aide-de-Camp, I consider myself obliged, for their prompt execution of my orders.'] [*London Gazette*]. Severely wounded, the Nive, 10 Dec. 1813, while serving as Capt., 5th Caçadores [*London Gazette*]. In Portuguese Service Oct. 1809 to April 1814. MGS. *Challis, Portuguese Army*, p. 53.

+BUNTING, James, Capt., 60th Foot: Lt., 60th Foot, 7 April 1797; Capt., 60th Foot, 25 June 1803. Killed, storming of Badajoz, 6 April 1812.

BUNWORTH, Peter, Ensign, 53rd Foot: Ensign, 53rd Foot., 29 Jan. 1812. Slightly wounded, Salamanca, 22 July 1812 ('Ensign') (2nd Battn.) [*London Gazette*]. Lt., 53rd Foot, 8 June 1814.

BUNWORTH, Richard, Capt., 88th Foot: Capt., 88th Foot, 30 May 1811. Slightly wounded, Orthes, 27 Feb. 1814 (1st Battn.) [*London Gazette*].

BURGES, Francis, Ensign, 83rd Foot: Ensign, 83rd Foot, 6 May 1813. Severely wounded, Nivelle, 10 Nov. 1813 ('Burgess') (2nd Battn.) [*London Gazette*].

+BURGESS, Wentworth Noel, Ensign, Coldstream Guards: Ensign, Coldstream Guards, 1 June 1809. Killed, siege of Burgos, 19 Oct. 1812 [*London Gazette*]. *Register of dead officers*: 'Killed before Burgos', 18 Oct. 1812. Return dated 25 Oct. 1812 [PRO: WO 25/2965].

BURGH, Ulysses, Capt., 54th Foot: Capt., Army, 4 Sept. 1806; Capt., 54th Foot, 9 Oct. 1806. Slightly wounded, Talavera, 28 July 1809, while serving as Aide-de-Camp to Sir Arthur Wellesley (92nd Regt.) [*London Gazette*]. ADC to Wellington at Busaco, 27 Sept. 1810, and carried Wellington's Busaco dispatch: 'I send this dispatch by my aide-de-camp Captain Burgh, to whom I beg to refer your Lordship for any further details, and I recommend him to your Lordship's notice.' [*London Gazette*]. Delivered to London Wellington's dispatches concerning the Affair at Majalahonda, 11 Aug. 1812, and the attack on the Retiro, 13 Aug. 1812 ['Downing-Street, September 4, 1812. Major Burgh, Aide-de-Camp to the Marquess of Wellington, has this day arrived at Lord Bathurst's office with dispatches addressed to his Lordship by Lord Wellington'] [*London Gazette*]. Gold Medal.

BURGOYNE, John Fox, Capt., Royal Engineers: 2nd Lt. 29 Aug. 1798; 1st Lt. 1 July 1800; 2nd Capt. 1 March 1805; Capt., Royal Engineers, 24 June 1809. Served in Egypt; engaged at Alexandria. Mentioned in Wellington's Badajoz dispatch, dated 7 April 1812 ['Lieutenant-Colonel Fletcher continued to direct the works ... which were carried on by Major Squire and Major Burgoyne, under his directions ... the latter attended the attack of the 3rd division on the castle.'] [*London Gazette*]. Bvt. Lt. Col., Royal Engineers, 27 April 1812. Mentioned in Wellington's dispatch concerning the siege and storming of the forts at Salamanca, dated Fuente la Pena, 30 June 1812 ['Major-General Clinton ... mentions in strong terms ... Lieutenant-Colonel Burgoyne, Lieutenant Reid, and the officers of the royal engineers'] [*London Gazette*]. Engaged at Vittoria. Slightly wounded, storming of San Sebastian, 31 Aug. 1813 [*London Gazette*]. Mentioned in Graham's San Sebastian dispatch, dated Oyarzun, 1 Sept. 1813 ['the

Engineer department [was commanded] by Lieutenant-Colonel Sir Richard Fletcher, 'till the moment of his much-lamented fall at the mouth of the trenches. Lieutenant-Colonel Burgoyne succeeded to the command... Lieutenant-Colonel Burgoyne was himself wounded, and only quitted the field from loss of blood; but I am happy to say he is able to carry on the duty of the department.'] [*London Gazette*]. Served at New Orleans. Gold Medal. MGS. Died 1871 aged 89, and is buried in St Peter's Church in the Tower of London. [*Mullen*, p. 645]. *Brotherton*, p. 23.

BURGWEDEL, Ernest von, Major, 3rd Light Dragoons/Hussars K.G.L.: *1829 Statement of Service for Retired Officers*: Aged thirty-one on his first appointment in the Army. Capt., 3rd Hussars K.G.L., 'Date not known, lost the commission in Spain' [No date given in Army List]; Major, 3rd Light Dragoons, 16 May 1806 [Army List gives 15 May 1806]; Half-pay, June 1811. 'Recommended to Half pay by a Medical Board in consequence of been wounded in the Battle of Benevente.' *Where serving when wounded*: 'In the Battle of Benevente.' *Family*: Married in Goldberg in Mecklenburg Schwerin, 27 March 1817. *Where generally resident during last five years*: 'Goldberg in Mecklenburg Schwerin.' [PRO: WO 25/751-f295]. Served in Peninsula 1808–9. Gold Medal. *Beamish*, vol. II, p. 621 ['Severely wounded 29th Dec. 1808 at Benevente ... placed upon half-pay 14th May 1811, [died] at Goldberg, grand dutchy of Mecklenburg, 16th Nov. 1832.'].

BURKE, Patrick John, Lt., 7th Foot: Lt., 7th Foot, 28 Oct. 1807. Slightly wounded, Orthes, 27 Feb. 1814 (1st Battn.) [*London Gazette*]. 'John Patrick Burke' in *Challis, Index*, p. 79.

+BURKE, Richard, Capt., 3rd Foot: Capt., Army, 23 Oct. 1806; Capt., 3rd Foot, 9 April 1807. Killed, Albuera, 16 May 1811 [*London Gazette*]. Return dated 25 May 1811 [PRO: WO 25/2965]. *Register of officers' effects*: 'In debt'. [PRO: WO 25/2963].

BURKE, Richard, Lt., 45th Foot: Lt., 45th Foot, 14 Nov. 1805. Slightly wounded, Rolica, 17 Aug. 1808 [*London Gazette*].

BURKE, Stephen, Ensign, 47th Foot: *1829 Statement of Service for Retired Officers*: Aged nineteen on first appointment to the Army. Ensign, Galway Militia, 24 Dec. 1810; Lt., Galway Militia, 17 Feb. 1812; Ensign, 47th Foot, 11 June 1812, 'Volunteered from Galway Militia'; Lt., 47th Foot, 26 May 1814; Half-pay, 24 Oct. 1814, by reduction. *Where serving when wounded*: 'Spain, Severely Wounded at the assault of St Sebastian on the 31st August 1813. Ball passed through the right thigh.' No pension. *Family*: Married in Galway, 5 May 1824. Three children by 1829. *Title and nature of civil employment*: 'Chief Constable'. *Where generally resident during last five years*: 'Bantry County Cork 4 years, Killarney County Kerry one year.' [PRO: WO 25/751 f341]. Severely wounded, storming of San Sebastian, 31 Aug. 1813 (2nd Battn.) [*London Gazette*]. MGS.

BURKE, Thomas, Capt., 4th Foot: *1829 Statement of Service for Retired Officers*: Aged seventeen on his first appointment in the Army. Ensign, 4th Foot, 1 Oct. 1794, by 'Raising 25 men'; Lt., 87th Foot, 1798; Lt., 4th Foot, 1799; Capt., 4th Foot, 1804; Major, 4th Foot, 1813 [Army List gives 22 July 1813]. Half-pay 'by the Reduction of the 2 Battn.' 'Extremely desirous to serve, as far as the nature of my wounds will admit, not being fit for any thing, or other professions, but the Army.' 'Retired on Half Pay [25 Feb. 1816] by decision of a Medical Board in consequence of wounds received at the storming of Badajoz the 6th of April 1812, where I commanded the Forlorn Hope of General Leith's Division.' *Where serving when wounded*: 'In Spain, Assault of Badajoz, commanded the Forlorn hope of Genl. Leith's Division.' *Details of pension*: One hundred pounds, commencing 1814. Family: Married Carugaline Church, County Cork, 30 April 1807. He had seven children by 1829. *Where generally resident during last five years*: 'Prospect Villa, Co. Cork, Ireland.' [PRO: WO 25/750 f336]. Severely wounded, storming of Badajoz, 6 April 1812 [*London Gazette*]. MGS. Major-General, 20 June 1854. *1858 Hart's Army List* ['Served in Jamaica and St Domingo, 1796–7... Served in Holland in 1809, where he volunteered at the taking of the Island of Schouwen. Served in the Peninsula 1810–12. Was present at the battle of Fuentes d'Onor; was slightly wounded at the affair of Barba del Puerco; volunteered the Forlorn Hope of Sir James Leith's 5th Division at the taking of Badajoz, where he received several severe wounds "which have rendered him incapable of following his profession." ']. Temporary pension of one hundred pounds per annum, 'for wounds' received at Badajoz, 1812, commencing 7 April 1813 [*1818 Pension Return*, pp. 4–5].

+BURN, Henry, Ensign/Adjutant, 27th Foot: Killed, Pyrenees, 28 July 1813 ('Adjutant Burne') (3rd Battn.) [*London Gazette*]. Return dated 28 July 1813. [PRO: WO 25/2965]. 'Ensign ... Burn', in 'Deaths', *1814 Army List*. 'Henry Burn' in *Challis, Index*, p. 100.

BURN, Henry John, Lt., 28th Foot: Lt., 28th Foot, 11 Oct. 1810. Slightly wounded, Vittoria, 21 June 1813 ('Burne') [*London Gazette*].

BURN, William, Capt., 3rd Dragoons: Lt., Army, 1 Sept. 1807; Lt., 3rd Dragoons, 18 Jan. 1810; Capt., 3rd Dragoons, 28 Jan. 1813. Slightly wounded, Toulouse, 10 April 1814 [*London Gazette*].

BURNS, John, Ensign, 39th Foot: Ensign, 39th Foot, 25 Aug. 1813. Slightly wounded, the Nive, 13 Dec. 1813 (1st Battn.) [*London Gazette*].

+BURRARD, Paul Henry D., Ensign, 1st Foot Guards: Ensign, 1st Foot Guards, 5 Sept. 1805. Killed, 'in the Army lately in Spain' (1st Battn.) [*March 1809 Army List*, p. 105]. Obituary, *The Gentleman's Magazine*, Feb. 1809, p. 185 ['21 [Jan.]... The eldest son of Sir Harry Burrard, and aide-de-camp to Sir John Moore. He was severely wounded in the battle of Corunna, on the 16th; put on-board the Audacious man of war, where he died this day (the 21st).']. *Haythornthwaite, Armies*, p. 25.

+BURRARD, William, Ensign, 1st Foot Guards: Ensign, 1st Foot Guards, 17 Jan. 1811. Severely wounded, 'since dead', storming of San Sebastian, 31 Aug. 1813 [*London Gazette*]. Died of wounds, 2 Sept. 1813. Return dated Sept. 1813 [PRO: WO 25/2965]. Son of General Sir Harry Burrard. [*Haythornthwaite, Armies*, p. 25]. Obituary, *The Gentleman's Magazine*, Nov. 1813, p. 504 ['Of wounds received in the assault of St Sebastian, Ensign Burrard, 1st guards, son of Gen. B. (being the third gallant son of that officer who has fallen in the service of his country) whose own death is noticed in a succeeding page.'].

+BURROUGHS, William, Lt. and Capt., Coldstream Guards: Adjutant, Coldstream Guards, 23 April 1810; Lt. and Capt., Coldstream Guards, 28 Sept. 1809. Severely wounded, sortie from Bayonne, 14 April 1814 (1st Battn.) [*London*

Gazette]. *Register of dead officers*: Died of wounds, 26 April 1814. Return dated May 1814. [PRO: WO 25/2965]. *Hurt*, p. 75 ['Bayonne, D.O.W. Apl. 26 [1814]']. Buried in St Etienne, near Bayonne. *Fletcher, Fields of Fire*, p. 164 ['Coldstream Guards cemetery, Bayonne ... those who lie here include ... Burroughs'].

BURROWES, Robert, Cornet, 4th Dragoons: Cornet, 4th Dragoons, 25 Feb. 1813. Slightly wounded, Toulouse, 10 April 1814 [*London Gazette*].

BURROWS, John, Capt./Major, 57th Foot: Capt., 57th Foot, 14 May 1804. Slightly wounded, Pyrenees, 28 July 1813 ('Burrows') (1st Battn.) [*London Gazette*]. Bvt. Major, 57th Foot, 26 Aug. 1813; Major, 57th Foot, 10 Nov. 1813. Severely wounded, Nivelle, 10 Nov. 1813 ('John Burrowes, (Major)') (1st Battn.) [*London Gazette*]. Temporary pension of two hundred pounds per annum, commencing 11 Nov. 1814, 'for wounds' received at 'Anhoe', 1813 [*1818 Pension Return*, pp. 14–15]. MGS. 'Burroes' and 'Burrows' in Army List. *Mullen*, p. 374 ['Burrowes'].

BURY, George, Capt., 88th Foot: Lt., 88th Foot, 11 July 1805. Slightly wounded, Busaco, 27 Sept. 1810 (1st Battn.) [*London Gazette*]. MGS.

+BUSHE, Richard, Major, E.O.P.S.; Lt. Col., 20th Portuguese Regt: Capt., Army, 4 July 1803; Capt., 7th Foot, 6 Sept. 1804; Major, E.O.P. S., 16 Feb. 1809, 'Serving with the Portuguese Army'. 'Dangerously wounded', Barossa, 5 March 1811, as Lt. Col in 20th Portuguese Regt. [*London Gazette*]. Mentioned in Graham's Barossa dispatch of 6 March 1811 ['Lieutenant-Colonel Barnard (twice wounded) and the Officers of his flank battalion, executed the duty of skirmishing in advance with the enemy in a

masterly manner, and were ably seconded by Lieutenant-Colonel Bushe, of the 20th Portuguese, who (likewise twice wounded,) fell into the enemy's hands, but was afterwards rescued. The detachment of this Portuguese regiment behaved admirably throughout the whole affair.'] [*London Gazette*, 25 March 1811]. Lt. Col., 20th Portuguese Regt. 'Died of wounds received at the Battle of Barossa on 5 March.' 'Date of Decease: 20 April 1811'. Return dated 25 April 1811. [PRO: WO 25/2965]. In Portuguese Service from March 1809 to April 1814. Gold Medal. *Challis, Portuguese Army*, p. 53. *Surtees*, pp. 115, 116, 120–1 [Barossa: 'In this action, Colonel Bush [sic] was almost absurdly brave and conspicuous. As soon as he got his Portuguese fairly into action, he rode slowly backward and forward among them, with his spectacles on, crying out as the balls whistled past him, "Que bella musica!" what delightful music! Poor fellow, he did not ride there many minutes; for, being within a very short distance of the enemy's tirailleurs so conspicuous an object, it was not to expected he could escape. He died a few days after the action.'].

BUSSCHE, Augustus Frederick von dem, Major, 2nd Light Dragoons/Hussars K.G.L.: Major, 2nd Light Dragoons, 1 Aug. 1810. Mentioned in Abercromby's dispatch dated Merida, 5 Jan. 1812, concerning the action near Fuente del Maestre, 3 Jan. 1812 ['Suffice it to say, that on this occasion the hussars under Major Busche [sic] upheld the high military character they are so universally known to possess.'] [*London Gazette*]. Slightly wounded, Arroyo dos Molinos, 28 Oct. 1811 [*London Gazette*]. Thanked in Hill's dispatch of 30 Oct. 1811, for Arroyo do Molinos [*London Gazette*]. Gold Medal. Served in the Peninsula 1808-12. *Beamish*, vol. II, p. 622

['half-pay 9th March 1813, lieut. general h. p. commandant at Stade.'].

BUTLER, James, Lt., 40th Foot: Lt., 40th Foot, 14 Dec. 1809. Wounded in the trenches before Badajoz, 8–15 May 1811 [*London Gazette*]. Severely wounded, storming of Badajoz, 6 April 1812 (1st Battn.) [*London Gazette*].

+BUTLER, John O'Brien, Ensign, 32nd Foot: Ensign, 32nd Foot, 24 Aug. 1812. Killed, Nivelle, 10 Nov. 1813 ('Ensign John O'Brien Buller') [*London Gazette*].

BUTLER, Robert, Lt., 47th Foot: Lt., 47th Foot, 9 Oct. 1811. Pension of seventy pounds per annum, commencing 8 Oct. 1814, 'for wounds' received at 'Bidassoa, 1812'. A second, temporary pension of seventy pounds per annum, commencing 25 Dec. 1815, for 'injury sustained on service, Bidassoa' [*1818 Pension Return*, pp. 12–13]. Presumably this refers to the crossing of the Bidassoa, 7/9 Oct. 1813.

+BUTLER, Theobald, Ensign, 87th Foot: Ensign, 87th Foot, 25 Aug. 1808. Severely wounded, Talavera, 27 July 1809 [*London Gazette*]. *Register of officers' effects*: 'Died of wounds', 24 May 1811. Single. 'Acct. settled previous when taken Prisoner, 3 Aug. 1809.' 2nd Battn. [PRO: WO 25/2964].

BUTLER, William, Capt., 27th Foot: *1829 Statement of Service for Retired Officers*: Aged eighteen on his first appointment to the Army. Ensign, 27th Foot, 16 Aug. 1804; Lt., 27th Foot, 27 June 1805; Capt., 27th Foot, 25 June 1812 [Army List gives 24 June]; Half-pay by reduction 2nd Battn. 'Is not desirous of again entering the service.' *Where serving when wounded*: 'Spain, on the Pyrenees.' *Details of pension*: One hundred pounds per annum

commencing 1 Aug. 1814. *Family*: Married in London, 17 July 1827. *Where generally resident during last five years*: 'Ballybar House'. [PRO: WO 25/751 f332]. Severely wounded, Pyrenees, 1 Aug. 1813 (3rd Battn.) [*London Gazette*]. *1818 Pension Return*, pp. 8–9 ['for wounds' received at Lezaca, 1813]. Mentioned in the 1830 Statement of Service of William Boyle ['1st August 1813 was ordered with Captain Butler and two Companies of the 3rd Battalion 27th Regiment to attack a Body of French Troops on a height adjoining the Village of Lesaka in the Pyrenees at the Comencement Captain Butler was severely wounded and Borne to the rear.'] [PRO: WO 25/789 f82]. MGS.

BUTLER, William, Lt., 31st Foot: Lt., 31st Foot, 25 March 1808. Severely wounded, Albuera, 16 May 1811 (2nd Battn.) [*London Gazette*]. MGS.

BUTTERWORTH, Henry, Lt., 32nd Foot: *1829 Statement of Service for Retired Officers*: Aged twenty-four on his first appointment to the Army. Ensign, 32nd Foot, 25 Oct. 1807; Lt., 32nd Foot, 27 April 1809; Half-pay 35th Foot, 'at my own request ... from ill health either in June or July 1820'. 'Cannot serve again from ill health.' *Where serving when wounded*: 'Wounded several times at Salamanca & Waterloo.' 'Never applied' for pension. Not married in 1829. *Where generally resident during last five years*: 'Rochdale, Lancashire.' [PRO: WO 25/751 f369]. Severely wounded, Salamanca, 22 July 1812 [*London Gazette*]. MGS. *Mullen*, p. 260 ['A native of Rochdale, Lancs.'].

BYAM, Edward, Ensign, 38th Foot: Ensign, 38th Foot, 14 Nov. 1811. Severely wounded, Salamanca, 22 July 1812 (1st Battn.) [*London Gazette*]. Severely wounded by a grape shot while carrying the regimental colours of the 38th Foot at

Salamanca. Lt., 15th Light Dragoons, 9 April 1813. Wounded, Waterloo. MGS. *Dalton*, p. 76 [Born 1794... Maj.-Gen 11 Nov. 1851; Col.-in-Chief, 18th Hussars, 1858. Died 9 Sept. 1864].

BYRNE, Arthur, Lt., 27th Foot: *1829 Statement of Service*: Born 8 June 1784, Ireland. Aged sixteen on first appointment to the Army. 'Non Comd. Officer 7th Royal Fusiliers from 1799 to July 1811'; Ensign, 27th Foot, 18 July 1811; Lt., 27th Foot, 25 Aug. 1813; Adjutant, 27th Foot, 21 April 1814. *Battles, sieges and campaigns*: 'At the Siege of Copenhagen as a Non Commd. Officer in 1807... At the taking of the Island of Martinique in February 1809 as Non Commd. Officer... At the Battle of Busaco in 1810 as Non Commd. Officer... At the Battle of Albuhera in 1811 as Non Commd. Officer 7th Royal Fusiliers... At the Siege and Storming of Badajos 1812 Ensign 27th Regt... At the Affair on the 18th July 1812 with the advance guard of the French as Ensn. 27th Regt. near Carasal... At the Battle of Salamanca 22d July 1812... At the Battle of Vittoria 21 June 1813... At the Battle of the Pyrenees 26 July 1813... At the Nivelle 10 Novr. 1813, Lieut... At the Battle of Orthes 27 Feb. 1814... At the Battle of Thoulouse 10th April 1814... At the Affair with the Americans at Plattsburgh in 1814... July 1815 At the capture of Paris.' *Wounds received in action*: 'Severely wounded on the 26 July 1813 [Pyrenees] in Action with the Enemy; received one years pay as Ensign for that Wound. Severely Wounded in Action with the Enemy at the Battle of Thoulouse on the 10th of April 1814, when in Command of a company, received one years pay as Captain for the above wound. Permanent Pension of £70 per annum commencing in 1824.' *Service abroad*: '1800 to Nov. 1801, America. Decr. 1801 to Novr. 1805, West Indies. June 1807 to decr. 1808, America. 1 Jan. 1809 to 20 Apl. 1809, West Indies. Apl. 1809 to May 1810, America. June 1810 to 4 June 1814, France, Spain and Portugal. July 1814 to May 1815, America. June 1815 to April 1817, France. Jan. 1819 to Decr. 1823, Gibraltar. Jany. 1824 to 31 Decr. 1829, West Indies.' *Family*: Married Frances Doyle, 5 Aug. 1819, Gibraltar. They had four children by 1830. [PRO: WO 25/790 f115]. Slightly wounded, Pyrenees, 26 July 1813 (3rd Battn.) [*London Gazette*]. Severely wounded, Toulouse, 10 April 1814 (3rd Battn.) [*London Gazette*].

+BYRNE, Thomas, Ensign, 28th Foot: Ensign, 28th Foot, 28 Nov. 1811. Severely wounded, Vittoria, 21 June 1813 ('Burn') (1st Battn.) [*London Gazette*]. Died 'of wounds, Spain', 30 July 1813. Return dated July 1813 [PRO: WO 25/2965].

C

CADELL, Charles, Capt., 28th Foot: *1829 Statement of Service*: Born 6 July 1789, Cockenzie, near Edinburgh. Aged fifteen years and two months on his first entrance into the Army. Ensign, 28th Foot, 1 Sept. 1804; Lt. 1 Aug. 1805; Capt. 9 March 1809; Major 26 Dec. 1826. *Battles, sieges and campaigns*: 'Served at the Siege of Copenhagen in 1807 under Earl Cathcart. The expedition to Sweden in 1808, afterwards to Portugal in August of the same year. Went to Spain in October 1808 under Sir John Moore, was on the retreat and at the Battle of Corunna. Served in the Expedition to Walcheren in 1809, a Captain. Went with the Regiment to Gibraltar in February 1810, was at the Battle of Barrossa 5th March 1811, under Lord Lyndock. Served a short time at the siege of Cadiz, was at the following actions with the Regt. under the Duke of Wellington, in Spain & South of France viz at the surprize of Arrio Molina 28th October 1811. The Reduction of the Forts of Almarez 19th May 1812. Battle of Vittoria 21st June 1813. Battle of the Pyrennees from 25th to 31st July 1813. Battle of Nivelle 10th Nov. 1813. The Battle of the Nieve 9th & 13th Decr. 1813. The action of St Palais 15th Feby. 1814. The Battle of Orthes 27th Feby. 1814. The action of Lambego 18th March 1814. Then I commanded the right wing of the Regt. in the attack of that village. Battle of Toulouse 10th April 1814, all the Campaign of 1814, being second in command of the Regiment I did the duty of Major. Served at the Battle of Waterloo & commanded the Regt. for upwards of Two months afterwards, & at the second reduction of Paris. I have had the honor of serving in every action where the 1st Battn. 28th Regt. has been in during the last war a period of nearly 26 years.' *Distinguished conduct*: 'Was commended for Promotion by Brevet, on the two occasions, hereafter expressed. Was thanked by the late Lieutenant General Sir Wm. Stewart at the head of the 2nd Division (which was then commanded by him) for my services on the 13th December 1813. Again thanked for my service at the action of Lambego on the 18th March 1814 by Lt. Genl. Sir Wm. Stewart. The Senior Captains being Bt. Majors, & both wounded were promoted to the rank of Lieutenant Colonels.' *Wounds received in action*: 'Slightly wounded at the Battle of Barrossa on the 5th March 1811, but received no grant of Pay.' *Titles, honorary distinctions and medals*: 'Received a Medal for the Battle of Waterloo.' *Service abroad*: '24th July 1807 to 21st Novr. 1807, Copenhagen. June 1808 to Jany. 1809, Sweden, Portugal & Spain. 27th July 1809 to Octr. 1809, Walcheren. 27th Jany. 1810 to 12 Jan. 1814, Gibraltar & Peninsula. 27th April 1815 to 17th Decr. 1815, Netherlands & France. 7th Decr. 1817 to 3rd April 1827, Ionian Islands.' *Family*: Married Miss McDonald of Boisdale, 10 Nov. 1829, Guernsey. [PRO: WO 25/790 f170]. MGS. *Blakeney*, pp. 2, 84–5 [Retreat to Corunna, Jan. 1809: 'the whole reserve presented a rather curious appearance, in consequence of their being partially clad with the raiment which they had snatched from the Spanish carts the previous night. I recollect that Lieutenant Cadell, of the 28th Regiment (now lieutenant-colonel), cut a hole in a blanket, through which he thrust his head, and thus marched the whole day. Being a tall man, a grenadier, his appearance was afterwards called to mind when we saw the shepherds clad in sheepskins crossing the Pyrenean mountains on stilts.'], p. 205 [Wounded, Barossa, 5 March 1811]. Author of *Narrative of the Campaigns of the 28th Regiment from 1802 to 1832*, (London, 1835).

+**CADOGAN, Hon. Henry, Lt. Col., 71st Foot**: Lt. Col., Army, 22 Aug. 1805; Lt. Col., 71st Foot, 7 Jan. 1808. Born 26 Feb. 1780, seventh son of Charles, 1st Earl Cadogan. Mentioned in Wellington's Fuentes de Onoro dispatch, 8 May 1811 [concerning the fighting on 3 May: 'having observed the repeated efforts which the enemy were making to obtain possession of the Village... I reinforced the Village successively with the 71st regiment under the Honourable Lieutenant-Colonel Cadogan ... [who] at the head of the 71st regiment, charged the enemy, and drove them from the part of the Village of which they had obtained a momentary possession... [5 May:] Lieutenant-Colonel Cameron was severely wounded in the afternoon, and the command in the Village devolved upon the Honourable Lieutenant-Colonel Cadogan... I particularly request your Lordship's attention to the conduct of ... the Honourable Lieutenant-Colonel Cadogan'] [*London Gazette*, 26 May 1811]. Mentioned in Hill's Almaraz dispatch, 21 May 1812 [*London Gazette*]. Mentioned in Lt.-Gen. Hamilton's dispatch of 11 Nov. 1812, concerning the Affair at Alba de Tormes, 10–11 Nov. 1812 ['The enemy's light troops advanced close to the walls we had hastily thrown up; but from the cool and steady conduct of the ... 71st Regiment, the Honourable Colonel Cadogan ... the enemy dared not attempt the town.'] [*London Gazette*]. Killed, Vittoria, 21 June 1813 [*London Gazette*]. *Register of officers' effects*: 'Died of wounds, 21 June 1813, Vittoria.' Single. Value of effects 'not asertained.' [PRO: WO 25/2964]. *Sherer*, p. 240 [Vittoria: 'The 71st suffered severely, losing 400 men, and their gallant commander, the Honourable Colonel Cadogan. This brave officer, it is reported, mortally wounded, and fully aware of his situation, begged to be carried to a higher point than that on which he fell, that he might see how the battle went, and gaze to the last, on the advance of our victorious troops.'].

+**CADOUX, Daniel, Capt., 95th Foot**: Capt., 95th Foot, 10 July 1807. Mentioned in Skerrett's dispatch concerning the capture of Seville on 27 Aug. 1812 ['I must ... mention the detachment of 95th, [led] by Captain Cadoux'] [*London Gazette*]. Killed, 'in the Operations of the Army', 31 Aug. 1813 (3rd Battn.). [*London Gazette*]. *Simmons*, p. 311 [Vera: 'A captain of ours, who stood upon the bridge rallying his men round him, fell like a soldier, covered with wounds'], p. 314 ['Captain Cadoux brought his company to the bridge and tried to drive the enemy back, or prevent more from passing. They fought most heroically; he soon fell, after having received several musket-balls in his breast.']. *Leach*, p. 339 [Vera: 'The French, completely routed, fell back towards the Bidassoa; but heavy rains having swollen the river and rendered the fords impassable since the morning, they had no resource but to force the bridge of Vera about midnight of the 31st. This post was defended by two companies only of our 2d battalion, who, although they inflicted a severe loss on the enemy, as their dead bodies on and near the bridge plainly told the next morning, could not stop 10,000 Frenchmen. Captain Cadoux, who commanded the two companies, was killed in the gallant defence of the bridge, with many of his men.']. *Harris*, p. 74 ['I remember there was an officer, named, I think, Cardo [sic], with the Rifles. He was a great beau; but although rather effeminate and ladylike in manners, so much so as to be remarked by the whole regiment at that time, yet he was found to be a most gallant officer when we were engaged with the enemy in the field. He was killed whilst fighting bravely in the Pyrenees; and amongst other jewellery he wore, he had a ring on his finger worth one hundred and fifty guineas. As he lay dead on the field, one of our Rifleman, named Orr, observed the sparkling gem, and immediately resolved to make prize of it. The ring, however, was so firmly fixed that Orr could not draw it from the finger, and whipping out his knife cut the finger off by the joint. After the battle Orr offered the ring for sale amongst the officers, and, on inquiry, the manner in which he had obtained it transpired. Orr was in consequence tried by court-martial, and sentenced to receive five hundred lashes, which sentence was carried into execution.']. *Brett-James*, p. 72 ['When Richard Henegan arrived at Lesaca, just in time for the sale of belongings of a Captain Cardew [sic], who had been killed with the 95th at Vera, only his sword and watch were reserved as momentoes for relatives; otherwise everything went piecemeal to those who had lived and worked with the deceased. "As I entered, the half worn-out jacket, and still glittering chacot [shako] were held up to view by the military auctioneer. Such objects usually go to the regiment, and bidders were not slack in their endeavours to obtain some relic of their lamented comrade. In some short moments, the limited wardrobe was dispersed in divers hands." ']. *Fletcher, Fields of Fire*, p. 144 ['Today, Cadoux's bridge at Vera is still in a good state of repair and a plaque, erected in 1921, records the heroic stand by him and his men on August 31st 1813.'], plate 31a ['The Cadoux memorial plaque at Vera. "To the Glory of God / and in Memory of / CAPTAIN DANIEL CADOUX / and his gallant riflemen / of the 2nd Bn 95th (Rifle Brigade) / who on 1

September 1813 / fell gloriously / defending this bridge / against the furious attack of a French Division / His fame can never die." '].

CAIRNCROSS, Alexander, Capt., 94th Foot: *1829 Statement of Service*: Born in Dundee, County of Forfar, Scotland, 29 Aug. 1783. Aged nineteen '& ten months' on 'his first Entrance into the Army.' Ensign, 94th Foot, 25 June 1803. Lt., 94th Foot, 15 Sept. 1804. 'Lieut. & Adj.', 94th Foot, 17 Aug. 1809. Capt., 94th Foot, 7 June 1810. Half-pay, 25 Dec. 1818, 'Reduction of the Regiment.' Capt., 8th Royal Veterans Battn., 24 Feb. 1820. Capt., 2nd Royal Veterans Battn., 25 Dec. 1821. Capt., 96th Foot, 29 Jan. 1826. Major, 96th Foot, 10 June 1826. *Battles, sieges and campaigns*: 'Seige of Cadiz. Masena retreat from Portugal in March & April 1811. Fuentes D'Onor 3 & 5 May 1811. Seige & Blocade of Badajoz in May & June 1811. el Bedon & Guinaldo 25th Sepr. 1811. Seige Capture & Storm of Ciudad Rodrigo 19 Jany. 1812. Battle of Salamanca 22 July 1812. Madrid & Retiro 12th Aug. 1812. Retreat to Portugal Octo. & Nov. Battle of Vitoria 21st June 1813.' *Wounds received in action*: 'Wounded in the head while in Command of the Left Wing of the Regt. at the Storm of C. Rodrigo 19th Jany. 1812. No grant of Pay. Gun Shot wound thro' the right elbow joint when Commanding the Right Wing of the Regt. separated from the other at Battle of Vitoria 21st June 1812, received a years Pay & Pension to 25th decemr. 1816 as Major, since which received £100 pension permanent.' *Service abroad*: '24 July 1804 to 12 April 1808, East Indies. 1st Jany. 1810 to 6th June 1810, seige of Cadiz. 7th June 1810 to 1st Octo. 1813, Peninsula. 1st July 1824 to 9th June 1826, N. Scotia & Bermuda. 10 June 1826 to 1st June 1827, Bermuda. 1st June 1829 to 31st Decemr. 1829, Nova Scotia.' [PRO:

WO 25/804 f5]. Slightly wounded, storming of Ciudad Rodrigo, 19 Jan. 1812 [*London Gazette*]. Severely wounded, Vittoria, 21 June 1813 [*London Gazette*]. *1818 Pension Return*, pp. 20–1.

+CAIRNES, Allan Billingham, Lt., 34th Foot: Lt., 34th Foot, 21 Dec. 1812. Slightly wounded, Vittoria, 21 June 1813 (2nd Battn.) [*London Gazette*]. Died 'of fever, Cambo, France', 19 Jan. 1814 [PRO: WO 25/2965].

CAIRNES, Robert Macpherson, Capt., Royal Artillery: 2nd Capt., Royal Artillery, 1 Feb. 1808; Capt., Army, 12 April 1814. Wounded, by the explosion of the magazine in Seville, 29 Sept. 1812. Killed by a cannon ball at Waterloo, while serving in Major Bull's Troop RHA. Memorial tablet in Canterbury Cathedral ["Sacred to the Memory of Robert Macpherson Cairnes, Major of Royal Horse Artillery, who was taken from this sublunary scene June the 18th 1815, aged 30. Brief, but most noble, was his career, and his end was glorious, bravely asserting the cause of an injured monarch, he fell on the plains of Waterloo. His rare endowments, his high qualities, attractions of his character as son, as brother, and as friend, are indelibly impressed on the hearts of all who had the happiness of possessing his esteem, and who now feel the exquisite anguish inflicted by his early death. This humble monument erected by the hand of friendship, is a faithful, but very inadequate, testimony of affection, and grief which no language can express, of affection which lives beyond the tomb, of grief which will never terminate till those who now deplore his loss shall rejoin him in the blest realms of everlasting peace.']. *Webber*, p. 89 [wounded, Seville, 1812], pp. 142, 152–4, 158. *Dalton*, p. 212 ['Had seen much action in the Pa.'].

+CALDER, James, Lt., 79th Foot: Lt., 79th Foot, 23 April 1805. Slightly wounded, Fuentes de Onoro, Evening 3 May 1811 (1st Battn.) [*London Gazette*]. *Register of officers' effects*: Died, 25 July 1812, Abrantes. Married. Effects sold for £60.14s.9d. [PRO: WO 25/2964].

CALLANDER, Alexander James, Capt., 91st Foot: Capt., Army, 19 Oct. 1804; Capt., 91st Foot, 10 Oct. 1811. Slightly wounded, Toulouse, 10 April 1814 (1st Battn.) [*London Gazette*]. Bvt. Major 4 June 1814. Waterloo.

CAMERON, Alexander, Lt., 79th Foot: Lt., 79th Foot, 12 May 1807. Severely wounded, Fuentes de Onoro, 5 May 1811 (1st Battn.) [*London Gazette*]. Capt., 79th Foot, 19 July 1815; Bvt. Major, Jan. 1819. Died at Tobago, Oct. 1820. Waterloo.

CAMERON, Alexander, Capt./Major, 95th Foot: *1829 Statement of Service for Retired Officers*: Aged eighteen on his first appointment to the Fencibles, twenty when appointed to the 92nd Foot. 'In Nov. 1797 to an Ensigncy in the Breadalbane Fencibles. On 22d Octr. 1799 to an Ensigncy in the 92d. Regt. In Augt. 1800 to a Lieutcy. in the Rifle Corps. In May 1805 to a Company in the same corps [Army List gives 6 May 1805]. In May 1811 to a Brevet Majority in Do. On 27 April 1812 to a Brevet Lieut. Colonelcy in Do. And on 14 May of same year to a Majority in the Regiment... Placed on half pay of the Greek Light Infantry in March 1817.' 'Appointment to an Ensigncy in the 92nd Regt. from being a volunteer in Holland. Lieutenantcy in Rifle Corps by volunteering to serve with that corps from the 92nd. Company by regular promotion in Rifle Corps. Bt. Majority by recommendation of the Duke of Wellington. Bt. Lt. Colonelcy by recommendation of the Duke of Wellington for assault of Badajoz. Majority in the Regiment by the death of Major O'Hare at Badajoz at the recommendation of the Duke of Wellington.' Half-pay 'From ill health in consequence of wounds.' *Where serving when wounded*: 'In Egypt in 1800, severely wounded in the arm and side. Severely wounded at Vittoria. Dangerously wounded at Waterloo.' *Details of pension*: 'Two pensions amounting to £500... Grants made in 1816 and 1817 in consequence of the Reports of the Medical Boards of London & Edinburgh when placed on half-pay from bad health occasioned by wounds.' *Family*: Married in 'Barrisdale in the County of Inverness.' Five children by 1829. *Where generally resident during last five years*: 'Inverness Shire... [and] Ross Shire.' [PRO: WO 25/752 f75]. Severely wounded, Vittoria, 21 June 1813 (Brevet Lieutenant-Colonel) (1st Battn.) [*London Gazette*]. Gold Medal with 2 clasps (Ciudad Rodrigo, Badajoz, Salamanca). Served through most of the Peninsular War, until severely wounded at the battle of Vittoria, 21 June 1813. Severely wounded in the throat at Waterloo. Major-General, 1838. MGS. Died 26 July 1850. *Dalton*, p. 197 [Born in 1781 in Inverallert, co. Argyll.]. *Blakeney*, pp. 102–4 [Retreat to Corunna, at El-Burgo, Jan. 1809: 'Having a sumptuous dinner on this day, we invited Captain Cameron, commanding the Highland company of the 95th, who were on piquet in the house opposite, to come over and dine with us. Cameron was an excellent fellow and a gallant and determined soldier; he willingly accepted the invitation, but hesitated as to crossing the street, not thinking himself justified in risking his life for a dinner when employed upon duty so important. But I told him that if he would wait until three shots had been fired at the window from which I was speaking (but standing at a respectful distance from it), he

would be safe in running across the street. I then put my cap upon the point of my sword, pushing it gradually out of the window, at the same time cautiously, as it were, moving forward a musket. The three shots were soon fired at the cap. Cameron then bolted across the street; but just as he was entering the door a fourth shot was fired, which I did not expect, and, as well as I can remember, passed through the skirts of his greatcoat without doing any other injury. The danger was not here finished, for as soon as he arrived within three steps of the top of the stairs he was obliged to crawl on all fours, and continue that grovelling movement until he arrived within the sanctum sanctorum.']. *Leach*, p. 391 [Waterloo: 'Sir Andrew Barnard received a wound early in the action, and the command of our battalion then devolved on Lieutenant-Colonel Cameron. That officer was likewise severely wounded some time afterwards']. *Kincaid, Adventures*, pp. 104, 115–16 [Trying to restore order amongst the British troops following the Storming of Ciudad Rodrigo: '... the voice of Sir Thomas Picton, with the power of twenty trumpets, began to proclaim damnation to every body, while Colonel Barnard, Colonel Cameron, and some other active officers, were carrying it into effect with a strong hand; for seizing the broken barrels of muskets, which were lying about in great abundance, they belaboured every fellow, most unmercifully, about the head who attempted either to load or fire, and finally succeeded in reducing them to order.'], pp. 130–1 [Storming of Badajoz: 'Colonel Cameron and myself had reconnoitred the ground so accurately by day-light, that we succeeded in bringing the head of our column to the very spot agreed on, opposite to the left breach ... without a word being spoken.'], pp. 139–40, 225–6 [Vittoria, 21 June 1813: 'Among the evil chances of that glorious day, I had to regret the temporary loss of Colonel Cameron, – a bad wound in the thigh having obliged him to go to England. Of him I can truly say, that, as a friend, his heart was in the right place, and, as a soldier, his right place was at the head of a regiment in the face of an enemy. I never saw an officer feel more at home in such a situation, nor do I know any one who could fill it better.'], p. 337 [Wounded at Waterloo]. *Kincaid, Random Shots*, p. 183 [April 1811: 'The garrison of Almeida was blockaded with a fortnight's provision only, and two companies of ours under Colonel Cameron were immediately dispatched to shoot their bullocks while grazing on the ramparts, which still further contracted their means of subsistence.'], p. 285 [Following storming of Badajoz: 'profiting by his experience at Ciudad, our commandant (Colonel Cameron) took the necessary measures to keep his battalion together ... he addressed them, and promised that they should have the same indulgence as others, and that he should not insist upon keeping them together longer than was absolutely necessary; but he assured them that if any man quitted the ranks until he gave them permission he would cause him to be put to death on the spot. That had the desired effect.'], pp. 333–4.

CAMERON, Charles, Capt., 3rd Foot: Capt., 3rd Foot, 1 Dec. 1804. Recorded as having been severely wounded and taken prisoner, Albuera, 16 May 1811 [*London Gazette*]. Severely wounded, Nivelle, 10 Nov. 1813 [*London Gazette*]. Bvt. Major, 3rd Foot, 22 Nov. 1813. Slightly wounded, the Nive, 13 Dec. 1813 (1st Battn.) [*London Gazette*]. Severely wounded, 'in Action with the Enemy', 14 Feb. 1814 (1st Battn.) [*London Gazette*]. Gold Medal. Pension of one hundred pounds per annum, commencing 25 dec. 1816, 'for wounds' received at Egmont-op-Zee, 1799, Albuera, 1811, Nivelle, 1813, Bayonne, 1813, and France, 1814 [*1818 Pension Return*, pp. 4–5].

CAMERON, Donald, Lt., 7th Foot: *1829 Statement of Service for Retired Officers*: Aged twenty-four on first appointment to the Army. Lt., 7th Foot, 7 May 1811, 'volunteer from the 3rd Lancashire Militia'; Half-pay, Oct. 1919, 'the request of the officer, from ill health.' *Where serving when wounded*: 'Wounded at the battle of Orthes.' No pension. *Family*: Married, 'parish of Kilmaillie, Inverness Shire', 11 Sept. 1820. Four children by 1829. *Title and nature of civil employment*: 'Captain in the Renfrew Militia, since 1820.' *Where generally resident during last five years*: 'in Edinburgh till May 1827 and at Strone near Fortwilliam N.B. [Scotland] since.' [PRO: WO 25/752 f174]. Slightly wounded, Orthes, 27 Feb. 1813 (1st Battn.) [*London Gazette*]. MGS.

CAMERON, Donald, Lt., 79th Foot: Lt., 79th Foot, 13 May 1807. Severely wounded, Toulouse, 10 April 1814 (1st Battn.) [*London Gazette*]. Killed, Waterloo.

+CAMERON, Duncan, Lt., 79th Foot: Lt., 79th Foot, 2 April 1812. Killed, Toulouse, 10 April 1814 (1st Battn.) [*London Gazette*].

+CAMERON, Ewen, Capt., 43rd Foot: Capt., 43rd Foot, 14 Aug. 1804. Killed, Coa, 24 July 1810 [*London Gazette*].

CAMERON, Ewen, ('Sr.'), Lt., 79th Foot: Ensign, 79th Foot, 16 March 1809; Lt., 79th Foot, 29 May 1811. Severely wounded, Toulouse, 10 April 1814 ('senior') (1st Battn.) [*London Gazette*]. Temporary pension of seventy pounds per annum, commencing 11 April 1815, 'for wounds' received at Toulouse

[*1818 Pension Return*, pp. 18–19]. Wounded, Waterloo. Died, Ireland, 1822 'of brain fever, through the effects of a blow from a stone thrown by a peasant.' [*Dalton*, p. 191]

+CAMERON, Ewen, ('Jr.'), Ensign/ Lt., 79th Foot: Ensign, 79th Foot, 26 July 1810. Slightly wounded, Fuentes de Onoro, 5 May 1811 ('W. Cameron') (1st Battn.). Lt., 79th Foot, 1 Oct. 1812. Severely wounded, 'since dead', Toulouse, 10 April 1814 ('junior') (1st Battn.) [*London Gazette*]. *Register of dead officers*: Died of wounds, 11 April 1814. Return dated April 1814. [PRO: WO 25/2965].

CAMERON, Hector, Capt., 9th Foot: *1829 Statement of Service for Retired Officers*: Aged sixteen on first appointment to the Army. Ensign, 41st Foot, 11 Oct. 1794; Lt., 41st Foot, 27 Feb. 1796; Capt., 9th Foot, 25 Aug. 1804; Bvt. Major, 21 Sept. 1813, 'By volunteering an attack during the Siege of St Sebastian.'; Half-pay, Aug. 1817. *Where serving when wounded*: 'St Sebastian.' *Details of pension*: One hundred pounds, commencing 1824. *Family*: Married in Nov. 1797. Seven children by 1829, including his eldest son, Hector, born 1798, who 'Died in Jamaica an Ensign 33rd Regt.' [PRO: WO 25/752 f76]. *London Gazette*, 4 Sept. 1813 ['Admiral Lord Keith has transmitted to Mr Croker dispatches from Captain Sir George Collier, dated from Passages the 27th and 28th ult. [Aug.], announcing that a successful attack was made upon the island of Santa Clara, at the mouth of the harbour of Saint Sebastian, at three o'clock on the morning of the 27th, by the boats of the squadron, under the command of Lieutenant the Honourable James Arbuthnot, of His Majesty's ship Surveillance. The boats were manned by the seamen and marines, and by a party of soldiers,

under the command of Captain Cameron, of the 9th regiment. The only landing-place was under a flight of steps, commanded by a small entrenchment thrown up on the west point, and completely exposed to the fire from grape of the whole range of works on the west side of the rock and walls of St Sebastian's. These local circumstances enabled a very small garrison, of an officer and twenty-four men, to make a serious resistance, by which two of our men were killed, and one officer of the army, and another of the marines, and fifteen seamen and marines, were wounded. The conduct of the officers and men was highly meritorious; each was anxious to be foremost. Lieutenant Bell, of the royal marines, had the good fortune first to succeed in getting on shore, and was immediately followed by Captain Cameron, of the 9th, and Captain Henderson, of the engineers.']. Slightly wounded, 'at the Siege of St Sebastian,' 7–27 July 1813 (1st Battn.) [*London Gazette*].

+CAMERON, John, Capt., 1st Foot: Capt., 1st Foot, 26 April 1809. Killed, 'at the Siege of St Sebastian,' 7–27 July 1813 (3rd Battn.) [*London Gazette*].

CAMERON, John, Lt. Col., 9th Foot: Lt. Col., Army, 28 May 1807; Lt. Col., 9th Foot, 3 Sept. 1807. Mentioned in Graham's report to Wellington, concerning the taking of the convent of San Bartolome, dated 18 July 1813 [17 July: '... supported by the 9th regiment, under Lieutenant-Colonel Cameron.'] [*London Gazette*]. Slightly wounded, storming of San Sebastian, 31 Aug. 1813 (1st Battn.) [*London Gazette*]. Slightly wounded, 'at the Siege of St Sebastian,' 7–27 July 1813 (1st Battn.) [*London Gazette*]. Gold Medal.

CAMERON, John, of Fassiefern, Lt. Col., 92nd Foot: Lt. Col., Army, 25

April 1808; Lt. Col., 92nd Foot, 23 June 1808. Slightly wounded, Arroyo dos Molinos, 28 Oct. 1811 (1st Battn.) [*London Gazette*]. Mentioned in Hill's Almaraz dispatch, 21 May 1812 [*London Gazette*]. Mentioned in Hamilton's dispatch of 11 Nov. 1812, concerning the Affair at Alba de Tormes, 10–11 Nov. 1812 ['The enemy's light troops advanced close to the walls we had hastily thrown up; but from the cool and steady conduct of the ... 92nd, Colonel Cameron ... the enemy dared not attempt the town.'] [*London Gazette*]. Wounded, Pyrenees, 25 July 1813 (1st Battn.) [*London Gazette*]. Killed at Quatre Bras. Waterloo. An illustration of the incident involving him at Alba de Tormes in November 1812 is illustrated in Haythornthwaite, *Armies of Wellington*, between pp. 224–5 ['The morality of war: when a French officer was seen reconnoitring the British position at Alba de Tormes in November 1812, prior to the French attack, Lieutenant-Colonel John Cameron of Fassiefern of the 92nd specifically ordered his men not to fire, as deliberately shooting at an individual was considered dishonourable. Tradition asserts that the Frenchman thus saved was Marshal Soult himself.']. An engraved portrait of him in the uniform of the 92nd Highlanders, is illustrated in Haythornthwaite, *Armies*, between pp. 97–8 ['... a man admired throughout the army for his soldierly qualities, though a harsh disciplinarian. This portrait includes the Waterloo Medal which he did not live to receive, being killed at Quatre Bras.']. Born 1771. Revered by his men in the manner of an old clan chief, but a stern disciplinarian: 'the very devil' in the punishment of dirty or drunken soldiers according to one of his men (quoted in Gardyne, C. G., *The Life of a Regiment* (London, 1929) I, p. 359). Clerk, Rev. A., *Memoir of*

Colonel John Cameron, Fassiefern (Glasgow, 1858).

+CAMERON, John, Capt., 79th Foot: Lt., 79th Foot, 11 May 1807; Capt., 79th Foot, 13 Jan. 1814. Killed, Toulouse, 10 April 1814 (1st Battn.) [*London Gazette*].

CAMERON, Kenneth, Lt./Adjutant, 79th Foot: *1829 Statement of Service*: Born in the Parish of Kilmanivaig, Invernesshire, 20 Feb. 1788. Aged seventeen on first appointment to the Army. Ensign, 79th Foot, 22 April 1805; Lt., 79th Foot, 10 April 1806; Adjutant, 79th Foot, 21 Feb. 1811; Capt., 79th Foot, 18 May 1814; Half-pay, 25 Feb. 1816, by reduction; Capt., 79th Foot, 15 May 1817. *Battles, sieges and campaigns*: 'Expedition to Gottenburgh in 1808: Lieut. of Light C... Campaigns of 1808 & 9 in Portugal & Spain. Battle of Corunna 16 Jany. 1809, Lieut. of Light Co... Expedition to Walcheren, Siege of Flushing &c 1809 Lieut. of Light Co... Campaign of 1810: Peninsula, defence of Cadiz & Isla de Leon from 12 Febry. to 17 Augt. & Castle of Matagorda 15 & 16 March, during a projected attack on the French Post at Trocadero, Lt. of Light Co... held an apptmt. in the Qr.Mr. Gl's. dept. during a short period of this service... battle of Busaco 27 Sepr. & affair near Sobral 14 Octr. Lt. of Light Co... Campaign of 1811: affair of Foz d'Aronce 15 March, Lt. of Light Co. Battles of Fuentes d'Onor 3 & 5 May & skirmish 4th May, Adjutant. Campaign of 1812: with the Army covering the siege of Badajos in March & April. Battle of Salamanca 22 July. Advance to Madrid in August, & Siege of Burgos in Septr. & October, Adjutant. Campaign of 1813: Blockade of Pamplona in July. Battles of the Pyrenees 28 & 30 July. Passage of the Nivelle 10th Novr. Passage of the Nive 9th December. Bayonne 13th Decr. Regiment detached against Parties of the Enemy which threatened the rear of the Army. Adjutant. Campaign of 1814. Battle of Toulouse 10th April. Adjutant. Never absent a single day throughout the above services.' *Distinguished conduct*: 'Made the Colonel of the 39th French regt. a Prisoner in the affair of Foz d'Aronce on the 15th March 1811. At Fuentes d'Onor 3d & 5th May 1811; & Toulouse 10th April 1814, as per particulars specified in the prefixed extracts of letters from Lt. Cols. Brown, Cameron, Campbell & Marshall who were present on those occasions.' [see later] *Wounds received in action*: 'Wounded in the Battle of Toulouse 10th April 1814: received one year's pay, & the usual compensation as Adjutant of Inftry. for a charger killed in the same action.' *Service abroad*: '29 April 1808 to 25 Jany. 1809, At Sea, Sweden, Portugal & Spain. 15 July 1809 to 10 Sept. 1809, At Sea, & before Flushing, Island of Walchern, &c. 28 Decr. 1809 to 25 July 1814, At Sea, Portugal, Spain & France. 17 June 1817 to 30 Octr. 1818, France. 26 Augt. 1825 to 31 Decr. 1829, At sea, & Canada.' [PRO: WO 25/800 f236]. *Extracts of various testimonials*: 'Extract of Letter from Colonel Andrew Brown C.B. late of the Regiment... "Since the year 1805 you & I have been seldom separated... As for your Conduct in the Field, it has been equally gallant & judicious in the several actions we have together engaged in; & I remember particularly those of Fuentes d'Onor on the 3d 5th May 1811 & Toulouse on the 10th April 1814, where you were wounded & had a horse shot under you. The Regt. on these occasions expereienced a great, & you an irreparable loss in the death of your Brother, who was killed in the latter action..." Extract of a letter from Lieut. Colonel Duncan Cameron C.B. late of the Regiment... "I had many opportunities of witnessing your firm, judicious & gallant conduct, more particularly in the affair of Foz d'Aronce in March 1811, and in the action of Fuentes d'Onor on the 3d & 5th May 1811, & at Toulouse on the 10th April 1814, where you were wounded in the shoulder, had your horse shot under you, & on the same hard contested occasion you sustained an irreparable loss in the death of your Brother, whose gallant conduct with the Light Co. in the attack of the Redoubt 'Le Tour des Augustins' excited the admiration of Sir Dennis Pack & others." ... Extract of a letter from Lieut. Colonel Marshall late of 79th Regiment "... I have also great pleasure in bearing testimony to his distinguished Bravery in the Field – of which the following two instances are within my immediate recollection, viz: In the action of Foz d'Aronce in Portugal, 15th March 1811, the Commg. officer of the French 39th Regt. surrendered himself Prisoner to Capt. Cameron (then Lieut. of Light Infantry) in consequence of the vigorous attack which he made on that part of the French rear guard immediately opposed to him. In the Battle of Toulouse 10th April 1814, when the Redoubt called 'Le Tour des Augustins' was carried with great loss by the 79th Regt. Capt. Cameron, being then Adjutant, was among the first who entered the work, receiving then a wound, & having a Brother killed by his side." [Also letter from Lt. Col. Donald Campbell] [PRO: WO 25/800 f235]. Slightly wounded, Toulouse, 10 April 1814 (1st Battn.) [*London Gazette*]. MGS.

+CAMERON, Philip, Lt. Col., 79th Foot: Capt. 6 June 1794; Lt. Col., 79th Foot, 19 April 1804. Recorded as wounded at Fuentes de Onoro, 5th May 1811, and died on the 13th May 1811 [*London Gazette*]. Mentioned in Wellington's Fuentes de Onoro dispatch, dated Villa Formosa, 8 May 1811 [at first commanding the 79th, then taking over command of the various units involved in the fighting on 3 May following the wounding of Lt. Col. Williams; 5 May: 'Lieutenant-Colonel Cameron was severely wounded in the afternoon, and the command in the Village devolved upon the Honourable Lieutenant-Colonel Cadogan... I particularly request your Lordship's attention to the conduct of... Lieutenant-Colonel Cameron'] [*The Gentleman's Magazine*]. *Register of officers' effects*: 'Phillip Cameron'. Died of Wounds, 13 May 1811, Villa Formosa. Single. Effects sold for £594. 3s. 6d. [PRO: WO 25/2962]. *Register of dead officers*: Return dated 25 May 1811. [PRO: WO 25/2965]. Obituary, *The Gentleman's Magazine*, June 1811, p. 602 ['13 May... In Portugal, of the wound he received in the action of Fuentes d'Honor, Lieut.-col. Cameron, 76th reg. [sic] His funeral was attended by Lord Wellington, with many general officers, and the whole of his lordship's personal staff. (See pp. 578, 580.)']. *Brotherton*, p. 42 ['We buried him [Capt. Knipe, 14th Dragoons] in the same grave with another gallant soldier who fell that day, Colonel Cameron of the 79th Highlanders.']. *Pearson*, p. 89 [Fuentes de Onoro: 'Early in the encounter, Colonel Cameron was mortally wounded, and three regiments were driven back to the lower part of the village by an attacking column of tremendous strength... The highlanders thirsted to take vengence for the fall of the noble Cameron, and ultimately the French were driven from the village, leaving nothing but their dead and badly wounded.']

CAMERON, William Gordon, Ensign, 1st Foot Guards: *1829 Statement of Service for Retired Officers*: Aged seventeen on his first appointment in the Army. Ensign, 1st Foot Guards, 19 Aug. 1809; Lt. and Capt., 1st Foot Guards, 10 Jan. 1813; 'Student at the Senr. Dept. of the Military College'; 'Depty. Asst. Qr. Master General in Flanders, 14 April 1815'; Bvt. Major, 21 Jan. 1819, 'From services in the Qr. Mr. Genl. Department at Waterloo'; Half-pay, Lt. Col., unattached, 7 June 1825, 'purchased as a channel of Promotion.' 'Desirous of service.' *Where serving when wounded*: 'At Barrossa. At Waterloo.' *Details of pension*: 'Two Pensions £200.' 'Barrossa Pension [commenced] 6 March 1812. Waterloo Pension [commenced] 11 Nov. 1816.' *Where generally resident during last five years*: 'In England.' [PRO: WO 25/752 f83]. Severely wounded, Barossa, 5 March 1811 (Ensign) [*London Gazette*]. *1818 Pension Return*, pp. 2–3. MGS.

CAMERON, William, Lt., 79th Foot: *1829 Statement of Service for Retired Officers*: Aged twenty-five on first appointment to the Army. Ensign, 79th Foot, 1 April 1805; Lt., 79th Foot, 8 April 1806; Capt., 79th Foot, 17 June 1813; Half-pay, 25 Dec. 1815, 'By the reduction of the 2nd Battalion.' 'Not desirous [to serve], being from severe injuries unfit for Service.' *Where serving when wounded*: 'In Spain in 1812. Severe injuries received.' *Details of pension*: Seventy pounds, commencing 25 March 1813. *Family*: Married in Strone near Fort-William, Scotland, 9 Jan. 1817. Six children by 1829. *Where generally resident during last five years*: 'Camathy near Fort-William N.B. [Scotland]' [PRO: WO 25/752 f141].

CAMPBELL, Alexander, Lt-General: Major-General, 26 Feb. 1795; Lt.-General, 29 April 1802; Col., 13th Foot, 11 July 1804. Slightly wounded, Talavera, 28 July 1809 [*London Gazette*]. Gold Medal. Father of Lt. Col. Allan W. Campbell, 74th Foot, and is mentioned in his son's obituary, *The Gentleman's Magazine*, Nov. 1813, p. 506. For biography, see *Royal Military Calendar*, vol. II, pp.

406–10 ['At the memorable battle of Talavera, where he was wounded through the thigh by a grape shot, he commanded the division which formed the right wing of the British army'].

CAMPBELL, Alexander, Lt., 38th Foot; Lt., 3rd Portuguese Line: Ensign, 38th Foot, 3 Jan. 1811; Lt., 38th Foot, 26 Nov. 1812. Severely wounded, the Nive, 11 Dec. 1813, while serving as Lt., 3rd Portuguese Line [*London Gazette*]. In Portuguese Service Dec. 1811 to April 1814. Pension of one hundred pounds per annum, commencing 17 March 1815, 'for wounds' received at Bayonne, 1814 [*1818 Pension Return*, pp. 10–11]. MGS. *Challis, Portuguese Army*, p. 53.

CAMPBELL, Alexander, Lt., 91st Foot: Ensign, 91st Foot, 15 Aug. 1805; Lt., 91st Foot, 12 May 1808. Severely wounded, Orthes, 27 Feb. 1813 (1st Battn.) [*London Gazette*]. Waterloo. Capt., 91st Foot, 3 Sept. 1818; Half-pay, 16 Dec. 1821. Died 1 May 1835. Letter from him to Lord Fitzroy Somerset, 2 July 1834 ['My Lord, I most respectfully take the liberty of addressing your Lordship to represent that as there appears little or no chance of my being again reinstated on full Pay, your lordship would be pleased to recommend to the proper quarter that a reasonable sum would be allowed me in lieu of my half Pay, to enable me if possible to enter upon some business by which I may support myself and family with greater comfort. I entered the service in the year 1805 in the 1st Battn. 91st Regt. with which I regularly served in all its campaigns, until I was put on Half Pay in 1821, being a period of about sixteen years & three months. I served with that Battalion in Holland, Portugal, Spain and France, and had a Musket Ball through my left cheek bone which came out under my Ear, in the Battle of Orthes. I had always been anxious of being reinstated on full pay and had stated that anxiety in the circular sent to Officers on Half Pay some years since. I am 44 years of age. I therefore very respectfully beg that your Lordship may be pleased to intimate to me what allowance would be made in lieu of Half Pay that I may decide on either alternative of accepting the commuted allowance or remain as I am. I have the Honor to be, My Lord, Your Lordship's most Obt. & most Humble Servant, Alexander Campbell.'] [*Spink & Son Ltd., London, 1997*]. *Dalton*, p. 245 ['Alexander Campbell (1st Batt.)'], p. 247 ['H.p. 1821. D. 1835.'].

+CAMPBELL, Alexander, 2nd Lt., 95th Foot: 2nd Lt., 95th Foot, 13 May 1812. Killed, Crossing the Bidassoa, 7/9 Oct. 1813 (2nd Battn.) [*London Gazette*]. *Register of officers' effects*: 'Killed in Action, 7 Oct. 13, Vera'. Single. Effects totalled £21. 11s. 6d. 2nd Battn. [PRO: WO 25/2964]. *Simmons*, p. 318 [Lt. Campbell, 2nd Battn., killed, Vera, 7 Oct. 1813]. Note: Alexander Campbell was carried on the rolls of both the 1st and 2nd battalions, and so confusingly at times is indicated as two different men. The Register of Deceased Officers [PRO: WO 25/2965], for example, indicates two different officers with the same name and rank, suggesting that one fell on the 7th and the other on the 9th. In fact, 2nd Lt. Alexander Campbell, of the 1st Battn. 95th Foot, was serving with the 2nd Battn. when killed at Vera on 7th Oct. 1813.

+CAMPBELL, Allan William, Major, 74th Foot, Lt. Col., 4th Portuguese Regt.: Major, 74th Foot, 5 April 1810. Wounded, Pyrenees, 25–28 July 1813, while serving as Lt. Col., 4th Portuguese Line [*London Gazette*]. *Register of officers' effects*: 'Died of wounds, 9 Oct. 1813'. Single. 'Was attached to Portuguese service.' [PRO: WO

25/2964]. In Portuguese Service June 1810 to Oct. 1813. Gold Medal. Obituary, *The Gentleman's Magazine*, Nov. 1813, p. 506 ['At Bilboa, Spain, in his 28th year, Lieut.-col. Allan Campbell, major of the 74th Foot, and commandant of the 3d reg. of Portuguese Infantry (sic). He had served four years in the Peninsula, and received the wound, which, after much suffering, caused his death, in the battle of the Pyrenees. The gallant manner in which he led his corps into action, upon that memorable day, was rewarded with a promotion that he has not lived to enjoy. The elder brother of Lieut.-col. Campbell was killed in India ... on the celebrated plains of Assaye. Lieut.-col. A. Campbell was the only surviving son of Sir Alex. Campbell, Commander-in-chief at the Isle of France. That distinguished officer, who was severely wounded at the battle of Talavera, in which he commanded the British centre, must feel deeply the loss of a son who was so endeared to him and to all his family by his virtues, and by the early fame he acquired in the service of his Country.']. *Challis, Portuguese Army*, p. 53 ['Lt.-Col. 4 Line... Wd. Pyrenees 30 July '13... Died of Wounds 9 Oct. '13'].

+CAMPBELL, Archibald Argyle, Major, 42nd Foot: Major, 42nd Foot, 9 July 1803. Obituary, *The Gentleman's Magazine*, Feb. 1809, 187 ['27 [Jan.]... At Plymouth, of the wounds... received in Spain, Major Archibald-Argyle Campbell, of the 42d Royal Highlanders'].

CAMPBELL, Archibald, Major, 46th Foot; Major, 15th Portuguese Line: *1829 Statement of Service*: 'Born Kruek, Isle of Mull, Argyleshire, in 1777. Aged 20 years on his first Entrance into the Army. Ensign, 25th Regiment, 9th Nov. 1797. Lieutenant, 46th Regiment, 20 June 1798. Captain, 10th Reserve, [22 Dec.] 1803. Captain, 46th Regi-ment, 3rd Feby. 1804. Major, 46th Regiment, 3 Septr. 1812. Lieut. Colonel, 46th Regiment, 17th Feb. 1814. Bt. Colonel in India, 46th Regiment, 5th June 1829.' *Battles, sieges and campaigns*: 'When Captain of Grenadiers of the 46th Regiment he was present under the Command of Major General Prevost at the Attack of Dominica in the West Indies on the 22nd Feby. 1805 by the French. On his return from the West Indies as Major of the 15th Portuguese served and was present during the several campaigns in Spain, Portugal, and the South of France from Sept. 1811 until 1814. Was present at the Battle of Salamanca on the 22nd July 1812, in that of Victoria on the 21st June 1813, at the Surrender of Saint Sebastian and Commanding the 15th Portuguese Infantry in crossing the Bidassoa into France, Forcing the Enemy's Lines on the 10th of November, and the Attacks of the 9th, 10th & 11th of December in the same year. Appointed to the Command of the Hyderabar Subsidiary Force in the East Indies on the 16th April 1828 – which he now holds.' *Distinguished conduct*: 'Was mentioned in the public dispatch of Major General Prevost for his conduct as Captain of the Grenadiers 46th Regt. when the Island of Dominica was attacked by a French Force on the 22d February 1805. Was mentioned in Brigade Orders by Major General Spry for his conduct in the Battle of Victoria on which occasion he commanded the Advance of his Brigade amounting to 300 Men in the Attack of the Village of Gomarah Mayor when he and two Capts under his Command were severely Wounded. Commanded the 15th Portuguese in the Attacks of the 9th, 10th & 11th December 1813 in the South of France when he was rewarded with the Rank of Lieut. Colonel in the Portuguese Service for what Field Marshal Beresford was pleased to term in General

Orders his distinguished Conduct.' *Wounds received in action*: 'Was wounded in the Battle of Victoria on the 21st June 1813, for which he received one years Pay.' *Titles, honorary distinctions and medals*: 'Was honoured with a Gold Medal by His Majesty for the Actions of the Nive in the South of France on the 9th, 10th & 11th Decr. 1813.' *Service abroad*: 'March 1804 to June 1811, West Indies. Sept. 1811 to Jany. 1814, Spain, Portugal and France. June 1818 to 31 Decr 1829, Madras Presidency, east Indies.' *Family*: Married Anne Blackford, Rowner, Hampshire, in 1817. They had four children by 1826. Ann was not living in 1830. [PRO: WO 25/794 f1]. Severely wounded, Vittoria, 21 June 1813, as Major, 15th Portuguese Line [*London Gazette*]. Lt. Col., 46th Foot, 17 Feb. 1814. In Portuguese Service Oct. 1811 to Dec. 13. Gold Medal. *Challis, Portuguese Army*, p. 53.

CAMPBELL, Archibald, Lt., 59th Foot: Lt., 59th Foot, 28 March 1811. Severely wounded, storming of San Sebastian, 31 Aug. 1813 (2nd Battn.) [*London Gazette*]. Adjutant, 59th Foot, 24 Sept. 1813. Severely wounded, the Nive, 9 Dec. 1813 ('Lieutenant Archibald Campbell') [*London Gazette*]. Waterloo.

CAMPBELL, Charles Stewart, Capt., 26th Foot; Major, 3rd Portuguese Line: : Born in New York, America, 12 April 1779. Aged seventeen on first appointment to the Army. Ensign, 26th Foot, Dec. 1796; Lt., 26th Foot, Dec 1797; Capt., 26th Foot, 14 May 1804; Bvt. Major, 26th Foot, 1813; Major, 26th Foot, 1822; Lt. Col., 26th Foot, 25 April 1828; Lt. Col., 1st Foot, 24 Jan. 1829. *Battles, sieges and campaigns*: Battle of Corunna; Siege of Flushing; campaign in Walcheren; Battle of Vittoria as Major commanding 3rd Portuguese Line; siege and assault of St Sebastian, as Major commanding 3rd

Portuguese Line. *Distinguished conduct*: 'Commanding Picquets of the Brigade at Battle of Corunna. – Assault of St Sebastian, Lord Lyndock's dispatch – and Marshal Lord Beresford's order of the day.' *Wounds received in action*: '31 Aug. 1813 Thigh, storming of St Sebastian, one years pay, Pension 250 Pounds Temporary from 1814 – Permanent from 28th Nov. 1825.' *Titles, honorary distinctions and medals*: 'A Medal for Battle of Vittoria, commanding 3rd Regt. Portuguese Infy. A clasp for Commanding above regt. assault St Sebastian & for which service was appointed a Major by Brevet in the British and Lt. Col. in the Portuguese Army.' *Service abroad*: 1796–1800, Canada; 1801–2, Egypt; 1808–9, Spain; 1809, Walcheren; 1811–14, Portugal and Spain; 1815–21, Gibraltar; 1828–9, India. *Family*: Married in Ireland in 1805. They had three children by 1830. [PRO: WO 25/785 f7]. Severely wounded, storming of San Sebastian, 31 Aug. 1813, while serving as Major, 3rd Portuguese Line [*London Gazette*]. Mentioned in Graham's San Sebastian dispatch, Oyarzun, 1 Spt. 1813 ['Major-General Sprye mentions in terms of high praise ... Major Charles Stuart Campbell, commanding the 3rd regiment in Colonel M'Crae's absense on general duty'] [*London Gazette*]. In Portuguese Service June 1812 to Oct. 1813. Gold Medal. *1818 Pension Return*, pp. 8–9. MGS. *Challis, Portuguese Army*, p. 5.

CAMPBELL, Colin, Major, 1st Foot: Major, 1st Foot, 27 Sept. 1810; Lt. Col., Army, 17 Aug. 1812. Severely wounded, Vittoria, 21 June 1813 (3rd Battn.) [*London Gazette*]. Gold Medal. Severely wounded at Quatre Bras. Died, Inverery, 1 Feb. 1833.

CAMPBELL, Colin, Lt., 9th Foot; Capt., 60th Foot: *1829 Statement of Service*: Born 20 Oct. 1792, Island of

Isla. Aged fifteen on his first Entrance into the Army. Ensign, 9th Foot, 26 May 1808; Lt., 9th Foot, 29 June 1808; Capt., 60th Foot, 9 Nov. 1813; Capt., 21st Foot, Nov. 1818; Major 26 Nov. 1825. *Battles, sieges and campaigns*: '1808 Battle of Vimeiro, 21st August... Advance and Retreat of the Army of Spain under the Orders of Sir Jn. Moore... 1809 Battle of Corunna, 16th January... Expedition to Zealand... 1811 Battle of Barrossa, 5th March, Rank Lieut., In Command of the two Flank Companies 9th Regt. the latter part of the Action with all the other Officers havg. been wounded... Defence of Tarifa, 1811 ... 1812 Spring of this year in the Expedition under the Orders of Col. Skerret 47th Regt. for the Relief of Tarragona, and during the Autumn and Winter Months attached as Aide-de-Camp to Brigad. General Livesay of the Spanish Army in Andalusia under the Order of the Capt. General Ballasteros. Present at the Affairs of Posts of Alhaurin and Coin in the valley of Malaga. 1813 Affair at Osma, 18th June. Battle of Vitoria, 21st June. Seige of San Sebastian, Assault of the Outworks, 17th July, and Body of the Fortress, 25th July. In these Assaults led columns of Attack – The first with the Light Company of the 9th Regimt. and the latter with 23 Men of the same Company and Light Infantry Company 3rd Battn. Royal Regiment... Passage of the Bidassoa and Assault of the Intrenched Position on that River on the 7th Oct. Rank Lieut., Commandg. Light Company 9th Regt.' *Distinguished conduct*: 'Extract of a Dispatch from Lieut. Genl. Sir Thos. Graham Commandg. the Corps beseiging San Sebastian to Lord Wellington, reporting the Assault and Capture of the Fortified Convent of Saint Bartolemeo and adjoining Outworks. Extract: "Ernani July 18th 1813. But in justice to the distinguished Gallantry of those Officers who led their men to over-come the variety of Obstacles that were opposed to them, I beg leave to mention Major Snodgrass, 13th Portuguese, and Lieut. Colin Campbell, 9th Regt." From the same Officer to Lord Wellington, reportg. the Failure of the Assault upon San Sebastian on the Morng. of the 25th July 1813. Extract: "Ernani July 25th 1813. I beg leave also to mention Lieut. Campbell, 9th Regt., who led the Forlorn Hope, and who was severely wounded in the Breach." ' *Wounds received in action*: 'Received Two Wounds at the Assault of San Sebastian – One through the Right Hip, and one thro' the Left Thigh. At the Assault of the Intrenched Position on the Bidassoa – a musket Shot through the Right Thigh, immediately above the knee. Two years Pay and a temporary Pension which expired in 1820.' *Service abroad*: '18th July 1808 to January 1809, Portugal & Spain. July 1809 to September 1809, South Boveland. December 1809 to January 1814, Spain, Portugal and France. August 1814 to August 1815, America. January 1817 to September 1818, Gibraltar. April 1819 to March 1826, West Indies.' Unmarried in 1830. [PRO: WO 25/789 f2]. Severely wounded, 'at the Siege of St Sebastian,' 7–27 July 1813 (1st Battn.) [*London Gazette*]. Mentioned in Graham's dispatch to Wellington, dated 27 July 1813 concerning the failed Assault on St Sebastian on 25 July 1813 ['I beg too to recommend to your Lord-ship, Lieutenant Campbell, of the 9th, who led the forlorn hope, and who was severely wounded on the breach.'] [*London Gazette*]. Slightly wounded, Crossing the Bidassoa, 7/9 Oct. 1813 (1st Battn.) [*London Gazette*]. *1818 Pension Return*, pp. 6–7. MGS. *Mullen*, p. 179 ['Later Lord Clyde']. Mentioned in the Statement of Service of James Fitz William Miller [PRO: WO 25/768 f76]. His real name was Macliver, having adopted the name

Campbell in tribute to a maternal uncle who financed his education and obtained a commission for him in the 9th Foot. He is best remembered for leading the Highland Brigade in the Crimea, and for commanding the forces which suppressed the Indian Mutiny, for which he became Field-Marshal and 1st Baron Clyde. Died 1863. Burne, Sir Owen, *Clyde and Strathnairn* (London, 1895); Forbes, A., *Colin Campbell, Lord Clyde* (London, 1895); Shadwell, L., *Life of Colin Campbell, Lord Clyde* (Edinburgh, 1881).

CAMPBELL, Colin, Major, 70th Foot: Major, 70th Foot, 15 Dec. 1808; Lt. Col., Army, 3 May 1810. Slightly wounded, Busaco, 27 Sept. 1810, while serving on the Staff as AAG. [*London Gazette*]. Gold Medal. KCB. Colonel, Coldstream Guards, in 1817 A/L. *Kincaid, Adventures*, p. 137 [Storming of Badajoz, 6 April 1812: 'Colonel Barnard and Sir Colin Campbell had a piquet of our men, drawn across the street, on the point of sending a volley into us, thinking that we were a rallied body of the enemy.'].

CAMPBELL, Donald, Volunteer, 57th Foot: *1829 Statement of Service for Retired Officers*: Aged seventeen on his first appointment to the Army. 'Left the Highlands as a gentleman volunteer, at my own expenses, in September 1812, joined the 57th Regt. as such, in Spain, beginning of the Campaign of 1813.' Ensign, 57th Foot, 16 Sept. 1813; Lt., 57th Foot, 8 Dec. 1814. 'Obtained my Ensigncy through the recommendation of Lieut. General Sir John Byng, in consequence of his being as good as to commend my conduct at the battle of Vitoria, in the presence of his Brigade, on the field after the battle. Got my lieutenacy in the regular course of promotion in the Regiment.' 'Placed on Half-pay in consequence of the Peace and the reduction of

the second Battalion, which I joined in consequence of having received my Lieutenancy, and on the return of the 1st Batt. from Canada, 1815.' 'Desirous of service in the event of a war – not otherwise. Would prefer an appointment to Cavalry (being no bad rider and not at all fit to march on foot from the effects of a wound in the thigh) in the event of being required on service.' *Where serving when wounded*: 'Near Pampaluna in Spain.' [Battle of Sorauren, 28 July 1813]. *Details of pension*: Fifty pounds per annum, commencing 28 July 1813. 'Applied for the Pension in 1820 and was allowed to receive it from the day on which I was wounded as above marked.' *Family*: Married in Appin, Argyleshire, 27 May 1819. Five children by 1829. *Where generally resident during last five years*: 'Newark Castle near Air North Britain.' [PRO: WO 25/752]. MGS.

CAMPBELL, Donald, Lt., 71st Foot: *1829 Statement of Service for Retired Officers*: Aged twenty-six on his first appointment to the Army. Ensign, Ray Fencibles, Oct. 1798, 'reduced Aug. 1802'; Ensign, 92nd Foot, July 1803; Lt., 14th Reserve Battn., April 1804; Lt., 71st Foot, Aug. 1804; Capt., 71st Foot, 22 June 1809; 'Removed to 2nd R.V. Battn.', Oct. 1820; 'Placed on Retired List', June 1821. *Where serving when wounded*: 'Vemeira, Aug. 1808, slightly. Waterloo, slightly.' No pension. *Family*: Married in Galway, Ireland, 14 Feb. 1801. *Where generally resident during last five years*: 'Castle Town, Isle of Man.' [PRO: WO 25/752 f197]. MGS.

CAMPBELL, Dugald, Capt., 91st Foot; Capt., 2nd Portuguese Line: Capt., 91st Foot, 23 Nov. 1809. Severely wounded, Nivelle, 10 Nov. 1813, while serving as Capt., 2nd Portuguese Line [*London Gazette*]. *Challis, Portuguese Army*, p. 53

['P/S Apr. to Dec. '11' (sic)]. Waterloo. Died 1825.

CAMPBELL, Dugald, Capt., 92nd Foot: Capt., 92nd Foot, 13 June 1805. Severely wounded, Pyrenees, 31 July 1813 [*London Gazette*]. Pension of two hundred pounds per annum, commencing 1 Aug. 1814, 'for wounds' received at Pampeluna [*1818 Pension Return*, pp. 20–21]. Wounded, Waterloo.

+CAMPBELL, Duncan, Capt., 42nd Foot: Capt., 42nd Foot, 9 July 1803. Regimental Muster, 1st Battn., 25 Dec. 1808–24 March 1809: 'Died of Wounds on Bd. Ship 18 Jany.' [PRO: WO 12/5489]. Obituary, *The Gentleman's Magazine*, Feb. 1809 ['Jan... On-board the Resolution, on his passage from Corunna, of the wounds he received in the battle before that place, on the 16th, Capt. Duncan Campbell, of the 42d Royal Highlanders.'].

CAMPBELL, Duncan, Lt., 91st Foot: *1829 Statement of Service for Retired Officers*: Aged twenty on his first appointment to the Army. Ensign, 91st Foot, 12 Oct. 1804; Lt., 91st Foot, Decr. 1806; Capt., 91st Foot, 3 March 1814. 'Acting Adjt. Acting Major of Brigade.' Half-pay, 'Reduction of the 2nd Battn. [1816]' *Where serving when wounded*: 'Spain.' *Family*: Married in Edinburgh, 4 Feb. 1822. Three children by 1829. *Where generally resident during last five years*: 'Hawich, Roxburgh Shire.' [PRO: WO 25/752 f121].

CAMPBELL, Francis B., Lt. Col., 58th Foot: Major, 58th Foot, 29 March 1810. Severely wounded, Pyrenees, 2 Aug. 1813 (2nd Battn.) [*London Gazette*]. Gold Medal (Orthes), for command of a Provisional Battalion.

CAMPBELL, Guy, Major, 6th Foot: Capt., 6th Foot, 14 Sept. 1804; Major, 6th Foot, 1 April 1813.

Severely wounded, Pyrenees, 2 Aug. 1813 (1st Battn.) [*London Gazette*]. Gold Medal. Lt. Col., AAG at Waterloo. MGS. Died, Kingstown, Ireland, 25 Jan. 1849. *Dalton*, p. 30.

CAMPBELL, J., Ensign, 51st Foot: Severely wounded, Vittoria, 21 June 1813 ('Ensign J. Campbell') (1st Battn.) [*London Gazette*].

CAMPBELL, James, Capt., 45th Foot: Capt., 45th Foot, 29 Dec. 1808. Slightly wounded, storming of Badajoz, 6 April 1812, while serving on the Staff as Brigade Major [*London Gazette*]. Bvt. Major, 45th Foot, 3 March 1814. Wounded, Waterloo.

CAMPBELL, James, Ensign, 71st Foot: Ensign, 71st Foot, 21 Jan. 1808. Slightly wounded, Vimeiro, 21 Aug. 1808 [*London Gazette*].

CAMPBELL, James, Capt., 79th Foot: Capt., 79th Foot, 5 Sept. 1805. Severely wounded, Toulouse, 10 April 1814 (1st Battn.) [*London Gazette*].

CAMPBELL, James, Lt. Col., 94th Foot: Lt. Col., 94th Foot, 27 Sept. 1804. Mentioned in Wellington's Ciudad Rodrigo dispatch, 20 Jan. 1812 [Storming of Ciudad Rodrigo, 19 Jan. 1812: 'Major Ridge, of the 2d battalion of the 5th Regiment, having escalated the fausse braye wall, stormed the principal breach in the body of the place, together with the 94th Regiment, commanded by Lieutenant-Colonel Campbell, which had moved along the ditch at the same time, and had stormed the breach in the fausse braye... I beg particularly to draw your attention to the conduct of ... Lieutenant-Colonel Campbell, of the 94th Regiment'] [*London Gazette*, 5 Feb. 1812]. Mentioned in Wellington's Badajoz dispatch, 7 April 1812 ['Lieutenant-General Picton ... particularly reported the good conduct of Colonel Campbell of the 94th, commanding the Honourable Major-General Colville's brigade during his absence in command of the 4th division, whose conduct I have so frequently had occasion to report to your Lordship.']. Severely wounded, Salamanca, 22 July 1812 [*London Gazette*]. Mentioned in Wellington's Salamanca dispatch, 24 July 1812 ['Lieutenant-Colonel Campbell, of the 94th, commanding a brigade in the 3rd division']. Severely wounded, Vittoria, 21 June 1813 [*London Gazette*]. Gold Medal.

+CAMPBELL, James, Lt., 94th Foot; Capt., 19th Portuguese Line: Lt., 94th Foot, 25 Nov. 1808; Adjutant, 94th Foot, 7 June 1810. Killed, Pyrenees, 31 July 1813, while serving as Capt., 19th Portuguese Line [*London Gazette*]. In Portuguese Service June 1812 to July 1813. *Challis, Portuguese Army*, p. 53.

CAMPBELL, John, Lt., 48th Foot: Lt., Army, 8 Oct. 1805; Lt., 48th Foot, 26 Nov. 1807. Slightly wounded, Toulouse, 10 April 1814 (1st Battn.) [*London Gazette*].

+CAMPBELL, John, Ensign, 47th Foot: Killed, storming of San Sebastian, 31 Aug. 1813 (2nd Battn.) [*London Gazette*]. *Challis, Index*, p. 141.

+CAMPBELL, Leckie, 1st Lt., 95th Foot: Ensign, 47th Foot, 11 Dec. 1806; Lt., Army, 5 July 1809; 1st Lt., 95th Foot, 28 Sept. 1809. Killed, Vittoria, 21 June 1813 ('Lieutenant L. Campbell') (3rd Battn.) [*London Gazette*]. *Register of officers' effects*: Not known if married or single. Effects totalled £88. 0s. 5d. [PRO: WO 25/2964].

CAMPBELL, Norman, Lt., 71st Foot: *1829 Statement of Service for Retired Officers*: Aged twenty-four on his first appointment to the Army. Ensign, 71st Foot, 27 June 1811; Lt., 71st Foot, 14 April 1813; Half-pay, 24 Dec. 1818, 'By Reduction.' 'Not capable for active service; from wound.' *Where serving when wounded*: 'Vittoria 1813.' *Details of pension*: Seventy pounds per annum, commencing 26 Dec. 1820. *Family*: Married in St George's Church, Hanover Square, London, 31 Oct. 1816. Five children by 1829. *Where generally resident during last five years*: '1 in Aberdeen. 4 in France. 6 months in England.' [PRO: WO 25/752 f36]. Severely wounded, Vittoria, 21 June 1813 (1st Battn.) [*London Gazette*]. Waterloo.

CAMPBELL, Patrick, Capt., 52nd Foot: *1829 Statement of Service for Retired Officers*: Aged twenty on first appointment to the Army. Ensign, 53rd Foot, 31 Aug. 1797; Lt., 52nd Foot, 1 March 1800; Capt., 52nd Foot, 16 Aug. 1804; Bvt. Major, 52nd Foot, 21 June 1813; Half-pay, [4 May 1818], 'at the request of the officer from wounds & ill health.' *Where serving when wounded*: 'Portugal, Spain & France.' *Details of pension*: One hundred pounds per annum 'for loss of sight of right eye, & wounds' commencing 25 June 1819. *Family*: First married, London, 1 Dec. 1814. From this marriage he had two sons, the latter born in 1817. He remarried on 2 Oct. 1828. *Where generally resident during last five years*: 'London.' [PRO: WO 25/752 f42]. Severely wounded, 'not dangerously', during 'several affairs with the French Army', 18 March–7 April 1811 (1st Battn.) [*London Gazette*]. Mentioned in Wellington's dispatch, dated Villa Formosa, 1 May 1811 ['The enemy had on the 23d [April] attacked our piquets on the Azava, but were repulsed. Captains Dobbs and Campbell, of the 52d regiment, and Lieutenant Eeles, of the 95th regiment, distinguished themselves upon this occasion, in which the allied troops defended their post against very superior numbers of the enemy.'] [*London Gazette*, 18 May 1811]. Slightly wounded, Crossing the Bidassoa, 7/9 Occt. 1813 (1st Battn.) [*London Gazette*]. Slightly wounded, Orthes, 27 Feb. 1814 (1st Battn.) [*London Gazette*]. Gold Medal. Waterloo. Lt. Col., half pay, 1830. CB. MGS.

CAMPBELL, Robert, Capt., 52nd Foot: *1829 Statement of Service for Retired Officers*: Aged sixteen on first appointment to the Army. Lt, Royal Novia Scotia Regt., 1 Dec. 1795 'till commencement 1799'; Ensign, 92nd Foot, 22 Oct. 1799; Lt., 52nd Foot, 2 March 1800; Capt., 52nd Foot, 24 Aug. 1804; Bvt. Major, 52nd Foot, 21 Sept. 1813; Capt., 13th Foot, 2 July 1818; Half-pay, 28th Foot, 20 Aug. 1818, 'in consequence of ill health caused by frequent wounds.' 'Not desirous [of service] having been obliged from the severity & number of wounds to Exchange from the 52d Regt. when senior Captain of that Corps.' *Where serving when wounded*: 'Spain & Portugal.' *Details of pension*: Two hundred pounds per annum, commencing 1 Sept. 1814. *Where generally resident during last five years*: 'Near Longtown, Cumberland.' [PRO: WO 25/752 f37]. Wounded, 'in the Army lately in Spain' (1st Battn.) [*March 1809 Army List*, p. 105]. Slightly wounded, Coa, 24 July 1810 [*London Gazette*]. Severely wounded, storming of Badajoz, 6 April 1812 (1st Battn.) [*London Gazette*]. Severely wounded, storming of San Sebastian, 31 Aug. 1813, while serving with a 'Detachment 52nd Foot, 1st Batt.' [*London Gazette*]. Gold Medal. Pension 'for wounds' received at St Sebastian [*1818 Pension Return*, pp. 14–15]. *Moorsom*, p. 108 ['The 52nd sustained the following casualties at Corunna... Captain Robert Campbell... severely wounded.'], p. 415 ['Served in the 52nd from 1800 to 1813, and was present in most of the battles and affairs in which the

regiment was engaged in the Peninsula, and received a medal for the assault of St Sebastian, at which he commanded the detachment of 52nd stormers.'].

CAMPBELL, Robert P., 1st Lt., Royal Marines Artillery: 1st Lt., Royal Marines Artillery, 18 Nov. 1807. Severely wounded, 'not dangerously', Heights of Ordal, 12/13 Sept. 1813, while serving as DAAG on the General Staff [*London Gazette*].

CAMPBELL, William, Capt., 36th Foot: Capt., 36th Foot, 22 Dec. 1804; Bvt. Major, 36th Foot, 26 Aug. 1813. Severely wounded, Toulouse, 10 April 1814 (1st Battn.) [*London Gazette*].

+**CAMPBELL, William, Lt., 71st Foot**: Lt., 71st Foot, 22 June 1809. Killed, the Nive, 13 December 1813 (1st Battn.) [*London Gazette*]. *Register of officers' effects*: Single. Effects totalled £29.14s. [PRO: WO 25/2964].

CAMPBELL, William, 1st Lt., 95th Foot: 1st Lt., 95th Foot, 6 June 1809. Severely wounded, Barossa, 5 March 1811 (3rd Battn.) [*London Gazette*]. Temporary pension of seventy pounds per annum, commencing 6 March 1812, 'for wounds' received at Barossa [*1818 Pension Return*, pp. 22–3].

CANCH, Thomas, Ensign/Lt., 5th Foot: *1829 Statement of Service*: Born 23 Jan. 1786, Govan, Lanarkshire. Aged 23 years and 249 days on his first entrance into the Army. Ensign, 5th Foot, 28 Sept. 1809; Adjt. 26 March 1812; Lt. 13 May 1813. 'Permitted to resign the Adjutancy only, 5th August 1829.' *Battles, sieges and campaigns*: 'Busaco, 27 Septr. 1810... Redinha, 12 March 1811... Sabugal, 3 April 1811... Siege of Badajoz, From 8th to 21st May 1811... Fuentes d'honore, 5th May 1811... El Bodon,

25 Septr. 1811... Ciudad Rodrigo, 19 January 1812... Siege & Capture of Badajoz, 6 April 1812... Salamanca, 22 July 1812... Nivelle, 10 Novr. 1813... Orthez, 27th Feby. 1814... Toulouse, 10 April 1814... Platsburgh, September 1814...' *Distinguished conduct*: 'Had the honor of carrying the King's Colour at the assault and Capture of Ciudad Rodrigo on the night of the 19th Jany. 1812 and after entering the Breach with the Colours displayed led the way over two wide Ditches Cut between the Breach and the Ramparts for which I received the verbal thanks of my then Commanding officer – Major afterwards Lt Col. Ridge. Was selected to lead the 5th Regt at the Escalade and assault on the Castle of Badajoz on the night of the 6th April 1812 – and having succeeded in making footing at the Top of the Wall was soon joined by Lt. Colonel Ridge and a sufficient force to beat off whatever were immediately opposed. I then led the way over newly constructed works and towards the high part of the Citadel and Ramparts and was close to Lt. Col. Ridge when he fell – and afterwards led on the men till the Castle was taken – for which I received the Verbal thanks of Colonel Campbell 94th Foot Commg. the Brigade and who on that night succeeded to the Command of the Division after Sir J. Picton & Genl. Kemp were wounded.' *Wounds received in action*: 'Received a severe blow in the right thigh from a Musket Ball (which passed through my Trousers and Shirt) at Sabugal 3 April 1811. Received a severe contusion in the Chest from the hit of part of a shell at the siege of Badajoz, 14 May 1811. Wounded in the right thigh at the assault and Capture of Ciudad Rodrigo on the night of the 19th Jany. 1812, for which I received a Compensation of one year's full pay. Received a severe blow in the neck from a

Musket Ball (which passed through the folds of my handkerchief & shirt) at the assault & capture of Badajoz on the night of the 6th April 1812. Had a Horse killed under me at the Battle of Salamanca 22 July 1812. Had a Horse wounded under me at the Battle of Toulouse 16 April 1814.' *Titles, honorary distinctions, etc*: 'None.' *Service abroad*: '28 Septr. 1809 to 30 Decr 1812, Spain & Portugal; 10 Octr. 1813 to 30 May 1814, France & Spain; 31 May 1814 to 1 Novr. 1818, At Sea – Canada & France; 4 Feby. 1819 to 22 April 1826, At Sea and the West Indies.' *Family*: Married Agnes Rowan, 15 July 1816, Govan, Lanarkshire. She was still alive on 24 July 1830, at which date they had two children. [PRO: WO 25/785 f431]. Slightly wounded, storming of Ciudad Rodrigo, 19 Jan. 1812 [*London Gazette*]. MGS.

+CANDLER, Robert, Capt., 50th Foot: Capt., 50th Foot, 2 Jan. 1806. Killed, 'at the Storm and Capture of Fort Napoleon, and the Enemy's other works,' near Almaraz, 19 May 1812 ('Chandler') [*London Gazette*]. Mentioned in Hill's Almaraz dispatch, 21 May 1812 ['Our loss has not been severe, considering the circumstances under which the attack was made ... Captain Candler, of the 50th Regiment (the only officer killed in the assault), has, I am sorry to say, left a large family to deplore his loss. He was one of the first to mount the ladder, and fell upon the parapet, after giving a distinguished example to his men.']. Obituary, *The Gentleman's Magazine*, Supplement 1812 Part I, p. 668 ['May 19... In Spain, in his 34th year, Capt. Caudler, 50th foot, son of the late Mr S. C. of Colchester. In the memorable assault by Gen. Hill, on Fort Napoleon, near the bridge of Almarez, he was the first to ascend the ladders, and after giving to his men an example worthy of so brave an officer, fell gloriously while leading them to victory.']. Army List gives variously as 'Candler' and 'Chandler'.

CANE, James Frederick, Lt., 23rd Foot: *1829 Statement of Service for Retired Officers*: Aged fourteen on his first appointment to the Army. Ensign, Northampton Fencibles, Feb. 1799, 'disbanded 1802'; Ensign, 67th Foot, 9 July 1803; Lt., 23rd Foot, 1804 [Army List gives 24 April 1804]; Captain, 23rd Foot, [Army List gives 16 June 1811]; 'Retired upon Half Pay ... from incapacity to serve in consequence of a remarkably severe wound.' [Army List gives 1814]. *Where serving when wounded*: 'Spain.' *Details of pension*: One hundred pounds per annum, commencing 1814. *Family*: Married in Cheltenham, 18 Oct. 1818. One child by 1829. *Where principally resident during previous five years*: 'Bath & Weymouth.' [PRO: WO 25/752 f105]. MGS.

CANNING, Charles Fox, Capt. and Lt. Col., 3rd Foot Guards: Capt. and Lt. Col., Army, 19 Aug. 1813; Capt. and Lt. Col., 3rd Foot Guards, 31 March 1814. Mentioned in Wellington's Badajoz dispatch, 7 April 1812 ['This dispatch will be delivered to your Lordship by my Aide-de-Camp, Captain Canning, whom I beg leave to recommend to your protection. He has likewise taken the colours of the garrison and the colours of the Hesse D'Armstadt's Regiment, to be laid at the feet of His Royal Highness the Prince Regent. The French battalions in the garrison had no eagles.'] [*London Gazette*]. Served as ADC to Wellington in the Peninsula, and served on his personal staff at Waterloo, where he was killed. The elder brother of the famous statesman Stratford Canning, Viscount Stratford de Redcliffe.

CANNON, William, Ensign/Lt., 94th Foot: *1829 Statement of Service*:

Born in 'Baittle, Co. Galloway, N. Britain', 10 March 1784. Aged twenty-three 'on his first Entrance into the Army.' Ensign, 94th Foot, 10 Aug. 1807. Lt., 94th Foot, 7 April 1810. Half Pay, 25 Dec. 1818, 'on Reduction of the 94th Foot.' Lt., 97th Foot, 25 March 1824, 'on formation of the 97th Foot.' Capt., 97th Foot, 7 April 1825. *Battles, sieges and campaigns*: 'Was present as Ensign with the 94th Foot at the Siege of Fort Matagorda in front of Cadiz in 1810, during the tremendous bombardment that lasted for two months under the command of Captain M'Lean 94th Foot commanding the said fort. With the 94th in the Lines of Torres Vedras before the commencement of the Retreat of the French army, and with my Regt. following up the Enemy's Retreat. Was present as Lieut, in the 94th at the Battle of Fuentes D'Onor, 1st Siege of Badajoz from June 6th to June 14th 1811, affair of Elbaden, Storm of Ciudad Rodrigo, Battles of Salamanca, Vittoria & Pyrenees. Entrance into France Novr. 10th 1813 & at the Battles of Orthes and Toulouse. The various affairs in which the 3rd Division were engaged under Sir Thomas Picton and which are not termed General Actions I was also present with.' *Distinguished conduct*: 'My Conduct at the Siege of Fort Madagorda was published in General Orders and in the Dispatches sent to England by Lieut. General Sir Thomas Graham.' *Wounds received in action*: 'Was severely wounded under the chest at the storming of Ciudad Rodrigo on the 19th January 1812, for which I received one years pay as Captain having had a Command of a Company that Evening, also slightly wounded in the cap of the right knee at the Battle of Vittoria on the 21st June 1813.' *Service abroad*: 'Jany. 1810 to April 1814, Spain, Portugal and France. 11th Aug. 1825 to 29th May

1830, Ceylon.' *Family*: Married Margaret Muire Smith, 12 April 1824, 'North Britain.' They had two children by 1830. [PRO: WO 25/804 f90]. Severely wounded, storming of Ciudad Rodrigo, 19 Jan. 1812 [*London Gazette*]. Slightly wounded, Vittoria, 21 June 1813 [*London Gazette*]. Brevet Major 1838; Major 1841; retired 1842; died 1851. MGS.

+CAPEL, Thomas, Lt./Capt., 43rd Foot: Lt., 43rd Foot, 11 Dec. 1806. Severely wounded, storming of Badajoz, 6 April 1812 ('Capell') (1st Batt.) [*London Gazette*]. Killed, Nivelle, 7/10 Nov. 1813 ('Captain Thomas Capel') [*London Gazette*].

+CAREW, Robert, Lt./Capt., 18th Light Dragoons: Lt., 18th Light Dragoons, 27 June 1805; Capt., 18th Light Dragoons, 19 Sept. 1811. Severely wounded, 'since dead', Vittoria, 21 June 1813 [*London Gazette*]. *Brett-James*, pp. 71–2 ['As in many wars, when an officer was killed, his effects, apart from personal, sentimental and valuable items, were put up for auction among his companions. After Captain Carew of the 18th Light Dragoons was killed at Vitoria, brother officers paid high prices, such as 35s for two bottles of sauce, 63s 6d for seven pounds of cheese, and 27s for two tongues. Lord Worcester bid 34s for a pair of bronze spurs.'].

CAREY, Michael, Ensign, 83rd Foot: *1829 Statement of Service for Retired Officers*: Aged twenty on his first appointment to the Army. Ensign, South Cork Militia, May 1808; Ensign, 83rd Foot, 27 Oct. 1808; Lt., 83rd Foot, 7 March 1811; Half-pay, 24 Dec. 1818, by reduction. *Where serving when wounded*: 'Talavera, Spain, July 28th 1809.' Received one year's pay as Ensign. *Family*: Married in Killarney, 1 Nov. 1828. *Where generally resident during last five years*: 'Cork.' [PRO:

WO 25/752 f35]. Severely wounded, Talavera, 28 July 1809 (Ensign) [*London Gazette*]. MGS.

CARGILL, William, Lt., 74th Foot: Lt., 74th Foot, 23 Sept. 1803. Severely wounded, Busaco, 27 Sept. 1810 ('Cargell') [*London Gazette*]. MGS.

CARLETON, Hon. George, Lt. Col., 44th Foot: Lt. Col., Army, 28 Jan. 1808; Lt. Col., 44th Foot, 22 Aug. 1811. Severely wounded, storming of Badajoz, 6 April 1812 (2nd Battn.) [*London Gazette*]. Mentioned in Wellington's Badajoz dispatch, 7 April 1812 [Commanding 44th Foot: Lieutenant-Colonel 'Carlton'] [*London Gazette*]. Born 25 Sept. 1781, fourth son of Sir Guy Carleton, 1st Baron Dorchester (famous for his services in America). Killed at Bergen-op-Zoom with the 44th in 1814 [*London Gazette*, 14 March 1814].

+CARLISLE, Robert, Lt., 38th Foot: Lt., 38th Foot, 122 Sept. 1811. Killed, 'at the Siege of St Sebastian,' 7–27 July 1813 (1st Battn.) [*London Gazette*]. Severely wounded, the Nive, 9 dec. 1813 (2nd Battn.) [*London Gazette*].

CARMICHAEL, Lewis, Lt., 59th Foot: *1829 Statement of Service*: 'Born Invernesshire, Scotland, 26th June 1793. Aged 16 years on his first Entrance into the Army. Ensign, 59th Regt., 8th June 1809. Lieutenant, 59th Regt., 7th Mar. 1812. Captain, 59th Regt., 5th Decr. 1826.' *Battles, sieges and campaigns*: 'Battle of Vittoria 1813. Battle of St Sebastian 1813. Battle of Nivelle 1813. Battle of Nieve 1813. Battle of Waterloo 1815. And several Skirmishes as Lieut... Campaign of 1817 & 1818 as Lieutenant under the Command of the Marquis of Hastings. Ceylon 1819 as Lieutenant under the Command of Sir Robert Browning. Bhurtpore 1826 as Brevet Captain and Aide De Camp to Major General Jasper Nicolls' *Distinguished conduct*: 'Volunteered to Support the forlorn hope at the Storming of St Sebastian & became the only remaining Officer of the 13 who accompanied the Light Companies and the forlorn hope, and remained in Command of the whole until the Town was taken, after having received three wounds and two contusions. Noticed particularly by Sir Neil Campbell in a Skirmish before Cambray in 1815. Examined the interior defences of the Breach the day previous to the Storming of Bhurtpore, and was the first person that entered the Citadel. Mentioned in Division Orders by Major General Jasper Nicolls.' *Wounds received in action*: '1813. Received three wounds at the Storming of St Sebastian and one at the Battle of Nieve. One years pay, and a permanent Pension of £70 per annum.' *Titles, honorary distinctions and medals*: 'Received A Medal for Waterloo.' Service abroad: '26 Augt. 1812 to 1 Feby. 1814, Spain. 2nd May 1815 to 14 Jany. 1816, France. 18 Feby. 1817 to 19 May 1829, East Indies.' Not married by 1830. [PRO: WO25/796 f236]. Slightly wounded, storming of San Sebastian, 31 Aug. 1813 (2nd Battn.) [*London Gazette*]. Severely wounded, the Nive, 9 Dec. 1813 (2nd Battn.) [*London Gazette*]. Pension 'for wounds' received at Bayonne, 1813 *1818 Pension Return*, pp. 14–15.

CARR, Henry William, Major, 83rd Foot: Major 17 Sept. 1807. Mentioned in Wellington's Fuentes de Onoro dispatch, 8 May 1811 (commanding the 2nd Batt. 83rd, during the fighting of 3 May). [*London Gazette*, 26 May 1811]. Mentioned in Wellington's Badajoz dispatch, 7 April 1812 ['Lieutenant-General Picton has reported to me particularly the conduct of ... Major Carr of the 83rd'] [*London Gazette*]. Bvt. Lt. Col., 27 April 1812. Severely wounded, Orthes, 27 Feb. 1813 (2nd

Battn.) [*London Gazette*]. Lt. Col., 83rd Foot, 22 Sept. 1814. Gold Cross with 3 clasps (Fuentes d'Onor, Ciudad Rodrigo, Badajoz, Salamanca, Vittoria, Nivelle, Orthes), in command 2nd Battn. 83rd Foot. KCB. *Colville*, p. 170 [Letter from John Keane to Sir Charles Colville, 17 March 1814: 'Greenwell severely, Carr ditto – ball entered the chin and lodged in the roots of his tongue.'].

+CARROLL, Alexander, Lt., 82nd Foot: Ensign, 82nd Foot, 11 Jan. 1810. Killed, Vittoria, 21 June 1813 ('Lieutenant Carrol') (1st Battn.) [*London Gazette*].

+CARROLL, John, Capt., 28th Foot: Capt., 28th Foot, 17 May 1810. Slightly wounded, Albuera, 16 May 1811 ('2nd Battn.') [*London Gazette*]. Severely wounded, 'in Action with the Enemy', 18 March 1814 (1st Battn.) [*London Gazette*]. *Hurt*, p. 77 ['Capt. Carrol, D.O.W., Lembeye, Apl. 7']. Died, France, 7 April 1814 [PRO: WO 25/2965].

CARROLL, Morgan, Lt., 87th Foot: Lt., Army, 10 Dec. 1806; Lt., 87th Foot, 10 Dec. 1807. Severely wounded, Talavera, 27 July 1809 [*London Gazette*]. Slightly wounded, Tarifa, 31 Dec. 1811 [*London Gazette*].

CARROLL, Richard, Ensign, 43rd Foot: *1829 Statement of Service for Retired Officers*: Aged eighteen on his first appointment to the Army. Ensign, 43rd Foot, 18 Oct. 1809; Lt., 43rd Foot, 14 March 1811; Capt., 16 March 1816; Half-pay 1817, 'by the reduction of the 2d. Bn.'; 'Appointed Sub-Inspr. of Militia in the Ionian Islands in 1820 and returned to Half pay from ill health in 1821.' *Where serving when wounded*: 'In Portugal & Spain.' No pension. Not married. *Where generally resident during last five years*: 'In the Pays Bas.' [PRO: WO 25/752 f14]. Severely wounded, during 'several Affairs with the French Army', 14 March 1811 [*London Gazette*].

+CARROLL, William Henry, Lt., 4th Foot: Lt., 4th Foot, 27 May 1809. Killed, storming of San Sebastian, 31 Aug. 1813 ('Carrol') [*London Gazette*].

+CARSS, John, Adjutant/Lt., 53rd Foot: Adjutant, 53rd Foot, 25 Sept. 1803; Lt., 53rd Foot, 13 March 1805. Slightly wounded, Salamanca, 22 July 1812 (2nd Battn.) [*London Gazette*]. Died, St Jean de Luz, 5 March 1814, as Capt. [PRO: WO 25/2965].

CARTER, Dansie, Lt., 58th Foot: *1829 Statement of Service for Retired Officers*: Aged twenty-one on first appointment to the Army. Ensign, 15th Foot, 14 July 1808; Lt., 15th Foot, 7 Sept., 1809; Lt., 58th Foot, 9 Aug. 1810; Capt., 58th Foot, 4 Aug. 1814; Half-pay, 25 Feb. 1816, 'by reduction'; Capt., 95th Foot, 1 Dec. 1823; Half-pay, 15 Nov. 1827, 'unattached, in consequence of ill health.' *Where serving when wounded*: 'Burgos.' *Details of pension*: Seventy pounds, commencing 1821. *Where generally resident during last five years*: 'Malta & Lowestoft, Suffolk.' [PRO: WO 25-752-147]. Severely wounded, storming of Fort St Michael, 19 Sept. 1812 (2nd Battn.) [*London Gazette*]. MGS.

CARTER, Nathan Truman, Lt., 40th Foot: Lt., 40th Foot, 1 March 1810. Slightly wounded, Pyrenees, 28 July 1813 (1st Battn.) [*London Gazette*]. Slightly wounded, Nivelle, 10 Nov. 1813 (1st Battn.) [*London Gazette*].

CARTHEW, Charles, Capt., 39th Foot: Capt., 39th Foot, 12 Sept. 1805. Slightly wounded, Vittoria, 21 June 1813 (1st Battn.) [*London Gazette*]. *Royal Military Calendar*, vol. V, pp. 364–5 ['Albuhera... 16th

May, 1811, he commanded the light infantry companies of the brigade. He received the thanks of L.-Gen. the Hon. Sir W. Stewart, in front of his reg. for his conduct during the action... Was at the battle of Vittoria, where he received a severe contusion in both thighs, from a spent shot... was with the expedition against Plattsburg.'].

+CARY, Arthur, 1st Lt., 95th Foot: Lt., Army, 9 Feb. 1809; 1st Lt, 95th Foot, 8 March 1810. Killed, storming of Badajoz, 6 April 1812 ('Carey') (3rd Battn.) [*London Gazette*]. *Register of officers' effects*: Died of wounds, 7 April 1812, Badajoz. Effects totalled £48. 8s. 5d. [PRO: WO 25/2964]. *Simmons*, p. 232 [killed]. *Surtees*, p. 138 [Badajoz: 'I was then in the mess of the senior captain of my battalion, who commanded it on this occasion; and my other messmates were poor little Croudace and Cary, both lieutenants, the latter acting adjutant, and another. We had taken a farewell glass before we got up from dinner, not knowing which of them would survive the bloody fray that was likely soon to commence.'] p. 140 ['It was now dawn of day, and the firing had ceased at every point... Cary had fallen, but they could not tell what had become of him.'], pp. 145–6 ['It was now between twelve and one o'clock, and though we had a great many removed, a much greater number lay groaning in the ditch... But my lamented friend and messmate, poor Cary, was still to search for, and, after a considerable time, he was found beneath one of the ladders by which they had descended into the ditch. He was shot through the head, and I doubt not received his death-wound on the ladder, from which in all probability he fell. He was stripped completely naked, save a flannel waistcoat which he wore next his skin. I had him taken up and placed upon a shutter (he still breathed a little, though quite insensible,) and carried him to the camp. A sergeant and some men, whom we had pressed to carry him, were so drunk that they let him fall from off their shoulders, and his body fell with great force to the ground. I shuddered, but poor Cary, I believe, was past feeling, or the fall would have greatly injured him. We laid him in bed in his tent, but it was not long ere my kind, esteemed, and lamented friend breathed his last. Poor Croudace had also died... Thus I lost two of my most particular and intimate acquaintances, from both of whom I had received many acts of kindness and friendship. They will long live in my memory. Cary was buried next day behind our tents, one of the officers (my other messmate) reading the funeral service.']. Arthur's brother, George Marcus Cary, joined the 95th as a Volunteer in June 1812, serving with the 3rd Battn. until the close of the Peninsular War, and at New Orleans. George went on to receive an MGS. See PRO: WO 25/752 f38. *Surtees*, p. 256.

CASHEL, James, Lt., 31st Foot: Lt., 31st Foot, 23 Aug. 1809. Severely wounded, Albuera, 16 May 1811 ('Cashell') (2nd Battn.) [*London Gazette*].

CASTLE, Robert, 2nd Lt., 23rd Foot: 2nd Lt., 23rd Foot, 19 Jan. 1809. Slightly wounded, Albuera, 16 May 1811 ('Castles') [*London Gazette*].

+CASTLE, Thomas, Lt., 34th Foot: Lt., 34th Foot, 6 Dec. 1809. Killed, Albuera, 16 May 1811 [*London Gazette*].

CATOR, William, Capt., Royal Artillery: 2nd Capt., Royal Artillery, 1 May 1809. Slightly wounded, Barossa, 5 March 1811 [*London Gazette*]. Wounded, explosion of the magazine at Seville, 29 Sept. 1812. Major 12 April 1814 (Army).

MGS. *Webber*, p. 89 [Wounded, Seville], p. 117.

CATTANACH, John, Lt./Capt., 92nd Foot: *1829 Statement of Service for Retired Officers*: Aged twenty-six on his first appointment to the Army. Ensign, 92nd Foot, 25 Oct. 1803; Lt., 92nd Foot, 5 Sept. 1805 [Army List gives 16 Sept. 1805 ('Catenaugh')]; Capt., 92nd Foot, 10 Feb. 1814; Half-pay 'by the reduction of the 2nd Battalion.' *Where serving when wounded*: 'Five times wounded in the Peninsula and in France, but never applied for a Pension.' *Where generally resident during last five years*: 'Strone House' in Scotland. [PRO: WO 25/752 f103]. Slightly wounded, siege of Badajoz, 31 March–2 April 1812, while serving as Acting Engineer [*London Gazette*]. Wounded, storming of Badajoz, 6 April 1812, while serving as an Assistant Engineer ('Cattenhaugh') [*London Gazette*]. Slightly wounded, the Nive, 13 Dec. 1813 (1st Battn.) [*London Gazette*]. Half pay upon the reduction of the regiment in 1814 ['Cattanach'] [Army List]. MGS.

CAVANAGH, W. G., Lt./Capt., 87th Foot: Lt., 87th Foot, 8 Oct. 1807 ['Cavenagh']. Slightly wounded, Talavera, 27 July 1809 ('Kavanah') [*London Gazette*]. Capt., 87th Foot, 22 Nov. 1810.

CAVENDISH, Hon. Henry F. Compton, Lt., 7th Foot: *1829 Statement of Service*: Born 5 Nov. 1789, London. Aged eighteen on his first Entrance into the Army. Lt., 7th Fusiliers, 26 May 1808; Lt., 10th Hussars, 22 June 1808; Lt., 24th Light Dragoons, 26 July 1810; Capt., 103rd Foot, 6 June 1811; Capt., 25th Foot, Half Pay, 9 Jan. 1812; Capt., 96th Foot, 8 Jan. 1818; Major, 75th Foot, 2 April, 1818; Major, 9th Lancers, 24 Sept. 1818; Major and Lt. Col., 1st Life Guards, 12 July 1821. *Battles, sieges and* *campaigns*: 'Campaigns in Portugal & Spain in 1808 & 1809 under Sir Hew Dalrymple & Lt. General Sir John Moore (as Lieutenant). Battle of Corunna, Aide de Camp to Major General Lord William Bentinck (as Lieutenant).' *Wounds received in action*: 'Musket Shot through the wrist at the Battle of Corunna. No grant of Pay or Pension.' *Service abroad*: 'July 1808 to Jany 1809, Portugal & Spain.' *Family*: His first wife, Sarah Fankaner, whom he married 24 Oct 1811, St George's Westminster, died. He married his second wife, Frances Susan Howard, 15 June 1819, St James', Westminster. In 1830 he had eight children, three of them by his first marriage. [PRO: WO 25/780 f7]. MGS. Born 5 Nov. 1789, the third son of George Augustus Henry, 1st Earl of Burlington. He married a third time, to Susanna Emma Byerlie, 28 Jan. 1873, and died on 5 April following. He became a general and colonel of the 2nd Dragoon Guards [*Burke's Peerage*].

+CHADWICK, John, Lt., 9th Foot: Lt., 9th Foot, 22 Sept. 1808. Wounded, 'at the Assault upon the Island of Santa Clara ... at the mouth of the harbour of Saint Sebastian', 27 Aug. 1813 [*London Gazette*]. Severely wounded, 'since dead', in the siege of San Sebastian, 29 Aug. 1813 (1st Battn.) [*London Gazette*]. Presumably he died on the 29th of wounds received on the 27th, making him the only British Army officer killed in the Peninsula in an amphibious landing. *London Gazette*, 4 Sept. 1813 ['Admiral Lord Keith has transmitted to Mr Croker dispatches from Captain Sir George Collier, dated from Passages the 27th and 28th ult., announcing that a successful attack was made upon the island of Santa Clara, at the mouth of the harbour of Saint Sebastian, at three o'clock on the morning of the 27th, by the boats of the squadron, under the command of Lieutenant the Honourable James Arbuthnot, of His Majesty's ship Surveillance. The boats were manned by the seamen and marines, and by a party of soldiers, under the command of Captain Cameron, of the 9th regiment. The only landing-place was under a flight of steps, commanded by a small entrenchment thrown up on the west point, and completely exposed to the fire from grape of the whole range of works on the west side of the rock and walls of St Sebastian's. These local circumstances enabled a very small garrison, of an officer and twenty-four men, to make a serious resistance, by which two of our men were killed, and one officer of the army, and another of the marines, and fifteen seamen and marines, were wounded. The conduct of the officers and men was highly meritorious; each was anxious to be foremost. Lieutenant Bell, of the royal marines, had the good fortune first to succeed in getting on shore, and was immediately followed by Captain Cameron, of the 9th, and Captain Henderson, of the engineers.'].

CHADWICK, Nicholas, Ensign, 59th Foot: *1829 Statement of Service*: Born 27 Feb. 1787, County Tipperary. Aged Twenty-one years and six months on his first entrance into the Army. Ensign, 59th Foot, 21 Sept. 1808; Lt., 59th Foot, 5 Dec. 1811; Capt., 59th Foot, 29 April 1824; Capt., 13th Light Infantry, 3 August 1826. 'Died in England, 4 June 1838.' *Battles, sieges and campaigns*: 'Campaign in Spain under Sir David Baird in 1808, as Ensign 59th Regiment. Battle of Corunna under Sir John Moore 16 Jany. 1809... Expedition to Walcheren under Lord Chatham in 1809... Served on the Staff in the Island of Java in the years 1812–13 – & part of 1814 under Generals Gillespie & Nightingale. Served at the Capture of Palambang under General Gillespie in June 1813... Campaign in the

Netherlands in 1815... was present at the Storm and Capture of Cambray in June 1815... Served at the siege and Capture of Bhurtpore in 1825 and 1826 under Lord Combermere.' *Distinguished conduct*: 'Noticed in General Orders 21st February 1814, by the Commander of the Forces in Java (General Nightingale) for Meritorious and zealous conduct whilst holding the appointment of Station Staff Officer at Wattevreeden – Cornelius – & Reswick.' *Wounds received in action*: 'Wound in the Right Thigh by a Grape shot at the Battle of Corunna in January 1809 – Received a Grant of one years pay.' *Titles, honorary distinctions and medals*: 'Waterloo Medal.' *Service abroad*: '5 October 1808 to 28 Jany. 1809, Spain. 10 July 1809 to 1 Sept. 1809, Walcheren. 15 Jany. 1811 to 20 July 1814, east Indies. 6 May 1815 to 10 August 1815, France. 10 Feby. 1817 to 31 Decr. 1829, east Indies. For Waterloo Two Years. 1 Jan. 1830 to 12 Jan. 1838, E.I.' Not married in 1830. [PRO: WO 25/787 f178]. Wounded, 'in the Army lately in Spain' (2nd Battn.) [*March 1809 Army List*, p. 105].

+CHADWICK, William, Ensign, 3rd Foot: Ensign, 3rd Foot, 28 Sept. 1809. Killed, Albuera, 16 May 1811 [*London Gazette*]. Register of officers' effects: Effects totalled £9. 16s. 0½. [PRO: WO 25/2963].

CHALMERS, William, Lt./Adjutant/Capt., 52nd Foot: *1829 Statement of Service for Retired Officers*: Aged sixteen on first appointment to the Army. 'Ensign, 52nd Foot, 1803; Lt., 52nd Foot, 1804; Adjutant, 52nd Foot, 1804; Capt., 52nd Foot, 1807; Bvt. Major, 52nd Foot', 'At the recommendation of the Duke of Wellington, after the actions of the Pyrenees in 1813'; Bvt. Lt. Col., 18 June 1815, 'At the recommendation of the Duke of Wellington after the Battle of Waterloo.' 'I have not stated the months in which my

appointments are dated, as I do not recollect them exactly.' [Army List gives: Lt., 52nd Foot, 25 Oct. 1803; Adjutant, 52nd Foot, 14 Sept. 1804; Capt., 52nd Foot, 27 Aug. 1807; Bvt. Major, 26 Aug. 1813; Bvt. Lt. Col., 18 June 1815]. 'In October 1817 I was placed on half pay ... being obliged to retire from the activity of my profession, on account of Infirmities & ill health contracted on constant foreign service, & particularly a concussion of the head which rendered me unfit to bear heat except of the most moderate temperature.' *Where serving when wounded*: 'In Spain.' 'I was inspected by the Medical Board in London and obtained a remuneration for a wound received in 1813, but no Pension.' *Family*: Married in Arbroath, Scotland, 30 Jan. 1826. Two children by 1829. *Title and nature of civil employment*: 'Clerk of the Peace & Regr ... for the County of Forfar, Scotland.' *Where generally resident during last five years*: 'Dundee, Forfarshire and Glenericht ... Perthshire, North Britain'. [PRO: WO 25/753 f58]. MGS.

CHAMBERS, James, Lt., 66th Foot: Lt., 66th Foot, 25 Feb. 1808. Slightly wounded, Albuera, 16 May 1811 (2nd Battn.) [*London Gazette*].

CHAMBERS, Thomas Walker, Capt., 30th Foot: Capt., 30th Foot, 2 April 1807. Severely wounded, storming of Badajoz, 6 April 1812 (2nd Battn.) [*London Gazette*]. Bvt. Major, 30th Foot, 16 Feb. 1815. Killed at Waterloo.

CHAMPAGNE, Forbes, Lt., 20th Foot: Lt., 20th Foot, 19 May 1808. Slightly wounded, Pyrenees, 25 July 1813 ('Champigny') [*London Gazette*].

CHANCELLEUR, Alexander, Capt., 38th Foot: Capt. 9 Feb. 1804. Slightly wounded, Talavera, 28 July 1809, while serving with 1st Batt.

Detachments ('Chanceller') [*London Gazette*].

CHANTRY, George, Adjutant/Lt., 4th Dragoons: Adjutant, 4th Dragoons, 23 May 1805; Lt., 4th Dragoons, 17 June 1807. Slightly wounded, Albuera, 16 May 1811 [*London Gazette*].

CHAPLIN, Thomas, Ensign, Coldstream Guards: Ensign, Coldstream Guards, 18 April 1811; Lt. 6 Oct. 1814. Severely wounded, storming of San Sebastian, 31 Aug. 1813 ('Chaplain') (1st Battn.) [*London Gazette*]. Pension of fifty pounds per annum, commencing 1 Sept. 1814, 'for wounds' received at St Sebastian [*1818 Pension Return*, pp. 2–3]. MGS.

CHAPMAN, James, Lt., 61st Foot: Lt., 61st Foot, 2 July 1807. Severely wounded, Salamanca, 22 July 1812 [*London Gazette*]. Pension of seventy pounds per annum, commencing 23 July 1813, 'for wounds' received in Salamanca [*1818 Pension Return*, pp. 16–17].

CHAPMAN, John, Capt., 14th Light Dragoons: Capt., 14th Light Dragoons, 25 June 1803. Severely wounded, Talavera, 28 July 1809 [*London Gazette*].

CHAPMAN, William, Lt., 95th Foot; Capt., 1st Caçadores: *1829 Statement of Service for Retired Officers*: Aged thirty-one on his first appointment to the Army. Ensign, Leicester Militia, 4 March 1806; Lt., Leicester Militia, 6 April 1807; 2nd Lt., 95th Foot, 4 April 1809, 'Volunteering from Leicester Militia with 127 men'; 1st Lt., 95th Foot, 10 March 1810 [Army List gives 26 April]; Capt., 'Portuguese Caccadores', 1 Feb. 1811; Lt., Half-pay, 12 April 1819, 'Retired in consequence of wounds.' *Where serving when wounded*: 'At Redinha, Portugal, 12 March 1811. Quatre Bras, Belgium, 15th June 1815.' No

pension. *Family*: Married, London, 10 Oct. 1825. Children recorded as 'dead.' *Where generally resident during last five years*: 'Atherton, Warwickr. London. Latterly at St Peters, Isle of Thanet, Kent.' [PRO: WO 25/753 f15]. Wounded, during 'several Affairs with the French Army' (at Redinha), 12 March 1811, while serving as a Capt. in 1st Caçadores [*London Gazette*]. In Portuguese Service Feb. 1811 to Feb. 1812. Waterloo. MGS. Died at Leamington, 12 Feb. 1854. *Challis, Portuguese Army*, p. 53. *Simmons*, p. 141 [wounded, Redinha]. *Harris*, pp. 166–7 [Following Corunna: 'We reached Hastings that same night, where we found that the volunteering of the Leicester Militia (who were quartered there) had commenced, and that one hundred and twenty-five men and two officers had given their names to the 7th Fusileers, and these Adams and I determined to make change their minds in our favour if we could. The appearance of our Rifle uniform, and a little of Sergeant Adams' blarney, so took the fancies of the volunteers, that we got everyone of them for the Rifle Corps, and both officers into the bargain... The names of these two officers were Chapman and Freere.'].

CHARLES, John, Ensign/Lt., 36th Foot: Ensign, 36th Foot, 2 March 1809; Lt., 36th Foot, 20 Jan. 1812. Slightly wounded, Pyrenees, 30 July 1813 (1st Battn.) [*London Gazette*].

CHARLTON, Edward, Capt., 61st Foot: *1829 Statement of Service*: Born in Hexham, Northumberland, 8 July 1783. Ensign, 61st Foot, 8 Oct. 1804; Lt., 61st Foot, Aug. 1806; Capt., 61st Foot, 22 June 1809. *Battles, sieges and campaigns*: 'Battles of Talavera fought the 27th & 28th July 1809... Battles of the Pyrenees fought the 28th & 29th & 30th July 1813... Battle of Anoa fought the 10 Novr. 1813... Passage of the Nive on the 9th Decr. 1813, commg. during the greater part of the affair, the Light Infy. Cos. of the left Brigade 6th Divn. Battle of Orthes fought 27 Feby. 1814... Engaged with the Enemy at Tarbes, 20 March 1814... The Battle of Toulouse fought 10 April 1814, Commanding the 61st Regt. during part of the action. The campaign of 1809, part 1810, 1813, & 1814 in the Peninsula.' *Wounds received in action*: 'Wounded on the 28th July 1813 in the actions of the Pyrenees. Wounded at the Passage of the Nive the 9th December 1813, when in Command of the Light Infantry Cos. of the left Brigade 6th Division. Twice severely Wounded in the action fought near Toulouse on the 10th April 1814, the second wound received when commanding the 61st Regiment. Received a grant of one years pay of a Major of Infantry.' *Titles, honorary distinctions and medals*: 'A Gold Medal for Commanding the 61st Regiment rank Captain during a part of the actions fought near Toulouse on the 10th April 1814, under the Duke of Wellington.' *Service abroad*: '16 August 1805 to 11 June 1809, Mediterranean. 12 June 1809 to 8 Feby. 1810, Peninsula. 30 March 1813 to 2 July 1814, Peninsula. 26 Octr. 1816 to 27 May 1822, Jamaica. 1 July 1828 to 31 Decr. 1829, Ceylon.' *Family*: Married Elizabeth Kosse, 18 Oct. 1825, in Plymouth, Devon. They had one child by 1830. [PRO: WO 25/797 f7]. Slightly wounded, Pyrenees, 28 July 1813 (1st Battn.) [*London Gazette*]. Wounded, the Nive, 9 Dec. 1813 (1st Battn.) [*London Gazette*]. Severely wounded, Toulouse, 10 April 1814 (1st Battn.) [*London Gazette*]. Gold Medal.

+**CHAUNER, Andrew, Lt., 61st Foot**: Lt., 61st Foot, 18 Dec. 1806. Killed, Salamanca, 22 July 1812 (1st Battn.) [*London Gazette*]. *Register of officers' effects*: Single. Effects totalled £31.6s.8d. [PRO: WO 25/2964].

CHESSLYN, William W., Lt., 48th Foot: Lt., 48th Foot, 18 April 1805; Adjt. 25 June 1806. Severely wounded, Talavera, 28 July 1809 ('Cheslyn') [*London Gazette*].

CHETHAM, Isaac, Lt./Adjutant, 40th Foot: *1829 Statement of Service for Retired Officers*: Aged sixteen years on first appointment to the Army. '1797–8, Entered the 29th Regt. and was 3 years 6 months a private soldier, two years a corporal, 8 years 6 months a Serjeant, and three months Serjt. Major. Promoted to an Ensigncy 79th Regt. 6 August 1811. Promoted to a Lieutenancy 79th Regt. 10th December 1812 and immediately removed to the 40th Regiment as Adjutant' [Army List gives Lt., 40th Foot, 10 Dec. 1812. Adjutant, 40th Foot, 17 Dec. 1812]; Half-pay, 'By Reduction of the additional Lieutenants... I think on the 24th February 1817, and not by any wish of my own in any shape whatever.' 'Having served in Holland in 1799 under the command of His late Royal Highness the Duke of York. Landed on the 27th Augt. with the first Division and was engaged with the enemy the whole of that day, and subsequently in the Battles of the 19th September 2nd and 6th October. Had the Honor of Serving under His Grace the Duke of Wellington during the whole of the Peninsular War, and was present in every action in which the Regt. was engaged. Was at the Battles of Roleia, Vemerio, Oporto, Talavera, Busaco, Albuhera, Salamanca, Siege of Burgos, Siege of Badajos, Orthes, Vittoria, Pampalona, Zarria, Storming the Heights near Lasaca and of Toulouse. Was in the Peninsula under the command of His Grace the Duke of Wellington, when the first and last guns were fired. Have been three times very severely wounded and was present with my Regt. on all occasions when it was engaged with the enemy.' 'Notwithstanding my much impaired state of Health, from long foreign service, and severe wounds I received, still I should be most happy to spend the last day of my life in His Majesty's Service.' *Where serving when wounded*: [blank] *Details of pension*: 'I have no Pension, altho' three times severely wounded.' *Family*: Married in Halifax, Nova Scotia, 7 Dec. 1802. Three children by 1829. *Where generally resident during last five years*: 'Resided in Nottingham during the last 5 years and indeed ever since the commenct. of my being reduced to half pay.' [PRO: WO 25/753 f49]. Slightly wounded, Nivelle, 10 Dec. 1813 ('Adjutant Isaac Cheetham') (1st Battn. [*London Gazette*].

+**CHEVERS, Lawrence, Lt., 26th Foot**: Lt., 26th Foot, 3 May 1806. Killed, 'in the Army lately in Spain' (1st Battn.) [*March 1809 Army List*, p. 105].

+**CHILCOT, Charles M., Lt., 48th Foot**: Lt., 48th Foot, 28 Aug. 1807. Killed, storming of Badajoz, 6 April 1812 ('Chilcott') [*London Gazette*].

CHIPCHASE, John, Lt., 61st Foot: Lt., 61st Foot, 15 Oct. 1807. Slightly wounded, Salamanca, 22 July 1812 [*London Gazette*]. MGS.

CHISHOLM, James John, Lt., 92nd Foot: Lt., 92nd Foot, 4 Feb. 1808. Slightly wounded, Pyrenees, 25 July 1813 ('Chisholme') (1st Battn.) [*London Gazette*]. Severely wounded, the Nive, 13 Dec. 1813 (1st Battn.) [*London Gazette*]. Killed at Waterloo.

CHOISEUL, Octavius, Lt., Chasseurs Brittanniques: Lt., Chasseurs Brittanniques, 10 Oct. 1811. Severely wounded, 'in the Operations of the Army', 31 Aug. 1813 [*London Gazette*].

CHOISEUL, Xavier, Capt., Calabrian Free Corps: *1829 State-*

ment of Service for Retired Officers: Aged twenty on first appointment to the Army. 2nd Lt., 'Royal foreign artillery', 20 March 1807; Lt., 27th Foot, 3rd May 1811 [Army List gives 2 May]; 'Did duty in Spain as Captain and Adjt. Major in 1813 and 1814, Calabrian free corps.' 'Temporary rank of Captain and adjt. major.' 'After serving two years in Spain as Captain and Adjt. Major in the Calabrian free corps, prefered taking his half pay to doing duty as a Lieutenant.' *Whether desirous of service*: 'Not as Lieutenant.' *Where serving when wounded*: 'Wounded in Spain.' *Family*: Married in Southampton, 3 June 1811. Three children by 1829. *Title and nature of civil employment*: 'Employed as secretary general of the Department of the Bas Rhin.' *Where generally resident during last five years*: 'Strasburg.' [PRO: WO 25/753 f19].

+**CHOLWICH, William Francis, Capt., 7th Foot**: Capt., 7th Foot, 21 Aug. 1804. Slightly wounded, Albuera, 16 May 1811 (1st Battn.) [*London Gazette*]. Killed, storming of Badajoz, 6 April 1812 ('Cholwick') [*London Gazette*]. *Haythornthwaite, Die Hard*, p. 186 [Badajoz: 'Next morning ... [Harry Smith] ... found a party of 7th Fuzileers at work... He asked about his other companion, Captain Cholwich, and was told that he had been wounded climbing over a palisade, had fallen into the inundation and been seen no more.'].

CHRISTIAN, James, Lt., 11th Foot: *1829 Statement of Service for Retired Officers*: Aged 'about eighteen' on first appointment to the Army. Ensign, South Down Militia, 19 July 1806; Lt., South Down Militia, 7 Nov. 1806; Ensign, 11th Foot...; Lt., 11th Foot,... 'relative to the dates of those commissions in the 11th Regt. I can give no certain information as the commissions to the best of my recollection never were received by me.' [Army List gives Lt., 11th Foot, 19 Feb. 1811]. Half-pay, by reduction, 'at the conclusion of the war.' 'Lieutenant Christian is desirous of resuming the active duties of his profession ... he takes the liberty of stating that he is well adapted for the recruiting department having been in that service under General Sir Charles Asgill whose death he now sincerely regrets.' *Where serving when wounded*: 'Spain, wounded severely at Pampeluna, being shot through both thighs by a Musket ball.' No pension. *Where generally resident duriing last five years*: 'County Down, Ireland.' [PRO: WO 25/753 f51]. Severely wounded, Pyrenees, 28 July 1813 (1st Battn.) [*London Gazette*].

CHRISTIE, Braithwaite, Lt., 5th Dragoon Guards: Lt., 5th Dragoon Guards, 3 Oct. 1811. Severely wounded, Salamanca, 22 July 1812 [*London Gazette*]. ADC to Major-General Ponsonby at Waterloo. Died 23 Sept. 1825.

CHRISTIE, Charles Maitland, Lt. and Capt., Coldstream Guards: Lt. and Capt., Coldstream Guards, 16 Aug. 1804. Wounded, 'severely but not dangerously', Talavera, 28 July 1809 [*London Gazette*]. MGS. *Mullen*, p. 112 ['Wounded and taken prisoner at Talavera. Ret 20/6/10'].

+CHÜDEN, Paul Gottlieb, Major, 2nd Line Battn. K.G.L.: Major, 2nd Line Battn. K.G.L., 7 Dec. 1809. Killed, sortie from Bayonne, 14 April 1814 [*London Gazette*]. Served in Peninsula 1808–14. *Beamish*, vol. II, p. 632 ['severely wounded, 27th Feb. 1814, before Bayonne.'].

CLARK, John, Lt., 28th Foot: *1829 Statement of Service for Retired Officers*: Aged eighteen on first appointment to Army. Ensign, 28th Foot, 1 Feb. 1810; Lt., 28th Foot, 4

March 1813; 'Went on Half Pay from Wounds and ill health, 4 Apr. 1816.' 'Served previously in 19th Dragoons from 1800 till the return of Regiment from India.' *Where serving when wounded*: 'Vittoria, and slightly at Assaye.' *Details of pension*: Seventy pounds per annum, commencing 22 June 1813. *Family*: Married in St Anne's, Lime-house, 27 Sept. 1817. No children by 1829. *Where generally resident during last five years*: 'Plymouth and London.' [PRO: WO 25/753 f138]. Slightly wounded, Vittoria, 21 June 1813 ('Clark') [*London Gazette*]. Lt., Toulouse, 10 April 1814 ('John Thomas Clarke') (1st Battn.) [*London Gazette*]. *1818 Pension Return*, pp. 8–9.

CLARK, Robert, Lt., 68th Foot: *1829 Statement of Service for Retired Officers*: Aged twenty-two on first appointment to the Army. Ensign, 68th Foot, 12 April 1809; Lt., 68th Foot, 26 Dec. 1811; Half-pay, 29 March 1819, 'in Consequence of Wounds – Right leg amputated.' *Where serving when wounded*: 'At St Pee, France.' *Details of pension*: Seventy pounds, commencing 12 Nov. 1814, 'being a year and a day after being wounded.' *Where generally resident during last five years*: 'At Ardyne House by Rothesay N.B. [Scotland]' [PRO: WO 25/753 f90]. Severely wounded, Nivelle, 10 Nov. 1813 [*London Gazette*]. Pension for 'loss of a leg' at St Pe, 1813 ('Clarke') [*1818 Pension Return*, pp. 16–17]. MGS.

CLARKE, George, Capt., 5th Foot: Capt., 5th Foot, 28 Aug. 1804. Severely wounded, Nivelle, 10 Nov. 1813 (1st Battn.) [*London Gazette*].

CLARKE, John, Lt. Col., Spanish Service: Temporary pension of three hundred pounds per annum, commencing 2 June 1813, 'for a wound' received at 'Guadelete', 1812 [*1818 Pension Return*, pp. 26–7].

CLARKE, John, Lt., 66th Foot: *1829
Statement of Service*: 'Born
Newtown Butter, Fermanah,
Ireland, 12 May 1792. Aged 16 on his
first Entrance into the Army.
Ensign, 66th Foot, 21 July 1808.
Lieut., 66th Foot, 4 Octr., 1809.
Captain, 66th Foot, 13 Jany. 1825.'
Battles, sieges and campaigns:
'Oporto 12 May 1809. Talavera 27th
& 28th July 1809. Torres Vedras.
Aroyo de Milina. Campo Mayor.
Albuhera 16th May 1811. Badajos,
on Duty. Vittoria 21st June 1813.
Pyrenees, 25, 26, 27, 28, 30, 31 July 2d
Augt. 1813. Nivelle 10th Novr. 1813.
Nive 9th Decr. 1813. Bayonne 13th
Decr. 1813. St Palais 15 Feby. 1814.
Orthes 27 Feby. 1814. Toulouse 10
April 1814. Skirmishes too
numerous for insertion.' *Distin-
guished conduct*: 'On the 13 Decr.
1813 at Bayonne from my knowledge of the country brought the
Regt. into action half an hour
sooner than they otherwise would
have been. Commanded some skirmishers same day which took 2
Guns (not noticed in orders, the
Regt. at the time forming part of a
Provisional Battn. On four occasions was selected by Genl. Officers
for particular duties and received
their thanks. Was the only officer of
the Reg. who was present at every
action and skirmish in which the
regt. fired a shot. Commanded a
Company in all except Oporto.'
Wounds received in action: 'At the
Battle of Albuhera when in the
Command of a Compy. of Flankers
was struck down by a Polish Lancer,
taken Prisoner, but made his escape
in a Charge of Cavalry. Was so much
bruised as to be unable to walk for a
fortnight.' *Service abroad*: '29
March 1809 to July 1814, Portugal,
Spain, France. 16 Jany. 1816 to June
1821, St Helena. June 1827 to 31
Decr. 1829, Canada.' *Family*:
Married Susana Marcia Blood, 12
May 1827, Limerick. They had one
child by 1830. [PRO: WO 25/798 f9].
MGS. *Simmons*, p. 351 ['Dined with
Clerk [sic], 66th regiment'].

+CLARKE, Samuel, Lt., 1st Foot:
Lt., 1st Foot, 28 June 1810. Severely
wounded, Salamanca, 22 July 1812
[*London Gazette*]. Killed, 'at the
Siege of St Sebastian,' 7–27 July
1813 (3rd Battn.) [*London Gazette*].

CLARKE, William, Lt., 1st Foot: Lt.,
1st Foot, 21 June 1810. Severely
wounded, storming of San Sebastian, 31 Aug. 1813 (3rd Battn.)
[*London Gazette*]. Waterloo.
Pension for wounds received at
Quatre Bras [*1818 Pension Return*,
pp. 4–5].

**CLARKE, William, Ensign/Lt., 4th
Foot:** *1829 Statement of Service*:
Born 1 Sept. 1794, Cork. Aged 16
years 180 days on his first entrance
into the Army. Ensign, 4th Foot, 28
Oct. 1810; Lt. 28 June 1813. *Battles,
sieges and campaigns*: 'Salamanca
22d July 1812, Ensign, Duke of
Wellington. Commdg. – Burgos in
1812, Duke of Wellington. Palencia,
Ens. Oct 25th 1812, Duke Well.
Vittoria, 21 June 1813, Duke of
Wellington, Lieut. – St Sebastian
31st August 1813 Lieut, Duke of
Wellington. Bidasoa, 7th Oct. 1813,
Lieut., Duke of Wellington. Nivelle,
10th Nov. 1813, Lieut, Duke of
Wellington. Nive, 9th 10th & 11th
Decr. 1813, Lieut, Duke of
Wellington. Waterloo, 18th June
1815, Lieut., Duke of Wellington.'
Distinguished conduct: 'Command-
ed Light Infantry, Waterloo, 18th
June 1815.' *Wounds received in
action*: 'Severely wounded, St
Sebastian, 31st Augt. 1813. Severely
wounded, Nive. Medal, Waterloo.'
Service abroad: 'Campaigns 1812,
1813, 1814, Spain & Portugal; 10th
June 1815 to 25th Decr. 1816, Nether-
lands; 4th Feby. 1820 to 1 Apl 1826,
West Indies; 9 Apl. 1827 to 29 Apl.
1828, Portugal.' Unmarried by 1830.
[PRO: WO 25/785 f354]. Severely
wounded, the Nive, 11 Dec. 1813 (1st
Battn.) [*London Gazette*]. Waterloo.

**CLEARY, Richard Stanton, Lt.,
76th Foot; Capt., 13th Portuguese**

Line: *1829 Statement of Service for Retired Officers*: Aged twenty-one on first appointment to the Army. Ensign, 76th Foot, 2 June 1808; Lt., 76th Foot, 23 March 1809; Capt., 13th Portuguese Line; Half-pay, 29 Sept. 1819, 'at my own request, from private motives.' *Where serving when wounded*: 'Sortie of Bayonne, when Captain in the 13th Portuguese Infantry.' No pension. *Family*: Married in Swanlinbar, Ireland, 21 March 1827. One child by 1829. *Where generally resident during last five years*: 'Haldimand & Cramalie, near Enniskillen, Ireland, and in France.' [PRO: WO 25/753 f91]. MGS.

CLEEVES, Andrew, 2nd Capt., K.G.L. Artillery: 2nd Capt., K.G.L. Artillery, 5 June 1807; 1st Capt., K.G.L. Artillery, 26 March 1814. Served in Peninsula 1808–14. Waterloo. *Beamish*, vol. II, p. 122 [Madrid, 31 Oct. 1812: 'Finding that the rear-guard was halted at a short distance from the town, Hartmann applied for general Hill's permission to attempt the explosion of the mine which had failed. This was the more important as a quantity of musquets and small arms had been placed near it for the purpose of being destroyed at the same time. General Hill having assented, the operation was entrusted to captain Cleeves, who, accompanied by four mounted men, and protected by the cavalry picquets, returned to the arsenal, and quickly renewing the train, effected the explosion. Unfortunately, owing to the too rapid ignition of the port-fire, the gallant officer was severely burned in the hands and face, and suffered serious injuries in the head.'], p. 533 ['Severely wounded, 31st October 1812, at the Retiro... [Died] at Selby, county of York, in England, 8th June, 1830']. 'Cleves' in Army List.

CLERKE, St John Augustus, Lt. 77th Foot: Ensign, Army, 13 Oct. 1808; Ensign, 94th Foot, 24 May 1810; Lt., 77th Foot, 6 June 1811. Severely wounded, storming of Badajoz, 6 April 1812 ('Clark') [*London Gazette*]. Temporary pension of seventy pounds per annum, commencing 7 April 1813, 'for wounds' received at Badajoz [*1818 Pension Return*, pp. 18–19]. Later Lt. Col. on Staff in Ireland. MGS.

CLERKE, Thomas Henry Shadwell, Lt., 5th Foot: *1829 Statement of Service for Retired Officers*: Aged fifteen on first appointment in the Army. Ensign, 28th Foot, 30 July 1805; Lt., 5th Foot, 12 March 1807; Capt., 1st Garrison Battn., 22 Aug. 1811; Capt., 57th Foot, 10 June 1813; Half-pay, 25 Feb. 1816, 'Reduced with the 2nd Battn.' 'N.B. I refused a Company of Veterans offered me in the first instance; foregoing the advantages of Retirement with a view to more active service.' 'I have desired nothing more than to serve in a suitable situation. Since I quitted the Military College in 1806 up to the year 1823 I have constantly held military employment; and from the latter period to the present have repeatedly applied for and been promised employment on the Staff.' *Where serving when wounded*: 'In the Peninsula, wounded in action with the French Army on the 12th March 1811. Right leg amputated.' *Details of pension*: One hundred pounds, commencing 13 March 1812. *Where generally resident during last five years*: 'London & vicinity.' [PRO: WO 25/753 f142]. Severely wounded, during 'several Affairs with the French Army', 12 March 1811 ('Clarke') (2nd Battn.) [*London Gazette*]. Pension for 'loss of a leg' at Redinha, 1811, *1818 Pension Return*, pp. 4–5. MGS.

CLITHEROW, John, Lt. and Capt./Capt. and Lt. Col., 3rd Foot Guards: Ensign, 3rd Foot Guards, 19 Dec. 1799 ('Clithero'). Served in

Egypt. ADC to Gen. Burton. Lt. and Capt., 3rd Foot Guards, 24 Feb. 1803. Served at Walcheren. Slightly wounded, Fuentes de Onoro, 5 May 1811 [*London Gazette*]. Capt. and Lt. Col., 3rd Foot Guards, 8 Oct. 1812. Later Lt.-General. MGS.

+CLITHEROW, William Henry, Lt and Capt., 3rd Foot Guards: Lt. and Capt., 3rd Foot Guards, 11 Dec. 1806. Severely wounded, siege of Burgos, 5–10 Sept. 1812 ('Captain') [*London Gazette*]. Slightly wounded, the Nive, 13 Dec. 1813, while serving as ADC to Major-General Byng [*London Gazette*]. Severely wounded, 'in Action with the Enemy', 15 Feb. 1814, 'since dead', while serving as ADC to Major-General Byng [*London Gazette*].

+CLUFFE, James, Adjutant/Lt., 1st Foot: Adjutant, 1st Foot, 24 Jan. 1805. Lt., 1st Foot, 3 July 1806. Killed, 'at the Siege of St Sebastian,' 7–27 July 1813 (3rd Battn.) [*London Gazette*].

CLUNES, Richard, Ensign, 27th Foot: Ensign, 1st Foot, 25 Feb. 1813. Severely wounded, Pyrenees, 28 July 1813 (Ensign) (3rd Battn.) [*London Gazette*]. Lt., 27th Foot, 11 Aug. 1814.

CLUNES, William, Capt., 50th Foot: Capt., 50th Foot, 20 Sept. 1797. Wounded, 'in the Army lately in Spain' (1st Battn.) [*March 1809 Army List*, p. 105].

CLYDE, John, 2nd Lt., 23rd Foot: 2nd Lt., 23rd Foot, 20 June 1811. 1st Lt., 23rd Foot, 14 May 1812. Severely wounded, Salamanca, 22 July 1812 ('Cloyde') [*London Gazette*]. Died from wounds, Waterloo.

+COANE, Alexander, 1st Lt., 95th Rifles: 1st Lt., 95th Rifles, 2 Aug. 1805. Severely wounded, Coa, 24 July 1810 ('Alexander Coane') [*London Gazette*]. *Register of offi-*

cers' effects: Died, 14 Feb. 1812, Lisbon. Single. 'In debt'. [*Public Record Office*: WO25/2964]. *Simmons*, p. 82 [wounded, Coa: 'I then dressed the wound of Lieutenant Coane, who was shot in the side; he was in the same company as myself.'].

COCHRANE, Robert, Lt., 47th Foot: *1829 Statement of Service*: 'Born in Clones, Ireland, 4th June 1794. Aged 15 years on his first Entrance into the Army. Ensign, 47 Regt., 6th July 1809. Lieutenant, 47 Regt., 26th June 1811. Half Pay, 27th April 1826, Ill Health. Half Pay, 4th Regt. Lieutenant, 55th Regt., 22d Decr. 1828.' *Battles, sieges and campaigns*: 'Siege of Cadiz. Battle of Vittoria 21st June 1813. Storming of Saint Sebastian 31st August 1813. Sortie of Bayonne 14th April 1814, and during all the operations in France, and Spain in the Campaigns of 1811, 1812, 1813, and 1814. Lost two "Brothers" in the Service.' *Wounds received in action*: 'Wounded at the Storming of Saint Sebastian, but not included in the Returns. Never received any compensation.' *Service abroad*: '10th Decr. 1811 to 9th Augt. 1814, Peninsula. 10th Decr. 1816 to 9th June 1822, East Indies.' *Family*: Married Catherine Henderson, 11 Oct. 1824, Sligo. They had three children by 1830. [PRO: WO 25/795 f360]. MGS.

COCHRANE, Robert, 1st Lt., 95th Foot: *1829 Statement of Service*: Born in Gibraltar, 8 Aug. 1794. Aged fifteen 'on his first Entrance into the Army.' 2nd Lt., 95th Foot, [9] Nov. 1809. 1st Lt., 95th Foot, 8 May 1812. Capt., Rifle Brigade, 22 May 1825. *Battles, sieges and campaigns*: 'At Cadiz August 1811 and during the Siege. At Aranjuez 29 Octr. 1812... St Manios 17th Novr. 1812... San Milan 18th June 1813... Vittoria 21st June 1813... Bridge of Vera, 31st Augt. 1813... Waterloo 18th June 1815.' *Wounds received in*

action: 'Wounded severely in left
arm at the Bridge of Vera on the
31st August 1813. Wounded in left
Breast at Waterloo on the 18th June
1815. Received a Years Pay as 1st
Lieut. viz. £118.12.6 & a tempy.
Pension of £70 fm. 1st Septr. 1814 to
24th June 1817 for the wounds
received on the 31st Augt. 1813.'
*Titles, honorary distinctions and
medals*: 'A Waterloo Medal.' *Service
abroad*: Augt. 1811 to July 1814,
Peninsula. Decr. 1814 to 31st Octr.
1818, Holland, Netherlands &
France. 12th Jany. 1826 to Feby.
1828, Malta.' [PRO: WO 25/804
f342]. Severely wounded, 'in the
Operations of the Army', 31 Aug.
1813 ('Cochran') [*London Gazette*].
Waterloo. MGS.

**COCHRANE, Thomas, 2nd Lt./1st
Lt., 95th Foot**: 2nd Lt., 95th Foot,
1808; 1st Lt., 95th Foot, 22 Feb.
1809. Slightly wounded, Rolica, 17
Aug. 1808 ('Cortman') [*London
Gazette*]. Severely wounded,
Barossa, 5 March 1811 (2nd Battn.)
[*London Gazette*]. Waterloo.
Dalton, p. 203 ['D. as lt. in this regt.
1823 at Kinsale.']. *Leach*, pp. 47–8
[Rolica: 'Having driven the enemy
from one of the highest mountains,
and in the act of collecting our men
on its summit to renew the attack
on a second position, to which they
had retired, one of my brother-officers, whilst holding his canteen to
my mouth, to give me some wine,
well mulled by the sun, received a
musket shot through his hand, and
through the canteen, which latter it
split, splashed my face thoroughly
with wine, spoiled my draught, gave
me a sharp blow, which cut my
mouth, and spun me round like a
top. For a few moments I concluded
I was wounded; but the mystery
was soon explained by seeing my
friend on the ground, bleeding
profusely, and the broken canteen
at his side. I sent a soldier with him
to the rear; and, notwithstanding
that his wound was for a length of
time afterwards painful and trou-

blesome, we had the pleasure to see
him rejoin us in a few weeks. A more
gallant soldier, sincere friend, or a
more independent, straightforward, manly fellow than Cock-
rane [sic], never wore His Majesty's
uniform. In proof of the high estimation in which he was held by his
corps, suffice it to say, that his
brother-officers erected a moument
to his memory in Ireland, where he
died a few years after the termination of the war in the Peninsula and
Waterloo, in both of which he was
actively engaged.']. *Harris*, p. 179.

**COCKBURN, Patrick Heron, Lt.,
88th Foot**: Lt., Army, 25 Feb. 1808;
Lt., 88th Foot, 17 Aug. 1808.
Severely wounded, storming of
Badajoz, 6 April 1812 ('Colborn')
[*London Gazette*].

**COCKBURN, William Horton,
Ensign, 9th Foot**: *1829 Statement of
Service for Retired Officers*: Aged
twenty-three on his first appointment to the Army. Ensign and Lt.,
3rd Somerset Militia, 1807; Ensign,
9th Foot, 9 April 1809; Lt., 9th Foot,
25 June 1812; Capt., 9th Foot, 2
June 1825; Half-pay, 1828 'from ill
health, having for the last eight
years served in the West Indies.'
Where serving when wounded:
'Tarifa.' [Dec. 1811–Jan. 1812] No
pension. *Family*: Married in Dublin,
10 Aug. 1811. One child by 1829.
*Where generally resident during
last five years*: 'In Bangor ... for the
last 9 months since retirement to ½
pay.' [PRO: WO 25/753 f187].

**+COCKS, Hon. Edward Charles
Somers, Capt./Major, 16th Light
Dragoons; Major, 79th Foot**: Some
of his diaries are published under
the title *Intelligence Officer in the
Peninsula*. Lt., 16th Light
Dragoons, 1 Aug. 1805; Capt., 16th
Light Dragoons, 12 March 1807;
Major, Army, 30 May 1811.
Mentioned in Cotton's Llerena
dispatch, 11 April 1812 ['I have
great pleasure in assuring you of

the good conduct of ... the Honourable Major Cocks, commanding detachments of the 12th and 14th light dragoons.']. Mentioned in Wellington's dispatch of 21 Sept. 1812 regarding the capture of Fort St Michael, Burgos, 19 Sept. 1812 ['As soon as the 1st division crossed the Arlanzon on the 19th, the enemy's outposts were driven in by the light infantry battalion of Colonel Sterling's brigade, under the command of the Honourable Major Cocks... As soon as it was dark the same troops ... attacked and carried by assault the hornwork which the enemy had occupied in strength. In this operation Brigadier-General Pack ... and the Honourable Major Cocks of the 79th Regiment, commanding light infantry battalion, distinguished themselves; the latter, in particular, led the attack of the enemy's posts in the morning, and entered the hornwork by its gorge at night.'] [*London Gazette*]. Killed, siege of Burgos, 5–10 Oct. 1812 [*London Gazette*]. *Register of officers' effects*: 'Killed in Action, 8 Octr. 1812, Burgos.' Single. effects sold for £86.0s.2d". [PRO: WO 25/2964]. Obituary, *The Gentleman's Magazine*, Feb. 1813, p. 182 ['At Burgos, the Hon. Lieut.-col. Cocks, eldest son of Lord Somers.']. *Webber*, p. 88 [Burgos, 8 Oct. 1812: 'the enemy had made a sortie and had been driven in with loss of 30 men in killed and wounded. We suffered also and amongst the officers killed was Major Cocks of the 15th Dragoons [sic], whose death has occasioned universal regret throughout the army and will be felt by the Service at large'; n40: 'The Hon Edward Charles Cocks, sometimes styled Somers-Cocks, was one of Wellington's most skilled intelligence officers. He served in the 16th Light Dragoons (not 15th as recorded here) and had joined the 79th Highlanders at the time of his death at Burgos on 8th October 1812]. *Rice Jones*, p. 65 ['August 15

[1810]. The Telegraph at Guarda reports a skirmish to have taken place in front of the city, in which Capt. Cocks, 16th Lt. Dragoons, aided by the peasantry of the country had killed 4 and taken 18 of a party of the enemy.']. *Haythornthwaite, Armies of Wellington*, pp. 30–1, ['very exceptional was Hon. Edward Cocks, one of the most intelligent officers of his generation; his library is known to have included not only military works and history from Saxe to Adye's Bombardier and Pocket Gunner, but classics, poetry, science and mathematics; with the Sermons and Lectures on Rhetoric of Hugh Blair ... and Adam Ferguson's Lectures on philosophy and politics.'], pp. 34–5 ['Edward Cocks, one of the wisest and most knowledgeable officers in the army (one of the "observing officers" used on intelligence missions) had little opinion of the conventional education provided by officers' schools, which he thought produced officers of sergeant-majors' mentality, military pendants more concerned with drill than practical operations. He believed that all a young man required was a determination to do well and make the best of his situation, and a spare habit, as for every one "who falls sick from want, a dozen die from the gross habits of eating and drinking". Military training, he thought, should be left until the officer joined his regiment, and that all the education needed was a knowledge of history, inspirational military anecdotes, French, Latin (the foundation of the Romance languages), mathematics and the elements of fortification; tactics and strategy, he thought, could only be appreciated after experience of active service.']. *Cocks*, pp. 13–17 ['Edward Charles Cocks was born on 27 July 1786 in Great Marlborough Street, London, to John Sommers Cocks, heir to the Somers barony... Charles (the Edward was never used) came into the world burdened with clubfeet ... the residual deformity presumably being hidden by his boots... The peace of Amiens may have delayed his joining the army but when war again appeared likely his father purchased a cornetcy for him in the 16th (Queen's) Light Dragoons ... he was gazetted in April 1803... He sat on the Commons benches from 1807–9 as a passionate, albeit silent, Whig... Charles became a captain, by purchase, in the 48th Foot on 25 December 1806, but by 12 May 1807 had exchanged back into the 16th.'], p. 199 ['27 September [1812], Camp before Burgos ... I received a slight wound by a musket ball the day of the storm, but it was so trifling I did not return it.'], p. 204 [Killed, Burgos, 7/8 Oct. 1812: 'In pouring rain on the night of 7 October, Cocks took over as field officer in the trenches ... just after 3am the enemy made a sortie and succeeded in driving both the workmen and the covering party to the foot of the breach. After reforming, he led the way back up the slope to regain the outer wall but had no sooner reached the top than one of the French, standing not five yards off, fired straight at him, and the ball entered "between the 4th and 5th rib on the right side, passing through the main artery above the heart and so out at the left side, breaking an arm", and killing him instantly. The men fought on until the enemy was pushed back into the covered way and when morning broke his body was returned under a flag of truce "to be buried with military honours in compliment to his distinguished service"... They buried him the next morning under a cork tree in the 79th's ground at Bellima. "Lord Wellington, Sir Stapleton Cotton, Generals Pack and Anson and the whole of their staff and the officers of the 16th Light Dragoons and the 79th Regiment attended him to his grave," Tomkinson continued. "He is regretted by the whole army and in those regiments in which he has been, not a man can lament a brother more than they do him." "He is on every ground the greatest loss we have yet sustained," Wellington wrote to Beresford.'], p. 206 ['However, possibly Wellington spoke the tribute Charles would have appreciated most: "D'Urban," he said at last, to the officer next to him at the funeral, "had Cocks outlived the campaigns, which from the way he exposed himself was morally impossible, he would have become one of the first Generals in England." ']. *Brett-James*, pp. 237–8.

CODD, John, Lt., 66th Foot: Lt., 66th Foot, 5 Oct. 1809. Severely wounded, Albuera, 16 May 1811 (2nd Battn.) [*London Gazette*].

COEN, John, Lt., 28th Foot: Lt., 28th Foot, 29 Jan. 1810. Slightly wounded, Vittoria, 21 June 1813 (1st Battn.) [*London Gazette*]. Wounded, Waterloo.

COGHLAN, James, Lt., 45th Foot: Ensign, 45th Foot, 3 April 1810; Lt., 45th Foot, 3 March 1812. Slightly wounded, Salamanca, 22 July 1812 [*London Gazette*]. Severely wounded, Orthes, 27 Feb. 1814 (1st Battn.) [*London Gazette*]. Pension of seventy pounds per annum, commencing 28 Feb. 1815, 'for a wound' received at Orthes [*1818 Pension Return*, pp. 12–13].

+COGHLAN, James R., Major/Lt. Col., 61st Foot: Major, 61st Foot, 9 Jan. 1806. Severely wounded, Talavera, 27 July 1809 [*London Gazette*]. Bvt. Lt. Col., 30 May 1811; Lt. Col., 61st Foot, 13 June 1811. Killed, Toulouse, 10 April 1814 (1st Battn.) [*London Gazette*]. *Register of officers' effects*: 'Coghlan, K. John, Lt. Col.' 'Killed in Action, Toulouse, 10 April 1814.' Single. Effects totalled £155.16s.1d. [PRO: WO 25/2964]. *Pearson*, p. 82 ['In the course of our engagements, Major Coghlan and Adjutant Drew, two of the most acute and valiant of our officers, had been lost to us, – the former having been wounded at Talavera and taken prisoner... Major Coghlan speedily recovered, under the careful treatment of the French doctors, and, being declared convalescent, was sent to one of their prisons, from which he escaped a few months afterwards and returned to England... Of the former officer [Coghlan] we heard nothing... One morning, however, the two officers appeared in our midst, glad to be with us again, and we were as happy to receive them.'], pp. 89–90 [Fuentes de Onoro: 'Major Coghlan commanded us'].

COLBORNE, Sir John, Lt. Col., 52nd Foot: Portrait of him in *Haythornthwaite, Wellington's Military Machine*, p. 128 ['Sir John Colborne of the 52nd, later Baron Seaton (1778–1863), unequalled as a regimental commander.']. Born 16 Feb. 1778. Capt., 20th Foot, 12 Jan. 1800; Lt. Col., Army, 2 Feb. 1809; Lt. Col., 52nd Foot, 18 July 1811. Severely wounded, storming of Ciudad Rodrigo, 19 Jan. 1812 [*London Gazette*]. Mentioned in Wellington's Ciudad Rodrigo dispatch of 20 Jan. 1812 ['I have already reported in my letter of the 9th instant, my sense of the conduct of Major-General Craufurd, and of Lieutenant-Colonel Colborne, and of the troops of the light division in the storm of the Redoubt of St Francisco, on the evening of the 8th instant. The conduct of these troops was equally distinguished throughout the siege, and in the storm nothing could exceed the gallantry with which these brave officers and troops advanced and accomplished the difficult operation allotted to them... I particularly request your Lordship's attention to the conduct of ... Lieutenant-Colonel Colborne'] [*London Gazette*, 5 Feb. 1812]. Gold Medal. Waterloo. MGS. *Dalton*, pp. 169–71. *Simmons*, pp. 218, 222

[badly wounded, storming of Ciudad Rodrigo, 19 Jan. 1812], p. 317. *Leach*, p. 249 [Ciudad Rodrigo], pp. 341–3 [Vera, Oct. 1813: 'From the hill we were able to reconnoiter the whole of the French entrenchments in the higher mountains beyond it. Art and nature combined had certainly given it a formidable appearance, particularly that portion allotted to the 2d brigade of the Light Division to assault, commanded by Lieutenant-Colonel Colbourne, of the 52d regiment, an officer possessing the most cool and determined courage, coupled with excellent judgement and considerable experience... During these operations, Colonel Colbourne's brigade had a much more arduous task to perform. His opponents could not be taken in flank, and he was therefore obliged to advance straight against them, entrenched up to their chins. The impetuosity of the attack made with the bayonet by this brigade, headed by Colonel Colbourne, and its brilliant success, are like many other conflicts which took place during the Peninsular war, not coming under the head of general actions, but imperfectly known except to those engaged in the operations on the spot. A succession of redoubts and field-works were carried by the bayonet, and those who defended them were either shot, bayoneted, or driven off the mountain. The 52d regiment, the 2d battalion of the 95th, and the 1st Caçadores, which composed this brigade, suffered very severely.']. *Kincaid, Adventures*, p. 101 [Storming of Fort San Francisco, Ciudad Rodrigo, 8 Jan. 1812: 'We lay by our arms until dark, when a party, consisting of a hundred volunteers from each regiment, under Colonel Colborne, of the fifty-second, stormed and carried the Fort of St Francisco, after a short sharp action, in which the whole of its garrison were taken or destroyed.']. *Brett-James*, pp. 26,

261-2 ['No more gallant officer campaigned under Wellington's command than Colonel John Colborne, afterwards a field-marshal. At the storming of Ciudad Rodrigo while in command of the 52nd a bullet struck his right shoulder and passed some way down the arm, carrying part of the gold wire of his epaulette into the wound. He could not lie on his left side, as it hurt the other to be raised, and the pain of lying on his back became so dreadful that his bed had to be lifted off the ground on one side to give him ease. The day after the battle a surgeon cut the wound across and across, probing for the ball, but he could not find it, and fifteen months were to elapse before it was extracted. Harry Smith, who knew him well, wrote long afterwards: "The pain Colborne suffered in the extraction of the ball was more even than his iron heart could bear. He used to lay his watch on the table and allow the surgeons five minutes' exertions at a time, and they were three or four days before they wrenched the bone from its ossiffied bed ... of course the shoulder-joint was anchylosed, but he had free use of the arm below the elbow." At one stage of the journey to Coimbra, whither he was carried on twenty men's shoulders, Colborne felt so weak and his nerves were so upset that he used to be obliged to say "Give me a glass of wine, I am going to cry". "I could not help crying continually. Once I felt it coming on as I was being carried across a stream in my journey and a good many soldiers were looking on, but I was so ashamed of their seeing me and thinking I was crying because I was hurt, that that, I think, prevented me." ']. *Bruce*, p. 78 [Letter from Lt. Col. Macleod to William Napier, La Encina, 21 Jan. 1812: 'Poor Colborne's wound was at first thought to be slight, but to-day the surgeons say that they fear it will be very troublesome: the ball entered his shoulder and was lodged deep in, and they are afraid to try to extract it.'], pp. 79-80 [Macleod to W. Napier, El Bodem, 4 Feb. 1812: 'Colborne's wound is still giving him a great deal of pain, but I hope from what I heard is going on as favorably as can be expected; the ball had worked its way towards his elbow from the shoulder, and they have by this time, I dare say, extracted it; when this occurs his case will be easy.']. *Kincaid, Random Shots*, pp. 273-4 ['At the storming of the heights of Bera, on the 8th of October, 1813, Colonel, now Sir John Colbourne, who commanded our second brigade, addressed his men before leading them up to the enemy's redoubt with, "Now, my lads, we'll just charge up to the edge of the ditch, and if we can't get in, we'll stand there and fire in their faces." They charged accordingly, the enemy fled from the works, and in following them up the mountain, Sir John, in rounding a hill, accompanied only by his brigade-major and a few riflemen, found that he had headed a retiring body of about 300 of the French, and whispering to his brigade-major to get as many men together as he could, he without hesitation rode boldly up to the enemy's commander, and demanded his sword! The Frenchman surrendered it with the usual grace of his countrymen, requesting that the other would bear witness that he had conducted himself like a good and valiant soldier! Sir John answered the appeal with an approving nod; for it was no time to refuse bearing witness to the valour of 300 men, while they were in the act of surrendering to half a dozen.']. Colborne executed the manoeuvre which led to the defeat of the attack of the Imperial Guard at Waterloo. He was later C-in-C and Governor-General of Canada at the time of the 1837-8 rebellions, became Baron Seaton in 1839 and field-marshal in 1860.

Moore Smith, G. C., *The Life of John Colborne, Field-Marshal Lord Seaton* (London, 1903).

COLCLOUGH, Guy, Lt., 3rd Foot: Lt., 3rd Foot, 30 May 1805. Slightly wounded, Pyrenees, 30 July 1813 [*London Gazette*].

COLE, Hon. Galbraith Lowry, Major-General/Lt.-General: Colonel, 27th Foot, 1 Jan. 1801; Major-General 25 April 1808. Slightly wounded, Albuera, 16 May 1811 [*London Gazette*]. Lt.-General, 'having local rank', Spain and Portugal, 6 Sept. 1811. Severely wounded, 'not dangerously', Salamanca, 22 July 1812 [*London Gazette*]. Lt.-General, 4 June 1813. Gold Medal. For biographical details see *Royal Military Calendar*, vol. II, pp. 305–14 ['In 1809 he was appointed to the Staff of the army serving in Spain and Portugal, and was present in command of a division (the 4th) at the battles of Albuhera, Salamanca, Vittoria, Pyrenees, Nivelle, Orthes, and Toulouse']. *Bruce*, p. 106 [Letter from William Napier to his wife, Florres de Avila, 25 July 1812: 'I am sorry to say that Cole has been wounded in the arm.']. 'George Lowrey Cole' in Army List.

COLE, John, Lt., 45th Foot: Lt., 45th Foot, 5 June 1805. Slightly wounded, Talavera, 28 July 1809 [*London Gazette*].

COLEMAN, George, Capt., 31st Foot: Capt., 31st Foot, 8 Aug. 1804. Severely wounded, Talavera, 27 July 1809 [*London Gazette*]. Pension of one hundred pounds per annum, commencing 25 Dec. 1811, 'for wounds' received at Talavera [*1818 Pension Return*, pp. 8–9].

+COLLIER, W. George, Lt. and Capt./Capt. and Lt. Col., Coldstream Guards: Lt., Army, 14 May 1801; Lt. and Capt., Coldstream Guards, 25 Dec. 1802. Slightly wounded, Talavera, 28 July 1809 [*London Gazette*]. Capt. and Lt. Col., Coldstream Guards, 3 Oct. 1811. Severely wounded, sortie from Bayonne, 14 April 1814 ('George Colyer') (1st Battn.) [*London Gazette*]. *Register of dead officers*: Died of wounds, 10 May 1814. Return dated May 1814. [PRO: WO 25/2965]. *Hurt*, p. 75 ['George Collier, Bayonne, D.O.W. May 10']. *Fletcher, Fields of Fire*, p. 164 ['Coldstream Guards cemetery, Bayonne... The cemetery, which lies literally in the corner of a field, was the site of the Coldstream Guards' camp and those who lie here include ... Lt. Col. W. G. Collier'].

+COLLINS, Bassett, Capt., 74th Foot: Capt., 74th Foot, 20 Aug. 1805. Slightly wounded, storming of Ciudad Rodrigo, 19 Jan. 1812 ('Colling') [*London Gazette*]. Killed, siege of Badajoz, 26 March 1812 [*London Gazette*]. *Register of officers' effects*: 'Baset Collins'. 'Killed in Action, 25 Mar. 12, Badajoz'. Single. Effects sold for £48. 1/10. [PRO: WO 25/2964]. *Register of dead officers*: 'Killed before Badajos', 25 March 1812. Return dated 25 April 1812 [PRO: WO 25/2965].

COLLINS, Charles, Ensign/Lt., 50th Foot: Ensign, 50th Foot, 24 May 1810. Severely wounded, Pyrenees, 25 July 1813 (1st Battn.) [*London Gazette*]. MGS.

+COLLINS, George Trelawny, Lt., 23rd Foot: Lt., 23rd Foot, 14 June 1807. Killed, storming of Badajoz, 6 April 1812 (1st Battn.) [*London Gazette*]. Obituary, *The Gentleman's Magazine*, June 1812, p. 594 ['Mortally wounded by a musket-ball through the body, in advancing to the main breach of Badajoz, while gallantly leading the light company of the Welsh Fusileers to the storm of that fortress, aged 24, Lieut. George Trelawny Collins, eldest son of G. C.

esq. of Ham, Devon. Of the many victims who have fallen a sacrifice to these afflicting times, not one has left a brighter fame behind him, or been lamented with more poignant grief, than this most amiable youth, who from his infancy, sweet-tempered, modest, and affectionate, gave an early promise of that sterling excellence of character... At the siege of Copenhagen, at the taking of Martinique and Olivenza, at Albuera, Aldea de Ponte, Ciudad Rodrigo, and Badajoz, he nobly supported the character of a British officer, with the distinguished regiment to which he belonged; and it had pleased God to protect him through these many severe conflicts, as well as to preserve his health amidst the privations and hardships of his arduous campaigns; but alas! while his beloved family were bending with grateful hearts for past mercies, an eternal termination was given to all their earthly hopes in this dear son... He received the fatal wound while cheering on his men, and his last words to the officer who succeeded him in the command were, "Take care of my company." '].

COLLINS, Graves Chamney, Lt., 61st Foot: *1829 Statement of Service for Retired Officers*: Aged fifteen on first appointment to the Army. Ensign, 91st Foot, 20 May 1799; Lt., 91st Foot, 8 Oct. 1801; Half-pay, Dec. 1802; Lt., 61st Foot [Army List gives 25 Feb. 1804; Capt., 61st Foot; Half-pay, by reduction. 'In consequence of the very severe and afflicting wound I received at the battle of Talavera de la Reyna, which occasioned the Amputation of my left-arm from the shoulder-joint, which causes me excessive pain either in cold or Hot weather, I find myself totally inadequate to perform the duties of a military life.' *Where serving when wounded*: 'Spain.' *Details of pension*: One hundred pounds per annum,

commencing 25 Dec. 1811, 'as Lieutenant. Increase as Captain from June 25th 1816'; Not married in 1829. *Where generally resident during last five years*: 'Parsonstown, King's County, Ireland.' [PRO: WO 25/754 f30]. Severely wounded, Talavera, 28 July 1809 [*London Gazette*]. Pension for 'loss of an arm' at Talavera [*1818 Pension Return*, pp. 16–17].

+COLLINS, Richard, Lt. Col., 83rd Foot; Col., Portuguese Staff: Lt. Col., Army, 25 April 1808; Lt. Col., 83rd Foot, 17 Aug. 1809. Wounded, Albuera, 16 May 1811, while serving as Col. on the Portuguese Staff [*London Gazette*]. Slightly wounded, Salamanca, 22 July 1812, while serving as Col. on the Portuguese Staff [*London Gazette*]. In Portuguese Service Oct. 1810 to Feb. 1813. Gold Medal. Obituary, *The Gentleman's Magazine*, April 1813, p. 386 ['Feb. 18. At his station in Gouves, province of Beira, Portugal, aged 38, Lieut.-col. Rochard Collins, 83d reg. colonel in the Portuguese service, and commanding a brigade in the 7th division... He spoke the German, French, Spanish, and Portuguese languages; not only fluently, but eloquently; he was a good draftsman, and well read in the military history of all the great Generals who flourished in the last century. He commenced his military career in the West Indies in the year 1795–6... At the storming of Morne Fortunee, in St Lucie ... he was struck by a musket-ball in the breast, and was, after lying for some hours on the spot, taken up as dead; he was, however, present at the capture of the island of Trinidad soon afterwards... He commanded his regiment at the capture of the Cape of Good Hope... At the memorable and sanguinary battle of Albuera, his leg was taken off by a cannon-ball, and, in consequence of a succeeding mortification, his thigh was obliged to be amputated

very high up; he languished for some time, but the resources of a mind never to be subdued turned the balance; his stump healed, and here he gave an instance of heroism never paralleled, perhaps, in military annals: he returned to this country in the month of July 1812, in this mutilated state; and was found again at the head of his brigade, as active as any man in the Peninsula, with a cork leg and thigh, in the beginning of the month of October following... The brigade which he had the honour to command, as a mark of their high opinion of his talents and worth, have agreed to erect a monument to his memory.'].
Challis, Portuguese Army, p. 53. *Haythornthwaite, Armies of Wellington*, p. 30.

COLLINS, Stephen, Ensign/Lt., 48th Foot: Ensign, 48th Foot, 10 Aug. 1809. Slightly wounded, Albuera, 16 May 1811 ('Collin') [*London Gazette*]. Lt., 48th Foot, 20 June 1811. Severely wounded, Nivelle, 10 Dec. 1813 (1st Battn.) [*London Gazette*].

COLLIS, Charles, Capt., 24th Foot: *1829 Statement of Service for Retired Officers*: Aged sixteen on first appointment to the Army. Ensign, 5th Foot, 23 Jan. 1800; Half-pay, Lt., 12th Foot, 24 June 1802; Lt., 5th Foot, 17 Sept. 1803; Capt., 24th Foot, 23 Oct. 1805 [Army List gives 31 Oct. 1805]; Bvt. Major, 24th Foot, 12 Aug. 1819; Capt., Half-pay, 84th Foot, 9 Dec. 1819, 'at my request in consequence of a Wound.' *Where serving when wounded*: 'Spain.' *Details of pension*: One hundred pounds, commencing 24 Dec. 1811. *Family*: Married in Lympston, Devonshire, 2 Aug. 1825. Two children by 1829. *Where generally resident during last five years*: 'Lympston, Taunton...' [PRO: WO 25/753 f203]. Severely wounded, Talavera, 28 July 1809 [*London Gazette*]. *Royal Military Calendar*, vol. V, p. 366.

COLLIS, John, Lt., 61st Foot: *1829 Statement of Service for Retired Officers*: Aged seventeen years seven months on first appointment to the Army. Ensign, 6th Garrison Battn., 1 Dec. 1806, 'immediately joined & continued to serve with it in Ireland untill promoted'; Lt., 61st Foot, 16 June 1808, 'joined the 2d Battn. of 61st on Guernsey in Augt. 1808 where he served till ordered to join 1st Battn. in the Peninsula & wounded at Salamanca 22d July 1812. Placed at his own Request on the retired list 21st April 1814.' 'Incapable of serving having lost both eyes.' *Where serving when wounded*: 'in Spain at the Battle of Salamanca 22nd July 1812.' *Details of pension*: '£140 – being £70 for each eye... Can not state now when the Pension comenced but believes from the day of the wound. Passed the Medical Board in London about March 1813.' *Where generally resident during last five years*: 'at his mother's House Mountford Lodge... County of Cork, Ireland.' John Collis has signed the document with a cross ['his X mark'], while his father, Will Collins, filled out the form and signed as a witness. [PRO: WO 25/753 f215]. Severely wounded, Salamanca, 22 July 1812 [*London Gazette*]. *1818 Pension Return*, pp. 16–17.

+COLLYER, George, 2nd Capt., Royal Engineers: 1st Lt., Royal Engineers, 1 May 1807; 2nd Capt., Royal Engineers, 5 March 1812. Killed, storming of San Sebastian, 31 Aug. 1813 ('Captain') [*London Gazette*].

+COLQUHOUN, Archibald, Capt., 40th Foot: Capt., 40th Foot, 10 March 1804. Slightly wounded, Talavera, 28 July 1809 [*London Gazette*]. Died, Peninsula, 19 Aug. 1812 [PRO: WO 25/2965].

+COLQUHOUN, George, Capt., 2nd Foot: Capt., Army, 28 Sept. 1804; Capt., 2nd Foot, 28 Aug. 1806.

Killed in the siege of the Forts of St Vincente, St Cayetano, and La Merced, Salamanca, 18–24 June 1812 [*London Gazette*].

+COLQUITT, John Scope, Capt. and Lt. Col., 1st Foot Guards: Capt. and Lt. Col., 1st Foot Guards, 14 Sept. 1809. Severely wounded, Barossa, 5 March 1811 [*London Gazette*]. Mentioned in Skerrett's dispatch concerning the capture of Seville, 28 Aug. 1812 ['I am also much indebted to Lieutenant-Colonel Colquit, commanding a detachment of the 1st Regiment of Guards'] [*London Gazette*]. Obituary, *The Gentleman's Magazine*, Feb. 1813, p. 182 ['Lately... At Seville, of his wounds, Lieut.-col. Colquhit, whose meritorious services were recently noticed by Col. Skerret. (See our last volume, p. 480.)']. Died, Seville, 4 Sept. 1812 [PRO: WO 25/2965].

COLTHURST, Nicholas, Lt., 83rd Foot: Lt., 83rd Foot, 29 March 1808. Slightly wounded, Busaco, 27 Sept. 1810 (2nd Battn.) [*London Gazette*]. In Portuguese Service (Capt., 21st Line) March 1811 to April 1814. MGS. *Challis, Portuguese Army*, p. 53.

COLVILLE, Hon. Charles, Major-General: Lt. Col., 13th Foot, 26 Aug. 1796; Major-General 25 July 1810. Severely wounded, 'not dangerously', storming of Badajoz, 6 April 1812 (77th Foot) [*London Gazette*]. Mentioned in Wellington's Badajoz dispatch, 7 April 1812 ['The arrangements made by Major-Genral Colville for the attack by the 4th division, were very judicious, and he led them to the attack in the most gallant manner.']. Slightly wounded, Vittoria, 21 June 1813 [*London Gazette*]. Gold Medal. Temporary pension of three hundred and fifty pounds per annum, commencing 7 April 1813, 'for wounds' received at Badajoz [*1818 Pension Return*, pp. 24–5]. Commanded the Reserves at

Hal, 18 June 1815, and was not present at Waterloo. *Dalton*, p.16. For biographical details, see *Royal Military Calendar*, vol. III, pp. 16–19. Also John Colville, *The Portrait of a General: A Chronicle of the Napoleonic Wars*. Letter from Colville to the Rev. Roger Frankland, 'Camp before Badajos', 8 April 1812: 'I think myself very fortunate in having escaped in the assault with the loss of the upper joint of my third finger, and a musket shot through the thick part of my thigh, which has most providentially kept clear of the bone' [*Colville*, p. 97]. Letter from Colville to his brother, John, following Vittoria: 'I had another instance of providential escape, for which I cannot be sufficiently grateful: for it appears to me that had the ball pierced only a line or two deeper, I must have lost my thumb and with it most probably my hand. The bruised flesh sloughed off two days since and wholesome granulations are throwing themselves out, which by the bye is the most painful part of the process of the wound, but only occasionally felt. In another fortnight I should hope it will entirely have healed over. Rest would be preferable, but still having the use of my fingers, I dress myself and go on much as usual, and with my hand generally in a sling of my sash... I had the scabbard of my sword in my hand at the time I received the blow, which came sideways, and which probably by swelling out the muscles accounts for the depth of the wound without material injury. I was at the time on foot' [*Colville*, p. 120]. *Haythornthwaite, Die Hard*, p. 180 [Storming of Badajoz: 'Before he was able to get down into the ditch, Colville was hit twice... For some time he appears to have lain where he fell, endeavouring to command his division through his staff.'].

COMBERMERE, Lord, Lt.-General: see Cotton, Stapleton.

COMBREMENT, A. Le Theur, Major, Chasseurs Britanniques: Major, Chasseurs Britanniques, 7 March 1811. Slightly wounded, Pyrenees, 30 July 1813 ('Combre Lont') [*London Gazette*].

COMMELINE, Thomas, Lt., 71st Foot: Lt., 71st Foot, 15 April 1813. Severely wounded, Vittoria, 21 June 1813 (1st Battn.) [*London Gazette*].

+COMMERELL, William Henry, Ensign, 1st Foot Guards: Ensign, 1st Foot Guards, 27 April 1809. Killed, Barossa, 5 March 1811 [*London Gazette*].

+CONNELL, John J., 1st Lt., Royal Artillery: 1st Lt., Royal Artillery, 1 Sept. 1811. *Register of dead officers*: 'Killed Trenches Badajos', 28 March 1812. Return dated 25 April 1812. [PRO: WO 25/2965].

CONNELL, John, Ensign, 68th Foot: Ensign, 68th Foot, 7 Oct. 1812. Severely wounded, 'arm amputated', Pyrenees, 30 July 1813 ('O'Connel') [*London Gazette*].

CONNOR, Charles, Volunteer, 18th Light Dragoons; Lt., 20th Foot: *1829 Statement of Service*: Born 10 Aug. 1784, Sandymount, County Down. Aged twenty-four years and 197 days on his first entrance into the Army. Ensign, 20th Foot, 23 Feb. 1809; Lt. 27 June 1811; Capt., unattached, 7 Aug. 1827; Capt., 20th Foot, 9 Aug. 1829. *Battles, sieges and campaigns*: 'Expedition to Walcheren in 1809 ... served the Champaign of 1813 and 14 in the Peninsula with the Regiment at the Battles of Vittoria, 21st June 1813; Pass of Toucesvalles, 25th July 1813; Battle of Pyrenees, 28th July 1813; Battle of Eschalar, 2 Aug. 1813; Battle of Nivelle, 10th Novr. 1813; Battle of Nive, December 1813; Battle of Orthes, 27th February 1814... Served during Sir J. Moores Champaign in Spain with the 18th Hussars, as a Volunteer at Rueda,

12th December 1808, and Benevente, 29th December 1808.' Wounds received in action: 'Wounded Severely at Orthes on the 27th February 1814, when in command of a Company. Received one years Pay as Captain.' Service abroad: '16th July 1809 to 16th Sept. 1809, Walcheren. 7th January 1813 to 7th July 1814, Portugal, Spain & France. 1st January 1819 to 15th November 1825, St Helena and East Indies.' Unmarried in 1830. [PRO: WO 25/788 f328]. Slightly wounded, Pyrenees, 28 July 1813 [*London Gazette*]. Severely wounded, Orthes, 27 Feb. 1814 [*London Gazette*]. It appears that it was indeed this officer who was, according to the *London Gazette*, wounded in the Pyrenees, even though, strangely, he made no record of it in his Statement of Service.

+CONNOR, William Shewbridge, Lt., 7th Foot; Capt., 8th Portuguese Regt: Lt., 7th Foot, 28 Feb. 1811. Slightly wounded, as Capt. 8th Portuguese Regt., in the siege of the Forts of St Vincente, St Cayetano, and La Merced at Salamanca, 18–24 June 1812 ('Conner') [*London Gazette*]. Severely wounded, 'in the Operations of the Army', 31 Aug. 1813, as Capt., 8th Portuguese Line [*London Gazette*]. *Register of dead officers*: Died of wounds, 25 Nov. 1813. Return dated Dec. 1813. [PRO: WO 25/2965]. In Portuguese Service May 1810 to April 1813. *Challis, Portuguese Army*, p. 53 ['Wd. San Sebastian 31 Aug. '13 (sic), Bidassoa 7 Oct. '13'].

CONROY, Patrick, Lt., 4th Foot: Lt., Army, 26 July 1804; Lt., 4th Foot, 13 Feb. 1805. Slightly wounded, storming of Badajoz, 6 April 1812 ('Convoy') [*London Gazette*].

CONSIDINE, James, Ensign/Lt., 43rd Foot: *1829 Statement of Service*: 'Born Taullamore, King's

135

County, Ireland, 7th June 1794. Aged 14 years and Eleven Months, on his first Entrance into the Army. Ensign, 5th W.I. Regt., 18 May 1809. Ensign, 43d Lt. Infantry, 25 July 1809. Lieutenant, 43rd Lt Infantry, 27 December 1810. Captain, 43d Lt. Infantry, 29 August 1822. Major, 43d Lt. Infantry, 11 July 1826. Lieut. Colonel, Unattached, Half Pay, 1 July 1828. Lieut. Colonel, 53d Regiment, 2 April 1829.' Note added: 'Lieut. Colonel, 53d Regiment, Half Pay, 1836.' *Battles, sieges and campaigns*: 'Ensign. Coa, 24th July 1810. Busaco, 27 September 1810. Lieutenant. Redinha, 12 March 1811. Condeixa, 14 March 1811. Sabugal, 3 April 1811. Fuentes D'Onor 5 May 1811. Ciudad Rodrigo, 8 January 1812. Rodrigo Assault & Capture 19 Jan. 1812. Badajoz Siege 17 March 1812. Badajoz Assault & Capture 6 April 1812. Salamanca, 22 July 1812. Bidassoa, 7 October 1813. Nivelle, 10 November 1813. And sundry skirmishes in which the Light Division were engaged, in the years 1810, 11, 12 and 13... New Orleans, 8 January 1815.' *Wounds received in action*: 'Wounded very severely at the Assault of Badajoz, 6 April 1812. Very severely at Nivelle 10 November 1813. Two years pay and Pension as Lieutenant of seventy pounds per Annum, from 11th November, 1814, Permanent.' *Titles, honorary distinctions and medals*: 'Knight of the Hanoverian Guelphic Order January 1832.' *Service abroad*: 'May 1810 to February 1814, Peninsula. December 1814 to June 1815, America. June 1815 to October 1818, Flanders & France. May 1823 to January 1827, Gibraltar. January 1827 to March 1828, Portugal. March 1828 to July 1828, Gibraltar. 2 December 1829 to 31 December 1829, Gibraltar. 1 January 1830 to 6 April 1834, Gibraltar. 7 April 1834 to 6 May 1836, Malta.' *Family*: Married Miss Stewart, 24 Aug. 1819, Belfast. They had two children by 1830. [PRO:

WO 25/795 f156]. Severely wounded, storming of Badajoz, 6 April 1815 ['Consadine'] (1st Battn.) [*London Gazette*]. Severely wounded, Nivelle, 10 Nov. 1813 (1st Battn.) [*London Gazette*]. Temporary pension of seventy pounds per annum, commencing 11 Nov. 1814, 'for wounds' received at Badajoz and Nivelle [*1818 Pension Return*, pp. 12–13].

CONYERS, Charles Edward, Major, 82nd Foot: Major, 82nd Foot, 16 Feb. 1809. Severely wounded, Orthes, 27 Feb. 1814 (1st Battn.) [*London Gazette*]. Gold Medal. Temporary pension of two hundred and fifty pounds per annum, commencing 18 Feb. 1815, 'for wounds' received at Orthes, as 'Major Comg.' the regiment [*1818 Pension Return*, pp. 18–19]. *Royal Military Calendar*, vol. V, p. 20 ['This officer served with the 82d foot at Gibraltar and in the West Indies, and was the only officer of those who went out with that reg. who returned to England with it ... in Egypt; at the storming of Rosetta, where he received a severe contusion ... on the Staff as Brigade Maj. in Spain, and present at the battle of Orthes'].

COOKE, James, Capt., 94th Foot: Lt., 94th Foot, 31 Dec. 1805; Capt. 94th Foot, 27 Feb. 1812. Severely wounded, Salamanca, 22 July 1812 ('Captain') [*London Gazette*]. Pension of one hundred pounds per annum, commencing 23 July 1813, 'for a wound' received at Salamanca [*1818 Pension Return*, pp. 20–1].

COOKE, John Henry, Lt., 43rd Foot: Lt., 43rd Foot, 19 April 1810. Slightly wounded, storming of Badajoz, 6 April 1812 ('Cook') (1st Battn.) [*London Gazette*].

+COOKSEY, Walter C., Capt., 79th Foot; Capt., 24th Portuguese Line: Capt., 79th Foot, 30 April 1807. In Portuguese Service Nov. 1810 to

Jan. 1811. *Challis, Portuguese Army*, p. 53 ['Capt. 24 Line... K/A Villa del Ponte 11 Jan. '11.'].

+COOKSON, George Parker, Ensign, 3rd Foot Guards: Ensign, 3rd Foot Guards, 29 June 1809. Killed, Fuentes de Onoro, 5 May 1811 (1st Battn.) [*London Gazette*].

COOPER, Leonard Morse, Ensign, 47th Foot: *1829 Statement of Service*: Born 25 Dec. 1798, London. Aged fourteen years and eleven months on his first entrance into the Army. Ensign, 34th Foot, Nov. 1813; Ensign, 47th Foot, Jan. 1814; Half Pay Sept. 1814; Ensign, 1st Foot, Dec. 1814; Half Pay Jun 1816; Lt., 66th Foot, Jn. 1817; Lt., 20th Dragoons, Sept. 1818; Half Pay Dec. 1818; Lt., 11th Dragoons, Jan. 1819; Capt. 25 Feb. 1831. *Battles, sieges and campaigns*: 'Siege and Sortie of Bayonne 14th April 1814... Battle of Waterloo 16th & 18th June 1815... Siege and Capture of Bhurtpore, 18th Jany. 1826.' *Wounds received in action*: 'Slightly at the Siege and Sortie of Bayonne, 14th April 1814. Five wounds at the Battle of Waterloo 18th June 1815. One years Pay, and Permanent Pension as Lieut. from 18th June 1815.' *Titles, honorary distinctions and medals*: 'Waterloo Medal.' *Service abroad*: 'Jany. 1814 to Aug. 1814, South of France. April 1815 to Octr. 1815, Wounded at Brussells. Feby. 1819 to Decr. 1829, Bengal.' *Family*: Married Emma, Daughter of Rt. Hon. Walter Esq., 1 March 1831, Trinity Church, St Mary-le-bone, London. [PRO: WO 25/783 f294].

+COOTE, Arthur Gethin, Capt., 50th Foot: Lt., 10th Foot, 6 Jan. 1796; Capt., Army, 30 Dec. 1803; Capt., 50th Foot, 2 Aug. 1804. Killed, Vimeiro, 21 Aug. 1808 ('Capt. A. G. Cooke') [*London Gazette*]. Monthly Returns, 1st Battn., Return dated 1 Sept. 1808: 'Vacant Commissions – One Company... By the Death of Capn. Coote in the action of 21

August.' [PRO: WO 17/164]. He was the only officer from the 50th Foot killed at Vimeiro. *Harris*, pp. 55–6 [Vimeiro: 'After the battle I strolled about the field in order to see if there was anything to be found worth picking up amongst the dead... A little further off lay an officer of the 50th regiment. I knew him by sight, and recognised him as he lay. He was quite dead, and lying on his back. He had been plundered, and his clothes were torn open. Three bullet-holes were close together in the pit of his stomach: beside him lay an empty pocket-book, and his epaulette had been pulled from his shoulder. I had moved on but a few paces when I recollected that perhaps the officer's shoes might serve me, my own being considerably the worse for wear, so I returned again, went back, pulled one of his shoes off, and knelt down on one knee to try it on. It was not much better than my own; however, I determined on the exchange, and proceeded to take off its fellow... The dead and the dying lay thickly all around'].

COOTE, Thomas Gethin, Capt., 24th Foot: Capt., 24th Foot, 22 Feb. 1810. Severely wounded, 'in the assault and capture of the exterior line of the castle of Burgos on the evening of the 4th October, 1812' [*London Gazette*].

COPPINGER, Thomas G., Lt., 97th Foot: Lt., 97th Foot, 21 Feb. 1805. Severely wounded during the repulse of a sortie from Badajoz, 10 May 1811 [*London Gazette*]. Temporary pension of one hundred pounds per annum, commencing 11 May 1812, 'for a wound' received at St Christoval, 1811 [*1818 Pension Return*, pp. 22–3]. MGS.

CORDEMANN, Ernest, Lt., 1st Light Dragoons K.G.L.: Lt., 1st Light Dragoons, 6 June 1810. Slightly wounded, Salamanca, 22 July 1812 ('Cordeman') [*London*

CORDEMANN

Gazette]. 'Cordeman' in Army List. Served in Peninsula 1809–14. Waterloo. *Beamish*, vol. II, p. 549 [Died 'at Langenhagen in Han. 27th Sept. 1833'].

COSBY, Philip Stopford, Lt., 45th Foot: Lt., 45th Foot, 11 April 1811. Severely wounded, Orthes, 27 Feb. 1814 (1st Battn.) [*London Gazette*]. Temporary pension of seventy pounds per annum, commencing 28 Feb. 1815, 'for wounds' received at Orthes [*1818 Pension Return*, pp. 12–13]. *Colville*, p. 170 [Letter from John Keane to Sir Charles Colville, 17 March 1814, regarding Orthes: 'Golby [sic] was wounded in this affair, but from his known zeal Sir Thomas allowed me to recommend his name ... to the Lord's consideration for the battle of Orthez.'].

COTHER, Charles, Major, 71st Foot: Capt., 71st Foot, 25 March 1803; Major, 71st Foot, 9 March 1809. Mentioned in Hill's Almaraz dispatch, 21 April 1812 ['Lieutenant-Colonel Stewart, and Major Harrison, of the 50th, and Major Cother of the 71st, commanded the three attacks, and led them in a most gallant and spirited manner.'] [*London Gazette*]. Lt. Col., Army, 19 June 1812. Slightly wounded, Vittoria, 21 June 1813 ('Brevet Lieutenant-Colonel Cothen') [*London Gazette*]. Lt. Col., 71st Foot, 13 Oct. 1814. Gold Medal. MGS.

COTMAN, Samuel, Assistant Surgeon, 38th Foot: Assistant Surgeon, 38th Foot, 18 Feb. 1813 ('Cottnam'). Severely wounded, Nivelle, 10 Nov. 1813 ('Cotman'") (1st Battn.) [*London Gazette*].

COTTER, William, Lt., 83rd Foot; Capt., 9th Portuguese Line: Lt., 83rd Foot, 12 March 1808. Temporary pension of two hundred pounds, commencing 22 June 1814, 'for a wound' received at Vittoria, 1813, while serving as Capt., 9th Portuguese Line [*1818 Pension Return*, pp. 24–5]. *Challis, Portuguese Army*, p. 53 ['P/S July '10 to Dec. '13.' Does not record wound].

COTTINGHAM, Edward, Lt., 28th Foot: *1829 Statement of Service for Retired Officers*: Aged nineteen on first appointment to the Army. Ensign, 28th Foot, 20 April 1809; Lt., 28th Foot, 19 July 1810; Capt., 85th Foot, 25 Jan. 1813; Capt., York Chasseurs, 23 June 1814; Half-pay, 2 March 1815, 'in consequence of Wounds.' *Where serving when wounded*: 'Spain at Albuera 16 May 1811.' *Details of pension*: One hundred pounds, commencing June 1812. *Family*: Married in Dublin, 30 March 1826. One daughter by 1829. *Where generally resident during last five years*: 'England 2 years. Ireland 3 years.' [PRO: WO 25/754 f62]. Slightly wounded, Albuera, 16 May 1811 (2nd Battn.) [*London Gazette*]. Temporary pension of one hundred pounds per annum, commencing 10 May 1812, for 'loss of the use of an arm' at Albuera [*1818 Pension Return*, pp. 8–9]. MGS.

+COTTON, Edward, Lt., 88th Foot: Lt., 88th Foot, 16 March 1809. *Register of officers' effects*: Died of wounds, 8 April 1812, Badajoz. Single. 'Balance supposed to have been paid to ... Friends, or lodged with the Agents.' [PRO: WO 25/2964]. Return dated 25 April 1812 ('Cottin') [PRO: WO 25/2965].

+COTTON, John, Lt., 10th Light Dragoons: Cornet, 10th Light Dragoons, 14 Dec. 1809; Lt., 10th Light Dragoons, 28 March 1811. Killed, 'in Action with the Enemy's Rear Guard, near Morales', 2 June 1813 [*London Gazette*]. Mentioned in Grant's Morales dispatch, 2 June 1813 ['It is with much satisfaction I acquaint your Lordship, that nothing could exceed the steadiness and bravery of the troops in this affair. I have, however, to regret the loss of a very promising young officer, Lieutenant Cotton, of the 10th Hussars, who was killed in the midst of the enemy's ranks.'] [*London Gazette*]. Obituary, *The Gentleman's Magazine*, 1813 Supplement Part I, p. 662 ['June 2. At Morales, near Toro, in his 18th year, Lieutenant Cotton, 10th reg. hussars. In a most resolute and successful charge against the 16th French dragoons (which was completely destroyed), this amiable and gallant young officer was first wounded by a sabre over the forehead, which rather stunned him, and almost immediately afterwards was shot through the right breast, and killed on the spot. His conduct during the charge and pursuit was, to use the expression of his commanding officer, "the admiration of the regiment." ']. *Webber*, p. 154 ['we were informed of a gallant affair... On our part we lost Lieut Cotton, a fine young man of the 10th Dragoons, and a few men.']. 'Cottin' in Army List.

COTTON, Stapleton, (Lord Combermere), Lt.-General: 2nd Lt. 26 Feb. 1790; Lt. 16 March 1791; Capt. 28 Feb. 1793. Served in Flanders in 1793–4. Major 28 April 1794; Lt. Col., Army, 9 March 1794. From 1794–1800 in India in the Mysore War, including Seringapatam. Col., Army, 1 Jan. 1800; Lt. Col., 16th Light Dragoons, 14 Feb. 1800. Major-General 30 Oct. 1805; Lt.-General 1 Jan. 1812. Severely wounded, Salamanca, 22 July 1812 [*London Gazette*]. Gold Medal. MGS. Hart's *1840 Army List* ['In the Peninsula and South of France, in command of a brigade of cavalry, from 1808–14, including the operations at Oporto; battle of Talavera, and various actions in covering the retreat from Almeida to Torres Vedras; battle of Busaco; cavalry action at Villa Garcia, Castrajon, Fuentes d'Onor, Salamanca (severely wounded), El Bodon, the

Pyrenees and Orthes. Gold Medal with one clasp. Gen. 27 May 1825. Present at the siege and capture of Bhurtpore in 1825–6 as Commander-in-Chief. Col., 1st Life Guards, 16 Sept. 1829.']. He was Sir Stapleton, Bart., after inheriting the family baronetcy in 1809. The injury at Salamanca occurred on the night of the battle when he was shot accidentally by a sentry whose challenge he had failed to answer. His success at Bhurtpore led him to be created Viscount; became Fieldmarshal Oct. 1865. During his Peninsular service he was also MP for Newark (1806–14). *Memoirs and Correspondence of Field-Marshal Viscount Combermere, from his Family Papers*, ed. Mary, Viscountess Combermere & W. W. Knollys (London, 1866).

+COTTON, Thomas D'Avenant, Capt., 7th Foot: Capt., 7th Foot, 30 Aug. 1810. Severely wounded, Nivelle, 10 Nov. 1813, while serving as Brigade-Major [*London Gazette*]. *Register of dead officers*: Died of wounds, 13 Nov. 1813. Return dated Nov. 1813. [PRO: WO 25/2965]. Obituary, *The Gentleman's Magazine*, Dec. 1813 ['Nov. 13... At the village of Anhoue, near Bayonne, in his 30th year, T. D'Avenant Cotton, esq. (youngest son of the very Rev. the Dean of Chester, and first cousin of Lieut.-gen. Sir Stapylton C. bart K.B.) a captain in the Royal Fusileers, and major of Brigade to Major-gen Byng, 2d division of the British Army in France. After having been engaged in the taking of Copenhagen and Martinique, he embarked with his regiment in 1810 for Portugal, and has been in active service during the whole campaign. He distinguished himself in most of the great battles in the Peninsula, particularly in those of Salamanca and the Pyrenees. His person was miraculously spared in every engagement until the battle of the 10th, when he recieved a mortal wound at the head of his brigade, in the act of carrying a redoubt on the left of the Enemy's intrenchments before Anhoue.'].

+COULTER, William, Ensign, 66th Foot: Ensign, 66th Foot, 29 May 1809. Severely wounded, Talavera, 28 July 1809 ('Cotter') [*London Gazette*]. Killed, Albuera, 16 May 1811 (2nd Battn.) [*London Gazette*]. *Register of officers' effects*: Single. Effects totalled £32. 2s. 3d, 'Paid to his Mother.' [PRO: WO 25/2964]. *Register of dead officers*: Died of wounds, 18 May 1811. Return dated 25 May 1811 [PRO: WO 25/2965].

COURTENAY, William Allan, Ensign, 39th Foot: *1829 Statement of Service for Retired Officers*: Aged eighteen on his first appointment to the Army; Ensign, 39th Foot, 21 June 1809 [Army List gives 14 June 1809]; Lt., 39th Foot, 23 Aug. 1813; Half-pay, 4 April 1816, 'in consequence of wounds.' *Where serving when wounded*: 'Spain, at the pass of Maya in the Pyrenees.' *Details of pension*: Fifty pounds per annum, commencing 22 Aug. 1814. *Where generally resident during last five years*: 'Ireland.' [PRO: WO 25/754 f17]. Slightly wounded, Pyrenees, 25 July 1813 (1st Battn.) [*London Gazette*]. Temporary pension of fifty pounds per annum, commencing 26 July 1814, 'for wounds' received in the Pyrenees [*1818 Pension Return*, pp. 10–11]. MGS.

COWELL, William, Major., 42nd Foot: Capt., Royal Regt. of Malta, 8 Dec. 1804; Major, Royal Regt. of Malta, 16 March 1809; Major, 42nd Foot, 30 May 1811. Severely wounded, Orthes, 27 Feb. 1814 (1st Battn.) [*London Gazette*]. Gold Medal. *Anton*, p. 68 ['On the 9th of October [1813] we again advanced. Major Cowell, at the head of the light-infantry companies of the brigde, drove back the enemy's picquets and established our advances on the defiles of the

mountains looking down towards France.'], p. 107 [Orthes, 27 Feb. 1814: 'The light-infantry companies of the brigade, under the command of Major Cowel (afterwards brevet lieutenant-colonel), were skirmishing in front. The major was severely wounded and carried to the rear.'].

COWPER, John, Ensign, 59th Foot: *1829 Statement of Service*: 'Born Carlton, Cumberland, January 18th 1791. Aged 17 years on his first Entrance into the Army. Ensign, 59th Foot, 28th April 1808. Lieut., 59th Foot, 7th June 1809. Captain, 59th Foot, 10th May 1820.' Note added: 'Died at Gibraltar 2 Nov 1835 of apoplexy.' *Battles, sieges and campaigns*: 'In Campaign of 1808 & 09 in Spain, and Battle of Corunna 16 Jany. 1809, under Sir Jon Moore as Ensign. The Campaign of 1815 in Netherlands and France, Battle of Waterloo, Storming of Cambray & Paris as Lieutenant.' *Wounds received in action*: 'Wounded severely at the Battle of Corunna 16 Jany. 1809. Pension granted of 50£ pr. Annm. Papers lost in the shipwreck off Ireland and [so unable] to give dates. Pension increased to 70£ pr. Annm. in 1824, and permanently granted.' *Titles, honorary distinctions and medals*: 'Medal for Waterloo.' Service abroad: 'Septr. 1808 to Jany. 1809, Spain. May 1815 to Jany. 1816, France. Febry. 1817 to May 1823, Bengal & Ceylon, East Indies. NB. Shipwrecked in the Sea Horse Transport in Tramore Bay 30th January 1816, when 363 Men Women & Children perished.' [PRO: WO 25/796 f223]. Wounded, 'in the Army lately in Spain' ('Cooper') (2nd Battn.) [*March 1809 Army List*, p. 105].

+COWSELL, John, Lt., 71st Foot: Lt., 71st Foot, 25 Aug. 1806. Killed, Fuentes de Onoro, evening of 3 May 1811 (1st Battn.) [*London Gazette*]. *Register of officers' effects*: Single.

Effects totalled £1. 2s. 3d. [PRO: WO 25/2964]. 'Consell' in Army List.

COX, Charles, Ensign/Lt., 39th Foot: Ensign, 39th Foot, 25 May 1809. Severely wounded, Albuera, 16 May 1811 (2nd Battn.) [*London Gazette*]. Lt., 39th Foot, 1 Oct. 1812. Severely wounded, Pyrenees, 25 July 1813 (1st Battn.) [*London Gazette*]. Severely wounded, 'in Action with the Enemy', 18 March 1814 (1st Battn.) [*London Gazette*].

COX, Charles Thomas, Ensign/Lt., 71st Foot: *1829 Statement of Service for Retired Officers*: Aged twenty-one on first appointment to Army. Ensign, 71st Foot, 29 June 1809; Lt; 71st Foot, 29 May 1811; Half-pay, 25 Oct. 1821, 'By reduction; at the same time being disabled by the change of position of a ball, which still remains lodged.' *Where serving when promoted*: 'Spain, at the Battle of Vittoria.' *Details of pension*: Seventy pounds, commencing 'Believed it to have been in June 1814; the grant of a years pay being considered equivelant for the first year after the wound was received.' Not married. *Where generally resident during last five years*: Gloucestershire. [PRO: WO 25/753 f164]. Slightly wounded, Fuentes de Onoro, 5 May 1811 (1st Battn.) [*London Gazette*]. Wounded, 'severely and missing', Vittoria, 21 June 1813 (1st Battn.) [*London Gazette*]. Waterloo. MGS. Died in 1875. *Dalton*, p. 183 ['At Vittoria he was severely wounded, a musket ball having passed through the lungs and lodged in the body. He was taken prisoner, but the enemy being hard pressed, he was left on the field.'].

COX, John, 2nd Lt./1st Lt., 95th Foot: *1829 Statement of Service*: Born in St Anne's Parish, Dublin, 22 May 1790. Aged seventeen years and ten months 'on his first Entrance into the Army.' 2nd Lt., 95th Foot, 16 March 1808; 1st Lt.,

95th Foot, 8 June 1809; Capt., Rifle Brigade, 23 Dec. 1819; Major, Rifle Brigade, 19 Aug. 1828. Note added: 'Lt. Col., Half Pay, Unattd., 17 [Dec?] 1837.' *Battles, sieges and campaigns*: '1st Campaign, 1808. At Obidos, 15th August. At Roleia, 17th August. At Vimiera, 21st August. 2nd Campaign, 1808. At Bridge of Benevento, 28th Decr. 3rd Campaign, 1809. In front of Talavera 30th July. 4th Campaign, 1810. At Barba del Puerco, 19th March. At Galligos, 4 July. At Burguillo, 11th July. At Almaida, 24th July. At Mora Mosta, 25th Septr. Near Sula, 26 Sept. At Busaco, 27 Sept. At Alenquier, 10th Oct. Near Santarem, 20th Novr. 5th Campaign, 1811. Near Pombal, 9th March. At Pombal, 11th March. At Redinha, 12th March. At Candeixa, 13th March. At Cuza Nova, 14th March. At Foz de Aroce, 15th March. At Ponte de Murcella, 18th March. At Fruxadas, 28th March. At Sabugal, 3rd April. At Almeida on 10th 11th 12th 13th & 14th April. At Marialva Bridge 30th April. At Fuentes de Onor, 3rd & 5th May. Near Naves de Avar, 6th June. At Forcaylos, 27th Sept. 6th Campaign, 1812. Siege & Stormg. of Ciudad Rodrigo fm. 8th to 19th Jany. 7th Campaign, 1813. At St Milan, 18th June. At Vittoria, 21st June. At Echanianos, 23rd June. Near Pampluna, 24th June. Heights of Santa Barbara, 15th July. Pass of Echallar, 3rd August. At Vera, 1st Septr. Attack on Pass of Vera, 7th Octr. At Nivelle, 10th Novr. In affair of Outposts near Aroanquis, 20th Novr. In affair of Outposts near Bassissurry, 30th Novr. Outposts affairs frm. 10th to 12th Decr. 8th Campaign, 1814. At Tarbes, 20th March. 9th Campaign, 1815. Outpost affairs, 17th June. At Waterloo, 18th June.' *Wounds received in action*: 'Wounded by a Musket Ball in Right Shoulder at the Battle of Vimiera, 21st Augt. 1808, for which the Patriotic Fund presented me with £20. Wounded in

COX

the left arm by a Musket shot at the Storming of Ciudad Rodrigo, 19th Jany. 1812. Received a Years Pay as 1st Lieut. for it. Left leg badly fractured by a Musket shot at Tarbes on 20th March 1814. Received a Years Pay as 1st Lieut. and £50 from Patriotic Fund & was granted a temporary Pension as Captain of £100 on 21st March 1815 having been filling that situation when disabled which was reduced to that of 1st Lieut. on 24th Decr. 1816. This Pension was made permanent on 30th July 1825 having been twice inspected in the intermediate time by the Army Medical Board, London.' *Titles, honorary distinctions and medals:* 'A Waterloo Medal.' *Service abroad:* '8th June 1808 to 1st Feby. 1809, Portugal and North of Spain. 25th May 1809 to July 1812, Peninsula. Octr. 1812 to 22nd July 1814, Peninsula. 8th Novr. 1814 to Novr. 1818, Holland, Netherlands, France. 28th July 1825 to 21st Decr. 1827, North America.' Note added: "Oct. 1831 to 1834, Malta & Ionian Islands.' *Family:* Married Miss Caroline Wolfe, 17 June 1830, Lymstone, Devon. [PRO: WO 25/804 f314]. Severely wounded, storming of Ciudad Rodrigo, 19 Jan. 1812 (1st Battn.) [*London Gazette*]. Severely wounded, 'in Action with the Enemy', 20 March 1814 (1st Battn.) [*London Gazette*]. Temporary pension of seventy pounds per annum, commencing 21 March 1815, 'for wounds' received at Ciudad Rodrigo, 1812, and Tarbes, 1814 [*1818 Pension Return*, pp. 22–3]. Waterloo. MGS. *Dalton*, pp. 197, 199 ['Afterwards Maj.-Gen. John Cox, K.H... Had a compound fracture of his left arm at the storming of Ciudad Rodrigo.... D. at Cheltenham, 7th Feb., 1863. There were two officers of this name in the Rifles in 1815, who appear to have been brothers, and of the same family as Sir Richard Fox, Bart., Lord Chancellor of Ireland.']. *Simmons*, p. 223 [wounded, Ciudad Rodrigo], p. 314.

COX, William, 1st Lt./Capt., 95th Foot: 2nd Lt., 95th Foot, 6 June 1805; 1st Lt., 95th Foot, 19 Nov. 1807. Severely wounded, Vittoria, 21 June 1813 (1st Battn.) [*London Gazette*]. Capt., 95th Foot, 16 Sept. 1813. Slightly wounded, Nivelle, 10 Nov. 1813 (2nd Battn.) [*London Gazette*]. Severely wounded, 'in Action with the Enemy', 20 March 1814 (3rd Battn.) [*London Gazette*]. MGS. Probably brother of John Cox, 95th Foot. *Simmons*, p. 318. *Harris*, p. 13 [At Copenhagen], p. 65 [Lisbon, 1808: 'Captain Leech and Lieutenant Cox ... were good-looking men, and, in their Rifle uniform, with the pelisse hanging from one shoulder, and hessian-boots then worn, cut a dash, I thought'], pp. 67–8, 148 [retreat to Corunna: 'Whilst we lay exhausted in the road, the rear guard, which was now endeavouring to drive on the stragglers, approached, and a sergeant of the Rifles came up and stopped to look at us... Whilst he was urging me to endeavour to rise up, the officer in command of the rear guard also stepped up. The name of this officer was Lieutenant Cox; he was a brave and good man, and observing that the sergeant was rough in his language and manner towards me, he silenced him, and bade the guard proceed, and leave me. "Let him die quietly, Hicks," he said to the sergeant. "I know him well; he's not the man to lie here if he could get on. I am sorry, Harris," he said, "to see you reduced to this, for I fear there is no help to be had now." He then moved on after his men, and left me to my fate.'], p. 157 [Vigo: 'I was the very last of the retreating force to reach the beach... I made out a boat which seemed the last that had put off... I took off my cap, and placed it on the muzzle of my rifle as a signal, for I was totally unable to call out. Luckily, Lieutenant Cox, who was aboard the boat, saw me, and ordered the men to return.'].

CRABBE, Eyre John, Lt., 74th Foot: *1829 Statement of Service*: Born Tamerton Folliott, Devonshire, 5th September 1791. Aged fifteen years nine Months on first appointment to the Army. Ensign, 74th Foot, 11 June 1807; Lt., 74th Foot, 11 March 1808; Capt., 74th Foot, 19 May 1814; Major, 74th Foot, 31 Jan. 1828. *Battles, sieges and campaigns*: 'As Lieutenant the whole of the retreat to the Lines of Torres Vedras, including the Battle of Busaco, the advance of the Allies from the Lines to Guarda in the Spring of 1811. The Siege of Badajos, from 30th June to 14th July 1812 [sic], & the remainder of the Campaign of that year. The Siege & Storming of Ciudad Rodrigo in Jany. 1812, the Siege and Storming of Badajos in 1812. Battle of Salamanca, Capture of Madrid, & the whole of the Campaign of that year including the retreat thro' Spain until the Army retired to Winter Quarters in Novr. The whole of the Campaign of 1813 & 1814 from 1st Augt. 1813 up to the Battle of Toulouse including the entrance into France on 10th Novr., the Actions of Nivelle, Nive, Vic, Tarbes & Orthes & the whole of the various minor affairs during that period.' *Wounds received in action*: 'Wounded on the 13th March 1811 when Commanding a Party at Foz d'aronce, ordered to drive a French Picquet from the said Village in which I succeeded – received no renumeration for it. Wounded on the 10th April [1814] at Toulouse when attacking the Tete du Pont in Command of a Company for which I received one years Pay as Gratuity.' *Service abroad*: '24th Jany. 1810 to 31st Decr. 1812, Peninsula. 4th June 1813 to 19th July 1814, France. 18th June 1818 to 5th Novr. 1819, New Brunswick, North America. 20th April 1824 to 24th Augt. 1828, Nova Scotia. 25th Augt. 1828 to 3d June 1829, Bermuda.' [PRO: WO 25/799 f224]. Slightly wounded, during 'several Affairs with the French Army', 14 March 1811 ('Crabb') [*London Gazette*]. Slightly wounded, Toulouse, 10 April 1814 ('Eyre John Crab') (1st Battn.) [*London Gazette*]. MGS.

CRAIG, Henry, Capt., Sicilian Regt. of Foot: *1829 Statement of Service for Retired Officers*: Aged sixteen on first appointment to the Army. Ensign, 30th Foot, 31 Dec. 1799; Lt., 89th Foot, 3 Sept. 1801; Half-pay, 25 Aug. 1802, by reduction. Lt., 35th Foot, 31 Oct. 1804; Capt., Sicilian Regt., 11 Feb. 1808; Capt., 30th Foot, 15 Nov. 1809; Capt., '102d (afterwards 100th)', 2 April 1815; Half-pay, 18 May 1818, by reduction. Brevet Major, 27 May 1825; 'Promoted to Lieutenant Colonel 24th July 1828, By Brevet on appointment to be Depy. Adjt. General in the West Indies.' *Where serving when wounded*: 'Wounded at Talavera in Spain 28 July 1809.' No pension. *Family*: Married in Portsmouth, Hampshire, Aug. 1810. Three children by 1829. *Where generally resident during last five years*: 'Ireland, Portugal & the West Indies on the Staff in each country.' [PRO: WO 25/754 f181]. Slightly wounded, Talavera, 28 July 1809, while serving as ADC to General Sherbrooke [*London Gazette*].

CRAMMER, James Henry (Samuel), Lt., 28th Foot: Note: Army Lists give name as Samuel Crammer. It is clear from his Statement of Service, however, that he went by James Henry. *1829 Statement of Service*: Born 31 Oct. 1792, Athlone, County Roscommon. Aged twelve years and seven months when he first joined the Army. Volunteer, 28th Foot, June 1805; Ensign July 1805; Lt. 2 July 1807; Capt. July 1815. *Battles, sieges and campaigns*: 'Siege of Copenhagen 1807... Battle of Busaco 27th Septr. 1810... Campa Mayor 25th March 1811... 1st Siege of Badajos May 1811... Albuhera 16th May 1811, Lieut. Commanding a Company... Vittoria 21st June 1813. Puerte d'Ispegey 7th July 1813, Lieutent. Commandg. a Compy... Pyrennees July 1813, Lieutent. Commandg. a Compy. Nivelle 10th Novr 1813, Ditto ditto. Nive 9th Decr. 1813, Do. Do. Bayonne 13th Decr. 1813, Do. Do. St Palais 15 Feby. 1814, Do. Do. Orthes 27th Feby. 1814, Do. Do. Lambage 18th March 1814... Toulouse 10th April 1814... Les Quatre Bras 16th June 1815... Waterloo 18th June 1815... Lieutenant Comg. a Compy. on the above occasions... Acted as Brigade Major to the British Brigade from the Battle of Waterloo till the Capture of Paris, vice Capt. Eeles 95th Rifles Killed in action on the 18th June 1815.' *Distinguished conduct*: 'Employed on the night of the 5th March 1811, by Major General Sir William Lumley, Commanding 2nd Brigade 2nd Division to carry Despatches from Almeyrion, on the left bank of the Tagus, to Lord Wellington whose Head Quarters were then at Cartaxo, giving information of the intended retreat of the French Army from the lines of Santorem. Employed on the 24th April 1811 by Major General Sir William Stewart Commanding the 2nd Division to carry despatches from Almandrelego in Estremadurato the Spanish Governor of Merida announcing the advance of a British Division in support of that place threatened by a forward movement of the Enemy. Employed on the night of the 15th May 1811, by Marshal Beresford to carry Despatches from the Field of Albuhera to Major General Sir Lowry Cole then in command of the Troops in the lines before Badajos by the prompt execution of which mission a considerable part of the Forces under the Major General's orders were enabled to reach the Position of Albuhera on the following morning, in time to take a decisive part in the action of that day.' *Wounds received in action*: 'wounded Severely in Action, Albuhera, 16th May 1811. Received one year's Pay as Captain. Wounded severely in action, Pyrenees 25th July 1813. Received one year's Pay as Captain.' 'A medal for Waterloo.' *Service abroad*: "July 1807 to Novr. 1807, Island of Zealand. June 1809 to Septr. 1811, Portugal & Spain. July 1812 to June 1814, Spain & France. May 1815 to Febry. 1816, Netherlands & France. Decr. 1817 to Octr. 1818, Ionian Islands. October 1821 to Octr. 1828, Ionian Islands.' *Family*: Married Catherine, only daughter of George Plefson, 17 Feb. 1827, Government House, Calamos, with the ceremony performed by a priest of the Greek Church. The couple had two children by 1830. [PRO: WO 25/790 f174]. Slightly wounded, Albuera, 16 May 1811 [*London Gazette*]. Slightly wounded, Pyrenees, 25 July 1813 (1st Battn.) [*London Gazette*]. MGS. *Dalton*, pp. 135, 138 ['Jas. Henry Crummer [sic]... Was severely wounded in the left leg at Albuera. In 1832, when serving as senior capt. in this regt., the old wound broke out afresh and caused much suffering. Applied for a pension for wounds to which he had been entitled, but it was refused on the ground of the lapse of years since the said wound was received.'].

+**CRAMPTON, Jeremiah, Capt., 95th Rifles**: Capt., 95th Rifles, 20 June 1805. Severely wounded, storming of Badajoz, 6 April 1812 (1st Battn.) [*London Gazette*]. *Register of officers' effects*: Died of wounds, 18 Sept. 1812, Ciudad Rodrigo. Single. No details of Effects. [PRO: WO 25/2964]. *Harris*, p. 97. *Simmons*, p. 232 [wounded, storming of Badajoz].

CRASTER, Warton Thomas, Lt., 4th Foot: Lt., Army, 7 Feb. 1811; Lt., 4th Foot, 27 June 1811. Severely wounded, storming of Badajoz, 6 April 1812 [*London Gazette*].

'Thomas Wharton Crastor' in *Challis, Index*, p. 71.

+**CRAUFURD, Robert, Major-General**: The famous 'Black Bob', commander of the Light Brigade, later Division, one of the legendary figures of the British Army. Col., Army, 26 Jan. 1797; Maj.-Gen. 25 Sept. 1803; Col., 2nd Dragoon Guards, 18 Sept. 1807; Lt.-Gen. 25 July 1810. Wounded, 'dangerously', storming of Ciudad Rodrigo, 19 Jan. 1812 [*London Gazette*]. Mentioned in Wellington's Ciudad Rodrigo dispatch of 20 Jan. 1812 ['Major-General Craufurd likewise received a severe wound while he was leading on the light division to the storm, and I am apprehensive that I shall be deprived for some time of his assistance.']. *Register of dead officers*: 'Craufurd, R.,... Died of wounds received at Ciudad Rodrigo', 24 Jan. 1812. [PRO: WO 25/2965]. Obituary, *The Gentleman's Magazine*, Feb. 1812, p. 191 ['Jan. 24... In consequence of the wounds received at the head of his brigade, in gallantly entering the breach of Ciudad Rodrigo, Major-General Craufurd. On the 25th, his remains were interred in the breach. Lord Wellington, and every officer in the neighbourhood, followed him to the grave. At the time he was wounded, he was considerably advanced before his division, animating them to storm the breach. There cannot be a stronger proof of the regard the light division bore him than the following circumstances:– Upon his return to Portugal last spring, he joined his division, when the army was drawn up to receive Massena's attack at Fuente d'Honore, and as soon as he appeared at their head, the whole division gave him three cheers in presence of the Enemy... In private life, he was one of the best and most estimable of men. The loss that the country sustains in him is very great; and to his wife and four children it is irreparable.'].

Report of his death, from Wellington to Earl of Liverpool, *London Gazette*, 22 Feb. 1812 ['My Lord, – Major-gen. Craufurd died on the 24th ult. of the wounds received on the 19th... I cannot report his death to your Lordship, without expressing my sorrow and regret, that his Majesty has been deprived of the services, and I of the assistance, of an officer of tried talents and experience, who was an ornament to his profession']. *Hay*, pp. 27, 33–4 [1811: 'One afternoon we had to witness an act of diabolical tyranny. On the road was a stream... The general, from his position on the bridge, observed two or three of the 95th take some water in their hands to cool their parched mouths; instantly the halt was sounded, the brigade ordered to retrace their steps, the whole division formed into hollow square, and these unfortunate men paraded, stripped, and flogged. Such scenes, alas! were of almost daily occurrence, and disgusted me beyond measure.'], pp. 35, 42, 84 ['our tyrannical General Crawford']. *Leach*, p. 249 [Storming of Ciudad Rodrigo, 19 Jan. 1812: 'General Crawford received a mortal wound whilst bravely leading his division to the assault, and was buried near the spot where he fell.']. *Kincaid, Adventures*, p. 118 [Ciudad Rodrigo: 'General Crawford fell on the glacis, at the head of our division, and was buried at the foot of the breach which they so gallantly carried. His funeral was attended by Lord Wellington, and all the officers of the division, by whom he was, ultimately, much liked. He had introduced a system of discipline into the light division which made them unrivalled. A very rigid exaction of the duties pointed out in his code of regulations made him very unpopular at its commencement, and it was not until a short time before he was lost to us for ever, that we were capable of appreciating his merits, and fully sensible of the incalculable advantages we derived from the perfection of his system.']. *Brett-James*, pp. 25–6 ['Sir John Colborne ... confirms that Craufurd was the first man to introduce a proper system of marching. "Sit down in it, sir! Sit down in it," he used to call out if he saw a soldier stepping across a puddle. "That was the way he got them to march so beautifully." '], pp. 182, 193, 205, 237. Craufurd, Rev. A. H., *General Craufurd and his Light Division* (London, n.d.).

+**CRAUFURD, Henry, Major, 9th Foot**: Major, 9th Foot, 1 Aug. 1804; Lt. Col., Army, 25 April 1808. Mentioned in Graham's report to Wellington, concerning the capture of the convent of San Bartolome, dated 18 July 1813 ['three companies of the 9th regiment, under the command of Lieutenant-Colonel Crauford [sic]'] [*London Gazette*]. Killed, storming of San Sebastian, 31 Aug. 1813 ('Crawfurd') (1st Battn.) [*London Gazette*].

+**CRAWFORD, Charles, Lt., 27th Foot**: Lt., 27th Foot, 23 Nov. 1809. Severely wounded, 'since dead', Pyrenees, 26 July 1813 (3rd Battn.) [*London Gazette*]. *Register of dead officers*: Died of wounds, 27 July 1813. Return dated Aug. 1813. [PRO: WO 25/2965].

+**CRAWFURD, George Douglas, Lt., 91st Foot; Capt., 23rd Portuguese Line**: Lt., 91st Foot, 18 May 1808. Slightly wounded, Salamanca, 22 July 1812, as Capt. in 23rd Portuguese Line [*London Gazette*]. In Portuguese Service Sept. 1811 to July 1813. *Challis, Portuguese Army*, p. 54 ['K/A Sauroren 28 July '13']. Obituary, *The Gentleman's Magazine*, Dec. 1813, p. 621 ['Aug. 31. In his 22d year, Capt. Geo. Douglas Craufurd, of the 91st British and 23d Portuguese regiments of the Line. He entered the Army at the age of 15; shared in the glorious battles of Vimeira, Corunna, Talavera, Salamenca, Vittoria, and the Pyrenees; in the sieges of Ciudad Rodrigo and Badajos, and most powerfully contributed, by his distinguished bravery, and the spirit he infused into his little band, to arrest the progress of the Enemy's forces, when they threatened to force our brave Army from the assault of St Sebastian – the most important result of their hard-fought campaign; and fell in the moment of repulsing the Enemy from a most important Pass of the Pyrenees. The affectionate gratitude of his men induced them to erect a little stone, to mark the spot where the remains of their revered commander were deposited.'].

CRAWFURD, John, Lt., 6th Foot: *1829 Statement of Service*: Born 1790, Newfield, near Kilmarnock. Aged twenty-two on his first entrance into the Army. Volunteer, 79th Foot, Jan. 1812; Ensign, 45th Foot, April 1812, 'Obtained by serving as Volunteer in the Peninsula'; Lt., 6th Foot, Sept. 1813; Capt. 17th May 1821. *Battles, sieges and campaigns*: 'Operations of Covering Army during the Siege of Badajoz 1812 as Volunteer 79th Regt. – Battle of Salamanca. Capture of Madrid, and whole of the Campaign of 1812, as Ensign 45th Regiment. Operations in the Pyrenees & South of France 1813 & 1814. Battle of Nivelle Novr. 1813. Battle of Nive Decr. 1813. Battle of Orthez Feby. 1814 as Ensign 45th Regt. and Lieutenant 6th Regt.' *Wounds received in action*: 'Severe Gun Shot Wound in action at Orthez 27th Feby. 1814. Received Grant of One Year's Pay as Lieutenant for above Wound.' *Service abroad*: '1st Jany 1812 to March 1813, and June 1813 to July 1814, Peninsula & South of France; Aug. 1814 to July 1815, Jersey; July 1815 to Octr. 1818, France; July 1821 to March 1825, Capri; March 1825 to Dec. 1828, India.' Not married by

1830. [PRO: WO 25/786 f13]. Slightly wounded, Orthes, 27 Feb. 1814 ('Crawford') (1st Battn.) [*London Gazette*].

CRAWLEY, Lawrence, Lt., 48th Foot: Lt., 48th Foot, 28 May 1806. Slightly wounded, Albuera, 16 May 1811 [*London Gazette*]. MGS.

CRAWLEY, Thomas, Ensign/Adjutant, 59th Foot: *1829 Statement of Service for Retired Officers*: Aged thirty-one on his first appointment to the Army. Ensign, 59th Foot, 24 Sept. 1813. 'Joined the 59th in October 1807 and promoted from Serjt. Major Sept. 24th 1813 was placed on half pay in 1816.' 'Ensn. & Adjt. Lt. & Adjt.' Half-pay 'in consequence of a severe Gun shot wound.' [Army List gives: Ensign and Adjutant, 59th Foot, 24 Sept. 1812; Lt., 59th Foot, 24 May 1814; Half-pay, 25 May 1816]. *Where serving when wounded*: 'Before St Sebastian.' *Details of pension*: Seventy pounds per annum, commencing 25 July 1814. *Family*: Married in Dublin, 23 April 1810, 'but a widower since Augt. 1824.' Five children born by 1823, one of whom had died by 1829. *Where generally resident during last five years*: 'In Engd. 4 yrs. Parsontown 1 yr.' [PRO: WO 25/754 f143]. Severely wounded, 'at the Siege of St Sebastian,' 7–27 July 1813 ('Adjutant') (2nd Battn.) [*London Gazette*]. *1818 Pension Return*, pp. 14–15.

+CRAWSTON, John, Volunteer, 27th Foot: Killed, storming of San Sebastian, 31 Aug. 1813 (3rd Battn.) [*London Gazette*].

CREAGH, Andrew, Capt., 29th Foot: *1829 Statement of Service*: Born in Limerick, Ireland. He indicated that his date of birth was 'not known to a certainty', and that he did not know how old he was on his first Entrance into the Army. He was also uncertain as to his first commission, indicating that he had

been an Ensign, but that he knew neither the regiment nor the date of commission. Lt., Irish Brigade, 1 Oct. 1799. Capt., Irish Brigade, 26 Oct. 1796. Capt., 29th Foot, 21 Oct. 1798. Bvt. Major, 29th Foot, 1808. Major, 95th Rifles, May 1809. Major, 93rd Foot, Oct. 1810. Bvt. Lt. Col., 93rd Foot, June 1814. 'Effective' Lt. Col., 93rd Foot, 6 Sept. 1814. Lt. Col., 81st Foot, 7 March 1822. 'Colonel & Aide de Camp to the King', 81st Foot, 22 July 1830. *Battles, sieges and campaigns*: 'Served with the Troops in the Island of St Domingo in 1797 & 1798... Served in Holland under the Duke of York... Present at the action of the 27th August on Landing. Present at the action on 19th Septr. Present at the action on 2nd Octr. Present at the action on 6th Octr. and returned with the army to England. Present at the Battle of Rolea & Vimieria ... at New Orleans 25th Decr. 1814 & 1st Jany. 1815 and 8th Jany. 1815.' *Wounds received in action*: 'Wounded at the Battle of Vimeria as Brevet Major in 29th Regiment while in the Command of a Light Brigade on the 21st August 1808. Permanent Pension of £200 per annum, & one years Full Pay.' *Titles, honorary distinctions and medals*: 'Obtained a Medal as Brevet Major in 29th Rgiment for Commanding a Light Brigade at the Battle of Rolea & Vimeria.' *Service abroad*: 'End of 1795 to Octr. 1798, West Indies. Aug. 1799 to Novr. 1799, North Holland. Octr. 1800 to March 1801, Guernsey. June 1802 to June 1807, Halifax, Nova Scotia. Decr. 1807 to Octr. 1808, Gibraltar, Spain, Portugal. Dec. 1810 to Apl. 1814, Cape of Good Hope. Ser. 1814 to May 1815, West Indies & New Orleans. May 1822 to 24th Augt. 1826, Nova Scotia. 31st Augt. 1826 to 14th Novr. 1829, New Brunswick. 15th Novr. 1829 to 31st Decr. 1829, Bermuda.' *Family*: Married Mary Head, 20 Dec. 1804, Halifax, Nova Scotia. They had five

CREAGH

children by 1830. [PRO: WO 25/801 f1]. Wounded, Vimeiro, 21 Aug. 1808, while serving on the staff as Brigade Major [*London Gazette*]. Gold Medal. *1818 Pension Return*, pp. 8–9.

+CREAGH, Jasper, Capt., 95th Foot: Capt., 95th Foot, 19 June 1805. Slightly wounded, Rolica, 17 Aug. 1808 [*London Gazette*]. Severely wounded, 'since dead', Coa, 24 July 1810 (1st Battn.) [*London Gazette*]. *Register of officers' effects*: Died, 24 July 1810. Single. His Effects were given to 'Major Creagh, 5th Foot'. [PRO: WO 25/2964]. *Simmons*, p. 82 [Coa: 'shot through the lower part of his body, died the night of the action']. *Leach*, p. 124 [commanding a company at Barba del Puerco].

+CREIGHTON, John, Lt., 43rd Foot: Lt., 43rd Foot, 5 Oct 1808. Severely wounded during 'several affairs with the French Army', 18 March–7 April 1811 (1st Battn.) [*London Gazette*]. Died, Portugal, 12 May 1811 [PRO: WO 25/2965].

+CRESPIGNY, George Champion, Major, 68th Foot: Capt., Army, 14 May 1807; Capt., 68th Foot, 17 Nov. 1808; Major, 68th Foot, 8 Oct. 1812. Killed, Pyrenees, 30 July 1813 [*London Gazette*]. *Register of officers' effects*: Single. Effects totalled £377. 17s. [PRO: WO 25/2964]. *Green, Vicissitudes*, p. 171 [14 July 1813: 'about two o'clock in the afternoon began to ascend a mountain, which had a very steep ascent for nearly six miles... I found it hard work to ascend these lofty hills, for I was then labouring under a complaint to which we were very subject, and had often to leave the ranks. What added to my distress, was the unnecessary strictness of our second major [Crespigny], who refused me liberty to fall out. I at last told him that I really must have liberty; he then ordered a serjeant, of a tyrannical spirit like himself, to

remain with me, who constantly urged me to move forwards, notwithstanding I was so exceedingly ill.'], p. 181 [30 July 1813: 'we then, as on other occasions of the kind, began to enquire who was killed and who was wounded: the first person mentioned was our second major [Crespigny]; he had received a ball in his neck, or rather in his wind-pipe, which killed him instantly. As soon as this was generally known amongst us, joy was seen in every countenance, and I verily thought we should have had three cheers, for several of the men began to cry "hip ! hip !" which was always the signal for cheering. He was a cruel man to us, and his death was considered as a happy release.'].

CRESSWELL, George, Lt., 88th Foot: *1829 Statement of Service for Retired Officers*: Aged twenty-seven on first appointment to the Army. Ensign and Adjutant, 74th Foot, 3 Sept. 1807; Lt. and Adjutant, 1 Dec. 1808; Lt., 88th Foot, 25 April 1811; 'Ensn. & Lieutenant', Half-pay, 3rd Foot Guards, 30 April 1820, 'in consequence of ill health, the effects of a wound recd. in 1814.' 'Thirty-five years in the service, and actively employed during the whole of the war, from 1793. Fourteen years of which in 103rd Reg. & 3rd Foot Guards, up to appointment as Adjutant of the 74th Regt.' *Where serving when wounded*: 'Battle of Orthes 27th February 1814.' *Details of pension*: Seventy pounds, commencing 28 Feb. 1815. *Family*: Married in Chelmsford, 28 June 1804. *Where generally resident during last five years*: 'Dunkirk, France.' [PRO: WO 25/754 f96]. Severely wounded, Orthes, 27 Feb. 1814 (1st Battn.) [*London Gazette*]. *1818 Pension Return*, pp. 20–1. MGS.

CRESWELL, William, Capt., 36th Foot: Capt., Army, 5 Feb. 1806; Capt., 36th Foot, 27 Nov. 1806;

148

Capt., 8th Veteran Batt., 8 April 1813 ('Cresswell'). *Harris*, pp. 187–8 [Following Walcheren: 'I was appointed to the 8th Veteran Battalion, with others, and sent to Fort Cumberland. Here I joined Captain Creswell's company – an officer who had lost one eye whilst in the 36th regiment in Spain.'].

CREWE, Frederick, Lt., 27th Foot: Lt., 27th Foot, 13 Feb. 1806. Severely wounded, Pyrenees, 28 July 1813 ('Drew') (3rd Battn.) [*London Gazette*]. Note: This attribution is tentative. The obvious choice of officer wounded in the Pyrenees that day would be Edward Ward Drewe, Lt., 27th Foot, 8 Feb. 1808. However, in Drewe's *1829 Statement of Service* he lists various wounds, including 13 March and 13 Sept. 1813, but not one for the Pyrenees on 28 July [PRO: WO 25/803 f297]. He is so clear about the location and date of his various wounds, that I find it unlikely that he would have forgotten one he received in the Pyrenees. In my judgement it was Crewe, not Drewe, who was the casualty recorded in the *London Gazette*. The *Statement of Service* was, however, written seventeen years after the events in question and so it is possible that Drewe was confused or mistaken.

CRIGAN, Charles, Major, 81st Foot: Major, 6th Garrison Battn., 26 Nov. 1806. Died, 1 Feb. 1809, from wounds received during Corunna campaign. Obituary, *The Gentleman's Magazine*, Feb. 1809, p. 188 ['Feb. 1... At Plymouth, of his wounds, received in Spain, Major Crigan, of the 81st Foot.'].

CROFT, James William, Lt., 3rd Dragoons: Lt., 3rd Dragoons, 6 June 1811. *Bragge*, p. 107 ['Col. Grant's Brigade Major is James Croft of the 15th; if you ever saw the Parties you will not think the Black Giant and Red Dwarf bad names.'], p. 135

['Croft, James, Cornet 3rd D.G. 1810. Capt. 1811. Ret. 1814.'].

CROFTON, William Edward, Ensign/Lt., 50th Foot: *1829 Statement of Service*: Born in Ireland, 21 May 1793. Aged sixteen 'on his first Entrance into the Army.' Ensign, 50th Foot, [19] Oct. 1809. Lt., 50th Foot, 17 Dec. 1812. Half Pay, 24 March 1817, 'Reduction of the supery. Lieutenant.' Lt. and Adjt., 50th Foot, Oct. 1819. Capt., 91st Foot, 2 April 1826. Note added: 'Retired 29 Nov. 1833.' *Battles, sieges and campaigns*: 'Joined the Army in the Penninsular, in the Spring of 1811, and continued with it till the latter end of 1813 during which period he was at Aroya de Molino in Spain. At the Storming of Fort Napoleon near Almara on the 19th May 1812. In the Covering Army of the Siege of Badajos. At the Battle of Vittoria on the 21st June 1813, and at the pass of Maya in the Pyrenees, besides various affairs & skirmishes.' *Distinguished conduct*: 'Was appointed by General Lord Hill to act as Engineer at Bejar in N. Castille having assisted in throwing up temporary works at that advanced post, on which occasion he was introduced to the notice of the General by the Asst. Qr. Master General of the Division.' *Wounds received in action*: 'Was wounded at the storming of Ft Napoleon and received a grant of a years pay as Ensign.' *Service abroad*: '11th May 1811 to 9th September 1813, Peninsula. 29 Novemr. 1820 to 19 May 1827, Jamaica.' *Family*: Married Alicia Moore, 15 Jan. 1816, Aughnasloy, Ireland. They had six children by 1830. [PRO: WO 25/803 f17]. Slightly wounded, 'at the Storm and Capture of Fort Napoleon, and the Enemy's other Works, in the Neighbourhood of Almaraz', 19 May 1812 [*London Gazette*]. MGS.

+CROFTON, Hon. William George, Lt. and Capt., Coldstream Guards:

Lt. and Capt., Coldstream Guards, 10 March 1808. Severely wounded, siege of Burgos, 19 Oct. 1812 [*London Gazette*]. Killed, sortie from Bayonne, 14 April 1814 (1st Battn.) [*London Gazette*]. Obituary, *The Gentleman's Magazine*, May 1814, p. 517 ['At Bayonne, Hon. Capt. W. G. Crofton.']. *Hurt*, p. 75. *Fletcher, Fields of Fire*, p. 164 ['Coldstream Guards cemetery, Bayonne... The cemetery, which lies literally in the corner of a field, was the site of the Coldstream Guards' camp and those who lie here include ... Captains Crofton and Burroughs']. 'Croften' in Army List. The fourth son of Sir Edward Crofton, 2nd Bart. [*Burke's Peerage*].

CROKAT, William, Lt., 20th Foot: *1829 Statement of Service for Retired Officers*: Aged eighteen on first appointment to the Army. Ensign, 20th Foot, 9 April 1807; Lt., 20th Foot, 30 June 1808; Capt., 20th Foot, 31 March 1814; Brevet Major, 20th Foot, 5 July 1821; Half-pay, Nov. 1826. *Where serving when wounded*: 'Pyrenees.' No pension. *Where generally resident during last five years*: 'East Indies. Scotland.' [PRO: WO 25/754 f128]. Slightly wounded, Pyrenees, 25 July 1813 ('Crockatt') [*London Gazette*]. Army List gives as 'Crockatt'. MGS.

CROKER, Richard, Capt., 18th Light Dragoons: *1829 Statement of Service for Retired Officers*: Aged nineteen on first appointment to the Army. Cornet, 18th Light Dragoons, 27 June 1805; Lt., 18th Light Dragoons, 2 Jan. 1806; Capt., 18th Light Dragoons, 9 July 1812; Half-pay, Portuguese Service, 16 Nov. 1820, 'at my own request from ill health'. *Where serving when wounded*: 'Wounded severely, Thoulouse.' No pension. *Family*: Married in Huddersfield, 23 July 1821. Three children by 1829. *Where generally resident during last five years*: 'Cheltenham.' [PRO: WO

25/754 f97]. Severely wounded, 'in Action with the Enemy', 8 April 1814 [*London Gazette*]. Waterloo. MGS. Died, Leamington, 15 Jan. 1854.

+CROMIE, James, Ensign, 36th Foot: Ensign, 36th Foot, 3 Sept. 1812. Killed, Toulouse, 10 April 1814 (1st Battn.) [*London Gazette*].

CROMPTON, George, Lt., 66th Foot: Lt., 66th Foot, 5 April 1810. Severely wounded, Albuera, 16 May 1811 (2nd Battn.) [*London Gazette*].

+CROPP, Lewis, Capt., 1st Light Battn. K.G.L.: Capt., 1st Light Battn. K.G.L., 26 Jan. 1811. Severely wounded, 'since dead', in an action near Tolosa, 25 June 1813 [*London Gazette*]. *Register of dead officers*: Died of wounds, 25 June 1813. Return dated July 1813. [PRO: WO 25/2965]. Served in Peninsula 1808–13. *Beamish*, vol. II, p. 638.

CROSS, John, Lt., 1st Foot: Lt., 1st Foot, 7 March 1811. Severely wounded, Vittoria, 21 June 1813 (3rd Battn.) [*London Gazette*].

CROSS, John, Lt., 52nd Foot: *1829 Statement of Service*: 'Born Darton, Parish of Tynen, Co. of Armagh, 17 January 1787. Aged 18 years 173 days on his first Entrance into the Army. Ensign, 52nd Foot, From 9th July 1805 to 28th May 1806. Lieut., 52nd, From 29th May 1806 to 30th Decr. 1812. Captain, 52nd, From 31st Decr. 1812 to 22d June 1825. Major, 52nd, From 23rd June 1825 to 31 Decr. 1829. Upon full pay the whole time with the exception of one year 241 days on half pay as Captain viz. from 15th Septr. 1816 to 13th May 1818. Placed on Half Pay 15th Septr. 1816, in consequence of the reduction of the 2nd Battn. which took place on the 31st May 1816, but serving as a Volunteer with the 1st Battn. in France, the order for being placed on Half

Pay did not affect him until the 15th September 1816.' *Battles, sieges and campaigns*: 'As Lieut. Corunna 16th Jany. 1819. Almeida on the Coa 24th July 1810. Busaco 27th Sept 1810. & the different actions & affairs in which the Light Division was engaged during Massina's retreat &c. Pombal 11th March 1811. Redinha 12th March 1811. Miranda do Coro 14th March 1811. Foz de Aronce 15th March 1811. Sabugal 5th April 1811. Fuentes d'Onor 3 & 5th May 1811. Ciudad Rodrigo 8th to 19th Jany 1812. San Munoz 17th Nov. 1812. As Capt.: San Millan 18th June 1813. Vittoria 21st June 1813. Lezacco Bridge, Bidassoa, 4 to 30 Augt. 1813. Vera, 7th Octr. 1813. Niville, 10th Novr. 1813. Nive 9th 10th, & 11th Decr. 1813. Orthes 27th Feby. 1814. Tarbes 20th March 1814. Thoulouse 10th April 1814. Waterloo 18th June 1815. Served the Campaign of 1808, & the Greatest part 1809, & the Campaigns of 1810, 1811, 1812, 1813, 1814, 1815, with the Light Division.' *Distinguished conduct*: 'Served with the 1st Battn. 52d. Regiment as a volunteer, when effective in the 2nd Battalion, from the 31st Decr. 1812 to 25th July 1816, as a Captain.' *Wounds received in action*: 'Wounded at the affair of Redinha in 1811. Received a severe contusion at Waterloo, but not obliged to leave the field. Received no grant of Pay or Pension never having applied for any.' *Titles, honorary distinctions and medals*: 'Waterloo Medal.' *Service abroad*: '30th April 1808 to 14th Feby. 1809, Passage to Gottinbug & from thence to the coast of Portugal & in Portugal & Spain. 25th May 1809 to 28th June 1814, Portugal, Spain, & the South of France. 5th Jany. 1815 to 25th July 1816, Netherlands & France. 20th Oct. 1818 to 26th Novr. 1818, France. 9th June 1823 to 23rd July 1824, North America. 22nd July 1827 to 31st Decr. 1829, North America.' Not married by 1830. [PRO: WO 25/795 f83]. Wounded,

during 'several Affairs with the French Army', 12 March 1811 (1st Battn.) [*London Gazette*]. Waterloo. MGS.

CROSS, Richard, Lt., 38th Foot: Lt., 38th Foot, 4 Nov. 1807. Severely wounded, storming of San Sebastian, 31 Aug. 1813 (1st Battn.) [*London Gazette*].

CROSS, William, Major, 36th Foot: Major, 36th Foot, 8 Dec. 1808; Bvt. Lt.Col., 36th Foot, 22 Nov. 1813. Severely wounded, Toulouse, 10 April 1814 (1st Battn.) [*London Gazette*]. *Royal Military Calender, 1820*, vol. V, pp. 5–7 ['1328. Lieutenant-Colonel William Cross, C.B. ENTERED the army in 1799, as Ensign in the 62d ... autumn of 1805, when the 36th reg. being ordered on service, he resigned his staff appointment, and accompanied his corps to Germany, under Lord Cathcart. In 1806 he embarked for South America, and commanded the left wing of his reg. at the storming of Buenos Ayres; in 1808 he served in Portugal, and was detached in charge of three companies in the affair of Roleia; was in the battle of Vimiera; and in all the subsequent operations of that army in Spain, until its embarkation at Corunna, in Jan. 1809. During this campaign, viz. on the 8th Dec. 1808, he was promoted to the Maj. of his reg.; the remainder of 1809 and 1810 he was principally in charge of the 2d batt. of his corps in England; in Jan. 1811, he joined and accompanied the 1st batt. to Portugal; he was in the pursuit of Massena from Santarem, in March, 1811; the blockade of Almeida, where the reg. protected the bridge of Almeida; at the battle of Fuentes d'Onor; and at the evacuation of Almeida on the 11th May. He was likewise at the affair of Especca, near Ciudad Rodrigo, 24th Sept., and the subsequent one near Ronda. He was in command of the 36th, from Oct. this year, to May,

1812, which period comprises the investment of Badajos, and the expedition under Sir T. Graham, which, after the affairs of Usagre, Llerena, Berlonga, and Usuaga, effected the expulsion of the enemy from Spanish Estremadura. This army returned with a view to the support of the besiegers of Badajos, and reached Albuhera the 6th April, on which night the place fell. He was also present and in command of the reg. from Sept. 1813, until the return of the army from France, in July, 1814, which includes the affair of the 7th of Oct. at Ordax; the battle of Nivelle, on the 10th Nov., when it was the proud lot of the 36th to charge and carry the enemy's principal redoubt on the heights of Andya, for which this officer received the brevet of L.-Col.; he was at the forcing of the passage of the Nive on the 9th and the 13th Dec.; the blockade of Bayonne; battle of Orthes; with the subsequent affairs of Vic and Tarbes. He likewise commanded the reg. at the battle of Toulouse, which commenced with the attack of the 6th division, and in which the reg. with only 250 firelocks in the field, lost, in killed and wounded, of all ranks, upwards of 150. On this day the L.-Col. was so severely wounded through the neck, as to be pronounced in the commencement without hope of recovery; and from which he is still a considerable sufferer. The 36th reg. landed at Cork in July, 1814; and in July, 1815, joined the army under the Duke of Wellington, before Paris, and with which they served until the treaty of Nov. and arrived in England in December. L.-Col. C. has received a cross for the battles of Nivelle, Nive, Orthes, and Toulouse, and is a Companion of the Bath.'].

+CROUDACE, Christopher, 1st Lt., 95th Foot: 2nd Lt., 95th Foot, 4 May 1809; 1st Lt., 95th Foot, 30 May 1811. Killed, storming of Badajoz, 6 April 1812 (3rd Battn.) [*London Gazette*]. *Register of officers' effects*: 'Crondace' [sic]. His effects totalled a mere 1s. 8d. [PRO: WO 25/2964]. *Simmons*, p. 232 [Killed]. *Surtees*, p. 138 [Badajoz: 'I was then in the mess of the senior captain of my battalion, who commanded it on this occasion; and my other messmates were poor little Croudace and Cary... We had taken a farewell glass before we got up from dinner, not knowing which of them would survive the bloody fray that was likely soon to commence. Poor Croudace, a native of the county of Durham, and consequently a near countryman, put into my hand a small leather purse, containing half a doubloon, and requested me to take care of it for him, as he did not know whose fate it might be to fall or to survive. I took it according to his wish, and put it into my pocket, and, after a little more conversation, and another glass, for the poor little fellow liked his wine, we parted, and they moved off.'], p. 140 ['Croudace had been shot through the body, and carried to the rear'], p. 146 ['Poor Coudace had also died immediately after reaching the hospital, whither he had been carried when he was shot. Thus I lost two of my most particular and intimate acquaintances, from both of whom I had received many acts of kindness and friendship. They will long live in my memory.'], pp. 319–20 ['after dark, he or they lifted up a part of the tent where the box was standing, and, pulling it out, set off with it bodily... [I lost] my papers and books, public and private, about £19 in money, an old silver watch, and, among other things, the half doubloon which poor Croudace had given me to take care of for him on the evening previous to his death at Badajos, and which I was preserving as a memorial for his afflicted friends.'].

CROWDER, John, Capt., 7th Foot: Capt., 7th Foot, 5 Nov. 1806. Slightly wounded, Albuera, 16 May 1811 (1st Battn.) [*London Gazette*]. Mentioned in Wellington's Salamanca dispatch, 24 July 1812 ['I must also mention Lieutenant-Colonel Woodford, commanding the light battalion of the brigade of guards, who, suported by two companies of the fusileers, under the command of Captain Crowder, maintained the village of Aripiles against all the efforts of the enemy, previous to the attack upon their position by our troops.'] [*London Gazette*]. Severely wounded, Pyrenees, 28 July 1813 (1st Battn.) [*London Gazette*]. *Cooper*, p. 99 [Following Battle of Pampeluna, July 1813: 'Here for several days I had an ague fit every afternoon. While in one, Major Crowder, who was wounded in the late battle, called to see the two officers that I had in charge [Lt. James Baillie Fraser and Capt. Charles J. Fraser, both of the 7th Foot, who had died of their wounds]. He gave me a few words also which were encouraging.']. *Royal Military Calendar*, vol. V, p. 204.

CRUISE, Richard, Lt., 84th Foot: Lt., 84th Foot, 8 Sept. 1808. Slightly wounded, the Nive, 11 Dec. 1813 (2nd Battn.) [*London Gazette*].

+CUEILLE, Arnet Charles de., Capt., Chasseurs Britanniques: Capt., Chasseurs Britanniques, 19 Sept. 1811. Severely wounded, Orthes, 27 Feb. 1814 ('Charles de Cueille') [*London Gazette*]. *Register of dead officers*: 'Cueiller de Chas'. Died of wounds, 8 March 1814. Return dated March 1814. [PRO: WO 25/2965].

+CULLEN, Ensign, 42nd Foot: Killed, siege of Burgos, 20–26 Sept. 1812 (1st Battn.) [*London Gazette*].

CULLY, James, Capt., 5th Foot: Capt., 5th Foot, 24 Jan. 1805. Severely wounded, 'in Action with the Enemy', 24 Feb. 1814 ('James Culley') (1st Battn.) [*London Gazette*].

CUMMING, Henry John, Lt. Col., 11th Light Dragoons: Lt. Col., 11th Light Dragoons, 17 Feb. 1803. Slightly wounded, El Bodon, 25 Sept. 1811 [*London Gazette*]. Gold Medal (Salamanca). *Bragge*, p. 10 ['Belem, Septr 6th 1811... Officers of the 11th, amongst whom Col. Cumming is so troublesome that Diggens and several others have entered the Portuguese Service.'], p. 135 ['(?-1856)... Commanded the Regt. in Peninsula May 1811–March 1813. Wounded at El Bodon Sept. 1811, where conduct of Regt. was praised by Wellington. Col. 1812. Lt.-Gen. 1830. K.C.H. 1833. Col. 12th Lancers 1837. Gen. 1846.'].

+CUMMINS, William G., Lt., 83rd Foot; Capt., 9th Caçadores: Lt., 83rd Foot, 28 March 1809. In Portuguese Service July 1811 to Oct. 1813. Obituary, *The Gentleman's Magazine*, Nov. 1813, p. 506 ['Oct. 8. Fell by a musket-ball, whilst commanding two companies, in an attack on the Enemy's out-posts in front of Auboa, Capt. W. G. Cumming, 9th Caçadores.']. *Challis, Portuguese Army*, p. 54 ['Capt. 9 Caçad... K/A Bidassoa 7 Oct. '13.'].

CURRAN, John, Ensign, 38th Foot: *1829 Statement of Service for Retired Officers*: Aged twenty-two on first appointment to the Army. Ensign, 38th Foot, April 1813 [Army List gives 23 April 1813]; Lt., 38th Foot, July 1814 [Army List gives 15 July 1814]; Half-pay, Nov. 1814, by reduction; Lt., 97th Foot, July 1815; 'number of Regt. changed to 96, and disbanded on 24 Dec. 1818.' Half-pay, 24 Dec. 1814. '... being recommended for promotion from the severity of my wounds, though they were not considered equal to the loss of a limb by the Medical

Board.' *Where serving when wounded*: 'Was twice wounded by musquet balls, in attacking the Bridge of Gomarrah Mayor at the Battle of Vittoria on the 21st of June 1813 – vouchers of which were regularly transmitted to the Secretary at War from Staff Surgeon Ryan, who dressed my wounds on the field...' 'No pension, no grant.' *Family*: Married in the Parish of Kilcomick, County of Longford, Ireland, May 1816. Five children by 1829. *Where generally resident during last five years*: 'Glanmore, Ballymahon, County Longford, Ireland.' [PRO: WO 25/754 f215]. Severely wounded, Vittoria, 21 June 1813 ('Curren') (1st Battn.) [*London Gazette*].

CURREY, John, Capt., 6th Foot: Capt., Army, 22 July 1797; Capt., 6th Foot, 18 Feb. 1804. Slightly wounded, Rolica, 17 Aug. 1808 [*London Gazette*].

+CURRIE, James Hunter, Capt., 52nd Foot: Capt., 52nd Foot, 11 July 1805. Slightly wounded, during operations, 15–19 Nov. 1812 (1st Battn.) [*London Gazette*]. Killed, Vittoria, 21 June 1813 ('Curry') (1st Battn.) [*London Gazette*].

CURRIE, John, Lt., 60th Foot: Ensign, 60th Foot, 2 Oct. 1811; Lt., 60th Foot, 22 Dec. 1812. Slightly wounded, Orthes, 27 Feb. 1814 (5th Battn.) [*London Gazette*].

CURZON, Hon. William, Lt., 9th Foot: Lt., 9th Foot, 8 Aug. 1808. Severely wounded, during 'movements of the Army' [Retreat from Burgos], 25 Oct. 1812 ('Curzons') [*London Gazette*]. Capt., 69th Foot, 17 Dec. 1812. Killed, Waterloo, as DAAG. *Dalton*, p. 32 ['He met his fate at Waterloo with almost "military glee". In falling from his horse, he called out gaily to Lord March, who had been galloping by his side, "Good-bye, dear March"'].

CUSTANCE, Holman, Lt., 50th Foot: *1829 Statement of Service for Retired Officers*: Aged eighteen on first appointment to the Army. Ensign, 50th Foot, 20 Oct. 1808; Lt., 50th Foot, 22 Feb. 1810; Capt., 50th Foot, 26 May 1814; Half-pay, 25 Dec. 1814, 'by reduction 2d Battn.'; Capt., 102nd Foot, 23 March 1815; Half-pay, 45th Foot, 29 June 1815; Capt., 50th Foot, 6 July 1815; Major, 50th Foot, 2 Sept. 1824; Lt. Col., Half-pay, unattached, 12 Dec. 1826.' *Where serving when wounded*: 'Before Bayonne.' *Details of pension*: One hundred pounds, commencing in 1814. *Where generally resident during last five years*: '3 years with 50th Regt. in West Indies & the last 2 years in England.' [PRO: WO 25/754 f199]. Severely wounded, the Nive, 13 Dec. 1813 (1st Battn.) [*London Gazette*]. Slightly wounded, Aire, 2 March 1814 (1st Battn.) [*London Gazette*]. *1818 Pension Return*, pp. 14–15. MGS.

CUTHBERT, Kingston, Lt., 82nd Foot: Lt., 82nd Foot, 13 Oct. 1808. Severely wounded, Nivelle, 10 Nov. 1813 (1st Battn.) [*London Gazette*].

+CUTHBERT, Robert, Capt., 7th Foot: Capt., 7th Foot, 3 Feb. 1809. Severely wounded, ('since dead'), siege of Badajoz, 19 March 1812, while serving as ADC to Lt.-General Picton [*London Gazette*]. Died of wounds, 'camp at Badajos'. Return dated 25 March 1812. [PRO: WO 25/2965].

CUTHBERTSON, John, Lt., 48th Foot: Lt., 48th Foot, 28 Jan. 1808. Slightly wounded, Talavera, 28 July 1809 [*London Gazette*]. Slightly wounded, storming of Badajoz, 6 April 1812 [*London Gazette*]. Severely wounded, Pyrenees, 28 July 1813 (1st Battn.) [*London Gazette*]. Pension of seventy pounds per annum, commencing 29 July 1814, 'for wounds' received at Pampeluna, 1813 [*1818 Pension Return*, p. 12–13].

CUYLER, George, Lt. Col., 11th Foot: Lt. Col., Army, 28 Jan. 1808; Lt. Col., 11th Foot, 16 Nov. 1809. Severely wounded, Salamanca, 22 July 1812 [*London Gazette*]. Severely wounded, Talavera, 10 April 1814 (1st Battn.) [*London Gazette*]. Temporary pension of three hundred pounds per annum, commencing 23 July 1813, 'for wounds' at Salamanca [*1818 Pension Return*, pp. 6–7]. Gold Medal.

D

+DACHENHAUSEN, Ernest Gottlieb von, Lt., 5th Line Battn. K.G.L.: Lt., 5th Line Battn. K.G.L., 3 Jan. 1806. Served in the Peninsula 1808–9. *Beamish*, vol. II, p. 634 ['Killed in the battle of Talavera de la Reyna, 28th July 1809'].

+DAHMAN, William, Lt., 83rd Foot: Lt., 83rd Foot, 31 March 1808. Killed, Talavera, 28 July 1809 [*London Gazette*].

DALE, James, Ensign/Lt., 45th Foot: Ensign, 45th Foot, 4 April 1810. Slightly wounded, storming of Badajoz, 6 April 1812 ('Lieut.') [*London Gazette*].

DALE, Richard, Lt., 9th Foot: Lt., 9th Foot, 30 Aug. 1807. Slightly wounded, storming of San Sebastian, 31 Aug. 1813 (1st Battn.) [*London Gazette*]. Severely wounded, Crossing the Bidassoa, 7/9 Oct. 1813 (1st Battn.) [*London Gazette*].

DALLAS, Robert William, Lt., 9th Foot: *1829 Statement of Service for Retired Officers*: Aged eighteen on first appointment to Army. Ensign, 9th Foot, Sept. 1808; Lt., 9th Foot, 1811 [Army List gives 13 Oct. 1811]; Capt., York Chasseurs, 1814; 'Exchanged to H.P. 4th W. I. Regt. for a few weeks as a means of returning to the 9th Foot'; Capt., 9th Foot, 1817; Half-pay, 14th Foot, 1818, 'Partly for family reasons & partly from being rendered incapable of much fatigue by a severe wound.' *Where serving when wounded*: 'Severely wounded at Bidart in France.' No pension. *Family*: Married in St George's Church, Bloomsbury, London, May 1818. Five children by 1829. *Where generally resident during last five years*: 'London and the vicinity.' [PRO: WO 25/755 f42]. Severely wounded, the Nive, 10 Dec. 1813 (1st Battn.) [*London Gazette*]. MGS.

+DALMANN, John William von, Lt., 60th Foot: Lt., Army, 21 Feb. 1811; Lt., 60th Foot, 29 Aug. 1811. Killed, Pyrenees, 25 July 1811 ('Von Dahlmon') (5th Battn.) [*London Gazette*].

DALMER, Thomas, Major, 23rd Foot: Major, 23rd Foot, 10 Dec. 1807. Severely wounded, Salamanca, 22 July 1812 [*London Gazette*]. Gold Medal. Waterloo. MGS.

+DALRYMPLE, Robert, Capt., 3rd Foot Guards: Lt. and Capt., 3rd Foot Guards, 24 March 1803. Killed, Talavera, 28 July 1809 [*London Gazette*]. Illustration including him in *Fletcher, Regiments*, p. 44 ['The 3rd Foot Guards at the battle of Talavera, July 28th 1808 [sic]. The bareheaded officer in the centre is Robert Dalrymple who was killed during the battle.'].

DALTON, Aylmer, Ensign, Chasseurs Britanniques: Ensign, Chasseurs Britanniques, 15 Oct. 1812. Severely wounded, Orthes, 27 Feb. 1814 [*London Gazette*].

DALTON, Mathew Aylmer, Lt., Chasseurs Britanniques: *1829 Statement of Service for Retired Officers*: Aged twenty-seven on first appointment to the Army. Lt., Chasseurs Britanniques, 15 Dec. 1812; Half-pay, 25 Dec. 1814; Lt., Sicilian Regt., 10 Aug. 1825; Half-pay, 25 March 1826, 'reduction of the Sicilian Regt.' *Where serving when wounded*: 'Peninsula, Orthes.' *Family*: Married in Cloughran Church, Dublin, May 1818. Two children by 1829. *Title and description of civil employment*: 'Chief Constable of Pol[ ]' *Where gener-*

ally resident during last five years: 'Co. Cork.' [PRO: WO 25/755 f66].

DALY, Francis Dermot, Lt., 84th Foot: *1829 Statement of Service*: Born 5 June 1794, Galway. Aged fifteen on his first entrance into the Army. Ensign, 84th Foot, 5 Dec. 1811; Lt. 19 Nov. 1812; Lt., 76th Foot, June 1814; Half Pay 25 Mrch 1817; Lt., 4th Dragoons, 19 Feb. 1818; Capt. 26 June 1824. *Battles, sieges and campaigns*: 'Served in Spain & Portugal in Two Campaigns in the 84th Regt. with the 2nd Brigade of 5th Division. At the close of the war, proceeded with the expedition from Burdaux to Quebec and served in the 76th Regt. at the Siege and Battle of Platsburg.' *Wounds received in action*: 'Wounded at Bayonne on the 13th Decr. 1813. Received neither grant of Pay or Pension.' *Service abroad*: 'May 1813 to June 1814, Spain & France. June 1814 to Decr. 1816, Canada. Augt. 1822 to 31 Decr. 1829, East Indies.' *Family*: Married Mary McIntosh, Jan. 1819, Isle of Wight. They had two children prior to her death in the East Indies, 19 June 1823 [PRO: WO 25/782 f180]. MGS.

DALZELL, Robert, Capt., 43rd Foot: *1829 Statement of Service for Retired Officers*: Aged eighteen on his first appointment to the Army. Cornet, 29th Light Dragoons, 1798; Lt., 29th Light Dragoons, 1801; Capt., 43rd Foot, 1804 [Army List gives 26 Aug. 1804]; Bvt. Major, 43rd Foot, 1814 [Army List gives 12 April 1814]; Major, 43rd Foot, 1819; Lt. Col., Half-pay, unattached, 1822. *Where serving when wounded*: 'With the army under the Duke of Wellington in Portugal.' *Details of pension*: 'One hundred pounds per annum, commencing 1812.' *Where generally resident during last five years*: 'England, Scotland, France.' [PRO: WO 25/755 f28]. Slightly wounded, during 'several Affairs with the French Army', 14 March

1811 (1st Battn.) [*London Gazette*]. Severely wounded during 'several Affairs with the French Army', 18 March–7 April 1811 [*London Gazette*]. Pension commencing 3 April 1812, for 'loss of the use of an arm' in Portugal, 1811 [*1818 Pension Return*, pp. 12–13]. Later Major-General. MGS. Died 24 April 1848.

+DANE, Martin, Lt., 4th Foot: Lt., 4th Foot, 14 Feb. 1805. Severely wounded, storming of Badajoz, 6 April 1812 ('Dean') [*London Gazette*]. Recorded as having died, *1813 Army List*.

DANIEL, Holland, Lt., 61st Foot: Lt., 61st Foot, 25 June 1807. Pension of one hundred pounds per annum, commencing 23 July 1813, 'for a wound' received at Salamanca, 1812 [*1818 Pension Return*, pp. 16–17].

DANIELL, Richard, Lt., 11th Foot: *1829 Statement of Service*: Born 31 May 1791, City of Armagh. Aged sixteen years and seven months 'on his first Entrance into the Army.' Ensign, Wicklow Militia, 28 Dec. 1807; Ensign, 11th Foot, 24 Oct. 1808; Lt. 28 Dec. 1809; Capt., attached to the Portuguese service, 25 Oct. 1814; Half Pay 1 Jan. 1817; Capt., 21st Foot, 9 March 1821. *Battles, sieges and campaigns*: 'Ensign at the Seige of Flushing... Was present at the Battle of the Pyrenees 28th July 1813... Also was while attached to the Portuguese service at the Assault of San Sebastian, 31 August 1813... at blockade of Bayonne.' *Wounds received in action*: 'Wounded on the 28 July in the cheek the ball still remaining in the neck, in the battle of the Pyrenees. Wounded also twice thro' the body at San Sebastian on 31st Aug. 1813. Received two years Pay, but no pension.' *Titles, honorary distinctions and medals*: 'A Portuguese Medal for two Campaigns.' *Service abroad*: 'July

1809 to Sep. 1809, Walcheren. Jany 1810 to July 1810, Portugal. March 1811 to Sepr. 1812, Gibraltar. Sepr. 1812 to August 1820, Spain & Portugal. August 1821 to March 1827, West Indies.' Unmarried in 1830. [PRO: WO 25/789 f14]. Slightly wounded, Pyrenees, 28 July 1813 ('Daniel') (1st Battn.) [*London Gazette*].

DANIELL, Walter, Lt., 11th Foot: Lt., 11th Foot, 15 Sept. 1808. Slightly wounded, Salamanca, 22 July 1812 ('Daniel') (1st Battn.) [*London Gazette*].

DANSEY, Charles C., Capt., Royal Artillery: 2nd Capt., Royal Artillery, 1 Oct. 1809. Slightly wounded, siege of Burgos, 20–26 Sept. 1812 ('Dancey') [*London Gazette*]. *Webber*, p. 83 [wounded, Burgos, 30 Sept. 1812; Webber seems to believe, incorrectly, that Dansey had been killed: 'it is intended to make a breach in the fort in the town of Burgos... Two attempts to enter have already been made and failed with the loss of 45 officers and 700 men, killed and wounded; amongst the former Captain Williams... Dansey another,... of the Artillery']. Severely wounded, Waterloo. MGS. Died 21 July 1853.

DANSEY, George Henry, Capt., 88th Foot: *1829 Statement of Service for Retired Officers*: Aged sixteen on his first appointment to the Army. Ensign, 8th Foot, 22 Aug. 1805; Lt., 88th Foot, 22 July 1806; Capt., 88th Foot, 3 Aug. 1809; Bvt. Major, 88th Foot, 4 Dec. 1815; Major, 88th Foot, 25 July 1825; Major, 27th Foot, 6 Oct. 1813; Half-pay, unattached, 22 March 1827, 'at his own request for private affairs.' *Where serving when wounded*: 'At Buzaco Sept. 27 1810' No pension. *Family*: Married in Bath, Somerset, May 1821. No children by 1829. *Where generally resident during last five years*: 'On Duty with the 88th and 27th Regiments until July 1827

when he returned from the West Indies, and has since resided in France.' [PRO: WO 25/755 f1]. Slightly wounded, Busaco, 27 Sept. 1810 (1st Battn.) [*London Gazette*].

D'ARCEY, Edward, Lt., 43rd Foot: Lt., 43rd Foot, 22 Aug. 1810. Slightly wounded, Nivelle, 10 Nov. 1813 ('D'Arcy') (1st Battn.) [*London Gazette*]. Two pensions, each for one hundred pounds, commencing 9 Jan. 1816, for 'loss of both legs' at New Orleans. [*1818 Pension Return*, pp. 12–13].

DAUBRAYA, Beyrimhof de, Lt., 3rd Dragoon Guards; Capt., 8th Caçadores: Lt., 3rd Dragoon Guards, 10 Oct. 1811. Severely wounded, Salamanca, 22 July 1812, while serving as Capt., 8th Caçadores ('Daubrawa') [*London Gazette*]. In Portuguese Service July 1810 to April 1814. *Challis, Portuguese Army*, p. 54.

DAUNT, George Digby, Lt., 97th Foot: Lt., 97th Foot, 28 Sept. 1809. Slightly wounded during the repulse of a sortie from Badajoz, 10 May 1811 [*London Gazette*]. MGS.

DAVERN, John, Lt., 88th Foot: Lt., 88th Foot, 11 Nov. 1807. Slightly wounded, storming of Badajoz, 6 April 1812 ('Dauern') (1st Battn.) [*London Gazette*]. Severely wounded, Orthes, 27 Feb. 1814 (1st Battn.) [*London Gazette*]. Capt., 88th Foot, 31 Aug. 1815. MGS.

DAVIDSON, George, Capt., 42nd Foot: Capt., Army, 5 April 1801; Capt., 42nd Foot, 25 Sept. 1807. Slightly wounded, storming and capture of Fort St Michael, Burgos, 19 Sept. 1812 (1st Battn.) [*London Gazette*]. Major, Army, 4 June 1813. Waterloo. Mortally wounded at Quatre Bras. *Anton*, p. 193 [Quatre Bras: 'Colonel Dick assumed the command on the fall of Sir Robert Macara, and was severely wounded. Brevet-mjor Davidson succeeded, and was mortally wounded; to him succeeded Brevet-major Campbell... Thus in a few minutes, we had been placed under four different commanding-officers.']

+**DAVIDSON, Sinclair, Capt., 79th Foot**: Capt., 79th Foot, 14 Feb. 1811. Severely wounded, 'since dead', Fuentes de Onoro, 5 May 1811 (1st Battn.) [*London Gazette*]. *Register of officers' effects*: 1st Battn. 'Kill'd in Action, 7 May, Villa Formosa'. Single. Effects sold for £95. 14s. 6d. [PRO: WO 25/2964]. Also listed with 2nd Battn., however, which indicated 'Died of Wounds, 10 May 1814, Villa Formosa... Serving with 1st Battn.' [PRO: WO 25/2964]. *Register of dead officers*: Died of wounds, 7 May 1811. Return dated 25 May 1811. [PRO: WO 25/2965].

DAVIES, Edward Phineas, Lt., 82nd Foot: *1829 Statement of Service*: Born in Oswestry, Shropshire, 19 Jan. 1782. 'Temporary Rank of Lieutenant, 36th Regt., 1st Octr. 1799, Volunteered with Quota of Men fm. 2d Battn. Shropshire Militia. Left the Regt. in 1800 in consequence of not being allowed to Purchase.' Ensign, 82nd Foot, 7 Sept. 1807, 'From Rl. Denbigh Militia without Purchase'. Lt., 82nd Foot, 27 Oct. 1808. Capt., 82nd Foot, 8 April 1825. *Battles, sieges and campaigns*: 'Passage of the Douro 11th & 12th May 1809. Talavera 27th & 28th July 1809. As Lieut... Vittoria 21st June 1813. Pass of Mayo 25th July 1813. Pampeluna 30th & 31st July 1813. Lesacca 31st August 1813. Nivelle & St. Vee 10th Novr. 1813, as Lieut... Campaigns in Spain and Portugal.' *Wounds received in action*: 'Received a severe contusion on the left Shoulder from a Nine pound Cannon Shot at the Battle of Vittoria on the 21st June 1813.' Note added by Lt. Col. W. Balfour, 82nd Foot: 'This appears to me very exhausting. W.B.' *Service abroad*: 'Novr. 1808 to Novr. 1809, Lisbon, Talavera. Novr. 1812 to Feby. 1814,

Peninsula. Septr. 1814 to Jany. 1816, America & France. June 1819 to Decr. 1829, Mauritius.' *Family*: Married Miss Ann Llewelyn, 27 Jan. 1800, Llanymynach. They had no children by 1830. [PRO: WO 25/801 f88]. MGS.

DAVIES, Francis John, Lt., 52nd Foot: Lt., 52nd Foot, 26 Jan. 1809. Slightly wounded, storming of Badajoz, 6 April 1812 ('Davis') [*London Gazette*]. MGS.

+**DAVISON, James, Lt./Adjutant, 27th Foot**: Lt., 27th Foot, 15 Jan. 1807. Severely wounded, storming of Badajoz, 6 April 1812, while regimental adjutant ('Davidson') (3rd Battn.) [*London Gazette*]. Killed, Salamanca, 18 July 1812 ('Adjutant Davidson') [*London Gazette*].

DAWKINS, Henry, Lt. and Capt., Coldstream Guards: *1829 Statement of Service for Retired Officers*: Aged fifteen years and three months on his first appointment to the Army. Ensign, Coldstream Guards, 10 March 1804; Lt. and Capt., Coldstream Guards, 25 Aug. 1808; Adjutant, Coldstream Guards, 14 April 1808 to 24 May 1810; Capt. and Lt. Col., Coldstream Guards, 25 July 1814; Half-pay, 31 Aug. 1826. *Where serving when wounded*: 'Wounded at the sortie from Bayonne April 1814.' No pension. *Family*: Married 15 Sept. 1821. Four children by 1829. *Where generally resident during last five years*: 'London.' [PRO: WO 25/755 f37]. Slightly wounded, sortie from Bayonne, 14 April 1814, while serving on the General Staff as Brigade Major [*London Gazette*]. Waterloo. MGS. Died Nov. 1864. *Dalton*, p. 109. *Royal Military Calendar*, vol. V, pp. 73–4.

DAWSON, Charles, Lt., 52nd Foot: Lt., 52nd Foot, 21 June 1810. Severely wounded, storming of Badajoz, 6 April 1812 [*London Gazette*]. *Moorsom*, p. 416 ['Served in the Peninsula, and died of wounds received at Waterloo.'].

+DAWSON, Henry, Lt./Capt., 52nd Foot: Lt., 52nd Foot, 14 Nov. 1805. Killed, during operations, 15–17 Nov. 1812 (1st Battn.) [*London Gazette*]. Obituary, *The Gentleman's Magazine*, March 1813, p. 284 ['Jan. 17 [sic]. Struck in the breast by a musket-ball, in the retreat near the river Huerta, in his 24th year, Capt. Henry Dawson, 52d foot, fourth son of Pudsey D. esq. of Liverpool. His fall has renewed in his family those griefs which had scarcely subsided for the loss of another son, Capt. Wm. D. of the Piedmontaire, who lately died in the East Indies."']. *Simmons*, p. 258 [killed, Huebra, 17 Nov. 1812: 'A Brigade of Swiss wanted to reconnoitre the river, opposite where the 52nd were posted, but were put back handsomely. Captain Dawson, a friend of mine, was killed.']. *Moorsom*, p. 121 [Almeida, 24 July 1810: 'The half-company under Lieutenant Dawson, being unable to retreat at speed with the horse artillery guns, had been cut off in the tower by the rapid advance of Ney's right; finding his post passed by the enemy and not attacked, Dawson remained quiet till nightfall, and then drew off his men under the glacis of Almeida and along the right bank of the Coa, and, without being observed by the enemy, rejoined his regiment by Pinhel, – a fine example of coolness and daring.'], p. 416 ['Served with the 52nd in the Peninsula, distinguished himself at the combat of Almeida in 1810, and was present with the regiment in the succeeding engagements until 1812, when he was killed in defending the position on the banks of the river Huebra, on the retreat from Madrid.']. Note that the obituary provides the wrong month and year for his death [17 Jan. 1813, rather than 17 Nov. 1812].

+DAWSON, Robert, Ensign, 45th Foot: Ensign, 45th Foot, n.d. [*1808 Army List*]. Killed, Rolica, 17 Aug. 1808 [*London Gazette*].

DAY, James, 1st Lt., Royal Artillery: 1st Lt., Royal Artillery, 1 Feb. 1808. Severely wounded, Nivelle, 10 Nov. 1813 ('Royal Horse Artillery') [*London Gazette*]. Waterloo. *Buckland, Dix & Wood*, catalogue, 12 May 1993 ['James Day was wounded at the siege of St Sebastian and severely at Nivelle... He retired on half pay as 2nd Captain, on 3 February, 1828, and died in Jersey, 1 August 1842.'].

+DAY, John, Lt./Adjtutant, 34th Foot: Lt., 34th Foot, 26 June 1810; Adjutant, 34th Foot, 24 Oct. 1811. Recorded as 'Killed', Pyrenees, 25 July 1813 (2nd Battn.) [*London Gazette*]. *Bell*, p. 83 [Pyrenees, 25 July 1813: 'the Adjutant, severely hit, tumbled off his horse and was left for dead (more about him hereafter).'], pp. 141–2 [Bordeaux, following the end of the war: 'The kind landlord ... had little music parties of an evening. On one of those occasions a French officer came up to me and looked at my buttons, being, as he said, familiar with the No. 34, and asked me if there was an officer named Day in the regiment, and if I knew anything of him. "Oh, yes! he was our Adjutant, but was unfortunately killed on the Pyrenees on the 25th of July last, when you paid us that most unfriendly visit." "Not so," he said, "but was mortally wounded. I found him on the battlefield after he had been plundered, and spoke to him. He gave me the sign and token of a brother of our craft, and, being a Freemason myself, I took him from that moment under my charge. I was sent to Bayonne with our wounded and many of your prisoners. Poor Day was my special care – I got him so far, and made his wasting life as quiet to him as possible. He wanted for many things that I had not in my power to provide. I got him cash for a bill on England, which I may say was duly honoured, but he did survive over a couple of weeks or so, and was buried with Masonic honours." '.].

DEANE, Hon. John Thomas Fitz-maurice, Major, 38th Foot: Bvt. Lt. Col., 38th Foot, 2 Oct. 1806; Major, 38th Foot, 8 Feb. 1807. Slightly wounded, sortie from Bayonne, 14 April 1814 (1st Battn.) [*London Gazette*]. Bvt. Colonel, 38th Foot, 4 June 1814.

DEARES, James, Lt., 28th Foot: Lt., 28th Foot, 25 April 1811. Slightly wounded, Toulouse, 10 April 1814 (1st Battn.) [*London Gazette*]. Taken prisoner and severely wounded, Waterloo.

DE BORGH, Anthony Philip, Lt., 60th Foot; Capt., 11th Caçadores: Lt., 60th Foot, 18 April 1811. In Portuguese Service Sept. 1811 to April 1814. Temporary pension of one hundred pounds per annum, commencing 4 Jan. 1815, 'for a wound' received at 'Asperne', 1814, while serving as Capt., 11th Caçadores [*1818 Pension Return*, pp. 26–7]. *Challis, Portuguese Army*, p. 54 ['De Burgh'].

+DE BREUNIG, Anthony Francis, Lt., York Light Infantry Volunteers; Capt., 8th Portuguese Line Regt: Lt., York Light Infantry, 25 July 1811. Killed, storming of Badajoz, 6 April 1812, while serving as Capt., 8th Portuguese Line ('de Bruning') [*London Gazette*]. In Portuguese Service March 1811 to April 1812. 'de Bruiney' in Army List. *Challis, Portuguese Army*, p. 54 ['De Breunig, Anthony Francis'].

DE BURGH, John Henry, Lt., 47th Foot: *1829 Statement of Service for Retired Officers*: Aged seventeen on first appointment to the Army. Ensign, Royal York Rangers, 7 Nov.

1807; Lt., 47th Foot, 1 March 1810; Lt., Half-pay, 21st Light Dragoons, 13 Sept. 1821. *Where serving when wounded*: 'Bejere Spain. Tarrifa Spain. Bayonne France.' No pension. Not married in 1829. *Where generally resident during last five years*: 'Shanonbridge, Ireland and London.' [PRO: WO 25/755 f185]. Slightly wounded, Tarifa, 30 Dec. 1811 (2nd Battn.) [*London Gazette*]. Slightly wounded, sortie from Bayonne, 14 April 1814 (2nd Battn.) [*London Gazette*].

DECHAIR, Henry, Lt., 6th Foot: Ensign, 6th Foot, 18 April 1811; Lt., 6th Foot, 8 Feb. 1814. Slightly wounded, Orthes, 27 Feb. 1814 ('Ensign Henry de Chain') [*London Gazette*]. 'Delhair' in *1812 Army List*.

DECKEN, Benedix von der, Lt., 1st Dragoons K.G.L.: Lt., 1st Dragoons K.G.L., 5 March 1811. Wounded, during 'movements of the Army' [Retreat from Burgos], 23 Oct. 1812 ('Deeken') [*London Gazette*]. Waterloo. *Beamish*, vol. II, p. 541 ['slightly wounded 23d Oct. 1812, at Venta del Poco'].

DECKEN, Claus Friederich von der, Lt., 2nd Line Battn. K.G.L.: *1829 Statement of Service for Retired Officers*: Aged fifteen years eight months on first appointment to the Army. Ensign, 2nd Line Battn. K.G.L., 24 Jan. 1806; Lt., 2nd Line Battn. K.G.L., 17 Nov. 1807; Capt., 2nd Line Battn. K.G.L., 25 June 1815; Half-pay, 25 April 1816, by reduction. *Where serving when wounded*: 'Memorandum. The undersigned was wounded several times in the Campaigns of the Peninsula and in France, seriously even at the Battle of Talavera de la Reyna, severely however at the Battle of Waterloo. From the Conse-quences of those Wounds he suffers continually and in a growing degree. Notwithstanding he never enjoyed the benefit of a Pension or any other allowance whatsoever for such Wounds.' *Family*: Married 'in the Bailiwick of Thedinghausen, Dukedom of Brunswick', 22 Sept. 1819. Three children by 1829. *Where generally resident during last five years*: 'near Freyburg in the County of Kehdingen, Kingdom of Hanover.' [PRO: WO 25/756 f268]. Slightly wounded, Nivelle, 10 Nov. 1813 [*London Gazette*]. Letter from him to Sulivan, War Office, dated 'Oerichsheil, near Freyburg', 7 Jan. 1829: 'Sir, It having in a memorandum of mine, inserted in the return transmitted to you with my letter of 26th Unlto., been represented that I was wounded on several occasions whilst serving in the Campaigns of Spain and France without having received any allowance whatsoever on that account, I have to recitify such insertion made by a mistake of mine in that manner, and so state that I received a full years pay for the wound received at the Battle of Waterloo, from government, and had a reward of £50 paid to me by the Waterloo Committee, besides £70 travelling expences granted and paid to me in Septr. 1823, when I had repaired in London to be inspected by a Medical Board. A Pension however never has been granted to me notwithstanding my continually suffering – as is stated in the said memorandum – from the consequences of these wounds. I have the honor to be ... Claus von der Decken'. [PRO: WO 25/776 p. 405 (between f381 and f382)]. Served in Peninsula 1808–14. Waterloo. *Beamish*, vol. II, p. 577 ['slightly wounded 10th Nov. 1813, at Uragne; slightly wounded, 27th Feb. 1814 before Bayonne; severely wounded, 18th June 1815 at Waterloo... [Died] at Oerichsheil near Stade, 15th Sept. 1834.'].

DECKEN, Frederick von der, Capt., 1st Light Dragoons K.G.L.: Capt., 1st Light Dragoons K.G.L., 18 Nov. 1811. Slightly wounded, Salamanca,

22 July 1812 [*London Gazette*]. Served in Peninsula 1809–14. Waterloo. *Beamish*, vol. II, p. 549.

DECKEN, George von der, Capt., 1st Light Dragoons K.G.L./1st Hussars K.G.L.: *1829 Statement of Service for Retired Officers*: Aged sixteen on first appointment to the Army. Cornet, 1st Light Dragoons K.G.L., 11 Feb. 1804; Lt., 1st Light Dragoons K.G.L., 27 Feb. 1806; Capt., 1st Light Dragoons K.G.L., 'in the year 1811' [Army List gives 11 July 1811]; Half-pay, by reduction. *Where serving when wounded*: 'In France wounded the first time on the Hights of Biddart the 10th of Decr. 1813, in France the second time on the 27th Feb. 1814, near Orthes, for the last Wound the Pension was granted me.' *Details of pension*: One hundred pounds per annum, commencing 28 Feb. 1815. Not married in 1829. *Where generally resident during last five years*: 'generally at Hannover.' [PRO: WO 25/756 f269]. Severely wounded, the Nive, 10 Dec. 1813, while serving as Aide-de-Camp to Lieutenant-General Sir Stapleton Cotton [*London Gazette*]. Severely wounded, Orthes, 27 Feb. 1814, while serving as ADC to Lt.-General Sir S. Cotton ('Dukin') [*London Gazette*]. Served in Peninsula 1809–14. Waterloo. *Beamish*, vol. II, p. 548 ['severely wounded, 10th Dec. 1813 at Bidart; severely wounded 27th Feb. 1814 at Orthes'].

+DECKEN, Gustavus, von der, Capt., 1st Dragoons K.G.L.: Joined the K.G.L. 7–17 Nov. 1803. Capt., 1st Dragoons K.G.L., 24 Sept. 1804. Severely wounded, in an Affair with the Enemy's Rear-Guard near La Serna, 23 July 1812 [*London Gazette*]. *Kincaid, Random Shots*, p. 338 ['The day after the battle of Salamanca a brigade of heavy German dragoons, under the late Baron Bock, made one of the most brilliant charges in history'].

Hanover campaign, 1805. Peninsular campaign of 1812. *Beamish*, vol. II, p. 616 [Died 'at Salamanca 16th Sept. 1812, of wounds he received in the combat of Garcia Hernandez, 23d July 1812.'].

DECKEN, William von der, Capt., 2nd Line Battn. K.G.L.: *1829 Statement of Service for Retired Officers*: Aged thirty-one on first appointment to the Army. Lt., 2nd Line Battn. K.G.L., 4 Feb. 1804; Capt., 2nd Line Battn. K.G.L., 13 Dec. 1806; Bvt. Major, 2nd Line Battn. K.G.L., 18 June 1815; Half-pay, 25 Feb. 1816, by reduction. *Where serving when wounded*: 'With the Army in Spain, with the 2nd Line Battalion K.G.L., at the Battle of Fuentes d'Honore.' *Details of pension*: One hundred pounds per annum, commencing 5 May 1812. *Family*: Married at Rotenburg, Hanover, 4 Feb. 1826. *Where generally resident during last five years*: 'At Hannover.' [PRO: WO 25/755 f215]. Severely wounded, Fuentes de Onoro, 5 May 1811 [*London Gazette*]. Served in Peninsula 1808-14. Waterloo. MGS. *Beamish*, vol. II, p. 576.

+DEIGHTON, William, Lt., 50th Foot: Lt., 50th Foot, 28 Sept. 1809. Killed, Pyrenees, 25 July 1813 (1st Battn.) [*London Gazette*]. Obituary in *Newcastle Courant*, 4 Sept. 1813 ['Lieutenant Deighton, late of the 1st batt. of the 50th regt. who fell, on the 25th July, in the Pyrenees, was son of the Rev. Wm Deighton, of East Dereham, in Norfolk, and nephew of Mr Wilson, of Percy-street, in this town. Though only in his 24th year, he had suffered many hardships, and had been in several conflicts, viz. at Corunna, under Gen. Sir John Moore, at Walcheren, and in various sieges and skirmishes with Field Marshal Lord Wellington; and had met with distinguished proofs of approbation from the general of the division of the army to which he belonged.'].

+DELACHEROIS, Nicholas, Ensign, 47th Foot: Ensign, 47th Foot, 30 March 1809. Killed, Barossa, 5 March 1811 (2nd Battn.) [*London Gazette*].

+DELATRE, F. Ensign/Lt., Regt. of Dillon: Ensign, Regt. of Dillon, 13 May 1811. Killed, at the taking of Fort St Phillippe, Tarragona, 3-7 June 1813 [*London Gazette*].

DELIUS, Carl August, Lt./Adjutant, 7th Line Battn. K.G.L: *1829 Statement of Service for Retired Officers*: Aged '27 years & 337 days' on first appointment to the Army. Lt., 7th Line Battn. K.G.L., 19 Jan. 1806; Adjutant, 7th Line Battn. K.G.L., May 1806 [Army List gives 17 May 1806]; Half-pay, 1810, 'on own request after being disabled for active service by the loss of an arm &c.' '... received in 1820 from His Hanoverian Majesty the brevet Rank of a Major which he still holds without any Rank in the Army though.' *Where serving when wounded*: 'In Spain at Talavera de la Reyna.' *Details of pension*: Seventy pounds per annum, commencing 25 Dec. 1811. *Family*: Married in Slade, Hanover, 30 June 1810. Six children by 1829. *Title and description of civil employment*: 'Captain of His Majesty's Hanoverian Guard Ship at the station of the Customs of the River Elbe.' *Where generally resident during last five years*: 'Stade in the Kingdom of Hanover.' [PRO: WO 25/755 f230]. Severely wounded, Talavera, 27 July 1809 ('Adjutant') [*London Gazette*]. Served in Peninsula 1808-9. *Beamish*, vol. II, p. 656 ['Charles Delius... severely wounded (arm amputated) 27th Jan. 1809, at Talavera. Placed upon half-pay, 27th Jan. 1810.'].

+DELMAR, John, Ensign, 28th Foot: Ensign, 28th Foot, 23 July 1812. Killed, Pyrenees, 25 July 1813 (1st Battn.) [*London Gazette*].

DENECKE, George, Surgeon, K.G.L.; Staff Surgeon, Hospital Staff: *1829 Statement of Service for Retired Officers*: Aged twenty-nine on his first appointment to the Army. Assistant Surgeon, K.G.L., 12 Jan. 1805; Surgeon, K.G.L., 25 May 1805; Staff Surgeon, Hospital Staff, 6 July 1809; Physician, Hospital Staff, 17 June 1813; Bvt. Deputy Inspector, Hospital Staff, 22 Feb. 1816; Half-pay, 15 July 1824; Deputy Inspector, Hospital Staff, 28 Oct. 1827; Half-pay, 6 Nov. 1827. 'Ill health contracted in Service in Walcheren, Peninsula and France, wounded at Salamanca and Waterloo.' *Where serving when wounded*: 'Salamanca. Waterloo.' No pension. *Family*: Married in Newport, Isle of Wight, 4 Feb. 1819. Two children by 1829. *Where generally resident during last five years*: 'Cape of Good Hope and Isle of Wight.' [PRO: WO 25/755 f212]. *Peterson and Johnson*, vol. I, p. 163 ['Copenhagen 1807. Walcheren 1809. Peninsula 1808, 1811–14. Waterloo (slightly wounded at Quatre Bras). M.D., Wurzburg 1801. Died in Isle of Wight, 19 Aug. 1838.'].

DERENZY, Bartholomew Vigors, Lt., 81st Foot; Capt., 7th Caçadores: *1829 Statement of Service*: Born 10 Dec. 1791, Clobemon Hall, Co. Wexford, Ireland. Aged fourteen years six months on his first entrance into the Army. Ensign, 81st Foot, 13 May 1806 [Army List gives 26 May]; Lt. 16 March 1808; Capt., Portuguese Service, 8 Sept. 1811; Major, Portuguese Service, 11 April 1814; Captain, unattached, 25 Dec. 1814; Capt., Half Pay, 28 Sept. 1818 ('Anglo-Portuguese Officers placed on Half Pay'); Capt., 11th Foot, 8 March 1821. *Battles, sieges and campaigns*: 'Campaign and Battle of Corunna... 1808–9. Expedition, Siege & Capture of Flushing, Walcheren 1809... Affairs of Redinha & Pombal, 1811; recapture of Campo Maior 1811; Capture of Olivenca 1811; 1st Siege of Badajos; Battle of Albuera 1811; Siege & Capture of Ciudad Rodrigo 1812; 3rd Siege and Capture of Badajos 1812; Battle of Salamanca 1812. Affair of Aldeiu da Ponte 1811. Retreat from Madrid (Burgos) in October & November 1812. Affairs of Gona & Jocaua and Battle of Vittoria 1813; Blockade of Pampeluna; Affairs of Roncesvalles; Zubisi, Battle of Pampeluna 28th July, and the Pyrenees 30th July 1813; Affairs of Eschallar, St Estevan, &c. 1813. Capture of St Sebastian; Passage of the Bidassoa, & Battles of the Nivelle & Nive 1813; Affairs of Baslide de la Chasence and Gary d'Olero 1814; Battle of Orthes and of Toulouse 1814... During the above Services he has had, on fourteen different occasions, detached & Separate Commands of personal responsibility of one, two and three Companies until the Command of the Battalion 17th Caçadores 4th Division finally devolved upon him at the Battle of Toulouse; and of which he retained the Command for two years, when he was appointed to the 12th Caçadores of which he was generally in command until the Revolution of 1820 in Portugal placed all the British Officers then serving there, on the half pay of that Service, on which they still continue. The Anglo-Portuguese Officers were placed on the British Half Pay in September 1818, but continued actually serving on full pay in the Portuguese Army until December 1820; & were still retained on full pay up to December 1824, when placed on Half Pay.' *Distinguished conduct*: 'Promoted to the Rank of Major "on the Field for distinction" in General Orders dated 20th April 1814, when in Command of the 7th Caçadores, 4th Division at the Battle of Toulouse, he having been previously recommended for that Rank by the Lieutenant General Commanding the Division on three former occasions; Viz: Pampeluna, Nivelle, & Orthes; but objected to in consequence of his then extreme youth! he being then in his twenty-second year of Age.' *Wounds received in action*: '1st. Severely Wounded in both knees at the Battle of Corunna 1809. Received a year's pay as Lieutenant, and £50 from Lloyds patriotic fund. – 2nd. Slightly wounded at Flushing in Left Arm. – 3rd. Dangerously wounded (reported killed) through the Body at the Battle of Nivelle – received a year's pay (Captain). – 4th. Twice slightly; by Musket Ricochet ball in left arm, & by a splinter of a Shell in Chest at the Battle of Toulouse 10th April 1814; but did not quit the field.' *Titles, honorary distinctions and medals*: 'Received the British and Portuguese Medals of Command for the Battle of Toulouse, as well as the Portuguese Gold Cross for "four Campaigns and afterwards." – Recommended also for the Spanish Cross for "personal distinction" given by the King of Spain for the battle of Vittoria, by Lieut. General Stubbs, Commanding the Brigade on that occasion.' *Service abroad*: 'July 1808 to Jany. 1809, Spain. June 1809 to Decr. 1809, Walcheren. Decr. 1810 to Jany 1821, Portugal, Spain, and France. 12 Jan. 1827 to 29 March 1828, Portugal. 30 March 1828 to 31 Decr. 1829, Corfu.' *Family*: 'Married Sarah Martha, eldest daughter of Lieut. General Richard Nelson, Sept. 1821, Devonport.' No children by 1830. [PRO: WO 25/787 f5]. Wounded, 'in the Army lately in Spain' (2nd Battn.) [*March 1809 Army List*, p. 105]. Severely wounded, Nivelle, 10 Nov. 1813, as Capt., 7th Caçadores ('Captain B. K. De Rendze') [*London Gazette*]. Gold Medal. MGS. *Challis, Portuguese Army*, p. 54 ['Derinzy'].

DERENZY, George Webb, Lt., 82nd Foot: *1829 Statement of Service for Retired Officers*: Aged twenty-one on first appointment to the Army. Ensign, 6th Garrison Battn., 27 Nov. 1806; Lt., 82nd Foot, 25 Dec. 1807; Capt., 82nd Foot, 20 April 1815; Half-pay, 'By reduction of 2nd Battalion 82nd Regt.' 'Quite willing to serve if required to do so.' *Where serving when wounded*: 'Spain.' *Details of pension*: One hundred pounds per annum, commencing 24 June 1814. *Title and nature of civil employment*: 'Unattached Barrackmaster.' *Where generally resident during last five years*: 'London and Ireland.' [PRO: WO 25/756 f200]. Severely wounded, Vittoria, 21 June 1813 (1st Battn.) [*London Gazette*]. Pension of one hundred pounds per annum, commencing 22 June 1814, for 'loss of an arm' at Vittoria [*1818 Pension Return*, pp. 18–19]. A portrait of him, an engraving by Turner after I. G. Strutt, is illustrated in *Haythornthwaite, Armies*, between pp. 224–5 ['Even the loss of a limb did not necessarily disqualify an officer from service. George Webb Derenzy lost his right arm as a lieutenant in the 82nd at Vittoria, but continued to serve despite his disability, and later transferred to the 4th Dragoons. He became barrack-master at Exeter.']. MGS. *Mullen*, p. 460 ['De Rency... Leg amputated' (sic)].

+DE SALABERRY, Edward A., Lt., Royal Engineers: 1st Lt., Royal Engineers, 1 March 1811. Killed, storming of Badajoz, 6 April 1812 ('De Salabury') [*London Gazette*].

DESBARRES, Joseph Frederick, Major, 87th Foot: Capt., 87th Foot, 29 Dec. 1804; Major, 87th Foot, 11 April 1811. Severely wounded, Orthes, 27 Feb. 1814 (2nd Battn.) [*London Gazette*]. Bvt. Lt. Col., 87th Foot, 3 March 1814. Gold Medal.

DESHON, Peter, Capt., 43rd Foot: Capt., 43rd Foot, 25 June 1803. Slightly wounded, Coa, 24 July 1810 [*London Gazette*]. Gold Medal.

+DESPARD, William, Major, 7th Foot: Capt., 7th Foot, 14 May 1804; Bvt. Major, 7th Foot, 20 June 1811; Major, 7th Foot, 15 Aug. 1811. Severely wounded, Pyrenees, 28

July 1813 [*London Gazette*]. Died of
wounds, 16 Aug. 1813. Return dated
Aug. 1813 [PRO: WO 25/2965]. Obituary, *The Gentleman's Magazine*,
Nov. 1813, p. 504 ['At Vittoria, of
wounds received in the battle of the
Pyrenees on the 26th July, Lieut.-
col. Despard, 7th or Royal
Fusileers.'].

+**DETTMERING, Charles, Capt.,
1st Line Battn. K.G.L.**: Lt., 1st Line
Battn. K.G.L., 3 Jan. 1804.
Promoted to Capt., 1st Line Battn.
K.G.L., replacing Wurmb, in 'Alter-
ations while Printing', *1809 Army
List*. Killed, Heights of Grijon, 11
May 1809 ('Captain Delanring')
[*London Gazette*]. Served in Penin-
sula 1808–9. *Beamish*, vol. II, p. 632
['Killed in action before Oporto,
11th May 1809.'].

DEVEY, Henry Fryer, Lt., 7th Foot:
*1829 Statement of Service for
Retired Officers*: Aged twenty-two
on first entrance to the Army.
Ensign, 2nd Battn. Staffordshire
Militia, 5 Nov. 1804; Ensign, Worcestershire Militia, 10 May 1806; Lt.,
Worcestershire Militia, 4 April 1807;
Lt., 7th Foot, 30 Aug. 1807, 'Volunteering from the Worcestershire
Militia'; Capt., 7th Foot, 8 Sept.
1813; Half-pay, 'my own request
from wounds & ill health, after the
Battle of Toulouse.' *Where serving
when wounded*: 'Badajos'. *Details
of pension*: One hundred pounds
per annum, commencing '7th Apl.
1813 as a Lieut., 18th June 1815 as a
Capt.' *Family*: Married in Hagley,
Worcestershire, 25 April 1816. Eight
children by 1829. *Where generally
resident during last five years*:
'Handsworth nr. Birmingham.'
[PRO: WO 25/755 f252]. Severely
wounded, storming of Badajoz, 6
April 1812 [*London Gazette*]. *1818
Pension Return*, pp. 4–5.

+**DEVONISH, J. A., Lt., 53rd Foot**:
Lt., 53rd Foot, 1 Feb. 1810. Severely
wounded, 'since dead', in the siege
of the Forts of St Vincente, St

Cayetano, and La Merced at Salamanca, 18–24 June 1812 (2nd
Battn.) [*London Gazette*]. *Register
of dead officers*: Died of wounds, 24
June 1812. Return dated 25 June
1812. [PRO: WO 25/2965].

**DICENTA, Francis, Lt., Watteville's
Regt.**: *1829 Statement of Service for
Retired Officers*: Aged twenty-four
on first appointment to the Army.
Sergeant Volunteer, Watteville's
Regt., 1 May 1801; Sergeant Major,
Watteville's Regt., 1807; Ensign,
Watteville's Regt., 1810 [Army List
gives 6 Sept. 1810]; Lt., Watteville's
Regt., 18 Aug. 1811. 'Town and Fort
Adjutant in Zante Ionian Islands.
Deputy Assistant Adjutant General
in the Upper Province of Canada.'
Where serving when wounded:
'Cadiz'. No pension. *Family*:
Married in Cadiz, 16 Feb. 1813. Four
children by 1829. *Title and nature of
civil employment*: 'Clark in a public
account office in Zaragosa.' *Where
generally resident during last five
years*: 'Zaragosa'. 'The above
signed Officer has not been able to
state the date of his appointment
to Ensign to the Watteville Regiment, on account of having been
deprived of his Brevet by the unfortunate accident of the House where
Mrs Dicenta lived in at Montreal in
the lower Province of Canada was
destroyed by fire, on the 12th of
January 1814, and all they
possessed lost; at which time the
above signed suffered the lamentable situation of a hostage Prisoner in the Gaols of the United
States.' [PRO: WO 25/756 f78].

+**DICKENS, Frederick J., Capt.,
12th Light Dragoons**: Capt., Army, 4
Aug. 1804; Capt., 12th Light
Dragoons, 16 Aug. 1804. Mentioned
in Cotton's Llerena dispatch, 11
April 1812 ['I have great pleasure in
assuring you of the good conduct of
... Captain Dickens, commanding
12th light dragoons']. Killed, Salamanca, 22 July 1812 [*London
Gazette*]. Obituary, *The Gentle-*

man's *Magazine*, Sept. 1812, p. 297 ['At the battle of Salamanca, Captain Dickins, 12th Light Dragoons, second son of F. D. esq. of Wohaston-house, co. Northampton, and nephew to the Archbishop of Canterbury.'].

DICKENS, Thomas M., Capt., Royal Engineers: 2nd Capt., Royal Engineers, 3 Jan. 1808; Capt., Royal Engineers, 21 July 1813. Severely wounded, sortie from Bayonne, 14 April 1814 [*London Gazette*].

+DICKENSON, Sebastian, Capt., Royal Engineers: 1st Lt., Royal Engineers, 1 March 1805; 2nd Capt. 29 May 1810. Killed, in the trenches before Badajoz, 8–15 May 1811 [*London Gazette*].

DICKSON, Hugh, Lt., 60th Foot: Lt., 60th Foot, 4 Aug. 1813. Slightly wounded, the Nive, 9 Dec. 1813 (5th Battn.) [*London Gazette*].

+DIGBY, Robert, Capt., 81st Foot: Capt., 81st Foot, 26 March 1807. Killed, 'in the Army lately in Spain' (2nd Battn.) [*March 1809 Army List*, p. 105]. *Regimental Pay List*, 2nd Battn., 25 Dec. 1808–24 March 1809: 'Killed, 16 Jan. 1809' [PRO: WO 12/8593].

+DIGGLE, Thomas A., Capt., 95th Foot: 1st Lt., 95th Foot, 13 Aug. 1805; Capt., 95th Foot, 10 Oct. 1811. Killed, storming of Badajoz, 6 April 1812 [*London Gazette*]. *Register of officers' effects*: 3rd Battn. Effects totalled £41. 14s. 5d. [PRO: WO 25/2964]. *Simmons*, p. 232 [killed].

DIGHTON, Robert, Lt., 38th Foot: *1829 Statement of Service*: Born 14 April 1786, London. Aged twenty-three on first appointment to the Army. Ensign, 38th Foot, 27 April 1809; Lt. 38th Foot, 7 Sept. 1807; Lt., 71st Foot, July 1815 [Army List gives 23 June 1815]; Lt., 16th Lancers, 9 July 1829. *Battles, sieges and campaigns*: 'Messena's Re-

treat, Peninsula &c &c. 5th Division of the Army Commanded by Genl. Leith. Acting Engineer, 1810. Bayonne &c... 1814.' *Wounds received in action*: 'Bayonne, April 1814. Wounded slightly.' 'A Years Pay granted.' *Service abroad*: 'April 1st 1810 to July 1812, Spain & Portugal. 1814, France &c. 1830 to 1832, East Indies, Bengal.' *Family*: His wife 'died in Lisbon Decr. 1st 1810.' They had one daughter, Victoire, who was born 12 Aug. 1809, 'Juernsey.' [PRO: WO 25/784 f304]. Enclosed memorandum: '1834. Near Portsmouth. Memorandum. The Statement which I filled up and signed when present with the Regiment, I did under the instruction of the Adjutant, and as I have not been able to find some documents which would greatly assist me here, if I am incorrect as to a few months, it is that my memory is not sufficient after so many years! but I trust the statement which I now forward will answer the purpose required, and is not materially wrong! Robt. Dighton, 8 NP, lte 16th Lancers (Bt. Captain India). [PRO: WO 25/784 304a]. Slightly wounded, sortie from Bayonne, 14 April 1814 (1st Battn.) [*London Gazette*]. Son of the artist and caricaturist Robert Dighton Sr. (1752–1814), brother of the military artist Denis Dighton (1792–1827) and the caricaturist Richard Dighton (1795–1880). Robert Dighton was also an accomplished artist; he died 1865.

+DINWOODY, Samuel, Ensign, 2nd Foot: Ensign, 2nd Foot, 9 Nov. 1809. Killed, Salamanca, 22 July 1812 ('Denwoody') [*London Gazette*].

DIX, Thomas, Lt., 57th Foot: Lt., 57th Foot, 5 March 1807. Slightly wounded, Albuera, 16 May 1811 [*London Gazette*]. Slightly wounded, Vittoria, 21 June 1813 (1st Battn.) [*London Gazette*]. Severely wounded, the Nive, 13 Dec. 1813 (1st Battn.) [*London Gazette*].

167

DIXON, Francis, 1st Lt., 95th Foot: 1st Lt., 95th Foot, 4 Jan. 1810. Severely wounded, 'in Action with the Enemy', 20 March 1814 (2nd Battn.) [*London Gazette*]. Waterloo. Half-pay 80th Foot, 11 Dec. 1817. Died in Jersey, 1832. *Simmons*, pp. 351–2.

DIXON, John William, Ensign/Adjutant, 48th Foot: *1829 Statement of Service for Retired Officers*: Aged twenty on first appointment to the Army. Ensign and Adjutant, 48th Foot, 2 Nov. 1809, 'By Merit'; Lt. and Adjutant, 48th Foot 14 Aug. 1811; Half-pay, 'Ill health from long service in different climates.' *Where serving when wounded*: 'Wounded at Talavera but receiving no Pension for it.' *Family*: Married in Norwich, 19 Nov. 1797. Four children by 1829. *Where generally resident during last five years*: 'Blantisham near St Ives, Huntingdon Shire.' [PRO: WO 25/756 f96].

+DOBBIN, Robert Brown, Lt., 66th Foot: Lt., 66th Foot, 22 Sept. 1808. Slightly wounded, Pyrenees, 30 July 1813 (2nd Battn.) [*London Gazette*]. Severely wounded, Nivelle, 10 Nov. 1813 ('Dobbins') (2nd Battn.) [*London Gazette*]. *Register of dead officers*: Died of wounds, 10 Dec. 1813. Return dated Dec. 1813. [PRO: WO 25/2965]. *Hurt*, p. 80 ['D.O.W., Nivelle, Nov. 10'].

DOBBIN, William, Lt., 27th Foot; Capt., 3rd Caçadores: Lt., 27th Foot, 17 March 1808. Slightly wounded in the trenches before Badajoz, 8–15 May 1811 ('Dobbins') (3rd Battn.) [*London Gazette*]. Wounded, storming of Badajoz, 6 April 1812, while serving as a Capt. in the 3rd Caçadores [*London Gazette*]. In Portuguese Service May 1811 to April 1814. Temporary pension of one hundred pounds per annum, commencing 7 April 1813, 'for a wound' received at Badajoz [*1818 Pension Return*, pp. 26–7]. *Challis, Portuguese Army*, p. 54.

DOBBS, John, Lt., 52nd Foot; Capt., 5th Caçadores: Lt., 52nd Foot, 14 Feb. 1809. Severely wounded, sortie from Bayonne, 14 April 1814, as Capt., 5th Caçadores ('Dobb') [*London Gazette*]. In Portuguese Service Sept. 1813 to April 1814. MGS. *Challis, Portuguese Army*, p. 54.

+DOBBS, Joseph, Capt., 52nd Foot: Capt., 52nd Foot, 26 Aug. 1804. Mentioned in Wellington's dispatch, dated Villa Formosa, 1 May 1811 ['The enemy had on the 23d [April] attacked our piquets on the Azava, but were repulsed. Captains Dobbs and Campbell, of the 52nd regiment, and Lieutenant Eeles, of the 95th regiment, distinguished themselves upon this occasion, in which the allied troops defended their post against very superior numbers of the enemy.'] [*London Gazette*, 18 May 1811]. Killed in the storming of Ciudad Rodrigo, 19 Jan. 1812 [*London Gazette*]. Mentioned in the obituary of Major-General McKinnon, *The Gentleman's Magazine*, Feb. 1812, p. 190 ['Capt. Dobbs was buried within a yard of his gallant General.']. *Moorsom*, pp. 139–40 [Azava, 23 April 1811: 'Captain Dobbs received four shots through various parts of his clothing.'], pp. 155–6 [Storming of Ciudad Rodrigo: 'The forlorn hope was led by Lieutenant Gurwood, of the 52nd, with twenty-five volunteers. The storming-party, consisting of 100 volunteers from each regiment; those of the 52nd under Captain Joseph Dobbs... The 1st battalion, commanded by Lieut.-Colonel Colborne, had Captain Joseph Dobbs, and eight rank and file killed.'], p. 417 ['Served as a volunteer in the expedition to Ferrol in 1800, and received a commission in the 52nd for his conduct on that occasion. He was with the 52nd at Copenhgen in 1807;

in the expedition to Sweden in 1808; in Portugal and Spain with Sir John Moore, and in the retreat and battle of Corunna. He returned to Portugal with the 52nd in 1809, and was present at the battle of Busaco, the combats of Pombal, Redinha, Foz d'Aronce, Sabugal, and particularly distinguished in the defence of the bridge of Marialva. He was present at the battle of Fuentes d'Onor, at the storming of the redoubt of San Francisco, and at the storming of Ciudad Rodrigo, where he lost his life gallantly in the little breach in 1812.'].

DOBBS, William, Volunteer/Ensign, 1st Foot: *1829 Statement of Service for Retired Officers*: Aged nineteen on first appointment to the Army. 'As a Volunteer from the County Limerick Militia retaining the Rank & Pay in said Corps having previously obtained His late Royal Highness the Duke of York's permission.' Ensign, 1st Foot, 22 Aug. 1813; Lt., 1st Foot, 29 Sept. 1814; Half-pay, 'By the Reduction of the 4th and subsequently 3rd Bn. of The Royals in both of which I had served.' *Where serving when wounded*: '18 June 1813. 21 May 1813. 31 Sept. 1813 at St Sebastian. 18th June 1815 at Waterloo.' *Details of pension*: Fifty pounds, commencing 1 Oct. 1814. No pension for wound received at Waterloo. *Family*: Married in Dublin, 24 June 1822. No children by 1829. *Where generally resident during last five years*: 'Kingstown, Dublin & Douglas, Isle of Wight.' [PRO: WO 25/756 f150]. Slightly wounded, 'in operations', 12–19 June 1813, ('Volunteer') [*London Gazette*]. Severely wounded, Vittoria, 21 June 1813 ('Volunteer') (3rd Battn.) [*London Gazette*]. Severely wounded, storming of San Sebastian, 31 Aug. 1813 ('Volunteer Dobb') (3rd Battn.) [*London Gazette*].

+DOBBYNS, Alexander, Ensign, 40th Foot: Ensign, Army, 28 July 1813; Ensign, 40th Foot, 24 Aug.

1813. Killed, Nivelle Nov. 1813 ('Alexander Dobbin') [*London Gazette*].

+DODD, Robert, Lt., 51st Foot: Ensign, 51st Foot, 17 Aug. 1809. Severely wounded, 'in the Operations of the Army', 31 Aug. 1813 [*London Gazette*]. *Register of dead officers*: Died of wounds, 13 Sept. 1813. Return dated Sept. 1813. [PRO: WO 25/2965]. *Wheeler*, p. 142 [30th Aug. 1813: 'At Lezaca we were joined by Lieut. Dodd and 30 men from England.'], p. 144 [31 Aug. 1813: 'Our loss was severe... It is worthy of notice that Lieut. Dodd and every man of his party were either killed or wounded.']

DODGIN, Daniel, Major, 66th Foot: Major, 66th Foot, 29 June 1809. Slightly wounded, Pyrenees, 30 July 1813 (2nd Battn.) [*London Gazette*]. Severely wounded, Aire, 2 March 1814 ('Major Daniel Dodgen (Lieutenant-Colonel)') (2nd Battn.) [*London Gazette*]. Gold Medal.

DODWELL, James, Cornet, 23rd Light Dragoons: Slightly wounded, Talavera, 28 July 1809 ('Cornet Dodvile') [*London Gazette*]. Lt., 23rd Light Dragoons, 17 Aug. 1809. *Challis, Index*, p. 242 [Capt., 6th Portuguese Cavalry].

DOLPHIN, John, Lt., 11th Foot: Lt., 11th Foot, 8 Aug. 1809. Slightly wounded, the Nive, 9 Dec. 1813 (1st Battn.) [*London Gazette*]. Severely wounded, Toulouse, 10 April 1814 (1st Battn.) [*London Gazette*].

+DONAHUE, Daniel, Capt., 44th Foot; Major/Lt. Col., 11th Portuguese Line: Capt., Army, 15 May 1806; Capt., 44th Foot, 7 Aug. 1806. Slightly wounded, Vittoria, 21 June 1813, as Major, 11th Portuguese Line ('Donahoe') [*London Gazette*]. Severely wounded, Orthes, 27 Feb. 1814, as Lt. Col., 11th Portuguese Line

('David Donohue' [*London Gazette*]. In Portuguese Service Oct. 1810 to Nov. 1811 and March 1812 to Feb. 1814. *Challis, Portuguese Army*, p. 54 ['Wd. Vittoria 21 June '13, Orthes 27 Feb. '14; Died of wounds.'].

DONALD, William, Ensign, 94th Foot: *1829 Statement of Service for Retired Officers*: Aged twenty-three on first appointment to the Army. Ensign, 94th Foot, 21 Dec. 1809;Lt., 12th Foot, 12 March 1812; Capt., Half-pay, unattached, 31 Dec. 1825, 'owing to a contusion & loss of health contracted by over-exertion as a sapper at the sieges in the Peninsula.' *Where serving when wounded*: 'At Badayos.' *Details of pension*: 'Nothing of the kind was then thought of.' [PRO: WO 25/756 f160].

+DONAVAN, Daniel, Lt., 11th Foot: Lt., Army, 25 Sept. 1804; Lt., 11th Foot, 26 Feb. 1805. Slightly wounded, Salamanca, 22 July 1812 ('Donovan') (1st Battn.) [*London Gazette*]. Died of wounds, 22 Aug. 1812. Return dated 25 Sept. 1812 ('Donevan'). [PRO: WO 25/2965].

DONAVAN, Daniel, Ensign, 27th Foot; Lt., 14th Portuguese Line: Ensign, 27th Foot, 13 May 1812. Wounded, the Nive, 13 Dec. 1813, as Lt., 14th Portuguese Line ('Daniel Domewer') [*London Gazette*]. In Portuguese Service May 1812 to April 1814. *Challis, Portuguese Army*, p. 54 ['Wd. Nive 13 Dec. '13.'].

DONELLAN, Charles, Lt. Col., 48th Foot: Lt. Col., Army, 28 Sept. 1804; Lt. Col., 48th Foot, 14 Nov. 1804. Severely wounded, Talavera, 28 July 1809 [*London Gazette*]. *Fletcher, Regiments*, pp. 44–5 ['The 48th (Northamptonshire) Regiment at Talavera, July 28th 1809. Colonel Donellan, seriously wounded, takes off his hat and gives command of the regiment to Major Middlemore saying, "You will

have the honour of leading the 48th to the charge." '].

+DONKIN, Robert, Lt., 82nd Foot: Lt., 82nd Foot, 7 Aug. 1806. Killed, Vimeiro, 21 Aug. 1808 [*London Gazette*].

DONNELLAN, Hugh S., Lt., 82nd Foot: Lt., 82nd Foot, 8 March 1810. Slightly wounded, 'in the Operations of the Army', 31 Aug. 1813 ('Donnelan') [*London Gazette*].

DONOVAN, Daniel, Ensign, 27th Foot; Lt., 14th Portuguese Line: *1829 Statement of Service for Retired Officers*: Ensign, 6th Irish Brigade, 1796, 'By raising men at my own expence for that corps'; Lt., 6th Irish Brigade, 'I think in Nine or twelve months.' Dates uncertain 'being shipwrecked on my passage to North America & our lives only saved by the Porcupine Frigate I consequently lost my commissions and papers.' Lt., 35th Foot, 'I think ... in 99'; 'In 1802 or 3 retired from the service'; 'joined the Portuguese service under Marshal Beresford in 1810, 1809'; 'recommended by His Grace the Duke of Wellington for a commission in 27th Regt. Ensigncy, dated 13th May 1812'; 'Lt., 27th Foot, 9 Feb. 1814'; Half-pay, by reduction. 'I was first gazetted in the 6th Irish Brigade as Ricd. O'Donovan which was subsequently rectified to Danl. Richd. O'D at the War Office ... an Ensigncy to the 27th Regt. 3rd Battn. by the name of Danl. Donovan'. '[Joined 35th Foot in] Malta, proceeding from that Island in 1801 I was with some other officers captured ... in the Gulph of Lions and conveyed to Alais in Languedoc where we were detained for 8 months.' *Where serving when wounded*: 'In the Peninsula, slightly at Salimanca in the 12th Portuguese and after at la Nieve or Nivelle ... on the 13th December 1813 very badly by a musquet Ball in the right thigh hiting the bone in its passage, then serving as Lieutenant in the 14th Portuguese... No pension, tho' many besides myself justly thought me intitled to one. No grant or pension save a years pay altho' my old commanding General the Duke of Kent thought me intitled to one and would have essayed to procure it had God in his mercy spared me the patronage of so Enlightened and Illustrious a Prince.' *Family*: 'No marriage yet tho' I have been some time thinking about it.' *Where generally residing during last five years*: 'I have been residing at Kilovinogue ... these nine years back and my agent is Hopkinson and Co. Regent Street, London.' [PRO: WO 25/756 f153].

+DOUGLAS, Charles Aytoyne, Capt., 51st Foot: Capt., Army, 3 Dec. 1803; Capt., 51st Foot, 25 April 1806. Killed, 'in the Operations of the Army', 31 Aug. 1813 [*London Gazette*]. Obituary, *The Gentleman's Magazine*, Nov. 1813, p. 499 ['Aug. 31. In the action on the Pyrenees, Capt. Charles A. W. Douglas, 51st Light Inf. who, on this day, closed a life devoted to the service of his country. This distinguished officer served in the East Indies, Egypt, the first campaign in Spain, in Walcheren, and for the last three years in the Peninsula. During a great part of the latter period he served with great credit on the Staff of his cousin Sir Howard Douglas, in his important mission to the Northern provinces of Spain. Capt. Douglas died in the very act of displaying one of the noblest qualities of our nature. The brigade was ordered to retire, having suffered much from bravely maintaining its ground against a very superior body of the Enemy. Capt. Douglas, who was ever where he could be most useful, and where most was going on, was in the act of encouraging some of the skirmishers to return for the purpose of carrying off a wounded man, when he was shot through the heart. So much was he beloved by his men, that although under a heavy fire, four soldiers of the 51st endeavoured to remove the body; persisting in this attempt, two of them were killed and one wounded; when the other, being hardly pressed by the Enemy, was obliged to relinquish his precious charge, which was plundered of every thing valuable. Captain Douglas was the only son of the late Col. Robert Douglas, and nephew to the late Admiral Sir Charles Douglas.']. *Wheeler*, pp. 64, 144 [Killed, near Lezaca, 31 Aug. 1813], p. 145 ['The name of Douglas and courage are so closely connected in British history, it will only be necessary to say, he stood high as a brave soldier, but he was in possession of another virtue, rarely to be met with to so great a degree in any man – it was a noble generosity and good will that he extended to all about him. He had acquired the appelation of "Father" by his company, by whom he was almost idolized. By the Regiment at large he was highly beloved and respected. Notwithstanding he was a strict disciplinarian, but somehow, he never had any trouble in keeping his men in order, as a look or a word from him had more effect then 500 lashes would from some officers. Our regret for his loss can be much easier imagined then described.'].

DOUGLAS, James, Lt. Col., E.O.P.S.; Col., 8th Portuguese Line: *1829 Statement of Service for Retired Officers*: Aged sixteen on first appointment to the Army. Ensign, 45th Foot, April 1800; Lt., 45th Foot, May 1800; Capt., 45th Foot, Sept. 1802; Major, Portuguese Service, Feb. 1809; Lt. Col., Portuguese Service, May 1811; 'Colonel July 1821, DQM Genl in Scotland & in Ireland'. 'Removed from Portuguese Service to half pay.' *Where serving when wounded*: 'Commanding a Brigade in France.' *Details of pension*: Three hundred and fifty pounds, commencing 1815.

DOUGLAS

Family: Married in Hampstead, 7 Sept. 1815. Six children by 1829. *Where generally resident during last five years*: 'Dublin. Albury.' [PRO: WO 25/756 f127]. Slightly wounded, 'in the Operations of the Army', 31 Aug. 1813, as Col., 8th Portuguese Line [*London Gazette*]. Wounded, Nivelle, 10 Nov. 1813. Severely wounded, Toulouse, 10 April 1814, as Col., 8th Portuguese Line [*London Gazette*]. Served in Portuguese Army April 1809 to April 1814. Gold Medal. Three hundred and fifty pounds per annum pension, commencing 11 April 1815, for 'loss of a leg' at Toulouse [*1818 Pension Return*, pp. 24–5]. MGS. *Challis, Portuguese Army*, p. 54. *Anton*, p. 84 [Late 1813: in command of a brigade consisting of three Portuguese regiments].

+DOUGLAS, John Graham, Capt., 52nd Foot: Capt., 52nd Foot, 27 Aug. 1804. Severely wounded, Crossing the Bidassoa, 7/9 Oct. 1813 [*London Gazette*]. Severely wounded, the Nive, 10 Dec. 1813 ('Captain Graham Douglas') (1st Battn.) [*London Gazette*]. *Register of dead officers*: Died of wounds, 23 Dec. 1813. Return dated Dec. 1813. [PRO: WO 25/2965]. *Hurt*, p. 79 ['D.O.W., Nive, Dec. 10']. *Hay*, p. 19 ['I was attached to the company of Captain Douglas, a most worthy, excellent man, and a brave soldier.'].

DOUGLAS, Joseph, Lt., 45th Foot: Lt., Army, 20 Dec. 1810; Lt., 45th Foot, 10 April 1811. Slightly wounded, Toulouse, 10 April 1814 ('Joshua Douglas') (1st Battn.) [*London Gazette*]. MGS.

DOUGLAS, Neil, Capt., 79th Foot: *1829 Statement of Service*: Born in Glasgow, Feb. 1783. Aged 18 on his first Entrance into the Army. 2nd Lt., 21st Foot, 28 Jan. 1801. Lt., 9th Foot, 16 July 1802. Half Pay, 25 Dec. 1802, by reduction. Lt., 42nd Foot, 9 July 1803. Lt., 95th Rifles, 2 Dec. 1803. Capt., 79th Foot, 19 April

1804, 'By raising a quota of Men.' Major, 79th, 31 Jan. 1811. Lt. Col., 79th Foot, 3 Dec. 1812. Colonel, ADC. to the King, 27 May 1825. *Battles, sieges and campaigns*: 'Siege of Copenhagen in 1807 as Captain in the 79th... Campaigns in Sweden, Portugal, & Spain, & Battle of Corunna, in 1808 & 1809 as Captain in the 79th... Siege of Flushing and Campaign in Holland in 1809... Siege of Cadiz & Campaign in Portugal, & Battle of Busaco in 1810, as Brigade Major & Captain in the 79th... Campaigns in Spain & France, & Battles of the Pyrenees, Nivelles, Nive, & Toulouse, in 1813 & 1814 as Lt. Col. Commanding the 79th... Battle of Waterloo and Campaign in Belgium in 1815 Commanding 79th Regt.' *Distinguished conduct*: 'The Piquet of the Regt. having been Cut off during the Battle of Busaco, Captn. Douglas was selected to try & recover it. In executing this Service he was severely wounded but he succeeded in extricating the Lieut. & about 2/3ds of the Piquet, the Captain having been killed. At the Battle of Toulouse the 79th Regt. under Lt. Colonel Douglas carried by Storm the largest of the Enemy's Redoubts, & when another highly distinguished Corps was driven from a Redoubt, which they had carried at the same time, they retreated upon the 79th which was thus also thrown into some confusion, & both Regiments obliged to retire but in a few minutes Lt. Col. Douglas succeeded in Rallying the 79th, & retook not only his own former Position, but the redoubt which the other Regt. had lost. For this he received on the Field the thanks of Sir Henry Clinton, & Sir Denis Pack Commanding the Brigade & Division; he was also directed to retain possession of it, & which he did, until the Capture of the Town. In the Official Account of this Battle, the 79th is one of only Four regiments stated to have been "highly distinguished throughout the whole day." At the Battles of Quatre Bras, & Waterloo, the 79th under Lt. Col. Douglas had thirty one officers & a Volunteer, among its Killed & Wounded, & was again One of only Four Regiments, particularly mentioned in the Official Dispatch. The 79th was the Highland Regiment selected by the Duke of Wellington to remain in France with the Army of Occupation.' *Wounds received in action*: 'A Ball through the Left Shoulder Joint, & another in the Left Arm on the 27 Sepr. 1810 at Busaco. One hundred a year Pension. A Ball through the Right Knee & a Contusion from a Ball hitting a Button at Quatre Bras on 16 June 1815. Pension raised to £300 a year in all.' *Titles, honorary distinctions and medals*: 'A Gold Medal each for the Battles of the Pyrenees, the Nivelle, the Nive & Toulouse. A Companions Cross of the Bath for General Service. A Medal for the Battle of Waterloo, also another Companions Cross of the Bath & thus twice gazetted for that distinction. The Cross of Maria Theresa from the Emperor of Austria for Waterloo. The Cross of St Vladimir of the 3d Class from the Emperor of Russia for Waterloo.' *Service abroad*: 'July 1807 to Novr. 1807, Denmark. April 1808 to Jany. 1809, Sweden, Portugal & Spain. July 1809 to Octr. 1809, Holland. Decr. 1809 to Jany. 1811, Spain & Portugal. April 1813 to Augt. 1814, Spain & France. April 1815 to Novr. 1818, Belgium & France. Augt. 1825 to date, Canada & continuing to serve in that Colony.' *Family*: Married Barbara Robertson, Aug. 1816, Grunorh. They had five children by 1830. [PRO: WO 25/800 f228]. Severely wounded, Busaco, 27 Sept. 1810 (1st Battn.) [*London Gazette*]. Gold Medal. Temporary pension of three hundred pounds per annum, commencing 25 Dec. 1811, 'for a wound' received at Busaco [*1818 Pension Return*, pp. 18–19]. MGS.

DOUGLAS, Robert, Lt., 7th Light Dragoons: Lt., 7th Light Dragoons, 17 June 1813. Slightly wounded, Orthes, 27 Feb. 1814 [*London Gazette*]. Wounded, Waterloo.

DOWKER, Thomas, Lt., 53rd Foot: *1829 Statement of Service for Retired Officers*: Aged eighteen on first appointment into the Army. Ensign, 53rd Foot, 20 April 1809; Lt., 53rd Foot, 10 March 1810; Half-pay, 38th Foot, 'think it was... Decr. 1814', 'in consequence of ill health ... contracted during the five years served in Spain, Portugal and France.' *Where serving when wounded*: 'Slightly wounded on the 28 July 1813 but never received a pension, in the Pyreneas.' *Family*: Married in York, 5 Dec. 1820. Four children by 1829. *Where generally resident during last five years*: 'Huntington, near York.' [PRO: WO 25/756 f156]. MGS.

DOWLING, Thomas, Lt., 87th Foot: Lt., 87th Foot, 21 Feb. 1810. Slightly wounded, Vittoria, 21 June 1813 (2nd Battn.) [*London Gazette*].

+DOWMAN, William, Ensign, 97th Foot: Ensign, 97th Foot, 26 Oct. 1807. Wounded, 'lost an arm', during the repulse of a sortie from Badajoz, 10 May 1811 [*London Gazette*]. *Register of dead officers*: Died of wounds, 4 June 1811. Return dated 25 June 1811. [PRO: WO 25/2965].

DOWNIE, John, Brigadier-General, Spanish Service: No rank in the British Army. Pension of £350, commencing 28 Aug. 1813, for 'loss of an eye and ear' in Seville, 1812 [*1818 Pension Return*, pp. 26–7].

DOWNING, Adam Gifford, Capt., 81st Foot: *1829 Statement of Service for Retired Officers*: Aged seventeen on first appointment to the Army. Ensign, 34th Foot, 1799; Lt., 34th Foot; Capt., 81st Foot, 1805; Major, 81st Foot, 1815; Half-pay, by reduction 2nd Battn. [Army List gives: Ensign, 34th Foot, 26 June 1799; Lt., 34th Foot, 7 March 1800; Capt., 81st Foot, 26 Dec. 1805; Major, 81st Foot, 21 Dec. 1815; Half-pay, 25 Feb. 1816]. *Where serving when wounded*: 'Corrunna'. *Details of pension*: One hundred pounds commencing 1809, increased to two hundred on 25 Dec. 1823. Not married in 1829. *Where generally resident during last five years*: 'Ireland'. [PRO: WO 25/756 f139]. Wounded, 'in the Army lately in Spain' (2nd Battn.) [*March 1809 Army List*, p. 105]. *Monthly Return*, 2nd Battn., dated 25 Feb. 1809: 'Wounded, in Naval Hospl. Plymouth' [PRO: WO 17/202].

+DOWNING, James, Major, 61st Foot: Major, 61st Foot, 8 Oct. 1807. Severely wounded, Salamanca, 22 July 1812 [*London Gazette*]. *Register of officers' effects*: Died of wounds, 13 Aug. 1812, Salamanca. Married. Effects totalled £78. 3s. 8 1/2d. [PRO: WO 25/2964]. *Register of dead officers*: Died of wounds, 13 Aug. 1812. Return dated 25 Aug. 1812. [PRO: WO 25/2965].

DOWNING, John, Ensign, 97th Foot: Ensign, 97th Foot, 20 July 1809. Severely wounded during the repulse of a sortie from Badajoz, 10 May 1811 [*London Gazette*].

+DOWSON, William, Capt., 6th Dragoons: Capt., 6th Dragoons, 9 July 1807. Severely wounded, Salamanca, 22 July 1812, while serving as extra ADC to Lt.-General Leith ('Dawson') [*London Gazette*]. Obituary, *The Gentleman's Magazine*, Supplement 1814 Part I, p. 700 ['At Liverpool, in his 27th year, W. Dowson, esq. captain in the 6th or Inniskillen dragoons, who was severely wounded at the battle of Salamanca, when serving as aide-de-camp to Maj.-gen. Leith.'].

+DOYLE, John, 2nd Lt., 95th Foot: 2nd Lt., 95th Foot, 10 Oct. 1811.

Severely wounded, Nivelle, 10 Nov. 1813 (2nd Battn.) [*London Gazette*]. 1st Lt., 95th Foot, 25 Nov. 1813 (though he had apparently died prior to being gazetted at this new rank). *Register of dead officers*: Died of wounds, 10 Nov. 1813. Return dated Nov. 1813. [PRO: WO 25/2965]. *Hurt*, p. 82 ['D.O.W., Nivelle, Nov. 10']. *Kincaid, Adventures*, pp. 266–7 ['A curious fact occurred in our regiment at this period. Prior to the action of the Nivelle, an owl had perched itself on the tent of one of our officers (Lieut. Doyle). This officer was killed in the battle, and the owl was afterwards seen on Capt. Duncan's tent. His brother-officers quizzed him on the subject, by telling him that he was the next on the list; a joke which Capt. D. did not much relish, and it was prophetic, as he soon afterwards fell at Tarbes.']. *Surtees*, p. 248 [Killed, Nivelle: 'little Lieutenant Doyle was killed.'].

DOYLE, John, Capt., 47th Foot: *1829 Statement of Service*: 'Born Killmaculla, County Clare, Ireland, 26 Septr. 1788. Aged Sixteen on his first Entrance into the Army. Ensign, 47th Regt., 28 Sept. 1804. Lieut., 47th Regt., 5 Novr. 1805. Captain, 47th Regt., 29 Septr. 1813. Half Pay, 24 Octr. 1814, by Reduction of 2nd Battalion. Captain, 72nd Regt., 25 June 1818.' *Battles, sieges and campaigns*: 'As Lieut. Siege of Montevideo. Sortie from Montevideo. Storming, by the Enemy, of Colonia, in 1807. As Captain, last Campaign in the Peninsula. Siege of Bayonne. Sortie from Bayonne, 1814.' *Wounds received in action*: '[Sortie from Bayonne] Contusion in left Arm, no advance of Pay.' *Service abroad*: 'May 1806 to Augt. 1810, South America, Cape of Good Hope & East Indies. Decr. 1813 to Augt. 1814, South of France. Decr. 1818 to June 1822, Cape of Good Hope.' *Family*: Married his first wife, Miss Gonnell, 30 July 1816, in Cork. They had one daughter, born in Oct. 1817. He remarried, Miss O'Brien, 29 Nov. 1827, Newry. They had no children by 1830. [PRO: WO 25/799 f84].

DOYLE, Michael Taylor, Lt./Capt., 5th Foot: *1829 Statement of Service for Retired Officers*: Aged twenty-two on first appointment to the Army. Ensign, 5th Foot, 3 July 1805; Lt., 5th Foot, 10 July 1806; Capt., 5th Foot, 1 Feb. 1810; Half-pay, by reduction. *Where serving when wounded*: 'Roleia. Badajos'. *Details of pension*: One hundred pounds, commencing 7 April 1813. *Family*: Married in Glanmire, Cork, 18 April 1816. *Title and nature of civil employment*: 'Barrack master of Yaughal'. *Where generally resident during last five years*: 'Yaughal'. [PRO: WO 25/756 f142]. Slightly wounded, Rolica, 17 Aug. 1808 [*London Gazette*]. Severely wounded, storming of Badajoz, 6 April 1812 [*London Gazette*]. Pension 'for wounds' received at Badajoz [*1818 Pension Return*, pp. 4–5]. MGS.

DRAKE, William, Capt., 23rd Dragoons: Capt., 23rd Dragoons, 25 June 1803. Recorded as wounded and missing, Talavera, 28 July 1809 [*London Gazette*].

+DRECHSELL, Frederick von, Brigade-Major, K.G.L. Staff: Capt., Army, 18 July 1810; Brigade-Major, K.G.L., Staff, 18 July 1810. Killed, sortie from Bayonne, 14 April 1814, while serving as Brigade Major, Permanent Staff K.G.L. ('Dreschell') [*London Gazette*]. 'Dreschell' in Army List. *Beamish*, p. 611.

+DREW, Francis, Lt., 48th Foot: Lt., 48th Foot, 22 June 1810. Killed, Albuera, 16 May 1811 (2nd Battn.) [*London Gazette*].

DREW, Richard, Lt./Adjtutant, 61st Foot: *1829 Statement of Service*: 'Born in Collumpton, 21st Novr.

1780. Aged Twenty four on his first Entrance into the Army. Ensign, 35th Foot, 18th Augt. 1805. Lieut & Adjt., 61st, 22d Augt. 1805. Captain, 73rd, 12th May 1812. Major, 91st, 10th June 1826. Major, 73rd, 13 July 1826.' *Battles, sieges and campaigns*: 'Talavera 1809. Busaco 1810. Sabugal 1811. Fuentes D'Onor, 1811.' *Wounds received in action*: 'Severely and dangerously wounded through the body at Talavera 29th July 1809 and taken Prisoner. Received one years pay.' *Service abroad*: '1800 to 1805, Malta and Porto Ferrajo. 1805 to 1807, Italy, Sicily. 1809 to 1812, Spain, Portugal. 1813 to 1816, Germany, Flanders. 1817 to 1820, Ceylon. 1827 to 1829, Gibraltar.' *Family*: Married Isabella Alicia Downing, 28 July 1823, Morpeth. They had no children by 1830. [PRO: WO 25/799 f155]. Severely wounded, Talavera, 28 July 1809 [*London Gazette*]. *Pearson*, pp. 82–3 ['In the course of our engagements, Major Coghlan and Adjutant Drew, two of the most acute and valiant of our officers, had been lost to us ... the latter having received a musket ball in the abdomen, which passed through the bowels and came out at the loins... I remember when the adjutant was wounded I assisted two drummers to carry him to the rear, and then went for a doctor of the German legion, who at once came along with me to dress the wound of our favourite officer. After an examination, the doctor inquired when he had last tasted food. The adjutant, in his usual happy way, replied, "Nothing for three days, my dear fellow; but it is through the gut and I cannot live." The doctor replied that in consequence of there being no food in that part, it was quite possible for him to recover under careful treatment. Of the former officer [Coghlan] we heard nothing; and as to the latter, after his removal to the hospital at Talavera, nothing was known. One morning, however, the two officers appeared in our midst, glad to be with us again, and we were as happy to receive them.'].

DREWE, Edward Ward, Lt., 27th Foot: *1829 Statement of Service*: Born in Castle Ward, Ireland, 24 Dec. 1786. Aged seventeen 'on his first Entrance into the Army.' Ensign, 'South Downshire Militia', 4 April 1803 to 4 Oct. 1806. Ensign, 27th Foot, 5 Oct. 1806. Lt., 27th Foot, 8 Feb. 1808. Capt., Royal African Corps, 7 Jan. 1824. Capt., 95th Foot, 18 May 1825. *Battles, sieges and campaigns*: "Landing on & taking the Island of Ischea from the French 3 Augt. 1809... Siege of the Castle of Ischea 7 to 11 Augt. 1809... Almost complete destruction of French flotilla Cape Messina Bay of Naples 12 Augt. 1809... The several engagements with French... 10, 11 & 12 June 1810... British Army flotilla under Genl. Sir J. Stewart. Engagement with French flotilla Battery off porto del Pizzo 12 Augt. 1810... Several officers with Sir J. Stewart on the Coasts of Naples & Calabria... Sept. & Oct. 1810.... [various other actions, then] Battle of Castalla (Spain) 13 March 1813 D.A.Q. Mr. Genl. under Sir Murray. Siege of Tarragona (Spain) June 1813 D.A.Q. Mr. Genl. Engagement with French Army & taking the Fort & Pass of Ballequer June 1813 D.A.Q. Mr. Genl. Battle of Col D'Ordal (Spain) 13 Sept. 1813... Blockade of Barcelona & several skirmishes with the French Garrison to the end of 1813 & to 14 Apl. 1814... Siege of Platsburgh (America) from 10th to 21st Septr. 1814... several affairs with the American Troops near Mobil, latter end of 1814... Battle of Waterloo 18 June 1815... Part of the Campaign against the Ashantees (Africa) latter end of 1824 & beginning of 1825, Captain...' *Distinguished conduct*: 'At the taking of Eschia & destruction of French flotilla noticed in Genl. Orders by Sir John Stewart & was in consequence

shortly after appointed Major of Brigade to the Combined British & Sicilian flotillas. Was honorably mentioned in Genl. Orders for the Destruction of French Positions on the Coast of Arcadia ... when in Command of the flotilla ship ... & was in consequence appointed some time after to the Qr. Mr. Genls. Depart. & accompanied the portions of the Army from Sicily to Spain by Order of Genl. Wm. Bentinck in that capacity.' *Wounds received in action*: 'Wounded (slightly) in the Bay of Naples Augt. 1809. Wounded (slightly) Battle of Castalla 13 March 1813. Wounded Severely Battle of Col D'Ordal 13 Septr. 1813. Wounded (Slightly) Crossing the Saranac (America) 12 Septr. 1814. Wounded Severely Battle of Waterloo 18 June 1815. Recd. two years pay as Capt. for Commg. Companies at the Col D'Ordal (Spain) & at Waterloo. Receives a permanent Pension of £70 annually for wounds recd. in Action.' *Titles, honorary distinctions and medals*: 'Waterloo Medal for Battle of Waterloo 18 June 1815.' *Service abroad*: 'Augt. 1807 to May 1817, Gibraltar, Sicily, Malta, Sicily, Ionian Islands, Sicily, Spain, France, America, West Indies, Belgium & France. May 1824 to Novr. 1825, Africa. 1 Augst. 1826 to 4 Octr. 1828, Malta.' *Family*: Married E. C. Eustace, 18 Feb. 1817, in Brussels. They had no children by 1830. [PRO: WO 25/803 f297]. Severely wounded, 'not dangerously', Heights of Ordal, 12/13 Sept. 1813 (2nd Battn.) [*London Gazette*]. See also Crewe, Frederick.

DREWE, John Ringrove, Lt., 27th Foot: Ensign, 27th Foot, 15 Nov. 1810; Lt., 27th Foot, 25 Feb. 1813. One hundred pounds per annum pension, commencing 29 July 1814, for 'loss of an arm' at Pampeluna, 1813 [*1818 Pension Return*, pp. 8–9].

+DROEGE, Robert, Cornet, 2nd Dragoons K.G.L.: Cornet, 2nd

Dragoons K.G.L., 11 Feb. 1811. Recorded as 'Missing', during 'movements of the Army' [Retreat from Burgos], 23 Oct. 1812 ('Droege') [*London Gazette*]. 'Droegge' in Army List. Served in the Peninsula only in the campaign of 1812. *Beamish*, vol. II, p. 615 ['Killed in an affair with the enemy's cavalry, near Venta del Poco, in Spain, 23d October 1812.'].

DROUGHT, Bartholomew Edward, Lt./Capt., 48th Foot: *1829 Statement of Service for Retired Officers*: Aged twenty-two on first appointment to the Army. Ensign, 50th Foot, 2 Sept. 1802; Lt., 48th Foot, 4 July 1804 [Army List gives 6 July]; Capt., 48th Foot, 21 June 1810; Half-pay, Oct. 1814, 'By Reduction of the 2nd Battn.' 'In consequence of wounds, and ill health sustained in the service, is incapacitated from serving again.' *Where serving when wounded*: 'in Spain, at Talavera and Albuera, six different wounds.' *Details of pension*: One hundred pounds per annum, commencing 17 May 1812. *Family*: Married in Clonfert, 4 May 1819. No children by 1829. *Where generally resident during last five years*: 'King's County, Ireland.' [PRO: WO 25/756 f194]. Severely wounded, Talavera, 28 July 1809 [*London Gazette*]. Slightly wounded, Albuera, 16 May 1811 [*London Gazette*]. Pension 'for wounds' received at Albuera [*1818 Pension Return*, pp. 12–13].

+DRUMMOND, George Duncan, Lt. Col., 24th Foot: Lt. Col., 24th Foot, 11 Feb. 1808; Col., Army, 25 October 1809. Severely wounded, Talavera, 28 July 1809 [*London Gazette*]. Died, Portugal, 8 Sept. 1811 [PRO: WO 25/2965]. *Simmons*, p. 136 [8 Feb. 1811: 'Colonel Drummond took command of the 2nd Brigade of the Light Division', p. 166. *Leach*, pp. 229–30 [August 1811: 'Many officers and soldiers died whilst we were in this neighbourhood, having undoubtedly brought the malignant fever with them from

that unhealthy camp on the Caya, in Alemtejo. Amongst the number were Colonel Drummond of the 24th regiment, (who commanded a brigade in the Light Division during Colonel Beckwith's absence in England, from ill-health)'].

DRUMMOND, John McGregor, Lt., 82nd Foot: *1829 Statement of Service for Retired Officers*: Aged thirty-one on first appointment to the Army. Ensign, 82nd Foot, 15 Dec. 1808; Lt., 82nd Foot, 23 April 1811; Capt., 82nd Foot, 4 Dec. 1823; Half-pay, 'By reduction of the 9th Compy.' *Where serving when wounded*: 'at Orthes in France.' *Where generally resident during last five years*: 'Chiefly Perth Shire N.B. [Scotland]'. [PRO: WO 25/756 f186]. Severely wounded, Orthes, 27 Feb. 1814 (1st Battn.) [*London Gazette*]. MGS.

DRYSDALE, William, Lt., 1st Line Battn. K.G.L.: Lt., 1st Line Battn. K.G.L., 19 Aug. 1813. Served in Peninsula 1813–14. Waterloo. *Beamish*, vol. II, p. 573 ['slightly wounded, 27th Feb. 1814, before Bayonne... [Died] in London, 13th April 1823.'].

DUBOURDIEU, Arthur, Capt., 5th Foot: *1829 Statement of Service*: Born 17 Dec. 1781, Anahilt Glebe, County Down. Aged eighteen on his first entrance into the Army. Ensign, 5th Foot, 15 Aug. 1799; Lt. 10 Dec. 1800; Lt., 6th West India Regt., 21 April 1803; Lt., 5th Foot, 25 June 1803; Capt., 7th Garrison Batt., 26 Nov. 1806; Capt., 5th Foot, 2 June 1808; Major, Army, 12 Aug. 1819. *Battles, sieges and campaigns*: 'Campaign in Holland, 1799, Commander in Chief His Royal Highness Frederick Duke of York. Rank of Ensign 5 Regiment. Battles. 19 September 1799, 6 October 1799, 2 October 1799, 10 October 1799. – Expedition to Hanover, 1804, Commander in Chief Lord Cathcart, Rank Lieutenant 5

Regiment. – Expedition to South America which sailed in 1806, Commander in Chief Brigadier General Crawford, Rank Captain 7th Garrison Battalion. – Joined the troops in the Rio Plata in 1807, Commander in Chief Lieut. General Whitelock, Rank Captain 7th Garrison Battalion, landing at and march from Ensenada de Bavragon to Buenos Ayres. Investment and storming Buenos Ayres. – Peninsular Campaigns, Battles: Busaco, 27 Sept. 1810; Radigna, 12 March 1811; Foz de Roy, 15 March 1811; Sabugal, 3 April 1811; Fuentes d'Onor, 5 May 1811; Siege of Badajoz, from 30 March 1811 to 17 June 1811; El Bodon, 25 Sept. 1811; Siege and Capture of Ciudad Rodrigo, from 8 Jan. 1812 to 19 Jan. 1812.' *Distinguished conduct*: 'In the Expedition to Hanover under Lord Cathcart in 1804, the vessel in which the Right Wing of the Regiment was embarked was drawn on a Bank of the Mouth of the Wiser out of Sight of Land in a gale of Wind the only means of saving the men had the vessel gone to pieces were seizing some coasting vessels which were going up the river. I volunteered to do so and with those Individuals who came with me, was lowered down in the Ship's Boat, and with difficulty (on account of the heavy Sea) succeeded in Boarding and bringing along side two of them, and anchoring them under the lee of the Vessel, in consequence of this I was personally recommended by Lieut. Colonel Davis who commanded the Regiment to His Royal Hiness the Duke of York Commander in Chief, and promoted to a Company in the 7th Garrison Battalion, being at that time the 3 Lieutenant of the Regiment. – At the Battle of El Bodon commanding the Grenadiers of the 2nd Battalion 5 Regiment, after the Regiment had charged and retaken the Guns of the division from the Enemy's Cavalry, the Regiment being charged when in line by the

Cavalry, and at the time defending themselves by an intensive fire, I threw back the right subdivision of my company and by that movement covered and Protected the Right flank of the Regiment which was not protected at that point. – At the Storming of Ciudad Rodrigo commanding the Grenadiers of the 2nd Battn. 5 Regiment, I was the first who placed a scaling ladder and entered the Enemy's Works, and the first of the Enemy who fell that night at the Escalade was by my hand in making my way over one of the Guns placed on the embrazure of the fasisse Braze. I was wounded afterwards in the side and arm on the Ramparts of the Town after the Regiment succeeded in carrying the main Breach.' Wounds received in action: 'Wounded in the side and arm at the Storming of Ciudad Rodrigo on the 19th January 1812. Received one year's pay. Pension £100 per annum 20 January 1813 permanent.' *Service abroad*: 'Sept. 1799 to Decr 1799, North Holland; June 1800 to July 1802, Gibraltar; Decemr 1804 to April 1805, Hanover; March 1805 to Decr 1807, Expedition to the Rio Plata; June 1809 to June 1812, Peninsula; Aug. 1816 to Oct. 1818, France; April 1819 to May 1821, West Indies; May 1822 to March 1826, West Indies.' *Family*: Married Mary Flattery, 26 March 1809, Park House, King's County. Wife still alive on 25 Sept 1830. At that date they had seven children. [PRO: WO 25/785 f411]. Slightly wounded, storming of Ciudad Rodrigo, 19 Jan. 1812 [*London Gazette*]. *1818 Pension Return*, pp. 4–5. Brother of Saumarez Dubourdieu, Royal Artillery. Mentioned in his brother's obituary as having 'lost his left arm' at Ciudad Rodrigo, though the Pension Return suggests that he received an award only 'for wounds', while his Statement of Service does not indicate that he suffered an amputation.

+**DUBOURDIEU, Saumarez, 2nd Capt., Royal Artillery**: 2nd Capt., Royal Artillery, 7 July 1805. Mentioned in Wellington's Vittoria dispatch, dated 22 June 1813 ['The Lieutenant-General [Sir T. Graham] then proceeded to attack the village of Abechuco, with the 1st division, by forming a strong battery against it, consisting of Captain Dubourdieu's brigade and Captain Ramsay's troop of horse artillery, and, under cover of this fire, Colonel Halkett's brigade advanced to the attack of the village, which was carried'] [*London Gazette*]. Mentioned in Sir Thomas Graham's dispatch concerning the action near Tolosa, 24–25 June 1813 ['A general attack began between six and seven in the evening ... two nine-pounders of Captain Dubourdieu's ... were brought rapidly forward on the Chaussee, and fired with effect against several formed bodies of the enemy in the plain near the town'] [*London Gazette*]. Severely wounded, 'since dead,' 'at the Siege of St Sebastian,' 7–27 July 1813 [*London Gazette*]. *Register of dead officers*: Died of wounds, 22 July 1813. Return dated June 1813. [PRO: WO 25/2965]. Obituary, *The Gentleman's Magazine*, Nov. 1813, p. 504 ['By the explosion of a shell in the breaching of St Sebastian, Capt. Dubordieu, Royal Artillery. Although a young officer, he was highly esteemed for his professional talents. He had distinguished himself during a series of 10 years' service in the West Indies, particularly at the recapture of Martinique, and had just arrived in Spain to take part in the battle of Vittoria, and the siege of St Sebastian. He was the son of Rev. John D. of the North of Ireland; another of whose sons, Capt. D. 5th reg. lost his left arm in leading the grenadiers into the breach at the storming of Ciudad Rodrigo.'].

DU CHATELET, Maximilian, 5th Batt. 60th Foot: Lt., 60th Foot, 3 Dec. 1807. Slightly wounded, Fuentes de Onoro, Evening 3 May 1811 (5th Battn.) [*London Gazette*].

+**DUCKWORTH, George Henry, Lt. Col., 48th Foot**: Lt. Col., Army, 14 Jan. 1808; Lt. Col., 48th Foot, 16 June 1808. Killed, Albuera, 16 May 1811 (1st Battn.) [*London Gazette*]. Obituary, *The Gentleman's Magazine*, 1811 Supplement, Part I, p. 679 ['In the battle of Albuera, aged 23, Col. Duckworth, son of Adm. Sir J. D. The circumstances of his death are thus described in a letter from an Officer high in rank in Gen. Beresford's army: "Lieut.-col. Duckworth was first severely wounded in the left breast by a musket-ball, while gallantly leading his regiment to the charge; but, the same noble blood which runs in the veins of the father flowing equally warm in those of the son, he could not be induced to quit the field. Shortly after another shot struck him in the throat, when he expired without a groan." – Thus did this brave young Officer, well knowing the effect of example to his followers, choose rather to die upon the field, than retire at such a moment, though it were to stanch the life-blood which was flowing from his brave heart. It is an interesting fact, that his horse, which had carried him during all the campaign, shared his master's fate. He died, the day after the battle, of the wounds he had received. – The Colonel married, at a very early age, Miss Fanshawe, daughter of Commissioner F. of Plymouth Dockyard. On the day the afflicting news of the Colonel's death arrived at Plymouth, their only son, four years old, lay dead in the house, and was buried the following day.']. *Haythornthwaite, Armies of Wellington*, p. 33 ['it was still possible for very young men to attain high rank: the son of Admiral Duckworth, lieutenant-colonel of the 1/48th, who was killed at Albuera, was apparently aged only

23 when shot in the left breast in
that action; he refused to leave his
battalion and was killed by a shot
through the throat.']. *Haythornthwaite, Die Hard*, p. 153 [Albuera:
'The 1/48th went into action with 33
officers and 464 other ranks; they
lost sixteen and 258 respectively,
plus six men missing, a casualty-
rate of more than 56 per cent.'

DUDGEON, Peter, Capt., 58th Foot:
*1829 Statement of Service for
Retired Officers*: Aged seventeen at
first appointment to the Army.
Ensign, Southern Fencibles, 19 July
1797; Ensign, 58th Foot, 4 April
1800; Lt., 58th Foot, 3 Sept. 1801;
Capt., 58th Foot, 19 March 1807;
Bvt. Major, 58th Foot, 19 July 1821;
Half-pay, unattached, 4 May 1826. 'I
served in the Fencible Corps above
mentioned from the date of my
appointment until its Reduction
which took place on the 24th
February 1799.' *Where serving when
wounded*: 'Burgos, Spain.' *Details
of pension*: One hundred pounds,
commencing 25 Dec. 1817. *Family*:
Married in 'County of Waddington',
10 May 1813. Five children by 1829.
[PRO: WO 25/756 f213]. Slightly
wounded, storming of Fort St
Michael, Burgos, 19 Sept. 1812 (2nd
Battn.) [*London Gazette*]. Severely
wounded, 'in the assault and
capture of the exterior line of the
castle of Burgos on the evening of
the 4th October, 1812' (2nd Battn.)
[*London Gazette*]. MGS.

DUDGEON, Peter, Lt., 66th Foot:
Lt., 66th Foot, 10 Feb. 1808.
Severely wounded, Talavera, 28 July
1809 (2nd Battn.) [*London
Gazette*].

DUDGEON, Ralph, Lt., 71st Foot:
*1829 Statement of Service for
Retired Officers*: Aged eighteen on
first appointment to the Army.
Ensign, 71st Foot, 'some time in the
year 1805' [Army List gives 22 April
1805]; Lt., 71st Foot, 1 Jan. 1807;
Capt., 71st Foot, 'in Augt. or Septr.

1813'; Half-pay, 'By Reduction of
the 2nd Battn. of my Regiment.' 'I
served at the Cape of Good Hope in
Spanish America and the whole of
the War in the Peninsula from the
first landing of the British Army
until the close of the War and had
the Honour of being more than
once employed By Order of Lord
Hill on a Particular Service.' *Where
serving when wounded*: 'Received
one years pay for wounds received
at the Battle of Vimera through the
Hand & Leg.' *Family*: Married in
Monaghan Church, Ireland, 24 June
1816. Seven children by 1829. *Title
and nature of civil employment*:
'Magistrate for Co. Monaghan.'
*Where generally resident during
last five years*: 'Rosefield,
Monaghan, Ireland.' [PRO: WO
25/756 f242]. Ensign, 71st Foot, 22
April 1805. Slightly wounded,
Vimiero, 21 Aug. 1808 [*London
Gazette*].

+DUFF, Alexander, Lt., 71st Foot:
Lt., 71st Foot, 12 Nov. 1807. Slightly
wounded, Vittoria, 21 June 1813
(1st Battn.) [*London Gazette*].
Killed, Pyrenees, 25 July 1813 (1st
Battn.) [*London Gazette*].

DUFFEY, John, Capt., 43rd Foot:
Capt., 43rd Foot, 12 Aug. 1804.
Mentioned in Wellington's Ciudad
Rodrigo dispatch, 20 Jan. 1812
['The conduct of Captain Duffey of
the 43d ... [has] likewise been
particularly reported to me']
[*London Gazette*, 5 Feb. 1812]. Bvt.
Major, 43rd Foot, 6 Feb. 1812; Major,
43rd Foot, 17 June 1813. Slightly
wounded, Vittoria, 21 June 1813
('Captain Duffey (Major)') (1st
Battn.) [*London Gazette*]. Gold
Medal. MGS.

+DUGUID, William, Lt., 29th Foot:
Lt., 29th Foot, 7 Feb. 1808. Killed,
Albuera, 16 May 1811 [*London
Gazette*].

**DUHIGG, Bartholomew Thomas,
Lt., 27th Foot**: Lt., 27th Foot, 9 Nov.

1806. Severely wounded, Castalla, 12-13 April 1813 (2nd Battn.) [*London Gazette*].

DUKE, John William, Lt., 48th Foot: *1829 Statement of Service*: 'Born Whatlington, Sussex, 26th August 1782. Aged Twenty Four on his first Entrance into the Army. Ensign, 48th, 29th May 1806. Lieutenant, 48th, 10th Feby. 1808. Captain, 48th, 24th March 1824.' *Battles, sieges and campaigns*: 'Talavera 28th July 1809. Busaco 27th Sptr. 1810. Albuhera 16 May 1811. Seiges of Rodrigo and Badajos 7th April 1812 Pampeluna 27th & 28th July 1813 Pyrenees 10th Novr 1813 Orthes 27th Feby 1814 Tolouse 10th April 1814.' *Wounds received in action*: 'Wounded, [indicates Albuhera], one years full pay as lieutenant. Wounded, [indicates Pampeluna?], one years full pay as Captain.' *Service abroad*: '1806 to 1808, Ireland. 1808 to 1809, Gibraltar. 1809 to 1814, Portugal, Spain & France. 1814 to 1817, Ireland. 1817 to 3rd March 1828, England. 3rd March 1828 to 31st Decr. 1829, East Indies.' *Family*: Married Leonora-de-Castro, 1823, Isle of Wight. They had no children by 1830. [PRO: WO 25/794 f163]. Slightly wounded, Albuera, 16 May 1811 [*London Gazette*]. Severely wounded, Pyrenees, 28 July 1813 (1st Battn.) [*London Gazette*].

DUMARESQ, Henry, Lt., 9th Foot: Lt., 9th Foot, 9 Aug. 1808. Severely wounded, siege of Burgos, 5–10 Oct. 1812, while serving as Assistant Engineer ('Dumareusq') (1st Battn.) [*London Gazette*]. Wounded, Waterloo, as ADC to Major-General Byng. Dalton, p. 20 ['Fought in 13 battles during the Pen. War. Also at the sieges of Burgos and Badojoz, and assaults on forts of Salamanca. On the two former occasions served as a volunteer with the Engineers, and on the latter was again a volunteer ... Shot

through the lungs at Hougoumont... Ball never extracted. D. in New South Wales 5th March, 1838, age 46'].

DUNBAR, Robert Nugent, Capt., 92nd Foot: Capt., 92nd Foot, 28 April 1804; Major, Army, 25 April 1808. Slightly wounded, Arroyo dos Molinos, 28 Oct. 1811 (1st Battn.) [*London Gazette*].

+DUNCAN, Alexander, Major, Royal Artillery: Major, Royal Artillery, 17 Nov. 1809; Lt. Col., Army, 6 March 1811. Mentioned in Graham's Barossa dispatch, 6 March 1811 ['Major Duncan soon opened a powerful battery of ten guns in the centre... I owe too much to Major Duncan, and the Officers and corps of the Royal Artillery, not to mention them in terms of the highest approbation; never was artillery better served... I cannot conclude this dispatch without earnestly recommending to His Majesty's gracious notice for promotion... Major Duncan, royal artillery'] [*London Gazette*, 25 March 1811]. Obituary, *The Gentleman's Magazine*, Feb. 1813, p. 182 ['Lately... At Seville, by an accidental explosion, Col. Duncan, R.A.']. Killed by the explosion of a magazine in Seville, 29 Sept. 1812. *Webber*, pp. 89–90 ['We received in the evening the melancholy intelligence of the death of Colonel Duncan of the Artillery, who was blown up by an explosion of the magazine at Seville... Everyone in the Regiment must sincerely lament the loss of Colonel Duncan, for he was an excellent officer and one who always upheld the character of the Corps and assisted the right of its officers whenever it may have been disputed. A man of great independence of spirit, a noble and brave mind. In my opinion his loss to us is almost irreparable, at least for the present.'], n42 [had been Commander Royal Artillery at Cadiz].

DUNCAN, Edward, Lt., 59th Foot: *1829 Statement of Service*: 'Born in Sutherlandshire, 1792. Aged 16 years on his first Entrance into the Army. Ensign, 59th Regt., 3rd Sept. 1806. Lieutenant, 59th Regt., 28th Feby. 1811. Captain, 59th Regt., 24th July 1817.' *Battles, sieges and campaigns*: 'Siege of Flushing in 1809... Battle of Vittoria 21 June 1813... Siege of San Sebastian 31 Augt. 1813... The Campaign of 1815, in the Netherlands and France. Battle of Waterloo, Storming of Cambray, & Paris'. *Wounds received in action*: 'Severely wounded at San Sebastian on the 31 August 1813. The Ball being lodged in the region of the Liver. Pension £100 a year Permanent.' *Titles, honorary distinctions and medals*: 'Received a Medal for Waterloo.' *Service abroad*: May 1809 to Septr. 1809, Flushing. Augt. 1812 to Octr. 1813, Spain. April 1815 to Jany. 1816, France. Jany. 1821 to June 1822, East Indies. June 1827 to 28th June 1829, East Indies.' [PRO: WO 25/796 f224]. Severely wounded, storming of San Sebastian, 31 Aug. 1813 (2nd Battn.) [*London Gazette*]. *1818 Pension Return*, pp. 14–15.

+DUNCAN, John, Capt., 95th Foot: Capt., Army, 19 Sept. 1800; 1st Lt., 95th Foot, 15 June 1804; Capt., 95th Foot, 27 April 1809. Severely wounded, 'in Action with the Enemy', 20 March 1814 (2nd Battn.) *Register of officers' effects*: Killed in Action, 20 March 1814, Tarbes. Single. Effects totalled £259. 6s. 8d, out of which regimental debts of £209. 19s. 3d were subtracted. [PRO: WO 25/2964]. *Hurt*, p. 82 ['D.O.W., Tarbes, Mar. 20']. *Simmons*, pp. 336, 341 [Killed. 2nd Battn.]. *Kincaid, Adventures*, pp. 266–7 ['A curious fact occurred in our regiment at this period. Prior to the action of the Nivelle, an owl had perched itself on the tent of one of our officers (Lieut. Doyle). This

officer was killed in the battle, and the owl was afterwards seen on Capt. Duncan's tent. His brother-officers quizzed him on the subject, by telling him that he was the next on the list; a joke which Capt. D. did not much relish, and it was prophetic, as he soon afterwards fell at Tarbes.'].

DUNCOMBE, Francis Harold, Lt., 74th Foot: *1829 Statement of Service for Retired Officers*: Aged fourteen on first appointment to Army. Ensign, 89th Foot, 23 May 1808, 'at the recommendation of His Grace the Duke of Northumberland'; Lt., 74th Foot, 1 Jan. 1811, 'at the recommendation of Lt. Genl. Sir Alexr. Hope'; Half-pay, 52nd Foot, 'in consequence of wounds.' *Where serving when wounded*: 'Pyrenees, Spain.' *Details of pension*: Two at £70 each', commencing 30 July 1814. *Family*: Married in St Mary's, Dover, 26 May 1827. One child by 1829. *Where generally resident during last five years*: 'London & Boulogne sur mer.' [PRO: WO 25/756 f247]. Severely wounded, Pyrenees, 30 July 1813 ('Duncomb') (1st Battn.) [*London Gazette*]. *1818 Pension Return*, pp. 18–19.

DUNDAS, William, 2nd Capt., Royal Artillery: 2nd Capt. 11 July 1811. Mentioned in Wellington's Ciudad Rodrigo dispatch, 20 Jan. 1812 ['The rapid execution produced by the well-directed fire kept up from our batteries, affords the best proof of the merits of the officers and men of the royal artillery... But I must particularly mention ... Captains ... Dundas, of the royal artillery'] [*London Gazette*, 5 Feb. 1812]. Severely wounded, 'lost an arm,' at the siege of Badajoz, 31 March–2 April 1812 [*London Gazette*] MGS.

DUNKIN, John Henry, Lt. Col. 77th Foot: Lt. Col., 77th Foot, 15 Nov. 1809. Slightly wounded, storming of

Badajoz, 6 April 1812 ('Duncan') [*London Gazette*]. Gold Medal.

+DUNKLEY, William, Lt., 11th Foot: Ensign, 11th Foot, 7 June 1810. Killed, Toulouse, 10 April 1814 (1st Battn.) [*London Gazette*]. *Haythornthwaite, Armies of Wellington*, p. 256 [16 Jan. 1814, before Bayonne: 'The grenadier captain of the 11th Foot, Francis Guley, decided to beat-up the French outpost in his front... Lieutenant William Dunkley and Sergeant Pike then jumped the moat and killed the inlying sentry, who was almost asleep; then they assisted the rest of the raiding-party to clamber in and out of the moat. Securing the Frenchmen's weapons, which were in a rack outside the barn, they took the whole lot prisoner, less six who were killed resisting; the officers were captured in an upstairs room, where they were entertaining a lady. The French arms and accoutrements were flung into the moat, and more than 200 prisoners were escorted to the British lines. For this unusual enterprise, Gualey received a brevet rank of major, but enjoyed it only briefly; he was mortally wounded at Toulouse, where Dunkley was killed.'].

DUNLEVIE, William, Lt., 87th Foot: Lt., 87th Foot, 15 Sept. 1808. Severely wounded, 'in Action with the Enemy', 19 March 1814 (2nd Battn.) [*London Gazette*].

DUNLOP, Robert Graham, Lt., Royal Navy: Lt., Royal Navy, 7 Feb. 1812. Severely wounded, 'at the Siege of St Sebastian,' 7–27 July 1813, while serving with a 'Detachment of Seamen' [*London Gazette*]. Serving on board HMS *Porcupine*, stationed 'North of Spain', Jan. *1814 Navy List*. Commander, Royal Navy, 20 July 1822. Died 28 Feb. 1841. D. Syrett ed., *The Commissioned Sea Officers of the Royal Navy, 1660–1815* (1994), p. 136.

DUNN, William, Ensign, 66th Foot: *1829 Statement of Service*: Born 10 Oct. 1794, Drumsna, Co. Leitrum, Ireland. Aged Seventeen on his first entrance into the Army. Ensign, 66th Foot, 15 July 1812; Lt., 2nd Garrison Batt., 21 Sept. 1815; Half Pay 24 July 1816; Lt., 25th Foot, 2 Nov. 1820; Half Pay 25 Oct. 1821; Lt., 6th Foot, 17 Nov. 1825; Lt., 44th Foot, 10 May 1826; Lt., 12th Foot, 10 May 1827; Adjutant 15 June 1830; 'Resigned the Adjutantcy only, 25th Jany. 1831.' *Battles, sieges and campaigns*: 'Vittoria 21st June 1813. Pyrenees 25th July 1813. Nevelle 10th Novr. 1813. Nive 9 to 13 Decr. 1813. Campaign of 1813 and 1814 in Spain and France.' *Wounds received in action*: 'Wounded on the Pyrenees on the 25th July 1813. Received a years Pay.' *Service abroad*: '29th Sept. 1812 to 28th Sept. 1814, Portugal, Spain & France. 28 Decr. 1827 to 31 Decr. 1829, Gibraltar.' *Family*: Married Emily, 'only daughter of John Willock Esqr, of Killeney Park Co. Dublin,' 9 Feb. 1824, Dublin. No children by 1830. [PRO: WO 25/787 f113]. MGS.

DUNN, William, Lt., Royal Horse Artillery: 1st Lt. 20 July 1804. Severely wounded, 'not seriously', in 'an Affair with the Enemy, near Aldea de Ponte', 27 Sept. 1811 [*London Gazette*].

DURIE, John A., Lt., 92nd Foot: Lt., 92nd Foot, 18 Sept. 1805. Slightly wounded, Pyrenees, 25 July 1813 ('Dwire') (1st Battn.) [*London Gazette*]. Slightly wounded, Aire, 2 March 1814 (1st Battn.) [*London Gazette*].

DÜRING, Albrecht von, Capt., 2nd Light Battn. K.G.L.: Capt., 2nd Light Battn. K.G.L., 12 Nov. 1803. Slightly wounded, Talavera, 27 July 1809 ('Rifle Corps K.G.L.') [*London Gazette*]. Served in Peninsula 1808-9. *Beamish*, vol. II, p. 652 ['Retired on an allowance of 3s. per day, 7th May 1811. [Died] in Hanover, 7th June 1820'].

DÜRING, Christian Henry von, Lt., 1st Line Battn. K.G.L.: Lt., 1st Line Battn. K.G.L., 17 Aug. 1809. Slightly wounded, Busaco, 27 Sept. 1810 [*London Gazette*]. Served in Peninsula 1808–14. Waterloo. *Beamish*, vol. II, p. 572.

DÜRING, Ernest von, Lt., 5th Line Battn. K.G.L.: *1829 Statement of Service for Retired Officers*: Aged fifteen and a half 'when engaged as soldier at Stade 1805.' Ensign, 5th Line Battn. K.G.L., 26 Jan. 1806; Lt., 5th Line Battn. K.G.L., 'in the month of April or May 1809'; Capt., 5th Line Battn. K.G.L., 13 May 1815; Half-pay, by reduction; Capt., Half-pay, 'in the 7th Regt. of Infantry in the Hannoverian Army.' *Where serving when wounded*: 'in Spain at the Battle of Talavera de la Reyna 28th July 1809.' *Details of pension*: 'from the years 1812 to 1825 £70 p. an. from June 1825 till now £100.' Commenced 'in the year 1812 the date can not be accurately stated the first Papers being lost.' *Family*: Married in Celle, Kingdom of Hanover, 16 Aug. 1818. One child by 1829. *Title and nature of employment*: 'Captain in the 7th Regt. of Infantry Hannoverian Army.' *Where generally resident during last five years*: 'Verden, Kingdom of Hannover.' [PRO: WO 25/756 f218]. Severely wounded, Talavera, 28 July 1809 [*London Gazette*]. Waterloo. Served in Peninsula 1808–9, 1814. *Beamish*, vol. II, p. 591 ['severely wounded, 28th July 1809, at Talavera, where he was taken prisoner; leg amputated in consequence of a wound in 1831.'].

DUTTON, Thomas, Lt., 6th Foot: *1829 Statement of Service*: 'Born in Birmingham, 1st Jany. 1790. Aged 19 Years on his first Entrance into the Army. Previously served 12 Months in the Warwick Militia. Ensign, 6th Foot, 9th Sept. 1809,

From Warwick Militia. Lieutenant, 6th Foot, 14th April 1813. Half Pay, 24th March 1816. Lieutenant, 71st Foot, 8th April 1825. Dutton returned to England from the Army of occupation in France in Feby. 1816, at which time he found his Mother dangerously ill and said to be in a dying state by her Physician. He consequently applied at the Horse Guards for Leave of Absence, which could not then be granted, but he was told by the Adjt. Genl. that if he went on Half Pay, his doing so under such peculiar circumstances, should not militate against his being re-employed when his family affairs were arranged. Lieut. Dutton made many applications for a reappointment, but did not succeed till the Augmentation in 1815 [sic. ie 1825].' *Wounds received in action*: 'Slightly wounded on the Pyrenees 25 July 1813, but did not receive any grant of Pay, not having been returned in the list of wounded.' *Service abroad*: "Novemr. 1812 to May 1814, Portugal, Spain and France. May 1814 to June 1815, Canada. July 1815 to March 1816, France.' *Family*: Married Mrs Sarah Walker, Widow, 19 Nov. 1821, St Hiliers, Jersey. They had no children by 1830. [PRO: WO 25/799 f31].

DYNELY, Thomas, 2nd Capt., Royal Artillery: 2nd Capt., Royal Artillery, 22 May 1808. Slightly wounded, siege of Ciudad Rodrigo, 19 Jan. 1812 [*London Gazette*]. Mentioned in Wellington's Ciudad Rodrigo dispatch, 20 Jan. 1812 ['The rapid execution produced by the well-directed fire kept up from our batteries, affords the best proof of the merits of the officers and men of the royal artillery... But I must particularly mention ... Captains ... Dynely'] [*London Gazette*]. Recorded as 'Missing', in 'an Affair with the Enemy's Cavalry, in Front of the Village of Majalahonda,' 11 Aug. 1812 ('Royal Horse Artillery') [*London Gazette*]. Served in Lt.

Col. Gardiner's Troop at Waterloo. MGS. Born 1782, died 1860 as lieutenant-general. His letters from the Peninsula published in the *Proceedings of the Royal Artillery Institution XXIII, 1896,* and reprinted as *Letters written by Lieut.-General Thomas Dyneley CD, RA, while on Active Service between the Years 1806 and 1815,* ed. Col. F. A. Whinyates (London, 1984). The wound mentioned at Rodrigo he described as 'a thump on the head from the splinter of a shell', and he said it was on 15 Jan.; 'for the next eight and forty hours I felt a little queer, but since then have not found the least inconvenience' [p.16]. He escaped from captivity within a week when captured in Aug. 1812.

E

EASON, George, Lt., 32nd Foot: Lt., 32nd Foot, 14 Nov. 1805. Severely wounded, Salamanca, 22 July 1812 (1st Battn.) [*London Gazette*].

EASTER, Jeremiah, Ensign/Lt., 24th Foot: *1829 Statement of Service for Retired Officers*: Aged eighteen on first appointment to the Army. Ensign, Warwick Militia, Aug. 1805; Lt., Warwick Militia, 1806; Ensign, 24th Foot, March 1808; Lt., 24th Foot, 26 July 1809; Lt., 23rd Light Dragoons, 1811; Half-pay, 1814, 'at reduction of two Troops.' *Where serving when wounded*: 'Spain. In 1809, 1810 & 1811.' No pension. Not married in 1829. *Where generally resident during last five years*: 'Paris & London.' [PR: WO 25/757 f4]. MGS.

EATON, Charles, Lt., 95th Foot: *1829 Statement of Service for Retired Officers*: Aged 'between 17 & 18' on first appointment to the Army. Ensign, 4th Garrison Battn., 'about Decr. 1806'; 2nd Lt., 95th Foot, 'about February 1807'; 1st Lt., 95th Foot, 'about August 1808'; Capt., 95th Foot, 'about April 1814'; Half-pay, 10th Foot, 13 Aug. 1823, 'From ill health, at the request of the officer.' [Army List gives: 1st Lt., 95th Foot, 7 June 1808; Capt., 95th Foot, 21 April 1814]. *Where serving when wounded*: 'Wounded at L'Urune, afterwards had a paralytic stroke supposed to have arisen from the wound as per certificate from the surgeon of the Regiment sent to Lord Palmerston in 1823.' *Details of pension*: One hundred pounds per annum, commencing Dec. 1822. *Family*: Married in St Mary's, Dover, 30 Dec. 1826. No children by 1829. *Where generally resident during last five years*: 'Dover.' [PRO: WO 25/757 f8]. Severely wounded, Nivelle, 10 Nov. 1813 (2nd Battn.) [*London Gazette*]. Waterloo. MGS. *Simmons*, p. 348.

EBERSTEIN, Franz Botho von, Baron, Lt., 60th Foot: *1829 Statement of Service for Retired Officers*: Aged eighteen years five months at first appointment to the Army. Ensign, 60th Foot, 28 Nov. 1805; Lt., 60th Foot, 10 Dec. 1807; Lt., 13th Royal Veteran Battn., 25 Jan. 1813; Retired List, Full-pay, 7th Royal Veteran Battn., 26 Aug. 1815. 'Invalid and not able to serve'. *Where serving when wounded*: 'In the Peninsula at Buscaco'. *Details of pension*: Seventy pounds per annum, commencing 25 Dec. 1811. *Family*: Married in 'Schoenefeld near Leipzig', 17 Dec. 1815. Two children by 1829. No employment. *Where generally resident during last five years*: 'Schoenefeld near Leipzig'. [PRO: WO 25/776 f350]. Severely wounded, Busaco, 27 Sept. 1810 (5th Battn.) [*London Gazette*]. 'Francis, Baron Eberstein' in Army List.

ECCLES, Cuthbert, Ensign, 61st Foot: *1829 Statement of Service for Retired Officers*: Aged twenty on first appointment to the Army. Ensign, 61st Foot, 19 Nov. 1812; Lt., 61st Foot, 20 May 1814; Half-pay 24 Oct. 1814, on reduction; Lt., 83rd Foot, 10 Aug. 1815; Half-pay, 25 March 1817, on reduction. 'Having recd. three wounds at the Battle of Thoulouse, two through my feet & one in my back while lying on the field of action, I am rendered unable by the former wounds, to walk any distance without considerable pain. I have likewise been afflicted for these 3 years past with a weakness in my back which still continues to cause me excruciating agony at times, (which the surgeon who attends me can certify). Under these circumstances I feel totally unfit for active service, which I would choose were I able, as the increase of pay would be a great object to me in supporting a Wife & five Children, having no situation whatever Civil or Military under government or any private employment, my half pay being my chief support, which if diminished by any means, will reduce me to great distress. I receive nor never did receive any pension for my wounds although for 2 years I was lame. Notwithstanding I place myself at the disposal of the Government.' *Where serving when wounded*: 'At Thoulouse in the South of France.' *Family*: Married in St George's Parish Church, Dublin, 30 April 1819. Five children by 1829. *Where generally resident during last five years*: 'Dublin. 43 Eccles St.' [PRO: WO 25/757 f17]. Letter from Thomas Bolton, Member of the Royal College of Surgeons in Ireland, dated Dublin, 2 Dec. 1828: 'I certify that Mr Cuthbert Eccles 83rd Regt. is affected with pain, & great weakness of his legs & feet, produced always by walking or over exertion, in consequence of the wounds he received in action at Thoulouse, this thro' 2 feet, which shattered the bones. From a personal knowledge of Lieutenant Eccles for these last three years, I can certify that he is constantly affected with pains in the lumbar region, which when aggravated by any exciting cause, or almost standing erect, in consequence of which I consider Lt. Eccles unfit for general or active service.' [PRO: WO 2/5-757 f17 encl.]. Severely wounded, Toulouse, 10 April 1814 (1st Battn.) [*London Gazette*]. MGS.

ECCLES, Hugh, Capt., 61st Foot: Lt., 61st Foot, 14 Aug. 1806; Capt., 61st Foot, 15 April 1813. Severely wounded, Nivelle, 10 Nov. 1813 (1st Battn.) [*London Gazette*]. Temporary pension of one hundred pounds per annum, commencing 11 Nov. 1814, 'for a wound' received at

Bayonne, 1813 [*1818 Pension Return*, pp. 16–17].

+ECCLES, Thomas, Lt., 60th Foot: Ensign, 34th Foot, 2 Nov. 1809; Lt., 34th Foot, 5 March 1812. Exchanged to 60th Foot in 1813. Killed, Nivelle, 10 Nov. 1813 (5th Battn.) [*London Gazette*].

EDGELL, James Charles, Capt., 4th Foot: Capt., 4th Foot, 5 Sept. 1805. Severely wounded, Vittoria, 21 June 1813 ('Edgel') (1st Battn.) [*London Gazette*]. Temporary pension of one hundred pounds per annum, commencing 22 June 1814, 'for wounds' received at Vittoria [*1818 Pension Return*, pp. 4–5]. Waterloo. Died, 1821, on passage to Barbados.

EDGELL, W. B. C., Lt., 4th Foot: Lt., 4th Foot, 5 Sept. 1805. Severely wounded, during 'movements of the Army' [Retreat from Burgos: Villa Muriel], 25 Oct. 1812 (1st Battn.) [*London Gazette*].

EDMONDS, Hamilton, Lt., 66th Foot: *1829 Statement of Service*: Born in Dublin, May 1790. Aged eighteen 'on his first Entrance into the Army.' Ensign, 66th Foot, 6 Feb. 1808. Lt., 66th Foot, 23 Feb. 1809. apt., Half Pay, Unattached, 13 Feb. 1827. Capt., 98th Foot, 3 Jan. 1828. Note added: 'To H. Pay 18 Nov. 1831.' *Battles, sieges and campaigns*: 'In all the Campaigns and in the several Battles &c. &c. (as Lieutenant) in which the 2nd Division of the Peninsular Army ... was Engaged from May 1809 to the Conclusion of the Peace in 1814 with the Exception of such as I was prevented from being present at in consequence of Sickness or being on Duty in the rere.' *Wounds received in action*: 'Slightly at the Battle of Talavera on the 28th July 1809.' *Service abroad*: 'March 1809 to August 1814, Portugal, Spain & France. June 1817 to Septr. 1821, St Helena.' [PRO: WO 25/804 f171].

EDMONDS, John Connell, Ensign, 45th Foot: *1829 Statement of Service for Retired Officers*: Aged nineteen upon first appointment to the Army. 'Served as a Volunteer, obtained Promotion as Ensign in May 1813' [Army List gives: Ensign, 45th Foot, 13 May 1813; Lt., 45th Foot, 8 June 1815]; Half-pay, Aug. 1816, 'at my own desire, in consequence of a Matrimonial arrangement.' 'The undersigned would feel happy of employment whether Civil or Military to assist in supporting educating and otherwise providing for a young family'. *Where serving when wounded*: 'In the Peninsula & South of France: Viz. Vittoria, Thoulouse. Was in every action, skirmish or affair from Vittoria to Thoulouse.' *Details of pension*: Seventy pounds per annum, commencing 'in the early part of 1815'. *Family*: Married in Co. Kilkenny, Ireland, 8 Nov. 1816. Six children by 1829. *Where generally resident during last five years*: 'Chiefly in the West Indies as a Barrack Master, & latterly at Wexford, Ireland, since June 1828.' [PRO: WO 25/757 f38]. Severely wounded, Vittoria, 21 June 1813 (1st Battn.) [*London Gazette*]. Severely wounded, Toulouse, 10 April 1814 (1st Battn.) [*London Gazette*]. Pension 'for wounds' received at Toulouse [*1818 Pension Return*, pp. 12–13].

EDWARDS, Benjamin Hutchins, Ensign, 9th Portuguese Line; Ensign, 43rd Foot: *1829 Statement of Service*: Born in Antigua, 15 March '1794 or 1795.' Aged seventeen 'on his first Entrance into the Army.' Subaltern, 9th Portuguese Line, 1811. Ensign, 43rd Foot, 14 May 1812. Lt., 43rd Foot, 21 Oct. 1819. Half Pay, 25 Dec. 1818, 'By Reduction.' Lt., 98th Foot, 12 March 1829. *Battles, sieges and campaigns*: 'Siege of Badajoz 1812. Salamanca 1812. Nivelle 1813. Nive 1813. Toulouse 1814.' *Wounds received in action*: 'Wounded at

Badajoz 1812. Wounded at Nivelle 1813.' *Service abroad*: '1811 to 1812, Spain. 1812 to 1818, Spain & France.' *Family*: Married Elizabeth Bigmaiden, 2 Oct. 1817, Liverpool. They had four children by 1830. [PRO: WO 25/804 f204]. In Portuguese Service Dec. 1811 to July 1812. MGS. *Challis, Portuguese Army*, p. 54 ['Wd. Badajos 6 Apr. '12.'].

EDWARDS, Wright, Ensign, 59th Foot: Ensign, 59th Foot, 2 Sept. 1812. Severely wounded, storming of San Sebastian, 31 Aug. 1813 ('Ensign') (2nd Battn.) [*London Gazette*]. Lt., 59th Foot, 10 Nov. 1813. MGS.

EELES, Charles, 1st Lt., 95th Foot: 1st Lt., 95th Foot, 9 June 1808. Severely wounded while skirmishing, 9–14 Oct. 1810, ['Lieutenant Eccles'] [*London Gazette*]. Mentioned in Wellington's dispatch, dated Villa Formosa, 1 May 1811 ['The enemy had on the 23d [April] attacked our piquets on the Azava, but were repulsed. Captains Dobbs and Campbell, of the 52d regiment, and Lieutenant Eeles, of the 95th regiment, distinguished themselves upon this occasion, in which the allied troops defended their post against very superior numbers.'] [*London Gazette*, 18 May 1811]. Adjutant, 95th Foot, 30 May 1811. Killed at Waterloo while serving as Major of Brigade under Maj.-Gen. Sir James Kempt. *Dalton*, pp. 4, 19, 204. Brother of William Eeles. *Simmons*, p. 109 [sick], p. 112 [wounded, Sobral, 12 Oct. 1810: 'A body of the enemy's infantry moved against the 1st Division near Sobral, but were repulsed in good style, leaving a number of dead. Lieutenant C. Eeles, who had quitted the detachment and joined his company when I passed through, was shot through the body and put on the road to Lisbon.'], p. 379. *Kincaid, Random Shots*, p. 290 ['At the close of the war ... Eeles minus a thumb'], pp. 332-3. See Crammer, James Henry.

EELES, William, 1st Lt., 95th Foot: *1829 Statement of Service*: Born in Wilmington, Kent, 12 Oct. 1783. Aged twenty-four 'on his first Entrance into the Army.' 2nd Lt., 95th Foot, 12 Dec. 1805; 1st Lt., 95th Foot, 17 Dec. 1807; Adjutant, 95th Foot, 2 Nov. 1809; Capt., 95th Foot, 7 Dec. 1813. Bvt. Major, 95th Foot, 18 June 1815. Major, Rifle Brigade, 8 Jan. 1824. *Battles, sieges and campaigns*: 'Served as 2nd Lieut. with the Army at the attack of Buesnes Aryres in 1806, was engaged with the Enemy three days viz. on 3d 4th & 5th July. Embarked the next year being 1st Lieutenant and went to Sweden with the Army under the Command of Lt. General Sir John Moore, remained under his Command until the Army returned to England after the Battle of Corunna, having been severely wounded during the Retreat. Went again to Portugal with the 1st Battn. of the Regt. in the Spring of 1809, and was obliged to return to England in the Autumn of the same year in consequence of extreme ill health contracted on the Retreat to Corunna. Remained at Home till 1813, when I went with Lord Lyndock to Holland, being then a Captain, was severely wounded at the 2nd Attack on the village of Meuxem near Antwerp, remained with the Army under the Command of the Prince of Orange, and was present at the Battle of Waterloo.' *Wounds received in action*: [see previous section: wounded on retreat to Corunna and in Holland] 'I appeared before a Medical Board, at Bruxelles in the summer of 1814, and received a Gratuity of two Years Pay, as far as I can recollect, viz. One Year as Lieut. and one Year as Captain. On my return to England His Majesty was pleased to grant me a permanent Pension of £100 a Year from 3d February 1815, in consequence of wounds received

while serving in the Rifle Brigade.' *Titles, honorary distinctions and medals*: 'Waterloo Medal, and Brevet Rank of Major.' *Service abroad*: '26th July 1806 to 9th Novr. 1807, Bueonos Aryes South America and on the voyage to and from. 8th April 1808 to 21st Jany. 1809, Sweden, Portugal & Spain. May 1809 till about Octr. 1809, Portugal & Spain. Decr. 1813 to Octr. 1818, Netherlands and France. 21st May 1828 to 31st Decr. 1829, North America.' Not married in 1830. [PRO: WO 25/804 f312]. Waterloo. Died in command of the 1st Battn. Rifle Brigade. K. H. *Dalton*, p. 19 ['Lt.-Col. Wm. Eeles, K. H., who d. in command of 1st Batt. Rifle Brigade in 1837.'], p. 204 ['Afterwards lt.-col. 1st Batt... H.p. 1850.']. Note the contradiction in dates given by Dalton, however, which has him going on half pay thirteen years after he died. *Royal Military Calendar*, vol. V, p. 324.

EGERTON, Richard, Capt., 34th Regt: Capt., Army, 28 Sept. 1804; Capt., 34th Foot, 14 April 1808. Slightly wounded, Albuera, 16 May 1811, while serving as Deputy Assistant Adjutant-General [*London Gazette*]. Waterloo Medal. Military General Service Medal (8 bars – Busaco, Albuhera, Vittoria, Pyrenees, Nivelle, Nive, Orthes, Toulouse). *Bell*, pp. 16, 63–4 ['My Captain, Egerton, or, as the girls called him, "Senor quatro-ojos", or four eyes, as he wore spectacles, was a fine specimen of a Cheshire gentleman and a brave soldier. He had gone on General Hill's staff as chief aide-de-camp, and was always my friend, until he finished off his campaign, a general officer on his native ground.'], p. 82. *Webber*, p. 44. *Dalton*, pp. 13–14 ['As a subaltern served in North America with 29th Foot, and in South America with the 89th Foot. Served with the 2nd Batt. 34th Foot in the Pa., in 1809. In 1810 was appointed to the Staff of Wellington's army. In 1812 was A.D.C. to Lord (then Sir Rowland) Hill, and served in that capacity at Waterloo, and with the army of occupation in France... D. at Eaton Banks, Cheshire, aged 72, 21st Nov., 1854.'].

EGERTON, Thomas, Major, 29th Foot: Capt., Army, 6 March 1795; Capt., 29th Foot, 20 Oct. 1796; Major, Army, 25 April 1808; Major, 29th Foot, 2 Sept. 1808. Wounded, Rolica, 17 Aug. 1808 [*London Gazette*].

ELDER, George, Lt. Col., E.O.P.S.; Lt. Col., 3rd Caçadores: Capt., 95th Foot, 23 May 1805; Bvt. Major, 95th Foot, 13 April 1809; Lt. Col., E.O.P.S., 30 May 1811 'attached to Portuguese Army'. Mentioned in Wellington's Ciudad Rodrigo dispatch, 20 Jan. 1812 ['Lieutenant-Colonel Elder, and the 3d Caçadores, were likewise distinguished upon this occasion.'] [*London Gazette*, 5 Feb. 1812]. Wounded, storming of Badajoz, 6 April 1812, while serving as the Lt. Col. of the 3rd Caçadores [*London Gazette*]. Mentioned in Wellington's Badajoz dispatch, 7 April 1812 ['Lieutenant-Colonel Elder of the 3rd'] [*London Gazette*]. Gold Medal. In Portuguese Service June 1809 to April 1814. Pension of three hundred pounds per annum, commencing 7 April 1813, 'for wounds' received at Badajoz [*1818 Pension Return*, pp. 24–5]. *Challis, Portuguese Army*, p. 54. *Harris*, p. 6 [Following Buenos Ayres: 'Captain Eleder']. *Simmons*, p. 112 [commanding 3rd Caçadores, 13 Oct. 1810]. *Kincaid, Random Shots*, pp. 68–9 [Coa, July 1810: '[Rogers] found himself among some skirmishers of the 3d Caçadores, and within a few yards of a rocky ridge, rising out of the ground ... and he sheltered himself accordingly... This happened to be the first occasion in which the Caçadores had been under fire; they had the highest respect for the bravery of their British officers, and had willingly followed where their colonel had led; but having followed him into the field, they did not see why they should not follow another out of it, and when they saw a red coat take post behind a rock, they all immediately rushed to take advantage of the same cover ... their colonel (Sir George Elder) rode furiously at him with his drawn sword, exclaiming "who are you, you scoundrel, in the uniform of a British officer, setting an example of cowardice to my men? get out of that instantly, or I'll cut you down!" '].

+ELDERHORST, George, Lt., 1st Light Battn. K.G.L.: Joined the K.G.L. 28 Jan. 1806. Lt., 1st Light Battn. K.G.L., 30 Nov. 1810. Slightly wounded, the Nive, 9 Dec. 1813 [*London Gazette*]. Served in the Peninsula 1808–14. *Beamish*, vol. II, p. 635 ['slightly wounded, 9th Dec. 1813, before Bayonne; killed in action before Bayonne, 28th of Feb. 1814.'].

ELGEE, William, Lt., Royal Artillery: 1st Lt., Royal Artillery, 20 May 1808. Slightly wounded, siege of Burgos, 5–10 Oct. 1812 ('Elgie') [*London Gazette*]. MGS.

+ELIGE, John P., Capt., Royal Artillery: Capt., Army, 11 Oct. 1804; Capt., Royal Artillery, 5 Sept. 1811. Killed in the siege of the Forts of St Vincente, St Cayetano, and La Merced at Salamanca, 18–24 June 1812 ('Elijie') [*London Gazette*].

ELLEY, John, Lt. Col., Royal Horse Guards: Lt. Col., Royal Horse Guards, 6 March 1806. Mentioned in Cotton's Llerena dispatch, 11 April 1812 ['Major-General Le Marchant's brigade (which I had sent Colonel Elley to conduct under cover of the heights)... To Lieutenant-Colonel Elley, my Assistant Adjutant-General, I am much indebted for the very great assistance which I derived from him, particularly in conducting my right column to the point of attack.'] [*London Gazette*]. Slightly wounded, Salamanca, 22 July 1812, while serving as AAG [*London Gazette*]. Gold Medal. Wounded, Waterloo, as DAG. Died, Chalderton Lodge, 23 Jan. 1839. *Dalton*, pp. 29-30 ['This distinguished general entered the Army as a private soldier and rose by his own merits. He commanded the rear guard of the cavalry at Talavera.'].

ELLIOT, Gilbert, Capt., 83rd Foot: Capt., 83rd Foot, 14 June 1810. Severely wounded, Orthes, 27 Feb. 1814 (2nd Battn.) [*London Gazette*]. Gold Medal. *Colville*, p. 170 [Letter from John Keane to Sir Charles Colville, 17 March 1814: 'Elliott severely [wounded] in the belly, but also doing well.'].

ELLIOT, Theod. Henry, 1st Lt., Royal Engineers: *1829 Statement of Service for Retired Officers*: 'Appointed Cadet between 14 & 15, first Commission as 2d Lieut. between 17 & 18 years of age.' Cadet, Ordnance, 'Early in 1807'; 2nd Lt., Royal Engineers, 7 May 1810; 1st Lt., Royal Engineers, 1 May 1811; 2nd Capt., Royal Engineers, 18 Nov. 1820; Half-pay, 7 April 1821, by reduction; 2nd Capt., Royal Engineers, 22 March 1825; Capt., 40th Foot, 18 Jan. 1827; Major, unattached, Half-pay, 20 March 1827. *Where serving when wounded*: 'Severely at Badajoz. Severely at Mahidpore E. Indies.' No pension. *Family*: Married in St George's, Hanover Square, 31 Oct. 1823. No children by 1829. *Where generally resident during last five years*: 'Perthshire.' [PRO: WO 25/757 f87].

ELLIS, Conyngham, Capt., 40th Foot: Capt., 40th Foot, 30 Nov. 1809. Severely wounded, Vittoria, 21 June 1813 (1st Battn.) [*London Gazette*]. Waterloo.

ELLIS, Henry Walton, Lt. Col., 23rd Foot: Major, 23rd Foot, 23 Oct. 1804; Lt. Col. 23 April 1807. Slightly wounded, Albuera, 16 May 1811 (1st Battn.) [*London Gazette*]. Wounded during the siege of Badajoz, 1812 [see Wellington's Badajoz dispatch, 7 April 1812: 'Captain Leaky, who commanded the 23rd Regiment, Lieutenant-Colonel Ellis having been wounded during the previous operations of the siege.'] [*London Gazette*]. Severely wounded, Salamanca, 22 July 1812 [*London Gazette*]. Mentioned in Wellington's Salamanca dispatch, 24 July 1812 ['Lieutenant-Colonel Ellis, of the 23rd, commanding General the Honourable Edward Packenham's brigade in the 5th division, during his absence in the command of the 3rd division']. Colonel, Army, 4 June 1814. *Dalton*, p. 129 ['Was severely wounded at Waterloo, in the breast, by a shot from a carbine. On his way to the rear he was thrown from his horse, whilst attempting to jump a ditch, and one of his men carried him to a small outhouse, where his wound was dressed. On the night of 19th June the hovel took fire, and he was with difficulty rescued by Assistant-Surgeon Munro, of the above regt. He died the next day. This gallant and universaally lamented officer was son of Maj.-Gen. John Joyner Ellis, and was a native of Worcester. He had served in Holland, Egypt, America, the West Indies, Spain, Portugal, and France. Monumental inscription in Worcester Cathedral. Buried at Braine L'Alleud, within a few hundred yards of the place where he fell.']. *Speeckaert*, p. 34 [Memorial plaque, located in 'Le Musée Wellington', Waterloo: 'To the memory of / Colonel Sir H. W. Ellis K.C.B. / 25th Reg. R. Welsh Fusiliers/killed in action at Waterloo / 18 June 1815']. *Haythornthwaite, Die Hard*, p. 157 [Albuera: 'Lieutenant-Colonel Henry Walton Ellis of the 23rd had the third and little fingers of his right hand shattered as he was holding his bridle (he survived to fall at Waterloo)'].

ELLIS, Theophilus Thomas, Lt., 14th Light Dragoons: Lt., 14th Light Dragoons, 18 Aug. 1808. Severely wounded, Talavera, 28 July 1809 [*London Gazette*]. Not in 1815 A/L.

ELLIS, William Richard, Cornet, 14th Light Dragoons: Cornet, 14th Light Dragoons, 23 Aug. 1810. Slightly wounded, Fuentes de Onoro, 5 May 1811 [*London Gazette*].

ELLISON, John Montague, Lt., 61st Foot: Ensign, 61st Foot, 28 Feb. 1812. Slightly wounded, Toulouse, 10 April 1814 ('Lieutenant J. H. Ellison') (1st Battn.) [*London Gazette*].

ELLWOOD, Charles William, Lt., 48th Foot: Lt., 48th Foot, 18 May 1808. Recorded as 'Missing', Albuera, 16 May 1811 (2nd Battn.) [*London Gazette*]. Temporary pension of seventy pounds per annum, commencing 17 May 1812, 'for wounds' received at Albuera ('Elwood') [*1818 Pension Return*, pp. 12–13].

ELPHINSTONE, Howard, Capt., Royal Engineers: Capt., Army, 1 July 1800; Capt., Royal Engineers, 1 March 1805. Severely wounded, Rolica, 17 Aug. 1808 [*London Gazette*]. Gold Medal.

+ELWIN, Henry, Ensign/Lt., 44th Foot: Ensign, 44th Foot, 28 Sept. 1809. Wounded, 'dangerously', during 'movements of the Army' [Retreat from Burgos: Villa Muriel], 25 Sept. 1812 ('Elwis') (2nd Battn.) [*London Gazette*]. *Register of dead officers*: Died of wounds, 14 Nov. 1812. Return dated 25 Nov. 1812. [PRO: WO 25/2965]. Obituary, *The Gentleman's Magazine*, Jan. 1813 ['Nov. [1812] At Ciudad Rodrigo, of a wound received in the retreat

from Burgos, Lieut. H. Elwin, 44th Foot.'].

EMES, Thomas, Major, 5th Foot: Capt., 5th Foot, 8 Oct. 1803; Major, 5th Foot, 8 May 1806. Slightly wounded, Rolica, 17 Aug. 1808 [*London Gazette*]. Bvt. Lt. Col., 5th Foot, 4 June 1813. Gold Medal. *Royal Military Calendar*, vol. IV, p. 447.

EMMETT, Anthony, Lt., Royal Engineers: First commissioned in 1808. Lt., Royal Engineers, 24 June 1809. Severely wounded, storming of Badajoz, 6 April 1812 [*London Gazette*]. 2nd Capt., Royal Engineers, 21 July 1813. Served in the expedition to New Orleans. Commanding Royal Engineer on St Helena during Napoleon's captivity. MGS. Maj.-General Emmett died in 1872, aged 82.

ENOCH, John, 2nd Lt./1st Lt., 23rd Foot: *1829 Statement of Service*: Born 1 March 1785, Carmarthen, Wales. Aged twenty-four on his first entrance into the Army. 2nd Lt., 23rd Foot, 30 March 1809; 1st Lt. 15 Aug. 1811; Adjt. 16 Feb. 1813 to 2 Jan. 1823. *Battles, sieges and campaigns*: 'At Walcheren in 1809 & 1810... Siege of Badajos in May 1811... At Fuenta Guinalda, 25, 26 & 27 Sept. 1811... Siege of Ciudad Rodrigo Jany 1812... Siege of Badajos March & April 1812... Battle of Salamanca 22 July 1812... Waterloo 18 June 1815... Storming of Cambray, 24 June 1815.' *Wounds received in action*: 'Slightly at Albuera 16 May 1811. Severely at Salamanca 22 July 1812. One years grant of Pay as Adjutant.' *Titles, honorary distinctions and medals*: 'Medal for Battle of Waterloo.' *Service abroad*: 'Part of 1809 and Part of 1810, Walcheren. 1810 to 1813, Spain & Portugal. 1815 to 1818, France.' *Family*: Married Anne Far, 26 Feb. 1816, Arras, France. They had two children by 1830. [PRO: WO 25/789 f193].

Severely wounded, Salamanca, 22 July 1812 [*London Gazette*]. MGS.

+ENRIGHT, Volunteer, 94th Foot: Killed, Vittoria, 21 June 1813 (1st Battn.) [*London Gazette*].

+ERCK, Gasper, Capt., 7th Foot: Capt., 7th Foot, 25 April 1809. Killed, Albuera, 16 May 1811 (2nd Battn.) [*London Gazette*].

ERSKINE, James, Major/Lt. Col, 48th Foot: Major, Army, 15 Dec. 1803; Major, 48th Foot, 14 Feb. 1805. Slightly wounded, passage of the Douro, 12 May 1809 [*London Gazette*]. Bvt. Lt. Col., 48th Foot, 25 July 1810; Lt. Col., 48th Foot, 20 June 1811. Severely wounded, storming of Badajoz, 6 April 1812 (1st Battn.) [*London Gazette*]. Gold Medal. Pension of three hundred pounds per annum, commencing 7 April 1813, 'for wounds' received at Badajoz [*1818 Pension Return*, pp. 12–13].

ERSKINE, William Howe, Major, 27th Foot: *1829 Statement of Service for Retired Officers*: Aged twelve on first appointment to the Army. 'In consequence of my Father's services, His late Royal Highness the Duke of York was pleased to grant me an Ensigncy at a very early age.' Ensign, 27th Foot, 1794; Lt., 27th Foot, Sept. 1795; Capt., 27th Foot, 1800; Major, 27th Foot, 1805; Bvt. Lt. Col., Army, 1812. 'In consequence of a severe wound which I received at the assault and capture of Badajoz, which materially affected my health, I ... obtained permission to retire upon half pay ... in 1813.' *Where serving when wounded*: 'Badajoz.' *Details of pension*: 'None. I received one years full pay for my wound.' *Family*: Married in St Martin's, London, 12 Aug. 1812. Two children by 1829. *Where generally resident during last five years*: 'Aberdeenshire N.B. [Scotland], and occasionally in England.'

[PRO: WO 25/757 f107]. Severely wounded, storming of Badajoz, 6 April 1812 (3rd Battn.) [*London Gazette*]. Gold Medal.

ESTORFF, Hermann Segeband Gotthelf Friedrich August von, Lt., 2nd Light Dragoons/Hussars K.G.L.: Lt., 2nd Light Dragoons, 11 July 1811. Served in Peninsula in 1811. Waterloo. *Beamish*, vol. II, p. 529 ['Brigade Major... severely wounded, 29th Dec. 1811, at La Nava... [Died] at Osnabruck, 28th April 1827'].

+EUSTACE, Alexander, Capt., 20th Light Dragoons: Capt., Army, 25 June 1803; Capt., 20th Light Dragoons, 3 July 1805. Recorded as 'Missing', Vimeiro, 21 Aug. 1808 [*London Gazette*]. Obituary, *The Gentleman's Magazine*, Feb. 1809 ['15 [Jan.]... At Lisbon, in consequence of the wounds he had received at the battle of Vimiera, on the 21st of August, Capt. Eustace, of the 20th Dragoons, son of the late Lieutenant-General Eustace.']. *Harris*, pp. 53–4 [Vimeiro: 'Tired and overweighted with my knapsack ... I lay where I had fallen for a short time, and watched the cavalry as they gained the enemy. I observed a fine, gallant-looking officer leading them on in that charge. He was a brave fellow, and bore himself like a hero; with his sword waving in the air, he cheered the men on, as he went dashing upon the enemy, and hewing and slashing at them in tremendous style. I watched for him as the dragoons came off after that charge, but saw him no more; he had fallen. Fine fellow! his conduct indeed made an impression upon me that I shall never forget, and I was told afterwards that he was a brother of Sir John Eustace.'].

EUSTACE, William Cornwallis, Lt. Col., Chasseurs Britanniques: *1829 Statement of Service for Retired*

Officers: Lt., Half-pay, 32nd Foot, 27 Sept. 1783; Lt., 6th Foot, 1 Jan. 1797; Capt., Half-pay, 81st Foot, 24 Dec. 1802; Capt., 81st Foot, 25 May 1803; Major, 96th Foot, 17 March 1808; Lt. Col., Chasseurs Britanniques, 23 Aug. 1810; Half-pay, 1814, by reduction; Lt. Col., Grenadier Guards, 25 March 1818; Bvt. Col, 12 Aug. 1819; Half-pay, unattached, 18 May. 1826. *Where serving when wounded*: 'Le Secca near St Sebastian & Salamanca'. *Details of pension*: Three hundred pounds, commencing 1814 '& Renewed 23 July 1825'. *Family*: Married in Marylebone in 1809, and Hanover Square in 1819. Three children by the first marriage, three more by the latter. *Where generally resident during last five years*: 'London'. [PRO: WO 25/757 f134]. Mentioned in Wellington's Fuentes de Onoro dispatch, 8 May 1811 [5 May: 'The main body [of French cavalry] were checked and obliged to retire by the fire of Major-General Houston's division; and I particularly observed the Chasseurs Britanniques, under Lieutenant-Colonel Eustace as behaving in the most steady manner... I particularly request your Lordship's attention to the conduct of ... Lieutenant-Colonel Eustace, of the Chasseurs Britanniques'] [*London Gazette*, 26 May 1811]. Slightly wounded, Heights of Villares, 20–22 June 1812 [*London Gazette*]. Severely wounded, 'in the Operations of the Army', 31 Aug. 1813 [*London Gazette*]. Gold Medal. Pension of three hundred pounds per annum, commencing 1 Sept. 1814, 'for a wound' received at St Sebastian, 1813 [*1818 Pension Return*, pp. 24–5]. *Wheeler*, p. 68 [Sept. 1811: 'Colonel Custis [sic] and Captain Napier are the only British in the Regiment.'].

+EVANS, Edward, Ensign, 38th Foot: Ensign, 38th Foot, 18 Jan. 1810. Killed, storming of Badajoz, 6 April 1812 [*London Gazette*].

EVANS, George De Lacy, Lt., 3rd Dragoons: *1829 Statement of Service for Retired Officers*: Aged 'about 18' on first appointment to the Army. Ensign, 22 Foot, 1 Feb. 1807; Lt., 22nd Foot, 'end of 1808' [Army List gives 1 Dec. 1808]; Lt., 3rd Dragoons [Army List gives 26 March 1812]; Capt., 5th West India Regt., 12 Jan. 1815; Bvt. Major, 'April or May 1815'; Bvt. Lt. Col., 18 June 1815. 'Placed on the half pay during his staff service with the army in France... Subsequently the 5th W. I. Regt. was reduced, before the Duke of Wellington's several staff in France was dissolved. In 1820 served for a short time on the staff in Scotland.' *Where serving when wounded*: 'America & Peninsula.' No pension or grant. *Where generally resident during last five years*: 'London'. [PRO: WO 25/757 f111]. Served in the American War of 1812, including the battle at Bladensburg. With a very small force of infantry he captured the Congress House in Washington. Also fought at Baltimore and New Orleans. Waterloo. Commanded the British Legion in Spain, 1835–7, and the 2nd Division during the Crimean War. MGS. NGS. *Dalton* [Born Moig, Ireland, 1787. Educated at the Military Academy, Woolwich. Col.-in-Chief, 21st Fusiliers, 1853. Lt.-Gen. 20 June 1854. Died 9 Jan. 1870, and is buried in Kensal Green Cemetery.] Famous for leading the British Legion in the Carlist War and the 2nd Division in the Crimea; became General in 1861. Spiers, E. M., *Radical General: Sir George De Lacy Evans 1787-1870* (Manchester, 1983).

+EVANS, John, Capt., 24th Foot: Ensign, 24th Foot, 27 May 1796; Lt., 24th Foot, 7 June 1797; Capt., 24th Foot, 13 Jan. 1806. Severely wounded, 'since dead', Talavera, 28 July 1809 [*London Gazette*]. *Register of officers' effects*: Died of wounds, 31 July 1809, Talavera. Single. Effects totalled £57. 2s. 10d, 'ordered to J. Evans Esq. 12 Aug. 1811'. [PRO: WO 25/2963].

EVANS, John, Lt., 28th Foot: Ensign, 28th Foot, 1 March 1810. Slightly wounded, Vittoria, 21 June 1813 (Lieutenant) (1st Battn.) [*London Gazette*]. MGS.

EVANS, John, Lt., 83rd Foot: Lt., 83rd Foot, 21 June 1810. Slightly wounded, Salamanca, 22 July 1812 (2nd Battn.) [*London Gazette*]. MGS. *Mullen*, p. 465 ['HP 23/7/20'].

EVATT, J. H., Lt., 57th Foot: Lt., 57th Foot, 28 Sept. 1804. Slightly wounded, Albuera, 16 May 1811 (1st Battn.) [*London Gazette*].

EVEREST, Henry Bennett, Lt., 6th Foot: Lt., 6th Foot, 1 March 1807. Slightly wounded, Pyrenees, 2 Aug. 1813 (1st Battn.) [*London Gazette*]. MGS.

EVERNDERN, Thomas, Ensign, 3rd Foot: Ensign, 3rd Foot, 21 May 1812. Slightly wounded, the Nive, 13 Dec. 1813 ('Everdern') (1st Foot) [*London Gazette*].

+EVERT, George, Lt., 5th Line Battn. K.G.L.: Capt., 5th Line Battn. K.G.L., 7 Dec. 1805. Served in the Peninsula 1808-9. *Beamish*, vol. II, p. 634 ['Killed in the battle of Talavera de la Reyna, 28th July 1809.'].

EWART, John F., Capt., 52nd Foot: *1829 Statement of Service*: Born in Berlin, 29 July 1787. Aged sixteen years three months 'on his first Entrance into the Army.' Ensign, 52nd Foot, 1 Nov. 1803. Lt., 52nd Foot, May 1806. Capt., 3rd Garrison Battn., April 1806. Capt., 52nd Foot, June 1806 [Army List gives Capt., Army, 17 April 1806; Capt., 52nd Foot, 8 May 1806]. Major, Royal York Rangers, Nov. 1812. Lt. Col., 'Y. Chasseurs', Sept. 1814. Lt. Col., Half Pay, 5th West India Regt., April 1817, 'in consequence of temporary ill health on returning from West Indies.' Lt. Col., 67th Foot, Feb. 1818. Lt. Col., Inspecting Field Officer Coventry District, May 1826. *Battles, sieges and campaigns*: 'Capt. 52nd Light Infantry. 1807. Copenhagen ... 1808. Battle of Vimiera ... 1808-9. Campaigns under General Sir John Moore. 1809. Expedition to the Scheldt ... 1811-12. Campaigns with the Light Division... Battles of Fuentes D'Onor, Siege of Ciudad Rodrigo, last Siege of Badajoz, and Battle of Salamanca. 1815. Lieut. Colonel 67th Foot, Siege of Asseirgur, East Indies, as Brigadier under General Sir J. Doveton.' *Distinguished conduct*: 'Captain 52nd Foot, with the Light Division at the storming of Ciudad Rodrigo, also with the Party that captured Fort Peinrine in front of Badajoz, 1812. Lieut. Colonel York Chasseurs, Guadaloupe, named in Despatches by General Sir J. Leith, 1815. Lieut. Colonel 67th Foot, named in Despatches by General Sir J. Doveton, and General Sir J. Malcolm, Siege of Asseirgur, 1819. Named in General Orders on Commanding Sholapoor Brigade with Descan, East Indies for 15 Months, by General Sir Charles Colville, 1821-1822.' *Wounds received in action*: 'Wounded in the right Leg at the Battle of Vimiera 21st August 1808, and Wounded through the right arm at the Siege of Badajoz, March 1812. One Year's Pay as Captain was granted for the above wounds.' *Titles, honorary distinctions and medals*: 'French Order of the Fleur de Lis, transmitted by General Sir J. Leith, after the Capture of Guadaloupe in 1815. Appointed Companion of the Most Honorable Military Order of the Bath, by His late Majesty, George the 4th, October 1818.' *Service abroad*: 'July 1807 to October 1807, Copenhagen. July 1808 to Feby. 1809, Portugal & Spain. July 1809 to Novr. 1809, Walcheren. Feby. 1811 to Jan. of 1813, Portugal & Spain. June 1813 to Septr. 1814, West Indies. Jan. of 1815 to Septr. 1816, West Indies. May 1818 to June 1823, East

Indies.' *Family*: Married Lasinia Isabella, 'Daughter of the late Admiral Sir Chas. Brisbane K.C.B.', 1 Jan. 1816, St Vincent, West Indies. They had five children by 1830. [PRO: WO 25/805 f53]. Wounded, Vimeiro, 21 Aug. 1808 [*London Gazette*]. Slightly wounded, siege of Badajoz, 26 March 1812 [*London Gazette*]. MGS.

+**EWART, Walter, Lt., 36th Foot**: Ensign, 36th Foot, 13 Nov. 1805; Lt., 36th Foot, 20 April 1807. Slightly wounded, Vimeiro, 21 Aug. 1808 (Lt. 'Edwards') [*London Gazette*]. Severely wounded, Salamanca, 22 April 1812 ('Hewart') [*London Gazette*]. *Register of dead officers*: Died of wounds, 27 July 1812. Return dated 25 Aug. 1812. [PRO: WO 25/2965].

+**EWING, Daniel, Lt., 74th Foot**: Lt., 74th Foot, 7 June 1810. Severely wounded, Salamanca, 22 July 1812 [*London Gazette*]. Severely wounded, Orthes, 27 Feb. 1814 [*London Gazette*]. *Register of dead officers*: 'Ewing, Dan., 7th Foot [sic]'. Died of wounds, France, 2 March 1814. Return dated March 1814. [PRO: WO 25/2965].

EWING, James, Ensign, 47th Foot: Ensign, 47th Foot, 23 Sept. 1812. Slightly wounded, the Nive, 10 Dec.

1813 (2nd Battn.) [*London Gazette*].

EYRE, Charles, Lt., 1st Foot: *1829 Statement of Service for Retired Officers*: Aged fifteen on first appointment to the Army. Ensign, 1st Foot, 18 July 1809; Lt., 1st Foot, 18 Oct. 1810; Capt., 1st Foot, 23 Nov. 1823; Half-pay, 2 June 1827. *Where serving when wounded*: 'St Sebastian on the Peninsula & East Indies. Disabled from wounds received on the Peninsula.' *Details of pension*: '70 Pounds a year from the 25th December 1813 to the 25th June 1826, and from that period made one Hundred.' *Where generally resident during last five years*: 'Came home in 1826 from the East Indies disabled, since in London generally.' [PRO: WO 25/757 f138]. Recorded as 'Missing', 'at the Siege of St Sebastian', 7–27 July 1813 (3rd Battn.) [*London Gazette*].

+**EYRE, Gervase Anthony, Ensign, 1st Foot Guards**: Ensign, 1st Foot Guards, 9 Feb. 1809. Killed, Barossa, 5 March 1811, while serving on the Staff as Acting ADC to Col. Wheatly [*London Gazette*]. Obituary, *The London Gazette*, April 1811, p. 396 ['March 5. At the battle of Barrosa, in his 20th year, Ensign Eyre, only son of A. H. E. esq. M.P. for Notts.'].

F

FAHLE, William, Ensign/Adjutant, 1st Light Battn. K.G.L.: Ensign and Adjutant, 1st Light Battn. K.G.L., 22 Feb. 1810. Slightly wounded, Albuera, 16 May 1811 [*London Gazette*]. Served in Peninsula 1808-14. *Beamish*, vol. II, p. 609 ['severely wounded, 27th Feb. 1814, before Bayonne.'].

FAIR, David, Lt., 81st Foot: Ensign, 81st Foot, 20 March 1806; Lt., 81st Foot, 7 Jan. 1808. Wounded, 'in the Army lately in Spain' (2nd Battn.) [*March 1809 Army List*, p. 105]. *Monthly Return*, 2nd Battn., dated 25 Feb. 1809: 'Wounded, in the Naval Hospl. Plymouth' [PRO: WO 17/202].

+FAIRTLOUGH, Edward, Lt., 5th Foot: Ensign, 5th Foot, 2 Nov. 1808; Lt., 5th Foot, 10 Oct. 1811. Slightly wounded, storming of Ciudad Rodrigo, 19 Jan. 1812 [*London Gazette*]. Killed, siege of Badajoz, 24 March 1812 ('Fairclough') (2nd Battn.) [*London Gazette*]. 'Killed before Badajos, 25 March 1825.' Return dated 25 April 1812. [PRO: WO 25/2965].

FALCK, Neil, Lt., 1st Foot: Lt., 1st Foot, 21 July 1809. Severely wounded, Salamanca, 22 July 1812 ('Falk') [*London Gazette*].

FALKINER, Samuel, Lt., 61st Foot: *1829 Statement of Service for Retired Officers*: Aged sixteen on first appointment to the Army. Ensign, 61st Foot, 25 Sept. 1806; Lt., 61st Foot, 11 June 1807; Capt., 61st Foot, 5 Feb. 1818; Half-pay, 7 June 1819, by reduction; Capt., 23rd Foot, 20 Nov. 1823; Half-pay, unattached, 22 Feb. 1827, 'at my own request feeling from wounds & climate unfit for foreign service.' *Where serving when wounded*: 'Spain.' *Details of pension*: Seventy

pounds, commencing '1813 or 14'. *Where generally resident during last five years*: 'Since placed on H.P. at Brighton.' [PRO: WO 25/758 f7]. Severely wounded, Salamanca, 22 July 1812 ('Falkener') [*London Gazette*]. Temporary pension of seventy pounds per annum, commencing 23 July 1813, 'for a wound' received at Salamanca [*1818 Pension Return*, pp. 16–17]. MGS.

+FANE, Charles, Lt. Col., 59th Foot: Lt. Col., 59th Foot, 20 June 1805. Wounded, 'in the Army lately in Spain' (2nd Battn.) [*March 1809 Army List*, p. 105]. Severely wounded, Vittoria, 21 June 1813 (2nd Battn.) [*London Gazette*]. *Register of officers' effects*: Died of wounds, 21 June 1813, Vittoria. Single. 'Colonel Fane's Effects in Spain were left to his Servants.' [PRO: WO 25/2964]. Obituary, *The Gentleman's Magazine*, July 1813, p. 94 ['At Vittoria, of the wound he received in the great battle, Lieut.-col. Fane, 59th reg. He was one of the most promising officers in the service. Early in life he went over to Germany, where he studied the military science; from thence he proceeded to Egypt, and served with distinguished credit under General Abercrombie. He was in the expedition to the Scheldt, and under Sir John Moore in Spain. In the battle of Corunna he was dangerously wounded in the head, part of his skull being carried away. Just before he embarked for Spain to join his regiment under Lord Wellington, he was advised to be trepanned; but he preferred joining his regiment, saying, that when he returned the operation should be performed! – Gallant spirit! he returned no more. In the battle of Vittoria he had his leg and part of his thigh carried off, but survived the wound some days. He wrote to some of his relations after he had received his wound. His last moments were easy and quiet. He was buried at Vittoria, the scene of his latest glory and of his death. But Government will, probably, cause a monument to be erected in this country to his memory.']. Buried in the garden of a convent in Vittoria: see obituary of Lt. Col. John L. Wier, *The Gentleman's Magazine*, Nov. 1813, p. 504.

+FANE, George A. S., Lt., 59th Foot: Lt., 59th Foot, 15 Oct. 1812. Killed, storming of San Sebastian, 31 Aug. 1813 (2nd Battn.) [*London Gazette*]. *Register of officers' effects*: 'Effects left to His Cousin Ens. Fane.' [PRO: WO 25/2964].

FARIS, George F., Lt., 88th Foot: Lt., 88th Foot, 11 July 1809. Severely wounded, storming of Ciudad Rodrigo, 19 Jan. 1812 ('Fairris') [*London Gazette*]. Severely wounded, siege of Badajoz, 18 March 1812 ('Farris') [*London Gazette*]. Slightly wounded, Vittoria, 21 June 1813 ('Faires') (1st Battn.) [*London Gazette*].

FARMER, Thomas, Lt., 23rd Foot: 1st Lt., 23rd Foot, 29 Oct. 1805. Severely wounded, storming of Badajoz, 6 April 1812 [*London Gazette*]. Capt., 23rd Foot, 16 April 1812. Killed, Waterloo.

FARMER, William John George, 2nd Lt./1st Lt., 95th Foot: *1829 Statement of Service for Retired Officers*: 2nd Lt., 95th Foot, '1811 or 1812'; 1st Lt., 95th Foot, '1811 or 1812'; Half-pay, 9th Foot, 'at the request of the officer viz. private motives.' [Army List gives: 2nd Lt., 95th Foot, 31 Oct. 1811; 1st Lt., 95th Foot, 6 Dec. 1813]. Five years service on full-pay. *Where serving when wounded*: 'Severe wounded at Tarbes, and New Orleans.' *Family*: Married in the British Embassy, Paris, 17 Feb. 1827. No children by

1829. *Where generally resident during last five years*: 'Paris'. [PRO: WO 25/758 f26]. Severely wounded, 'in Action with the Enemy', 20 March 1814 (3rd Battn.) [*London Gazette*]. MGS. See Firman, Walter.

+FARQUHARSON, Donald, Ensign/ Lt., 42nd Foot: Ensign, 42nd Foot, 25 Oct. 1810; Lt., 42nd Foot, 17 March 1813. Severely wounded, Toulouse, 10 April 1814 (1st Battn.) [*London Gazette*]. *Hurt*, p. 78 ['D.O.W., Toulouse, Apl. 10']. *Anton*, pp. 64–5, 70 ['I set about constructing a hut that should be proof against wind and rain. One of my officers (Lieutenant D. Farquharson) very kindly made an offer of any pecuniary assistance I might require, and gave me a blanket to replace that which was lost. The latter I accepted gratefully, it was more than money could purchase, the former I declined, as I was far from being in want; but the offer, which I am certain was sincerely intended for my acceptance, impressed me with the most sincere regard for that officer."], pp. 125, 136 [Toulouse: 'I had occasion to remark, before entering France, of Lieutenant Farquharson... He fell this day, by my side, on the road skirting the redoubt, and before we entered it. It was impossible to render him any assistance at the time, we were so closely engaged; but when the action closed, I returned and found him where he fell. He had been for a few minutes in the power of the enemy, and had been stripped of his sash, sword, epaulettes, and money, but no other violence had been offered to him. I got him conveyed to a house which was enclosed in another redoubt, and now filled in every place with our wounded. From this he was removed on the morning of the 12th, to Toulouse, where he died of his wounds. In him, I may say, I lost a friend.'].

**FARRINGTON, Charles Henry, Lt.,
4th Foot:** Lt., 4th Foot, 29 July 1813.
Slightly wounded, the Nive, 11 Dec.
1813 (1st Battn.) [*London Gazette*].

**FAUNCE, Edmund, Lt. Col., 4th
Foot:** *1829 Statement of Service*:
Born 28 Nov. 1775, Quebec, Canada.
Aged twenty on his first entrance
into the Army. Ensign, 4th Foot, 2
Dec. 1795; Lt. 13 Oct. 1796; Adju-
tant 19 Oct. 1800; Capt. 6 Aug. 1803;
Major 14 Feb. 1811; Lt. Col., Army,
4 June 1811; Lt. Col., 4th Foot, 1
Aug. 1811. *Battles, sieges and
campaigns*: 'As Lieut in the Battles
of the 2nd & 6th Oct. 1799 in
Holland under the Duke of York. As
Captain with the Army in Hanover
in 1805 & 1806 under Lord Cathcart.
At Copenhagen in 1807 under Lord
Cathcart. With the expedition to
Sweden in 1808 under Sir John
Moore. With the Army in Portugal
and Spain, & Retreat to Corunna in
1808 and 1809 under Sir John
Moore. With the Army in Walcheren
in 1809 under Lord Chatham. As
Major, in Portugal and Spain during
the Campaigns of 1811 and 1812
under the Duke of Wellington. At
the storming of Badajoz 6th April
1812, at the Battle of Salamanca
22d July 1812. With the Army in
France in 1814 under the Duke of
Wellington at the Siege of Bayonne.
At the Battle of Bladensberg and
capture of Washington the 24th
August 1814 under Major General
Ross. In action near Baltimore in
1814 under Genl. Ross and Col.
Brooke. At New Orleans in 1814 and
1815 under Major General Beane
and Pakenham. With the Army of
occupation in France from 1816 to
1818 under the Duke of Wellington.
Served with the Regiment in the
West Indies, latterly as Lt. Colonel.
As Lt. Colonel in Portugal from 1826
to 1828 under William Clinton.'
Distinguished conduct: 'Recommended by Major General Pringle
to the Duke of Wellington for his
conduct in the command of the
Light Infantry Companies of the

Brigade in the Battle of Salamanca,
22d July 1812. Commanded the
Regiment at the Battle of Bladens-
bergh, was mentioned in Major
Genl. Ross's despatch and recommended for promotion. Commanded the Regiment in Action
wth the Enemy on the 12th Sept.
1814 near Baltimore, and was
mentioned by Colonel Arthur
Brooke in his official letter.' *Wounds
received in action*: 'Wounded at the
storming of Badjoz on the 6th April
1812 when in command of the party
carrying the Escalading ladders.
Received a years pay. Severely
wounded in action with the Enemy
at New Orleans on the 8th January
1815, received a year's pay, and a
temporary Pension of £200, last
date 19th Sept. 1826.' *Titles,
honorary distinctions and medals*:
'Received a Medal for Commanding
a Light Infantry Battn. at the Battle
of Salamanca on the 22d July 1812,
and nominated a Companion of the
Bath.' *Service abroad*: '10 April
1796 to 28 Oct. 1797, Quebec &
Montreal; 15 Sept. 1799 to 30 Nov.
1799, Holland; 17 Nov. 1805 to 18
Feby. 1806, Hanover; 1 Augt. 1807 to
6 Nov. 1807, Copenhagen; 17 May
1808 to 20 July 1808, Sweden; 25
Augt. 1808 to 31 Jany. 1809,
Portugal & Spain; 1 Augt. 1809 to 16
Sept. 1809, Walcheren; 4 Novr. 1810
to 23 Feby 1813, Portugal & Spain;
16 March 1814 to 30 May 1815,
France & America; 12th April 1816
to 8 Novr. 1818, France; 1st April
1819 to 30 Sept. 1820, Trinidad; 11
Augt. 1822 to 24 Sept. 1823, Barba-
does; 6 Augt. 1825 to 16 March 1826,
Antigua; 27 Decr. 1826 to 29 April
1828, Portugal.' *Family*: Married, 12
Oct. 1805, Miss Goddard, in
London. Wife still living as of 19 July
1830, by which date they had seven
children. [PRO: WO 25/785 f328].
Slightly wounded, storming of
Badajoz, 6 April 1812 [*London
Gazette*]. Gold Medal.

**+FAVELL, Samuel, Capt., 61st
Foot:** Capt., 61st Foot, 6 April 1809.

Severely wounded, 'since dead', Salamanca, 22 July 1812 ('Faville') [*London Gazette*].

+**FAVELL, William Anthony, Ensign, 61st Foot:** Ensign, 61st Foot, 18 Nov. 1812. Severely wounded, 'since dead', Toulouse, 10 April 1814 (1st Battn.) [*London Gazette*]. *Hurt*, p. 79 ['D.O.W., Toulouse, Apl. 10']. *Register of dead officers*: 'Faville'. Died of wounds, 24 July 1812. Return dated 24 July 1812 [PRO: WO 25/2965].

+**FAWCETT, Ralph, Capt., 57th Foot:** Capt., 57th Foot, 13 Dec. 1810. Killed, Albuera, 16 May 1811 (1st Battn.) [*London Gazette*]. *Haythornthwaite, Die Hard*, p. 153 [Albuera: 'Emulating his commanding officer [William Inglis], Captain Ralph Fawcett refused to be carried away when wounded but lay by his company, calling on them to fire low and steadily; but unlike Inglis, who survived, Fawcett died of his injuries.'].

+**FAWSON, Jonas, Lt., 4th Foot:** Lt., 4th Foot, 4 June 1807. Killed, storming of San Sebastian, 31 Aug. 1813 [*London Gazette*].

+**FEARON, Peter, Capt., 31st Foot; Lt. Col., 6th Caçadores:** Capt., 31st Foot, 17 Aug. 1809. Severely wounded, 'since dead', 'in Action with the Enemy', 15 Feb. 1814, as Capt., 6th Caçadores ('Pedro Fearon') [*London Gazette*]. *Register of officers' effects*: 'Captn. 31st, Lt. Col. Portuguese Service'. Died of wounds, 16 Feb. 1814. Single. [PRO: WO 25/2963]. *Hurt*, p. 77 ['Bt. Maj. Fearon, D.O.W., Garris, Feb. 15 [1814]']. In Portuguese Service July 1810 to Feb. 1814. Gold Medal. *Challis, Portuguese Army*, p. 54 ['Lt.-Col. 6 Cacad... K/A Garris 15 Feb. '14.'].

FEHRZEN, Oliver George, Capt., 53rd Foot: Capt., 53rd Foot, 31 Oct. 1805. Severely wounded, Salamanca, 22 July 1812 ('Fehrsen') (2nd Battn.) [*London Gazette*].

FEILDING, George, 1st Lt., 23rd Foot: *1829 Statement of Service*: Born 14 Jan. 1792, Hartforth, County of York. 2nd Lt., 23rd Foot, 24 May 1810; 1st Lt., 23rd Foot, 7 Nov. 1811; Capt., 23rd Foot, 6 June 1822. *Battles, sieges and campaigns*: 'Portugal 1811 Fuente Guinal. Spain 1812 Badajos Siege & Capture. Pyrennees 1813 Bera Nivelle Nive. France 1814 Orthes & Toulouse. Netherlands & France 1815 Waterloo & Cambray.' *Wounds received in action*: 'At Badajos severely in breast & Shoulder. At Waterloo slightly.' *Titles, honorary distinctions and medals*: 'Waterloo Medal.' *Service abroad*: 'July 1811 to July 1812, Portugal. August 1813 to June 1814, Pyrenees & France. March 1815 to Novr. 1818, Netherlands & France. Decr. 1823 to Jany. 1827, Gibraltar. Jany 1827 to March 1828, Portugal. March 1828 to Decr. 1829, Gibraltar.' Unmarried in 1830. [PRO: WO 25/789 f173] Severely wounded, storming of Badajoz, 6 April 1812 ('Fielding') [*London Gazette*].

FENNELL, James Gubbins, Lt., 87th Foot: Lt., 87th Foot, 3 Dec. 1807. Severely wounded, Barossa, 5 March 1811 (2nd Battn.) [*London Gazette*].

FENSHAM, Daniel, 1st Lt., 95th Foot: *1829 Statement of Service for Retired Officers*: Aged twenty-three on his first appointment to the Army. 2nd Lt., 95th Foot, 28 March 1811; 1st Lt., 95th Foot, 29 Oct. 1812 [Army List gives 22 Oct. 1812]; Half-pay, 25 Dec. 1818, by reduction. *Where serving when wounded*: 'South of France'. *Details of pension*: Seventy pounds per annum, commencing 11 Nov. 1813. Not married in 1829. *Where generally resident during last five years*: 'No general residence.' [PRO: WO 25/758 f63]. Severely wounded,

Nivelle, 10 Nov. 1813 ('Daniel Fendam') (1st Battn.) [*London Gazette*]. Pension of seventy pounds per annum, commencing 11 Nov. 1814, for 'loss of an eye' in 'Navarre' (sic), 1813 [*1818 Pension Return*, pp. 22–3]. 'David Fensham' in Army List.

+FENWICK, Joseph, Lt., 3rd Foot; Capt., 7th Portuguese Line: Ensign, 3rd Foot, 27 Nov. 1806; Lt., 3rd Foot, 10 Dec. 1807. 'Died of wounds... Date of Decease: not stated'. Return dated 25 Jan. 1811. [PRO: WO 25/2965]. Obituary, *The Gentleman's Magazine*, Supplement 1810, p. 669 ['Lately... In Portugal, in attacking about 100 French with only 30 Portuguese chasseurs, Major Fenwick, of the Buffs. He beat the Enemy, and took from them a considerable convoy of cattle, but was mortally wounded, and seven men killed.']. Wellington's dispatch, Cartaxo, 15 Dec. 1810 ['I am concerned to forward the enclosed report from Marshal Sir William Beresford, of the death of Captain Fenwick, the late Commandant of Obidos. During the last two months he had been engaged more than twenty times with the enemy's foraging parties, and I have had several opportunities of reporting his success. Upon this last occasion he had made an attack upon, and had driven in, a party, consisting of eighty grenadiers, in the neighbourhood of Evora, near Alcobaca, which had come there in search of provisions, having under his command a detachment of the same number of the militia of the Garrison of Obidos, and was pursuing them when he was mortally wounded, and he died on the 10th: we have thus sustained a great loss, and he is lamented by all who had any knowledge of his gallantry and exertions.']. Beresford's dispatch, Carlaxo, 11 Dec. 1810 ['My Lord, It is with much regret that I communicate to you

the loss of Captain Fenwick (Lieutenant in the Buffs,) who died the following day of the wounds he received in the attack he made upon the enemy at Evora, on the 8th instant. Your Lordship will equally feel with me the loss of this enterprising gallant young officer, who, since the enemy's being in their late and present position, has been of so much service, and who has in such various instances given proof of his talents and undaunted courage.' [*London Gazette*, 1 Jan. 1811]. In Portuguese Service July 1809 to Dec. 1810. *Challis, Portuguese Army*, p. 54 ['Capt. 7 Line... K/A Obidos 4 Dec. '10']. *Cocks*, pp. 92, 96 ['Poor Fenwick has died of his wounds.'].

FENWICK, William, Lt. Col., 34th Foot: Lt. Col., 34th Foot, 15 Dec. 1808. Severely wounded, Pyrenees, 25 July 1813 [*London Gazette*]. Gold Medal. Three hundred pounds per annum pension, commencing 26 July 1814, for 'loss of a leg' in the Pyrenees. [*1818 Pension Return*, pp. 10–11]. *Sherer*, p. 258 [Aretesque, Pass of Maya, 25 July 1813: 'Among other brave victims... our colonel desperately wounded']. Haythornthwaite introduction to 1996 ed. of *Sherer*, n.p. [Aretesque: 'the battalion's commanding officer, Lieut. Col. William Fenwick, who was grievously wounded when shot from his horse as he led the uphill scramble in an attempt to relieve the picquet.'].

+FERGUSON, Dugald, Capt., 95th Foot: 1st Lt., 52nd Foot, 16 Aug. 1804; Capt., 95th Foot, 23 Nov. 1809. Wounded, Salamanca, 22 July 1812. *Register of dead officers*: 2nd Battn. Died, 16 Aug. 1812, at Salamanca. Return dated: 25 Aug. 1812 [PRO: WO 25/2965]. *Register of officers' effects*: 2nd Battn. 'Ferguson, Dond.' 'Died of sickness, 6 April 12, Badajoz [sic].' 'Effects sold by Col. Ware and amount paid his Mother.' [PRO: WO 25/2964]. *Brett-James*, p.

71 ['A clear notion of the extensive kit an officer might have with him while campaigning is given by the following list of effects belonging to Captain Dugold Ferguson of the 2/95th Rifle Corps, who died from wounds received at the battle of Salamanca. His effects, auctioned on 17 August 1812, and shared among fifteen officers, were as follows: 1 tarpaulin bed, 1 pair saddle bags, a set of handkerchiefs, 1 portmanteau, 1 pair gloves and braces, 1 morning gown, 1 writing case, 1 pair spurs and hooks, 6 old towels, 1 silver watch, 1 horse, 1 mule, 2 pairs trousers, 1 saddle and bridle, 1 set of old boots, 1 boat cloak, 2 boots, 8 silk handkerchiefs, 1 belt, 1 pair boots, 1 pair gloves, 1 canteen, 1 waistcoat, 1 spy glass, 1 sword, 6 shirts, flannel drawers and waistcoat, 1 sash, 1 looking-glass, 11 pairs socks, dressing brushes, 1 shaving case. From this total of 467.5 dollars, the equivalent of £100 at the time, were deducted funeral expenses amounting to 14.5 dollars: "Paid nurse, 3 dollars. For digging grave, 3 dollars. Batman, 2 dollars. Coffin and other funeral expenses, 6.5 dollars." ']. Note: the *Register of Officers' Effects* is not accurate: Dugold, not Donald, Ferguson, died in Salamanca, not Badajoz, on 16 Aug., not 6 April.

FERGUSSON, James, Capt., 43rd Foot: *1829 Statement of Service*: 'Born in Cork, Ireland, 17th March 1788. Aged 13 years 150 days on his first Entrance into the Army. Ensign, 18th Foot, 20th Augt. 1801. Lieut, 18th Foot, 9th Feby. 1804. Lieut., 43rd Foot, 7th Aug. 1804. Captain, 43rd Foot, [1] Decr. 1806. Major, 79th Foot, 3rd Decr. 1812. Major, 85th Foot, 25th Jany. 1813. Lieut. Coll., 3rd Foot, 16th May 1814. Half Pay, 25th Feby. 1816, by Reduction of the 2nd Battalion Buffs. Lieut. Coll., 88th Foot, 12th Aug. 1819. Lieut. Coll., 52nd Foot, 2nd June 1825.' *Battles, sieges and campaigns*: 'As Captain: Vimeira

21st Aug. 1808. Corunna 16th Jany. 1809. Walcheren & Islands in the Scheld 15th Aug. 1809. Almeida on the Coa 24th July 1810. Battle of Busaco 27th Sept. 1810. Massina's retreat with the Light division. Pombal 11th March 1811. Redinha 12th March 1811. Miranda de Co[ ] 14th March 1811. Foz de Aronce 17th March 1811. Sabugal 3rd April 1811. Fuentes d'Onoro 3rd & 5th May 1811. San Francisco out work of Ciudad Rodrigo 8th Jany. 1812. Storm of Ciudad Rodrigo 19th Jany. 1812. Storm of Badajoz 6th April 1812. Salamanca 22nd July 1812. San Munoz 17th Novr. 1812. As Major: Biddassoa 7th Octr. 1813. Niville 10th Nov. 1813. Nive from 9th to 13th Decr. 1813. Investment Bayonne 26 Feby. 1814. Served in the Campaigns of 1808, part of 1809, 1810, 1811, 1812, 1813, & 1814, in Spain, Portugal & South of France & Walchareen in 1809.' *Distinguished conduct*: 'Volunteered with my Company at the Escalade of the San Francisco out work of Ciudad Rodrigo, 8th Jany. 1812. Commanded as a volunteer the Storming Party of the 43rd Regt. at the Storm of Ciudad Rodrigo, 19th Jany. 1812. Appointed to the Command of the Buffs, by the Duke of Wellington, Vide. Genl. order issued by his Grace in May 1814.' Wounds received in action: 'Slightly wounded at Vimeira 21st Augt. 1808. Severely wounded in the body & slightly in the foot at the Storm of Ciudad Rodrigo 19th Jany. 1812. Slightly wounded from the splinter of a Shell in the side in the trenches at Badajoz 29th March 1812. Wounded in the Head at the Storm of Badajoz 6th April 1812. Received a Grant of three years pay as Captain.' *Titles, honorary distinctions and medals*: 'A Medal as Senior surviving Officer of the Storming Party of the Light Division at Badajoz.' *Service abroad*: '17th May 1808 to 14th Feby. 1809, Portugal & Spain. 15th July 1809 to

26th Sept. 1809, Walchareen. 4th March 1810 to 24th March 1813, Portugal & Spain. 7th May 1813 to 27th June 1814, Spain & South of France. 1st June 1826 to 31st Dec. 1829, North America.' [PRO: WO 25/795 f79]. Wounded, Vimeiro, 21 Aug. 1808 [*London Gazette*]. Severely wounded, storming of Ciudad Rodrigo, 19 Jan. 1812 ('Ferguson') [*London Gazette*]. Slightly wounded, siege of Badajoz, 26 March 1812 ('Ferguson') [*London Gazette*]. Slightly wounded, storming of Badajoz, 6 April 1812 ('Ferguson') [*London Gazette*]. Gold Medal. Temporary pension of one hundred pounds per annum, commencing 20 Jan. 1813, 'for wounds' received at Ciudad Rodrigo [*1818 Pension Return*, pp. 12–13]. Later Major-General. MGS. Died 4 Sept. 1865. *Bruce*, p. 77 [Letter from Lt. Col. Macleod to Major William Napier, La Encina, 21 Jan. 1812: 'Ferguson behaved beautifully; he is turning out one of the best soldiers extant.'], p. 80 [Macleod to Napier, El Bodem, 4 Feb. 1812: 'Poor Jim Ferguson is wounded nearly where you were, by a musket-ball, as near as it could be with any safety to the backbone, and it is uncertain whether the ball is in or out, but the surgeons say it is of little importance which; he is recovering, which I am truly glad of, very fast.'], pp. 83–4 [He is quoted in detail, concerning the storming of Ciudad Rodrigo], p. 112 [Napier: 'A braver and more zealous officer never entered the field, and I hold his services before my own.']. *Haythornthwaite, Die Hard*, p. 173 ['James Fergusson of the 43rd had been severely wounded leading the stormers at Ciudad Rodrigo; with a ball still lodged under his spine he insisted on serving at Badajoz, was wounded again on 26 March, yet with his wounds still open he declared himself fit again to lead the stormers. (He was wounded again, but survived).'].

FERNANDEZ, John, Capt., 53rd Foot: Capt., 53rd Foot, 3 Oct. 1811. Severely wounded, Salamanca, 22 July 1812 (2nd Battn.) [*London Gazette*].

+FERNIE, Andrew, Capt., 7th Foot: Capt., 7th Foot, 26 April 1809. Killed, Pyrenees, 28 July 1813 (1st Battn.) [*London Gazette*].

FERNS, William, Capt., 66th Foot: Capt., Army, 15 Sept. 1808; Capt., 66th Foot, 4 Jan. 1810. Slightly wounded, Albuera, 16 May 1811 (2nd Battn.) [*London Gazette*]. Pension of one hundred pounds per annum, commencing 17 May 1812, 'for wounds' received at Albuera [*1818 Pension Return*, pp. 16–17].

FERRARS, Thomas, Capt., 9th Foot: Capt., 9th Foot, 3 Aug. 1804. Severely wounded, storming of San Sebastian, 31 Aug. 1813 ('Thomas Ferrars') (1st Battn.) [*London Gazette*].

+FERRIS, Jones, Lt., 83rd Foot: Lt., 83rd Foot, 29 March 1809 (' – Ferries'). Killed, Fuentes de Onoro, 5 May 1811 (2nd Battn.) [*London Gazette*].

FETHERSTONE, Francis, Capt., 47th Foot: Capt., 47th Foot, 25 April 1805. Slightly wounded, Barossa, 5 March 1811 (2nd Battn.) [*London Gazette*].

FFENNELL, James, Lt., 11th Foot: Lt., 11th Foot, 2 May 1811. Severely wounded, Nivelle, 10 Nov. 1813 (1st Battn.) [*London Gazette*].

FIDDES, Thomas, Assistant Surgeon, 9th Foot: *1829 Statement of Service*: Born in 'Mogheoboy, Ennisluillen, Co. Fermanagh', 8 Oct. 1788. Hospital Assistant, 16 June 1808. Asst. Surgeon, 7th Foot, 14 Nov. 1809. Surgeon, 38th Foot, 26 May 1814. Half Pay, 24 Dec. 1814, 'By reduction of the 2d Battn.' Surgeon, 10th Foot, 20 April 1815. Surgeon,

85th Foot, 17 Aug. 1815. *Battles, sieges and campaigns*: 'Was Present on the Peninsular Campaigns of 1808, 1809, 1811, 1812, 1813, and 1814... As Hospital assistant was present at the following Actions in Portugal.– O'Bidos 15th August 1808. Roleia, 17th August 1808. Vimeria, 21st August 1808. 10th & 11th May 1809 in the advance to Oporto. 12th at the Capture of Oporto. As Asst. Surgeon in Spain.– Cuidad Rodrigo, 19th Jany. 1812. Badajos, 7th April 1812. Salamanca, 22nd July 1812. Burgos, 1812. Armandrillos, 1813. Vittoria, 21st June 1813. St. Sebastian, 1813. Bidossoa, 1813. In France – St Jean De Luz, 1813. 9th 10th 11th 12th & 13th Decr. Near Bayone, and at the investment of Bayone, 1814.' *Distinguished conduct*: 'Received the thanks of Major General Hay Commanding the 5th Division, and the inspector General of Hospitals. Also the officer in command of the 2d Battn. 47th Regiment for Reestablishing the health of that Corps while in winter quarters after the retreat from Burgos.' *Wounds received in action*: 'Received a deep flesh wound through the left shoulder on the retreat to Corunna. At Salamanca, a slight flesh wound in the left hand. At Vittoria a severe contusion in the left Eye by the wadding of a cannon Ball by which the Vision was seriously impaired. No grant of pay or Pension received or applyed for.' *Service abroad*: '16th June 1808 to 27th April 1809, Portugal. 28th April 1809 to Feby. 1811, Gibraltar & Cadiz. August 1811 to 2d Augt. 1814, Peninsula. 3d August 1814 to 27th Sept. 1814, America. 14th June 1821 to 10th Febry. 1827, Malta. 11th Febry. 1827 to 4th April 1828, Gibraltar. 5th April 1828 to 31st Decr. 1829, Malta.' *Family*: Married Anne Galland, 15 Jan. 1827. They had two children by 1830. [PRO: WO 25/801 f354].

FIELDE, William Henry, Ensign, 1st Foot Guards: Ensign, 1st Foot Guards, 10 May 1809. Slightly wounded, Barossa, 5 March 1811 ('Field') [*London Gazette*].

FIELDING, James Campbell, Lt., 3rd Foot: Lt., 3rd Foot, 3 Aug. 1809. Severely wounded, the Nive, 13 Dec. 1813 (1st Battn.) [*London Gazette*].

FINCH, Hon. John, Lt., 15th Light Dragoons: Lt., 15th Light Dragoons, 20 Dec. 1810. Slightly wounded, Vittoria, 21 June 1813 [*London Gazette*]. Military Secretary to Lord Combermere. MGS.

FINCKE, Frederik, Ensign, Lt., 1st Light Battn. K.G.L.: *1829 Statement of Service for Retired Officers*: Aged twenty-four on first appointment to the Army. 'Private Soldier (Cadet)', 1st Light Battn. K.G.L., 'End of July 1810'; Ensign, 1st Light Battn. K.G.L., 4 May 1811 [Army List gives 30 Nov. 1810]; Lt., 1st Light Battn. K.G.L., 20 March 1812; Lt., 1st Foreign Veteran Battn. K.G.L., 20 Aug. 1815; Half-pay, 25 April 1816, by reduction. 'On the 22 November 1817 the Rank as a Captain was conferred to me but without a Augmentation of Pay.' *Where serving when wounded*: 'In Spain (at Toloza)'. *Details of pension*: 'I received this Pension of £70 per annum, since being wounded, the 25th June 1813. The grant of the Permanency of this Pension is from the 18th June 1818.' *Family*: Married in 'Dusseldorff, In the beginning of the month of July 1818.' No children by 1829. *Where generally resident during last five years*: 'at Potsdam.' [PRO: WO 25/758 f78]. Severely wounded, in an action near Tolosa, 25 June 1813 [*London Gazette*]. Served in Peninsula 1811–13. Waterloo. *Beamish*, vol. II, p. 609 ['Frederick von Fincke'].

+FINCKE, W. Philip Augustus von, Ensign/Lt., 2nd Light Battn. K.G.L: Ensign, 2nd Light Battn. K.G.L., 15 Oct. 1810. Killed, Salamanca, 22

July 1812 ('Lieutenant Fincke') [*London Gazette*]. Served in Peninsula 1811–12. *Beamish*, vol. II, p. 636.

+FINUCANE, Frederick, Ensign/ Lt., 68th Foot: Ensign, 68th Foot, 22 Sept. 1808. Killed, Salamanca, 22 July 1812 ('Lieutenant') (1st Battn.) [*London Gazette*]. *Green, Vicissitudes*, pp. 99–100 ['About three o'clock ... we immediately marched off to join the division. About this time the cannonading commenced... The shot of the foe now began to take effect on us. As we were marching in open column to take our position, one of our supernumary sergeants, whose name was Dunn, had both his legs shot from under him, and died in a few minutes. Shortly after, a shot came and took away the leg and thigh, with part of the body, of a young officer named Finukin [sic]: to have seen him, and heard the screams of his servant, would have almost rended a heart of stone: he was a good master, an excellent officer, and was lamented by all who knew him.'].

FIRMAN, Brook, Capt., 82nd Foot: *1829 Statement of Service*: Born in Westow, Yorkshire, 13 Feb. 1778. Aged twenty-one on his first Entrance into the Army. Ensign, 82nd Foot, 6 Aug. 1799. Lt., 82nd Foot, 29 Nov. 1799. Captain, 82nd Foot, 28 Nov. 1805. Bvt. Major, 82nd Foot, 12 Aug. 1819. *Battles, sieges and campaigns*: 'With the army during the retreat from Madrid Novr. 1812. Vittoria 21st June 1813. Pass of Mayo 25th July 1813.' *Wounds received in action*: 'Twice wounded at the Pass of Mayo 25th July 1813. Received One Years Pay.' *Service abroad*: 'July 1800 to July 1802, Minorca. Feby. 1810 to Novr. 1813, Gibraltar and Peninsula. June 1815 to Jany. 1816, France. June 1819 to May 1829, Mauritius.' *Family*: Married Tryphera A. Biggs, 29 Novr. 1831, Terryglass. [PRO: WO 25/801 f77]. Severely wounded,

Pyrenees, 25 July 1813 (1st Battn.) [*London Gazette*].

+FIRMAN, Walter, 2nd Lt., 95th Foot: 2nd Lt., 95th Foot, 6 Feb. 1812. Wounded, storming of Badajoz, 6 April 1812 ('Farmer') (3rd Battn.) [*London Gazette*]. *Simmons*, p. 232 [wounded, Badajoz, as 'Farmer']. Note: the officer wounded at Badajoz seems to have been Firman, as 2nd Lt. Farmer was apparently not serving there. Died, Peninsula, 15 Nov. 1812 [PRO: WO 25/2965]. The *1813 Army List* records that Allan Stewart became 2nd Lt., 95th Foot, 10 Dec. 1812, replacing Firman, 'dead.' *Simmons*, pp. 254–5 [died of injuries, Salamanca; 13 Nov. 1812: 'Finding the stairs very slippery and the place very dark... I left him, got a candle from a neighbouring house, and returned. I went up three or four stairs, when I heard a slip and in a moment, poor Firman fell through. In his progress downwards his feet repeatedly struck one side and his head the other. He came with a tremendous force to the bottom, which was a flagged pavement in the cellar. I directly retraced my steps and found him almost dashed to pieces, his skull frightfully fractured and several ribs broken... He remained for two days in a state of insensibility and died.'].

+FISCHER, John Christian Diedrich, Major, 1st Dragoons K.G.L.: Major, 1st Dragoons K.G.L., 16 Feb. 1809. Recorded as 'Missing', during 'movements of the Army' [Retreat from Burgos], 23 Oct. 1812 [*London Gazette*]. Served in Peninsula in 1812. *Beamish*, vol. II, p. 616 [Died 'in French captivity at Burgos, 27th Oct. 1812, of the wounds he received in a combat with the enemy's cavalry near Venta del Poco, 23d October 1812.'].

FITZCLARENCE, George, Lt., 10th Light Dragoons: Lt., 10th Light Dragoons, 9 March 1809 ('Fitz Clarence'). Slightly wounded,

Fuentes de Onoro, 5 May 1811, while serving as ADC to Major-General Stewart [London Gazette]. Bvt. Capt., 10th Light Dragoons, 2 Aug. 1811. Severely wounded, Toulouse, 10 April 1814 ('Fitz-Clarence') [London Gazette]. Capt., 10th Light Dragoons, 12 Nov. 1814. Born 1794, an illegitimate son of the Duke of Clarence (later King William IV); became major-general, died 1842; 1st Earl of Munster June 1831 [Burke's Peerage].

FITZGERALD, Charles John, Lt., 82nd Foot; Brigade-Major, Portuguese Staff: Lt., 82nd Foot, 4 Feb. 1808. Slightly wounded, Vittoria, 21 June 1813, while serving as Brigade Major on Portuguese Staff [London Gazette]. In Portuguese Service April 1809 to April 1814. Challis, Portuguese Army, p. 54 ['Maj. 13 Line'].

FITZGERALD, Edward, Capt., 6th Foot: Capt., Army, 26 Nov. 1806; Capt., 6th Foot, 25 Dec. 1806. Severely wounded, Orthes, 27 Feb. 1814, while serving as Brigade-Major [London Gazette]. MGS.

FITZGERALD, Frederick, Lt., 20th Foot: Lt., 20th Foot, 9 Feb. 1809. Slightly wounded, Pyrenees, 1 Aug. 1813 [London Gazette].

FITZGERALD, Gerald, Assistant Surgeon, 27th Foot: Asst. Surgeon, 27th Foot, 25 April 1811. Slightly wounded, Heights of Ordal, 12/13 Sept. 1813 (2nd Battn.) [London Gazette]. 'Gerrard Fitzgerald' in revised casualty list [London Gazette, 23 Oct. 1813]. Waterloo.

FITZGERALD, James, Ensign, 77th Foot: Ensign, 77th Foot, 21 Nov. 1811. Slightly wounded, storming of Ciudad Rodrigo, 19 Jan. 1812 [London Gazette]. Lt., 77th Foot, 21 April 1814. MGS.

FITZGERALD, James, Lt., 87th Foot: Lt., 87th Foot, 24 June 1812.

Killed, Orthes, 27 Feb. 1814 (2nd Battn.) [London Gazette].

FITZGERALD, John Forster, Major, 60th Foot: Major, 60th Foot, 9 Nov. 1809. Bvt. Lt. Col., 60th Foot, 25 July 1810. Slightly wounded, storming of Badajoz, 6 April 1812 (5th Battn.) [London Gazette]. Mentioned in Wellington's Badajoz dispatch, 7 April 1812 ['Lieutenant-General Picton has reported to me particularly the conduct of ... Lieutenant-Colonel Fitzgerald of the 60th'] [London Gazette]. Recorded as 'Missing', Pyrenees, 31 July 1813 (5th Battn.) [London Gazette]. Gold Cross (Badajoz, Salamanca, Vittoria, Pyrenees), in command of a Light Battn., then a Brigade.

+FITZGERALD, Robert Uniacke, Ensign, 32nd Foot: Ensign, 32nd Foot, 31 Oct. 1810. Killed, in the siege of the Forts of St Vincente, St Cayetano, and La Merced at Salamanca, 25–27 June 1812 [London Gazette].

FITZGERALD, William Edward, Major, 82nd Foot: Capt., 82nd Foot, 25 June 1803; Major, 82nd Foot, 4 June 1813. Severely wounded, Pyrenees, 30 July 1813 [London Gazette]. Pension of two hundred pounds per annum, commencing 31 July 1814, 'for wounds' received at Pampeluna, 1813 [1818 Pension Return, pp. 18–19]. MGS.

FITZGERALD, William Villiers, Lt., 5th Foot: 1829 Statement of Service: Born in Limerick. No date of birth given. Aged sixteen 'on his first Entrance into the Army.' Ensign, 5th Foot, 15 Sept. 1808. Lt., 5th Foot, 13 June 1811. Capt., Half Pay, 13 Feb. 1827. Capt., 2nd West India Regt., 23 March 1827. Battles, sieges and campaigns: 'Busaco, Redinha, Foz D'Aronce, Sabugal, El Bodon, Fuentes D'Onor, Cuidad Rodrigo, Badajos, Salamanca, Pyrenees, Nivelle, Platsburg, Ensign & Lieut. in the 5th Foot.' Wounds *received in action*: 'Wounded at the storming of Ciudad Rodrigo, Granted a year Pay.' *Service abroad*: 'June 1809 to June 1814, Peninsula. June 1814 to June 1815, America. July 1815 to November 1818, Flanders & France. February 1819 to June 1826, West Indies. With the Fifth or Northumberland Regt. of Foot. October 1827 to 31 December 1832, West Indies. With the 2 W. I. Regt.' [PRO: WO 25/805 f135]. Slightly wounded, storming of Ciudad Rodrigo, 19 Jan. 1812 [*London Gazette*].

FITZGIBBON, W., Ensign, 83rd Foot: Ensign, 83rd Foot, 29 May 1811. Slightly wounded, storming of Badajoz, 6 April 1812 ('Fitzgibbons') [*London Gazette*]. Lt., 83rd Foot, 16 Sept. 1813.

FITZMAURICE, John George, 2nd Lt., 95th Foot: *1829 Statement of Service*: Born Duogh, County of Kerry, 23 June 1792. Aged eighteen years ten months 'on his first Entrance into the Army.' 2nd Lt., 95th Foot, 25 April 1811; 1st Lt., 95th Foot, 14 Jan. 1813; Half-pay, 25 Nov. 1818, by reduction; Lt., 68th Foot, 19 May 1825; Capt., Half-pay, unattached, 16 June 1825; Capt., Rifle Brigade, 19 Dec. 1826. Note added: 'Major, Half Pay, Unattd., 30 March 1832.' *Battles, sieges and campaigns*: 'The different actions during the Retreat of the French Army from Portugal in 1811. Action at Sabugal 3d April 18111. Battle of Fuentes d'Onoro 5 May 1811. Siege & assault of Ciudad Rodrigo 8th to 19th Jan. 1812. Seige & assault of Badajos 17 March to 6 April 1812. San Milan 18 June 1813. Vittoria 21 June 1813. Bridge of Yanzi 1 Aug. 1813. Vera 7 Oct. 1813. Nivelle 10 Nov. 1813. Nive 9, 10 & 11th Decr. 1813. Tarbes 20 March 1814. Toulouse 10 April 1814. Waterloo 18 June 1815.' *Wounds received in action*: 'Leg broken at the Storming of Badajos, 6th April 1812. Received one years pay and a permanent

pension of £50 per ann. A Ball in the thigh at Waterloo, 18th June 1815. received one years Pay as Captain having Command of the Company on that occasion.' *Titles, honorary distinctions and medals*: 'Waterloo Medal.' *Service abroad*: '25 April 1811 to June 1814, Portugal, Spain and France. May 1815 to Octr. 1818, Belgium & France. Sept. 1828 to 31st Decr. 1829, Malta.' *Family*: Married Frances Maria Watkyn, 3 Nov. 1824, Barnborough, Yorkshire. They had three children by 1830. [PRO: WO 25/804 f338]. Slightly wounded, storming of Badajoz, 6 April 1812 ('Fitzmorrice') (1st Battn.) [*London Gazette*]. Temporary pension of fifty pounds per annum, commencing 7 April 1813, 'for a wound' received at Badajoz [*1818 Pension Return*, pp. 22–3]. Waterloo. MGS. *Simmons*, p. 232 [wounded, Badajoz]. *Du Cane*, p. 758 ['was put on half-pay on the reduction of the 3rd Battalion Rifle Brigade at the end of the war. On applying to the Duke to be restored to full pay, he told him to send him a memorial every month until he got a reply. Eventually he was put into the corps of Gentlemen-at-Arms on full pay over the heads of many others.']. *Dalton*, pp. 197, 200 ['Aftds. major-general and K.H.D. 24th Dec., 1865.']. *Haythornthwaite, Wellington's Military Machine*, p. 85 [Illustration of Fitzmaurice's heroic action at Arinez: 'individual acts of heroism occurred throughout the period: at Arinez, near Vittoria, Lt. John G. Fitzmaurice of the 1/95th with only two men intercepted a French battery and captured a gun and team. (Print after Harry Payne, executed about 80 years after the event).'].

FITZPATRICK, John, Lt., 88th Foot: *1829 Statement of Service for Retired Officers*: Aged twenty-one on first appointment to the Army. Ensign, 8th Foot, 7 Dec. 1806; Lt., 88th Foot, Dec. 1807 [Army List gives 3 July 1806]; Capt., 88th Foot,

8 Sept. 1814; Half-pay, 25 March 1816, by reduction. *Where serving when wounded*: 'Busaco. Orthes. Also wounded at Talavera, Vittoria.' *Details of pension*: One hundred pounds 'for wounds' at Busaco, commencing 25 Dec. 1811; one hundred pounds for 'loss of eye' at Orthes, commencing 28 July 1814. *Family*: Married in St Martin's Church, London, 5 Nov. 1820. Three children by 1829. *Where generally resident during last five years*: 'Montreuil'. [PRO: WO 25/758 f90]. Severely wounded, Busaco, 27 Sept. 1810 (1st Battn.) [*London Gazette*]. Slightly wounded, Vittoria, 21 June 1813 (1st Battn.) [*London Gazette*]. Severely wounded, Orthes, 27 Feb. 1814 (1st Battn.) [*London Gazette*]. *1818 Pension Return*, pp. 20–1.

FITZPATRICK, Mathew, Ensign, 39th Foot: *1829 Statement of Service for Retired Officers*: Aged twenty-one on first appointment to the Army. Ensign, 39th Foot, 24 July 1813; Lt., 39th Foot, 20 July 1815; Lt., 97th Foot, '1815 or 1816'; Half-pay, 1817, by reduction. *Where serving when wounded*: 'In the Peninsula, France, & on board H.M.S. Confiance on Lake Champlain off Platsburgh, N. America.' *Details of pension*: Fifty pounds per annum, commencing 25 Dec. 1820. *Family*: Married in Winchester, 11 Feb. 1818. Five children by 1829. *Title and nature of civil employment*: 'Chief Constable of Police'. *Where generally resident during last five years*: 'Dunmanday, Ireland.' [PRO: WO 25/758 f104].

FLACK, William, Lt., 88th Foot: Ensign, 88th Foot, 1805; Lt., 88th Foot, 29 May 1806. Wounded, 'dangerously', siege of Ciudad Rodrigo, 16 Jan. 1812 [*London Gazette*]. Pension of one hundred pounds per annum, commencing 17 Jan. 1813, 'for wounds' received at Ciudad Rodrigo [*1818 Pension Return*, pp. 20–1]. MGS.

FLEISCH, Ernest August Jonas, Lt., 2nd Line Battn. K.G.L.: Ensign, 2nd Line Battn. K.G.L., 28 Nov. 1807; Lt., 2nd Line Battn., 17 March 1812. Slightly wounded, sortie from Bayonne, 14 April 1814 ('Fleish') [*London Gazette*]. Waterloo. 'Fleish' in Army List. *Beamish*, vol. II, p. 577 [Died 'at Buxtehude in Han. 21st December 1817.'].

FLEMING, Edward, Capt., 31st Foot: *1829 Statement of Service*: Born 1786, Belville, County Cavan. Aged sixteen on his first entrance into the Army. Ensign, 31st Foot, 24 June 1802; Lt. 6 July 1804; Capt. 30 May 1807; Major, 2nd West India Regt., 1 April 1813; Lt. Col. 18 July 1816; Half Pay 24 Dec. 1818; Lt. Col., 2nd Ceylon Regt., 12 Aug. 1819; Lt. Col., 53rd Foot, 24 Feb. 1820; Half Pay 24 Sept. 1823; Lt. Col., 24th Foot, 6 Nov. 1823. *Battles, sieges and campaigns*: 'Action as Adjt. to a Grendr. Battalion at Reggio L. Calabria... Alexandria & Rosetta in Egypt 31st March 1807... Talavera 27 & 28 July 1809... Albuera 16 May 1811... Cumberland Island North America, May 1815.' *Wounds received in action*: 'Albuera, in the Head, from a charge made by the Polish Lancers. One year's pay – no pension.' *Service abroad*: 'April 1806 to 1807, Sicily, Calabria, Egypt. 1807 to 1808, Egypt & Sicily. 1808 to 1811, Peninsula. 1814 to 1815, Bahamas Islands & North America. 1816 to 1818, Jamaica. 1820 to 1823, East Indies. 30 July 1829 to 31 Dec. 1829, Canada.' *Family*: Married Charlotte St Leger, 19 Dec. 1819. They had three children by 1830. [PRO: WO 25/789 f246]. Severely wounded, Albuera, 16 May 1811 (2nd Battn.) [*London Gazette*]. MGS.

FLEMING, Hugh, Ensign/Adjutant, 24th Foot: Ensign, 24th Foot, 11 Jan. 1810. Adjutant, 24th Foot, 11 Jan. 1810. Slightly wounded, Pyrenees, 2 Aug. 1813 (2nd Battn.) [*London Gazette*]. MGS.

FLETCHER, J. Wynne, Capt., 4th Foot: Capt., 4th Foot, 4 June 1807. Severely wounded, Storming of San Sebastian, 31 Aug. 1813 (1st Battn.) [*London Gazette*].

+FLETCHER, Richard, Lt. Col., Royal Engineers: Lt. Col., Royal Engineers, 24 June 1809. Mentioned in Wellington's Ciudad Rodrigo dispatch, 20 Jan. 1812 ['I likewise request your Lordship's attention to the conduct of Lieutenant-Colonel Fletcher, the chief engineer, and of Brigade-Major Jones, and the officers and men of the royal engineers. The ability with which these operations were carried on exceeds all praise; and I beg leave to recommend those officers to your Lordship most particularly.'] [*London Gazette*]. Slightly wounded, siege of Badajoz, 19 March 1812 [*London Gazette*]. His wound at Badajoz was unusual, a musket-shot striking his purse and driving a dollar into his groin. Mentioned in Wellington's Badajoz dispatch, 7 April 1812 ['Lieutenant-Colonel Fletcher continued to direct the works (notwithstanding that he was wounded in the sortie made by the enemy on the 19th March), which were carried on by Major Squire and Major Burgoyne, under his directions.'] [*London Gazette*]. Mentioned in Wellington's Vittoria dispatch, 22 June 1813 ['I am likewise indebted ... to Lieutenant-Colonel Sir Richard Fletcher, and the Officers of the Royal Engineers.'] [*London Gazette*]. Slightly wounded, 'at the Siege of St Sebastian,' 7–27 July 1813 [*London Gazette*]. Killed, storming of San Sebastian, 31 Aug. 1813 [*London Gazette*]. Mentioned in Wellington's San Sebastian dispatch ['Colonel Sir Richard Fletcher, of the Royal Engineers, was killed by a musket-ball at the mouth of the trenches. In this officer ... His Majesty's service has sustained a serious loss.'] [*London Gazette*].

Obituary, *The Gentleman's Magazine*, Nov. 1813, p. 499 ['Aug. 30. At the storming of St Sebastian, Col. Sir R. Fletcher. He had long served as chief engineer under Lord Wellington, and gave constant proofs of superior skill and abilities. He had been wounded several times before: the fatal shot entered the spine of his back, and occasioned his instant death; which, however, did not happen till it was certain that St Sebastian was gained. Sir R. F. married a sister of Capt. Madge, R.N. By this lady, who died before him, he has left five daughters and one son.']. Born 1768. He was the principal designer of the Lines of Torres Vedras.

+FLOOD, Francis, Lt., 83rd Foot: Ensign, 83rd Foot, 11 Feb. 1807; Lt., 83rd Foot, 15 March 1808. Killed, Talavera, 28 July 1809 [*London Gazette*].

FLOOD, James, Lt., 88th Foot: Lt., 88th Foot, 26 June 1806. Slightly wounded, Vittoria, 21 June 1813 (1st Battn.) [*London Gazette*].

FLOOD, Ross, Ensign, 74th Foot: *1829 Statement of Service for Retired Officers*: Aged nineteen on first appointment to the Army. Ensign, Galway Militia, 8 Oct. 1809; Lt., Galway Militia, 16 Aug. 1811; Ensign, 74th Foot, 26 March 1812, 'By volunteering from the militia'; Lt., 74th Foot, 31 March 1814; Adjutant, 74th Foot, 2 Jan. 1817; Half-pay, 4th Foot, 22 April 1824, 'in consequence of ill health.' *Where serving when wounded*: 'South of France'. *Details of pension*: Fifty pounds, commencing 24 June 1822. *Family*: Married in 'Fredericton, N.B.', 16 Dec. 1820. One child by 1829. *Where generally resident during last five years*: 'England'. [PRO: WO 25/758 f130]. Severely wounded, 'in Action with the Enemy', 19 March 1814 ('Ross Hood') [*London Gazette*].

209

+**FOLLIETT, George, Ensign/Lt., 43rd Foot:** Ensign, 43rd Foot, 22 Aug. 1810. Severely wounded, 'in the Operations of the Army', 31 Aug. 1813, 'since dead' ('Geo. Foillett') ('Lieutenant') (1st Battn.) [*London Gazette*]. Obituary, *The Gentleman's Magazine*, Oct. 1813, p. 401 ['Aug. 31. Immediately after a severe wound received in the battle before St Sebastian, Lieut. G. Follett, eldest son of B. F. esq. of Topsham.']. 'George Folliett' in *Challis, Index*, p. 131.

+**FORBES, Thomas, Major/Lt.Col., 45th Foot:** Major, 45th Foot, 20 Oct. 1808; Lt. Col., Army, 25 April 1808. Mentioned in Wellington's Badajoz dispatch, 7 April 1812 ['Lieutenant-General Picton has reported to me particularly the conduct of ... Lieutenant-Colonel Forbes of the 45th regiment'] [*London Gazette*]. Slightly wounded, Salamanca, 22 July 1812 ('Lieutenant-Colonel') [*London Gazette*]. Lt. Col., 45th Foot, 7 Oct. 1813. Slightly wounded, Orthes, 27 Feb. 1814 (1st Battn.) [*London Gazette*]. Killed, Toulouse, 10 April 1814 (1st Battn.) [*London Gazette*].

FORD, John Butler, Lt., 9th Foot: Lt., 9th Foot, 31 Aug. 1808. Severely wounded, during 'movements of the Army' [Retreat from Burgos], 25 Oct. 1812 (1st Battn.) [*London Gazette*].

+**FORDYCE, Alexander, Capt., 81st Foot:** Capt., Army, 10 June 1804; Lt., 81st Foot, 19 July 1804. Killed, Talavera, 27 July 1909, while serving on the General Staff as Deputy Adjutant-General [*London Gazette*]. Obituary, *The Gentleman's Magazine*, August 1809 ['Captain Fordyce, Deputy-adjutant-general, who was also killed in the battle of Talavera, was a son of the late John Fordyce, esq. of Ayton.'].

FORNERET, Cuthbert A. W., Lt., 60th Foot: Ensign, 60th Foot, 17 Oct. 1811; Lt., 60th Foot, 6 Feb. 1813. Slightly wounded, 'in Action with the Enemy', 19 March 1814 (5th Battn.) [*London Gazette*]. MGS.

FORSTER, Jonathan Gustavus, 1st Lt., 95th Foot: 2nd Lt., 95th Foot, 18 April 1809; 1st Lt., 95th Foot, 30 April 1811. Severely wounded, storming of Badajoz, 6 April 1812 (1st Battn.) [*London Gazette*]. *Simmons*, p. 232 [wounded, Badajoz]. *Wheeler*, p. 6 [12 April 1809: 'Upwards of 90 men [from the 2nd Royal Surrey Militia] volunteered to the 95th Rifle Regiment. I was near going to this Regt. myself for it was always a fancy Corps of mine, and another cause was that Lieut Foster a good officer beloved by every man in the Corps I had left, volunteered into the 95th. But I had made up my mind'].

+**FORSTER, William, Lt., Royal Engineers:** 1st Lt., Royal Engineers, 1 March 1808. Severely wounded, 'since dead', siege of Badajoz, 6–11 June 1811 [*London Gazette*]. *Colville*, p. 60 [Quoting Sir Charles Colville: 'I went upon the duty of trenches again that evening and had ... the mortification to witness the failure of the assault made by the 7th Divn. on Fort Christopher's... Lt. Foster of the Engineers with some small numbers of men had actually surmounted the breach. He, I fear, is since dead of the wound received, I understand, as he descended from it.'].

FOSTER, Charles, 1st Dragoons: Lt., 1st Dragoons, 18 Nov. 1807 ('Forster'). Mentioned in Wellington's dispatch of 27 March 1811 ['I have received the report of a gallant action of one of our patroles yesterday evening, between Alverca and Guarda, under the command of Lieutenant Perse [sic], of the 16th light dragoons, and Lieutenant Foster, of the royals, who attacked a detachment of the enemy's cavalry ... and killed and wounded several of them, and took the officer and thirty-seven men prisoners.'] [*London Gazette*]. Slightly wounded, Fuentes de Onoro, 5 May 1811 ('Forster') [*London Gazette*]. Killed at Waterloo.

+**FOSTER, W. H., Cornet, 18th Light Dragoons:** Cornet, 18th Light Dragoons, 9 July 1812. Severely wounded, Vittoria, 21 June 1813 ('Forster') [*London Gazette*]. Obituary, *The Gentleman's Magazine*, Nov. 1813, p. 504 ['of wounds, recieved in the battle of Vittoria ... Lieut. Forster, of the 18th.'].

+**FOTHERGILL, John, Lt./Capt., 59th Foot:** Ensign, 59th Foot, 18 Dec. 1806; Lt., 59th Foot, 28 April 1808. Wounded, 'in the Army lately in Spain' (2nd Battn.) [*March 1809 Army List*, p. 105]. Capt., 59th Foot, 15 Oct. 1812. Severely wounded, storming of San Sebastian, 31 Aug. 1813 (2nd Battn.) [*London Gazette*]. *Register of officers' effects*: Died of wounds, 1 Sept. 1813, St Sebastian. Single. His effects totalled $177.3 Reals. [PRO: WO 25/2964]. Obituary, *The Gentleman's Magazine*, Oct. 1813, p. 402 ['Sept. 7... Of wounds received in the assault of the town of St Sebastian, Capt. J. Fothergill, 59th foot, second son of Col. F. of Kingthorpe, near Pickering, co. York.']. Second obituary notice, *The Gentleman's Magazine*, Dec. 1813, p. 621 ['Sept. 7. In his 23d year, of wounds received in the assault on S. Sebastian... Walcheren, Corunna, Vittoria, and St Sebastian, form a lasting wreath on the brow of the youthful Hero.'].

FOTHERINGHAM, Thomas, Lt. and Capt., 3rd Foot Guards: Lt. and Capt., 3rd Foot Guards, 19 Dec. 1799; Bvt. Major, 3rd Foot Guards, 1 Jan. 1805. Slightly wounded, Talavera, 28 July 1809 [*London Gazette*].

FOULKES, John, Lt., 40th Foot: *1829 Statement of Service for Retired Officers*: Aged twenty-four on first appointment to the Army. Ensign, 40th Foot, 22 Nov. 1810; Lt., 40th Foot, 14 May 1812; Half-pay, 58th Foot, 26 Oct. 1820, 'in consequence of ill health.' 'Is desirous of returning to Service but from Wounds and privations in the service in the Peninsula New Orleans and Waterloo his health renders him incapable.' *Where serving when wounded*: 'In the Pyrenees thirtieth July Eighteen Hundred and thirteen when commanding a Company.' No pension. *Where generally resident during last five years*: 'Sunderland in the County of Durham.' [PRO: WO 25/758 f205]. Slightly wounded, Pyrenees, 30 July 1812 ('Foulks') (1st Battn.) [*London Gazette*].

FOWKE, Francis, Lt., 14th Light Dragoons: Lt., 14th Light Dragoons, 6 Dec. 1810. Slightly wounded, Salamanca, 18 July 1812 [*London Gazette*].

FOWKE, John, Ensign/Lt., 68th Foot: *1829 Statement of Service for Retired Officers*: Aged twenty on first appointment to the Army. Ensign, 68th Foot, 20 Feb. 1812; Lt., 68th Foot, 19 Aug. 1813; Half-pay, 25 Dec. 1818, by reduction. *Where serving when wounded*: 'Wounded at the Battle of Vitoria by a gun shot wound through the thigh.' No pension. *Family*: Married in Belfast, 1 Feb. 1822. Two children by 1829. *Where generally resident during last five years*: 'Boughood South Wales and Antrim Ireland.' [PRO: WO 25/758 f198]. Severely wounded, Vittoria, 21 June 1813 ('Ensign Fawke') (2nd Battn.) [*London Gazette*]. MGS.

+**FOWLER, Robert J., Lt., 7th Foot:** Lt., 7th Foot, 14 Sept. 1809. Killed, storming of Badajoz, 6 April 1812 [*London Gazette*].

+FOX, Arthur, Lt., 3rd Dragoon Guards: Lt., 3rd Dragoon Guards, 27 Dec. 1810. Killed, Albuera, 16 May 1811 [*London Gazette*].

+FOX, Charles James, Ensign/Lt., 66th Foot; Capt., 16th Portuguese Line: Ensign, 66th Foot, 21 Sept. 1808. In Portuguese Service April to Sept. 1810. *Challis, Portuguese Army*, p. 55 ['Capt. 16 Line... K/A Busaco 27 Sep. '10']. *Sherer*, p. 109 [Busaco: 'The first wounded man I ever beheld in the field was carried past me, at this moment: he was a fine young Englishman, in the Portuguese service, and lay help-lessly in a blanket, with both his legs shattered by cannon-shot. He looked pale, and big drops of perspiration stood on his manly forehead; but he spoke not – his agony appeared unutterable. I secretly wished him death; a mercy, I believe, that was not very long withheld.'].

+FOX, Humphrey, Lt., 71st Foot: Lt., 71st Foot, 17 March 1808. Severely wounded, Fuentes de Onoro, evening 3 May 1811 (1st Battn.) [*London Gazette*]. Severely wounded, 'since dead', Vittoria, 21 June 1813 (1st Battn.) [*London Gazette*]. *Register of officers' effects*: Died of wounds, 22 June 1813, Vittoria. Single. [PRO: WO 25/2964].

FOX, J., Ensign, 40th Foot: Ensign, 40th Foot, 26 Sept. 1811. Severely wounded, Vittoria, 21 June 1813 (1st Battn.) [*London Gazette*].

FOX, John, Capt., 36th Foot: Capt., 36th Foot, 4 Aug. 1804; Major, Army, 4 June 1811. Slightly wounded, Salamanca, 22 July 1812 [*London Gazette*].

FOX, William A., Ensign, 48th Foot: Ensign, 48th Foot, 18 June 1812. Severely wounded, 'left leg ampu-tated', Toulouse, 10 April 1814 (1st Battn.) [*London Gazette*].

FRAGSTEIN, Franz von, Major, Duke of Brunswick Oels' Corps (Infantry): Major, Duke of Brunswick Oels' Corps, 26 Sept. 1809. Slightly wounded, Crossing the Bidassoa, 7/9 Oct. 1813 [*London Gazette*].

FRAMINGHAM, Hoylet, Lt. Col., Royal Artillery: Lt. Col., Royal Artillery, 29 Dec. 1805. Slightly wounded, Talavera, 28 July 1809 [*London Gazette*]. Mentioned in Wellington's Badajoz dispatch, 7 April 1812 ['Major Dickson conducted the details of the artillery service during the siege, as well as upon former occasions, under the general superintendance of Lieutenant-Colonel Fram-ingham, who, since the absence of Major-General Borthwick, has commanded the artillery with this army.' [*London Gazette*]. Mention-ed in Wellington's dispatch concerning the siege and storming of the forts at Salamanca, dated Fuente la Pena, 30 June 1812 ['Major-General Clinton ... mentions in strong terms Lieu-tenant-Colonel May, who commanded the artillery under the direction of Lieutenant-Colonel Framingham'] [*London Gazette*]. Mentioned in Wellington's Sala-manca dispatch, 24 July 1812 ['The royal and German artillery, under Lieutenant-Colonel Framingham, distinguished themselves by the accuracy of their fire, wherever it was possible to use them; and they advanced to the attack of the enemy's position with the same gallantry as the other troops.'] [*London Gazette*]. Gold Medal. KCB.

FRANCHINI, Ignatius (John), Lt., 60th Foot: *1829 Statement of Service for Retired Officers*: Aged eighteen on first appointment to the Army. Volunteer, 97th Foot, 25 Dec. 1798; Town Adjutant of Rosetta, Egypt, 1801; Ensign, 60th Foot, Dec. 1802; Lt., 60th Foot, 8

Nov. 1804; Capt., 60th Foot, 28 Jan. 1813; Half-pay, 7 July 1827, 'in consequence of an Order issued from the Horse Guards, he believes 1825, directing that all foreign officers of the 60th should either sell or retire on half pay ... he chose the latter'. *Where serving when wounded*: 'In the West Indies & Peninsula'. 'He is disabled in consequence of Wounds received viz. In 1806 he was stabbed in the West Indies, while (as Actg. Adjutant) in the act of reading the sentence of a Regl. Court Martial, for which the prisoner was executed; was severely wounded at the Battle of Busaco 27th Sept. 1809; at Vittoria in Spain 21st June 1813; received two musket Ball Wounds at Orthes 27th Feby. 1814; has not the proper use of his Right Arm & right Leg, for which wounds he passed the Army Medical Board, besides in Consequence of his services in different hot Climates his Constitution being impaired, having been sent twice to England from the West Indies] by a Medical Board for Chronic Disease'. *Details of pension*: No pension. Received one year's pay for the 'two wounds he received at Orthes in France' *Where generally resident during last five years*: '2 years and a half with the 2d. Batt. 60th Reg. in Demerara, one year 2 months in England & the last 15 month in France'. [PRO: WO 25/776 f205]. Slightly wounded, Busaco, 27 Sept. 1810 ('Franheine') (5th Battn.) [*London Gazette*]. Slightly wounded, Vittoria, 21 June 1813 ('Captain Franchiny') (2nd Battn.) [*London Gazette*]. Slightly wounded, Orthes, 27 Feb. 1814 ('Captain Ignace Franchini') (5th Battn.) [*London Gazette*]. 'John Franchini' in Army List.

FRANCIS, George, Lt., 57th Foot: *1829 Statement of Service for Retired Officers*: Aged twenty-five on first appointment to the Army. Ensign, 57th Foot, 12 April 1809; Lt., 57th Foot, 20 June 1811; Lt., Half-pay, 10th Foot, 7 Feb. 1822, 'at my own request from private motives.' *Where serving when wounded*: 'at the Battle of Vittoria in Spain.' No pension. *Where generally resident during last five years*: 'Thornbury in Gloucestershire, Plymouth Bristol & London.' [PRO: WO25/758-f227]. Slightly wounded, Vittoria, 21 June 1813 ('Frances') (1st Battn.) [*London Gazette*].

FRANKLAND, James William, Capt., 23rd Light Dragoons: Capt., Army, 27 June 1805; Capt., 23rd Foot, 14 April 1808. Severely wounded, Talavera, 28 July 1809 [*London Gazette*]. Listed amongst 'officers who have resigned and retired' in *1811 Army List*. MGS.

FRANKLYN, Thomas Demicus, Lt., 40th Foot: Ensign, 40th Foot, 16 Jan. 1806; Lt., 40th Foot, 11 Feb. 1807. Slightly wounded, Vimeiro, 21 Aug. 1808 ('Frankley') [*London Gazette*]. Severely wounded, Toulouse, 10 April 1814 (1st Battn.) [*London Gazette*]. Capt. 40th Foot, 10 Nov. 1814. Waterloo. Died, 3 Nov. 1857. MGS.

+FRASER, Alexander, Ensign, 52nd Foot: Severely wounded, Crossing the Bidassoa, 7/9 Oct. 1813. (1st Battn.) [*London Gazette*]. *Hurt*, p. 79 ['Ens. A. Frazer, D.O.W., Bidassoa, Oct. 7 [1813]']. Obituary, *The Gentleman's Magazine*, Dec. 1813, p. 621 ['Oct. 20. At Beara, after undergoing two operations from a wound received on the 8th inst. while storming the Enemy's lines in entering France, aged 18, Ensign Alex. John Fraser, 52d reg. youngest son of the late Capt. John Grant Fraser, R.A. ... an amiable and promising youth.'].

+FRASER, Archibald, Lt., 79th Foot: Lt., 79th Foot, 23 Oct. 1806. Slightly wounded, Fuentes de Onoro, 5 May 1811 (1st Battn.) [*London Gazette*]. Died, Portugal, 15 Sept. 1811 [PRO: WO 25/2965].

FRASER, Charles Mackenzie, Lt. and Capt., Coldstream Guards: Ensign, 78th Foot, 18 Dec. 1806; Capt., Army, 22 March 1810; Lt. and Capt., Coldstream Guards, 16 Aug. 1810 ('Frazer'). Severely wounded, siege of Burgos, 20–26 Sept. 1812 ('Frasier') (1st Battn.) [*London Gazette*]. One hundred pound pension, commencing 24 Sept. 1813, for 'loss of a leg', Burgos, 1812 ('Frazer') [*1818 Pension Return*, pp. 2–3]. MGS. *Mullen*, p. 112 ['Ret 16/3/14']. *Moorsom*, p. 418 ['Fraser, Captain, Charles (Mackenzie). – Served with the 52nd in 1808, and accompanied the 2nd battalion to the Peninsula. In 1809 he served with the 52nd in the Walcheren expedition, and was appointed to the Staff. He subsequently served in the Peninsula with the Coldstream Guards in 1812, was wounded at Burgos, lost a leg, and retired in 1814; and is now Honorary Colonel of the Ross, etc., Militia.'].

+FRASER, Erskine Alexander, Lt., 9th Foot: Lt., Army, 2 Nov. 1809; Lt., 9th Foot, 28 Dec. 1809. Killed, Storming of San Sebastian, 31 Aug. 1813 (1st Battn.) [*London Gazette*]. Memorial tablet to his father in Canterbury Cathedral ['Sacred to the memory of GEORGE FRASER, Esqr., Many years Paymaster to the 2nd Battalion, 9th Regt. of Foot. The loss of his much beloved son Erskine Alexander Fraser, Lieutenant in the same Regiment, whose early distinguished talents promised a bright ornament to the profession, and who gallantly fell at the Storming of San Sebastian, in Spain, on the 31st of August, 1813, before he had completed his 18th year. This severe dispensation so preyed on the mind of his afflicted father that he became the victim of unceasing grief, and expired on the 4th of December in the following year, in the 54th year of his age...'].

FRASER, Hugh Andrew, Lt., 42nd Foot: *1829 Statement of Service*: Born in 'Kelso, North Britain', 14 Oct. 1793. Aged thirteen on first appointment to the Army. Ensign, 42nd Foot, 4 June 1806; Lt., 8 Feb. 1809; Capt., 12 Dec. 1822; Major, 42nd Foot, 3 Dec. 1829. *Battles, sieges and campaigns*: 'Ensign at the Battle of Corunna, 16th January 1809... Lieutenant on the Expedition to Walcheren 1809... Lieutenant in the Campaigns of 1810, 1811, 1812, & 1814 on the Peninsula... Battles of Busaco 27th Sept 1810, Fuentes D'Honor 5th May 1811, Siege of Ciudad Rodrigo 19th Jany 1812, Battle of Salamanca 22d July 1812, Siege of Burgos 19th Septr. 1812, Battle of Toulouse 10th April 1814. As Lieutenant at the battle of Waterloo 16th & 18th June 1815.' *Wounds received in action*: 'Wounded at Burgos 19th Sept. 1812, very severely through the body, by gun shot. At Toulouse very severely by gun-shot, in the right thigh, grazing the bone, and at Waterloo slightly. Two years pay as Captn. and Permanent Pension as Lieutenant from 10th April 1815.' *Titles, honorary distinctions and medals*: 'Waterloo Medal, 18th June 1815.' *Service Abroad*: 10th Augt. 1807 to 19th Feb. 1809, Gibraltar, Portugal, and Spain. 28th July 1809 to 10th Sept. 1809, Holland. 7th Augt. 1810 to 5th Decr. 1812, Peninsula. 13th Feb. 1814 to 11th July 1814, Spain & France. 18th May 1815 to 19th Decr. 1815, Flanders & France. 27th Oct. 1825 to 2d July 1828, Gibraltar.' [PRO: WO 25/793 f91]. Severely wounded, storming of Fort St Michael, Burgos, 19 Sept. 1812 ('Frazer') (1st Battn.) [*London Gazette*]. Severely wounded, Toulouse, 10 April 1814 ('Frazer') (1st Battn.) [*London Gazette*]. MGS.

+FRASER, James Baillie, Lt., 7th Foot: Lt., 7th Foot, 21 June 1810. Slightly wounded, Albuera, 16 May 1811 ('Frazer') (2nd Battn.) [*London Gazette*]. Severely wounded, Pyrenees, 28 July 1813

(1st Battn.) [*London Gazette*]. Obituary, *The Gentleman's Magazine*, Sept. 1813, p. 298 ['July 28. In Spain, killed by a musket-ball, in battle, aged 20, Lieut. J. B. Fraser, 7th Royal Fuzileers, and of Ballindown, Ireland, eldest son of the late Capt. J. Grant Fraser, R.A. Educated at the Military College at Marlow, he entered the Army at 17, and immediately embarked for Spain. In a very few days after he landed, he was engaged in the battle of Busaco, and afterwards that of Albuera. In the latter he was shot through the thigh, and all the officers and men in his company (except four) were either killed or wounded. In 1811 he returned to England, with several other officers, to recruit the regiment, and was on the recruiting service to Leicester. In 1812 he again embarked for Spain, and was in most of the actions since that time. Though dreadfully afflicted with the ague in the spring of this year, yet, with the noble spirit of a brave soldier, anxious to do his duty, he declined Gen. Cole's permission to return home for the benefit of his health, being determined, if possible, to serve another campaign. He was engaged in the battle of Vittoria, where he escaped unhurt. In the late battles his regiment formed part of the 4th division, which, as Lord Wellington says, "has so frequently been distinguished in the army, and which, on this occasion, surpassed their former good conduct, and charged with the bayonet four different times; their officers setting them the example."']. *Cooper*, pp. 97-98 [Following the Battle of Pampeluna, 28 July 1813: 'Looking about, I saw a surgeon that formerly belonged our regiment. I told him my case, and was directed to go to a large house close by and take charge of a captain and a lieutenant who were both mortally wounded. "They are your own officers, and both will die," said he. "See that their servants do not rob them." I went accordingly. The captain was wounded in the left side, and so was the lieutenant, but the shot had gone quite through the lieutenant's body. Lieutenant Frazer [sic] died on the second or third day after the battle; Captain Wemyss on the fourth or fifth... A coffin was made of some old furniture, and the captain was buried in a garden beside the lieutenant.'].

FRASER, James, Lt., 79th Foot: Lt., 79th Foot, 16 March 1809. Severely wounded, Toulouse, 10 April 1814 ('Frazer') (1st Battn.) [*London Gazette*]. Wounded, Waterloo. MGS. Died 1849.

+FRASER, John, Lt., 4th Foot: Lt., 4th Foot, 21 Nov. 1809. Severely wounded, the Nive, 9 Dec. 1813 (1st Battn.) [*London Gazette*]. Hurt, p. 83 [Concerning the memorial porch in the New English Church, Biarritz, 1887: 'Slabs have been added for Lt. J. Fraser, 4th Ft. K. O. Nive, D.O.W., Dec. 1813'].

FRASER, John, Capt., 42nd Foot: Capt., 42nd Foot, 8 July 1803. Wounded, 'in the Army lately in Spain' (1st Battn.) [*March 1809 Army List*, p. 105]. *Monthly Return*, 1st Battn., dated 25 Feb. 1809: 'Left wounded at Plymouth' [PRO: WO 17/152]. Pension of one hundred pounds per annum, commencing 25 Dec. 1811, 'for wounds' received at Corunna, 1809 [*1818 Pension Return*, pp. 12-13].

FRASER, John, Ensign/Lt., 53rd Foot: *1829 Statement of Service*: 'Born Kirkton, Golspie, Sutherlandshire, 21st January 1792. Aged 17 Years and 4 Months on his first Entrance into the Army. Ensign, 53rd Regt., 29th May 1809. Lieutenant, 53rd Regt., 12th January 1812.' *Battles, sieges and campaigns*: 'Lieutenant. Siege and Capture of the Fortified Convents at Salamanca, 17th to 27th June 1812. Salamanca, 22d July 1812.

215

FRASER

Siege of the Castle of Burgos, 23d September to 21st October 1812. Vittoria, 21st June 1813. Pyrenees, 26th July 1813. Nivelle, 10th November 1813. Toulouse, 10th April 1814.' *Distinguished conduct*: [This section appears to have been completed by James Considine, Lt. Col. of the 53rd in 1830] 'On the evening of the 4th October 1812 Lieut Fraser was detached in command of a party to carry ladders &c for the storming of some out-works at the Castle of Burgos, and having performed this duty by placing the ladders he was the first to *lead the way* up one of them. His present Commanding officer finding this Gallant conduct mentioned with records of the Regiment has great pleasure in inserting it here. Jas. Considine. Lt Colonel 53rd.' *Wounds received in action*: 'Wounded severely at Pampluna, on the 26th of July 1813 – received a grant of one years Pay, and a temporary Pension on the 25th December 1824 of Seventy Pounds a Year.' *Service abroad*: '21st August 1811 to 6th July 1814, Peninsula. 16th October 1815 to 12 October 1817, St Helena. 13th October 1817 to 7th July 1823, East Indies. 2d December 1829 to 31st December 1829, Gibraltar.' [PRO: WO 25/795 f180]. Severely wounded, Pyrenees, 26 July 1813 ('Lieut. Frazer') [*London Gazette*]. MGS.

FRASER, Malcolm, Capt., 79th Foot: Capt., 79th Foot, 29 Nov. 1810. Slightly wounded, Fuentes de Onoro, 5 May 1811 (1st Battn.) [*London Gazette*]. Wounded at Waterloo. Died in Ireland, 1822.

+FRASER, Thomas, Major, 1st Foot: Major, 1st Foot, 6 July 1809. Killed, Siege of St. Sebastian, 7–27 July 1813 (3rd Battn.) [*London Gazette*]. Mentioned in Graham's dispatch to Wellington, dated 27 July 1813, concerning the failed Assault on St Sebastian on the morning of 25 July 1813 ['Major

Frazer ... commanding the royal Scotch ... greatly distinguished themselves. Major Frazer lost his life on the breach, with many of his brave comrades.'] [*London Gazette*].

FRASER, William, Ensign, 92nd Foot: *1829 Statement of Service*: 'Born Woodhill, Inverary, Aberdeenshire, 21st November 1796. Aged Sixteen years and four months on his first Entrance into the Army. Ensign, 92nd Regt., 8th April 1813. Lieutenant, 92d Reg. 19th Jany. 1814. Lieutenant, 93d Regt., 1 June 1815... Lieutenant, Rifle Brigade, 16th May 1818. Lieutenant, 43rd Regt., 6 July 1820... Captain, 43rd Regt., 9th Decr. 1824.' *Battles, sieges and campaigns*: 'Duke of Wellington's Army, Campaign 1813, as Ensign in the 92d Regiment.' *Wounds received in action*: 'Wounded severely at the Battle of the Nive 13th Decr. 1813. Received one years Pay as Ensign.' *Service abroad*: 'Octr. 1813 to Apl. 1814, Spain and France. Septr. 1822 to Jany 1826, Gibraltar. Jany. 1829 to 31 Decr. 1829, Gibraltar.' [PRO: WO 25/793 f170]. Severely wounded, the Nive, 13 Dec. 1813 (1st Battn.) [*London Gazette*]. MGS.

FREDERICK, Edward, Lt./Capt., 51st Foot: Born 6 Aug. 1788. Lt., 51st Foot, 7 May 1807. Severely wounded, 'in the Operations of the Army', 31 Aug. 1813 [*London Gazette*]. Capt., 51st Foot, 28 April 1814. Waterloo. Retired, Half-pay, as Capt., 7 April 1826. Died in 1846. *Wheeler*, pp. 143–4 [near Lezaca, 31 Aug. 1813: 'General English had ridden to the front to become better acquainted with the ground, when by some unforseen accident he became separated from his men and would have been made prisoner but for the little band who at a great disadvantage rescued him. Captain Frederick saw the danger his general was in, ordered his buglar to sound the charge, the sound was answered by three cheers, and off his company went... In a moment they were mixed with the enemy and down the hill they went together, pel mel, into the wood. The General was rescued... Our loss was severe... Wounded,... [Capt] Fredrick [sic] (severely)'].

FREDERICK, Roger, Lt., 43rd Foot: Lt., 43rd Foot, 18 Oct. 1809. Severely wounded, Coa, 24 July 1810 [*London Gazette*].

FREEBAIRN, William, Ensign, 50th Foot: Ensign, 50th Foot, 9 April 1812. Severely wounded, the Nive, 13 Dec. 1813 (1st Battn.) [*London Gazette*].

+FREER, Edward, Ensign, 43rd Foot: Lt., 43rd Foot, 12 July 1810. Severely wounded, storming of Badajoz, 6 April 1812 (1st Battn.) [*London Gazette*]. Killed, Nivelle, 10 Nov. 1813 [*London Gazette*]. Obituary, *The Gentleman's Magazine*, Dec. 1813, p. 623 ['In his 19th year, Lieut. Edw. Freer, a native of Coventry, third son of Mr. Thos. F. surgeon of the Leicestershire militia. He had a commission in the 43d reg. at a very early age. At Walcheren he displayed that contempt of danger which has since so eminently shone in his military conduct. He joined the army under Marquis Wellington at the battle of the Bridge of the Coa; since which period, he has been in every engagement with that distinguished regiment. He was of the storming-parties at Ciudad Rodrigo, Badajos, Salamanca, and St Sebastian. At Badajos, having gained the summit of a high wall, and his companions being all killed or wounded, unable alone to descend amongst the French, yet unwilling to retreat, he was observed by the combatants on both sides, from the flashes of the guns, standing most gallantly, and contemptuously picking stones from the wall and throwing them at the Enemy, till at length, having received three shots, he fell, and was carried to a tent and laid by the side of his brother, who was also severely wounded at the breach. Soon recovering, he twice volunteered to conduct the forlorn hope, at the storming of the two last-mentioned fortress; and terminated his gallant career ... in storming the redoubts at St Pe.']. *Haythornthwaite, Die Hard*, pp. 178-9 [Storming of Badajoz: 'Two of the 43rd's lieutenants were William Freer and his younger brother, 19-year-old Edward... In the indescribable confusion, [Harry] Smith found some troops intent on climbing back out of the ditch (hardly any other mention is made of troops attempting to escape from the fiery pit); little Freer and Smith were determined to stop them retreating: "Let us throw down the ladders; the fellows shan't go out." The men in the trench had other ideas, saying "Damn your eyes, if you do we will bayonet you," and such was the crush that the officers were forced back up the ladder... Young Freer seems then to have ascended the ravelin – or at least some high point before the defences – and by the flash of gunfire and the light of burning debris was observed by both sides, unwilling to withdraw but unable to reach the French, picking up and hurling stones at the defenders of the breach. He was hit at least once – one account says three times – it was said in the abdomen, and he was carried off and laid in the same tent as his injured brother [William]. By Edward Freer's own account, the shot he received was in the testicles, but when writing home he reported that it had not done any material damage; thus he survived, only to fall, lamented by all, in the following year at Nivelle.']. *Bruce*, p. 135 [Quoting Napier's *History*: 'low in rank, for he was but a lieutenant; rich in honour, for he bore many scars; was young of days – he was only nineteen, and had seen more combats and sieges than he could count years. So slight in person, and of such surpassing and delicate beauty that the Spaniards often thought him a girl disguised in man's clothing, he was yet so vigorous, so active, so brave, that the most daring and experienced veterans watched his looks on the field of battle, and implicitly following where he led, would like children obey his slightest sign in the most difficult situations. His education was incomplete, yet were his natural powers so happy that the keenest and best furnished intellects shrunk from an encounter of wit; and every thought and aspiration was proud and noble, indicating future greatness if destiny had so willed it. Such was Edward Freer of the 43rd. The night before the battle he had that strange anticipation of coming death so often felt by military men; he was struck with three balls at the first storming of the Rhune rocks, and the sternest soldiers wept, even in the middle of the fight, when they saw him fall.'], p. 137 ['The night before the battle of the Nivelle, Major Napier was stretched on the ground under a large cloak, when young Freer came to him and crept under the cover of his cloak, sobbing as if his heart would break. In his endeavours to soothe and comfort the boy, Napier learnt from him that he was firmly persuaded he should lose his life in the approaching battle, and his distress was caused by thinking of his mother and sisters in England.']. *Haythornthwaite, Armies of Wellington*, p. 33, ['Extreme youth, indeed, was no hindrance to being a good officer. Edward Freer of the 43rd was an ensign at sixteen... he was ... a perfect casting for the heroine Peggy in the play *Raising the Wind* performed by the officers of the Light Division at Gallegos in March 1813. Despite his youth and frail

appearance he was the most intrepid of men, a veteran in his teens and with an unfailingly cheerful spirit.'], 294 n67. See N. Scarfe, *Letters from the Peninsula: The Freer Family Correspondence, 1807-1814* (Leicester, 1953).'].

FREER, George, Ensign/Lt., 38th Foot: Ensign, 38th Foot, 13 Feb. 1812. Slightly wounded, Salamanca, 22 July 1812 (1st Battn.) [*London Gazette*]. Slightly wounded, storming of San Sebastian, 31 Aug. 1813 ('Lieutenant') (1st Battn.) [*London Gazette*]. Lt., 38th Foot, 22 Sept. 1813. Severely wounded, the Nive, 9 Dec. 1813 ('Frier') (1st Battn.) [*London Gazette*]. Temporary pension of seventy pounds per annum, commencing 10 Dec. 1814, 'for wounds' received at St Sebastian and Bayonne, 1813 [*1818 Pension Return*, pp. 10–11]. MGS.

FREER, Richard Bruin, 1st Lt., 95th Foot: *1829 Statement of Service for Retired Officers*: Aged twenty-four on first appointment to the Army. 2nd Lt., 95th Foot, 6 April 1809; 1st Lt., 95th Foot, 21 Aug. 1810; Lt., 89th Foot, 1819; Lt., 2nd Royal Veteran Battn., 1820; Barrack Master of Jamaica, 5 Feb. 1824. *Where serving when wounded*: 'At the seige of Badagos 1812.' *Details of pension*: Seventy pounds per annum, commencing 1813. *Family*: Married in the 'village of Alvestoke, Hants', 20 Aug. 1821. One child by 1829. *Title and nature of employment*: 'Barrack Master of Jamaica'. *Where generally resident during last five years*: 'Jamaica'. [PRO: WO 25/758 f210]. Wounded, siege of Badajoz, 20 March 1812 (1st Battn.) [*London Gazette*]. *Simmons*, p. 232 [wounded, Badajoz, 6 April 1812: 'wounded in the trenches upon the day of the sortie']. *Harris*, p. 167 [following Corunna: 'we reached Hastings that same night, where we found that the volunteering of the Leicester Militia (who were quartered there) had commenced, and that one hundred and twenty-five men and two officers had given their names to the 7th Fusileers, and these Adams and I determined to make change their minds in our favour if we could. The appearance of our Rifle uniform, and a little of Sergeant Adams's blarney, so took the fancies of the volunteers, that we got everyone of them for the Rifle corps, and both officers into the bargain... The names of these two officers were Chapman and Freere [sic], and I believe they are living now.'].

FREER, William Gardner, Lt., 43rd Foot: *1829 Statement of Service:* Born 27 July 1791, Coventry. Aged Fourteen 'on his first Entrance into the Army.' Ensign, 43rd Foot, 25 Dec. 1805; Lt., 43rd Foot, 5 Feb. 1807; Capt., 43rd Foot, 1 Dec. 1813; Half Pay March 1817; Capt., 43rd Foot, 13 Dec. 1817; Major, unattached, Sept. 1825; Major, 10th Foot, 8 June 1826. Note added: 'Lt. Col. 24 May 1833. Died at Corfu, 2 August 1836.' *Battles, sieges and campaigns:* 'Campaigns of 1808 and 1809. Battle of Vimeiro 21 Aug... Battle of Corunna 16 Janry... Campaign of 1809. Talavera. Campaign of 1810 to Lines of Torres Vedras. Redinha 12th March... Condeixa 13 & 14 March... Foz de Arouse 15 March... Sabugal 3rd April... Battle of Fuentes de Onoro 6th May... Campaign of 1812. Siege and Assault of Badajoz 17 March to 6 April... Campaign of 1813. Battle of Vittoria 21st June... Pyrenees August... Heights of Vera 7 October... Battle of Nive 10 Nov... Battle of Nivelle 10-11 & 12 Decr... Campaign 1814 in France. Battle of Thoulouse 10th April... Also numerous Affairs and Skirmishes with Light Dragoons.' *Wounds received in action:* 'Wounded above the left hip at Sabugal 3rd April 1811. Wounded when storming the Breach at Badajoz 6th April 1812, in the back and right knee – right Arm amputated, One years pay as Lieut.

Pension of £100 permanent.' *Service abroad:* 'Aug. 1808 to June 1814, Portugal, Spain & France. Decr 1817 to Sepr 1818, France. Oct 1822 to Sepr 1825, Gibraltar. July 1828 to Decr 1829, Ionian Islands.' Not married in 1830. [PRO: WO 25/786 f309]. Slightly wounded during 'several affairs with the French Army', 18 March-7 April 1811 ('Frier') [*London Gazette*]. Severely wounded, 'right arm amputated', storming of Badajoz, 6 April 1812 (1st Battn.) [*London Gazette*]. Pension for 'loss of an arm' at Badajoz [*1818 Pension Return*, pp. 12–13]. Haythornthwaite, *Die Hard*, p. 178 [Badajoz: 'Two of the 43rd's lieutenants were William Freer and his younger brother, 19-year-old Edward... In the assault William lost his right arm, shattered by a musket-ball (he also suffered a bruised knee from a stone thrown from the breaches, and a slug in the backside which worked out several days later)'].

+FREEZE, George Fraser, Lt., 59th Foot: Ensign, 59th Foot, 6 June 1809; Lt., 59th Foot, 5 March 1812. Severely wounded, storming of San Sebastian, 31 Aug. 1813 (2nd Battn.) [*London Gazette*]. *Register of officers' effects:* 'Freese'. Died of wounds, 5 Sept. 1813, St Sebastian. Single. 'Effects left to Lt. O'Hara.' [PRO: WO 25/2964]. Obituary, *The Gentleman's Magazine*, Oct. 1813, p. 402 ['Sept. 6. In Spain, of wounds received on the 31st of August, deeply regretted for his private worth, as well as public virtues, in his 22d year, George Fraser Freere, 59th foot. He was a most gallant young officer, highly esteemed by his superiors in the service, and adored by his men. His military career was short but active. As an ensign he partook of the perils of the Walcheren expedition. In the memorable battle of Vittoria, as lieutenant, his intrepidity was highly conspicuous, and claimed the particular attention of his honourable commander Fane, now no more; and at the storming of St Sebastian he was mortally wounded, having his arm and shoulder carried away by a cannon-ball, whilst gallantly leading and cheering the brave company he had the honour to command, and which was one of the first that stormed the breach.'].

+FRENCH, William Fry, Capt., 48th Foot: Capt., 48th Foot, 19 Sept. 1804. Slightly wounded, Talavera, 28 July 1809 [*London Gazette*]. Slightly wounded, Albuera, 16 May 1811 [*London Gazette*]. Severely wounded, storming of Badajoz, 6 April 1812 [*London Gazette*]. *Register of dead officers*: Died of wounds, 12 April 1812. Return dated 25 May 1812. [PRO: WO 25/2965].

FREULLER, Fridolin de, Capt., Chasseurs Britanniques: Capt., Army, 2 Sept. 1806; Capt., Chasseurs Britanniques, 11 June 1807. Slightly wounded, Fuentes de Onoro, 5 May 1811 ('Freuler') [*London Gazette*]. Slightly wounded, Pyrenees, 30 July 1813 ('Treuller') [*London Gazette*].

FREYTAG, Clamor Ludwig Ernst Leo von, Lt., 7th Line Battn. K.G.L.: Lt., 7th Line Battn. K.G.L., 24 June 1806. Severely wounded, Talavera, 28 July 1809 ('1st Line Battn.' (sic)) [*London Gazette*]. Served in Peninsula 1808-9. *Beamish*, vol. II, p. 662 ['slightly wounded, 28th July 1809, at Talavera. Resigned 2d April 1811. [Died] at Estorf, amt. Stolzenau in Han. 16th Nov. 1825'].

+FREYTAG, Ernestus von, Lt., 3rd Line Battn. K.G.L.: Lt., 3rd Battn. K.G.L., 5 Feb. 1808. Severely wounded, Castalla, 12-13 April 1813 [*London Gazette*]. *Beamish*, vol. II, p. 639 [Died 'at Alicante, 13th June 1813 of the wounds he received in action near Castalla, 13th April 1813.'].

+FRY, George, Capt., 83rd Foot: Capt., 83rd Foot, 26 July 1810. Killed, storming of Badajoz, 6 April 1812 (2nd Battn.) [*London Gazette*].

FRY, John, 1st Lt., 95th Foot: *1829 Statement of Service*: Born in the Parish of Boyle, Ireland, 16 June 1795. Aged sixteen 'on his first Entrance into the Army.' 2nd Lt., 95th Foot, 21 June 1811; 1st Lt., 95th Foot, 12 May 1812. *Battles, sieges and campaigns*: 'Battle of Salamanca, 22d July 1812. Vittoria, 21st June 1813. Waterloo.' *Wounds received in action*: 'Left leg fractured by a Musket Shot in the Attack of the Heights of Vera on the 7th October 1813, for which received a Grant of One years Pay and a further Grant of one year's Pension as Lieut. but do not remember the date of either Grant. Again wounded at Waterloo 18th June 1815.' *Titles, honorary distinctions and medals*: 'Waterloo Medal.' *Service abroad*: 'May 1812 to Augt. 1814, Peninsula. March 1815 to May 1818, France, Flanders and France.' [PRO: WO 25/804 f354]. Severely wounded, Crossing the Bidassoa, 7/9 Oct. 1813 (2nd Battn.) [*London Gazette*].

FRYER, Charles, 2nd Lt., 23rd Foot: 2nd Lt., 23rd Foot, 27 June 1811. Severely wounded, Salamanca, 22 July 1812 [*London Gazette*].

FULLARTON, Archibald, Lt., 38th Foot: *1829 Statement of Service for Retired Officers*: Aged nineteen on first appointment to the Army. Ensign, 38th Foot, 15 March 1801; Lt., 38th Foot, 15 Oct. 1803; Capt., 38th Foot, 2 April 1812; Capt., 6th Royal Veteran Battn., Sept. 1815. 'Disabled from wounds.' *Where serving when wounded*: 'Spain.' *Details of pension*: One hundred pounds per annum, commencing 13 July 1813. *Family*: First married in Ayr, 25 Dec. 1816. Second marriage in Edinburgh, 13 Aug. 1821. One child from the first, three more from the latter prior to 1829. *Where generally resident during last five years*: 'Edinburgh and its vicinity.' [PRO: WO 25/758 f281]. Slightly wounded, Talavera, 28 July 1809, while serving with 1st Battn. Detachments ('Fullerton') [*London Gazette*]. Severely wounded, Salamanca, 22 July 1812 ('Captain Fullarton' (1st Battn. 38th Foot) [*London Gazette*]. Pension for 'loss of a leg' at Salamanca [*1818 Pension Return*, pp. 10–11].

FULLER, Francis, ('Sr.'), Capt., 59th Foot: *1829 Statement of Service*: 'Born Salisbury, Wiltshire, 28th October 1787. Aged 16 Years on his first Entrance into the Army. Ensign, 59th Regt., 23 June 1803. Lieutenant, 59th Regt., Oct. 1804. Captain, 59th Regt., 5 Octr. 1809. Major, 59th Regt., 17 July 1817. Lieut. Colonel., 59th Brevet, 19 Jany. 1826. Lieut. Colonel, Half Pay, Unattached, 18 Decr. 1827. Lieut. Colonel, 59th Regt., 25 Novr. 1828.' Note added: 'Retired 22 Aug. 1834.' *Battles, sieges and campaigns*: 'Cape of Good Hope in 1806 as Lieutenant... Battle of Vittoria in 1813. Battle of San Sebastian in 1813. Battle of Nivelle in 1813. Battle of Nieve in 1813. And Waterloo in 1815. Storming of Cambray and Paris in 1815 as Captain... Bhurtpore in 1826 as Major Commanding 59th Regiment.' *Distinguished conduct*: 'Omitted by mistake in the Dispatch of the Capture of San Sebastian; received a Medal on representation of the fact to the Marquis of Wellington. Noticed in Public Orders for the Storming of Bhurtpore.' *Wounds received in action*: 'Nieve, Shoulder and Thigh, One Years pay. Bhurtpore slightly in the arm, no gratuity of pay or Pension.' *Titles, honorary distinctions and medals*: 'Received a Gold Medal for Commanding the Regiment at San Sebastian. Received a Medal for Waterloo. Received 3rd Class of the Order of the Bath for

Bhurtpore.' *Service abroad*: 'Septr. 1805 to Septr. 1812, Cape of Good Hope and East Indies. Decr. 1812 to Febr. 1814, Spain & Portugal, France. July 1818 to Novr. 1827, East Indies.' *Family*: Married Emelia Fuller, Jan. 1818, Paris, at the British Ambassador's. They had seven children by 1830. [PRO: WO 25/796 f216]. Slightly wounded, the Nive, 9 Dec. 1813 (2nd Battn.) [*London Gazette*]. Gold Medal (St Sebastian). Waterloo. Severely wounded, the Nive, 11 Dec. 1813 (2nd Battn.) [*London Gazette*]. MGS. *Mullen*, p. 383.

FULLER, Thomas Trayton, Capt., 52nd Foot: Capt., 52nd Foot, 11 Aug. 1808. Severely wounded, 'not dangerously', in operations, 15–19 Nov. 1812 (1st Battn.) [*London Gazette*].

FUMETTE, Augustus, Lt., 2nd Dragoons K.G.L.: Cornet, 2nd Dragoons K.G.L., 27 Feb. 1809; Lt., 2nd Dragoons, 24 March 1812. Slightly wounded, in 'an Affair with the Enemy's Rear-Guard near La Serna', 23 July 1812 [*London Gazette*]. 'Furnetti, Aug.' and 'Fumette, Augustus' in Army Lists. Served in Peninsula 1812–14. Waterloo. MGS. *Beamish*, vol. II, p. 545 ['Joannes Justinus von Fumetty ... slightly wounded, 23d July, 1812, at Garcia-Hernandez'].

+FURNACE, Edward, Ensign, 29th Foot: Ensign, 29th Foot, 18 Jan. 1810. Killed, Albuera, 16 May 1811 [*London Gazette*]. *Haythornthwaite, Die Hard*, p. 153 [Albuera: 'one of their [the 29th Foot] Colourbearers, Ensign Edward Furnace (or Furness) refused to go to the rear when severely wounded, and was hit again and killed.']. Brother of Norbury and William.

FURNACE, Norbury, Lt., 61st Foot: *1829 Statement of Service for Retired Officers*: Aged sixteen on first appointment to the Army.

Ensign, 61st Foot, Dec. 1806; Lt., 61st Foot, 16 March 1808; Capt., 61st Foot, 30 Dec. 1819; Capt., Half-pay, 60th Foot, 3 April 1823, 'at my own request in consequence of the death of my mother which rendered my retirement indispensible to arrange some private property and family affairs.' *Where serving when wounded*: 'Was wounded at the Battles of Salamanca and Toulouse. Served my Corps in the Peninsula from the Battle of Tallavera to that of Toulouse (both inclusive) and was present in every action & affair in which the Regiment was Engaged during that period. Also served six years in the West Indies. Lost two Brothers in the peninsula service Viz. Captn. [William] Furnace when senior of his Rank in the Corps killed at the Battle of Nivelle and Ensign Edward Furnace 29th Regt. killed at Albuhera.' No pension. *Family*: Married in Dublin, 18 Nov. 1822. No children by 1829. *Where generally resident durig last five years*: 'Tallavra House near Beldoyle County of Dublin.' [PRO: WO 25/758 f283]. Severely wounded, Salamanca, 22 July 1812 [*London Gazette*]. Severely wounded, Toulouse, 10 April 1814 (1st Battn.) [*London Gazette*]. MGS.

+**FURNACE, William H., Capt., 61st Foot:** Capt., 61st Foot, 28 Aug. 1804. Slightly wounded, Talavera, 28 July 1809 ('Furnase') [*London Gazette*]. Killed, Nivelle, 10 Nov. 1813 ('Captain W. H. Furnace') (1st Battn.) [*London Gazette*]. *Register of officers' effects*: Single when killed. 'Effects delivered to his Brother Lt. Norbury Furnace.' [PRO: WO 25/2964].

FYFE, William, Lt./Capt., 92nd Foot: Lt., 92nd Foot, 29 Aug. 1805. Slightly wounded, Pyrenees, 25 July 1813 (1st Battn.) [*London Gazette*]. Capt., 92nd Foot, 16 Sept. 1813. Severely wounded, Aire, 2 March 1814 (1st Battn.) [*London Gazette*].

G

GAIRDNER, James Penman, 1st Lt., 95th Foot: 2nd Lt., 95th Rifles, 23 Aug. 1810; 1st Lt. 12 May 1812. Severely wounded, Vittoria, 21 June 1813 (1st Battn.) [*London Gazette*]. Wounded, Waterloo. MGS.

GALBRAITH, John, Ensign, 27th Foot: Ensign, 27th Foot, 13 April 1813. Severely wounded, Nivelle, 10 Nov. 1813 (3rd Battn.) [*London Gazette*].

GALBRAITH, Morgan, Lt., 5th Foot: *1829 Statement of Service*: Born 4 Feb. 1789, Elphin, County Roscommon. Aged nineteen on his first entrance into the Army. Ensign, 5th Foot, 13 Feb. 1808; Lt. 27 Sept. 1809; Capt. 7 April 1825; Capt., 27th Foot, 18 Jan. 1827; Capt., unattached, 10 Sept. 1830 ['in consequence of ill health & urgent Private affairs']. *Battles, sieges and campaigns*: 'Ensign at Roleia 17 Aug. 1808... Ensign at Vimeria 21 Augt. 1808... Sahagun Benevente &c Dec. 1808 & Janry 1809... Corunna 16 Janry 1809... Walcheren, Siege of Flushing 1809... Lieut. at Ciudad Rodrigo Janry & Febry 1812... Salamanca 22d July 1812... Vittoria 21 June 1813... Lieut. at the Pyrenees 28 July to 2d Augt. 1813... Nivelle 10 Novr. 1813... Nive 9th to 13th Decr. 1813... Orthes 27 Feby 1814... Toulouse 10 April 1814... Lieut. at Plattsburgh N. America Septr. 1814.' *Wounds received in action*: 'At the Siege of Flushing 1809. At Vittoria 21 June 1813. One years Pay as Ensign, no Pension.' *Service abroad*: 'April 1808 to Janry 1809, Peninsula. July 1809 to Septr. 1809, Walcheren. June 1812 to June 1814, Peninsula. June 1814 to June 1815, America. July 1813 to April 1818, France. Febry 1819 to April 1826, west Indies.' Not married in 1830. [PRO: WO 25/790 f111]. Wounded, 'very slightly'", Vittoria, 21 June 1813 [*London Gazette*].

GALBRAITH, William, Ensign, Lt., 51st Foot; Lt., 21st Portuguese Line: Ensign, 51st Foot, 11 July 1811. Wounded, Vittoria, 21 June 1813, while serving as Lt., 21st Portuguese Line [*London Gazette*]. Lt., 51st Foot, 22 July 1813. Slightly wounded, Orthes, 27 Feb. 1814, while serving as Lt., 21st Portuguese Line [*London Gazette*]. In Portuguese Service Nov. 1810 to April 1814. *Challis, Portuguese Army*, p. 55. 'Galbreath' in Army List.

+GALE, Arthur, Capt., 28th Foot: Capt., 28th Foot, 19 Oct. 1804. Severely wounded, Albuera, 16 May 1811 (2nd Battn.) [*London Gazette*]. Severely wounded, 'in Action with the Enemy', 15 Feb. 1814 (1st Battn.) [*London Gazette*]. *Register of dead officers*: Died of wounds, 17 Feb. 1814. Return dated Feb. 1814. [PRO: WO 25/2965].

GALIFFE, John P., Major, 60th Foot: Capt., Army, 31 Oct. 1796; Capt., 60th Foot, 30 Dec. 1797; Bvt. Major, 60th Foot, 25 April 1808; Major, 60th Foot, 15 March 1810. Slightly wounded, Talavera, 28 July 1809 ('Garliff') [*London Gazette*]. Severely wounded, Salamanca, 22 July 1812 [*London Gazette*]. Bvt. Lt. Col., 3 March 1814. Gold Medal. MGS. *Royal Military Calendar*, Vol. V, p. 20 ['From 1785 to 1792, this officer was in the French service; he then entered the Dutch service in the hussar reg. of Timorman, in which he made part of the campaigns of 1793, and the whole of 1794. At the time the French took possession of Holland, he came over to England, and was appointed Lieut. in the 6th West India reg.: he joined in the West Indies in 1796; and on the York Rangers being disbanded, was appointed to the 5th batt. of the 60th reg. 30th Dec. 1797. He served in Portugal and Spain, and was slightly wounded at the battle of Talavera; he also served in the battles of Nivelle, Orthes, and Toulouse.'].

GALLEE, John Lockhart, Capt., 38th Foot: *1829 Statement of Service for Retired Officers*: Aged fifteen on first appointment to the Army. Ensign, 60th Foot, 5 March 1796; Lt., 60th Foot, 11 July 1800; Capt., 38th Foot, 27 Sept. 1804 [Army List gives 27 Sept. 1807]; Bvt. Major, 4 June 1814; Half-pay, 83rd Foot, Feb. 1820, 'solely on account of ill health'. 'Is most desirous of being employed on account of having an unprovided for family.' *Where serving when wounded*: 'Battle of Salamanca'. No pension. *Family*: Married in the 'Parish Church of Shuttingdon Shire of Warwick', 31 May 1806. Five children by 1829. *Where generally resident during last five years*: 'In the vicinity of Dundee.' [PRO: WO 25/759 f56]. Slightly wounded, Salamanca, 22 July 1812 ('Gallie') [*London Gazette*].

+GALWAY, Anthony, Ensign/Lt., 40th Foot: Ensign, 40th Foot, 27 April 1809. Killed, Pyrenees, 28 July 1813 (Lieutenant) (1st Battn.) [*London Gazette*].

GAMBLE, Andrew William, Ensign/Lt., 31st Foot: Slightly wounded, Talavera, 27 July 1809 [*London Gazette*]. Lt., 31st Foot, 24 Aug. 1809. MGS.

GAMMELL, William, Lt., 85th Foot: Lt., 85th Foot, 25 Jan. 1809. Slightly wounded, siege of Badajoz, 6-11 June 1811 [*London Gazette*].

+GARDINER, Daniel, Capt., 43rd Foot: Capt., 43rd Foot, 27 Aug. 1804. Killed, Talavera, 28 July 1809, while serving as Brigade Major to Brig.-Gen. R. Stewart ('Gardner') [*London Gazette*].

GARDINER, James, Ensign, 4th Foot: *1829 Statement of Service for Retired Officers*: Aged sixteen on first appointment to the Army. 'Served as a volunteer in the 88th Regt. in the Peninsula'; Ensign, 4th Foot, Dec. 1813 [Army List gives 20 Oct. 1813]. 'Dismissed the Service for being absent without leave, but reappointed in Yorkshire Light Infantry Volunteers on memorialing His Late R.H. the Duke of York shewing that I was severely wounded at the time of the absence, & also in consequence of the strong recommendation of the Court Martial, & of Commanding officer. Paid difference to 6th Dragoon Guards in (I believe) 1815; remained with them until my wife's health was such as to induce me to leave in (I believe) 1816'. Half-pay, 'on account of ill health in family.' *Where serving when wounded*: 'Severely Wounded in action near the Mayor's House at Biantry, in France; received a year's pay but have no pension.' *Family*: Married in Dublin, 20 April 1815. 'No children living.' *Where generally living during last five years*: 'England, Ireland, Wales, Jersey and the Continent.' [PRO: WO 25/759 f34]. Severely wounded, the Nive, 11 Dec. 1813 ('Gardner') (1st Battn.) [*London Gazette*]. MGS. *Haythornthwaite, Armies*, p. 141 ['Ensign Gardner of the 1/4th was desperately wounded at the Nive on 11 December 1813, having been on active service only some three weeks and thus presumably scarcely familiar with routine. Following this wound he left the army to recoup his health, but immediately upon rejoining his battalion in early April 1814 was court-martialled for absenting himself without leave, even though in his injured state he could have been of no use to his battalion, and indeed his absence presumably actually reduced the demands on the medical department. Despite recommendations for clemency on account of his "youth and inexperience", he was cashiered.']. *The Times*, 27 Oct. 1814.

GARDINER, James Ballard, Capt., 50th Foot: Capt., 50th Foot, 20 July 1809. Severely wounded, Vittoria, 21 June 1813 (1st Battn.) [*London Gazette*]. MGS.

GARDINER, John, 1st Lt., 95th Foot: 1st Lt., 95th Foot, 30 Aug. 1810. Severely wounded, storming of Badajoz, 6 April 1812 ('Gardner') (1st Battn.) [*London Gazette*]. Waterloo. Later Capt. and Bt.-Major 82nd Foot. MGS. Died 18 June 1852, at Jock's House, Kinnoull, on the anniversary, and at the same hour, on which he was wounded at Waterloo. [*Dalton*, p. 197]. *Simmons*, p. 232 [wounded, Badajoz]. *Kincaid, Adventures*, pp. 269–70 [November 1813: 'The only instance of a want of professional generosity that I ever had occasion to remark was that of a French officer, which occurred on one of these occasions. We were about to push in their out-posts, for some particular purpose, and I was sent with an order for Lieutenant Gardiner of ours, who was on piquet, to attack the post in his front, as soon as he should see a corresponding movement on his flank, which would take place almost immediately. The enemy's sentries were so near, as to be quite at Mr. Gardiner's mercy, who immediately said to me, "Well, I won't kill these unfortunate rascals at all events, but shall tell them to go in and join their piquet." I applauded his motives, and rode off; but I had only gone a short distance when I heard a volley of musketry behind me; and seeing that it had come from the French piquet, I turned back to see what had happened, and found that the officer commanding it had no sooner got his sentries so generously restored to him, than he instantly formed his piquet and fired at Lieutenant Gardiner, who was walking a little apart from his men, waiting for the expected signal. The balls all fell near, without touching him, and, for the honour of the French army, I was glad to hear afterwards that the officer alluded to was a militiaman'].

GARRETT, Robert, Ensign, 2nd Foot; Lt., 7th Foot: *1829 Statement of Service for Retired Officers*: Aged eighteen on first appointment to the Army. Ensign, 2nd Foot, March 1811 [Army List gives 6 March 1811]; Lt., 2nd Garrison Battn., Sept. 1812; Lt., 7th Foot, Sept. 1812; Capt., '97th afterwards 96th', July 1814; Half-pay, Dec. 1818, by reduction; Capt., 20th Foot, June 1826; Major, Half-pay, unattached, 19 Sept. 1826. *Where serving when wounded*: 'Peninsula'. No pension. 'I have taken the liberty of making a remark in the pension Column relative to wounds I received in the Peninsula – two at the storming of the Forts at Salamanca, in June 1812 – & the last, from which I still suffer considerable inconvenience, a gun shot wound through the wrist joint of the left arm, received at the Battle of the Pyrenees, in front of Pampeluna on the 28th July 1813.' *Family*: Married in 'Mary le bone, London', 10 Feb. 1821. One child by 1829. *Where generally resident during last five years*: 'Updown Nr Margate'. [PRO: WO 25/759 f45]. Slightly wounded in the siege of the Forts of St Vincente, St Cayetano, and La Merced at Salamanca, 18–24 June 1812 [*London Gazette*]. Severely wounded, Pyrenees, 28 July 1813, as Lt. in 7th Foot (1st Battn.) [*London Gazette*]. MGS.

GARVEY, John, Lt., 30th Foot: Lt., 30th Foot, 19 July 1810. Slightly wounded, Salamanca, 22 July 1812 (2nd Battn.) [*London Gazette*].

GASCOYNE, Thomas Bamber, Lt., 83rd Foot: Lt., 83rd Foot, 25 March 1809. Severely wounded, Salamanca, 22 July 1812 ('Gascoigne') (2nd Battn.) [*London Gazette*]. MGS.

+**GAUNTLETT, Samuel, Capt., 29th Foot:** Capt., 29th Foot, 25 June 1803. Severely wounded, Talavera, 28 July 1809 [*London Gazette*]. Obituary, *The Gentleman's Magazine*, Sept. 1809, p. 886 ['30 [July]. In Spain, in consequence of a wound received at the battle of Talavera, Capt. Samuel Gauntlett, of the 29th Foot.'].

GAWLER, George, Ensign/Lt., 52nd Foot: *1829 Statement of Service*: 'Born in London, 21 July 1795. Aged 15 years and 3 months on his first Entrance into the Army. Ensign, 52nd, 4 Oct. 1810. Lieut. 52nd, 12 May 1812. Captain, 52nd, 9 June 1825.' *Battles, sieges and campaigns*: 'Ensign, Campaign 1812 at Badajos. Lieutenant, in the advance to Madrid and Salamanca retreat. In the Campaign of 1813 including Vittoria, the Pass of Vera & the Nive. In the campaign of 1814 including the Nivelle, Orthes & Toulouse. In the campaign of 1815 includg. Waterloo. With various intervening skirmishes.' *Distinguished conduct*: 'Volunteer with the storming party at the breaches of Badajos 6th April 1812 as per Regimental Record book.' *Wounds received in action*: 'Musket shot below right knee, Badajos 6 April 1812. One years pay as Ensign. Musket shot neck, San Munoz 17 Novr. 1812.' *Titles, honorary distinctions and medals*: 'Waterloo Medal.' *Service abroad*: 'Novr. 1811 to 1814, Peninsula and France. Jany. 1815 to Augt. 1818, Embarked for North America & in Flanders & France. July 1823 to Octr. 1826, New Brunswick.' *Family*: Married Maria, daughter of J. Cox Esq., 22 Sept. 1820, Derby. They had three children by 1830. [PRO: WO 25/795 f89]. Slightly wounded, storming of Badajoz, 6 April 1812 ('Gowler') [*London Gazette*]. Waterloo. MGS.

Dalton, p. 172. *Moorsom*, p. 167 [Storming of Badajoz: 'The buglers of the reserve were then sent to the crest of the glacis to sound the retreat... Cool generosity did not forsake the British soldier to the last, – one of them made a wounded officer of the 52nd take hold of his accoutrements that he might drag him up a ladder, "or," said he, "the enemy will come out and bayonet you." The fine fellow was just stepping on to the covered way, when a thrill was felt by the hand which grasped his belts and the shot which stretched him lifeless, threw his body backward into the ditch again, while the officer whom he had thus rescued crawled out upon the glacis. (This man's name is unknown, even to the officer thus saved – the present Colonel Gawler, K.H.).'], pp. 168–9 ['Officers who volunteered for the Storming Party... Ensign George Gawler.'].

GAYNOR, Brian, Ensign/Lt., 7th Portuguese Line: *1829 Statement of Service*: Born in Dublin, 19 May 1796. Aged thirteen on his first Entrance into the Army. 'Ensn. & Lieut., Portuguese Service, From 1809 to 1814.' Ensign, 63rd Foot, May 1814. Half Pay, n.d., 'reduction of 2nd Batt.' Ensign, 99th Foot, March 1815. Lt., York Chasseurs, 20 April 1815. Half Pay, 24 Decr. 1818, 'reduction of Corps.' Lt., 99th Foot, 25 March 1824. Capt., 99th Foot, 7 April 1825. Note added: 'Sold out 18 July 1834.' *Battles, sieges and campaigns*: 'Braga, Oporto, Naval Carneira, Bauhas, Arroyo del Puerco.' *Distinguished conduct*: 'Employed and almost constantly employed on the reconnoitreing Service until taken prisoner on the 12th March 1810.' *Wounds received in action*: 'Received a wound on the left knee at arroyo del puerco on March 12 1810. Neither pension nor year's pay was received.' *Service abroad*: '1809 to 1814, Portugal, Spain & France. 1815 to 1818, West Indies. Novr. 1825 to Decr. 1828,

Mauritius.' *Family*: Married Anna Maria Sherurro, 29 April 1819, Dublin. They had six children by 1830. [PRO: WO 25/804 f243]. Note: he was still aged only fourteen when wounded and captured at Arroyo Del Puerco, 12 March 1810, having been 'constantly employed' in the 'reconnoitring Service'. In Portuguese Service 1813 to April 1814. *Challis, Portuguese Army*, p. 55 ['Lt. 7 Line... Wd. and P/W Arroyo del Puerco '13'].

GAYNOR, Edward, Ensign/Lt., 61st Foot: *1829 Statement of Service:* Born in Dublin, Oct. 1792. Aged sixteen 'on his first Entrance into the Army.' Ensign, 61st Foot, 5 May 1808. Lt., 61st Foot, 13 June 1811. Capt., 61st Foot, 12 June 1823. *Battles, sieges and campaigns*: 'Busaco 27th Septemr. 1810. Fuentes d'Onor 5 May 1811. Pyrenees from 28th July to 2nd August 1813. Nivelle 10th Novr. 1813. Nive from 9th to 13th Decr. 1813. Orthes 27th Feby. 1814. Tarbes March 1814. Toulouse 10th April 1814. Campaigns 1810, 1811, 1812, 1813 and 1814.' *Wounds received in action*: 'Wounded, in the Right Shoulder, Toulouse 10th April 1814. A Pension of £70 per Annum from 25th June 1825 – Permanent, for the loss of Vision of the Right Eye.' *Service abroad*: '4th Octr. 1809 to 12th Novr. 1811, Peninsula. 10th Augt. 1812 to 12th July 1814, Peninsula. 13th Octr. 1816 to 22nd May 1822, Jamaica. 30th June 1828 to 22nd Octr. 1829, Ceylon.' [PRO: WO 25/797 f13]. Severely wounded, Toulouse, 10 April 1814 (1st Battn.) [*London Gazette*].

+GEALE, Frederick, Lt., 13th Light Dragoons: Lt., 13th Light Dragoons, 3 March 1808. Slightly wounded, Campo Mayor, 25 March 1811 ('Gale') [*London Gazette*]. *Register of officers' effects*: Killed, 27 Feb. 1814, Geta, France. Single. 'His Effects taken charge of by his Mother with the Regt.' [PRO: WO 25/2963].

+GEARY, Henry, Capt., Royal Artillery: Capt., Royal Artillery, 12 April 1802. Killed, Rolica, 17 Aug. 1808 [*London Gazette*]. Obituary, *The Gentleman's Magazine*, Sept. 1808 ['17... Capt. Geary, of the Royal Artillery, who was also killed in the same action, by a ball striking him on the head while pointing a gun, was the last officer who embarked at Portsmouth to join Sir A. Wellesley's army. He was a son of the late Capt. G. of the Royal Navy, and a native of the Isle of Wight; and married Miss Jolliffe, dau. of Dr J. of Newport, Hants, who is left, with four young children, to lament him.'].

GEDDES, James, Ensign, 42nd Foot: *1829 Statement of Service for Retired Officers*: Aged twenty-two on first appointment to the Army. 'From June 1808 to 1813 I served as Ensign and Lieutenant in the Tochabers Volunteers and Elginshire Local Militia'; Ensign, 42nd Foot, 17 March 1813; Lt., 42nd Foot, 1 June 1814; Half-pay, 24 Oct. 1814, by reduction. *Where serving when wounded*: 'Wounded at the Battle of Toulouse. On appearing at the Medical Board at London I received a years pay.' *Family*: Married at Garmouth, Scotland, 22 Nov. 1819. Four children by 1829. *Where generally resident during last five years*: 'Near Elgin in Scotland.' [PRO: WO 25/759 f69]. Severely wounded, Toulouse, 10 April 1814 (1st Battn.) [*London Gazette*]. MGS.

GEDDES, John, Capt., 27th Foot: *1829 Statement of Service*: Born 30 Oct. 1787, Edinburgh. Aged seventeen on his first entrance into the Army. Ensign, 72nd Foot, Aug. 1804; Lt., 27th Foot, 25 Oct. 1805; Capt. 1 Dec. 1808; Major 25 Feb. 1825. *Battles, sieges and campaigns*: 'Served as Lieut. in Calabria 1806. Captain at Procida 1809... Captain in Sicily 1810... Captain in 1813 & 1814 under the Duke of Wellington. 7 Oct. 1813. Nivelle 10 Novr 1813.

Nive Decr 1813. Orthes 27 Feby 1814. Thoulouse 10 Apl. 1814.' *Wounds received in action*: 'Commanded 4 companies at Thoulouse 10 April 1814 and was severely wounded by a musquet shot which broke the left thigh near the hip joint. One years pay and permanent pension of £100 per annum.' *Service abroad*: 'May 1806 to Augt. 1814, Mediterranean, Peninsula & France. July 1815 to Apl. 1817, France. Jany. 1819 to June 1823, Gibraltar. Novr. 1825 to Aug. 1828, West Indies.' Not married in 1830. [PRO: WO 25/790 f91]. Severely wounded, Toulouse, 10 April 1814 (3rd Battn.) [*London Gazette*]. *1818 Pension Return*, pp. 8–9. MGS.

GEILS, Thomas, Lt. and Capt., 3rd Foot Guards: Capt., Army, 7 Aug. 1800; Lt. and Capt., 3rd Foot Guards, 2 Dec. 1800. Slightly wounded, Talavera, 28 July 1809 [*London Gazette*]. Temporary pension of one hundred pounds per annum, commencing 25 Dec. 1811, 'for wounds' received at Talavera [*1818 Pension Return*, pp. 2–3].

GEORGE, John, Lt., 7th Foot: *1829 Statement of Service for Retired Officers*: Aged sixteen on first appointment to the Army; Ensign, 44th Foot, 28 Feb. 1810; Lt., 7th Foot, 7 Nov. 1811; Half-pay, 22 June 1817, by reduction; Lt., 21st Foot, Dec. 1818; Capt., Royal African Corps, 25 April 1825; Capt., 66th Foot, June 1826; Half-pay, 5 Dec. 1827, 'on the score of lameness, the effect of a wound thro' the Right foot, received at the Storming of Badajos & long services ... particularly in the West Indies'. *Where serving when wounded*: 'Received a pension of £70 per annum, for a wound thro' the right foot, received at the Storming of Badajos when serving with the 7th Fusiliers, but this pension was unfortunately withdrawn on the 24th June 1817.' *Where generally resident during last five years*: 'Demerary, t. Vincent, London, Dublin, Limerick'. [PRO: WO 25/759 f61]. Severely wounded, storming of Badajoz, 6 April 1812 [*London Gazette*]. MGS.

+GERBER, Detlef, Capt., 5th Line Batt. K.G.L.: Capt., 5th Line Battn. K.G.L., 31 Oct. 1803. Slightly wounded, Talavera, 28 July 1809 [*London Gazette*]. 'Died of wounds', Peninsula, 19 Sept. 1812. Return dated 25 Sept. 1812 [PRO: WO 25/2965]. Served in Peninsula 1808–12. *Beamish*, vol. II, p. 644 [Died of sickness or accident, 'at Majados in Spain, 19 Sept. 1812.'].

GETHIN, Richard, Lt., 31st Foot: *1829 Statement of Service*: Born in Carrick, Ireland, Oct. 1790. Aged fifteen 'on his first Entrance into the Army.' Ensign, 31st Foot, 19 March 1806. Lt., 31st Foot, 27 Oct. 1808. Capt., 31st Foot, 27 April 1813. Half Pay, Dec. 1814, 'Reduction of Regt. 2d. Battalion.' Capt., 20th Foot, Dec. 1817. Capt., 96th Foot, 29 Jan. 1824. Note added: 'Retd. to H.P. unattd. 31 Jan. 1834.' *Battles, sieges and campaigns*: 'Talavera 27th 28th & 29th July 1809, Lieutenant. Sierra de Busaco 27th Sep. 1810. Retreat of the Army from Portugal in March & April 1811, Lieutenant. Albuhera 16th May 1811, Lieut. in Commd. of Compy. Arroyo de Molino 28th Octobr. 1811, Lieutenant. Toulouse April 1814.' *Wounds received in action*: 'Wounded through the neck in the Battle of Albuhera while in the Commd. of the Light Compy. & flankers of the Regiment. Received one years pay as Captain.' *Service abroad*: 'Sept. 1808 to March 1812, Spain & Portugal. Feby. 1814 to Augt. 1814, France. Decr. 1818 to Decr. 1820, St Helena. 1 July 1824 to 10 June 1826, Nova Scotia. 1 June 1829 to 31 Decr. 1829, Nova Scotia.' *Family*: Married Jane South, 1 Nov. 1819, St Helena. They had four children, the last in Sept. 1828, prior to her death in or before 1830. [PRO:

WO 25/804 f9]. Lt., 'Gethen' in Army List. Severely wounded, Albuera, 16 May 1811 (2nd Battn.) [*London Gazette*].

GETHIN, Richard, Lt., 11th Foot; Capt., 60th Foot: Lt., 11th Foot, 30 Aug. 1810 ('Gethins'). Slightly wounded in the siege of the Forts of St Vincente, St Cayetano, and La Merced at Salamanca, 25–27 June 1812 ('Gethen') [*London Gazette*]. Severely wounded, Salamanca, 22 July 1812 ('Gethen') (1st Battn.) [*London Gazette*]. Mentioned in Graham's report to Wellington concerning the storming of San Sebastian, 31 Aug. 1813 ['P.S... I have omitted to mention the gallant conduct of Lieutenant Gethin, 11th regiment, acting Engineer, who conducted a Portuguese column to the attack, and took the enemy's colours from the Cavalier.'] [*London Gazette*]. Severely wounded, Nivelle, 10 Nov. 1813 (1st Battn.) [*London Gazette*]. Capt., 60th Foot, 12 Nov. 1813.

GEYER, Julius, Ensign, Duke of Brunswick Oels' Corps (Infantry): Ensign, Duke of Brunswick Oels' Corps, 16 Dec. 1812. Severely wounded, Pyrenees, 2 Aug. 1813 ('Guyer') [*London Gazette*].

GIBBONS, Frederick, Lt., 7th Foot: Lt., Army, 21 Aug. 1806; Lt., 7th Foot, 1 Sept. 1808. Slightly wounded, Albuera, 16 May 1811 (1st Battn.) [*London Gazette*]. Temporary pension of seventy pounds, commencing 17 May 1812, 'for a wound' received at Albuera [*1818 Pension Return*, pp. 4–5].

+GIBBONS, George, Capt., 34th Foot: Capt., Army, 19 Dec. 1806; Capt., 34th Foot, 5 Nov. 1807. Killed, Albuera, 16 May 1811 (2nd Battn.) [*London Gazette*].

+GIBBONS, George, Capt., 95th Foot: Capt., Army, 12 Jan. 1809; Capt., 95th Foot, 26 July 1810.

Severely wounded, 'since dead', Crossing the Bidassoa, 7/9 Oct. 1813 (2nd Battn.) [*London Gazette*]. Obituary, *The Gentleman's Magazine*, Nov. 1813, pp. 505–6 ['Fell bravely this day, by a wound from a musket-ball, on the heights above Vera, whilst gallantly leading his company through the French entrenchments, Capt. Geo. Gibbons, 2d batt. 95th foot, a brave officer, as well as a most accomplished and amiable young man, who distinguished himself at the taking of the Island of Martinique in 1809, and shared in the glories attending our late battles in Spain.']. *Hurt*, p. 82 ['D.O.W., Bidassoa, Oct. 7 [1813]']. *Simmons*, pp. 317–18 [killed, Vera, 7 Oct. 1813].

GIBBS, Edward, Major, 52nd Foot: Major, 52nd Foot, 4 Feb. 1808. Mentioned in Wellington's Ciudad Rodrigo dispatch, 20 Jan. 1812 ['I particularly request your Lordship's attention to the conduct of ... Major Gibbs... of the 52d'] [*London Gazette*, 5 Feb. 1812]. Severely wounded, storming of Badajoz, 6 April 1812 [*London Gazette*]. Mentioned in Wellington's Badajoz dispatch, 7 April 1812 ['I must likewise mention Lieutenant-Colonel Gibbs of the 52nd Regiment, who was wounded'] [*London Gazette*]. Lt. Col., Army, 6 Feb. 1812; Lt. Col., 52nd Foot, 8 April 1813. Gold Medal. Three hundred pounds per annum pension, commencing 7 April 1813, for 'loss of an eye' at Badajoz, 1812 [*1818 Pension Return*,, pp. 14–15]. *Hay*, pp. 13–14 ['After drill Colonel Ross and my kind friend, then Major Gibbs (afterwards Lieutenant-General and Lieutenant-Governor of Jersey), were ready to receive Hamilton and myself... The colonel told us the major had something to communicate. He then left us with that kindest and best of men in command, and from him we received an admonition as to our misconduct ... an admonition which

GIBBS

went far deeper than a much more severe censure would have done.'], pp. 34–6 ['the excellent, gentlemanly, and kind-hearted man'], pp. 38, 42 ['I rode up to my good friend Major Gibbs. He received me with his wonted kindness, and said no apology was needed for being a few minutes late for parade']. *Moorsom*, p. 168 [Badajoz: '*Officers Wounded. Major and Brevet Lieut.-Colonel Edward Gibbs* (severely, lost an eye).'], pp. 418–19 ['Gibbs, Lieut.-General Sir Edward, K.C.B. – Entered the 52nd in 1798. Served in the expedition to Ferrol, in Sicily, in Spain and Portugal, and was present at the sieges of Ciudad Rodrigo and Badajoz, and at the battle of Vittoria, for which he received the war-medal with two clasps. Whilst serving as a regimental officer in the 52nd, Sir Edward was repeatedly mentioned in the Duke of Wellington's despatches, and more especially on occasion of the assault of Ciudad Rodrigo and of Badajoz.'].

GIBBS, John, Paymaster, 51st Foot: *1829 Statement of Service*: 'Born in London, 18 October 1787. Aged Twenty two years & four months on his first Entrance into the Army. Paymaster, 51st Regt., 15 Feby. 1810.' *Battles, sieges and campaigns*: 'Present with his Regiment during the whole of the period of its Service abroad, both in the Peninsula and France & the Netherlands. NB. Mr Gibbs was in the Adjutant Generals Office, Horse Guards, from about Feby or March 1805, to the day preceeding his appointment as Paymaster of the 57th regiment, a period of 5 years, and whilst so employed was attached to the Department of the Adjutant General, with the expedition under General the Earl of Chatham, and accompanied said expedition to Walcheren. The above will make his Total Service to 31st Decr. 1829, 24 years and 10 months.' *Wounds received in action*:

'Severely wounded in an advance on Llerena, in the South of Spain, on the 26th March 1812, Lt Gen Sir T Graham Comp. 1 years Pay Received but no Pension.' *Titles, honorary distinctions and medals*: 'Waterloo Medal.' *Service abroad*: '25 June 1811 to 26 June 1814, Peninsula & France. 30 March 1815 to 2 Jany. 1816, Netherlands & France. 3 July 1821 to 31 Decr. 1829, Ionion Islands.' [PRO: WO 25/795 f68]. Waterloo. Half-pay 1846, and died the same year. *Wheeler*, p. 83 [Near Llerena, March 1812: 'several officers who should have been with their Companys were at the head of the column, and as our advance was very slow they had imperceptably gained several paces – or more properly speaking we had lost ground. They had got up unperceived near to one of the enemy's pickets, this caused them to fall back on the column. It being very dark this caused some confusion at the head of the Regiment which soon spread through the whole Division. The Chassuers [sic] [Britanniques] followed us, and began firing, our paymaster and an Hospital Assistant who was in the rear of our Regt. received the fire of the Chasseures. The Hospl. Assistant was killed and our paymaster was severely wounded in the shoulder.']

GIBSON, Edgar, Ensign, 1st Light Battn. K.G.L.: *1829 Statement of Service*: Born 1794, London. Aged eighteen on his first entrance into the Army. Ensign, 1st Light Battn. K.G.L., 5 Dec. 1812; Lt., 1st Light Battn., 26 March 1814; 'Kings German Legion Disembodied 24 Jany. 1816'; Cornet, Staff Corps of Cavalry, May 1816; Lt., Staff Corps of Cavalry, n.d.; Half-pay, 24 Dec. 1818; Lt., 4th Dragoons, Dec. 1821. *Battles, sieges and campaigns*: 'Ensign at the Siege of Saint Sebastian. An action in the Pyrenees at the Crossing of the Bidassoa and the subsequent actions in which

GILBERT

the left wing of the Army were engaged till the Peace of 1814... Lieutenant at the Battle of Waterloo.' *Wounds received in action*: 'Slightly wounded at the Passage of the Bidassoa, also at Waterloo.' *Titles, honorary distinctions and medals*: 'Waterloo.' *Service Abroad*: 'Augt. 1813 to 24th July 1814, Spain & France. Septr. 1814 to Jany. 1816, Flanders, France & Germany. 1st June 1816 to 24th Nov. 1818, France. 1st Jany. 1822 to Decr. 1829, India.' Not married in 1830. [PRO: WO 25/782 f192]. Slightly wounded, Crossing the Bidassoa, 7/9 Oct. 1813 [*London Gazette*]. Served in Peninsula 1813–14. Waterloo. *Beamish*, vol. II, p. 563 ['slightly wounded, 7th Oct. 1813, on the Bidassoa; slightly wounded, 18th June 1815, at Waterloo.'].

GIBSON, John, Ensign, 68th Foot: Ensign, 68th Foot, 28 July 1813. Slightly wounded, 'in the Operations of the Army', 31 Aug. 1813 [*London Gazette*]. Slightly wounded, Nivelle, 10 Nov. 1813 ('Joseph Gibson') [*London Gazette*].

GICHARD, Edward, Lt., 4th Foot: *1829 Statement of Service for Retired Officers*: Aged twenty-two on first appointment to the Army. Ensign, 4th Foot, 26 Aug. 1806; Lt., 4th Foot, 'Gazetted ... in December 1808, but commission antedated July 1808, cannot state the precise date' [Army List gives 28 July 1808]; Half-pay, April 1816, 'From severe wounds.' 'Incapable from my disabled state to perform active duty in the field.' *Where serving when wounded*: 'In France, at the Battle of the Nive.' *Details of pension*: '£70 per ann.' commencing 11 Dec. 1814. Increased to one hundred pounds, commencing 11 April 1816, 'in consequence of commanding a company at the time of receiving the Wound and for a considerable time before.' [Note

added in pencil that states: 'Not so – the Thirty Pounds was given in consideration of the injury ... more than equal to loss of a limb.'] 'Reduced to £70, 25 Decr. 1817.' *Family*: Married in Penryn, Cornwall, 18 Jan. 1819. Four children by 1829. *Where generally resident during last five years*: 'In Cornwall generally at Penryn.' [PRO: WO 25/760 f188]. Severely wounded, the Nive, 10 Dec. 1813 ('Guichard') (1st Battn.) [*London Gazette*]. 'Guichard' in Army List. *1818 Pension Return*, pp. 4–5. MGS.

+GIFFORD, Theophilus, Lt., 52nd Foot: Lt., 52nd Foot, 1 July 1805. Killed, during 'several Affairs with the French Army', 14 March 1811 (1st Battn.) [*London Gazette*]. *Moorsom*, p. 133 [Cazal Novo, 14 March 1811: 'Captain William Jones's and Captain George Thomas Napier's companies were the first sent out to force back the enemy's light troops, which were posted behind some stone enclosures ... and as the bugles repeated the sound to advance, the companies pressed forward, although engaged against vastly superior sorces, and the enemy gave way; but in gaining this first ridge ... Lieutenant Theophilus Gifford [was] killed.'].

GILBERT, Roger Pomeroy, Lt., 28th Foot: *1829 Statement of Service for Retired Officers*: Aged 'early 15' on first appointment to the Army. Ensign, 28th Foot, 1806; Lt., 28th Foot, 1809 [Army List gives 27 April 1809]; Capt., 28th Foot, 1817; Major, Half-pay, unattached, 1826. *Where serving when wounded*: 'At Grijon 1809. Near Oporto. At Talavera 1809. Near Tarbes 18 March 1814. At Waterloo 18 June 1815... Never in receipt of Pension.' Not married in 1829. *Where generally resident during last five years*: 'Corfu.' [PRO: WO 25/759 f117]. Severely wounded, Talavera, 28 July 1809, while serving with 1st Battn.

231

Detachments [*London Gazette*]. Slightly wounded, 'in Action with the Enemy', 18 March 1814 (1st Battn.) [*London Gazette*]. MGS.

GILDER, Matthew William, Lt., 6th Foot: *1829 Statement of Service for Retired Officers*: Aged seventeen on first appointment to the Army. 'Was appointed in 1809 at the age of 16 to an Ensigncy in the Royal Montgomery Militia, and from that Corps to the 6th Foot.' Ensign, 6th Foot, 19 July 1810; Lt., 6th Foot, 20 Aug. 1813; Half-pay, March 1817, by reduction. *Where serving when wounded*: 'Wounded at Orthes, but not in the receipt of a pension.' *Family*: Married in 'St Mary le Bone, London', 22 Sept. 1821. Three children by 1829. *Where generally resident during last five years*: 'Jersey & France'. [PRO: WO 25/759 f105]. Slightly wounded, Orthes, 27 Feb. 1813 ('Gelder') (1st Battn.) [*London Gazette*].

GILL, William, Lt., 48th Foot: *1829 Statement of Service for Retired Officers*: Aged twenty-two on first appointment to the Army. Ensign, 48th Foot, 9 July 1803; Lt., 48th Foot, 14 July 1804; Capt., 48th Foot, 20 June 1811; Half-pay, 24 Oct. 1814; Capt., 24th Foot, Dec. 1815; Half-pay, 27th Foot, March 1824, 'on account of ill health on my return from India with the 24th Regt.' *Where serving when wounded*: 'Wounded at Talavera but do not receive any pension. Allowed one years pay as Subaltern for the wound received at Talavera.' *Family*: Married in Crawbrook, Kent, 17 Dec. 1815. Five children by 1829. *Title and nature of employment*: 'Barrack Master of Rathkeale County of Limerick, Ireland.' *Where generally resident during last five years*: 'Have resided at Rathkeale since my appointment as Bk. Master in May 1824.' [PRO: WO 25/759 f88]. Slightly wounded, Talavera, 28 July 1809 ('Giles') [*London Gazette*].

GILLAM, William, Capt., 36th Foot: Lt., 17th Foot, 5 Feb. 1807. Capt., Army, 21 Nov. 1811. Severely wounded, Nivelle, 10 Nov. 1813, as Capt., 36th Foot ('Wm. Gillam') (1st Battn.) [*London Gazette*]. MGS.

GILLIES, John, Major, 40th Foot: *1829 Statement of Service for Retired Officers*: Aged seventeen on first appointment to the Army. Ensign, 40th Foot, 13 Sept. 1795; Lt., 40th Foot, 1796; 'Captain Lieutenancy the 5 April 1801, a Captain of a Company in 1803', 40th Foot; Major, 40th Foot, 8 Feb. 1808 [Army List gives 8 Feb. 1807]; Lt. Col., Army, 1813 [Army List gives 4 June 1813]. *Where serving when wounded*: 'Commanding the 1st Battalion of the 40th Regt. of Foot at the Storming of Badajos the 5th April 1812.' *Details of pension*: Three hundred pounds, commencing 5 April 1813. *Where generally resident during last five years*: 'Kenloch Moror House'. [PRO: WO 25/759 f111]. Severely wounded, storming of Badajoz, 6 April 1812 (1st Battn.) [*London Gazette*]. Gold Medal. *1818 Pension Return*, pp. 10–11.

GILLMAN, Henry, Lt., 3rd Foot: *1829 Statement of Service*: 'Born in St. Lucie [sic], West Indies, 4th August 1793. Aged 1 Year 8 Months on his first Entrance into the Army.' Ensign, 27th Foot, 1 April 1795; Half-pay, 1800, 'Unable to serve from youth.' Ensign, 3rd Foot, 1808; Lt., 3rd Foot, Decr. 1809 [Army List gives 18 Dec. 1808]; Capt., 3d Foot, Nov. 1817; Major, 3rd Foot, 14 Nov. 1827; Major, 69th Foot, 20 March 1828. Note added: 'Lt. Colonel, Half Pay, Unattached, 26th Octr. 1830.' *Battles, sieges and campaigns*: 'Ensign 3d Foot, Surrender of the Island of Maderia in 1808, Forts St Julian &c, Cascies, Mouth of the Tagus 20th Aug. 1808, under the Command of Marshal Beresford. Campaign in Spain & Portugal under Sir John Moore in 1808 &

1809. Advance to Oporto & passage of the Douro, & Storming of Oporto 11th & 12th May 1809. In front of Placeretia 26 July 1809. Advance to Chaes 15 & 16 May 1809. Lieutenant 3d Foot. Talavera 27 & 28 July 1809. Retreat from the Frontiers of Portugal in August 1809. Battle of Busaco 27 Septr. 1809. From this period to the Retreat of the French from the Lines in various Skirmishes at Ahandra. Camp at ahor near Badajos in March & April 1811 under Lord Hill. Albuerar 12 May 1811... Surprise of a French Corps under General Gerard, at Arios Das Molina in Octr. 1811... Almaraz 19 May 1811 & various affairs at Villafranca, Almandralgo, Ilsuegre &c. &c. in June & July 1812 under Lord Hill. Entry into Madrid 14 Aug. 1812, frequently Engaged with Light Compys during the Retreat from Madrid, Vittoria 21 June 1813. Pampeluna 27 & 28 June 1813. Pyrenees 25 & 26 June 1813, and Retreat of the French into France 29th & 30 June 1813 under Lord Wellington. Various Skirmishes between this period & Novr. with Light Compys. Biddassoa 7 Octr. 1813, Nivelle 10 Novr. 1813. Cambo 20th & 21 Novr. Nive 9th & 10 Decr. Bayonne 13 Decr. 1813. Orthes 27 Feby. 1814. Toulouse 10 April 1814.' *Distinguished conduct*: 'Noticed in Orders for conduct as Adjutant of the Light Companies, on the 25th & 26th July 1813.' *Wounds received in action*: 'Lieutenant Light Infantry at Talavera on 27 & 28 July. Recd. one Years Pay as Lieutenant. Bayonne 13 Decr. 1813, received one years Pay and Pension as Lieutenant.' *Service abroad*: '1808 to June 1814, Island of Maderia, Spain, Portugal & France. July 1815 to 1818, N. America & France. 1822 to Nov. 1827, New South Wales.' *Family*: Married Clare Winter, 4 April 1816, Putney. They had five children by 1830. [PRO: WO 25/798 f218]. Severely wounded, the Nive, 13 Dec. 1813 (1st Battn.) [*London Gazette*].

GILSE, Frederick de, Adjutant/ Ensign/Lt., 60th Foot: Adjutant, 60th Foot, 6 Feb. 1806; Ensign, 60th Foot, 15 May 1806. Slightly wounded, Rolica, 17 Aug. 1808 ('Adjt. de Gilso') (5th Battn.) [*London Gazette*]. Lt., 60th Foot, 26 Sept. 1809. Slightly wounded, storming of Badajoz, 6 April 1812 ('Gilsa') (5th Battn.) [*London Gazette*]. MGS.

GIRDLESTONE, James, Lt./Capt., 31st Foot: Lt., 31st Foot, 25 Dec. 1807. Slightly wounded, Talavera, 28 July 1809 ('Girdelstone') [*London Gazette*]. Capt., 31st Foot, 20 Dec. 1810. Severely wounded, Vittoria, 21 June 1813 (2nd Battn.) [*London Gazette*]. Severely wounded, Pyrenees, 30 July 1813 (2nd Battn.) [*London Gazette*]. Severely wounded, Nivelle, 10 Nov. 1813 (2nd Battn.) [*London Gazette*]. Pension of one hundred pounds per annum, commencing 11 Nov. 1814, 'for wounds' received at St Jean de Luz, 1813 ('John') [*1818 Pension Return*, pp. 8–9]. MGS. *Blakeney*, pp. 329–30 [Returned to Britain after being wounded, Nov. 1813: 'we were removed to los Pasages and there embarked in a transport bound for Portsmouth; but ... we were compeled to put into Bantry Bay in Ireland... I sent for the driver and immediately concluded a bargain; he engaged to carry us to Bandon in the hearse ... the whole party, consisting of Captain Taylor, 28th, with a broken thigh, Captain Girlston [sic], 31st, a broken arm ... [etc] entered the hearse... Our appearance must have been extraordinary; for as we moved along in the carriage of death ... the country folk, abandoning their legitimate avocations, ran after us for miles.'].

+GIRSEWALD, Carl von, Capt., Duke of Brunswick Oels' Corps (Infantry): Capt., Duke of Brunswick Oels' Corps, 29 Aug. 1811. Severely wounded, storming of Badajoz, 6 April 1812 ('Girswald') [*London Gazette*]. Died of wounds, 30 April 1812. Return dated 25 May 1812 ('Grieswald') [PRO: WO 25/2965].

GITTERICK, John, Adjutant/Lt., 12th Light Dragoons: Ensign and Adjutant, 12th Light Dragoons, 14 Nov. 1804; Lt., 12th Light Dragoons, 8 Dec. 1808. Severely wounded, Salamanca, 18 July 1812 ('Adjutant Gettrick') [*London Gazette*].

GIVEN, James, Lt., 61st Foot: Lt., 61st Foot, 1809. Slightly wounded, Talavera, 28 July 1809 ('Gwan') [*London Gazette*]. Slightly wounded in the siege of the Forts of St Vincente, St Cayetano, and La Merced at Salamanca, 18–24 June 1812 [*London Gazette*]. Temporary pension of seventy pounds per annum, commencing 25 Dec. 1811, 'for a wound' received at Talavera [*1818 Pension Return*, pp. 16–17].

GLEDSTANES, Nathaniel, Capt., 68th Foot: *1829 Statement of Service*: 'Born in London, 6th November 1787. Aged Fourteen on first appointment to the Army. Ensign, 68th Foot, 3 Oct. 1801; Lt., 68th Foot, 25 Oct. 1803; Capt., 68th Foot, 13 July 1809; Bvt. Major, 68th Foot, 21 June 1817.' Note Added: 'Died at Athlone 7 Oct. 1830.' *Battles*: 'Taking of St. Lucia 20th June 1803... 1st 3rd & 5th Augt. 1800 before Flushing... Moresco, 20th June 1812, Dy. A. Qr. Mr. Gl. Heights above Moresco, 21 June D.A.Q.M.G. Fort El-Reterio, 13th Augt. 1812, D.A.Q.M.G. Olmas, 20th October 1812, D.A.Q.M.G. Jaun Munoz, 7th Novr. 1812, D.A.Q.M.G. Vittoria, 21st June 1813, Captain. Ostes, 30th July 1813, Captain. Zara, 31st July 1813, Captain. Echelar, 2d Aug. 1813, Captain. Lazacea, 31st Augt. 1813, Captain. Nivelle, 10th Novr. 1813, Captain.' *Wounds received in action*: 'Wounded severely in the right Leg at Nivelle on 10th Novr. 1813, Received one years Pay.' *Titles, honorary distinc-* *tions and medals*: 'Brevet Major for particular Services performed in the Peninsula.' *Service abroad*: '23rd Decr. 1801 to 26th Septr. 1806, West Indies. 30th July 1809 to 27th Novr. 1809, Walcheren. 28th June 1811 to 26th July 1814, Peninsula. 3rd July 1818 to 7th March 1820, Canada. 22nd June 1824 to 7th Augt. 1828, Canada.' *Family*: Married Ann Garner, 1 May 1816, in Belfast. They had two children prior to her death on 10 April 1828. [PRO: WO 25/798 f153]. Severely wounded, Nivelle, 10 Nov. 1813 [*London Gazette*]. *Green*, pp. 179, 189–90 [31 Aug. 1813, Pyrenees: 'My shirt and trowsers were drenched with blood. In this condition I started to the rear, assisted by the men above mentioned. I had not proceeded more than fifty yards, before I was deserted by them. The shots from the enemy at this period flew so exceedingly fast, that the men were afraid of being killed, so that I was left to take care of myself; but Captain Gledstanes being near the spot, I said, "Sir, am I to be left in this condition, to be killed or taken by the enemy?" "No, my man," said this amiable officer, "I will assist you:" and immediately seizing hold of my right arm, and giving me a stick in my left hand, conducted me out of the reach of the enemy's balls... I never think of Captain Gledstane but with pleasure: I was indebted to him for my life'.].

GLOSTER, Thomas, Lt., 61st Foot: *1829 Statement of Service*: 'Born Limerick, Co. Limerick, in 1787. Aged Twenty years on his first Entrance into the Army. Ensign, 61st Foot, 1st April 1807. Lieut., 61st Foot, 17 March 1808. Captain, 61st Foot, 7 April 1825.' Note added: 'Major Unattached 8 Oct 1830.' *Battles, sieges and campaigns*: 'Busaco 27th September 1810. Fuentes d'onor 5 May 1811. Forts of Salamanca June 1812. Salamanca 22nd July 1812. Pyrenees 28th July to 2nd August 1813. Nivelle 10th November 1813. Nive 9th to 13th

December 1813. Orthes 27th February 1814. Toulouse 10th April 1814. Campaigns 1809, 1810, 1811, 1812, 1813 and 1814.' *Distinguished conduct*: 'After being Wounded in the Arm at the Battle of Salamanca, continued to perform his Duty.' *Wounds received in action*: 'Wounded in the left Arm at the Battle of Salamanca and through the Right Breast at Toulouse, the Ball passing through the right lobe of the Lungs, and out at the Back. Grant a years Pay as Captain. Pension £70 per year Permanently.' *Service abroad*: '21st Febry. 1808 to 8 Sept. 1808, Gibraltar. 4th October 1809 to 5th July 1814, Peninsula. 14th Octr. 1816 to 12th Augt. 1821, Jamaica.' [PRO: WO 25/797 f15]. Slightly wounded, Salamanca, 22 July 1812 [*London Gazette*]. Severely wounded, Toulouse, 10 April 1814 (1st Battn.) [*London Gazette*]. MGS.

+GLOVER, George Henry, Lt., 1st Foot: Lt., Army, 21 Jan. 1808; Lt., 1st Foot, 17 Nov. 1808. Severely wounded, Vittoria, 21 June 1813 (3rd Battn.) [*London Gazette*]. *Register of dead officers*: Died of wounds, 28 June 1813. Return dated June 1813. [PRO: WO 25/2965].

GLYNN, Andrew Eugene, Lt., 40th Foot: *1829 Statement of Service for Retired Officers*: Aged twenty on first appointment to the Army. Ensign, 40th Foot, April 1809, 'from the Militia'; Lt., 40th Foot, Sept. 1811 [Army List gives 19 Sept. 1811]; Half-pay, 44th Foot, 'about October 1816'. *Where serving when wounded*: 'Near Pampeluna in Spain... I have served from 1810 untill after the Battle of Waterloo and previous to which in America.' No pension. *Family*: Married near Kenmar, County Kerry, 20 March 1817. Six children by 1829. *Where generally resident during last five years*: 'In and near the Town of Killarney County Kerry.' [PRO: WO

25/759 f141]. Slightly wounded, Pyrenees, 28 July 1813 (1st Battn.) [*London Gazette*]. Waterloo. MGS.

GLYNN, James, Ensign, 40th Foot: Ensign, 40th Foot, 8 Oct. 1812. Severely wounded, Toulouse, 10 April 1814 (1st Battn.) [*London Gazette*]. Temporary pension of seventy pounds per annum, commencing 11 April 1815, 'for wounds' received at Toulouse [*1818 Pension Return*, pp. 10–11].

GODDARD, George Anthony, Ensign, 50th Foot: *1829 Statement of Service for Retired Officers*: Aged nineteen on first appointment to the Army. Ensign, 50th Foot, 14 Dec. 1809; Lt., 50th Foot, 21 Jan. 1813. Six years on full-pay. *Where serving when wounded*: '19th May 1812. Spain.' No pension. *Family*: Married in 'Westbury on Trym in the County of Gloucester', 15 April 1816. Four children by 1829. *Where generally resident during last five years*: 'Bristol'. [PRO: WO 25/759 f173]. Severely wounded, 'at the Storm and Capture of Fort Napoleon, and the Enemy's other Works, in the Neighbourhood of Almaraz', 19 May 1812 [*London Gazette*].

GODFREY, Edward Lee, Lt., 20th Foot: Ensign, 20th Foot, 13 April 1809; Lt., 20th Foot, 25 Aug. 1813. Slightly wounded, Orthes, 27 Feb. 1814 [*London Gazette*]. MGS.

GODFREY, John, Ensign, 50th Foot: Ensign, 50th Foot, 25 Aug. 1809. Slightly wounded, 'at the Storm and Capture of Fort Napoleon, and the Enemy's other Works, in the Neighbourhood of Almaraz', 19 May 1812 [*London Gazette*].

GODWIN, Henry, Capt., 9th Foot: *1829 Statement of Service for Retired Officers*: Aged nineteen on first appointment to the Army. Ensign, 9th Foot, 30 Oct. 1799; Lt.,

9th Foot, 21 June 1803; Capt., 9th Foot, 28 March 1808; Major, 5th West India Regt., 26 May 1814; Major, 41st Foot, 15 Nov. 1815; Lt. Col., 41st Foot, 26 July 1821; Lt. Col., 87th Foot, March 1829; Half-pay, 24 June 1829, by reduction. *Where serving when wounded*: 'Spain'. *Details of pension*: Two hundred pounds, commencing 1812. *Family*: Married in Waltham-stow, 14 Jan. 1812. One child by 1829. *Where generally resident during previous five years*: 'India and England.' [PRO: WO 25/759 f168]. Severely wounded, Barossa, 5 March 1811 (1st Battn.) [*London Gazette*]. Two hundred pounds per annum pension, commencing 6 March 1812, for 'loss of the use of a hand' at Barrosa, 1811 [*1818 Pension Return*, pp. 6–7]. MGS. *Blakeney*, pp. 146–8 [Gibraltar, April 1810: '[Upon arrival from Tarifa] the first person who addressed me on landing was Lieutenant Taylor, 9th Regiment (afterwards shot through the body at Barossa), demanding, without any prelude whatever, if Captain Godwin of his regiment was wounded. I dryly answered, "Yes." "Where?" "In the shoulder."... This was sufficient to extricate me from the surrounding crowd... During my absence Godwin had been told that I had reported his having been wounded in the back of his shoulder; but although he taxed me with the report in a laughing way, still he appeared not well pleased. His usual good-humour returned when I assured him that I never made use of such an expression; and certainly Godwin was one of the last to whom I should attribute a wound in the back. The fact was that he had been hurt in the shoulder a short time previously by his horse running with him against a tree.'].

GOEBEN, Christian von, Lt., 5th Line Battn. K.G.L.: Lt., 5th Line Battn. K.G.L., 19 July 1808.

Severely wounded, siege of Burgos, 5–10 Oct. 1812 [*London Gazette*]. Served in Peninsula 1808–12. MGS. *Beamish*, vol. II, p. 608.

GOEBEN, Frederick von, Lt., 1st Line Batt. K.G.L.: Lt., 1st Line Battn. K.G.L., 9 Jan. 1806. Severely wounded, Talavera, 28 July 1809 ('Gorben Sr') [*London Gazette*]. Served in Peninsula 1808–9. Waterloo. MGS. *Beamish*, vol. II, p. 571.

GOEBEN, William von, 2nd Lt., Artillery, K.G.L.: 2nd Lt. 8 Nov. 1808. Severely wounded, storming of Badajoz, 6 April 1812 [*London Gazette*]. Served in Peninsula 1809–14. Waterloo. *Beamish*, vol. II, p. 535 ['severely wounded 7th May 1812 [sic], at assault of Badajos, severely wounded 16th June 1815 at Quatre-bras'].

GOLDIE, George Leigh, Captain, 66th Foot: *1829 Statement of Service*: 'Born Goldie Leigh, near Dumfries NB, 27 May 1789. Aged 14 Years on his first Entrance into the Army. Cornet, 6 Dr Guards, 3 Sept. 1803. Lieut., 6 Dr Guards, 5 March 1805, by raising men. Captain, 5 Gn Battn., 4 Decr 1806. Captain, 66 Foot, 21 Jany 1808. Bt. Major, 66 Foot, 20 June 1811. Bt. Lt Colonel, Army, 12 August 1819. Major, Half Pay, unattached, May 1821. Major, 50 Regt., 12 Decr. 1826. Lt. Colonel, Half Pay, unattached, 25 Feby. 1831. Lt. Colonel, Half Pay, Inspecting Field Officer of Militia, 27 Sept. 1833.' *Battles, sieges and campaigns*: 'Crossing the Duro 12 May 1809 and frequent skirmishes before and after. At Talavera commanded light Company of his Corps which suffered *very* severely. At Busaco. Frequent skirmishes at the lines at Torres Vedras. At Albuera the Comm of his Corps devolved upon him for some hours – during the most arduous period of the Battle, Commd the *remains* of two other Regiments of the

Brigade. At Vittoria Commanded 3 Companies posted in advance to protect the Guns under a most destructive Fire which killed or wounded 1/2 the detachments in a few minutes. Received the thanks of Major Gen. Byng on the field. During the operations in the Pyrenees was intrusted with several distinct & important Commands. On the night of 25 July covered the retreat of the whole of that part of the Army at Ronces Valles.' *Distinguished conduct*: 'Crossing the Duro 12 May 1809 – on which occassion I commanded 2 Companies and received personally the expressions of approbation from The Duke of Wellington.' *Wounds received in action*: 'Whilst in advance commanding 300 Men on 30 July 1813 recd. a most dangerous Wound by a Musket Ball (long considered Mortal) which is still lodged in his lungs. For this Wound he received one year's Pay and a Pension as Major Commanding.' *Titles, honorary distinctions and medals*: '[Albuhera] For his conduct on this occasion – received a Gold Medal.' *Service abroad*: '1 March 1809 to Novr. 1813, Peninsula. February 1818 to August 1821, St Helena.' [PRO: WO 25/794 f338]. Gold Medal. Severely wounded, Pyrenees, 30 July 1813 [*London Gazette*]. Temporary pension of two hundred and fifty pounds per annum, commencing 30 July 1814, 'for wounds' received in the Pyrenees, 1813 [*1818 Pension Return*, pp. 16–17]. MGS.

+GOLLAND, Ensign, 45th Foot: Killed, storming of Badajoz, 6 April 1812 ('Gollins') [*London Gazette*]. 'Died... Ensign Golland... 45th Foot' in *1813 Army List*. 'Golland' in *Challis, Index*, p. 137.

GOMERSALL, John, Capt., 58th Foot; Lt. Col., 2nd Portuguese Regt: Capt., 58th Foot, 25 Dec. 1804. Slightly wounded, the Nive, 13 Dec. 1813, while serving as Lt.

Col., 2nd Portuguese Line ('Joao Gomersall') [*London Gazette*]. In Portuguese Service May 1810 to Jan. 1814. Gold Medal. *Challis, Portuguese Army*, p. 55.

GOMM, Henry, Major, 6th Foot: Major, 6th Foot, 18 May 1809. Severely wounded, Pyrenees, 25 July 1813 (1st Battn.) [*London Gazette*].

GOMM, William Maynard, Major, 9th Foot: Lt., 9th Foot, 16 Nov. 1794. Capt., 9th Foot, 25 June 1803. Major, 9th Foot, 10 Oct. 1811. Lt. Col., Army, 17 Aug. 1812. Mentioned in Wellington's Vittoria dispatch, 22 June 1813 ['Major-General Oswald reports ... Lieutenant-Colonel Gomm, of the Quarter Master-General's department.'] [*London Gazette*]. Slightly wounded, the Nive, 9 Dec. 1813, while serving as AQMG ('9th Foot – Lieutenant-Colonel William Gomm') [*London Gazette*]. Capt. and Lt. Col., Coldstream Guards, 25 July 1814. Gold Medal. Waterloo. Pension of three hundred pounds per annum, commencing 10 Dec. 1814, 'for a wound' received at Bidart, 1813 [*1818 Pension Return*, pp. 6–7]. MGS. *Royal Military Calendar*, vol. IV, pp. 430–1. *Dalton*, p. 35 ['Commander-in-chief in India, and received a Field-Marshal's baton in Jan., 1868. He died at Brighton, 15th March 1875, full of years and good works.']. *Blakeney*, p. 96 [Retreat to Corunna: 'Captain Gomm, General Disney's major of brigade'].

GOODIFF, James Maynard, Lt., 31st Foot: *1829 Statement of Service for Retired Officers*: Aged twenty-one on first appointment to the Army. Ensign, 31st Foot, 15 Aug. 1809; Lt., 31st Foot, 16 Jan. 1812; Half-pay, 'July or August' 1817; Lt., 98th Foot, Aug. 1824; Lt., 7th Foot, 'December 1824 or Jany. 1825'; Lt., 48th Foot, March 1825; Lt., 66th Foot, April 1825; Lt. & Cornet, Half-pay, 18th Light Dragoons, 30 April 1827. *Where serving when wounded*: 'Badajoz a Bayonet wound in the head.' No pension. *Family*: First married in 'Cove of Cork, Autumn 1814.' Second marriage in Boyle County of Roscommon, 19 July 1825. Four children from the first marriage, one from the latter, by 1829. *Where generally resident during last five years*: 'Marching with his Regt. in Ireland & latterly resident at Burrisakome.' [PRO: WO 25/759 f170]. MGS.

GOODSMAN, David, Capt., 61st Foot: *1829 Statement of Service for Retired Officers*: Aged nineteen on first appointment to the Army. Ensign, 9th Foot, Aug. 1799; Lt., 9th Foot, March 1800; Half-pay, Nov. 1802, by reduction; Lt., 61st Foot, July 1803; Adjutant, 61st Foot, July 1803; Capt., 61st Foot, Nov. 1808 [Army List gives 28 Nov.]; Bvt. Major, 61st Foot, May 1825; Major, Half-pay, unattached, June 1826, by reduction. *Where serving when wounded*: 'Battle Talavera'. No pension. Not married by 1829. *Where generally resident during last five years*: 'Ireland & England'. [PRO: WO 25/759 f205]. Slightly wounded, Talavera, 28 July 1809 [*London Gazette*]. MGS.

GORDON, Hon. Alexander, Lt. Col., 3rd Foot Guards: Lt. and Capt. 3 April 1806; Major, Army, 26 May 1810. Mentioned in Wellington's Ciudad Rodrigo dispatch, 20 Jan. 1812 ['I transmit this dispatch by my Aide-de-Camp the Honourable Major Gordon, who will give your Lordship any further details you may require; and I beg leave to recommend him to your protection.'] [*London Gazette*, 5 Feb. 1812]. Lt. Col., Army, 6 Feb. 1812. Severely wounded, Pyrenees, 28 July 1813 ['Lieut.-Col. the Hon. A. Gordon, Aide-de-Camp to the Commander of the Forces'] [*London Gazette*]. Capt. and Lt. Col., 3rd Foot Guards, 25 Dec. 1813.

K.C.B. Killed at Waterloo while serving as ADC to the Duke of Wellington. *Dalton*, p. 10 ['It is said that when Wellington was roused from sleep by Dr. Hume early on the morning after Waterloo and told that Gordon had died from the effect of his wounds, he burst into tears. Alex. Wm. Gordon was 3rd son of George, Lord Haddo, by Charlotte, youngest daughter of Wm. Baird, of Newbyth. He had served as A.D.C. to his uncle, Sir David Baird, at the capture of the Cape of Good Hope and in several subsequent campaigns.']. Gordon's family raised a monument to him at Plancenoit. *Speeckaert*, pp. 17–18 [The text of the memorial reads: 'Sacred to the Memory of/Lieutenant-Colonel the Honourable Sir Alexander Gordon / Knight Commander of the most Honourable Order of the Bath / Aide-de-Camp to Field-Marshal the Duke of Wellington/And also Brother to George Earl of Aberdeen / Who in the twenty-ninth year of his age / Terminated a short but glorious career / On the 18th of June 1815 / Whilst executing the orders of his great Commander / In the battle of Waterloo / Distinguished for gallantry and Good Conduct in the Field / He was Honoured with repeated marks of Approbation / By the Illustrious Hero / With whom he shared the Dangers of every Battle / In Spain Portugal and France / And received the most flattering proof of his Confidence / On many trying Occasions/His Zeal and activity in the Service obtained the reward / Of ten medals / And the honourable distinction of the Order of the Bath / He was justly lamented by the Duke of Wellington / In his public Despatch / As an Officer of High Promise / And a serious Loss for the Country / Not less worthy of record for his Virtues in private life / His unaffected respect for Religion / His high sense of Honour / His scrupulous integrity / And the most amiable Qualities / Which secured

the attachment of his Friends / And the love of his own Family / In testimony of Feelings which no language can express / A disconsolated Sister and Five surviving Brothers / Have erected this simple Memorial / To the object of their tenderest Affection.']

+GORDON, Alexander, Lt. Col., 83rd Foot: Lt. Col., Army, 28 Aug. 1804; Lt.Col., 83rd Foot, 16 May 1805. Killed, Talavera, 28 July 1809 [London Gazette]. Obituary, The Gentleman's Magazine, Aug. 1809, p. 780 ['Col. Alex. Gordon, of the 83d Regiment, who fell so nobly at the battle of Talavera, was wounded in the neck by a musketball, charging the Enemy at the head of his Regiment; and when carrying off the field, a shell fell on him and killed him instantaneously. Colonel Gordon was very severely wounded in Holland, under the Marquis of Huntly, in whose Regiment he was at that time a Captain. He served in the same Regiment in Egypt, and was subsequently appointed Aide-de-Camp to the Earl of Hardwicke, during his Viceroyship in Ireland. He was son to the late Lord Rockville, and the Countess of Dumfries, and brother to Wm. Gordon, Member for Worcester, one of the partners of the respectable house of Gordon and Murphy, in London. Colonel Gordon was scarcely more than 33 years old.']. Brett-James, p. 72 ['After Talavera Commissary Schaumann watched several auctions held in regimental bivouacs and from the effects of Colonel Gordon, who had been killed by a howitzer, he bought very cheaply a fine pair of dark blue overalls with two rows of buttons, which he wore for a very long time.'].

GORDON, Alexander, Lt., 92nd Foot: Lt., 92nd Foot, 3 March 1808. Perhaps slightly wounded, Pyrenees, 25 July 1813 ('Gordon') (1st

Battn.) [London Gazette] [or perhaps Thomas Alexander]. Waterloo.

GORDON, Arthur, Capt., 3rd Foot: Capt., 3rd Foot, 14 April 1808. Severely wounded, Albuera, 16 May 1811 [London Gazette].

+GORDON, Charles John, Capt., 10th Light Dragoons: Capt., 10th Light Dragoons, 29 June 1809. Killed, Toulouse, 10 April 1814 [London Gazette].

GORDON, George, Lt., 92nd Foot: 1829 Statement of Service for Retired Officers: Aged nineteen on first appointment to the Army. Ensign, 92nd Foot, 27 May 1809; Lt., 92nd Foot, 25 Feb. 1813; 'Placed on Half Pay 24 Decr. 1814. Removed to Full Pay 25 May 1815. To Half Pay 24th of March 1817... By reduction.' 'Rendered unfit by wound.' Where serving when wounded: 'Spain'. Details of pension: Seventy pounds, commencing 26 July 1814. Family: Married in 'Kingussie N.B.' [Scotland], 5 June 1820. Three children by 1829. Where generally resident during last five years: 'Edinburgh & County of Inverness.' [PRO: WO 25/759 f189]. Slightly wounded, the Pyrenees, 25 July 1813 (1st Battn.) [London Gazette]. Pension 'for wounds' received at Pampeluna, 1813 [1818 Pension Return, pp. 20–1].

+GORDON, Philip, Lt., 27th Foot: Lt., 27th Foot, 8 Nov. 1806. Slightly wounded in the trenches before Badajoz, 8–15 May 1811 (3rd Battn.) [London Gazette]. Slightly wounded, storming of Badajoz, 6 April 1812 (3rd Battn.) [London Gazette]. Slightly wounded, Salamanca, 22 July 1812 (3rd Battn.) [London Gazette]. Wounded, Vittoria, 21 June 1813 (3rd Battn.) [London Gazette]. Register of dead officers: Died of wounds, 28 Aug. 1813. Register dated Sept. 1813. [PRO: WO 25/2965].

GORDON, Robert, Lt., 42nd Foot: Lt., 42nd Foot, 29 Aug. 1811. Severely wounded, Toulouse, 10 April 1814 (1st Battn.) [*London Gazette*]. Killed, Quatre Bras.

+GORDON, Stephen, Lt., 28th Foot: Lt., 28th Foot, 18 May 1809. Slightly wounded, Vittoria, 21 June 1813 (1st Battn.) [*London Gazette*]. Slightly wounded, Pyrenees, 25 July 1813 (1st Battn.) [*London Gazette*]. Slightly wounded, 'in Action with the Enemy', 15 Feb. 1814 (1st Battn.) [*London Gazette*]. Killed, 'in Action with the Enemy', 18 March 1814 (1st Battn.) [*London Gazette*].

GORDON, Theodore, Surgeon, 4th Foot: Surgeon, Army, 6 July 1809; Surgeon, 4th Foot, 28 March 1811. Severely wounded, Crossing of the Bidassoa, 7/9 Oct. 1813 ('Surgeon J. Gordon') (1st Battn.) [*London Gazette*].

GORDON, Thomas William, Lt. Col., 3rd Foot Guards: Capt. and Lt. Col., 3rd Foot Guards, 22 May 1806. Slightly wounded, Talavera, 28 July 1809 [*London Gazette*].

GORDON, William, Lt., 2nd Foot; Capt., 10th Portuguese Line: *1829 Statement of Service for Retired Officers*: Aged sixteen on first appointment to the Army. Lt., Perthshire Regt. of Militia, 1 Aug. 1804; Ensign, 78th Foot, 25 Aug. 1807; Lt., 2nd Foot, 20 June 1809 [Army List gives 21 June]; Capt., 'unattached British Service', 25 Oct. 1814. Half-pay, 'by reduction while attached to the Portuguese Army.' 'Not equal to active service in consequence of wounds.' Twelve years on full-pay. *Where serving when wounded*: 'Peninsula at the battle of Salamanca, 22 July 1812. Peninsula at the battle of Nivelle, 10th Nov. 1813.' *Details of pension*: For the former, one hundred pounds, commencing '23rd July 1813 as Lieutenant'. For the latter, a

pension commencing '11th Nov. 1814 was made 100£ as Capt. and deprived of my pension as Lieut. though I am still suffering from the effects of both wounds.' *Family*: Married in Antrim, 18 Nov. 1817. Three children by 1829. *Where generally resident during last five years*: 'In Aberdeen since I returned from Portugal in 1821.' [PRO: WO 25/759 f197]. Severely wounded, Salamanca, 22 July 1812 [*London Gazette*]. Severely wounded, Nivelle, 10 Nov. 1813, as Capt., 10th Portuguese Line ('Guilherme Gordon') [*London Gazette*]. In Portuguese Service Oct. 1813 to Feb. 1814. *1818 Pension Return*, pp. 24–5. *Challis, Portuguese Army*, p. 55.

+GORDON, William, Lt., 42nd Foot: Lt., 42nd Foot, 29 Oct. 1812. Killed, Toulouse, 10 April 1814 (1st Battn.) [*London Gazette*].

GORDON, William Alexander, Capt., 50th Foot: *1829 Statement of Service for Retired Officers*: Aged nineteen on first appointment to the Army. Ensign, 112th Foot, Nov. 1794; Lt., 112th Foot, 1795; Lt., 26th Foot, 'unknown'; Lt., 92nd Foot, 1799; Capt., 85th Foot, 2 Oct. 1801; Half-pay, by reduction; 'Served in Aberdeen shire Militia after being placed on H.P. 85 Foot'; Capt., 50th Foot, 23 Oct. 1806; Bvt. Major, 50th Foot, 4 June 1813; Bvt. Lt. Col., 50th Foot, 26 Dec. 1813; Captain, Half-pay, 26 Nov. 1818, 'At my own request in consequence of ill health'. 'I entered the Army in November 1794, and have been on full & Half Pay ever since, but cannot with certainty ascertain the precise dates, having lost severall of my Commissions when taken Prisoner by the Enemy when on Passage to Canada to join 26 Foot in 1796.' *Where serving when wounded*: 'At Vittoria. At Bayonne. At Haspern.' No pension. *Family*: Married in Aberdeen, 12 Sept. 1823. Three children by 1829. *Where* generally resident during last five years: 'Scotland'. [PRO: WO 25/759 f184]. Severely wounded, Vittoria, 21 June 1813 ('A. Gordon') (1st Battn.) [London Gazette]. Slightly wounded, 'in Action with the Enemy', 14 Feb. 1814 (1st Battn.) [London Gazette]. MGS.

GORMAN, Constantine, Ensign/Lt., 40th Foot: 1829 Statement of Service for Retired Officers: Aged sixteen on first appointment to the Army. Ensign, 40th Foot, 2 Nov. 1809; Lt., 40th Foot, 3 Sept. 1811 [Army List gives 12 Sept.]; Half-pay, 'about Augt. 1818', 'By his own request from private motives & ill health'. Where serving when wounded: 'In the Peninsula.' Details of Pension: Seventy pounds. 'The Pension was granted about 14th May 1814, but antedated from the 7th April 1813. The Pension renewed in 1827.' Where generally resident during last five years: 'Lieut. Gorman has resided chiefly in London for the last two years & a half, & in Ireland previously.' [PRO: WO 25/759 f183]. Slightly wounded, storming of Badajoz, 6 April 1812 (1st Battn.) [London Gazette]. Severely wounded, Vittoria, 21 June 1813 (1st Battn.) [London Gazette].

+GOUGH, Hugh, Lt., 27th Foot: Lt., 27th Foot, 18 July 1811. Killed, Toulouse, 10 April 1814 (3rd Battn.) [London Gazette].

GOUGH, Hugh, Major, 87th Foot: 1829 Statement of Service for Retired Officers: Aged fifteen on first appointment to the Army. Ensign, 119th Foot, 11 Oct. 1794; Lt., 119th Foot, 11 Oct. 1794; Adjutant, 119th Foot, 1795; Lt., 78th Foot, May 1795; Lt., 87th Foot, 23 Dec. 1795; Capt., 87th Foot, June 1803; Major, 87th Foot, 8 Aug. 1805; Bvt. Lt. Col., 29 July 1809; Lt. Col., 87th Foot, 25 May 1815; Half-pay, 1 April 1817, by reduction; Bvt. Colonel, 12 Aug. 1819; Lt. Col., 22nd Foot, 22 Aug. 1819; Half-pay, Oct.

1826. Where serving when wounded: 'Talavera'. Details of pension: Three hundred pounds, commencing 1811. Family: Married in Plymouth, 3 June 1807. Five children by 1829. [PRO: WO 25/759 f203]. Severely wounded, Talavera, 28 July 1809 (2nd Battn.) [London Gazette]. Mentioned in Graham's Barossa dispatch, 6 March 1811 ['The left wing now advanced firing; a most determined charge by the three companies of guards, and the 87th regiment... The eagle of the 8th regiment of light infantry, which suffered immensely, and a howitzer, rewarded this charge, and remained in possession of Major Gough, of the 87th regiment... I must equally recommend to your Lordship's notice ... Major Gough... The animated charges of the 87th regiment were most conspicuous... I cannot conclude this dispatch without earnestly recommending to His Majesty's gracious notice for promotion ... Major Gough, of the 87th'] [London Gazette, 25 March 1811]. Mentioned in Skerrett's dispatch concerning Tarifa, 1 Jan. 1812 ['The conduct ... of Lieutenant-Colonel Gough, and the 2nd battalion of the 87th Regiment, exceeds all praise.'] [London Gazette]. Mentioned in Lt. Gen. Campbell's dispatch dated Gibraltar, 3 Jan. 1812 [Tarifa: 'On the 31st [Dec. 1811], between eight and nine o'clock in the morning, the enemy (having effected a breach in the east wall of the town) advanced with two thousand picked men, grenadiers and light infantry, to assault the place. Eight companies of the 87th Regiment, under the orders of Lieutenant-Colonel Gough, were stationed on the walls in that district of the town. The enemy was received by them, when near the breach, with three cheers, under a steady discharge of musketry. From the spirited behaviour of this corps ... the enemy was broken and dispersed with great slaughter.']. Severely wounded,

Nivelle, 10 Nov. 1813 ('Major Hugh Gough (Lieutenant-Colonel)') (2nd Battn.) [*London Gazette*]. Gold Medal. *1818 Pension Return*, pp. 20–1. *Colville*, p. 151. He became a field-marshal in 1862, and was c-in-c of British forces in the 1st China War (1841–2) and in India (1843–9, including notable victories in the Gwalier and First Sikh Wars). Became viscount June 1849; born 1779, died 1869. Was brother of William Gough of the 68th. Rait, R. S., *Life and Campaigns of Hugh, 1st Viscount Gough* (London, 1903).

GOUGH, William, Capt., 68th Foot: Capt., 68th Foot, 13 May 1804. Severely wounded, Vittoria, 21 June 1813 (2nd Battn.) [*London Gazette*]. Temporary pension of one hundred pounds per annum, commencing 22 June 1814, 'for a wound' received at Vittoria [*1818 Pension Return*, pp. 16–17]. Green, *Vicissitudes*, pp. 35, 89, 165 [Wounded, Vittoria]. Brother of Hugh Gough of the 87th. Was lost off Kinsale Head in 1822.

GRADY, Richard, Lt., 87th Foot: Ensign, 87th Foot, 25 Jan. 1810; Lt., 87th Foot, 25 June 1812. Slightly wounded, Orthes, 27 Feb. 1814 ('Richard Gready') (2nd Battn.) [*London Gazette*]. Brother of Walter Grady.

+GRADY, Walter, Ensign, 87th Foot: Killed, Vittoria, 21 June 1813 ('Gready') (2nd Battn.) [*London Gazette*]. *Register of officers' effects*: Single. Effects totalled £12. 10s 'Paid to his Brother Lt. Rd. Grady.'

+GRAEFFE, Charles, Lt., 4th Line Battn. K.G.L.: Ensign, 4th Line Battn. K.G.L., 29 March 1809. Initially recorded as severely wounded, 'since dead', Heights of Ordal, 12/13th Sept. 1813 ('Lieutenant Graaffe') ('Rifle Company 4th King's German Legion') [*London Gazette*, 9 Oct. 1813].

Recorded only as 'severely' wounded in the revised casualty list ('Graiffe') [*London Gazette*, 23 Oct. 1813]. Served in Peninsula 1812–13. *Beamish*, vol. II, p. 640 [Died '14th Sep. 1813, of the wounds he received in action on the night of the 12th and morning of the 13th Sep. 1813, in the pass of Ordal in Spain.'].

GRAHAM, Hector, Ensign, 90th Foot; Lt., 77th Foot: *1829 Statement of Service for Retired Officers*: Aged fourteen on first appointment to the Army. 'Entered a Volunteer the 4th Septr. 1794'; Quarter Master, 90th Foot, 17 April 1806; Ensign, 90th Foot, 26 Oct. 1809; Lt., 77th Foot, 8 June 1811; Half-pay, 18 Nov. 1819, 'in consequence of ill health, caused by wounds, and long residence in warm climates ... being actively engaged in the most arduous struggles connected with the late war.' *Where serving when wounded*: 'On board ships in the west Indies, Menorca, Egypt & the Peninsula.' No pension. *Family*: Married in Tarbert, County Kerry, Ireland, 28 Jan. 1817, 'the daughter of the Reverand John Parker.' *Title and nature of employment*: 'Barrack Master of Mallow.' 'Holding for the last two years an Employment in the Barrack department' *Where generally resident during last five years*: 'Rushy Park, County Kerry, and Mallow, County Cork.' [PRO: WO 25/760 f20]. MGS.

GRAHAM, Henry Charles Edward Vernon, Major, 2nd Foot: *1829 Statement of Service for Retired Officers*: Aged nineteen on first appointment to the Army. Cornet, 10th Light Dragoons, 28 Nov. 1798; Lt., 10th Light Dragoons, 26 Sept. 1799; Capt., 8th West India Regt., 17 July 1801; Capt., 10th Light Dragoons, 1 Aug. 1801; Half-pay, 1802, 'By reduction of the additional Troops of Cavalry, after the Treaty of Amiens'; Capt., 15th Light Dragoons, 25 May 1803; Capt., 26th

Foot, 6 March 1806; 'Appointed to the Staff in S.W. District as Brigade Major'; '1808, Appointed to the Staff of the Army in Spain as Deputy Assistant Adjt. General. So continued to act in the Peninsula till' Major, 66th Foot, 13 June 1811, 'Joined the Battn. under Lord Hill'; Major, 2nd Foot, 5 March 1812, 'Joined it on March to the Northern Army, & was severely wounded in command of it at the Battle of Salamanca'; Appointed Inspectg. Field Officer of Militia, Nova Scotia, with the rank of Lieut. Colonel', 4 June 1813; Lt. Col., 2nd Foot, 24 Aug. 1815, 'Joined & proceeded in command of the Regt. to the West Indies where I experienced two attacks of yellow Fever'; 'Inspecting Field Officer in Ionian Islands, 5 Nov. 1818'; Lt. Col., Half-pay, unattached, 25 Feb. 1828, 'to enable him to arrange Family Affairs ... having last year been left a Widower with a Family'. *Where serving when wounded*: 'In Spain'. No pension. *Family*: Married in 'St Mary le Bowne Church, Do. Parish, London', 28 Feb. 1804. 'Wife Died 3 Octr. 1827, at Geneva, Switzerland, and is buried in the Church Yard of La Petite Saconex, near Geneva.' Four children prior to his wife's death. *Title and nature of employment*: 'Justice of the Peace in the County of Stafford.' *Where generally resident during last five years*: 'In the Ionian Islands.' [PRO: WO 25/760 f117]. Severely wounded, Salamanca, 22 July 1812 [*London Gazette*]. Gold Medal. Detailed biography in *Royal Military Calendar*, vol. IV, pp. 463-5 ['in the battle of Salamanca ... the command of the 2d Foot devolved upon him... Maj. G. on this occasion had the satisfaction, though wounded slightly in the early part of the day, to see his reg. in possession of the enemy's position, and rapidly following up the advantages they had gained, when a severe wound at that moment stopped his further progress.'].

+GRAHAM, William, Lt., 71st Foot: Lt., 71st Foot, 5 Nov. 1807. Killed, Fuentes de Onoro, 5 May 1811 (1st Battn.) [*London Gazette*].

GRAHAM, William, Lt., 74th Foot: *1829 Statement of Service*: Born near Enniskillen, 15th December 1784. Aged twenty-five on first appointment to the Army. Ensign, 74th Foot, 23 Feb. 1809; Lt., 74th Foot, 28 Dec. 1810. Note added: 'Capt., 91st Regt., 8 Oct. 1830. Capt., 74th Regt., 9 Nov. 1830. Retired on Half Pay 4 Decr. 1832.' *Battles, sieges and campaigns*: 'Rodrigo 19th Jany. 1812. Badajos 6th April 1812. Nivelle 10th Novr. 1813. Orthes 27th Feby. 1814. Toulouse, 10th Apr. 1814.' *Wounds received in action*: 'Twice wounded on 10th April 1814, and received a Years Pay extra as Lieutenant Commanding a Company at the time.' *Service Abroad*: '25th Jany. 1810 to 25th July 1814, Portugal, Spain, and France. 18th June 1818 to 15th May 1822, N. America. 16th Octr. 1825 to 15th May 1827, N. America.' *Family*: Married Charlotte Blake, 23 June 1815, Galway. They had five children by 1830. [PRO: WO 25/799 f248]. Slightly wounded, Toulouse, 10 April 1814 (1st Battn.) [*London Gazette*].

GRANT, Alexander, Lt./Capt., 71st Foot: *1829 Statement of Service*: 'Born Inverness Shire, 10th January 1787. Aged Seventeen years & seven Months on his first Entrance into the Army. Ensign, 71st Regt., 16 Aug. 1804. Lieut., 71st Foot, 25 March 1806. Captain, 71st Foot, 15 April 1813.' *Battles, sieges and campaigns*: 'As Ensign. Cape of Good Hope 6th & 8th Jany. 1806... As Lieut. at Buenos Ayres 26 & 27th June, 1st 11th & 12th Aug. 1806... Roleia, Vimeria 1808... Lugo & Coruna 8th & 13th Jany. 1809... Walcheren 30 & 31 July 1809. As Captain, Vittoria 20 June 1813, Pyrenees 4th, 6th, 25th, 30 & 31 July 1813. Cambo 12 Nov. Nive 9 Decr.

Bayonne 13 Decr. 1813 & several skirmishes to Feby. 1814. Orthes 27 Feby. Nive 2d March. Torbes 21 March, & Toulouse 10 April 1814. Waterloo 18 June 1815.' *Wounds received in action*: 'Wounded at Vittoria 21 June, Mayo 25 July, & Bayone 13th Decr. 1813. No grant of Pay or Pension Claimed.' *Titles, honorary distinctions and medals*: 'Has a Medal for the Battle of Waterloo.' *Service abroad*: '10 Jany. 1806 to 5 Sep. 1807, Cape of Good Hope and Boneuse Ayres. 1 Augt. 1808 to 16 Jany. 1809, Portugal & Spain. 30 July 1809 to 24 Decr. 1809, Walcheren. 28 Sep. 1810 to 24 July 1814, Portugal, Spain, and France. 5 Apr. 1815 to Oct. 1818, Netherlands and France. 24 June 1824 to 31 Decr. 1829, Canada.' [PRO: WO 25/799 f9]. Slightly wounded, Vittoria, 21 June 1813 (1st Battn.) [*London Gazette*]. Slightly wounded, Pyrenees, 25 July 1813 (1st Battn.) [*London Gazette*]. Slightly wounded, the Nive, 13 Dec. 1813 (1st Battn.) [*London Gazette*].

+GRANT, Alexander, Lt., 74th Foot: Lt., 74th Foot, 20 Dec. 1810. Severely wounded, storming of Badajoz, 6 April 1812 [*London Gazette*]. *Register of dead officers*: Died 'of his wounds at Badajos', 10 April 1812. Return dated 25 April 1812. [PRO: WO 25/2965].

GRANT, Charles, Capt., 50th Foot: *1829 Statement of Service for Retired Officers*: Aged nineteen on first appointment to the Army. Ensign, 96th Foot, 5 July 1804; Lt., 78th Foot, 17 Sept. 1804; Capt., 50th Foot, 8 June 1809; Half-pay, 45th Foot, 6 July 1815. 'Unable from the loss of a leg in action with the Enemy to Serve'. *Where serving when wounded*: 'Spain'. *Details of pension*: One hundred pounds per annum, commencing 25 July 1814, 'to the best of my recollection.' *Family*: Married in 'Mortlach, County of Banff, Scotland', 23 Jan. 1816. Two children by 1829. *Where generally resident during last five years*: 'At Tombrechachie & at Durn in the County of Banff N.B. [Scotland]'. [PRO: WO 25/760 f34]. Severely wounded, Pyrenees, 25 July 1813 (1st Battn.) [*London Gazette*]. Pension for 'loss of a leg' in the Pyrenees [*1818 Pension Return*, pp. 14–15]

GRANT, Colquhoun, Lt. Col., 15th Light Dragoons: Lt. Col., 15th Hussars, 25 Aug. 1808; Col., Army, 4 June 1811. *Porter*, p. 218 [Sahagun, 21 Dec. 1808: 'Colonel Grant and Captain Jones, of the 15th, were the only officers wounded; and very few men fell on our side']. Mentioned in Wellington's Morales dispatch, 6 June 1813 [2 June: 'The English hussars, being in the advanced guard, fell in, between Toro and Morales, with a considerable body of the enemy's cavalry, which were immediately attacked by the 10th, supported by the 18th and 15th. The enemy were overthrown, and pursued for many miles, and two hundred and ten prisoners, with many horses, and two officers, fell into our hands. I enclose Colonel Grant's report of this gallant affair, which reflects great credit upon ... Colonel Grant, under whose direction they acted.' Grant's dispatch: 'Morales, June 2, 1813. My Lord... It is with much satisfaction I acquaint your Lordship, that nothing could exceed the steadiness and bravery of the troops in this affair... I have the honour to be, &c. C. GRANT.'] [*London Gazette*]. Slightly wounded, 'in Action with the Enemy's Rear Guard, near Morales', 2 June 1813 [*London Gazette*]. 'Aide-de-Camp to His Royal Highness the Prince Regent', *1814 Army List*. Gold Medal. KCB. Waterloo.

GRANT, Francis, Ensign, 24th Foot: Lt., 24th Foot, 22 July 1809. Severely wounded, Talavera, 28 July 1809 [*London Gazette*].

+GRANT, Hugh, Lt., 79th Foot: Lt., 79th Foot, 30 April 1807. Severely wounded, storming of Fort St Michael, Burgos, 19 Sept. 1812 (1st Battn.) [*London Gazette*]. *Register of dead officers*: Died of wounds, 20 Sept. 1812. Return dated 25 Sept. 1812 [PRO: WO 25/2965].

GRANT, James, Lt., 85th Foot: Lt., 85th Foot, 24 Oct. 1809. Slightly wounded, siege of Badajoz, 6–11 June 1811 [*London Gazette*].

+GRANT, James, Lt., 2nd Light Battn. K.G.L.: *Beamish*, vol. II, p. 636 ['killed in action when reconnoitering before Badajoz, on the 22d April 1811.'].

GRANT, John, Major, E.O.P.S.; Major, Portuguese Service: *1829 Statement of Service*: Born in Elgin, Murrayshire, in 1782. Aged eighteen on first appointment to the Army. Lt., 4th Foot, 1799, 'Having volunteered from the Royal Glamorgan Militia'; Half-pay, 1802; Major, 'Portuguese Service, 1808, Full Pay British Service, By order of Govt.'; Cornet, 3rd Dragoon Guards, 1810; Lt., 3rd Dragoon Guards, 24th July 1811; 'Retired on full pay, 1816'; Paymaster, 56th Foot, 24th March 1829. *Battles, sieges and campaigns*: 'Part of the campaign of 1808 in Portugal. Whole of the campaigns in the Peninsula of 1809, 10, 11, 12, 13, & 14, in the respective ranks of Major, Lieut. Colonel and Colonel, Portuguese Service, Cornet & Lieutenant B. Service. Was present in the Battles of Talavera and Busaco, in the latter Commanding a Battn., Loyal Lusitanian Legion, and in the action at Spanish Alcantara, also commanded a Battn. as second in command.' *Distinguished conduct*: 'In 1809, in the action of Spanish Alcantara, mentioned in Marshal Beresford's general orders of the 27th May 1809. By Sir Arthur Wellesley, now Duke of Wellington, in his Dispatches from Spain of 21st August 1809, and from those in Portugal of the 9th & 11th February

1811.' *Wounds received in action*: 'Wounded in the interior part of the thigh by a rifle Ball in the action at Spanish Alcantara, on the 14th of May 1809. Subsequently by a slight sabre cut in the face, near Salamanca in March 1809. No Pension.' *Titles, honorary distinctions and medals*: 'The Spanish Alcantara Medal and Cross, having been second in Command in the action of Alcantara. Recommended for the Cross of the Portuguese Order of the Tower and Sword in consequence of services rendered to that Country during the campaigns from 1808 to 1815.' *Service abroad*: 'September 1808 to March 1815, Spain and Portugal.' *Family*: Married Sarah Sophia Moore, July 1815, London. They had two children by 1830. [PRO: WO 25/796 f61]. Note: he also completed an *1829 Statement of Service for Retired Officers*, presumably completed prior to his being appointed Paymaster, 56th Foot, 24 March 1829. A few of the details he gives are slightly different: Married, London, 24 Jan. 1820; 'Wounded at three different periods in the Peninsula, and once considerably disabled by fracture in the Chest in the Peninsula. No Pension.' [PRO: WO 25/760 f7]. In Portuguese Service Sept. 1808 to April 1814. *Challis, Portuguese Army*, p. 55 ['Wellington's famous scout.'].

GRANT, John, Ensign/Lt., 92nd Foot: Ensign, 92nd Foot, 5 Oct. 1809; Lt., 92nd Foot, 15 April 1813. Slightly wounded, Pyrenees, 25 July 1813 ('Lt') (1st Battn.) [*London Gazette*]. MGS.

+GRANT, Lewis, Capt., 71st Foot: Lt., 71st Foot, 13 June 1805; Capt. 6 July 1809. Wounded, 'dangerously (since dead)', 'at the Storm and Capture of Fort Napoleon, and the Enemy's other Works, in the Neighbourhood of Almaraz', 19 May 1812 [*London Gazette*]. *Register of officers' effects*: 1st Battn. Died of

GRANT

wounds, 19 May 1812, Almarez. Single. Effects sold for £102. 9/-. [PRO: WO 25/2964]. *Register of dead officers*: Died of wounds, 20 May 1812. Return dated 25 May 1812. [PRO: WO 25/2965].

GRANT, Maxwell, Capt./Major, 42nd Foot; Lt. Col., 6th Portuguese Regt: Capt., 42nd Foot, 9 July 1803. Wounded, 'in the Army lately in Spain' (1st Battn.) [*March 1809 Army List*, p. 105]. *Monthly Return*, 1st Battn., dated 25 Feb. 1809: 'Left wounded at Plymouth' [PRO: WO 17/152]. Major, 42nd Foot, 10 Oct. 1811. Slightly wounded, Pyrenees, 30 July 1813, while serving as Lt. Col., 2nd Portuguese Line [*London Gazette*]. Severely wounded, the Nive, 13 Dec. 1813, while serving as Lt. Col., 6th Portuguese Line [*London Gazette*]. In Portuguese Service Aug. 1809 to April 1814. Wounded, Pyrenees, 30 July 1813. Gold Medal. *Challis, Portuguese Army*, p. 55.

GRANT, Peter, Major, 92nd Foot: Major, 92nd Foot, 23 June 1808. Severely wounded, 'left arm amputated', Fuentes de Onoro, 5 May 1811 (1st Battn.) [*London Gazette*]. Pension of two hundred pounds per annum, commencing 5 May 1812, for 'loss of a leg' at Villa Formosa, 1811 [*1818 Pension Return*, pp. 20–1].

GRANT, William, Lt., 50th Foot: Lt., 50th Foot, 19 April 1810. Slightly wounded, Fuentes de Onoro, evening 3 May 1811 (1st Battn.) [*London Gazette*].

GRANT, William, Lt. Col., 82nd Foot: Lt. Col., Army, 9 July 1803; Lt. Col., 82nd Foot, 15 Aug. 1805. Severely wounded, Vittoria, 21 June 1813 [*London Gazette*]. Slightly wounded, Pyrenees, 25 July 1813 (1st Battn.) [*London Gazette*]. Severely wounded, Pyrenees, 30 July 1813 [*London Gazette*]. Gold Medal. Pension of three hundred

pounds per annum, commencing 22 June 1814, 'for wounds' received at Vittoria [*1818 Pension Return*, pp. 18–19]. Later Major-General.

GRANT, William Alexander, Capt., 71st Foot: Capt., 71st Foot, 12 Oct. 1809. Slightly wounded, Pyrenees, 31 July 1813 (1st Battn.) [*London Gazette*]. Wounded, Waterloo.

GRATTAN, William, Ensign/Lt., 88th Foot: *1829 Statement of Service for Retired Officers*: Aged seventeen on first appointment to the Army. Ensign, 88th Foot, 6 July 1809; Lt., 88th Foot, 30 April 1812; Half-pay, 25 March 1816, by reduction. 'Is unfit for active service in consequence of the wound'. *Where serving when wounded*: 'Storming of Badajoz in Spain, and at Battle of Salamanca in Spain.' *Details of pension*: Fifty pounds, commencing 6 April 1813, discontinued 25 Dec. 1816. *Family*: Married in Dublin, 13 May 1819. Three children by 1829. *Where generally resident during last five years*: 'For the last two years in Paris, and for the ten years preceeding at Athy Ireland.' [PRO: WO 25/760 f128]. Severely wounded, storming of Badajoz, 6 April 1812 ('Gratton') [*London Gazette*]. MGS. Later, the famous historian, author of *Adventures with the Connaught Rangers, 1808–14* (London, 1847), and *Reminiscences* (London, 1853).

GRAVES, Anthony, Lt., 32nd Foot: *1829 Statement of Service for Retired Officers*: Aged fifteen on first appointment to the Army. Ensign, 1st West India Regt., July 1801; Ensign, 6th West India Regt., 1802; Ensign, 31st Foot, 3 Feb. 1803; Lt., '12th Battn. Royal Reserve', 24 March 1804; Lt., 32nd Foot, 7 Aug. 1804; 'Appointed Major of Brigade, Staff of the Army in Spain, July 1812'; Capt., 32nd Foot, 13 April 1813; Half-pay 'in consequence of the reduction of the 2nd Battn.' Served fourteen years on full-pay.

'From service in Walcheren and injury from Wounds – three fingers of the right hand disabled, and right thigh fractured – does not feel equal ... of general service'. *Where serving when wounded*: 'In the Peninsula at the Battle of Salamanca 1812, as Brigade Major.' *Details of pension*: One hundred pounds, commencing 23 July 1813. *Family*: Married in Norton, near Stockton on Tees, 20 May 1822. Four children by 1829. *Where generally resident during last five years*: 'York.' [PRO: WO 25/760 f168]. Severely wounded, Salamanca, 22 July 1812 ('Greaves') (1st Battn.) [*London Gazette*]. *1818 Pension Return*, pp. 8-9. *Haythornthwaite, Armies*, p. 23 ['The most obvious abuse was the commissioning of children... Anthony Graves, who served in the Peninsula with the 31st Foot [sic]. Born in 1789, he was commissioned as ensign in the Somerset Militia before his fourth birthday, his father being that regiment's adjutant. He later received two commissions in the 1st and 6th West India Regiments by the influence of the lamentable Whitelocke (a friend of Graves senior), in both cases being given indefinite leave to allow him to remain at school. He finally joined the 31st in 1804, five months before his 15th birthday.'].

GRAY, Charles George, Capt., 95th Fot: Capt., 95th Foot, 6 May 1809. Slightly wounded, storming of Badajoz, 6 April 1812 (1st Battn.) [*London Gazette*]. Waterloo. Retired, 1837. MGS. *Simmons*, pp. 228-9, 378-9.

+GRAY, George, Major, 30th Foot: Major, 30th Foot, 1 Dec. 1804; Lt. Col., Army, 4 June 1811. Severely wounded, 'since dead', storming of Badajoz, 6 April 1812 (2nd Battn.) [*London Gazette*]. Mentioned in Wellington's Badajoz despatch, 7 April 1812 ['I must likewise mention... Lieutenant-Colonel Grey of the 30th, who was unfortunately

killed.'] [*London Gazette*]. Died 'of his wounds at Badajos', 7 April 1812. Return dated 25 April 1812. [PRO: WO 25/2965].

GRAY, John F., Lt., 40th Foot: Lt., 40th Foot, 26 Aug. 1807. Severely wounded, storming of Badajoz, 6 April 1812 ('Grey') (1st Battn.) [*London Gazette*]. Severely wounded, Salamanca, 22 July 1812 [*London Gazette*]. *Register of dead officers*: Died of wounds, 7 Oct. 1812. Return dated 25 Oct. 1812. [PRO: WO 25/2965].

GRAY, Loftus, Capt., 95th Foot: *1829 Statement of Service for Retired Officers*: Aged eighteen on first appointment to the Army. Ensign, 46th Foot, 26 Sept. 1799; 2nd Lt., 95th Foot, 4 Nov. 1800; 1st Lt., 95th Foot, 25 June 1803; Capt., 95th Foot, 16 April 1807; Bvt. Major, 95th Foot, 12 April 1814; Half-pay, 'ill health from wounds.' Served twenty-two years on full-pay. *Where serving when wounded*: 'South of France'. *Details of pension*: One hundred pounds per annum, commencing 1814. *Family*: Married in Sidmouth, Devon, 10 Sept. 1824. Two children by 1829. *Where generally resident during last five years*: 'Sidmouth, Devon'. [PRO: WO 25/760 f62]. Severely wounded, 'in Action with the Enemy', 20 March 1814 (1st Battn.) [*London Gazette*]. Pension, commencing 21 March 1815, 'for a wound' received at Tarbes, 1814 [*1818 Pension Return*, pp. 22-3]. *Kincaid, Random Shots*, p. 290 ['At the close of the war, when we returned to England ... the officers commanding companies on the day of inspection, viz ... Loftus Gray with a gash in the lip and minus a portion of one heel, which made him march to the tune of dot and go one']. See Charles George Gray.

GRAY, Robert, Capt., 48th Foot: Capt., 48th Foot, 10 Aug. 1809. Slightly wounded, storming of San

GRAY

Sebastian, 31 Aug. 1813, while serving with a 'Detachment 48th Foot, 1st Batt.' [*London Gazette*]. MGS.

+GRAYDON, John, Lt., 88th Foot: Lt., Army, 15 March 1802; Lt., 88th Foot, 5 Aug. 1804. Killed, Talavera, 27 July 1809 [*London Gazette*]. Obituary, *The Gentleman's Magazine*, Sept. 1809, p. 886 ['27 [July]. Among the heroes of Talavera, his 23d year, John Graydon, esq. captain in the 88th Foot, and third son of the late Robert G. esq. of Killishee, co. Kildare, in Ireland, whose services in Parliament, for a long series of years, received distinguished marks of approbation from the different Guilds of the city of Dublin. On his entrance into the Army, this young Officer served with much credit in the West Indies. In the hopeless attack on Buenos Ayres, sharing the fate of the brave Grenadiers of the 88th Regiment, he was carried, severely wounded, from the mouths of the Enemy's guns. In the glorious conflict of Talavera, this gallant young Officer was among the first who fell, displaying to his heroic companions an animating example of that enthusiastic bravery for which he was ever conspicuous. With talents the most promising, with manners the most attractive, he associated every quality which could adorn the gentleman, ennoble the hero, exalt the Christian, or endear the friend.'].

GREEN, John, Lt., 28th Foot: Lt., 28th Foot, 13 Nov. 1806. Severely wounded, Toulouse, 10 April 1814 ('Greene') (1st Battn.) [*London Gazette*]. 'Grene' and 'Green' in Army List.

GREEN, Joshua W., Capt., 4th Foot; Major, 10th Caçadores: Capt., 4th Foot, 1 Nov. 1810. In Portuguese Service Aug. 1809 to Sept. 1812 and April 1813 to Feb. 1814. *Challis, Portuguese Army*, p. 55 ['Bt. Maj.

E.O.P.S.; Maj. 10 Cacad... Wd. Pyrenees 27 July '13.'].

GREEN, Samuel, Ensign, 1st Foot: Ensign, 1st Foot, 31 Oct. 1810. Slightly wounded, Vittoria, 21 June 1813 (3rd Battn.) [*London Gazette*].

GREEN, William, Capt., 61st Foot: Capt., Army, 18 Dec. 1806; Capt., 61st Foot, 11 June 1807. Severely wounded, Salamanca, 22 July 1812 ('Green') [*London Gazette*]. Slightly wounded, the Nive, 9 Dec. 1813 ('Greene') (1st Battn.) [*London Gazette*]. Bvt. Major, 61st Foot, 3 March 1814. Severely wounded, Toulouse, 10 April 1814 ('Greene') (1st Battn.) [*London Gazette*]. Gold Medal. Temporary pension of one hundred pounds per annum, commencing 11 April 1815, 'for wounds' received at Toulouse, 1814 [*1818 Pension Return*, pp. 16–17]. MGS.

+GREENSHIELS, James, Lt., 40th Foot: Ensign, 40th Foot, 19 April 1809; Lt. 13 June 1811. Killed, storming of Badajoz, 6 April 1812 ('Greenshuld') [*London Gazette*].

GREENWELL, Leonard, Major, 45th Foot: *1829 Statement of Service for Retired Officers*: Aged twenty on first appointment to the Army. Ensign, 45th Foot, 1801; Lt., 45th Foot, '1802–3'; Capt., 45th Foot, 1804; Major, 45th Foot, 1810, 'vice Smith killed in action at Battle of Busaco' [Army List gives 25 Oct. 1810]; Bvt. Lt. Col., 1812, 'For conduct in the Field at the Battle of Salamanca'; Lt. Col., 45th Foot, 1814, 'vice Forbes, killed in action at the Battle of Toulouse'; Bvt. Col., 1825, 'By appointment of Aide de Camp to the King'; Half-pay, unattached, 8 Nov. 1827, 'by request, in consequence of ill health arising from the influence of a Tropical Climate on his wounds... He was thereby compelled to relinquish a lucrative Command in India.' *Where serving when wounded:*

248

'Buenos Ayres, South America. Peninsula.' *Details of pension*: '£200 increased to £300', commencing '1812 or 1814 not having his accounts in possession is not certain of the date'. *Title and nature of employment*: 'Aide de Camp to the King.' *Where generally resident during last five years*: 'Ceylon, England, France.' [PRO: WO 25/760 f29]. Severely wounded, Salamanca, 22 July 1812 [*London Gazette*]. Slightly wounded, Orthes, 27 Feb. 1814 (1st Battn.) [*London Gazette*]. Temporary pension of two hundred pounds per annum, commencing 23 July 1813, 'for wounds' received at Salamanca [*1818 Pension Return*, pp. 12–13]. Gold Medal. Letter from him, see James MacPherson. Detailed military biography, *Royal Military Calendar*, vol. IV., pp. 429–30 ['On the 1st Aug, 1808, he disembarked with his reg. in Portugal, and served with it during the whole of the Peninsular war, except on two occasions when he was absent in consequence of wounds... L.-Col. G. has been shot through the neck, the body, both arms, and wounded in one leg at the battle of Orthes'].

+GREGORSON, Dugald, Lt., 42nd Foot: Lt., 42nd Foot, 29 Dec. 1804. Killed, assault and capture of Fort St Michael, Burgos, 19 Sept. 1812 (1st Battn.) [*London Gazette*]. *Register of dead officers*: 'Killed before Burgos', 19 Sept. 1812. Return dated 25 Sept. 1812. [PRO: WO 25/2965].

GREY, John, Major, 5th Foot: Major, Army, 27 Nov. 1806; Major, 5th Foot, 13 June 1811. Slightly wounded, siege of Ciudad Rodrigo, 12 Jan. 1812 [*London Gazette*]. Severely wounded, storming of Ciudad Rodrigo, 19 Jan. 1812 [*London Gazette*]. Mentioned in Wellington's Ciudad Rodrigo dispatch, 20 Jan. 1812 ['I beg particularly to draw your Lordship's attention to the conduct of ... Major Grey, of the 2d

battalion 5th foot, who has been twice wounded during the siege.'] [*London Gazette*, 5 Feb. 1812]. MGS.

+GRIERSHEIM, Albert von, Lt., Duke of Brunswick Oels' Corps (Infantry): Lt., Duke of Brunswick Oels' Corps, 27 Aug. 1811. Slightly wounded, Salamanca, 22 July 1812 ('Griesham') [*London Gazette*]. Slightly wounded, Crossing the Bidassoa, 7/9 Oct. 1813 ('Greisheim') [*London Gazette*]. Severely wounded, Pyrenees, 25 July 1813 ('Gresham') [*London Gazette*]. *Register of dead officers*: 'Grierham'. Died of wounds, 22 Aug. 1813. Register dated Sept. 1813. [PRO: WO 25/2965].

+GRIFFIN, Thomas, Ensign, 81st Foot: Ensign, 81st Foot, 17 Oct. 1807. Wounded, 'in the Army lately in Spain' (2nd Battn.) [*March 1809 Army List*, p. 105]. *Monthly Return*, 2nd Battn., dated 25 Feb. 1809: 'Wounded, in Naval Hospl. Plymouth' [PRO: WO 17/202]. *Monthly Return*, 2nd Battn., dated 25 March 1809: 'Died of wounds' [PRO: WO 17/202]. Obituary, *The Gentleman's Magazine*, March 1809, p. 284 ['2 [March]... At the Royal Naval Hospital at Plymouth, in consequence of a wound he received at the battle of Corunna, Ensign Thomas Griffin, of the 31st Foot [sic]. He has left a wife and child to deplore him.'].

GRIFFITH, Matthew C. Darby, Capt. and Lt. Col., 1st Foot Guards: Capt. and Lt. Col., 1st Foot Guards, 3 July 1801. Wounded, 'in the Army lately in Spain' ('Griffiths') (3rd Battn.) [*March 1809 Army List*, p. 105].

GRIFFITH, Moses, Assistant Surgeon, 94th Foot: *1829 Statement of Service*: Born 19 March 1789, Pointz Castle, Pembrokeshire. Aged twenty years seven months and sixteen days on his first entrance into the Army. Hospital Mate, Staff, 4 Nov. 1809; Assistant Surgeon, 94th Foot, 24 Oct. 1811; Asst. Surgeon, 47th Foot, 27 Nov. 1817; Asst. Surgeon, 20th Foot, 5 Nov. 1824; Surgeon 8 Feb. 1827. *Battles, sieges and campaigns*: 'Campaigns in the Peninsula and France... 1810 – Battle of Bassucco, 27th September. 1811 – Massena's Retreat in March. Battle of Fuentes de Onor, 5th May. 1812 – Siege of Ciudad Rodrigo & Assault, 19th January. Siege of Badajos & Assault, 6th April. Battle of Salamanca, 22nd July. 1813 – Battle of Vittoria, 21st June. Battle of Pyrenees, 27th & 28th July. Battle of Neville, 10th November. Battle of Nive, 9th 10th 11th and 14th December. 1814 – Battle of Orthes 27th February. Affair of Via Bijore, 19th March. Battle of Thoulouse, 10th April. India 1819 – Siege of Afsurghur, March & April... Persian Gulph, Siege of Rassel Kyma & Zaia in December... 1820 India – Siege of Dwarka & Assanti 26th November... Arabia 1821 – Affair of Biniaboa Ali, 2nd March... 1825 Burmese Empire – Assault of a Ford on Banks of Pesjer River 11th January. Assault of Syrian Pagoda 12th January. Siege of Donaber, March and April. Battle near Prosne on 2d and 3d December.' *Wounds received in action*: 'Was wounded at the affair of Via Bijore on the 19th March 1814 for which I received one years pay as Assistant Surgeon.' *Service abroad*: '31st December 1809 to 24th July 1814, Peninsula and France. 2d May 1818 to 31st December 1829, India, Arabia, Burmese Empire.' Unmarried in 1830. [PRO: WO 25/788 f394]. Slightly wounded, 'in Action with the Enemy', 19 March 1814 ('Moses Griffiths') [*London Gazette*]. MGS.

GRIFFITHS, John Charles, Lt., 94th Foot: *1829 Statement of Service for Retired Officers*: Aged seventeen on first appointment to

the Army. Ensign, 4th Garrison Battn., 15 Oct. 1807; Lt., 4th Garrison Battn., 21 July 1809; Lt., 94th Foot, 30 Nov. 1809; Capt., 94th Foot, 7 July 1814; Half-pay, 94th Foot, 24 Dec. 1818, by reduction. *Where serving when wounded*: 'Salamanca'. No pension. *Family*: Married in 'Banff N.B.' [Scotland], 3 Aug. 1818. No children 'at present' by 1829. *Where generally resident during last five years*: 'Banff N.B.' [PRO: WO 25/760 f144]. Severely wounded, Salamanca, 22 July 1812 [*London Gazette*].

GRIFFITHS, William A., 1st Lt., 23rd Foot: *1829 Statement of Service*: Born 14 Feb. 1792, Wrexham, Denbighshire. Aged nineteen on his first entrance into the Army. 2nd Lt., 23rd Foot, 11 March 1811; 1st Lt. 13 May 1812. *Battles, sieges and campaigns*: 'Siege and Storming of Badajos 6 April 1812. Battle of Salamanca 22nd July 1812. Battle of Waterloo 18th June 1815.' *Wounds received in action*: 'Received a Gun Shot Wound in left arm at Salamanca 22nd July 1812. Received a Gun Shot Wound at Waterloo in the right thigh 18th June 1815. One years pay received.' *Titles, honorary distinctions and medals*: 'Waterloo Medal.' *Service abroad*: 'Jany 1812 to Sept. 1813, Spain and Portugal. March 1815 to Nov. 1818, Belgium & France. Decr. 1823 to Nov. 1825, Gibraltar.' Not married in 1830. [PRO: WO 25/789 f195]. Slightly wounded, storming of San Sebastian, 31 Aug. 1813 (1st Battn.) [*London Gazette*]. Waterloo. Note: he was not recorded as having been wounded as Salamanca, as he indicated in his Statement of Service, but he was wounded at San Sebastian.

GRIMES, Robert, Lt., Royal Artillery: 2nd Lt., Royal Artillery, 4 March 1809. Wounded, siege of Badajoz, 26 March 1812 [*London Gazette*]. MGS.

+GRUBEN, Charles von, Lt., 2nd Light Dragoons/Hussars K.G.L.: Lt., 2nd Light Dragoons, 19 Nov. 1807. Served in Peninsula 1811–12. *Beamish*, vol. II, pp. 131–2 [1 Aug. 1812: 'The skirmishers had to sustain a severe and unequal contest, and many times it was found necessary to form up and charge the advancing horsemen, which was always done with success. Lieutenant Charles von Gruben directed these operations, and with such a degree of judgement and gallantry, that the enemy failed in every attempt to drive back the hussars. This fatiguing contest had continued for several hours, and the skirmishes were relieved, but their zealous officer, disdaining repose, insisted on continuing his exertions... Gruben now redoubled his labours; made the men take steady aim at their opponents, and being himself a good marksman, exemplified his instructions by a few well-directed shots at the opposing line. This drew upon him the attention of the enemy; his horse was soon hit, and shortly after, a fatal bullet struck the gallant youth to the earth!... The officer, lieutenant von Gruben was a most promising young man, of great natural ability, and who, on this day, had particularly distinguished himself. The esteem in which he was held was fully testified by the attendance of nearly all the officers of General Hill's corps at his interment on the following day.'], p. 615 ['Killed in a skirmish with the enemy in front of Ribeira in Spain, 1st August 1812.'].

GRUBEN, Gustav von, Lt./Adjutant, 2nd Light Dragoons/Hussars K.G.L.: Lt., 2nd Light Dragoons K.G.L., 16 July 1810. Served in Peninsula in 1811. *Beamish*, vol. II, p. 619 ['slightly wounded, 25th June 1811, at Quinta de Gremezia... [Died by illness] 14th Oct. 1811, at Castello Branco in Portugal.'].

GRUBEN, Philip Moritz von, Capt., 1st Light Dragoons/Hussars, K.G.L.: Capt., 1st Light Dragoons K.G.L., 8 Nov. 1803. Severely wounded, Fuentes de Onoro, 5 May 1811 [*London Gazette*]. Bvt. Major, 1st Light Dragoons K.G.L., 25 Feb. 1812; Major, 1st Light Dragoons KGL, 12 Jan. 1813. Gold Medal. 'Philip' and 'Frederick' in Army Lists. Served in Peninsula 1809–14. Waterloo. *Beamish*, vol. II, p. 548 [Died 'at Diepholz in Han. 13th Oct. 1828, a major-gen. in H.S. & colonel comm. 2d regiment of hussars.'].

GRUTTEMANN, Augustus, Lt., Duke of Brunswick Oels' Corps (Infantry): *1829 Statement of Service for Retired Officers*: Born 10 Aug. 1787. Aged twenty-three on first appointment to the Army. 'October 1810 joined the Army in Portugal, as Volunteer'; Ensign, Duke of Brunswick Oels' Corps, 22 July 1812; Lt., Duke of Brunswick Oels' Corps, 10 Dec. 1812; Half-pay, by reduction. Served on full-pay for four and a half years. *Where serving when wounded*: 'In Spain, Seventh Division, at the Passage of the Bidassoa the 9 of October 1813.' *Details of pension*: Seventy pounds, commencing 1814, 'permanently 1818.' *Family*: Married in the Parish of Shoreditch, London, 11 April 1815. No children by 1829. *Where generally resident during last five years*: 'In France.' [PRO: WO 25/760 f139]. Severely wounded, Crossing the Bidassoa, 7/9 Oct. 1813 ('Lieutenant Gruttemann (2d)') [*London Gazette*].

+GUALEY, Francis, Capt., 11th Foot: Capt., 11th Foot, 25 Nov. 1808. Severely wounded, Salamanca, 22 July 1812 ('Gualy') (1st Battn.) [*London Gazette*]. Severely wounded, Toulouse, 10 April 1814 (1st Battn.) [*London Gazette*]. *Haythornthwaite, Armies*, p. 256 [16 Jan. 1814, before Bayonne: 'The grenadier captain of the 11th Foot, Francis Gualey, decided to beat-up the French outpost in his front; for this he obtained official sanction from Beresford, so it would be unfair to ascribe this somewhat unfriendly spirit to the fact that Gualey was himself a Frenchman, though as an emigrant he might have more reason to feel antagonistic towards his French enemies. The French picquet, more than 200 strong, was stationed in a barn, behind a dry moat; Gualey's party was much smaller. Gualey sent forward Sergeant James Duffy and two grenadiers to deal with the outlying sentries; Duffy approached them by claiming to be a deserter, and both sentries were then bayoneted. Lieutenant William Dunkley and Sergeant Pike then jumped the moat and killed the inlying sentry, who was almost asleep; they then assisted the rest of the raiding-party to clamber in and out of the moat. Securing the Frenchmen's weapons, which were in a rack outside the barn, they took the whole lot prisoner, less six who were killed resisting; the officers were captured in an upstairs room, where they were entertaining a lady. The French arms and accoutrements were flung into the moat, and more than 200 prisoners were escorted to the British lines. For this unusual enterprise, Gualey received the brevet rank of major, but enjoyed it only briefly; he was mortally wounded at Toulouse, where Dunkley was killed.'].

GUANTER, James, Lt., Chasseurs Britanniques: *1829 Statement of Service for Retired Officers*: Aged twenty-five on first appointment to the Army. 'Volunteer, Asst. Qr. Mr. Gl.', Chasseurs Britanniques, 28 March 1806; Ensign, Chasseurs Britanniques, 25 Nov. 1806; Lt., Chasseurs Britanniques, 4 April 1810; Capt., 2nd Greek Light Infantry, 27 May 1813; Capt., Royal Corsican Rangers, 1 June 1813; Half-pay, 16 Jan. 1817, 'the Regiment being disbanded.' *Where*

serving when wounded: 'Defence of Tarifa, lost his Right Eye.' *Details of pension*: One hundred pounds, commencing 30 Dec. 1812. *Where generally resident during last five years*: 'Narbonne, Departement of the Aude.' [PRO: WO 25/760 f184]. Severely wounded, Tarifa, 29 Dec. 1811 [*London Gazette*]. Mentioned in Skerrett's dispatch from Tarifa, 30 Dec. 1811 ['A constant fire of musketry is interchanged. I have particularly to regret the loss of the service of Lieutenant Guanter, deputy assistant Quarter-Master-General, a very intelligent and brave officer, who is severely wounded.'] [*London Gazette*].

GUARD, William, Lt. Col., 45th Foot: Lt. Col., 45th Foot, 3 Oct. 1799. Severely wounded, Talavera, 27 July 1809 [*London Gazette*].

GUISE, John Wright, Capt and Lt. Col., 3rd Foot Guards: Capt. and Lt. Col., 3rd Foot Guards, 25 July 1805. Mentioned in Wellington's Fuentes de Onoro dispatch, 8 May 1811 [5 May: '[The French] attempted to push a body of light infantry down the ravine of the Turon to the right of the 1st division, which were repulsed by the light infantry of the guards, under Lieutenant-Colonel Guise, aided by five companies of the 95th, under Captain O'Hare.'] [*London Gazette*, 26 May 1811]. Gold Medal. MGS. General, 11 Nov. 1851.

GUN, William, Capt., 91st Foot: Lt., 51st Foot, 24 Nov. 1803; Capt., Army, 30 Nov. 1809; Capt., 91st Foot, 7 June 1810. Severely wounded, Orthes, 27 Feb. 1814 ('Gunn') (1st Battn.) [*London Gazette*]. Temporary pension of one hundred pounds per annum, commencing 28 Feb. 1815, 'for a wound' received at Orthes ('Gunn') [*1818 Pension Return*, pp. 20–1].

GUNN, John, Lt., 5th Foot: Lt., Army, 14 Aug. 1805; Lt. 5th Foot, 1

Oct. 1806. Severely wounded, Salamanca, 22 July 1812 (1st Battn.) [*London Gazette*].

GURWOOD, John, Lt./Capt., 52nd Foot: Lt., 52nd Foot, 3 Aug. 1809. Severely wounded, 'not dangerously', during 'several affairs with the French Army', 18 March–9 April 1811 [*London Gazette*]. Recorded as 'slightly' wounded, storming of Ciudad Rodrigo, 19 Jan. 1812 [*London Gazette*]. In fact he was wounded in the head while commanding the Forlorn Hope at the lesser breach, Ciudad Rodrigo, but carried on to take Governor Barrie prisoner. Mentioned in Wellington's Ciudad Rodrigo dispatch, 20 Jan. 1812 ['The conduct of ... Lieutenant Gurwood of the 52d Regiment, who was wounded, has likewise been particularly reported to me'] [*London Gazette*, 5 Feb. 1812]. Capt., Army, 6 Feb. 1812; Capt., 10th Light Dragoons, 12 Nov. 1814. Waterloo. *Dalton*, p. 16 ['Came of poor but honest parents in the East Riding of Yorkshire.' Later Deputy Lieutenant of the Tower of London. Died at Brighton, 25 Dec. 1843, and is buried in the Tower]. Rose to the rank of bvt. Col. and achieved fame as the editor of Wellington's dispatches (having been Wellington's private secretary). The date of his death given by Dalton, 1843, is evidently wrong; it was 1845 and his obituary appeared in Colburn's *United Service Magazine* 1846, I, p. 298. Gurwood took his own life, which the aforementioned obituary blamed on the work of collating the dispatches, and the Ciudad Rodrigo wound. It lamented that he should meet such an end, and that all his experience 'should have proved unavailing against the delusions of a harassed and distempered mind'; and that his work on the dispatches with its 'drudgery and excitement ... acting on a brain rendered more susceptible of irritation by a wound in the head, received at the storming of Ciudad Rodrigo, no doubt occasioned the desponding state of mind which led to the fatal result... Colonel Gurwood was endeared to his friends by his frank and generous characters; he was an upright gentleman and a brave soldier.' Gurwood was born in 1790.

GWYN, William, Major, 45th Foot: Ensign, 45th Foot, 1 Aug. 1788; Lt., 45th Foot, 27 Oct. 1789; Capt., 45th Foot, 3 Sept. 1795; Major, 45th Foot, 2 Aug. 1804. Slightly wounded, Talavera, 28 July 1809 (1st Battn.) [*London Gazette*]. Severely wounded, Busaco, 27 Sept. 1810 [*London Gazette*].

GWYNNE, John, Lt., 14th Light Dragoons: Cornet, 14th Light Dragoons, 7 Nov. 1805; Lt., 14th Light Dragoons, 14 Jan. 1808. Slightly wounded, Fuentes de Onoro, 5 May 1811 [*London Gazette*]. Slightly wounded, Salamanca, 18 July 1812 [*London Gazette*]. MGS.

H

HAASMANN, George, Capt., 2nd Light Battn. K.G.L.: Capt., 2nd Light Battn. K.G.L., 18 July 1809. Slightly wounded, Salamanca, 22 July 1812 ('Haassman') [*London Gazette*]. 'Haasman' in Army List. Waterloo. *Beamish*, vol. II, p. 566.

+HACKETT, Isaac, Ensign, 83rd Foot: Ensign, 83rd Foot, 18 July 1811. Wounded, 'dangerously', siege of Badajoz, 26 March 1812 [*London Gazette*]. *Register of dead officers*: 'Hackett, Ens. 88th F 1 Bn. [sic]' Died of wounds, 29 March 1812. [PRO: WO 25/2965].

HAGEMANN, John George, Capt., 5th Line Battn. K.G.L.: *1829 Statement of Service for Retired Officers*: Aged twenty-one on first appointment to the Army. Ensign, 6th Line Battn. K.G.L., 17 Jan. 1806; Lt., 5th Line Battn. K.G.L., 26 March 1807; Capt., 5th Line Battn. K.G.L., 16 Dec. 1812; Half-pay, 25 July 1815, 'from ill health.' *Where serving when wounded*: 'Peninsula.' *Details of pension*: 'A Pension of £70 per annum was granted from the 25th December 1814; a further increased pension of £100 per annum from the 25 December 1817, and lastly £200 [commencing] 25 December 1820.' *Family*: Married in Lisbon, 2 Aug. 1814. Six children by 1829. *Where generally resident during last five years*: 'City of Hanover.' [PRO: WO 25/761 f65].

HAGGUP, William, 2nd Lt./1st Lt., 95th Foot: *1829 Statement of Service for Retired Officers*: Aged fifteen on first appointment to the Army. Ensign, Northumberland Militia, 24 March 1809; Volunteer, 7th Foot, 24 March 1810; 2nd Lt., 95th Foot, 30 Aug. 1810; 1st Lt., 95th Foot, 12 May 1812; Half-pay, 25 Dec. 1818, by reduction; Lt. and Adjutant, 11th Foot, 3 Aug. 1820; Half-

pay, unattached, 14 Feb. 1828, 'Own request, from the effects of wounds'. 'From the nature and extent of his Wounds he is rendered incapable of active Field Service'. *Where serving when wounded*: 'Portugal, at Sabugal 3 Apl. 1811. Spain, 18 June 1813, at San Millan. France, 10th Nov. 1813, Passage of the Nivelle.' *Details of pension*: Seventy pounds per annum, commencing 25 Dec. 1822. *Where generally resident during last five years*: 'With 11th Regt. at Dublin, Belfast, Cork; Carmarthen, London.' [PRO: WO 25/761 f80]. Slightly wounded during 'several affairs with the French Army', 18 March–7 April 1811 [*London Gazette*]. Severely wounded, 'in operations', 12–19 June 1813 [*London Gazette*]. Severely wounded, Nivelle, 10 Nov. 1813 (1st Battn.) [*London Gazette*]. Waterloo. MGS. *Simmons*, p. 162 [wounded, Sabugal, 3 April 1811], 259, 288 [wounded, Villa Nana, 18 June 1813: 'My friend Haggup was shot directly across his stomach.'].

HALL, Alexander, Ensign, 47th Foot: Ensign, 47th Foot, 6 Feb. 1812. Severely wounded, storming of San Sebastian, 31 Aug. 1813 (2nd Battn.) [*London Gazette*]. Recorded as dead, *1814 Army List*.

HALL, Charles, Ensign, 3rd Foot Guards: Ensign, 3rd Foot Guards, 6 April 1809. Slightly wounded, siege of Burgos, 20–26 Sept. 1812 (1st Battn.) [*London Gazette*]. MGS. *Aitchison*, p. 206 [Burgos: 'The enemy attempted to regain the work ... at 4 in the afternoon they renewed this attempt with their whole garrison and aided by the most tremendous fire, which I ever saw of cannon, they succeeded in driving us out of both breaches and they levelled our works and carried off the intenching tools – but a small party of about 30 of our men maintained themselves behind a breastwork (the enemy being on the near side and stabbing at each other with bayonets) and from their spirited conduct the work was regained and we were completely re-established in it before dark. An officer of our regiment (the only one present) was wounded and our whole loss was, I believe, about 120.'].

+HALL, Charles, Ensign, 38th Foot: Ensign, 38th Foot, 28 Aug. 1807. Died, 27 Jan. 1809, of wounds received during Corunna campaign. Obituary, *The Gentleman's Magazine*, Feb. 1809, p. 187 ['27 [Jan.]... At Plymouth, of the wounds ... received in Spain ... Ensign Hall, of the 38th Foot.'].

HALL, Francis, Lt., 14th Light Dragoons: Cornet, 14th Light Dragoons, 28 June 1810; Lt., 14th Light Dragoons, 28 March 1811. Slightly wounded, El Bodon, 25 Sept. 1811 [*London Gazette*].

HALL, George, Ensign, 52nd Foot: *1829 Statement of Service*: 'Born Parish of Egham, Surry, 10th July 1794. Aged 16 on his first Entrance into the Army. Ensign, 52nd Regt., 3d May 1810. Lieutenant, 52nd Regt., 9th May 1812. Captain, 52nd Regt., 30th August 1821. Half Pay, 24th October 1821, By reduction. Captain, 72nd Regt., 5th July 1822. Major, 72nd Foot, 19th Novemr. 1825.' *Battles, sieges and campaigns*: 'Ensign at Fuentes d'Onor, Ciudad Rodrigo and Badajos. Lieut. at the Nive, Orthes, Tolouse and Waterloo.' *Wounds received in action*: 'Wounded severely at the Siege of Badajos in 1812, received a grant of one year's pay as Ensign.' *Service abroad*: 'January 1811 to 6th June 1812, Peninsula. October 1813 to 29th June 1814, South of France. January 1815 to November 1818,

Netherlands and France. 4th July 1828 to 31st Decemr. 1829, Cape of Good Hope.' [PRO: WO 25/799 f80]. Severely wounded, siege of Badajoz, 22 March 1812 (1st Battn.) [*London Gazette*]. MGS.

+HALL, Henry G., Capt., 71st Foot: Capt., 71st Foot, 26 Feb. 1807. Killed, Vittoria, 21 June 1813 (1st Battn.) [*London Gazette*].

+HALL, Revis, 2nd Lt., 23rd Foot: 2nd Lt., 23rd Foot, 25 Nov. 1808. Killed, Albuera, 16 May 1811 [*London Gazette*].

+HALL, Richard, 47th Foot: Lt., 47th Foot, 9 Nov. 1809. Killed, Tarifa, 31 Dec. 1811 (2nd Battn.) [*London Gazette*]. *Register of dead officers*: Return dated 25 Jan. 1812. [PRO: WO 25/2965].

+HAMELBERG, Ernest von, Capt., 5th Line Battn. K.G.L.: Capt., 5th Line Battn. K.G.L., 19 Oct. 1803. Severely wounded, Talavera, 28 July 1809 ('Hamelberg') [*London Gazette*]. Served in Peninsula 1808–9. *Beamish*, vol. II, p. 637 [Died '11th August 1809, of the wounds he received in the battle of Talavera de la Reyna, 28th July 1809.'].

HAMERTON, William Meadows, Capt., 7th Foot: *1829 Statement of Service for Retired Officers*: Aged sixteen on first appointment to the Army. Ensign, 61st Foot, 26 Dec. 1806; 2nd Lt., 95th Foot, 19 Jan. 1807; Lt., 7th Foot, 19 March 1807; Capt., 7th Foot, 16 Jan. 1812; Bvt. Major, 21 Jan. 1819; Half-pay, 22 April 1819, 'in consequence of the last wounds'. *Where serving when wounded*: 'Salamanca, twice. Pampaluna, very badly.' No pension. *Family*: Married in Paris, 24 Dec. 1818. One child by 1829. *Where generally resident during last five years*: 'Cheltenham'. [PRO: WO 25/761 f215]. Slightly wounded at Salamanca, 22 July 1812

HAMERTON

('Hammerton') [*London Gazette*]. Severely wounded, Pyrenees, 28 July 1813 [*London Gazette*]. MGS.

HAMILTON, Alexander, Assistant Surgeon, 42nd Foot: *1829 Statement of Service for Retired Officers*: Aged nineteen on first appointment to the Army. Hospital Mate, 6 May 1806; Regimental Assistant Surgeon, 42nd Foot, 7 March 1808; Staff Surgeon, 'under Marshal Beresford', 3 June 1813; Surgeon to the Forces, British Hospital Staff, 25 Oct. 1814; Half-pay 25 Dec. 1814, by reduction. *Where serving when wounded*: 'Portugal'. *Details of pension*: Seventy pounds, commencing 1 Dec. 1812. *Family*: Married in Edinburgh, 9 April 1817. *Where generally resident during last five years*: 'Edinburgh'. [PRO: WO 25/761 f69].

HAMILTON, Andrew, Capt., 4th West India Regt.: Capt., 4th West India Regt., 19 Dec. 1811. Severely wounded, Pyrenees, 2 Aug. 1813, while serving as ADC to Major-General Barnes [*London Gazette*]. Severely wounded, the Nive, 13 Dec. 1813, while serving as ADC to Major-General Barnes [*London Gazette*]. Brother of James Hamilton. ADC to Major-General Barnes at Waterloo. Died 1821.

+HAMILTON, George, Capt., Royal Engineers: Lt., Royal Engineers, 2 Jan. 1804. *Rice Jones*, pp. 8, 11 ['Lisbon, April 5, 1809... On Sunday ... Lt. Hamilton ... arrived here from England'], p. 23 ['Oporto, May 13th, 1809... Poor Hamilton of our Corps was very badly wounded yesterday; I understand a musquet ball entered one of his thighs and lodged in the other; the ball is extracted; I am now endeavouring to find him, to render him what assistance I can'], p. 54 ['poor Capt. Hamilton who had been wounded at Oporto, died on May 20, and was buried in the new Factory Burying Ground; the 2nd grave from the

Hospital, on the South side of the centre walk, near a young Cyprus Tree.'], p. 69 ['died at Lisbon'].

+HAMILTON, Henry Stewart, Ensign/Lt., 74th Foot: Ensign, 74th Foot, 21 Nov. 1811. Severely wounded, Vittoria, 21 June 1813 [*London Gazette*]. Lt., 74th Foot, 11 Nov. 1813. Severely wounded, Toulouse, 10 April 1814 (1st Battn.) [London Gazette]. Died of wounds, 16 April 1814. Return dated April 1814. [PRO: WO 25/2965]. *Hurt*, p. 80 ['D.O.W., Toulouse, Apl. 16 [1814]'].

HAMILTON, James Banbury, Ensign, 5th Foot: Ensign, 5th Foot, 25 Sept. 1809. Slightly wounded, Salamanca, 22 July 1812 [*London Gazette*].

HAMILTON, James, Lt., 53rd Foot: Lt., 53rd Foot, 14 March 1810. Slightly wounded in the siege of the Forts of St Vincente, St Cayetano, and La Merced at Salamanca, 18–24 June 1812 (2nd Battn.) [*London Gazette*]. Severely wounded, Toulouse, 10 April 1814 (2nd Battn.) [*London Gazette*].

HAMILTON, James, Lt., 4th West India Regt.: Slightly wounded, the Nive, 13 Dec. 1813 [*London Gazette*]. Brother of Andrew, same regtiment.

HAMILTON, John, Capt., 11th Foot: Capt., Army, 18 Aug. 1808; Capt., 11th Foot, 13 Sept. 1808. Severely wounded, Salamanca, 22 July 1812 (1st Battn.) [*London Gazette*].

+HAMILTON, John, Lt., 60th Foot: Ensign, 60th Foot, 7 Oct. 1811; Lt., 60th Foot, 31 Dec. 1812. Severely wounded, sortie from Bayonne, 14 April 1814 (5th Battn.) [*London Gazette*]. *Hurt*, p. 79 ['D.O.W., Bayonne, Apl. 14 [1814]']. *Fletcher, Fields of Fire*, p. 164 ['Coldstream Guards cemetery, Bayonne... The

256

cemetery, which lies literally in the corner of a field, was the site of the Coldstream Guards' camp and those who lie here include ... Lieutenant Hamilton of the 60th Regiment'].

HAMILTON, Thomas, Capt., 27th Foot: *1829 Statement of Service for Retired Officers:* Aged twenty-four on first appointment to the Army. Ensign, 27th Foot, 29 Aug. 1804; Lt., 27th Foot, 7 Sept. 1805; Capt., 27th Foot, 24 Sept. 1812; Half-pay, May 1817, by reduction. *Where serving when wounded:* 'Wounded at Pampelona.' No pension. *Family:* Married at Queen Square Chapel, Bath, 14 Dec. 1815. Four children by 1829. *Where generally resident during last five years:* 'At Liverpool' [PRO: WO 25/761 f148]. Slightly wounded, Pyrenees, 28 July 1813 (3rd Battn.) [*London Gazette*].

HAMILTON, Thomas, Ensign, 29th Foot: *1829 Statement of Service for Retired Officers:* Aged eighteen on first appointment to the Army. Ensign, 29th Foot, Aug. 1810 [Army List gives 2 Aug.]; Lt., 29th Foot, Oct. 1811 [Army List gives 31 Oct.]; Half-pay, March 1818. *Where serving when wounded:* 'Wounded at Albuera.' No pension. *Family:* Married in St Paul's Chapel, Edinburgh, 14 Nov. 1820. No children by 1829. *Where generally resident during last five years:* 'Edinburgh.' [PRO: WO 25/761 f55]. Severely wounded, Albuera, 16 May 1811 [*London Gazette*].

+HAMILTON, William A., Capt., 3rd Foot: Capt., 3rd Foot, 13 Dec. 1810. Severely wounded, the Nive, 13 Dec. 1813 (1st Battn.) [*London Gazette*]. *Register of officers' effects:* Died of wounds, 29 Dec. 1813, 'Cambo nr. Bayonne'. Single. 2nd Battn. 'on duty with 1st Battn.' [PRO: WO 25/2963]. *Register of dead officers:* 2nd Battn. Died of wounds, 29 Dec. 1813. Return dated Jan. 1814. [PRO: WO 25/2965].

HAMILTON, William, 2nd Lt., 95th Foot: 2nd Lt., 95th Foot, 26 Sept. 1811. Severely wounded, storming of Ciudad Rodrigo, 19 Jan. 1812 (1st Battn.) [*London Gazette*]. Severely wounded, storming of San Sebastian, while serving with a 'Detachment 95th Foot' (1st Battn.) [*London Gazette*]. 1st Lt., 95th Foot, 22 Oct. 1813. Pension of seventy pounds per annum, commencing 1 Sept. 1815, 'for wounds' received at St Sebastian [*1818 Pension Return*, pp. 22–3]. *Simmons*, p. 223 [wounded, storming Ciudad Rodrigo, 19 Jan. 1812], p. 301 [volunteered for the storming party, San Sebastian], p. 316 [wounded, storming of San Sebastian, 31 August 1813: 'seriously wounded in two places']. *Kincaid, Adventures*, p. 248 [San Sebastian: 'the works were now reduced to such a state as to justify a second attempt, and our division sent forth their three hundred volunteers to join the storming party. (Lieutenants Percival and Hamilton commanded those from our battalion, and were both desperately wounded.)']. *Kincaid, Random Shots*, pp. 257–60 ['For the storming of St Sebastian, the number from our battalion were limited to ... a subaltern's command of twenty-five men; and as the post of honour was claimed by the senior lieutenant, (Percival,) it in a manner shut the mouths of all the juniors; yet were there some whose mouths would not be shut, - one in particular (Lieutenant H.) who had already seen enough fighting to satisfy the mind of any reasonable man, for he had stormed and bled at Ciudad Rodrigo, and he had stormed at Badajos, not to mention his having had his share in many, and not nameless battles, which had taken place in the interim; yet nothing would satisfy him but that he must draw his sword in that also. Our colonel was too heroic himself to check a feeling of that sort in those under him, and he very readily obtained the necessary permission to be a volunteer along with the party. Having settled his temporal affairs, namely willing away his pelisse, jacket, two pairs of trousers, and sundry nether garments... The prejudice against will-making by soldiers on service is so strong, that had H. been a rich man in place of a poor one, he must have died on the spot for doing what was accounted infinitely more desperate than storming a breach; but his poverty seemed to have been his salvation, for he was only half killed, – a ball entered under his eye, passed down the roof of the mouth, through the palate, entered again at the collar-bone, and was cut out at the shoulder-blade. He never again returned to his regiment, but I saw him some years after, in his native country (Ireland), in an active situation, and, excepting that he had gotten an ugly mark on his countenance, and his former manly voice had dwindled into a less commanding one, he seemed as well as ever I saw him ... he had been my messmate and companion at the sieges and stormings of both Ciudad and Badajos – and on the morning after the latter, he told me that he had had a presentiment that he would have fallen the night before, though he had been ashamed to confess it sooner – and yet to his credit be it spoken, so far from wishing to avoid, he coveted the post of danger – as his duty for that day would have led him to the trenches, but he exchanged with another officer, on purpose to ensure himself a place in the storm.'].

+**HAMMOND, Abel, Cornet, 12th Light Dragoons:** Killed, Vittoria, 21 June 1813 [*London Gazette*]. Recorded as dead, *1814 Army List* [Cornet 'Hammond 12Dr']. 'Abel Hammon' in *Challis, Index*, p. 29.

HANBY, Fethuston, Ensign/Lt., 27th Foot: *1829 Statement of Service for Retired Officers*: Aged seventeen on first appointment to the Army. Ensign, 27th Foot, 26 Feb. 1808; Lt., 27th Foot, 10 July 1811; Half-pay 'about Nov. 1815 ... from Ill Health in consequence of wounds – Examined by the Medical Board in Dublin.' *Where serving when wounded*: '1st. 10th May 1810, at Badajoz. 2nd. at Badajoz 6th April 1812. 3rd. Pampelona 28th July 1813.' No pension. *Family*: Married in Dublin, 'Ann's Church', 15 Aug. 1814. Three children by 1829. *Where generally resident during last five years*: 'Dumlish Co. Longford, Newton Forbes, Williamstown, Dublin'. [PRO: WO 25/761 f232]. Wounded during the repulse of a sortie from Badajoz, 10 May 1811 (3rd Battn.) [*London Gazette*]. Slightly wounded, storming of Badajoz, 6 April 1812 ('Hanley') (3rd Battn.) [*London Gazette*]. Severely wounded, Pyrenees, 28 July 1813 (3rd Battn.) [*London Gazette*].

HANCOT, Horatio, Lt., 43rd Foot: Slightly wounded, Coa, 24 July 1810 [*London Gazette*].

HANCOX, Skinner, Capt., 15th Light Dragoons: Capt., 15th Light Dragoons, 11 May 1809. Slightly wounded, Vittoria, 21 June 1813. [*London Gazette*]. Commanded the regt. by close of day at Waterloo.

HAND, Francis, Lt., 66th Foot: Lt., 66th Foot, 26 Oct. 1809. Severely wounded, Albuera, 16 May 1811 (2nd Battn.) [*London Gazette*].

+**HANMER, Thomas Hardy, Ensign, 81st Foot:** Ensign, 81st Foot, 30 July 1807. Killed, 'in the Army lately in Spain' (2nd Battn.) [*March 1809 Army List*, p. 105]. *Regimental Pay List*, 2nd Battn., 25 Dec. 1808–24 March 1809: 'Killed, 16 Jany.' [PRO: WO 25/8593].

HANNAM, Pitt, Lt., 7th Foot: Lt., 7th Foot, 20 April 1808. Slightly wounded, Salamanca, 22 July 1812 [*London Gazette*].

+HANSING, Adolphus, Lt., 2nd Line Battn. K.G.L.: Lt., 2nd Battn. K.G.L., 21 Jan. 1809. Killed, siege of Burgos, 20–26 Sept. 1812 [*London Gazette*]. Served in Peninsula 1808–12. *Beamish*, vol. II, pp. 101, 635 ['killed in the attack of the exterior line of defence of the castle of Burgos, 22d Sep. 1812.']. See Ernest Scharnhorst.

+HANSON, William, Capt., 20th Light Dragoons: Capt., Army, 12 May 1808; Capt., 20th Light Dragoons, 31 May 1810. Killed, Heights of Ordal, 12/13 Sept. 1813 [*London Gazette*]. Obituary, *The Gentleman's Magazine*, Nov. 1813, pp. 499–500 ['Sept. 13. Aged 25, in action, with the French cavalry near Villa Franca, on the East Coast of Spain, Capt. William Hanson, of the 20th Light Dragoons, eldest son of John H. esq. of Woodford and Great Bromley-Hall, Essex. We have been favoured with the following extract of a letter from Lieut.-col. Hawker, commanding the 20th Light Dragoons, dated Tarragona, 16th September, 1813, to John Hanson, esq. communicating the death of his son, Capt. H. "Dear Sir, it is with the deepest concern I communicate to you, and to your family, the afflicting intelligence of the death of Capt. Hanson, of the 20th Light Dragoons, who fell in action with the Enemy's Cavalry, near Villa Franca, on the 12th instant. In his fall, myself and other officers of the regiment have to deplore the loss of a friend, who possessed the most amiable and the most excellent private virtues; and our Country is deprived of an officer of the first promise. Capt. H. fell at the head of his troop at a moment of the most brilliant success, which his gallant example had much contributed to obtain... I saw Capt. Hanson in his last moments, and ... he expired free from pain. His death was occasioned by a carbine-shot, which entered his right breast, and he died in a few minutes after he was struck. His body has been interred. Thomas Hawker." ']. His sister was married to Richard Bogue, who was killed commanding the British Rocket Troop at Leipzig.

HARCOURT, Charles Amedee, Lt. Col. 40th Foot: Lt. Col., Army, 1 Nov. 1804; Lt. Col., 40th Foot, 25 Jan. 1810. Slightly wounded during the repulse of a sortie from Badajoz, 10 May 1811 [*London Gazette*]. Mentioned in Wellington's Ciudad Rodrigo dispatch, 20 Jan. 1812 ['In my dispatch of the 15th, I reported to your Lordship the attack on ... the Convent of Saint Francisco, on the 14th instant ... by Lieutenant-Colonel Harcourt, with the 40th Regiment. This regiment remained from that time in the suburb of Saint Francisco, and materially assisted our attack on that side of the place.'] [*London Gazette*, 5 Feb. 1812]. Severely wounded, storming of Badajoz, 6 April 1812 (1st Battn.) [*London Gazette*]. Mentioned in Wellington's Badajoz dispatch, 7 April 1812 ['Lieutenant-Colonel Harcourt of the 40th, likewise wounded, was highly distinguished']. Colonel, 4 June 1813. Gold Medal. Pension of three hundred pounds per annum, commencing 7 April 1813, 'for a wound' received at Badajoz [*1818 Pension Return*, pp. 10–11]. Later Major-General. *Royal Military Calendar*, vol. IV, pp. 8–10.

HARDCASTLE, William Augustus, Ensign, 31st Foot; Capt., 10th Caçadores: *1829 Statement of Service for Retired Officers*: Aged twenty-two on first appointment to the Army. Ensign, 31st Foot, 7 March 1811; Lt., 31st Foot, 29 April 1819; Half-pay, 75th Foot, 14 March 1822, 'by request.' 'Served by His Majesty's Permission in the Portuguese Army.' 'Ensign, Loyal

Lusitanian Legion, July 1810; Lt., 10th Caçadores, 4 June 1811; Capt., 10th Caçadores, 9 Nov. 1813.' 'Retired from the Portuguese Service on the 22 of Octr. 1814 the Army being put on a Peace Establishment.' *Where serving when wounded*: 'Aire in France, Captain in the 10th Caçadores.' *Details of pension*: One hundred pounds, commencing 3 March 1815. *Family*: Married three times: the first, in Manchester, 11 April 1820; the second, in East Dawson, 11 Jan. 1822; the third, in Belfast, 22 Oct. 1828. He had one child from each of the first two marriages. *Where generally resident during last five years*: 'Castle Dawson, Scotland, now Belfast.' [PRO: WO 25/761 f39]. MGS. In Portuguese Service August 1810 to April 1814. *1818 Pension Return*, pp. 26–7. *Challis, Portuguese Army*, p. 55 ['Wd. Aire 2 Mar. '14'].

HARDING, Benjamin, Capt, 10th Light Dragoons: Capt., 10th Light Dragoons, 25 Jan. 1810. Severely wounded, in Action with the Enemy, 28 Feb. 1814 [*London Gazette*]. Capt., 20th Light Dragoons, 12 Nov. 1814. MGS.

+HARDING, Frederick, Ensign/Lt., 27th Foot: Ensign, 27th Foot, 1 Sept. 1808. Killed, storming of San Sebastian, 31 Aug. 1813 ('Lieutenant Hardinge') (3rd Battn.) [*London Gazette*].

HARDING, George, Major, 44th Foot: Major, 44th Foot, 16 Aug. 1805; Bvt. Lt. Col., 44th Foot, 1 Jan. 1812. Slightly wounded, during 'movements of the Army' [Retreat from Burgos: Villa Muriel], 25 Oct. 1812 (2nd Battn.) [*London Gazette*]. *Lawrence*, p. 93.

HARDINGE, Henry, Capt., 57th Foot; Lt. Col., E.O.P.S.; Lt. Col., Portuguese Staff: Third son of Rev. Henry Hardinge, Rector of Stanhope, Durham. Capt., 57th Foot, 7

April 1804. Wounded, Vimeiro, 21 Aug. 1808, while serving on the General Staff as DAQMG [*London Gazette*]. Bvt. Lt. Col. E.O.P.S., 30 May 1811, 'Serv. with the Portug. Army'. Mentioned in Wellington's dispatch, 27 March 1812 [Storming of Fort Picurina, Badajoz, 26 March 1812: 'Major-General Kempt ... particularly mentions Lieutenant-Colonel Hardinge, of the staff of the Portuguese Army, who attended him on this occasion'] [*London Gazette*]. Severely wounded, Vittoria, 21 June 1813, while serving as DQMG in Portuguese Army [*London Gazette*]. Gold Medal. Capt. and Lt. Col., 1st Foot Guards, 25 July 1814. Waterloo. Later Governor-General of India. MGS. *Challis, Portuguese Army List*, p. 55. *Dalton*, p. 101 ['Afterwards Viscount Hardinge, G.C.B., and K.T.S... D. 24th Sept., 1856.']. He became Field-Marshal Viscount Hardinge of Lahore, following distinguished service as governor-general of India; field-marshal 1855. Commander-in-Chief 1852–6; British commissioner to the Prussian HQ in the Waterloo campaign, he lost his left hand at Ligny. His most outstanding Peninsular service was in persuading Lowry Cole to advance at Albuera to reinforce 'the heights'; had also been Moore's ADC at Corunna. Born 1785, died 1856. Wellington's appraisal: 'quoted in Griffiths, A. J., *The Wellington Memorial* (London, 1897), p. 304). His brother, Capt. George Nicholas Hardinge (1781–1808) was a noted hero of the Royal Navy, killed commanding HMS *San Fiorenzo* when capturing the French frigate *La Piedmontaise*. Harding, C., *Viscount Hardinge and the Advance of the British Dominions in the Punjab* (London, 1900).

+HARDY, James, Ensign, 31st Foot: Ensign, 31st Foot, 20 Feb. 1812. Severely wounded, 'right thigh amputated', the Nive, 13 Dec. 1813

(2nd Battn.) [*London Gazette*]. *Register of officers' effects*: Died of wounds, 5 Jan. 1814, 'Cambo'. Single. [PRO: WO 25/2963]. *Hurt*, p. 77 ['D.O.W., Nive, Dec. 13'].

+HARDYMAN, Robert, Capt., 45th Foot: Capt., 45th Foot, 7 Nov. 1811. Killed in the storming of Ciudad Rodrigo, 19 Jan. 1812 [*London Gazette*].

+HARLEY, John, Lt., 47th Foot: Lt., 47th Foot, 7 Sept. 1809. Killed, Vittoria, 21 June 1813 (2nd Battn.) [*London Gazette*].

HARNETT, John Crosbie, Lt., 27th Foot: *1829 Statement of Service for Retired Officers*: Aged 'abt. 17' on first appointment to the Army. Ensign, 27th Foot, 20 March 1806; Lt., 27th Foot, 27 Oct. 1807; Half-pay, 21 Jan. 1819, 'Ill health caused by 12 years Service in foreign climate.' *Where serving when wounded*: 'Severely wounded at Toulouse.' No pension. *Family*: Married in Camp Haven church, 31 Jan. 1919. Two children by 1829. *Where generally resident during last five years*: 'Kinsale'. 'I served his late & his present Majesty 12 years on foreign service & one year on the home service: during the former period I served in the Mediteranean in Sicily Malta &c. Having got leave to return I joined & served in the army under the Duke of Wellington in Spain & France in the 27th ... having been in the different actions with my Regiment for the last eight months of the campaign & severely wounded at Toulouse. I then served in Canada, a short time in the West Indies Flanders & France... I always commanded a company in action & when serving in Lord Wellington's army & generally for the last few years whilst on full pay.' [PRO: WO 25/761 f219]. Severely wounded, Toulouse, 10 April 1814 (3rd Battn.) [*London Gazette*].

HARRIS, Isaac Watkins, 2nd Lt./1st Lt., 23rd Foot: *1829 Statement of Service for Retired Officers*: 'Cannot possitively say' how old he was on first appointment to the Army, 'but think about 20 years.' 2nd Lt., 23rd Foot, 10 Dec. 1808 [Army List gives 8 Dec.]; 1st Lt., 23rd Foot, 20 June 1811; Capt., 23rd Foot, 7 April 1825; Half-pay, 'and was obliged in consequence of ill health to leave the Regt. while serving with them at Gibraltar.' Served seventeen and a half years on full-pay. *Where serving when wounded*: 'Severely wounded through both thighs on the 16th of May 1811 in the Battle of Albuera. Received a contusion in the breast on the 28th of July 1813 in the Battle of Pampluna. Severely wounded in the right thigh on the 27th of February 1814 in the Battle of Orthes. No Pension.' *Family*: Married in County Wexford, 19 March 1806. One child by 1829. *Where generally resident during last five years*: 'Since I got out on half pay residing at Sheaf near Bandon Co. Cork, Ireland.' [PRO: WO 25/761 f47]. Slightly wounded, Albuera, 16 May 1811 [*London Gazette*]. Slightly wounded, Pyrenees, 28 July 1813 (1st Battn.) [*London Gazette*]. Severely wounded, Orthes, 27 Feb. 1814 ('William Harris') (1st Battn.) [*London Gazette*]. Waterloo. MGS.

HARRIS, James, Lt., 61st Foot: *1829 Statement of Service*: Born Clonmel, June 1788. Aged twenty-two on first appointment to the Army. Ensign, 61st Foot, 12 July 1810; Lt., 61st Foot, 26 July 1812. *Battles, sieges and campaigns*: 'Forts of Salamanca June 1812. Seige of Burgos 1812. Battle Pyrenees 28th July to 2nd August 1813. Nivelle 10th Novr. 1813. Nive from 9 to 13th Decr. 1813. Orthes 27th Febry. 1814. Tarbes March 1814. Toulouse 10th April 1814. Campaigns 1812, 1813 and 1814.' *Distinguished conduct*: 'On the

10th November 1813 Received his Commanding Officers thanks (Lieut. Col. Coghlan) and the future Command of the Flankers whenever they were opposed to the Enemy.' *Wounds received in action*: 'Wounded Severely at Toulouse through the Right Shoulder. Grant a years Pay made up to a Captain.' *Service abroad*: '1st April 1812 to 11th July 1814, Peninsula. 13th October 1816 to 31st May 1822, Jamaica.' [PRO: WO 25/797 f27]. Severely wounded, Toulouse, 10 April 1814 (1st Battn.) [*London Gazette*].

HARRIS, John, Lt., 45th Foot: Lt., 45th Foot, 5 June 1806. Severely wounded, Busaco, 27 Sept. 1810 (1st Battn.) [*London Gazette*].

HARRIS, Thomas Noel, Cornet, 13th Light Dragoons; Lt., 18th Light Dragoons: Lt., 18th Light Dragoons, 15 Aug. 1811. 'Very slightly' wounded, storming of Badajoz, 6 April 1812, while serving as ADC to Major-General Walker [*London Gazette*]. Waterloo. MGS. *Dalton*, p. 28. See article about him by Philip Haythornthwaite, *Military Illustrated*, No. 9, 1987. Portrait of him in *Haythornthwaite, Wellington's Military Machine*, p. 20.

HARRISON, John Christopher, 1st Lt., 23rd Foot: *1829 Statement of Service*: Born 5 April 1788, County of Worcester. 2nd Lt., 23rd Foot, 7 March 1805; 1st Lt., 23rd Foot, 27 May 1806; Capt., 23rd Foot, 20 May 1812; Major, 23rd Foot, 29 Oct. 1825; Lt. Col., 23rd Foot, 22 July 1830. *Battles, sieges and campaigns*: 'Campaign in Island of Zealand & Siege of Copenhagen 1807... Campaign in Martinique & Siege of Fort Bourbon in 1809... Part of Peninsula Campaign of 1810. All the Peninsula Campaign of 1811. Part of the Peninsula Campaign of 1812, 1st Lieutenant Commg. a Company... Battle of Redinha, on Massina's retreat 12th March 1811, 1st Lieut.

Commg. a Company... Siege of Olivenza 9th April 1811, 1st Lieut. Commg. a Company... Siege of Badajos 7 May 1811, 1st Lieut. Commg. a Company... Battle of Albuhera 16th May 1811, 1st Lieut. Commg. a Company... Siege of Ciudad Rodrigo 1812, 1st Lieut. Commg. a Company... Siege & Storming of Badajos, March & April 1812, 1st Lieut. commanding a Compy.' *Wounds received in action*: 'Received a Gun Shot Wound above left knee at Albuhera 16th May 1811 in action with the French. Received One Gun Shot Wound thro' Right shoulder a Second thro' the Right Elbow and a third in the right leg, at the storming of the Breach of Badajos, 6th April 1812. Grant of two years pay. Pension £100 per annum – Date from 7th April 1813.' *Service abroad*: '29th Oct. 1805 to 11th Feby. 1806, Hanover. 25 July 1807 to Oct. 1807, Copenhagen. 4 Feby. 1808 to 29th Nov. 1808, Nova Scotia. 29th Nov. 1808 to 6 April 1809, West Indies. 6 April 1809 to 10 Oct. 1810, Nova Scotia. 10 Oct. 1810 to June 1812, Peninsula. Nov. 1815 to Nov. 1818, France. Decr. 1823 to 7 Jany. 1827, Gibraltar. 7 Jany. 1827 to 12 March 1828, Portugal. 12 March 1828 to 12 May 1828, Gibraltar.' *Family*: Married Miss Roche, 11 Oct. 1820, Ennistymon, County Clare. They had no children by 1830. [PRO: WO 25/789 f169] Slightly wounded, Albuera, 16 May 1811 [*London Gazette*]. Severely wounded, storming of Badajoz, 6 April 1812 [*London Gazette*]. Pension 'for wounds' received at Badajoz [*1818 Pension Return*, pp. 6–7]. MGS.

+HARRISON, John Mellish, Lt., 38th Foot; Capt., 9th Caçadores: Lt., 38th Foot, 1 April 1807. Killed, the Nive, 9 Dec. 1813, while serving as Capt., 9th Caçadores ('Captain Joao Mellish Harrison') [*London Gazette*]. In Portuguese Service Aug. 1809 to Dec. 1813. *Challis, Portuguese Army*, p. 55 ['Capt. 38

Ft; Bt. Maj. 9 Cacad... Bt. Majority for Pyrenees'].

HARRISON, John William, Capt., 60th Foot: Capt., Army, 15 Oct. 1807; Capt., 67th Foot, 1 Oct. 1809; Capt., 60th Foot, 12 Aug. 1812. Two pensions, each for two hundred pounds, commencing 28 Feb. 1815, for 'loss of both eyes' at Bayonne, 1814, plus a third for 'loss of smell and taste' also at Bayonne [*1818 Pension Return*, pp. 16–17].

HARRISON, William, Lt., 38th Foot: Lt., 38th Foot, 7 March 1811. Slightly wounded, 'at the Siege of St Sebastian', 7–27 July 1813 (1st Battn.) [*London Gazette*].

HART, Francis Henry, Lt., 39th Foot: *1829 Statement of Service for Retired Officers*: 'In his 17th yr.' on first appointment to the Army. Ensign, 39th Foot, 5 Jan. 1805; Lt., 39th Foot, 15 Jan. 1807; Capt., 39th Foot, 8 April 1825; Half-pay, 84th Foot, 'I was ... considered by my Commg. Offr. and Surgeon of the 39th Regt. as unfit for Service, from ill health occasioned by Wounds recd. in Action.' 'Capt. Hart feels every wish to serve his King, but is prevented from applying by his disabled state from the Wounds he has received and constant ill health arising therefrom.' *Where serving when wounded*: 'at Albuhera on the 16th May 1811. Pass of Mayo in Spain, 25th July 1813.' *Details of pension*: Seventy pounds for the first wound, commencing 17 May 1812. Seventy pounds for the second wound, commencing 25 Dec. 1826. *Where generally resident during last five years*: 'From the period of being placed on Half Pay in different parts of Somerset & Devon. Residence in Bristol.' [PRO: WO 25/761 f137]. Severely wounded, Albuera, 16 May 1811 (2nd Battn.) [*London Gazette*]. Severely wounded, Pyrenees, 25 July 1813 (1st Battn.) [*London Gazette*]. Temporary Pension of seventy

pounds per annum, commencing 17 May 1812, 'for wounds' received at Albuera and the Pyrenees [*1818 Pension Return*, pp. 10–11]. MGS.

HART, Henry Scott, Lt., 36th Foot: *1829 Statement of Service for Retired Officers*: Aged twenty-five on first appointment to the Army. Ensign, 36th Foot, 15 Oct. 1803; Lt., 36th Foot, Jan. 1805; Capt., 36th Foot, 7 Feb. 1811; Half-pay, 75th Foot, 1824, 'in consequence of ill health sustained in the Service'. *Where serving when wounded*: 'Slightly wounded as Lieut. 36th Reg. in Peninsula.' No pension. *Family*: Married in Alderney, 23 Jan. 1816. No children by 1829. *Where generally resident during last five years*: 'Alderney.' [PRO: WO 25/761 f224]. Slightly wounded, Vimeiro, 21 Aug. 1808 [*London Gazette*].

HART, John Blackburn, Capt., 95th Foot: Lt., Army, 22 Jan. 1801; Lt., 95th Foot, 22 Dec. 1803; Capt., 95th Foot, 1 Feb. 1809. Slightly wounded, 'in the Operations of the Army', 31 Aug. 1813 [London Gazette]. Severely wounded, Crossing the Bidassoa, 7/9 Oct. 1813 (2nd Battn.) [*London Gazette*]. Pension of one hundred pounds per annum, commencing 8 Oct. 1814, 'for wounds' received at Vera, 1813 [*1818 Pension Return*, pp. 22–3]. *Harris*, pp. 84–7 ['Thomas Mayberry was ... a sergeant... Whilst in the town of Hythe, he got the fingering of about two hundred pounds for the purpose of paying for necessaries purchased for the men of his company... Captain Hart, who then commanded the company Mayberry belonged to, was not a little thunderstruck, some little time after, at finding that the several tradesmen who furnished the articles for the men had never been settled with, and, sending for Mayberry, discovered the delinquency. Mayberry was a prisoner in a moment; and Captain Hart was as much astonished as if his own father had committed a fraud, so well and so much was Mayberry thought of... He was sentenced to receive seven hundred lashes... Mayberry after this was much scouted by his fellow-soldiers, and also ill-thought of by the officers; and on a detachment being sent to Portugal, he volunteered for the expedition. Captain Hart, however, would fain have declined taking him, as he had so bad an opinion of him after this affair; but Mayberry showed himself so desirous of going, that at last he consented and took him. At the seige of Badajoz, Mayberry wiped off, in a measure, all his former ill-conduct. He was seen by Captain Hart to behave so bravely in the breach that he commended him on the spot. "Well done, Mayberry!" he said; "you have this day done enough to obliterate your disgrace; and, if we live, I will endeavour to restore you to your former rank. Go now to the rear; you have done enough for one day." Mayberry, however, refused to retire, although covered with wounds... He accordingly continued in front of all, till at last he was seen to be cut down'], pp. 171, 183.

HARTFORD, Henry, Lt., 59th Foot: Ensign, 59th Foot, 19 July 1810. Lt., 59th Foot, 12 March 1812. Severely wounded, storming of San Sebastian, 31 Aug. 1813 (2nd Battn.) [*London Gazette*]. Waterloo.

HARTLEY, Andrew, Capt., 61st Foot: Capt., 61st Foot, 9 July 1803. Slightly wounded, Talavera, 28 July 1809 [*London Gazette*].

HARTLEY, Thomas, Lt., 7th Foot: Lt., Army, 3 Dec. 1807; Lt., 7th Foot, 3 Aug. 1809. Severely wounded, Salamanca, 22 July 1812 ('Hartly') [*London Gazette*].

HARTLEY, William, Lt., 71st Foot: Lt., 23rd Foot, 5 April 1801; Lt., 71st Foot, 26 Aug. 1804. Slightly wounded, Vimeiro, 21 Aug. 1808

[*London Gazette*]. Capt., 62nd Foot, 22 Dec. 1808. MGS.

HARTMANN, George Julius, Major, K.G.L. Artillery; O.C., Portuguese Artillery: Major, K.G.L. Artillery, 12 April 1806. Mentioned in Hill's dispatch of 30 Oct. 1811, concerning Arroyo dos Molinos, 28 Oct. 1811 ['I must also express my obligations to ... Major Hartmann, commanding the artillery'] [*London Gazette*]. Slightly wounded, sortie from Bayonne, 14 April 1814 ('Major and Lieutenant-Colonel') [*London Gazette*]. Served in Peninsula 1808-14. In Portuguese Service Jan. 1811 to April 1814. Gold Medal. Waterloo. Later Lt.-General. MGS. *Webber*, p. 120 ['Col. Hartman']. *Beamish*, vol. II, p. 532. *Challis, Portuguese Army*, p. 55 ['O.C. Port. Arty.'].

+HARTWIG, Carl, Lt., Duke of Brunswick Oels' Corps (Infantry): Lt., Duke of Brunswick Oels' Corps (Infantry), 1 Aug. 1811. Killed, during 'movements of the Army' [Retreat from Burgos: Villa Muriel], 25 Oct. 1812] [*London Gazette*].

HARTWIG, Frederick William von, Major, 1st Light Battn. K.G.L.: Major, 1st Light Battn. K.G.L., 4 April 1809. Slightly wounded, Albuera, 16 May 1811 [*London Gazette*]. Served in Peninsula 1811-14. Waterloo. *Beamish*, vol. II, p. 561 [Died 'at Hameln, 16th Nov. 1822.'].

HARTWIG, John Frederick Lewis von, Lt., 1st Light Battn. K.G.L.: *1829 Statement of Service for Retired Officers*: Aged sixteen on first appointment to the Army. Ensign, 1st Light Battn. K.G.L., 28 Sept. 1809; Lt., 1st Light Battn. K.G.L., 17 April 1811; Capt., 1st Light Battn. K.G.L., 16 Aug. 1815; Half-pay, 25 Feb. 1816, by reduction of K.G.L. *Where serving when wounded*: 'In the Battle of Albuera on the 16th May 1811 & in the Battle of Salamanca on the 22nd

July 1812 (in Spain).' *Details of pension*: Seventy pounds, commencing 25 Dec. 1821. *Family*: Married in Frenhagen, Province of Luneburg, Hanover, 27 Sept. 1818. Three children by 1829. *Where generally resident during last five years*: 'in Emden.' [PRO: WO 25/755 f132]. Letter from de Hartwig, dated Emden 26 Dec. 1828, enclosed with Statement of Service: 'I am appointed as Captain in the Regiment of Eastfriesland' [PRO: WO 25/755 f132 encl.]. Slightly wounded, Albuera, 16 May 1811 [*London Gazette*]. Severely wounded, Salamanca, 22 July 1812 [*London Gazette*]. Served in Peninsula 1811–14. Waterloo. *Beamish*, vol. II, p. 562 ['Frederick von Hartwig'].

+HARVEST, Augustus, Lt., 52nd Foot: Lt., 52nd Foot, 6 Jan. 1808. Killed, storming of San Sebastian (1st Battn.) [*London Gazette*].

+HARVEST, Horatio, Lt., 43rd Foot: Lt., 43rd Foot, 9 Dec. 1805. Killed, storming of Badajoz, 6 April 1812 [*London Gazette*]. *Surtees*, pp. 151–2 [Badajoz: 'It is well known, I believe, to be the rule in all services like the assault of fortresses, &c., that those, both officers and men, who form the forlorn hope and the storming party, are volunteers, these being services of extreme danger, and which generally procure for the officers who survive a step of promotion; but it might as well have gone (in the light division at least) as a tour of duty, for on all occasions of this nature, with only one or two exceptions, the senior officers of each rank insisted upon being sent on duty. Nay, in one instance this heroic feeling was carried to an almost censurable excess. Lieutenant Harvest of the 43d having been some time the senior of his rank in that regiment, and there being a vacancy for a captain, he had been recommended for the company; and although he

had not been gazetted, yet it had been intimated to him through his commander-officer that his name should shortly appear as captain. Thus his promotion was perfectly secure; notwithstanding, when volunteers were called for for the storming party, he insisted on his right of going as senior lieutenant; so over scrupulous was he that his permitting a junior officer to occupy this post might be construed to the detriment of his honour. He went, and fell; and thus not only lost his company but his life, and by his too refined sense of honour deprived another officer, probably, of that promotion which would have been the consequence of going on this duty had he survived.'].

+HARVEY, Edward, Lt. and Capt., Coldstream Guards: Lt. and Capt., Coldstream Guards, 17 Aug. 1809. Slightly wounded, Fuentes de Onoro, 5 May 1811 ('Hervey') (1st Batt.) [*London Gazette*]. Killed, siege of Burgos, 18 Oct. 1812 [*London Gazette*]. Obituary, *The Gentleman's Magazine*, Feb. 1813, p. 182 ['At Burgos, Capt. Hervey, son of Adm. H. late member for Essex.'].

HARVEY, James Vickers, Lt. and Capt., Coldstream Guards: Lt. and Capt., Coldstream Guards, 7 Jan. 1811. Slightly wounded, sortie from Bayonne, 14 April 1814 (1st Battn.) [*London Gazette*].

HARVEY, Robert John, Bvt. Major, E.O.P.S.; Portuguese Staff: Bvt. Major, E.O.P.S., 25 July 1811, 'Serv. with the Portug. Army'; Bvt. Lt. Col., E.O.P.S., 21 June 1813. In Portuguese Service June 1809 to April 1814. Gold Medal. MGS. General, 31 Aug. 1855. *Challis, Portuguese Army*, p. 55 ['Bt. Lt.-Col. E.O.P.S.; Bt. Col. Staff... Wd. Badajos 6 Apr. '12, Pyrenees July '13']. *Mullen*, p. 670 ['AQMG, Portuguese Service'].

HARVEY, Thomas John, Lt., 66th Foot: Lt., 66th Foot, 2 Feb. 1808. Slightly wounded, Albuera, 16 May 1811 (2nd Battn.) [*London Gazette*]. Adjutant, 66th Foot, 13 Aug. 1811. Recorded as 'missing', the Nive, 13 Dec. 1813 (2nd Battn.) [*London Gazette*].

+HARVEY, William Maundy, Major, 79th Foot; Brigadier-General/ Major-General, Portuguese Staff: Major, 79th Foot, 27 Feb. 1806; Bvt. Lt. Col., 79th Foot, 17 Dec. 1803. Severely wounded, storming of Badajoz, 6 April 1812, while serving as a Brigadier-General on the Portuguese Staff [*London Gazette*]. Mentioned in Wellington's Badajoz dispatch, 7 April 1812 ['I have also to mention Major-General Harvey, of the Portuguese service, commanding a brigade in the 3rd division'] [*London Gazette*]. Obituary, *The Gentleman's Magazine*, 1813 Supplement Part I, p. 663 ['June 10... At sea, on his return from the Peninsula (where he had been for the recovery of his health) much and deservedly lamented in his 39th year, Wm. Maundy Harvey, esq. colonel in the army, lieut.-col. of the 79th Foot, and a brigadier-general in the Portuguese service, for whose meritorious services in that kingdom the Prince Regent of Portugal conferred on him the honour of a knight commander of the Order of the Tower and Sword. He was the only son of Samuel H. esq. of Ramsgate, Kent.']. In Portuguese Service Aug. 1809 to June 1813. Gold Medal. *Challis, Portuguese Army*, p. 55 ['Harvey, William Munday... Wd. Affair of outposts at Dos Portas 13 Oct. '10'].

HASSARD, Jason, Lt., 74th Foot: Lt., Army, 6 Sept. 1809; Lt., 74th Foot, 18 Oct. 1810. Slightly wounded, Toulouse, 10 April 1814 (1st Battn.) [*London Gazette*].

+HASSELBACH, Frederick, Lt., 3rd Line Battn. K.G.L.: Lt., 3rd Line Battn. K.G.L., 1 May 1810. Killed, near Castalla, 12 April 1813 ('Rifle Company... Hazlebach') [*London Gazette*]. 'Hasselback' in Army List. Served in Peninsula 1812–13. *Beamish*, vol. II, p. 635 ['killed in action near Castalla in Spain, 13th April 1813.'].

HATTORF, Henry George von, Capt., 1st Dragoons K.G.L.; Capt., 1st Light Dragoons K.G.L.: *1829 Statement of Service for Retired Officers*: Aged twenty on first appointment to the Army. Cornet, 1st 'Heavy Dragoons' K.G.L., 8 Feb. 1804; Lt., 1st Dragoons K.G.L., 1805 [Army List gives 25 Sept. 1804]; Capt., 1st Light Dragoons K.G.L., 25 Feb. 1812 [Army List gives: Capt., 1st Heavy Dragoons, 8 June 1807; recorded in 1st Dragoons until *1813 Army List. 1814 Army List* notes as Capt., 1st Light Dragoons K.G.L., 25 Feb. 1812]; Half-pay, by reduction. Served at Waterloo. Served fourteen years on full pay. *Where serving when wounded*: '1st at Las Roses in Spain on the 11th of August 1812. 2nd at Waterloo, June 18th 1815.' *Details of pension*: One hundred pounds per annum, commencing 25 Dec. 1825. *Family*: Married in 'Schnarenburg, Kingdom of Hannover', 5 Sept. 1817. Two children by 1829. *Where generally resident during last five years*: 'at Feldersheim in the Kingdom of Hannover.' Signed 'Henry George Hattorf'. [PRO: WO 25/761 f12]. Severely wounded, in 'an Affair with the Enemy's Cavalry, in Front of the Village of Majalahonda,' 11 Aug. 1812 [*London Gazette*]. 'Geo. Henry de Hattorff' in Army List. Served in Peninsula 1812–14. Waterloo. *Beamish*, vol. II, p. 540 ['George Henry von Hattorf ... severely wounded, 11th Aug. 1812, at Majalahonda; severely wounded, 18th June 1815, at Waterloo.'].

HAUTOY, Charles Louis Alexis Comte du, Major, Chasseurs

Britanniques: *1829 Statement of Service for Retired Officers*: Aged thirty-six years five months on first appointment to the Army. Capt., Chasseurs Britanniques, 1 May 1801; Major, Chasseurs Britanniques, 10 Aug. 1809; Bvt. Lt. Col., Army, 21 June 1813. Half-pay, by reduction. *Where serving when wounded*: 'Wounded at Rosett in Egypt 31st March 1807 [sic]. In the Pyrenees, 31st August 1813.' No pension. *Family*: Married in 'Bellem near Lisbon, Portugal', 7 Aug. 1811. No children by 1829. *Where generally resident during last five years*: 'Etain, Département de la Meuse.' [PRO: WO 25/756 f11]. Severely wounded, 'in the Operations of the Army', 31 Aug. 1813 ('Major Duhantoy (Lieutenant-Colonel)') [*London Gazette*]. Gold Medal. 'Duhautoy' in Army List.

HAVERFIELD, John, Capt., 43rd Foot: Capt., 43rd Foot, 15 Aug. 1804. Wounded, Vimeiro, 21 Aug. 1808 [*London Gazette*].

+HAWKER, Edmund, Lt., Royal Artillery: 1st Lt., Royal Engineers, 28 March 1806. Killed during the seige of Badajoz, 30 May–5 June 1811 [*London Gazette*]. Mentioned in Wellington's dispatch of 6 June 1811 ['I am sorry to say that Lieutenant Hawker, of the royal artillery, an officer who has distinguished himself in these operations, was killed this morning.'].

HAWKER, James, Capt., Royal Artillery: Capt., Army, 16 July 1799; Capt., Royal Artillery, 12 Sept. 1803. Slightly wounded, Albuera, 16 May 1811 [*London Gazette*]. Bvt. Major, Royal Artillery, 4 June 1811. Mentioned in Hill's dispatch, Merida, 30 Dec. 1811, regarding the action at La Nava, 27 Dec. 1811 ['the enemy retired ... and he effected his retreat with the loss of about twenty killed, and as many wounded, from four nine-pounders, which, by the great exertion of

Major Hawker and his officers and men, got within range, and followed him for some distance']. Gold Medal. Waterloo.

HAWKER, Peter, Capt., 14th Light Dragoons: Capt., 14th Light Dragoons, 4 Aug. 1804. Slightly wounded, passage of the Douro, 12 May 1809 [*London Gazette*]. Slightly wounded, Talavera, 28 July 1809 [*London Gazette*]. MGS. Portrait of him in *Fletcher, Regiments*, between pp. 44–5 ['Colonel Peter Hawker, 14th Light Dragoons, 1812. Hawker fought at Talavera and was wounded at Oporto in 1809. He later wrote *Instructions to Young Sportsmen*.']. Author of *Journal of the Campaign of 1809* (London, 1810).

HAWKER, Samuel, Lt. Col., 14th Light Dragoons: Lt. Col., 14th Light Dragoons, 12 June 1800; Bvt. Col., 14th Light Dragons, 25 April 1808. Portrait of him, *Perrett*, p. 17. The 14th Light Dragoons' first Commanding Officer in the Peninsular War. *Perrett*, pp. 16, 17 [Talavera, 28 July 1809: 'Colonel Hawker, who was among the wounded, was awarded a gold medal. He returned home shortly after the battle and command passed to Lt-Colonel Neil Talbot.']. There is an obituary of his wife, *The Gentleman's Magazine*, Nov. 1809, p. 1077 ['9. [Oct.]... At a village near Elvas, in the South of Portugal, Mrs Hawker, wife of Lieut.-col. H. of the 14th Light Dragoons. This lady, when much indisposed, accompanied by her daughter, set off for Oporto, to join the Colonel, who was stated to be wounded in battle, and very narrowly escaped being made a prisoner by the Enemy. The fatigue and anxiety brought on a rapid decline, of which she died.'].

HAWKINS, John P., Capt., 68th Foot: Capt., Army, 24 Aug. 1804; Capt., 68th Foot, 5 July 1806. Slightly wounded, Heights of

Villares, 20–22 June 1812 [*London Gazette*].

HAWKSHAW, Edward, Major, E.O.P.S.; Major, 7th Caçadores or Lt. Col., Loyal Lusitanian Legion: Major, E.O.P.S., 16 Nov. 1809, ('Staff officer with permanent rank in the Army, not holding regimental commission... Serving with Portuguese Army'). Wounded, Albuera, 16 May 1811, while serving as Lt. Col., Loyal Lusitanian Legion (1st Battn.) [*London Gazette*]. In Portuguese Service April 1809 to June 1813. Bvt. Lt. Col., 4 June 1814. Half-pay, 'late serving with the Portuguese Army', *1815 Army List*. Pension of three hundred pounds per annum, commencing 16 May 1812, 'for a wound' received at Albuera, while serving as Major, 7th Caçadores [*1818 Pension Return*, pp. 26–7]. Gold Medal. MGS. *Challis, Portuguese Army*, p. 55 ['Lt. Col. 2 Line']. Note the confusion over his regt. and rank when wounded at Albuera.

+HAWKSLEY, Rutherford, Lt., 95th Foot: 2nd Lt., 95th Foot, 22 Feb. 1810. Severely wounded, 'but not dangerously', 'in carrying a Redoubt before Ciudad Rodrigo', 8 Jan. 1812 (1st Battn.) [*London Gazette*]. Mentioned in Wellington's dispatch of 15 Jan. 1812 ['N.B. – Lieutenant Hawkesley, 95th, wounded on the 8th, since dead.'] [*London Gazette*]. *Register of dead officers*: Died of wounds, 11 Jan. 1812. Return dated 25 Jan. 1812. [PRO: WO 25/2965]. Obituary, *The Gentleman's Magazine*, May 1812, p. 498 ['Lately... At head-quarters, Gallegos, having been severely wounded on the night of the 8th of Jan. in storming the redoubt of Francisco, before Ciudad Rodrigo, in his 20th year, Lieut. Rutherford Hawksley, of the 95th Rifle Regiment, second son of Archibald H. esq. of Dublin. The ardour and enthusiasm for his profession, felt by this gallant young soldier,

offered the brightest prospect for his future career; and his most estimable private character and numerous virtues strongly endeared him to his brother officers and a large circle of friends.'].

HAWTYN, Joseph, Capt., 23rd Foot: Capt., 23rd Foot, 11 Sept. 1806. Slightly wounded, storming of Badajoz, 6 April 1812 [*London Gazette*]. Bvt. Major, 17 Aug. 1812. Killed, Waterloo.

+HAY, Andrew, Lt. Col., 1st Foot; Major-General: Lt. Col., Army, 1 Jan. 1798; Lt. Col., 1st Foot, 19 March 1807. Wounded, 'in the Army lately in Spain' (3rd Battn.) [*March 1809 Army List*, p. 105]. Major-General, 4 June 1811. Killed, sortie from Bayonne, 14 April 1814 [*London Gazette*]. Report of Colville to Wellington, Baucaut, 14 April 1814:. 'I much regret to have to mention the death of Major-General Hay, general officer of the night. His last words were (a minute before he was shot) an order to hold the Church of St Etienne, and a fortified house adjoining, to the last extremity.' [*London Gazette*, 27 April 1814]. Report of K. A. Howard to Colville, dated 'Camp near Bayonne', 15 April 1814: 'Major-General Hay was the General Officer of the day, in command of the line of outposts, and I regret much to say, was killed shortly after the attack commenced... In Major-General Hay, who was well known to you, His Majesty's service has lost a most zealous and able officer, who has served a considerable time in this army with great distinction.'] [*London Gazette*, 27 April 1814]. Obituary, *The Gentleman's Magazine*, May 1814, p. 517 ['a most zealous and able officer, whose whole life was spent in the service of his country, and who in every situation entitled himself to the esteem of his commanders, to the friendship of his brother officers, and to the care of his men. He has left a widow, two sons, and four daughters: a third son, his eldest, fell in battle by his side.']. This, however, does not accord with the opinion of Frederick Robinson, who held an equivalent command in the Peninsula: 'a fool and I verily believe, with many others on my side, an arrant Coward. That he is a paltry, plundering old wretch is established beyond doubt. That he is no Officer is clear, and that he wants spirit is firmly believed, ergo, he ought not to be a General' ('A Peninsular Brigadier', ed. G. T. Atkinson, *Journal of the Society for Army Historical Research*, XXXIV (1956), p. 168). Hay was born in 1762.

HAY, Andrew Leith, Lt., 29th Foot: Lt., 29th Foot, 15 April 1808. Slightly wounded, Salamanca, 22 July 1812, while serving as Aide-de-Camp to Lt.-General Leith [*London Gazette*]. MGS.

+HAY, George, Capt., 1st Foot: Capt., 1st Foot, 7 May 1807. Severely wounded, Vittoria, 21 June 1813, while serving as ADC to Major-General Hay [*London Gazette*]. *Register of dead officers*: Died of wounds, '1 June 1813 [sic]'. Return dated 25 June 1813. [PRO: WO 25/2965]. Obituary, *The Gentleman's Magazine*, July 1813, p. 91 [June 24. At Vittoria, of a wound received on the 21st inst. when leading the column to storm the bridge at Guimarra Major, Capt. G. Hay, Royal Scots, eldest son and aide-de-camp to Major-gen. And. H.'].

HAY, James, Lt./Adjutant, 7th Foot: *1829 Statement of Service*: Born 12 June 1775, Aberdeenshire. Aged nineteen on his first Entrance into the Army. Private, 109th Foot, 11 April 1794; 'Serjt. and Serjt. Major until 19 August 1809, when appointed to Act as Adjt. to the 7th Roy. Fus.'; Lt., 7th Foot, 3 May 1810; Lt. and Adjt. 22 Nov. 1810; 'Lt. Acting Pay Master to Reserve Company,' 24 June 1825; sold out, 8 Oct. 1830. *Battles, sieges and campaigns*: 'Capture of St Lucia. Reduction of St Vincent. Capture of Trinidad. Attack on Portorino ... in the years 1796 and 7. Passage of Douro, 12 May 1809. Battle of Talavera, 27–28 July 1809. Battle of Busaco, 27 Sep 1810. Affair of Burtada, 13 Oct. 1810. Seige of Elivenere, 5 April 1811. Battle of Albuera, 16 May 1811. Affair of Aldea de Ponte, 27 Sep 1811. Siege of Ciudad Rodrigo, 19 Jan. 1812. Sieges of Badajoz, Ap. & May 1811, 6 Ap 1812. Affair of Fuenta de la Penna, 18 July 1812. Battle of Salamanca, 22 July 1812. Battle of DiHoria, 21 June 1813. Affair of Romesvalles, 25 July 1813. Battle of Pampeluna, 28 July 1813. Affair of Eschalar, 2 Aug. 1813. Battle of Nivelle, 10 Nov. 1813. Battle of Toulouse, 10 Ap 1814... Besides the above Lieut Hay was present on every occasion (Battle of Orthes) excepted in which the Fusiliers were engaged during the Peninsular Campaigns.' *Distinguished conduct*: 'Had a Horse shot under him at Albuera on the 16 May 1811, and another at Pampeluna on the 28 July 1813.' *Wounds received in action*: 'Severely wounded at the Battle of Salamanca on the 22 July 1812. received a grant of One year's Pay and a Permanent Pension of 70£ per Annum.' *Service abroad*: '10 Oct. 1796 to 20 Jany 1802, West Indies. 6 April 1809 to 28 June 1814, Peninsula. 18 June 1815 to 2 Nov. 1818, France.' *Family*: Married Mary Jane Dobbin, 26 Oct. 1819, Dublin. In 1830 he had one child, James, born in 1806: 'This son by a former marriage is at present Ensign & Adjt in the 15th Regiment of Foot.' Extract from the 'Book of Merit', attached to his Statement of Service: 'At the close of these Campaigns (Peninsular under His Grace the Duke of Wellington) justice to an Individual, whose long and unwearied exertions from the Commencement of the Peninsular War, to its final termination, require that his name should be recorded, and held forth as a model of strict Attention to Duty and zealous endeavours for the credit and Interest of the Corps to which he belongs. In recording the name of Lieutenant and Adjutant Hay, his Commanding Officer, and Brother Officers, who have served with him, will, with pleasure bear testimony to his Zeal and constant anxiety for the fulfillment of the Arduous duties, which his situation required, during so many long and fatiguing Campaigns, in which, on all occasions, he manifested the same promptitude and ready wish to second the views of his Commanding Officer as he had evinced at the Commencement, the most severe marches never relaxed his performance of duty, nor was he ever absent from his Corps but from Wounds. It is impossible to convey here fully an adequate idea of his rigorous exactitude, but those Officers who have served with him, will always be ready to witness it, and such exemplary conduct ought to stimulate the Soldier and urge him to the performance of his own duty in the above manner, the continuance of which will merit the approbation, esteem and reward of his Commanding Officer and also entitle him to the distinction of a good soldier. Signed, E. Blakeney, Colonel.' [PRO: WO 25/786 f106]. Severely wounded, Salamanca, 22 July 1812 ('Adjutant') [*London Gazette*]. MGS.

HAY, James, Ensign, 66th Foot: Ensign, 66th Foot, 20 July 1809. Severely wounded, Albuera, 16 May 1811 (2nd Battn.) [*London Gazette*]. Temporary pension of seventy pounds per annum, commencing 17 May 1812, 'for wounds' received at Albuera [*1818 Pension Return*, pp. 16–17]. *Haythornthwaite, Die Hard*, p. 149 [Albuera: 'Ensign James Hay was run through by a lance, but struggled to his feet to continue the

fight; he was run through a second time and was found sitting on the field in the evening, remarking to those who sought to help him that there were many in a worse plight. He servived his injuries but died of a lung complaint some years later.'].

HAY, John, Lt., 34th Foot: Lt., 34th Foot, 9 March 1809. Wounded, Albuera, 16 May 1811 (3rd Battn.) [*London Gazette*].

HAYTON, Thomas, Lt., 58th Foot: *1829 Statement of Service for Retired Officers*: Aged twenty-six on first appointment to the Army. Ensign, 4th Foot, 1804; Lt., 58th Foot, 28 May 1807; Half-pay, upon reduction and 'for ill-health'. Served eleven and a half years on full-pay. *Where serving when wounded*: 'Spain'. No pension. *Where generally resident during last five years*: 'Hull'. 'On Service ... as Ensign 4th or King's Own with General Lord Cathgart. Five years on Service in Spain & Portugal as Lieut. 58th Regiment Commanding a Company 2d Battn. with General Duke Wellington. Returned to England 1814.' [PRO: WO 25/761 f186]. Slightly wounded, Pyrenees, 2 Aug. 1813 (2nd Battn.) [*London Gazette*].

HEALY, John, Lt., 7th Foot: Lt., 7th Foot, 8 Sept. 1808. Severely wounded, Albuera, 16 May 1811 (2nd Battn.) [*London Gazette*]. Seventy pounds per annum pension, commencing 17 May 1812, for 'loss of an arm' at Albuera, 1811 [*1818 Pension Return*, pp. 4–5]. MGS.

HEARN, Daniel James, Major, 43rd Foot: Major, 43rd Foot, 25 March 1808. Wounded, Vimeiro, 21 Aug. 1808 [*London Gazette*].

HEATLEY, Charles, Lt., 50th Foot; Capt., 15th Portuguese Line: Lt., 50th Foot, 27 Dec. 1807. In Portuguese Service Nov. 1814 to

Aug. 1813. *Challis, Portuguese Army*, p. 55 ['Capt. 15 Line... Wd. Pyrenees July '13.'].

+HEDEMANN, Charles von, Lt., 1st Light Battn. K.G.L.: Ensign, 1st Light Battn. K.G.L., 25 Nov. 1809; Lt., 1st Light Battn. K.G.L., 17 Dec. 1811. Slightly wounded, Vittoria, 21 June 1813 [*London Gazette*]. Died of wounds, 30 March 1814. Return dated April 1814. [PRO: WO 25/2965]. Served in Peninsula 1811–14. *Beamish*, vol. II, p. 640 [Died '30th March 1814, of the wounds he received that day in action before Bayonne'].

HEIMBRUCH, Gottlieb von, Cornet, 1st Light Dragoons K.G.L.: Cornet, 1st Light Dragoons, 6 Aug. 1805. Severely wounded 'in the arm', Talavera, 27 July 1809 ('Heimbruck') [*London Gazette*]. 'Gottlieb de Heimburg' in Army List. Served in Peninsula 1809–10. *Beamish*, vol. II, p. 626 ['resigned 22d Sept. 1810... [Died] at Stelligte, in Han. 6th June 1822, captain Han. 8th regt. infantry.'].

+HEIMBRUCH, Henry von, Lt., 1st Light Battn. K.G.L.: Lt., 1st Light Battn. K.G.L., 27 Sept. 1809. Served in Peninsula 1808–14. *Beamish*, vol. II, p. 639 [Died '2d March 1814, of the wounds he received in action before Bayonne, 27th of Feb. 1814.'].

HEIMBRUCH, William von, Capt., 1st Light Battn. K.G.L.: Capt., 1st Light Battn. K.G.L., 1 March 1806. Severely wounded, 'left arm amputated', Nivelle, 10 Nov. 1813 ('Wm. Humbruck') [*London Gazette*]. Served in Peninsula 1808–9, 1813–14. *Beamish*, vol. II, p. 656 ['severely wounded (arm amputated) 10th Nov. 1813, at Uragne. Placed upon half-pay 25th June 1815. [Resident] at Stellichte near Walsrode, in Han'.].

+HEINE, Frederick, Capt., 1st Line Battn. K.G.L.: Lt., 1st Line Battn. K.G.L., 25 Jan. 1806; Capt., 1st Line Battn. K.G.L., 30 Oct. 1812. Severely wounded, storming of San Sebastian, 31 Aug. 1813 [*London Gazette*]. Died of wounds, 3 Sept. 1813. Return dated Sept. 1813. [PRO: WO 25/2965]. Served in Peninsula 1808–13. *Beamish*, vol. II, p. 638.

HEISE, Augustus, Capt., 2nd Light Battn. K.G.L.: Capt., Army, 27 Jan. 1808; Capt., 2nd Light Battn. K.G.L., 17 July 1809. Wounded, Albuera, 16 May 1811 [*London Gazette*]. Bvt. Major, 2nd Light Battn. K.G.L., 21 June 1813. Severely wounded, the Nive, 9 Dec. 1813 ('brev. Major Aug. Heisse') [*London Gazette*]. Served in Peninsula 1808–14. Waterloo. *Beamish*, vol. II, p. 566 [Died 'at Tubingen in Wurtemberg, 1st Aug. 1819'].

HEISE, Christoph, Lt., 1st Light Battn. K.G.L.: Ensign, 1st Light Battn. K.G.L., 5 April 1810; Lt. 1st Light Battn. K.G.L., 20 March 1812. Slightly wounded, 'in an action near Tolosa,' 25 June 1813 [*London Gazette*]. Served in Peninsula 1811–14. Waterloo. *Beamish*, vol. II, p. 562 ['severely wounded, 18th June 1815, at Waterloo.'].

+HEISE, George Arnold, Capt., 2nd Light Battn. K.G.L.: Lt., 2nd Light Battn. K.G.L., 24 Jan. 1804. *Register of dead officers*: 'Heise, Arnold'. Died of wounds, 10 June 1811. Return dated 25 June 1811. [PRO: WO 25/2965]. Served in Peninsula 1808–11. *Beamish*, p. 638 [Died '10th June 1811 at Elvas in Portugal, of the wounds he received in the battle of Albuera, 16th of May 1811.'].

+HELDERITT, Charles von, Capt., 2nd Line Battn. K.G.L.: Capt., 2nd Line Battn. K.G.L., 21 April 1804. Slightly wounded, Talavera, 28 July 1809 ('Heldtrith') [*London Gazette*]. Served in Peninsula 1808–9. *Beamish*, vol. II, p. 638

[Died '3d Aug. 1809, of the wounds he received in the battle of Talavera de la Reyna, 28th July 1809.'].

HELY, Price, Capt., 57th Foot: Capt., 57th Foot, 15 Feb. 1810. Slightly wounded, Albuera, 16 May 1811 (1st Battn.) [*London Gazette*]. MGS.

+HEMMELMANN, George, Lt., 5th Line Battn. K.G.L.: Lt., 5th Line Battn. K.G.L., 27 Jan. 1806. Served in Peninsula 1808–9. *Beamish*, vol. II, p. 634 ['killed in the battle of Talavera de la Reyna, 28th July 1809.']. 'Hemelman' in Army List.

+HEMNS, Daniel James, Lt., 61st Foot: Lt., 61st Foot, 25 Oct. 1805. Killed, 28 July 1809 ('Haimes') [*London Gazette*].

HEMSWORTH, William John ('Thomas'), Lt., 50th Foot: *1829 Statement of Service for Retired Officers*: Aged sixteen on first appointment to the Army. Ensign, 9th Garrison Battn., 25 Nov. 1826 [sic. ie 1806]; Lt., 50th Foot, 28 Dec. 1827 [sic. Army List gives 28 Dec. 1807]; Half-pay, 'in Consequence total inability to do duty from the effects of a severe wound.' 'Unfit for service from the effects of a Wound received in Action.' Served eight years on full-pay. *Where serving when wounded*: 'Storming of Fort Napoleon near the Bridge of Almarez in Spain, on the morning of the 19th July 1812.' *Details of pension*: Seventy pounds per annum, commencing 1814. *Where generally resident during last five years*: 'Chatham & London.' [PRO: WO 25/761 f305]. Severely wounded, 'at the Storm and Capture of Fort Napoleon, and the Enemy's other Works, in the Neighbourhood of Almarez', 19 May 1812 [*London Gazette*]. *1818 Pension Return*, pp. 14–15. Army List gives as 'Thomas Hemsworth'. *Challis, Index*, p. 146, gives 'Thomas Hemsworth' as the only Hemsworth who served with

the 50th Foot in the Peninsula. It is clear, however, that Thomas and William John were one and the same.

+HENDERSON, Charles, Lt., 71st Foot: Ensign, 71st Foot, 7 Dec. 1809. Killed, the Nive, 13 Dec. 1813 ('Lieutenant') (1st Battn.) [*London Gazette*].

+HENDERSON, John, Capt., 42nd Foot: Capt., 42nd Foot, 21 Feb. 1811. Severely wounded, Toulouse, 10 April 1814 (1st Battn.) [*London Gazette*]. *Hurt*, p. 78 ['D.O.W., Toulouse, July 8 [1814]'].

HENDERSON, John William, Capt., 50th Foot: *1829 Statement of Service for Retired Officers*: Aged fifteen on first appointment to the Army. Ensign, 8th West India Regt., March 1800; Lt., 8th West India Regt., 1801; Capt., 8th West India Regt., 12 March 1807; Capt., 50th Foot, Feb 1809; Half-pay, 'about June 1817', 'in consequence of wound not allowing him to accompany the 50th Regt. to West Indies'; Bvt. Major, 12th Foot, Nov. 1821; Half-pay, 41st Foot, 'about July or August 1825', 'in consequence of the heat of Gibraltar acting on his Wound in the Head and rendering him unable to do duty in the hot season.' *Where serving when wounded*: 'Capture of Aire in France, wounded on the 2nd March 1814.' *Details of pension*: One hundred pounds, commencing 'About 1816 or 1817 but the exact time not known. The Pension made permanent by Lord Palmerston's Letter dated 2nd Aug. 1825.' *Family*: Married in 'St Mary le bone', 3 June 1809. No children by 1829. *Where generally resident during last five years*: 'With the 12th Regt. in Guernsey, England, & Gibraltar 'till 1825 then on 1/2 pay at Hucclecote near Gloucester.' [PRO: WO 25/761 f281]. Severely wounded, Aire, 2 March 1814 (1st Battn.) [*London Gazette*]. Temporary pension of one hundred pounds per annum, commencing 3 March 1815, 'for wounds' received at Toulouse [*1818 Pension Return*, pp. 14–15]. MGS.

HENRY, George, Lt., 7th Foot: Lt., 7th Foot, 25 Oct. 1807. Slightly wounded, Albuera, 16 May 1811 [*London Gazette*]. Slightly wounded, storming of Badajoz, 6 April 1812 [*London Gazette*]. Slightly wounded, Salamanca, 22 July 1812 [*London Gazette*]. Capt., 7th Foot, 9 Sept. 1813.

HEPBURN, Francis, Lt. Col., 3rd Foot Guards: Lt. and Capt., 3rd Foot Guards, 28 May 1798; Capt. and Lt. Col. 23 July 1807. Severely wounded, Barossa, 5 March 1811 [*London Gazette*]. Second Major, 3rd Foot Guards, 25 July 1814; Bvt. Col., 4 June 1814. Gold Medal. Waterloo.

+HEPPENSTALL, Leigh, Lt., 88th Foot: Lt., 88th Foot, 15 Dec. 1808. Slightly wounded, during 'several Affairs with the French Army', 12 March 1811 (1st Battn.) [*London Gazette*]. Killed, during 'several Affairs with the French Army', 15 March 1811 ('Heppinstall') [*London Gazette*].

+HERBERT, Arthur, Lt., 3rd Foot: Lt., 3rd Foot, 26 Nov. 1806. Killed, Albuera, 16 May 1811 [*London Gazette*]. *Register of officers' effects*: Effects totalled £15.0s.0½d. [PRO: WO 25/2963].

+HERRICK, Henry M., Capt., 45th Foot: Lt., 45th Foot, 7 Aug. 1806; Capt., 45th Foot, 13 July 1809. Killed, storming of Badajoz, 6 April 1812 [*London Gazette*].

HERRIES, William Lewis, Capt. Meuron's Regt.: 9th Dragoons 1806; Capt., 1st Dragoon Guards, 19 Oct. 1809; Capt., Meuron's Regt., by Feb. 1814. Severely wounded, and 'missing', sortie from Bayonne, 14

April 1814, while serving on the General Staff as AQMG [*London Gazette*]. Major, Army, 2 June 1814; Major, Permanent AQMG, 'Not holding Regimental Commission', 28 July 1814. Pension of three hundred pounds per annum, commencing 15 April 1815, for 'loss of a leg' at Bayonne, 1814, while serving as Capt. Meuron's Regt. [*1818 Pension Return*, pp. 24–5]. MGS. *Mullen*, p. 14 ['Left leg amputated from wound received at Bayonne. Lt-Gen 20/6/54, KCH, CB'].

HERRING, Robert, Lt., 48th Foot: *1829 Statement of Service for Retired Officers*: Aged eighteen on first appointment to the Army. Ensign, 48th Foot, Nov. 1804; Lt., 48th Foot, 1806 [Army List gives 29 May 1806]; Capt., 48th Foot, 1813; Half-pay, by reduction. Served eleven years on full-pay. 'Incapable [of service] from a wound thro the body.' *Where serving when wounded*: 'Albuera'. *Details of pension*: One hundred pounds per annum, commencing 1811. Not married, no children. *Where generally resident during last five years*: 'Norwich and Bath'. [PRO: WO 25/761 f284]. Wounded, Albuera, 16 May 1811 [*London Gazette*].

HERTSBERG, Frederick Augustus von, Lt. Col., Duke of Brunswick Oels' Corps (Infantry): Major, Duke of Brunswick Oels' Corps, 25 Sept. 1809; Lt. Col., Duke of Brunswick Oels' Corps, 28 May 1812. Slightly wounded, Pyrenees, 2 Aug. 1813 ('Hertzberg') [*London Gazette*].

HERVEY, Felton Bathurst, Major, 14th Light Dragoons: Major, 14th Light Dragoons, 8 May 1806. 'Major Hervey lost his right arm, but doing well', passage of the Douro, 12 May 1809 [*London Gazette*]. Lt. Col., 14th Light Dragoons, 12 July 1810. Mentioned in Cotton's Llerena dispatch, 11 April 1812 ['I have great pleasure in assuring you of the good conduct of Lieutenant-Colonel Hervey, commanding 14th Light Dragoons']. Mentioned in Wellington's Castrejon dispatch, 21 July 1812 ['In these affairs ... Lieutenant-Colonel Arentschildt of the 1st Hussars, and Hervey of the 14th Light Dragoons ... distinguished themselves.'] [*London Gazette*]. Mentioned in Wellington's Salamanca dispatch, 24 July 1812 [*London Gazette*]. Gold Medal. Pension of three hundred pounds per annum, commencing 25 Dec. 1811, for 'loss of an arm' at Douro, 1809 [*1818 Pension Return*, pp. 2–3]. Waterloo. *Brotherton*, p. 42 [Fuentes d'Onor, 5 May 1811: 'Colonel Hervey escaped losing his right leg by having put a thick book [*Quenado's Works*] ... into his sabretache. An eight-pound shot entering his sabretache, went through his horse, and just appeared on the other side of his body, without coming through the skin, and it was evident that the thick book prevented it from going through and taking off Colonel Hervey's leg. Poor fellow, he had already lost his right arm; and his leg, from the blow, immediately swelled to an immense size, but though the horse fell down dead, and in the fall again hurt him, he would not leave the field, but had himself placed under a tree, where he remained during the remainder of the battle.'], pp. 55, 62 ['Colonel Hervey, who, the night before, going his rounds with this orderly, went by mistake (the night being very dark and the enemy's picquets and ours very close together) up to a French picquet, and finding his mistake galloped off; but his gallant orderly, in order to save him from his pursuers – he, Colonel Hervey, having only one arm – sacrificed himself and kept sabring with the enemy to give time to Colonel Hervey to escape, which he did, though with difficulty.'], p. 70. *Dalton*, p. 34. *Perrett*, p. 16 [Crossing the Douro, 12 May 1812: 'The Regiment, commanded by Colonel

Samuel Hawker ... had meanwhile been ordered to provide two squadrons for a move against the enemy's flank. These, under Major Felton Hervey, led the advance... The attack was made in column up a narrow lane, the walls on either side of which had been lined by the French with sharpshooters... The French rearguard, seeing that its fire could not halt the squadrons, disintegrated at the last moment and an instant later the troopers were among them, hacking and slashing. The impetus of the attack can be gauged by the fact that both French general officers present were roughly handled; one Moy, was cut down while the other, Delaborde, was bowled over. It is not known how many of the enemy were killed and wounded but it is thought that about 300 surrendered. The Fourteenth sustained the loss of twelve killed, one missing and twenty-two wounded, the last including four officers. Major Hervey lost his right arm, but insisted on remaining with the Regiment.'] p. 18 [Following the death of Lt. Col. Talbot, 11 July 1811: 'Major Hervey took over the Regiment and remained in command throughout the war, being promoted Lt-Colonel on 4th June 1811.'] p. 24 [Affair in Sept. 1811: 'In another of this brisk series of actions, "a French officer, while striking at Felton Hervey, perceived he had only one arm, and with a rapid change brought his sword down into a salute and passed on." ']. *Kincaid, Random Shots*, pp. 99–101 [Nov. 1810: 'I was amused to see General Slade, who commanded the brigade of cavalry attached to us, order up his sumpter mule, and ... undid several packages, and presently displayed a set-out which was more than enough to tempt the cupidity of the hungry beholders ... the commanders of the twelfth and fourteenth light dragoons, (Colonels Ponsonby and Harvey [sic],) whose olfactory nerves, at a distance of some hundred yards, having snuffed up the tainted air, eagerly followed the scent, and came to a dead point before the general and his panniers. But although they had flushed their game they did not succeed in bagging it; for while the general gave them plenty of his own tongue, the deuce take the slice did he offer of the bullock's – and as soon as he had satisfied his appetite he very deliberately bundled up the fragments, and shouted to horse']. *Bragge*, p. 10 ['Belem, Septr. 6th 1811... General Slade ... was in conversation with Col. Hervey when a spent Shot struck the latter's Sabretache, which together with the Shot and a Volume of "Tristram Shandy" lodged in the Horse's side and was afterwards cut out, Col. H. having received no injury but the loss of his Horse and a slight Bruise on his own Leg.' n6 'His leg on this occasion was certainly saved by a thick book, although the Regimental historian ascribes the honour to Quinedo's Works.'], p. 73 [Castrillo], p. 91 ['Soure, 24th March 1813... The Affair of Col. Hervey and his orderly... The Coll had been dining with the Division left as the Rear Guard and returning in the Dark accidently rode up to the Enemy's Vidette who was a German. The Officer of the Picquet was at that Moment visiting his outposts with a few Followers and some conversation about his (the Col.) deserting took place between them before the Coll perceived his Mistake. He immediately made his Escape but the Orderly's Bridle was seized and the man made Prisoner. This Account Col. Hervey gave Sir S. Cotton. I should add that the 14th are brigaded with the Germans and that the Colonel speaks the Language.'], pp. 137, 145.

HESSE, Adolphus, Lt., 2nd Line Battn. K.G.L.: *1829 Statement of Service for Retired Officers*: Aged sixteen on first appointment to the Army. Cadet, 8th Line Battn. K.G.L., 16 Oct. 1806; Ensign, 2nd Line Battn. K.G.L., 30 Dec. 1807 Army List gives 30 Nov. 1807]; Lt., 2nd Line Battn. K.G.L., 17 March 1812; Adjutant, 2nd Line Battn. K.G.L., 17 June 1814; Half-pay, by reduction. Served nine and a half years on full-pay. *Where serving when wounded*: 'With the British Army on the Peninsula, and severely wounded on the 18 October 1812 at the assault of the Castle of Burgos, & on the 7 October 1813, when crossing the Bidassoa.' *Details of pension*: Seventy pounds per annum, commencing 25 Dec. 1819. *Family*: Married in 'Hannover', 4 July 1827. One child by 1829. *Where generally resident during last five years*: 'Hannover'. [PRO: WO 25/761 f274]. Severely wounded, siege of Burgos, 18 Oct. 1812 ('Hesse') [*London Gazette*]. Severely wounded, Crossing the Bidassoa, 7/9 Oct. 1813 ('Hesse') [*London Gazette*]. Army List gives variously as 'Heise', 'Heisse', 'Hess' and 'Hesse'. Served in Peninsula 1808–14. Waterloo. *Beamish*, vol. II, pp. 108–9 [Burgos, 18 Oct. 1812: 'Lieutenant Hesse of the second line battalion commanded the forlorn hope of the German stormers, and, the mine having been sprung at the appointed hour, this intrepid officer led his detachment up the breach in the most gallant style... The distinguished gallantry of lieutenant Hesse in leading the German attack, obtained for him the tardy, but well merited acknowledgement, of promotion in the Hanoverian army at the end of the war.'], p. 579.

+HEUGEL, Charles von, Lt., 1st Dragoons K.G.L.: Cornet, 1st Dragoons K.G.L., 19 Feb. 1810. Killed, in an Affair with the Enemy's Rear-Guard near La Serna, 23 July 1812 ('Lieut. Heugell') [*London Gazette*]. 'Charles de Hengel' in Army List. Served in Peninsula in

HEUGEL

1812. *Beamish*, vol. II, p. 615 ['lieutenant Charles von Heugel ... killed in the combat of Garcia Hernandez, 23d July 1812.']. *Kincaid, Random Shots*, p. 338 ['The day after the battle of Salamanca a brigade of heavy German dragoons, under the late Baron Bock, made one of the most brilliant charges in history'].

HEUGEL, William von, Lt., 1st Light Battn. K.G.L.: *1829 Statement of Service for Retired Officers*: Aged twenty-one on first appointment to the Army. Ensign, 1st Light Battn. K.G.L., 30 Oct. 1811; Lt., 1st Light Battn. K.G.L., 20 March 1812; Half-pay, 24 Feb. 1816, by reduction. Served at Waterloo. *Where serving when wounded*: 'In the 1st Light Infantry Battalion K.G.L. at the action before Tolosa in Spain, June 25th 1813.' *Details of pension*: Seventy pounds per annum, commencing 'June 25th 1813 or 1814. I really do not know exactly, because an allowance of one year's pay was issued to me by Warrant dated the 21st December 1813.' *Family*: Married in Breslau, Silesia, 15 May 1827. *Where generally resident during last five years*: 'Breslau, Mondschutz (village) in Silesia.' [PRO: WO 25/755 f131]. Severely wounded, 'arm amputated', in an action near Tolosa, 25 June 1813 [*London Gazette*]. Served in Peninsula only in 1813. Waterloo. *Beamish*, vol. II, p. 563 ['severely wounded (arm amputated) 25th June 1813, at Toloza.'].

HEWAN, Michael, Capt., 95th Foot: Capt., 95th Foot, 13 May 1812. Severely wounded, Toulouse, 10 April 1814 (2nd Battn.) [*London Gazette*]. Temporary pension of one hundred pounds per annum, commencing 11 April 1815, 'for a wound' received at Toulouse [*1818 Pension Return*, pp. 22-3].

HEYBERG, Frederick Augustus de, Major/Lt. Col., Duke of Brunswick Oels' Corps (Infantry): *1829 State-ment of Service for Retired Officers*: Aged thirty on first appointment to the Army. Major, Duke of Brunswick Oels' Corps, 25 Sept. 1809; Lt. Col., Duke of Brunswick Oels' Corps, 28 May 1812; Half-pay, 25 Dec. 1814, by reduction of regt. *Where serving when wounded*: 'In Spain in the fighting of Echelar in the left-hand, but having lost no limb, no pension was granted.' *Family*: Married in Wendelsen, near Brunswick, 7 March 1819. Three children by 1829. *Where generally resident during last five years*: 'at Brunswick.' [PRO: WO 25/755 f108].

HEYDE, Frederick John Adrian von der, (William Frederick), Lt., Duke of Brunswick Oels' Corps (Infantry): *1829 Statement of Service for Retired Officers*: 'William Frederick von Heyde. Remark: the real Christian and surnames of the officer are "Frederick John Adrian von der Heyde", but by a mistake in his first appointment his names were altered as above mentioned, and his application for the amendment had no consequences, he therefore thought it necessary to keep the names inserted in the Commission'. Aged nineteen on first appointment to the Army. Lt., Duke of Brunswick Oels' Corps (Infantry), 27 Sept. 1809; Half-pay, 24 Dec. 1814, by reduction. 'No higher rank in the British Army since his reduction, but promoted Captain in the Duke of Brunswick own service'. *Where serving when wounded*: 'Wounded at Vittoria in Spain and near Bayonne in France, but having lost no eye or limb, no pension was granted to him'. *Family*: Married in the 'Town of Brunswick', 9 Jan. 1817. Four children by 1829. *Where generally resident during last five years*: 'At the Town of Brunswick'. [PRO: WO 25/776 f370]. Slightly wounded, the Nive, 11 Dec. 1813 ('V. D. Heyde') [*London Gazette*]. 'Wilhelm von Heyde' in Army List. MGS.

HEYLAND, Arthur Rowley, Capt. 40th Foot: Capt., 40th Foot, 7 Aug. 1804. Wounded in the trenches before Badajoz, 8–15 May, 1811 (1st Batt.) [*London Gazette*]. Severely wounded, Pyrenees, 26 July 1813 (1st Battn.) [*London Gazette*]. Bvt. Major, 40th Foot, 26 Aug. 1813; Major, 40th Foot, 10 Nov. 1814. Killed at Waterloo. *Dalton*, p. 153. *Lawrence*, p. 208 [Waterloo, 18 June 1815: 'At the commencement the commanding officer was killed by a musket-shot, but his place was soon filled up.']. *Speeckaert*, p. 33 [Memorial plaque, originally located in the garden of the 'Cheval Blanc', but now in Le Musée Wellington in Waterloo: 'Sacred / to the memory of / Major Arthur-Rowley Heyland / of his Britannic Majesty's / fortieth Regiment of foot / who was buried on this spot / He fell gloriously in the Battle of Waterloo / on the 18th June 1815 / At the moment of victory / and in command of the regiment / age 34 years.'].

HEYLIGER, Peter Augustus, Capt., 7th Light Dragoons: Capt., Army, 9 March 1809; Capt., 7th Light Dragoons, 2 Aug. 1810. Severely wounded, Orthes, 27 Feb. 1814 [*London Gazette*]. Waterloo. MGS.

HEYWOOD, George, Lt., 4th Foot: Lt., 4th Foot, 29 May 1809. Severely wounded, Storming of San Sebastian. 31 Aug. 1813 ('Haywood') (1st Battn.) [*London Gazette*].

HICKIE, Bartholomew, Lt./Capt., 51st Foot: *1829 Statement of Service for Retired Officers*: Aged twenty-three upon first appointment to the Army. Ensign, 51st Foot, 2 June 1804; Lt., 51st Foot, 18 April 1805; Capt., 51st Foot, 31 Dec. 1812; Capt., 13th Royal Veteran Battn., 25 Jan. 1813, 'afterwards numbered 7th Royal Vetn. Battn. and reduced 1816.' 'Health ... is very much impaired, occasioned chiefly by the severe Wound in my Breast and the

loss of my Right Arm from the shoulder joint, which a certificate in my possession dated 23 April 1813 from Army Medical Board Office London, will testify.' *Where serving when wounded*: 'Valladolid, Spain.' *Details of pension*: One hundred pounds per annum, commencing '29th October 1813. A Warrant was issued in June 1816 by Order of His Majesty that my Pension should be increased from £70 to £100 per year commencing the 18th June 1815.' *Family*: Married in Rochdale, Lancashire, 25 April 1807. No children by 1829. *Where generally resident during last five years*: 'Willow Bank, Limerick.' 'I beg leave to state that from the Age of seventeen years I was serving as Ensign and Lieutenant in the Royal County of Limerick Militia commencing from 19th October 1798, to the reduction of the Militia being about three years. Did not insert this in the Columns with my Services in the Regular Army fearing it might be incorrect in specifying the two services in the same Columns.' [PRO: WO 25/762 f50]. Severely wounded, 'arm amputated', during 'movements of the Army' [Retreat from Burgos], 28 Oct. 1812 [*London Gazette*]. Pension for 'loss of an arm' at Valladolid, 1812 [*1818 Pension Return*, pp. 14–15]. MGS. *Wheeler*, p. 111 [Near Validolid: 'The Regiment defended the bridge until everything was cleared and the army was on the move then blew it up and retired. The loss of the Regiment at the bridge was Lieut. Hickey severely wounded, his right arm amputated'].

HICKIN, Thomas Bennett, Lt., 66th Foot: *1829 Statement of Service*: Born 11 Dec. 1787, English Bicknor, County of Gloucester. Aged seventeen years and four months on his first entrance into the Army. Ensign, 38th Foot, 4 May 1805; Lt., 2nd West India Regt., 31 Oct. 1805; Lt., 66th Foot, 'about January 1808' [28 Jan. 1808]; Capt., 66th Foot, 9

May 1816; Half-pay, 24 Nov. 1817; Capt., 29th Foot, 28 Jan. 1819. *Battles, sieges and campaigns*: 'Oporto 12th May 1809. Talavera 27th & 28th July 1809. Busaco 27th Sept. 1810. Albuhera 16th May 1811. Vittoria 21st June 1813. Ronces Villas 25th July 1813. Pampluna 28th & 30th July 1813. Nivelle 10th Novmr. 1813. Nive December 1813. Bayonne 13th December 1813. Aire 1814. Heights of Garis 1814. Orthes 27th February 1814. Toulouse 10th April 1814.' *Wounds received in action*: 'Wounded at Albuhera on 16 May 1811 and again (severely) at Pampluna on 30th July 1813. Received for the last wound a Year's pay as Captain.' *Service abroad*: 'About March 1806 to Septr. 1807, Jamaica. 10th April 1809 to July 1814, Peninsula and France. Feby. 1815 to June 1817, St Helena. 25th Septr. 1826 to June 1829, Mauritius.' Not married in 1830. [PRO: WO 25/790 f249]. Slightly wounded, Albuera, 16 May 1811 ('Hicken') (2nd Battn.) [*London Gazette*]. Severely wounded, Pyrenees, 30 July 1813 ('Hicken') (2nd Battn.) [*London Gazette*].

HICKS, Richard, Lt., 51st Foot: *1829 Statement of Services for Retired Officers*: Aged sixteen years upon first appointment to the Army. Ensign, 51st Foot, 21 Dec. 1807; Lt., 51st Foot, 21 Sept. 1809; Half-pay, 10th Foot, 25 Jan. 1815, 'From ill health in consequence of wounds and injuries received on service.' *Where serving when wounded*: 'At the siege of Badajos, Spain, Storming Fort San Christoval 1811.' *Details of pension*: Seventy pounds per annum, commencing 25 Dec. 1826. *Family*: Married in 'Ottery St Mary Devonshire', 20 Oct. 1813. Six children by 1829. *Where generally resident during last five years*: 'Harpford in Sidmouth, Devonshire.' [PRO: WO 25/762 f61]. Duplicate *1829 Statement of Service for Retired Officers*, but with additional service informa-tion: 'He did duty with his regiment in Spain with the forces under the command of the late General Sir John Moore; He was present at the siege of Flushing in the Islands of Walcheren and returned with his regiment in September 1809. He ... accompanied a detachment of his regiment a second time to Walchereen where he remained to the end of the year 1809. In the beginning of 1811 he disembarked with his regiment at Lisbon, followed up the retreat of Massena, was present at the battle of Fuentes de Honore on the 5th of May 1811. On the 9th of June of the same year acted as Adjutant to the detachment ordered to Storm Fort San Christoval (Badajos) where in the discharge of his duty he was wounded severely in the left leg with a bayonet also received many bodily injuries and severe contusions. He was ordered to England for the recovery of his health and wounded limb, but continuing lame and in a precarious state of health, he was placed on the half pay...' [PRO: WO 25/762 f62]. Severely wounded, siege of Badajoz, 6–11 June 1811 [*London Gazette*]. MGS. *Wheeler*, p. 65 [Wounded, Badajoz, 9 June 1811].

+HICKS, William, Capt., 39th Foot: Lt., Army, 30 Oct. 1799; Lt., 39th Foot, 9 July 1803. Severely wounded, Vittoria, 21 June 1813 (1st Battn.) [*London Gazette*]. Died, Spain, 3 July 1813 [PRO: WO 25/2965].

+HIGGINS, Thomas, Lt., 5th Foot: Lt., 5th Foot, 26 Sept. 1805. Severely wounded, Vittoria, 21 June 1813 (1st Battn.) [*London Gazette*]. *Register of dead officers*: Died of wounds, 15 July 1813. Return dated July 1813 [PRO: WO 25/2965].

HIGGINSON, Philip, Lt., 87th Foot: Lt., 87th Foot, 23 Sept. 1807. Severely wounded, Vittoria, 21 June 1813 (2nd Battn.) [*London Gazette*].

HILL, Charles, Major/Lt. Col., 50th Foot: Ensign, 50th Foot, 27 Dec. 1778; Lt. 13 Sept. 1780; Capt. 17 Feb. 1794; Major, Army, 25 Sept. 1803; Major, 50th Foot, 1 Aug. 1804. Wounded, Vimeiro, 21 Aug. 1808 [*London Gazette*]. *Monthly Return*, 1st Battn., dated 1 Sept. 1808: 'Wounded (on board), 21 Aug. 1808' [PRO: WO 17/164]. Bvt. Lt. Col., 50th Foot, 25 July 1810; Lt. Col., 50th Foot, 13 June 1811. Severely wounded, Pyrenees, 25 July 1813 (1st Battn.) [*London Gazette*]. Gold Medal. Pension of three hundred pounds per annum, commencing 26 July 1814, 'for wounds' received in the Pyrenees [*1818 Pension Return*, pp. 14–15]. *Leach*, pp. 50–1 [Vimiero: 'The night before the battle I belonged to a picket of about two hundred rifleman, of our own regiment [95th] and the 60th, under the command of Major Hill, of the 50th regiment. We were posted in a large pine wood, to the right and front of General Fane's brigade. About eight or nine o'clock in the morning of the 21st, a cloud of light troops, supported by a heavy column of infantry, entered the wood, and assailing the pickets with great impetuosity, obliged us to fall back for support on the 97th regiment. In our retrograde movement, Major Hill, who commanded the pickets, was severely wounded.']

HILL, Clement, Lt., Royal Horse Guards: *1829 Statement of Service*: Born 6 Dec. 1782, Prees, Shropshire. Aged twenty-two years and eight months 'on his first Entrance into the Army.' Cornet, Royal Horse Guards, 22 Aug. 1805; Lt. 6 March 1806; Capt. 4 April 1811; Bvt. Major, 19 Dec. 1811; Bvt. Lt. Col., 30 Dec. 1813; Major, Royal Horse Guards, 21 June 1820; Lt. Col., Royal Horse Guards, 24 July 1823; Col., Army, 21 June 1827. 'Promoted to Major General 10 Jany 1837.' *Battles, sieges and campaigns*: 'Joined the Staff of Major General [Rowland]

Hill as Aide-de-Camp in August 1808 in Portugal a few days after the Battle of Vimiera:– Continued as Aide-de-Camp to the General to the end of the Peninsular War. Was sent Home with the Dispatches from the Duke of Wellington after the Action of Arroyo-del-Molino, 28th October 1811, and received the Rank of Brevet Major; again sent Home with Dispatches after the Battle of the Nive 13th december 1813 and received the Rank of Brevet Lieut. Colonel. Reappointed Aide-de-Camp to Lieut. General Lord Hill 16th April 1815 in Flanders. The Regiment having arrived in that Country in May, I gave up my Staff appointment and joined my own Troop, and was present with it at the Battle of Waterloo.' *Wounds received in action*: 'Slightly Wounded at Oporto on the Passage of the Duoro – May 12th 1809. Severely at Waterloo: received 1 year's Pay as Captain.' *Titles, honorary distinctions and medals*: 'Waterloo Medal.' *Service abroad*: '10th August 1808 to 7 Decemr 1814, Peninsula and France. 16th April 1815 to 2d Februy. 1816, Flanders and France.' Not married in 1830. [PRO: WO 25/780 f160]. Waterloo. *Dalton*, pp. 2, 13 ['Brother to [Lt.-General (Rowland) Lord Hill. Bn 6th Dec., 1781. As a Maj.-Gen. commanded the forces at Madras. Equerry to H.R.H. the Duchess of Kent. D. unm., 20th Jan., 1845.'], p. 50.

HILL, Dudley St. Leger, 1st Lt., 95th Foot; Capt., Royal West India Rangers; Major, 8th Caçadores: *1829 Statement of Service for Retired Officers*: Aged seventeen on first appointment to the Army. Ensign, 82nd Foot, 6 Sept. 1804; 1st Lt., 95th Foot, 10 Oct. 1805; Capt., Royal West India Rangers, 16 Aug. 1810; Bvt. Major, 27 April 1812; Bvt. Lt. Col., 21 June 1813; 'Bt. Lieut. Colonel and Colonel attached to the Portuguese Army'; Half-pay, Major, 'being incapable of serving in consequence of ill health occasioned by many wounds.' 'The wounds recd. at St Sebastian rendering it painful & almost impossible to ride.' *Where serving when wounded*: 'Monte Video & Rolica. 2 Battle of Salamanca. Attack at the Carrior. 2 Assault at St Sebastian. Sortie at Bayonne. Total number of Wounds: 8.' *Details of pension*: Two hundred and fifty pounds, commencing 25 Dec. 1819, augmented to three hundred pounds 25 Dec. 1824. 'NB Granted previous to 1819 3 years pay at different perriods for the cure of the severest wounds.' *Family*: Married in 'Mary le bone Church', London, 15 June 1819. Five children by 1829. *Title and nature of employment*: 'Served in the Portuguese Army untill 1821'. *Where generally resident during last five years*: 'In Carlow & Dublin, Ireland, and In Bath, Hampshire and Surry, England.' [PRO: WO 25/762 f48]. Slightly wounded, Rolica, 17 Aug. 1808 [*London Gazette*]. Wounded, Vimiero, 21 Aug. 1808 [*London Gazette*]. Mentioned in Wellington's Badajoz dispatch, 7 April 1812 ['In the 5th division I must mention Major Hill, of the 8th Caçadores, who directed the false attack upon the fort Pardelera. It was impossible for any men to behave better than these did.'] [*London Gazette*]. Severely wounded, Salamanca, 22 July 1812, as Major in 8th Caçadores [*London Gazette*]. Slightly wounded, during 'movements of the Army' [Retreat from Burgos: Villa Muriel], 25 Oct. 1812, as Major, 8th Caçadores [*London Gazette*]. Severely wounded, storming of San Sebastian, 31 Aug. 1813, while serving as Lt. Col. in 8th Caçadores [*London Gazette*]. Gold Medal. MGS. Detailed military biography in *Royal Military Calendar*, vol. IV, pp. 475–7 ['Buenos Ayres, where he received a wound in the thigh, and was taken prisoner... The battle of Roleia, where he was wounded in the leg... Commanded the 8th Caçadores, at the battle of Sala-manca, and took possession of the last hill position of the enemy; where he was severely wounded in the breast by a shell, and a musket shot through the centre of the arm... On the 25th Oct. [1811] he defended the passage of the river Carrion ... being himself wounded and taken prisoner; but afterwards effected his escape... Commanded the 8th Caçadores at the sorties and attacks of [St Sebastian]. During the service in this siege, he was twice wounded in the body... He has been wounded seven different times.']. *Challis, Portuguese Army*, p. 55. *Harris*, pp. 112–13, 123 [Retreat to Corunna: 'We were now upon the mountains; the night was bitter cold, and the snow falling fast. As day broke, I remember hearing Lieutenant Hill say to another officer (who, by the way, afterwards sank down and died): "This is New Year's Day; and I think if we live to see another we shall not easily forget it." '], p. 128 ['Lieutenant Hill had a black servant with him in this retreat, a youth he had brought with him from Monte Video, where, I heard, the Rifles had found him tied to a gun they had captured there. This lad came and aroused me as I lay in the mule-stable, and desired me to speak with his master in the adjoining room. I found the lieutenant seated in a chair by the fire when I entered. He was one of the few amongst us who rejoiced in the possession of a tolerably decent pair of boots, and he had sent for me to put a few stitches in them, in order to stop them from flying to pieces. I was so utterly wearied... I fell asleep as I worked, the awl and wax ends falling to the ground ... they all saw it was in vain to urge me to mend Lieutenant Hill's boots. He therefore put them on again with a woeful face and a curse, and dismissed me to my repose.'], pp. 146–7 ['I remember Sir Dudley Hill passing me on a mule this day. He wore a Spanish straw-hat, and had his cloak on. He looked back when he had passed, and addressed me. "Harris," said he, "I see you cannot keep up." He appeared sorry for me, for he knew me well. "You must do your best," he said, "my man, and keep with us, or you will fall into the hands of the enemy." '], pp. 162-3 ['After the disastrous retreat to Corunna, the Rifles were reduced to a sickly skeleton... The captain of my company was sick, and Lieutenant Hill commanded the three men who answered for No. 4 on this occasion. I remember he smiled when he looked at me. "Harris," he said, "you look the best man here this morning. You seem to have got over this business well." '], p. 171. *Mullen*, p. 520 ['Wounded at Vimiera'].

HILL, Edward Embury, Ensign, 28th Foot: Ensign, 28th Foot, 14 Nov. 1811. Slightly wounded, Pyrenees, 25 July 1813 (1st Battn.) [*London Gazette*]. Lt., 28th Foot, 9 Sept. 1813. Waterloo. *Dalton*, pp. 135, 138 ['Capt. 7th March, 1822. H. p. 17th Aug., 1822.'].

+HILL, George, Lt., 47th Foot: Lt., 47th Foot, 17 Oct. 1811. Killed, Vittoria, 21 June 1813 (2nd Battn.) [*London Gazette*].

HILL, John, Lt., 3rd Foot: Lt., 3rd Foot, 16 Aug. 1810. Reported as 'Missing', Albuera, 16 May 1811 [*London Gazette*].

HILL, John, Lt., 47th Foot: Lt., 47th Foot, 21 July 1808. Slightly wounded, Tarifa, 31 Dec. 1811 (2nd Battn.) [*London Gazette*].

HILL, John, Lt., 92nd Foot: Lt., 92nd Foot, 9 July 1803. Severely wounded, Fuentes de Onoro, Evening 3 May 1811 (1st Battn.) [*London Gazette*].

+HILL, John, 2nd Lt., 95th Rifles: 2nd Lt., 95th Rifles, 11 May 1812. Killed, Crossing the Bidassoa, 7/9 Oct. 1813 [*London Gazette*].

Simmons, p. 318 [killed, 1813]. Obituary, *The Gentleman's Magazine*, Nov. 1813, p. 505 ['Oct. 7... Shot through the breast, during an attack on the Enemy's position to the North of Vera, and expired in a quarter of an hour, Lieut. John Hill, 2d batt. 95th foot, second son of Mr John H. of Rotherhithe.'].

HILL, Joseph, Lt., 27th Foot: *1829 Statement of Service for Retired Officers:* Aged twenty-five on first appointment to the Army. Ensign, 27th Foot; Lt., 27th Foot, 'cannot state the exact time as I have lost my Commissions out of my Baggage' [Army list gives: Ensign, 27th Foot, 25 Nov. 1808; Lt., 27th Foot, 14 May 1812]; Half-pay, 'by Reduction and by the loss of my leg and thigh.' 'I am anxious for a situation, as my Income is not adequate to support me.' Served on full-pay for six years ('Service on Peninsula'). *Where serving when wounded:* 'Vittoria, Leg and Thigh'. *Details of Pension:* Seventy pounds, commencing 'January 1813, cannot exactly tell the day of the month.' *Family:* Married in Dublin, 6 Nov. 1816. Three children by 1829. *Where generally resident during last five years:* 'Mullingar'. [PRO: WO 25/762 f23]. Wounded, Vittoria, 21 June 1813 (3rd Battn.) [*London Gazette*]. Seventy pounds per annum pension, commenced 22 June 1814, for 'loss of an arm' at Vittoria [*1818 Pension Return*, pp. 8-9].

HILL, Richard, Lt., 45th Foot: *1829 Statement of Service for Retired Officers:* Aged sixteen on first appointment to the Army. Ensign, 45th Foot, 30 Dec. 1809; Lt., 45th Foot, 2 March 1812, 'by the siege of Ciudad Rodrigo'; Half-pay, 43rd Foot, 11 Feb. 1818. *Where serving when wounded:* 'At the Battle of Toulouse on the 10th April 1814. No pension or remuneration as explained in note below.' *Family:* Married in St Mary's Church, Manchester, 5 Jan. 1822. Four children by 1829. *Where generally resident during last five years*: 'North Wales and Isle of Man'. 'N.B. In reference to the letter of, dated War Office 10th Septr. 1828 ... wherein the grounds of the refusal of my claim to a year's full pay is stated as owing to the slightness of the wound received at the Battle of Toulouse on the 10th April 1814, I beg most respectfully to submit to the consideration of the Rt. Honble. the Secretary at War, it was for family reasons, and on account of the infirm state of health, of an only, aged, and respected parent at my own earnest request that my name was returned as only slightly wounded; for the correctness of this statement, I beg respectfully to refer to Surgeon Smyth late 45th Regt. Slightly as the wound has been represented it deprived me of all recollection for a considerable time, and of the use of my left arm for upwards of one month afterwards. In respect to any expence not being incurred in the case of my wound I beg respectfully to observe, that being with my Regiment at the time, I must have been at the same expence as others similarly wounded and who have received remuneration. For the length of time I suffered to elapse since the wound was received, I have only to repeat, that at that time I was in possession of a Patrimony of £300 per annum and rejected the idea of claiming compensation, or being a burthen on my Country – and but for my misfortunes and the distress of my children, I had still been satisfied with having done my duty. Under these circumstances the nature of the grounds of refusal, become more particularly distressing, as I must ever consider my claim a just one.' [PRO: WO 25/762 f28]. Slightly wounded, Toulouse, 10 April 1814 (1st Battn.) [*London Gazette*]. MGS.

HILL, Rowland, Major-General: Major-General, 30 Oct. 1805.

Slightly wounded, Talavera, 28 July 1809 [*London Gazette*]. Lt.-General, 1 Jan. 1812. Gold Medal. Waterloo. Portrait of him in *Haythornthwaite, Wellington's Military Machine*, p. 125 ['General Sir Rowland Hill (1772–1842) was Wellington's most trustworthy deputy in the Peninsular War, universally liked and nicknamed "Daddy" for his concern for his men.']. He became 1st Viscount Hill, General (1825) and was commander-in-chief from 1828 until shortly before his death. Born 1772, died 1842; nephew of the famous preacher Rev. Rowland Hill (1744–1833, joint founder of the British & Foreign Bible Society and London Missionary Society). Wellington's senior deputy in the later stages of the Peninsular War, about whom Wellington wrote that 'nothing ever occurred to interrupt for one moment the friendly and intimate relations which subsisted between us' (quoted in Griffiths, A. J., *The Wellington Memorial* (London, 1897), p. 295). Sidney, Rev. E., *Life of Lord Hill* (London, 1845); Teffeteller, G. L., *The Surpriser* (Newark N. J., 1983).

HILL, William Henry, Ensign, 59th Foot: *1829 Statement of Service*: Born 26 Feb. 1796, Portarlington, Queens County. Aged 16 when he first Entered the Army. Ensign, 59th Foot, 3 Dec. 1812; Lt., 59th Foot, 25 May 1814. Half Pay 25 July 1816. Lt., 1st R.V. Battalion, 4 Nov. 1823; Lt., 9th Foot, 8 April 1825. *Battles, sieges and campaigns*: 'Peninsula, Biddassoa, 10th Novr. 1813. Nivelle, 11th November 1813. Nive 9th December 1813, as Ensign. Flanders Waterloo 18th June 1815. Cambray 14th June 1815. 2nd Surrender of Paris 7th July 1815.' *Wounds received in action*: 'Dangerously 9th December 1813 charging the Enemy, one Years Pay as Ensign £95–16/3 Pension £50 per Annum 24th March 1817 Temporary received for Two Years.' *Service* *abroad*: 'October 1813 to February 1814, Peninsula. May 1815 to January 1816, Flanders & France.' Not married in 1830. [PRO: WO 25/786 f264]. Severely wounded, the Nive, 9 Dec. 1813 (2nd Battn.) [*London Gazette*]. Waterloo. MGS.

+HILL, William, Ensign/Adjutant, 3rd Portuguese Line: No commission in the British Army. Slightly wounded, 'at the Siege of S. Sebastian', 7–27 July 1813, while serving as Adjutant, 3rd Portuguese Line [*London Gazette*]. Killed, storming of San Sebastian, 31 Aug. 1813, as Adjutant, 3rd Portuguese Line [*London Gazette*]. Served in Portuguese Army from June 1810 to Aug. 1813. *Challis, Portuguese Army*, p. 56 ['Ens. 3 Line... Wd. San Sebastian 15 July '13; K/A San Sebastian 25 Aug. '13'].

HILLIARD, Christopher, Lt., 5th Foot: Lt., 5th Foot, 22 Feb. 1810. Slightly wounded, Salamanca, 22 July 1812 (2nd Battn.) [*London Gazette*]. MGS.

+HILLIARD, Morgan, Ensign, 87th Foot: Killed, Nivelle, 10 Nov. 1813 (2nd Battn.) [*London Gazette*].

HILSON, Gavin, Assistant Surgeon, 4th Dragoons: *1829 Statement of Service for Retired Officers*: Aged twenty on first appointment to the Army. Hospital Mate, 15 April 1808; Assistant Surgeon, 4th Dragoons, 17 May 1810; Staff Surgeon, 'Under Lieut. Genl. Lord Beresford', 26 May 1814; Half-pay, Dec. 1814; Full-pay, 24 June 1815; Half-pay, Jan. 1816, by reduction. *Where serving when wounded*: 'At Toulouse. No pension.' *Where generally resident during last five years*: 'In Jedburgh, North Britain.' [PRO: WO 25/762 f68]. Slightly wounded, Toulouse, 10 April 1814 [*London Gazette*].

HILTON, Thomas, Capt., 45th Foot: Capt., Army, 26 Jan. 1809; Capt.,

45th Foot, 23 Aug. 1810. Severely wounded, Toulouse, 10 April 1814 (1st Battn.) [*London Gazette*].

HINDS, John, Adjutant/Lt., 68th Foot: Adjutant, 68th Foot, 3 Dec. 1807; Lt. 7 Nov. 1809. Severely wounded, Vittoria, 21 June 1813 (Adjutant) [*London Gazette*].

HINGSTON, James, Lt., 83rd Foot: Lt., Army, 22 April 1807; Lt., 83rd Foot, 21 April 1808. Slightly wounded, 'in Action with the Enemy', 19 March 1814 ('James Kingston') (1st Battn.) [*London Gazette*].

HINGSTON, Richard Thomas, Lt., 87th Foot: Lt., 87th Foot, 12 Nov. 1807. Severely wounded, Talavera, 27 July 1809 ('Kingston') [*London Gazette*].

HITCHEN, John, Capt., 30th Foot: Capt., 30th Foot, 13 June 1805. Slightly wounded, storming of Badajoz, 6 April 1812 (2nd Battn.) [*London Gazette*]. Slightly wounded, during 'movements of the Army' [Retreat from Burgos], 25 Oct. 1812 ('Hitchins') (2nd Battn.) [*London Gazette*]. Capt., 13th Royal Veteran Batt., 25 Jan. 1813.

+HOBART, Paul Minchin, Capt., 36th Foot: Capt., 36th Foot, 5 Aug. 1804. Slightly wounded, Vimeiro, 21 Aug. 1808 ('Herbert') [*London Gazette*]. Severely wounded, while serving as Brigade Major, in the siege of the Forts of St Vincente, St Cayetano, and La Merced at Salamanca, 18–24 June 1812 [*London Gazette*]. Mentioned in Wellington's dispatch concerning the storming of the forts at Salamanca, dated Fuente la Pena, 30 June 1812 ['Major-General Clinton ... mentions in strong terms of commendation the conduct of ... Brigade-Major Hobart'] [*London Gazette*]. *Register of dead officers*: Died of wounds, 1 Sept. 1812.

Return dated 25 Sept. 1812. [PRO: WO 25/2965].

HOBKIRK, Samuel, Capt., 43rd Foot: Lt., 43rd Foot, 7 April 1808. Capt., 43rd Foot, 3 Dec. 1812. Recorded as 'missing ... wounded and taken prisoner', in a skirmish near Bayonne involving advancement of outposts of the Light Division, 23 Nov. 1813 [*London Gazette*]. *Surtees*, p. 254 [Arcangues, 23 Nov. 1813: 'The 43rd ... was selected for the purpose of driving in the enemy's picquets... They accordingly attacked and carried the houses without a moment's delay; but unfortunately, Captain Hobkirk of that regiment, advancing with his company beyond the line at which it was intended to halt, got immediately in front of some of their intrenchments, from which he could not extricate himself, in consequence of which our first battalion was ordered to advance to cover his retreat; but he had by this time fallen into the hands of the enemy, with a considerable number of his men: his lieutenant was killed, and altogether the company suffered great loss.'], pp. 257–8 ['The French officers were extremely polite, and asked us many questions of the news of the day... They told us also how Hobkirk was situated, and were astonished at the extent and splendour of his equipage, (for he was a great dandy,) and could scarcely be persuaded he was only a captain.']. *Bruce*, p. 162 [Letter from William Napier to his wife, dated Arcangues, 24 Nov. 1813: 'We have had an affair yesterday which has caused me much mortification... Some young sanguine officers who are more vain than good, concluded that with three or four companies they could drive the whole French army before them; the result was that I lost 75 men – more than I did in the last action... Hopkirk dangerously wounded, and is taken prisoner with a good many men.'], p. 163 [Napier to his wife, dated Arbonne, France,

27 Nov. 1813: 'I have heard from Hopkirk, who is not badly wounded, and whom I hope we shall be able to get exchanged: he has been as usual very well treated by the French, who, I am sorry to say, exceed us considerably in their attention to officers who are made prisoners.']. *Haythornthwaite, Armies of Wellington*, p. 27 ['some officers spent vast sums on their uniform: Captain Hobkirk of the 43rd, for example, was reputed to spend almost £1,000 per annum on his uniform, which was so rich that when dining with Soult on the evening of his capture in November 1813 he was mistaken for a field marshal.'].

+HOBSON, Samuel Meade, Lt./Adjutant, 58th Foot: Lt., 58th Foot, 22 Nov. 1810. Killed, siege of Burgos, 5–10 Oct. 1812 ('Adjutant') [*London Gazette*]. *Register of officers' effects*: Killed in action, 8 Oct. 1812, Burgos. Single. 'Effects taken charge of by his Executors'. [PRO: WO 25/2963].

HODENBERG, Ernest von, Lt., 1st Line Battn. K.G.L.: Lt., 1st Line Battn. K.G.L., 25 March 1807. Severely wounded, Talavera, 28 July 1809 [*London Gazette*]. Capt., 1st Line Battn. K.G.L., 22 Sept. 1813. Served in Peninsula 1808–10, 1813–14. MGS. *Beamish*, vol. II, p. 572.

+HODENBERG, Frederick von, Lt., 2nd Line Battn. K.G.L.; Lt., 1st Line Battn. K.G.L: Lt., 2nd Line Batt. KGL., 21 April 1804. Severely wounded, Talavera, 28 July 1809, while serving as Lt., 1st Line Batt. K.G.L. [*London Gazette*]. Served in Peninsula 1808–9. *Beamish*, vol. II, p. 639 [Died '30th July 1809, of the wounds he received in the battle of Talavera de la Reyna, 28th July 1809.'].

+HODENBERG, George Henry von, Lt., 1st Line Battn. K.G.L:

Ensign, 1st Line Battn. K.G.L., 27 Jan. 1806. Killed, Talavera, 28 July 1809 ('Captain, 1st Light Battn. K.G.L.' (sic) [*London Gazette*]. Served in Peninsula 1808–9. *Beamish*, vol. II, p. 635 ['lieut. George Henry von Hodenberg ... killed in the battle of Talavera de la Reyna, 28th July 1809.'].

HODGE, Peter, Capt. 29th Foot: Lt., 29th Foot, 31 May 1798; Capt., 29th Foot, 2 May 1800. Wounded, Rolica, 17 Aug. 1808 [*London Gazette*]. Slightly wounded, Albuera, 16 May 1811 [*London Gazette*]. Major, 29th Foot, 29 Aug. 1811. Temporary pension of one hundred pounds per annum, commencing 25 Dec. 1813, 'for wounds' received at Rolica [*1818 Pension Return*, pp. 8–9]. *Royal Military Calendar*, vol. V, p. 133 ['Served in America, in 1814, and was honorably mentioned in the despatches on the capture of Machias.'].

+HODGES, William Arthur, Capt., 47th Foot: Capt., 14th Foot, 22 Dec. 1808; Capt., 47th Foot, 18 Oct. 1810. Slightly wounded, Vittoria, 21 June 1813 (2nd Battn.) [*London Gazette*]. Killed, storming of San Sebastian, 31 Aug. 1813 (2nd Battn.) [*London Gazette*].

+HODGSON, Augustus Theodore, Lt., 43rd Foot: Lt., 43rd Foot, 16 Oct. 1809. Slightly wounded, storming of Badajoz, 6 April 1812 (1st Battn.) [*London Gazette*]. *Register of dead officers*: Died of his wounds, 8 April 1812. Return dated 25 April 1812. [PRO: WO 25/2965].

+HOEY, William R., Capt., 99th Foot: Lt., 18th Light Dragoons, 28 Aug. 1806; 'Charles Rowlls, Lieut., vice Hoey, 99F, 14 Mar. 11' [*1811 Army List*]. Severely wounded during the advance of the French army towards the position of Busaco, 25–26 Sept. 1810, while serving as DAAG ('99th Regt ... Capt. Hoey') [*London Gazette*].

Recorded as dead in the *1811 Army List* ('Capt. Hoez 99F'). *Rice Jones*, p. 72 [Busaco: 'On the afternoon of the 25th, the enemy advanced upon Mortagao and drove our advance into the position, taking up their own ground on the opposite hill. Hoey of the Adjt.-Genl.'s Depart. severely wounded whilst looking out in the front.'].

HOGAN, Ensign, 88th Foot: Severely wounded, Fuentes de Onoro, 5 May 1811 (1st Battn.) [*London Gazette*].

+HOGAN, William, Capt., 88th Foot: Capt., 88th Foot, 28 March 1805. Killed, Salamanca, 22 July 1812 (1st Battn.) [*London Gazette*].

+HOGG, George, Lt., 85th Foot: Lt., 85th Foot, 16 June 1808. Severely wounded, Fuentes de Onoro, 5 May 1811 [*London Gazette*]. Killed at the siege of Badajoz, 6–11 June 1811 [*London Gazette*]. *Register of officers' effects*: 'Married, 1 Child'. Effects sold for £4. 0s. 6d. 'Paid to Miss Man in part of his Demand.' [PRO: WO 25/2964]. *Register of dead officers*: Died of wounds, 10 June 1811. Return dated 25 June 1811 [PRO: WO 25/2965].

HOGG, John, Lt., 20th Foot: Lt., 20th Foot, 1 Aug. 1805. Wounded, Vimeiro, 21 Aug. 1808 [*London Gazette*]. MGS. 'Hogge'.

+HOGHTON, Daniel, Major-General: Lt. Col., 8th Foot, 22 Nov. 1804; Major-General 25 July 1810. Killed, Albuera, 16 May 1811 [*London Gazette*]. Obituary, *The Gentleman's Magazine*, Supplement 1811, Part I, p. 679 ['In the battle of Albuera, Major-gen. Hoghton, second son of the late Sir Henry H. bart. of Hoghton Tower and Walton Hall, Lancashire, M.P. for Preston, brother to the present Baronet. He served for several years in the East Indies under his friend

Lord Wellington, and was sent over to England with dispatches from Marquis Wellesley. Before his constitution had recovered from the effects of that climate, he was sent to the West Indies, where he commanded under Gen. Beckwith, at the capture of Martinique. In the last year he was sent to Cadiz, from whence he joined Lord Wellington's army. From thence he was detached, under Marshal Beresford, to the siege of Badajoz. He was Lieut.-col. of the 8th regiment of foot. A monument in St Paul's to his memory has been voted by Parliament.']. Mentioned in the obituary for Lt. Col. Daniel White, 29th Foot, *The Gentleman's Magazine*, July 1811, p. 88. *Pearson*, p. 94 [Albuera: 'Houghton's brigade, the next of the two brigades which had been sent forward to recover possession of the ridge, soon reached the summit, joined the 31st, and maintained a most desperate struggle against an immensely superior force. Houghton's men, however, fell fast, and his ammunition, expended in a rapidly sustained fire, began to fail. While Houghton was in the act of cheering on his men he fell, and died from the numerous wounds he had received.']

+HOLBOURNE, Francis, Lt. and Capt./Adjutant, 3rd Foot Guards: Lt., Army, 7 April 1808; Ensign, 3rd Foot Guards, 22 June 1809. Severely wounded, siege of Burgos, 18 Oct. 1812 ('Lieutenant Holborn') [*London Gazette*]. Slightly wounded, the Nive, 12 Dec. 1813 ('Lieutenant Holborne') (1st Battn.) [*London Gazette*]. Adjutant, 3rd Foot Guards, 25 Dec. 1813. Severely wounded, sortie from Bayonne, 14 April 1814 (1st Battn.) [*London Gazette*]. *Register of dead officers*: Died of wounds, 23 April 1814. Return dated April 1814. [PRO: WO 25/2965]. *Hurt*, p. 46 [Illustration of his grave-stone, as it appeared in 1854], pp. 48, 49 ['in gilt letters:–

"Burial-place of the Officers of the Third Guards who fell before Bayonne on 14th April, 1814. This ground forming part of the site of the camp of their regiment, was enclosed by Miss Holburne, of Bath, A.D. 1876." '], p. 50 ['On the middle terrace ... is the fine granite obelisk to the memory of Captain Holburne, sent out from Aberdeen by his sister... On the base is inscribed in gold letters: "Sacred to the memory of Francis R. T. Holburne, Captain and Adjutant of 3rd Regiment of Guards, eldest son of Sir Francis Holburne, Bart., who was severely wounded while gallantly leading his men against the sortie made by the French from Bayonne, April 14, 1814, and died of his wounds April 23, 1814. He lies buried in this cemetery. His loss was greatly deplored by his afflicted family, and all who knew him. This monument is erected as a tribute of affection by his only surviving sister." ']. *Fletcher, Fields of Fire*, p. 164. *Fletcher, Gentlemen's Sons*, p. 185.

HOLDEN, John Fish, Lt. 7th Foot: Lt., 7th Foot, 12 July 1810. Slightly wounded, Albuera, 16 May 1811 (2nd Battn.) [*London Gazette*]. Temporary pension of seventy pounds per annum, commencing 17 May 1812, 'for wounds' received at Albuera [*1818 Pension Return*, pp. 4–5].

HOLDSWORTH, Samuel, Lt./Adjt., 82nd Foot: *1829 Statement of Service*: Born near Bradford, Yorkshire, 14 Feb. 1779. Aged 20 on his first Entrance into the Army. Sgt., 82nd Foot, 11 Oct. 1799, 'From the East York Militia'; Sgt.-Major, 82nd Foot, 25 Sept. 1804; Ensign and Adjutant, 82nd Foot, 31 Dec. 1807; Lt., 82nd Foot, 1 Nov. 1809; Paymaster, 82nd Foot, 22 Sept. 1825. 'NB Regained the Adjutancy 18th Novr. 1818.' 'Service in the East York Regt. of Militia not included above, Viz. Private 5th July 1795,

Age 16 years. Corporal April 1798. Serjeant July 1798.' *Battles, sieges and campaigns*: 'In the expedition against Belleisle June 1800 under the Command of Major General Sir . Paget – then in the situation of Serjeant. Siege and Capture of Flushing Commencing 3rd Augt. 1809... In the Campaign of 1812, 1813, and 1814, in Spain and France and was present in the Battles of Vittoria 21st June 1813. Pass of Mayo 25th July 1813. Heights of Pampeluna 30th & 31st July 1813. Heights of Lesacca 31st Augt. 1813. Nevelle 10th Novr. 1813. Orthes 27th Feby. 1814 ... during the above period in the Situation of Lieut. and Adjutant.' *Wounds received in action*: 'Received a Wound in the wrist by a Musquet Ball, as also a Contusion on the Shoulder by a half spent Ball on the 30th July 1813 on the heights of Pampeluna in driving the enemy from a strong position on the right of the French line, and on acct. of which received one years Pay.' *Service abroad*: 'June 1800 to June 1802, Minorca. 16th July 1809 to 18th Septr. 1809, Walcheren. 23rd Feby. 1810 to 10th June 1812, Gibraltar. 11th June 1812 to 3d May 1814, Portugal, Spain, & France. 4th May 1814 to 30th June 1815, Canada. 1st July 1815 to 31st Decr. 1815, France, Paris. 11th Feby. 1820 to 9th Augt. 1822, New South Wales & East Indies. 10th Augt. 1822 to 31st Decr. 1829, Mauritius.' *Family*: Married Miss J. B. Becker, 2 July 1816, Kinsale, Ireland. They had five chiildren by 1830. [PRO: WO 25/801 f135]. Slightly wounded, Pyrenees, 30 July 1813 ('Adjutant') (1st Battn.) [*London Gazette*]. MGS.

HOLEBROOKE, John Tracey, Lt., 1st Foot: *1829 Statement of Service*: Born in Ireland, 29 Oct. 1790. Aged 17 when he first entered the Army. Unmarried by 1830. Ensign, 1st Foot, 10 March 1808; Lt. 11 Jan. 1810; Capt. 22 May 1826. *Battles, sieges and campaigns*: 'Peninsula campaigns of 11, 12 and 13. Capture

of Badajoz. Seige & capture of San Sebastian. Campaigns of 1815, 16, 17 & 18 with the Army Commd by Maj. Gen. Daviton. Battle & seige of Magpore 1817 in the East Indies.' *Wounds received in action*: 'Wounded through the lung and the right breast and through the right ear at the storming of San Sebastian 31 Aug. 1813. Received a years pay of a captain.' *Service abroad*: 'June 1811 to Oct. 1813, Peninsula. Jan. 1815 to Sept. 1819, East Indies. Feb. 1826 to July 1829, West Indies.' [PRO: WO 25/785 f33]. Severely wounded, storming of San Sebastian, 31 Aug. 1813 ('Holbrooke') (3rd Battn.) [*London Gazette*].

HOLFORD, James Price, Lt., 52nd Foot: Lt., 52nd Foot, 5 July 1810. Slightly wounded, Orthes, 27 Feb. 1814 (1st Battn.) [*London Gazette*].

HOLLAND, Richard, Lt., 88th Foot: Ensign, 88th Foot, 11 April 1811; Lt., 88th Foot, 12 Nov. 1813. Severely wounded, Orthes, 27 Feb. 1814 (1st Battn.) [*London Gazette*].

HOLLE, Charles von, Lt., 1st Line Battn. K.G.L: Lt., 1st Line Battn. K.G.L., 27 Jan. 1806. Severely wounded, Talavera, 27 July 1809 ('Rifle Corps K.G.L.') [*London Gazette*]. Served in Peninsula 1808–14. Waterloo. *Beamish*, vol. II, p. 634 ['severely wounded, 28th July 1809, at Talavera ... killed in the battle of Waterloo, 18th June 1815.'].

HOLLE, Ferdinand Adolphus von, Lt., 2nd Line Batt. K.G.L.: *1829 Statement of Service for Retired Officers*: Aged seventeen on first appointment to the Army. Ensign, 1st Line Battn. K.G.L., 19 Aug. 1805; Lt., 2nd Line Battn. K.G.L., 16 Nov. 1807; Capt., 2nd Line Battn. K.G.L., 28 May 1815; Half-pay, 24 Feb. 1816, by reduction. *Where serving when wounded*: '28th July 1809, Battle of Talavera. 25th June 1813, at Tolosa in Spain.' *Family*: Married in

Goltern, Hanover, 13 Jan. 1824. Three children by 1829. *Where generally resident during last five years*: 'Hanover'. [PRO: WO 25/762 f138]. Severely wounded, Talavera, 28 July 1809 [*London Gazette*]. Severely wounded, in an action near Tolosa, 25 June 1813 [*London Gazette*]. Served in Peninsula 1808–14. *Beamish*, vol. II, p. 577.

HOLLMAN, Charles, Lt., Portuguese Service: Lt., 52nd Foot, 11 Nov. 1813. In Portuguese Service Jan. 1812 to April 1814. Waterloo. Half-pay 25 Dec. 1818. MGS. *Challis, Portuguese Army*, p. 56 ['Lt. 2 Line... Wd. Salamanca 22 July '12, Pyrenees July '13']. *Mullen*, p. 671 ['8th Portuguese']. *Dalton*, p. 170 ['Holman'].

HOLLOWAY, William, Capt., Royal Engineers: 2nd Capt., Royal Engineers, 24 June 1809. Severely wounded, siege of Badajoz, 26 March 1812 [*London Gazette*]. Mentioned in Wellington's dispatch, 27 March 1812 [Storming of Fort Picurina, 26 March 1812: 'Major-General Kempt ... particularly mentions ... Captain Holloway ... of the Royal Engineers, who conducted the several detachments to the points of attack'] [*London Gazette*]. MGS.

HOLLZERMAN, Frederick, Lt., 1st Light Dragoons K.G.L.: *1829 Statement of Service for Retired Officers*: Aged twenty-four on first appointment to the Army. Cornet, '1st Hussars' K.G.L., 8 July 1811; Lt., '1st Hussars' K.G.L., 20 June 1813; Half-pay, by reduction. Served five years on full-pay. *Where serving when wounded*: 'Near Salamanca in Spain on the 16th of June 1812.' *Details of pension*: Fifty pounds, commencing 25 Dec. 1824. *Family*: Married twice: first in Linden, Hanover, 21 Feb. 1816; second in Osnabruck, 7 Dec. 1824. One child by the first marriage, two by the second by 1829. *Where generally resident during last five years*: 'At Osnabruck'. [PRO: WO 25/762 f77]. Slightly wounded, during the advance from Fuente Guinaldo to Salamanca, 16–18 June 1812 ('Holtzermann') [*London Gazette*]. Army List gives as 'Hobzermann'. Served in Peninsula only in 1812. *Beamish*, vol. II, p. 550.

HOLMES, David, Ensign, 9th Foot: *1829 Statement of Service for Retired Officers*: Aged seventeen on first appointment to the Army. Ensign, 9th Foot, 21 Oct. 1812; Lt., 9th Foot, 20 Jan. 1814; Half-pay, 1817, by reduction. *Where serving when wounded*: 'Nive, Pyrenees'. *Details of pension*: Fifty pounds per annum, commencing 11 Dec. 1814. *Family*: Married in Richmond, Surrey, 29 April 1823. One child by 1824. *Where generally living during last five years*: 'France and Italy'. [PRO: WO 25/762 f183]. Severely wounded, the Nive, 11 Dec. 1813 (1st Battn.) [*London Gazette*]. Pension 'for wounds' received in the Pyrenees [*1818 Pension Return*, pp. 6–7]. MGS.

HOLMES, George W., Capt., 92nd Foot: Capt., 92nd Foot, 28 March 1805. Wounded, Pyrenees, 25 July 1813 (1st Battn.) [*London Gazette*]. Severely wounded, Pyrenees, 30 July 1813 (1st Battn.) [*London Gazette*]. Severely wounded, the Nive, 13 Dec. 1813 (1st Battn.) [*London Gazette*]. Major, 92nd Foot, 18 June 1815. Waterloo. MGS.

HOLMES, Henry Hayes, Volunteer, 36th Foot: Severely wounded, Toulouse, 10 April 1814 ('Homes') (1st Battn.) [*London Gazette*]. Ensign, 36th Foot, 19 May 1814. Pension of fifty pounds per annum, commencing 11 April 1815, for 'loss of a leg' at Toulouse, 1814, while serving as a Volunteer [*1818 Pension Return*, pp. 24–5].

HOLMES, James, Capt., 4th Dragoons: Capt., 4th Dragoons, 28

April 1808. Slightly wounded, Albuera, 16 May 1811 [*London Gazette*].

HOLMES, Joseph, Lt., 84th Foot: Lt., 84th Foot, 26 April 1810. Severely wounded, the Nive, 10 Dec. 1813 ('Joshua Homes') (2nd Battn.) [*London Gazette*]. Temporary pension of seventy pounds per annum, commencing 11 Dec. 1814, 'for a wound' received at Bayonne, 1813 [*1818 Pension Return*, pp. 20–1].

HOLMES, Robert Pattison, 1st Lt., 23rd Foot: *1829 Statement of Service*: Born 3 Oct. 1790, Alconbury, Huntingdownshire. Aged twenty on his first entrance into the Army. 2nd Lt., 23rd Foot, 14 Feb. 1811; 1st Lt., 23rd Foot, 12 Dec. 1811; Capt., 23rd Foot, 4 Sept. 1823. *Battles, sieges and campaigns*: '1812 Siege of Ciudad Rodrigo... 1812 Siege of Badajos... 1813 Battle of Nivelle... 1813 Battle of Nive... 1814 Battle of Orthes... 1814 Battle of Toulouse... 1815 Battle of Waterloo... 1815 Storming of Cambray... 1815 Capture of Paris.' *Wounds received in action*: 'At the Storming of Badajos in 1812 by a Musket Shot in the right hand. One years pay as First Lieutenant a Pension of £70 per annum permanent 1813. Contusion in the Head at Waterloo by a Musket Ball.' *Titles, honorary distinctions and medals*: 'Medal for the Battle of Waterloo.' *Service abroad*: 'Nov 1811 to July 1812, Portugal. Oct 1813 to June 1814, Spain & France. March 1815 to Nov 1818, Belgium & France. Decr. 1823 to May 1826, Gibraltar.' Not married in 1830. [PRO: WO 25/789 f175]. Severely wounded, storming of Badajoz, 6 April 1812 [*London Gazette*]. Pension 'for wounds' received at Badajoz [*1818 Pension Return*, pp. 6–7]. MGS.

HOLMES, Samuel, Lt./Adjutant, 13th Light Dragoons: Adjutant, 13th Light Dragoons, 17 Sept. 1801;

Lt., 13th Light Dragoons, 24 Feb. 1804. Slightly wounded, Campo Mayor, 25 March 1811 [*London Gazette*]. Capt., 13th Light Dragoons, 10 Sept. 1812.

+HOLMES, Samuel, Lt., 85th Foot: Lt., 85th Foot, 3 March 1804. Killed, Fuentes de Onoro, 5 May 1811 [*London Gazette*].

HOME, John, Lt., 3rd Foot: Ensign, 3rd Foot, 11 Oct. 1810. Lt., 3rd Foot, 26 Nov. 1812. Severely wounded, the Nive, 13 Dec. 1813 (1st Battn.) [*London Gazette*].

HOMEWOOD, Edward, Lt., 3rd Dragoon Guards: Lt., 3rd Dragoon Guards, 30 May 1811. Recorded as 'Missing', Maguilla, 11 June 1812 [*London Gazette*]. Mentioned in Slade's Maguilla dispatch, 11 June 1812 ['I am concerned to say Lieutenant Windsor of the Royals, and Homewood of the 3rd Dragoon Guards, have fallen into the enemy's hands, the former having his horse shot, and the latter being wounded.'] [*London Gazette*].

+HOOD, Hon. Francis Wheler, Lt. Col., 3rd Foot Guards: Lt. Col., 3rd Foot Guards, 16 May 1811. Killed, Aire, 2 March 1814, while serving as AAG [*London Gazette*]. Letter from Wellington to The Earl Bathurst, dated St Sever, 4 March 1814: 'The enemy had collected a corps at Aire... Sir Rowland Hill attacked this corps on the 2d, and drove them from their post with considerable loss... I am sorry to report that we lost the Honourable Lieutenant-Colonel Hood on this occasion, an officer of great merit and promise.' [*London Gazette*]. R. Hill to Wellington, Aire, 3 March 1814: 'I have to regret the loss of a valuable officer in the death of Lieutenant-Colonel Hood, Assistant-Adjutant-General to the 2d division, who was unfortunately killed during the contest of yesterday.' [*London Gazette*]. Obituary, *The Gentle-*

HOOD

man's *Magazine*, April 1814, p. 413
['2 March... While engaged in
driving the Enemy from Aire, in his
33d year, Hon. Lieut.-col. F. W.
Hood, eldest son and heir-apparent
of Lord Hood, of Catherington, and
Whitley Abbey, near Coventry,
assistant-adjutant-general to the
2d division. He was a most amiable
young man, and an excellent officer.
He married the daughter of Sir A.
Hammond, late comptroller of the
Navy, whom he has left with a
young family.']. Eldest son of Henry,
2nd Viscount Hood, and thus
grandson of the great admiral
Samuel, 1st Viscount Hood.
[*Burke's Peerage*].

HOOD, James, Lt., 91st Foot: *1829
Statement of Service for Retired
Officers*: Aged twenty on first
appointment to the Army. Ensign,
'38th Ayr Militia', 25 April 1804;
Ensign, 91st Foot, 28 Aug. 1807,
'having raised 60 men'; Lt., 91st
Foot, 3 Aug. 1809; Lt., 9th Royal
Veteran Battn., 24 March 1821, 'in
consequence of extreme Bad health
incurred in Walcheren & Wounds
received in Spain & France'; Capt.,
'Royal Regiment of Ayr', 15 March
1825. *Where serving when wounded*:
'91 Regt. on 10th April 1814 In front
of Thoulouse.' *Details of pension*:
'None altho entitled to it by being
Engaged at Waterloo when the 12
Mos Expired after wounded viz.
Medical Board Regulation.' *Family*:
Married in Aberdeen, 6 Jan. 1819.
One child by 1829. *Title and nature
of employment*: 'Captain in His
Prince Regents Royal Regt. of Ayr
when called upon.' *Where generally
resident during last five years*:
'Fanfield House near Aberdeen.'
[PRO: WO 25/762 f188]. Slightly
wounded, Toulouse, 10 April 1814
(1st Battn.) [*London Gazette*].
Waterloo. MGS. Died, Jersey, 1853.

HOOPER, Richard, Lt., 3rd Foot:
*1829 Statement of Service for
Retired Officers*: Aged nineteen on
first appointment to the Army.

Ensign, 3rd Foot [Army List gives 28
Aug. 1807]; Lt., 3rd Foot, [Army List
gives 4 Jan. 1810]; Capt., 3rd Foot;
Half-pay, 3rd Dragoon Guards, 1822,
'in consequence of ill health.' *Where
serving when wounded*: 'Spain'.
Details of pension: Seventy pounds,
commencing 16 May 1811. *Family*:
Married in Bristol, April 1814. One
child by 1829. *Where generally resident during last five years*:
'London.' [PRO: WO 25/762 f101].
Slightly wounded, Albuera, 16 May
1811 [*London Gazette*]. Pension 'for
wounds' received at Albuera [*1818
Pension Return, pp. 4–5*].

**HOPE, Isaac, ('James'), Lt., 92nd
Foot:** *1829 Statement of Service for
Retired Officers*: Aged twenty on
first appointment to the Army.
'Accompanied 92nd Regt. as a
volunteer on the Expedition to
Holland in 1809'; Ensign, 92nd Foot,
1 Nov. 1809; Lt., 92nd Foot, 7 Jan.
1813; Half-pay, 24 March 1817, by
reduction. *Where serving when
wounded*: 'Peninsula 31st July 1813
and Belgium 18th June 1815.'
Details of pension: Seventy pounds,
commencing 25 Dec. 1821. *Family*:
Married in 'Keith, County of Banff',
27 Aug. 1816. Six children by 1829.
*Where generally resident during
last five years*: 'In Edinburgh'.
[PRO: WO 25/762 f178]. Severely
wounded, Pyrenees, 31 July 1813
[*London Gazette*]. MGS. *Mullen*, p.
505 ['James']. 'James' in Army List.

HOPE, Hon. John, Lt.-General:
Col., 92nd Foot, 3 Jan. 1806; Lt.-
General, 25 April 1808. Gold Medal.
Recorded as 'missing', sortie from
Bayonne, 14 April 1814 ('Sir J. Hope
K.B.') [*London Gazette*]. Report
from K. A. Howard to C. Colville,
dated 'Camp near Bayonne', 15
April 1814 ['It was towards the right
that Lieutenant-General Sir John
Hope was taken. In endeavouring
to bring up some troops to the
support of the picquets, he came
unexpectedly in the dark on a party
of the enemy; his horse was shot

290

dead and fell upon him, and not being able to disengage himself from under it, he was unfortunately made prisoner. I regret to say that from a letter I have received from him, I find he was wounded in two places, but in neither of them dangerously; you will easily conceive, Sir, that only one feeling, that of the greatest regret, pervades all the troops at the Lieutenant-General's misfortune.'] [*London Gazette*, 27 April 1814, p. 425]. Report of Colville to Wellington, Baucaut, 14 April 1814 ['Sir John Hope's horse was shot and fell upon him, which prevented his extricating himself. We hear that he is wounded in the arm, and a French officer speaks also of a wound in his thigh, but we trust this may have reference to his former injury. The boot of his left leg was found under his horse.'] [*London Gazette*, 27 April 1814].

HOPE, John Charles, 1st Lt., 95th Foot: *1829 Statement of Service*: Born in Laytonstone, Essex, 7 Feb. 1791. Aged sixteen 'on his first Entrance into the Army.' Ensign, 26th Foot, 7 Jan. 1807; 2nd Lt., 95th Foot, May 1807; 1st Lt., 95th Foot, Feb. 1808 [Army List gives 2 Feb. 1809]; Capt., Rifle Brigade, 9 Nov. 1820. *Battles, sieges and campaigns*: 'Served as as 2d Lieut. in the 95th regt. at the Seige of Copenhagen in 1807... and in Sweden and Portugal under Sir John Moore ... in 1808 and in 1809 in the Reserve during the Retreat and in the Battle of Corunna. Served as 1st Lieut. in the Expedition to the Scheldt in 1809... Served at Cadiz during the Seige in 1810 and 1811 and was present in the Battle of Barrosa in 1811 ... also in Holland and the Netherlands in 1814 and 1815... Served in the Netherlands and France in 1815 ... was present at the Battle of Waterloo & commanded the 3rd Battalion 95th Regiment during the rest of the Campaign until after the capture of Paris. Served also in the Army of Occupation during 1815, 16, 17 & 18 and as Captain in North America during 1826, 27, 28 & 29.' *Wounds received in action*: 'Severely wounded at Barrosa. One year's Pay as Lieutenant. Permanent Pension of £70, 1812.' *Titles, honorary distinctions and medals*: 'Waterloo Medal.' *Service abroad*: 'July 1807 to Decr. 1807, Denmark. April 1808 to Feby. 1809, Sweden, Portugal, Spain. July 1809 to Octr. 1809, Islands in the Scheldt. March 1810 to Augt. 1811, Spain, Holland. Feby. 1814 to 20th June 1815, Netherlands. 21st June 1815 to Novr. 1818, France. June 1826 to 25th Decr. 1829, North America, New Brunswick.' [PRO: WO 25/804 f318]. Severely wounded, Barossa, 5 March 1811 (2nd Battn.) [*London Gazette*]. *1818 Pension Return*, pp. 22–3. Waterloo. Died, 2 Oct. 1842. *Simmons*, p. 379. *Kincaid, Random Shots*, p. 290 ['At the close of the war, when we returned to England ... the officers commanding companies on the day of inspection, viz ... Hope with a grape-shot lacerated leg'].

HOPKINS, Charles, Volunteer, 36th Foot: *1829 Statement of Service for Retired Officers*: Aged twenty-five on first appointment to the Army. 'As a Volunteer at the Storming of Rodrigo my Ensigncy and Lieutcy. at Salamanca'; 'Ensigncy & Lieutcy', 36th Foot, 21 Jan. 1812 [Army List gives: Ensign, 36th Foot, 22 Jan. 1812; Lt., 36th Foot, 9 Dec. 1812]; Half-pay, by reduction. Served five years on full-pay. *Where serving when wounded*: 'Wounded at Rodrigo but no pension.' Not married, no children. *Where generally resident during last five years*: '10 Blackhall St. Dublin'. [PRO: WO 25/762 f175].

HOPKINS, Elers Pernell, Lt., 4th Foot: Lt., 4th Foot, 10 Jan. 1805. Slightly wounded, Vittoria, 21 June 1813 [*London Gazette*].

HOPKINS

+HOPKINS, Henry Lewis, Lt., 5th Foot: Lt., 5th Foot, 21 May 1807. Killed, Orthes, 27 Feb. 1814 (1st Battn.) [*London Gazette*].

HOPKINS, John Paul, Lt., 43rd Foot: *1829 Statement of Service*: Born in London, 11 July 1787. Aged seventeen 'on his first Entrance into the Army.' Ensign, 61st Foot, 12 Oct. 1804. Ensign, 43rd Foot, 7 Nov. 1804. Lt., 43rd Foot, 19 June 1805. Capt., 43rd, 29 Aug. 1811. Major, Half Pay, unattached, 5 Nov. 1825. Major, 98th Foot, 25 June 1829. Note added: 'Retired 18 Oct. 1831.' *Battles, sieges and campaigns*: 'Battle of Kioge in Denmark 1807. Siege of Copenhagen 1807... Present when a Lt. of the 43d. Campaign of Talavera 1809. Campaign of Corruna 1809. Battle of Almeida 1810. Battle of Busaco 1810. Battle of Redinha 1811. Battle of Pombal 1811. Battle of Conduxo 1811. Battle of Foz de Avronz 1811. Battle of Sabugal 1811. Battle of Fuentes de Onor 1811. And several skirmishes as Lieut. of the 43rd. Siege & Storm of Ciudad Rodrigo 1812. Siege and Storm of Badajoz 1812. Battle of Salamanca 1812. Campaign of Madrid and retreat from Burgos 1812. Battle of Vittoria 1813. The Battles and Skirmishes in the Pyrenees. As Captain of the 43rd.' *Distinguished conduct*: 'Thanked on the Field during the action of Sabugal and recommended for Promotion by General Sir Sidney Beckwith to His Grace the Duke of Wellington.' *Wounds received in action*: 'Two wounds at the action of Almeida while Lieut. of the 43rd. The grant of a Twelve months pay as a Captain given for it.' *Service abroad*: 'The summer of 1807 to the end of the year, Denmark. October 1808 to Feby. 1809, Spain. July 1809 to the end of the year 1813, Portugal and Spain. June 18 1815 to 1818, Belgium and France. Septr. 1822 to Novr. 1825, Gibraltar.' *Family*: Married Miss Wallace, 1814, London. They had no children by 1830. [PRO: WO 25/804 f161]. See also his *1829 Statement of Service for Retired Officers*, which was completed prior to his being appointed as Major in the 98th Foot [PRO: WO 25/762 f168]. Severely wounded, Coa, 24 July 1810 [*London Gazette*]. MGS.

HOPKINS, William Randolph, Ensign, 5th Foot: *1829 Statement of Service for Retired Officers*: Aged sixteen on first appointment to the Army. Ensign, 27th Foot, 14 Sept. 1808; 'Exchanged to 5th Regiment in March 1810' [Army List gives 14 June 1810]; Lt., 5th Foot, 5 Oct. 1813; Half-pay, 24 July 1816, 'from the state of my wound and contrary to my wishes.' *Where serving when wounded*: 'In Spain at the Storming of Badajoz'. *Details of pension*: Seventy pounds, commencing 'I believe in June 1813 but am not certain.' *Family*: Married in Christ Church, Cork, 9 Feb. 1819. Three children by 1829. *Where generally resident during last five years*: 'Bandon'. [PRO: WO 25/762 f154]. Severely wounded, storming of Badajoz, 6 April 1812 [*London Gazette*]. Temporary pension of fifty pounds per annum, commencing 7 April 1813, 'for wounds' received at Badajoz [*1818 Pension Return*, pp. 4–5]. MGS.

HOPPER, Edward, Lt., 38th Foot: Lt., 38th Foot, 21 March 1811. Severely wounded, storming of San Sebastian, 31 Aug. 1813 (1st Battn.) [*London Gazette*]. Slightly wounded, the Nive, 9 Dec. 1813 (1st Battn.) [*London Gazette*]. MGS.

HOPPER, George, Ensign, 89th Foot: *1829 Statement of Service for Retired Officers*: Aged twenty-five on first appointment to the Army. Ensign, 89th Foot, 22 July 1809; Lt., 89th Foot, 25 June 1812; Adjutant, 89th Foot, 1814; Lt., Nova Scotia Regt., 31 Aug. 1815; Half-pay, 25 Sept., 1816. 'I am not desirous of Service, being incapacitated from the severity of the wounds I have received.' *Where serving when wounded*: 'In Spain on the 15th of October 1810. I was wounded in three places, in the left leg and in the left Groin, these balls were both extracted. The last wound I received on that day, shattered my right ancle and completely incapacitated me from a longer performance of my duty in the field where I was left for dead, of these wounds. I can never expect to recover, both my legs being at present in such a state that it is with difficulty I can walk at all, and for which as Commanding the Light Company of the 89th Regt. I received a Captains years pay. I was on this occasion taken prisoner of War. On the 25th of July 1814 at Lundys Lane in America, I received a Ball in my right arm, a severe contusion on my right side, and had my Charger killed under me, for these wounds I received an Adjutants years pay. I was induced from severe suffering, in March 1816, at the instigation of my friends to make application for a Medical board, neither the report of this, or the one subsequently obtained in February 1824 realised my perhaps too sanguine expectations, the intimation of the ill success of my memorial, was accompanied by an assurance from my kind friend the Earl of Dalhousie that my claims should be remembered, and the appointment to my present situation almost immediately followed.' No pension. *Family*: Married in Cornwall, Upper Canada, 30 June 1814. No children by 1829. *Title and nature of employment*: '30th of April 1825 appointed Store Keeper and Clerk of Works, on the Grenville Canal, Lower Canada...' *Where generally resident during last five years*: 'Since the 16th of May 1825 in Grenville Camp Lower Canada, previously in Coteau Du Lac, Lower Canada.' [PRO: WO 25/762 f155].

+HOPPER, William, Adjutant/Lt., 38th Foot: Adjutant, 38th Foot, 4 June 1807. Lt., 38th Foot, 2 June 1808. Severely wounded, 'since dead', 'at the Siege of St Sebastian', 7-27 July 1813 ('Adjutant Hopper') (1st Battn.) [*London Gazette*]. *Register of dead officers*: Died of wounds, 25 July 1813. Return dated Aug. 1813. [PRO: WO 25/2965].

+HOPWOOD, John, 1st Lt., 95th Foot: 1st Lt., 95th Foot, 6 Feb. 1811. Wounded, 'in the several Affairs with the French Army', 11 March 1811 (1st Battn.) [*London Gazette*]. Severely wounded, Vittoria, 21 June 1813 [*London Gazette*]. Killed, the Nive, 10 Dec. 1813 (1st Battn.) [*London Gazette*]. Simmons, p. 323 [10 Dec. 1813: 'Marshal Soult advanced with a large force by the high road from Bayonne and formed up near Bassussarry, which is directly opposite the church and chateau of Artcangues, and made an attack upon the left of our line. Lieutenant Hopwood and Sergeant Brotherwood were killed. A ball passed through both their heads, happening to be standing a little behind one another. They were both capital soldiers and were put in the same grave.']. Leach, pp. 352-3 [10 Dec. 1813: 'During the remainder of the day, Marshal Soult confined his operations to a cannonade on the posts of the Light Division in the churchyard of Arcanguez, and a continual fire of light troops. One of my subalterns, Lieut. Hopwood, was killed on this occasion. He was a good and gallant soldier, and a worthy fellow.']. *Harris*, pp. 53, 163 ['I myself started off with Lieutenant Pratt, Sergeant-major Adams, and William Brotherwood, the latter of who was afterwards killed at Vittoria [sic] by a cannon-ball, which at the same moment ended Patrick Mahon and Lieutenant Hopwood. The manner in which these three soldiers met with their death is extraordinary. As they were creeping from their cover to try and shoot one of the French generals, who was much exposed, the enemy pointed a gun at them, and succeeded in sweeping down all three as they crawled along.' Note: Harris was not present]. *Kincaid, Adventures*, pp. 273–4 [10 Dec. 1813: 'An officer of ours, Mr Hopewood [sic], and one of our serjeants, had been killed in the field opposite, within twenty yards of where the enemy's skirmishers now were. We were very anxious to get possession of their bodies, but had not force enough to effect it. Several French soldiers came through the hedge, at different times, with the intention, as we thought, of plundering, but our men shot every one who attempted to go near them, until towards evening, when a French officer approached, waving a white handkerchief and pointing to some of his men who were following him with shovels. Seeing that his intention was to bury them, we instantly ceased firing, nor did we renew it again that night.'].

HORT, Josiah George, Lt., 81st Foot: *1829 Statement of Service for Retired Officers*: Aged twenty-one on first appointment to the Army. Ensign, 81st Foot, 19 Sept. 1805; Lt., 81st Foot, 26 Feb. 1807; Capt., 5th Garrison Battn., 23 Aug. 1810, 'in consequence of the loss of a leg in action at Corunna'; Capt., 12th Royal Veteran Battn., 21 Feb. 1811. 'Not desirous of Service, having lost a leg in action and being charged with a family consisting of a Wife and seven children.' *Where serving when wounded*: 'Corunna in Spain with the Army under the late Sir John Moore.' *Details of pension*: One hundred pounds per annum, 'for the loss of a leg.' Commenced '25 Decemr. 1811. Original Amt. of pension as Lieut. £70 per annum on the Order dated War-Office 20 June 1812. Increased to £100 from the 25th Decemr. 1811 agreeably to the Order dated War-Office 31st July 1815.' *Family*: Married in Letterkenny, County Donegal,

Ireland, 25 Sept. 1809. Seven children by 1829. *Where generally resident during last five years*: 'City of Dublin'. Signed and addressed: '16 Russell Street, Dublin'. [PRO: WO 25/762 f189]. Wounded, 'in the Army lately in Spain' (2nd Battn.) [*March 1809 Army List*, p. 105]. *Monthly Return*, 2nd Battn., dated 25 Feb. 1809: 'Wounded, in Naval Hospl. Plymouth' ('Hart') [PRO: WO 17/202]. *Monthly Return*, 2nd Battn., dated 25 Aug. 1809: 'Loss of leg. Dublin'. *1818 Pension Return*, pp. 18–19. MGS.

HORTON, George William, Lt., 71st Foot: Lt., Army, 25 July 1811; Lt. 71st Foot, 23 Jan. 1812. Slightly wounded, Orthes, 27 Feb. 1814 (1st Battn.) [*London Gazette*]. Waterloo. MGS.

HORTON, James, Capt., 61st Foot: Lt., Army, 16 May 1801. Lt., 61st Foot, 24 Feb. 1803. Capt., 61st Foot, 23 July 1807. Severely wounded, Nivelle, 10 Nov. 1813 (1st Battn.). MGS.

+HORTON, P. B. Posthumus, Capt., 61st Foot: Capt., 61st Foot, 21 Aug. 1806. Killed, Salamanca, 22 July 1812 (1st Battn.) [*London Gazette*]. *Register of officers' effects*: Single. Effects totalled £222. 19s. 6d. [PRO: WO 25/2964].

HOSKINS, Joseph, Ensign/Lt., 1st Foot: *1829 Statement of Service for Retired Officers*: Aged twenty-one on first appointment to the Army. Ensign, 1st Foot, March 1812 [Army List gives 2 April 1812]; Lt., 1st Foot, Sept. 1813 [Army List gives 22 Sept.]; Half-pay, 1817, by reduction, 'but serving in India at the time did not return to England before October 1819'. *Where serving when wounded*: 'Spain 1813'. *Details of Pension*: Fifty pounds, 'Granted Jany. 1820, Commencing Decr. 1818'. *Where generally resident during last five years*: 'England & Jersey'. [PRO: WO 25/762 f196].

Severely wounded, 'at the Siege of St Sebastian,' 7–27 July 1813 (3rd Battn.) [*London Gazette*].

HOTHAM, Beaumont, Ensign, Coldstream Guards: Ensign, Coldstream Guards, 27 June 1810. Slightly wounded, Salamanca, 22 July 1812 [*London Gazette*]. Lt. and Capt., Coldstream Guards, 13 Jan. 1814. Waterloo. MGS. Died, 12 Dec. 1870.

HOUGHTON, Richard, Lt., 3rd Foot: Lt., 3rd Foot, 14 April 1808. Severely wounded, Albuera, 16 May 1811 [*London Gazette*]. Slightly wounded, the Nive, 13 Dec. 1813 ("Haughton")(1st Battn.) [*London Gazette*]. MGS.

HOULTON, George, Lt., 43rd Foot: Lt., 43rd Foot, 6 Oct. 1808. Severely wounded, Vittoria, 21 June 1813 (1st Battn.) [*London Gazette*]. MGS. Died 15 Sept. 1862.

+HOUSTON, William, Lt., 71st Foot: Lt., Army, 12 Nov. 1807; Lt., 71st Foot, 28 July 1808. Killed, Fuentes de Onoro, 5 May 1811 ('Houstoun') (1st Battn.) [*London Gazette*].

HOVENDEN, Nicholas, Lt., 59th Foot: *1829 Statement of Service*: 'Born in the County of Dublin, August 1793. Aged 16 years on his first Entrance into the Army. Ensign, 59th Regt., 6 April 1809. Lieutenant, 59th Regt., 11th Decr. 1811. Captain, 59th Regt., 19 Jany. 1826.' Note added: 'Major, 59th Regt., 22 Aug. 1834. Died at Leeds 30 Sept. 1845.' *Battles, sieges and campaigns*: 'Battle of Vittoria 21st June 1813. Storming of St Sebastian 31 Augt. 1813... Campaign of 1815 in the Netherlands and France, Battle of Waterloo, Storming of Cambray & Paris... Maharatta Campaign in 1817 & 1818... Siege & Storming of Bhurtpore 18 Jany. 1826, as Bt. Captain' *Wounds received in action*:

'Wounded Severely at the Storming of St Sebastian. One years pay as Captain. No pension.' *Titles, honorary distinctions and medals*: 'Medal for Waterloo.' *Service abroad*: 'Augt. 1812 to Novr. 1813, Spain & Portugal. May 1815 to Decr. 1815, France. May 1816 to 28th Jan. 1829, Bengal, Ceylon, East Indies.' Note added: '12 April 1835 to 27 June 1836, Gibraltar. 28 June 1836 to 18 Oct. 1838, Malta. 30 Novr. 1842 to 17 Dec. 1843, West Indies.' Not married in 1830. [PRO: WO 25/796 f234]. Severely wounded, storming of San Sebastian, 31 Aug. 1813 (2nd Battn.) [*London Gazette*].

+HOVENDEN, Tarleton, 1st Lt., 95th Rifles: 1st Lt., 95th Rifles, 16 Nov. 1809. Slightly wounded, Barossa, 5 March 1811 [*London Gazette*]. Killed, storming of Badajoz, 6 April 1812 [*London Gazette*]. *Simmons*, p. 232 [killed]. 3rd Battn.

HOWARD, Thomas Phipps, Capt., 23rd Light Dragoons: Lt., Royal York Hussars, 25 Nov. 1795; Capt., Royal York Hussars, 4 June 1798; Capt., 23rd Light Dragoons, 4 July 1798. Severely wounded, Talavera, 28 July 1809 [*London Gazette*]. Bvt. Major, 23rd Light Dragoons, 15 March 1810. Pension of two hundred pounds per annum, commencing 25 Dec. 1811, 'for a wound' received at Talavera [*1818 Pension Return*, pp. 2–3]. Bvt. Lt. Col., 23rd Light Dragoons, 12 Aug. 1819. MGS. *Royal Military Calendar*, vol. V, p. 157.

HOWELL, John, Surgeon, 61st Foot; Surgeon to the Forces: *1829 Statement of Services for Retired Officers*: Aged twenty-four on first appointment to the Army. Hospital Mate, 11 June 1801; Assistant Surgeon, 61st Foot, 28 Aug. 1802; Surgeon, 'Grenadier Battn. Sicily', 22 Sept. 1805; Surgeon, Royal Sicilian Regt., 17 March 1808; Surgeon, 61st Foot, 11 May 1809;

'Surgeon to the Forces', 16 April 1811; Half-pay, 'by reduction in 1816, from ill Health 25 Feby 1818.' 'Ill Health the Ball remaining in the side.' *Where serving when wounded*: 'Peninsula.' *Details of pension*: One hundred pounds, commencing 1811. *Family*: Married in Dawlish, Devon, 7 Sept. 1818. Two children by 1829. *Where generally resident during last five years*: 'Clifton'". [PRO: WO 25/762 f124]. MGS.

HOYSTED, Frederick William, Major, 59th Foot: Capt., 59th Foot, 5 Jan. 1805. Major, 59th Foot, 17 June 1813. Severely wounded, the Nive, 10 Dec. 1813 (2nd Battn.) [*London Gazette*]. Bvt. Lt. Col., 59th Foot, 26 Dec. 1813. Temporary pension of two hundred and fifty pounds per annum, commencing 11 Dec. 1814, 'for wounds' received at Bayonne, 1813 [*1818 Pension Return*, pp. 14–15]. Waterloo.

HUDSON, James E., Lt., 2nd Foot: Lt., Army, 29 May 1806. Lt., 2nd Foot, 17 Aug. 1809. Severely wounded, Salamanca, 22 July 1812 [*London Gazette*].

HUDSON, Richard, Lt., 40th Foot: Lt., 40th Foot, 7 Nov. 1811. Severely wounded, Salamanca, 22 July 1812 [*London Gazette*]. Waterloo. *Dalton*, pp. 153, 155 ['H. p., 22nd Foot, 21st March, 1822. D. in 1827.'].

HUGHES, John, Lt., 57th Foot: Lt., 57th Foot, 6 Feb. 1808. Slightly wounded, Albuera, 16 May 1811 [*London Gazette*]. Severely wounded, Nivelle, 10 Nov. 1813 (1st Battn.) [*London Gazette*]. MGS.

HUGHES, Philip I., Capt., Royal Artillery: Capt., Army, 12 Sept. 1803; Capt., Royal Artillery, 1 Feb. 1808. Slightly wounded, Barossa, 5 March 1811 [*London Gazette*].

HUGHES, Robert, Lt., 30th Foot; Lt., 9th Portuguese Line: Ensign, 30th Foot, 11 April 1811; Lt., 30th Foot, 29 Oct. 1812. In Portuguese Service Dec. 1810 to Oct. 1813. Waterloo. MGS. Lt. Col., 1st West India Regt., 3 March 1843. Died, Sept. 1855. *Challis, Portuguese Army*, p. 56 ['Lt. 9 Line... Wd. Vittoria 21 June '13.']. *Dalton*, pp. 140, 142.

HUGO, Brandano Henry Frederick William Ludolphus de, Lt., 2nd Dragoons K.G.L.: *1829 Statement of Service for Retired Officers*: Aged 'nearly 15 or 16 years of age' on first appointment to the Army. Ensign, 7th Line Battn. K.G.L., 29 Nov. 1805; Cornet, 2nd Dragoons K.G.L., 12 Nov. 1806; Lt., 2nd Dragoons, 24 March 1812; Half-pay, 24 April 1816, by reduction. *Where serving when wounded*: 'In the engagement of La Venta del Pozo or Villadrigo near Quintailla de la Puente between Burgos and Valladolid in Spain, on the 23rd of October 1812. I received a lance wound in the sword-arm, and a hurt in the calf of the leg, caused by the hoof-iron of a horse, entering the flesh – sundry sabre cuts on the fingers etc – also a severe contusion on the breast, produced by the fall of the enemy's horse on my body in a heavy charge of cavalry, which occasioned spitting of blood during several years, and an asthmatic affection, which still remains.' *Details of pension*: 'No pension or gratification whatever, notwithstanding the Medical Board, assembled at Osnabruch in Hanover on the 6th Day of May 1816, deemed it proper to grant me an order for one years pay, which was subsequently refused by Command of His Lordship the Secretary at War, dated 28th of May 1816.' *Family*: 'Un-married and prevented entering the state of matrimony – (after having concluded a contract of Marriage under faith of the Order or Warrant dated 18th of June 1818, which inconditionally granted pension to the Widows of Officers, who have served longer than three years) – in consequence of the prejudice to the Widows interest by the subsequent Order or Warrant, dated 13th June 1826, which excludes her from any share of pension.' *Where generally resident during last five years*: 'At Aurich near Embden in the Province of East Friesland in the Kingdom of Hanover.'" He signed the form 'Ludolphus de Hugo'. [PRO: WO 25/755 f200]. Wounded, during 'movements of the Army' [Retreat from Burgos], 23 Oct. 1812 [*London Gazette*]. Served in Peninsula 1812-14. Waterloo. MGS. *Beamish*, vol. II, p. 545 ['Ludolph von Hugo ... slightly wounded, 23d Oct. 1812, at Venta del Poco'].

+HULL, Edward, Lt. Col., 43rd Foot: Lt. Col., 43rd Foot, 10 Aug. 1804. Killed, Coa, 24 July 1810 (1st Battn.) [*London Gazette*]. Obituary, *The Gentleman's Magazine*, Aug. 1810, p. 192 ['At the head of his regiment in the late hard-fought engagement at Almeida, Lieut.-col. Hull. This most deservedly lamented officer was the only son of Trevor Hull, esq. of Southampton. In him his Majesty has lost a most deserving and meritorious officer; his country a sincere and fervent friend; whose loss cannot be more deeply lamented in his profession, to which he did the greatest honour, than it is from his private worth by his numerous friends and relatives'].

HULL, James Watson, Capt., 43rd Foot: Capt., 43rd Foot, 11 June 1807. Severely wounded, Coa, 24 July 1810 ('J. W. Hail') (1st Battn.) [*London Gazette*]. Temporary pension of one hundred pounds per annum, commencing 25 Dec. 1811, 'for wounds' received at Coa [*1818 Pension return*, pp. 12–13].

HULLESSEN, Charles Gerhard Baron Meerscheid von, Lt., Duke of Brunswick Oels' Corps (Infantry): *1829 Statement of Service for Retired Officers*: Aged sixteen on first appointment to the Army.

Ensign, Duke of Brunswick Oels' Corps (Infantry), 27 Sept. 1809; Lt., Duke of Brunswick Oels' Corps (Infantry), 16 Aug. 1810; Half-pay, 28 Dec. 1814, by reduction. Note added: 'Died 25 April 1829'. *Where serving when wounded*: 'a severe wound through the breast at the storming of St Sebastian in the Peninsula in the year 1813.' *Details of pension*: Seventy pounds per annum, commencing 1 Sept. 1814. *Family*: Married in Brunswick, 27 April 1824. Four children by 1829. *Where generally resident during last five years*: Brunswick. [PRO: WO 25/776 f354]. 'Gustavus von Hulsen' in Army List. Wounded, storming of San Sebastian, 31 Aug. 1813 ('Hulsen') [*London Gazette*].

HULME, William Brown, Capt., Royal Staff Corps: *1829 Statement of Service for Retired Officers*: Aged thirty-nine on first appointment to the Army. Lt., 7th Foot, 11 Oct. 1796; Half-pay, 6th Irish Brigade, 20 Sept. 1799; Lt., 2nd Garrison Battn., 26 Sept. 1805; Lt., Royal Staff Corps, 3 Oct. 1805; Capt., Royal Staff Corps, 30th Feb. 1809; Half-pay, 14 Feb. 1814, 'in consequence of severe injuries received while on Actual [sic] Service in Spain.' 'Being now in my 72nd year and labouring under severe Bodily Infirmities rendors me totally incapable of Service. Remarks: I was removed from the Drawing room in the town in 1780 and employ'd as an asst. Engineer and a Draftsman till 1784. Appointed Asst. Engineers at Halifax Nova-Scotia June 25th 1795, and continued as such to 1896 [sic] when I join'd the Royl. Staff Corps.' *Where serving when wounded*: 'In Spain'. *Details of pension*: One hundred pounds, commencing 24 March 1817. *Family*: Married in Chelsfield Church, Kent, 3 Aug. 1811. Two children by 1829. *Where generally resident during last five years*: 'Oxford, 1 year. Exeter, 1 year, and 3 years in the Parish of Camberwell, Surry.' [PRO: WO 25/762 f223].

HÜLSEMANN, Henry Frederick, Capt., 1st Light Battn. K.G.L.: Capt., Army, 17 July 1809; Capt., 1st Light Battn. K.G.L., 5 Feb. 1810. Severely wounded, Salamanca, 22 July 1812 ('Hulseman') [*London Gazette*]. Slightly wounded, Crossing the Bidassoa, 7/9 Oct. 1813 [*London Gazette*]. Severely wounded, sortie from Bayonne, 14 April 1814 ('Frederick Hulseman') [*London Gazette*]. Served in Peninsula 1808–9, 1811–14. Waterloo. *Beamish*, vol. II, p. 561.

HUMBLEY, William, Lt., 95th Foot: 1st Lt., 95th Foot, 13 Oct. 1808. Slightly wounded, 'in Action with the Enemy', 20 March 1814 ('Humbly') (2nd Battn.) [*London Gazette*]. Severely wounded at Waterloo, serving with the 2nd Batt. Attained the rank of Lt. Col., unattached, 1851. MGS. Died at Eyresbury, 26 Oct. 1857.

+HUMBLY, Philip, Lt., 66th Foot: Lt., 66th Foot, 4 Dec. 1808. Severely wounded, Talavera, 28 July 1809 (2nd Battn.) [*London Gazette*]. Obituary, *The Gentleman's Magazine*, Oct. 1809, p. 984 ['Sept... Lieutenant Steel and Humbly, of the 66th Foot. These officers were returned severely wounded in the battle of Talavera.'].

HUMFREY, Benjamin Geale, Lt., 45th Foot: Lt., 45th Foot, 20 Oct. 1808. Severely wounded, storming of Ciudad Rodrigo, 19 Jan. 1812 ('Humphrey') [*London Gazette*]. Severely wounded, Pyrenees, 30 July 1813 (1st Battn.) [*London Gazette*]. MGS. There is a photograph of him illustrated in *Haythornthwaite, Armies of Wellington*, between pp. 96–7 ['Few officers who served in the storming parties at both Ciudad Rodrigo and Badajoz can have survived into the age of photography. This is one: Lieutenant-Colonel Benjamin Geale Humfrey, who was a lieutenant in the 45th's light company in both actions, was wounded by falling off a scaling-ladder at Rodrigo and virtually lost the use of his right hand at Pampelona.'].

+HUMPHREY, John, Capt., 29th Foot: Lt., 29th Foot, 17 Sept. 1804; Capt., 27 July 1809. Killed, Albuera, 16 May 1811 [*London Gazette*]. *Sherer*, p. 159 [Albuera: 'I remember well, as we moved down in column, shot and shell flew over and through it in quick succession; we sustained little injury from either, but a captain of the twenty-ninth had been dreadfully lacerated by a ball, and lay directly in our path. We passed close to him, and he knew us all; and the heart-rendering tone in which he called to us for water, or to kill him, I shall never forget. He lay alone, and we were in motion, and could give him no succour; for on this trying day, such of the wounded as could not walk lay unattended where they fell'.].

HÜNICKEN, John Charles Christoph, Lt., 1st Line Battn. K.G.L.: Lt., 1st Line Battn. K.G.L., 27 Jan. 1811. Severely wounded, 'lost both legs', siege of Ciudad Rodrigo, 14 Jan. 1812 ('Hunecken') [*London Gazette*]. Served in Peninsula 1808–12. *Beamish*, vol. II, p. 656 ['Retired on full pay of his rank, 17th Aug. 1814. [Died] at Goslar in Han. 4th June 1824.'].

HUNT, John Philip, Major, 52nd Foot: Major, 52nd Foot, 8 Sept. 1808. Severely wounded, storming of San Sebastian, 31 Aug. 1813 ('Major Hunt (Lieut. Col.)') ('Detachment, 52d Foot, 1st Batt.') [*London Gazette*]. Mentioned in Graham's San Sebastian dispatch, dated Oyarzun, 1 Sept. 1813 ['Major-General Hay likewise expresses his great satisfaction with ... Lieutenant-Colonel Hunt, commanding the detachment of the left division, who was severely wounded'] [*London Gazette*]. MGS. *Surtees*, p.

238 [Storming of San Sebastian: 'The volunteers who went from our division to assist in the storm or assault, sustained their full share in the casualties attendant thereon. The field-officer, Colonel Hunt of the 52d, was severely wounded.']. *Royal Military Calendar*, vol. IV, pp. 412–13 [Extensive military biography. 'On the 31st Aug. [1813] he commanded the volunteers of the light division at the assault of St Sebastian, where he was twice severely wounded; one of which wounds has lamed him for life, the ball being lodged under his left knee.'].

+**HUNT, Richard, Lt., Royal Engineers:** 1st Lt., Royal Engineers, 1 Aug. 1809. Killed at the siege of Badajoz, 6–11 June 1811 [*London Gazette*].

HUNT, Vere, Lt., 4th Foot: *1829 Statement of Service for Retired Officers*: Aged twenty on first appointment to the Army. Ensign, 58th Foot, 1803; Lt., 4th Foot, 20 Oct. 1804; Capt., 4th Foot, 12 May 1812; Half-pay, by reduction. *Where serving when wounded*: 'Corunna'. *Details of pension*: Seventy pounds per annum, commencing 25 Dec. 1824. Not married. *Where generally resident during last five years*: 'Askeaton'. [PRO: WO 25/762 f217]. Wounded, 'in the Army lately in Spain' ('Vero Hunt') (1st Battn.) [*March 1809 Army List*, p. 105].

HUNTER, John, Lt., 53rd Foot: Lt., 53rd Foot, 28 May 1809. Severely wounded, Salamanca, 22 July 1812 (2nd Battn.) [*London Gazette*].

HUNTER, William, Ensign/Lt., 52nd Foot: *1829 Statement of Service*: 'Born in Forfar, Scotland, 10th March 1797. Aged 16 years on his first Entrance into the Army. Ensign, 52nd Regt., 24th March 1812. Lieutenant, 52nd Regt., 28th April 1813. Half Pay 24th Octr. 1818, by Reduction of two Lieutenants in

the Army. Lieutenant, 34th Regt., 13th March 1827. Captain, 96th Regt., 28th Novr. 1828. Captain, 55th Regt., 4 Decr. 1828.' *Battles, sieges and campaigns*: 'Present as Lieutenant in the 52d Regt. on the 7th October 1813 at the crossing of the Bidessoa. At the Battles of Bayonne [sic] 10th, 11th & 12th of December 1813, and the Battle of Orthes and Toulouse on the 27th of February 1814 and 14th April 1814.' *Wounds received in action*: 'Severely wounded by a Musket Shot through the Body on the 7th October 1813 at the crossing of the Bidissoa. And slightly on the 10th December 1813 at the Battle of Bayonne [sic]. Received one years pay.' *Service abroad*: '24th Feby. 1813 to 24th Octr. 1818, Spain, Portugal, France and Netherlands.' *Family*: Married Mary Taylor, 21 Nov. 1821, in Montrose. They had five children by April 1830. [PRO: WO 25/795 f337]. Note: it appears that he has confused Bayonne with the Nive. Presumably it was at the Nive where he was wounded on 10 Dec. 1813. Severely wounded, Crossing the Bidassoa, 7/9 Oct. 1813 (1st Battn.) [*London Gazette*].

HURFORD, William Lewin, Capt., 23rd Foot: Capt., 23rd Foot, 25 Oct. 1804. Slightly wounded, Albuera, 16 May 1811 (1st Battn.) [*London Gazette*]. Temporary pension of three hundred pounds, commencing 17 May 1812, 'for wounds' received at Albuera ('Herford, William Lewis') [*1818 Pension Return*, pp. 6–7].

HUSSEY, George, Lt./Capt., 38th Foot: Lt., 38th Foot, 7 Aug. 1804; Capt. 10 Sept. 1812. Severely wounded, storming of San Sebastian, 31 Aug. 1813 (1st Battn.) [*London Gazette*].

HUTCHISON, Joseph, Lt., 7th Foot: *1829 Statement of Service*: Born 29 July 1793, Isle of Bermuda. Aged seventeen on his first

Entrance into the Army. Lt., 26 April 1810; Capt. 8 April 1825. *Battles, sieges and campaigns*: 'Sieges of Badajoz, Ap. & May 1811. Battle of Albuera, 16 May 1811. Affair of Fuenta de la Penna, 18 July 1812. Battle of Salamanca, 22 July 1812. Affair of Asma, 19 June 1813. Battle of Vittoria, 21 June 1813. Affair of Romesvallos, 25 July 1813. Battle of Pampeluna, 28 July 1813. & Affairs untill 2 Aug. 1813. Assault at St. Sebastian, 31 Aug. 1813. Attack of New Orleans on the 8th January 1815...' *Distinguished Conduct*: 'At the Assault of St Sebastian 31 Aug 1813 served as a Volunteer with a Detachment of the Fusiliers in the course of the Assault succeeded to the Command of the Volunteers of the Fusilier Brigade by the Death of Major Rose of the 20 Regt. was thanked by Major General Ross for his Conduct on that day and strongly recommended to the late Sir H. Torrens. – At the Assault of the Lines at New Orleans 8 January 1815 was Subaltern of one of the 3 Comps which succeeded in entering the enemy's Works, preceeding which by the death of the Captain, the Command of the Comps devolved upon him, was thanked by Sir Edwd. Blakeney then Commg. the Fusiliers for his conduct on the occasion.' *Wounds received in action*: 'On the 22 July 1812 was severely wounded at the Battle of Salamanca, for which he received a grant of One year's pay and a pension of 70£ per annum which pension he resigned in 1816 in Consequence of finding himself no longer inconvenienced from the Bullet which had lodged in his shoulder, he received a Letter of high approbation from His Royal Highness the Prince Regent.' *Service abroad*: 'February 1811 to 7 October 1813, Peninsula. 12 March 1814 to 28 June 1814, Peninsula. 4 October 1814 to June 1815, America. 16 August 1815 to 2 Novem. 1818, France. 29 Decem.

1826 to 10 April 1828, Portugal (As Aide de Camp to Maj: General Sir Edwd Blakeney).' *Family*: Married Harriett White, 8 Jan. 1829, Exeter. No children in 1830. [PRO: WO 25/786 f92]. Severely wounded, Salamanca, 22 July 1812 ('Hutchinson') [*London Gazette*].

HUTTON, William, Lt., 2nd Foot: *1829 Statement of Service for Retired Officers*: Aged twenty-four on first appointment to the Army. Ensign, 2nd Foot, 12 April 1809; Lt., 2nd Foot, 6 Oct. 1812; Half-pay, 2 Oct. 1817, 'the Army Medical Board considering me unfit for further actual service.' *Where serving when wounded*: 'Spain, 26 July 1813 in Pyrenees'. *Details of pension*: Seventy pounds per annum, from July 1814 to 21 July 1825. *Where generally resident during last five years*: 'Sunderland, Durham, except last three months residence Rothbay Northumberland for recovery of health.' [PRO: WO 25/762 f227]. Severely wounded, Pyrenees, 28 July 1813 [*London Gazette*]. Pension 'for wounds' received at Pampeluna, 1813 [*1818 Pension Return*, pp. 4–5].

HYDE, Frederick, Lt., 4th Foot: *1829 Statement of Service for Retired Officers*: Aged twenty-two on first appointment to the Army. Ensign, 4th Foot, 29 Oct. 1810; Lt., 4th Foot, 16 Sept. 1813; Half-pay, 'Reduced by the Peace Establishment.' *Where serving when wounded*: 'France, severely wounded.' No pension, no grant. *Family*: Married in 'Tadley, County of Hants', 31 Jan. 1822. Four children by 1829. *Where generally resident during last five years*: 'Tadley Lodge, County of Hants, and Seven Oaks county of Kent.' [PRO: WO 25/762 f274]. Severely wounded, Storming of San Sebastian, 31 Aug. 1813 (1st Battn.) [*London Gazette*]. Severely wounded, the Nive, 10 Dec. 1813 (1st Battn.) [*London Gazette*]. MGS.

I

ILLINS, William, Volunteer, 83rd Foot: Slightly wounded, storming of Badajoz, 6 April 1812 ('Volunteer Illers') [*London Gazette*]. Ensign, 83rd Foot, 30 April 1812; Lt., 83rd Foot, 29 July 1813.

ILTEN, Adolphus George Hermann von, Lt., 1st Light Dragoons/Hussars K.G.L.: Lt., 1st Light Dragoons KGL, 15 July 1811. Slightly wounded, Pyrenees, 30 July 1813 [*London Gazette*]. Served in Peninsuula 1809–14. Waterloo. *Beamish*, vol. II, p. 550 ['Slightly wounded, 30th July, 1813, near Pampelona... [Died] at Harburg, 3d of Nov. 1829, a captain Han. garde du corps.'].

+IMLACH, William, Capt., 79th Foot: Capt., 79th Foot, 14 March 1805. Killed, Fuentes de Onoro, evening of 3 May 1811 (1st Battn.) [*London Gazette*].

IMPETT, Thomas, Lt., 53rd Foot: Lt., 53rd Foot, 26 July 1810. Severely wounded, Toulouse, 10 April 1814 (2nd Battn.) [*London Gazette*].

INCE, William, Lt., 38th Foot: Lt., Army, 4 Dec. 1806; Lt., 38th Foot, 6 Aug. 1807. Slightly wounded, Salamanca, 22 July 1812 (1st Battn.) [*London Gazette*].

INGERSLEBEN, von, Lt., 60th Foot: Lt., 60th Foot, 31 Oct. 1810 ('de Ingersleben'). Slightly wounded, Albuera, 16 May 1811 (5th Battn.) [*London Gazette*].

INGLIS, William, Lt. Col., 57th Foot; Major-General: Lt. Col., 57th Foot, 16 Aug. 1804; Bvt. Col., 57th Foot, 25 July 1810. Slightly wounded, Albuera, 16 May 1811 [*London Gazette*]. Brigadier-General, 21 Jan. 1813; Major-General, 4 June 1813. Temporary pension of three hundred pounds per annum, commencing 17 May 1812, 'for wounds' received at Albuea [*1818 Pension Return*, pp. 14–15]. Gold Medal. *Royal Military Calendar*, vol. III, pp. 231–4 ['On the 16th of May, 1811, he commanded his regiment in the hard-contested battle of Albuhera, at the commencement of which he had his horse shot under him, and at the close was very severely wounded ... on the 10th of November [1813, in command of a brigade] ... he received a contusion on the foot by a musket-ball.']. Memorial tablet in Canterbury Cathedral, where he is buried ['Within the Chapter House of this Cathedral, rest the remains of Lieutenant General Sir William Inglis, K.C.B. Governor of Core; and Colonel of the 57th Regiment. During many years of active service in this gallant corps, he rose through all the various ranks, to that of its Lieutenant Colonel, and was at length appointed its Colonel, as a just tribute to the gallantry which he had displayed, at its head, in the sanguinary battle of Albuhera, (where he was severely wounded,) and to his subsequent services as a General officer, during the Peninsular War. He died at Ramsgate the 29th of November 1835, in the 72nd year of his age, and the 57th of his service.']. *Haythornthwaite, Die Hard*, p. 152 [Albuera: 'Daniel Hoghton ... was mortally wounded early in the action, and command of the brigade devolved temporarily upon William Inglis of the 57th. His battalion went into action with 31 officers and 616 other ranks, of whom 23 officers and 405 men were killed or wounded, a casualty-rate of more than 66 per cent. Inglis himself was grievously wounded by grapeshot which entered his left breast and lodged in his back, but he refused to be carried to the rear, lying in front of his battalion's Colours and calling upon his men with the immortal exhortation, "Die hard, 57th, die hard!" '].

INGRAM, George, Ensign., 28th Foot: Ensign, 28th Foot, 29 Jan. 1810. Slightly wounded, Albuera, 16 May 1811 (2nd Battn.) [*London Gazette*]. Died of wounds, Waterloo. *Dalton*, p. 138 ['Distinguished himself at the battle of Albuera. Had his leg amputated after Waterloo; the tourniquet shifted in the night and he bled to death.'].

INGRAM, John A., Capt., 24th Foot: Capt., 24th Foot, 3 Oct. 1811. Severely wounded, Orthes, 27 Feb. 1814 ('James Ingram') (2nd Battn.) [*London Gazette*].

INNES, Alexander, Lt., 42nd Foot: Lt., 42nd Foot, 15 Oct. 1812. Severely wounded, Toulouse, 10 April 1814 (1st Battn.) [*London Gazette*]. Waterloo. MGS. Half-pay, 24 Nov. 1828.

+INNES, Gordon C., Lt., 94th Foot: Lt., 94th Foot, 31 Aug. 1809. Killed, Salamanca, 22 July 1812 [*London Gazette*]. *Register of officers' effects*: Single. 'Effects paid to his Uncle, Capt. Innes 79th Reg.' [PRO: WO 25/2964].

+INNES, John W., Lt./Adjt., 42nd Foot: Lt., 42nd Foot, 2 July 1806; Adjt. 8 Dec. 1808. Killed, Orthes, 27 Jan. 1814 (1st Battn.) [*London Gazette*]. *Anton*, p. 57 ['Lieutenant Innes performed the duty of adjutant; he was an excellent officer, particularly correct in the management of regimental business and arrangement of duties. I cannot be mistaken in saying that he was a good man, for I never heard a bad one speak well of him, for he was an enemy of bad men; but the most worthless could not but allow afterwards, when he fell on the battle-field, that he left not a braver behind.'], p. 107 [Orthes, 27 Jan. 1814: 'There is a small village consisting of one street on that brow of the hill towards the north, upon which the enemy was driven back, and from this kept up a destructive fire of musquetry from garden walls, windows, and loopholes. Our regiment was ordered to drive him from that annoying post... The bearer of this order was Lieutenant Innes, who was then acting brigade-major to Sir D. Pack; he preceeded the regiment, and may be said to have led it on. The word of command to advance at the charge was received with loud animating cheers.'], pp. 108–9 ['Lieutenant Innes (our adjutant) was doing the duty of brigade-major. It was near the close of this day's contest that he carried the orders of the general for the regiment to drive the enemy from the village situated on the north brow of the hill; he might have retired after delivering the orders, without throwing a blot on his good name, but his heart was with the regiment, and he advanced to the charge in person; not with a fearful heart or a half-shut eye, to watch the distant motions, but spurring forward his steed in the blazing front of battle, led the way to victory. It was amidst the animating shouts which arose around him, that the last hostile and fatal bullet pierced his brain, and laid him in the dust. He fell amidst our foremost ranks, and breathed his last between the saddle and the ground.'].

INNES, Peter, Capt., 79th Foot: Capt., 79th Foot, 4 Sept. 1805. Slightly wounded, Toulouse, 10 April 1814 (1st Battn.) [*London Gazette*]. Waterloo. Died, Tunnach, 1822.

+IRBY, Hon. Edward Methuen, Lt. and Capt./Adjt., 3rd Foot Guards: Lt. and Capt., 3rd Foot Guards, 14 May 1804. Killed, Talavera, 18 July

1809, while serving as Adjt. [*London Gazette*]. Obituary, *The Gentleman's Magazine*, Aug. 1809, p. 780 ['The Hon. Edward Methuen Irby, aged 22, likewise slain in the [battle of Talavera], was the sixth son of Lord Boston, and an ensign in the 3d Regiment of Guards. In him his afflicted parents have lost a most aimiable and affectionate son, and the service a most zealous and promising officer, deservedly lamented by all who knew him.'].

+IRELAND, Edmund Kelly, Lt., 24th Foot: Lt., 24th Foot, 20 June 1809. Killed, Fuentes de Onoro, 3 May 1811 (2nd Battn.) [*London Gazette*]. Mentioned in an obituary for his brother(s), *The Gentleman's Magazine*, Feb. 1813, p. 182 ['Lately... In Spain, on the retreat of the army, of fatigue, Lieut. De Courcy Ireland, and Ensign W. Ireland, 87th reg. brother to Lieut. E. I. 24th reg. who fell before Fuente D'Onore, sons of R. Ireland, esq. of the county of Mayo, and nephews of the Hon. Sir Edmund Stanley.'].

IRELAND, Samuel, Ensign, 27th Foot: Ensign, 27th Foot, 25 Aug. 1813. Severely wounded, Nivelle, 10 Nov. 1813 (3rd Battn.) [*London Gazette*]. Killed, Waterloo.

IRONSIDE, George Edward, Lt., 74th Foot: Lt., 74th Foot, 31 Jan. 1811. Slightly wounded, storming of Badajoz, 6 April 1812 [*London Gazette*]. Slightly wounded, Orthes, 27 Feb. 1814 [*London Gazette*].

+IRWIN, Edward, Lt., 7th Foot: Lt., 7th Foot, 1 Dec. 1808. Severely wounded, Albuera, 16 May 1811 (2nd Battn.) [*London Gazette*]. Died of wounds, 27 May 1811. Return dated 25 June 1811. [PRO: WO 25/2965]. *Register of officers' effects*: Single. Effects totalled £23.2s.10½d. [PRO: WO 25/2963].

+IRWIN, Henry Bury, Lt./Capt., 68th Foot: Lt., 68th Foot, 23 June 1804. Severely wounded, Pyrenees, 30 July 1813 ('Captain Irvin') [*London Gazette*]. Killed, Nivelle, 10 Nov. 1813 [*London Gazette*].

IRWIN, William, Ensign/Lt., 28th Foot: *1829 Statement of Service*: Born 14 May 1784, Ballinihil, County of Sligo. Aged twenty-three on his first entrance into the Army. Ensign, 28th Foot, Nov. 1807; Lt. 20 July 1809; Capt. May 1816. *Battles, sieges and campaigns*: 'Passage of the Douro May 1809... Battle of Talavera July 1809... Did duty with Battn. Detachments, Busaco 27th Septr. 1810, Lieutenant Commg. a Company. Campa Mayor 25th March 1811. Albuhera, May 1811, Lieutenant commanding a Comp. with the 2nd Battn. 28th Regt... Aroya des Molinos 28th Octr. 1811. Almarez 1812. Vittoria 21st June 1813. Nivelle 10th Novr. 1813. Nieve from 9th to 13th Decr. 1813. Orthes 27th Feby. 1814. Toulouse 10th April 1814. Waterloo from 16th to 18th June 1815. Commanding a Company on the above occasions.' *Distinguished conduct*: 'At Aroya des Molinos, made 8 Prisoners, in consequence of having succeeded in knocking 2 of them down with stones. At Toulouse the Regiment was ordered by Lord Hill to carry a mill occupied by the Enemy the possession of which would expose the left of those opposed to Sir Thos. Picton's Division on the opposite bank of the Garonne but notwithstanding the determined manner in which the attack was made (would have failed as the men were falling fast) had I not thrown myself with great force against a *wall* which yielded to the exertion, leaving a breach through which the men entered, and ultimately enabling them to expel the Enemy at the point of the bayonet, from the mills after the Officer commg. the Party surrendered himself. This was a high dry brick wall, and looped, erected purposely, as an advanced work to the mill.' *Wounds* *received in action*: 'Slightly 28th July 1809, Talavera. Severely 21st June 1813, Vittoria. One year's Pay as Captain. Slightly 10th April 1814, Thoulouse. Severely 16th June 1815, Waterloo. One year's pay as Captain.' *Titles, honorary distinctions and medals*: 'A medal for Waterloo.' *Service abroad*: 'May 1808 to May 1810, at Gottenburg and in the Peninsula. May 1815 to December 1815, Netherlands & France. Decr. 1817 to June 1827, Ionian Islands. Decr. 1828 to Decr. 1829, Ionian Islands.' *Family*: Married Susan Blackman, 29 May 1816, Sligo. They had no children by 1830. [PRO: WO 25/790 f176].

Severely wounded, Vittoria, 21 June 1813 ('Irving') (1st Battn.) [*London Gazette*]. Waterloo.

+IRWINE, Christopher Thomas, Capt., 88th Foot: Capt., 88th Foot, 15 May 1806. Killed, Fuentes de Onoro, 5 May 1811 ('Irwin') (1st Battn.) [*London Gazette*].

ISSENDORFF, William von, Lt., 2nd Light Dragoons K.G.L.: Lt., 2nd Light Dragoons K.G.L., 10 May 1806. Slightly wounded 'in Action with the Enemy near La Nava', 29 Dec. 1811 [*London Gazette*]. Served in Peninsula 1811–13. *Beamish*, vol. II, p. 553.

J

JACKSON, Edward, Capt., 20th Foot: Capt., 20th Foot, 20 Aug. 1807. Severely wounded, Pyrenees, 28 July 1813 [*London Gazette*].

JACKSON, James, Ensign, 57th Foot: *1829 Statement of Service*: 'Born Newtownards, Co. Down, 11th March 1791. Aged 18 years on his first Entrance into the Army. Ensign, 57th Foot, 2nd March 1809. Lieutenant, 57th Foot, 19th June 1811. Captain, 57th Foot, 5 April 1825.' Note added: 'Bt. Major, 57th Foot, 28 June 1838.' *Battles, sieges and campaigns*: 'Spanish Campaign of 1810 as Ensign... Spanish Campaign of 1811 as Ensign. Battle of Albuera 16th May... Campaign in Canada as Lieutenant 1814, Army Commanded by Lieut General Sir George Provost.' *Wounds received in action*: '16th May 1811 Battle of Albuera through the left breast and in the Right and Left Arms. Received One years Pay.' *Service abroad*: 'Decr 1809 to Decr 1811, Spain & Portugal. Jany. 1814 to Novr. 1818, Spain, France & the Canadas. Nov. 1827 to 31 Decr. 1829, N. S. Wales.' Note added: '1 Jan 1830 to 14 May 1831, N. S. Wales. 13 May 1831 to 29 April 1833, India. 29 Aug. 1839 to 25 June 1841, India.' [PRO: WO 25/796 f80]. Slightly wounded, Albuera, 16 May 1811 [*London Gazette*]. *Haythornthwaite, Die Hard*, p. 152 [Albuera: 'The very Colours were riddled, the Regimental Colour receiving 21 bullet-holes and the King's Colour seventeen and a broken staff; Ensign James Jackson, who carried the latter, was wounded in three places and handed it to Ensign James Veitch; when Jackson returned from having his wounds dressed he found that Veitch, though himself wounded, refused to give up the precious burden.'].

JACKSON, James, Ensign/Adjutant, 94th Foot: Ensign, 94th Foot, 12 May 1812; Adjutant, 94th Foot, 12 May 1812. Severely wounded, Vittoria, 21 June 1813 (Adjutant) [*London Gazette*].

+JAMES, Francis, Capt., 81st Foot: Capt., 81st Foot, 3 March 1808. Severely wounded, 'not dangerously', storming of Badajoz, 6 April 1812, serving on the staff as AAG [*London Gazette*]. Died of wounds, 14 April 1812. Return dated 25 April 1812. [PRO: WO 25/2965]. Obituary, *The Gentleman's Magazine*, Aug. 1812, p. 192 ['At Badajoz, of wounds received at the assault of that place, aged 24, Captain James, 81st reg. and Assistant Adj.-gen. to Maj.-gen. Colville's brigade in Portugal. This promising young officer was the eldest son of Sir W.-J. James, bart. and nephew of Earl Camden. Although born to affluence, he chose a military profession. He had seen service in the West Indies, in Denmark, in Egypt, at the battle of Maida, and in the Peninsula; and had been successively aid-de-camp to Sir Jas. Craig, Sir John Stuart, Maj.-gen. Meade, Lieut.-gen. Cole, and the Earl of Wellington. Major-gen. Colville, in whose brigade Capt. James served, was severely wounded, and wrote, after the assault, to the Earl of Wellington, in the following terms: "When totally disqualified myself from giving superintendance, I was delighted to see the exertions of Capt. James, assistant adjutant-general, to maintain order and bring on the troops, and whatever duty I had to employ him upon." The remains of this gallant young officer were interred, by the leave of the governor of Badajoz, in the bastion, close to the breach he was one of the first to ascend'.].

+JAMES, Henry, Capt., 61st Foot:
Capt., 61st Foot, 9 April 1807.
Killed, Talavera, 28 July 1809
[*London Gazette*]. Obituary, *The Gentleman's Magazine*, Sept. 1809, p. 886 ['28 [July]. At the dreadful battle of Talavera, Capt. Henry James, of the 61st Foot, who fell gloriously among the foremost heroes of the conflict.'].

JAMESON, J. K., Lt., 27th Foot: Lt., 27th Foot, 12 Sept. 1808. Slightly wounded, Castalla, 12–13 April 1813 [*London Gazette*].

+JAMESON, John Putland, Lt., 4th Foot: Lt., 4th Foot, 28 May 1809. Killed, storming of San Sebastian, 31 Aug. 1813 (1st Battn.) [*London Gazette*].

JAUNCEY, Henry Tyge, Lt., 50th Foot: Lt., 50th Foot, 7 July 1808. Slightly wounded, Aire, 2 March 1814 (1st Battn.) [*London Gazette*].

JENKIN, James, Capt., 84th Foot: Capt., 84th Foot, 20 May 1808. Slightly wounded, the Nive, 10 Dec. 1813 (2nd Battn.) [*London Gazette*]. Bvt. Major, 84th Foot, 26 Dec. 1813. Gold Medal. MGS.

JENKINS, John, Lt., 11th Light Dragoons: *1829 Statement of Service*: Born 6 Jan. 1789, Jedbury, Devonshire. Aged eighteen on his first entrance into the Army. Cornet, 11th Light Dragoons, 31 Jan. 1807; Lt., 31 Dec. 1807; Capt. 22 Dec. 1814. *Battles, sieges and campaigns*: '21st April 1811 ... in front of Elvas. In 1812 ... on the Banks of the Aduoda ... at Torre de Sillas ... and ... at Castrizon for 8 hours. At Badajoz, upon the Douro at Salamanca, Monestero, Burgos, & Torguenad. In Flanders ... on the 16th and 17th June 1815 and at the Battle of Waterloo. At the Seige and Capture of Bhurtpore 18th Jany. 1826 under Lord Combermere, Commanded 2 Squadrons.' *Wounds received in action*: 'Wounded at Badajoz.' *Titles, honorary distinctions and medals*: 'Medal for Waterloo.' *Service abroad*: 'May 1811 to July 1814, Peninsula. April 1815 to Novr. 1818, France. 7 Feby. 1819 to 31st Decr. 1829, Bengal.' *Family*: Married Sophia Isabella Patton, 11 Nov. 1819, Cawnpore. They had four children by 1831. [PRO: WO 25/783 f274]. Died, 31 Oct. 1840.

+JENKINS, John, Capt., 95th Foot: Capt., 95th Foot, 17 Dec. 1807. Slightly wounded, Vittoria, 21 June 1813 (2nd Battn.) [*London Gazette*]. Died, Spain, 17 July 1813 [PRO: WO 25/2965].

JENKINSON, F. Edward, Capt., Coldstream Guards: Ensign, Coldstream Guards, 26 May 1803. Lt. and Capt., Coldstream Guards, 29 May 1806. Severely wounded, Talavera, 28 July 1809 [*London Gazette*].

JENKINSON, George, 2nd Capt., Royal Artillery: 2nd Capt., Royal Artillery, 1 June 1806; Bvt. Major, Royal Artillery, 21 June 1813. *Webber*, p. 143 ['Lt.']. *Kincaid, Adventures*, pp. 155–7 [Guerrena, 19 July 1812: 'Lord Wellington, with his staff, and a cloud of French and English dragoons and horse artillery intermixed, came over the hill at full cry, and all hammering at each others' heads in one confused mass... It appeared that his Lordship had gone there to reconnoitre, covered by two guns and two squadrons of cavalry, who, by some accident, were surprised, and charged by a superior body of the enemy, and sent tumbling in upon us in the manner described... General Alten, and his huge German orderly dragoon, with their swords drawn, cursed the whole time, to a very large amount; but as it was in German, I had not the full benefit of it. He had an opposition swearer in Captain Jenkinson, of the artillery, who commanded the two guns, and whose oaths were chiefly aimed at himself for his folly, as far as I could understand, in putting so much confidence in his covering party, that he had not thought it necessary to unfix the catch which horse-artillerymen, I believe, had to prevent their swords quitting the scabbards when they are not wanted, and which, on this occasion, prevented their jumping forth when they were so unexpectedly called for.'].

+JERMYN, John, Capt., 57th Foot: Capt., 57th Foot, 7 Sept. 1804. Slightly wounded, Albuera, 16 May 1811 (1st Battn.) [*London Gazette*]. Died of wounds, 23 May 1811. Return dated 25 June 1811. [PRO: WO 25/2965].

+JERMYN, Samuel Beresford, Lt., 57th Foot; Capt., 21st Portuguese Line: Lt., 57th Foot, 5 Feb. 1808. Killed, Orthes, 27 Feb. 1814, while serving as Capt., 21st Portuguese Line ('Samuel Germin') [*London Gazette*]. In Portuguese Service April 1810 to Feb. 1814. *Challis, Portuguese Army*, p. 56.

+JERVIS, Humphrey, Ensign, 84th Foot: Ensign, 84th Foot, 19 Dec. 1811. Severely wounded, the Nive, 9 Dec. 1813 ('J. Jervise') (2nd Battn.) [*London Gazette*]. Died of wounds, 11 Dec. 1813. Return dated Dec. 1813 [PRO: WO 25/2965]. Obituary, *The Gentleman's Magazine*, Supplement 1813 Part II, p. 701 ['10 Dec... At Bidart, in consequence of a severe wound in the leg (after suffering amputation) received while accompanying his regiment in a charge made upon the Enemy in the action of the 9th, under the Marquis of Wellington, near Bayonne, Ensign Humphrey Jervis, 84th reg.; a young officer of the greatest promise, admired and beloved.'].

+JERVOISE, Francis B., Capt., 44th Foot: Capt., 44th Foot, 30 March 1809. Severely wounded, storming of Badajoz, 6 April 1812 ('Jervoice') (2nd Battn.) [*London Gazette*]. Died of wounds, 25 Aug. 1812. Return dated 25 Sept. 1812 [PRO: WO 25/2965]. Obituary, *The Gentleman's Magazine*, Feb. 1813, p. 182 ['Lately... At Seville, of their wounds... Capt. Jervoise.'].

JERVOISE, Isaac, Capt., 9th Foot: Capt., 9th Foot, 29 June 1809. Slightly wounded, at the Siege of St Sebastian, 7–27 July 1813 (1st Battn.) [*London Gazette*]. Slightly wounded, Crossing of the Bidassoa, 7/9 Oct. 1813 (1st Battn.) [*London Gazette*].

JESSEMAN, Alexander, Ensign, 24th Foot: Ensign, 24th Foot, 17 Aug. 1808. Severely wounded, Talavera, 28 July 1809 ('Jessamin') [*London Gazette*].

JOBIN, Marius T. H., Lt., 2nd Light Battn. K.G.L.: Ensign, 2nd Light Battn. K.G.L., 25 Sept. 1810; Lt., 2nd Light Battn. K.G.L., 24 Dec. 1811. Served in Peninsula 1811–14. Waterloo. *Beamish*, vol. II, p. 568 ['slightly wounded, 27th Feb. 1814, before Bayonne; slightly wounded, 18th June 1815, at Waterloo... [Died] at Surinam in 1825.'].

JOHNSON, Arthur, Ensign, 24th Foot: Ensign, 24th Foot, 18 Aug. 1808. Severely wounded, Talavera, 28 July 1809 [*London Gazette*].

JOHNSON, Arthur England, Lt., 5th Foot: Lt., 5th Foot, 31 Aug. 1809. Severely wounded, Vittoria, 21 June 1813 [*London Gazette*].

JOHNSON, David England, Lt./ Adjutant, 5th Foot: *1829 Statement of Service*: Born Jan. 1788, Bettyville, Limerick. Aged sixteen on first appointment to the Army. Ensign, 5th Foot, 9 Feb. 1804; Lt., 5th Foot, 30 Dec. 1804; Adjutant, 5th Foot, 18 Aug. 1808; Capt., 5th Foot, 12 March 1812. *Battles, sieges and* *campaigns*: 'Buenoes Ayres, 6 July 1806... Roleia, 17 August 1808... Vimiera, 21 August 1808... Lugo, 6 and 7th Jany 1809... Corunna, 16 January 1809... Busaco, 27 Sept. 1809... Sabugal, 3 April 1810... Fuentes d'Onor, 3 May 1810... El Bodon, 25 Sept. 1810... Ciudad Rodrigo, 19 Jany 1812... Badajoz, 6 April 1812... Salamanca, 22 July 1812.' *Wounds received in action*: 'At Sabugal, Slightly, 3 April 1810 in action with French under Massena. Storming Ciudad Rodrigo, Severely, 19th January 1812 – Compensation, one year's pay.' *Service abroad*: 'Sept. 1804 to March 1805, Holland; Novr. 1806 to Decr. 1807, Buenoes Ayres; June 1808 to Jany 1809, Peninsula; June 1809 to Decr. 1812, Peninsula; Decr. 1819 to Decr. 1822, West Indies, Novr. 1823 to Oct. 1824, West Indies.' *Family*: Married Sarah Ellis Bates, 10 May 1823, Lambeth, Surrey. Wife still living on 25 Sept. 1830. At that date they had three children. [PRO: WO 25/785 f415]. Slightly wounded, storming of Ciudad Rodrigo, 19 Jan. 1812 ('Johnston') [*London Gazette*]. MGS.

JOHNSON, Edward, Assistant Surgeon, 28th Foot: Assistant Surgeon, 28th Foot, 19 Nov. 1807. Pension of one hundred pounds per annum, commencing 29 Jan. 1812, 'for wounds' received in Spain, 1811 [*1818 Pension Return*, pp. 8–9]. MGS.

JOHNSON, Henry Cavendish, 1st Lt., 23rd Foot: *1829 Statement of Service for Retired Officers*: Aged twenty-three on first appointment to the Army. 2nd Lt., 23rd Foot, 6 July 1805, 'from the Shropshire Militia'; 1st Lt., 23rd Foot, 26 May 1806; Capt., 23rd Foot, 14 May 1812; Half-pay, 7th Dragoons, 'from ill health from Wounds received in the service'. Served fifteen years on full-pay. 'I will be most happy to serve... I have recovered my Health, and find Half pay a very poor support for such a family.' *Where serving*

when wounded: 'Five severe gun shot wounds at Badajos, and one at Waterloo.' *Family*: Married in King's County, Ireland, 19 March 1802. Six children by 1829. *Where generally resident during last five years*: 'Queen's County, Ireland.' [PRO: WO 25/763 f163]. Severely wounded, storming of Badajoz, 6 April 1812 ('Johnstone') [*London Gazette*]. Waterloo. MGS. *Dalton*, pp. 128, 130 ['At the siege of Badajoz, Johnson fell from the breach pierced with gunshot wounds, which prevented his doing any regimental duty until 1815, when he served at Waterloo and was again wounded. D. in Ireland, 19th Feb., 1853, aged 78.'].

+JOHNSON, Henry, Lt., 88th Foot: Lt., 88th Foot, 25 July 1806. Killed, Busaco, 27 Sept. 1810 (1st Battn.) [*London Gazette*].

+JOHNSON, Hugh, Lt., 74th Foot: Ensign, 74th Foot, 25 May 1809; Lt. 29 Dec. 1810. Killed, Fuentes de Onoro, 3 May 1811 [*London Gazette*]. Died of wounds, 8 May 1811. Return dated 25 May 1811. [PRO: WO 25/2965].

+JOHNSON, James, Capt., 28th Foot: Capt., 28th Foot, 2 July 1807. Killed, storming of Badajoz, 6 April 1812, while serving on the Staff as ADC to Major-General Bowes ('Johnstone') [*London Gazette*]. Mentioned in the obituary for Major-General Foord Bowes, *The Gentleman's Magazine*, Oct. 1812, p. 403 ['At the storming of Badajoz he ... had his aide-de-camp, Capt. Johnson, killed by his side.']. *Blakeney*, pp. 2, 266 [Badajoz, 6 April 1812: 'General Bowes ... being severely wounded, and his aide-de-camp, my old comrade and brother officer Captain Johnson, 28th Regiment, being killed, as I had no duty to perform (my regiment not being present), I attended the general as he was borne to his tent. He enquired anxiously about poor

Johnson, his relative, not being aware that this gallant officer received his death-shot while he was being carried to the rear in consequence of a wound which he had received when cheering on a column to one of the breaches.'].

JOHNSON, James, Ensign, 48th Foot: Ensign, 48th Foot, 13 June 1811. Slightly wounded, storming of Badajoz, 6 April 1812 [*London Gazette*]. Lt., 48th Foot, 6 Jan. 1814.

JOHNSON, James, Lt., 50th Foot: Lt., 50th Foot, 30 Aug. 1810. Slightly wounded, storming of Badajoz, 6 April 1812, while serving as ADC to Major-General Walker [*London Gazette*].

JOHNSON, Ralph, Lt., 87th Foot: Lt., 87th Foot, 18 Nov. 1807. Severely wounded, Talavera, 27 July 1809 [*London Gazette*]. MGS.

JOHNSON, Richard, Lt., 7th Foot: Lt., 7th Foot, 28 July 1808. Slightly wounded, Salamanca, 22 July 1812 [*London Gazette*].

JOHNSON, Samuel, Ensign, 48th Foot: *1829 Statement of Service for Retired Officers*: Aged thirty-six on first appointment to the Army. Ensign, 48th Foot, 13 June 1811; Lt., 48th Foot, 6 Jan. 1814; Half-pay, 24 Oct. 1814, by reduction. 'Unfit for service through Wounds.' 'Joined the 48th Regt. in the year 1794 & Removed in the said Regiment till Reduced the 24 October 1814.' *Where serving when wounded*: 'Storming of Badajoz'. *Details of pension*: Fifty pounds per annum, commencing 3 April 1813. *Family*: Married in Sheffield, Yorkshire, 18 Dec. 1797. No children in 1829 ('none living'). *Where generally resident during last five years*: 'City of Coventry.' [PRO: WO 25/763 98]. *1818 Pension Return*, pp. 12–13.

JOHNSON, William McKenzie, Ensign/Lt., 47th Foot: Ensign, 47th

Foot, 7 Sept. 1809. Severely wounded, storming of San Sebastian, 31 Aug. 1813 ('Lieutenant') (2nd Battn.) [*London Gazette*].

+JOHNSON, William Yates, Capt., 84th Foot: Capt., Army, 28 Nov. 1806. Capt., 84th Foot, 15 Aug. 1808. Killed, the Nive, 11 Dec. 1813 ('Captain Yates Johnson') (2nd Battn.) [*London Gazette*].

+JOHNSTON, Arthur, Ensign, 68th Foot: Killed, Nivelle, 10 Nov. 1813 [*London Gazette*]. Not in *Challis, Index*.

JOHNSTON, Francis, Ensign, 83rd Foot: *1829 Statement of Service*: Born near Ballybay, Monaghan, 1 Feb. 1791. Aged 'sixteen years, 348 Days' on his first Entrance into the Army. Ensign, 83rd Foot, 14 Jan. 1808. Lt., 83rd Foot, 27 March 1809. Capt., 83rd Foot, 7 April 1825. 'Sold out 7 Apl. 1834.' *Battles, sieges and campaigns*: 'Was present at the taking of Oporto in the year 1809, held the Rank of Lieut. at the time... Was present at the Battle of Talavera in the year 1809, held the Rank of Lieut. at the time... Served during the Rebellion in Ceylon in the year 1817 & 1818' *Wounds received in action*: 'Wounded in the Head at the Battle of Talavera (and taken Prisoner.) did not receive any grant of pay or pension in consequence.' *Service abroad*: '6th Apl. 1809 to 24 July 1814, Portugal, Spain & France. 16 Novr. 1817 to Mar. 1822, Ceylon.' *Family*: Married Mary Downing, 30 June 1827, Ryton, Durham. They had two children by 1830. [PRO: WO 25/801 f156]. 'Johnson' in *Army List*. Slightly wounded, Talavera, 28 July 1809 ('Johnson') (2nd Battn.) [*London Gazette*]. MGS.

JOHNSTON, George, Capt., 43rd Foot: *1829 Statement of Service*: Born in 'Chirnside, Beswickshire', January 1784. Aged twenty on first appointment to the Army. Ensign,

43rd Reg., 23 Oct. 1804; Lt., 43rd Foot, 29 May 1805; Capt., 16 Aug. 1810. *Battles, sieges and campaigns*: 'Copenhagen in 1807. Sir John Moores campaign in 1808–9. Passage of the Coa 24th July 1810. Busaco 27th Sept 1810. In the various skirmishes in Massena's Retreat from the lines of Torres Vedras. Fuentes d'Onor 5th May 1811, Ciudad Rodrigo, Jan. 1812. Badajos 6 April 1812. Salamanca 22d July 1812. New Orleans.' *Wounds received in action*: 'Wounded in the left arm at the Passage of the Coa. The Groin, trenches, Badajos.' *Service abroad*: 'July 1807 to Oct 1807, Copenhagen. Sept. 1808 to 19th Jan. 1809, Spain. June 1809 to Nov. 1812, Peninsula. 14th March 1814 to 8th July 1814, Spain & France. Oct. 1814 to April 1815, America. 18th June 1815 to Nov. 1818, France. 19th Sept. 1822 to 1st Jan. 1826, Gibraltar. 19th Feb. 1828 to 11 March 1828, Portugal. 23rd March 1828 to 31st Decr. 1829, Gibraltar.' [PRO: WO 25/793 f168]. Slightly wounded, Coa, 28 July 1809 ('Johnstone') [*London Gazette*]. Slightly wounded, siege of Badajoz, 21 March 1812 ('Johnstone') [*London Gazette*]. MGS.

JOHNSTON, James, Lt., 40th Foot; Capt., 5th Portuguese Line: *1829 Statement of Service*: Born at Simprin, Berwickshire, 5 Dec. 1788. Aged sixteen years nine months 'on his first Entrance into the Army.' Ensign, 40th Foot, 29 Aug. 1805; Lt., 40th Foot, 21 Aug. 1806; Capt., 5th Portuguese Line, 7 May 1810; Capt., 'Staff Portgse. Army', 11 Dec. 1811; Capt., 40th Foot, 24 Feb. 1814; Capt., 'attached to Portgse. Service', 1815. 'Gave up his Company in the 40th Regiment to remain attached to the Portuguese Service on British full pay, but afterwards was placed on Half Pay by order of the British Government.' Half Pay, 25 Dec. 1816. Bvt. Major, 4 Sept. 1817. Lt. Col., 24th Portuguese Regt., 1818. Half Pay, 13 April 1826. Bvt. Major, 99th Foot, 25 March 1824. Major, 99th Foot, 17 Nov. 1825. Lt. Col., 99th Foot, 11 June 1829. Note added: 'Retired 17 Oct. 1839.' *Battles, sieges and campaigns*: 'Siege and Assault of Monte Video, 40th Regiment in January and February 1809... Roliosa 17 Aug. 1808. Vimiera 2 Aug. 1808. Talavera 28 July 1809 in the 40th Regiment... 1st Siege of Badajoz May 1811. Albuhera 16th May 1811, 5 Regiment Portuguese Foot... Badajoz 6th April 1812. Salamanca 22 July 1812. Vittoria 21st June 1813. Pyrenees 26th 27th and 30th July 1813. Nivelle 10 Novr. 1813, as Aide-de-Camp to Major General Sir Manly Power Commanding 8th Portuguese Brigade 3rd Division.' *Distinguished conduct*: 'At the Battle of Vittoria where he was promoted to the effective Rank of Major in the Staff of the Portuguese Army, 3rd Division 8th Brigade of Portuguese Infantry, and his name published in General Orders 1st July 1813 by Marshal General Lord Beresford, as promoted for good conduct.' *Wounds received in action*: 'At the Assault of Monte Video 3rd Feby. 1807. At Albuhera 16th May 1811. Having no documents in this Country he cannot exactly say what pay he received – believes a years pay. He was granted a Pension of £100 per Annum since May 1811, which has been renewed twice since and is now considered as permanent.' *Titles, honorary distinctions and medals*: 'The Portuguese Campaign Cross, for 3 Campaigns, and the Battle Medal No. 3 as a Field Officer with Staff. Also the Order of the Tower and Swords decreed by the Portugues Cortes of 1820, and afterwards confirmed by His late Majesty King John 4th.' *Service abroad*: 'January 1807 to November 1807, South America. August 1808 to December 1820, Portugal, Spain and France. 23 Feby. 1826 to 15 April 1829, Mauritius.' *Family*: Married Jane Trotter, 21 May 1821,

Dunse, Berwickshire. They had six children by 1838. [PRO: WO 25/804 f233]. Wounded, Albuera, 16 May 1811, while serving as Capt., 5th Portuguese Regt. [*London Gazette*]. In Portuguese Service May 1810 to Dec. 1813. MGS. *Challis, Portuguese Army*, p. 56.

JOHNSTON, James W., 1st Lt., Royal Artillery: 1st Lt., Royal Artillery, 29 July 1804. Wounded, during 'movements of the Army' [Retreat from Burgos: Villa Muriel], 25 Oct. 1812 ('Johnstone') [*London Gazette*].

JOHNSTON, Robert, Lt., 7th Foot: Lt., 7th Foot, 13 Dec. 1810. Slightly wounded, Albuera, 16 May 1811 ('Johnstone') (1st Battn.) [*London Gazette*].

+JOHNSTON, Stephen B., Lt., 7th Foot: Lt., 7th Foot, 8 Jan. 1807. Severely wounded, 'since dead', Albuera, 16 May 1811 ('Johnstone') (1st Battn.) [*London Gazette*]. Died of wounds, 17 May 1811. Return dated 25 May 1811 ('Johnson') [PRO: WO 25/2965].

+JOHNSTON, William, Ensign, 57th Foot: Ensign, 57th Foot, 18 July 1811. Killed, the Nive, 13 Dec. 1813 ('Johnson') (1st Battn.) [*London Gazette*].

JOHNSTON, William, Lt. Col., 68th Foot: Lt. Col., Army, 25 April 1808. Lt. Col., 68th Foot, 13 July 1809. Severely wounded, Vittoria, 21 June 1813 ('Johnson') (2nd Battn.) [*London Gazette*]. Temporary pension of three hundred pounds per annum, commencing 22 June 1814, 'for wounds' received at Vittoria [*1818 Pension Return*, pp. 16–17]. *Green*, p. 24 ['Colonel William Johnson, who was an officer that loved his men, and by whom he was respected in return.'], pp. 56, 111 [Aug. 1812: 'Colonel Johnson came from Madrid, and took command... Although the colonel

was an Irishman, yet he was as good an officer as ever commanded a regiment: he was very hot in his temper, but was soon appeased: he was an officer that loved his men, and could not be happy unless they were comfortable; indeed he has often been known to shed tears when we were short of provisions, and could not obtain them for money.'], p. 163 [Vittoria: 'On the other side of the wood, there was a division of the enemy's infantry drawn up ready to receive us, and when we came within a short distance, they poured a volley upon us which did great execution, wounding Colonel Johnson in two places, and killing several of the men.'], p. 165 ['Colonel Johnson, wounded in the body and arm'].

+JOHNSTONE, Edward, Ensign, 40th Foot: Ensign, 40th Foot, 7 Nov. 1811. Severely wounded, storming of Badajoz, 6 April 1812 ('Johnson') [*London Gazette*]. Died of wounds, 11 April 1812. Return dated 25 April 1812 ('Johnson') [PRO: WO 25/2965].

JOHNSTONE, Edward, Ensign/Lt., 48th Foot: *1829 Statement of Service*: 'Born Moffat, County of Dumfries N.B. [North Britain], 17th June 1791. Aged Nineteeen on his first Entrance into the Army. Ensign, 48th Foot, 21st June 1810. Lieutenant, 48th, 4th June 1812. Half Pay, 24th Decr 1814, by Reduction. Lieutenant, 58th, April 1818. Lieutenant, 50th, 25th Decr. 1818. Captain, 50th, 7th April 1825.' Note added: 'Bt. Major, 28 June 1838. Sold out 20 July 1838.' *Battles, sieges and campaigns*: 'Albuhera... Badajoz, Salamanca, Vittoria, Pyrenees, Nivelle, Orthes, Toulouse, and Ciudad Rodrigo.' *Wounds received in action*: 'Salamanca. Pyrenees. Received for the above One years Pay as Captain.' *Service abroad*: 'August 1810 to July 1814, Peninsula. 20th January 1820 to 31st Augt. 1826, Jamaica.' Note added: '1

July 1834 to 20 July 1838, NS Wales.' *Family*: Married Anne Rae, 20 Nov. 1826, Moffat. They had four children by 1830. [PRO: WO 25/794 f346]. Severely wounded, Salamanca, 22 July 1812 ('Johnson') [*London Gazette*]. Slightly wounded, Pyrenees, 28 July 1813 ('Johnston') (1st Battn.) [*London Gazette*]. MGS.

+**JOHNSTONE, George, Lt. 88th Foot:** Lt. 29 June 1809. Severely wounded, storming of Ciudad Rodrigo, 19 Jan. 1812 ('Johnston') [*London Gazette*]. Killed, siege of Badajoz, 26 March 1812 ('Johnson') [*London Gazette*].

JOHNSTONE, Hugh, Ensign, 50th Foot: Ensign, 50th Foot, 25 June 1812. Severely wounded, the Nive, 13 Dec. 1813 (1st Battn.) [*London Gazette*].

JOHNSTONE, James, Ensign/Lt., 48th Foot: *1829 Statement of Service*: 'Born Kirk Patrick, Dumfrieshire, 19th October 1784. Aged 22 years on his first Entrance into the Army. Ensign, 4th Foot, 19th June 1806. Lieutenant, 48th Foot, 11th Feby. 1808. Captain, 4th Gn. Batt., 15th July 1813. Half Pay, 2d Gn. Batt. formerly 4th, 24th Octr. 1816, Reduction. Captain, 58th Foot, 4th June 1818. Half Pay, 6th H. I. Regt., Sepr. 1818, Exchange in Consequence of Ill Health'. 'Paymaster, 70th Foot, 17th July 1823.' *Battles, sieges and campaigns*: 'Siege of Copenhagen 1807... Aviero, May, Oporto 12th May, Talavera, Dela Ryna 27th & 28 July 1809... Busaco 27th Septr. 1810... In the Lines of Torres Vedras, Engaged in 4 different Skirmishes, 2 of them severe, during the time the army remained there... Taking of Campo Mayor, date not certain 1811... At the taking of Ilivencea in 1811... Skirmishes at Zafra St D'Martha in 1811... 1st Siege of Badajos in 1811... Albuhera 16th May 1811... Present during the Campaigns of 1812 up to the taking

of Madrid.' *Distinguished conduct*: 'On or about 5th Octr. 1810 Volunteered with the Company I commanded together with two other companies of the Regiment (the whole) under the Command of Captn. Wood to drive back the Out Posts of the Enemy on the Heights of Alahandra in front of the Lines, which we fully Effected & remained in possession of the ground gained until recalled by order of Lieut. Col. Cockburne then in Command of the 1st Brigade of the 2d Division of the Army. On the Retreat of the French Army from the Lines, I also volunteered with the company I commanded to storm the Works which the Enemy had thrown up at Villa Nova, on the Banks of the Tagus. In Command of a Company during the period of my Service on the Peninsula.' *Wounds received in action*: 'At the Battle of Talavera the 28th July 1809. Several severe and dangerous wounds at the Battle of Albuhera 16th May 1811 for which I received a Gratuity of 12 Months Pay and a permanent Pension as Lieutenant Commencing 17th May 1811.' *Service Abroad*: 'Augt. 1807 to Novr. 1807, Copenhagen. March 1809 to Octr. 1811, Spain and Portugal. Feby. 1812 to Feby. 1813, Spain & Portugal. Octr. 1813 to Septr. 1815, Bermuda. Octr. 1815 to Decr. 1815, Ostend. 24th Octr. 1823 to 11th Sepr. 1827, Upper & Lower Canada.' *Family*: Married Mary Harrison, 7 May 1818, Christ Church, Surrey. As far as children, he noted that they had 'none living' in 1830. [PRO: WO 25/798 f362]. Slightly wounded, Talavera, 28 July 1809 ('Johnson') (2nd Battn.) [*London Gazette*]. Severely wounded, Albuera, 16 May 1811 [*London Gazette*]. *1818 Pension Return*, pp. 12–13 ('Johnston').

+**JOHNSTONE, Thomas, Major, 27th Foot:** Major, Army, 3 March 1808; Major, 27th Foot, 21 Jan. 1813. Killed, Nivelle, 10 Nov. 1813 ('Major

Thomas Johnstone') [*London Gazette*]. 'Charles Mills, Major, vice Johnston, killed, 23 Dec. 13' in 'Alterations and Additions while printing', *1814 Army List*.

JOHNSTONE, William, 1st Lt., 95th Foot: Lt., Army, 6 Feb. 1806; 1st Lt., 95th Foot, 20 Nov. 1806. Severely wounded, storming of Badajoz, 6 April 1812 (1st Battn.) [*London Gazette*]. Pension of seventy pounds per annum, commencing 7 April 1813, 'for wounds' received at Badajoz [*1818 Pension Return*, pp. 22–3]. Wounded, Waterloo. *Dalton*, p. 199 ['An interesting memoir of this gallant soldier appeared in the *United Service Journal* for 1837. He was a native of Dumfriesshire, where his father had a small property of his own. In 1805 he joined the 52nd L. I. as an ensign, and in the year following was appointed to a lieutenancy in the Rifle Brigade (as the old 95th is now styled). As a lieut, he had the good fortune to command one of the four companies of the Rifles which, under Sir S. Beckwith, at the Pass of Barba del Puerco, on the 19th March 1810, so gallantly repulsed 600 chosen French troops who attempted to surprise them at mid-night. I extract the following from the above memoir :– "On the 19th Jan., 1812, he was one of the officers who volunteered and led the stormers at the taking of Ciudad Rodrigo, and was fortunate enough to come out unscathed, although one of the first to enter that deadly pass. At the storming of Badajoz on the 6th April, 1812, his name again stood on the list of volunteers for the Forlorn Hope, but as it was claimed by a senior officer of the division, he was obliged to limit his expectations to one of the posts of honour with the storming party. Sir Andrew Barnard, however, who commanded the Light Division, knowing how peculiarly well qualified he was for desperate enterprise, assigned him

a post in front of the Forlorn Hope, in the command of a party carrying ropes prepared with nooses to throw over the sword-blades which formed the chevaux-de-frise, in the hope of being able to displace it by dragging it down the breach, but Johnstone and all his party were stricken down before they got within throwing distance."... Promoted maj. 24th Dec., 1829. Quitted the service in 1831. Was Colonial Sec. at Cape of Good Hope, and d. at sea 6th April, 1836.']. *Simmons*, pp. 77, 232 [wounded, storming of Badajoz], p. 379. *Du Cane*, p. 754 ['Johnson [sic] was, in point of fact, the first man to get into Ciudad Rodrigo, though he did not get the credit. He was a very active man, and some days before the assault he marked a place, apart from the breach, where he would get in. He did so, and some men followed. Gurwood led the forlorn hope of the Light Division, and his party, who came in by the breach, found Johnson and his party already inside. But Gurwood went straight to the Commandant's house and got his sword.']. *Kincaid, Adventures*, p. 108 [Storming of Ciudad Rodrigo: 'The storming party, consisting of three officers and one hundred volunteers from each regiment, the officers from ours were Captain Mitchell, Mr Johnstone, and myself, and the whole under the command of Major Napier, of the fifty-second.']. *Kincaid, Random Shots*, pp. 280–1 [Badajoz: 'Major (then Lieutenant) Johnston [sic], of ours, who was peculiarly calculated for desperate enterprize, preceded the forlorn hope, in command of a party carrying ropes, prepared with nooses, to throw over the sword blades, as the most likely method of displacing, by dragging them down the breach; but he and his whole party were stricken down before one of them had got within throwing distance... When an officer, as I have already mentioned, with a presentiment of death upon him, resigned a safe duty to take a desperate one ... these, I say, ... will shew that there was no want of daring leaders or desperate followers.'], pp. 287–8 [Following storming of Badajoz: 'The first tent that I entered was Johnston's, with his shattered arm bandaged; he was lying on his boat-cloak fast asleep; and, coupling his appearance with the recollection of the daring duty he had been called on to perform but a few hours before, in front of the forlorn hope, I thought that I had never set my eyes on a nobler picture of a soldier. His whole appearance, even in sleep, shewed exactly as it had been in the execution of that duty; his splendid figure was so disposed that it seemed as if he was taking the first step on the breach – his eyebrows were elevated – his nostrils still distended – and altogether, he looked as if he would clutch the castle in his remaining hand. No one could have seen him at that moment without saying, "there lies a hero !" '], p. 290 ['At the close of the war, when we returned to England, if our battalion did not shew symptoms of its being a well-shot corps, it is very odd... Johnston, in addition to other shot holes, a stiff elbow, which deprived him of the power of disturbing his friends as a scratcher of Scotch reels upon the violin'].

JOLLIFFE, Charles, Capt., 23rd Foot: Capt., 23rd Foot, 18 June 1811. Severely wounded, Orthes, 27 Feb. 1814 (1st Battn.) [*London Gazette*]. Killed, Waterloo. *Dalton*, pp. 129–30 ['Youngest son of T. S. Jolliffe, of Ammerdown, co. Somerset... Served at Copenhagen, in North America, and the West Indies. Served several campaigns in the Pa. Sev. wnded at Orthes. Had not entirely recovered from his wound when the tocsin of war once more summoned him to the field of battle.'].

JONES, Alexander, Lt., 6th Foot: *1829 Statement of Service for Retired Officers*: Aged nineteen on first appointment to the Army. Ensign, 6th Foot, 13 Sept. 1804; Lt., 6th Foot, 18 Sept. 1805; Capt., 8 Dec. 1814; Half-pay, 25 Dec. 1815, by reduction. 'I might possibly be mistaken in the dates of my commissions.' *Where serving when wounded*: 'at the Battle of Orthes in France in 1814 I received a wound in my leg – for which I received twelve months pay, as lieutenant commanding a company, on my return from Canada in 1815, but never received any pension.' *Where generally resident during last five years*: 'I have been residing at Blois in France the last 6½ years without quitting it.' [PRO: WO 25/763 f151]. Severely wounded, Orthes, 27 Feb. 1814 (1st Battn.) [*London Gazette*].

JONES, Arthur, Capt., 71st Foot: *1829 Statement of Service*: Born Vellore, East Indies, 14th November 1777. Aged Seventeen on his first Entrance into the Army. Ensign, 36th Foot, 1 Jan. 1795; Lieut., 71st Foot, 5 Oct. 1795; Capt., 71st Foot, 24 March 1803; Major, 71st Foot, 23 June 1809; Bvt. Lt. Col., 71st Foot, 4 June 1814; Lt. Col., 71st Foot, 2 June 1825. *Battles, sieges and campaigns*: 'As Captain in the 71st Regt. was present at the Action of Bleuberg on 8th Jany. 1806, & at Capture of Cape Town... At the Action of Quelines 26th June & the taking of Buenas Ayres... The Battles of Roleia 17th Augt. 1808, and Vimiera 21 Augt. 1808... at the Battle of Carunna 18th January 1809... when Major was at the taking of Flushing in 1809... The Battle of Toulouse 10th April 1814 and Waterloo 18 June 1815.' *Wounds received in action*: 'Wounded 21st June 1808 at the Battle of Vimiera, received no Pay or Pension for it. Wounded in the Left Knee upon the 18th June 1815 at the Battle of Waterloo, for which received a grant of £292 being a Years Pay as Major.'

Titles, honorary distinctions and medals: 'Appointed a Companion of the Order of the Bath for the Action of Waterloo by the recommendation of Major General Sir Fred. Adam, Commandg. the Brigade; has also the Waterloo Medal.' *Service abroad*: '1st Jany. 1795 to Oct. 1797, East Indies. Augt. 1805 to Decemr. 1807, Cape of Good Hope & South America. Augt. 1808 to Jany. 1809, Peninsula. July 1809 to Decemr. 1809, Flushing. March 1814 to July 1814, France. April 1815 to October 1818, France. June 1824 to 31 Decemr. 1829, Canada.' *Family*: Married Mary, 'daughter of the late John Johnston Esq., County Tyrone, Ireland', 7 Dec. 1801, Parish of St Paul's, Dublin. They had five children by 1830. [PRO: WO 25/799 f1]. Slightly wounded, Vimiero, 21 Aug. 1808 [*London Gazette*].

JONES, Benjamin Orlando, Capt., 36th Foot; Capt., 13th Portuguese Line: *1829 Statement of Service for Retired Officers*: Aged sixteen on first appointment to the Army. Ensign, 36th Foot, 29 May 1805; Lt., 36th Foot, 30 Oct. 1806; Capt., 36th Foot, 9 Sept. 1812; Bvt. Major, 36th Foot, 4 Sept. 1817; Capt., 12th Foot, 19 Sept. 1822; Major, unattached, 6 July 1826. 'Captn. unattached whilst in the Portuguese Service from December 1816 to 17th Sept. 1822, when restored to full pay in the 12th Regt.' 'Placed upon the h.p. in consequence of arrangements having been entered into with the British Government to allow a certain number of British Officers to remain under Lord Beresford Comd. in the Portuguese Service.' *Where serving when wounded*: 'Lascano, Spain'. *Family*: Married in 1806. One child by 1829. *Title and nature of employment*: 'Major reformado, Portuguese Service ... not paid since December 1826'. *Where generally resident during last five years*: 'Gibraltar & England'. [PRO: WO 25/763 f132]. Severely wounded, in an action near Tolosa, 24 June 1813, while serving as Capt., 13th Portuguese Line [*London Gazette*]. In Portuguese Service April 1809 to April 1814. *Challis, Portuguese Army*, p. 56 ['Maj. 5 Line... Wd. Sge. Salamanca Forts June '12, Villa Franca June '13']. MGS.

JONES, Charles, Adjutant/Lt., 15th Light Dragoons: Adjutant, 15th Light Dragoons, 27 Aug. 1807; Lt. 15th Light Dragoons, 10 March 1808. Wounded, Sahagun, 21 Dec. 1808. *Porter*, p. 218 [Sahagun, 21 Dec. 1808: 'Colonel Grant and Captain Jones, of the 15th, were the only officers wounded; and very few men fell on our side']. Waterloo, as Major of Brigade under Major-General Grant. *Dalton*, p. 24.

JONES, Edward, Lt./Adjutant, 77th Foot: *1829 Statement of Service*: 'Born in the Parish of Cumytydour, County of Rodnor, 5th December 1784. Aged Twenty years on his first Entrance into the Army. Ensign, South Essex Militia, 1804. Ensign, West Kent Militia, 1805. Lieutenant, West Kent Militia, 1806. Ensign, 77th Regt., 26th Augt. 1807. Adjutant, 77th Regt., 1809 till 1815 [Army List gives 2 Feb. 1809]. Lieutenant, 77th Regt., 10th Novr. 1810. Captain, 77th Regt., 1822. Major, 77th Regt., 10th June 1826.' *Battles, sieges and campaigns*: 'At Walcheren... At the Affair of Albedon 25th September 1811. At the Storming of Ciudad rodrigo in 1812. At the Storming of Badajos on 6th April 1812, as Lieutenant and Adjutant.' *Wounds received in action*: 'Severely wounded at the Storming of Ciudad rodrigo in 1812. No grant of pay has been received.' *Service abroad*: 'June 1809 to Septr. 1809, Walcheren. 12th July 1811 to Septr. 1814, Portugal, Spain & France. 27th March 1824 to 31st Decr. 1829, Jamaica.' *Family*: Married Sarah Jones, 6 June 1804, Rhayader. They had no children by 1830 [PRO: WO 25/800 f77]. Slightly wounded, storming of Ciudad Rodrigo, 19 Jan. 1812 ('Adjutant Jones') [*London Gazette*]. Slightly wounded, storming of Badajoz, 6 April 1812 ('Adjutant Jones') [*London Gazette*]. Note: Returned as having been wounded at Badajos, though he fails to mention this in his Statement of Service.

JONES, Harry David, 1st Lt., Royal Engineers: 1st Lt., Royal Engineers, 24 June 1809. Recorded as 'Missing', 'at the Siege of St. Sebastian', 7–27 July 1813 [*London Gazette*]. Mentioned in Graham's dispatch to Wellington dated 27 July 1813, concerning the failed Assault on St Sebastian on the morning of 25 July 1813 ['The conduct throughout the whole of the operations of the siege hitherto, of the officers and men of the ... engineers, never was exceeded in indefatigable zeal, activity, and gallantry... The three officers of this corps, employed to conduct different parts of the columns of attack, behaved admirably, but suffered severely. Captain Lewis has lost his leg, Lieutenant Jones was wounded in the breach, and taken; and Lieutenant Machell, after his return, was killed in the trenches.'] [*London Gazette*]. MGS. *Mullen*, p. 655 ['Commissioned 17/9/08. At capture of Flushing. Distinguished at Vittoria. Wounded and taken prisoner at St Sebastian. 1st Lt 24/6/09, 2nd Capt 12/11/13 for distinguished service at Nivelle. Expedition against New Orleans, capture of Paris. 1st Capt 1826. Chairman of the Board of Public Works in Ireland 1845. Brig-Gen 1854 in command of land forces in the Baltic. Maj-Gen Dec 1854, Commanding Royal Engineer in the Crimea. Severely wounded during the assault on the Redan 18/6/55. KCB, 1st Class Military Order of Savoy, 2nd Class Order of the Medjidie. Governor of RMA Sandhurst May 1856. Lt-Gen 6/6/60. Died 2/8/66, buried at RMA Sandhurst.'].

+JONES, Henry Ireson, Lt., 7th Foot: Lt., 7th Foot, 29 Oct. 1807. Severely wounded, Albuera, 16 May 1811 (1st Battn.) [*London Gazette*]. Obituary, *The Gentleman's Magazine*, March 1812, p. 300 ['Lately... At Elvas, of wounds received at the battle of Albuera, aged 20, universally beloved and sincerely regretted, Lieut. Henry Ireson Jones, of the 9th Fusileers [sic]; a most promising officer, possessing the highest principles of honour and liberality.']. Died, Portugal, 7 Aug. 1811 [PRO: WO 25/2965].

JONES, John Gibson, Lt., 43rd Foot: *1829 Statement of Service for Retired Officers*: Aged sixteen on first appointment to the Army. Lt., City of Dublin Militia, 6 March 1806; Ensign, Royal West India Rangers, 26 March 1808; Lt., Royal West India Rangers, 6 Aug. 1809; Lt., 43rd Foot, 11 April 1811; Lt., 1st Garrison Battn., Nov. 1814; Half-pay, by reduction. Served eight years and six months on full-pay. 'Is now home on sick leave of absence and under medical care.' *Where serving when wounded*: 'Spain'. No pension. *Family*: Married in Kensington Square, London, 10 Nov. 1814. Five children by 1829. *Title and nature of employment*: 'Barrack Master in the West Indies, 18th of August 1824'. *Where generally resident during last five years*: 'Trinidad'. [PRO: WO 25/763 f145].

JONES, John Thomas, Capt., Royal Engineers: Capt., Army, 1 March 1805; Capt., Royal Engineers, 24 June 1809. Mentioned in Wellington's Ciudad Rodrigo dispatch, 20 Jan. 1812 ['I likewise request your Lordship's attention to the conduct of Lieutenant-Colonel Fletcher, the chief engineer, and of Brigade-Major Jones, and the officers and men of the royal engineers. The ability with which these operations were carried on exceeds all praise; and I beg leave to recommend those officers to

your Lordship most particularly.']
[*London Gazette*, 5 Feb. 1812].
Mentioned in Wellington's Badajoz
dispatch, 7 April 1812 ['I have likewise to report the good conduct of
Major Jones ... of the Royal Engineers.'] [*London Gazette*]. Bvt. Lt.
Col., Royal Engineers, 27 April 1812.
Severely wounded, during 'the
assault and capture of the exterior
line of the castle of Burgos on the
evening of the 4th October, 1812'
('Brevet Lieutenant-Colonel') [*London Gazette*].

**+JONES, John Fitzwilliam, Ensign,
45th Foot:** Ensign, 45th Foot, 15
Nov. 1810. Severely wounded,
storming of Badajoz, 6 April 1812
[*London Gazette*]. Obituary, *The
Gentleman's Magazine*, Aug. 1812,
p. 187 ['June 18. In consequence of
wounds received at the storming of
Badajoz, Lieut. John-Fitzwilliam
Jones, 45th foot.'].

**JONES, Joseph Allingham, Capt.,
39th Foot:** *1829 Statement of
Service for Retired Officers*: Aged
twenty-two on first appointment to
the Army. Ensign, 39th Foot, 4 Oct.
1804; Lt., 39th Foot, 9 Oct. 1806;
Capt., 39th Foot, 3 June 1813; Half-
pay, 1816, by reduction, 'contrary to
his wishes'. 'Unfortunately disqualified for Active Service By Wounds,
received in Action: and A Rupture,
originating from Exertions in The
Field.' *Where serving when
wounded*: 'At Puerto de Mayo, in
the Pyrenees, 25th July 1813.'
Details of pension: 'Nothing, the
undersigned not having hitherto
applied for one. But his Private
resources, having latterly, in a great
measure failed; and now having an
invalid wife and Two Children,
entirely dependant on him for their
support (not to speak of an Aged
and widowed Mother who has long
looked to him for occasional Assistance) He fears, that he must
shortly be under the painful necessity, of making a humble Appeal to
His Royal Majesty's munificence,

for the Pension, graciously granted
to Disabled Officers similarly situated.' *Family*: Married in Walcot
Church, Bath, 16 Dec. 1817. Two
children by 1829 [one born 15 Dec.
1818, the other 1 Nov. 1828, just
three weeks before he completed
this statement]. *Where generally
resident during the last five years*:
'in Bath'. [PRO: WO 25/763 f153].
Severely wounded, Pyrenees, 25
July 1813 (1st Battn.) [*London
Gazette*].

**JONES, Loftus Frances, 1st Lt.,
95th Foot:** *1829 Statement of
Service*: Born in Birmingham, 21
Aug. 1796. Aged fifteen 'on his first
Entrance into the Army.' 2nd Lt.,
95th Foot, 7 Feb. 1811; 1st Lt., 95th
Foot, 1 Oct. 1812; Half-pay, 25 Nov.
1818, 'By reduction of 3d Battn.';
Lt., 59th Foot, 26 Dec. 1822; 'Lieut.
& Adjt.', 2nd Foot, 13 March 1823;
Lt., 96th Foot, 29 Jan. 1824, 'on the
formation of the 96th Foot.' *Battles,
sieges and campaigns*: '1812. Battle
of Salamanca, San Munos, as 2nd
Lieut. 1813, San Milan, Vittoria,
Heights of Suida Badbura, Guneg
Bridge, Mountain of Echelar, Vera
Bridge, Vera Heights (Bidassoa), La
Petite La Rhune (Nivelle), as Lieu-
tenant. 1814, Orthes, Tarbes,
Tournfeuille, Toulouse, as Lieutenant. Was present with a detachment of five Companies of the Rifle
Brigade during the whole of the
operations against New Orleans
and was constantly engaged with
the Enemy particularly on the 23rd
Decr. 1814 and 1st & 8th Jan. 1815.'
Distinguished conduct: Note
written by Major General John
Ross: 'I certify that this officer
served under my command in the
Rifle Brigade in nearly all the
actions stated in the adjoining
column & that I had many occasions to remark his gallant & skilful
conduct.' Note written by Gen. A. F.
Barnard: 'I certify that I am well
acquainted with the gallant and
meritorious conduct of Lt. Jones as
an officer during the period that he

served in the Rifle Brigade.' *Wounds received in action*: 'Wounded severely at the attack on La Petite La Rhune (Nivelle) on the 10th November 1813. Received one years pay as Lieut. and a Pension of £70 a year from 25th Decr. 1821 to 24th June 1826, and from 25th Decr. 1826 it was renewed to 24th June 1832 which by the late Regulations is now Permanent.' *Service abroad*: '7th June 1812 to 19 July 1814, Peninsula. 16th Septr. 1814 to 2d June 1815, With the Expedition to New Orleans. 16th Oct. 1815 to 24 Decr. 1815, France. 17 July 1824 to 2 Decr. 1825, Nova Scotia.' *Family*: Married Louisa Beddik, 'Daughter of Richd. Beddik Esq. late Regent of the Royal Naval Hospital Plymouth'", 2 Oct. 1830, St Andrew's Church, Plymouth. They had no children prior to 1831. [PRO: WO 25/804 f27]. Severely wounded, Nivelle, 10 Nov. 1813 (3rd Battn.) [*London Gazette*]. MGS.

JONES, Richard, Lt., 50th Foot: Lt., 50th Foot, 18 May 1809. Severely wounded, Pyrenees, 25 July 1813 (1st Battn.) [*London Gazette*]. Slightly wounded, the Nive, 13 Dec. 1813 ('Lieutenant R. Jones') (1st Battn.) [*London Gazette*]. Severely wounded, 'in Action with the Enemy', 15 Feb. 1814 (1st Battn.) [*London Gazette*]. MGS.

+JONES, Thomas, Capt., 27th Foot: Capt., 27th Foot, 8 Oct. 1806. Killed, storming of Badajoz, 6 April 1812 (3rd Battn.) [*London Gazette*].

JONES, Timothy, Capt., 4th Foot: Capt., 4th Foot, 11 Aug. 1804. Severely wounded, the Nive, 10 Dec. 1813 ('Captain Timothy Jones (Major)') (1st Battn.) [*London Gazette*]. Gold Medal. Killed in action at New Orleans.

JONES, William, Ensign/Lt./Adjutant, 51st Foot: *1829 Statement of Service for Retired Officers*: Aged 'between 16 & 17 years' on first appointment to the Army. 'Entered the service in the 43d Regiment in 1799'; Ensign, 51st Foot, 21 Feb. 1811; Lt., 51st Foot, 16 April 1813; Half-pay, 60th Foot, on reduction. 'Having had the honor to serve His late Majesty at Copenhagen in 1807 and in 1808 in the Peninsula and in 1809 at Flushing again in 1811–1812–1813 and 1814 in the Peninsula and in 1815 at the battle of Waterloo and through the Campaigne to Paris. Having a rising family and England being at Peace he obtained His Late Royal Highnesses permission to retire on Half pay'. Served twenty years on full-pay. *Where serving when wounded*: 'Corunna. Vittoria'. *Family*: Married in Vale Parish, Guernsey, 2 April 1809. Nine children by 1829. *Where generally resident during last five years*: 'Guernsey'. [PRO: WO 25/763 f119]. Severely wounded, Vittoria, 21 June 1813 ('52d [sic] Foot, 1st Batt.') ('Adjutant Jones') [*London Gazette*]. Waterloo. Half-pay, 60th Rifles, 25 Feb. 1819. *Wheeler*, p. 135 [Vittoria: 'Wounded, Lieut. and Adjt. Jones (severely)']. Note: the published *London Gazette* casualty returns confuses his regiment.

+JONES, William ('Jack'), Capt., 52nd Foot: Capt., 52nd Foot, 15 Aug. 1804. Severely wounded, during 'several Affairs with the French Army', 14 March 1811 [*London Gazette*]. Killed, storming of Badajoz, 6 April 1812 [*London Gazette*]. *Rice Jones*, p. 84 ['Dec. 16 [1810]... Returned to dinner (Xmas Day) and just sitting down to it with the Brigade Major, when the Col. came from Lord Wellington's where he was to dine, to desire the bridge in the Causeway leading to Santarem to be mined immediately... Procured a few men from the inlying picket commanded by Capt. Jones of the 52nd Regt. Began about midnight; although close to the abattis that separated our sentries from the French, and the noise reverberated on the arch, the enemy gave us little interruption. Brig.-Major Jones relieved me at 4 o'clock, and completed the mine soon after light.']. *Moorsom*, p. 124 [Busaco, 27 Sept. 1810: 'When the head of Simon's column appeared in the act of deploying, and the 52nd advanced to charge, Captain John Jones, more commonly known in the division by the name of "Jack Jones," a fiery Welshman, rushed upon the Chef de Bataillon, who was in the act of giving the word to his men, and killed him on the spot with a blow of his sword. Jones immediately cut off the medal with which the major was decorated, and appropriated it to himself.'], p. 159 [Storming of Ciudad Rodrigo: 'Captain William Jones ("Jack Jones" of Busaco celebrity) made himself remarkable immediately after the assault of Ciudad Rodrigo. A French officer having surrendered to Jones, Jack made use of him ... to show quarters for his men, – and having placed some of them in a large store, the French officer led the way into the church, in front of which Lord Wellington and some staff were collected. Some fire had been lighted already (supposed by Portuguese soldiers) on the pavement, and the Frenchman entering, and seeing the fire, instantly started back, exclaiming, "Sacré bleu!" and ran out with looks of the utmost horror. Jones, not understanding French, did not catch the idea: "Sacré bleu" puzzled him, until going further in, he saw powder about the floor and powder-barrels near the fire. "Sacré bleu" became at once identified with *powder*, and he immediately got the help of two or three of his men (whose names are not known), and carried with his own hands the powder-barrels out of the way of immediate danger. This deed passed unrequited at the time: let the memory of it now receive our admiration!'], p. 168 [Killed, Badajoz], p. 421 ['Served with the 52nd in the Peninsula, and was

distinguished at Busaco and at Ciudad Rodrigo, and fell gallantly in the breach at Badajoz in 1812.'].

JOYCE, John, Lt., 60th Foot: Lt., 60th Foot, 5 Oct. 1809. Severely wounded, Busaco, 27 Sept. 1810 ('Joice') (5th Battn.) [*London Gazette*]. Slightly wounded, Vittoria, 21 June 1813 (5th Battn.) [*London Gazette*]. Inaccurately recorded as killed, Pyrenees, 25 July 1813 (5th Battn.) [*London Gazette*]. One hundred pounds per annum pension, commencing 26 July 1814, for wounds received in the Pyrenees, 1813 [*1818 Pension Return*, pp. 14–15].

JULIANI, John, Ensign, Chasseurs Britanniques: *1829 Statement of Service for Retired Officers*: Aged eighteen on first appointment to the Army. 'The 5th December 1805, begin my service in the Chasseurs Britanniques regiment as a soldier'; Ensign, Chasseurs Britanniques, 12 Aug. 1812, 'from Serjeant'; Lt., Chasseurs Britanniques, Feb. 1814; Half-pay, 25 Dec. 1814, 'when the Chasseurs Britanniques was disbanded'; Lt., Roll's Regiment, 2 Nov. 1815; Half-pay, 25 July 1816, 'when the Roll's Regiment was disbanded'. *Where serving when wounded*: 'Wounded twice in the Chasrs. Britanniques Regt. the 5th May 1811 at Fuentes d'Honore in Portugal as Serjeant, and also was wounded another time at Orthez in France as a Lieutenant the 27 February 1814, having received after a Medical Board for such wounds a year full-pay in England.' *Family*: Married in Palermo, Sicily, 10 Aug. 1818. One child by 1829. *Where generally resident during last five years*: 'At Naples'. [PRO: WO 25/763 f197]. Severely wounded, Orthes, 27 Feb. 1814 ('Ensign John Geulanis') [*London Gazette*].

JULL, William, Ensign, 50th Foot: *1829 Statement of Service*: Born in Newnham, near Feversham, Kent,

13 June 1795. Aged seventeen on first appointment to the Army. Volunteer, 94th Foot, March 1813; Ensign, 50th Foot, 22 Oct. 1813; Lt., 50th Foot, 11 Aug. 1814; Half-pay, 24 Oct. 1814, by reduction; Lt., 50th Foot, May 1815; Half-pay, 24 Oct. 1817, by reduction; Lt., 64th Foot, Jan. 1819; Adjutant, 64th Foot, Oct., 1822; Capt., 64th Foot, 23 Sept. 1823. *Battles, sieges and campaigns*: 'Battles of Vittoria 21st June 1813, Pyrenees 25th July to 1st August 1813, Nivelle 10 November 1813 as Volunteer in 94 Regiment... Battle of Nive 9th Decr. 1813. Bayonne 13th Decr 1813. Orthez 28th Feby. 1814. Aize 2nd March 1814. Tarbes 20th March 1814. Toulouse 10th April 1814, as Ensign 50th Regiment.'

Wounds received in action: 'Severely wounded at Toulouse on 10th April 1814, received a Gratuity of One Years Pay.' *Service abroad*: 'Octr. 1813 to June 1814, Portugal, Spain and France. Augt. 1819 to March 1820, Gibraltar. March 1821 to Jany. 1825, Gibraltar.' *Family*: Married Clara Skyring, 'Daughter of Major Skyring, Royal Artillery,' 16th April 1823, in Gibraltar. They had two children by 1830. [PRO: WO 25/797 f250]. Severely wounded, Toulouse, 10 April 1814 (1st Battn.) [*London Gazette*].

JUXON, William, Lt., 3rd Foot: Lt., 3rd Foot, 14 Nov. 1805. Slightly wounded, Albuera, 16 May 1811 [*London Gazette*].

K

KEARNEY, Edward, Ensign, 29th Foot: Ensign, 29th Foot, 25 Oct. 1810. Severely wounded, Albuera, 16 May 1811 [*London Gazette*]. Lt., 29th Foot, 6 Aug. 1812. Pension of fifty pounds per annum, commencing 17 May 1812, 'for wounds' received at Albuera [*1818 Pension Return*, pp. 8–9].

+KEARNS, Donald John, Ensign, 71st Foot: Ensign, Army, 14 Sept. 1809; Ensign, 71st Foot, 14 Oct. 1809. Wounded, 'dangerously', Fuentes de Onoro, Evening 3 May 1811 ('Kearne') (1st Battn.) [*London Gazette*]. Died of wounds, 9 May 1811. Return dated 25 May 1811. [PRO: WO 25/2965]. *Register of officers' effects*: 'Kearn'. Died of wounds, 8 May 1811. Single. Effects sold for £16. 15/8. [PRO: WO 25/2964].

KEATING, George, Cornet, 16th Light Dragoons: Cornet, 16th Light Dragoons, 10 Nov. 1808. Slightly wounded during the advance of the French Army towards the position of Busaco, 25–26 Sept. 1810 [*London Gazette*].

KEDDLE, Robert, Lt., 50th Foot: Lt., 50th Foot, 7 Jan. 1808. Severely wounded, the Nive, 13 Dec. 1813 (1st Battn.) [*London Gazette*].

KEEP, William Thornton, Lt., 28th Foot: *1829 Statement of Service for Retired Officers*: Aged seventeen on first appointment to the Army. Ensign, 77 Foot, 21 April 1808; Ensign, 28th Foot, 29 Aug. 1811; Lt., 28th Foot, 8 Sept. 1813; Half-pay, 1814, by reduction. *Where serving when wounded*: 'Bayonne, in Command of a company of the 28th Regt.' *Details of Pension*: Seventy pounds per annum, commencing 13 Dec. 1813, 'renewed in July 1826 by letter from the War Office.' *Where*

generally resident during last five years: 'England during the whole period.' [PRO: WO 25/764 f66]. Severely wounded, the Nive, 13 Dec. 1813 ('W. Kepp') (1st Battn.) [*London Gazette*]. MGS. His letters are to be published as *In the Service of the King*, ed. Ian Fletcher.

KELLETT, Alexander, Lt., 1st Foot: Lt., 1st Foot, 21 July 1808. Severely wounded, Salamanca, 22 July 1812 [*London Gazette*].

+KELLETT, Christopher, Ensign/Lt., 61st Foot: Ensign, 61st Foot, 18 July 1811. Killed, Nivelle, 10 Nov. 1813 (Lieutenant) (1st Battn.) [*London Gazette*].

KELLY, Edward, Capt., 51st Foot: *1829 Statement of Service for Retired Officers*: Aged twenty-one on first appointment to the Army. Ensign, 22nd Foot, 1800; Lt., 22nd Foot, 1802; Capt., 51st Foot, 1808 [Army List gives: Capt., Army, 11 Feb. 1808. Capt., 51st Foot, 21 April 1808]; Half-pay, 'by a severe wound, the thigh bone being broken.' Served sixteen years on full pay. *Where serving when wounded*: 'St Sebastian, 31st August 1813.' *Details of pension*: One hundred pounds per annum, commencing 2 Sept. 1814. *Family*: Married in Cornwall, 19 Jan. 1819. One child by 1829. *Where generally resident during last five years*: 'Lamerton, Devon.' [PRO: WO 25/764 f85]. Severely wounded, 'in the Operations of the Army', 31 Aug. 1813 [*London Gazette*]. Wheeler, p. 144 [Severely wounded, near Lezaca, 31 Aug. 1813]. *1818 Pension Return*, pp. 14–15.

KELLY, John, Lt., 87th Foot: *1829 Statement of Service for Retired Officers*: Aged nineteen on first appointment to the Army. Ensign, 87th Foot, Dec. 1807, 'obtained by bringing volunteers from the militia'; Lt., April 1811 [Army List gives 10 April]; Half-pay, 87th Foot, 'Ill Health in consiguence of Wounds without the difference.' Served nine years on full-pay. *Where serving when wounded*: 'South of France under His Grace the Duke of Wellington.' *Details of pension*: Seventy pounds, commencing 'in the year 1814'. *Family*: Married in Dublin, April 1824. One child by 1829. *Where generally resident during last five years*: 'Ireland'. [PRO: WO 25/764 f52]. Severely wounded, Nivelle, 10 Nov. 1813 (2nd Battn.) [*London Gazette*]. Pension of seventy pounds per annum, commencing 11 Nov. 1814, for 'loss of a leg' at St Pe, 1813 [*1818 Pension Return*, pp. 20–1].

KELLY, Richard, Capt., 66th Foot: Capt., 66th Foot, 6 March 1806. Slightly wounded, Talavera, 28 July 1809 (2nd Battn.) [*London Gazette*].

+KELLY, Robert, Major, 47th Foot: Major, Army, 25 July 1810; Major, 47th Foot, 13 June 1811. Killed, storming of San Sebastian, 31 Aug. 1813 (2nd Battn.) [*London Gazette*].

KELLY, Robert, Lt./Capt., 60th Foot: Lt., 60th Foot, 17 Oct. 1800. Capt., 60th Foot, 16 Aug. 1810. Severely wounded, 'in Action with the Enemy', 19 March 1814 (5th Battn.) [*London Gazette*]. Temporary pension of one hundred pounds per annum, commencing 20 March 1815, 'for wounds' received at Tarbes, 1814 [*1818 Pension Return*, pp. 16–17]. Lt. Col., unattached list, half-pay, 15 Jan. 1829. Fort Major, Dartmouth. MGS. *Simmons*, pp. 351–2.

KELLY, William, Lt. Col., 24th Foot: Lt. Col., Army, 1 Jan. 1805. Lt. Col., 24th Foot, 22 Feb. 1810. Mentioned in Wellington's Fuentes de Onoro dispatch, 8 May 1811 ['I particularly request your Lordship's attention to the conduct of ... Lieutenant-Colonel Kelly, of the 24th regiment'] [*London Gazette*, 26 May 1811]. Col., Army, 4 June 1813. Severely wounded, Pyrenees, 2 Aug. 1813 (2nd Battn.) [*London Gazette*]. Gold Medal.

KELLY, W., Lt., 40th Regt: Lt., 40th Foot, 13 Aug. 1807. Wounded during the repulse of a sortie from Badajoz, 10 May 1811 [*London Gazette*]. Slightly wounded, Salamanca, 18 July 1812 [*London Gazette*]. Slightly wounded, Pyrenees, 26 July 1813 (1st Battn.) [*London Gazette*]. *Lawrence*, p. 139 ['I had been fortunate enough to get [a sheep] and bring it into camp, and was proceeding to kill it by putting my bayonet through the neck, when Lieutenant Kelly of our company happening to pass, "Hullo, Lawrence," he said, "you seem a capital butcher." I said, "Would you like a piece of it?" "I certainly should very much," he answered, "for I am devilish hungry;" so I took out my knife and cut off one of the quarters just as it was, without even skinning it, and gave it to him, saying, "There, sir, you must skin it yourself." He thanked me, and said, "Never mind the skin, I will manage that." '].

KEMPT, James, Major-General; Lt. Col., 81st Foot, 23 July 1803; Col., 81st Foot, 9 March 1809; Major-General 1 Jan. 1812. Slightly wounded, storming of Badajoz, 6 April 1812 [*London Gazette*]. Slightly wounded, Nivelle, 10 Nov. 1810 [*London Gazette*]. Wounded, Waterloo. *Dalton*, p. 18 ['Bn. in Edinburgh about 1764 ... Entd. army 1783. A.D.C. to Abercrombie in Holland ... Served under Lord Hutchinson in Egypt ... Commanded a Brigade in the 3rd Division in the Pa ... Died in London 20th Dec. 1854']

KENDALL, William, Lt., 47th Foot: Lt., 47th Foot, 12 April 1810. Slightly wounded, storming of San Sebastian, 31 Aug. 1813 (2nd Battn.) [*London Gazette*]. Slightly wounded, sortie from Bayonne, 14 April 1814 (2nd Battn.) [*London Gazette*].

KENNEDY, Ewen, Ensign, 92nd Foot: Ensign, 92nd Foot, 26 Nov. 1812. Slightly wounded, Pyrenees, 25 July 1813 (1st Battn.) [*London Gazette*].

KENNELLY, James, Ensign/Lt., 87th Foot: *1829 Statement of Service:* Born in 'Ballendenesk, Coy. Cork', 25 Dec. 1793. Aged sixteen on 'his first Entrance into the Army.' Ensign, 103rd Foot, 11 Jan. 1809. Ensign, 87th Foot, 19 March 1812, 'at the recommendation of Genl. Sir Jas. Doyle Bart.' Lt., 87th Foot, 15 Nov. 1813. Capt., 87th Foot, 12 April 1826. *Battles, sieges and campaigns*: 'Vittoria 21st June 1813. Present at the investment & throwing up of the works before Pampoluna June & July 1813. Pyrenees 27, 28, & 29 of July 1813. Zagree Murdy 31st Augt. 1813. Nivelle 10th Novr. 1813: as Ensign. Toulouse 10 April 1814 as Lieutenant... At the Siege of Hatrus in Bengal in Feb. 1817... The Campaign in India in 1817 & 1818... The Campaign in Burmese Country in 1825 & 1826.' *Wounds received in action*: 'At Nivelle 10th Decr. 1813. Received One Years full pay as Ensign.' *Service abroad*: 'July 1812 to July 1814, Peninsula. Decr. 1815 to May 1822, Bengal. Decr. 1823 to June 1827, Bengal & Ava.' [PRO: WO 25/802 f88]. Severely wounded, Nivelle, 10 Nov. 1813 (2nd Battn.) [*London Gazette*].

+KENNION, George, Volunteer, 27th Foot: Killed, storming of San Sebastian, 31 Aug. 1813 (3rd Battn.) [*London Gazette*].

KENNY, Charles, Lt., 52nd Foot: Lt., 52nd Foot, 13 Sept. 1810.

Slightly wounded, Nivelle, 10 Nov. 1813 (1st Battn.) [*London Gazette*]. Waterloo. MGS.

+KENNY, Courtney Crowe, Capt., 9th Foot: Capt., 9th Foot, 28 Aug. 1804. 'Dangerously' wounded, siege of Burgos, 20–26 Sept. 1812, while serving as Acting Engineer [*London Gazette*]. Died of wounds, 30 Sept. 1812. Return dated 25 Oct. 1812. [PRO: WO 25/2965]. His daughter later married Edward Kenny, who had served as a Volunteer and Ensign with the 9th Foot in the Peninsular. See *Statement of Service* of Edward Kenny [PRO: 25/802 f254].

KENNY, Edward, Ensign, 9th Foot: *1829 Statement of Service*: Born in Johnstown, County Kilkenny, Ireland, 13 Dec. 1793. Aged 'Nineteen years, six months' on his 'first Entrance into the Army.' Ensign, 9th Foot, 17 June 1813. Ensign, 89th Foot, 3 March 1814. Lt., 89th Foot, 1 Nov. 1819. Adjutant, 89th Foot, June 1823. 'Resigned the Adjutancy 10th June 1830 having been obliged to return from India a second time on medical certificate in consequence of severe constitutional injury contracted during the Burmese War in 1824 & 1825.' *Battles, sieges and campaigns*: 'Served in the Peninsula ... in the campaigns of 1813 and 1814. Was present in Action on 17 June 1813, as a volunteer attached to the 9th at Osma in Spain. Received an Ensigncy with that date. In Action at Vittoria 21st June 1813. At the Siege of St Sebastian till its Capture. At the passage of the river Bidassoa into France, 7th October 1813. St Jean de Luz, and the series of actions which took place between the 9th & 13th December 1813 in front of the intrenched camp near Bayone, prior to the Citadel being closely invested. Served with the Army in Ava... 1824–1825. as Adjutant of the 89th Regt. was present in action 9 & 10

KENNY

June 1824. At Kymenderee, at seven stockades 8th July. At the storming of Mergui on the Tenassorim Coast, and the other operations of the seperate Force ... from August to November 1824, In action on the 7th December & 9th Decr. at Dalla, 1824. Tantabein 5th February 1825. Panlang 19th February, and Yangonchinya 1st March 1825. Donabien 4 & 7th March to 1 April 1825, including the several attacks made by the Enemy on the Flotilla from 17th to 24th March inclusive.' *Distinguished conduct*: 'Not particularized in General Orders.' *Wounds received in action*: 'Wounded severely above left hip in October 1813 after passing the river Bidasoa into the French Territory. Applied for a years pay some years subsequently but owing to the absence of a document did not receive it.' *Service abroad*: '17th June 1813 to April 1814, Peninsula and on passage home. July 1814 to September 1815, Canada & on passage. 10th November 1815 to 8 July 1826, East Indies & on passage. 3rd March 1828 to 3d March 1830, East Indies & on passage.' *Family*: Married Mary Anne Evans Kenny, 'daughter of the late Captain Courtney Crowe Kenny 9th Foot Killed at Burgos 1812', 5 Nov. 1827, St Luke's Church, Parish of Chelsea. They had one child, a son, by 1831. [PRO: WO 25/802 f254]. Severely wounded, Crossing the Bidassoa, 7/9 Oct. 1813 (1st Battn.) [*London Gazette*]. MGS.

KENT, James D., Lt./Adjutant, 60th Foot: Lt., 60th Foot, 2 Sept. 1812; Adjutant, 60th Foot, 31 Dec. 1812. Slightly wounded, Pyrenees, 30 July 1813 (5th Battn.) [*London Gazette*]. 'Michael Kent' in *1812 Army List*.

KENT, John, Lt., 50th Foot: Lt., 50th Foot, 28 Aug. 1804. Wounded, Vimeiro, 21 Aug. 1808 [*London Gazette*]. *Monthly Return*, 1st Battn., dated 1 Sept. 1808: 'Wounded (on board) 21 Aug. 1808'

[PRO: WO 17/164]. Capt., 95th Foot, 10 May 1809. Later 53rd Foot. MGS.

KEOGH, Francis Gethings, Lt., 14th Light Dragoons; Lt., 57th Foot: *1829 Statement of Service*: Born in 'Pillow, Co. of Carlow', 13 Sept. 1793. Aged '15 1/2 years' on his 'first Entrance into the Army.' Cornet, 14th Light Dragoons, 9 Feb. 1809. Lt., 14th Light Dragoons, 29 March 1810. Lt., 57th Foot, 7 March 1811. Half Pay, Aug. 1818, 'urgent private affairs.' Lt., 94th Foot, April 1824. Half Pay, 60th Foot, 9 Nov. 1825, 'ill health.' Lt., 86th Foot, Feb. 1829. *Battles, sieges and campaigns*: 'Present with the 14th Lt. Dragoons during Massenas retreat from Portugal in March 1811. Joined the 57th Foot on the field of Battle at Albuhera, on 17th May 1811. Was present in the following Engagements – Vittoria. The Pyrenees. The Nivelle. The Nieve. Orthes. Thoulouse. Besides many other minor actions, such as – A'Royos Molinos, Ronces Valles, and Ellasonda &c &c &c. Served 4 Campaigns in Spain, and accompanied the Army to America.' *Distinguished conduct*: 'Commanded 23 men of the 14th Lt. Dragoons on Massenas Retreat and fell in with and captured a Convoy guarded by Infantry in presence of a French Brigade within shot. Not noticed in general orders. On another occasion, after the Battle of the Pyrenees, owing to the good conduct of the 57th Lt. Company, captured a very large convoy, guarded by a French Brigade. Sir John Byng Commanded.' *Wounds received in action*: 'Was severely wounded by a Grape Shot at Bayonne 13th Decr. 1813. Recd. for that wound the Grant of Full Pay as Capt. commanding a Compy., £191: 12: 6d. Recd. five shares of Prize Money for the Peninsular Campaigns.' *Service abroad*: '1810 to 1818, Portugal, America and France. April 1824 to Novr. 1825, in Gibraltar.' *Family*: Married Ann Getling, June 1816, St

324

Mary's, City of Dublin. They had no children by 1830. [PRO: WO 25/802 f47]. Severely wounded, the Nive, 13 Dec. 1813 (1st Battn.) [*London Gazette*]. MGS.

KESSLER, Frederick Theodore, Lt., 2nd Light Battn. K.G.L.: *1829 Statement of Service for Retired Officers*: Aged sixteen on first appointment to the Army. Ensign, 2nd Light Battn. K.G.L., 7 May 1809; Lt., 2nd Light Battn. K.G.L., 12 Dec. 1809; Capt., 2nd Light Battn. K.G.L., 28 June 1815; Half-pay, 25 Feb. 1816, by reduction. *Where serving when wounded*: 'In the Peninsula and at Waterloo.' *Details of pension*: Seventy pounds, commencing 25 June 1824. No married. *Where generally resident during last five years*: 'City of Hanover'. [PRO: WO 25/764 f35]. Slightly wounded, in an action near Tolosa, 24 June 1813 [*London Gazette*]. 'G. T. Kessler' in Army List. Served in Peninsula 1811–14. Waterloo. *Beamish*, vol. II, p. 567 ['slightly wounded, 24th June 1813, at Villa-franca; slightly wounded, 18th June 1815, at Waterloo... [Died] at Hanover, 28th January 1833'].

KETTLEWELL, Evans, Lt., 97th Foot: *1829 Statement of Service for Retired Officers*: Aged twenty-four on first appointment to the Army. Ensign, 97th Foot, 1807; Lt., 97th Foot, 1808 [Army List gives 21 April 1808]; Half-pay, by reduction. Served twelve years on half-pay. *Where serving when wounded*: 'Wounded at Vimiera & Badajos'. No pension. *Family*: Married in St George's Church, Dublin, 2 Feb. 1826. No children by 1829. *Where generally resident during last five years*: 'At 51 Dorset St., Dublin & Thomastown County Meath.' [PRO: WO 25/764 f60]. Wounded, Vimeiro, 21 Aug. 1808 [*London Gazette*]. Wounded during the repulse of a sortie from Badajoz, 10 May 1811 [*London Gazette*]. MGS.

KEYT, John Thomas, Capt., 51st Foot: *1829 Statement of Service*: Born in the Parish of Wendlebury, Oxfordshire, April 1778. Aged 20 on his first Entrance into the Army. Ensign, 51st Foot, 6 Sept. 1798. Lt., 51st Foot, 21 Feb. 1800. Capt., 51st Foot, 24 June 1804. Bvt. Major, 51st Foot, 4 June 1814. Bvt. Lt. Col., 51st Foot, 18 June 1815. Major, 51st Foot, 24 April 1817. Lt. Col., unattached, Nov. 1825. Lt. Col., 84th Foot, 29 May 1828, *Battles, sieges and campaigns*: 'Employed in the Kandian War in Ceylon in 1803... North of Spain in 1808/9... The Walcheren expedition in 1809... Portugal and Spain 1811, 1812 & 1813... Siege of Badajoz 1812. Battle of Vittoria 1813. Battle of Orthes 1814. Several Skirmishes near Peyrehorade, advancing Bourdeaux &c. Battle of Waterloo. escalade of Cambray.' *Wounds received in action*: 'Severe Wound in the Arm on the heights of Lezaca (Pyrenees) on the 31st August 1813. One years Pay; granted.' *Titles, honorary distinctions and medals*: 'Companion of the Order of the Bath, and a Waterloo Medal.' *Service abroad*: 'May 1799 to Sept. 1807, Madras & Ceylon. Sept. 1808 to Jany. 1809, Spain. July 1809 to Nov. 1809, Walcheren. Mar 1811 to Nov 1811, Portugal. Decr. 1812 to July 1814, Portugal, Spain and France. Mar 1815 to any. 1816, Netherlands & France. 8th Decr. 1828 to 31 decr. 1829, Jamaica.' *Family*: Married Miss King, Oct. 1820, in Newbury. They had one child, a son, by 1830. [PRO: WO 25/801 f214]. Severely wounded, 'at the Operations of the Army', 31 Aug. 1813 [*London Gazette*]. Waterloo. *Wheeler*, p. 144 [Wounded, 'severely', near Lezaca, 31 Aug. 1813, 'Keyts'], p. 199 [Waterloo: 'Major Keyt commanded the light troops in advance'], p. 201.

+KILSHAW, Charles, Capt., 77th Foot; Lt. Col., 11th Caçadores: Lt., 77th Foot, 2 April 1800; Capt., 77th

Foot, 30 Nov. 1809. Killed, Orthes, 27 Feb. 1814, while serving as Lt. Col., 11th Caçadores [*London Gazette*]. In Portuguese Service Nov. 1810 to Feb. 1814. Gold Medal. *Challis, Portuguese Army,* p. 56 ['Kilsha'].

KINCAID, John, Lt., 95th Foot: Author of *Adventures in the Rifle Brigade* (1830), and *Random Shots from a Rifleman* (1835). Born at Dalbeath, near Falkirk, Jan. 1787. Served first as Ensign in a Stirling-shire local militia, then in the North York militia. 2nd Lt., 95th Foot, 27 April 1809 ('Kincaird'). Served in Walcheren in the Spring of 1809, where he became sick with fever. Joined 1st Battn. in Peninsula in Spring 1810. Slightly wounded, during 'several Affairs with the French Army', 15 March 1811 (Foz de Aronce) [*London Gazette*]. 1st Lt., 95th Foot, 23 May 1811. Was one of the officers who led the storming party of the Light Division at Ciudad Rodrigo, 19 Jan. 1812. Waterloo. MGS. Died at Hastings, 22 April 1862. *Simmons,* pp. 141, 145 [Slight wound, Foz de Aronce, 15 March 1811: 'shot through his cap, which grazed the top of his head. He fell as if a sledge hammer had hit him'], pp. 378–9.

KING, Charles, Lt., 11th Light Dragoons: *1829 Statement of Service for Retired Officers:* Aged seventeen on first appointment to the Army. Cornet, 11th Light Dragoons, 9 May 1805; Lt., 11th Light Dragoons, 30 Jan. 1806; Capt., 16th Light Dragoons, 18 Feb. 1813; Major, 16th Light Dragoons, 2 June 1825; Lt. Col., Half-pay, unattached, 18 Oct. 1827. *Where serving when wounded:* 'El Bodon near Ciudad Rodrigo'. *Details of pension:* One hundred pounds per annum, commencing 1812. *Family:* Married in Marylebone, London, 24 Jan. 1822. Four children by 1829. *Where generally resident during last five years:* 'With the 16th Lancers in the

East Indies.' [PRO: WO 25/764 f102]. Severely wounded, El Bodon, 25 Sept. 1811 [*London Gazette*]. *1818 Pension Return,* pp. 2–3.

KING, Charles, Lt., 74th Foot: *1829 Statement of Service for Retired Officers:* Aged twenty-one on first appointment to the Army. Ensign, 74th Foot, 18 June 1808, 'volun-teered from the Fumanagh Militia'; Lt., 74th Foot, 27 Dec. 1810; Capt., Half-pay, unattached, 26 April 1817. *Where serving when wounded:* 'At the Storming of Badajos, 6 April 1812'. No pension. *Family:* Married in Saint Peter's Church, Dublin, 15 Feb. 1825. No children by 1829. *Where generally resident during last five years:* 'Serving with the 74 Rgt. in Newfoundland and Halifax and the Depot of the Regt. and on the Recruiting Service, also on leave of absence for the recovery of health and since placed upon Half Pay in Edinburgh and Dublin.' [PRO: WO 25/764 f104]. Severely wounded, storming of Badajoz, 6 April 1812 [*London Gazette*].

+KING, Francis, Ensign, 29th Foot: Ensign, 29th Foot, 5 Oct. 1809. Killed, Albuera, 16 May 1811 [*London Gazette*].

KING, James, Capt., 87th Foot: *1829 Statement of Service for Retired Officers:* Aged eighteen on first appointment to the Army. Ensign, 54th Foot, 25 Sept. 1806; Lt., 54th Foot, 10 Dec. 1806; Capt., 4th Garrison Battn., 28 Feb. 1811; Capt., 87th Foot, 4 July 1811; Half-pay, 73rd Foot, 1 Jan. 1818, 'At my own request in consequence of Wounds and general ill Health and without the difference.' 'Disabled and unfit for active service.' *Where serving when wounded:* 'Spain'. *Details of pension:* One hundred pounds, commencing 22 June 1814. *Where generally resident during last five years:* 'Anglesey, N. Wales'. [PRO: WO 25/764 f128]. Severely wounded, Vittoria, 21 June 1813

(2nd Battn.) [*London Gazette*]. Pension 'for wounds' received at Vittoria *1818 Pension Return*, pp. 20-1. MGS.

+KING, John, Lt., 23rd Light Dragoons: Lt., 23rd Foot, 5 Aug. 1796. Killed, Talavera, 28 July 1809 [*London Gazette*].

KING, John Duncan, Lt., 1st Foot; Lt., 7th Foot: *1829 Statement of Service*: 'Born in the City of Waterford, Ireland, 4th November 1788. Aged Seventeen on his first Entrance into the Army. Ensign, 71st Regt., 28th Augt. 1806. Lieutenant, 71st Regt., 18 Feby. 1808. Lieutenant, 3d Battn. 1st Royals [1st Foot], 1808 [Army List gives 28 July 1808]. Lieutenant, 7th Royal Fusiliers, 13th June 1811. Half Pay, 8th Foot, April 1820. Lieutenant, 75th Regt., 14 May 1829. Captain, 75th Regt., 10th March 1830.' Note added: 'Capt Unattd. 28 Decr. 1830.' *Battles, sieges and campaigns*: 'As Lieutenant at the taking of the Island of Walcheren in August 1809, and the seige of Flushing with the 3d Battalion of the Royals... Lieutenant in the 3d Battalion of the Royals at the Battle of Busaco in Portugal 27th Septr. 1810. Lieutenant in the 7th Fusiliers, at Fuento Guinaldo, in Spain, and the subsequent affairs at Aldea del Ponte Septr. 1811. At the Battle of Vittoria in Spain with the 7th Fusiliers 21st June 1813. At the Battles of the Pyrenees of the 25th 26th 27th & 28th July 1813... At the taking of Paris in 1815.' *Wounds received in action*: 'Wounded Severely in the right shoulder on 28th July 1813 at the Pyrenees, received a grant of One years additional Pay as Lieutenant, and one year and a half temporary pension at £70 pr. year.' *Service abroad*: 'July 1809 to July 1814, Holland, Portugal & Spain. May 1815 to Octr. 1818, France.' *Family*: Married Sally, 7 Jan. 1815, Chelmsford, Essex. They had four children by 1830. [PRO:

WO 25/799 f341]. Also, note his *1829 Statement of Service for Retired Officers*, completed prior to his taking up the appointment in the 75th Foot. Duplicate information, but states as his place of residence during previous five years: 'at Paris & Boulogne Sur Mer'. [PRO: WO 25/764 f101]. Severely wounded, Pyrenees, 28 July 1813 (1st Battn.) [*London Gazette*]. MGS.

KING, John Grant, Lt., 48th Foot; Capt., 23rd Portuguese Line: Lt., 48th Foot, 8 Feb. 1808. Severely wounded, Orthes, 27 Feb. 1814, as Capt., 23rd Portuguese Line [*London Gazette*]. In Portuguese Service April 1810 to April 1814. Gold Medal. *Challis, Portuguese Army*, p. 56.

+KING, Samuel Dikes, Lt., 13th Light Dragoons: Lt., Army, 9 March 1808; Lt., 13th Light Dragoons, 20 Sept. 1810. *Register of officers' effects*: 'Killed when returning with a flag of Truce from Badajoz, 21 Nov. 1811, between Badajoz & Campe Mayor'. Single. Effects totalled £121. 5s. 5½d, plus £173. 16s. 4d. 'Allowed by Board of Claims for losses sustained at Olivenza 7 April 1811. [PRO: WO 25/2963]. Obituary, *The Gentleman's Magazine*, 1811 Supplement, II, p. 658 ["Lately [Nov.]... Killed by a Guerilla mistaking him for a Frenchman, whilst escorting a French captain exchanged for an English one, Lieut. King, 13th Light Drag. son of Mrs. K. wine-mechant, Ipswich. His remains were conveyed to Badajoz, and interred by the French General Philipon, with all the honours of war."]. *The Gentleman's Magazine*, Jan. 1812, p. 76 ['The death of Lieut. King, of the 13th Light Dragoons ... was attended with circumstances peculiarly afflicting and extraordinary. Appointed to command the escort of a French captain in exchange for Capt. [Brinsley] Nixon [85th Foot], taken at the siege of Badajoz, he met the French escort, each attended by trumpets as flags of truce, and was inducted, by civility to the French officer, to accompany them further towards Badajoz; about three miles from which place they fell in with a party of mounted Spaniards, who commenced a fire upon the party, especially upon the French trumpeter, some little way to the rear, owing to his being mounted on a lame horse, which they shot. Lieut. King instantly galloped up to the Spaniards, and in their own language would have explained the nature of the service they were upon, but they would not listen. They shot him through the heart. Thus fell as brave a youth as ever carried arms.'].

KINGSBURY, John, Major, 2nd Foot: Major, 2nd Foot, 15 Dec. 1800; Bvt. Lt.Col., 2nd Foot, 25 April 1808. Severely wounded, Salamanca, 22 July 1812 [*London Gazette*]. Obituary, *The Gentleman's Magazine*, Nov. 1813, p. 504 ['After an illness of only two hours, Lieut.-col. Kingsbury, who had served in the Army 33 years, and 25 of that period in the 2d or Queen's Royal Regiment of Infantry. He was wounded at the siege of Gibraltar, under Gen. Elliot; served in Holland under the Duke of York; in the West Indies under Gen. Sir R. Abercrombie; in the Rebellion in Ireland, under the Marquis Cornwallis; in Egypt under Sir R. Abercrombie; in Portugal under Sir J. Moore; and lastly in Spain and Portugal, under the Marquis of Wellington, where he was severely wounded, and had his horse shot under him at the battle of Salamanca.'].

KINGSCOTE, Nigel, Major, 53rd Foot: Major, 53rd Foot, 1806. Slightly wounded, Talavera, 28 July 1809 (2nd Battn.) [*London Gazette*].

KINGSMILL, Parr, Lt., 88th Foot: Lt., 88th Foot, 8 May 1811. Slightly wounded, Salamanca, 22 July 1812 (2nd Battn.) [*London Gazette*]. His account of Badajoz, from his journal, was published in *With Fife and Drum*, ed. A. H. Miles (London, n.d.).

KINGSMILL, William, Lt., 88th Foot: *1829 Statement of Service for Retired Officers*: Aged twenty on first appointment to the Army. Ensign, 88th Foot, 15 Sept. 1808; Lt., 88th Foot, 30 May 1811; Half-pay, 4th Foot, 29 Aug. 1816, 'At my own Request having lost my Right Leg on Service'; Lt., 10th Royal Veteran Battn., 24 Feb. 1820; 'Retired on Full Pay', 10th Royal Veteran Battn., 24 March 1821. *Where serving when wounded*: 'At Ciudad Rodrigo in Spain.' *Details of pension*: Seventy pounds, commencing 20 Jan. 1813. *Family*: Married in Glenville, Ireland, 18 April 1815. Three children by 1829. *Where generally resident during last five years*: 'City of Limerick'. [PRO: WO 25/764 f107]. Severely wounded, storming of Ciudad Rodrigo, 19 Jan. 1811 [*London Gazette*]. Pension for 'loss of a leg' at Ciudad Rodrigo [*1818 Pension Return*, pp. 20–1. MGS.

KINLOCK, Charles, Lt., 52nd Foot: Lt., 52nd Foot, 12 Feb. 1808. Slightly wounded, storming of Badajoz, 6 April 1812 ('Kinloch') [*London Gazette*]. Capt., Army, 18 March 1813; Capt., 52nd Foot, 22 July 1813.

KIPPING, John Easton, Capt., 4th Foot: Capt., 4th Foot, 8 Aug. 1804. Severely wounded, Vittoria, 21 June 1813 ('Kepping') [*London Gazette*].

+KIRBY, George, Capt., 57th Foot: Capt., 57th Foot, 1 March 1810. Slightly wounded, Albuera, 16 May 1811 (1st Battn.) [*London Gazette*]. Died of wounds, 10 June 1811. Return dated 25 June 1811. [PRO: WO 25/2965]. Obituary, *The Gentleman's Magazine*, July 1811, p. 90 ['Lately... At Elvas, from the wound he received on the 10th of May [sic], at the battle of Albuera, Captain Kirby, 57th regiment, second son of the late Rev. John K. of Mayfield, Sussex.'].

+**KIRK, Daniel, Lt., 32nd Foot; Capt., 3rd Caçadores:** Lt., 32nd Foot, 8 Nov. 1807. Severely wounded, 'since dead', the Nive, 10 Dec. 1813, while serving as as Capt., 3rd Caçadores [*London Gazette*]. In Portuguese Service May 1812 to Dec. 1813. Died 14 Dec. 1813 [PRO: WO 25/2965].

KIRKMAN, James, 1st Lt., 95th Foot: 1st Lt., 95th Foot, 25 Aug. 1809. Slightly wounded, Nivelle, 10 Nov. 1813 (3rd Battn.) [*London Gazette*]. Later Barrack Master, Dublin. MGS.

KIRWAN, Richard, Lt., 7th Foot: Lt., 7th Foot, 27 Oct. 1807. Severely wounded, Talavera, 28 July 1809 ('Kerwan') [*London Gazette*]. MGS.

+**KLENCK, Frederick von, Lt., 1st Light Battn. K.G.L.:** Lt., 1st Light Battn. K.G.L., 18 Jan. 1811. Killed, Crossing of the Bidassoa, 7/9 Oct. 1813 ('Klanck') [*London Gazette*]. Served in Peninsula 1808–13. *Beamish*, vol. II, p. 636 ['killed in action, on fording the river Bidassoa, south of France, 7th Oct. 1813.'].

KLINGSÖHR, George, Lt., 5th Line Battn. K.G.L.: *1829 Statement of Service for Retired Officers*: Aged sixteen on first appointment to the Army. Ensign, 5th Line Battn. K.G.L., 6 Jan. 1812; Lt., 5th Line Battn. K.G.L., 16 Dec. 1812; Half-pay, 5th Line Battn. K.G.L., 25 April 1816, by reduction. *Where serving when wounded*: 'At Bayonne in France on 27th Febr. 1814. At the Battle of Waterloo 18th June 1815.' *Details of pension*: Seventy pounds, commencing 25 Dec. 1821. *Where generally resident during last five years*: 'Hanover.' [PRO: WO 25/764

f141]. Served in Peninsula 1813–14. Waterloo. *Beamish*, vol. II, p. 592.

KNIPE, George Frederick, Lt., 11th Light Dragoons: *1829 Statement of Service for Retired Officers*: Aged sixteen on first appointment to the Army. Cornet, 22nd Dragoons, 29 May 1796; Lt., 22nd Dragoons, 16 July 1800; Half-pay, 1802; Lt., 11th Dragoons, 23 June 1804; Capt., 11th Dragoons, 2 July 1813; Half-pay, 1814; Capt., full-pay, 23rd Dragoons, 6 Oct. 1814; Capt., 60th Foot, 19 Jan. 1815; Half-pay, 23rd Foot, 1815, 'at my own request on Acct. of ill health'. *Where serving when wounded*: 'Near Burgos in Spain'. No pension. *Family*: Married in St John's, near Worcester', 19 Oct. 1808. Ten children by 1829. *Where generally resident during last five years*: 'Caernarvon 6 months at Worcester & 2½ years in Hereford'. [PRO: WO 25/764 f144]. Wounded, during 'movements of the Army' [Retreat from Burgos], 23 Oct. 1812 [*London Gazette*].

+**KNIPE, Robert, Lt./Capt., 14th Light Dragoons:** Lt., 14th Light Dragoons, 5 Jan. 1805. Slightly wounded, passage of the Douro, 12 May 1809 [*London Gazette*]. Capt., 14th Light Dragoons, 28 Dec. 1809. Severely wounded, Fuentes de Onoro, 5 May 1811 [*London Gazette*]. Died of wounds, 18 May 1811. Return dated 25 May 1811. [PRO: WO 25/2965]. Obituary, *The Gentleman's Magazine*, Supplement 1811, p. 675 ['Lately... At Villa Fermosa, of the wounds he received in the action of the 5th, Capt. Knipe, 14th dragoons.']. *Brotherton*, pp. 41–2 [Fuentes de Onoro: 'We had a very fine fellow, Captain Knipe, killed through his gallant obstinacy, if I may call it so. we had the night before been discussing the best mode for cavalry to attack batteries in the open field. He maintained, contrary to us all, that they ought to be charged in front, instead of the usual way in gaining

their flanks, and thereby avoiding their fire. Poor fellow, the experiment next day, in support of his argument, was fatal to him. He had the opportunity of charging one of the enemy's batteries, which he did by attacking it immediately in front, and got through the discharge of round-shot with little loss; but the enemy having most rapidly reloaded with grape, let fly at his party, at a close and murderous distance, almost entirely destroying it; he himself receiving a grape-shot, passing through his body. The shot went through his lungs. I was with the poor fellow the next morning, as long as he survived. He could speak distinctly, and was most composed and resigned, and even argued the point over again. His chief anxiety, however, was to be permitted to write a line to his mother, and he expired in the very act of attempting it. We buried him in the same grave with another gallant soldier who fell that day, Colonel Cameron of the 79th Highlanders.'].
Perrett, pp. 20, 24.

+KNIPE, William Henry, Capt., 95th Foot: Capt., 11th Foot, 8 Sept. 1808; Capt., 95th Foot, 5 May 1809. Killed, Barossa, 5 March 1811 (3rd Battn.) [*London Gazette*].

+KNOWLES, Robert, Lt., 7th Foot: Lt., 7th Foot, 8 May 1811. Slightly wounded, storming of Badajoz, 6 April 1812 [*London Gazette*]. Slightly wounded, Salamanca, 22 July 1812 [*London Gazette*]. Killed, Pyrenees, 25 July 1813 (1st Battn.) [*London Gazette*]. His letters were published in *Letters of Lieut. Robert Knowles, 7th Fusiliers, during the Campaigns of 1811–13*, ed. Sir Lees Knowles Bt. (Bolton, 1909).

KNOX, Edward, Capt., 31st Foot: *1829 Statement of Service for Retired Officers*: Aged eighteen on first appointment to the Army. Ensign, 31st Foot, Oct. 1804; Lt.,

31st Foot, 5 March 1805; Capt., 31st Foot, 5 Nov. 1807; Bvt. Major, 21 June 1817; Capt., Half-pay, 2nd Garrison Battn., March 1823, 'for the arrangement of private affairs.' *Where serving when wounded*: 'Peninsula.' *Details of pension*: 'Original grant £100 per annum, From February 1814 to June 21st 1817. From June 21st 1817 to the present time £200 pr. ann.' Not married. *Where generally resident during last five years*: 'In England & Ireland.' [PRO: WO 25/764 f149]. Slightly wounded, Albuera, 16 May 1811 (2nd Battn.) [*London Gazette*]. Severely wounded, 'in Action with the Enemy', 15 Feb. 1814 (1st Battn.) [*London Gazette*]. Two hundred pounds per annum pension, commencing 16 Feb. 1815, for 'loss of an arm' at St Palais, 1814 [*1818 Pension Return*, pp. 8–9]. MGS.

+KNOX, George, Lt., 57th Foot: Lt., 57th Foot, 11 Feb. 1808. Killed, Nivelle, 10 Nov. 1813 [*London Gazette*].

KNOX, John H., Ensign, 3rd Foot Guards: Lt., Army, 21 Jan. 1808; Ensign, 3rd Foot Guards, 24 Aug. 1809. Severely wounded, siege of Burgos, 18 Oct. 1812 ('Lieutenant') [*London Gazette*]. Pension of seventy pounds per annum, commencing 18 Oct. 1813, 'for wounds' received at Burgos [*1818 Pension Return*, pp. 2–3]. MGS.

KNOX, Wright, Ensign/Lt., 87th Foot: Ensign, 87th Foot, 15 Sept. 1808. Severely wounded, Talavera, 27 July 1809 ('Ensign') [*London Gazette*]. Lt., 87th Foot, 16 Aug. 1810.

KOCH, Charles W. H., Lt., 60th Foot: Lt., 60th Foot, 2 Aug. 1800. Wounded, Vimeiro, 21 Aug. 1808 ('Charles Kirk') [*London Gazette*].

KOCH, William von, Capt., Duke of Brunswick Oels' Corps (Infantry):

Lt., Duke of Brunswick Oels' Corps, 25 Sept. 1809. Capt., Duke of Brunswick Oels' Corps, 10 Sept. 1812. Severely wounded, Nivelle, 10 Nov. 1813 [*London Gazette*].

+KÖHLER, Charles, Ensign/Lt., 5th Line Battn. K.G.L.: Ensign, 5th Line Battn. K.G.L., 21 Feb. 1809. Severely wounded, Talavera, 28 July 1809 ('Ensign') [*London Gazette*]. Lt., 5th Line Battn. K.G.L., 21 Sept. 1810. Killed, sortie from Bayonne, 14 April 1814 [*London Gazette*]. Served in Peninsula 1808–14. *Beamish*, vol. II, p. 635.

+KOHLSTEDT, Frederick William, Cornet, 2nd Dragoons K.G.L.: Cornet, 2nd Dragoons, K.G.L., 12 May 1810. Killed, 'in an Affair with the Enemy's Cavalry in Front of the Village of Majalahonda,' 11 Aug. 1812 [*London Gazette*]. Served in Peninsula in 1812. *Beamish*, vol. II, p. 616.

KORSCHANN, Joseph, Lt., 5th Line Battn. K.G.L.: Lt., 5th Line Battn. K.G.L., 25 Sept. 1812. Served in Peninsula 1808–9, 1813–14. *Beamish*, vol. II, p. 657 ['slightly wounded, 27th Feb. 1814, before Bayonne. Placed upon half-pay, 25th July 1815. [Resident] at Znaim in Moravia.'].

+KOSEHENBAR, Ernst von, Lt., Duke of Brunswick Oels' Corps (Infantry): Lt., Duke of Brunswick Oels' Corps, 25 Sept. 1809. Severely wounded, Pyrenees, 2 Aug. 1813 ('Koskenbar') [*London Gazette*]. Killed, Orthes, 27 Feb. 1814 ('Koshenahr') [*London Gazette*].

+KOUGH, Edward E., Ensign, 87th Foot: Ensign, 87th Foot, 12 Oct. 1809. Killed, Barossa, 5 March 1811 (2nd Battn.) [*London Gazette*]. *Surtees*, p. 119 [Barossa: 'I understand, when the 87th charged, Ensign Keogh [sic] of that regiment made the first attempt to wrench the eagle from the officer who carried it; but in so doing he was run through by several of those who supported it, and fell lifeless to the ground. Sergeant Masterson of that regiment then dashed at it, and was more fortunate, he succeeded in securing it.'].

KRAUCHENBERG, George, Baron, Capt., 1st Light Dragoons/Hussars K.G.L.: Capt., 1st Light Dragoons K.G.L., 28 Jan. 1804. Slightly wounded, Fuentes de Onoro, evening 3 May 1811 [*London Gazette*]. Bvt. Major, 1st Light Dragoons K.G.L., 30 May 1811. Slightly wounded, Salamanca, 18 July 1812 ('Barrack-Master Kraukenberg') [*London Gazette*]. Major, 3rd Light Dragoons K.G.L., 20 June 1813. Served in Peninsula 1809–14. Waterloo. Later Major-General. *Beamish*, vol. II, p. 556 ['severely wounded, 1st Oct. 1810, at the passage of the Mondego; slightly wounded 5th May 1811 at Fuentes de Onoro; slightly wounded, 18th July 1812, at Canizal.']. *Leach*, p. 138 ['4th July [1810].– Being under arms, as usual, an hour before day-break, on the heights, some shots were heard from our cavalry pickets at Marialva, who shortly afterwards retired slowly and in excellent order, keeping up a continued skirmish. Captain Kraukenberg [sic], of the 1st German Hussars, an officer of the highest merit, distinguished himself on this occasion. Forming his squadron on some eligible ground near a small narrow bridge over a rivulet which runs through Gallegos, he waited until as many of the French dragoons had crossed as he thought proper to permit, when he instantly charged and put them into confusion, killing and wounding many of them, and bringing some prisoners with him to the heights, where General Crawford had drawn out the Light Division in line.']. *Kincaid, Random Shots*, p. 190 [March 1811: 'I was soon after ordered to join my battalion, which I found lodged in a stubble field about half way between Gallegos and Almeda, on a piece of rising ground which we had christened Krauchenberg's hill, in compliment to that gallant captain of German hussars, who, with his single troop, had made a brilliant and successful charge from it the year before on the enemy's advancing horsemen.'].

KRAUCHENBERG, Louis, Lt., 1st Light Dragoons/Hussars K.G.L: *1829 Statement of Service for Retired Officers*: Aged fifteen on first appointment to the Army. Ensign, 1st Light Battn. K.G.L., 15 Jan. 1804; Cornet, '1st Hussars K.G.L.', 15 Nov. 1804; Lt., '1st Hussars K.G.L.', 13 April 1807 [Army List gives 13 April 1808]; Capt., '1st Hussars K.G.L.'", 13 Jan. 1813; Half-pay, 'By reduction of the K. G. Legion' [Army List gives 24 Feb. 1816]. Served '15 years with Waterloo' on full-pay. *Where serving when wounded*: 'In Spain'. *Details of pension*: Seventy pounds per annum, commencing 6 May 1812. *Where generally resident during last five years*: 'City of Hannover'. [PRO: WO 25/764 f165]. Severely wounded, Fuentes de Onoro, 5 May 1811 [*London Gazette*]. Served in Peninsula 1809–11. Waterloo. MGS. *Beamish*, vol. II, p. 549 ['Lewis Krauchenberg'].

KUHLS, Augustus, Lt., 2nd Dragoons K.G.L.: Cornet, 2nd Dragoons K.G.L., 4 April 1809; Lt., 2nd Dragoons K.G.L., 28 May 1811. Severely wounded, in 'an Affair with the Enemy's Cavalry, in Front of the Village of Majalahonda,' 11 Aug. 1812 ('Lieutenant') [*London Gazette*]. Served in Peninsula 1812–14. *Beamish*, vol. II, p. 545.

KUNOWSKY, Frederich von, Lt., Duke of Brunswick Oels' Corps (Infantry): Lt., Duke of Brunswick Oels' Corps, 27 Sept. 1809. Slightly wounded, storming of Badajoz, 6 April 1812 [*London Gazette*].

KYLE, Alexander, Capt., 94th Foot: Capt., 94th Foot, 11 Oct. 1810. Slightly wounded, storming of Ciudad Rodrigo, 19 Jan. 1812 [*London Gazette*]. Severely wounded, siege of Badajoz, 26 March 1812 [*London Gazette*]. MGS.

KYNOCK, Volunteer, 79th Foot: Severely wounded, Pyrenees, 28 July 1813 (1st Battn.) [*London Gazette*]. Not in *Challis, Index*.

KYNOCK, John, Lt., 79th Foot: Lt., 79th Foot, 13 June 1811. Severely wounded, Toulouse, 10 April 1814 (1st Battn.) [*London Gazette*]. Killed, Waterloo.

L

LA BACHELLÉ, George William Ernst, Ensign, 7th Line Battn. K.G.L.: Ensign, 7th Line Battn. K.G.L., 18 Jan. 1810. Severely wounded, Fuentes de Onoro, 5 May 1811 [*London Gazette*]. Lt., 7th Line Battn. K.G.L., 23 March 1812. Served in Peninsula 1810–11. Waterloo. *Beamish*, vol. II, p. 600 ['severely wounded, 13th May 1813, at Zollenspiker... [Died] at Wilhelminenholz, near Aurich, 28th July 1825, captain Han. 1st regiment infantry.'].

LACY, Richard J. I., Capt., Royal Artillery: Capt., Army, 20 July 1804; Capt., Royal Artillery, 24 March 1809. Mentioned in Murray's Castalla dispatch, 14 April 1813 ['The different brigades of guns, under Captains Lacy, Thomson, and Gilmour ... and Lieutenant Patton, of the flying artillery, were extremely useful, and most gallantly served'] [*London Gazette*].

LACY, Samuel Walker, Ensign, 82nd Foot: Ensign, 82nd Foot, 4 Oct. 1810. Slightly wounded, Pyrenees, 25 July 1813 ('Lacey') (1st Battn.) [*London Gazette*]. Lt., 82nd Foot, 16 Sept. 1813. Half-pay, 24 June 1824. MGS.

LAING, John, Capt, 61st Foot: Capt., 61st Foot, 7 March 1805. Slightly wounded, Talavera, 28 July 1809 [*London Gazette*]. MGS.

LAING, Thomas, Capt., 94th Foot: Capt., 94th Foot, 24 Dec. 1804. Severely wounded, storming of Ciudad Rodrigo, 19 Jan. 1812 [*London Gazette*].

+LAKE, Hon. George A. F., Lt. Col., 29th Foot: Capt., Army, 17 Jan. 1799; Capt., 4th Foot, 5 Sept. 1799; Lt. Col., Army, 12 Nov. 1803; Lt. Col.,

29th Foot, 5 Nov. 1804. Killed, Rolica, 17 Aug. 1808 [*London Gazette*]. Obituary, *London Gazette*, Nov. 1808, p. 964 ['in the general engagement of the 21st of August, at Vimiera [sic] ... fell the Hon. Col. Lake, of the 29th foot, 2d son of the late Lord Lake']. *Leach*, p. 47 ['Battle of Roleia... The Honourable Colonel Lake of the 29th, and Colonel Stewart of the 9th, fell at the head of their regiments.']. *Harris*, p. 22 [Rolica: 'The 29th regiment received so terrible a fire, that I saw the right wing almost annihilated, and the colonel (I think his name was Lennox) lay sprawling amongst the rest.'], p. ix [Intro by Hon. Sir John Fortescue: 'At Rolica he saw the too impetuous colonel of the 29th shot dead as he hurried his battalion prematurely to the attack, and believed his name was Lennox. His real name was Lake, the son of Lord Lake, whose severe wound before his father's eyes at the battle of Laswari is not the least dramatic incident in the history of the Army.']

LALOR, Thomas, Lt., 43rd Foot: *1829 Statement of Service for Retired Officers*: Aged eighteen on first appointment to the Army. Lt., 1st Fencible Cavalry, 'cannot recall'; Cornet, 9th Light Dragoons, 'Three years after'; Ensign, 43rd Foot, Oct. 1808; Lt., 43rd Foot, Oct. 1808 [Army List gives 17 Oct. 1808]; Half-pay, 'July or August 1819', 'on account of a rhumatic complaint.' *Where serving when wounded*: 'In Spain'. *Details of pension*: Seventy pounds, commencing Dec. 1813. *Family*: Married in 'St Martin's in the Field', 19 Oct. 1827. *Where generally resident during last five years*: 'In France from February 1825.' [PRO: WO 25/765 f58]. Seventy pounds per annum pension, commencing 25 Dec. 1811, for 'loss of an eye' in Spain, 1809 [*1818 Pension Return*, pp. 12–13].

LAMBERT, Henry, Ensign, 1st Foot Guards: *1829 Statement of Service for Retired Officers*: Aged sixteen on first appointment to the Army. Ensign, 1st Foot Guards, 6 April 1809; Lt. and Capt., 1st Foot Guards, May 1813; Capt., 69th Foot, April 1815; Half-pay, May 1815, 'private motives'. 'Not desirous service, an open wound.' *Where serving when wounded*: 'Barrosa'. No pension. *Family*: Married in St George's Church, Hanover Square, London, 7 May 1821. Four children by 1829. *Where generally resident during last five years*: 'Oxfordshire'. [PRO: WO 25/765 f47]. Severely wounded, Barossa, 5 March 1811 [*London Gazette*]. MGS.

LAMBRECHT, John, Lt., 66th Foot: Lt., 66th Foot, 30 May 1809. Slightly wounded, 'in Action with the Enemy', 16 Feb. 1814 (2nd Battn.) [*London Gazette*].

LAMPHIER, William Wolsley, Lt., 87th Foot: Lt., Army, 18 Oct. 1810; Lt., 87th Foot, 30 May 1811. Slightly wounded, 'in Action with the Enemy', 24 Feb. 1814 (2nd Battn.) [*London Gazette*]. Slightly wounded, Toulouse, 10 April 1814 (2nd Battn.) [*London Gazette*].

LANE, Ambrose, Ensign, 83rd Foot: *1829 Statement of Service for Retired Officers*: Aged twenty-one on first appointment to the Army. Ensign, 83rd Foot, May 1811 [Army List gives 28 May]; Lt., 83rd Foot, 'June or July (I do not recollect which) 1813'; Half-pay, 1817, by reduction. 'Not now desirous of service, rendered by wounds inefficient for active duty.' *Where serving when wounded*: 'Is not in receipt of a Pension since 1822, until when he enjoyed one at £50 pr. annm. as compensation for a musket shot

wound in his temple received at the Escalade of the Castle of Badajos in 1812.' *Family*: Married in 'Balintemple Church in the Co. Tipperary', 23 June 1825. One child by 1829. *Where generally resident during last five years*: 'Clonmel in Ireland'. [PRO: WO 25/765 f74]. Severely wounded, storming of Badajoz, 6 April 1812 (2nd Battn.) [*London Gazette*]. Slightly wounded, 'in Action with the Enemy', 19 March 1814 (1st Battn.) [*London Gazette*]. *1818 Pension Return*, pp. 18–19. MGS.

LANE, John, Volunteer, 42nd Foot: Volunteer, 42nd Foot. Severely wounded, storming of Fort St Michael, Burgos, 19 Sept. 1812 (1st Battn.) [*London Gazette*]. Ensign, 42nd Foot, 13 Oct. 1812.

+LANG, John Sibbald, Ens., 94th Foot: Ensign, 94th Foot, 9 Nov. 1809. Killed, storming of Badajoz, 6 April 1812 ('Long') [*London Gazette*].

LANGLANDS, George, Capt., 74th Foot: Capt., 74th Foot, 28 Sept. 1803. Slightly wounded, storming of Ciudad Rodrigo, 19 Jan. 1812 [*London Gazette*]. Severely wounded, storming of Badajoz, 6 April 1812 [*London Gazette*]. Bvt. Major, 74th Foot, 27 April 1812; Major, 13th Royal Veteran Battalion, 25 Jan. 1813. Gold Medal. Temporary pension of two hundred pounds per annum, commencing 7 April 1813, 'for wounds' received at Badajoz ('Longlands') [*1818 Pension Return*, pp. 18–19]. MGS.

+LANGLEY, Roger, Lt., 59th Foot: Lt., 59th Foot, 6 June 1809. Severely wounded, Vittoria, 21 June 1813 (2nd Battn.) [*London Gazette*]. Died of wounds, 1 Aug. 1813. Return dated Aug. 1813. [PRO: WO 25/2965]. *Register of officers' effects*: Died, 1 Aug. 1813, of wounds received at 'Mayer' [Maya, 25 July]. Single. His effects totalled '134 dollars 2 Reals', which 'will be accounted for by Paymr. to relatives.' [PRO: WO 25/2964].

LANGREHR, Charles William, Capt./Major, 2nd Line Battn. K.G.L.: Capt., 2nd Line Battn. K.G.L., 3 Nov. 1803. Severely wounded, Heights of Grijon, 11 May 1809 ('Langrelin') [*London Gazette*]. Severely wounded, siege of Burgos, 5–10 Oct. 1812 [*London Gazette*]. Major, 2nd Line Battn. K.G.L., 21 June 1813. Severely wounded, in an action near Tolosa, 25 June 1813 [*London Gazette*]. Served in Peninsula 1808–13. *Beamish*, vol. II, p. 644 ['... severely wounded, 8th Oct. 1812 ... found drowned in the river Leine near Hanover, on the 5th of May 1814.'].

+LANGREHR, Frederick Ernest, Capt., 5th Line Battn. K.G.L.: Capt., 5th Line Battn. K.G.L., 3 Nov. 1803. Severely wounded, Salamanca, 22 July 1812 ('Langresher') [*London Gazette*]. Died of wounds, 12 Sept. 1812. Return dated 25 Sept. 1812. [PRO: WO 25/2965]. Served in Peninsula 1808–12. *Beamish*, vol. II, p. 637 [Died '12th Sep. 1812, at Salamanca, of the wounds he received in the battle near that place, 22d July 1812.'].

+LANGWERTH, Ernest Eberhard Kuno von, Col., 4th Line Battn.; Brigadier-General: Col., K.G.L., 16 Dec. 1804. Killed, Talavera, 28 July 1809, while serving on the General Staff ('Brig.-Gen ... Langworth') [*London Gazette*]. Served in Peninsula 1808–9. Gold Medal. *Beamish*, vol. II, p. 631 ['colonel commandant 4th line battalion ... brigadier-gen. 1808.'].

+LASCELLES, Thomas, Lt., Royal Engineers: 1st Lt., Royal Engineers, 18 Nov. 1807. Killed at the storming of Badajoz, 6 April 1812 ('Lacelles') [*London Gazette*].

+LA SERRE, Nicholas, Ensign, 87th Foot: Ensign, 87th Foot, 26

Aug. 1808. Killed, Talavera, 27 July 1809 [*London Gazette*].

LATHAM, Matthew, Lt., 3rd Foot: *1829 Statement of Service for Retired Officers*: Aged nineteen on first appointment to the Army. Ensign, 3rd Foot, Nov. 1805; Lt., 3rd Foot, April 1807 [Army List gives 8 April]; Capt., Canadian Fencibles, 11 Feb. 1813; Capt., 3rd Foot, 13 May 1813; Capt., Portuguese Service, 20 April 1820; Half-pay, by exchange. Served fifteen years on full-pay. 'Prevented [from service] by bad health.' *Where serving when wounded*: 'Spain'. *Details of pension*: One hundred pounds per annum, commencing 17 May 1813. *Family*: Married in Blingel, 31 Dec. 1816. Five children by 1829. *Where generally resident during last five years*: 'Blingel'. [PRO: WO 25/765 f33]. Recorded as 'slightly' wounded, Albuera, 16 May 1811 [*London Gazette*]. Capt., Army, 11 Feb. 1813; Capt., 3rd Foot, 13 May 1813. MGS. Pension for one hundred pounds per annum, commencing 17 May 1812, for 'loss of an arm' at Albuera. A second pension, for seventy pounds per annum, commencing 17 May 1812, 'for wounds' received at Albuera [*1818 Pension Return*, pp. 4–5]. *Haythornthwaite, Die Hard*, p. 148 [Albuera: 'The King's Colour was borne by Ensign Charles Walsh; its pike was broken by a roundshot, Walsh was wounded and about to be taken prisoner when Lieutenant Matthew Latham seized the Colour from him. Latham was immediately surrounded by French cavalry, one of whom dealt him a dreadful, disfiguring blow across the face; but he continued to defend himself with his sword until another massive sabre-blow severed his left arm. Dropping his sword, Latham seized what remained of the colour-pike with his right arm and continued to struggle until he was ridden down, trampled and speared by lancers endeavouring to capture the flag.

335

With the last of his strength he tore the fabric from the pike and concealed it in the breast of his coat.'], p. 160 ['After the battle, both the Buffs' lost Colours were recovered ... astonishingly Matthew Latham was found still alive, with the King's Colour in his coat. Originally, Charles Walsh was credited with saving this invaluable treasure, and was praised for it in the House of Commons; but when Walsh escaped from the French he confirmed the truth. Latham was accordingly promoted to captain (in February 1813) and presented by his regiment with a gold medal worth £100 which portrayed his act of heroism, and which he was permitted to wear in uniform. The Prince Regent defrayed the expenses of a leading surgeon who repaired Latham's facial injury, and on his retirement in 1820 he received a pension of £170 per annum.']. There is an illustration of the incident at Albuera in *Fletcher, Regiments*, p. 53 ['The 3rd Foot (The Buffs) at Albuera. Soult's Polish lancers make a devastating attack on Colborne's brigade under cover of a hailstorm. Caught in line the British infantry suffered horrific losses in the attack. Ensign [sic] Latham, of the 3rd, defied the enemy cavalry, who were desperately trying to snatch the King's Colour from him, a remarkable feat of bravery which cost him an arm and a whole series of terrible wounds.'].

+LATHAM, William, 2nd Capt., Royal Artillery: 2nd Capt., Royal Artillery, 1 Feb. 1808. Killed at the storming of Badajoz, 6 April 1812 ('Lathum') [*London Gazette*].

+LATTA, John, Ensign, 42nd Foot: Ensign, 42nd Foot, 11 Feb. 1813. Killed, Toulouse, 10 April 1814 (1st Battn.) [*London Gazette*]. *Anton*, p. 136 [Toulouse: 'The company in which I was doing duty lost four officers... Ensign Latta killed.'].

+LAUTOUR, James Oliver, Ensign, 1st Foot Guards: Ensign, 1st Foot Guards, 3 Oct. 1811. Severely wounded, the Nive, 11 Dec. 1813 ('Latour') (3rd Battn.) [*London Gazette*]. Recorded as severely wounded, 'since dead', in the casualty list for the Nive published in the *February 1814 Army List*. Died of wounds, 24 Dec. 1813. Return dated Dec. 1813. [PRO: WO 25/2965]. *Hurt*, p. 75 ['D.O.W., Nive, Dec. 24']. Obituary, *The Gentleman's Magazine*, Jan. 1814, p. 96 ['Lately... At St Jean de Luz, of a wound received in action with the Enemy on the 12th inst. near Bayonne, James O. Lautour, esq. 1st foot guards.'].

LAW, Robert, Ensign/Adjutant/Lt., 71st Foot: Ensign, 71st Foot, 8 June 1809; Adjutant, 71st Foot, 6 Dec. 1810. Slightly wounded, Fuentes de Onoro, Evening 3 May 1811, while Adjt. (1st Battn.) [*London Gazette*]. Slightly wounded again, Fuentes de Onoro, 5 May 1811 [*London Gazette*]. Lt., 71st Foot, 27 May 1811. Severely wounded, 'in Action with the Enemy', 20 March 1814 ('Robert Lowe') (1st Battn.) [*London Gazette*]. Wounded, Waterloo. Capt., 71st Foot, 18 Oct. 1821; Capt., 33rd Foot, 20 March 1823; Capt., Ceylon Rifles, 25 Sept. 1824. MGS. Major-General, 17 July 1859. KH.

+LAWRENCE, William D., ('Jr.'), Ensign, 38th Foot: Ensign, 38th Foot, 11 Sept. 1811. Slightly wounded, 'in the assault and capture of the exterior line of the castle of Burgos on the evening of the 4th October, 1812' [*London Gazette*]. Killed, storming of San Sebastian, 31 Aug. 1813 ('Lawrence, jun.') (1st Battn.) [*London Gazette*].

LAWRENCE, W. Dawson, Lt., ('Sr.'), 38th Foot: Ensign, 38th Foot, 9 Aug. 1810; Lt., 38th Foot, 22 Aug. 1811. Slightly wounded, storming of

Badajoz, 6 April 1812 (2nd Battn.) [*London Gazette*]. Severely wounded, storming of San Sebastian, 31 Aug. 1813 (1st Battn.) ('Lawrence, sen.') [*London Gazette*].

+LAWRIE, Andrew, Major, 79th Foot: Major, 79th Foot, 4 Oct. 1810. Killed, siege of Burgos, 20–26 Sept. 1812 (1st Battn.) [*London Gazette*]. Obituary, *The Gentleman's Magazine*, Oct. 1812, p. 402 ['Sept. 22... Whilst gallantly leading an attack on the outward wall of the citadel of Burgos, in which his conduct was the admiration of all present, aged 27, Major Lawrie, 79th foot, eldest son of A. L. esq. of the Adelphi, London, army agent, and of Sydenham, Kent, leaving a disconsolate widow with an infant son and numerous friends to deplore his loss. His remains were interred in the evening with every mark of respect.']. *Aitchison*, p. 202 ['Burgos, 26th September 1812 ... an attempt was made to carry the lower defences by assault a few nights since [22nd], but it unfortunately failed – Major Lawrie of the 79th, who commanded, was killed and our loss otherwise severe'].

+LAWS, William John, Lt., 38th Foot: Lt., 38th Foot, 14 Nov. 1811. Severely wounded, Salamanca, 22 July 1812 (1st Battn.) [*London Gazette*]. Died of wounds, 26 July 1812. Return dated 25 Aug. 1812. [PRO: WO 25/2965].

LAWSON, Robert, Capt., Royal Artillery: Capt., Army, 1 March 1804; Capt., Royal Artillery, 29 June 1808; Major, Army, 17 Aug. 1812. Mentioned in Wellington's Vittoria dispatch, dated 22 June 1813 ['the village of Gamarra Maior was most gallantly stormed and carried by Brigadier-General Robinson's brigade of the 5th division, which advanced in columns of battalions, under a very heavy fire of artillery and musquetry, without firing a shot, assisted by two guns of Major Lawson's brigade of artillery.'] [*London Gazette*]. Gold Medal.

LAWSON, Samuel Humble, Volunteer/2nd Lt., 95th Foot: *1829 Statement of Service for Retired Officers*: Aged nineteen on first appointment to the Army. 'Served five years (previous to entering the line) in the Irish Militia as Ensign and Lieutenant'; 2nd Lt., 95th Foot, 9 May 1812, 'obtained for having volluntered on the Forlorn Hope at Badajoz in Spain being then a Vollunteer with 3rd B. 95th Rifle Corps'; 1st Lt., 95th Foot, 21 April 1814; Half-pay, 2nd 'R.N.B. Dragoons', 15 Nov. 1814, 'in consequence of ill health contracted on service'. *Where serving when wounded*: 'Spain and France'. No pension. *Family*: Married in Bandan, Co. Cork, Ireland, 18 Jan. 1815. Eight children by 1829. *Title and nature of employment*: 'Chief Constable of Police, in Command of a certain number of men embodied for the purpose of more effectually executing Warrants & for the preservation of the Peace.' *Where generally resident during last five years*: 'Kinsall, Co. Cork, Ireland.' [PRO: WO 25/765 f71]. Slightly wounded, storming of Badajoz, 6 April 1812 [*London Gazette*]. MGS.

LEAF, John Walton, Lt., 52nd Foot: *1829 Statement of Service for Retired Officers*: Aged eighteen on first appointment to the Army. Ensign, 52nd Foot, 31 Dec. 1812; Lt., 52nd Foot, 7 Dec. 1813; Half-pay, 25 July 1816, by reduction. 'Not desirous of service, owing to a severe Wound above the ankle, received at the Battle of Orthez, March 27th 1814, and which by the least exertion in walking, occasions me great Pain and lameness.' *Where serving when wounded*: 'Wounded at Orthez in France March 27th 1814'. Not married. *Where generally resident during last five years*: 'Hall, Cheshire'. [PRO: WO 25/765

LEAF

f184]. Severely wounded, Orthes, 27 Feb. 1814 (1st Battn.) [*London Gazette*].

LEAKY, John Thomas, Major, 23rd Foot: *1829 Statement of Service*: Born Sept. 1783, Cork, Ireland. Aged sixteen on his first entrance into the Army. Ensign, 69th Foot, 18 June 1799; Lt., 4th Foot, Aug. 1799; Lt., 69th Foot, July 1802; Capt., 23rd Foot, Jan. 1805; Major, 23rd Foot, March 1812; Half-pay, 1814; Major, 7th Foot, 1815; Half-pay, 1816; Major, 21st Foot, April 1819; Lt. Col., 21st Foot, Aug. 1821. *Battles, sieges and campaigns*: 'Served in Holland in June 1799... At the capture and Seige of Copenhagen...1807... At the capture of Martinique in 1809 ... and the Seige of Fort Bourbon... At the affair of Redina in Portugal on the retreat of the French from the lines in 1811... At the seige of Badajos and Battle of Albuera in 1811... At the operations and with the divisions in support of the storming and capture of Ciudad Rodrigo in 1811 ... served with the Fusilier Brigade under General Packenham. At the affair of Albodam in 1811 in support of the Brigade under Sir C. Colville... The next day the command of the light cos. of the Fusilier Brigade and a company of the Brunswick's at the Aldea de ponte – devolved on me, Lieut. Col. Pearson having been wounded in the early part of the Day; which companies were reinforced by two cos. of the 7th and 2 Cos of the 23rd Fusiliers, on which Occasion the Honble. General Packenham expressed to me in person the Duke of Wellington's approbation of my conduct. Captain Commanding the 23rd Fusiliers during the Seige and Storming of Bajados in 1812.' *Distinguished conduct*: 'Mentioned in the Despatch of the Duke of Wellington as having Commanded the 23rd Fusiliers during the Operation and at Storming of Badajos in 1812.' *Wounds received in action*: 'Wounded at Badajos in March 1812. Received One years pay and a Pension of £200 per annum and permanently.' *Titles, honorary distinctions and medals*: 'A medal for Badajos in consequence of commanding the 23rd Royal Welsh Fusiliers.' *Service abroad*: 'July 1799 to 1799, Holland. 1802 to 1803, Jamaica and West Indies. 1807 to 1807, Copenhagen. 1807 to 1812, North America, West Indies, and Portugal. 1819 to 1824, West Indies.' Unmarried in 1830. [PRO: WO 25/789 f1]. Severely wounded, storming of Badajoz, 6 April 1812 ('Leckey') (1st Battn.) [*London Gazette*]. Mentioned in Wellington's Badajoz dispatch, 7 April 1812 ['likewise wounded, was ... Captain Leaky, who commanded the 23rd Regiment'] [*London Gazette*]. Temporary pension of one hundred pounds per annum, commencing 7 April 1813, 'for wounds' received at Badajoz, 1812 ('Leahy') [*1818 Pension Return*, pp. 6–7].

LE BLANC, Francis, Lt., 4th Foot: Lt., 4th Foot, 16 March 1809. Severely wounded, Storming of San Sebastian, 31 Aug. 1813 (1st Battn.) [*London Gazette*]. Mentioned in Graham's San Sebastian dispatch, dated Oyarzun, 1 Sept. 1813 ['Sir James Leith likewise particularizes... Lieutenant Le Blanc, of the 4th foot, who led the light infantry company of the regiment, immediately after the forlorn hope, and is the only surviving officer of the advance.'] [*London Gazette*]. Capt., 95th Foot, 1 Dec. 1814. Waterloo. MGS. *Dalton*, pp. 201, 202 ['Retd. in 1845. Living 1879.'].

+LEDWITH, Henry, 2nd Lt./1st Lt., 23rd Foot: 2nd Lt., 23rd Foot, 23 Feb. 1809. Slightly wounded, Albuera, 16 May 1811 (1st Battn.) [*London Gazette*]. 1st Lt., 23rd Foot, 11 July 1811. Slightly wounded, Pyrenees, 25 July 1813 (1st Battn.) [*London Gazette*]. Died of wounds, 3 Sept. 1813. Return dated Sept. 1813. [PRO: WO 25/2965].

LEE, James, Capt., 92nd Foot: *1829 Statement of Service for Retired Officers*: 'Major Jas. Lee took the name of Harvey only, By Royal Sign... 3rd February 1821.' Aged nineteen on first appointment to the Army. Ensign, 92nd Foot, 23 Feb. 1799; Lt., 92nd Foot, 7 Oct. 1799; Capt., 92nd Foot, 12 Oct. 1804; 'Obtained the Rank of Brevet Major after the Battle of Toulouse 12th Apl. 1814'; Major, 92nd Foot, 28 April 1814; Half-pay, 1814, 'In consequence of the Reduction of the 2nd Battn. of the 92nd Regt. which took place at Edinburgh Castle'. *Where serving when wounded*: 'At the taking of the Town of Aise in France'. No pension. *Family*: Married in 'Castle Temple, RenfrewShire, Scotland', 22 April 1816. Eight children born by 1829, though three had died. *Where generally resident during last five years*: 'Renfrewshire, Scotland.' [PRO: WO 25/761 f136]. Slightly wounded, Pyrenees, 31 July 1813 [*London Gazette*].

LEEBODY, William, Volunteer, 61st Foot: Severely wounded, Pyrenees, 28 July 1813 (1st Battn.) [*London Gazette*].

LEECH, James, Ensign/Adjutant, 8th Caçadores: Severely wounded, during 'movements of the Army' [Retreat from Burgos: Villa Muriel], 25 Oct. 1812, as Adjutant, 8th Caçadores [*London Gazette*]. Ensign, 86th Foot, 10 March 1814 ('Leche'). *Challis, Portuguese Army List*, p. 56 ['Ens. 8 Cacad.; P/S July '11 to Aug. '13.'].

LEEKY, David, Capt., 45th Foot: Capt., 45th Foot, 27 Aug. 1804; Major, Army, 1 Jan. 1805. Recorded as 'Missing', Talavera, 28 July 1809, while serving as brigade-major ('Leckey') [*London Gazette*].

+LEFEBURE, Charles, Capt., Royal Engineers: Capt., Army, 11 June 1800; Capt., Royal Engineers,

1 March 1805. Obituary, *The Gentleman's Magazine*, May 1810, pp. 497–8 ['22. [April]... During the defence of Fort Matagorda [Cadiz], Major Lefevre, royal engineers, by a cannon-ball. By his death the army has lost a most intelligent officer. Upon every occasion in which his services were demanded, he evinced the utmost bravery and zeal; but it was chiefly at the battle of Maida that he displayed those qualities. The talents he manifested in a district command which was entrusted to him in that ever-memorable battle, entitled him to the honour of a medal, which was intended to be conferred only on officers of superior rank; but his claims were undeniable, and the reward which was due to his gallant exertions was in justice granted as a fair distinction which he had earned on that glorious day. The reputation he had acquired attracted the notice of His Majesty's government; and he was, with great propriety, selected as an officer in every respect qualified to give the Spaniards the aide of his talents, and to obtain such intelligence respecting the state of things in Spain as could be relied upon for the extent and the accuracy of its details. In the performance of both these services, he gave the utmost satisfaction. Major Lefevre may be truly said to have existed only for the service. His passion for the Army, predominated over every other, and almost every thought of his mind was concentrated in that single point. He, at last, fell a victim to his heroic gallantry. General Graham, who entertained a just conception of his merit, had commanded him to bring off the detachment that had so long and so bravely defended the fortress of Matagorda... The evacuation was effected in good order; and Major Lefevre continuing in it to the last, was, at the moment of retiring from it, struck between the shoulders by a 32-pound shot, and instantly

killed.'], p. 475 [Reprinted from the *London Gazette*: 'Herewith I send a list of killed and wounded; and, among the former, I am sorry to return Major Lefebvre, of the Royal Engineers; he was killed close to me by a cannon-ball; the loss of such an excellent Officer is deeply to be lamented... A. MACLAIN, Cap. 94th reg. late Commander at Fort Matagorda.'].

LEITH, Alexander, Lt. Col., 31st Foot: *1829 Statement of Service for Retired Officers*: Aged seventeen on first appointment to the Army. Ensign, 42nd Foot, 8 Aug. 1792; Lt., 'Independent Company', 19 Nov. 1794; Capt., 109th Foot, 27 Nov. 1794; Capt., 31st Foot, 5 Sept. 1795; Major, 31st Foot, 1 Aug. 1804; Lt. Col., 31st Foot, 7 Feb. 1811; Half-pay, 48th Foot, 25 May 1815, 'Private motives'; Bvt. Col., 19 July 1821. *Where serving when wounded*: 'Holland 1799. France 1813.' *Details of pension*: One hundred pounds, commencing 1821. *Family:* Married in Mastrick, Aberdeenshire, 16 Sept. 1816. Four children by 1829. *Where generally resident during last five years*: 'Aberdeenshire'. [PRO: WO 25/765 f90]. Slightly wounded, the Nive, 13 Dec. 1813 (2nd Battn.) [*London Gazette*]. *Royal Military Calendar*, vol. IV, p. 330. ['He commanded the 31st foot at the battles of Vittoria, Pyrenees, Nivelle, Nive, and Orthes, for which he has the honor of wearing a Cross and one Clasp. He is Knight Commander of the Bath.'].

LEITH, James, Lt.-General: Colonel, 4th West India Regt., 1 Jan. 1801; Major-General 25 April 1808; Lt.-General, 'having local rank', Spain and Portugal, 6 Sept. 1811. K.B. Severely wounded, 'not dangerously', Salamanca, 22 July 1812 [*London Gazette*]. Severely wounded, storming of San Sebastian, 31 Aug. 1813 [*London Gazette*]. Mentioned in Graham's San Sebastian dispatch, dated Oyarzun, 1 Sept. 1813 ['Lieutenant-General Sir James Leith justified, in the fullest manner, the confidence reposed in his tried judgement and distinguished gallantry, conducting and directing the attack, till obliged to be reluctantly carried off, after receiving a most severe contusion on the breast, and having his left arm broken.'] [*London Gazette*].

+LEITH, James U. M., Lt., 68th Foot: Lt., 68th Foot, 24 July 1804. Slightly wounded, Pyrenees, 30 July 1813 [*London Gazette*]. Killed, 'in Action with the Enemy', 23 Feb. 1814 ('James W. M. Leith') [*London Gazette*]. *Register of officers' effects*: Killed in Action, Agarve, France, 25 Feb. 1814. Married. His effects totalled £1. 16s. 4d. [PRO: WO 25/2964]. Obituary, *The Aberdeen Journal*, 30 March 1814 ['Killed on the 23d ult. in action with the enemy, Captain James U. M. Leith, of the 68th Foot. He has left a widow, inconsolable for his loss, who, as a tribute of respect to his beloved memory, inserts the following extract of a letter received upon the mournful occasion: "The brigade to which he was attached was ordered to drive the enemy from the village, and entrenched camp, in front of Perion-hasse; and he, as usual the first man, had penetrated to the entrance of the town, and had the satisfaction to see them give way, when he received the fatal shot, which entered his left breast and passed through his body, allowing him only time to say to Lieutenant Stapleton, who was following him: 'Lead on, Stapleton, I am no more;' and who in emulating his noble example, is but too likely to share his fate, having received a wound immediately after, which I much fear will prove mortal. As a soldier and a companion, Captain Leith was respected and beloved in the division, and in his fall the service has lost an Officer, in whom knowledge, discretion, and real gallantry were happily combined – the most marked attention has been paid to his remains, by every officer and soldier of the corps, of which he was justly considered the brightest ornament." '].

+**LE MARCHANT, Carey, Lt. and Capt., 1st Foot Guards:** Ensign, Army, 28 May 1807; Ensign, 1st Foot Guards, 15 Sept. 1808; Lt. and Capt., 1st Foot Guards, 25 March 1813. Severely wounded, the Nive, 13 Dec. 1813, while serving as ADC to Lt.-General Sir W. Stewart [*London Gazette*]. Died of wounds, 12 March 1814. Return dated March 1814. [PRO: WO 25/2965]. Eldest son of John Gaspard Le Marchant. Born 1791. [*Burke's Peerage*].

+**LE MARCHANT, John Gaspard, Major-General:** Lt. Col., Army, 6 April 1797; Lt. Col. 2nd Dragoon Guards, 19 July 1799; Lt.-Gov. and Superintend. Gen. of the Royal Military College, 1807; Major-General, 4 June 1811; Lt. Col., 6th Dragoon Guards, 25 July 1811. Mentioned in Cotton's Llerena dispatch, 11 April 1812 ['I have to recommend strongly to your notice Major-General Le Marchant and the Honourable Lieutenant-Colonel Ponsonby, who commanded the two brigades with so much gallantry and judgement.'] [*London Gazette*]. Killed, Salamanca, 22 July 1812 [*London Gazette*]. *The Gentleman's Magazine*, Sept. 1812, p. 286 ['September 30... A handsome provision has been made for the family of the gallant General Le Marchant, who died with 36 balls in his body, while advancing and cheering at the head of his men. To the eldest son a pension is given of 200£. a year, to each of the four daughters 120£. a year, and to each of the three younger sons 100£. making in all 1200£. a year.']. Obituary, *The Gentleman's Magazine*, Oct. 1812, pp. 398–9 ['July 22. Fell, gallantly, at the head of his brigade, at the

battle of Salamanca, Major-gen. Le Marchant, a native of Guernsey. He embraced the military profession at an early period of life, and served principally in the cavalry. He was considered as an officer of great activity, and strictly attentive to all the duties connected with his station... He appears to have served his first campaign in the continental expedition of 1793 and 1794, under his Royal Highness the Duke of York. It was while employed on this service that he witnessed the great advantages to be derived in action from the skilful use of the cavalry sword, long practised by the Hungarian hussars... On his return from the Continent, he employed himself with great assiduity and perseverance in improving, and reducing into a system, all that his own experience had taught him... Major Le Marchant had ... the honour of first perfecting and digesting that system which was published at the War-Office in 1796, by his Majesty's command, and has since been adopted by the British cavalry... As a reward for his zeal and exertions, manifested in the foundation of this great national Academy [The Royal Military College], he was raised to be its Lieut.-governor, a situation of considerable honour and emoluments... [In 1811, as Major-General] he was appointed [to command] a brigade of cavalry, when on the eve of embarking for service in Portugal, for which country he immediately set out... Major-gen. Le Marchant was soon distinguished as an active and enterprizing officer... He had been but a short time in Portugal when he received the afflictive and most unexpected news of the death of Mrs. Le Marchant, whom the General had been obliged to leave far advanced in pregnancy. His grief, at so deplorable an event, was now only to be soothed by the bustle and activity of a fatiguing and protracted Campaign... He was not long in obtaining opportunities to distinguish himself, no less honourable to himself than useful to the service in which he was engaged. – A handsome provision has been made by Government, for the family of this gallant officer.']. *Leach*, p. 274 [Salamanca: 'General Le Marchant was killed, whilst gallantly leading a brilliant charge of cavalry.']. Le Marchant, Sir Denis, *Memoirs of the late Major-General Le Marchant* (London, 1841); Thoumine, R. H., *Scientific Soldier: A Life of General Le Marchant* (London, 1968).

+LE MESURIER, Havilland, Bvt. Lt. Col., E.O.P.S.; Col., 12th Portuguese Line: Bvt. Lt. Col., E.O.P.S., 3 Oct. 1811, 'Serv. with the Portug. Army'. Wounded, Pyrenees, 25–28 July 1813, while serving as Col., 12th Portuguese Line ('P. L. Measurier') [*London Gazette*]. In Portuguese Service April 1809 to Aug. 1813. Gold Medal. *Challis, Portuguese Army*, p. 56 ['Wd. Pyrenees 28 July '13; Died of Wounds Aug. '13']. Lengthy obituary, *The Gentleman's Magazine*, Jan. 1814, pp. 90–4 ['... at school at Salisbury, and afterwards at Westminster... His corps had scarcely entered into action on the 28th of July, when a musket-shot penetrated the back part of his head (or his temples, according to some accounts) and passed out at his eye, and he fell senseless; nor did he ever afterwards utter a word, or shew that he was sensible, though he lived till the 31st. By some strange chance, he was stated in the Gazette only simply as wounded; so that his friends were tantalized for more than three weeks before they obtained certain accounts of his fate ... he was little more than thirty years of age when he died... His constitution was not a good one, and he was subject to almost continued fevers and agues when in the Peninsula... The impetuosity of his temper, which certainly was

great, never troubled him, or any one else, but when he was in a state of inaction, either real or fancied. When employed, he was ever cool and collected. In him there was neither selfishness nor concealment. There was never a being more honourable or high-spirited and generous; more kind-hearted or liberal.']. Brother of Henry.

LE MESURIER, Henry, Ensign, 48th Foot: Ensign, 48th Foot, 13 May 1812. Severely wounded, 'right arm amputated', Salamanca, 22 July 1812 [*London Gazette*]. Seventy pounds per annum pension, commencing 23 July 1813, for 'loss of an arm' at Salamanca [*1818 Pension Return*, pp. 12–13]. MGS. Brother of Havilland. Obituary of his brother, *The Gentleman's Magazine*, Jan. 1814, p. 93 ['...that Brother whom he had induced to enter the Army, and who had lost his right arm by a cannon-shot at the Battle of Salamanca.'].

+LE MESURIER, Peter, Lt. 9th Foot: Lt., 9th Foot, 23 Nov. 1809. Slightly wounded, Crossing the Bidassoa, 7/9 Oct. 1813 ('Lemesurier') (1st Battn.) [*London Gazette*]. Killed, the Nive, 10 Dec. 1813 ('P. L. Lemesurier') (1st Battn.) [*London Gazette*].

LE MESURIER, William Abraham, Capt., 24th Foot: Capt., 24th Foot, 15 March 1810. Slightly wounded, Orthes, 27 Feb. 1814 (2nd Battn.) [*London Gazette*]. MGS.

LEMMERS, Nicholas, Lt., 2nd Light Battn. K.G.L: Lt., 2nd Light Battn. K.G.L., 3 March 1810. Severely wounded, Heights of Villares, 20–22 June 1812 [*London Gazette*]. Slightly wounded, Crossing the Bidassoa, 7/9 Oct. 1809 ('Lemers') [*London Gazette*]. Served in Peninsula 1811–14. *Beamish*, vol. II, p. 663 ['severely wounded, 22d June 1812, at Morisco; slightly wounded, 7th Oct.

1813, on the Bidassoa. Resigned 10th May 1814. [Died] in the West Indies, 1828.'].

+LEMPRIERE, Charles, Lt., 58th Foot; Capt., 16th Portuguese Line: Lt., 58th Foot, 29 April 1808. Severely wounded, Pyrenees, 2 Aug. 1813 ('Lamprier') (2nd Battn.) [*London Gazette*]. Severely wounded, the Nive, 10 Dec. 1813, 'since dead', while serving as Capt., 16th Portuguese Line ('Lamprier') [*London Gazette*]. Died of wounds, 12 Dec. 1813. Return dated Dec. 1813. [PRO: WO 25/2965]. *Register of officers' effects*: Died of wounds, 12 Dec. 1813, St. Jean de Luz. Single. Effects totalled £11. 14s. 1d. [PRO: WO 25/2963]. In Portuguese Service Sept. 1813 to Dec. 1813. *Challis, Portuguese Army*, p. 56 ['Died of wounds 20 Jan. '14'].

+LENHART, Lt., Chasseurs Britanniques: Lt., Chasseurs Britanniques, 26 April 1810. Severely wounded, Vittoria, 21 June 1813 [*London Gazette*]. Died of wounds, 25 June 1813. Return dated July 1813. [PRO: WO 25/2965].

+LENNON, William Fitzmaurice, Lt., 44th Foot: Lt., 44th Foot, 26 Feb. 1810. Killed, during 'movements of the Army' [Retreat from Burgos: Villa Muriel], 25 Oct. 1812 ('Lemon') [*London Gazette*].

LEONARD, Thomas, Ensign, 88th Foot: Ensign, 88th Foot, 11 Aug. 1808. Severely wounded, Busaco, 27 Sept. 1810 (1st Battn.) [*London Gazette*]. Recorded as having died. *1811 Army List.*

LEONHARDT, Georg Carl Friederich, Cornet, 1st Light Dragoons/Hussars K.G.L: *1829 Statement of Service for Retired Officers*: Aged 'near 26' on first appointment to the Army. Cornet, '1st Regt, of Hussars K.G. Legion', 31 Jan. 1812; Lt., 1st Hussars K.G.L., 13 Sept. 1814 [Army List

gives 31 Sept. 1814]; Half-pay, by reduction. Served six years on full-pay, 'including two years for the Battle of Waterloo.' *Where serving when wounded*: 'In Portugal & Spain.' *Details of pension*: Fifty pounds per annum, commencing 25 Dec. 1822. *Family*: Married in Moringen, Hanover, 9 April 1817. Two children by 1829. 'Allow me to remark that my wife is absent, without my permission, since 6th December 1825.' *Where generally resident during last five years*: 'Hannover'. [PRO: WO 25/765 f192]. Slightly wounded, during the advance from Fuente Guinaldo to Salamanca, 16–18 June 1812 [*London Gazette*]. Served in Peninsula 1809–14. Waterloo. *Beamish*, vol. II, p. 551 ['severely wounded, 16th Sept. 1810, at Corticao; severely wounded 8th May, 1812, at Castello Branco... [Died] at Hanover 4th May, 1833, a captain h.p.'].

LEONHART, Ernest Lewis Francis, Lt. Col. 1st Light Battn. K.G.L.: Lt. Col., 1st Light Battn. K.G.L., 8 Jan. 1805. Served in Peninsula 1808–12. Gold Medal. *Beamish*, vol. II, p. 644 ['severely wounded, 16th May 1811, at Albuera... [Died from illness or accident] at Escurial in Spain, 10th Sept. 1812.'].

LEPPER, James, Capt., 24th Foot: Capt., 24 Foot, 22 June 1809. Severely wounded, Pyrenees, 2 Aug. 1813 (2nd Battn.) [*London Gazette*]. MGS.

LERCHE, Gottlieb, Ensign/Lt., 60th Foot: *1829 Statement of Service for Retired Officers*: Aged twenty-two on first appointment to the Army. 'In the year 1798, I served in the Corps of 3d Lowenstein, the Campaign in Egypt and on returning to the Isle of Wight this Corps was disbanded and was transferred to the 5th Bn. 60th Rgt. and joined my Battn. in Halifax America.' Ensign, 60th Foot, 14 May 1812; Lt., 60th

Foot, 19 Aug. 1813; Half-pay, Royal Waggon Train, 'at my own request for ill-health.' Served five years on full-pay. Thirteen years 'as Private and Noncommissioned officer.' *Where serving when wounded*: 'in the Peninsula'. Seventy pounds, commencing 'from the date I lost my arm, 15 Feby. 1814.' *Family*: Married in Brunswick, Germany, 15 May 1815. One child by 1829. *Where generally resident during last five years*: '3 years in the Hanov. Country Salzquitter and 2 years in Brunswick.' [PRO: WO 25/765 f149]. Severely wounded, 'left arm amputated', 'in Action with the Enemy', 15 Feb. 1814 (5th Battn.) [*London Gazette*]. Seventy pounds per annum pension, commencing 16 Feb. 1814, for 'loss of an arm' at St Palais, 1814 [*1818 Pension Return*, pp. 14–15].

LEROUX, George Wilson, Lt., 48th Foot: Lt., 48th Foot, 3 Feb. 1808. Severely wounded, Salamanca, 22 July 1812 ['Leroux'] [*London Gazette*]. 'Leroo' in Army List.

LESLIE, Charles, Lt., 29th Foot; Capt., 60th Foot: *1829 Statement of Service*: 'Born Fetternea House, Aberdeenshire, April 1785. Aged twenty one years on his first Entrance into the Army. Ensign, 29th Foot, 18th Decr. 1806. Lieutenant, 29th Foot, [10] Feby. 1808. Captain, 60th Foot, 5 Novr. 1813. Half Pay, 25 Dec. 1818, on reduction of the 3rd Bn. 60th Regt. but retained on full pay doing duty with it until appointed. Captain, 60th regt., 17 May 1820. Major, 60th, 18 Dec. 1828.' Note added: 'Lt. Col., Half Pay, Unattd., 28 Decr. 32.' *Battles, sieges and campaigns*: 'Secret Expedition under Sir B. Spencer from the 7th Decr. 1807 to 6th August 1808. The Action of Rolica 17th Augt. 1808. The Battle of Vimiera 21st Augt. 1808. Taking of Oporto 12 May 1809. Battle of Talavera 27th and 28th July 1809. First Siege of Badajos May 1811.

Battle of Albuhera 16th May 1811 soon after which had the command of 29th Regt. for a short time when only a Lieut. in consequence of the severe loss of officers. Besides various Skirmishes and Affrays at Out Posts. Lieutenant 29th Regt. at the whole of the above actions.' *Wounds received in action*: 'severely wounded at the Battle of Talavera 28th July 1809. A Ball still lodged in the Right Leg. Received the usual Gratuity of one Years Pay as Lieut. No Pension.' *Titles, honorary distinctions and medals*: 'None' Note added: 'K H Jany 1836' *Service abroad*: 'Secret Expedition under Sir B. Spencer: 7 Dec. 1807 to 14th March 1808, at Sea. 15th March 1808 to 14th May 1808, Gibralter. 15th May 1808 to 3 July 1808, cruizing with the Fleet off Cadiz. 4th July 1808 to 20th July 1808, landed at St Marys. 21 July 1808 to 6 Augt. 1808, with the Fleet off Lisbon. 7th Augt. 1808 to 1st Decr. 1811, Portugal & Spain. 14th Feby. 1813 to 6 Decr. 1815, Spain, Cadiz, Tariffa, Gibralter. 12 Aug. 1816 to 16 July 1820, Halifax, North America. 9 June 1821 to 20 Augt. 1824, Canada.' *Family*: Married his first wife, Mary Halloway, daughter of Major General Sir Charles Halloway, Royal Engineers, on 24 Nov. 1826, in Plymouth. The couple had one son, born on 28 April 1832, prior to Mary's death on 30 Sept. 1832. Charles Leslie remarried in 1836, Lady Dorothy Eyre. [PRO: WO 25/796 f301]. Severely wounded, Talavera, 28 July 1809 [*London Gazette*].

+LESLIE, David. A., Lt., 50th Foot; Lt., 19th Portuguese Line: Lt., 50th Foot, 1 Aug. 1811. Killed, 'in the Operations of the Army', 31 Aug. 1813, while serving as Lt., 19th Portuguese Line [*London Gazette*]. In Portuguese Service Oct. 1812 to Aug. 1813. *Challis, Portuguese Army*, p. 56 [Lt. 19 Line... Wd. Pyrenees 30 July '13; K/A San Sebastian (sic) 31 Aug. '13'].

LESTER

+LESLIE, James, Capt., 45th Foot: Lt., 45th Foot, 13 Nov. 1805; Adjutant, 45th Foot, 26 March 1807; Capt., 45th Foot, 5 March 1812. Severely wounded, Orthes, 27 Feb. 1814 ('Captain James Lester') (1st Battn.) [*London Gazette*]. Died of wounds, 1 March 1814. Return dated March 1814. [PRO: WO 25/2965].

LESLIE, James, Ensign, 57th Foot: *1829 Statement of Service for Retired Officers*: Aged thirty on first appointment to the Army. Ensign, 57th Foot, 15 Feb. 1810, 'Obtained the Ensigncie at the Recommendation of the Duke of Wellington after having served 13 years in His Majesty's 3rd Regt. of Foot Guards'; Lt., 57th Foot, 21 Nov. 1811; Adjutant, 57th Foot, 20 May 1813; Half-pay, 5 Feb. 1818, 'on account of ill health occasioned by Wounds after returning to this Country from the Army in France.' *Where serving when wounded*: 'While leading a part of the Portuguese in the assault upon Fort St Christoval at the seige of Badajos in Spain in the night of the 9th June 1811 then an assistant-engineer, taken prisoner the same night but escaped the Enemy the 9th October 1811.' *Details of pension*: '10th June 1812 a Grant of £50 per annum being the allowance granted to an Ensign the Rank I heald at the time of being wounded but His Majesty was pleased to augment the grant to £70 per annum from the 25th June 1821'. *Family*: Married in St Ann, Westminster, 25 Sept. 1802. 'No children living'. *Where generally resident during last five years*: 'At Tents Hill Cottage, Mells Somersetshire.' [PRO: WO 25/765 f186]. Recorded as 'Missing', siege of Badajoz, 6–11 May 1811 [*London Gazette*]. Wounded, siege of Badajoz, 30 May–5 June 1811 [*London Gazette*]. *1818 Pension Return*, pp. 14–15.

LESLIE, Joseph, Ensign/Lt., 87th Foot: Ensign, 87th Foot, 26 April 1810. Lt., 87th Foot, 8 Oct. 1812. Severely wounded, Nivelle, 10 Nov. 1813 (2nd Battn.) [*London Gazette*].

LESLIE, Kevan Izod, Ensign/Lt., 79th Foot: *1829 Statement of Service for Retired Officers*: Aged eighteen on first appointment to the Army. Ensign, 79th Foot, 21 March 1811; Lt., 79th Foot, 1 April 1812; Capt., 60th Foot, 18 Oct. 1815; Half-pay, 25 March 1818, by reduction. *Where serving when wounded*: 'Severely wounded at the siege of Burgos.' 'I did not apply for Pension.' *Family*: Married in Halifax, Nova Scotia, 30 Oct. 1817. Two children by 1829. *Where generally resident during last five years*: 'In Ireland'. [PRO: WO 25/765 f177]. Severely wounded, 'in the assault and capture of the exterior line of the castle of Burgos on the evening of the 4th October, 1812' (1st Battn.) [*London Gazette*]. Waterloo Medal. *Dalton*, pp. 189, 191 ['Capt. 60th Rifles 18th Oct., 1815. H.p. 1817.'].

LESTER, Thomas Young, Lt., 7th Foot: *1829 Statement of Service for Retired Officers*: Aged twenty-four 'to the best of my Belief' on first appointment to the Army. Lt., 7th Foot, 30 May 1810; Half-pay, 'August or October 1821', 'By incapacity occasioned by wounds'. 'Perfectly desirous of serving but apprehensive that continual disability from wounds & subsequent ill Health occasioned by an almost constant confinement to House during the last seven years will ever prevent his being placed any situation of activity.' *Where serving when wounded*: 'In Spain'. *Details of pension*: Seventy pounds, commencing 7 April 1813. *Family*: 'Married in Dumbarton Castle N.B. [Scotland]', 9 Sept. 1822. Two children by 1829. *Where generally resident during last five years*: 'Toulouse in France & Barnwood near Gloster.' [PRO: WO 25/765

345

f114]. Severely wounded, storming of Badajoz, 6 April 1812 [*London Gazette*].

L'ESTRANGE, John, Lt., 66th Foot: Lt., 66th Foot, 3 Feb. 1808. Slightly wounded, Albuera, 16 May 1811 92nd Battn.) [*London Gazette*].

L'ESTRANGE, Thomas, Lt., 36th Foot: Lt., 36th Foot, 29 Feb. 1808. Slightly wounded, Nivelle, 10 Nov. 1813 (1st Battn.) [*London Gazette*]. Severely wounded, Toulouse, 10 April 1814 (1st Battn.) [*London Gazette*]. MGS.

LETOLLER, Henry, Ensign, 83rd Foot: Ensign, 83rd Foot, 16 March 1809. Slightly wounded, Talavera, 28 July 1809 [*London Gazette*].

+LEVINGE, Charles, Lt., 27th Foot: Lt., 27th Foot, 14 Sept. 1808. Wounded during the repulse of a sortie from Badajoz, 10 May 1811 [*London Gazette*]. Killed, storming of Badajoz, 6 April 1812 [*London Gazette*].

LEWIN, Carrique, Lt., 71st Foot: *1829 Statement of Service for Retired Officers*: Aged 'about 15 or 16' on first appointment to the Army. Ensign, Roscommon Militia, 6 March 1806; Lt., Roscommon Militia, 'latter end of 1807'; Ensign, 71st Foot, 3 Aug. 1809, 'By volunteering and procuring volunteers for the Lign'; Lt., 71st Foot, 27 June 1811; Half-pay, 'April or May 1822', 'to afford support to an aged, dependent, and infirm Father and Mother'. *Where serving when wounded*: 'No grant or pension from Wounds, nor have I at any time received any, though twice wounded, first, at Fuentes de Honour in Portugal, when I was not returned in the number of wounded in consideration of my parents then labouring under severe indisposition. Second wound at Waterloo when in command of a company'. Not married. *Where generally resi-*

dent during last five years: 'At Oakland... County of Galway.' [PRO: WO 25/765 f169]. Died, 1875.

LEWIN, Thomas Ross, Lt., 32nd Foot: See Ross-Lewin, Thomas.

LEWIS, Edward, Lt., 36th Foot: Ensign, 36th Foot, 18 July 1811; Lt., 36th Foot, 9 Sept. 1812. Severely wounded, Toulouse, 10 April 1814 (1st Battn.) [*London Gazette*].

LEWIS, Griffith George, 2nd Capt., Royal Engineers: 2nd Capt., Royal Engineers, 18 Nov. 1807. Severely wounded, 'at the Siege of St Sebastian,' 7–27 July 1813 [*London Gazette*]. Mentioned in Graham's dispatch to Wellington dated 27 July 1813, concerning the failed Assault on San Sebastian on the morning of 25 July 1813 ['The conduct throughout the whole of the operations of the siege hitherto, of the officers and men of the ... engineers, never was exceeded in indefatigable zeal, activity, and gallantry... The three officers of this corps, employed to conduct different parts of the columns of attack, behaved admirably, but suffered severely. Captain Lewis has lost his leg, Lieutenant Jones was wounded in the breach, and taken; and Lieutenant Machell, after his return, was killed in the trenches.'] [*London Gazette*]. MGS.

LEWIS, Roger Lambert, Lt., 20th Foot: Lt., 20th Foot, 10 Nov. 1808. Severely wounded, Pyrenees, 28 July 1813 [*London Gazette*].

+LIFFORD, Richard, Ensign, 52nd Foot: Ensign, 52nd Foot, 3 Aug. 1809. Wounded, during 'several Affairs with the French Army' [Redinha], 12 March 1812 (1st Battn.) [*London Gazette*]. *Moorsom*, p. 134 ['The 52nd, commanded by Lieutenant-Colonel John Ross, sustained the following casualties on the 12th, 14th, and 15th March... Ensign Richard

Lifford (severely)... Ensign Lifford afterwards died of his wounds.'].

+LIGHT, John, Lt., 1st Batt. 28th Foot: Lt., 28th Foot, 1 April 1806. 'Dangerously wounded', Barossa, 5 March 1811 [*London Gazette*]. *Haythornthwaite, Die Hard,* p. 138 ['two of the wounded officers died of their injuries: Lieutenant John Light of the 28th's grenadiers, and Blakeney's friend Bennett'].

LIGHTFOOT, Thomas, Capt./ Major, 45th Foot: Capt., 45th Foot, 15 Dec. 1804. Slightly wounded, siege of Badajoz, 26 March 1812 [*London Gazette*]. Slightly wounded, storming of Badajoz, 6 April 1812 [*London Gazette*]. Slightly wounded, Salamanca, 22 July 1812 [*London Gazette*]. Major, 45th Foot, 7 Oct. 1813. Severely wounded, Toulouse, 10 April 1814 (1st Battn.) [*London Gazette*]. Gold Medal. Later Major-General. MGS. *Royal Military Calendar,* vol. V, pp. 31–2 ['He served at the siege ... of Roderigo in 1812, where he stormed, at the head of the light and grenadier companies of the 3d division, the great breach, the storming party consisting of the flank companies of the 45th, 74th, and 88th regs. He was in the siege of Badajos in 1812, and stormed Fort Piccarini ... and was slightly wounded. He stormed the castle of Badajos, at the head of the flank companies of the 3d division, consisting as before, and was again slightly wounded... he was second in command of the 45th reg ... at the battle of Toulouse, where he was severely wounded.'].

LILLIE, John Scott, Lt., 6th Foot; Capt., 60th Foot; Major, 7th Caçadores: *1829 Statement of Service for Retired Officers*: Aged eighteen on first appointment to the Army. Ensign, 6th Foot, 3 March 1807; Lt., 6th Foot, 1810 [Army List gives 29 March 1810]; Capt., 60th Foot, 1813 [Army List gives 11 Nov.

1813]; Half-pay, 24 Dec. 1818, by reduction; Capt., 46th Foot, 1827, 'but being unable from the nature of his wounds to serve in a tropical climate he returned to half pay of the 31st Regt. in 1828.' *Where serving when wounded*: 'Toulouse'. *Details of pension*: Two hundred and fifty pounds, commencing '1815 or 1816'. *Family*: Married in the Parish of St George, Hanover Square, London, 22 Jan. 1820. Two children by 1829. *Where generally resident during last five years*: 'St John's, Fulham, Middx.' [PRO: WO 25/765 f193]. Severely wounded, Toulouse, 10 April 1814, as Major, 7th Caçadores ('John Scot Lillie') [*London Gazette*]. In Portuguese Service Dec. 1808 to April 1814. Gold Medal. *1818 Pension Return*, pp. 26–27. MGS. *Challis, Portuguese Army*, p. 56 ['Wd. Osma 19 June '13, Nivelle 10 Nov. '13, Toulouse 10 Apr. '14']. Co-author with Lt. Col. William Mayne of *Narrative of the Campaigns of the Loyal Lusitanian Legion* (London, 1812).

LILLIE, Thomas, 2nd Lt., 23rd Foot: *1829 Statement of Service*: 'Born Drimdos near Boyle, Ireland, 3rd November 1796. Was 16 Years of Age on first entering the Army. 2nd Lieut., 23d Fusileers, 1 October 1812. 1st Lieut., 23d Fusileers, 17 July 1815. Half Pay, 25 March 1817, Reduction. Lieut., 48 Foot, 26 March 1824. Lieut., 31 Foot, 25 January 1825. Lieut., 59 Foot, before Augt. 1828. Half Pay, Between March and June 1830, Reduction. Lieut., 58 Foot, 11 January 1831.' *Battles, sieges and campaigns*: 'Was present with the Army under His Grace the Duke of Wellington during the following operations, viz. 19 June 1813 driving the Enemy across the Zadino; 21 June 1813, Battle of Vittoria; 5th to 18 July employed in the Blockade of Pampeluna; 25 July, Pass of Rouncesvallies' 28th Battle of Pampeluna; 10 Novr. Nivelle; 9 to 13th Passage of the Nive; 27

February 1814 Battle of Orthes; 10 April Battle of Thoulouse; 18 June 1815 – Waterloo; 24 June – Storming Cambray.' *Wounds received in action*: 'Slightly wounded at the Battle of Orthes, in command of a Compy.' *Titles, honorary distinctions and medals*: 'Medal for Waterloo.' *Service abroad*: 'December 1812 to June 1814, Portugal, Spain, France. March 1815 to March 1817, France, Netherlands. May 1824 to April 1826, India. 27 June 1831, Ceylon.' *Family*: Married Elizabeth Hunter, 20 March 1817, in Paris. They had three children by 1830. [PRO: WO 25/796 f264].

+**LIMA, Martin, Lt., 48th Foot:** Lt., 48th Foot, 11 July 1811. Killed, Pyrenees, 28 July 1813 (1st Battn.) [*London Gazette*].

LINDSAY, George, Lt., 9th Foot: Lt., Army, 18 Jan. 1808; Lt., 9th Foot, 7 Dec. 1809. Severely wounded, Busaco, 27 Sept. 1810 (1st Battn.) [*London Gazette*]. Seventy pounds per annum pension, commencing 25 Dec. 1811, for 'loss of an arm' at Busaco [*1818 Pension Return*, pp. 6–7].

+**LINDSAY, Patrick, Capt., 88th Foot:** Capt., Army, 16 April 1807; Capt., 88th Foot, 15 Oct. 1807. Killed, storming of Badajoz, 6 April 1812 ('Lindsey') [*London Gazette*].

+**LINDSAY, Thomas, Lt., 83rd Foot:** Ensign, 83rd Foot, 7 March 1811. Killed, Vittoria, 21 June 1813 (2nd Battn.) ('Lieutenant') [*London Gazette*].

+**LINDSELL, John Peter, Lt., 11th Light Dragoons:** Lt., 11th Light Dragoons, 20 March 1806. Obituary, *The Gentleman's Magazine*, Oct. 1812, p. 400 ['Aug. 18. In Spain, of a gun-shot wound, Lieutenant Lindsell, of the 11th dragoons.'].

LINSINGEN, Charles von, Ensign/Lt., 5th Line Battn. K.G.L:

1829 Statement of Service for Retired Officers: Aged fourteen on first appointment to the Army. Ensign, 5th Line Battn. K.G.L., 7 Dec. 1805; Lt., 5th Line Battn. K.G.L., 14 Jan. 1808; Capt., 5th Line Battn. K.G.L., 16 April 1813; Half-pay, by reduction. Served eleven years on full pay. *Where serving when wounded*: 'before Bayonne in Pyranees'. *Details of pension*: One hundred pounds, commencing 28 Feb. 1815. *Family*: Married in Luneburg, Hanover, 21 Feb. 1816. Eight children by 1829. *Where generally resident during last five years*: 'near Bremen, Kingdom of Hannover.' [PRO: WO25/765-f211]. Severely wounded, Talavera, 28 July 1809 [*London Gazette*]. Served in Peninsula 1808–14. *Beamish*, vol. II, p. 590 ['severely wounded, 28th July 1809, at Talavera; severely wounded, 27th Feb. 1814, before Bayonne.'].

LINSINGEN, Ernest von, Capt., 1st Light Dragoons/Hussars K.G.L.: Capt., 1st Light Dragoons K.G.L., 17 Nov. 1804. Slightly wounded during skirmishing, 9–14 Oct. 1810 [*London Gazette*]. Served in Peninsula 1809–13. Later Major-General and Adjutant-General to the Hanoverian cavalry. *Beamish*, vol. II, p. 556 ['slightly wounded, 9th Oct. 1810, at Alcoentre'].

LISTER, William, 1st Lt., 95th Foot: 1st Lt., 95th Foot, 23 Aug. 1810. Slightly wounded, Vittoria, 21 June 1813 ('Lester') [*London Gazette*]. *Simmons*, p. 368 [killed, Quatre Bras, 16 June 1815: 'Poor Lister was killed the first day. He was wounded in the stomach, and died a few hours after.'].

+**LITTLE, George, Lt., 45th Foot:** Lt., 45th Foot, 7 Nov. 1811. Severely wounded, Vittoria, 21 June 1813 (1st Battn.) [*London Gazette*]. Severely wounded, Toulouse, 10 April 1814 (1st Battn.) [*London Gazette*]. Died of wounds, 11 April

1814. Return dated April 1814. [PRO: WO 25/2965]. *Hurt*, p. 78.

LIVESAY, Charles Edward, Capt., 47th Foot: Capt., 47th Foot, 30 Jan. 1806. Severely wounded, storming of San Sebastian, 31 Aug. 1813 (2nd Battn.) *[London Gazette]*. Mentioned in Graham's San Sebastian dispatch, dated Oyarzun, 1 Sept. 1813 ['Major-General Robinson ... commends highly Captain Livesay, who succeeded to the command of the 47th foot, on Major Kelly's being killed, and kept it till wounded'] *[London Gazette]*.

LIVINGSTONE, Alexander, Capt., 60th Foot: Served in Egypt as a Cornet with the 12th Light Dragoons. Capt., 60th Foot, 3 Aug. 1805. Severely wounded, storming of Ciudad Rodrigo, 19 Jan. 1812 ('Livingston') *[London Gazette]*. Capt., 1st Garrison Battn., 20 May 1813. One hundred pounds per annum pension, commencing 20 Jan. 1813, for wounds received at Ciudad Rodrigo, 1812 [*1818 Pension Return*, pp. 14–15]. MGS.

LLEWELYN, Edward, 2nd Lt., 23rd Foot: 2nd Lt., 23rd Foot, 17 Aug. 1810. Severely wounded, storming of Badajoz, 6 April 1812 *[London Gazette]*. *Challis, Index*, p. 94.

LLEWELLYN, Henry, 1st Lt., 95th Foot: 1st Lt., 95th Foot, 21 Nov. 1810. Slightly wounded, 'at the Capture of the City of Seville by Assault,' 27 Aug. 1812 *[London Gazette]*. Severely wounded, 'in the Operations of the Army', 31 Aug. 1813 *[London Gazette]*. Pension of seventy pounds per annum, commencing 1 Sept. 1814, 'for a wound' received in the Pyrenees, 1813 [*1818 Pension Return*, pp. 22–3]. *Simmons*, p. 314 [wounded, Vera, 31 Aug. 1813: 'had his jaw shattered.'].

LLOYD, Frederick. Volunteer/ Ensign, 32nd Foot: Slightly wounded, Pyrenees, 28 July 1813 ('Volunteer Lloyd') (1st Battn.) *[London Gazette]*. Ensign, 32nd Foot, 1 Sept. 1813.

LLOYD, James Richard Lewis, Capt., 10th Light Dragoons: Capt., 10th Light Dragoons (Hussars), 25 Aug. 1809. Recorded as 'missing', 'in Action with the Enemy's Rear Guard, near Morales', 2 June 1813 *[London Gazette]*. Mentioned in Grant's Morales dispatch, 2 June 1813 ['It is with much satisfaction I acquaint your Lordship, that nothing could exceed the steadiness and bravery of the troops in this affair. I have, however, to regret the loss of ... Lieutenant Cotton, of the 10th Hussars, who was killed... I am sorry to add, that Captain Lloyd, of the same regiment, is missing... P.S. Since writing the above, I have learnt that Captain Lloyd was wounded and taken prisoner, but has been left at Pedrosa del Rey, having given his parole to the enemy. His wound is severe, but not dangerous.'] *[London Gazette]*. Capt., 18th Light Dragoons, 12 Nov. 1814. Waterloo. MGS.

+LLOYD, Richard, Lt. Col., 84th Foot: Lt. Col., Army, 13 Nov. 1806; Lt. Col., 84th Foot, 22 Dec. 1808. Killed, the Nive, 10 Dec. 1813 (2nd Battn.) *[London Gazette]*. Mentioned in Wellington's Nive dispatch, *London Gazette*, 30 Dec. 1813 ['Lieutenant-General Hope reports most favourably of the conduct of ... Lieut. Col. Lloyd, of the 84th, who was unfortunately killed']. *Fletcher, Fields of Fire*, p. 159 ['Visitors to the small but charming village of Bidaut, on the Atlantic coast, will find a very peculiar oddity within the grounds of the local church. Within the churchyard lies the grave of Lieutenant Colonel Richard Lloyd, of the 84th Regiment, who was killed on December 11th 1813 during the battle of the Nive. The unusual feature about Lloyd's grave is that he was buried standing upright!'].

+LLOYD, Thomas, Capt., 43rd Foot; Major, 94th Foot: Capt., Army, 8 Oct. 1803; Capt., 43rd Foot, 10 Aug. 1804. Slightly wounded, Coa, 24 July 1810 [*London Gazette*]. Major, 94th Foot, 4 Oct. 1810. Lt. Col., Army, 17 Aug. 1812. Killed, Nivelle, 10 Nov. 1813 ('Major Thomas Lloyd, Lieutenant Colonel') [*London Gazette*]. Mentioned in Wellington's Nivelle dispatch ['we have lost in Lieutenant-Colonel Lloyd, of the 94th, an officer who had frequently distinguished himself, and was of great promise.'] [*London Gazette*, 25 Nov. 1813]. Mentioned in the *1829 Statement of Service* of Archibald Robertson: 'succeeded [to Lt., 94th Foot] by the death of Major (Brevet Lieut. Colonel) Lloyd, near to whom Ensign Robertson stood when his brave Commanding Officer fell 10th November 1813 (at the Nivelle).' [PRO: WO 25/804 f33]. *Bruce*, pp. 134–5 ['In this battle of the Nivelle was killed Napier's old and dear friend Lloyd, he being at the time lieutenant-colonel commanding the 94th Regiment.'], pp. 135–6 [Quotes from Napier's History: 'He ... had been a long time in the 43rd ... but in the course of the war, promotion placed Lloyd at the head of the 94th, and it was leading that regiment he fell. In him also were combined mental and bodily powers of no ordinary kind. Graceful symmetry, herculean strength, and a countenance frank and majestic, gave the true index of his nature; for his capacity was great and commanding, and his military knowledge extensive both from experience and study. Of his mirth and wit, well known in the army, it only need be said that he used the latter without offence, yet so as to increase the ascendency over those with whom he held intercourse; for though gentle, he was ambitious, valiant, and conscious of fitness for great exploits. And he, like Freer, was prescient of, and predicted his own fall, but with no

abatement of courage; for when he received the mortal wound, a most painful one, he would not suffer himself to be moved; and remained to watch the battle, making observations upon its changes until death came. It was thus at the age of thirty, that the good, the brave, the generous Lloyd died.'], p. 137 ['when the news arrived of the death of Lloyd ... Napier threw himself on the ground and cried like a child.']. *Colville*, pp. 150–1.

+LOCKHART, William, Lt., 16th Light Dragoons: Lt., 16th Light Dragoons, 28 June 1810. Wounded, 'since dead', during 'movements of the Army' [Retreat from Burgos], 23 Oct. 1812 [*London Gazette*]. Died of wounds, 28 Oct. 1812. Return dated 25 Nov. 1812. [PRO: WO 25/2965]. *Register of officers' effects*: Died of wounds, 23 Oct. 1812, at 'Olmedo'. Single. Effects totalled £215. 19s. 4½d. [PRO: WO 25/2963].

LOCKWOOD, William, Lt., 71st Foot: Lt., 71st Foot, 27 Aug. 1807. Wounded, 'in the Army lately in Spain' (1st Battn.) [*March 1809 Army List*, p. 105]. Severely wounded, 'at the Storm and Capture of Fort Napoleon, and the Enemy's other Works, in the Neighbourhood of Almaraz', 19 May 1812 [*London Gazette*].

LOCKYER, Henry Frederick, Ensign/Lt., 71st Foot: *1829 Statement of Service*: Born 8 April 1796, Plymouth. Entered the Army aged 16. Ensign, 71st Foot, 18 March 1813; Lt., 71st Foot, 19 Jan. 1814; Half-pay 'by reduction of the 2nd Batt.', Dec. 1815; Lt., 43rd Foot, May 1816; Half-pay 'by reduction of the 2nd Batt.', 25 Dec. 1816; Lt., 3rd Foot, 12 Aug. 1820; Capt., 3rd Foot, 20 June 1822. *Service abroad*: 'Aug. 1813–July 1814 – Peninsula; April 1823–June 1827 – New South Wales; 5 July 1829–31 Dec. 1829 – Bengal.' *Battles, sieges and campaigns*:

Nive, Nivelle, Orthes, 'Thoulouse'. *Wounds received in action*: 'Was severely wounded at Battle of Ayres on 2d March 1814 on left Wrist and elbow joint of same arm. Made no application for remuneration.' *Distinguished conduct*: 'Was noticed in Garrison Orders by Colonel Arthur, commanding at Van Diemen's Land, for his zeal and activity in carrying into effect the arrangements directed for the apprehension of Bush Rangers, 21 April 1826.' [PRO: WO 25/785 f247]. Severely wounded, Aire, 2 March 1814 ('H. T. Lockeyer') (1st Battn.) [*London Gazette*]. MGS.

LODDERS, Frederick August John Lewis, Lt./Capt., 5th Line Battn. K.G.L.: Lt., 5th Line Battn. K.G.L., 8 Dec. 1805. Wounded, Heights of Grijon, 11 May 1809 ('Rifle Corps' KGL) [*London Gazette*]. Capt., 5th Line Battn. K.G.L., 8 Dec. 1809. Severely wounded, siege of Burgos, 5–10 Oct. 1812 [*London Gazette*]. 'Lewis Lodders' in Army List. Served in Peninsula 1808–12. *Beamish*, vol. II, p. 655 ['severely wounded, 8th Oct. 1812, before Burgos. Placed upon half-pay 25th April, 1815. [Died] at Neuhaus on the Oste, in Han. 4th Oct. 1825.'].

+LODGE, William, Capt., 31st Foot: Capt., 31st Foot, 16 May 1805. Killed, Talavera, 27 July 1809 [*London Gazette*].

+LOFT, Harry Capel, Lt., 48th Foot: Lt., Army, 21 Nov. 1805; Lt., 48th Foot, 29 May 1809. Killed, Albuera, 16 May 1811 (2nd Battn.) [*London Gazette*]. Obituary, *The Gentleman's Magazine*, 1811 Supplement, Part I., p. 679 ['In the battle of Albuera, Lieut. H. C. Lofft, son of Capel L. esq. Troston, Suffolk.'].

LOGAN, Abraham, Capt., 1st Foot: Capt., 1st Foot, 25 April 1809. Slightly wounded, Salamanca, 22 July 1812 [*London Gazette*].

Severely wounded, 'right arm amputated,' 'at the Siege of St Sebastian,' 7–27 July 1813 (3rd Battn.) [*London Gazette*]. Pension of one hundred pounds per annum, commencing 24 July 1814, for 'loss of an arm' at St Sebastian [*1818 Pension Return*, pp. 2–3].

LOGGAN, George, Lt., 7th Foot: Lt., Army, 14 Jan. 1808; Lt., 7th Foot, 5 April 1809. Severely wounded, Pyrenees, 28 July 1813 ('Logan') (1st Battn.) [*London Gazette*]. Temporary pension of one hundred pounds per annum, commencing 29 July 1814, 'for wounds' received at Pampeluna, 1813 [*1818 Pension Return*, pp. 4–5]. MGS.

LONG, William, Lt., 71st Foot: *1829 Statement of Service*: Born Kilmore, Co. Mayo. He gives his date of birth as 'unknown'. 'Aged Eighteen on his first Entrance into the Army. Ensign, 71st Foot, 6 Oct. 1808. Lieut., 71 Foot, 14 June 1810. Captain, 71st Foot, 31 Octr. 1822.' *Battles, sieges and campaigns*: 'As Lieutenant was present in the following actions... Cambo 12 Novr. 1813. Nive 9 Dec. 1813. Bayonne 13 Decr. 1813 and several skirmishes to Feby. 1814. Orthes 27 Feby. 1814. Aire 2 March 1814. Tarbes 21 March 1814. Toulouse 10 April 1814. Waterloo 18 June 1815.' *Wounds received in action*: 'Wounded slightly at the Battle of Bayonne, received no grant of pay or pension.' *Titles, honorary distinctions and medals*: 'Has a medal for the Battle of Waterloo.' *Service abroad*: 'Septr. 1813 to July 1814, France. March 1815 to Octr. 1818, Flanders & France. June 1824 to 31 Decr. 1829, Canada.' *Family*: Married Catherine Aure Dobson, 11 Nov. 1810, St Mary's, Edge Hill, Liverpool. They had no children by 1830. [PRO: WO 25/799-f17]. Slightly wounded, the Nive, 13 Dec. 1813 (1st Battn.) [*London Gazette*]. Waterloo. MGS. Died, March 1860.

+**LONGLEY, Joseph, Lt., Royal Engineers:** 1st Lt., Royal Engineers, 24 June 1809. Killed, Tarifa, 31 Dec. 1811 [*London Gazette*].

+**LORD, John, Lt., 39th Foot:** Adjutant, 7 April 1804; Lt., 39th Foot, 17 Feb. 1806. Killed, Pyrenees, 25 July 1813 (1st Battn.) [*London Gazette*].

LORENTZ, Charles, Lt., 7th Foot: Ensign, 60th Foot, 1 Oct. 1807; Lt., Army, 8 Oct. 1809; Lt., 7th Foot, 2 Aug. 1810. Slightly wounded, Albuera, 16 May 1811 (2nd Battn.) [*London Gazette*]. Slightly wounded, Orthes, 27 Feb. 1814 (1st Battn.) [*London Gazette*]. MGS.

LORIMER, Charles Hunt, Lt., 1st Foot: Lt., Army, 28 April 1806; Lt., 1st Foot, 27 Dec. 1807. *Monthly Return*, 3rd Battn., dated 25 Feb. 1809: 'In Haslar Hospital, Wounded' [PRO: WO 25/96]. Wounded, 'in the Army lately in Spain' (3rd Battn.) [*March 1809 Army List*, p. 105]. MGS.

LORIMER, William, Lt., 42nd Foot: *1829 Statement of Service for Retired Officers*: Aged twenty-three on first appointment to the Army. Ensign, 42nd Foot, 25 July 1805; Lt., 42nd Foot, 18 June 1807; Half-pay, 24 Nov. 1814, 'In consequence of being thrown from the walls of Burgos which injured my left Testicle, producing a paralytic affliction of the left thigh and leg, so as to render me incapable of Active Service.' *Where serving when wounded*: 'Burgos'. *Family*: Married in Kingston, near Portsmouth, 13 Aug. 1816. No children. *Where generally resident during last five years*: 'Gosport, Plymouth, St Hiliers, Jersey.' [PRO: WO 25/765 f299].

LOUGHT, Lt., 36th Foot: Slightly wounded, Vimeiro, 21 Aug. 1808 [*London Gazette*].

LOVE, George Harley, Lt., 52nd Foot: Lt., 52nd Foot, 18 April 1811.

Slightly wounded, 'in Action with the Enemy', 20 March 1814 (1st Battn.) [*London Gazette*]. Waterloo.

LOVE, James, 2nd Lt., Royal Artillery: 2nd Lt., Royal Artillery, 6 Nov. 1809. Slightly wounded in the siege of the Forts of St Vincente, St Cayetano, and La Merced at Salamanca, 18–24 June 1812 [*London Gazette*]. MGS.

LOVELOCK, John B., Ensign/Lt., 29th Foot: *1829 Statement of Service for Retired Officers*: Aged twenty-two on first appointment to the Army. Ensign, 29th Foot, 2 Aug. 1809 [Army List gives 3 Aug.], 'having volunteered from the Mayo Militia'; Lt., 29th Foot, 4 July 1811; Half-pay, 24 Oct. 1821, by reduction. *Where serving when wounded*: 'Wounded four times at the Battle of Albuhera on the 16th May 1811.' No pension. *Family*: Married in Cookstown, County Tyrone, 15 Jan. 1820. No children. *Title and nature of employment*: 'Barrack Master at Castleban'. *Where generally resident during last five years*: 'Castleban'. [PRO: WO 25/765 f230]. Slightly wounded, Albuera, 16 May 1811 [*London Gazette*].

LOVETT, Verney Robert, Capt., 50th Foot: Lt., 50th Foot, 3 July 1806; Capt., 50th Foot, 3 Sept. 1812. Severely wounded, Aire, 2 March 1814 (1st Battn.) [*London Gazette*].

+**LOWRIE, Robert, Capt., 91st Foot:** Capt., 91st Foot, 26 Oct. 1804. Severely wounded, Pyrenees, 28 July 1813 (1st Battn.) [*London Gazette*]. Died of wounds, 3 Oct. 1813. Return dated Oct. 1813 [PRO: WO 25/2965]. 'Lawrie' in Army List. Obituary, *The Gentleman's Magazine*, Nov. 1813, p. 505 ['At Vittoria, after suffering severely from a wound received in the battle of the Pyrenees, July 28, and from subsequent amputation, Capt. R. Lowrie, 91st reg.'].

LOWRY, Armar, Ensign, 45th Foot: *1829 Statement of Service for Retired Officers*: Aged twenty-two on first appointment to the Army. Ensign, 45th Foot, 'either towards the end of 1812 or beginning of 1813' [Army List gives 31 Dec. 1812]; Lt., 45th Foot, July 1814 [Army List gives 28 July]; Half-pay, 1814, by reduction. Served one year and ten months on full-pay. 'Does not think he would be equal to active service on account of his wounds.' *Where serving when wounded*: 'at the Battle of Ortez in France'. *Details of pension*: 'None, as he did not apply for it, but thinks he should get one, having got a severe gun shot wound, through the *joint* of the left knee, from which he suffers at times after severe exercise.' Not married. *Where generally resident during last five years*: 'For the most part between Tyrone & Dublin'. [PRO: WO 25/765 f301]. Severely wounded, Orthes, 27 Feb. 1814 ('Arman Lowry') (1st Battn.) [*London Gazette*]. 'Arman Lowry' in Army List. MGS.

LUCAS, Samuel Alexander Hood, Cornet, 5th Dragoon Guards: Cornet, 5th Dragoon Guards, 28 May 1812. Slightly wounded, Toulouse, 10 April 1814 [*London Gazette*].

LUCAS, St John Wells, Lt., 29th Foot: Lt., 29th Foot, 29 Jan. 1807. Wounded, Rolica, 17 Aug. 1808 [*London Gazette*]. MGS. *Mullen*, p. 248 ['Taken prisoner at Roleia'].

LUCKE, Ensign, 60th Foot: Severely wounded, Salamanca, 22 July 1812 [*London Gazette*].

LUDER, Frideric Franz, Capt., Duke of Brunswick Oels' Corps (Infantry): Capt., Duke of Brunswick Oels' Corps (Infantry), 25 Sept. 1809. Severely wounded, Salamanca, 22 July 1812 ('Lueder') [*London Gazette*].

LUDEWIG, Frederick, Lt./Capt., 4th Line Battn. K.G.L.: *1829 Statement of Service for Retired Officers*: Aged thirty on first appointment to the Army. Ensign, 4th Line Battn. K.G.L., 25 Sept. 1804; Lt., 4th Line Battn. K.G.L., 20 Dec. 1804; Capt., 4th Line Battn. K.G.L., 29 Oct. 1812; Half-pay, 25 May 1815, 'from ill health.' *Where serving when wounded*: 'In Spain.' *Details of pension*: One hundred pounds, commencing 9 June 1817. Not married. *Where generally resident during last five years*: 'City of Hanover.' [PRO: WO 25/765 f339].

LUMLEY, Hugh, Lt., 31st Foot; Capt., 18th Portuguese Line: Lt., 31st Foot, 12 March 1806. Slightly wounded, the Nive, 13 Dec. 1813, while serving as Capt., 18th Portuguese Line [*London Gazette*]. In Portuguese Service Aug. 1809 to April 1814. *Challis, Portuguese Army*, p. 56 ['Maj. 7 Line'].

LUTMAN, John, Adjutant/Lt., 81st Foot: Adjutant, 81st Foot, 9 June 1803; Lt., 81st Foot, 4 April 1804. Wounded, 'in the Army lately in Spain' ('Lieut.') (2nd Battn.) [*March 1809 Army List*, p. 105]. Capt., 81st Foot, 2 Feb. 1809. *Monthly Return*, 2nd Battn., dated 25 Feb. 1809: 'Wounded, in Naval Hospl. Plymouth' (Adjutant) [PRO: WO 17/202]. *Monthly Return*, 2nd Battn., dated 25 July 1809: 'Capt. Lutman. Wounded & unable to do Duty.' [PRO: WO 17/202]. Note: there were two John Lutmans serving with the 81st at Corunna, and both were wounded: Adjutant and Lt. John Lutman, and Volunteer John A. Lutman. MGS.

LUTMAN, John A., Volunteer, 81st Foot: *1829 Statement of Service*: Born in London, 24 Oct. 1793. Aged Sixteen on first appointment to the Army. Volunteer, 81st Foot, 8 Sept. 1808; Ensign, 81st Foot, Feb. 1809 [Army List gives 1 Feb.]; Lt., 81st Foot, 13 May 1813; Half-pay, 17 April

1817, by reduction; Lt., 81st Foot, 16 July 1817. Note added: Capt., 24th Foot, 13 Feb. 1835; retired on Full-pay, 9 May 1844. *Battles, sieges and campaigns*: 'Volunteer in Campaign in the North of Spain and in action of Corunna 16th Jany. 1809, under Lt. Genl. Sir John Moore. Ensign at Walcheren and Siege of Flushing... Sicily from May 1810 to June 1812... Ensign & Lieut. Eastern Coast of Spain and Battle of Castalla 13th Apr. 1813. Siege of Tarragona July and August 1813... Blockade of Barcelona February to May 1814... Embarked at Bordeaux 4th June 1814 for North America and served in the Canadas ... and Michigan Territory under Lieut. Colonel McDonald to Augt. 1815. To France and remained with Army of occupation until placed on Half Pay by reduction of Establishment 17th April 1817. Embarked for North America 4th April 1821 and returned to England in September 1825 to join Reserve Companies. Rebellion in Upper & Lower Canada in 1837 & 1838.' *Wounds received in action*: 'Slightly wounded in Left Thigh at Corunna.' *Service abroad*: "8th Septr. 1808 to 28th Jany. 1809, North of Spain. 16th July 1809 to 1st Novr. 1809, Walcheren. 1st May 1810 to 4th June 1812, Sicily. 5th June 1812 to 4th June 1814, eastern Coast of Spain & France. 5th June 1814 to 26th Sept. 1815, Canadas and Michigan Territory. 2nd Octr. 1815 to 10th Feby. 1817, France. 4th April 1821 to 27th Septr. 1825, North America.' Note added: '10 June 1837 to 26 July 1841, Canada.' *Family*: Married 'Margaret Ivers, Daughter of Henry Blakely Esq. of Enniskillen', 30 March 1821, Enniskillen. They had four children by 1829 [PRO: WO 25/801 f25]. MGS.

LUTTRELL, Jonathan, Ensign, 74th Foot: Ensign, 74th Foot, 26 Aug. 1813. Slightly wounded, Orthes, 27 Feb. 1814 [*London Gazette*].

LUTYENS, Engelbert, Lt., 20th Foot: Lt., 20th Foot, 21 March 1805. Slightly wounded, Pyrenees, 2 Aug. 1813 [*London Gazette*]. Capt., 20th Foot, 25 Aug. 1813.

+LYDDON, John, Lt., 48th Foot: Lt., 48th Foot, 25 Feb. 1808. Killed, Albuera, 16 May 1811 ('Liddon') (2nd Batt.) [*London Gazette*].

LYE, Benjamin Leigh, Lt., 11th Light Dragoons: Cornet, 11th Light Dragoons, 4 Aug. 1808; Lt., 11th Light Dragoons, 30 June 1811. Wounded, during 'movements of the Army' [Retreat from Burgos], 23 Oct. 1812 [*London Gazette*]. Waterloo. Half-pay 5 June 1817. Adjutant, North Somerset Yeomanry Cavalry, 1821. MGS. Lt.-General, 20 June 1854.

LYGON, Hon. Henry Beauchamp, Capt., 16th Light Dragoons: *1829 Statement of Service*: Born in Wadersfield, Worcester. Cornet, 16th Dragoons, 1 July 1803; Lt. 24 May 1804; Capt. 50th Foot, 15 Jan. 1807; Capt., 16th Dragoons, 12 Feb. 1807; Major 14 May 1812; Major and Lt., 1st Life Guards, 18 June 1815; Lt. Col., 90th Foot, 12 July 1821; Lt. Col., 1st Life Guards, 17 July 1821; Col., 1st Life Guards, 24 March 1822. Wounded during a skirmish near Fraxedas, 28 Aug. 1810 [Wellington's dispatch, 29 Aug. 1810, *London Gazette*]. *Battles, sieges and campaigns*: 'Oporto. Talavera. Crossing of the Coa.' *Wounds received in action*: 'Wounded Severely in the Neck 28 August 1810 in Massena's advance to the Battle of Busaco. A Years Pay but no Pension.' *Service abroad*: 'March 1809 to September 1810, Peninsula. February 1814 to September 1814, Peninsula & France. June 1815 to September 1815, France.' *Family*: Married the Lady Susan Eliot, 8 July 1824, St George's Church. In 1830 the couple had four children. [PRO: WO 25/780 f5]. MGS. Born 1784, died 1863; third son of William, 1st Earl

Beauchamp, and brother of both William, 2nd Earl, and John, 3rd Earl; Henry Beauchamp rose to the rank of general and succeeded his brother as 4th Earl Beauchamp in 1853. [*Burke's Peerage*].

+LYNCH, Thomas, Lt., 101st Foot; Capt., 16th Portuguese Line: Lt., 101st Foot, 30 Aug. 1806. Killed, Vittoria, 21 June 1813, as Capt., 16th Portuguese Line [*London Gazette*]. In Portuguese Service Aug. 1812 to June 1813. *Challis, Portuguese Army*, p. 56.

+LYON, William John, Lt., 14th Light Dragoons: Lt., 14th Light Dragoons, 10 June 1813. Killed, 'in Action with the Enemy', 18 March 1814 [*London Gazette*]. Obituary, *The Gentleman's Magazine*, April 1814, p. 416 ['Killed in action, in France, Lieut. Wm. John Lyon, of the 14th Light Dragoons, third son of the late Joseph Lyon, esq. Bloomsbury-square.'].

LYSTER, Thomas St George, Capt., 74th Foot: *1829 Statement of Service for Retired Officers*: Aged eighteen on first appointment to the Army. Ensign, 2nd West India Regt., 24 April 1805; Lt., 74th Foot, 15 Aug. 1805 [Army List gives Lt.,

74th Foot, 11 May 1807]; Capt., 74th Foot, 11 Nov. 1813; Capt., 11th Foot, 27 March 1817; Half-pay, 'Portuguese Officers', 8 March 1821; Fort Major of Jersey. *Where serving when wounded*: 'Spain & France'. *Details of pension*: £100, commencing 27 Feb. 1815. *Family*: Married in London, 12 June 1805. Ten children by 1829. *Where generally resident during last five years*: 'London & Northampton.' [PRO: WO 25/765 f320]. Severely wounded, siege of Badajoz, 26 March 1812 ('Lister') [*London Gazette*]. Severely wounded, Orthes, 27 Feb. 1814 ('George Lester') [*London Gazette*]. Temporary pension of seventy pounds per annum, commencing 27 March 1813, 'for wounds' received at Badajoz, 1812. Second temporary pension, for one hundred pounds, commencing 25 Feb. 1815, 'for wounds' received at Orthes ('Lister') [*1818 Pension Return*, pp. 18–19]. MGS.

LYZNEWSKY, Julius, Lt., Duke of Brunswick Oels' Corps (Infantry): Lt., Duke of Brunswick Oels' Corps, 25 Sept. 1809. Slightly wounded, siege of Badajoz, 6–11 June 1811 [*London Gazette*]. Wounded, the Nive, 10 Dec. 1813 ('Lyzneusky') [*London Gazette*].

M

MACADAM, William, Lt., 9th Foot: *1829 Statement of Service for Retired Officers*: Aged sixteen on first appointment to the Army. Ensign, 9th Foot, 14 Jan. 1808; Lt., 9th Foot, 10 Aug. 1808; Capt., 9th Foot, 17 Nov. 1814; Half-pay, 24 Dec. 1815, by reduction; Capt., 3rd Garrison Battn., 3 March 1816, 'and Exchanged into the 75th Foot'; Half-pay, 3 July 1817, by reduction; Full-pay, 75th Foot; Major, 75th Foot, 24 Sept. 1824; Lt. Col., unattached, 22 April 1826. *Where serving when wounded*: '3 times wounded in Spain in the 9th Foot'. No pension. *Family*: Married in St Mary's, Bath, 18 July 1822. Two children by 1822. *Where generally resident during last five years*: 'In Bath since Promoted to a H.P. Lt. Colonelcy in Aprl. 1826.' [PRO: WO 25/766 f29]. Slightly wounded, storming of San Sebastian, 31 Aug. 1813 ('McAdam') (1st Battn.) [*London Gazette*]. Severely wounded, Crossing the Bidassoa, 7/9 Oct. 1813 ('McAdam') (1st Battn.) [*London Gazette*]. MGS.

McALPIN, Volunteer, 1st Foot: Severely wounded, Salamanca, 22 July 1812 [*London Gazette*]. Not in *Challis, Index*.

McALPIN, Robert, Ensign, 71st Foot: Severely wounded, Vimeiro, 21 Aug. 1808, while serving as Acting Adjutant ('McAlpine') [*London Gazette*]. Seventy pounds per annum pension, commencing 25 Dec, 1811, for 'loss of the use of an arm' at Vimiera, 1808 [*1818 Pension Return*, pp. 16–17].

MACALPINE, Robert, Ensign, 38th Foot: Ensign, 38th Foot, 24 Nov. 1812. Severely wounded, storming of San Sebastian, 31 Aug. 1813 ('McAlpin') (1st Battn.) [*London Gazette*].

+MACALPINE, Samuel, Lt., 88th Foot: Lt., 88th Foot, 28 June 1809. Slightly wounded, Fuentes de Onoro, 5 May 1811 ('McAlpine') (1st Battn.) [*London Gazette*]. Killed, storming of Badajoz, 6 April 1812 ('McAlpin') [*London Gazette*].

MACARA, Robert, Lt. Col., 42nd Foot: Major, 42nd Foot, 14 Nov. 1805; Bvt. Lt. Col., 42nd Foot, 1 Jan. 1812; Lt. Col., 42nd Foot, 16 April 1812. Severely wounded, Toulouse, 10 April 1814 (1st Battn.) [*London Gazette*]. KCB. Killed at Quatre Bras. Waterloo. *Anton*, pp. 56–7 [Sept. 1813: 'Colonel Stirling ... resigned the command, went to England, and was appointed major-general. On his leaving the regiment, the command devolved on Lieutenant-Colonel Macara, a brave man, who feared no personal danger, but was not well acquainted with field manoeuvres or military tactics. This might have been owing, in a great measure, to his predecessor seldom having been absent from the regiment; so that not having the command sooner, he had not the opportunity of perfecting himself, by that practice which is absolutely necessary for one about to lead a regiment into the field ... the detached state of the regiment, after all these had been squad drilled, left but few soldiers at head-quarters to enable the commanding officer to practise with. In this manner we continued until the battle of Waterloo, when his fall at Quatre-Bras threw a halo round his expiring command, which places him on the list of our bravest countrymen.'], p. 96 [Nive, 13 Dec. 1813: 'Sir Denis Pack ordered the 42nd to advance... Our colonel was as anxious to execute the order as the men were proud to have been selected to perform it, but he led us into such a brake of furze, thorns, and brambles, that it would have been impossible to have taken our bare thighed regiment through its impenetrable meshes. The general, observing our painful but ineffectual struggling, withdrew us from that spot, and pointed to another place by which we should have advanced'], pp. 111–13 ['Our colonel had just dismounted ... when the sudden rush of the men, after having piled their arms and thrown down their knapsacks, attracted his attention. He gazed upon them with astonishment ... the men were loaded with armful of sticks... The colonel ... called out to the marauders, as he was pleased to call them, to carry back their burdens; some obeyed, others dropped them at their feet, and a few, less obedient, persisted in bringing them along; but the whole seemed rather unwilling to comply. The colonel, dissatisfied at the apathy displayed in obeying his orders, darted among the offenders, and personally chastised those who seemed the most reluctant to obey. Among the most refractory of those wood foragers were two men of singular dispositions; their names were Henderson and Doury... The colonel ... strode hastily forward to enforce obedience ... the colonel overtook him ... seized him by the kilt, the pins of which yielded to the tug, and left his naked posteriors to some merited chastisement. This excited bursts of laughter from all the men... Had the colonel been a severe or strict disciplinarian, or even a harsh commanding officr, he might have had recourse to courts-martial and punishments, after this display of opposition or reluctant obedience to his command; but no other punishment followed the offence than that which he had inflicted himself.'], pp. 119–20, 128 [Toulouse: 'Our colonel was a brave man, but there are moments when a well-timed manoeuvre is of more advantage than courage ... the shot, shell, and musketry poured in with

deadly destruction; and in this exposed position we had to make a second countermarch... These movements consumed much time, and by this unnecessary exposure exasperated the men to madness. The word "Forward – double quick!" dispelled the gloom'], p. 131 ['our colonel ... was wounded as he gave the word of command, "Forward" '], p. 193 [Killed at Quatre Bras: 'Our skirmishers having been impressed with the same opinion, that these were Brunswick cavalry, fell beneath their lances, and few escaped death or wounds: our brave colonel fell at this time, pierced through the chin until the point of the lance reached the brain.'].

McARTHUR, Archibald, Lt., 94th Foot: Lt., 94th Foot, 29 Oct. 1806. Severely wounded, Vittoria, 21 June 1813 [*London Gazette*]. Pension of one hundred pounds per annum, commencing 22 June 1814, 'for wounds' received at Vittoria [*1818 Pension Return, pp. 20–1*].

McARTHUR, Charles, Lt., 79th Foot: Lt., 79th Foot, 17 Oct. 1811. Slightly wounded, Toulouse, 10 April 1814 (1st Battn.) [*London Gazette*]. Wounded, Waterloo. Died, Inverness, 1846.

MACAUSLAND, John, Ensign/Lt., Chasseurs Britanniques: *1829 Statement of Service*: Born 'Lellerkenny, Ireland', 25 Dec. 1791. Aged twenty on first appointment to the Army. Ensign, Chasseurs Britanniques, 11 June 1812; Lt., Chasseurs Britanniques, 9 Sept. 1813; Half-pay, 25 Oct. 1814, by reduction; Lt., 3rd Royal Veterans Battn., 25 March 1824; Lt., 89th Foot, 8 April 1825. *Battles, sieges and campaigns*: 'Ensign at Vittoria. Lieut. at Pyrenees, Bidassoa 31st Augt., Nivelle, Nive, Orthes.' *Wounds received in action*: 'Wounded at Vittoria, Pyrenees, Nivelle, Orthes.' *Service abroad*:

'1812 to Augt. 1814, Peninsula. Jany. 1815 to Aug. 1817, Gibraltar. Sept. 1817 to March 1819, Jamaica. March 1828 to Decr. 1829, East Indies.' *Family*: Married Miss L. M. Crause, 15 Sept. 1829. [PRO: WO 25/802 f262].

+McBARNETT, William, Lt., 79th Foot: Lt., 79th Foot, 1 Jan. 1807. Severely wounded, Toulouse, 10 April 1814 (1st Battn.) [*London Gazette*]. Died of wounds, 17 April 1814. Return dated March 1814. [PRO: WO 25/2965].

MACBEAN, Alexander, Lt., 2nd Light Battn. K.G.L.: Lt., 2nd Light Battn. K.G.L., 27 Nov. 1813. Served in Peninsula 1813–14. *Beamish*, vol. II, p. 569 ['slightly wounded, 9th Dec. 1813, before Bayonne.'].

McBEAN, William, Bvt. Lt. Col., E.O.P.S.; Col., 24th Portuguese Line: Bvt. Major, E.O.P.S., 16 Feb. 1809; Bvt. Lt. Col., E.O.P.S., 30 May 1811. In Portuguese Service March 1809 to Feb. 1813 and May 1813 to April 1814. Gold Medal. MGS. *Challis, Portuguese Army*, p. 56 ['Wd. Villa de Ponte 30 Dec. '10, Bayonne Apr. '14'].

McBEATH, William, Lt., 42nd Foot: Lt., 42nd Foot, 3 July 1806. Severely wounded, Talavera, 28 July 1809, while serving with 1st Batt. Detachments ('McBeth') [*London Gazette*].

McCABE, James, Ensign, 36th Foot: Ensign, 36th Foot, 8 Sept. 1812. Severely wounded, Nivelle, 10 Nov. 1813 ('McAbe') (1st Battn.) [*London Gazette*]. Severely wounded, Toulouse, 10 April 1814 (1st Battn.) [*London Gazette*]. Pension of fifty pounds per annum, commencing 11 April 1815, 'for a wound' received at Toulouse [*1818 Pension Return*, pp. 10–11].

+McCABE, John, Capt., 51st Foot: Lt., Army, 13 May 1802; Lt., 51st Foot, 12 Aug. 1803; Capt., 51st Foot, 7 Dec. 1809. Killed, 'during operations with Army', 15–19 Nov. 1812 [*London Gazette*]. *Wheeler*, p. 112 ['At Salamanca on the 16th November our regiment was sharply engaged near a river (the cork wood of the village, St Munos). Capt. McCabe was killed and many men wounded.'].

+McCARTHY, C. F., Lt., 88th Foot: Lt., Army, 12 Feb. 1807; Lt., 88th Foot, 11 June 1807. Killed, Talavera, 27 July 1809 [*London Gazette*].

McCARTHY, Charles, Ensign/Lt., 66th Foot: Ensign, 66th Foot, 18 Aug. 1808. Slightly wounded, Talavera, 28 July 1809 [*London Gazette*]. Lt., 66th Foot, 4 Oct. 1809. Slightly wounded, Albuera, 16 May 1811 (2nd Battn.) [*London Gazette*].

McCARTHY, John Edward Connor, Lt., 50th Foot: *1829 Statement of Service for Retired Officers*: Aged thirty-two on first appointment to the Army. Ensign, 30th Foot, 9 July 1803; Lt., 30th Foot, 2 April 1805; Lt., 50th Foot, 19 March 1807; Capt., 50th Foot, 4 Feb. 1813; Capt., 3rd Garrison Battn., 11 May 1815; Capt., 2nd Veteran Battn., 8 Nov. 1815; 'Retired List', Nov. 1819. Served on full-pay for twenty-five and a half years. *Where serving when wounded*: 'Wounded in left knee at Corunna 16th Jany. 1809. Badajos 6th April 1812 Asst. Engineer & volunteered to conduct, & conducted 3d Division to escalade the Castle.' *Details of pension*: One hundred pounds, commencing 7 April 1813, for latter wound. *Family*: Married Sarah Ball in Soho, London, 28 Nov. 1789. Four children, including a son, Edward Dennis, 'a Lieut. 2d Wst. India Regt. died at Cape-Coast Castle soon after the massacre of Sir Charles MacCarthy.' Both of his other sons were serving officers: William Justin, 2nd Lt., Ceylon Rifles; and

James, Lt., 35th Foot in Dominica. *Where generally resident during last five years*: 'Bruges'. [PRO: WO 25/766 f115]. Wounded, 'in the Army lately in Spain' (1st Battn.) [*March 1809 Army List*, p. 105]. Severely wounded, storming of Badajoz, 6 April 1812, while serving as Acting Engineer [*London Gazette*]. *1818 Pension Return*, pp. 12–13. Author of *The Storm of Badajoz, with a Note on the Battle of Corunna* (London, 1836). MGS.

McCARTNEY, Lawrence, Lt., 81st Foot: Lt., 81st Foot, 29 Oct. 1807. Wounded, 'in the Army lately in Spain' (2nd Battn.) [*March 1809 Army List*, p. 105].

+McCOARD, James, Ensign, 27th Foot: Ensign, 27th Foot, 17 Feb. 1808. Wounded during the repulse of a sortie from Badajoz, 10 May 1811 (3rd Battn.) [*London Gazette*]. Died of wounds, 27 May 1811. Return dated 25 June 1811. [PRO: WO 25/2965].

McCRAW, William, Lt., 71st Foot: *1829 Statement of Service for Retired Officers*: Aged twenty-four on first appointment to the Army. Ensign, 71st Foot, 27 Aug. 1806; Lt., 71st Foot, 10 Feb. 1808; Half-pay, 38th Foot, 23 June 1815, 'ill health'. *Where serving when wounded*: 'At Fuentes de Honor in Spain, wounded.' No pension. *Family*: Married in Limerick, Ireland, 11 Dec. 1814. Five children by 1829. *Where generally resident during last five years*: 'Peebles, N. Britain'. [PRO: WO 25/766 f117]. Slightly wounded, Fuentes de Onoro, Evening 3 May 1811 [*London Gazette*].

+McCREA, Rawdon, Capt., 87th Foot: Capt., 87th Foot, 11 July 1807. Severely wounded, Talavera, 27 July 1809 ('Macrea') [*London Gazette*]. Obituary, *The Gentleman's Magazine*, Sept. 1809, p. 886 ['Aug. 2. Of his wounds, and buried in the field of battle, among the heroes of Talavera, in his 21st year, Capt. Rawdon McCrea, of the 87th or Prince of Wales's Irish Regiment, and eldest son of Major McC. of the 5th Royal Veteran Battalion. This gallant young man, who had been five times severely wounded at the storming of Monte Video, a veteran in conduct and example, in the act of encouraging his men, at the head of his light company, was wounded on the evening of the 27th of July, and taken prisoner. The ball, a rifle one, pierced both cases of his watch, and with part of the works, lodged in his groin. He was sent into Talavera, by a flag of truce, on the morning of the 30th; his wound looked well, and he was in good spirits, having been treated with the greatest humanity and attention by the French; but unexpected bleeding, caused by some parts of the watch having been carried deeper into the wound, and among the large blood-vessels, than was supposed, almost instantaneously put a period to his life.'].

+McCREMMEN, Donald, Ensign, 42nd Foot: Ensign, 42nd Foot, 5 Jan. 1814. Killed, Toulouse, 10 April 1814 ('McCrummen') (1st Battn.) [*London Gazette*].

McCROHAN, Denis Eugene, Volunteer/Ensign/Lt., 4th Foot: *1829 Statement of Service for Retired Officers*: Aged twenty on first appointment to the Army. 'Volunteer at Badajoz 4th foot'; Ensign, 4th Foot, 16 May 1812; Lt., 4th Foot, 21 Oct. 1813; Half-pay 'by the reduction of the 2nd Battn. 4th Foot. Removed from the half pay to the 3d Veteran Battn. Placed on the retired list of that Battalion from the effects of wounds received.' 'Unfit for active service'. *Where serving when wounded*: 'Badajoz & Vittoria 22nd June 1814 [sic]'. *Details of pension*: Fifty pounds. *Where generally resident during last five years*: 'Ireland'. [PRO: WO

25/766 f128]. Severely wounded, Vittoria, 21 June 1813 (1st Battn.) [*London Gazette*]. MGS.

MACCULLOCH, William, Lt./Capt., Royal Engineers: Lt., Royal Engineers, 1 Dec. 1805; 2nd Capt. 1 May 1811. Severely wounded, siege of Ciudad Rodrigo, 16 Jan. 1812 [*London Gazette*].

McCULLOCK, John Garlies, 1st Lt., 95th Foot: 1st Lt., 95th Foot, 16 Dec. 1807. Recorded as 'missing', Coa, 24 July 1810 (1st Battn.) [*London Gazette*]. Severely wounded, during 'several Affairs with the French Army', 15 March 1811 (Foz De Aronce) [*London Gazette*]. Capt., 95th Foot, 21 Oct. 1813. Pension of two hundred pounds per annum, commencing 16 March 1812, for 'loss of the use of an arm' at Puenta de Marulla, 1811. Second, temporary pension of seventy pounds per annum, commencing 19 June 1816, 'for a wound' at Waterloo ('McCullock') [*1818 Pension Return*, pp. 22–3]. Waterloo. *Dalton*, p. 202 ['majority in the 2nd Garrison Battalion in Dec., 1815, and d. in London in 1818.']. *Simmons*, pp. 75, 82 [Coa, 24 July 1810: 'Lieutenant McCullock taken prisoner.'], p. 108 ['The officer that was taken on the 24th of July was wounded; he was very ill-used by the French, nearly stripped and put in a common prison. He contrived to make his escape, and is again with the regiment.'], p. 145 [Foz De Aronce, 15 March 1811: 'Lieutenant McCullock was shot through the shoulder']. *Kincaid, Random Shots*, pp. 64–7 [Coa, July 1810: 'Mr. Rogers ... had, the day before, arrived from England, as an officer of one of the civil departments, and ... he was full of curiosity and excitement ... he was dancing about with his budget of inquiries, when chance threw him in the way of the gallant and lamented Jock Mac Culloch, at the time a lieutenant in the Rifles, and who was in the act of marching off a company to relieve one of the picquets for the night. Mac Culloch, full of humour, seeing the curiosity of the fresh arrival, said, "Come, Rogers, my boy, come along with me, you shall share my beefsteak, you shall share my boat-cloak, and it will go hard with me but you shall see a Frenchman, too, before we part in the morning." The invitation was not to be resisted, and away went Rogers on the spur of the moment... As usual, an hour before day-break, Mac Culloch, resigning the boat-cloak to his dosing companion, stood to his arms, to be ready for whatever changes daylight might have in store for him: nor had he to wait long, for day had just begun to dawn when the sharp crack from the rifle of one of the advanced sentries announced the approach of the enemy, and he had just time to counsel his terrified bedfellow to make the best of his way back to the division, while he himself waited to do battle... Four thousand horsemen, and a powerful artillery swept the plain, and Loison's division coming up at a charging pace, made towards the centre... Mac Culloch, almost instantly, received several bad sabre wounds, and, with five-and-twenty of his men, was taken prisoner.'] pp. 73–8 ['John Mac Culloch was from Scotland, (a native, I believe, of Kirkudbright;) he was young, handsome, athletic, and active; with the meekness of a lamb, he had the heart of a lion, and was the delight of every one. At the time I first became acquainted with him he had been several years in the regiment, and had shared in all the vicissitudes of the restless life they then led. I brought him under the notice of the reader in marching off to relieve the advanced picquet on the night prior to the action of the Coa... From the manner in which the French approached on the occasion referred to, it may be readily imagined that my gallant friend had but little chance of escape – it was, therefore, only left to him to do his duty as an officer under the circumstances in which he was placed. He gave the alarm, and he gave his visitors as warm a reception as his fifty rifles could provide for them, while he gallantly endeavoured to fight his way back to his battalion, but the attempt was hopeless; the cavalry alone of the enemy ought to have been more than enough to sweep the whole of the division off the face of the earth – and Mac Culloch's small party had no chance; they were galloped into, and he, himself, after being lanced and sabred in many places, was obliged to surrender. Mac Culloch refused to give his parole, in the hope of being able to effect his escape before he reached the French frontier; he was, therefore, marched along with his men a close prisoner as far as Valladolid, where fortune, which ever favours the brave, did not fail him. The escort had found it necessary to halt there for some days, and Mac Culloch having gained the goodwill of his conductor, was placed in a private house under proper security, as they thought; but in this said house there happened to be a young lady... She quickly put herself in communion with the handsome prisoner – made herself acquainted with his history, name, and country, and as quickly communicated it, as well as her plans for his escape, to a very worthy countryman of his, at that time a professor in one of the universities there. Need I say more than that before many hours had passed ... he found himself equipped in the costume of a Spanish peasant, the necessary quantity of dollars in his pocket, and a kiss on each cheek burning hot from the lips of his preserver, on the high road to rejoin his battalion, where he arrived in due course of time, to the great joy of every body – Lord Wellington himself was nót the least delighted of the party, and kindly invited him to dine with him that day, in the costume in which he had arrived. Mac Culloch continued to serve with us until Massena's retreat from Portugal, when, in a skirmish which took place on the evening of the 15th March 1811, I, myself, got a crack on the head which laid me under a tree, with my understanding considerably bothered for the next night, and I was sorry to find, as my next neighbour, poor Mac Culloch, with an excruciatingly painful and bad wound in the shoulder joint, which deprived him of the use of one arm for life, and obliged him to return to England for the recovery of health. In the meantime, by the regular course of promotion, he received his company, which transferred him to the 2d battalion, and, serving with it at the battle of Waterloo, he lost his sound arm by one of the last shots that were fired in that bloody field. As soon as he had recovered from this last wound he rejoined us in Paris, and, presenting himself before the Duke of Wellington in his usual straightforward manly way, said, "Here I am, my Lord; I have no longer an arm left to wield for my country, but I still wish to be allowed to serve it as I best can!" The Duke duly appreciated the diamond before him, and as there were several captains in the regiment senior to Mac Culloch, his Grace, with due regard to their feelings, desired the commanding officer to ascertain whether they would not consider it a cause of complaint if Mac Culloch were recommended for a brevet majority, as it was out of his power to do it for every one, and, to the honour of all concerned, there was not a dissentient voice. He, therefore, succeeded to the brevet, and was afterwards promoted to a majority, I think, in a veteran battalion. He was soon after on a visit in London, living at a hotel, when one afternoon he was taken suddenly ill; the feeling to him was an unusual one, and he immediately sent for a physician, and told him that he cared not for the consequences, but insisted on having his candid opinion on his case. The medical man accordingly told him at once that his case was an extraordinary one – that he might within an hour or two recover from it, or within an hour or two he might be no more. Mac Culloch, with his usual coolness, gave a few directions as to the future, and calmly awaited the result, which terminated fatally within the time predicted – and thus perished, in the prime of life, the gallant Mac Culloch, who was alike an honour to his country and his profession.'].

+McDERMID, John, Lt., 43rd Regt: Lt., 43rd Foot, 26 June 1806. Severely wounded, Coa, 24 July 1810 ('McDearmaid') (1st Battn.) [London Gazette]. Killed, during 'several affairs with the French Army', 18 March–7 April 1811, mentioned in Wellington's dispatch, 9 April 1811 [London Gazette], as 'Lieutenant J. McDearmaid'. Simmons, p. 88 [wounded, Coa, 1810], p. 188 [7 June 1811: 'We bivouacked in a wood of chesnut-trees, where several of our brave fellows had been buried, and whose bones had been dug up by wolves and were strewn above their graves. A gallant young fellow, Lieutenant and Adjutant McDiarmid [sic], 43rd Light Infantry, who was wounded with myself at Almeida, and who joined again when I did, had fallen in fight here. I went to see if his grave had escaped the general disturbance. I found his skull lying at some distance; I was convinced that it must be so, as the hair was still in patches on it. There was no mistaking it; his hair, when alive, was auburn and very curly. His bones were partly eaten and thrown about in the same way. This appearance of a friend whom I had esteemed and had so often associated with, and so recently too, produced many gloomy reflections. I collected the straggling relics and

replaced them and covered them over as the last tribute I could pay him.'].

McDERMID, John, Capt., 95th Rifles: Capt., 95th Rifles, 21 Aug. 1810. Slightly wounded, storming of Badajoz, 6 April 1812 ('McDermed') [London Gazette]. Simmons, p. 232 [wounded, Badajoz, 'McDiarmid'].

+McDERMOTT, Henry, Capt., 88th Foot: Capt., 88th Foot, 13 July 1809. Severely wounded, Busaco, 27 Sept. 1810 (1st Battn.) [London Gazette]. Severely wounded, Vittoria, 21 June 1813 ('McDermot') (1st Battn.) [London Gazette]. Killed, Orthes, 27 Feb. 1814 (1st Battn.) [London Gazette]. Colville, p. 170 [Quoting letter from John Keane to Sir Charles Colville, 17 March 1814: 'Capt. McDermot, 88th, only joined the day before, with his Vitoria wound open, was killed.'].

+McDONALD, Alexander, Ensign/Lt., 92nd Foot: Ensign, 92nd Foot, 2 Nov. 1809. Slightly wounded, Pyrenees, 25 July 1813 (1st Battn.) [London Gazette]. Register of officers' effects: Died of wounds, 5 Oct. 1813, Vittoria. Single. 'The produce of his Effects paid to his Brother Lt. Col. J. McDonald 88 Foot.' [PRO: WO 25/2964]. See John McDonald.

+McDONALD, Allan, Lt., 92nd Foot: Ensign, 92nd Foot, 30 May 1811. Killed, the Nive, 13 Dec. 1813 ('Lieutenant Allan Macdonald') (1st Battn.) [London Gazette]. Register of officers' effects: Single. Effects totalled £19. 18s. 2d [PRO: WO 25/2964].

McDONALD, Angus, Lt., 1st Foot: Lt., 1st Foot, 13 Nov. 1806. Slightly wounded, storming of San Sebastian, 31 Aug. 1813 ('Macdonald') (3rd Battn.) [London Gazette].

MACDONALD, Angus, Capt., 57th Foot; Capt., 4th Portuguese Line: Capt., 57th Foot, 21 Nov. 1811.

Slightly wounded, the Nive, 13 Dec. 1813, while serving as Capt., 4th Portuguese Line [*London Gazette*]. In Portuguese Service April 1810 to April 1814. *Challis, Portuguese Army*, p. 57.

+MACDONALD, Angus, Lt., 79th Foot: Lt., 79th Foot, 17 March 1808. Recorded as wounded, 'severely (since dead)', storming of Fort St Michael, 19 Sept. 1812 ('M'Donald') (1st Battn.) [*London Gazette*]. Died of wounds, 20 Sept. 1812. Return dated 25 Sept. 1812. [PRO: WO 25/2965].

McDONALD, Charles Alexander, Ensign, 58th Foot: Ensign, 58th Foot, 2 July 1812. Slightly wounded, Orthes, 27 Feb. 1814 ('Charles Alexander McDonnell') (2nd Battn.) [*London Gazette*]. MGS. *Foster*, p. 397. *Mullen*, p. 379 ['HP 25/6/18'].

MACDONALD, Colin, Capt., 23rd Foot: Capt., 23rd Foot, 5 Jan. 1805. Slightly wounded, Albuera, 16 May 1811 ('McDonald') (1st Battn.) [*London Gazette*].

McDONALD, Donald, Ensign, 40th Foot: NCO, 92nd Foot; Ensign, 40th Foot, 22 Oct. 1812. Slightly wounded, Toulouse, 10 April 1814 (1st Battn.) [*London Gazette*]. Lt., 40th Foot, 7 June 1815. Waterloo. Half-pay, 25 Feb. 1816. MGS.

MACDONALD, Donald, Capt., 42nd Foot: *1829 Statement of Service for Retired Officers*: Aged sixteen on first appointment to the Army. Ensign, 42nd Foot, 8 April 1801; Lt., 42nd Foot, 9 July 1803; Capt., 42nd Foot, 25 January 1810; Half-pay, 27 May 1819. *Where serving when wounded*: 'Fuentes D'Honor. Quatre Bras.' No pension. *Family*: Married in the Isle of Skye, 8 Feb. 1826. Two children by 1829. *Where generally resident during last five years*: 'Ord, Isle of Skye'. [PRO: WO 25/766 f135]. Severely wounded,

Fuentes de Onoro, evening 3 May 1811 (2nd Battn.) [*London Gazette*]. Waterloo. MGS. *Dalton*, pp. 157, 159 ['McDonald ... D. at Musselburgh, 1865.'].

+McDONALD, Donald, Lt., 71st Foot; Capt., 1st Caçadores: Lt., 71st Regt., 9 Feb. 1808. Severely wounded, storming of Badajoz, 6 April 1812, while serving as a Capt. in the 1st Portuguese Caçadores [*London Gazette*]. *Register of officers' effects*: Died of wounds, 19 April 1812, Badajoz. Single. Effects sold for £50.15/7. [PRO: WO 25/2964].

+McDONALD, Donald, Capt., 91st Foot; Lt. Col., 11th Portuguese Line: Capt., 91st Foot, 31 March 1803; Bvt. Major, 91st Foot, 25 April 1808. Killed, storming of Badajoz, 6 April 1812, while serving as Lt. Col. in 11th Portuguese Line ('McDonnell') [*London Gazette*]. In Portuguese Service Aug. 1809 to April 1812. *Challis, Portuguese Army*, p. 57.

MACDONALD, Donald, Capt., 92nd Foot: *1829 Statement of Service for Retired Officers*: Aged sixteen on first appointment to the Army. 'Quarter Master, 2nd Battn. 42nd, afterwd. 73rd, 100th Reg.', '16 Novemr. 1785, 1787/8'; Ensign, Edinburgh R. Volunteers, 10 March 1797; Lt., Edinburgh R. Volunteers, 31 Aug. 1797; Adjutant, 92nd Foot, 23 Nov. 1798; Ensign, 81st Foot, 22 Feb. 1799; Lt., 92nd Foot, 20 March 1799; Capt., 92nd Foot, 8 July 1803; Major, 92nd Foot, 26 Nov. 1812; Bvt. Lt. Col., 18 June 1815; Half-pay, Malta Regt., 26 Nov. 1818, 'in consequence of wounds'. 'Unfit for any active service in consequence of the effects of very severe wounds'. *Where serving when wounded*: 'Holland, 2nd October 1799. Egypt, 13 March 1801. Arroyo Molino, Spain 28 Octr. 1811'. *Details of pension*: One hundred pounds, commencing 29 Oct. 1812; three hundred pounds, commencing 18 June 1815; two hundred pounds, commencing 25 June 1820. *Where generally resident during last five years*: 'residing Dundas Street, Edinburgh for the last five years & upward.' [PRO: WO 25/767 f236]. Severely wounded, Arroyo dos Molinos, 28 Oct. 1811 ('McDonald') [*London Gazette*]. *1818 Pension Return*, pp. 20–1. Commanded the regiment at Waterloo.

MACDONALD, Donald, Lt., 92nd Foot: Lt., 92nd Foot, 10 Feb. 1808. Slightly wounded, Pyrenees, 25 July 1813 ('D. M'Donald') (1st Battn.) [*London Gazette*]. Waterloo. *Dalton*, pp. 193, 195 ['H.p. 2nd July, 1818.'].

+McDONALD, Duncan, Lt., 50th Foot: Lt., 50th Foot, 29 Dec. 1807. Slightly wounded, Pyrenees, 25 July 1813 ('McDonnell') (1st Battn.) [*London Gazette*] Killed, Aire, 2 March 1814 ('Duncan McDonnell') (1st Battn.) [*London Gazette*].

McDONALD, Duncan, Lt. Col., 57th Foot: Lt. Col., 57th Foot, 28 Aug. 1804. Col., Army, 4 June 1811. Severely wounded, Nivelle, 10 Nov. 1813 (1st Battn.) [*London Gazette*].

+MACDONALD, John, 1st. Lt., 23rd Foot: 1st Lt., 23rd Foot, 10 Oct. 1811. Slightly wounded, Salamanca, 22 July 1812 [*London Gazette*]. Died of wounds, 23 May 1811. Return dated 25 June 1811. [PRO: WO 25/2965].

McDONALD, John, Lt., 50th Foot: Lt., 50th Foot, 19 Dec. 1805. Wounded, 'in the Army lately in Spain' (1st Battn.) [*March 1809 Army List*, p. 105].

McDONALD, John, Capt., 88th Foot; Lt. Col., 14th Portuguese Line: *1829 Statement of Service*: Born in Dalchosnie House, Perthshire, 10 Sept. 1788. Aged fifteen on first appointment to the Army. Ensign, 88th Foot, 17 Dec. 1803; Lt., 88th Foot, 21 March 1805; Capt., 88th Foot, 7 Sept. 1809; Bvt. Major, 88th Foot, 26 Aug. 1813; Half-pay, unattached, 24 Oct. 1815; Bvt. Lt. Col., half-pay, unattached, 4 Sept. 1817; Major, 91st Foot, 29 Nov. 1821; Lt. Col., 91st Foot, 23 Sept. 1824; Lt. Col., Half Pay, unattached, 26 April 1827; Lt. Col., 92nd Foot, 21 Nov. 1828. *Battles, sieges and campaigns*: '1806. Lieutenant in the Expedition under Br. General Robert Crawford. 1807. Assault of Buenos Ayres, 5 July ... 1808. Secret Expedition ultimately under Major General Sherbrooke. 1809. Captain in the Campaigns in Portugal and Spain ... 1810. Major Commanding a Battalion at the Battle of Busaco 27th Sept. Lines of Torres Vedras ... 1811. In the affairs in the pursuit of Massena at Redinha, Pombal &c. at Campo Maior, 1st Siege of Badajos and Battle of Albuera 16 May. 1812. Lieut. Colonel Commanding a Regt. Seige of Badajos and at the assault by order of Lord Wellington to rally the 4th and Light Divisions at the breach 5th April. In the affairs advancing to and retreating from Madrid. Alva del Tormes 13th November. 1813. Battle of Vittoria 21st June Pyrenees 25th July Commanding a Brigade 30th and 31st July. 1814. Commanding a Brigade at the Battle of Tolouse, 10th April.' *Distinguished conduct*: 'Vide Lord Wellington's Dispatches 1st August and 9th Octr. 1813, Published in the *London Gazette* with the reports of Major General Sir William Pringle, Sir Archd. Campbell, and Lord Hill, as referring to the occasion. For repulsing a Sortie by night from the Garrison of Badajoz on the right of the Guadiana. Thanked by Major General Hays orders and promoted in the Portuguese Army.' *Wounds received in action*: '5th July 1807, in the head and right thigh, at the assault of Buenos Ayres. No grant of pay or pension. 30th July 1813, Left leg and right groin in the Pyrenees. No grant of pay or pension. 2nd Octr. 1813, Right shoulder and lungs, when Commanding the assault of the fortified rock on the mountain "Arollo" and surprising the Enemy's posts in the valley of Banca Pyrenees. Received a years pay and a permanent pension of £300 per annum.' *Titles, honorary distinctions and medals*: 'A **Cross** Bearing the word "Albuera"... From His Majesty Ferdinand the 7th, King of Spain. Commanding 1st Battalion 2nd Portuguese Regiment which was separated from its own Brigade and attached to the 2d British Division during the Battle of Albuera. **A Medal** Bearing the word "Vittoria". Lieut. Colonel Commanding 14th Portuguese Regiment at the Battle of Vittoria, and **A Clasp** Bearing the word "Pyrenees". Lieut. Colonel Commanding 14th Portuguese Regiment on the 25th July and a Brigade on the 30th and 31st July in the Battles of the Pyrenees... **A Medal** Bearing the words "Vittoria" and "Pyrenees", and **A Gold Cross** Bearing the words "Guerra Peninsular" with the figures "VI" to denote being engaged in six General Actions, and having served in six campaigns in the Peninsula, from His Majesty John the Sixth of Portugal. **Jewel & Ribband**. The Jewel and Ribband of the most honorable Military Order of the Bath, of which he was apointed Knight Companion by His Majesty King William the Fourth at the recommendation of the Commander in Chief for "Services during the war." ' *Service abroad*: 'Sept. 1806 to Novr. 1807, Porto Praya, Cape of Good Hope & St Helena. Novr. 1808 to Novr. 1813, Off Cadiz, Peninsula & France. March 1814 to Nov. 1815, France & Peninsula. 1 Feby. 1822 to 8th May 1824, Jamaica. Augt. 1824 to Octr. 1825, Jamaica.' *Family*: Married Adriana McInroy, 12 Sept. 1826, Lude House, Perthshire. They had three children by 1830. [PRO: WO 25/803 f74]. Brother of Alexander

McDonald, 92nd Foot, who died of wounds, 5 Oct. 1813. In Portuguese Service April 1809 to April 1814. *1818 Pension Return*, pp. 24–5. *Challis, Portuguese Army*, p. 57.

MACDONALD, Robert, Capt., 1st Foot: Capt., 1st Foot, 8 Feb. 1810. Brevet Major, Army, 21 Sept. 1813. Severely wounded, 'at the Siege of St Sebastian,' 7–27 July 1813 [*London Gazette*]. Waterloo. MGS. *Dalton*, pp. 117–18 ['Brother to Gen. Sir John Macdonald, Adjt.-Gen. of the British Army, and cousin to Etienne Macdonald, Duke of Tarentum and Marshal of France, whose father fought at Culloden in 1746. Robert Macdonald did good service in the Pa., and was present at five general actions. Was severely wounded at the assault on the Convent of St Sebastian, and, although suffering from the effects of his wounds, was present, and engaged, at the assault on town of St Sebastian, where he commanded two companies ordered to the breach in advance of the 1st Bde. of the 5th Division, and was at the surrender of the castle... At his death, which occurred 14th Nov., 1860, a very eulogistic paragraph appeared in a Belize newspaper containing these words: "Col. Macdonald's conversation was like reading a page of history." '].

MACDONALD, Robert, Capt., Royal Artillery: Capt., Army, 1 June 1806; Capt., Royal Artillery, 6 April 1802. Mentioned in Wellington's dispatch concerning the Affair at Majalahonda, 11 Aug. 1812 ['The conduct of the brave German cavalry, was, I understand, excellent, as was that of Capt. M'Donald's troop of horse artillery.'] [*London Gazette*]. *Webber*, p. 116 [wounded, San Munoz, 17 Nov. 1812, as Major serving with E Troop R.H.A.].

MACDONALD, Ronald, Capt., 92nd Foot: Capt., 92nd Foot, 23 May 1805.

Wounded, Pyrenees, 25 July 1813 ('McDonald') (1st Battn.) [*London Gazette*]. Severely wounded, the Nive, 13 Dec. 1813 (1st Battn.) [*London Gazette*].

McDONALD, Ronald, Lt., 92nd Foot: Lt., 92nd Foot, 17 Sept. 1805. Wounded, 'in the Army lately in Spain' (1st Battn.) [*March 1809 Army List*, p. 105].

MACDONALD, Ronald, Lt., 92nd Foot: *1829 Statement of Service for Retired Officers*: Aged sixteen on first appointment to the Army. Ensign, 92nd Foot, 25 March 1807; Lt., 92nd Foot, 5 May 1808; Capt., 92nd Foot, 3 Dec. 1818; Major, half-pay, unattached, 24 Jan. 1828. *Where serving when wounded*: 'South of France, Battle of the Nieve, December 1814 [sic], and Battle of Waterloo, June 1815.' *Details of pension*: Seventy pounds, commencing 19 June 1816. Not married. No civil employment. *Where generally resident during last five years*: 'On Service in the West Indies (Jamaica)'. [PRO: WO 25/767 f246]. Severely wounded, the Nive, 13 Dec. 1813 (1st Battn.) [*London Gazette*]. *1818 Pension Return*, pp. 20–1. Died, Bombay, 31 May 1845. *Dalton*, p. 195 ['his proper name was "Reginald Ronald MacDonald".']

McDONELL, Allan, Ensign/Lt., 79th Foot: *1829 Statement of Service*: Born in 'Glenturret, Inverness Shire', Feb. 1794. Aged '18 years on his first Entrance into the Army.' Ensign, 79th Foot, 12 April 1812. Lt., 79th Foot, 6 Jan. 1814. *Battles, sieges and campaigns*: 'Sarauren 26 & 27 July 1813. Nivelle 10 Novr. 1813. Nive 10th Decr. 1813. Toulouse 10th April 1814.' *Wounds received in action*: '10th April 1814, in the Right foot, at the Battle of Tolouse. Received a Gratuity of one years Pay £118.' *Service abroad*: 'Feby. 1813 to May 1814, Portugal, Spain & France. July 1815 to Augt.

1817, France.' Not married in 1830. [PRO: WO 25/800 f251]. Slightly wounded, Toulouse, 10 April 1814 ('Macdonell') (1st Battn.) [*London Gazette*].

+MACDONNELL, Alexander, Lt., 1st Foot: Lt., 1st Foot, 5 April 1810. Slightly wounded, the Nive, 10 Dec. 1813 (3rd Battn.) [*London Gazette*].

+MACDONNELL, Alexander, 1st Lt., 95th Foot: 1st Lt., 95th Foot, 5 Oct. 1809. Severely wounded, storming of Badajoz, 6 April 1812 ('Macdonald') (3rd Battn.) [*London Gazette*]. Died, Peninsula, 7 Aug. 1812 [PRO: WO 25/2965]. *Simmons*, p. 232 [wounded, storming of Badajoz, 6 April 1812: 'MacDonnel'].

+McDONNELL, George, Ensign, 45th Foot: Ensign, 45th Foot, 28 Feb. 1811. Killed, storming of Badajoz, 6 April 1812 [*London Gazette*].

+McDONNELL, Robert I., Lt., 28th Foot: Ensign, 28th Foot, 28 Jan. 1810. Severely wounded, Vittoria, 21 June 1813 (Lieutenant) (1st Battn.) [*London Gazette*]. Died of wounds, 22 June 1813. Return dated July 1813. [PRO: WO 25/2965].

MACDONNELL, Randolph William, Lt., 47th Foot: Ensign, 47th Foot, 14 March 1811; Lt., 47th Foot, 28 July 1813. Recorded as 'missing', the Nive, 10 Dec. 1813 ('McDonell') (2nd Battn.) [*London Gazette*]. Waterloo.

McDONNELL, Richard, Lt., 92nd Foot: Lt., 92nd Foot, 1 Nov. 1809. Slightly wounded, 'in Action with the Enemy', 14 Feb. 1814 (1st Battn.) [*London Gazette*]. Slightly wounded, Aire, 2 March 1814 (1st Battn.) [*London Gazette*].

+MACDOUGAL, Alexander, Capt., 5th Foot: Capt., Army, 19 Dec. 1805; Capt., 5th Foot, 1 March 1810. Killed in the storming of Ciudad

Rodrigo, 19 Jan. 1812 ('M'Dougal') [London Gazette].

+McDOUGALL, Colin, Lt., 91st Foot: Lt., 91st Foot, 16 Jan. 1806. Killed, Talavera, 27 July 1809, while serving with the 1st Batt. Detachments ('McDougal') [London Gazette].

McDOUGALL, Colin, Lt., 91st Foot: Ensign, 91st Foot, 12 Oct. 1809; Lt., 91st Foot, 19 July 1813. Slightly wounded, Toulouse, 10 April 1814 (1st Battn.) [London Gazette]. ' – McDougall' and ' – Macdougall' in Army Lists. MGS.

MACDOUGALL, Duncan, Capt., 53rd Foot; Capt., 85th Foot: 1829 Statement of Service for Retired Officers: Aged sixteen on first appointment to the Army. Ensign, 71st Foot, 6 April 1804; Lt., 71st Foot, 23 April 1805; Capt., '[Capers?] Regt.', 19 June 1806; Capt., 53rd Foot, 1811; Capt., 85th Foot, 1813; Bvt. Major, 85th Foot, 1814; Half-pay, 1817; Lt. Col., Half-pay, 21 April 1825, 'by being appointed ... Field Officer in Nova Scotia 21st April 1825.' Where serving when wounded: 'Spain.' Family: Married in Castleton, Isle of Man, 20 March 1817. Two children by 1829. Where generally resident during last five years: 'Nova Scotia employed on the Staff.' [PRO: WO 25/766 f190]. Severely wounded, Salamanca, 22 July 1812 ('McDougal') (2nd Battn.) [London Gazette]. MGS.

MACDOUGALL, John, Lt., 91st Foot: 1829 Statement of Service for Retired Officers: Aged nineteen on first appointment to the Army. Ensign, Argyle Militia, 29 Aug. 1804; Lt., Argyle Militia, 5 Feb. 1805; Ensign, 91st Foot, 27 Aug. 1807, 'By bringing Volunteers from the Argyle Militia to the 91st Regt.'; Lt., 91st Foot, 15 June 1809; Half-pay, 39th Foot, 7 Sept. 1820, 'on account of Ill Health.' Served

sixteen years on full-pay, plus two for Waterloo. Where serving when wounded: 'at Tolouse severely in the left thigh.' No pension. Not married. Where generally resident during last five years: 'Argyle shire.' [PRO: WO 25/766 f36]. Slightly wounded, Toulouse, 10 April 1814 ('McDougall') (1st Battn.) [London Gazette].

McDOUGALL, Kenneth/Kennett, Lt., 42nd Foot: Ensign, 42nd Foot, 16 March 1809; Lt. 42nd Foot, 12 Feb. 1812. Severely wounded, Nivelle, 10 Nov. 1813 (1st Battn.) [London Gazette]. Temporary pension of seventy pounds per annum, commencing 11 Nov. 1814, 'for wounds' received at St Jean de Luz, 1813 [1818 Pension Return, pp. 12–13]. Waterloo. Died in Skye, 1827. Anton, p. 76 [Nivelle: 'The regiment's loss this day did not exceed twenty-seven killed and wounded; among the latter ... Lieutenant Kenneth McDougall.'].

+McDOUGALL, Neil, Lt., 75th Foot: Lt., 75th Foot, 28 July 1808. Mentioned in an 'Extract of a Letter from Lieutenant-General Sir J. Murray to General the Marquess of Wellington, dated Castalla, March 23, 1813' ['a reconnoitring party on the same day, conducted by Major-General Donkin ... and Lieutenant M'Dougall, of the Adjutant-General's Department, had an opportunity of making a spirited attack on an enemy's post, which was carried in the presence of a battalion drawn up as spectators. We suffered no loss on this occasion, but killed some of the enemy, and took a few prisoners.'] [London Gazette]. Severely wounded, 'since dead', Castalla, 12 April 1813 ('Dy. Ass. A. Gen.') [London Gazette]. Obituary, The Gentleman's Magazine, Aug. 1813, p. 194 ['April 13. Near Alicant, of wounds received in the action of the preceeding day, Lieut. Niel McDougal, 75th regt. and assistant-adjutant-general of the allied

Army in that place, son of the late Capt. McDougal, of Ardenrive.'].

MACDOUGALL, Patrick, Ensign, 48th Foot: *1829 Statement of Service for Retired Officers*: Aged twenty-three on first appointment to the Army. Ensign, 48th Foot, 28 Dec. 1809; Half-pay, 1814, by reduction. 'Not willing [to serve] but owing to be subject to delirium and vertigo in the head especially in warm weather.' *Where serving when wounded*: 'Serving in Portugal at the battle of Albuera wounded by both leg & Head'. No pension. Not married. No employment. *Where generally resident during last five years*: 'I have resided at Leith for these five years past.' [PRO: WO 25/767 f174]. Wounded, Albuera, 16 May 1811 ('McDougall') (2nd Battn.) [*London Gazette*].

MACDOUGALL, Peter, Lt., 57th Foot: Lt., 57th Foot, 15 June 1809. Slightly wounded, Albuera, 16 May 1811 ('McDougal') [*London Gazette*].

McDOWALL, John, Ensign, 11th Foot: Ensign, 11th Foot, 31 Oct. 1811. Severely wounded, 'right arm amputated', during 'the assault and capture of the exterior line of the castle of Burgos on the evening of the 4th October, 1812' ('M'Dowell') [*London Gazette*].

McENNALLY, John, Assistant Surgeon, 28th Foot: *1829 Statement of Service for Retired Officers*: Aged twenty-five on first appointment to the Army. Hospital Mate, Hospital Staff, May 1810; Assistant Surgeon, 28th Foot, Aug. 1811 [Army List gives 29 Aug. 1811]; Half-pay, 6th Garrison Battn., Feb. 1815, 'in consequence of my wound.' 'I am not able to serve in consequence of my wound'. *Where serving when wounded*: 'at Pampalon in the Peninsula'. *Details of pension*: Seventy pounds per annum, commencing 1815. *Family*: Married

in Monaghan, 26 June 1815. *Where generally resident during last five years*: 'Monaghan'. [PRO: WO 25/766 f118].

McFARLANE, George, Lt., 57th Foot: Lt., 57th Foot, 6 Feb. 1806. Slightly wounded, Albuera, 16 May 1811 [*London Gazette*].

MACFARLANE, Peter, Lt., 91st Foot: Ensign, 91st Foot, 23 May 1811; Lt., 91st Foot, 23 July 1813. Slightly wounded, Pyrenees, 28 July 1813 (1st Battn.) ('Ensign M'Farlain') [*London Gazette*]. MGS.

+McGEACHY, Alexander, Capt., 11th Foot; Major, 17th Portuguese Regt: Capt., Army, 1 July 1802; Capt., 11th Foot, 10 June 1804. Killed while commanding the storming party, 9 June 1811, during the second failed attempt to take Fort San Cristoval, Badajoz. Killed at the siege of Badajoz, 6–11 June 1811, while serving as Capt., 17th Portuguese Line [*London Gazette*]. In Portuguese Service Sept. 1809 to June 1811. *Challis, Portuguese Army*, p. 57. *Wheeler*, pp. 61, 64 ['Major McGeechy was killed, the few that remained of his party carried on and followed him to the grave.'].

McGIBBON, Dugold, Lt., 57th Foot; Capt., 2nd Portuguese Line: Lt., 57th Foot, 9 April 1807. Killed, Pyrenees, 30 July 1813, while serving as Capt., 2nd Portuguese Line [*London Gazette*]. In Portuguese Service April 1810 to July 1813. *Challis, Portuguese Army*, p. 57.

McGIBBON, Walter, Capt., 57th Foot: Capt., Army, 22 Jan. 1804; Capt., 57th Foot, 28 April 1804. Slightly wounded, Albuera, 16 May 1811 (1st Battn.) [*London Gazette*]. Temporary pension of one hundred pounds per annum, commencing 17 May 1812, 'for a wound' received at Albuera [*1818 Pension Return*, pp. 14–15].

McGLASHAN, James, Lt., 2nd Light Battn. K.G.L: Lt., 2nd Battn. Light Infantry K.G.L., 24 April 1811 ('Macklashan'). Severely wounded, Heights of Villares, 20–22 June 1812 ('McGlashon') [*London Gazette*]. Served in Peninsula 1811–12. ADC to Major-General Lyon at Waterloo. *Beamish*, vol. II, p. 669 ['Appointed captain of a company, 1st Ceylon regiment, by exchange with captain George Richter. [Died] on his passage to the East Indies, 2d Dec. 1817.'].

McGREGOR, Alexander, 1st Lt., 95th Foot; Capt., 4th Caçadores: 1st Lt., 95th Foot, 29 May 1811. Severely wounded, Salamanca, 22 July 1812, as Capt., 4th Caçadores [*London Gazette*]. Severely wounded, Vittoria, 21 June 1813, as Capt. in 4th Caçadores [*London Gazette*]. In Portuguese Service Jan. 1812 to April 1814. Pension of one hundred pounds per annum, commencing 23 July 1813, 'for wounds' received at Salamanca [*1818 Pension Return*, pp. 26–7]. *Challis, Portuguese Army*, p. 57.

+McGREGOR, George, Major, 59th Foot: Major, 59th Foot, 30 May 1805. Wounded, 'in the Army lately in Spain' (2nd Battn.) [*March 1809 Army List*, p. 105]. Obituary, *The Gentleman's Magazine*, Feb. 1809 ['Jan ... At Plymouth, of wounds he also received in Spain, Major McGregor, of the 59th Regiment of Foot.'].

McGREGOR, James, Lt., 59th Foot: Lt., 59th Foot, 3 June 1808. Severely wounded, Vittoria, 21 June 1813 (2nd Battn.) [*London Gazette*]. Capt., 59th Foot, 25 Sept. 1813. Waterloo. Drowned in the wreck of the *Seahorse*, 30 Jan. 1816.

McGREGOR, Robert B., Major, 88th Foot: Capt., 88th Foot, 12 Dec. 1798; Major 23 Nov. 1809. Severely wounded, Busaco, 27 Sept. 1810 (1st Battn.) [*London Gazette*].

McGREGOR, William Gordon, Major, 11th Foot: Major, 11th Foot, 26 Nov. 1807. Severely wounded, Salamanca, 22 July 1812 (1st Battn.) [*London Gazette*]. Pension of two hundred pounds per annum, commencing 23 July 1813, 'for wounds' received at Salamanca ('Mac Gregor') [*1818 Pension Return*, pp. 6–7].

+McGUCHIN, Charles Averill, Lt., 38th Foot: Lt., 38th Foot, 27 Aug. 1807. Killed, storming of San Sebastian, 31 Aug. 1813 (1st Battn.) [*London Gazette*].

+MACGUIRE, Francis, Lt., 4th Foot: Lt., 4th Foot, 6 June 1805. Killed, storming of San Sebastian, 31 Aug. 1813 ('Macquire') [*London Gazette*]. Killed on his 21st birthday while leading the Forlorn Hope of the 4th Foot. This incident is illustrated in *Fletcher, Regiments*, p. 91 ['Lieutenant Macguire, of the 4th (King's Own), leads the forlorn hope into the breach at San Sebastian. In order to make himself more conspicuous Macguire wore a white feather in his cap. It evidently made him too conspicuous, however, as he was shot dead soon afterwards. Another version of this painting by Beadle shows him wearing a cocked hat.']. 'Maguire, Francis' in Army List.

+MACHELL, Lancelot, 1st Lt., Royal Engineers: 1st Lt., Royal Engineers, 1 March 1811. Killed, Siege of St Sebastian, 7–27 July 1813 [*London Gazette*]. Died of wounds, 25 July 1813. Return dated Aug. 1813. [PRO: WO 25/2965]. Mentioned in Graham's dispatch to Wellington dated 27 July 1813, concerning the failed Assault on St Sebastian on the morning of 25 July 1813 ['The conduct throughout the whole of the operations of the siege hitherto, of the officers and men of the ... engineers, never was exceeded in indefatigable zeal, activity, and gallantry... The three officers of this corps, employed to

MACHELL

conduct different parts of the columns of attack, behaved admirably, but suffered severely. Captain Lewis has lost his leg, Lieutenant Jones was wounded in the breach, and taken; and Lieutenant Machell, after his return, was killed in the trenches.'] [London Gazette].

MACHELL, Richard, Capt. 30th Foot: Capt., Army, 2 June 1808; Capt., 30th Foot, 27 Oct. 1808. Severely wounded, storming of Badajoz, 6 April 1812, while serving on the Staff as a Brigade Major [London Gazette].

McINNES, Duncan, Lt., 42nd Foot: Lt., 42nd Foot, 26 July 1804. Wounded, 'in the Army lately in Spain' (1st Battn.) [March 1809 Army List, p. 105]. Monthly Return, 1st Battn., dated 25 Feb. 1809: 'Left wounded at Plymouth' [PRO: WO 17/152].

McINTOSH, Aeneas, Major, 85th Foot: Major 7 April 1808. Mentioned in Wellington's Fuentes de Onoro dispatch, 8 May 1811 [commanding the regt: 'I particularly request your Lordship's attention to the conduct of ... Major McIntosh of the 85th regiment'] [London Gazette, 26 May 1811]. Commanded the storming party, Badajoz, 6 June 1811, during the failed attempt to storm Fort San Cristoval [Ensign Dyas commanded the forlorn hope]. Not in 1815 A/L. Wheeler, p. 60 ['We were commanded by Major MacIntosh, 85th Regt... We advanced up the glacies close to the walls... Heaps of brave fellows killed and wounded, ladders shot to pieces, and falling together with the men down upon the living and the dead.']

MACINTOSH, Alexander, Lt., 48th Foot: Lt., 48th Foot, 18 June 1807. Slightly wounded, Albuera, 16 May 1811 ('M'Intosh') [London Gazette].

McINTYRE, Augustus Johnson, Capt., 71st Foot: Ensign, 71st Foot, 1804; Lt., 71st Foot, 4 July 1805; Capt., 71st Foot, 17 May 1810. Slightly wounded, Vimeiro, 21 Aug. 1808 [London Gazette]. Wounded, Waterloo. Half-pay, 56th Foot, 31 Dec. 1818. Died in 1834.

+McINTYRE, David, Capt., 91st Foot: Capt., 91st Foot, 9 March 1809. Killed, Nivelle, 10 Nov. 1813 ('M'Intire') [London Gazette].

+McINTYRE, James, Capt., 71st Foot: Ensign, 71st Foot,14 July 1800, joining from the Breadalbane Fencibles; Lt. and Adjutant, 71st Foot, 28 Sept. 1801; Capt., 71st Foot, 25 Feb 1808. Served in South America, 1806–7. Portugal 1808. Walcheren, Holland, 1809. Peninsula, 1810–14. Severely wounded, Fuentes de Onoro, evening 3 May 1811 [London Gazette]. Transferred to 13th Royal Veteran Battalion, 25 Jan. 1813. Died in Lisbon, 27 Jan. 1814. [PRO: WO 17/283]. Register of officers' effects: 13th Royal Veteran Battn. Died, Lisbon, 27 Jan. 1814. Effects totalled £47. 0s. 0d. [PRO: WO 25/2964].

McINTYRE, John, Lt./Adjutant, 71st Foot: Ensign, 71st Foot, 22 June 1809. Walcheren, where he became very sick. Lt., 71st Foot, 28 May 1811. Severely wounded, Vittoria, 21 June 1813 (1st Battn.) [London Gazette]. Adjutant, 71st Foot, 25 Nov. 1813. Slightly wounded, the Nive, 13 Dec. 1813 (1st Battn.) [London Gazette]. Half-pay, 25 Feb. 1816. [PRO: WO 17/192, 265, 280, 294, 309].

MACK, Thomas, Ensign/Lt., 66th Foot: Ensign, 66th Foot, 4 April 1810. Slightly wounded, Albuera, 16 May 1811 (2nd Battn.) [London Gazette]. Lt., 66th Foot, 7 Oct. 1813.

MACKAY, Honeyman, Lt., 68th Foot: 1829 Statement of Service: Born in Bighouse, Sutherland, 19 Dec. 1792. Aged fifteen on 'his first Entrance into the Army.' Ensign,

96th Foot, June 1807. Lt., 96th Foot, 30 June 1808. Lt., 68th Foot, 18 May 1809. Capt., '5th W.I.', 30 May 1816. Capt., 90th Foot, 10 Oct. 1816. Major, 90th Foot, 22 July 1830. *Battles, sieges and campaigns*: 'Expedition to Walcheren and at the taking of Flushing, 1809 as Lieut. 68th... Peninsula 1811 to 1814. Salamanca, 1812. Retreat from Burgos, 1812. Vittoria, 1813. Pyrenees, 1813. Nivelle, 1813. Orthes, 1813, as Lieut. 68th.' *Wounds received in action*: 'Wounded in the Head at Vittoria on 1st June 1813. No remuneration or pay on that account was received.' *Service abroad*: 'June 1809 to Octr. 1809, Walcheren. June 1811 to June 1814, Peninsula. Oct. 1820 to March 1824, Mediteranean. June 1826 to 31st Decr. 1829, Mediteranean.' [PRO: WO 25/802 f315]. Slightly wounded, Vittoria, 21 June 1813 ('Lieutenant McKay') (2nd Battn.) [*London Gazette*]. MGS. *Mullen*, p. 410 ['Honeymoon [sic]... To 5th WIR. Maj unatt. HP 29/5/35. *Green*, pp. 57, 212 (John Green, *Vicissitudes of a Soldier's Life*, 1827)].

MACKAY, James, Capt., 53rd Foot: Capt., 53rd Foot, 22 March 1810. Severely wounded, Nivelle, 10 Nov. 1813 (2nd Battn.) [*London Gazette*]. Slightly wounded, Toulouse, 10 April 1814 (2nd Battn.) [*London Gazette*].

MACKAY, John F., Lt., 82nd Foot: *1829 Statement of Service*: Born 'Lock-geel, Antrim, Ireland', 16 Sept. 1785. Aged Nineteen on his first Entrance into the Army. Ensign, 82nd Foot, 19 Dec. 1804. Lt., 82nd Foot, 19 Feb. 1807. Capt., 82nd Foot, 16 Aug. 1813. *Battles, sieges and campaigns*: 'Copenhagen August 1807, as Lieut... Roleia 17th Augt. 1808. Vimiera 21st Aug. 1808... Corunna 16th Jany. 1809 as Lieut... Flushing 1809, Lieut... Barrosa 5th March 1811. Vittoria 21st June 1813. Pass of Mayo 25th July 1813. Pampeluna 30th July 1813, Lieut.' *Wounds received in*

action: '5th March 1811 Severely wounded at Barrosa for which received One Years Pay. 30th July 1813 Severely wounded at Pampeluna for which received One Years Pay.' *Service abroad*: 'Augt. 1807 to Novr. 1807, Copenhagen. Decr. 1807 to Feby. 1809, Gibraltar, Cadiz, Spain, and Portugal. July 1809 to Jany. 1810, Walcheren. Feby. 1810 to Decr. 1813, Gibraltar & Peninsula. Septr. 1815 to Jany. 1816, France. June 1819 to Decr. 1829, Mauritius.' [PRO: WO 25/801 f83]. Severely wounded, Barossa, 5 March 1811 ('McKoy') [*London Gazette*]. Severely wounded, Pyrenees, 30 July 1813 ('M'Kay') (1st Battn.) [*London Gazette*].

MACKAY, William, Capt., 68th Foot: *1829 Statement of Service for Retired Officers*: Letter dated 19 Dec. 1828, Waterloo Street, Lower Stoke, near Devonort, to the Secretary of War: 'Sir, Having observed in the newspapers a call made upon officers receiving half-pay and pension to make certain statements and not having had the honour to receive any form for such statements I trust the following will be deemed satisfactory: Commissions – "Ensigncy dated 24th November 1803; Lieutenantcy 25th May 1804; Company 9th January 1812; Bt. Majority 21st January 1819 – 68th or Durham Regt. of Light Infantry. The last commission for services performed in the Field in action with the Enemy near Salamanca on the 21st June 1812. I commenced receiving a pension of £100 pr. annum in 1813 but my papers being in Scotland I am unable to particularize what month of that year. I was permitted by the kind indulgence of the late lamented Duke of York to continue with the 68th Regt. until 1821 when in consequence of the severe effects of the Canadian climate upon my shattered constitution I was reluctantly obliged to retire upon half-pay and relinquished a profession to which I was ardently attached. I believe I may venture to say that my case has no parallel in the service having received *twenty-two Bayonet wounds*. A second pension of £100 pr. annum was granted in 1823. I was married 23d August 1820 but have no children. For the last five years I have resided chiefly near Inverness but during the winter have been obliged to remove for a milder climate.'" [PRO: WO 25/768 f317]. Wounded, 'dangerously', Heights of Villares, 20–22 June 1812 ('Mackry') [*London Gazette*]. Pension of one hundred pounds per annum, commencing 22 June 1813, 'for wounds' received at Salamanca, 1812 [*1818 Pension Return*, pp. 16–17]. *Surtees*, pp. 162–3 [June 1812: 'about three days after [the French] arrival, they made a very brisk and vigorous attack upon a conical hill immediately in front of our position, and a little to the right of Morisco... The 68th regiment distinguished itself greatly, but in their pursuit of the beaten enemy, they advanced too far into the plain, and which the French observing, a forward movement was made again by them, and before our people could recover the high ground, Captain M'Kay and Lieutenant M'Donald, with a considerable number of their men, were made prisoners. Poor M'Kay received I know not how many bayonet wounds on this occasion, I believe not less than ten or twelve, but none of them very serious of course, or he could not have survived. He, with the others, were taken into the French lines, but he was so ill when they retired a few days after, that they were obliged to leave him in Morisco.'].

MACKENZIE, Alexander, Capt., 42nd Foot: Lt., 42nd Foot, 16 May 1805; Capt., 42nd Foot, 6 Jan. 1814. Severely wounded, Toulouse, 10 April 1814 (1st Battn.) [*London Gazette*].

+MACKENZIE, Colin, Ensign/Lt., 71st Foot: Ensign, Army, 10 Aug. 1809; Ensign, 71st Foot, 25 June 1811. Slightly wounded, 'at the Storm and Capture of Fort Napoleon, and the Enemy's other Works, in the Neighbourhood of Almaraz', 19 May 1812 [*London Gazette*]. Killed, Vittoria, 21 June 1813 ('Lieutenant C. McKensey') (1st Battn.) [*London Gazette*].

McKENZIE, Donald, Lt., 42nd Foot: Lt., Army, 3 Dec. 1806; Lt., 42nd Foot, 23 July 1807. Severely wounded, Toulouse, 10 April 1814 (1st Battn.) [*London Gazette*]. *Anton*, p. 136 [Toulouse: 'The company in which I was doing duty lost four officers... Lieutenant D. McKenzie severely wounded']. Wounded, Waterloo. Died, Edinburgh, 5 Dec. 1838.

+MACKENZIE, George, Lt., 36th Foot: Lt., 36th Foot, 21 April 1807. Killed in the siege of the Forts of St Vincente, St Cayetano, and La Merced at Salamanca, 18–24 June 1812 ('McKenzie') [*London Gazette*].

+MACKENZIE, John, Lt. Col., 5th Foot: Lt. Col., 5th Foot, 8 May 1806. Wounded, 'since dead', 'in the Army lately in Spain' (1st Battn.) [*March 1809 Army List*, p. 105]. *Blakeney*, p. 112 ['On the evening of the 15th [Jan. 1809] a smart skirmish took place between our piquets on the left and a party sent forward on the French right, in the neighbourhood of Palavia Abaxo. Laborde sent forward two guns to strengthen his party. Lieutenant-Colonel M'Kenzie, of the 5th, with some companies rushed forward, endeavouring to seize the battery; but a strong line of infantry who lay concealed behind some walls started up and poured in such a sharp fire that the piquets were driven back, carrying their lieutenant-colonel mortally wounded.']. *Moorsom*, p. 105 [Corunna: 'On the 14th the enemy

MACKIE

cannonaded the left of the British line, and on the 15th his whole army made a forward movement, and took up a strong position in front of the British; this evening an affair took place in which Colonel Mackenzie, of the 5th regiment, fell in endeavouring to take two of the enemy's guns.'].

MACKENZIE, John Holland, Lt., 5th Foot: Lt., 5th Foot, 21 April 1808. Wounded, 'dangerously', storming of Ciudad Rodrigo, 19 Jan. 1812 [*London Gazette*].

+McKENZIE, John Randoll, Major-General: Lt. Col., 78th Foot, 27 Feb. 1796; Col., Army, 1 Jan. 1801; Major-General, 25 April 1808. Killed, Talavera, 28 July 1809, while serving on the General Staff [*London Gazette*]. Obituary, *The Gentleman's Magazine*, Aug. 1809, p. 780 ['Major-general John Randoll McKenzie, who so gloriously fell, in the battle of Talavera ... whose patrimonial estate (Suddie) lies in that part of the county of Ross called the Black Isle. He fell in or about his 47th year ... he was removed to the command of a brigade in Portugal in 1808. He was in Parliament four years, first for the Sutherland district of boroughs, and latterly for the shire of Sutherland... In 1805 ... [in the] 2d Battalion of the 78th, which, when but recruits in fact, beat the chosen troops of France on the plains of Maida... He was a zealous, steady, cool, soldier; a mild and most friendly man. The Service loses in him a most excellent officer; his friends an estimable and amiable man. The 78th adored him, and will long lament him. His estate called Suddie devolves to an only sister, Mrs Potts, a widow lady, without children.'].

+MACKENZIE, Maxwell, Capt./ Major, 71st Foot: Capt., 71st Foot, 25 June 1803. Major, Army, 30 May 1811. Slightly wounded, Vimeiro, 21

Aug. 1808 [*London Gazette*]. Severely wounded, Pyrenees, 25 July 1813 ('M'Kenzie') (1st Battn.) [*London Gazette*]. Killed, the Nive, 13 Dec. 1813 ('Major M. M'Kenzie (Lieutenant-Colonel)') (1st Battn.) [*London Gazette*]. Obituary, *The Gentleman's Magazine*, March 1814 ['Dec. 13... Lieut.-col. Maxwell Mackenzie, major of the 71st regt. son of John M. esq. of Kincraig, Ross-shire. This gallant officer received his mortal wound in the engagement with the Enemy near Bayonne, while nobly cheering and leading on his men; and thus terminated an honourable life in a glorious death.'].

+MACKENZIE, Murdock, Capt., 20th Foot: Capt., 20th Foot, 9 Feb. 1809. Killed, Pyrenees, 28 July 1813 ('McKenzie') [*London Gazette*].

McKENZIE, William, Capt., 42nd Foot: Capt., 42nd Foot, 8 Aug. 1805. Severely wounded, storming and capture of Fort St Michael, Burgos, 19 Sept. 1812 (1st Battn.) [*London Gazette*].

MACKIE, William, Lt./Capt., 88th Foot: *1829 Statement of Service for Retired Officers:* Aged eighteen years on first appointment to the Army. Ensign, 88th Foot, 21 March 1805; Lt., 88th Foot, May 1806 [Army List gives 24 June 1806]; Capt., 88th Foot, 24 May 1812; Half-pay, Jan. 1816, by reduction; Capt., full-pay, 88th Foot, 24 March 1818; Half-pay, 6th Dragoon Guards, 'private affairs'. Served twenty-one years on full-pay. *Where serving when wounded:* 'Wounded.' *Where generally present during last five years:* 'In England since placed on H. pay.' [PRO: WO 25/766 f15]. Volunteered for the Forlorn Hope, storming of Ciudad Rodrigo. His bravery was, however, long overlooked. *Haythornthwaite, Armies of Wellington*, p. 248 [Salamanca, 22 July 1812: 'The colonel of the leading French regiment (22eme

Ligne), endeavouring to hearten his men, seized a musket and ran forward towards the advancing 88th Foot, led by Major Barnaby Murphy and the adjutant, Captain William Mackie, both mounted ... the French officer fired at Murphy, killing him on the spot... At the same moment someone from the 88th shot the French colonel through the head, who threw up his arms and fell forward; as Murphy, his foot caught in a stirrup, was dragged by his frightened horse along the front of the battalion, a sight which threw the 88th into a frenzy of rage. Pakenham rode up at this moment and called to Wallace, "Let them loose"; the brigade charged and the French, astonished at the sight of a two-deep line running towards superior numbers, broke and fled. After some bloody bayonet-work among the bolting Frenchmen, the brigade rallied in a state of exhaustion; except Adjutant Mackie who, seeing the infantry fight had ended, joined a cavalry charge from which he returned covered in dust, with only the hilt of his sword left, and that reeking of blood.'].

McKILLIGAN, John, Lt., 1st Foot: Lt., 1st Foot, 30 Nov. 1809. Slightly wounded, Salamanca, 22 July 1812 [*London Gazette*]. Severely wounded, Vittoria, 21 June 1813 ('McKellegane') [*London Gazette*]. Recorded as 'missing', the Nive, 10 Dec. 1813 ('McKilligam') (3rd Battn.) [*London Gazette*].

+MACKINNON, Henry, Capt. and Lt. Col./Col., Coldstream Guards; Major-General: Capt. and Lt. Col. 18 Oct. 1799; Col., Army, 25 Oct. 1809; Maj.-Gen. 1 Jan. 1812. Mentioned in Wellington's Fuentes de Onoro dispatch, 8 May 1811 [5 May: 'Colonel Mackinnon's brigade ... the 88th, with the 71st and 79th, under the command of Colonel Mackinnon, charged the enemy, and drove them through the

Village... I particularly request your Lordship's attention to the conduct of ... Colonel MacKinnon'] [*London Gazette*, 26 May 1811]. Killed in the storming of Ciudad Rodrigo, 19 Jan. 1812 [*London Gazette*]. Mentioned in Wellington's Ciudad Rodrigo dispatch of 20 Jan. 1812 ['Major-General Mackinnon was unfortunately blown up by the accidental explosion of one of the enemy's expense magazines, close to the breach, after he had gallantly and successfully led the troops under his command to the attack.']. Obituary, *The Gentleman's Magazine*, Feb. 1812, p. 190 ['Jan. 19... Fell gloriously on the breach of Ciudad Rodrigo, Major-gen. McKinnon. He was descended from one of the most antient families in Scotland; being a younger son of the late W. McKinnon, esq... At an early age he entered into the Coldstream guards; and served his first campaign under the Duke of York in Holland. During the rebellion in Ireland, he was Brigade-major to Gen. Sir G. Nugent, where he was remarkable for his courage, humanity, and good conduct. The Gazette of that time particularly notices him. He served in the expedition to Egypt. In the year 1805, he served with his regiment in Germany, under Lord Cathcart; as well as at the taking of Copenhagen, in 1807. He again embarked at the end of 1808 for the Peninsula; where an action was fought under Lord Wellington, in which his name was mentioned with the highest praise in the dispatches. The General married in 1804, the youngest daughter of the late Sir J. Colt, bart. who is left with two infants. After the fall of Ciudad Rodrigo, the body of Major-gen. McKinnon was found, and with difficulty recognised; and his regiment shewed all the respect possible to the remains of so brave and meritorious an officer.']. *Leach*, p. 249 [Storming of Ciudad

Rodrigo: 'Whilst the 3d Division was engaged at the large breach, one of the enemy's expense magazines exploded with a terrible crash, which blew up a great number of both parties, amongst whom was Major-General M'Kinnon, who commanded a brigade in the 3d Division.']. *Simmons*, p. 222 [Ciudad Rodrigo: 'General McKinnon, who commanded a Brigade in the 3rd Division, was blown up and his body sadly mutilated, but being a very tall man, it was not difficult to make him out.']. *Brett-James*, pp. 75, 237 ['Two generals perished in the storming of Ciudad Rodrigo: Henry Mackinnon and Robert Craufurd. The former was extricated from under other bodies in the ditch and carried by a sergent's party to Espeja, where he was buried with full military honours, his remains being followed by his brother officers of the Guards to a grave dug in the village market-place. Ensign Stepney had previously cut off a lock of hair to send to Mackinnon's widow.'].

McKINNON, Ranold Angus, Lt., 42nd Foot: *1829 Statement of Service for Retired Officers*: Aged twenty-three on first appointment to the Army. Ensign, 54th Foot, 30 Jan. 1806; Ensign, 42nd Foot, 17 Feb. 1807; Lt., 42nd Foot, 16 Nov. 1809; Half-pay, 13 July 1815, 'being considered unfit for farther service in consequence of severe wounds & by a decision of the Army Medical Board to that effect.' 'Totally unfit for any farther service'. *Where serving when wounded*: 'Burgos in Spain & Toulouse in France'. *Details of pension*: Seventy pounds for each wound, the first commencing 11 April 1815, the latter on 25 Dec. 1818. *Family*: Married in St Mary, Lambeth, Surrey, London, 8 Nov. 1819. No children. *Where generally resident during last five years*: 'London'. 'Springfield, Wandsworth Road,

London'. [PRO: WO 25/766 f120]. Severely wounded, siege of Burgos, 20–26 Sept. 1812 ('M'Kinnon') (1st Battn.) [*London Gazette*]. Severely wounded, Toulouse, 10 April 1814 ('Roderick A. McKinnon') (1st Battn.) [*London Gazette*]. *1818 Pension Return*, pp. 12–13 ('Ranold'). Army List gives as 'Ronald A. McKinnon'.

MACKINTOSH, Aeneas, Major, 85th Foot: Major, 85th Foot, 7 April 1808; Lt. Col., Army, 30 May 1811. Obituary, *The Gentleman's Magazine*, April 1814, p. 422 ['He was stationed many years in the West Indies; and survived several of his comrades, who fell victims to the baneful effects of that climate ... He was then ordered, with other forces, to join the expedition for Walcheren; had his share of the difficulties and dangers the troops there underwent, and returned in safety. His regiment was now again called into service, and joined Lord Wellington in the Peninsula ... Lord Wellington selected him to command a storming-party, which failed only through the efficiency of the scaling-ladders. Though the party was half destroyed, yet he again escaped... He had received many wounds in different actions, though none dangerously. When returned again to England, he found himself persecuted by cabals in the regiment, and brought to court-martial; ... he was fully and honourably acquitted of [all charges] ... the Lieut.-colonel was appointed to the same rank in the 79th, which he was on the point of joining, when his sudden and untimely fate took place, deeply and justly lamented by all his friends and relations ... The circumstances of his untimely fate were peculiarly distressing to his relations, who would have been more open to comfort and consolation, had he perished in that field of honour in which he had so often exposed himself.'].

MACKINTOSH, Donald, Sergeant, 79th Foot; Ensign/Lt., 88th Foot: *1829 Statement of Service*: Born in the 'Parish of Moy, County of Inverness', 23 Dec. 1784. Aged sixteen 'on his first Entrance into the Army.' 'Private, Corporal & Serjeant, 79th Foot, From October 1804 to the 10th May 1811.' Ensign, 88th Foot, 11 May 1811. Lt., 88th Foot, 21 April 1814. Half Pay, 25 March 1816, 'By the Reduction of the 2nd Battn.' 'Lieutenant and Adjutant', 97th Foot, 25 March 1824. *Battles, sieges and campaigns*: 'Siege of Copenhagen 1807 as Serjt. in 79th Foot... Oporto 10th & 12th May 1809 & Talavera de la Reyna 27 & 28th July 1809, as Serjt. 1st Batt. Detmts... Siege of Cadiz in 1810 as Serjt. in 79th... Busaco 27th Sept. 1810. Fuentes de Onor 3rd & 5th May 1811 as Serjt. in 79th... Nivelle 10th Novr. 1813, Orthez 27th Feby. 1814 and Toulouse 10th April 1814, as Ensign in 88th Foot... Massena's retreat from Torres Vedras as Serjt. in 79th. Retreat from Madrid in 1812 as Ensn. in 88th. Served in all the Campaigns on the peninsular and several affairs and skirmishes not mentioned.' *Distinguished conduct*: 'Recommended by Sir Brent Spencer on the 5th May 1811 to the Duke of Wellington and was appointed an Ensign in the 88th a few days after.' *Wounds received in action*: 'Wounded from the fragment of a Shell at Orthez on the 27th February 1814 and received One years Pay as Ensign.' *Service abroad*: '1807 to 26th March 1816, Zealand Expedition to Gottenburgh, Portugal, Spain, France, N. America, France. 15th April 1825 to 31st Decr. 1829, Ceylon.' [PRO: WO 25/804 f110].

MACKINTOSH, Robert, Lt., 4th Foot; Capt., 1st Portuguese Line: Lt., 4th Foot, 20 Sept. 1810. Wounded at Barba del Puerco, 11 May 1811 ('McIntosh') (1st Battn.) [*London Gazette*]. In Portuguese Service Feb. 1812 to April 1814. One

hundred pounds per annum pension, commencing 25 Dec. 1815, for 'loss of an eye' in Spain, 1814, while serving as Capt., 1st Portuguese Line ('Mac Intosh') [*1818 Pension Return*, pp. 24–5]. MGS. Challis, *Portuguese Army*, p. 57.

+MACKINTOSH, William Henry, Lt., 4th Foot; Capt., 1st Portuguese Line: Lt., Army, 28 Aug. 1801; Lt., 4th Foot, 19 July 1804. In Portuguese Service April 1809 to Sept. 1810. Challis, *Portuguese Army*, p. 57 ['Capt. 1 Line... K/A Busaco 27 Sep. '10'].

McLACHLAN, Donald, Lt., 57th Foot: Lt., 57th Foot, 1 Dec. 1804. Severely wounded, Albuera, 16 May 1811 [*London Gazette*].

McLACHLAN, Peter, Capt., 77th Foot: Capt., 77th Foot, 15 Feb. 1810. Slightly wounded, storming of Ciudad Rodrigo, 19 Jan. 1812 ('M'Laughlin') [*London Gazette*].

MACLAINE, Archibald, Major, 87th Foot: First appointment to the Army on 16 April 1794; Capt., 94th Foot, 22 Dec. 1804. Commanded Fort Matagorda, Cadiz, during its lengthy and heroic defence prior to its evacuation on 22 April 1810. Major, 87th Foot, 4 Oct. 1810. Severely wounded, Barossa, 5 March 1811 (2nd Battn.) [*London Gazette*]. Mentioned in Skerrett's dispatch concerning the capture of Seville, 28 Aug. 1812 ['I am also much indebted to ... Major Maclain, commanding a detachment 87th Regiment.'] [*London Gazette*]. Dispatch written by him as 'late Commander at Fort Matagorda', dated Cadiz, 23 April 1810, originally in the *London Gazette*, is reprinted in *The Gentleman's Magazine*, May 1810, p. 474. See Lefebure, Charles. Lt. Col., 7th West India Regt., 25 Jan. 1813; Half-pay, 25 April 1816. Col., Army, 22 July 1830; Major-General, 23 Nov. 1841; Col.,

52nd Foot, 8 Feb. 1847; Lt.-General, 11 Nov. 1851; General, 5 June 1855. Temporary pension of two hundred pounds per annum, commencing 6 March 1812, 'for wounds' received at Barrosa [*1818 Pension Return*, pp. 20–1]. *Hart's 1860 Army List*, pp. 7, 270 ['Sir Archibald Maclaine's services:– Mysore campaign of 1799 against Tippoo Sultan, including the battle of Mallavelly, siege and storming of Seringapatam, where he received three wounds, from the effects of which he was confined in hospital for upwards of a year. Capture of the Danish settlement of Tranquebar, and the Polygar war in 1801, including the battle of Ardingy, and affair of Serungapore, where he was wounded. Mahratta war of 1802, 3, and 4, ... including ... siege of Asseerghur (wounded)... Ordered home in 1804, in consequence of severe wounds received in the different actions from 1799 to 1804. Peninsular campaigns of 1810, 11, and 12, including the defence of Cadiz, the defence of Matagorda (an outwork of Cadiz, and a ruined redoubt when taken possession of from the enemy), from 22nd February to 22nd April 1810, during which long period Sir Archibald, then a Captain in the old 94th Regiment, with a very small force under his command, most gallantly kept at bay 8,000 of the enemy under Marshal Soult, who conducted the siege, and did not evacuate until ordered to do so by Lieut. General Sir Thomas Graham, his men being nearly all either killed or wounded. Served also at the battle of Barrosa (dangerously wounded, and his horse killed) and capture of Seville.']. MGS.

MACLAINE, Hector, Capt., 57th Foot: *1829 Statement of Service for Retired Officers*: Aged seventeen on first appointment to the Army. Ensign, 64th Foot, '24th or 25th September 1803'; Lt., 46th Foot, 24 Dec. 1804; Lt., 64th Foot, 'Removed immediately in 1805'; Capt., 9th

Garrison Battn., 1 Dec. 1806; Capt., 57th Foot, [21 Jan.]1808; Major, 57th Foot, May 1819; Half-pay, 3rd Ceylon Regt., 'May or June 1822', 'By Request for Private affairs'; Major, 21st Foot, July 1824; Lt. Col., unattached, 9 Sept. 1824. *Where serving when wounded*: 'Nivelle, France'. One hundred pounds, commencing 25 Dec. 1825. *Family*: Married in Thornbury, Gloucestershire, 29 Aug. 1816. One child by 1829. *Where generally resident during last five years*: 'Thornbury, Gloucestershire.' [PRO: WO 25/766 f7]. Severely wounded, Nivelle, 10 Nov. 1813 ('Maclaine') (1st Battn.) [*London Gazette*].

McLAINE, Murdoch Hugh, Capt., 77th Foot: Capt., 77th Foot, 3 July 1805. Severely wounded, storming of Ciudad Rodrigo, 19 Jan. 1812 ('McLean') [*London Gazette*]. Pension of two hundred pounds per annum, commencing 20 Jan. 1813, for 'loss of a leg' at Ciudad Rodrigo ('Maclaine') [*1818 Pension Return*, pp. 18–19].

McLAREN, Charles, Lt., 42nd Foot: Lt. Army, 28 April 1808; Lt., 42nd Foot, 2 June 1808. Severely wounded, Toulouse, 10 April 1814 (1st Battn.) [*London Gazette*]. Temporary pension of seventy pounds per annum, commencing 11 April 1815, 'for wounds' received at Toulouse [*1818 Pension Return*, pp. 12–13]. *Anton*, pp. 141–2 [Following Toulouse: 'Here fell Cunningham, a corporal in the grenadier company, a man much esteemed in the regiment; he was a married man.. she now stood a lonely unprotected being... In this instance, the officer who commanded the company to which Cunningham belonged having been severely wounded, sent for the widow; she became his sicknurse, and under his protection was restored in decent respectability to her home. Worthy generous McLaren, thou art now no more; the wounds of that day preyed upon thy frame, shortened thy brief career, and bereaved the regiment of one of its best subalterns. Thou wert always the soldier's friend, as well as the widow's protector. Shade of the brave, forgive this poor apostrophe to thy memory! it is the only offering a soldier can present; he plants it as a flower upon the green turf that covers thy cold remains; may it take root, and its blossoms excite some abler florist to grace the spot with greater beauty.'].

MACLEAN, Allan, Ensign, 79th Foot: Ensign, 79th Foot, 9 Dec. 1812. Severely wounded, Toulouse, 10 April 1814 (1st Battn.) [*London Gazette*]. Lt., 79th Foot, 28 July 1814.

MACLEAN, Allen Thomas, Cornet/Lt., 13th Light Dragoons: *1829 Statement of Service*: Born in Argylshire, Scotland, 1 May 1794. Aged sixteen on first appointment to the Army. Ensign, 2nd West India Regt., 4 Jan. 1810; Cornet, 13th Light Dragoons, 23 Aug. 1810; Lt., 13th Light Dragoons, 11 July 1811; Capt., 13th Light Dragoons, 23 Dec. 1818; Major, 13th Light Dragoons, 29 Oct. 1830; Lt. Col., 13th Light Dragoons, 11 July 1834; Half-pay, 31 May 1840. *Battles, sieges and campaigns*: 'Present with my corps in any action in which it was engaged from Decr. 1810 to the end of the Peninsula War and at the Battle of Waterloo. Present in the Campaign in E. Indies in 1839 in command of the Cavalry Brigade.' *Distinguished conduct*: 'Thanked by Sir John Byng for my conduct in the Pyrenees 25th of Augt. 1813 and by Sir Henry Fane for my behaviour at an affair a few days previous to the Battle of Orthes.' *Wounds received in action*: '13th March 1814 at Conches in France & taken Prisoner. A years pay.' *Service abroad*: Decr. 1810 to 1814, Peninsula. May 1815 to 1816, France. 14 June 1819 to 31 Decr. 1829, India.'

Not married by 1830. [PRO: WO 25/784 f62]. Recorded as 'missing', 'in Action with the Enemy', 13 March 1814 ('Alan McLean') [*London Gazette*]. Waterloo Medal. MGS. *Dalton*, p. 78 ['Allan T. Maclean'], p. 80 ['Bn. 1793. Attained the rank of lt.-gen.']

+McCLEAN, Allen, Lt., 91st Foot: Lt., 91st Foot, 15 May 1808. Severely wounded, Pyrenees, 28 July 1813 ('Maclean') (1st Battn.) [*London Gazette*]. Died of wounds, 24 Dec. 1813. Return dated Dec. 1813. [PRO: WO 25/2965].

MACLEAN, George, Lt./Capt., 61st Foot: Lt., 61st Foot, 15 Aug. 1805. Slightly wounded, Talavera, 28 July 1809 ('McLean') [*London Gazette*]. Slightly wounded, Pyrenees, 30 July 1813 ('Captain M'Lean') (1st Battn.) [*London Gazette*].

MACLEAN, John, Lt. Col., 27th Foot: Major, 27th Foot, 2 Aug. 1804; Lt. Col., 27th Foot, 9 June 1808. Wounded in the trenches before Badajoz, 8–15 May 1811 ('M'Lean') (3rd Battn.) [*London Gazette*]. Mentioned in Wellington's Castrejon dispatch, 21 July 1812 ['In these affairs ... Lieutenant-Colonel Maclean of the 27th [and others] ... distinguished themselves.'] [*London Gazette*]. Severely wounded, Toulouse, 10 April 1814 (3rd Battn.) [*London Gazette*]. Gold Medal. Pension of three hundred pounds per annum, commencing 11 April 1815, 'for wounds' received in Holland and at Fort St Christoval [*1818 Pension Return*, pp. 8–9]. *Royal Military Calendar*, vol. IV, pp. 215–16 ['In 1799 he accompanied his regiment [100th Foot, later 92nd] to Holland, and was present at ... 2nd Oct., near Alkmaar, where he was severely wounded in two places ... at every action that took place in Egypt during the campaign of 1801... In Aug. 1808, he took command of the 3rd battalion of the 27th regiment ...

and embarked with it for the Peninsula; and although a young battalion, being chiefly composed of recruits, his unremitting attention to the discipline and interior arrangements, soon made his corps not inferior to any with the army ... at the siege of Badajos in May, 1811, where he was severely wounded ... and near Pampluna, on the 26th July, 1813, where he was wounded... He was present at ... Toulouse, on the 10th April, 1814, where he was wounded severely, being the fifth wound he received in the service of his country; he had one horse killed under him, and another wounded, at the battle of Toulouse.'].

MACLEAN, John, Ensign/Lt., 43rd Foot: *1829 Statement of Service*: Born 6 Oct. 1794, Berwick upon Tweed. Aged sixteen on first appointment to the Army. Ensign, 43rd Foot, 2 May 1811; Lt., 43rd Foot, 10 Oct. 1812; Half-pay, 24 Dec. 1818; Lt., 20th Foot, 22 Nov. 1821. *Battles, sieges and campaigns*: 'Was in the action on the 11th Nov. 1812, on the retreat from Salamanca... Vittoria 21st June 1813, Nivelle 10th Novr. 1813. Nive 12th December 1813. Toulouse 10th April 1814... New Orleans, 8th January 1815.' *Wounds received in action*: 'Slightly wounded at the Battle of the Nivelle, on the 10th November 1813.' *Service abroad*: 'June 1812 to December 1812, Peninsula. Decr. 1812 to July 1814, Peninsula & South of France. Octr. 1814 to May 1815, New Orleans, & on the Passage. June 1815 to Septr. 1818, France.' Unmarried in 1830. [PRO: WO 25/788 f336]. Slightly wounded, Nivelle, 10 Nov. 1813 ('John M'Clean, junior') (1st Battn.) [*London Gazette*].

MACLELLAN, 1st Lt./Adjutant, 23rd Foot: 1st Lt., 23rd Foot, 22 Oct. 1807; Adjutant, 23rd Foot, 17 March 1808. Wounded, Albuera, 16 May 1811, while serving as Adjutant ('McLellan') (1st Battn.) [*London*

Gazette]. Severely wounded, Pyrenees, 28 July 1813 ('M'Lellan') (1st Battn.) [*London Gazette*].

+MACLEOD, Charles, Major/Lt. Col., 43rd Regt: Lt., 62nd Foot, 21 March 1800; Major, 43rd Foot, 1807; Lt. Col. 16 Aug. 1810. Mentioned in Wellington's Ciudad Rodrigo dispatch, 20 Jan. 1812 ['I particularly request your Lordship's attention to the conduct of ... Lieutenant-Colonel M'Leod of the 43d.'] [*London Gazette*, 5 Feb. 1812]. Killed, storming of Badajoz, 6 April 1812 ('M'Leod') [*London Gazette*]. Mentioned in Wellington's Badajoz dispatch, 7 April 1812 ['In Lieutenant-Colonel M'Leod, of the 43rd Regiment, who was killed in the breach, His Majesty has sustained the loss of an officer who was an ornament to his profession, and was capable of rendering the most important services to his country.'] [*London Gazette*]. *Simmons*, p. 93 [Coa, 24 July 1810: 'A party of the 43rd, with Major McLeod at their head and several of their officers, as well as our men and officers, ran up the hill, exposed to a desperate fire, as the enemy had a strong wall to fire over. They did us much mischief before we got at them. It was a grand sight. Our brave boys would face anything.']. *Leach*, pp. 149–50 [Coa: 'If any are now living of those who defended the little hill above the bridge, they cannot fail to remember the gallantry displayed by Major M'Leod, of the 43rd, who was the senior officer on the spot. How either he or his horse escaped being blown to atoms, when, in the most daring manner, he charged on horseback, at the head of a hundred or two skirmishers of the 43rd and of our regiment mixed together, and headed them in making a dash at a wall lined with French infantry, which we soon dislodged, I am at a loss to imagine. It was one of those extraordinary escapes tending strongly to implant in the mind some faith in the doctrine of fatality. This gallant officer was killed afterwards whilst heading his regiment at the storming of Badjoz, and was sincerely regretted by all who knew him']. *Bruce*, pp. 77–81 [Two of his letters to his good friend, Major William Napier, who was recuperating in England, dated 21 Jan. 1812 and 4 Feb. 1812, concerning the storming of Ciudad Rodrigo], p. 87 ['On reaching Lisbon [Napier] heard of the bloody assault and capture of Badajoz, and learnt that his dearest friend, Lieutenant-Colonel Charles Macleod of the 43rd regiment, had been killed in the breach. Napier was terribly affected by the loss of his friend... Letter to his Wife. "Lisbon, 17th April 1812. Macleod is dead, and I am grovelling in misery and wretchedness – my temples ache with the painful images that are passing before me. He was the best and will be the last of my friends, for I cannot endure the torture that I feel again, and where can I find another like him?" '], p. 88 [Quotes Napier: 'Officers of all ranks ... were seen to start out as if struck by sudden madness and rush into the breach... In one of these attempts Colonel Macleod of the 43rd, a young man whose feeble body would have been quite unfit for war if it had not been sustained by an unconquerable spirit, was killed. Wherever his voice was heard his soldiers had gathered, and with such a strong resolution did he lead them up the fatal ruins, that, when one behind him in falling plunged a bayonet into his back, he complained not, but continuing his course was shot dead within a yard of the sword-blades.' ('Peninsular War, book xvi., chap. v.')], pp. 89, 90 [Letter from William Napier to his wife, La Encina, 29 April 1812: 'My poor friend was struck down from the breach twice before he was killed, once with a stone, once with a bayonet wound in the head;

nevertheless he persevered in his attempts till a shot went through his right breast and finished his career in the only manner that was worthy of his life.']. *Haythorn-thwaite, Die Hard*, p. 178 [Badajoz: '[Harry] Smith got into the ditch, where he found the commander of the stormers, Charles Macleod, leaning upon a ladder with his hands on his breast. The young man, "whose feeble body would have been quite unfit for war, if it had not been sustained by an unconquerable spirit" [Napier], had already been injured when a man behind him had been hit and in falling had run his bayonet into Macleod's back, but he had carried on until he was shot. He gasped, "Oh, Smith, I am mortally wounded. Help me up the ladder." Smith replied, "Oh no, dear fellow." "I am," said Macleod, "be quick." Smith helped him out of the ditch, but to no avail; the wound was mortal.'], p. 188 ['Lieutenant-Colonel Macleod of the 43rd was buried in a cornfield on the slope of a hill overlooking the regimental camp. Only six officers of the 43rd were fit to attend the interment, but his brother James, of the Royal Artillery, was also present; all were overcome with grief, and even the privates who carried the body were sobbing aloud. One of Macleod's men, Sergeant Thomas Blood, gave the most remarkable testimony: "There was not a man in that corps [the 43rd] but would have stood between him and the fatal ball that struck him dead, so esteemed was he by all, and only twenty-seven years of age." He was commemorated by a marble monument in Westminster Abbey, erected by his brother officers and executed by the great sculptor Joseph Nollekins.']. Biography appears in *Oxfordshire Light Infantry Chronicle*, vol. IV (1895).

+McLEOD, Donald, Lt., 95th Foot: 1st Lt., 95th Foot, 23 May 1805.

Killed, Coa, 24 July 1810 [*London Gazette*]. *Simmons*, p. 82 [killed, Coa: 'shot through the heart'].

MACLEOD, George, Capt., Royal Engineers: Capt., Army, 1 July 1806; Capt., Royal Engineers, 1 May 1811. Mentioned in Wellington's Ciudad Rodrigo, 20 Jan. 1812 ['It is but justice also to the 3d division to report, that the men who performed the sap belonged to the 45th, 74th, and 88th Regiments, under the command of Captain M'Leod, of the royal engineers ... and they distinguished themselves not less in the storm of the place, than they had in the performance of their laborious duty during the siege.'] [*London Gazette*, 5 Feb. 1812]. Major, Army, 6 Feb. 1812. Severely wounded, siege of Badajoz, 26 March 1812, while serving as Brigade Major ('M'Leod') [*London Gazette*]. MGS.

+MACLEOD, Roderick, Lt., 38th Foot: Lt., 38th Foot, 25 Aug. 1807. Severely wounded, 'at the Siege of St Sebastian', 7–27 July 1813, while serving as Assistant-Engineer (1st Battn.) [*London Gazette*]. Died of wounds, 25 July 1813. Return dated Aug. 1813. [PRO: WO 25/2965].

McLEOD, William, Capt., 61st Foot: *1829 Statement of Service for Retired Officers*: Aged twenty-eight on first appointment to the Army. Ensign, 24th Foot, 24 June 1796; Lt., 61st Foot, 5 March 1797; Capt., 61st Foot, 11 Sept. 1806; Capt., 13th Royal Veteran Battn., 25 Feb. 1813, 'the No. of this Battn. was changed to 7th in 1815. Disbanded 24th May 1816'; Capt., 6th Royal Veteran Battn., Dec. 1819, 'disbanded 24th March 1821'; Capt., 2nd Royal Veteran Battn., Dec. 1821, 'disbanded 24th April 1826'. Served thirty-two years on full-pay. *Where serving when wounded*: 'Battle of Salamanca, 22nd July 1812.' *Family*: Married on 5 Dec. 1789. Three children, all born before 1796. *Where*

generally resident during last five years: 'Lifford County Donegal, Ireland.' [PRO: WO 25/766 f110]. Severely wounded, Salamanca, 61st Foot [*London Gazette*].

+McNAB, Alan, Lt., 92nd Foot: Lt., 92nd Foot, 11 Dec. 1806. Severely wounded, 'right arm amputated', Fuentes de Onoro, 5 May 1811 (1st Battn.) [*London Gazette*]. Died of wounds, 9 May 1811. Return dated 25 May 1811 ('McNabb') [PRO: WO 25/2965]. *Register of officers' effects*: 'McNabb'. Died of wounds, 9 May 1811, Villa Formosa. Single. [PRO: WO 25/2964].

McNAIR, James, Lt./Capt., 52nd Foot: *1829 Statement of Service*: 'Born near Glasgow, Scotland, 24th September 1787. Aged 17 years 6 months on his first Entrance into the Army. Ensign, 52nd Foot, 14 March 1805. Lieut., 52nd, 330 June 1805. Captain, 52nd, 11 May 1812. Major, 52nd, 25 April 1822.' Note added: 'Lt Col., 73R, 3 Aug. 1830.' *Battles, sieges and campaigns*: '*Battles* Corunna 16 Jany. 1809. Busaco 27th Sept. 1810. Fuentes D'Onor 5 May 1811. Salamanca 22d July 1812. Waterloo 18 June 1815. *Sieges* Badajoz 6 April 1812. The Coa, Sabugal, and various minor Skirmishes with the Lt. Division. *Campaigns* 1808, Sir John Moore. 1809, 1810, 1811, 1812, Duke of Wellington. 1814, Lord Lyndoch. 1815, Duke of Wellington. 1816, 1817, 1818, Army of Occupation.' *Distinguished conduct*: 'Volunteer with the Storming Party at Badajoz.' *Wounds received in action*: 'Wounded in the head at the Storming of Badajoz, 6 April 1812. One years Pay as Lieut.' *Titles, honorary distinctions and medals*: 'Waterloo Medal.' *Service abroad*: 'Septr. 1806 to Jany. 1808, Sicily. May 1808 to Augt. 1808, Sweden. Aug. 1808 to Jany. 1809, Portugal & Spain. July 1809 to Octr. 1812, Spain. March 1813 to Novr. 1814, Belgium. Jany. 1815 to April 1815, on Bd. Ship at Cove of Cork bound for America. April 1815 to 24 Novr. 1818, Belgium & France. June 1823 to ctr. 1826, N. America.' *Family*: Married Ellen Stanser, 'Daughter of the Rt. Revd. Dr Stanser, Lord Bishop of Nova Scotia,' 31 July 1824, St. Mary's Fredericton N. Brunswick. They had three children by 1830. [PRO: WO 25/795 f81]. Slightly wounded, storming of Badajoz, 6 April 1812 [*London Gazette*]. Waterloo. *Dalton*, p. 171 ['K.H. Of Greenfield, near Glasgow. D. there, 15th April, 1836']. *Kincaid, Random Shots*, pp. 286–7 [Following the storming of Badajoz: 'As soon as a glimpse of day-light permitted I went to take a look at the breach, and there saw a solitary figure, with a drawn sword, stalking over the ruins and the slain, which, in the grey dawn of morning, appeared to my astonished eyes like a headless trunk, and concluded that it was the ghost of one of the departed come in search of its earthly remains. I cautiously approached to take a nearer survey, when I found that it was Captain M'Nair, of the 52d, with his head wrapped in a red handkerchief. He told me that he was looking for his cap and his scabbard, both of which had parted company from him in the storm, about that particular spot; but his search proved a forlorn hope. I congratulated him that his head had not gone in the cap, as had been the case with but too many of our mutual companions on that fatal hour.'].

MACNEILL, Donald, Major, 91st Foot: Major, Army, 23 Nov. 1809. Major, 91st Foot, 1 Aug. 1811. Severely wounded, Pyrenees, 30 July 1813 ('M'Niel') 91st Battn.) [*London Gazette*]. Temporary pension of three hundred pounds per annum, commencing 31 July 1814, 'for a wound' received in the Pyrenees, while serving as 'Major Comg.' his regiment ('McNeill') [*1818 Pension Return*, pp. 20–1].

McNIEL, Donald, Bvt. Major, E.O.P.S.; Lt. Col., 10th Portuguese Line: Slightly wounded, Nivelle, 10 Nov. 1813, while serving as Lt. Col., 10th Portuguese Line ('Donald McNeal') [*London Gazette*]. In Portuguese Service Aug. 1809 to April 1814. MGS. *Challis, Portuguese Army*, p. 57 ['Maj. E.O.P.S.'].

McNIVEN, Thomas William Ogilvy, Lt., 42nd Foot: *1829 Statement of Service*: Born in Banff, Scotland, 18 Sept. 1793. Aged nineteen on first appointment to the Army. Ensign, 42nd Foot, 13 July 1812 [Army List gives 23 July]; Lt., 42nd Foot, 27 Feb. 1814; Half-pay, 25 Oct. 1814, by reduction; Lt., 42nd Foot, June 1815; Half-pay, Feb. 1817, by reduction; Lt., 26th Foot, Feb. 1818; Capt., 29th Foot, 31 Oct. 1825; Capt., 80th Foot, 29 Nov. 1825. *Battles, sieges and campaigns*: 'Served as Ensign and Lieut. in the 42d Regt. in the Peninsula. was employed in the investment of Bayonne in 1813. Carried the Regt. Colour of the Regt. at the Battle of Orthes on the 27th Feb. 1814, and upon this occasion I succeeded to my Lieutenantcy by the death of Lieut. & Adjutant [John] Innes, who was killed. Was afterwards present in an affair on the 2d March near Aire, & again on the Evening of the 19th of the same month near Tarles. Was present at the Battle of Toulouse fought on 10 of April 1814. Served throughout these operations under Lieut. Col. Sir Robert Macara, then Comg. the 42nd & killed at Quatre Bras.' *Wounds received in action*: 'Severely wounded at the Battle of Toulouse on the 10th April 1814, while bearing the Regl. Colour of the 42d Regt. on that day, by a Musket Ball near the groin which compelled me to quit the Field, for which a year's Pay was granted to me, and from the effects of the Wound proving of a dangerous & suffering nature, a temporary Pension was granted in

1816.' *Service Abroad*: '1813 to 1816, Continent. 1818 to 1822, Gibralter. 1826 to 1829, Malta & Corfu.' [PRO: WO 25/800 f320]. Severely wounded, Toulouse, 10 April 1814 (1st Battn.) [*London Gazette*]. Temporary pension of seventy pounds per annum, commencing 11 April 1815, 'for a wound' received at Toulouse [*1818 Pension Return*, pp. 12–13]. MGS.

MACPHERSON, Aeneas, Ensign/ Lt., 59th Foot: *1829 Statement of Service for Retired Officers*: Aged nineteen on first appointment to the Army. Ensign, 59th Foot, May 1812; Lt., 59th Foot, Sept. 1813 [Army List gives 26 Sept.]; Half-pay, 1816, on reduction. 'He lost two ... brothers ... viz. Captain Evan Macpherson 59th Regt. killed at Java & Lieut. Duncan Macpherson 79th Regt. killed at Waterloo – his only surviving Brother Lieut. Colonel Alexander Macpherson was twice severely wounded.' *Where serving when wounded*: 'at St Sebastian, received two wounds, and at the Heights of Bidarte near Bayone, and this wound most dangerous one it is [sic]'. *Details of pension*: Seventy pounds per annum, commencing Dec. 1814. Not married. No employment. *Where generally resident during last five years*: 'Clune in the Glen of Stratheleen County of ... N.B.' [PRO: WO 25/767 f229]. Severely wounded, the Nive, 11 Dec. 1813 ('MacPherson') (2nd Battn.) [*London Gazette*]. Pension 'for wounds' received at Bayonne, 1813 [*1818 Pension Return*, pp. 14–15]. MGS. Waterloo.

MACPHERSON, Alexander, Lt., 59th Foot: Ensign, 59th Foot, 24 Aug. 1808; Lt., 59th Foot, 21 Dec. 1809. Severely wounded, Vittoria, 21 June 1813 ('McPherson') (2nd Battn.) [*London Gazette*]. Temporary pension of seventy pounds per annum, commencing 22 June 1814, 'for a wound' received at Vittoria

('McPherson') [*1818 Pension Return*, pp. 14–15]. Waterloo.

MACPHERSON, Alexander, Major, 59th Foot: Capt., Army, 1799; Capt., 59th Foot, 31 Dec. 1803; Bvt. Major, 4 June 1811; Major, 59th Foot, 26 Aug. 1811; 'Insp. F.O. Rec. District' in 1814 and 1815 Army List; Half-pay, 25 March 1816; Lt. Col., Half-pay, 12 Aug. 1819. Brother of Aeneas Macpherson, who states that he was 'twice severely wounded.' [PRO: WO 25/767 f229].

McPHERSON, Donald, Lt./Capt., 92nd Foot: Lt., 92nd Foot, 15 Sept. 1805. Perhaps slightly wounded, Pyrenees, 25 July 1813 ('Macpherson') (1st Battn.) [*London Gazette*] (though this could have referred to Duncan McPherson). Capt., 92nd Foot, 21 Oct. 1813. Severely wounded, the Nive, 13 Dec. 1813 (1st Battn.) [*London Gazette*].

+McPHERSON, Donald, 1st Lt., 95th Foot: 1st Lt., 95th Foot, 8 Nov. 1809. Severely wounded, storming of Badajoz, 6 April 1812 (1st Battn.) [*London Gazette*]. Died of wounds, 7 May 1812. Return dated 25 May 1812. [PRO: WO 25/2965]. *Register of officers' effects*: Died of wounds, 7 May 1812, at Elvas. Single. [PRO: WO 25/2964]. *Simmons*, p. 232 [wounded, storming of Badajoz, 6 April 1812]. *Kincaid, Random Shots*, pp. 288–9 [On the morning following the storming of Badajoz: 'Of the doomed, who still survived, was poor Donald Mac Person, a gigantic highlander of about six feet and a half, as good a soul as ever lived; in peace a lamb – in war a lion. Donald feared for nothing either in this world or the next; he had been true to man and true to his God, and he looked his last hour in the face like a soldier and a Cristian! Donald's final departure from this life shewed him a worthy specimen of his country, and his methodical arrangements, while they prove what I have stated, may, at the same time, serve as a model for Joe Hume himself, when he comes to cast up his last earthly accounts. Donald had but an old mare and a portmanteau, with its contents, worth about £15, to leave behind him. He took a double inventory of the latter, sending one to the regiment by post, and giving the other in charge of his servant – and paying the said worthy his wages up to the probable day of his death; he gave him a conditional order on the paymaster for whatever more might be his due should he survive beyond his time – and, if ever man did, he certainly quitted this world with a clear conscience. Poor Donald! peace be to thy manes, for thou wert one whom memory loves to dwell on!'].

McPHERSON, Duncan, Lt., 27th Foot: *1829 Statement of Service*: Born 4 Dec. 1791, Gordon Hall, Badenoch. Aged fourteen on his first entrance into the Army. Ensign, 27th Foot, 19 Sept. 1805; Lt. 10 Nov. 1806; Capt. 25 March 1824. *Battles, sieges and campaigns*: 'Ensign at Calabria 1806... Lieut. at Ischia 1809... Lieutenant Sicily 1810... Lieut. at Biar 12 April 1813... Castella 13 April 1813... Tarragona June 1813... Tarragona Augt. 1813... Ardell 13 Sept. 1813... Barcelona March 1814... Platsburgh Septr. 1814.' *Distinguished conduct*: 'At Briar and Castella 12 & 13 April 1813, and was noticed in General Orders.' *Wounds received in action*: 'At Ardell 13 Sept. 1813 through the Body and left Arm. One years Pay, Pension £70 per annum in June 1819, now permanent.' *Service abroad*: 'July 1806 to Decr. 1812, Meditaranean. Decr. 1812 to June 1814, Peninsula. June 1814 to June 1815, America. June 1815 to June 1817, Franc. March 1820 to Decr. 1823, Gibraltar. Janry. 1824 to June 1826, West Indies.' Not married in 1830. [PRO: WO 25/790 f99]. Severely wounded, 'not danger-

ously', Heights of Ordal, 12/13 Sept. 1813 (2nd Battn.) [*London Gazette*].

McPHERSON, Duncan, Lt., 79th Foot: Lt., 79th Foot, 19 July 1810. Severely wounded, Toulouse, 10 April 1814 (1st Battn.) [*London Gazette*]. Killed, Waterloo.

+McPHERSON, Duncan, Lt., 92nd Foot: Lt., 92nd Foot, 15 Dec. 1808. Perhaps wounded in the Pyrenees (see Donald McPherson). Killed, the Nive, 13 Dec. 1813 ('Duncan M'Pherson') (1st Battn.) [*London Gazette*]. *Register of officers' effects*: Killed in Action, 13 Dec. 1813, near Bayonne. Single. Effects totalled £19. 5s. 7d. [PRO: WO 25/2964].

MACPHERSON, Duncan, Ensign, 92nd Foot: *1829 Statement of Service for Retired Officers*: Aged thirty-four on first appointment to the Army. Ensign, 92nd Foot, 23 Dec. 1813; Lt., 92nd Foot, 22 Oct. 1818; Capt., 92nd Foot, 22 Sept. 1825; Half-pay, 27 April 1826, 'Sent home from Jamaica in March 1826, by a Medical Board, being considered at the time unfit for Service, in consequence of severe wounds received in His Majesty's Service and ill-health.' Served nineteen years 'Previous to obtaining my first appointment.' *Where serving when wounded*: 'Wounded in Holland in 1792, in Egypt 1802, & 4 wounds in Spain & France.' No pension. *Family*: Married in 'Cluny, Badenoch, Parish of Laggan', 26 Sept. 1826. No children by 1829. *Where generally resident during last five years*: 'Jamaica & North Britain.' [PRO: WO 25/766 f16]. Waterloo.

McPHERSON, Evan, Capt., 92nd Foot: Capt., Army, 12 Aug. 1799. Capt., 92nd Foot, 31 May 1804. Major, Army, 4 June 1811. Severely wounded, 'not dangerously', storming of Badajoz, 6 April 1812, while serving on the Staff as Brigade Major [*London Gazette*]. Perhaps severely wounded, Pyrenees, 31 July 1813 ('Major Macpherson') [*London Gazette*]. See John Macpherson.

MACPHERSON, James, Ensign/Lt., 45th Foot: *1829 Statement of Service*: Born 4 June 1790, Parish of Laggan, Inverness Shire. Aged seventeen 'on his first Entrance into the Army.' Ensign, 45th Foot, 1 March 1808; Lt. 28 Feb. 1810; Capt., 2nd Garrison Batt., 25 April 1815; Capt., 13th Foot, 7 March 1816. *Battles, sieges and campaigns*: 'Septr. *1808* – Landed in Portugal. 23rd Decr. joined the first Battn. 45th Foot in Almeda, proceeded with the Brigade, under Sir A. Cameron, across the Duro, to join the Army, under Sir John Moore, retreated to Lisbon... *1809.* Advanced with the Army into Spain an Ensign in the 45th Foot... The Affair at Talavera, 22nd July. Alberehe 24th July. Battle of Talavera 27th & 28th July. Retreated to Portugal. *1810.* 27th Septr. Battle of Busacco, Lieut. 45th Foot... Retreated to the lines of Lisbon. *1811.* The Affairs on Massena's Retreat from the lines. Lieut. 45th Foot, Commanding the Sharp Shooters of his Corps, consisting of an hundred men selected for bravery & as the best shots... Sabugal, 3rd April. Fuentes d'Honor from 3rd to 5th May. 2nd Siege of Badajos from 25th May to 15th June. Fuente Guinaldo, 26th June. *1812.* Lieut. 45th Foot. In Command of the Sharp Shooters... Siege and Storming of Badajos, from 16th March to 6th April... Selected to observe & report to Sir Thomas Picton, the movement and operations of the enemy. The enemy expecting an attack placed their troops for defence; a part of the castle was left unprotected, which Lieut. Macpherson reported to Sir Thomas Picton, the Castle was subsequently carried by

escalade, at that point. Salamanca 22nd July. Entered Madrid 12th August. Affairs of the retreat from Madrid to Portugal. During the campaign selected as intelligent, or orderly officer, to the Brigade. *1813.* Lieut. 45th Foot, Commanding Sharp Shooters. Orderly or intelligent officer of the Brigade... Battle of Victoria, 23rd June. Pampeluna, from 27th to 31st July. Affairs in the Pyrenees; crossed the Bidasoa. Stormed the enemy's fortified entrenchments, 7th & 9th Octobr. Nivelle 10th Novr. *1814.* Lieut. 45th Foot, Commanding Sharp Shooters. Battle of Orthez 27th Febry... *1815.* Captain, 2nd Garrn. Battn. Flanders... Employed in command of the main Guard, as Captain of the day, to quell a riot of the Hanoverian troops, on which occasion severely wounded. *1816.* Returned to England. *1824.* May. Rangoon. Commander in Chief, Brigadier General Sir A. Campbell. Captain 13th Foot. 28th May. Storming the stockades, with his company forced the gate, killed or drove the Enemy out with the bayonet. Thanked in the field by Sir A. Campbell. Mentioned in despatches, & promised promotion. 10th June Commanding the advanced Guard of the Army, at the attack of the stockades of Remmindire, drove the enemy into the works & repulsed their charge on the battering guns. 1st Decembr. the Attack on the enemy's Army in front of Rangoon; 5th Decr. Storming the Enemy's entrenchments near Rangoon. 15th December storming the stockades, in command of the Escalading party, severely wounded, but was first to enter. *1825.* 26th May. Capture of Baseen, commanding the advanced Guard, under Brigadier Sale. *1826.* 11th Febry. at Mowa, in command of a small party, attacked a body of the enemy; recaptured from them 14 Rowboats containing stores & ammunition belonging to Sir A. Campbell's

Army; Received his thanks and a promise of a special report to Government. Returned after the treaty of Peace at Yandaboo, to Bengal.' *Distinguished conduct*: '6th April 1812. Storm of Badajos. Though wounded at the Escalade, was the first who entered the tower of the castle and captured the Enemy's standard. Received the personal thanks of Sir Thomas Picton & Lord Wellington. Not mentioned in the despatches. Near Rangoon, 28th May 1824. Received the personal thanks of Sir A. Campbell on the field & mentioned in the despatches. 2nd Feby. 1826. With very few men under my command not altogether amounting to twenty, principally natives, attacked a force consisting of several hundred men & captured from them 14 Row Boats containing stores and ammunition for the Army, which the Enemy had previously captured from other parties. Received the thanks of Sir A. Campbell & a promise of a special report to Government.' *Wounds received in action*: '19th Janry. 1812. Storm of Roderigo, received a Contusion, not mentioned. Asked for no remuneration. Storm of Badajos, 6th April. Wounded on mounting at the Escalade, in the breast. Received one year's pay as Lieutenant. Battle of Orthez 27th Febry. 1814. Received one shot in the right fore arm & a second through my body; for which I received a donation of a year's pay and a permanent pension of £100 per annum. Ostend, June 1815. Received a severe bayonet wound in the leg – never applied for remuneration. 15th Decr. 1824. Wounded severely in the breast near Rangoon, applied for remuneration too late.' *Titles, honorary distinctions and medals*: 'None.' *Service abroad*: '1808 to 1814, Portugal, Spain, France. 1815 to 1816, Flanders. 1817 to 1822, Gt. Britain. 1823 to 1829, Bengal and Ava.' Unmarried by 1830. [PRO: WO 25/787 f168;

WO 25/787 f164A]. Copies of various letters, attached to his Statement of Service: 'London, 1st April 1820. I certify that Captain Macpherson of the 13th Regiment of Foot served in the Brigade under my Command, as Lieutenant of the 45th Regiment, during the Operations against Badajos, and was selected by me, as one of the most intelligent and zealous of the Subaltern Officers of the Brigade, to take charge of a post of Observation, to watch the Enemy's motions during the Siege. I also certify, that Captain Macpherson ws reported to me as having particularly distinguished himself in the Escalade of the Castle, and as being the person who struck the French Colour on the Tower on which they were displayed. Signed, James Kempt, Major General.' [PRO: WO 25/787 f165]. 'Extract of a letter from Lieut. Col. Ridewood. Lieutenant Macpherson, of the 45th Regiment, was among the first, who mounted the Walls, and although *wounded*, at the time, in the most gallant manner, climed up the Flag Staff, and struck the French Colour, which he afterwards, presented to the Earl of Wellington. Lieutenant Macpherson has I believe, been recommended, by the General of the Division, to the Commander of the Forces in this Country, that his name may be submitted to His Royal Highness for promotion, which I trust renderes any more I could say in his favor, unecessary. Signed, Henry Ridewood, Lieut. Col. Comg. 1st. Battn. 45th Regt. Renhados, 12 May 1812. To the Adjutant General of the Forces.' [PRO: WO 25/787 f165]. 'I am glad of the opportunity afforded me of testifying to Captain Macpherson's zeal and gallantry when in the 45th Regt.... He joined the 45th Regiment previous to the Battle of Talavera in which action he was present with his Corps, as well as in every siege, and action, in which the Regiment served, in the Peninsula, until the Battle of Orthez, where he was severely wounded. During the Siege of Badajos, he was employed to observe the Enemy's works & at the storming, and capture, of it, although previously wounded at the Escalade of the Castle, he struck the French Flag from the Flag staff, and was in consequence desired by the late Sir Thomas Picton to present it to the Duke of Wellington. Signed, Leonard Greenwell, Lieut. Col. 45th Regiment. London, March 29th 1820.' [PRO: WO 25/787 f167]. 'Extract of a Document, written by the late Sir Thomas Picton. Lieut. Macpherson served seven years as a Subaltern officer in the 45th Regiment, he was personally engaged in every Battle, Siege & Skirmish, which took place in the Peninsula, from the Battle of Talavera, to that of Orthez. Lieut. Macpherson was wounded on mounting the Ladder at the assault of the Castle of Badajos, & notwithstanding, was one of the first to get into the place, & actually struck the Enemy's Colour, which he had the honor of presenting to the Duke of Wellington. He was engaged in every affair from the Siege of Badajos to the Battle of Orthez, where he was wounded through the Body & Arm, & his life for several months despaired of.' [PRO: WO 25/787 f167]. Also, detailed accounts of his actions in Burma [PRO: WO 25/787 f167; WO25–787–166]. Slightly wounded, storming of Badajoz, 6 April 1812 ('McPerson') [*London Gazette*]. Severely wounded, Orthes, 27 Feb. 1814 (1st Battn.) [*London Gazette*].

MACPHERSON, John, Lt., 5th Foot: Lt., Army, 2 July 1803; Lt., 5th Foot, 6 March 1805. Severely wounded, Salamanca, 22 July 1812 [*London Gazette*]. MGS.

+McPHERSON, John, Lt., 38th Foot: Lt, 38th Foot, 4 Jan. 1810. Severely wounded, Salamanca, 22 July 1812 (2nd Battn.) [*London Gazette*]. Severely wounded, 'since dead', 'in the assault and capture of the exterior line of the castle of Burgos on the evening of the 4th October, 1812' ('Captain') [*London Gazette*].

+MACPHERSON, John, Capt./ Major, 92nd Foot: Capt., 92nd Foot, 24 Nov. 1803. Severely wounded, 'but not dangerously', Arroyos dos Molinos, 28th Oct. 1811 ('M'Pherson') (1st Battn.) [*London Gazette*]. Major, 92nd Foot, 31 May 1804. Wounded, Pyrenees, 25 July 1813 (1st Battn.) [*London Gazette*]. Severely wounded, Pyrenees, 31 July 1813 ('Major Macpherson') [*London Gazette*]. Severely wounded, the Nive, 13 Dec. 1813 (1st Battn.) [*London Gazette*]. Died of wounds, 1 Jan. 1814. Return dated Jan. 1814. [PRO: WO 25/2965]. *Register of officers' effects*: 'McPherson', John. Major and Bvt. Lt. Col. Died of wounds, 1 Jan. 1814, Cambo. Single. Effects 'delivered to his cousin Capt. McPerson 39 Regt.' [PRO: WO 25/2964]. *Hurt*, p. 82.

McPHERSON, Loughlan, Ensign, 74th Foot: *1829 Statement of Service*: 'Born in Badenoch, Invernesshire, 7th August 1787. Aged Twenty years on his first Entrance into the Army. Private, 74th Regt., 4th Sept. 1807. Serjeant, 74th Regt., 25th Septr. 1807. Serjt. Major, 74th Regt., 25th Septr. 1812. Ensign, 74th Regt., 31st March 1814. Lieutenant, 74th Regt., 7th Apl. 1825.' Note added: 'Capt., Half Pay, Unattd. 19 May 1837.' *Battles, sieges and campaigns*: 'Busaco 27th Septr. 1810. Fuentes d'Onor 5th May 1811. 1st Siege of Badajos 1811. Rodrigo 19th Jany. 1812. Badajos 6th April 1812. Vittoria 21st June 1813. Pyrenees 30th July 1813. Orthes 27th Feby. 1814. Nivelle 10th Novr. 1813. Toulouse 10th April 1814.' *Wounds received in action*: 'At Vittoria a severe wound in the Head. At Toulouse wounded in the left knee for which he received a years pay as Ensign.' *Service abroad*: '25th Jany. 1810 to 25th July 1814, Portugal, Spain and France. 8th July 1818 to 5th Decr. 1824, N. America.' *Family*: Married Miss Roberts, 8 May 1809, Glasgow. They had five children by 1830. [PRO: WO 25/799 f256]. MGS.

MACPHERSON, Mungo, Capt., 42nd Foot: Capt., 42nd Foot, 9 Feb. 1809. Severely wounded, Nivelle, 10 Nov. 1813 ('McPherson') (1st Battn.) [*London Gazette*]. Pension of one hundred pounds per annum, commencing 11 Nov. 1814, 'for wounds' received at St Jean de Luz, 1813 [*1818 Pension Return*, pp. 12–13]. Wounded, Waterloo. Died at Hastings, Nov. 1844. *Anton*, p. 76 [Nivelle: 'The regiment's loss this day did not exceed twenty-seven killed and wounded; among the latter were Captain Mungo McPherson'].

MACPHERSON, Mungo, Ensign, 42nd Foot: *1829 Statement of Service*: 'Born Strathbane by Dunkeld [?], 15th September 1797. Aged 15 on his first Entrance into the Army. Ensign, 42nd Regt., 14 Octr. 1812. Lieutenant, 42nd Regt., 19 May 1814. Half Pay, 25th Octr. 1814, upon reduction 2d Battn. Lieutenant, 48 Regt., 26 March 1824.' *Battles, sieges and campaigns*: 'Nive 10th December 1813... Orthes 27th Feby. 1814... Toulouse 10 April 1814.' *Wounds received in action*: '10th April 1814. Left arm. Toulouse. One years Pay.' *Service abroad*: '1st Octobr. 1813 to 1st July 1814, Peninsula. 25th Feby. 1825 to 31st Decemb. 1829, India.' [PRO: WO 25/794 f191]. Severely wounded, Toulouse, 10 April 1814 ('McPherson') (1st Battn.) [*London Gazette*].

McPHERSON, Phineas, Capt., 35th Foot: *1829 Statement of Service for Retired Officers*: Aged fifteen on first appointment to the Army. Ensign, 47th Foot, 29 July 1795; Lt., 47th Foot, 7 Sept. 1795; Lt., 40th Foot, 'about 18th Jany. 1800'; Lt., 52nd Foot, 'about 21st March 1800'; Lt., 42nd Foot, 9 July 1803; Capt., 35th Foot, 21 May 1805; Capt., unattached, 10 Oct. 1826. *Where serving when wounded*: 'Peninsula'. No pension. *Where generally resident during last five years*: 'West Indies and in Gt. Britain'. [PRO: WO 25/766 f163]. Severely wounded, Talavera, 28 July 1809, while serving with 1st Battn. of Detachments [*London Gazette*].

McQUEEN, Donald John, Capt., 74th Foot: *1829 Statement of Service*: Born in Applecross, Rosshire, 4th May 1786. Ensign, 74th Foot, 14th July 1800; Lt., 74th Foot, 25 June 1803; Capt., 74th Foot, 26 April 1810. *Battles, sieges and campaigns*: 'As Captain the whole of the retreat from the Frontier of Portugal to the Lines of Torres Vedras including the Battle of Busaco. The advance of the Allies from the lines to the Battle of Fuentes d'Onor, including the various Skirmishes during the whole of the period. In the Campaign of 1812 including the Battle of Salamanca, the Capture of Madrid, and the retreat for Fuentes Grimalda. The whole of the Campaigns of 1813 & 1814 including the Battles of Vittoria, Pyrenees, Nivelle, Nive, Tarbes and Toulouse; and various minor affairs during the entire of that period.' *Wounds received in action*: 'At Fuentes d'Onor on 5th May 1811, received no Gratuity. Three times wounded at Vittoria, 21st June 1813, then in Command of two Companies from the Regiment, but received no Gratuity. Wounded at Toulouse when Commanding three Companies of the Regiment at the attack on the Tete du Pont for which he received a Gratuity of a years Pay, and has now a Permanent Pension for the same, as granted on 21st Novr. 1829, by His Majesty's Warrant.' *Service abroad*: '24th Jany. 1810 to 20th Sept. 1811, Portugal. May 1812 to 15th June 1814, Peninsula. 18th June 1818 to 29th Septr. 1824, N. America. 5th Octr. 1825 to 24th Augt. 1828, N. America. 25th Augt. 1828 to 15th Septr. 1829, Bermuda.' *Family*: Married Miss Bliss, 21 Jan. 1819, Fredericton, New Brunswick. They had two children by 1830. [PRO: WO 25/799 f228]. Severely wounded, Fuentes de Onoro, 5 May 1811 ('MacQueen') [*London Gazette*]. Slightly wounded, Vittoria, 21 June 1813 [*London Gazette*]. Severely wounded, Toulouse, 10 April 1814 (1st Battn.) [*London Gazette*]. Temporary pension of one hundred pounds per annum, commencing 11 April 1815, 'for a wound' received at Toulouse ('Mac Queen') [*1818 Pension Return*, pp. 18–19]. MGS. 'Macqueen' in Army List.

MADDEN, Edward, 2nd Lt., 95th Foot: 2nd Lt., 95th Foot, 2 May 1811. 1st Lt., 95th Foot, 13 May 1813. Slightly wounded, Crossing the Bidassoa, 7/9 Oct. 1813 (2nd Battn.) [*London Gazette*]. Waterloo. Died, Chichester, 1819.

MADDEN, Monsoon Molesworth, Lt., 43rd Foot: *1829 Statement of Service for Retired Officers*: 'Cannot say' how old he was on first appointment to the Army, 'having been appointed when very young as a remuneration for my Fathers services in India. I joined the 43d Regt. in 1806 as a Lt. from Half Pay, at the age of 16'; Lt., 43rd Foot, 13 Nov. 1806 [Army List gives 30 Nov.]; Capt., 102nd Foot, 19 April 1809; Half-pay, May 1818, 'By reduction of 100th Reg. late 102nd'; Capt., 92nd Foot, 7 June 1821; Half-pay, Feb. 1826, 'for family affairs'. *Where serving when wounded*: 'Vimeira in Portugal.' *Details of pension*: Seventy pounds, commencing 25 Dec. 1824. *Family*: Married in 'St Andrews, Holbourn, London, 27 June 1811'. Five children by 1829. *Where generally resident during last five years*: 'Jamaica with 92nd Rgt. Isle of Wight with Depot 92nd.

Edinburgh with 92nd Regt. Leeds.' [PRO: WO 25/767 f58]. Wounded, Vimeiro, 21 Aug. 1808 [*London Gazette*].

+MADDEN, William S., Capt., 52nd Foot: Capt., 52nd Foot, 10 July 1805. Killed, storming of Badajoz, 6 April 1812 [*London Gazette*].

MADDEN, Wyndham C., Lt., 43rd Foot: Lt., 43rd Foot, 3 May 1809. Severely wounded, storming of Badajoz, 6 April 1812 (1st Battn.) [*London Gazette*]. Severely wounded, Nivelle, 10 Nov. 1813 (1st Battn.) [*London Gazette*]. Temporary pension of seventy pounds per annum, commencing 7 April 1813, 'for wounds' received at Badajoz [*1818 Pension Return*, pp. 12–13]. MGS. Died 13 May 1864.

MAGEE, Maurice, Ensign, 38th Foot: Ensign, 38th Foot, 22 Aug. 1811. Slightly wounded, Salamanca, 22 July 1812 ('Magie') (1st Battn.) [*London Gazette*].

MAGENNIS, Richard, Capt., 7th Foot: Capt., 7th Foot, 28 Feb. 1811. Severely wounded, 'left arm amputated', Albuera, 16 May 1811 ('Magenis') (2nd Battn.) [*London Gazette*]. One hundred pounds per annum pension, commencing 16 May 1812, for loss of arm at Albuera [*1818 Pension Return*, pp. 4–5]. MGS.

MAGILL, John, Lt., 38th Foot: Lt., 38th Foot, 30 March 1809. Slightly wounded, storming of Badajoz, 6 April 1812 (2nd Battn.) [*London Gazette*]. Slightly wounded, Vittoria, 21 June 1813 ('McGill') (2nd Battn.) [*London Gazette*]. Recorded as 'Missing', 'at the Siege of St Sebastian', 7–27 July 1813 ('McGill') (1st Battn.) [*London Gazette*].

MAGINNIS, William J., Ensign/Lt., 87th Foot: *1829 Statement of Service*: Born in Londonderry, Ireland, 10 Nov. 1796. Aged 'About Sixteen' on his first appointment to the Army. Ensign, 87th Foot, 19 July 1810; Lt., 87th Foot, 4 Aug. 1813; Lt., 80th Foot, 9 July 1818. *Battles, sieges and campaigns*: 'Barossa 5th March 1811. Tariffa 31st Decr. 1811. Vittoria 21st June 1813. Pyrenees 28th & 30th Augt. Nivelle Nive 10th Novr. 1813. Orthes, 27th Feby. 1814. Tolouse 10th April 1814.' *Distinguished conduct*: 'Thanked in Division Orders near Cambo 7th January 1814 by Lieut. Genl. Picton.' *Wounds received in action*: 'Vittoria 21st June 1813. Orthes 27th Feby. 1814. Years Pay. Near Tarbes during the operations between 17th and 20th March 1814.' *Service abroad*: 'Feby. 1811 to Augt. 1814, Peninsula. 1822 to Decr. 1829, Mediteranean.' [PRO: WO 25/800 f326]. Slightly wounded, Orthes, 27 Feb. 1814 ('Maginniss') (2nd Battn.) [*London Gazette*].

MAHER, John Pierce, Lt., 87th Foot; Portuguese Service: *1829 Statement of Service for Retired Officers*: Aged eighteen on first appointment to the Army. Ensign, 87th Foot, 25 June 1807; Lt., 87th Foot, Dec. 1807 [Army List gives 2 Dec.]; Capt., unattached, 1814; 'Majority Portuguese Service 1814'; Half-pay, 1815, 'when those officers attached to the Portuguese service were reduced from full to H.P.' 'Unable to serve from the bad effects of his wound.' *Where serving when wounded*: 'at the Battle of Tolouse 1814'. *Details of pension*: Two hundred pounds, commencing 1826. Not married. *Where generally resident during last five years*: 'Freshford, Ireland'. [PRO: WO 25/767 f163].

MAHON, Anthony, Lt., 47th Foot: Lt., 47th Foot, 27 June 1811. Severely wounded, the Nive, 10 Dec. 1813 (2nd Battn.) [*London Gazette*].

+MAHON, Luke, Lt. and Capt., 3rd Foot Guards: Lt. and Capt., 3rd Foot Guards, 27 June 1811. Severely wounded, sortie from Bayonne, 14 April 1814 (1st Battn) [*London Gazette*]. Died of wounds, 6 May 1814. Return dated May 1814. [PRO: WO 25/2965]. *Hurt*, p. 46 [Illustration of his original gravestone as it appeared in 1854, with the inscription: 'Capt. Mahon, 3 Guards, who died of wounds received in action before Bayonne 14 April 1814'], p. 49 ['...the new tomb to Captain Mahon. It is composed of a solid ridge-shaped block of Bidache stone, sloped off at the foot, placed on a base of the same material... "Beneath this stone lies the body of Captain Luke Mahon, 3rd Regiment of Foot Guards... Who died of wounds received before Bayonne, April 14, 1814." Round the base: "This stone was placed to his memory, and the footstone restored, by the only surviving sister of his bother officer, Captain Holburne, A.D. 1876."... At the foot of the grave stands the original foot-stone, placed there in 1814'] p. 75 ['D.O.W. Bayonne, May 6']. *Fletcher, Fields of Fire*, p. 164 ['Deep in the woods, close to the site of the Coldstream Guards cemetery, lies an even smaller one containing the graves of officers of the 3rd Foot Guards killed in the sortie from Bayonne on April 14th 1814. Amongst those buried here is Captain Luke Mahon. The cemetery was, for many years, maintained by the sister of Captain Holbourne, who is buried in the Coldstream Guards cemetery a short distance away. The cemetery marks the site of the camp of the 3rd Foot Guards at the time of the sortie']. *Fletcher, Gentlemen's Sons*, p. 185 ['later died of ... wounds'].

MAHON, Walter Gorges, Lt., 51st Foot: *1829 Statement of Service for Retired Officers*: Aged twenty-four on first appointment to the Army. Ensign, Galway Militia, 1807; Ensign, 51st Foot, 25 Oct. 1807; Lt., 51st Foot, 13 July 1809; Half-pay, 19 Sept. 1822, 'of his own request, from

Ill Health'; Lt., full-pay, 51st Foot, 16 June 1825; Capt., half-pay, unattached, 1 July 1828. *Where serving when wounded*: 'at St Pe'. *Details of pension*: Seventy pounds, commencing 11 Nov. 1814. *Family*: Married in Galway, 21 March 1824. One child by 1829. *Where generally resident during last five years*: 'Portsmouth'. [PRO: WO 25/767 f102]. Severely wounded, Nivelle, 10 Nov. 1813 (1st Battn.) [*London Gazette*]. Waterloo. *Dalton*, pp. 164, 166 ['Walter George Mahan'].

MAINWARING, John M., Lt. Col., 51st Foot: Lt. Col., Army, 23 Nov. 1804; Lt. Col., 51st Foot, 21 Apr. 1808; Col., Army, 4 June 1813; Half-Pay, 26 Foot, and Commandant of the Isle of Wight dept., 1815. *Wheeler*, p. 8 [12 April 1809: 'The Regiment is commanded by Lieut. Colonel Mainwaring, a very humane man. He is no advocate for the cat o'nine tails. I have more than once heard it remarked that if he could not stand fire better than witness flogging he would be the worst soldier in the Army.'], pp. 10–11, 17 [28 July 1809: 'the Colonel has just passed by and he has had a row with one of the men. I do not know what the offence was, but Colonel M– patted the Eaupulet [sic] on his shoulder, saying "If it was not for this." Then clenching his fist and putting it up to the man's nose, said "I would let you know that Colonel Mainwaring has got an iron fist." '], pp. 20–23, 24 [Letter dated 12 Aug. 1809, from Walcheren: 'Colonel M– charged at West Zuberg and took two guns'], pp. 28, 32, 34–9, 47 [arrived in Peninsula, March 1811], pp. 49, 53–4 [Fuentes D'Onor, 5 May 1811: 'The enemy had walked to the brow, and their trumpeter was sounding the Charge, when Colonel M– gave the words "Ready, Present, Fire." For the moment the smoke hindered us from seeing the effect of our fire, but we soon saw plenty of horses and men stretched not many yards from us... Thanks to

Colonel M– we came off safe, altho the shot was flying pretty thick, yet his superior skill baffled all the efforts of the enemy, he took advantage of the ground and led us out of the scrape without loss. I shall never forget him, he dismounted off his horse, faced us and frequently called the time "right, left" as he was accostomed to when drilling the regiment. His eccentricity did not leave him, he would now and then call out "That fellow is out of step, keep step and they cannot hurt us." '], p. 66 [Letter dated 16 July 1811: 'Colonel Mainwaring is gone to England, it is said for the benefit of his health.' 66n: 'Although Colonel Mainwaring had been quite genuinely invalided to Lisbon with a wound received in the trenches at Badajoz, he departed under a cloud, having been virtually relieved of his command by Wellington, who condemned his burning of the colours at a critical moment at Fuentes de Onoro.'], pp. 70–2 ['sometimes his fits of passion would lead or drive him into acts of violence... I could record many instances of petty tyranny, such as giving a man a dozen or two without trial ... the Colonel was as mad as a march hare ... if at times he was driven to excess by passion, he was in the whole a humane man. I hope his successor will not turn out worse.'], p. 79.

MAIR, John, Capt., 7th Foot: Lt., 7th Foot, 19 Feb. 1806. Slightly wounded, Busaco, 27 Sept. 1810 ('Marr') [*London Gazette*]. Capt., 7th Foot, 17 July 1811. Severely wounded, storming of Badajoz, 6 April 1812 [*London Gazette*]. Slightly wounded, Salamanca, 18 July 1812 [*London Gazette*]. Pension of one hundred pounds per annum, commencing 7 April 1813, 'for wounds' received at Badajoz [*1818 Pension Return*, pp. 4–5].

MAITLAND, Brownlow J., 1st Lt., Royal Artillery: 1st Lt., Royal

Artillery, 1 June 1806. Severely wounded, Barossa, 5 March 1811 [*London Gazette*].

MAJER, Philip, Capt., 60th Foot: Lt., 60th Foot, 5 Aug. 1800. Slightly wounded, Talavera, 28 July 1809 ('Captain B. Majer') [*London Gazette*]. Capt., 60th Foot, 23 Nov. 1809. Not in *Challis, Index*, p. 164.

MALCOLM, John, Ensign, 42nd Foot: Ensign, 42nd Foot, 6 Jan. 1814. Recorded as 'missing', Toulouse, 10 April 1814 (1st Battn.) [*London Gazette*]. *Anton*, p. 136 [Toulouse: 'There was one officer of the regiment taken prisoner this day: he had lately joined us from the 1st Royals, in which he had been cadet, and had not the uniform of the regiment, but his deficiency of the uniform betrayed no lack of personal courage; the charm of the bonnet and plume, though wanting, did not make him less the soldier; he fell, wounded, near to Lieutenant Farquharson, at the side of the redoubt, as we entered it, and when we fell back he was made prisoner.'], n138 ['Since writing these sketches, I have had the pleasure of reading "The Reminiscences of a Campaign, in the Pyrenees and South of France," by J. Malcolme, Esq., late of the 42d. It is contained in the twenty-seventh volume of Constable's Miscellany... Mr Malcolm was the officer formerly alluded to having been taken prisoner.'].

+MALLET, Elias, Capt., 30th Foot: Capt., 30th Foot, 21 April 1804. Killed, 'in the Operations of the Army', 31 Aug. 1813 ('Mallett') (2nd Battn.), while serving as DAAQMG attached to the Spanish army [*London Gazette*].

+MALONE, Anthony, Lt., 40th Foot: Lt., 40th Foot, 8 June 1809. Killed, Pyrenees, 26 July 1813 (1st Battn.) [*London Gazette*].

MANLY, Charles, Lt., 27th Foot: *1829 Statement of Service*: Born 1790, London. Aged sixteen on his first entrance into the Army. Ensign, 27th Foot, 7 Nov. 1806; Lt. 28 July 1808; Capt. 10 Sept. 1829. *Battles, sieges and campaigns*: 'Landing and capture of the Islands of Provida and Ischia, Bay of Naples, 1809 under Sir John Stewart... 1813 March at the Affair of Alcoy under Sir John Murray... 1813 April 12 & 13 Battle of Biar and Castalla... 1813 June Seige of Tarragona... 1813 Augt. Before Tarragona under Lord Wm. Bentick. 1813 Septr. at the Affair of Ordall under Lord Wm. Bentick... 1814, February at the Blockade of Barcelona under Sir Wm. Clinton... 1815 June at the Battle of Waterloo.' *Wounds received in action*: '1813 Sept. Received three wounds at Ordall. 1815 June, received one wound at Waterloo. Two years Pay as Captain. Permanent Pension, Seventy Pounds Per Annum. Date of Pension 14 Septr. 1814.' *Titles. honorary distinctions and medals*: 'One medal for Waterloo.' *Service abroad*: '1808 to 1812, Island of Sicily. 1813 to 1814, Spain & France. 1815 to 1817, Netherlands & France. 1822 to 1823, Gibraltar. 1824 to 1829, West Indies.' *Family*: Married Catherine Blair Maddock, 22 Jan. 1816, Dublin. They had three children by 1830. [PRO: WO 25/790 f113]. Severely wounded, 'not dangerously', Heights of Ordal, 12/13 Sept. 1813 (2nd Battn.) [*London Gazette*]. 'Charles Manley' in revised casualty list [*London Gazette*, 23 Oct. 1813]. *1818 Pension Return*, pp. 8–9 ('Manley'). *Dalton*, pp. 132-3 ['had a bullet through his thigh at Waterloo... Died in an apoplectic fit, 5th Nov. 1839, on board the SS *Barretta*, jun., when 17 days' sail from Cape of Good Hope.'].

MANNERS, Charles, Lt., Royal Artillery: 1st Lt., Royal Artillery, 24 Sept. 1808. Slightly wounded, Barossa, 5 March 1811 [*London Gazette*]. MGS.

MARCH

MANNERS, Henry Herbert, 1st Lt., 95th Foot: 1st Lt., 95th Foot, 1 Feb. 1809. Severely wounded, storming of Badajoz, 6 April 1812 (1st Battn.) [*London Gazette*]. Temporary pension of seventy pounds per annum, commencing 7 April 1813, 'for wounds' received at Badajoz [*1818 Pension Return*, pp. 22–3]. *Simmons*, p. 232 [wounded, Badajoz], pp. 378–9. *Kincaid, Random Shots*, p. 290 ['At the close of the war, when we returned to England ... the officers commanding companies on the day of inspection, viz ... Pemberton and Manners each with a shot in the knee, making them stiff as the other's tree one'].

MANNING, Thomas, Ensign, 81st Foot: Ensign, 81st Foot, 18 Oct. 1807. Wounded, 'in the Army lately in Spain' [*March 1809 Army List*, p. 105]. *Monthly Return*, 2nd Battn., dated 25 March 1809: 'Wounded, in Naval Hospital Plymouth' [PRO: WO 17/202].

MANSEL, Robert Christopher, Capt., 53rd Foot: *1829 Statement of Service for Retired Officers*: Aged sixteen on first appointment to the Army. Ensign, 10th Foot, 27 Jan. 1807; Lt., 10th Foot, 27 Jan. 1808; Capt., 4th West India Regt., 4 Feb. 1813; Capt., 53rd Foot, Aug. 1813; Capt., 93rd Foot, 'Jany. or Feby. 1820'; Bvt. Major, 93rd Foot, 21 July 1821; 'Capt. & Bt. Major', 96th Foot, 29 Jan. 1824; Major, 96th Foot, 9 June 1825; Lt. Col., Half-pay, unattached. *Where serving when wounded*: 'Toulouse, France'. *Details of pension*: One hundred pounds per annum, commencing April 1815. *Family*: Married in 'St Nicholas, Glamorganshire, So. Wales', 2 Sept. 1824. Two children by 1829. *Where generally resident during last five years*: 'Manchester with 96th Reg. with the Depot of 96th at Isle of Wight, Winchester and Plymouth, a short time at Cottrell Nr. Cardiff, and for nearly the last two years on the Staff at

Cork as A.D.C. to Sir George Bingham.' [PRO: WO 25/767 f63]. Severely wounded, Toulouse, 10 April 1814 (2nd Battn.) [*London Gazette*]. *1818 Pension Return*, pp. 14–15. MGS.

+MANSFIELD, Ralph, Lt., 88th Foot: Lt., 88th Foot, 14 July 1808. Killed, storming of Badajoz, 6 April 1812 [*London Gazette*].

MARCH, The Earl of, (Charles Lennon), Lt., 13th Light Dragoons; Capt., 92nd Foot; Capt., 52nd Foot: *1829 Statement of Service for Retired Officers*: 'Charles Lennon, commonly called the Earl of March, now Duke of Richmond'. Aged eighteen on first appointment to the Army. Ensign, 8th Garrison Battn., 8 June 1809. Lt., 13th Light Dragoons, 21 June 1810; Capt., 92nd Foot, 9 July 1812; Capt., 52nd Foot, 8 April 1813; Bvt. Major, 15 June 1815; Lt. Col., 25 July 1816; Half-pay, 25 July 1816, by reduction. 'Unfit for foreign service in consequence of wounds'. *Where serving when wounded*: 'Orthes – in the Peninsula campaign'. No pension. *Family*: Married in St James' Church, London, 10 April 1817. Eight children by 1829. *Title and nature of employment*: 'Colonel Sussex Lt. Infy. Militia. High Ltenant of City of Chichester'. *Where generally resident during last five years*: 'Goodwood nr. Chichester in County of Sussex'. [PRO: WO 25/772 f162]. Severely wounded, Orthes, 27 Feb. 1814 (1st Battn.) [*London Gazette*]. Waterloo. MGS. *Mullen*, p. 359 ['Later the Duke of Richmond... Principal spokesman in favour of the award of the MGS Medal.']. *Gronow*, p. 77 ['One of the most intimate friends of the Duke of Wellington was the Earl of March, afterwards Duke of Richmond. He was a genuine hard-working soldier, a man of extraordinary courage, and one who was ever found ready to gain laurels amidst the greatest dangers. When the 7th Fusiliers crossed the Bidassoa, the late duke left the staff and joined the regiment in which he had a company. At Orthes, in the thick of the fight, he received a shot which passed through his lungs; from this severe wound he recovered sufficiently to be able to join the Duke of Wellington, to whom he was exceedingly useful at the battle of Waterloo. On his return to England, he united himself to the most remarkably beautiful girl of the day, the eldest daughter of Lord Anglesea, and whose mother was the lovely Duchess of Argyle.']. *Moorsom*, p. 157 [Storming of Ciudad Rodrigo, 19 Jan. 1812: 'The young Earl of March (The present Duke of Richmond, K.G.), then a Lieutenant in the 13th Light Dragoons, and serving as aide-de-camp to the Earl of Wellington, also entered the breach as a volunteer with the storming-party of the 52nd. The Prince of Orange and Lord Fitzroy Somerset (the late Lord Raglan) were the companions of Lord March in this adventurous assault, and on the following morning, when taking their places at breakfast in the tent of the Commander of the Forces, they received a gentle reproof for adventuring into a position which, being officers of the staff, they were not called upon to undertake by the customs of the service.'], p. 429. *Bruce*, p. 171 [Letter of William Napier to his wife, dated Orthes, 28 Feb. 1814: 'Poor March was wounded very badly; I fear much that he will die. The only thing in his favour that I could see yesterday was that his face had no marks of immediate death about it; people mortally wounded have a very livid look about the lips, which he has not. It will be sad that the best of so large a family should die so young; and doubly sad that the only person of rank I ever saw with everybody his warm friend, and nobody envious of him, should fall before his age gave him time to do

that good which his noble disposition will lead him to.'], p. 172 [Napier to his wife, Château Papreon, 7 March 1814: 'March is declared out of all danger, although the wound is very severe; I am delighted; I cannot well tell you how much I felt when I saw him extended on the field with all the marks of death about him.'].

MARCHINGTON, Joseph, Ensign, 71st Foot; Lt., 60th Foot: *1829 Statement of Service for Retired Officers*: Aged sixteen on first appointment to the Army. Ensign, 61st Foot, 12 April 1807; Ensign, 71st Foot, 1811 [Army List gives 30 June]; Lt., 60th Foot, 7 May 1812; Lt., Nova Scotia Regt., 1813 [Army List gives 22 Oct. 1812]; Lt., 2nd Life Guards, 1814 [Army List gives 3 April 1815]; Half-pay, 13th Light Dragoons, Sept. 1816, 'from Ill health'. *Where serving when wounded*: 'Wounded on the Peninsula, but no Pension'. Not married. *Where generally resident during last five years*: 'British North America'. [PRO: WO 25/767 f121].

MARLAY, Edward Stephen George, Lt., 82nd Foot; Capt., 8th Portuguese Regt.: *1829 Statement of Service for Retired Officers*: Aged fifteen on first appointment to the Army. Ensign, 82nd Foot, 5 Dec. 1806; Lt., 82nd Foot, 8 Feb. 1808; Lt., '2d European Garrison Compy.', 25 Dec. 1816; 'Placed on the Retired List, upon 2d European Garrison Company being disbanded in 1817.' 'Incapacitated for active service, by the severity of his Wounds.' *Where serving when wounded*: 'At Salamanca in Spain, as Captain 8th Portuguese Infantry and Major of Brigade on the Staff of the Army.' *Details of pension*: One hundred pounds per annum, commencing 1814. *Family*: Married in Dublin, 25 Nov. 1815. Six children by 1829. *Title and nature of employment*: 'Barrack Master'. *Where generally resident during last five years*:

'Guernsey & Bantry.' [PRO: WO 25/767 f47]. Severely wounded, Salamanca, 22 July 1812, as Capt. in 8th Portuguese Line ('Marley') [*London Gazette*]. In Portuguese Service Oct. 1809 to May 1813. Pension of one hundred pounds per annum, commencing 23 July 1813, 'for wounds' received at Salamanca [*1818 Pension Return*, pp. 24–5]. *Challis, Portuguese Army*, p. 57.

MARLAY, Henry, Capt., 3rd Foot: Capt., 3rd Foot, 8 July 1807. Severely wounded, Albuera, 16 May 1811 ('Marley') [*London Gazette*].

MARSCHALCK, Ferdinand von, Capt., 1st Line Battn., K.G.L.: Capt., 1st Line Battn. K.G.L., 19 Dec. 1803. Severely wounded, Talavera, 28 July 1809 ('Marshall') [*London Gazette*]. Served in Peninsula 1808–11. 'Lewis, *Baron Marschalk*' in Army List. *Beamish*, vol. II, p. 585 [Died 'at Klinthoff, dutchy of Bremen, 29th May 1819.'].

MARSH, Hans Stevenson, Lt., 45th Foot: Lt., 45th Foot, 1 April 1810. Severely wounded, during 'several Affairs with the French Army', 12 March 1811, ('March') (1st Bttn.) [*London Gazette*]. Severely wounded, siege of Badajoz, 26 March 1812 [*London Gazette*].

MARSH, Robert, Ensign, 24th Foot: *1829 Statement of Service*: Born 15 Sept. 1795, Hoveton St John, Norfolk. Aged sixteen on his first entrance into the Army. Ensign, 24th Foot, 31 Oct. 1811; Lt. 13 Feb. 1817; Capt. 14 April 1829. *Battles, sieges and campaigns*: 'Part of 1812, Peninsula. 1813. Vittoria, June 21st. Pyrenees, July 28th, and Echalar, August 2nd. Nivelle Novr. 10th. 1814. Orthes February 27th... 1815 & 1816 Nepaul Campaign. Harriapore March 1st 1816... 1817 & 1818 Mahratta War.' *Wounds received in action*: 'Nivelle November 10th 1813. No Allowance whatever.' *Service abroad*: 'August 1812 to

July 1814, Portugal, Spain and France. February 1815 to June 1820, East Indies.' Not married in 1830. [PRO: WO 25/789 f268]. Slightly wounded, Nivelle, 10 Nov. 1813 (2nd Battn.) [*London Gazette*]. MGS,

MARSHALL, Anthony, 1st Lt., Royal Engineers: 1st Lt., Royal Engineers, 1 Aug. 1809. Slightly wounded, siege of Ciudad Rodrigo, 16 Jan. 1812 [*London Gazette*]. Severely wounded, storming of San Sebastian, 31 Aug. 1813 ("Marshal") [*London Gazette*]. MGS.

MARSHALL, George, Lt./Capt., 82nd Foot: *1829 Statement of Service*: Born in Adwick-le-Street, Yorkshire, 15 March 1783. Aged 'Sixteen years & Nine Months' on first appointment to the Army. Ensign, 82nd Foot, 6 Dec. 1799; Lt., 82nd Foot, 15 Aug. 1804; Capt., 82nd Foot, 27 Oct. 1808; Bvt. Major, 82nd Foot, May 1825. *Battles, sieges and campaigns*: 'Copenhagen Augt. 1807 as Lieut. & employed as Acting Engineer... Roleia 17th Augt. 1808, Vimiera 21st Augt. 1808, as Lieut... Corunna 16th January 1809, as Lieutenant... With the Army during the Retreat from Madrid November 1812. Vittoria 21st June 1813, Pass of Mayo 25th July 1813, Pampeluna 30 & 31st July 1813, 31st Augt. 1813, as Captain. Heights of St Pee 10th Novr. 1813... Niagara 17th September 1814 as Captain.' *Wounds received in action*: 'Wounded at the Pass of Mayo 25th July 1813. Wounded at St Pee 10th Novr. 1813 severely in the Head for which recd. One Years Pay. Slightly Wounded at Niagara 17th September 1814.' *Service abroad*: 'July 1800 to July 1802, Menorca. Augt. 1807 to Novr. 1807, Copenhagen. Decr. 1807 to Feby. 1809, Gibraltar, Cadiz, Roleia, Vimiera, Corunna. Novr. 1812 to May 1814, Peninsula. May 1814 to June 1815, America. June 1815 to Jany. 1816, France. June 1819 to Decr. 1829, Mauritius.' *Family*: Married Miss

Mary Hervey, 16 July 1824, Port Louis. They had three children by 1830. [PRO: WO 25/801 f79]. Slightly wounded, Pyrenees, 25 July 1813 (1st Battn.) [*London Gazette*]. Severely wounded, Nivelle, 10 Nov. 1813 (1st Battn.) [*London Gazette*].

MARSHALL, James, Lt., 4th Foot: Lt., 4th Foot, 23 Sept. 1813. Severely wounded, the Nive, 11 Dec. 1813 (1st Battn.) [*London Gazette*].

MARSHALL, John, Lt., 48th Foot: Lt., 48th Foot, 19 May 1808. Reported as 'Missing', Albuera, 16 May 1811 ('Marshal') (2nd Battn.) [*London Gazette*]. Severely wounded, Salamanca, 22 July 1812 [*London Gazette*].

MARSHALL, John, Lt., 91st Foot: Lt., 91st Foot, 23 Nov. 1809. Slightly wounded, Pyrenees, 28 July 1813 (1st Battn.) [*London Gazette*]. Severely wounded, Orthes, 27 Feb. 1814 ('Marshal') (1st Battn.) [*London Gazette*]. MGS.

MARSHALL, William, Capt., 79th Foot: *1829 Statement of Service*: Born at Fachabers, Banffshire, 18 Jan. 1780. Aged nineteen on his first Entrance into the Army. Ensign, 79th Foot, 10 Nov. 1799. Lt., 79th Foot, 25 June 1803. Adjt., 79th Foot, 21 April 1808. Capt., 79th Foot, 19 July 1810. Major, 79th Foot, 29 July 1824. *Battles, sieges and campaigns*: 'As Ensign, Descent on Ferrol. Expedition to Queberon Bay & Cadiz in 1800, Campaign of Egypt in 1801 ... including Battles of 13th & 21 of March 1801. Sieges of Grand Cairo & Alexandria. As Lieut, Expedition to & siege of Copenhagen autumn of 1807... Expedition to Gottenburg & Spain in 1808... Campaign of Portugal & Spain in 1808 & 1809 ... including retreat to & Battle of Corunna 18 Jany. 1809... Expedition to Walcheren ... autumn of 1809 including Siege of Flushing. As Lieut. & Captain, relief of Cadiz in 1810 when besieged by the French Army under Victor... As Captain, Campaigns of Portugal, Spain & France in 1810, 1811, 1812, 1813, & 1814... including battle of Busaco 27th Septr. 1810. Siege of Badajos in 1812 (with covering Army). Battle of Salamanca 22d July 1812. Siege of Burgos Sepr. & Octr. 1812, including capture of Hornwork by the Light Companies of Col. Sterling's Brigade, when in separate command of two Companies. Passage of the Nivelle 9 Novr. 1813. Passage of the Nive, 10th Decr. 1813. Battle of Bayonne 13 Decr. 1813 (during the action Regt. detached against parties of the enemy which threatened rear of the army). Battle of Toulouse 10th April 1814. As Captain, Campaign of the Netherlands in 1815 ... including Battle of Quatre Bras, 16 June 1815, when in command of three companies of the Regt. As Captain, with army of occupation in France in 1817 & 1818... N.B. Throughout the above services frequently detached from the Regt. & engaged in several skirmishes with the enemy (not herein stated) of a nature more or less severe; having belonged to the Light Company of the first Battalion during the whole period of his service as Captain & Subaltern, an interval of about 12 months excepted.' *Distinguished conduct*: 'At Burgos Castle 19th Septr. 1812, as will appear by the following extract of a letter from the late Major General Sir Denis Pack, dated 3d Feby. 1811 [sic], Viz. "I perfectly remember that honourable mention was made of Captain Marshalls name in carrying the Hornwork of Burgos Castle: I have also great pleasure in offering my testimony to his gallantry on frequent other occasions; his conduct as a Regtal. Officer while under my command was exemplary & his company always appeared in the best order & discipline." ' *Wounds received in action*: 'At siege of Burgos Castle Septr. & Octr. 1812 – twice slightly wounded. At Battle of Toulouse 10th April 1814 – once severely wounded. At Battle of Quatre Bras 16th June 1815 – twice severely with loss of right arm. Received grants of two years pay as Captain for wounds in action. Permanent pension of £100 per annum for loss of an arm 16 June 1815.' *Titles, honorary distinctions and medals*: 'Gold medal for Campaign of Egypt in 1801. Silver medal for Battle of Waterloo.' *Service abroad*: 'Augt. 1800 to Augt. 1802, At Sea, Egypt, Island of Minorca &c. Augt. 1807 to Septr. 1807, At Sea & before Copenhagen. 1808 to Jany. 16th 1809, At Sea, Cottenburg harbour, Portugal & Spain. 1809 to autumn of 1809, At Sea & before Flushing (Island of Walcheren) &c. Decr. 1810 to Augt. 1814, At Sea, Cadiz, Portugal, Spain & France. 1815 to Augt. 1815, Netherlands. 1817 to Octr. 1818, France with army of occupation.' [PRO: WO 25/800 f232]. Slightly wounded, siege of Burgos, 20-26 Sept. 1812 (1st Battn.) [*London Gazette*]. Waterloo. MGS.

MARSTON, Molyneux, Capt., 48th Foot: Capt., 48th Foot, 5 Sept. 1795; Major, Army, 1 Jan. 1805. Slightly wounded, Talavera, 28 July 1809 [*London Gazette*].

MARTIN, Alexander, Capt., 45th Foot: Capt., 45th Foot, 30 March 1809. Severely wounded, storming of Ciudad Rodrigo, 19 Jan. 1812 [*London Gazette*]. Pension of one hundred pounds per annum, commencing 20 Jan. 1812, 'for wounds' received at Ciudad Rodrigo [*1818 Pension Return*, pp. 12–13]. MGS.

MARTIN, Christopher Bernard, Ensign, 60th Foot: *1829 Statement of Service for Retired Officers*: Aged twenty on first appointment to the Army. Ensign, 60th Foot, 31 March 1812; Lt., 60th Foot, 3 Aug. 1813. 'I was obliged to go on half pay from very ill health being very severely

wounded.' Not 'adequate to active military service owing to the serious injury I received.' *Where serving when wounded*: 'Pyrenees (Spain)'. *Details of pension*: Seventy pounds per annum, commencing 18 June 1815. *Family*: Married in Ennis, 14 Feb. 1824. Three children by 1829. *Where generally resident during last five years*: 'Eyrecourt'. [PRO: WO 25/767 f118]. Severely wounded, Pyrenees, 26 July 1813 ('Ensign C. Martin') (5th Battn.) [*London Gazette*]. Temporary pension, commencing 27 July 1814 *1818 Pension Return*, pp. 14–15.

MARTIN, Henry, Lt., 51st Foot: Lt., 51st Foot, 21 Oct. 1813. Slightly wounded, Nivelle, 10 Nov. 1813 (1st Battn.) [*London Gazette*]. Waterloo. Died 1840.

+MARTIN, John G. 1st Lt., Royal Artillery: 1st Lt., Royal Artillery, 1 Feb. 1808. Slightly wounded, Fuentes de Onoro, 5 May 1811 ('Royal Foot Artillery') [*London Gazette*]. Obituary, *The Gentleman's Magazine*, 1811 Supplement, p. 657 ['Lately [Sept./Oct.]... At Castello Branco, Portugal, in his 22d year, Lieut. J. G. Martin, royal artillery, son of Rev. G. M. Great Ness, Salop, and nephew of the Duke of Athol.'].

+MARTIN, Samuel Coote, Capt. and Lt. Col., 1st Foot Guards: Lt. and Capt., 1st Foot Guards, 25 Nov. 1799; Bvt. Major, 1st Foot Guards, 4 June 1811; Capt. and Lt. Col., 1st Foot Guards, 30 July 1812. Killed, the Nive, 12 Dec. 1813 ('Captain S. Coote Martin (Lieutenant-Colonel)') (1st Battn.) [*London Gazette*]. Obituary, *The Gentleman's Magazine*, Supplement 1813 Part II, p. 701 ['Fell gallantly in an action near Bayonne, Lieut.-col. Samuel Coote Martin, 1st foot-guards, eldest son of the late Wm. Byam M. esq. of Whiteknights, Berks. The following is an extract from the letter of a brother officer: "Colonel Martin commanded the piquets which were attacked at day-light, on the 12th of December, by the Enemy in vast force. He repulsed them with great skill and gallantry; but at the conclusion of the contest he received a ball through the heart, which closed his honourable and virtuous life without a groan, deeply lamented by officers and men. He had greatly distinguished himself in the battle of the 9th." To his surviving parent, widow, and four infant children, his loss is indeed severe.'].

MASON, Edward H., Ensign, 82nd Foot: *1829 Statement of Service for Retired Officers*: Aged seventeen on first appointment to the Army. Ensign, 82nd Foot, 16 Aug. 1810; Lt., 82nd Foot, 1813 [Army List gives 15 Sept. 1813]; Half-pay, by reduction. Served seven years on full-pay. *Where serving when wounded*: '30th July 1813, Pyrenees'. *Details of pension*: Seventy pounds per annum, commencing 1814. *Family*: Married in Gosport, 11 April 1816. No children by 1829. *Where generally resident during last five years*: 'Tralee, Ireland'. [PRO: WO 25/767 f92]. Severely wounded, Pyrenees, 30 July 1813 (1st Battn.) [*London Gazette*]. Pension of fifty pounds per annum, commencing 31 July 1814, 'for a wound' received in the Pyrenees ('Mason, Edward Ussher') [*1818 Pension Return*, pp. 18–19].

MASON, William, Lt., 82nd Foot: *1829 Statement of Service for Retired Officers*: Aged twenty-nine on first appointment to the Army. Ensign, 82nd Foot, 23 Feb. 1809; Lt., 82nd Foot, 19 March 1812; Half-pay, 26 Nov. 1818. 'At his request placed on Half pay, from his health being impaired from the effects of Climate serving in the South of Spain the Continent and North America on active service, also suffered from severe Wounds Received at Nivelle a ball in the right hip. At Niagara a Ball in the front of his neck, a Ball in his right arm (remains in) a Ball in his Breast, and also several Buck shot Balls'. *Where serving when wounded*: 'at Nivelle severely and Niagara, severely'. No pension. *Family*: Married near Wexford, 12 May 1816. No children by 1829. *Where generally resident during last five years*: 'Newry, Ireland'. [PRO: WO 25/767 f129]. Severely wounded, Nivelle, 10 Nov. 1813 (1st Battn.) [*London Gazette*]. MGS.

+MASSEY, Francis, Lt., 1st Foot: Lt., 1st Foot, 26 July 1810. Killed, 'at the Siege of St Sebastian,' 7–27 July 1813 (3rd Battn.) [*London Gazette*].

MASSOW, Valentine von, Cornet, 2nd Dragoons K.G.L.: Cornet, 2nd Dragoons K.G.L., 6 May 1812. Wounded, during 'movements of the Army' [Retreat from Burgos], 23 Oct. 1812 ('Cornet De Massau') [*London Gazette*]. *Beamish*, vol. II, p. 626 ['severely wounded, 23d Oct., 1812 at Venta del Poco ... resigned, 16th May, 1813. Colonel, Prussian service, A.D.C. to his majesty the king of Prussia.'].

MASTERMAN, W. Thomas, Lt., 34th Foot: Lt., Army, 21 Feb. 1811; Lt., 34th Foot, 1 May 1811. Severely wounded, 'not dangerously,' while serving as an Acting Engineer, siege of Badajoz, 31 March–2 April 1812 [*London Gazette*]. Obituary, *The Gentleman's Magazine*, Nov. 1813, p. 504 ['Struck dead by a flash of lightning, whilst riding close to a section of his company through the mountains to Pampeluna, a few days after the battle of Vittoria, and killed on the spot, Lieut. Masterman, 34th reg. He formerly belonged to the Portsmouth Division of the Royal Marine Forces, and was shot through the body at the siege of Badajoz, when acting as engineer, from the effects of which he had but lately recovered.'].

MATHEWS, James, Surgeon, 3rd Foot; Surgeon, Hospital Staff: *1829 Statement of Service for retired officers*: Aged twenty-eight on first appointment to the Army. Hospital Mate, Hospital Staff, 8 July 1799; Assistant Surgeon, 52nd Foot, Sept. 1799; Assistant Surgeon, 4th Dragoons, 9 Nov. 1802; Surgeon, '1st Battn. of Reserve', 4 Aug. 1803; Half-pay, 24 Feb. 1805, by reduction; Surgeon, 8th West India Regt., 12 Sept. 1805; Surgeon, 3rd Foot, 7 July 1806; Surgeon, Hospital Staff, 14 Sept. 1813; Half-pay, 25 Aug. 1814, by reduction; Full-pay, Hospital Staff, 3 April 1815; Half-pay, 25 Oct. 1816, by reduction. 'Lameness prevents my accepting of Service except in an Hospital Station on Home Service, not being capable of riding on horse back.' *Where serving when wounded*: 'Spain'. *Details of pension*: One hundred pounds per annum, commencing 25 Dec. 1822. *Family*: Married in 'St Pancras Midx.', 6 May 1794. No children by 1829. *Where generally resident during last five years*: 'London and Margate, Kent.' [PRO: WO 25/767 f153]. Waterloo.

+MATHEWS, John, Lt., 2nd Foot: Lt., 2nd Foot, 25 Dec. 1807. Killed in the siege of the Forts of St Vincente, St Cayetano, and La Merced at Salamanca, 18–24 June 1812 [*London Gazette*].

MATHEWS, Joseph, Lt., 83rd Foot: *1829 Statement of Service for Retired Officers*: Aged twenty-six on first appointment to the Army. Ensign, 83rd Foot, 13 June 1809; Lt., 83rd Foot, 1811 [Army List gives 13 June 1811]; Half-pay, by reduction. Served seven years on full-pay. 'Lieut. Mathews would not be willing to join his Batallion in consequence of the loss of his arm, and his delicate state of health.' *Where serving when wounded*: 'Spain at the Siege of Ciudad Rodrigo.' *Details of pension*:

Seventy pounds per annum, commencing 1812. *Family*: Married in St Andrew's Church, Dublin, 26 June 1827. No children by 1829. *Where generally resident during last five years*: 'Dublin'. [PRO: WO 25/767 f170]. Severely wounded, siege of Ciudad Rodrigo, 12 Jan. 1812 ('Matthews') (2nd Battn.) [*London Gazette*]. Pension for 'loss of an arm' at Ciudad Rodrigo ('Matthews') [*1818 Pension Return*, pp. 18–19]. MGS.

MATHISON, John Augustus, Ensign, 77th Foot; Lt., 17th Portuguese Line: *1829 Statement of Service for Retired Officers*: Aged fifteen when he joined the Navy, and twenty-two when appointed to the Army. Ensign, 77th Foot, May 1811 [Army List gives 8 May]; Lt., 77th Foot, Aug. 1813 [Army List gives 12 Aug.]; Half-pay, 1817, by reduction. 'Served in the 17th Portuguese in the years 1812 & 1814, Light Division.' *Where serving when wounded*: 'Trafalgar when in the Navy. Badajos. Heights of Vera.' No pension. *Family*: Married in St Andrews, Lower Canada, 1 July 1822. Four children by 1829. *Title and nature of employment*: 'Justice of the Peace, in the District of Montreal. Commissioner for the trial of small causes'. *Where generally resident during last five years*: 'Montreal'. [PRO: WO 25/767 f87]. In Portuguese Service March 1813 to April 1814. MGS. *Challis, Portuguese Army*, p. 57 ['Wd. Bidassoa 5 June '11']. *Mullen*, p. 439, suggests service with 32nd Foot from Vittoria through Toulouse.

+MAW, J. H. L., Capt., 23rd Foot: Capt., Army, 3 Dec. 1806; Capt., 23rd Foot, 9 July 1807. Killed, storming of Badajoz, 6 April 1812 [*London Gazette*]. Obituary, *The Gentleman's Magazine*, June 1812, pp. 594–5 ['April 7. Fell gloriously in the arms of victory, at the storming of Badajoz, in his 29th year, Capt.

Maw, of the 23d reg. or Royal Welsh Fusileers, eldest son of John Henry M. esq. of Belle-Vue, near Doncaster. In him the service has lost a zealous and intelligent officer, and his friends have to lament a most honourable, well-disposed young man, a cheerful companion, and a good Christian. He served on the Quarter-master General's Staff, at the battles of Vimiera and Talavera, in the Peninsula, under the Earl of Wellington, and previously in the same department of the army under Lord Cathcart, in Scotland.'].

+MAXWELL, Robert, Lt., 74th Foot; Capt., 17th Portuguese Line: Lt., 74th Foot, 1 May 1804. Wounded during the repulse of a sortie from Badajoz, 10 May 1811, while serving as Capt., 17th Portuguese Line [*London Gazette*]. Severely wounded at the siege of Badajoz, 6–11 June 1811, while serving as Capt., 17th Portuguese Regt. [*London Gazette*]. Died of wounds, 16 June 1811. Return dated 25 June 1811. [PRO: WO 25/2965]. In Portuguese Service March 1810 to June 1811. *Challis, Portuguese Army*, p. 57 ['Wd. 2nd Sge. Badajos 5 June '11; Died of Wounds 11 June '11.'].

MAXWELL, William, Lt. Col., 26th Foot: Lt. Col., 26th Foot, 9 May 1805. Three hundred pounds per annum pension, commencing 25 Dec. 1811, for 'loss of an arm' at Corunna, 1809 [*1818 Pension Return*, pp. 8–9].

MAY, John, Capt., Royal Artillery: Capt., Royal Artillery, 1 June 1806. Mentioned in Wellington's Ciudad Rodrigo dispatch, 20 Jan. 1812 ['The rapid execution produced by the well-directed fire kept up from our batteries, affords the best proof of the merits of the officers and men of the royal artillery... But I must particularly mention Brigade-Major May ... of the royal artillery']

[*London Gazette*, 5 Feb. 1812]. Mentioned in Wellington's Badajoz dispatch, 7 April 1812 ['I cannot sufficiently applaud the officers and soldiers of the British and Portuguese artillery during the siege, particularly ... Major May'] [*London Gazette*]. Bvt. Lt. Col., Royal Artillery, 27 April 1812. Mentioned in Wellington's dispatch concerning the siege and storming of the Forts of St Vincente, St Cayetano, and La Merced at Salamanca, dated 30 June 1812 ['Major-General Clinton ... mentions in strong terms Lieutenant-Colonel May, who commanded the artillery under the direction of Lieutenant-Colonel Framingham'] [*London Gazette*]. Severely wounded, in an Affair with the Enemy's Rear-Guard near La Serna, 23 July 1812 ('Lieutenant-Colonel May, A.A.G.') [*London Gazette*]. Gold Medal. In Portuguese Service April 1809 to Aug. 1809. Waterloo. *Dalton*, pp. 209, 210 ['Son of John May, Esq., storekeeper of the Ordnance, Fort George, Guernsey... Bn. 1778... He recd. two musket balls through the left thigh when charging the French rearguard on the morning after the battle of Salamanca, and a violent contusion at Vittoria. D., 8th May, 1847, in London.']. *Challis, Portuguese Army*, p. 57. *Webber*, p. 150. *Kincaid, Random Shots*, p. 338 ['The day after the battle of Salamanca a brigade of heavy German dragoons, under the late Baron Bock, made one of the most brilliant charges in history... Lord Wellington, who was up with the advanced guard, no sooner observed the disposition of the enemy than he sent an order for the Baron to charge them. They charged accordingly – broke through the squares, and took the whole of the infantry – the enemy's cavalry and artillery having fled. Colonel May, of the British artillery, not satisfied with being the bearer of the order, gallantly headed the charge, and fell covered with wounds, from which he eventually recovered; but Lord Wellington, however much he must have admired the action, cut him for a considerable time in consequence, by way of marking his disapproval of officers thrusting themselves into danger unnecessarily.'].

MAYDELL, Charles von, Major, 1st Dragoons/Hussars, K.G.L.: Major, 1st Dragoons K.G.L., 16 May 1806. Wounded, during 'movements of the Army' [Retreat from Burgos], 23 Oct. 1812 ['Meydell'] [*London Gazette*]. Served in Peninsula 1812–14. Waterloo. *Beamish*, vol. II, p. 556 ['very slightly wounded, 23d Oct. 1812, at Venta del Poco, very slightly wounded, 18th June 1815, at Waterloo'].

MAYNE, William F., Lt., 59th Foot: Lt., 59th Foot, 4 Sept. 1808. Severely wounded, Vittoria, 21 June 1813 (2nd Battn.) [*London Gazette*]. Waterloo.

MEACHAM, John C., Capt., 24th Foot: Capt., 24th Foot, 28 March 1805. Slightly wounded, Busaco, 27 Sept. 1810 ('Meachan') (2nd Battn.) [*London Gazette*].

MEACHAM, William Prescott, Capt., 28th Foot: Capt., 28th Foot, 9 July 1803. Slightly wounded, Pyrenees, 25 July 1813 ('Meachem') (1st Battn.) [*London Gazette*]. Bvt. Major, 28th Foot, 4 June 1814. Killed, Waterloo. *Blakeney*, p. 144 [1811: 'Shortly after our occupation of Tarifa, a corps or civic guard, composed of young men, inhabitants of the town, was formed. The command of this body, called the Tarifa Volunteers, amounting to from forty to fifty individuals, was confided to Captain Meacham, 28th Regiment, not only because he was a gallant and experienced officer, but also on account of his knowledge of the Spanish language, acquired at an earlier period when the regiment was stationed in Minorca. This corps in its infancy imperfectly drilled, without any established uniform and not very imposing in appearance owing to their diversity of dress, could not be relied on as an efficient force. For these reasons perhaps it was that they got the name of "Meacham's Blind Nuts," so baptised, if I mistake not, by Captain Allen of the 10th Regiment.'], pp. 157, 166 ['Poor Meacham was sadly annoyed at being recommended to expose his Nuts to the sun for at least a fortnight to save them from perishing by mildew.'].

MEADE, Augustus, Major, 91st Foot: Major, 91st Foot, 28 Feb. 1812; Bvt. Lt.Col., 91st Foot, 4 June 1811. Slightly wounded, Toulouse, 10 April 1814 (1st Battn.) [*London Gazette*]. MGS.

MEADE, Frederick, Lt., 88th Foot: Lt., 88th Foot, 30 March 1809. Severely wounded, Salamanca, 22 July 1812 (2nd Battn.) [*London Gazette*]. MGS.

+MEADE, Hon. Michael. De Courcy, Lt., 39th Foot: Lt., 39th Foot, 5 Jan. 1805. Severely wounded, Vittoria, 21 June 1813 ('Mead') (1st Battn.) [*London Gazette*]. Obituary, *The Gentleman's Magazine*, Nov. 1813, p. 504 ['At Vittoria, of a wound received in that glorious battle, Lieut. Michael De Courcy Meade, 39th foot, son of Rev. Richard M. late rector of Innishannon, and nephew of Lord Baron Kinsale.'].

MEADE, William Henry, Lt., 44th Foot: Lt., 44th Foot, 27 Feb. 1810. Slightly wounded, Badajoz, 6 April 1812 ('Mead') (2nd Battn.) [*London Gazette*].

MEAGHER, Timothy, Lt., 7th Foot: Slightly wounded, Albuera, 16 May 1811, while serving as Acting Adjutant (2nd Battn.) [*London Gaz-*

ette]. Lt., 7th Foot, 17 July 1811. Adjutant, 7th Foot, 23 June 1814. *Challis, Index*, p. 80 ['To 43rd Ft'].

MEIN, William, Capt./Major, 52nd Foot: *1829 Statement of Service for Retired Officers*: Aged 'about 18' on first appointment to the Army. Ensign, 74th Foot, 20 Sept. 1797; Ensign, 52nd Foot, 18 Jan. 1798; Lt., 52nd Foot, 26 Nov. 1799; Capt., 52nd Foot, 14 Aug. 1804; Bvt. Major, 6 Feb. 1812; Bvt. Lt. Col., 7 Oct. 1813; Major 52nd Foot, 11 Nov. 1813; Half-pay, 25 July 1816, by reduction; Full-pay, 52nd Foot, 20 March 1817; Half-pay, 3rd Foot, 10 July 1818, 'in consequence of ill Health from Wounds.' *Where serving when wounded*: 'In Spain, Portugal and France from 1808 to 1814.' *Details of pension*: Three hundred pounds per annum, commencing 11 Dec. 1814. *Where generally resident during last five years*: 'Forge Cottage, Long Town, Cumberland'. [PRO: WO 25/766 f278]. Slightly wounded, during 'several Affairs with the French Army', 14 March 1811 [*London Gazette*]. Severely wounded 'in carrying a Redoubt before Ciudad Rodrigo', 8 Jan. 1812 [*London Gazette*]. Severely wounded, storming of Badajoz, 6 April 1812 [*London Gazette*]. Severely wounded, Crossing the Bidassoa, 7/9 Oct. 1813 ('Captain Mein (Major)') (1st Battn.) [*London Gazette*]. Severely wounded, the Nive, 10 Dec. 1813 (1st Battn.) [*London Gazette*]. Pension 'for wounds' received at Bayonne, 1813 [*1818 Pension Return*, pp. 14–15]. *Royal Military Calendar*, vol. V, pp. 1–3 ['... joined the army after the battle of Vimiera; and this officer served with it in the march through Spain, and at the battle of Corunna; in May, 1809, he again embarked with his reg. for the Peninsula, and the 52nd formed part of a light brigade under Maj. Gen. R. Crawfurd; he served with his company in the campaigns, from 1809, to 6th Feb. 1812, when he

received the brevet of Major, and was in the following battles, actions and sieges; Busaco, Fuentes d'Onor, Coa, La Lameida, Pombal, Redenhia, Cazalanovo, (where he received a severe wound from a musket ball, but continued at the head of his company,) Tose de Orouse, Sabugal, Fuentes, Guinaldo, siege of Ciudad Rodrigo, storming of fort St Francisco, (where he received a severe wound by a musket ball through the left thigh, being one of the first that entered this fort at the head of the storming party.) Immediately after the latter affair, the brevet of Major was conferred upon him, at the recommendation of the Duke of Wellington. From this date he constantly discharged the duty of a field officer with his corps; and in the campaigns of 1812 and 1813, was present at the following successes; siege of Badajoz, storming and capture of the same on the night of the 6th April, 1812, when, (though not recovered from his last wound) he received another severe wound by a musket shot through the right thigh; Castrajon, Guerrana, Salamanca, Sinminos, St Melian near Vittoria, Vittoria, Pyrenees, and Bidassoa, when the French army attempted to relieve and raise the siege of St Sebastian. About this period he succeeded to the command of his reg. and which he held on the 7th Oct. 1813, in the battle fought upon the heights near Beira. Major M. was on this day the first person, at the head of his corps, that entered a strong fort in possession of the enemy. Being in front, he leaped the ditch, and ascended the face of the redoubt, and on reaching the top, and leaping into it, a French soldier, at a few yards distance, presented his musket, and was upon the point of firing at him, when his presence of mind most probably saved his life; instantly stooping down, he took up a stone, and aimed so well at the head of the soldier, that he put him to the rout, and being now well supported by some of his men, completely drove the enemy from their strong hold. While at the head of his reg. and on the eve of carrying the last fortified position which the enemy held at this point in Spain, and upon the boundary of France, he received a severe and dangerous wound in the head, which, however, for a short time only compelled him to resign the command of his corps. In the despatches of the Duke of Wellington, announcing this victory, L.-Col. M. was particularly mentioned by name, as having, at the head of his corps, distinguished himself; at the recommendation of the Duke, the brevet of L.-Col. was conferred upon him; and on the 11th Nov. following, he succeeded to a Majority in his reg. He commanded it in the battle of the Nive; on the second day of the action he received another severe wound by a musket shot through the neck, while in command of the picquets of his brigade, and upon which occasion, although only in command of six companies, he defended a position which he took up, and maintained against a strong division of the French army. In consequence of the number and severity of the wounds which he had received, some of which were of so recent a date, and his health having suffered so much from the last six campaigns in which he had been constantly present with his corps, a medical board, in the ensuing year, strongly recommended his return to England... In July, 1818, he was compelled to retire upon half-pay, in consequence of his wounds.']. *Hay*, p. 18 ['another kind friend, Captain Mayne, senior captain of regiment']. *Moorsom*, pp. 151-2 [Storming of the Francisco redoubt, Ciudad Rodrigo, 8 Jan. 1812: 'Captain Mein of the 52nd came up with the escalading companies... The redoubt was entered ... by means of ladders at

the faces... Captain Mein was wounded, as was believed, by an accidental shot from one of our own companies as he was mounting on the rampart.'], pp. 424-5 [summary of career].

MEISTER, George, Lt., 2nd Light Dragoons/Hussars K.G.L.: Lt., 2nd Light Dragoons, 9 May 1806. Served in Peninsula only in 1811. *Beamish*, vol. II, p. 553 ['slightly wounded, June 13, 1811 at Los Santos. [Died] at Evensen in Han. 2d Dec. 1820.'].

+MELVILLE, David, 2nd Lt., Royal Engineers: 2nd Lt., Royal Engineers, 12 July 1809. Killed in the trenches before Badajoz, 8-15 May 1811 [*London Gazette*].

MENDHAM, William, Ensign/Lt., 68th Foot: Ensign, 68th Foot, 28 March 1811. Lt., 68th Foot, 30 Jan. 1812. Severely wounded, Nivelle, 10 Nov. 1813 [*London Gazette*].

MENZIES, Archibald, Capt., 42nd Foot: Capt., 42nd Foot, 5 June 1805. Temporary pension of two hundred pounds per annum, commencing 20 Sept. 1813, 'for wounds' received at Burgos, 1812 [*1818 Pension Return*, pp. 12-13]. Waterloo. MGS. Died in 1854. *Dalton*, pp. 157, 158-9 ['dangerously wounded at Quatre Bras... A pause in the battle permitted some men of the 42nd to carry their officer into the square of the 92nd, where he was found to have received sixteen wounds.'].

MERCER, Douglas, Lt. and Capt., 3rd Foot Guards: Lt. and Capt., 3rd Foot Guards, 20 March 1806. Slightly wounded while skirmishing, 9-14 Oct. 1810, while serving on the General Staff ('D. Merceo') [*London Gazette*]. Slightly wounded, Barossa, 5 March 1811, while serving on the Staff as ADC to Brig.-General Dilkes [*London Gazette*]. Capt. and Lt. Col., 3rd Foot Guards, 20 Dec. 1813. Waterloo. Third son of Lt. Col. George Mercer, by Jean, eldest daughter of Sir Robert Henderson, Bart. Lt.-Gen. 11 Nov. 1851. Col.-in-Chief 68th Foot. Assumed the additional surname of Henderson. MGS. Died at Naples, 21 March 1854. *Royal Military Calendar*, vol. V, p. 12 ['in 1805 accompanied the brigade to Hanover, in the expedition under Lord Cathcart. He returned with it, and, in March 1806, obtained a Lieutenancy: he accompanied the light infantry of his batt. to Beveland, in the Walcheren expedition: in the spring following, he was appointed A.-d-C to M.-Gen. Dilkes, and went with the brigade of guards under that officer's command to Cadiz. During the autumn of that year he passed over to Portugal, to visit the army under the Duke of Wellington, which he joined immediately after the battle of Busaco: he accompanied it to the Lines, where, while attending Sir B. Spencer, as A.-d.-C. near Sobral, he received a gun-shot wound, which caused his return to Lisbon, from whence, when recovered, he proceeded to Cadiz. In the spring following he was present at the battle of Barrosa, and was again wounded: the brigade of guards was shortly after ordered to England, where he remained a month, and then joined the 1st batt. of his reg. to which he had been appointed in Portugal: he continued with the army until the spring of 1814... Whilst in the Peninsula, he was present at the affair of El Boden, the sieges of Ciudad Rodrigo, and Badajos, the battle of Salamanca, the entrance to Madrid, the siege of Burgos, and subsequent retreat; the passage of the Bidassoa, and the battle of the Nive. He subsequently served in Flanders, and was present at the battles of Quatre Bras and Waterloo, for which, having commanded the batt. of guards, he received the 3d class of the Order of the Bath.'].

+MERCER, James, 2nd Lt., 95th Foot: 2nd Lt., 95th Foot, 13 March 1806. Killed, Barba del Puerco, 19

March 1810 [*London Gazette*]. *Simmons*, p. 53 [killed, Barba del Puerco: 'My friend, Lieutenant Mercer, who was putting on his spectacles, received a musket ball through his head, and fell dead close to my feet.'], pp. 62–3 ['an unlucky ball passed through poor Mercer's head just as he was saying, "Our brave fellows fight like Britons." ']. *Leach*, p. 129 [Barba del Puerco: 'We lost one officer killed (Mr. Mercer), and from fifteen to twenty sergeants and privates killed and wounded.'].

+MERRY, Augustus, Capt., 52nd Foot: Capt., 52nd Foot, 7 Jan. 1808. Severely wounded, storming of Badajoz, 6 April 1812. 'Since dead'. [*London Gazette*]. Died of wounds, 9 April 1812. Return dated 25 April 1812. [PRO: WO 25/2965]. *Register of officers' effects*: Single. [PRO: WO 25/2963].

MERVEDE, J. Charles, Baron, Lt., 2nd Light Battn. K.G.L.: Ensign, 2nd Light Battn. K.G.L., 8 May 1811; Lt., 2nd Light Battn. K.G.L., 25 March 1812. Slightly wounded, Crossing the Bidassoa, 7/9 Oct. 1813 ('Marweden') (1st Light Battn.) [*London Gazette*]. Served in Peninsula 1813–14. Waterloo. 'Merveden' in Army List. *Beamish*, vol. II, p. 568 ['severely wounded 27th Feb. 1814, before Bayonne; slightly wounded 7th Oct. 1813, on the Bidassoa.'].

MESSITER, Henry, Surgeon, 26th Foot: Surgeon, 26th Foot, 10 April 1806. Wounded, 'in the Army lately in Spain' (1st Battn.) [*March 1809 Army List*, p. 105]. Obituary, *The Gentleman's Gazette*, May 1809, p. 479 ['12 [April]. At Horsham, Sussex, Henry Messiter, esq. late of Wincanton, Somerset, and surgeon of the 26th Foot. He was wounded in the breast at the battle of Corunna, from which he had recovered, and fell a martyr to a fever which he caught in attending some soldiers of the regiment.'].

+METCALFE, John, Lt., 45th Foot:
Lt., 45th Foot, 16 June 1808.
Mentioned in Wellington's Ciudad
Rodrigo dispatch, 20 Jan. 1812 ['It
is but justice also to the 3d division
to report, that the men who
performed the sap belonged to the
45th, 74th, and 88th Regiments,
under the command of ... Lieutenant Metcalfe, of the 45th, and
they distinguished themselves not
less in the storm of the place, than
they had in the performance of their
laborious duty during the siege.']
[*London Gazette*, 5 Feb. 1812].
Slightly wounded, siege of Badajoz,
24 March 1812 [*London Gazette*].
Slightly wounded, siege of Badajoz,
26 March 1812 [*London Gazette*].
Severely wounded, storming of
Badajoz, 6 April 1812 ('Metcalf')
[*London Gazette*]. Killed, Orthes,
27 Feb. 1814 ('Metcalf') (1st Battn.)
[*London Gazette*].

MEYER, Augustus, Lt., 5th Line
Battn. K.G.L.: Lt., 5th Line Battn., 1
Dec. 1810. Served in Peninsula
1808–14. Waterloo. *Beamish*, vol. II,
p. 608 ['severely wounded, 27th Feb.
1814, before Bayonne... [Died] at
Tournay in Netherlands, 28th Sept.
1826.'].

+MEYER, Charles Gustavus, Lt.,
2nd Line Battn. K.G.L.: Lt., 2nd
Line Battn. K.G.L., 26 March 1807.
Served in Peninsula 1808-14.
Beamish, vol. II, p. 634 ['killed in
action before Bayonne, 27th Feb.
1814.'].

+MEYER, Conrad Victor,
Ensign/Lt., 1st Line Battn. K.G.L.:
Ensign, 1st Line Battn. K.G.L., 17
Feb. 1809. Severely wounded, 'in the
assault and capture of the exterior
line of the castle of Burgos on the
evening of the 4th October, 1812'
[*London Gazette*]. Died of wounds,
18 Oct. 1812. Return dated 25 Oct.
1812. [PRO: WO 25/2965]. Served in
Peninsula 1808-12. *Beamish*, vol. II,
p. 640 [Died '18th Oct. 1812, of the
wounds he received on the evening

of the 4th Oct. 1812, in the assault
and capture of the exterior line of
defence of the castle of Burgos.'].

MEYER, Frederick Lewis, Major,
1st Light Dragoons K.G.L.: Major,
1st Light Dragoons K.G.L., 25 Oct.
1810. Slightly wounded, Fuentes de
Onoro, 5 May 1811 [*London
Gazette*]. Lt. Col., 3rd Hussars
K.G.L., 10 Oct. 1813. Served in
Peninsula 1808–13. Waterloo.
Beamish, vol. II, p. 616 [Died 'at
Brussels, 6th July 1815, of the
wounds he received in the battle of
Waterloo, 18th June 1815.'].

MEYER, George, Lt., 2nd Light
Battn. K.G.L.: Joined the K.G.L. on
25 July 1809. Lt., 2nd Light Battn.
K.G.L., 29 March 1810. Severely
wounded, the Nive, 9 Dec. 1813
[*London Gazette*]. *Beamish*, p. 567
['severely wounded, 9th Dec. 1813,
before Bayonne; slightly wounded,
18th June 1815, at Waterloo.'].
Served in the Expedition to the
Scheldt, 1809; Peninsula, 1811–13;
South of France, 1813; North of
Germany, 1814, not present with
General Wallmoden's corps;
Netherlands, 1814. Waterloo. Died
at Otterndorf, Hanover, 16 March
1832, as Capt. on Half-pay.

MEYER, Johann Ludewig, Lt.,
Duke of Brunswick Oels' Corps
(Infantry): *1829 Statement of
Service for Retired Officers*:
'Remark: the Officer has a third
Christian Name, Martin, but he
allways made use only of the two
above mentioned.' Aged thirty
'when he entered in 1809 His
Majestys Service as Sergeant in the
Duke of Brunswick Light Infantry.'
Ensign, Duke of Brunswick Oels, 28
Feb. 1811; Lt., Duke of Brunswick
Oels, 25 July 1812; Half-pay, 24 Dec.
1814, on reduction. *Where serving
when wounded*: 'in Spain'. *Details
of pension*: Seventy pounds per
annum, 'first temporary granted on
the 19th June 1814; the permanent
Grant is the 16th February 1819'.

Family: Married in the 'Town of Brunswick', 8 May 1816. One child, born in 1817. *Where generally resident during the last five years*: 'at the Town of Brunswick'. [PRO: WO 25/766 f276].

+MEYER, John, Lt., 5th Line Battn. K.G.L.: Lt., 5th Line Battn. K.G.L., 6 Sept. 1809. Killed, sortie from Bayonne, 14 April 1814 [*London Gazette*]. Served in Peninsula 1808–14. *Beamish*, vol. II, p. 635.

MEYER, William, Lt., Duke of Brunswick Oels' Corps (Infantry): Ensign, Duke of Brunswick Oels' Corps (Infantry), 20 Feb. 1811; Lt., Duke of Brunswick Oels' Corps (Infantry), 23 July 1812. Severely wounded, in operations, 12-19 June 1813 ('Meger') [*London Gazette*].

MEYRICKE, John, Lt., 43rd Foot: Lt., 43rd Foot, 23 Aug. 1810. Slightly wounded, Nivelle, 10 Nov. 1810 (1st Battn.) [*London Gazette*].

MICHELET, Edward, Cornet, Duke of Brunswick Oels' Corps (Cavalry): Wounded, Heights of Ordal, 12/13 Sept. 1813 ('Cornet Micheler... Brunswick Hussars') [*London Gazette*, 9 Oct. 1813]. 'Michelet' in revised casualty list [*London Gazette*, 23 Oct. 1813]. 'Edward Missohlett' in *Challis, Index*, p. 273.

MICHELL, Edward, 1st Lt., Royal Artillery: 1st Lt., Royal Artillery, 13 Sept. 1803 [*London Gazette*]. Slightly wounded, Barossa, 5 March 1811 [*London Gazette*]. 2nd Capt. 11 Aug. 1811. Mentioned in Lt. Gen. Campbell's letter dated Gibraltar, 3 Jan. 1812 [Tarifa: 'On the 31st [Dec. 1811], between eight and nine o'clock in the morning, the enemy (having effected a breach in the east wall of the town) advanced with two thousand picked men, grenadiers and light infantry, to assault the place. Eight companies of the 87th Regiment, under the orders of Lieutenant-Colonel Gough, were stationed on the walls in that district of the town... From the spirited behaviour of this corps, aided by a well-directed fire from two field-pieces mounted on the north-east tower, under the command of Captain Mitchell, of the Royal Artillery, which flanked the column as it advanced, the enemy was broken and dispersed with great slaughter.'] [*London Gazette*]. Bvt. Major, Royal Artillery, 17 March 1814. *Blakeney*, p. 137 [Tarifa, 20 April 1810: 'This demonstration against Tarifa was attended with but few results or casualties, one man only, a gunner, being killed and a few more wounded. Lieutenant Mitchell, a gallant officer, commanded the artillery.'], pp. 154, 165–6 [Jan. 1811: 'In this expedition, as in all others which we made from Tarifa (too numerous to be mentioned), we were accompanied by Lieutenant Mitchell, Royal Artillery. In Tarifa he was an artilleryman, pointing the guns from the bastion most exposed; in the field he was a light bob, foremost in pricking for the foe; and on the occasion just mentioned he acted in a third capacity, for he reconnoitred the fort of Casa Vieja, guessed its capabilities from outward demonstration, ascertained the strength of its defences by personal observation and formally reported thereon with all the inherent pomp and acquired gravity of a Royal Engineer.'].

+MIDDLETON, Alexander, Capt., 36th Foot: Capt, 36th Foot, 26 Feb. 1807. Killed, Salamanca, 22 July 1812 [*London Gazette*].

MIDDLETON, Henry, Lt., 45th Foot: Lt., 45th Foot, 7 Oct. 1813. Slightly wounded, Orthes, 27 Feb. 1814 (1st Battn.) [*London Gazette*]. Lt., 35th Foot, 1 Dec. 1814. Waterloo.

MIDDLETON, William, Lt., 42nd Foot: *1829 Statement of Service*: Born in 'Kirkmichael Banffshire', 15 March 1787. Aged fifteen on first appointment to the Army. Ensign, 7th West India Regt., 18 Jan. 1802; Ensign, 42nd Foot, 9 July 1803; Lt., 28 June 1804; Capt., 13 May 1812; Half-pay, 24 Oct. 1814; Capt., 42nd Foot, 19 May 1819; Major, 42nd Foot, 15 Aug. 1826. Note added: 'Lt Col, 42nd Regt., 23 Oct. 1835. Retired from the service 23 Augt 1839.' *Battles, sieges and campaigns*: 'Campaigns 1808, 1809 and Battle of Corunna 16th Jany 1809... Walcheren 1809... Campaign 1812, Battle of Salamanca 22d July 1812, and subsequent operations' *Wounds received in action*: 'Dangerously wounded in the abdomen, slightly in left leg, and contusion left thigh, at Corunna 16th Jany 1809. Never applied for Pension, but received one year's pay as Lieutenant. Suffered much from Walcheren fever 1809, and still subject to attacks of it.' *Service abroad*: "Novr 1805 to Augt 1808, Gibralter. Augt 1808 to Jany 1809, Portugal & Spain. July 1809 to Octr 1809, Walcheren. March 1812 to Decr 1812, Spain. Novr 1825 to June 1829, Gibralter.' Then added: 'Decr '31 to 10 Decr '34, Malta. 11 Decr '34 to 8 Sepr. 1836, Cape.' *Family*: Married in Asketon, County Limerick, 28 July 1823. They had four children by 1829, with another noted in 1833. [PRO: WO 25/793 f89]. Wounded, 'in the Army lately in Spain' (1st Battn.) [*March 1809 Army List*, p. 105]. *Monthly Return*, 1st Battn., dated 25 Feb. 1809: 'Left wounded at Plymouth' [PRO: WO 17/152].

MIELMANN, Henry, 1st Lt., K.G.L. Artillery: 1st Lt., K.G.L. Artillery, 26 Nov. 1808. Served in Peninsula 1808–14. Waterloo. *Beamish*, vol. II, p. 535 ['slightly wounded, 22d July, 1812, at Salamanca; severely wounded, 17th July, 1813, before St Sebastian.'].

MILES, Edward, Major, 38th Foot: *1829 Statement of Service*: Born in Roach's Town, Tipperary, Ireland, March 1777. Aged seventeen on first appointment to the Army. Ensign, 38th Foot, May 1794; Lt., 38th Foot, 1 Sept. 1795; Capt., 38th Foot, Oct. 1802; Major, 38th Foot, March 1805 [Army List gives 21 March]; Bvt. Lt. Col., 38th Foot, [1] Jan. 1812; Lt. Col., 38th Foot, May 1818; Half-pay, 'by the Reduction of the 2d Lt. Colonel of Regiments not in the East Indies, but was immediately reappointed to a lieut. colonelcy in the 89th Regt. in India.' Lt. Col., 89th Foot, 12 Aug. 1819. Colonel, Army, 5 June 1829. *Battles, sieges and campaigns*: Campaigns in Holland in 1794 and 1795. 'At the Siege of St Lucia in the West Indies in April 1796... At the capture of Trinidad in 1797. Served during the Rebellion of Ireland in 1803. At the Battles of Roleia, Vimeria on the 17th & 21st August 1808 and at Lugo... At the Battle of Corrunna 16th Jany 1809... With the Expedition to Walcheren in 1809... At the Battle of Salamanca 22d July 1812 in Command of 38th Foot. At the Battles of Villa Muriel in July 1812. At Burgos. At Battles of Vitoria, Gormoria Mayor on 21 June 1813. At the Passage of Bidosoa and the Pyrenees from 28th July to 2nd August 1813. At the Siege of Saint Sebastian in August & Sept. 1813. At the Battle of Nivelle on the 10th Novr. 1813. At Nive from 9th to 13th December 1813. Bayone and at the Capture of Paris in 1815 under the Duke of Wellington. Served against the Caffres at the Cape of Good Hope. Proceeded in Command of a Brigade to Ava in April 1824 and was engaged in all the operations against the Enemy in that Country from June to 17th August 1824... Embarked and proceeded to the Eastward and commanded the Force at the Capture of Tavay 9th Sept. & Storm & Capture of Mergui 6th Oct. 1824. Returned to Rangoon in Novr. 1824 and served

MILES

during the investment of that town by the Enemy during the Month of Decr. 1824 and Commanded the Madras Forces in several attacks on the Enemy.' *Distinguished conduct*: 'Thanked by General Fox for leading Forlorn Hope at Nimegen [Oct. 1794]. Specially noticed by His late Royal Highness the Prince Regent for Valorous conduct at the Battle of Salamanca on the 23d July 1812 and for Exemplary and conspicuous conduct at the storm and capture of St Sebastian 32st August 1813. Noticed in General Orders by the Rt. Honorable the Governor Genl. and Commander in Chief of India and also by the Governor and Commander in Chief at Madras for the professional talents, judgement and skill with which the attacks on the Fortified Towns of Tavay and Mergui on the Tenasarim Coast in the Dominions of the King of Ava, were directed.' *Wounds received in action*: 'Severely and dangerously wounded on the 22d July 1812 in the Action at Salamanca. Dangerously wounded at St Sebastian 31st August 1813 when in command of the 38th Foot. One years Pay on each occasion. Pension £250 Per Annum permanent.' *Titles, honorary distinctions and medals*: 'Medal & Clasp. Companion of the Bath. Knight of the Tower & Sword and Knighted by His late Majesty George the Fourth. Special augmentation with armorial Bearings for distinguished conduct at St Sebastian.' *Service abroad*: 'May 1794 to 1795, Holland. 1 Sept. 1795 to 1801, West Indies. 12 July 1808 to 1811, and June 1812 to 1813, Portugal, Spain, Walcheren and Peninsula. 1815 to Dec. 1815, France. June 1818 to 17 March 1820, Cape of Good Hope and on Passage to India. 30 March 1820 to 8 Feby. 1825, India. 18 June 1829 to 31 Decr. 1829, India.' *Family*: He married his first wife, Maria Catherine Falconer, 'Daughter of Arch Deacon Falconer', 1802, in Thorpe, Stafford-

shire. They had three children prior to her death. He remarried, Mary Hopkins, in March 1828, in Islington. This couple had no children by 1830. [PRO: WO 25/802 f220]. Severely wounded, Salamanca, 22 July 1812 [*London Gazette*]. Gold Medal. *1818 Pension Return*, pp. 10–11. MGS.

MILES, John Marshal, Ensign, 43rd Foot: Ensign, 43rd Foot, 10 Dec. 1812. Slightly wounded, Nivelle, 10 Nov. 1813 (1st Battn.) [*London Gazette*].

MILL, Charles, Capt./Major, 27th Foot: *1829 Statement of Service*: 'Born Ferry Barn, Fifeshire, 22d February 1780. Aged Fourteen Years on his first Entrance into the Army. Ensign, 27th Regiment, 5 Octr. 1795. Lieut., 27th Regiment, 1 Septr. 1796. Captain, 27th Regiment, 4 Augt. 1804. Major, 27th Regiment, 10 Novr. 1813. Half Pay, 25 July 1817. Major, 55th Regimentm 11 Jany. 1821. Lt. Col., 55th Regiment, 10 Augt. 1826.' *Battles, sieges and campaigns*: 'Ensign 27 Regiment at the capture St Lucia... As Ensign on the 1 June 1796 embarked, and landed on the 10th in Grenada. Was present in Several Skirmishes in Subduing the Insurgents of that Island... Embarked and landed in Holland with the Division of the Army under Sir Ralph Abercrombie... As Lieut 27 Regiment commanding a Company landed in Egypt on the 9 March 1801 was present in the Battles of the 13th and 21st March, and on the 22d of August to the N. of Alexandria... In November 1812 Embarked and joined the Division of the Army under Sir J. Murray at Alicante in Spain, was present in the action at Castoria 14 April 1814 and at the Siege of Terragona which was raised in consequence of the advance of the French General Suchet's Army. In the Action at Ordal in Catalonia... On 13 September 1813, as Captain having rejoined the 2nd Battalion 27th Regiment in consequence of a Wound received was embarked in November 1813. In May 1814 embarked at Portsmouth and rejoined the 3rd Battalion 27th Regiment at Bourdoux in France. Joined as Major. Embarked in command of the Battalion at Poliack... June and arrived at Quebec on the 15 July 1814. Advanced with the Army under the Governor Sir G. Prevost to Platesburgh in the United States, and was present in the affairs which took place there on the 4 June 1815. Embarked with the Battalion and sailed for Long Island... Appointed to the 55th Regiment 11 Jany. 1821... On the 27 Augt. 1830 Embarked & landed at Madras 11 October 1830. On the 10 March 1834 marched in Command of the Right Wing and Head Quarters of the 55th Regiment to join a Force under Brigadier General Lindsey C.B. for the purpose of commencing Hostilities against His Highness the Rajah of Coorg. Was present at the Storming of Kissinhully on the 2nd April, and at the attack on Somarpett on the 3rd, at which latter place he was Killed at the Head of his Regiment. Killed in Action 3rd April 1834.' *Distinguished conduct*: 'Name Mentioned in General Orders by the Commander in Chief in India dated Head Quarters... 17 May 1834.' *Wounds received in action*: 'Wounded at Ordal in Spain, on the 13 September 1813, on which occasion recovered a gratuity of one years full pay as Captain.' *Titles, honorary distinctions and medals*: 'received a Subaltern's Medal for the Battle of the 21 March 1801 in Egypt.' *Service abroad*: [as detailed above] [PRO: WO 25/795 f316]. Severely wounded, Heights of Ordal, 12/13 Sept. 1813 (2nd Battn.) [*London Gazette*]. See letter of Capt. J. Waldron, 27th Foot, dated 15 Sept. 1813, published with the Tarragona dispatches in the *London Gazette*, 9 Oct. 1813 ['On

the night of the 12th instant, about twelve o'clock, the enemy in great force, attacked the position of the 2d battalion 27th regiment at Ordal; and shortly after, Lieutenant-Colonel Reeves and Captain Mills [sic] being wounded, the command of the battalion devolved upon me.'].

MILLAR, Henry, Lt., 40th Foot: Lt., 40th Foot, 5 Sept. 1810. Severely wounded, Badajoz, 6 April 1812 ('Miller') [*London Gazette*]. Waterloo. MGS.

MILLER, George, Capt., 95th Foot: Capt., 95th Foot, 21 Jan. 1808; Bvt. Major, 3 March 1814. Severely wounded, 'in Action with the Enemy', 20 March 1814 (2nd Battn.) [*London Gazette*]. Gold Medal. Waterloo. Died, 1843. *Simmons*, p. 336.

MILLER, James Fitz William, Volunteer, 1st Foot: *1829 Statement of Service for Retired Officers*: Aged sixteen on first appointment (as Ensign) into the Army. Volunteer, 1st Foot, 'in either January or February 1813'; Ensign, 1st Foot, 23 Aug. 1813; Lt., 1st Foot, 14 Oct. 1814 [Army List gives 6 Oct.]; Half-pay, 'early in 1816', by reduction; 'on full Pay ... in May same year'; 'was again reduced early in 1817'. 'Joined the 3d Battn. Royal Scots as a volunteer, under the Patronage of His late Royal Highness the Duke of Kent, to whom his Father was domestic Chaplain for twenty seven years, at Limago, in Portugal ... advanced with the army, was wounded on the 18th June same year at Osma, was present with the Battn. at the Battle of Vittoria, severely wounded at the first attack on St Sebastian July 31st. Sent to the rear to Bilbao was gazetted an Ensign... Joined the Battn. again on the Pyrennees and at the Crossing of the Bidassa, the advance on St Jean de Luz & subsequently the advance to Bayonne & engaged with the Battn. on the 9th of December commonly called the Mayor's House when he saved one of the Colours of the regt. & on every subsequent day until the sortie from Bayonne 14th April when he was on Picquet & saw General Hay fall close to the Convent of St Etienne. Was present with the Battn. until the return to Ireland in 1814. Was gazetted a Lieutenant ... went out with the same Batn. to Holland & was slightly wounded at Quatre Bras & severely at Waterloo.' 'Never unhealthy, nor any ailment ... saving what he suffers from wounds which occasionally break out'. *Where serving when wounded*: 'With the Forlorn Hope, commanded by Lieutenant [Colin] Campbell of the 9th Foot at the breach of St Sebastian when he received a musket shot thru the left arm which cut the tendons & broke the small bone and also wounded in the forehead by the bursting of a shell.' *Details of pension*: Fifty pounds, commencing 25 Dec. 1823. *Family:* Married in George's Church, Limerick City, 20 Sept. 1817. Five children by 1829. No employment. 'No other Property on earth to support his large family and Educate them but his H.P. Pension & Forty Eight Pounds Irish.' *Where generally resident during last five years*: 'Limerick'. [PRO: WO 25/768 f76]. Slightly wounded, in operations, 12–19 June 1813 ('Volunteer S. Miller') [*London Gazette*]. Severely wounded, 'at the Siege of St Sebastian,' 7–27 July 1813 ('Volunteer Miller') (3rd Battn.) [*London Gazette*].

+**MILLER, James, Capt., 68th Foot:** Capt., 68th Foot, 18 Jan. 1810; Major, Army, 25 July 1810. Severely wounded, Salamanca, 22 July 1812 ('Millar') [*London Gazette*]. Died of wounds, 12 Aug. 1812. Return dated 25 Aug. 1812. [PRO: WO 25/2965]. *Register of officers' effects*: Died, 12 Aug. 1812, Ciudad Rodrigo, of wounds received at Salamanca.

Married. His effects totalled £71. 15s. 7d. [PRO: WO 25/2964].

MILLER, James, Capt., 74th Foot: Capt., 74th Foot, 18 Jan. 1810; Bvt. Major, 74th Foot, 25 July 1810. Severely wounded, Toulouse, 10 April 1814 (1st Battn.) [*London Gazette*]. In Portuguese Service May 1810 to Dec. 1813. Gold Medal. *Challis, Portuguese Army*, p. 57 ['Lt. Col. 23 Line'].

+**MILLER, John, Lt., 38th Foot:** Lt., 38th Foot, 9 Nov. 1809. Slightly wounded, Busaco, 27 Sept. 1810 (2nd Battn.) [*London Gazette*]. Died 'of disease', St Sebastian, 31 Aug. or 9 Sept. 1813 [PRO: WO 25/2965].

MILLES, Thomas Potter, Capt., 14th Light Dragoons: Capt., 14th Light Dragoons, 9 July 1807. Slightly wounded, Fuentes de Onoro, 5 May 1811 [*London Gazette*]. Bvt. Major, 14th Light Dragoons, 12 April 1814. *Perrett*, p. 28 ['There were brushes with the French rearguard at Salamanca and at Burgos, where the fortifications were abandoned and blown up by the enemy. During the latter event, which took place on the 12th June, Captain Milles' squadron charged and captured a gun.'].

MILLING, Henry, Major, 81st Foot: Major, 81st Foot, 8 Jan. 1807, Wounded, 'in the Army lately in Spain' (2nd Battn.) [*March 1809 Army List*, p. 105]. *Monthly Return*, 2nd Battn., dated 25 Feb. 1809: 'Wounded, in Naval Hospl. Plymouth' [PRO: WO 17/202]. Temporary pension of three hundred pounds per annum, commencing 25 Dec. 1811, 'for a wound' received at Corunna, 1809 [*1818 Pension Return*, pp. 18–19].

+**MILLIUS, Charles, Capt., Chasseurs Britanniques:** Capt., Chasseurs Britanniques, 20 Feb. 1811. Slightly wounded, Vittoria, 21 June

1813 ('Millins') [*London Gazette*]. Killed, Orthes, 27 Feb. 1814 [*London Gazette*].

MILMAN, Francis Miles, Lt. and Capt., Coldstream Guards: Lt. and Capt., Coldstream Guards, 28 April 1804. Wounded, 'severely but not dangerously', Talavera, 28 July 1809 ('Millman') [*London Gazette*]. MGS.

+MILNE, Peter, Lt., 42nd Foot: Lt., 42nd Foot, 9 March 1809. Killed, storming and capture of Fort St Michael, Burgos, 19 Sept. 1812 (1st Battn.) [*London Gazette*].

MILNES, George Miles, Capt., 45th Foot: Capt., 45th Foot, 19 Sept. 1804. Slightly wounded, storming of Ciudad Rodrigo, 19 Jan. 1812 ('Milne') [*London Gazette*].

MINCHIN, Francis, Lt., 51st Foot: Lt., 51st Foot, 12 July 1809. Severely wounded, 'in the Operations of the Army', 31 Aug. 1813 [*London Gazette*]. Waterloo. Capt., 51st Foot, 22 June 1815. Died, 1865. MGS. *Wheeler*, p. 144 [Wounded, near Lezaca].

MITCHELL, George, Ensign/Lt., 92nd Foot: *1829 Statement of Service*: 'Born in Parson's Town, Ireland, 29 September 1794. Aged 16 2/12 years on his first Entrance into the Army. Ensign, 92nd Foot, 29 Novr. 1810. Lieut., 92nd Foot, 29 July 1813. Half Pay, 24 Decr. 1814, By Reduction of the 2nd Battn. Lieutenant, 78th Foot, 14 Feby. 1822.' *Battles, sieges and campaigns*: 'Was present at the Battle of Vittoria 21st June 1813, an Ensign in the 92nd Foot. Pyranees 25th 30th & 31st July, Nieve 10th & 13th Decr. 1813. Ayre 2d March, & Toulouse 10th April 1814, a Lieutenant in the 92nd Foot, also at all the skirmishes in which the 92nd Foot was engaged from 1st Mar. 1813 to 30th July 1814... Also at Orthes 27th Feby. 1814 a Lieut. in the 92d Foot.'

Wounds received in action: 'Was Wounded while the 92d Foot was engaged on the Pyranees on the 25th July, and at Nieve on the 13th Decr. 1813. Received no grant of Pay nor Pension.' *Service abroad*: '1st March 1813 to 28 July 1813, Peninsula. 29 July 1813 to 30 July 1814, Peninsula. 23d April 1826 to 31 Decr. 1829, Ceylon.' [PRO: WO 25/800 f181]. Slightly wounded, Pyrenees, 25 July 1813 (1st Battn.) [*London Gazette*]. Slightly wounded, the Nive, 13 Dec. 1813 (1st Battn.) [*London Gazette*]. MGS.

MITCHELL, James, Lt./Adjutant, 88th Foot: Ensign, 88th Foot, 8 May 1811; Adjutant, 88th Foot, 26 Sept. 1811; Lt., 88th Foot, 13 Nov. 1813. Severely wounded, Orthes, 27 Feb. 1814 (1st Battn.) [*London Gazette*].

MITCHELL, James, Major, 92nd Foot: Major, 92nd Foot, 30 March 1809. Wounded, Pyrenees, 25 July 1813 (1st Battn.) [*London Gazette*]. Gold Medal. Lt. Col., Army, 3 March 1814. Wounded, Waterloo.

MITCHELL, Robert, Ensign/Lt., 28th Foot: *1829 Statement of Service for Retired Officers*: Aged twenty on first appointment to the Army. Ensign, 28th Foot, 13 Feb. 1810 [Army List gives 15 Feb.]; Lt., 28th Foot, 11 Feb. 1813; Half-pay, [1817] by reduction. Served seven years on full-pay. *Where serving when wounded*: 'Wounded at Victoria in the Peninsula'. No pension. *Family*: Married in Parsonstown, King's County, 10 July 1821. Three children by 1829. [PRO: WO 25/768 f74]. Severely wounded, Vittoria, 21 June 1813 (1st Battn.) [*London Gazette*]. MGS. *Sherer*, pp. 243–4 ['It would be, perhaps, difficult to select a more painful anecdote connected with the battle of Vittoria, than the following: a paymaster of a regiment of British Infantry, had two sons, lieutenants in the corps in which he served; he was a widower, and had no relatives besides these youths;

they lived in his tent, were his pride and delight. The civil staff of a regiment usually remain with the baggage when the troops engage, and join them with it afterwards. In the evening, when this paymaster came up, an officer met him. "My boys," said the old man, "how are they? Have they done their duty?" "They have behaved most nobly, but you have lost" – "Which of them?" "Alas! both; they are numbered with the dead." ' In fact, though both Lt. Mitchells were recorded as severely wounded, only one appears to have died.

+MITCHELL, Robert Henry, Lt., 28th Foot: Ensign, 28th Foot, 17 May 1810. Severely wounded, Vittoria, 21 June 1813 (1st Battn.) [*London Gazette*]. Died of wounds, 27 July 1813. Return dated Aug. 1813. [PRO: WO 25/2965]. *Sherer*, pp. 243-4, quoted in Robert Mitchell.

MITCHELL, Robert, Lt., 60th Foot: Lt., 60th Foot, 22 Sept. 1808. Severely wounded, Talavera, 28 July 1809 [*London Gazette*].

MITCHELL, Samuel, Capt., 95th Foot; Major, 6th Caçadores: *1829 Statement of Service*: Born 14 June 1779, Campbelltown, Argyleshire. Aged twenty on his first appointment to the Army. Ensign, '71st Rifle Corps', May 1800; 2nd Lt., Nov. 1800; 1st Lt., Aug. 1801; Half-pay, June 1802; 1st Lt., 95th Foot, Aug. 1802; Adjutant, 95th Foot, Sept. 1803; Capt., 95th Foot, 9 May 1805; Bvt. Major, 95th Foot, 21 June 1813; Major, 95th Foot, Sept. 1813; Bvt. Lt. Col., 95th Foot, 21 Jan. 1819; Lt. Col., 31st Foot, 24 Dec. 1829. *Battles, sieges and campaigns*: 'Coa, 24th July 1810, Light Division, as Captain... Pombal 11th March, Redinha 12th, Miranda De Corva 14th, Forze De Ruze 15th March, Sabugal 3rd April, Fuentes De Onora. The Siege of Ciudad Roderigo, and as Major Commg.

the 6th Casadores under Lord Hill. Battle of Vittoria. Pyrenees, 1st–4th–25th–30th & 31 July, 1813. Major Commg. Rifle Brigade at New Orleans, 1814.' *Distinguished conduct*: 'A Volunteer Commanding 100 Men Rifle Corps, at the Storming of Fort Pickerine and the Citadel of Ciudad Rodrigo.' *Wounds received in action*: 'Very Severely wounded through the right arm at the Battle of Coa. Received One Year's Pay. Also severely wounded through the Leg, at the Storming of Ciudad Rodrigo. Slightly at the Battle of Vittoria, June 1813. Slightly at the Pyrennees Augt. 1813. Received One Year's pay for wound at Storming of Ciudad Rodrigo, with Pension to June 1817, when it was withdrawn.' *Titles, honorary distinctions and medals*: 'Medal for the Battle of Vittoria. Clasp for the Pyrenees. Ribbon and Cross of Companion of the Bath.' *Service abroad*: '1 May 1807 to 6 Oct. 1808, River Plate and Cape of Good Hope. May 1809 to Decr. 1813, Peninsula. May 1814 to May 1815, New Orleans. March 1829 to Decr. 1829, Malta.' *Family*: Married Sarah Penman, 27 Dec. 1807, Cape of Good Hope. They had no children by 1830. [PRO: WO 25/791 f3]. Incorrectly recorded as 'wounded, severely, since dead', Coa, 24 July 1810 ('Samuel Mitchell') [*London Gazette*]. Severely wounded, storming of Ciudad Rodrigo, 19 Jan. 1812 [*London Gazette*]. Gold Medal. In Portuguese Service April 1812 to Nov. 1813. *Challis, Portuguese Army*, p. 57. *Simmons*, pp. 88, 109 [Oct. 1810: 'Captain Mitchell, who was wounded through the elbow, came to live near us'], p. 113. *Kincaid, Adventures*, p. 108 [Storming of Ciudad Rodrigo: 'The storming party, consisting of three officers and one hundred volunteers from each regiment, the officers from ours were Captain Mitchell, Mr Johnstone, and myself, and the whole under the command of Major Napier, of the fifty-second.'].

+MITCHELL, Thomas, Ensign/Lt., 92nd Foot: Ensign, 92nd Foot, 28 June 1810. Slightly wounded, Pyrenees, 25 July 1813 ('F. Mitchell') (1st Battn.) [*London Gazette*]. Slightly wounded, Pyrenees, 31 July 1813 [*London Gazette*]. Killed, the Nive, 13 Dec. 1813 ('Lieutenant Thomas Mitchell') (1st Battn.) [*London Gazette*].

MODDEN, George, Ensign, 30th Foot: Ensign, 30th Foot, 24 Oct. 1811. Severely wounded, during 'movements of the Army' [Retreat from Burgos: Villa Muriel], 25 Oct. 1812 ('Madden') [*London Gazette*].

MOGRIDGE, James Edward, Lt., 34th Foot: Lt., 34th Foot, 28 June 1810. Severely wounded, Vittoria, 21 June 1813 ('Moggerige') (2nd Battn.) [*London Gazette*]. MGS.

MOLLE, George, Major, 9th Foot: Major, Army, 3 Sept. 1803. Major, 9th Foot, 2 June 1804. Wounded, Rolica, 17 Aug. 1808 [*London Gazette*]. Lt. Col., 9th Foot, 2 Sept. 1808. *Blakeney*, p. 147 [Gibraltar, April 1810].

+MONAGHAN, Thomas, Lt., 3rd Foot: Lt., 3rd Foot, 10 Oct. 1805. Slightly wounded, passage of the Douro, 12 May 1809 [*London Gazette*]. *Register of officers' effects*: 'Managhan, Thos.' Killed in Action, 25 July 1813, Spain. Single. [PRO: WO 25/2963].

+MONTAGUE, Frederick, Capt., 23rd Foot: Capt., 23rd Foot, 21 March 1805. Killed, Albuera, 16 May 1811 ('Montague') (1st Battn.) [*London Gazette*]. '–Montagu' in Army List. 'Frederick Montague' in *Challis, Index*, p. 94.

+MONTFORD, Charles, Ensign, 4th Foot: Ensign, 4th Foot, 7 March 1811. Killed, storming of San Sebas-tian, 31 Aug. 1813 (1st Battn.) [*London Gazette*].

MONTGOMERIE, Hugh Barnet, Ensign, 3rd Foot Guards: Ensign, 3rd Foot Guards, 28 March 1811. Severely wounded, the Nive, 12 Dec. 1813 ('Montgomery') (1st Battn.) [*London Gazette*]. Lt. and Capt., 3rd Foot Guards, 9 June 1814. Wounded, Waterloo. *Dalton*, p. 114 [Died '2nd May, 1817, from after effects of a wound received at Waterloo.']

+MONTGOMERY, J., Lt., 83rd Foot: Lt., 83rd Foot, 1 Dec. 1808. Killed, Talavera, 28 July 1809 [*London Gazette*].

+MOORE, George A., 1st Lt., Royal Artillery: 1st Lt., Royal Artillery, 24 March 1809. Killed, 'in Action with the Enemy', 15 Feb. 1814 [*London Gazette*]. *Webber*, p. 142 [21 March 1813: 'Moore joined the Brigade with 7 Gunners for the Company.'], p. 188 n2 ['Lt George A. Moore RA embarked for the Peninsula in February 1813 in charge of drafts. He joined Captain T. Hutchesson's Coy 3 Bn RA.'].

MOORE, James Thomas, Ensign/Lt./Adjutant, 87th Foot: *1829 Statement of Service*: Born in Dublin, 9 Aug. 1790. Aged eighteen on first appointment to the Army. Ensign, 87th Foot, 13 Oct. 1808; Lt., 87th Foot, 18 Feb. 1812; Adjutant, 87th Foot, 11 March 1812; 'Lost the Adjutancy on the reduction 2d Battn. 87 Regt. in Feb. 1817'; Capt., 87th Foot, 23 Aug. 1824. *Battles, sieges and campaigns*: 'Ensign at Talavera July 27 & 28th 1809. Ensign & Lieut. at the siege of Cadiz, served during the whole time. Adjutant at Vittoria 21 June 1813, had two horses shot that day, Adjutant at the Pyrenees July 1813. Adjutant at Nivelle 10th November 1813. Adjutant at Orthez 27 Feb. 1814, had a Horse Shot this day. Adjutant at Vic Biggoro, 19 March

1814. Adjutant at Toulouse 10 April 1814. Was also engaged in a number of Affairs during the War... Served as Lieutenant in the Mahratta Campaigns of 1817 & 1818... Served in the Burmese war in 1825 & 1826, as Major of Brigade under Sir Archd. Campbell.' *Wounds received in action*: 'At Talavera in the Right thigh: the Ball remains there. received a years pay as Ensign. At Vic Biggoro, 19th March 1814. Received a years pay as Adjutant.' *Service abroad*: 'December 1808 to July 1814, Peninsula. March 1817 to July 1828, Bengal. Jany. 1825 to June 1827, Bengal & Ava.' [PRO: WO 25/802 f84]. Slightly wounded, Talavera, 27 July 1809 [*London Gazette*]. Slightly wounded, 'in Action with the Enemy', 19 March 1814 (2nd Battn.) [*London Gazette*]. MGS.

+MOORE, John, Lt.-General: Col., Army, 21 Aug. 1795; Major-General, 18 June 1798; Col., 52nd Foot, 8 May 1801; Lt.-General, 30 Oct. 1805. Killed at Corunna, 16 Jan. 1809. Obituary, *The Gentleman's Magazine*, Jan. 1809, p. 94. *Blakeney*, pp. 121–3 [Corunna: 'he proudly sat erect on his war-steed, calmly casting a satisfied glance at the raging war around. It was at this moment that he was struck to the ground by a cannon-ball, which laid open the breast of as upright and gallant a soldier as ever freely surrendered life in maintaining the honour and glory of his king and country. He soon arose to a sitting position, his eyes kindling with their usual brilliancy when informed that the enemy were victoriously repulsed at all points... On placing Sir John Moore in the blanket in which he was borne to the rear, the hilt of his sword got into the wound; and as they tried to take it away, he declined having it moved, saying, "It may as well remain where it is, for, like the Spartan with his shield, the Briton should be taken out of the field with

his sword." The wound was of the most dreadful nature; the shoulder was shattered, the arm scarcely attached to the body, the ribs over his heart smashed and laid bare. Thus was Sir John Moore carried to the rear. As he proceeded, perceiving from the direction of the firing that our troops were advancing, he exclaimed, "I hope the people of England will be satisfied." On being taken to his house in Corunna, he again enquired about the battle, and being assured that the enemy were beaten at all points, exclaimed: "It is great satisfaction to me to know that the French are beaten. I hope that my country will do me justice."... He now enquired about the safety of several officers, those of his staff in particular; and he recommended several for promotion whom he considered deserving. This exertion caused a failing in his strength; but on regaining it in a slight degree, addressing his old friend Colonel Anderson, he asked if Paget was in the room. Upon being answered in the negative, he desired to be remembered to him, saying, "He is a fine fellow; 'tis General Paget, I mean." This was a noble testimonial to that gallant officer's high character, rendered sacred by the peculiar circumstances in which it was called forth; and it strongly marked the martial spirit and high mind of the dying hero, who, with his body writhing in torture, the veil of eternity fast clouding his vision and his lips quivering in the convulsive spasms of death, sighed forth his last words in admiration of the brave. The battle of Corunna terminated at the same moment that the British commander expired. He was buried in the citadel. As the enemy's last guns were firing his remains were lowered into the grave by his staff, simply wrapped in his military cloak.']. *Fletcher, Fields of Fire*, p. 90 ['The tomb of Sir John Moore lies in the garden of San Carlos, situated in the old part of the town of Corunna. This peaceful garden is enclosed within a high wall upon which is inscribed verses from the poem "The Burial of Sir John Moore at Corunna", written by Charles Wolfe and published iin 1817.'], 92. Bowrigg, B., *Life and Letters of Sir John Moore* (London, 1921); Maurice, Sir J. F., *Diary of Sir John Moore* (London, 1904); Oman, C., *Sir John Moore* (London, 1953); Parkinson, R., *Moore of Corunna* (London, 1976).

MOORE, Robert, Lt., 40th Foot: Lt., 40th Foot, 14 April 1808. Severely wounded, storming of Badajoz, 6 April 1812 (1st Battn.) [*London Gazette*]. Wounded, Waterloo. Died, 1845.

+MOORE, Robert, Ensign, 50th Foot: Ensign, 50th Foot, 3 Dec. 1807. Recorded as 'wounded' under 'Casualties' (1st Battn.) [*Feb. 1809 Army List*]. 'Died at Plymouth', 'casualties in the Army lately in Spain' (1st Battn.) [*March 1809 Army List*, p. 105].

MOORE, Samuel, Lt., 28th Foot: *1829 Statement of Service*: Born 22 Oct. 1793, Limerick. Aged fifteen years and five months on his first entrance into the Army. Ensign, 28th Foot, 31 March 1808; Lt. 28 Jan. 1810; Capt. 14 Dec. 1826. *Battles, sieges and campaigns*: 'Terifa in Spain April 1810... Barrossa 5th March 1811... Campaign of 1812... Vittoria 21st June 1813... Quatre Bras 16th June 1815... Waterloo 18th June 1815, Lieutenant commg. a compy.' *Wounds received in action*: '2 Wounds at Barrossa 5th March 1811. One years Pay as Lieut. £118–12s–6d.' *Titles, honorary distinctions and medals*: 'a Waterloo Medal.' *Service abroad*: 'Jany 1810 to April 1810, Gibraltar. April 1810 to March 1811, Terifa. March 1811 to June 1811, Cadiz. June 1811 to Feby. 1812, Gibraltar.

Feby. 1812 to Septr. 1814, Portugal & Spain. May 1815 to Decr. 1815, Netherlands & France. Decr. 1817 to March 1818, Malta. March 1818 to Febr. 1826, Ionian Islands.' Not married in 1830. [PRO: WO 25/790 f184]. Severely wounded, Barossa, 5 March 1811 [*London Gazette*]. MGS.

MOORE, Thomas, Lt., 27th Foot: *1829 Statement of Service*: Born 19 July 1788, Clonmel, Ireland. Aged nineteen on first appointment to the Army. Ensign, 27th Foot, 24 Nov. 1807; Lt., 27th Foot, 8 March 1810; Half-pay, 1813, 'In Consequence of wounds Received in the Peninsula'; Lt., 27th Foot, May 1815; Half-pay, 1816; Lt., 87th Foot, 21 Feb. 1816; Half-pay Feb. 1817; Lt., 18th Foot, 19 Aug. 1819; Capt., 98th Foot, 18 Feb. 1826; Capt., 18th Foot, 7 Nov. 1826. *Battles, sieges and campaigns*: 'At the Siege of Ciudad Rodrigo and Both Sieges of Badajos in the 27th Regt.' *Wounds received in action*: 'Severely wounded at the Storming of Badajos on the night of 6 April 1812. Received one years Pay and no Pension.' *Service abroad*: '1808 to 1813, Peninsula. 1821 to 1826, Mediterranean.' Not married in 1830. [PRO: WO 25/788 f179]. Slightly wounded, storming of Badajoz, 6 April 1812 (3rd Battn.) [*London Gazette*]. MGS.

MOORE, William, Lt., 11th Foot: *1829 Statement of Service*: 'Born Ballyhaise Cavan, Ireland, 28 June 1793. Aged fifteen on his first Entrance into the Army. Ensign, 11th Foot, 31st Decr. 1807. Lieutenant, 5th Jany. 1809. Captain, 45th Augt. 1825.' Note added: 'Died at Dublin, 6 July 1837.' *Battles, sieges and campaigns*: 'Lieutenant in 11th Foot at Busaco 27th February 1810. Fuentes D'Onor 5th May 1811. Was Engaged in the operations before and at the reduction and Capture of the Forts of Salamanca in the Month of June 1812.

Pyrenees 28th July 1813. Nive 9th & 13th Decemr. 1813. Orthes 27th February 1814. Tolouse 10th April 1814. Was present but not at the Assault and Capture of Ciudad Rodrigo and Badajor.' *Distinguished conduct*: 'Received the thanks of Lieut. General Sir Henry Clinton for the Manner in which I led the advance of the Light Infantry 11th Regiment to the attack and capture of a Party occupying a redoubt and Fortified House in front of the Position at Bayonne on some Night in January 1814 the same being noted in Division Orders.' *Wounds received in action*: 'Severely in the Body at the Battle of the Pyrenees on the 28th July 1813, when in command of the Light Company received a grant of a years Pay as Captain being wounded in the Command of it.' *Service abroad*: 'March 1808 to June 1809, Madeira. June 1809 to July 1814, Peninsula. March 1816 to January 1821, Gibraltar. June 1826 to 31st Decr. 1829, E. Indies.' Note added: '1 Jany. 1830 to 5 Jany. 1833, E. Indies.' *Family*: Married Cordelia Boswell, 3 Oct. 1815, in Drumreany, Co. Westmeath, Ireland. They had five children, all sons, born between 1816 and 1825. [PRO: WO 25/793 f328]. Severely wounded, Pyrenees, 28 July 1813 (1st Battn.) [*London Gazette*].

MOORE, William George, Lt., 52nd Foot: Ensign, 52nd Foot, 18 April 1811; Lt., 52nd Foot, 10 Sept. 1812. Severely wounded, and 'missing', sortie from Bayonne, 14 April 1814, while serving as ADC to Sir J. Hope [*London Gazette*].

MOORE, William, Capt., 74th Foot: Capt., 74th Foot, 25 Sept. 1806. Slightly wounded, Fuentes de Onoro, 5 May 1811 [*London Gazette*]. Bvt. Major, 74th Foot, 21 June 1813. Severely wounded, Pyrenees, 30 July 1813 ('Brevet-Major Moore') (1st Battn.) [*London Gazette*]. MGS.

MORGAN, Edward, Lt., 7th Foot: *1829 Statement of Service for Retired Officers*: Aged fifteen on first appointment to the Army. Lt., 7th Foot, 4 Feb. 1808; Capt., 7th Foot, 5 March 1812; Half-pay, 75th Foot, Aug. 1822, 'from ill health'. *Where serving when wounded*: 'Albuera in Spain'. *Details of pension*: Seventy pounds per annum, commencing May 1812. *Family*: Married in Genoa, 14 Feb. 1827. One child by 1829. No employment. *Where generally resident during last five years*: 'Milan & Florence in Italy'. [PRO: WO 25/768 f133]. Severely wounded, Albuera, 16 May 1811 (1st Battn.) [*London Gazette*]. MGS.

MORGAN, Herbert, Ensign, 66th Foot: Ensign, 66th Foot, 9 Feb. 1808; Lt., 66th Foot, 31 May 1809. Severely wounded, Talavera, 28 July 1809 ('Lt') [*London Gazette*].

+MORIARTY, James, Ensign/Lt., 88th Foot: Ensign, 88th Foot, 8 March 1810; Lt., 88th Foot, 13 May 1812. Killed, Orthes, 27 Feb. 1814 (1st Battn.) [*London Gazette*]. *Haythornthwaite, Armies of Wellington*, p. 248 [Salamanca, 22 July 1812: 'The colonel of the leading French regiment (22eme Ligne), endeavouring to hearten his men, seized a musket and ran forward towards the advancing 88th Foot, led by Major Barnaby Murphy and the adjutant, Captain William Mackie, both mounted, and the Colour-party, the King's Colour borne by Lieutenant John D'Arcy and the Regimental Colour by Lieutenant T. Moriarty. As the French colonel dashed forward, Moriarty remarked, "That fellow is aiming at me!"; "I hope so", said D'Arcy, "for I thought he had *me* covered." Instead, the French officer fired at Murphy, killing him on the spot, the ball passing through him, hitting the pole of the King's Colour and ricocheting to strike off part of D'Arcy's epaulette.'].

MORISSET, James Thomas, Capt., 48th Foot: *1829 Statement of Service for Retired Officers*: Aged fifteen on first appointment to the Army. Ensign, 80th Foot, 1 Feb. 1798; Lt., 80th Foot, 5 Nov. 1800; Capt., 48th Foot, 26 Dec. 1805; Bvt. Major, 48th Foot, 12 Aug. 1819; Major, 48th Foot, 8 June 1825; Half-pay, Lt. Col., unattached, 19 Dec. 1826. *Where serving when wounded*: 'Albuhera'. *Details of pension*: One hundred pounds per annum, commencing May 1817. *Family*: Married in New Church, Isle of Wight, 2 May 1826. *Title and nature of employment*: 'Military and Civil commandant of Norfolk Island'. *Where generally resident during last five years*: 'New South Wales, England, and Norfolk Island'. [PRO: WO 25/768 f183]. Slightly wounded, Albuera, 16 May 1811 ('Morrissett') [*London Gazette*]. 'Morisette' in Army List. *1818 Pension Return*, pp. 12–13. MGS.

MORPHETT, Mars, Volunteer 53rd Foot: *1829 Statement of Service*: 'Mars Morphett... Born in Dublin, Ireland, 8th July 1793. Aged Nineteen on his first Entrance into the Army. Volunteer, 53rd Regt., July 1812. Ensign, 36th Regt., 22nd July 1812, Appointed by Lord Wellington. Removed to 53rd on application of Lt. Col. Bingham, commission dated 1st October 1812. Ensign, 53rd Regt, 1st Octr. 1812. Lieutenant 53rd Regt, 29th June 1815. Lieutenant, 87th Regt., Octr. or Septr. 1823. Lieutenant 48th Regt., 26th March 1824. Adjutant, 48th Regt., 15th Decr. 1825.' Notes added: 'Lieut., 63rd Regt., 17 Sep. 33. Capt. 40th, 29 Jany. 36. Capt., 57th, 36. Retired by sale of Commission on 10 Decr. 1842.' *Battles, sieges and campaigns*: 'Salamanca 22nd July 1812. Volunteer ... Fort Jeytuck, India, May 1815.' *Wounds received in action*: 'Salamanca, Two slight wounds and one severe. One years Full Pay as Ensign.' *Service abroad*: 'May 1812

to Decr. 1812, Peninsula. May 1814 to May 1823, India. Septr. 1823 to Decr. 1829, India.' *Family*: Married Miss Vida Pohle, 4th April 1818, Trichinopoly, East Indies. They had six children by 1830, with an additional four noted by 1840. [PRO: WO 25/794 f193]. Severely wounded, Salamanca, 22 July 1812 ('Volunteer Morfshell') (2nd Battn. 53rd Foot) [*London Gazette*]. MGS.

+MORPHEW, Powell J., Lt., Royal West India Rangers; Capt., 3rd Caçadores: Lt., Royal West India Rangers, 16 Nov. 1809. Killed, storming of Badajoz, 6 April 1812, while serving as Capt., 3rd Caçadores [*London Gazette*]. In Portuguese Service Oct. 1811 to April 1812. *Challis, Portuguese Army List*, p. 57.

MORPHY, Richard, Ensign/Lt., 3rd Foot: *1829 Statement of Service for Retired Officers*: Aged twenty-one on first appointment to the Army. Ensign, 3rd Foot, 'March or April 1812'; Lt., 3rd Foot, Aug. 1813 [Army List gives 26 Aug. 1813]; Half-pay, March 1817, by reduction. 'I beg leave to state for the information of the Secretary at War that I had the Honor of serving three years as a midshipman on board His Majestys Ship Thetes, Captn. now Admiral Gage commanding, as also three years as an Ensign in the Kerry Militia Colonel Crombie commanding.' *Where serving when wounded*: 'before Bayonne in France 13th Decr. 1813.' No pension. *Family*: Married in Kilgarvan Church Co. Kerry, 14 July 1827. No children by 1829. No employment. *Where generally resident during last five years*: 'For the most part in Ireland, a short time in France and some time in England.' [PRO: WO 25/768 f138]. Severely wounded, the Nive, 13 Dec. 1813 ('R. Murphy') (1st Battn.) [*London Gazette*]. 'F. Murphy' in Army List. He clearly signed 'Morphy' in his Statement of Service. MGS.

+MORRANT, Robert, Ensign/Lt.,
9th Foot: Ensign, 9th Foot, 9 May
1811. Killed, San Sebastian, 31 Aug.
1813 ('Lieutenant R. Morant') (1st
Battn.) [London Gazette].

MORRIS, Apollos, Lt., 66th Foot:
Lt., 66th Foot, 6 Feb. 1808. Severely
wounded, Talavera, 28 July 1809
(2nd Battn.) [London Gazette].
Temporary pension of seventy
pounds per annum, commencing 25
Dec. 1811, 'for wounds' received at
Talavera, 1809 [1818 Pension
Return, pp. 16–17]. MGS.

MORRIS, Samuel, Lt., 28th Foot:
Lt., 28th Foot, 2 April 1806. Severely
wounded, Vittoria, 21 June 1813 (1st
Battn.) [London Gazette]. MGS.

MORTIMER, Charles, Lt., 82nd
Foot: Lt., 82nd Foot, 9 Feb. 1808.
Severely wounded, Nivelle, 10 Nov.
1813 (1st Battn.) [London Gazette].

MORTON, Harcourt, Lt., 85th Foot:
1829 Statement of Service for
Retired Officers: Aged twenty-three
on first appointment to the Army.
Ensign, 85th Foot, 21 April 1808; Lt.,
85th Foot, 10 Nov. 1808; Lt., 49th
Foot, 25 Jan. 1813; Capt., 14th Foot,
12 Jan. 1814; Half-pay, 25 March
1816, 'At my own request in conse-
quence of my private affairs
requiring my presence at Home'.
'Desirous but unequal to active
Service in consequence of a Wound
received at the Battle of Chrystler's
Farm in Upper Canada on the 11th
November 1813.' Where serving
when wounded: 'Spain and Upper
Canada'. Family: Married in 'St
Pancras Old Church, London', 15
Oct. 1814. Where generally resident
during last five years: 'Masham,
Yorkshire'. [PRO: WO 25/768 f200].
Slightly wounded, siege of Badajoz,
6–11 June 1811 [London Gazette].
MGS.

MOSES, Thomas, Lt., 7th Foot:
1829 Statement of Service for
Retired Officers: Aged sixteen on

first appointment to the Army.
Ensign, Royal Westmoreland
Militia, 1 Aug. 1803; Lt., Royal Westmoreland Militia, 1 Oct. 1803; Lt.,
7th Foot, 26 Aug. 1807, 'by volunteering with men'; Capt., 7th Foot,
20 Aug. 1812; Half-pay, Jan. 1817, by
reduction; Capt. 9th Royal Veteran
Battn., April 1820. 'Not capable of
active service on account of
wounds.' Where serving when
wounded: 'Spain, Ireland'. Details
of pension: One hundred pounds,
commencing 7 April 1813, 'withdrawn 24th Decr. 1817. Granted 3rd
Septr. 1821'. Family: Married in St
Faith's, London, 7 Feb. 1814. Seven
children by 1829. No employment.
Where generally resident during
last five years: 'Brampton,
Cumberland. Liverpool & the Isle of
Mann'. [PRO: WO 25/768 f121].
Slightly wounded, Albuera, 16 May
1811 (1st Battn.) [London Gazette].
Severely wounded, storming of
Badajoz, 6 April 1812 [London
Gazette]. Retired 1831. MGS.

+MOULTRIE, Thomas, Lt., 7th
Foot: Lt., 7th Foot, 5 Dec. 1805.
Slightly wounded, Albuera, 16 May
1811 ('Moultry') (1st Battn.)
[London Gazette]. Died of wounds,
10 June 1811. Return dated 25 June
1811. [PRO: WO 25/2965].

MOUNTGARRETT, William, Lt.,
87th Foot: Lt., 87th Foot, 6 Oct.
1808. Severely wounded, Vittoria, 21
June 1813 ('Mountgarret') (2nd
Battn.) [London Gazette]. Severely
wounded, Orthes, 27 Feb. 1814
('Moutgarrett') (2nd Battn.)
[London Gazette]. Pension of
seventy pounds per annum,
commencing 28 Feb. 1815, 'for
wounds' received in Egypt, 1807,
Vittoria, 1813, and Orthes, 1814
[1818 Pension Return, pp. 20–1].

MOWLDS, John David, Lt., 11th
Foot: Lt., 11th Foot, 28 Feb. 1811.
Slightly wounded, Nivelle, 10 Nov.
1813 ('Moulds') (1st Battn.)
[London Gazette].

MUNRO

+MULCASTER, Frederick W., Capt., Royal Engineers: Capt., Royal Engineers, 21 Sept. 1802; Bvt. Major, Royal Engineers, 25 July 1810. Slightly wounded, siege of Ciudad Rodrigo, 15 Jan. 1812 [London Gazette]. Killed, siege of Badajoz, 26 March 1812 [London Gazette].

MULLENS, Hon. Edward, Capt., 28th Foot: Capt., Army, 13 Nov. 1801; Capt., 28th Foot, 25 May 1803. Severely wounded, Barossa, 5 March 1811 (1st Battn.) [London Gazette]. Major, 28th Foot, 4 June 1813. Half-pay upon the reduction of the regt. in 1814.

MÜLLER, von, Capt., 1st Light Dragoons K.G.L: Slightly wounded, Salamanca, 18 July 1812 [London Gazette].

MÜLLER, August, Lt., 1st Line Battn. K.G.L.: Lt., 1st Line Battn. K.G.L., 22 Sept. 1813. Served in Peninsula 1809-11. Waterloo. Beamish, vol. II, p. 573 ['severely wounded, 28th July, 1809, at Talavera; very severely wounded, 18th June, 1815, at Waterloo.'].

MÜLLER, George, Capt., 2nd Line Battn. K.G.L: Capt., 2nd Line Battn. K.G.L., 2 Nov. 1803. Severely wounded, Fuentes de Onoro, 5 May 1811 [London Gazette]. Major, 2nd Line Battn. K.G.L., 18 Feb. 1813. Gold Medal. Served in Peninsula 1808-14. Waterloo. Later Major-General. MGS. Beamish, vol. II, p. 575.

+MÜLLER, Henry, Capt., 2nd Line Battn. K.G.L.: Lt., 2nd Line Battn. K.G.L., 20 Aug. 1805; Capt., 2nd Line Battn. K.G.L., 12 March 1812. Killed, sortie from Bayonne, 14 April 1814 [London Gazette]. Served in Peninsula 1808-14. Beamish, vol. II, p. 633.

MÜLLER, Moritz von, Capt., 1st Light Dragoons/Hussars K.G.L: Capt., 1st Light Dragoons K.G.L.,

14 Feb. 1804. Slightly wounded, Salamanca, 22 July 1812 [London Gazette]. 'Meriz de Muller' in Army List. Served in Peninsula 1809-14. Waterloo. Beamish, vol. II, p. 548 ['slightly wounded 18th June 1812 at Canizal; slightly wounded 22d July 1812 at Salamanca... [Died] at Hameln, 18th February 1835.'].

+MÜLLER, Paul, Lt., 5th Line Battn. K.G.L: Ensign, 5th Line Battn. K.G.L., 28 Jan. 1806. Severely wounded while skirmishing, 9-14 Oct. 1810 ('Lieutenant') [London Gazette]. Served in Peninsula 1808-10. Beamish, vol. II, p. 639 ['lieut. Paul Muller... [Died] 3d Nov. 1810, at Lisbon, of the wounds he received in a skirmish near Deteiro, on the 14th Oct. 1810.'].

MULLINS, Thomas Townsend Arenburg, Lt., 7th Foot: 1829 Statement of Service for Retired Officers: 'Lord Ventry'. Aged twenty-one on first appointment to the Army. Lt., 7th Foot, 7 Feb. 1807; Capt., 7th Foot, 8 Aug. 1811; Half-pay, 11 Dec. 1817. Where serving when wounded: 'Albuhera, Spain'. Details of pension: One hundred pounds, commencing Sept. 1812. Family: Married in Galway, 11 Aug. 1821. Two children by 1829. Where generally resident during last five years: 'Pringle, Ireland'. Signed simply "Ventry". [PRO: WO 25/776 f305]. Severely wounded, Albuera, 16 May 1811 (1st Battn.) [London Gazette]. 1818 Pension Return, pp. 4-5.

MUNRO, Charles, Ensign/Lt., 45th Foot: Ensign, 45th Foot, 6 April 1810. Slightly wounded, storming of Badajoz, 6 April 1812 ('Munroe') ('Lieut.') [London Gazette]. MGS.

MUNRO, David, Lt., 94th Foot: 1829 Statement of Service: Born in the County of Ross, Scotland, 17 Sept. 1786. Aged twenty on his first appointment to the Army. Ensign, 59th Foot, date 'not known'; Lt., 94th

419

Foot, 1 June 1807; Capt., 94th Foot, 11 Feb. 1814; Half-pay, 25 Dec. 1818, 'By Disbandment of the Regiment'; Capt., 94th Foot, Dec. 1823; Major, 94th Foot, 8 Dec. 1828. *Battles, sieges and campaigns*: 'Landed at Lisbon on 31st Decr. 1809, with the 94th Regt., re-embarked with the Regiment and landed at Cadiz in January 1810. Embarked again with the Regiment and landed at Lisbon in September same year. Joined the 3rd Division of the Army under General Picton, with the Regt. Oct. 1810, and was with it as Lieutenant. In the Lines Torres Vedras, General Massena's retreat from Portugal, the Sieges of Badajos in June 1811 and April 1812, Rodrigo Jany. 1811 and Battles of Salamanca, Victoria, Pyrenees, Nivelle... & Toulouse, besides all the minor Actions & Skirmishes during the whole of the above periood. Battle of Fuentes D'Onor, retreat from Madrid & Burgos, Battle of Orthes.' *Wounds received in action*: 'Was wounded in the Head & Body in action with the Enemy while Serving as Lieutenant in the 94th Regiment, at the Seige of Badajos in the year 1812. Received a years pay as Captain. Pension £70 per annum from April 1813, Permanent.' [PRO: WO 25/803 f218]. Slightly wounded, siege of Badajoz, 31 March-2 April 1812 ('Munroe') [*London Gazette*]. MGS.

MUNRO, Hector, Lt., 71st Foot: Ensign, 71st Foot, 26 June 1811; Lt., 71st Foot, 25 March 1813. Slightly wounded, Aire, 2 March 1814 (1st Battn.) [*London Gazette*].

MUNROE, Thomas, Lt., 42nd Foot: Lt., 42nd Foot, 8 Aug. 1805. Probably slightly wounded, Talavera, 28 July 1809, while serving with 1st Battn. Detachments ('Munroe') [*London Gazette*]. This could perhaps have referred to George Aylmer Munro (Lt., 25 Feb. 1804; Capt., though Thomas seems to have been referred to systematically in returns as 'Munroe' rather

than 'Munro'. Severely wounded, Toulouse, 10 April 1814 ('Thomas Munroe') (1st Battn.) [*London Gazette*]. 'Munro' in Army List. 'Munroe' in *Challis, Index*, p. 129.

+**MUNT, Frederick, Ensign, 36th Foot:** Ensign, 36th Foot, 10 Oct. 1812. Severely wounded, 'in the Operations of the Army', 31 Aug. 1813 (1st Battn.) [*London Gazette*]. Died of wounds, 6 Sept. 1813. Return dated Sept. 1813. [PRO: WO 25/2965].

MURALT, Rodolphe de, Capt., Chasseurs Britanniques: Capt., Chasseurs Britanniques, 11 June 1807; Capt., Army, 4 Sept. 1806. Slightly wounded, 'in the Operations of the Army', 31 Aug. 1813 [*London Gazette*].

+**MURCHISON, Robert P., Capt., 43rd Foot:** Capt., 43rd Foot, 8 March 1809. Severely wounded, 'since dead', Nivelle, 10 Nov. 1813 ('Murcheson') (1st Battn.) [*London Gazette*]. Died of wounds, 11 Nov. 1813. Return dated Nov. 1813. [PRO: WO 25/2965]. *Hurt*, p. 78 ['D.O.W., Nivelle, Nov. 11 [1813]']. *Bruce*, p. 158 [Letter from William Napier to his wife, dated 'France, Camp 1 league in front of San Pe' following Nivelle: 'Captain Murchison, another friend and companion of 11 years' standing, with every good quality, died in great agony yesterday from his wounds.'].

+**MURPHY, Barnaby, Capt., 88th Foot:** Capt., 88th Foot, 27 Aug 1804; Bvt. Major, 88th Foot, 21 Jan. 1808. Severely wounded, storming of Badajoz, 6–7 April 1812 [*London Gazette*]. Killed, Salamanca, 22 July 1812 ('Brevet Major') (1st Battn.) [*London Gazette*]. *Simmons*, pp. 110–11 [In charge of a detachment of wounded men returning to their regiments from Belem, 7–9 Oct. 1810: 'Major Murphy of the 88th Regiment; he had men belonging to every regiment in the country, amongst whom several who had much rather remained at Belem than have paraded their bodies in the field to be shot at... When we called the rolls, 100 out of 800 that had marched off were missing, which sadly annoyed Major Murphy... "Well, then sir, take the rear-guard to-morrow and make any straggler a prisoner, and I will bring him to a Drumhead Court-Martial"; which order he made known to the detachment... At the end of this day's march, another one hundred heroes had disappeared, which made our Commandant raving mad.']. *Haythornthwaite, Armies of Wellington*, p. 248 [Salamanca: 'The colonel of the leading French Regiment (22eme *Ligne*), endeavouring to hearten his men, seized a musket and ran forward towards the advancing 88th Foot, led by Major Barnaby Murphy and the adjutant, Captain William Mackie, both mounted... The French officer fired at Murphy, killing him on the spot, the ball passing through him, hitting the pole of the King's Colour and ricocheting to strike off part of D'Arcy's epaulette. At the same moment someone from the 88th shot the French colonel through the head, who threw up his arms and fell forward; as Murphy, his foot caught in a stirrup, was dragged by his frightened horse along the front of the battalion, a sight which threw the 88th into a frenzy of rage. Pakenham rode up at this moment and called to Wallace, "Let them loose"; the brigade charged and the French, astonished at the sight of a two-deep line running uphill towards superior numbers, broke and fled.'].

MURPHY, George Henry Edward, Lt., 87th Foot; Capt., Portuguese Staff: Born 25 Dec. 1795, London. Aged fifteen on hs first entrance into the Army. Ensign, 87th Foot, 27 Nov. 1805; Lt., 87th Foot, 2 July 1807; Capt., Army, 1814, 'Reduced to Half Pay as Captain in 1815, and remained so until appointed to the 6th Regiment 1821.' Capt., 6th Foot,

1821. 'Major, Portugal Staff, 1813; Major, Commanding 23d Portuguese Regt., 1814; Major, Portugueze Staff, From 1813 to 1820. Captain Portugueze Service from 1809 until Promoted to A Majority in that Service in December 1813 – Remained in Portugueze Service (on the Staff) until removed from it at the Revolution of 1820.' *Battles, sieges and campaigns*: 'Action at Albeigana 10th May 1809. Action at Grijo 11th May 1809. Passage of the Dourou. May 1809. Capture of Coimbre 1810, 1811 – and 1812. Employed in the South of Portugal with Generals Miller, Wilson and Grant. Siege and Capture of St Sebastian 1813. Passage and Action of the Bidasoa 1813. Action at Bidort 18th November 1813. Battle of the Nivelle 1813. Battle of the Nive 9th 10th 11th 12th and 13th December 1813. Blockade of Bayonne and Action at St Eltimo. Battle of Toulouse 18th April 1814. In the Actions of Albeigana, Grijo, and Passage of the Dourou in May 1809 Captain 16th Portuguese Regt. In the Remainder on the Staff A.D.C. to Major General Sir John Wilson untill he was Severely wounded in the Action 18th Novr. 1813. At Brevet at the Battle of Toulouse in Commnd of the 23rd Regiment Portugueze.' *Distinguished conduct*: 'Promoted with Field to A Majority in the Portugueze Service By Marshall Lord Beresford For my Services at the Battle of the Nive 9th 10th 11th 12th and 13th December 1813. Mentioned in General Orders on this occasion. In Command of the 23rd Portugueze Regt. at the Battle of Toulouse 10th April 1814 And Noticed in General Orders on this occasion.' *Wounds received in action*: 'Slightly wounded at the Battle of Bidort 18th November 1813. Slightly wounded again at the Battle of the Nive on the 10th December 1813. No Grant of Pay Received.' *Service abroad*: 'December 1808 until December 1830,

421

Spain, Portugal, France, Cape of Good Hope, India.' Unmarried as of 1830. [PRO: WO 25/786 f15]. Bvt. Major, 6th Foot, 10 Jan. 1837. MGS.

MURRAY, George Home, Capt./ Major, 16th Light Dragoons: *1829 Statement of Service*: Born 25 May 1777, 'Mid Lothian'. Aged twenty-three on first appointment to the Army. Ensign, 92nd Foot, 1800; Lt., 53rd Foot, 1800; Lt., 16th Light Dragoons, 1800; Capt., 16th Light Dragoons, 6 Nov. 1806; Bvt. Major, 16th Light Dragoons, 18 Feb. 1813; Bvt. Lt. Col., 16th Light Dragoons, 18 June 1815; Lt. Col., 16th Lancers, 1822; 'Brigadier 1825; Colonel 5 June 1829'. *Battles, sieges and campaigns*: '1809. Served this Campaign in Portugal as Captain commanding a Squadron in 16th Lt. Dns. was in all the affairs before and after crossing the Duoro in the North of Portugal... Commanded a squadron at the Battle of Talavera... 1810. Served this Campaign in the Peninsula – present at the Battle of Bussaco... 1811. Served this Campaign in the Peninsula present at the investment of Cuidad Rodrigo... 1812. Served this Campaign in Spain – 11th April commanded the 16th Lt. Drgns. at the General cavalry affair at Llerena South of Spain... 18th July commanded the 16th Lt. Drgns at the general cavalry affair at Castrahon ... 22nd July commanded the 16th Lt. Dragoons at the Battle of Salamanca. 1813. Served this campaign in the Peninsula. 21 June second in command of the 16th Lt. Drgns at the Battle of Vittoria. 1814. Served this Campaign in the Peninsula – commanded three Troops of the 16th Light Dragoons detached at the Battle of Nive. 1815. Served this Campaign in the Netherlands & France – 18th June commanded the 16th Light Dragoons at the Battle of Waterloo. 1825 & 1826. Commanded a Brigade of Cavalry and Horse Artillery at the Seige of Bhurtpore.' *Distinguished conduct*:

'1810. Oct. 5th. Was complimented in Cavalry Division Orders with 2 Squadrons of the 16th Lt. dragoons under his command for their conduct at Rio de Maudaville near Lyrea Portugal... Oct. 9th Noticed in General Orders in consequence of the gallant conduct of a squadron of the 16th Lt. Dragoons under his command at Alcuentra, Portugal... 1811. Jany. 24th. Had the conduct of three Troops of the 16th Lt. Dragoons detached at Reo Maior, which with 1 squadron of the 1st German Hussars opposed a large force of French Cavalry in reconnoissance under the Duc D'Abrautes who in this affair was grievously wounded and forced to retire. April 7. Was ordered by Major Genl. Slade to charge with his squadron the rear guard (formed in rallying square) a French Force retiring from the Fortress of Almeida, where 1 officer and 50 men were taken prisoners the rest cut to pieces... 1812. April 11th. Commanded the 16th Lt. Dragoons at the Cavalry Affair at llerena, South of Spain, and recommended in the dispatch... July 18th. Commanded the 16th Light Dragoons at the General Affair at Castrahon, many casualties in the Regiment. July 22nd. Commanded the 16th Light Dragoons at the Battle of Salamanca... July 23rd. Commanded the 16th Lt. dragoons in consort with the 11th Light Dragoons when an attack was made upon the enemy's retiring column when about 700 cavalry and infantry and a large quantity of cattle were taken... Oct. 22nd. Commanded a squadron of the 16th Dragoons on the first days retreat from Burgos when attacked by a superior force of Cavalry and Infantry, was complimented by Sir S. Cotton on the Field and ordered to thank his men for their intrepid conduct. Had many valuable men & horses killed of his squadron in this affair... 1825. Dec. 10th. Commanded a Brigade of Cavalry and Horse Artillery in a reconnoissance

MURRAY

upon the Fortress of Bhurtpore, surprised the Enemy encampment, drove him into the place, intercepting and killing about 90 of the enemy. Dec. 29th. The Enemy in considerable Force of Cavalry & Infantry endeavoured to cut their way thro' his Brigade. They were repulsed by HM 16th Lancers and 9th Light Cavalry leaving 30 men dead on the Field and 150 Prisoner. The Brigade thanked in Cavalry Division Orders. 1826. Jany. 18. Commanded a Brigade of Cavalry and Artillery at the Assault of Bhurtpore when about three thousand of the enemys fugitives, the usurper himself, were captured and cut up. Recommended in General Orders.' *Wounds received in action*: '1810. Septr. 25th, Wounded in the thigh by a musket when skirmishing and covering the Light Infantry retiring upon the position of Busacco... Oct. 5th, Wounded by a sabre in a mellee of Cavalry at the Rio de Maudarville near Lyria in Portugal. 1812. Oct. 23rd., Wounded by a Lance in an affair of Cavalry in the retreat from Burgos. 1813. Received one year's Pay in compenstion for the above wounds by order of the Medical Board.' *Titles, honorary distinctions and medals*: '1812. July 22nd. Medal conferred as commanding the 16th Lt. Drags. at the Battle of Salamanca. 1815. June 18th. Companion of the Bath, a Medal of Waterloo, as Commanding 16th Lt. Dragoons at Waterloo.' *Service abroad*: '1809 to 1814, Portugal, Spain, France. 1815, Netherlands and France. 1822 to 1829, Bengal, India.' [PRO: WO 25/784 f250]. Mentioned in Cotton's Llerena dispatch, 11 April 1812 ['I have great pleasure in assuring you of the good conduct of ... Captain Murray, commanding 16th light dragoons'] [*London Gazette*]. Wounded, during 'movements of the Army' [Retreat from Burgos], 23 Oct. 1812 [*London Gazette*]. Gold Medal (Salamanca). Waterloo. *Dalton*, pp. 86, 87 ['Made bt.-lt.-col.

and C.B. for Waterloo... D. at Cawnpore 15th Dec., 1833, whilst in command of above regt. and holding the rank of brig.-gen. at that station.'].

+MURRAY, James, Lt., 20th Foot: Ensign, 20th Foot, 19 Dec. 1811. Severely wounded, Orthes, 27 Feb. 1814 ('Lieutenant') [*London Gazette*]. Died of wounds, 7 March 1814. Return dated March 1814. [PRO: WO 25/2965]. *Hurt*, p. 76 ['Lt. J. Murray, D.O.W., Orthez, Mar. 7'].

MURRAY, James Patrick, Major, 66th Foot: *1829 Statement of Service for Retired Officers*: Aged 'fifteen years & nine months' on first appointment to the Army. Ensign, 44th Foot, 10 Nov. 1797; Lt., 44th Foot, 16 March 1798; 'Captain-Lieutenant', 9th Foot, 25 Dec. 1799; Half-pay, 25 Feb. 1802, by reduction; Capt., 66th Foot, July 1803; Major, 66th Foot, Feb. 1804 [Army List gives 9 Feb.]; Lt. Col., 66th Foot, 25 May 1809; Lt. Col., 5th Garrison Battn., 2 Nov. 1809; Half-pay, 6 Feb. 1815, by reduction; Bvt. Colonel, 12 Aug. 1819. 'I was on the Staff as an Assistant Adjutant General at Athlone in Ireland from February 1811 to the 24th August 1809. I was exchanged into the 5th Garrison Battalion at my own request, as my health had suffered so much from long confinement in consequence of my severe wound, that I was rendered unfit for Active Service in the Field.' *Where serving when wounded*: 'Major Commanding the 2d Battn. 66th Regiment of Foot, at the Battle of the Douro near Oporto, in Portugal, on the 12th of May 1809.' *Details of pension*: 'The first grant of the Pension for the loss of the use of my right arm, by a gun shot wound, was for £250 per annum but I do not recollect the date of the commencement of it & have mislaid the notificatin of it. The Pension was encreased to £300 per annum from the 18th June 1815'. *Family*: Married in Fresh-water Church, Isle of Wight, 31 Jan. 1803. Had twelve children, 'all living', by 1829. No employment. *Where generally resident during last five years*: 'Killimeure House near Athlone Ireland.' [PRO: WO 25/768 f254]. Severely wounded in the arm, passage of the Douro, 12 May 1809 (2nd Battn.) [*London Gazette*]. *1818 Pension Return*, pp. 16–17.

MURRAY, John, Capt., 20th Foot: Capt., 20th Foot, 31 Oct. 1806. Slightly wounded, storming of San Sebastian, 31 Aug. 1813 ('Detachment 20th Regiment') [*London Gazette*]. Slightly wounded, Pyrenees, 28 July 1813 [*London Gazette*]. Bvt. Major, 20th Foot, 21 Sept. 1813. Severely wounded, Orthes, 27 Feb. 1814 [*London Gazette*]. Major, 20th Foot, 30 March 1814. Pension of two hundred pounds per annum, commencing 28 Feb. 1815, 'for wounds' received at Orthes, 1814 [*1818 Pension Return*, pp. 6–7].

MURRAY, Hon. Richard, Capt., 5th Foot: *1829 Statement of Service*: 'Born in Liverpool, 19 October 1787. Aged 14 on his first Entrance into the Army. Ensign, 38th Foot, March 1801, By Volunteer from Manx Fencibles. Lieutenant, 38th, Half Pay, 1802. Lieutenant, 50th, 1805. Captain, 5th, 18 Apl. 1805. Capt., 5th, Half Pay, 18 June 1813, By report of the Medical board for injuries sustained in the Battle of Salamanca. Captain, 58th Foot, 26 May 1825. Brevet Major 12 Augt. 1819. Major, unattached, Half Pay, 11 May 1826. Major, 54th, 10 July 1828. Lt. Colonel, 54th, 25 Oct. 1829.' Note added: 'Half Pay 1 Feb. 1831'. *Battles, sieges and campaigns*: 'Expedition to Copenhagen 1807. Aid de Camp to Lt Gen Sir David Baird... Walcheren Expedition & Siege of Flushing as Capt. in the Fifth Foot... Capt. 5 foot in Spain. Battle of Salamanca.' *Wounds received in action*:

'Pension of £100 a year for four years and one years pay for injuries sustained in the Battle of Salamanca 22 July 1812.' *Service abroad*: '1 Augt. 1807 to November 1807, Copenhagen. 18 Jany. 1809 to March 1809, Portugal. July 1809 to Augt. 1809, Walcheren. May 1812 to Dec. 1812, Peninsula. Feby 1829 to 31 Dec. 1829, India.' *Family*: He married his first wife, Catherine Bacon, in April 1811, on the Isle of Man. They had three children prior to her death in 1817. He remarried, Margaret Tinison, in April 1819, also on the Isle of Man. They had one child by 1830. [PRO: WO 25/795 f227].

MURRAY, William, Volunteer: Temporary pension of fifty pounds per annum, commencing 22 June 1814, 'for a wound' received at Vittoria, 1813, while serving as a Volunteer (no regt. given) [*1818 Pension Return*, pp. 24–5].

+MUTER, James, Lt. Col., 3rd Foot: Lt. Col., 3rd Foot, 1 Dec. 1804. Severely wounded, 'since dead', Talavera, 28 July 1809 [*London Gazette*].

MUTER, Robert, Lt., 7th Foot: *1829 Statement of Service for Retired Officers*: Aged eighteen on first appointment to the Army. Ensign, 7th Foot, 4 March 1807; Lt., 7th Foot, 3 March 1808; Capt., 7th Foot, 27 May 1819; Half-pay, Dec. 1821, by reduction. *Where serving when wounded*: 'Severely wounded at Talavera 28th day of July 1809'. No pension. *Family*: Married in St Peter's Church, Dublin, 7 Jan. 1820. Six children by 1829. No employment. *Where generally resident during last five years*: 'Principally Isle of Man'. [PRO: WO 25/768 f247]. Severely wounded, Talavera, 28 July 1809 [*London Gazette*].

+MYERS, John, Lt., 57th Foot: Lt., 57th Foot, 24 May 1810. Slightly wounded, Albuera, 16 May 1811

[*London Gazette*]. Severely wounded, the Nive, 13 Dec. 1813 ('J. Meyers') (1st Battn.) [*London Gazette*]. Died of wounds, 23 Jan. 1814. Return dated Feb. 1814. [PRO: WO 25/2965].

+**MYERS, William James, Lt. Col., 7th Foot:** Lt. Col., Army, 24 May 1802; Lt. Col., 7th Foot, 15 Aug. 1804. Severely wounded, Albuera, 16 May 1811, 'since dead' [*London Gazette*]. Died of wounds, 17 May 1811. Return dated 25 May 1811 ('Myers, Sir Will. Bt.') [PRO: WO 25/2965]. Obituary, *The Gentleman's Magazine*, July 1811, p. 88 ['May 16. Of the wounds received at the battle of Albuera, aged 27, Sir Wm. James Myers, bart. Lieut.-col. of the 7th regiment of foot. He was born Nov. 27, 1783, succeeded his father, Sir William, in 1805, and deceased unmarried the baronetage becomes extinct. He was the only son of Sir William, 1st Baronet, Lieut.-gen. in the army ... [who] was created a baronet of Great Britain in 1801, which honour has become extinct in his only son, Sir William James, 2d baronet']. *Cooper*, pp. 21–2 [Talavera, 28 July 1809: 'We instantly retired upon our regiment, which sprung up and met the enemy on the rising ground, but our men being all raw soldiers, staggered for a moment under such a rolling fire. Our colonel Sir William Myers seeing this, sprang from his horse and snatching one of the colours, cried "Come on Fusiliers," 'Twas enough. On rushed the Fusiliers and 53rd regiment and delivered such a fire, that in a few

minutes the enemy melted away'], pp. 35, 36, 60 [Albuhera, 16 May 1811: 'Having arrived at the foot of the hill, we began to climb its slope with panting breath, while the roll and thunder of furious battle increased. Under the tremendous fire of the enemy our thin line staggers, men are knocked about like skittles; but not a step backward is taken. Here our Colonel and all the field-officers of the brigade fell killed or wounded'], p. 62. *Haythornthwaite, Armies of Wellington*, p. 25 ['Sir William Myers, Bt., lieutenant-colonel of the 7th, killed at Albuera at the age of 28, was the grandson of a builder from Whitehaven, whose son under the patronage of Lord Drogheda rose to the rank of lieutenant-general and colonelcy of the 2nd West India Regiment, 1795–1805.']

+**MYLES, John, Adjutant/Lt., 50th Foot:** Adjutant, 50th Foot, 17 Dec. 1807; Lt., 50th Foot, 3 May 1809. Slightly wounded, Pyrenees, 30 July 1813 (1st Battn.) [*London Gazette*]. Severely wounded, 'in Action with the Enemy', 15 Feb. 1814 ('Adjutant') (1st Battn.) [*London Gazette*]. Died of wounds, 16 March 1814. Return dated April 1814. [PRO: WO 25/2965]. *Hurt*, p. 79 ['D.O.W., Gave de Mauleon, Feb. 16'].

MYLNE, Thomas, Capt., 79th Foot: Capt., 79th Foot, 24 April 1805. Severely wounded, Toulouse, 10 April 1814 (1st Battn.) [*London Gazette*]. Wounded, Waterloo. Died, Edinburgh, 1832.

NAGLE, Michael, Volunteer, 1st Portuguese Regt.; Volunteer, 19th Portuguese Regt.; Ensign, 53rd Foot: *1829 Statement of Service*: 'Born Flemmingston, Ireland, 10 Nov. 1793. Aged 19 when he Entered the Army.' Volunteer, 1st Portuguese Regt. and 19th Portuguese Reg Regt., 9 May 1811; Ensign, 53rd Foot, 9 April 1812; Lt., Half Pay by reduction, 25 March 1817; Lt., 47th Foot, 26 Dec. 1822; Qr. Master 4 Nov. 1827. *Battles, sieges and campaigns*: 'Engaged with the Enemy at Aldewdiponde in Sept. 1811 when attached to the first Portuguese Regt... Present at the Seige of Kodre Jan. 1812 when attached to that Portuguese Regiment... Present at the seige of the Fortified Convent at Salamanca July 1812... Present at the Battle of Salamanca... Present at the seige of Burgos 1812... Present with the Army during the whole of the retreat from Burgos to Portugal in the Winter of 1812 and frequently Engaged during that Period... Vittoria... Present at the whole of the skirmishes which took place in the Pyrenees on the 24, 25th & 27 July 1813 also at the Battle of Pampeluna... and Engaged with the Enemy on the 1st & 2nd Aug. 1813 during the Retreat. Present at the carrying of the Enemy's Position in Front of Mount Marieal on the 7 & 8 Aug. 1813. Present at the Action which was fought on the 31 Aug. 1813 in front of St Sebastian. Present at the Battle of Nivelle which took place 10 Nov. 1813 the day the British Army entered France ... Toulouse... NB. I was present at several skirmishes in which the 2nd Battn. 53rd Regt. was engaged during the above campaigns, but too numerous to mention... Commanded a Division of Gun Boats on the Irrawaddy in the Burmese Empire also engaged with the Enemy on the 1st 2nd & 5th Dec. 1825'. *Distinguished conduct*: 'On the advance for Vittoria in June 1813 I was attached with a Party of Men from the 4th Division to the right of the column for the purpose of protecting the Inhabitants from some small parties of the Enemy who were plundering the Villages when I fell in with & after some smart resistance, succeeded in capturing the principal part of them; and for which service I was mentioned, and returned thanks in Division Orders by Lieut. General Sir Lowney Cole who then commanded the 4th Division to which I belonged. Returned thanks by the late Commodore Sir James Brisbane for my service whilst in command of the 1st Division Gun Boats on the Irawaddy and mentioned in his Despatches for the action of the 1–2 and 5 Decr 1825.' *Wounds received in action*: 'Wounded at the seige of Burgos and recd One years pay for it. Received a contusion on the right leg from a spent Musquet Ball at the Battle of Salamanca which leaves a mark 22d July 1812. Received a Ball through my Sash which lodged between my shirt and stomach at the Battle of Pampeluna 28th July 1813 received no pay for it.' *Service abroad*: '9 May 1811–19 Aug. 1814 – Peninsula; 1 Aug. 1815–2 Dec. 1816 – At St Helena with Buonaparte; 2 June 1823–29 Jan. 1829 – East Indies; 15 Oct. 1834–8 Feb. 1841 – Mediterranean'. *Family*: Married Miss Emma Valentine in Portsmouth, 30 July 1815. Five children by 1830. He is recorded as having 'Died of consumption at Malta, 8 Feby. 1841.' [PRO: WO 76/186 f13; WO 25/794 f151]. Slightly wounded, 'in the assault and capture of the exterior line of the castle of Burgos on the evening of the 4th October,

1812.' (2nd Battn. 53rd Foot)
[*London Gazette*].

**NAIRN, James Mellis D., Ensign,
94th Foot:** Ensign, 94th Foot, 16
April 1812. Severely wounded,
Vittoria, 21 June 1813 ('Nairne')
[*London Gazette*]. MGS.

NANTES, Richard, Lt., 7th Foot:
*1829 Statement of Service for
Retired Officers*: Aged 'between 15
& 16' on first appointment to the
Army. Lt., 7th Foot, 19 Oct. 1809,
'By presentation when at the Royal
Military College, Great Marlow, and
at least in a great measure thro' the
interest of a relative, M. General Sir
Thos. Pritzen now serving in India';
Half-pay, 'about the end of Decr.
1814', 'in consequence ... of a constitution impaired by Wounds & sickness'. 'Besides serving in the
situation of a Subaltern at Ciudad
Rodrigo, Orthes &c, a Company
had been commanded at the action
of Castrajon, at the Battles of Salamanca and Toulouse, and at other
times.' *Where serving when
wounded*: 'Castrajon, Salamanca, &
Vittoria'. 'No pension, tho' such
might have been had for one
Wound, a compound fracture of the
right arm, which for more than 9
years caused great suffering, but
money at that period was no object,
& a second application before the
Medical Board as directed did not
therefore follow, a Hundred Pounds
however had been awarded on the
first occasion which rather more
than covered some particular
expences incidental to a necessary
return to England &c in consequence of the Wound in question.'
Family: Married in Camberwell,
Surrey, 7 Sept. 1815, 'but became a
Widower Octr. 22nd 1828.' Two children before his wife's death. No
employment. *Where generally resident during last five years*: 'Exeter,
Plymouth, and Shilston ... Devonshire'. [PRO: WO 25/769 f3]. Slightly
wounded, Salamanca, 18 July 1812
[*London Gazette*]. Slightly wounded, Salamanca, 22 July 1812
[*London Gazette*]. Slightly wounded, Orthes, 27 Feb. 1814 (1st Battn.)
[*London Gazette*]. MGS.

**+NAPIER, Alexander, Lt. Col.,
92nd Foot:** Lt. Col., 92nd Foot, 5
April 1801. Killed, 'in the Army
lately in Spain' (1st Battn.) [*March
1809 Army List*, p. 105].

**NAPIER, Charles, Capt., Royal
Navy:** Born, 6 March 1786. Brother
of Thomas Erskine Napier of the
Chasseurs Britanniques. Entered
the Navy, 1 Nov. 1799; Lt., Royal
Navy, 30 Nov. 1805; Commander,
Royal Navy, 20 Nov. 1807; Captain,
Royal Navy, 22 May 1809. An officer
of great courage with a distinguished and lengthy career, he was
created a K.C.B, 4 Dec. 1840, and
promoted to Rear-Admiral of the
Blue, 19 May 1847. *Kincaid,
Random Shots*, p. 140 [Busaco, 27
Sept. 1810: 'the naval captain, (the
present admiral of that name,) was
there as an amateur, and unfortunately caught it on a spot where he
had the last wish to be distinguished, for, accustomed to face
broadsides on his native element,
he had no idea of taking a ball in
any other direction than from the
front, but on the shore we were
obliged to take them just as they
came!' *Bruce*, p. 55 [Busaco:
'another member of the family, his
cousin Charles Napier [Afterwards
Admiral Sir Charles Napier, K.C.B.],
was shot in the knee.']. For a
detailed biography see William R.
O'Byrne, *A Naval Biographical
Dictionary* (1849), pp. 802–4
['During the interval which elapsed
between his leaving the JASON and
his appointment to the THAMES,
Capt. Napier served a campaign
with the army in Portugal, as a
volunteer, and was again wounded.
He was present at the battle of
Busaco.']. He was cousin to the
military Napiers, Charles James,
George and William. Regarding his
wound at Busaco: he had borrowed

a very conspicuous white pony from his cousin, George, 'notwithstanding I told him it was very foolish for most certainly he would get hit, being the only person on horseback ... in less than half an hour he got a shot in the calf of his leg, but very slightly; and I was delighted at it, the obstinate dog, he deserved it well! ... he was very good-humoured and laughed as much as anyone at his own folly' [*Passages in the Early Military Life of General Sir George T. Napier*, ed. Gen. W. C. E. Napier (London, 1884) p. 147]. Napier, Maj. Gen. E., *Life and Correspondence of Admiral Sir Charles Napier* (London, 1862).

NAPIER, Charles James, Major, 50th Foot: One of the great heroes of the British Army, conquerer of Sind, brother of George Thomas and Sir William Francis Patrick Napier. Major, Army, 29 May 1806; Major, 50th Foot, 6 Nov. 1806. *Regimental Pay List*, 1st Battn., 25 Dec. 1808–24 March 1809: 'Pris. of War.' [PRO: WO 12/6113]. *Monthly Return*, 1st Battn., dated 25 April 1809: 'Prisoner of War, now on Parole in England' [PRO: WO 17/164]. Severely wounded, Busaco, 27 Sept. 1810 (1st Battn.) [*London Gazette*]. Gold Medal. Pension of three hundred pounds per annum, commencing 25 Dec. 1811, for wounds received at Corunna, 1809, and Busaco, 1810 [*1818 Pension Return*, pp. 14–15]. MGS. *Blakeney*, p. 121 [Battle of Corunna: 'Sir John Moore made straight for the village of Elvina, where the fight continued to be most bloody and most obstinately maintained. It had been repeatedly taken and retaken at the point of the bayonet. Just as the Commander of the forces arrived, the 50th Regiment, who were formed on the left of the village, commanded by Major Napier, and seconded by Major Stanhope, made a most desperate charge through the village; but Napier's impetuosity carrying him forward through some stone walls beyond the village, he was desperately wounded, and fell into the hands of the enemy; and Major Stanhope was killed. The general cheered the regiment during this charge, crying out, "Bravo, 50th, and my two brave majors!" ']. *Harris*, pp. 49–50 ['I remember meeting with General Napier before the battle of Vimeiro. He was then, I think, a major; and the meeting made so great an impression on me, that I have never forgotten him. I was posted in a wood the night before the battle, in the front of our army, where two roads crossed each other. The night was gloomy, and I was the very out-sentry of the British army. As I stood on my post, peering into the thick wood around me, I was aware of footsteps approaching and challenged in a low voice. Receiving no answer, I brought my rifle up to port, and bade the strangers come forward. They were Major Napier (then of the 50th foot, I think), and an officer of the Rifles. The major advanced close up to me, and looked hard in my face. "Be alert here, sentry," said he, "for I expect the enemy upon us to-night, and I know not how soon." I was a young soldier then, and the lonely situation I was in, together with the impressive manner in which Major Napier delivered his caution, made a great impression on me, and from that hour I have never forgotten him.']. *Rice Jones*, p. 58 ['July 16th [1810] [Almeida]... I walked around the works. Breakfasted at the Governor's and met Major Napier of the 50th Regt.; he went with a Flag of truce to Gallegos yesterday and saw General Loison there; he says Lord Wellington will not fight a battle to relieve Almeida.']. *Brett-James*, pp. 36, 48, 87 [Quotes a letter from Charles Napier to his mother, 21 March 1811: 'I make no apologies for the dirt of this note; for flead, bugged, centipeded, beetled, lizarded and earwigged, cleanliness is known to me only by name. Moreover a furze-bush makes a bad table for writing on, and a worse chair, when breeches are nearly worn out with glory, oh! oh!'], p. 110 [Napier to his mother, April 1811: 'We are on biscuits full of maggots, and though not a bad soldier, hang me if I can relish maggots.'], p. 182 ['Another "forced ride" was made by Charles Napier who, while recovering from a serious wound in Lisbon, heard that the French were retreating northwards from the Lines of Torres Vedras. Although his wound was still open, he rode all one night and having covered ninety-two miles with only one halt, he overtook the British army between Redinha and Condeixa.'], p. 262 ['When Charles Napier was wounded at Busaco, a musket ball entered one side of his nose, passed through, and lodged in the jawbone on the opposite side. It was extracted with great difficulty, a large part of the jaw coming away with the ball, as well as several teeth. During this long and painful operation Napier never uttered a word or winced while under the surgeon's hands, indeed, this surgeon told George Napier that he had never seen anyone beat pain so patiently and so manfully.']. Henry Hardinge commented: 'in his whole conduct there was displayed every quality which could adorn public and private life: bravery, humanity, and Christian feeling' [*Colburne's United Service Magazine*, 1844, I, p. 459]. Bruce, W. N., *Life of General Sir Charles Napier* (London, 1855); Lawrence, Lady Rosamond, *Charles Napier, Friend and Fighter* (London, 1952); Napier, Sir William, *Life and Opinions of General Sir Charles James Napier* (London, 1857).

NAPIER, George Thomas, Capt./ Major, 52nd Foot: *1829 Statement of Service for Retired Officers*: Aged 'fifteen & six months' on first appointment to the Army. Cornet, 24th Light Dragoons, 4 Jan. 1800; Lt., 46th Foot, 18 June 1800; Lt., 52nd Foot, 25 Dec. 1802; Capt., 52nd Foot, 5 Jan. 1804; Bvt. Major, 52nd Foot, 30 May 1811; Major, 52nd Foot, 27 June 1811; Bvt. Lt. Col., 6 Feb. 1812; Lt. Col., 71st Foot, 24 March 1814; Capt. and Lt. Col., 3rd Foot Guards, 25 July 1814; Lt. Col., 44th Foot, 22 Feb. 1821; Half-pay, Sicilian Regt., 19 April 1821; A.D.C. to the King, 27 May 1825. *Where serving when wounded*: 'Commg. Storming Party at the assault of Ciudad Rodrigo in Spain. Lost right arm'. *Details of pension*: '19th January 1812 as Major commg. & increased to three hundred per ann. at the date of Lt. Colonelcy 71st Regt. 24th March 1814.' *Family*: Married in Edinburgh, Oct. 1812. 'Widower in August 1819.' Four children prior to his wife's death. *Where generally resident during last five years*: 'Resided in England in the counties of Hertfordshire & Devonshire'. [PRO: WO 25/769 f20]. Slightly wounded, Busaco, 27 Sept. 1810 [*London Gazette*]. Severely wounded, during 'several Affairs with the French Army', 14 March 1811 [*London Gazette*]. Severely wounded, 'right arm amputated', storming of Ciudad Rodrigo, 19 Jan. 1812 [*London Gazette*]. Mentioned in Wellington's Ciudad Rodrigo dispatch, 20 Jan. 1812 ['Our loss was also ... severe... Major George Napier, who led the storming party of the light division, and was wounded on the top of the breach... I particularly request your Lordship's attention to the conduct of ... Major Napier of the 52d'] [*London Gazette*]. Three hundred pounds per annum pension, commencing 20 Jan. 1813, for 'loss of an arm' at Ciudad Rodrigo [*1818 Pension Return*, pp. 14–15]. MGS. *Lawrence*, p. 103 [Ciudad Rodrigo, 19 Jan. 1812]; *Simmons*, p. 223 [badly wounded, Ciudad Rodrigo]. *Leach*, pp. 249–50 [storming of Ciudad Rodrigo, 19 Jan. 1812: 'Major George Napier of the 52d regiment: lost an arm in command of the storming party of the Light Division, consisting of three hundred men of the 43d, 52d, and 95th regiments.']. *Bruce*, p. 77 [Letter from Lieut. Col. Macleod to William Napier, La Encina, 21 Jan. 1812: 'I have just been over to see your brother; he was asleep, and therefore I did not go into his room. Rob and all the surgeons who have attended him say that he is going on well, and that altogether he has supported himself better than anybody they ever saw in the same situation. I was with him yesterday for some time; he talked very composedly, and seemed to have made up his mind to his misfortune... He has covered himself with glory... He was hit by a grape-shot in the arm, the same as he was hit in the time before the two last times he was wounded, and the bone so shattered that the surgeons were all of opinion that it was impossible to save it, and George determined at once to have it amputated, which was done the same evening by Dr. Guthrie who is a clever man, and I have no doubt has performed the operation in a way that will prevent his feeling any inconvenience hereafter.']. *Kincaid, Adventures*, p. 108 [Storming of Ciudad Rodrigo]. *Kincaid, Random Shots*, p. 140 [Casal Nova, 14 March 1811: 'The two brothers [George and William Napier] in our division were badly wounded on this occasion, and, if I remember right, they were also at Busaco']. *Moorsom*, pp. 132–3 [Casal Novo, 14 March 1811: 'Captain William Jones's and Captain George Thomas Napier's companies were the first sent out to force back the enemy's light troops, which were posted behind some stone enclosures ... as the bugles repeated the sound to advance, the companies pressed forward, although engaged against vastly superior forces, and the enemy gave way; but in gaining this first ridge Captains Jones, Napier, and Mein, were wounded.'], p. 427 ['Napier, Lieut.-General Sir George Thomas,

K.C.B. – Entered the 52nd in 1802. Served at the capture of Martinique in 1809, was aide-de-camp to Sir John Moore, and subsequently served in Spain and Portugal at the siege of Ciudad Rodrigo in 1812, on which occasion he commanded the whole of the storming party from the Light Division, and was severely wounded. Sir George afterwards held the high situation of Governor of the Cape of Good Hope.']. *Aitchison*, pp. 55, 141 [Storming of Ciudad Rodrigo: 'At 7 p.m. the signal was given for the advance of the "Forlorn Hope" at the head of each storming party. The assault was made in silence and the breaches carried by the bayonet in the face of heavy fire from the defenders. Following close on the heels of the "Forlorn Hope", and two-thirds of the way up the left-hand breach, George Napier of the 52nd was wounded by a grape shot. Seeing him fall his men checked and began snapping their muskets. Napier called out: "Recollect you are not loaded; push on with the bayonet!" upon which they gave a loud Hurrah! and driving all before them carried the breach.'], pp. 277, 309. Brother to Charles James and William Francis Patrick Napier. Born 1784, died at Geneva in 1855. *Passages in the Early Military Life of General Sir George T. Napier*, ed. Gen. W. C. E. Napier (London, 1884). In this (p. 219) he describes staff-surgeon Guthrie's operation to amputate his arm, noting that his 'instruments were blunted, so it was a long time before the thing was finished, at least twenty minutes, and the pain was great. I then thanked him for his kindness, having sworn at him like a trooper while he was at it, to his great amusement, and I proceeded to find some place to lie down and rest'.

NAPIER, Thomas Erskine, Capt., Chasseurs Britanniques: *1829 Statement of Service for Retired*

Officers: Aged sixteen on first appointment to the Army. Ensign, 52nd Foot, 3 July 1805; Lt., 52nd Foot, 1 May 1806; Capt., Chasseurs Britanniques, 27 Oct. 1808; Bvt. Major, 26 Dec. 1813; Half-pay, by reduction; Bvt. Lt. Col., half-pay, 21 June 1817. Served nine years on full-pay. *Where serving when wounded*: 'In France as A.D.C. to the Earl of Hopetown.' *Details of pension*: Three hundred pounds, commencing 21 June 1817. *Family*: Married in Edinburgh, 19 Dec. 1820. One child by 1829. *Where generally resident during last five years*: 'Woodcot, Blackshiells'. [PRO: WO 25/769 f3]. Severely wounded, the Nive, 11 Dec. 1813, while serving as Aide-de Camp to Lieutenant-General Sir John Hope [*London Gazette*]. Major-General, 9 Nov. 1846. CB. MGS. *Wheeler*, p. 68 [Sept. 1811: 'Colonel Custis and Captain Napier are the only British in the Regiment.']. *Bruce*, p. 161 [Nive, Dec. 1813: '[William Napier's] cousin Tom Napier, who was on Sir John Hope's staff, lost his arm in this action... ("Lieutenant-General Thomas Napier, C.B.")'], p. 165 [Letter from William Napier to his wife, dated Arbonne, 14 Dec. 1813: 'Tom Napier is hit rather badly, his arm broke near the elbow, not in two, but the bone splintered; he will not lose it, however. I hope I have not been mistaken for him.'], p. 166 [Napier to his wife, Arbonne, 25 Dec. 1813: 'Poor Tom Napier has lost his arm, his left, above the elbow, but is doing as well as possible and is to get the brevet.'], 167 [Napier to his wife, dated 9 Jan. 1814: 'Send me, or buy at least, and keep till further orders, a knife and fork like George's. I want to buy one for Tom Napier; it is a silver fork with a cutting edge on the side for one-armed people.' Napier to his wife, Arauntz, 15 Jan. 1814: 'Tom Napier goes home shortly, and you must have a knife like George's ready for him when he calls upon you.']. Brother of Rear-Admiral

Charles Napier. Born 1790, rose to the rank of General, became Sir Thomas, died 1863. [*Burke's Peerage*].

NAPIER, William Francis Patrick, Capt., 43rd Regt: The great historian of the Peninsular War. *1829 Statement of Service for Retired Officers*: Aged fifteen on first appointment to the Army. 2nd Lt., Royal Irish Artillery, 1800; Lt., 62nd Foot, 1801; Half-pay, 1802; Cornet, Royal Horse Guards, 1803; Lt., 52nd Foot, 1804; Capt., 2nd West India Regt., 1804 [Army List gives 2 June]; Capt., '3rd Bn. of Army of Reserve', 1804; Capt., 43rd Foot, 1804 [Army List gives 11 Aug.]; 'Aide de Camp to the Lord Lieutenant of Ireland', 1809, 'never served this appointm. my regt. being in Spain'; 'Brigade Major Lt. Division', 1811, 'senior captain in ye. Brigade'; Bvt. Major, 43rd Foot, 1811, 'By good service during Massena's retreat'; Major, 43rd Foot, 1812, 'seniority'; Bvt. Lt. Col., 43rd Foot, 1813, 'By good service in the comd. of a Regt. at the Battles of Salamanca, Vera and the Nivelle.' *Where serving when wounded*: 'Three wounds. 1st At the Coa. 2d Miranda de Corvo. 3d Battle of the Nive'. No pension. *Family*: Married in Kensington, 14 March 1812. Ten children by 1829, though two had died. *Where generally resident during last five years*: 'London, Wiltshire'. [PRO: WO 25/769 f6]. Slightly wounded, Coa, 24 July 1810 [*London Gazette*]. Severely wounded, during 'several Affairs with the French Army', 14 March 1811 [*London Gazette*]. Gold Medal. MGS. Author of *History of the War in the Peninsula, and in the South of France from ... 1807 to ... 1814*, 6 vols (London, 1828–40). Biography of him, published in 1864 (2 vols), *Life of General Sir William Napier, K.C.B.*... Edited By H. A. Bruce, MP. *Bruce*, p. 1 ['Born at Celbridge, on the 17th of December, 1785, William Francis Patrick

Napier. Died at Clapham Park, on the 12th February, 1860, General Sir William F. P. Napier, K.C.B., Colonel of the 22nd Regiment, aged 74. The interval represents the life of a man of genius.']. *Simmons*, pp. 78–9 [wounded, 'in the side', Coa, 24 July 1810]. *Kincaid, Random Shots*, p. 139 [Casal Nova, 14 March 1811: 'When the shower [French shooting] ceased we found that they had also ceased to hold their formidable post, and, as quickly as may be, we were to be seen standing in their old shoes, mixed up with some of the forty-third, and among them the gallant Napier, the present historian of the Peninsular War, who there got a ball through his body which seemed to me to have reduced the remainder of his personal history to the compass of a simple paragraph: it nevertheless kept him but a very short while in the back-ground. I may here remark that the members of that distinguished family were singularly unfortunate in that way, as they were rarely ever in any serious action in which one or all of them did not get hit. The two brothers in our division [William and George] were badly wounded on this occasion, and, if I remember right, they were also at Busaco']. *Moorsom*, pp. 427–8 ['Napier, Lieut.-General Sir William F.P., K.C.B. – Entered the 52nd from the Royal Horse Guards in 1803, when the 52nd was forming as Light Infantry, and in 1804 he was promoted to a company in the 43rd Light Infantry. He served in the expedition to Copenhagen and action of Kioge, in the campaigns of 1808 and 1809 under Sir John Moore; in the subsequent Peninsular campaigns from 1809 till the end of the way in 1814, and was present at the action of the Coa, the battle of Busaco, the affairs during Massena's retreat, (and severely wounded at Casal Nova at the head of six companies supporting the 52nd,) the battles of Fuentes d'Onor, Salamanca, the Nivelle, the

Nive, and Orthes, and the intermediate affairs. He served also in the campaign of 1815. Sir William has received the Gold Medal and two clasps for Salamanca, Nivelle, and Nive, where he commanded the 43rd, and he has received the silver war-medal with three clasps for Busaco, Fuentes d'Onor, and Orthes. Sir William's admirable history of the Peninsular war is well known to the world.']. *Bruce*, p. 55 [Action on the Coa, 24 July 1810: 'Captain Napier was shot through the left hip towards the end of the action, but fortunately the bone, though injured, was not broken, and, although suffering considerably, he continued with his regiment until the battle of Busaco'], p. 56 [Cazal Noval: 'in his own words:– "... I had not made ten paces when a shot struck my spine, and the enemy very ungenerously continued to fire at me when I was down. I escaped death by dragging myself by my hands – for my lower extremities were paralyzed – towards a small heap of stones which was in the midst of the field, and thus covering my head and shoulders." '], p. 60 ['Major William Napier was, on rejoining the army with his wound still open and with a musket-bullet never extracted lodged near his spine, appointed brigade-major to the Portuguese brigade of the light division; he was present in that capacity at the battle of Fuentes Onoro, and until, after the raising of the second siege of Badajos, a fever he had caught in the Caya river attacked him... Ill as he was, he would not quit the army until Lord Wellington specially ordered him to do so, and sent his brother to carry him down to Lisbon... From Lisbon he was sent to England in the autumn of 1811; and in the spring of the following year he married Caroline Amelia, daughter of General the Honourable Henry Fox'], p. 114 [Dec. 1812: 'Major Napier obtained leave to go to England... He was at this time suffering severely from ... the commencement of neuralgic pains, caused by the bullet which had passed round his spine, fracturing one of the processes in its course, and which continued to lie near it during the remainder of his life, creating at times intolerable anguish.'], p. 128 ['Major Napier went to England in January 1813. He remained at home till the following August, when ... he returned to the Peninsula.'], pp. 160–1 [Arcangues, 10 Dec. 1813: 'Here he was twice wounded, once by a musket-ball in the right-hip, again by the explosion of a shell which drove his telescope against his face. He did not however quit the field, and defended the church and churchyard until the 13th, when the fighting terminated... Although his wound in the hip was not healed for six weeks, he did not return his name among the list of wounded, because he was fearful of alarming his wife who was on the point of being confined.'], p. 165 [Napier to his wife, dated Arbonne, 14 Dec. 1813: 'I was slightly wounded in the hip, a ball having glanced from a graveyard and struck me there. I would not return myself for fear of alarming you; but I assure you it is no more than what I say.'].

NASH, Henry, Ensign, 9th Foot: *1829 Statement of Service for Retired Officers*: Aged twenty-four on first appointment to the Army. Ensign, 9th Foot, 29 Oct. 1812; Lt., 9th Foot, 28 April 1814; Half-pay, 13 April 1817, by reduction. *Where serving when wounded*: 'severely wounded crossing the Biddasoa in the Right thigh'. No pension. *Family*: Married in the City of Cork, 23 Nov. 1826. One child by 1829. No employment. *Where generally resident during last five years*: 'City of Cork'. [PRO: WO 25/769 f10]. Severely wounded, Crossing the Bidassoa, 7/9 Oct. 1813 (1st Battn.) [*London Gazette*].

+NASON, John, Lt., 43rd Foot: Lt., 43rd Foot, 19 Oct. 1809. Killed, Coa, 24 July 1810 ('Nison') [*London Gazette*].

NASON, John Robert, Ensign/Lt., 47th Foot: Ensign, 47th Foot, 10 May 1810. Slightly wounded, in the siege of San Sebastian, 10 Aug. 1813 ('Lieutenant') (2nd Battn.) [*London Gazette*]. Severely wounded, storming of San Sebastian, 31 Aug. 1813 ('Lieutenant') (2nd Battn.) [*London Gazette*]. MGS.

NASSAU, Ludwig von, Capt., Duke of Oels' Corps (nfantry): Capt., Duke of Brunswick Oels' Corps, Infantry, 25 Sept. 1809. Wounded, during 'movements of the Army' [Retreat from Burgos: Villa Muriel], 25 Oct. 1812 [*London Gazette*].

NELSON, John Clark, Lt., 28th Foot: *1829 Statement of Service for Retired Officers*: Aged eighteen on first appointment to the Army. Ensign, 10th Foot, 4 Feb. 1808; 'resigned the 10th of April 1810'; Ensign, 28th Foot, 16 May 1811; Lt., 25 Aug. 1813; Half-pay, 28 May 1814, 'In consequence of a spitting of Blood from a wound through the lungs'. 'Not able to serve from a wound through the lungs and an injury in the knee'. *Where serving when wounded*: 'Bayonne'. *Details of pension*: Seventy pounds, commencing 13 Dec. 1814. *Family*: Married in St Peter's Church, Dublin, 19 June 1811. *Where generally resident during last five years*: 'Rathangan, Ireland'. [PRO: WO 25/769 f28]. Severely wounded, the Nive, 13 Dec. 1813 ('J. Clarke Nelson') (1st Battn.) [*London Gazette*]. MGS.

NEPEAN, William, Lt., 16th Light Dragoons: Cornet, 16th Light Dragoons, 11 July 1811. Lt., 16th Light Dragoons, 2 April 1812. Slightly wounded, Nive, 9 Dec. 1813 [*London Gazette*]. Waterloo. MGS. Died, 8 Dec. 1864.

NESTOR

NESTOR, Eugene, Capt., 29th Foot: Capt., 29th Foot, 19 Sept. 1804. Slightly wounded, Albuera, 16 May 1811 [*London Gazette*].

+NETHERY, James, Capt., 27th Foot: Capt., 27th Foot, 2 May 1811. *Register of officers' effects:* Died of wounds, 11 Aug. 1813, Alicante. Single. Effects totalled £6. 11s. 6d. [PRO: WO 25/2963].

NEVILL, Hon. John, 1st Lt., 23rd Foot: 1st Lt., 23rd Foot, 6 April 1809. Severely wounded, Pyrenees, 28 July 1813 ('Nevil') (1st Battn.) [*London Gazette*]. Third son of Henry, 2nd Earl of Abergavenny; born 1789, succeeded as 3rd Earl of Abergavenny 1843, died 1845; took holy orders after his military career. [*Burke's Peerage*].

NEVILLE, Parke Percy, Ensign/Lt., 30th Foot: *1829 Statement of Service:* Born York St., Dublin, 4 April 1794. Aged sixteen on his first entrance into the Army. Ensign, 30th Foot, 29 March 1810; Lt. 17 July 1811; Lt., 13th Light Dragoons, 9 Nov. 1826; Lt. 26th Foot, 14 Oct. 1830; Brevet Capt., in India, 29 March 1825. *Battles, sieges and campaigns:* 'Peninsula: Served part of the campaign of 1810, that of 1811, that of 1812, and to May 1813... At Torres Vedras, Oct. 6th 1810 to 27th March 1811; Engaged in the advance on Massena and Fuentes d'Honour, 3rd & 5th May 1811; Cuidad Rodrigo, 19th Jany. 1812; Salamanca, 22nd July 1812; Burgos to 4th October 1812. Holland: Campaign from December 1813 to April 1814; Engaged before Antwerp & Bergen op Zoom... Netherlands & France: Campaign of 1815, and Battle of Waterloo... India: Campaign of 1818 from 25th of Aug. and in the Mahratta War to the capture of Asseer Ghur 9th Apl. 1819... Attached to H.H. The Nizami troops' in the capture of the Predatory Force in the Deckan, 11th December 1820; with Captain Bissett; served in actions with 2nd & 1 Batt. 30th Regt., & sieges, as Asst. Engineer.' *Distinguished conduct:* 'Assistant Engineer in the Siege and Storm of Badajoz from 29th March to 6th April 1812. Asst. Engineer in the Siege of Burgos from 27th Septr. to 4th Octr. 1812. Asst. Engineer in Holland and the Netherlands, from 1814 to June 1815. In the siege of Asseer Ghur, India, repulsed a night attack with the Picket 17 March 1819. In the Deckan, with His Highness The Nizams Troops in the defeat of a Predatory Force 11 Decr. 1820. Note: During the above services noticed by distinguished officers in comd., Extracts of whose letters with other record, are placed on the back of the statement.' *Wounds received in action:* 'Severely, in the head and leg, at Badajoz, while employed as an Asst. Engineer placing Ladders for M. Genl. Sir Walkers Brigade, to Escalade the Bastion of St Vincent on the night of the 6th April 1812. Severely, through the left shoulder, when employed as Asst. Engr. with the 24th Regt. in the Storm of the 1st Line of the Castle of Burgos, on the Evening of the 4th of Octr. 1812. One years pay only received as Lieut.' *Titles, honorary distinctions and medals:* 'The Freedom of the City of Dublin for Badajoz & Burgos, conferred 16 July 1813. Waterloo Medal. Title of Merit granted by His late Highness The Nizam, for the Capture of a Predatory Force in the Deckan 11 Decemr. 1820.' *Service abroad:* 'July 1810 to Aug. 1810, Cadiz. Augt. 1810 to May 1813, Peninsula. Decr. 1813 to Feby. 1816, Holland, Netherlands, & France. Feby. 1818 to 4 Feby. 1831, India.' Not married by 1830. [PRO: WO 25/784 f96]. Note also that there are numerous extracts from letters of recommendation etc. on the reverse of his Statement of Service. For example: 'Be it Remembered, That, At a General Assembly of the Right Honble. The Lord Mayor's,

434

Sheriff's, Commons and Citizens of the City of Dublin, Held at the City Assembly House William St. on Friday the 16th Day of July 1813, The Freedom of the City was unanimously presented to Park P. P. de Neville Esqr., Lieutenant in His Majesty's 30th Regiment of Foot, In Token of Gallant conduct evinced by him upon many occasions, particularly at the Sieges of "Badajoz" and "Burgos"... Memorandum: The "de" is used in the original to denote descent from the Nevilles, formerly Earls of Westmoreland.' Extracts of letters from Col. Burgoyne, Commanding Engineer Dept.: 'I am so sensible of your zeal, spirit, & merits as an officer, that nothing would give me greater pleasure than to see you join the Engr. Depart. at any future siege' [Jan 14, 1814]; 'Your service at the sieges of Badajoz and Burgos was such as to reflect particular credit on yourself and was most beneficial to the service and I have only to express hope that you may get promotion, which is so peculiarly well deserved.' [17 July 1815]. [PRO: WO 25/784 f96]. Slightly wounded, storming of Badajoz, 6 April 1812 (2nd Battn.) [*London Gazette*]. Severely wounded, 'in the assault and capture of the exterior line of the castle of Burgos on the evening of the 4th October, 1812', while serving as Acting Engineer [*London Gazette*]. MGS. Died, Windsor Castle, 6 Feb. 1865.

NEWBOLD, Ambrose, Capt., 29th Foot: Lt., 29th Foot, 9 July 1803. Recorded as 'missing', Rolica, 17 Aug. 1808 [*London Gazette*]. Capt., 29th Foot, 8 June 1809. Slightly wounded, Talavera, 28 July 1809 ('Capt. Newbolt') [*London Gazette*].

NEWMAN, John, Lt., 36th Foot; Capt., 17th Portuguese Regt.: *1829 Statement of Service for Retired Officers*: Aged twenty on first appointment to the Army. Ensign,

36th Foot, July 1806; Lt., 36th Foot, 25 Nov. 1807; Capt., 17th Portuguese Regt., May 1813; Capt., 'In the British Army', Jan. 1815; Half-pay, Portuguese Service, 1818, by reduction. 'Desirous of Service but not able to march.' *Where serving when wounded*: 'Campo Maior in Portugal'. *Details of pension*: One hundred pounds per annum, commencing Sept. 1819. *Where generally resident during last five years*: 'London and Erdington near Birmingham'. [PRO: WO 25/769 f31].

NEWTON, Hibbert, Ensign/Lt., 32nd Foot: *1829 Statement of Service for Retired Officers*: Aged sixteen on first appointment to the Army. Ensign, 32nd Foot, 27 July 1809; Lt., 32nd Foot, 13 April 1813; Half-pay, Oct. 1814, by reduction; returned to full-pay, 25 May 1815; Half-pay, 'in October 1816 or January 1817'. 'In consequence of having received a Gun Shot wound in my left hip and the Ball not been extracted I am incapable of serving from constant weakness in that limb.' *Where serving when wounded*: 'At Salamanca, 22nd of July 1812'. *Family*: Married in the town of Wexford, co. Wexford, Ireland, 8 Jan. 1818. Five children by 1829. *Where generally resident during last five years*: 'Wicklow, Ireland'. [PRO: WO 25/769 f38]. Mentioned in Wellington's dispatch concerning the siege and storming of the Forts of St Cayetano, La Merced, and St Vincente at Salamanca, dated Fuente la Pena, 30 June 1812 ['Major-General Clinton ... mentions in strong terms of commendation the conduct of ... Ensign Newton of the 32nd Regiment, who distinguished himself in the attack of the night of the 23rd instant, and volunteered to lead the advanced party in the attack of the 27th.'] [*London Gazette*]. Severely wounded, Salamanca, 22 July 1812 ('Ensign Newton (2nd)') (1st Battn.) [*London Gazette*]. MGS.

+NEWTON, Hibbert, Ensign, 32nd Foot: Ensign, 32nd Foot, 27 April 1809. Killed, Salamanca, 22 July 1812 (1st Battn.) [*London Gazette*].

+NICHOLAS, William, Capt., Royal Engineers: 2nd Capt. 25 Aug. 1806. Severely wounded, storming of Badajoz, 6 April 1812 [*London Gazette*]. He died of these wounds eight days later. Mentioned in Wellington's Badajoz dispatch, 7 April 1812 ['I have likewise to report the good conduct of ... Captain Nicholas ... of the Royal Engineers.'] [*London Gazette*]. Letter from Gen. Colville to the Rev. Roger Frankland, 'Camp before Badajos', 8 April 1812: 'I exceedingly regret having to inform you, that there is hardly any possibility of the recovery of that very valuable young man and excellent officer, your nephew, Captain Nicholas of the Royal Engineers, who was attached to me on that night to lead the column to the assault. He met the various wounds he received in the ditch, where his voice in energetically doing his duty was the last heard previous to myself being knocked down in the Place d'Armes.' [*Colville*, p. 97]. *Haythornthwaite, Die Hard*, p. 181 [Storming of Badajoz: 'The engineer William Nicholas, after leaving Colville's side, had led two rushes but was incapacitated by a shot through the left arm, breaking it below the elbow, other balls injuring his left wrist and grazing a kneecap, and a bayonet spiking his right calf. Despite these injuries, when he heard soldiers asking who would lead them in the next assault, he had himself lifted up by two men and, in the company of Lieutenant James Shaw of the 43rd, led about seventy men up the rubble at the foot of the Santa Maria breach. Few got even part of the way; one of the men supporting Nicholas was killed and Nicholas was hit again, a musket-ball entering his left side, breaking two

ribs and exiting near the spine. He tumbled to the base of the ditch... Nicholas was dragged clear and taken for medical attention. He appeared to be recovering but died eight days later.']. The *Royal Military Chronicle*, February, 1813, pp. 271–2, gives a detailed account of Nicholas and his injuries.

NICHOLLS, George, Capt., 66th Foot: *1829 Statement of Service for Retired Officers*: Aged nineteen on first appointment to the Army. Ensign, 66th Foot, 26 June 1799; Lt., 66th Foot, 25 May 1803; Capt., 66th Foot, 23 Feb. 1809; Bvt. Major, 66th Foot, 5 July 1821; Half-pay, 11 May 1826. 'Perfectly willing to serve but laboring at present under ill-health & broken constitution from the effects of a Wounds [sic] received whilst serving in the 66th regiment.' *Where serving when wounded*: '66th regiment at Battle of Vittoria'. *Details of pension*: 'temporary Pension' of one hundred pounds, commencing 'in the year 1814'. *Where generally resident during last five years*: 'With 66th regiment until last 2 years, since which period he has resided in Devonshire'. [PRO: WO25/769-f89]. Severely wounded, Vittoria, 21 June 1813 (2nd Battn.) [*London Gazette*]. *1818 Pension Return*, pp. 16–17. MGS.

NICHOLLS, Samuel, Ensign/Lt., 9th Foot: Wounded, Rolica, 17 Aug. 1808 ('Nichols') [*London Gazette*]. Lt., 9th Foot, 11 Aug. 1808. MGS.

NICHOLSON, Elmes, S. L., Lt., 29th Foot: Ensign, 29th Foot, 27 March 1805; Lt., 29th Foot, 26 Feb. 1807. Slightly wounded, Talavera, 28 July 1809 [*London Gazette*].

NICHOLSON, John, Lt., 83rd Foot: Lt., 83rd Foot, 8 Feb. 1807. Severely wounded, Talavera, 28 July 1809 [*London Gazette*]. Pension of one hundred pounds per annum, commencing 25 Dec. 1811, for 'loss of a leg' at Talavera [*1818 Pension Return*, pp. 18–19]. MGS.

NICHOLSON, Joseph, Ensign/Lt., 53rd Foot: *1829 Statement of Service*: Born in Sunderland, County of Durham, 8 Nov. 1783. Aged twenty-four on his 'first Entrance into the Army.' Ensign, 53rd Foot ('2d Battalion'), 11 Aug. 1808. Lt., 53rd Foot ('2d Battn.'), 9 Aug. 1810. 'Staff Adjutant, Albany Barracks Isle of Wight', 22 June 1815. Capt., Albany Barracks, 15 March 1821. Half Pay, '25 November 1825 on Reduction of the Establishment.' Paymaster, 84th Foot, 7 Sept. 1826. *Battles, sieges and campaigns*: 'Talavera de la Reyna, 27th & 28th July 1809. Busaco, 27th Septr. 1810. Salamanca, 22nd July 1812.' *Wounds received in action*: 'Severely wounded when Commanding a Company in the Battle of Salamanca. Grant of a years Pay as Captain.' *Service abroad*: 'April 1809 to Augt. 1814, Peninsula of Spain & France. 17 March 1827 to 31st Dec. 1829, Jamaica.' *Family*: Married Ann Williams, May 1816, Carrisbrooke, Isle of Wight. They had three children by 1830. [PRO: WO 25/801 f273]. Severely wounded, Salamanca, 22 July 1812 (2nd Battn.) [*London Gazette*]. MGS.

NICHOLSON, Ralph, Ensign, 31st Foot: *1829 Statement of Service for Retired Officers*: Aged twenty on first appointment to the Army. Ensign, 31st Foot, 29 May 1810; Lt., 31st Foot, 9 Nov. 1812; Lt., 17th Foot, 'in 1815 or 1816'; Half-pay, 101st Foot, 20 June 1826, 'in consequence of ill health.' 'I should be very happy to serve it being the means of bettering my situation in life, but in consequence of one Ball not being extracted and the other disabling my right shoulder so much that it comes out of joint on very trifling exertion I am affraid my service at present would be of small benefit to His Majesty's service in

my present state thro' having a severe complaint, and having been in 16 different engagements with the enemies of my country little can be expected from me in the way of actual service.' 'NB there may be some mistakes in this ... not having any papers to go by, in consequence of being ship racked on my passage from India the ship went down 1400 miles from St Helena, we lost two Boats the first day we left the ship; we were then all in one Boat with which we made the island of St Helena in 13 days.' *Where serving when wounded*: 'Albuhera, Spain, two wounds one Ball not yet extracted. Jubbulpore, East Indies.' *Details of pension*: Fifty pounds, commencing 1824. *Family*: Married in Norham, county of Durham, 20 Jan. 1820. *Where generally resident during last five years*: 'Thornton, Parish of Norham, County of Durham.' [PRO: WO 25/769 f96]. Wounded, Albuera, 16 May 1811 (2nd Battn.) [*London Gazette*]. MGS.

NICKLE, Robert N., Capt., 88th Foot: Capt., 88th Foot, 1 June 1809. Severely wounded, Toulouse, 10 April 1814 (1st Battn.) [*London Gazette*]. Gold Medal. MGS. Major-General, 11 Nov. 1851.

NICKLE, William, Lt., 88th Foot: *1829 Statement of Service for Retired Officers*: Aged sixteen on first appointment to the Army. Ensign, 88th Foot, 21 Nov. 1805; Lt, 88th Foot, n.d. [Army List gives 1 Oct. 1807]; Capt., 88th Foot, 30 Aug. 1815; Half-pay, by reduction. Served ten years on full-pay. 'Having received severe Wounds and lost a Leg in the service I do not wish to be employed again as I fear I would not be equal to the duty.' *Where serving when wounded*: 'Salamanca'. *Details of pension*: One hundred pounds, commencing 22 July 1813. *Family*: Married in Dublin, 5 Oct. 1822. No children. *Title and nature of employment*:

'Barrack Master of Kinsale'. *Where generally resident during last five years*: 'Kinsale'. [PRO: WO 25/769 f80]. Severely wounded, Busaco, 27 Sept. 1810 (1st Battn.) [*London Gazette*]. Severely wounded, Salamanca, 22 July 1812 ('Nichols') ('2nd batt') [*London Gazette*]. *1818 Pension Return*, pp. 20–1.

NICOLLS, Thomas Samuel, Capt., 31st Foot: Capt. 20 March 1806. Slightly wounded, Talavera, 28 July 1809 ('Capt. Nicholls') [*London Gazette*].

NIGHTINGALL, Miles, Major-General: Lt. Col., Army, 9 Sept. 1795; Lt. Col., 38th Foot, 28 Oct. 1795; Lt. Col., 69th Foot, 8 May 1806; Col., Army, 25 Sept. 1803. Slightly wounded, Fuentes de Onoro, 5 May 1811 [*London Gazette*]. Mentioned in Wellington's Fuentes de Onoro dispatch, 8 May 1811 [5 May: 'Major-General Nightingall was wounded in the course of the cannonade, but I hope not severely.'] [*London Gazette*, 26 May 1811]. Lt.-Gen. 4 June 1814. Detailed biography, *Royal Military Calendar*, vol. II, pp. 379–85.

NISBET, Robert, Lt., 13th Light Dragoons: *1829 Statement of Service for Retired Officers*: Aged sixteen on first appointment to the Army. Cornet, 7th Dragoon Guards, 30 Nov. 1809; Lt., 13th Light Dragons, Dec. 1811 [Army List giives 26 Dec.]; Capt., 20th Light Dragoons, 'the exact date of commission does not recolect'; Half-pay, 'the 20th Lt. Dragoons disbanded in 1818 or 1819' [Army List gives: half-pay, 20th Light Dragoons, 19 Nov. 1818]. *Where serving when wounded*: 'At the Battle of Orthes in which engagement was twice wounded – stationed in France.' No pension. *Family*: Married in 'Marry le Bonne Chruch', London, Aug. 1819. One child by 1829. No employment. *Where generally resident during last five years*: 'Loughton, Berwickshire'. [PRO: WO 25/769 f105]. Slightly wounded, Orthes, 27 Feb. 1814 ('Nesbitt') [*London Gazette*]. Waterloo. MGS. 'Nisbett' in Army List.

NIXON, Alexander, Lt., 27th Foot: Lt., 27th Foot, 4 Nov. 1813. Slightly wounded, Orthes, 27 Feb. 1814 (3rd Battn.) [*London Gazette*]. MGS.

NIXON, Brinsley, Capt., 85th Foot: Capt., 85th Foot, 18 May 1809. Slightly wounded, Fuentes de Onoro, 5 May 1811 [*London Gazette*]. Recorded as 'Missing' at the siege of Badajoz, 6–11 June 1811 [*London Gazette*]. Exhanged for a French captain, Nov. 1811, see obituary of Lt. Samuel D. King [*The Gentleman's Magazine*, 1811 Supplement, II, p. 658, and Jan. 1812, p. 76], which describes the unfortunate events of the exchange, during which Spanish guerrillas killed King, mistaking him for a Frenchman.

NIXON, William Richmond, Ensign, 52nd Foot: *1829 Statement of Service for Retired Officers*: Aged seventeen on first appointment to the Army. Ensign, 52nd Foot, 26 July 1810; Lt., 52nd Foot, 11 May 1812; Half-pay, 25 Nov. 1819. *Where serving when wounded*: 'Portugal'. *Details of pension*: Fifty pounds per annum, commencing March 1813. *Where generally resident during last five years*: 'Dunkerque, Namur, Douai.' [PRO: WO 25/769 f104]. Severely wounded, siege of Badajoz, 26 March 1812 [*London Gazette*]. Severely wounded, Orthes, 27 Feb. 1814 (1st Battn.) [*London Gazette*]. Pension 'for wounds' received at Badajoz [*1818 Pension Return*, pp. 14–15]. Waterloo. MGS. *Moorsom*, p. 162 [Storming of Fort Picurina, 25 March 1812: 'One hundred men of the 52nd, under the command of Captain Ewart, headed the attacking parties, with ladders, grassbags, crowbars, and axes... The struggle was very fierce and prolonged, and Ewart fell wounded. Nixon, Ewart's subaltern, with his axemen broke through the gate of the palisades in rear, Nixon falling severely wounded within it. Another struggle in the narrow interior, and this most important fort, which was calculated to have held out for five days longer, was carried. Captain John Ewart and Ensign William Nixon were wounded, and thirty-four rank and file out of the 52nd hundred were killed or wounded.'], p. 428.

+**NOBLE, C., 1st Lt., 95th Foot:** 1st Lt., 95th Foot, 10 May 1805. 'in the Army lately in Spain' (1st Battn.) [*March 1809 Army List*, p. 105]. Obituary, *The Gentleman's Magazine*, Feb. 1809, p. 184 ['16 [Jan.]... At the battle of Corunna, in his 22d year, Lieut. Noble, of the 95th Rifle Regiment, only son of the late Mr N. of Wakefield, Yorkshire. He was bravely animating his men in the heat of the battle, when he received a shot through the head, and expired immediately.'].

NOLEKEN, George, Capt., 83rd Foot: *1829 Statement of Service*: Born in the County of Middlesex, 22 May 1786. Aged fourteen 'on his first Entrance into the Army.' Ensign, 3rd Foot Guards, 3 Jan. 1801. Lt. & Capt., 3rd Foot Guards, 4 Nov. 1804 [Army List gives 8 Nov.]. Capt., 83rd Foot, July 1808 [Army List gives 11 Aug. 1808]. Bvt. Major, 83rd Foot, June 1814. Bvt. Major, Half Pay, 57th Foot, 25 Feb. 1816, 'Reduced with 2nd Battalion.' Bvt. Major, 93rd Foot, 25 Nov. 1828. *Battles, sieges and campaigns*: 'Campaign in Zealand. Seige & Capture of Copenhagen, engaged under the Fire of Artillery and Gun boats on various occasions. Lieut. 3rd Guards... Campaigns in the Peninsula 1809, 1810, 1811. Battle of Talavera-de-la-Reyna 26th 27th & 28th July 1809. Capt. 83rd Regt. &

acting Brigade Major to Major Genl. Cameron's Brigade.' *Distinguished conduct*: 'In the charge on the 28 July 1809 received the thanks of Major Genl. Cameron Commanding the Brigade. Received the thanks of the Adj. General now Marquis of Londonderry for skilful conduct when in command of a Detachment of 900 men at Coimbra.' *Wounds received in action*: 'Musket shot above Right Knee slightly at Talavera-de-la-Reyna 28th July 1809.' *Service abroad*: 'July 1807 to Octr. 1807, Island of Zealand, Copenhagen. April 1809 to 1811, Portugal & Spain.' [PRO: WO 25/803 f163].

NORCLIFFE, Norcliffe., Lt., 4th Dragoons: *1829 Statement of Service for Retired Officers*: Aged sixteen on first appointment to the Army. Cornet, 4th Dragoons, 5 Feb. 1807; Lt., 4th Dragoons, 28 April 1808; Capt., 4th Dragoons, 29 Feb. 1816; Major, 4th Dragoons, 9 Aug. 1821; 'exchanged to full Pay 17 Lancers – a few months afterwards cannot charge my memory with the exact month & day'; Half-pay, 18th Light Dragoons, 22 May 1823, 'on peculiar private motives'. *Where serving when wounded*: 'Severely wounded at the Battle of Salamanca in 1812'. No pension, 'or ever applied for one.' *Family*: Married in York, 24 June 1824. One child by 1829. *Where generally resident during last five years*: 'at York and near Aberford in Yorkshire'. [PRO: WO 25/769 f125]. Severely wounded, Salamanca, 22 July 1812 [*London Gazette*]. MGS.

NORCOTT, Amos Godsill, Major, 95th Foot: *1829 Statement of Service*: Born in London, 3 Aug. 1777. Aged sixteen 'on his first Entrance into the Army.' Ensign, 1793; Lt., 33rd Foot, Nov. 1793; Capt., 33rd Foot, 28 Feb. 1794; Capt., 95th Foot, 22 June 1802; Bvt. Major, 95th Foot, Aug. 1803; Major, 95th Foot, Jan. 1809 [Army List gives 22 Dec. 1808]; Bvt. Lt. Col., 95th Foot, 22 July 1810 [Army List gives 25 July]; Lt. Col., Rifle Brigade, 9 Sept. 1819; Colonel, Rifle Brigade, 18 Aug. 1819; Major General, unattached, 22 July 1831. *Battles, sieges and campaigns*: 'As Captain the the Campaigns of 1794 & 5 on the Continent under H.R.H. the Duke of York. In the actions of Boxtel, Thuil, Geldermalsen, and Bureu & various affairs of lesser note in Holland in the above years. At the Cape of Good-Hope in 1796... In the East Indies from Feby. 1797 to Novr. 1799... On the expedition against the Manilla Islands... in 1797. In South America and at the Assault of Buenos Ayres 5th July 1807... In Sweden, Portugal and Spain in 1808 under Lt. Gen. Sir John Moore. In various Affairs and skirmishes during the retreat and at the Battle of Corunna 16th Jany. 1809. As Major Comg. 2 Comps. 2nd Batt. Rifle Brigade on the expedition to Walcheren. In several affairs before Flushing and at the Siege & capture of that place in 1809... As Bt. Lt. Col. Commg. 2 Comps. 2nd Batt. Rifle Brigade... at Cadiz, at the siege of that place in 1810, 11 & 12 and Battle of Barossa 5th March 1811. With the force ... at Seville in 1812. In Command of the 2nd Batt. Rifle Brigade during all the operations of the Army in the North of Spain and South of France in 1813 & 1814. At the Battles of the Nive, Orthes & Tarbes... In command of the 2nd Batt. Rifle Brigade in the Netherlands and at the Battle of Waterloo 18th June 1815.' *Wounds received in action*: 'Severely at the Battle of Tarbes in France, March 1814, for which one year's pay as a Major was granted. Severely, left arm broken at the Battle of Waterloo on the 18th June 1815 for which one year's pay as Lieut. Colonel was granted, and a temporary pension periodically until June 1830. A permanent pension as a Major Commg. has been since granted according to general

orders.' *Titles, honorary distinctions and medals*: 'A gold medal for the Battle of Barossa 5th March 1811. A gold clasp for the Battle of the Nive, Novr. 1813. The order of the 2nd Class of St Anne and the Order of Maximilian Joseph of Bavaria for service in the Netherlands and Battle of Waterloo. The Silver Medal for Waterloo 18th June 1815. The order of a Companion of the Bath for general services. The Honor & Knighthood, and the order and Star of a military Knight Comr. of the Royal Hanovarian Guelphic Order for General Services.' *Service abroad:* 'June 1794 to June 1795, Continent. April 1796 to June 1801, Cape of Good-Hope and East Indies. April 1806 to Feby. 1808, Cape of Good-Hope, St Helena, & South America. April 1808 to Augt. 1808, Sweden. Augt. 1808 to Jany. 1809, Portugal & Spain. July 1809 to Novr. 1812, Cadiz, Seville. Septr. 1813 to June 1814, Spain & France. April 1815 to Novr. 1818, Netherlands & France.' *Family*: Married Elizabeth Noble, 14 Nov. 1801, St John's Church, Wakefield, Yorkshire. They had seven children by 1830. [PRO: WO 25/804 f308]. Mentioned in Graham's Barossa dispatch, 6 March 1811 ['Lieutenant Norcott's two companies of the 2d rifle corps... I cannot conclude this dispatch without earnestly recommending to His Majesty's gracious notice for promotion... Brevet Lieutenant-Colonel Browne, Major of the 95th foot'] [*London Gazette*, 25 March 1811]. Severely wounded, 'in Action with the Enemy', 20 March 1814 (2nd Battn.) [*London Gazette*]. Waterloo. Temporary pension of two hundred and fifty pounds per annum, commencing 19 June 1816, 'for wounds' received at Tarbes, 1814, and Waterloo, 1815 [*1818 Pension Return*, pp. 22–3]. Later Major-General. Died at Cork, 1838. *Simmons*, p. 341 [wounded, Tarbes]. *Surtees*, p. 287 [Tarbes, 20 March 1814: 'We here found Colonel

Norcott, who then belonged to the 2d battalion, riding about on his large black mare; but he had not ridden long till he also was wounded through the shoulder, from which he still suffers.'].

NORMAN, John, Ensign, 34th Foot: *1829 Statement of Service*: 'Born in Hull, Yorkshire, 6th December 1788. Aged 23 years 6 months and 28 days on his first Entrance into the Army. Ensign, 34th Foot, 2nd July 1812, Volunteer from the Militia. Lieutenant, 34th Regt., 9th November 1815. Half Pay 14th September 1818. Lieutenant, 81st Regt., 19th Apl. 1821. Half Pay, 25th Octr. 1821. Lieutenant, 54th Regt., 28 Novr. 1821.' *Battles, sieges and campaigns*: 'Ensign at Vittoria 21 June and Pyrenees 25th July 1813.' *Wounds received in action*: '25th July 1813 in the Pyrenees. 12 months Ensign's pay.' *Service abroad*: 'February 1813 to October 1813, Peninsula. Feby. 1815 to Septem. 1818, East Indies. 16th May 1822 to 31st Decr. 1829, East Indies.' *Family*: Married Elizabeth Wriglesworth, 9 Sept. 1814, in Liverpool. They had no children by 1830. [PRO: WO 25/795 f253]. MGS.

NORMAN, William, Ensign, 48th Foot: *1829 Statement of Service for Retired Officers*: Aged eighteen on first appointment to the Army. Ensign, 48th Foot, 7 March 1810; Lt., 48th Foot, 14 May 1812; Lt., 100th Foot, 27 Aug. 1813; Half-pay, 24th Foot, 4 May 1815, 'from private motives'; Lt., 29th Foot, 13 June 1816; Half-pay, 25 March 1817, by reduction; Lt., 2nd Foot, 2 Oct. 1817; Half-pay, 4 July 1819, 'Reduced in West Indies'; Lt., 41st Foot, 26 Feb. 1819; Lt., 69th Foot, 3 April 1823; Half-pay, 25th April 1826; by reduction, 'Exchanged from ill health.' *Where serving when wounded*: 'Albuera'. No pension. 'A years Pay, 19th May 1815.' *Family*: Married in St Giles', London, 16th Feb. 1815. No children. *Where*

generally resident during last five years: 'East Indies and Woolwich'. [PRO: WO 25/769 f123]. Wounded, Albuera, 16 May 1811 (2nd Battn.) [*London Gazette*]. MGS.

NORMANN, Johann H. Ernst Gustav von, Lt./Adjutant, Duke of Brunswick Oels' Corps (Infantry): Aged nineteen years four months on first appointment to Army. Lt., Duke of Brunswick Oels' Corps, 27 Sept. 1809; Adjutant, Duke of Brunswick Oels' Corps, 18 April 1811; Capt., Duke of Brunswick Oels' Corps, 31 March 1814; Half-pay, 24 Sept. 1814, 'by reduction of the Brunswick Light Infantry.' *Where serving when wounded*: 'in Spain.' *Details of pension*: 'One hundred Pounds sterling ... from the day of my being wounded 18th of July 1813. 70£ per annum until the Day of the Battle of Waterloo and from 18th of June 1815 one hundred pounds sterling per annum.' *Family*: Married in 'Brunswick', 30 Nov. 1824, with Theresa Charlotte Henrietta Wilhelmine von der Muelle. No children by 1829. *Where generally resident during last five years*: 'at Brunswick.' [PRO: WO 25/755 f101].

+NORRIS, George, Ensign/Lt., 47th Foot: Ensign, 47th Foot, 5 Sept. 1809. Killed, storming of San Sebastian, 31 Aug. 1813 (Lieutenant) (2nd Battn.) [*London Gazette*].

NORTH, Roger, Capt., 50th Foot: Lt., 50th Foot, 8 Oct 1806; Capt., 50th Foot, 17 Dec. 1812. Slightly wounded, Pyrenees, 25 July 1813 (Captain) (1st Battn.) [*London Gazette*]. Severely wounded, the Nive, 13 Dec. 1813 (1st Battn.) [*London Gazette*].

+NORTH, Thomas, Lt., 88th Foot: Lt., 88th Foot, 4 Dec. 1806. Severely wounded, 'since dead', siege of Badajoz, 21 March 1812 (1st Battn.) [*London Gazette*]. Died of wounds,

22 March 1812. Return dated 25 March 1812. [PRO: WO 25/2965].

NORTH, William, Capt., 68th Foot: *1829 Statement of Service:* 'Born in Dublin, 8th July 1783. Aged Eighteen on his first Entrance into the Army. Ensign, 82nd Regt., 21st May 1801. Lieutenant, 68th Regt., 21st Decr. 1803. Captain, 68th Regt., 8th Novr. 1809.' *Battles, sieges and campaigns:* 'Moresco 20th June 1812... Heights above Moresco 21st June 1812... Salamanca 22d July 1812. Fort El-Reterio, 13th Augt. 1812. Munoz, 17 Novr. 1812.' *Wounds received in action:* 'Wounded in the face, Left hand, and left Thigh, at Salamanca, 22d July 1812.' *Service abroad:* '15th Septr. 1801 to 15th Augt. 1802, Minorca. 10 Aug. 1804 to 15th Feby. 1805, West Indies. 28th June 1811 to 10th Mar. 1813, Peninsula. 28th Decr. 1813 to 20th July 1814, Peninsula. 3d July 1818 to 24th July 1823, Canada. 10th July 1826 to 18th Nov. 1829, Canada.' *Family:* Married Sarah Marsh, 29 Aug. 1806, Clontarf, near Dublin. They had five children by 1830. [PRO: WO 25/798 f155]. Slightly wounded, Salamanca, 22 July 1812 [*London Gazette*]. MGS.

NORTHEY, Edward Richard, Lt., 52nd Foot: *1829 Statement of Service for Retired Officers:* Aged sixteen on first appointment to the Army. Ensign, 52nd Foot, 11 July 1811; Lt., 52nd Foot, 1 Oct. 1812; Capt., York Rangers, 24 June 1819; Half-pay, 24 June 1819, by reduction; Capt., 52nd Foot, 10 Aug. 1820; Capt., 3rd Foot Guards, 26 Sept. 1822; Capt., 25th Foot, 13 April 1826; Half-pay, 'Portuguese Service', 13 April 1826. *Where serving when wounded:* 'Wounded at Vittoria, but receive no Pension.' *Family:* Married in Brighton, 29 March 1828. *Where generally resident during last five years:* 'England.' [PRO: WO 25/769 f124]. Slightly wounded, Vittoria, 21 June 1813 ('57th Foot' sic) (1st Battn.) [*London Gazette*].

Waterloo. MGS. *Dalton*, pp. 169, 173 ['Of Woodcote House, Epsom, Surrey. Bn. 8th Feb., 1795.... D. in Dec., 1878.'].

NÖTTING, George, Capt., 5th Line Battn. K.G.L.: Lt., 5th Line Battn. K.G.L., 28 Jan. 1806; Capt., 5th Line Battn., 16 Oct. 1812. Slightly wounded, sortie from Bayonne, 14 April 1814 [*London Gazette*]. Served in Peninsula 1808–14. Waterloo. *Beamish*, vol. II, p. 590 [Died 'at Bremen, 11th Feb. 1837.'].

NOWLAN, William, Lt., 50th Foot: *1829 Statement of Service for Retired Officers:* Aged twenty-one on first appointment to the Army. Quartermaster, 5th Dragoons, Jan. 1796; Cornet, 18th Light Dragoons, 5 Jan. 1806, 'From Troop QrMr'; Ensign, 50th Foot, Sept. 1807 [Note added: 'Ensign, 3rd Garrn. Bn., 27 Aug. 1807']; Lt., 50th Foot, 12 Jan. 1809; Half-pay, 91st Foot, 22 June 1820, 'from severe ill health and the state of his private affairs.' 'On the Expedition to Holland in 1799.' 'The papers that would have enabled Lieut. Nowland to state with precision, the days of the month, of the ... appointments, were lost off the Escort, with the entire of his Baggage, & Bate Horse, on a night march, in the Peninsula, in 1814, for which he has not received any compensation.' 'Has been 3 times wounded, twice most severely, in Command of Companys.' 'Lieutenant Nowlan, applied for, & received his Colonels promise, to obtain for him, the Honor of leading the Forlorn Hope, at the Intended Siege of Pampluna had it been proceeded with, & was a volunteer for that or any similar duty till the close of the War, in the following year.' *Where serving when wounded:* 'On the Pyranees at the Pass of Maya 25th July 1813. Before Bayonne 13th December 1813. Per Certificate.' No pension. *Family:* Married in the Parish of Garvaghy, County Down, Ireland, 10 Nov. 1802.

Two children, the latter born in 1805. *Where generally resident during last five years*: 'Near Warrenport, County Down, Ireland, for near five years, the remainder in Dublin & Newry.' [PRO: WO 25/769 f117]. Attached to his Statement is a Doctor's Certificate: 'Toulouse, 13th May 1814. I do certify that Lieut. Nowlands 50th Regiment received a severe gun shot wound in the right thigh, when engaged with the Enemy on the 25th July 1813. The Ball passed near the femoral artery, the pulsation was easily felt by the finger when introduced by the would on the fore part of the thigh. And I do also certify that Lieut. Nowlands received a gun shot wound on the 13th December 1813. The Ball entered above the os pubis in the left side which appeared to me to have passed through the pelvis and os ilium of the same side. And at the time I saw him on the field I conceived his ultimate recovery very doubtful. Baillie Ross, Surgeon 50th Regt.' [PRO: WO 25/769 f116]. Slightly wounded, Pyrenees, 25 July 1813 (1st Battn.) [*London Gazette*]. Severely wounded, the Nive, 13 Dec. 1813 ('W. Nowland') (1st Battn.) [*London Gazette*]. Army List gives as 'Nolan'.

NUGENT, John, Lt. Col., 38th Foot: Lt. Col., 38th Foot, 8 Feb. 1807. Commanded the 2nd Battn. 38th Foot at the storming of Badajoz. Mentioned in Wellington's Badajoz dispatch, 7 April 1812 ['The 2nd battalion of the 38th, under Lieutenant-Colonel Nugent ... likewise performed their part in a very exemplary manner.'] [*London Gazette*].

NUGENT, Pierce Stephen, Volunteer/Ensign, 83rd Foot; Lt., 60th Foot: *1829 Statement of Service*: Born in the Parish of St Francis, Dublin, 26 Dec. 1788. Aged twenty-four on first appointment to the Army. Volunteer, 83rd Foot, Nov.

1812; Ensign, 83rd Foot, Feb. 1813; Lt., 8th Battn. 60th Foot, March 1814; Lt., 6th Battn. 60th Foot, Nov. 1816; Lt., 3rd Battn. 60th Foot, April 1818; Half-pay, 'about Feby. 1821', by reduction; Lt., 44th Foot, May 1822; Half-pay, 17th Foot, July 1823; Lt., 96th Foot, May 1824. *Battles, sieges and campaigns*: 'Vittoria, Nivelle, Orthes, Peninsula.' *Distinguished conduct*: 'On the 1st of July 1813. Ensign Nugent had the honor of receiving from Sir Charles Colville (who Commanded the Right Brigade of the 3d Division) a letter strongly expressive of his approbation of Ensign Nugents conduct in the Battle of Vittoria, which letter he transmitted to the late Sir H. Torrens on the 12th July 1814, and it remains still in the Commander in Chiefs Office.' *Wounds received in action*: 'At the Battle of Orthes by a Musket ball in the Right Arm, and by a Rifle ball in the Right side, for which injuries Lt. Nugent has received one years pay as Ensign, a temporary Pension from December 1826 to June 1831, and since June 1831 a permanent one of fifty pounds per annum.' *Service abroad*: '[Illegible] 1812 to June 1814, Portugal, Spain & France. June 1815 to Augt. 1816, Gibralter. Nov. 1816 to Nov. 1817, Jamaica. April 1818 to Novbr. 1820, Nova Scotia. May 1822 to July 1823, Bengal. Jany. 1824 to June 1828, Nova Scotia & Bermuda. April 1829 to Decbr. 1829, Nova Scotia & Prince E. Island.' [PRO: WO 25/804 f35]. Severely wounded, Orthes, 27 Feb. 1814 ('Pierse Nugent') (2nd Battn.) [*London Gazette*]. Colville, p. 170 [Letter from John Keane to Sir Charles Colville, 17 March 1814: 'Poor Nugent dangerously [wounded] in two places, but there are some hopes.'].

NUNN, John L., Lt., 7th Foot: *1829 Statement of Service*: 'Born Wexford, Ireland, 22nd August 1794. Aged 15 7/12 Years on his first Entrance into the Army. 2nd Lieut.,

443

4th Ceylon, 9th March 1810. Lieutenant, 7th Fusileers, 17th January
1811. Half Pay, 17th July 1828, In
consequence of ill health. Lieutenant, 66th Foot, 30th April 1827.'
Battles, sieges and campaigns: 'In
the Campaigns of 1813, Battle of
Vittoria 21 of June. Battles in the
Pyrenees 25 to 29 July. Taking the
heights of Vera 13 October. Passage
of the Nivelle in November. Passage
of the Nive 9th to 13th December
1813. Orthes 27th February 1814.
Toulouse 10 April 1814. Capture of
Paris 6th July 1815.' *Distinguished
Conduct:* 'In the affair on the 25th
July 1813, at Alta Bisea in the Pyrenees, ordered to the front in
Command of a Company to keep
the Enemy in check, remained skirmishing in a Wood for 3 or 4 hours
and performed the Service to the
Satisfaction of the Commanding
Officer. The same Service
performed at the Battle of Orthes
27th February 1814.' *Wounds receiv-
ed in action*: 'Wounded through the
Left Arm on the 28 July 1813 in the
General Action of the Pyrenees,
received one Years Pay for said
Wound.' *Service abroad*: '22nd
February 1811 to 24 July 1811,
[Peninsula]. 11th September 1812
to 23rd June 1814, [Peninsula,
South of France]. 17th June 1815 to
9th Novr. 1818, France.' *Family*:
Married Frances Butler, 31 May
1821. They had four children by
1830. [PRO: WO 25/798 f41].
Severely wounded, Pyrenees, 28

July 1813 (1st Battn.) [*London
Gazette*].

+NUNN, Joseph, Lt., 26th Foot: Lt.,
26th Foot, 18 Feb. 1806. Died, 30
Jan. 1809, from wounds received at
Corunna, 16 Jan. 1809. Obituary,
The Gentleman's Magazine, Feb.
1809, p. 188 ['30 [Jan.]... At Haslar
hospital, Gosport, in consequence
of the wounds he received at the
battle of Corunna, Lieut. Joseph
Nunn, of the 26th (or Cameronian)
Regiment.'].

NUNN, Loftus, Lt., 31st Foot: *1829
Statement of Service for Retired
Officers*: Aged sixteen on first
appointment to the Army.
'Previous to my appointment in the
Army, I served as a Midshipman in
His Majesty's Navy for a period of
five years and nine months.'
Ensign, 31st Foot, 24 Aug. 1809; Lt.,
31st Foot, 15 Jan. 1812; Half-pay, 24
Sept., 1817, by reduction; 'restored
to full Pay', Lt., 31st Foot, 18 Jan.
1818; Capt., 31st Foot, 16 June 1825;
Half-pay, 13 Feb. 1828, 'on account
of ill health returning from India.'
Where serving when wounded:
'Alba de Tormas'. *Details of
pension*: Seventy pounds, com-
mencing 13 Nov. 1813. *Family*:
Married in Carrickfergus, Ireland, 3
Dec. 1823. Two children by 1829.
*Where generally resident during
last five years*: 'In Ireland since
placed on Half Pay'. [PRO: WO
25/769 f132].

O

**OAKLEY, Richard C., Ensign/Lt.,
20th Foot:** *1829 Statement of Service*:
Born 31 January 1795, Wimborne
Minster, Dorset. Aged fifteen on first
appointment to the Army. Ensign,
36th Foot, 20 Dec. 1810; Ensign, 20th
Foot, 7 March 1811; Lt. 21 Oct. 1813;
Half Pay 25 March 1817; Lt., 20th
Foot, 3 Dec. 1818; Capt. 27 Dec. 1827.
Battles, sieges and campaigns:
'Served in the Campaigns of 1813
and 1814, in the Peninsula... Present
with the 20th Regt. in the following
Actions: at Vitoria 21 June 1813, in
the Pyrenees near Roncesvalles, 25
July 1813, at Orthes 27 Feby. 1814,
Toulouse 10 April 1814.' *Wounds
received in action*: 'Severely
wounded in the Action near Ronces-
valles, on the 25th July 1813, for
which he received a grant of One
year's pay as Ensign. Slightly
wounded at the Battle of Orthes,
27th Feby. 1814.' *Service abroad*:
'12th Octr. 1812 to 7th July 1814,
Peninsula. 13th March 1819 to 22nd
Jany. 1824, St Helena & India. 18th
Feby. 1828 to 13th March 1829,
India.' Unmarried in 1830. [PRO:
WO 25/788 f230]. Slightly wounded,
Pyrenees, 25 July 1813 [*London
Gazette*].

**OATES, James Poole, Capt., 88th
Foot:** *1829 Statement of Service for
Retired Officers*: 'Entered as a
Volunteer in His Majesty's Service,
in May 1787, in the 17th year of my
age, but only obtained my appointment as Ensign in the 49th Regt. on
the 3d of March 1797.' Lt., 49th
Foot, 12 May 1797; Lt., 88th Foot, 31
May 1798; Capt., 88th Foot, 19 Oct.
1804; Bvt. Major, 88th Foot, 3 March
1814; Half-pay, 26 March 1818,
'Retired in consiquence of Wounds
and ill health'. 'Is Not capable of
Serving'. 'NB. The above service
upon Full pay is exclusive of the
nine years Service as a Volunteer.'
Where serving when wounded:
'Twice severely wounded whilst
serving in the West Indies. Three
times severely wounded while
serving in the Peninsula and
France'. *Details of pension*: Two
hundred pounds per annum. 'Major
Oates's first Grant only £100 a year,
commencing 25th June 1816 – but
his being a Major more than 3 years
previous, and upon a subsequent
revision of his Claims with regard to
the permanent injuries he recd.
from the severity of his wounds, as
stated by the Medical Board, his
pension was encreased to that of a
Majors, but the last grant of £100 a
year in addition, only commenced
from 25th Decr. 1826.' *Family*:
Married in 'Mary le bone New
Church, London', 23 Oct. 1817. 'No
children of his own, but Major
Oates ... states that he has four
Orphan Children belonging to his
family entirely depending upon him
for support'. No employment.
*Where generally resident during
last five years*: 'Mill Hill, Harlow,
Essex.' [PRO: WO 25/770 f3].
Severely wounded, siege of
Badajoz, 26 March 1812 [*London
Gazette*]. Severely wounded,
Orthes, 27 Feb. 1814 (1st Battn.)
[*London Gazette*]. Pension of one
hundred pounds per annum,
commencing 25 June 1816, 'for
wounds' received at 'Buenos Ayres,
1807, St Domingo, 1794, Cape St.
Nicola, 1795, Talavera, 1809, and
Badajos, 1812, Orthes, 1814' [*1818
Pension Return*, pp. 20–1]. MGS.

OBINS, Hamlet, Capt., 20th Foot:
Capt., 'A Regiment at the Cape of
Good Hope', 22 Dec. 1808; Capt.,
20th Foot, 19 Dec. 1811. Severely
wounded, Toulouse, while serving
on the General Staff as Brigade-
Major ('Captain Hamlet Obins
(20th Foot)') [*London Gazette*].
Bvt. Major, 20th Foot, 12 April 1814.
MGS.

+**O'BRIEN, Volunteer, 40th Foot:**
Killed, storming of Badajoz, 6 April
1812 [*London Gazette*]. Not in
Challis, Index.

+**O'BRIEN, James, Capt., 87th
Foot:** Capt., 87th Foot, 11 April
1811. Severely wounded, Vittoria, 21
June 1813 (2nd Battn.) [*London
Gazette*]. Died of wounds, 8 July
1813. Return dated July 1813.
[PRO: WO 25/2965]. Obituary, *The
Gentleman's Magazine*, Nov. 1813,
p. 504.

**O'CALLAGHAN, Hon. Robert, W.,
Lt. Col., 39th Foot:** Lt. Col., 39th
Foot, 16 July 1803; Col., Army, 25
July 1810. Mentioned in
Wellington's Vittoria dispatch, 22
June 1813 ['the Honourable Lieutenant-Colonel O'Callagan [sic],
who maintained the village of Sabi-
jana de Alava against all the efforts
of the enemy to regain possession of
it'] [*London Gazette*]. Gold Cross
with 2 clasps (Maida, Vittoria, Pyrenees, Nivelle, Nive, Orthes), the first
as Lt. Col., Grenadiers, the
remainder as Col. commanding
39th Foot and a Brigade. K.C.B.
*Haythornthwaite, Armies of
Wellington*, p. 256 [quoting
'Ghunzee', 'Take the Hill Before
Dark', in *United Service Journal*,
1840, III, p. 530: 15 Feb. 1814, Garris,
'Colonel the Hon. R. W.
O'Callaghan, whose horse had been
shot from under him, and who was
now fighting on foot at the head of
the regiment, received one French
bayonet at the breast, and another
at the shin, at the same time.'].
Webber, p. 162.

+**O'CONNELL, John, Lt., 43rd
Foot:** Lt., 43rd Foot, 14 Dec. 1809.
Slightly wounded, storming of
Badajoz, 6 April 1812 (1st Battn.)
[*London Gazette*]. Killed, storming
of San Sebastian, 31 Aug. 1813 (1st
Battn.) [*London Gazette*]. Died of
wounds, 2 Sept. 1813. Return dated
Sept. 1813. [PRO: WO 25/2965].
Surtees, p. 238 [San Sebastian: 'a

lieutenant of the 43d, brother to Mr
O'Connell, the famous Roman
Catholic advocate, was killed'].
Bruce, p. 146 [Letter from William
Napier to his wife, Sept. 5, 1813:
'When I thought I was to have had
the command [of the storming
party], as I knew the eldest subaltern was old and stupid, I asked a
young man of the name of O'Connell who had led two storming
parties before, to volunteer,
thinking that I could get him a
company. He would not have done
so had it not been for my sake, and
he was killed, leaving a mother who
was supported by what he spared
her out of his pay. Is this not very
painful, and ought it not to
strengthen me in my disposition to
quit a service where friendship is a
curse and kindness kills?'].

O'CONNELL, John, Lt., 67th Foot:
Seventy pounds per annum
pension, commencing 31 July 1814,
for 'loss of an arm' at Pampeluna,
1813 [*1818 Pension Return*, pp.
16–17].

**O'CONNELL, Richard, Volunteer,
43rd Foot:** *1829 Statement of
Service*: Born in Ennis, co. Clare,
Ireland, 24 June 1794. Aged eighteen on first entrance into the
Army. Volunteer, 43rd Foot, 3 April
1812; Ensign, 43rd Foot, 12 May
1812; Lt., 43rd Foot, 12 July 1813;
Lt., 71st Foot, Half-pay, June 1816,
'on account of Family Affairs'; Lt.,
65th Foot, 6 Aug. 1828. *Battles,
sieges and campaigns*: 'At the
taking of Badajos on the night of
the 6 April 1812, then a Volunteer in
the 43rd Regiment... Present with
the above Regiment as an Ensign at
the Battle of Salamanca in June
1813... At the Battle of Vittoria as an
Ensn. ... 21st June 1813.' *Wounds
received in action*: 'Severely
wounded at the taking of Badajos
on the night of the 6th April 1812
when on the Storming Party, then a
Volunteer so no grant of Pay or
Pension for the Wound.' *Service*

abroad: '3rd April 1812 to October 1814, Elvas, Galligos, Madrid &c &c &c. 27th Decr. 1829 to 31st Decr. 1829, Demerara, West Indies.' *Family*: Married Frances Irving, 6 June 1816, St Mary's Church, Plymouth. They had no children by 1830. [PRO: WO 25/797 f355]. Severely wounded, storming of Badajoz, 6 April 1812 ['Volunteer O'Connell'] [*London Gazette*]. Note: wounded in the Storming Party at Badajos just three days after joining the regt. as Volunteer. MGS.

O'DELL, Henry Edward, Lt., 5th Foot: *1829 Statement of Service*: Born in Limerick, 1 May 1790. Aged sixteen on his 'first Entrance into the Army.' Ensign, 5th Foot, 8 July 1806. Lt., 5th Foot, 25 Feb. 1808. Capt., 5th Foot, 9 Jan. 1822. Capt., Half Pay, unattached, June 1826. Capt., 86th Foot, 3 July 1828. Note added: 'Capt., Half Pay, 67th, 4 Oct. 1831. Paymaster, 2d. 60th Rifles, 10 July 1835. Capt., Half Pay, 67th, 20 Sept. 1839.' *Battles, sieges and campaigns*: 'Busaco. Fuentes De Honore. Sabugal. El Bedon. Badajos 1st Siege. Salamanca. Vittoria. Nivelle. Orthes. Toulouse. Cuidad Rodrigo. Siege & Capture of Badajos.' *Wounds received in action*: '22d July 1812 at Salamanca. No grant of Pay or Pension.' *Service abroad*: 'June 1807 to March 1808, S. America. June 1809 to Oct. 1819, Peninsula & N. America & France. Jany. 1820 to Aprl. 1826, W. Indies. Jany. 1829 to Decr. 1829, W. Indies.' Note added: '10 Jan 1836 to 21 June 1839, Mediterranean.' *Family*: Married his first wife, M Hobson, 3 July 1823, St Vincent. They had one daughter prior to her death. He remarried, E. Townsend, 9 Jan. 1830, in Barbados. It is noted that they had three children by Nov. 1837. [PRO: WO 25/802 f21]. 5th Foot, 25 Feb. 1808. Severely wounded, Salamanca, 22 July 1812 (2nd Battn.) [*London Gazette*]. MGS.

O'DOGHERTY, Theobald, Lt., 40th Foot: Lt., 40th Foot, 28 Aug. 1807. Slightly wounded, Pyrenees, 28 July 1813 (1st Battn.) [*London Gazette*]. Severely wounded, Toulouse, 10 April 1814 ('O'Doherty') (1st Battn.) [*London Gazette*]. MGS.

O'DONAGHUE, John William, Capt., 47th Foot: *1829 Statement of Service*: 'Born near Mallow, Ireland, 8th Feby. 1777. Aged 17 years on his first Entrance into the Army. Ensign, 4th Regt. I. B., 1st Oct. 1794. Half Pay 25th Decr. 1797. Ensign, 63rd Regt., 23rd Feby 1800. Lieutenant, 9th Regt., 23rd April 1800. Half Pay 24 Octr. 1802. Lieutenant, 47th Regt., 9th July 1803. Captain, 47th Regt., 122th June 1806. Major, in the Army, 31st Decr. 1811. Lt. Colonel, in the Army, 12th Augt. 1819. Major, 47th Regt., 19th March 1824.' *Battles, sieges and campaigns*: 'At the attack on Ferrol on the 26th Augt. 1800 as Lieut. in the 9th Foot under Sir James Pultney. At the siege and capture of Monte Video in South America as Captain in the 47th Regt ... in Jany and Feby. 1807. At the defence of Cadiz in 1810 and 1811 as Capt. 47th Regt ... and on the Staff as Aide-de-Camp to Colonel Skerrett at the defence of Tarifa in Spain in Decr. 1811 and in the defeat of the French assault of that place in Decr. 1811. In 1817 & 18 with the Bombay Army ... the campaigns of those years against the Mahrattes as Bvt. Major 47th Regt. In 1824-25 Served with the Army under Sir A. Campbell against the Birmese as Bvt. Lt. Col. and Major 47th Regt.' *Distinguished conduct:* 'Was noticed and recommended by Colonel Skerrett in his Dispatches (which were published in the London Gazette) for his conduct at Tarifa in Decr. 1811. And also by Brigadier General Cotton, in his reports to Sir Archibald Campbell for his conduct on various occasions whilst serving under his seperate command against the Birmese in 1825.'

O'DONAGHUE

Wounds received in action: 'Was slightly wounded in Decr. 1811 at the defence of Tarifa.' *Titles, honorary distinctions and medals*: 'Obtained the Brevet rank of Major in 1812 for the defence of Tarifa on which occasion he brought home the dispatches. Was appointed a Companion of the Military Order of the Bath in Decr. 1826 for his services in Ava.' *Service abroad*: '1st Augt. 1800 to Feby. 1801, on an Expedition to Ferrol, Cadiz &c. May 1806 to Decr. 1807, Cape of Good Hope, South America &c. Oct. 1809 to May 1813, At Gibralter, Cadiz, Tarifa, and in the Peninsular. Feby. 1816 to Decr. 1826, In India Ava &c.' *Family*: Married Miss Brooks, in Liverpool, 4 July 1815. The couple had five children by July 1830. [PRO: WO 25/794 f88]. Slightly wounded, Tarifa, 22 Dec. 1811, while serving as Acting A.D.C. to Colonel Skerrett (2nd Battn., 47th Foot) [*London Gazette*]. Mentioned in Skerrett's dispatch of 5 Jan. 1812 ['I have the honour to dispatch this by my Acting Aide-de-Camp, Captain O'Donoghue, of the 47th Regiment, who is in possession of every information relative to my proceedings at this place, an officer of great merit and considerable length of service.']. *Blakeney*, p. 137 [Commanding four companies of the 28th Foot sent from Gibraltar to Tarifa, April 1810].

O'DONNELL, Pierce, Lt., 3rd Foot: Lt., 3rd Foot, 9 April 1807. Severely wounded, Albuera, 16 May 1811 [*London Gazette*]. 'Preise O'Donnell' in Army List. 'Pierce O'Donnell' in *Challis, Index*, p. 70. MGS.

O'DONOGHUE, Edward, Lt., 48th Foot: Lt., 48th Foot, 6 Feb. 1808. Slightly wounded, Albuera, 16 May 1811 ('O'Donaghue') [*London Gazette*].

OFFEN, Augustus von, Ensign, 7th Line Battn. K.G.L.: *1829 Statement of Service for Retired Officers*: Aged sixteen years five months on first appointment to the Army. Cadet Sergeant. Ensign, 7th Line Battn. K.G.L., 20 Dec. 1808; Lt., 7th Line Battn. K.G.L., 12 March 1811; Half-pay by reduction. *Where serving when wounded*: 'in the Battle of Tallavera in Spain, severly.' *Family*: Married in Stade, Hanover, 9 March 1825. Two children by 1829. *Where generally resident during last five years*: 'Emden, in Eastfreersland, Kingdom of Hannover.' [PRO: WO 25/755 f197]. Severely wounded, Talavera, 28 July 1809 ('1st Battn.') [*London Gazette*]. Served in Peninsula 1809–11. *Beamish*, vol. II, p. 599.

+OFFLEY, Francis Needham, Major, 23rd Foot: Major, 23rd Foot, 15 May 1806. Killed, Salamanca, 22 July 1812 [*London Gazette*].

O'FLAHERTY, Francis, 1st Lt., 23rd Foot: *1829 Statement of Service for Retired Officers*: Aged thirty-two on first appointment to the Army. 2nd Lt., 23rd Foot, Oct. 1808; 1st Lt., 23rd Foot, n.d. [Army List gives 6 Aug. 1807]; Capt., 23rd Foot, 17 July 1815; Half-pay, 15th Foot, 3 Aug. 1820, 'from ill health'. 'Would be desirous of service, if his health would permit him, but is constantly attacked with the gout and bad lungs since & before he quit the service, in consequence of a neglected cold in the Peninsula, & the effects of the Walcheren Fever & ague which he suffered very much from.' *Where serving when wounded*: 'Wounded in the Peninsula at Pampeloona'. No pension. *Family*: 'Widower'. One child. No employment. *Where generally resident during last five years*: 'Residing at Kingston near Galway'. [PRO: WO 25/770 f38]. Slightly wounded, Pyrenees, 25 July 1813 ('Flaherty') [*London Gazette*]. Waterloo.

O'FLAHERTY, John, Capt., 45th Foot: Capt., 45th Foot, 7 Jan 1808.

Slightly wounded, storming of Badajoz, 6 April 1812 ('O'Flaharty') [*London Gazette*]. Major, 45th Foot, 19 May 1814. Half-pay, 1814, by reduction. Gold Medal.

OGLANDER, Henry, Lt., 43rd Foot; Capt., 47th Foot: *1829 Statement of Service:* Born 12 Aug. 1788, Nunwell, Isle of Wight. Aged eighteen on his first entrance into the Army. Ensign, 43rd Foot, 20 Aug. 1806; Lt. 8 Sept. 1808; Capt., 47th Foot, 8 Sept. 1812; Bt. Major 31 Aug. 1813; Major, 2nd Garrison Battn., Sept. 1814; Half Pay Oct. 1814; Major, 40th Foot, May 1815; Lt. Col., De Watterville's, 14 Dec. 1815; Half Pay Jan. 1816; Lt. Col., 26th Foot, 23 Oct. 1817; Bt. Colonel in Indian Army 5 June 1829. *Battles, sieges and campaigns:* 'Ensign in the 43rd Lt. Regt. 1st Battn. during the campaigns in which Copenhagen was captured; present partly at the seige and partly engaged with the force commanded by Major Genl. Wellesley in the pursuit of the Danish Army which ended in their defeat at the battle of "Kioge." Lieut. in the 1st Battn. 43rd Lt. Regt. under Sir David Baird & Sir Jno. Moore in Gallicean 1808 & 9. Lieut. Comg. a compy. in 2d Battn. 43rd Lt. Regt. during the Campaign in 1809 which terminated in the capture of "Flushing." Lieut. serving with 1st Battn. 43rd Lt. Regt. from Augt. 1810 to April 1812; present at the affair on the "Coa" near "Almeda", at the battle of "Busaco", at the affair near "Redhina", at that near "Foz d'Aroce," & at "Sabugal"; at the battle of "Fuentes de Onor," at the seige and capture of Ciudad Rodrigo", and at the seige and capture of "Badajoz." Capt. in the 47th Foot from Feby. 1813 throughout the campaign till the capture of "St Sebastian", being present at the battle of "Vittoria", and the seige & capture of "St Sebastian". After recovering from wounds rejoined the 47th in front of Bayonne and remained in command of the Battn. with the blockading army till the peace, when the 47th returned to England.' *Wounds received in action:* 'Lost left arm at the assault of Badajoz, and wounded moreover in the arm and thigh and body. Lost first finger of right hand and wounded in the body at the assault of St Sebastian. Pension for the former £100 but increased to £300 per annum as Lt. Col. Pension for the latter £150 per annum.' *Titles, honorary distinctions and medals:* 'Received a Gold medal for the Capture of St Sebastian.' Not married in 1830. [PRO: WO 25/790 f4]. Severely wounded, 'left arm amputated', storming of Badajoz, 6 April 1812 (1st Battn. 43rd Foot) [*London Gazette*]. Severely wounded, storming of San Sebastian, 31 Aug. 1813 (2nd Battn.) [*London Gazette*]. Pension for 'loss of an arm' at Badajoz, and another 'for other wounds' at San Sebastian [*1818 Pension Return, pp. 12–13*].

OGLE, John, Lt., 9th Foot: Lt., 9th Foot, 12 Dec. 1807. Severely wounded, storming of San Sebastian, 31 Aug. 1813 (1st Battn.) [*London Gazette*].

O'HALLORAN, George, Major, 4th Foot: Major, 4th Foot, 1 Aug. 1811. Slightly wounded, Salamanca, 22 July 1812 (1st Battn.) [*London Gazette*].

+O'HARA, Marcus, Ensign, 59th Foot: Ensign, 59th Foot, 15 Oct. 1812. Killed, storming of San Sebastian, 31 Aug. 1813 (2nd Battn.) [*London Gazette*].

O'HARA, Patterson, Lt., 59th Foot: *1829 Statement of Service for Retired Officers:* Aged twenty-two when he was appointed to the Militia, twenty-five when first appointed to the Line. Ensign, Louth Militia, 8 Nov. 1807; Lt., Louth Militia, n.d.; Ensign, 59th

Foot, 8 Nov. 1810, 'having Volunteered from the Louth Militia'; Lt., 59th Foot, 2 Sept. 1812; Half-pay, 25 March 1816, 'by request in consequence of wounds received, and ill health contracted on Service'. 'Paymaster of the Cavan Militia'. *Where serving when wounded*: 'Anglette near Bayone, severely, and twice before at Vitoria & St Sebastian, but so slightly that they were not included in the returns.' 'No Grant except a years Pay for his wounds at Anglette.' *Family*: Married in Cavan [Ireland], 18 May 1816. One child by 1829. No civil employment, but Paymaster in the Cavan Militia. *Where generally resident during last five years*: 'Cavan'. [PRO: WO 25/770 f49]. Severely wounded, the Nive, 9 Dec. 1813 (2nd Battn.) [*London Gazette*]. MGS.

O'HARA, Walter, Lt., 47th Foot; Capt., 7th Caçadores: Lt., 47th Foot, 25 March 1811. Severely wounded, storming of Badajoz, 6 April 1812, while serving as Capt., 7th Caçadores [*London Gazette*]. Recorded as 'missing', the Nive, 10 Dec. 1813, while serving as Major, 1st Portuguese Line [*London Gazette*]. Capt., Half-pay, 1814, by reduction. In Portuguese Service June 1811 to April 1814. MGS. *Challis, Portuguese Army*, p. 58 ['P.W... Nive Dec. '13'].

+O'HARE, Peter, Major, 95th Foot: Capt., 95th Foot, 6 Aug. 1803; Major, 95th Foot, 11 April 1811. Mentioned in Wellington's Fuentes de Onoro dispatch, 8 May 1811 [5 May: '[The French] attempted to push a body of light infantry down the ravine of the Turon to the right of the 1st division, which were repulsed by the light infantry of the guards, under Lieutenant-Colonel Guise, aided by five companies of the 95th, under Captain O'Hare.'] [*London Gazette*, 26 May 1811]. Killed, storming of Badajoz, 6 April 1812 [*London Gazette*]. Mentioned in Wellington's Badajoz dispatch, 7 April 1812 ['I

must likewise mention ... Major O'Hare of the 95th, unfortunately killed in the breach'] [*London Gazette*]. *Register of officers' effects*: 1st Battn. Not known if married. His effects totalled £20. 5s. 3½d. [PRO: WO 25/2964]. *Simmons*, pp. 40–1, 52, 54, 61, 63, 65n1, 105 [injured], 111, 228, 231–2 [killed, Badajoz: 'I saw my poor friend Major O'Hare lying dead upon the breach. Two or three musket balls had passed through his breast... I called to remembrance poor O'Hare's last words just before he marched off to lead the advance. He shook me by the hand saying, "A Lieutenant-Colonel or cold meat in a few hours." I was now gazing upon his body lying stretched and naked amongst thousands more.']. *Leach*, p. 214 [Fuentes de Onoro], pp. 256–8 [Storming of Badajoz: 'Major O'Hare, of the 1st battalion 95th, commanded the storming party which headed the Light Division... Amongst the many whom our regiment had to lament, was Major O'Hare, who fell in the breach. The service boasted not a more truly gallant soldier.']. *Kincaid, Random Shots*, p. 54 [Barba del Puerco, 19 March 1810]: 'Ferey at the head of six hundred chosen grenadiers burst forth so silently and suddenly, that, of our double sentry on the bridge, the one was taken and the other bayonetted without being able to fire off their pieces. A sergeant's party higher up among the rocks had just time to fire off as an alarm, and even the remainder of the company on piquet under O'Hare had barely time to jump up and snatch their rifles when the enemy were among them. O'Hare's men, however, though borne back and unable to stop them for an instant, behaved nobly, retiring in a continued hand-to-hand personal encounter with their foes to the top of the pass, when the remaining companies under Sidney Beckwith having just started from their sleep, rushed forward to their support, and with a thundering discharge, tumbled the attacking column into the ravine below'].

O'HEHIR. Sylvester, Lt., 60th Foot: Lt., 60th Foot, 14 June 1810. Severely wounded, storming of Fort St Michael, Burgos, 19 Sept. 1812 ('O'Heher') (5th Battn.) [*London Gazette*].

OKE, John, Capt./Major, 61st Foot: Capt., Army, 1 Oct. 1802; Capt., 61st Foot, 9 July 1803. Severely wounded, Salamanca, 22 July 1812 [*London Gazette*]. Major, 61st Foot, 23 July 1812; Bvt. Lt. Col., 61st Foot, 22 Nov. 1813. Severely wounded, Toulouse, 10 April 1814 (1st Battn.) [*London Gazette*]. Gold Medal. Temporary pension of two hundred pounds per annum, commencing 11 April 1815, 'for wounds' received at Toulouse [*1818 Pension Return*, pp. 16–17]. *Royal Military Calendar*, vol. V, pp. 8–9 ['... battle of Salamanca, and wounded in both legs in this action... He has received a medal for the battle of Toulouse, at which the command of the 61st devolved on him in consequence of the death of his commanding officer. In this battle, when in the act of cheering his men on to one of the enemy's redoubts, in which he was the first who obtained a footing, L.-Col. Oke's horse was twice wounded, and himself very severely, by a musket ball entering in front of the right thigh, which passed through his groin, and lodged underneath the muscles of his left thigh, where it still remains, every attempt to extract it proving ineffectual, and which has occasioned him to retire on half-pay.'].

O'KEARNEY, Denis, Lt., 61st Foot: Lt., Army, 13 July 1808; Lt., 61st Foot, 13 Oct. 1808. Slightly wounded, Pyrenees, 28 July 1813 (1st Battn.) [*London Gazette*].

OLIVER, Andrew, Ensign, 38th Foot: Ensign, 38th Foot, 23 Sept. 1813. Slightly wounded, Nivelle, 10 Nov. 1813 (1st Battn.) [*London Gazette*].

+OLIVER, James Ward, Bvt. Major, E.O.P.S.; Lt. Col., 14th Portuguese Line: Bvt. Major, E.O.P.S., 16 Jan. 1809, 'Serv. with the Portuguese Army'. Severely wounded at the siege of Badajoz, 30 May-5 June 1811, while serving as Lt. Col., 14th Portuguese Line ('Olliver') [*London Gazette*]. In Portuguese Service April 1809 to June 1811. Obituary, *The Gentleman's Magazine*, July 1811 ['June 17. At Elvas, Portugal, in consequence of a wound received in the trenches before Badajos, on the 31st May, Lieut.-col. James Ward Oliver, 14th reg. Portuguese infantry, Major on the staff of the British army, and late Captain in the 4th or King's Own regiment of infantry.']. *Challis, Portuguese Army*, p. 58 ['Wd. 2nd Sge. Badajos 30 May and 6 June '11... Died of Wounds 6 June '11'].

OLIVER, Thomas Milward, Ensign, 38th Foot: *1829 Statement of Service for Retired Officers*: Aged twenty on first appointment to the Army. Royal Manx Militia. Ensign, 38th Foot, 20 July 1810; Lt., 38th Foot, 9 Sept. 1812; Half-pay, 1 May 1816, 'at my own request'. *Where serving when wounded*: 'Villa Morial Spain on the retreat from Burgos Castle'. *Family*: Married in Winchester, Hants., 3 March 1814. Four children by 1829. No employment. *Where generally resident during last five years*: 'Hagley, Worcestershire. West Bourne, Sussex.' [PRO: WO 25/770 f57].

O'NEALE, Thomas, Lt., 32nd Foot; Capt., 15th Portuguese Line: Lt., 32nd Foot, 26 Aug. 1807. Severely wounded, storming of Badajoz, while serving as a Capt., 15th Portuguese Line ('Thomas O'Neil') [*London Gazette*]. Severely wounded, storming of San Sebastian, 31 Aug. 1813, while serving as Capt.,

15th Portuguese Line ('O'Neil') [*London Gazette*]. In Portuguese Service April 1809 to April 1814. Temporary pension of one hundred pounds per annum, commencing 1 Sept. 1814, 'for wounds' received at Badajoz and St Sebastian ['O'Neill'] [*1818 Pension Return*, pp. 26–7]. *Challis, Portuguese Army*, p. 58.

O'NEIL, John E., Lt., 1st Foot: Lt., Army, 21 April 1808. Lt., 1st Foot, 8 June 1809. Slightly wounded, storming of Badajoz, 6 April 1812, while serving as an 'Acting Engineer' ('O'Neal') [*London Gazette*]. Severely wounded, Salamanca, 22 July 1812 [*London Gazette*]. Severely wounded, 'at the Siege of St Sebastian,' 7–27 July 1813 (3rd Battn.) [*London Gazette*]. Killed, Waterloo.

O'NEILL, Charles, Lt., 83rd Foot: *1829 Statement of Service for Retired Officers:* Aged eighteen on first appointment to the Army. 'Volunteered from the North Mayo Militia'. Ensign, 83rd Foot, 4 June 1808; Lt., 83rd Foot, 4 Jan. 1810; Half-pay, October 1819, by reduction 'of the Establishment in the Island of Ceylon'; Lt., 2nd Veteran Battn., October 1823; Lt., 33rd Foot, October 1825; Capt., Half-pay, 4 June 1827. *Where serving when wounded:* 'Severely wounded at the Storming of Badajos in Spain on the 6th April 1812. No pension. Received one year's Pay as a Lieut. commanding a Company.' Not married. No employment. *Where generally resident during last five years:* 'In Ballyshamon, since placed on H. Pay on the 4th June 1827'. [PRO: WO 25/770 f73]. Severely wounded, storming of Badajoz, 6 April 1812 ('O'Neal') (2nd Battn.) [*London Gazette*]. MGS.

O'REILLY, Dowell, Lt., Royal Navy: Lt., Royal Navy, 30 May 1807. Slightly wounded, 'at the Siege of St Sebastian', 7–27 July, while serving in a 'Detachment of Seamen' [*London Gazette*]. Commander, Royal Navy, 23 Sept. 1813; Captain, Royal Navy, 29 Aug. 1815. Died 28 May 1816. D. Syrett ed, *The Commissioned Officers of the Royal Navy, 1660–1815* (1994), p. 339.

O'REILLY, John, Ensign, 44th Foot: Ensign, 44th Foot, 12 Dec. 1811. Slightly wounded, storming of Badajoz, 6 April 1812 (2nd Battn.) [*London Gazette*]. 'O'Reiley' in Army List. 'O'Reilly' in *Challis, Index*, p. 135.

ORMISTON, John Andrew, Ensign, 91st Foot: Ensign, 91st Foot, 3 Oct. 1811. Slightly wounded, Pyrenees, 28 July 1813 ('J. Omarston') (1st Battn.) [*London Gazette*]. Lt., 91st Foot, 29 July 1813.

ORMSBY, James, Lt., 52nd Foot: Lt., 52nd Foot, 17 Dec. 1806. Wounded, 'in the Army lately in Spain' (1st Battn.) [*March 1809 Army List*, p. 105]. *Moorsom*, p. 108 ['The 52nd sustained the following casualties at Corunna... Lieutenant James Ormsby... severely wounded.'], p. 428 ['Served in the Peninsula.'].

+ORPEN, Henry Francis, Major, 61st Foot: Capt., Army, 27 May 1795; Capt., 61st Foot, 26 Jan. 1797. Killed, Talavera, 28 July 1809 [*London Gazette*].

ORR, John, Capt., 7th Foot: Capt., 7th Foot, 27 April 1809. Severely wounded, Albuera, 16 May 1811 (2nd Battn.) [*London Gazette*]. Severely wounded, Pyrenees, 28 July 1813 (1st Battn.) [*London Gazette*]. Temporary pension of two hundred pounds per annum, commencing 17 May 1812, 'for wounds' received at Albuera [*1818 Pension Return*, pp. 4–5]. MGS.

ORR, John, Ensign, 42nd Foot: *1829 Statement of Service for Retired*

Officers: Aged nineteen on first appointment to the Army. Ensign, 'ESL Militia', 21 July 1809; Ensign, Edinburgh Militia, 22 Nov. 1809; Lt., Edinburgh Militia, 19 July 1811; Ensign, 42nd Foot, 3 Oct. 1811; Lt., 42nd Foot, 29 April 1813; Half-pay, 25 Dec. 1816, by reduction; Lt., 94th Foot, 2 Aug. 1817; Half-pay, 25 Dec. 1818, by reduction; Lt., 8th Royal Veteran Battn., 6 July 1820. 'Lieutenant Orr was placed on the retired list when the 8th R.V. Battalion were disbanded at Belfast in 1821.' *Where serving when wounded*: 'At Burgos and Severely at Waterloo.' *Family*: Married in Glasgow, 2 Dec. 1816. Six children, though four had died in infancy prior to 1829. *Where generally resident during last five years*: 'Glasgow & Musselburgh'. [PRO: WO 25/770 f87]. MGS. Died, 7 Dec. 1879.

ORR, Martin, Lt., 7th Foot: *1829 Statement of Service*: Born in Paisley, 18 Oct. 1792. Aged eighteen on his first Entrance in the Army. Lt., 7th Foot, 28 June 1810; Adjutant, 7th Foot, 23 Oct. 1823; Capt., 88th Foot, 28 Oct. 1831. *Battles, sieges and campaigns*: 'Siege of Badajoz, Ap & May 1811. Battle of Albuera, 16 May 1811, Affair of Asma, 19 June 1813. Battle of Vittoria, 21 June 1813. Affair of Romesvalles, 25 July 1813. Battle of Pampeluna, 28 July 1813. and Affairs untill 2 Aug. 1813. Battle of Nivelle, 10 Nov. 1813. Battle of Orthes, 27 Feb. 1814. Battle of Toulouse, 10 April 1814.' *Distinguished conduct*: 'By Letter from the late Major Despard who succeeded in Command mentioning the Gallant Manner in which the Colors of the Regt. had been carried by me at Albuera on the 16th May 1811. Thanked by Lt. Col. Beatty Commg. for carrying & maintaining some Farm Houses and taking Prisoners at Orthes 27 Feb. 1814. Thanked by Lt. Colonel Achmuty Commg. Brigade of Lt.

Infy. Comps for gallant conduct during the 10 Ap 1814 at Toulouse having comd. of the Light Compy. in repelling several Attacks made by the enemy.' *Wounds received in action*: 'Wounded at Albuera 16th May 1811 thro' the left knee joint and the left Elbow. – Received a grant of one year's pay.' *Service abroad*: 'February 1811 to August 1811, Portugal & Spain. April 1812 to 28 June 1814, Portugal & Spain. 18 June 1815 to 2 Nov. 1818, France. 17 June 1825 to Dec. 1828, Ionian Islands and Malta. 7 March 1834 to 1836, Ionian Islands.' *Family*: Married Anna Dower, 17 Jan. 1829, Walmer, near Deal. No children by 1830. [PRO: WO 25/786 f108]. Severely wounded, Albuera, 16 May 1811 (2nd Battn.) [*London Gazette*]. MGS.

ORRELL, Andrew, Ensign, 34th Foot: Ensign, 34th Foot, 30 May 1811. Severely wounded, Pyrenees, 30 July 1813 ('Orrall') (1st Battn.) [*London Gazette*]. MGS.

+OSBOURNE, Keane, Capt., 5th Dragoon Guards: Capt., Army, 5 Jan. 1809; Capt., 5th Dragoon Guards, 9 Feb. 1809. Killed, Salamanca, 22 July 1812 ('Osborne') [*London Gazette*].

OSWALD, John, Major-General: Col., Greek Light Infantry Corps, 30 Oct. 1805; Major-General, 4 June 1811. Slightly wounded, storming of San Sebastian, 31 Aug. 1813 [*London Gazette*]. Mentioned in Graham's San Sebastian dispatch, dated Oyarzun, 1 Sept. 1813 ['Your Lordship will now permit me to call your attention to the conduct of that distinguished officer, Major-General Oswald, who has had the temporary command of the fifth division in Lieutenant-General Sir James Leith's absence, during the whole of the campaign, and who resigned the command of the division on Sir James Leith's arrival on the 30th ultimo. Having carried on with indefatigable attention all the laborious duties of the left attack, no person was more able to give Sir James Leith the best information and assistance. This Sir James Leith acknowledges he did with a liberality and zeal for the service in the highest degree praiseworthy, and he continued his valuable services to the last, by acting as a volunteer, and accompanying Lieutenant-General Sir James Leith to the trenches on the occasion of the assault. I have infinite satisfaction in assuring your Lordship of my perfect approbation of Major-General Oswald's conduct, ever since the 5th Division formed a part of the left column of the army.'] [*London Gazette*].

O'TOOLE, Bryan, Capt., 39th Foot; Lt. Col. 7th Caçadores: Capt., 39th Foot, 9 July 1803; Bvt. Major, 39th Foot, 25 April, 1808. Mentioned in Wellington's Ciudad Rodrigo dispatch of 20 Jan. 1812 [Commanding a Column under Picton at the storming of Ciudad Rodrigo: 'I beg particularly to draw your Lordship's attention to the conduct of Lieutenant-Colonel O'Toole, of the 2d Caçadores'] [*London Gazette*]. Severely wounded, Pyrenees, 25–28 July 1813, while serving as Lt. Col., 7th Caçadores ('Brien O'Toole') [*London Gazette*]. Mentioned in Hill's report to Wellington concerning operations before San Sebastian, dated 31 July 1813 ['I particularly observed Lieutenant-Colonel O'Toole, of the 7th Caçadores, in the charge upon the enemy, on our left, on the 28th'] [*London Gazette*]. Gold Medal. In Portuguese Service Nov. 1811 to April 1814. Temporary pension of three hundred pounds per annum, commencing 27 July 1814, 'for a wound' received at Pampeluna, 1813 [*1818 Pension Return*, pp. 26–7]. *Challis, Portuguese Army*, p. 58 ['Wd. Pyrenees 18 July '13' (sic)].

OUSELEY, Ralph, Capt., 63rd Foot; Lt. Col., 8th Portuguese Line: Capt., Army, 6 March 1805; Capt., 63rd Foot, 7 Sept. 1809. Severely wounded, 'in the Operations of the Army', 31 Aug. 1813, while serving as Lt. Col., 8th Portuguese Line [*London Gazette*]. Bvt. Major, E.O.P. S., 25 Nov. 1813, 'Serving with the Portug. Army'. In Portuguese Service Nov. 1809 to Sept. 1813. Gold Medal. Pension of three hundred pounds per annum, commencing 1 Sept. 1814, 'for wounds' received in the Pyrenees, 1813 [*1818 Pension Return*, pp. 24–5]. *Challis, Portuguese Army*, p. 58 ['Wd. San Sebastian 31 Aug. '13' (sic)].

+OUSELY, Ralph, Lt., 45th Foot: Ensign, 45th Foot, 17 Feb. 1808; Lt. 26 Oct. 1809. Killed, Busaco, 27 Sept. 1810 (1st Battn.) [*London Gazette*].

+OVENS, Edward, Capt., 38th Foot; Major, 3rd Portuguese Line: Capt., 38th Foot, 26 May 1808. Wounded, Heights of Grijon, 11 May 1809, while serving with the 1st battn. detachments ('Owens') [*London Gazette*]. In Portuguese Service Sept. 1810 to Oct. 1812. *Challis, Portuguese Army*, p. 58 ['Maj. 3 Line... K/A Villa Muriel 25 Oct. '12'].

OVENS, John, Ensign, 27th Foot: *1829 Statement of Service*: 'Born in Churchhill, Fermanagh, 21st April 1796. Aged 16²/12 years on his first Entrance into the Army. Ensign, 27th Foot, 2nd July 1812. Lieutenant, 27th Foot, 5 July 1814. Half Pay, 11th April 1816, By Reduction of the 3d. Battalion. Lieutenant, 20th Foot, 25th March 1824. Lieutenant, 57th Foot, 16th Decr. 1824.' *Battles, sieges and campaigns*: 'I performed my Regimental Duties, during the following Actions and was personally Engaged in them viz. Vittoria 21st June 1813. Pampeluna 28th July 1813. Nivelle

10th November 1813. Orthes 28th February 1814. Toulouse 10th April 1814. Platzburg in America 26th October 1814.' *Distinguished conduct*: 'After being wounded at the Battle of Pampeluna and Inspected by the Surgeon who ordered me to the rear, I continued in the Field, on which occasion Colonel McClean thanked me after the Action for not availing myself of the order I received and from seeing the nature of the Wound which I suffered much from at the time.' *Wounds received in action*: Wounded on the 28th July 1813 at the Battle of Pampeluna and I received One Years Pay as Ensign as a Remuneration.' *Service abroad*: 'November 1812 to June 1814, Peninsula. June 1814 to May 1815, America. June 1815 to January 1816, France. 24th May 1825 to 31st Decr. 1829, New South Wales.' [PRO: WO 25/796 f100]. Slightly wounded, Pyrenees, 28 July 1813 ('Ensign Ovens') (3rd Battn.) [*London Gazette*]. MGS.

OVENS, John, Capt., 74th Foot: Capt., 73rd Foot, 18 July 1811; Capt., 74th Foot, 8 Oct. 1812. Severely wounded, Vittoria, 21 June 1813 [*London Gazette*].

OWEN, John, Capt., 61st Foot: Capt., 61st Foot, 9 July 1803. Severely wounded, 'arm amputated', in the siege of the Forts of St Vincente, St Cayetano, and La Merced at Salamanca, 18–24 June 1812 [*London Gazette*]. Mentioned in Wellington's dispatch concerning the storming of the forts at Salamanca, dated Fuente la Pena, 30 June 1812 ['Major-General Clinton ... mentions in strong terms of commendation the conduct of ... Captain Owen of the 61st'] [*London Gazette*]. Two hundred pounds per annum pension, commencing 24 June 1813, for 'loss of an arm' at Salamanca [*1818 Pension Return*, pp. 16–17].

OWGAN, Joseph, Ensign, 88th Foot: *1829 Statement of Service*: 'Born near Kinsale, Ireland, 26th July 1792. Aged Seventeen on his first Entrance into the Army. Ensign, 88th Foot, 29th June 1809. Lieut., 88th Foot, 29th April 1812. Half Pay, March 1817, by Reduction. Lieut., 73rd Foot, 10th June 1825.' *Battles, sieges and campaigns*: 'Busaco 1810. Redinha, Sabugal, Fuentes D'Onor, 1811.' *Wounds received in action*: 'Severely Wounded through the Lungs at Fuentes D'Onor on the 5th May 1811. Received One Years Pay & a temporary Pension of Fifty pounds a year from the 6th May 1812 to 24th December 1816.' *Service abroad*: '1809 to 1811, Portugal. 1814 to 1817, Canada, France.' *Family*: Married Jane Morgan, 7 Nov. 1822, Cork. They had two children by 1830. [PRO: WO 25/799 f183].

P

PACK, Anthony Pierce, Lt., 71st Foot: *1829 Statement of Service*: Born in Kilkenny, Ireland, 21 May 1794. Aged seventeen on his first entrance into the Army. Ensign, 71st Foot, 12 Dec. 1811; Lt., 71st Foot, 3 June 1813; Half-pay, 24 Dec. 1818, by reduction; Lt., 55th Foot, March 1820; Lt., 84th Foot, Dec. 1821; Capt., 84th Foot, 20 May 1825. 'Aid-de-Camp to the late M. General Sir Denis Pack K.C.B. &c. from 12th Augt. 1819 to 25th July 1823 the date of the M. General's decease.' *Battles, sieges and campaigns*: 'Vittoria, 21st June 1813. Puerto Mayo, 25th July 1813.' *Distinguished conduct*: '25th July 1813. Conduct approved of by Lt. Colonel Cather then in Command of 71st Regt., lately Commg. 83rd Foot.' *Wounds received in action*: '25th July 1813, Severely wounded in command of a company in defending a particular rock, in front of the British positions. Recd. one years pay as Captain. The Ball still remains, & causes slight lameness.' *Service abroad*: 'Feby. 1813 to Novr. 1813, Peninsula. May 1816 to Decr. 1818, France. Decr. 1826 to Decr. 1829, Jamaica.' *Family*: Married Sarah Paterson, Jan. 1826, Kilrush, St Clare, Ireland. They had one child, a son, by 1830. [PRO WO25/801 f226]. Severely wounded, Pyrenees, 25 July 1813 ('Packe') (1st Battn.) [*London Gazette*]. MGS.

PACK, Dennis, Major-General: Colonel, Army, 25 July 1810; Major-General 4 June 1813. Slightly wounded, Pyrenees, 30 July 1813 [*London Gazette*]. Severely wounded, Toulouse, 10 April 1814 ('Denis Pack') [*London Gazette*]. In Portuguese Service July 1810 to April 1813. Gold Medal. Wounded, Waterloo. *Challis, Portuguese Army*, p. 58. *Dalton*, pp. 4, 21 ['The only son of the Very Rev. thos. Pack,

Dean of Ossory... Five times received the thanks of Parliament for his military services. Was one of the most dashing leaders of a brigade in the Par. War.' 'He was scarred with wounds and covered with glory.' Commanded the 71st Regt. at Buenos Ayres when that city was retaken by the Spaniards, and was sev. wnded. and taken prisoner. When he escaped from prison, Pack was appointed to the command of a provisional battalion stationed at Colonia. His fidgety and irascible temper somewhat tried those who had to serve under him. One morning there appeared written in chalk on the door of a barn the following distich:– 'The devil break the gaoler's back/That let thee loose, sweet Denis Pack.' For his services at Waterloo he was made Col.-in-Chf. of the York Chasseurs. M. 10th July, 1816, Lady Eliz. Beresford, youngest dau. of George, 1st Marquis of Waterford, and had issue... Sir Dennis d. 24th July, 1823.]'

PAGE, William Edward, Lt./Adjutant, 7th Foot: Lt. and Adjutant, 7th Foot, 29 Jan. 1807. Slightly wounded, Talavera, 28 July 1809 [*London Gazette*].

+PAGE, William, Lt., 48th Foot: Lt., 48th Foot, 15 Dec. 1804. Severely wounded, Talavera, 28 July 1809 (1st Battn.) [*London Gazette*]. Killed, Albuera, 16 May 1811 (1st Battn.) [*London Gazette*]. Obituary, *The Gentleman's Magazine*, 1811 Supplement, Part I., p. 679 ['In the battle of Albuera, Lieut. Page, a young gentleman of the highest promise, who was also wounded in the battle of Talavera. He was the son of Mr. D. P. of the Barrack Office, who has now lost his two eldest sons in the service of his country.'].

PAGET, Hon. Edward, Major-General: Lt. Col., 28th Foot, 30 April 1794; Col., 28th Foot, 1 Jan. 1798; Maj.-General, 1 Jan. 1805; Col., 80th Foot, 23 Feb. 1808. 'Lost his arm, but doing well', passage of the Douro, 12 May 1809 [*London Gazette*]. Lt.-General, 4 June 1811. Recorded as 'missing', in operations, 15–19 Nov. 1812 ('Lieutenant-General the Honourable Sir Edward Paget, K.B.') [*London Gazette*]. Pension of four hundred pounds per annum, commencing 25 Dec. 1811, for 'loss of an arm' in Portugal, 1809 [*1818 Pension Return*, pp. 18–19]. Brother of Henry Paget, 2nd Earl of Uxbridge and 1st Marquess of Anglesey, who famously lost a leg at Waterloo. *Haythornthwaite, Source Book*, p. 361 ['General Sir Edward Paget (1775–1849), one of Wellington's divisional commanders of considerable ability but no luck: he lost an arm at Oporto and was captured on the retreat from Burgos'].

PAKENHAM, Hon. Hercules Robert, Major, 7th West India Regt.: *1829 Statement of Service for Retired Officers*: Aged twenty-two on first appointment to the Army. Ensign, 40th Foot, Aug. 1803 [Army List gives 23 July 1803]; Lt., 2nd West India Regt., Jan. 1804 [Army List gives 3 Feb. 1804]; Lt., 95th Foot, March 1804 [Army List gives 28 April 1804]; Capt., 95th Foot, [2] Aug. 1805; Major, 7th West India Regt., Sept. 1810 [Army List gives 30 Aug. 1810]; Bvt. Lt. Col., [27] April 1812; Lt. Col., 26th Foot, [3] Sept. 1812; Capt. and Lt. Col., Coldstream Guards, [25 July] 1814; Half-pay, Portuguese Service, 1816, 'Being unequal to serve from suffering occasioned by my wounds'; Col., ADC to the King, 1825. 'The wound thro' my Hip bone, being still open, never having closed, & being frequently in a very inflamed state, I do not feel equal to active service. The first object of my life always was active employ-

ment in the service; I was forced into retirement by the severity of the wounds I received, during the time I was on full pay [thirteen years] I never had two months leave of absense from my corps.' *Where serving when wounded*: 'Badajoz'. *Details of pension*: Two hundred pounds, commencing April 1813. *Family*: Married in the British Embassy, Paris, 10 Nov. 1817. Five children by 1829. No employment. *Where generally resident during last five years*: 'London or Langford Lodge, Co. Antrim, Ireland.' [PRO WO25/770 f215]. Severely wounded, 'not dangerously,' storming of Badajoz, 6 April 1812, while serving on the staff as Assistant Adjutant-General [*London Gazette*]. Mentioned in Wellington's Badajoz dispatch, 7 April 1812 ['Lieutenant-General Picton has reported to me particularly the conduct of ... the Honourable Major Pakenham, Assistant Adjutant-General to the 3rd division.'] [*London Gazette*]. Gold Medal. Later Major-General. MGS. *Leach*, p. 45 ['On the 15th of August [1808], after a long march, a party of French cavalry and infantry were found near the town of Obidos, where there is a Moorish castle. Four companies of ours and of the 60th regiment instantly attacked and obliged them to retire. In the ardour of pursuit, our people pushed on a considerable distance from any support, and were met by a very superior body of the enemy, sent forward to support their advanced party. A sharp skirmish ensued, in which we lost some few in killed, wounded, and missing. The Honourable Captain Pakenham, of our regiment, was wounded, and Lieutenant Bunbury killed, the first British officer who fell in the Peninsular wars.']. *Simmons*, p. 10. *Harris*, p. 34 [Vimeiro], pp. 109–10 [Corunna retreat: 'The honourable Captain Pakenham (now Sir Hercules Pakenham), on the first sound of

PAKENHAM

the enemy being in sight, made a dash to get to the front, at the same moment I myself was scrambling up a bank on the road side. In the darkness and hurry the mule the captain was mounted on bore me to the ground, and, getting his fore-feet fast fixed somehow between my neck and my pack, we were fairly hampered for some moments. The captain swore, the mule floundered, and I bellowed with alarm'], p. 147. Third son of Edward, 2nd Baron Longford; born 1781, died 1850 as lieutenant-general Sir Hercules. Brother of Sir Edward Michael Pakenham, distinguished in the Peninsular War but best known for his death commanding the forces at New Orleans. Their sister Catherine married Wellington, so that during the Peninsular War Hercules was Wellington's brother-in-law. [Burke's Peerage].

PARK, Thomas, Lt., 71st Foot: *1829 Statement of Service*: Born 21 Oct. 1785, Parkhall, Stirlingshire, Scotland. Aged eighteen on first appointment to the Army. Ensign, 71st Foot, 21 June 1805; Lt. 3 Feb. 1808; Capt. 31 March 1814; Half Pay April 1816; Capt., 71st Foot, 8 April 1825; Capt., 26th Foot, 31 Aug. 1826. *Battles, sieges and campaigns*: 'Walcheren. Present at the Seige of "Flushing" in 1809, under Genl. Lord Chatham. Peninsula. At "Arroya de Molina," "Alba de Tormes," "Almarez," "Retreat from Burgos" to 4th October 1812. "Vittoria" 21 June 1813, and at the "Pyrenees" in July 1813. The whole as Lieutenant.' *Distinguished conduct*: 'Received strong testemonials from Major General Sir Dennis Pack, Major General Sir Thomas Reynell, and from Colonel Jones under all of whom I served in the 71st Regiment.' *Wounds received in action*: '25th July 1813, on the Pyrenees, in the breast; slightly. Nothing received.' *Titles, honorary distinctions and medals*:

'After being wounded in the Pyrenees, appointed by General Packenham to act as Commandant at Villarcayo and afterwards at St Andero. Remained in those situations for 13 months.' *Service abroad*: 'July 1809 to Decr. 1809, Walcheren. 1810 to 1814, Portugal & Spain.' *Family*: Married Miss Ann Robertson, 25 April 1816, Inverness. They had six children by 1830. [PRO: WO 25/790 f24]. Slightly wounded, Pyrenees, 25 July 1813 ('Parke') (1st Battn.) [London Gazette].

+PARKE, Robert, Ensign, 59th Foot: Ensign, 59th Foot, 29 Oct. 1812. Killed, storming of San Sebastian, 31 Aug. 1813 ('Pack') [London Gazette]. *Register of officers' effects*: Single. Effects totalled £64. 7s. [PRO: WO 25/2964].

PARKE, William, Capt., 2nd Foot: Capt., 2nd Foot, 27 Dec. 1797. Wounded, 'in the Army lately in Spain' [March 1809 Army List, p. 105]. MGS.

+PARKER, Arthur, Lt., 36th Foot: Lt., 36th Foot, 20 Feb. 1806. Killed, Salamanca, 22 July 1812 [London Gazette].

+PARKER, Edward, Capt., Royal Engineers: Capt., Royal Engineers, 24 June 1809. Killed, Orthes, 27 Feb. 1814 [London Gazette]. Colville, p. 170 [Letter from John Keane to Sir Charles Colville, 17 March 1814: 'Poor Parker was cut in two by a cannon shot close to the God of War.'].

+PARKER, Harry, Ensign, Coldstream Guards: Ensign, Coldstream Guards, 18 April 1805. Killed, Talavera, 28 July 1809 [London Gazette]. Son of Admiral Sir Hyde Parker (1739–1807). [Burke's Peerage].

+PARKER, John, Lt., 61st Foot: Lt., 61st Foot, 26 June 1807. Killed,

Salamanca, 22 July 1812 (1st Battn.) [*London Gazette*].

+**PARKINSON, John, Ensign, 74th Foot:** Ensign, 74th Foot, 21 Oct. 1813. Severely wounded and 'missing', Toulouse, 10 April 1814 (1st Battn.) [*London Gazette*]. Died of wounds, 11 April 1814. Return dated April 1814. [PRO: WO 25/2965].

PARRY, William Parry Jones, Capt., 48th Foot: *1829 Statement of Service for Retired Officers*: 'Wm Parry Yale, formerly Wm Parry Jones Parry'. Aged fifteen on first appointment to the Army. Ensign, 90th Foot, Sept. 1805; Lt., 4th Garrison Battn., 1807; Lt., 48th Foot, 1807; Capt., 48th Foot, May 1808 [Army List gives 17 May]; Bvt. Major, 48th Foot, May 1825; Major, Half-pay, unattached, June 1826. *Where serving when wounded*: 'Pampeluna'. One year's pay, but no pension. *Family*: Married in 'Launceston, Vandiemans Land', 16 Oct. 1821. *Title and nature of employment*: 'Magistrate'. *Where generally resident during last five years*: 'Hangollen'. [PRO: WO 25/779 f3]. MGS.

+**PARSONS, Edward, Capt., 48th Foot:** Capt., 48th Foot, 21 Nov. 1805. Severely wounded, Albuera, 16 May 1811 [*London Gazette*]. Died, Portugal, 4 June 1811 [PRO: WO 25/2965].

PARSONS, Henry, Capt., 47th Foot: Capt., 47th Foot, 13 June 1811. Slightly wounded, Vittoria, 21 June 1813 (2nd Battn.) [*London Gazette*].

+**PARSONS, Lucius, Ensign, 48th Foot:** Ensign, 48th Foot, 15 Aug. 1811. Killed, Pyrenees, 28 July 1813 (1st Battn.) [*London Gazette*].

+**PARVIN, John H., Ensign, 68th Foot:** Ensign, 68th Foot, 4 Oct. 1810. Killed, Vittoria, 21 June 1813 [*London Gazette*].

PASSLEY, John Panton, Lt., 60th Foot: *1829 Statement of Service for Retired Officers*: Aged eighteen on first appointment to the Army. Ensign, 60th Foot, 31 Oct. 1805; Lt., 60th Foot, 5 Dec. 1807; Capt., 60th Foot, 8 Jan. 1818; Half-pay, n.d. [1819], by reduction. Served thirteen years five months on full pay. *Where serving when wounded*: 'Peninsula'. *Details of pension*: Seventy pounds, commencing '17th Decr 1824 to take effect from 25th Decr. 1817.' *Family*: Married in Jamaica, 14 March 1820. Four children by 1829. No employment. *Where generally resident during last five years*: 'Jamaica principally, England occasionally'. [PRO WO 25/770 f194]. Severely wounded, Nivelle, 10 Nov. 1813 (5th Battn.) [*London Gazette*].

+**PATERSON, Charles, Major, 28th Foot:** Major, 28th Foot, 18 Jan. 1810; Bvt. Lt. Col., 28th Foot, 20 June 1811. Severely wounded, Vittoria, 21 June 1813 ('Patterson') [*London Gazette*]. Died of wounds, 18 Aug. 1813. Return dated Aug. 1813. [PRO: WO 25/2965]. Obituary, *The Gentleman's Magazine*, Oct. 1813, p. 401 ['Aug. 17. At Vittoria, in consequence of wounds received in the battle of the 21st of June, Lieut.-col. C. Paterson, 28th reg. fourth son of G. P. esq. of Castle Huntly.'].

PATERSON, Leeson, Lt., 57th Foot: Lt., 57th Foot, 4 Feb. 1808. Severely wounded, Albuera, 16 May 1811 ('Patterson') [*London Gazette*]. Temporary Pension of seventy pounds per annum, commencing 17 May 1812, 'for wounds' received at Albuera [*1818 Pension Return*, pp. 14-15].

PATISON, Andrew, Capt., 29th Foot: Lt., 29th Foot, 13 July 1798; Capt. 18 Dec. 1806. Wounded, Rolica, 17 Aug. 1808 [*London Gazette*].

PATRICKSON, Christopher C., Major, 43rd Foot: Major, 43rd Foot,

28 Sept. 1809. Slightly wounded during 'several affairs with the French Army', 18 March-7 April 1811 (1st Battn.) [*London Gazette*]. Lt. Col., Army, 30 May 1811; Lt. Col., 43rd Foot, 17 June 1813. Gold Medal. MGS.

PATRICKSON, Samuel, Lt., 95th Foot; Capt., 67th Foot: *1829 Statement of Service*: 'Born in Dublin, Ireland, 21 March 1785. Aged 18 years on his first Entrance into the Army. Ensign, 69th Foot, 9 July 1803. Lt., 69th Foot, March 1805. Lt., 95th Foot, June 1808. Captain, 67th Foot, 21 December 1809. Major, 67th Foot, 8 August 1816. Half Pay, 28 July 1817. Reduced with second Battalion. Major, 99th Foot, 25 Decr. 1824. Major, 66th Foot, 20 January 1825.' *Battles, sieges and campaigns*: 'Served with the Rifle Corps as Lieut. in the Campaigns under the late Sir J. Moore in Spain. Was present on the retreat and at the Battle of Caleavella and Corunna. Campaign under Lord Chatham to the Scheldt in 1809. Served with the 67th Foot as Captain at the Siege of Cadiz 1810. Battle of Barossa 5 March 1811. Campaign under Sir J. Murray. Was employed in the successful attack of the Fortress of Baliguer. Campaign under Lord W. Bentinck as Brigade Major in the South of Spain. Was present at the investment of the Fortress of Tarragona and Barcelona in 1813. Was a Volunteer on the expedition to Malago under Lord Blaney in 1810.' *Wounds received in action*: 'Severely Wounded at the Battle of Barosa, the left leg broken close under the knee. Received one years Pay and £100 Pension for Wounds and partial loss of Sight. Pension Permanent from 25 June 1824.' *Service abroad*: "July 1808 to January 1809, Spain. July 1809 to October 1809, Holland. July 1810 to November 1810, Gibraltar. December 1810 to April 1811, Cadiz, Spain. October 1812 to April 1813,

Carthagena, Spain. April 1813 to April 1814, Alicant, Catalonia. April 1814 to September 1816, Gibralter.' *Family*: Married Miss. M. Carter, 15 Aug. 1822. They had no children by 1830. [PRO: WO25/798 f3]. Severely wounded, Barossa, 5 March 1811 (2nd Battn. 67th Foot) [*London Gazette*].

PATTERSON, Cooke Tylden, Lt., 43rd Foot: Lt., 43rd Foot, 9 March 1809 ('Pattenson'). Severely wounded, storming of Ciudad Rodrigo, 19 Jan. 1812 [*London Gazette*]. MGS. *Bruce*, p. 80 [Letter from Lt. Col. Macleod to Major William Napier, El Bodem, 4 Feb. 1812: 'Ferguson and Patterson are both going on well; the latter was made a terrible figure of by the explosion of some gunpowder, whether placed there purposely or not is not easy to determine, but it was certainly a large quantity to have been left there accidentally. This scorched his face and one hand very badly, and he had scarcely recovered his astonishment at this summerset over the wall, when he received a pretty deep graze from the splinter of a shell or a ball in his *counterpart*, but he is likely to recover completely, and be as beautiful as ever.'].

PATTERSON, John, Lt., 50th Foot: *1829 Statement of Service for Retired Officers*: Aged eighteen on first appointment to the Army. Ensign, 7th Garrison Battn., 27 Nov. 1806; Ensign, 50th Foot, 6 Aug. 1807; Lt., 50th Foot, 22 Dec. 1808; Capt., 50th Foot, 19 Oct. 1820; Half-pay, 3 May 1821, 'on account of ill health arising from severe wounds, certified by a Medical Board'. 'Unable to serve in consequence of wounds'. *Where serving when wounded*: 'At the Pass of Maya in the Pyrenees while commanding a Company of the 50th foot, 25th July 1813'. *Details of pension*: Seventy pounds, commencing 26 July 1814. *Family*: Married in Enniskillen, 13

May 1816, Three children by 1829. No employment. *Where generally resident during last five years*: 'Chester, Sligo, Liverpool'. [PRO: WO 25/770 f157]. Severely wounded, Pyrenees, 25 July 1813 ('Paterson') (1st Battn.) [*London Gazette*].

PATTERSON, William, Lt., 50th Foot: Lt., 50th Foot, 31 Dec. 1807. Slightly wounded, 'at the Storm and Capture of Fort Napoleon, and the Enemy's other Works, in the Neighbourhood of Almarez', 19 May 1812 [*London Gazette*].

PATTISON, Alexander Hope, Lt., 74th Foot: Lt., 74th Foot, 26 April 1810. Slightly wounded, storming of Badajoz, 6 April 1812 [*London Gazette*]. Severely wounded, Pyrenees, 30 July 1813 (1st Battn.) [*London Gazette*]. Pension of seventy pounds per annum, commencing 1 Aug. 1814, 'for wounds' received at Pampeluna, 1813 [*1818 Pension Return*, pp. 18–19].

PATTON, Peter, Capt., Royal Engineers: Capt., Army, 1 March 1805; Capt., Royal Engineers, 24 June 1809. Severely wounded at the siege of Badajoz, 6–11 June 1811 [*London Gazette*].

+PATULLO, William, Lt., 6th Foot: Lt., 6th Foot, 4 March 1807. Killed, Orthes, 27 Feb. 1814 ('Pattulo') (1st Battn.) [*London Gazette*].

PAYNE, Capt., 23rd Foot: Severely wounded in 'an Affair with the Enemy near Aldea de Ponte', 27 Sept. 1811 [*London Gazette*].

PAYNE, Robert, Lt., 83rd Foot: Lt., 83rd Foot, 6 May 1805. Slightly wounded, Talavera, 28 July 1809 [*London Gazette*].

PEACOCKE, Nathaniel Levett, Lt. Col., 71st Foot: Lt. Col., 71st Foot, 25 June 1807; Colonel 4 June 1811. Slightly wounded, the Nive, 13 Dec. 1813 (1st Battn.) [*London Gazette*]. Haythornthwaite, *Armies of Wellington*, p. 254 [Nive, 13 Dec. 1813: 'The 1/71st was an excellent, experienced battalion, but had recently been inflicted with a new commander, Sir Nathaniel Peacocke, whom the brigade had already assessed as a tyrant off the battlefield and a coward on it. As the French advanced, Peacocke ordered his battalion to retire, leaving a gap in the centre of the British line, and took himself to the rear where he was found by Hill beating Portuguese ammunition-bearers, pretending to urge them forward while conveniently keeping himself out of danger.'].

PEACOCKE, Thomas Goodrick, Lt., 55th Foot; Capt. and Brigade Major, Portuguese Staff: 1829 Statement of Service for Retired Officers: Aged seventeen on first appointment to the Army. Ensign, 55th Foot, June 1807, 'obtained at the Royal Military College without Purchase'; Lt., 55th Foot, 3 March 1808; Capt., 55th Foot, Jan. 1818, 'and immediately after antidated to 25th Oct. 1814 in consequence of Portuguese services'; Half-pay, 36th Foot, 1823, 'in consequence of ill-health and sight much impaired'. 'I beg to state from 1810 to the close of the Peninsula War I served in the Portuguese Army as a Captain; then accompanied the expedition from Bordeaux to North America as Aide de Camp to M. Genl. Sir Manley Power on whose staff I remained until the termination of the Army of occupation in France when I rejoined the 55th Regiment, with which Corps I served until I retired to the Half Pay of the 36th Regt. by exchange with my Brother Captain William Lloyd Peacocke.' 'I should dread not being equal to a Foreign Climate in consequence of the effects of a Liver complaint and

PEACOCKE

very impaired sight. I beg to remark that I was twice wounded and had three Horses shot under me as A.D.C. to Major Genl. Sir Manley Power K.C.B.' *Where serving when wounded*: 'I was twice wounded with the Army in Spain and Portugal but I am not in rect. of any Pension'. *Family*: Married in the Parish of St James, Clerkenwell, Middlesex, 7 Nov. 1821. *Where generally resident during last five years*: 'County of Limerick, Ireland'. [PRO: WO 25/771 f13]. Severely wounded, Storming of Badajoz, 6 April 1812, while serving as Capt. and Brigade Major in the Portuguese Army [*London Gazette*]. MGS. *Challis, Portuguese Army*, p. 58.

PEACOCKE, William, Lt., 71st Foot: Ensign, Army, 25 Oct. 1809; Ensign, 71st Foot, 8 Nov. 1809; Lt., 71st Foot, 14 May 1812. Severely wounded, Pyrenees, 25 July 1813 (1st Battn.) [*London Gazette*].

+PEARSE, William, Lt., 45th Foot: Lt., 45th Foot, 1 Oct. 1807. Killed in the storming of Ciudad Rodrigo, 19 Jan. 1812 ('Persse') [*London Gazette*].

PEARSON, George, Lt., 81st Foot: Lt., 81st Foot, 21 May 1807. Wounded, 'in the Army lately in Spain' (2nd Battn.) [*London Gazette*]. Capt., 81st Foot, 25 June 1812; Half-pay 25 March 1816. MGS.

PEARSON, Thomas, Major, 23rd Foot: Major, 23rd Foot, 8 Dec. 1804; Lt. Col., Army, 4 June 1811. Severely wounded in 'an Affair with the Enemy near Aldea de Ponte', 27 Sept. 1811 [*London Gazette*].

PEDDIE, John, Lt., 38th Foot: *1829 Statement of Service for Retired Officers*: Aged 'between sixteen & seventeen' on first appointment to the Army. Ensign, 38th Foot, 26 Sept. 1805; Lt., 38th Foot, 26 Aug. 1807; Capt., 38th Foot, 23 Sept.

1813; Half-pay, 25 Oct. 1814, by reduction; Capt., 97th Foot, 25 March 1824; Major, 95th Foot, 16 June 1825; Half-pay, unattached, 25 Oct. 1826, 'from private motives'; Major, 56th Foot, 29 March 1827; Lt. Col., Half-pay, unattached, 28 Aug. 1827. 'Is most desirous of service, and has made several *very earnest* applications to be employed.' *Where serving when wounded*: 'Battle of Salamanca'. *Details of pension:* One hundred pounds per annum, commencing 23 July 1813. *Family:* Married in Guernsey, 15 March 1817. Three children by 1829. No employment. *Where generally resident during last five years*: 'When not employed he has been generally resident in France.' [PRO: WO 25/771 f37]. Severely wounded, 'right arm amputated', Salamanca, 22 July 1812 (1st Battn.) [*London Gazette*]. Pension for 'loss of an arm' at Salamanca [*1818 Pension Return*, pp. 10–11].

PELLY, Raymond, Major/Lt. Col., 16th Light Dragoons: Ensign, 27th Foot, 2 May 1800; Capt., Army, 6 Aug. 1802; Capt., 16th Light Dragoons, 25 Dec. 1802; Major 1 Nov. 1810; Lt. Col. 23 April 1812. Recorded as 'Missing', during 'movements of the Army', 23 Oct. 1812 [Retreat from Burgos] [*London Gazette*]. He had been wounded and taken prisoner. *Webber*, p. 106 [1 Nov. 1812: 'Here we heard that a severe skirmish had taken place on the banks of the Douro between the 16th Dragoons and the Hussars and several squadrons of the enemy's Cavalry, in which we had lost a great many men in killed and wounded, besides Colonel Parry [sic] of the 16th, taken prisoner.']. *Green, Vicissitudes*, p. 121 [23 Oct. 1812: 'At Torquemado our rear-guard had a most desperate action with the enemy, who pressed so hard upon them that we were in danger of losing a brigade of light dragoons; but Colonel Halket, with his brigade of German infantry, succeeded in beating the enemy back with very great loss. The colonel of the 16th light dragoons, however, was taken prisoner on this occasion.']. *Royal Military Calendar*, vol. IV, p. 410 ['... expedition to Ferrol, and thence to the Mediterranean... He served with the 27th during the whole of the campaign in Egypt in 1801 ... he served in Ireland during the disturbances in the years 1803, 4, and 5; in 1809 he embarked for the Peninsula, and served in that country during the campaigns of 1809, 10, 11, and 12. He was present at the battles of Oporto, Talavera, Busaco, and Fuentes d'Onor, and a number of other affairs of less note. On the retreat of the army to Torres Vedras, and the advance from thence to the frontiers of Spain, the 16th Light Drag, which this officer commanded during the latter, as well as on many former occasions, were with the 1st Hussar Reg. almost every day engaged with the enemy; they formed one of the corps of light cavalry composing the advance guard of the army... He commanded the rear-guard of the cavalry in the retreat from Burgos, and his horse being killed under him in one of the charges he made on that day, and himself wounded in two places, he was made prisoner. L.-Col. P. is a Companion of the Bath.'].

PEMBERTON, Andrew Wale, 1st Lt., 95th Foot: 1st Lt., 95th Foot, 6 June 1808. Severely wounded, Pyrenees, 2 Aug. 1813 (1st Battn.) [*London Gazette*]. Capt., 95th Foot, 9 Dec. 1813. Pension of one hundred pounds per annum, commencing 3 Aug. 1814, 'for wounds' received in the Pyrenees [*1818 Pension Return*, pp. 22–3]. *Simmons*, pp. 259, 300 [wounded, Santa Barbara, 2 Aug. 1813: 'Captain Pemberton ... received a severe wound, the ball passing directly under the ham.'], p. 308 ['This day I lost a valuable

friend. He was in the same company, and badly wounded in the knee, which I am afraid will finish his career of glory.'], pp. 378–9. *Kincaid, Random Shots*, p. 290 ['At the close of the war, when we returned to England ... the officers commanding companies on the day of inspection, viz ... Pemberton and Manners each with a shot in the knee, making them as stiff as the other's tree one'].

PENNEFATHER, Richard, Lt., 77th Foot: *1829 Statement of Service for Retired Officers*: Aged twenty-six on first appointment to the Army. Ensign, 'R. Tower H. Militia', 1801, 'from which I volunteered in 1809'; Ensign, 56th Regt., 'in the begining of the year 1810' [Army List gives 14 June 1810], 'by Volunteering from the Militia when I was Senr. Lieut. of the Regt.'; Ensign, 77th Foot, 10 Dec. 1810 [Army List gives 20 Dec.]; Half-pay, 87th Foot, Sept. 1817, 'in consequence of ill health from a Bilious and Rheumatic Fever contracted while on service with my Regt. in the Peninsula and which terminated in a chronic liver complaint that still periodically attacks me'. *Where serving when wounded*: 'Wounded at the siege of Badajos with a Bayonet in my side when scaling the Walls of the Castle on the night of the storm'. No pension. Not married. No employment. *Where generally resident during last five years*: 'Mostly London, Cheltenham, & Clonmel in Ireland'. [PRO: WO 25/771 f53]. Slightly wounded, storming of Badajoz, 6 April 1812 [*London Gazette*]. MGS.

PENNINGTON, James Masterson, Lt., 5th Foot: *1829 Statement of Service*: Born 13 July 1785, Kendal, Westmoreland. Aged twenty-one on first appointment to the Army. Ensign, 5th Foot, 5 Feb. 1807; Lt., 5th Foot, 31 March 1808; Paymaster, 5th Foot, 25 Jany. 1816; Half-pay, 17 Nov. 1840. *Battles, sieges and* *campaigns*: 'Busaco, 27 September 1810... Redinha, 12 March 1811... Foz de Roy, 15 March 1811... Sabugal, 3 April 1811... Fuentes d'Onor, 5 May 1811... Siege of Badajoz, from 30 May to 1st June 1811, siege razed... El'Bodon, 25 September 1811... Siege of Rodrigo, from 8th Jany to 19th Jany 1812... Siege of Badajoz, from 17th March to 6 April 1812... Salamanca, 22 July 1812... Vittoria, 21 June 1813... Nivelle, 10 November 1813... Orthes, 27 February 1814... Toulouse, 10 April 1814...' *Distinguished conduct*: 'At the Siege of Badajoz on the 9th June 1811 being on the covering Party at 10 p.m. the Engineers deeming it necessary to drive away a Picquet of the Enemy that were stationed to the left of the Breach in the Wall of the Citadel, a Subaltern of the 5 Regiment being required with a Serjeant and thirty men, I volunteered for the duty and having driven them from their Picquet House, maintained possession of it till daybreak, then retired to the trenches as directed by the Field Officer of the day. They attempted to dislodge me during the night but were repelled after a smart skirmish; my Serjeant and one man killed.' *Wounds received in action*: 'Siege of Rodrigo on the 11th January 1812 when on the Working Party in the Trenches, received two contusions from the Explosion of a 13 Inch Shell.' *Service abroad*: '19th June 1809 to 31st May 1814, Peninsula & France; 1 June 1814 to 10 June 1815, Canada; 11 June 1815 to 1 March 1816, France; 20 Feby. 1817 to 31 Oct. 1818, France; 3 Feby. 1819 to 22 Apr. 1826, West Indies; 9 Jan. 1832 to 26 Oct. 1834, Gibraltar; 27 Oct. 1834 to 28 March 1837, Malta; 3 April 1837 to 16 Nov. 1840, Ionian Islands.' *Family*: Married Harriott Livinia Hussey, 9 Oct. 1808, Banagher, King's County. His wife was still alive on 31 Dec. 1829, by which date they had four children. [PRO: WO 25/785 f471]. MGS.

PENNINGTON, John, Lt., 5th Foot: Lt., 5th Foot, 8 Feb. 1810. Severely wounded, storming of Badajoz, 6 April 1812 [*London Gazette*].

PENNINGTON, Rowland, Lt., 5th Foot: Lt., 5th Foot, 23 May 1811. Severely wounded, 'in Action with the Enemy', 24 Feb. 1814 (1st Battn.) [*London Gazette*]. Temporary pension of seventy pounds per annum, commencing 25 Feb. 1815, 'for wounds' received at Orthes, 1814 [*1818 Pension Return*, pp. 4–5]. MGS.

PENRICE, Edward, Lt., 7th Foot: Lt., 7th Foot, 10 April 1809. Slightly wounded, Albuera, 16 May 1811 (2nd Battn.) [*London Gazette*].

PEPPER, Theobald, Ensign, 87th Foot: Ensign, 87th Foot, 14 Sept. 1808. Slightly wounded, Talavera, 28 July 1809 [*London Gazette*]. MGS.

PERCEVAL, James, 1st Lt., 95th Foot: *1829 Statement of Service for Retired Officers*: Aged fifteen on first appointment to the Army. 2nd Lt., 95th Foot, 17 April 1806; 1st Lt., 95th Foot, 16 March 1808; Capt., 95th Foot, 8 Dec. 1813; Major, Half-pay, unattached, 29 Oct. 1825. *Where serving when wounded*: 'At the Siege and storming of St Sebastian as a Volunteer from the Light Division on 31st Augt. 1813.' *Details of pension*: Seventy pounds. 'My Pension was at first temporary commencing a year after I was wounded, from 1st Septr. 1814. The wound continued to Exfoliate bone for 4 years & pension permanently Granted in 1817.' Not married. No employment. *Where generally resident during last five years*: 'Being placed on Half Pay in 1825 I remained a year in America to visit the States & Canada by Permission of Sir James Kempt, and since my return have been residing on my property within 3 miles of Wexford'.

[PRO: WO 25/771 f62]. Severely wounded, storming of San Sebastian, 31 Aug. 1813, while serving with a 'Detachment 95th Foot, 1st Batt.' ('Percival') [*London Gazette*]. *Simmons*, p. 301 [volunteered for the storming party, San Sebastian, Aug. 1813: 'Lord Wellington paid the Light Division a high compliment by allowing a subaltern's party from each Battalion, total 250 men, to go as a storming party. My messmate Percival, a most worthy and brave fellow, being senior, took charge of the party from the 1st Battalion'], p. 316 [wounded, storming of San Sebastian, 31 August 1813: 'My poor friend Percival had been dreadfully wounded at the foot of one of the breaches, and in the evening he was carried away to a house in the neighbourhood. Today I paid him a visit, and was greatly shocked at his emaciated frame. However, he ultimately got better']. *Kincaid, Adventures*, pp. 247-8 [San Sebastian: 'the works were now reduced to such a state as to justify a second attempt, and our division sent forth their three hundred volunteers to join the storming party. (Lieutenants Percival and Hamilton commanded those from our battalion, and were both desperately wounded).'] *Kincaid, Random Shots*, p. 257 ['For the storming of St Sebastian, the numbers from our battalion were ... limited to a subaltern's command of twenty-five men; and ... the post of honour was claimed by the senior lieutenant, (Percival,)'], p. 290 ['At the close of the war, when we returned to England ... the officers commanding companies on the day of inspection, viz ... Percival with a shot through his lungs.']. 'Percival' in Army List.

PERCEVAL, Philip Joshua, Lt. and Capt., 1st Foot Guards: Ensign, 1st Foot Guards, 8 Aug. 1811; Lt. and Capt., 1st Foot Guards, 10 March 1814, Severely wounded, sortie from Bayonne, 14 April 1814 ('Percival') (3rd Battn.) [*London Gazette*]. Temporary pension of one hundred pounds per annum, commencing 19 May 1815, 'for wounds' received at Bayonne [*1818 Pension Return*, pp. 2-3].

PERCIVAL, William, Capt., 95th Foot: Capt., Army, 1 Nov. 1804; Capt., 95th Foot, 4 May 1809. Severely wounded, 'but not dangerously', while skirmishing, 9-14 Oct. 1810 [*London Gazette*]. Bvt. Major, 95th Foot, 21 June 1813. Severely wounded, Pyrenees, 31 July 1813 ('Major Perceval') (3rd Battn.) [*London Gazette*]. Pension of three hundred pounds per annum, commencing 25 Dec. 1811, for 'loss of the use of an arm' at 'Sobraul', 1811. An additional pension, of one hundred pounds per annum, commencing 25 Dec. 1811, 'for other wounds' received at Sobral [*1818 Pension Return*, pp. 22-23]. *Brotherton*, pp. 31-2 [wounded, Sobral, 12 Oct. 1810: 'At this moment Colonel (then Captain) Perceval [sic] fell close to me, pierced by two balls, one through his leg and another through his arm. He was on the point of falling into the hands of the enemy ... [I] put poor Perceval on my horse, and joined in the scramble on foot... It was a heartfelt satisfaction to have saved poor Perceval, who, to the last day of his life, was grateful for it. He died at Brussels in 1838, and his wife told me since that almost with his last breath he exclaimed, "Generous Bretherton; he once saved my life!" That is very gratifying to me.']. *Simmons*, p. 112 [wounded, Sobral: 'shot through the wrist'].

PERCY, Volunteer, 45th Foot: Slightly wounded, storming of Badajoz, 6 April 1812. [*London Gazette*].

+PERCY, John Samuel, Lt., 51st Foot: Lt., 51st Foot, 7 May 1809. Killed, Vittoria, 21 June 1813

[*London Gazette*]. *Wheeler*, p. 135 [killed, 'Percey'].

PERRY, Francis, Volunteer, 9th Foot: Severely wounded, Salamanca, 22 July 1812 (1st Battn.) [*London Gazette*]. MGS.

+PERRY, Henry, Lt., 28th Foot; Capt., 5th Caçadores: Lt., 28th Foot, 8 Jan. 1807. Killed, siege of Burgos, 5-10 Sept. 1812, while serving as Capt., 5th Caçadores [*London Gazette*]. In Portuguese Service March 1810 to Oct. 1812. *Challis, Portuguese Army List*, p. 58.

PERSSE, William, Capt., 16th Light Dragoons: *1829 Statement of Service*: Born Nov. 1788, County Galway, Ireland. Aged eighteen years on his first entrance into the Army. Cornet, 16th Light Dragoons, 10 Jan. 1806; Lt., Dec. 1806 [NB. Army Lists give 27 Nov. 1806]; Capt. 23 Jan. 1812; Major 25 May 1822. *Battles, sieges and campaigns*: 'Present with the Regt. during the Campaigns of 1809, 1810, 1811, 1812, 1813 & 1814. In August 1814 Embarked for America as Aide-de-Camp to Sir John Keane, was present with that Officer at New Orleans and the Service in America, at that period, returned to England with him in 1815 and remained on his Staff during the time of his Employment in France. Embarked for India in 1822 present at the taking of Bhurtpore in Command of the 16th Lancers under Lord Combermere.' *Distinguished conduct*: 'During Massena's Retreat in March 1811 with a Patrole of 24 Dragoons, came up with the Enemies Rear Guard and had a smart affair which terminated in capturing an Officer & 37 Men with a great quantity of Baggage & the whole of the Enemies Ovens – Vide Lord Wellington's Dispatch of March or Apl. 1811. During the Siege of Burgos in the year 1812 Repulsed a night attack made by the French

upon any Squadron and a Picquet of Brunswick Oels – The Post was in front of Monasterio. In 1814 had the honor of being mentioned by Major General Sir Jno. Keane in his Dispatch on the landing of our Troops at the Mouth of the River Mississippi.' *Wounds received in action*: 'Wounded by a Musket Shot in the arm 10th Decr. 1813, near Bayonne, for which I received 1 years Pay.' *Service abroad*: '1809 to 1818, Peninsula, France, America & France. 22 Nov. 1822 to 31 Decr. 1829, East Indies.' *Family*: Married Eliza Moore, 'eldest dughter of the Honble Mr Justice Moore', 6 Jan. 1819, Lamberton Park, Queens County, Ireland. They had two children by 1830. [PRO: WO 25/784 f254]. Mentioned in Wellington's dispatch dated 27 March 1811 ['I have received the report of a gallant action of one of our patrols yesterday evening, between Alverca and Guarda, under the command of Lieutenant Perse [sic], of the 16th Light Dragoons, and Lieutenant Foster, of the royals, who attacked a detachment of the enemy's cavalry ... and killed and wounded several of them, and took the officer and thirty-seven men prisoners.'] [*London Gazette*]. MGS. [*London Gazette*].

+PERY, Hon. William Cecil, Lt., 59th Foot: Lt., Royal Corsican Rangers, 31 Oct. 1811. Killed, storming of San Sebastian, 31 Aug. 1813, as Lt. 59th Foot, 2nd Battn. [*London Gazette*].

PESHALL, Charles John, Capt., 88th Foot: Capt., 88th Foot, 18 Sept. 1804. Wounded, 'very slightly', storming of Badajoz, 6 April 1812 ('Peschall') [*London Gazette*].

PESTER, Henry, 2nd Lt., Royal Artillery: 2nd Lt., Royal Artillery, 1 May 1809. Severely wounded, Barossa, 5 March 1811 [*London Gazette*]. MGS.

PETERSDORFF, Charles von, Capt., 1st Line Battn. K.G.L: *1829 Statement of Service for Retired Officers*: Aged thirty-two on first appointment to the Army. Capt., 1st Line Battn. K.G.L., 9 Nov. 1803; Major, 8th Line Battn. K.G.L., 6 May 1814; Bvt. Lt. Col., 'Battle of Waterloo'; Half-pay, 24 Feb. 1816, by reduction. *Where serving when wounded*: 'I have been twice wounded: 1. 28th July 1809, at the Battle of Talavera la Reyna in Spain. 2. 27th February 1814, before Bayonne in France.' No pension. *Family*: Married in Besenhausen, 19 April 1818. No children. 'My first wife died unfortunately for me, on the 24th June 1823 and I remarried', in Stiedenrode, 12 Feb. 1828. His second wife 'is with child' as of 19 Dec. 1828. No employment. *Where generally resident during last five years*: 'Witzenhausen, Electorate of Hesse.' [PRO: WO 25/771 f15]. Slightly wounded, Talavera, 28 July 1809 ('Petersdorf') [*London Gazette*]. Served in Peninsula 1808–14. Waterloo. *Beamish*, vol. II, p. 602 [Died 'at Witzenhausen, electorate of Hessia, 13th March, 1834.'].

PHELAN, George, Capt., 60th Foot; Capt., 6th Portuguese Line: *1829 Statement of Service for Retired Officers*: Aged eighteen on first appointment to the Army. Ensign, 48th Foot, 29 May 1809; Lt., 48th Foot, n.d. [Army List gives 14 June 1811]; Capt., 60th Foot, n.d. [Army List gives 13 Nov. 1813]; Half-pay, n.d., 'In consequence of ill health from Climate". Served fifteen years on Full-pay. *Where serving when wounded*: 'Wounded on 13 Decr. 1813 in front of Bayonne'. No pension. *Family*: Married at St Mary's Church, Lambeth, 15 May 1813. No children. No employment. *Where generally resident during last five years*: 'Bristol and Worthing'. [PRO: WO 25/771 f88]. Severely wounded, the Nive, 13 Dec. 1813, as Capt., 6th Portuguese Regt.

[*London Gazette*]. In Portuguese Service Oct. 1811 to April 1814. *Challis, Portuguese Army*, p. 58. ['Promoted Lt. 48 Ft. for Albuhera'].

PHIBBS, Harlow, Lt., 1st Dragoons K.G.L.: Lt., 1st Dragoons K.G.L., 20 Sept. 1811. Wounded, during 'movements of the Army' [Retreat from Burgos], 23 Oct. 1812 [*London Gazette*]. Served in Peninsula in 1812. *Beamish*, vol. II, p. 625 ['slightly wounded, 23d Oct. 1812, at Venta del Poco. Resigned 22d June 1813.'].

PHIBBS, William Harlow, Lt., 27th Foot: *1829 Statement of Service*: Born 25 Oct. 1791, Sligo. Aged nineteen on his first entrance into the Army. Ensign, 60th Foot, 30 Oct. 1810; Ensign, 27th Foot, 14 March 1811; Lt. 24 June 1813; Half Pay 14 June 1817; Lt., 2nd Royal Veteran Battn., 15 Jan. 1824; Lt., 89th Foot, Nov. 1824; Lt., 25th Foot, 5 May 1825. *Battles, sieges and campaigns*: 'In November 1813 joined as a Lieutenant the army in Spain ... was at the Battle of Lara or Niville, Orthes, and Toulouse & at several Skirmishes which were fought in Spain and France. At the conclusion of the Peninsuler War I embarked at Bourdeaux as a Lieutenant with the 27th Regt. for North America and was with the army ... at the taking of Platsburgh in Upper Canada.' *Wounds received in action*: 'Lost my left arm at the Battle of Lara or Neville on the 10th November 1813, and shot through both legs (only slight wounds), I received a full Years Pay and a permanent Pension of Seventy Pounds a Year Commencing in the Year 1814.' *Service abroad*: '6th Novr 1813 to 29th May 1814, Spain & France. July 1814 to Jany 1815, North America. 26th Jany 1826 to 24th Nov 1827, West Indies. 23rd Decr 1829 to 31st Decr 1829, West Indies.' Not married in 1830. [PRO: WO 25/789 f341]. Severely wounded,

Nivelle, 10 Nov. 1813 (3rd Battn.) [*London Gazette*]. *1818 Pension Return*, pp. 8–9. MGS.

+PHIFFEN, George, Lt., 3rd Foot; Capt., 11th Portuguese Line: Lt., 3rd Foot, 20 June 1811. In Portuguese Service Nov. 1809 to Oct. 1813. *Challis, Portuguese Army*, p. 58 ['Capt. 11 Line... Died of Wounds 21 Oct. '13'].

PHILLIPS, Hill, Lt., 45th Foot: Lt., 45th Foot, 21 July 1809. Severely wounded, storming of Ciudad Rodrigo, 19 Jan. 1812 [*London Gazette*].

PHILLIPS, Robert Jocelyn, Ensign, 27th Foot: *1829 Statement of Service for Retired Officers*: Aged twenty-three on first appointment to the Army. Lt., North Mayo Militia, n.d.; Ensign, n.d., 27th Foot [Army List gives 20 July 1809]; Lt., 27th Foot, 6 April 1812 [Army List gives 6 Oct. 1812]; Half-pay, n.d., 'from ill health, in consequence of wounds'. *Where serving when wounded*: 'Badajos in Spain'. *Details of pension*: Seventy pounds, commencing 7 April 1813. *Family*: Married in Dublin, 16 June 1815. Four children by 1829. *Title and nature of employment*: 'Barrack Master of Dundalk'. *Where generally resident during last five years*: 'Dundalk'. [PRO: WO 25/771 f65]. Severely wounded, storming of Badajoz, 6 April 1812 (3rd Battn.) [*London Gazette*]. *1818 Pension Return*, pp. 8–9. MGS.

PHILLIPS, Robert, Capt., 40th Foot: Lt., 40th Foot, 27 Feb. 1806; Capt., 40th Foot, 25 July 1811. Severely wounded, storming of Badajoz, 6 April 1812 (1st Battn.) [*London Gazette*]. Waterloo.

PICKETT, Sampson, Ensign, 34th Foot: Ensign, 34th Foot, 25 Feb. 1813. Slightly wounded, Pyrenees, 25 July 1813 ('Pickett') (2nd Battn.) [*London Gazette*]. Adjutant, 34th Foot, 14 Oct. 1813; Lt., 34th Foot, 20 Nov. 1816; Half-pay, 25 June 1817. MGS. *Mullen*, p. 267 ['Formerly a Sjt in the Regt.']

PICTON, Sir Thomas, Lt. General; Col., 77th Foot: Major-General 25 April 1808; Col., 77th Foot, 15 Oct. 1811. Slightly wounded, storming of Badajoz, 6 April 1812 [*London Gazette*]. Killed at Waterloo. *Speeckaert*, p. 16 [Monument at Waterloo: 'To the gallant memory of/Lt General Sir Thomas Picton/Commander of the 5th Division and the left wing/of the Army at the Battle of Waterloo/Born 1758/Died near this spot in the early afternoon/18th June 1815 leading his men against/Count Drouet d'Erlon's advance']. *Dalton*, pp. 2, 14. One of the great 'characters' of the army. Harvard, R., *Wellington's Welsh General* (London, 1996); Myatt, F., *Peninsular General* (Newton Abbot, 1980); Robinson, H. E., *Memoirs and Correspondence of Lieut. General Sir Thomas Picton* (London, 1836).

PIDGEON, Joseph Thomas, Lt./Capt., 71st Foot: *1829 Statement of Service*: 'Born in Dublin, 4th February 1787. Aged 17 Years on his first Entrance into the Army. Ensign, 71st Foot, March 1804. Lieutenant, 71st Foot, April 1805. Captain, 71st Foot, 1st Decr. 1808. Bt. Major, 71st Foot, 21st Jany. 1819. Major, 71st Foot, 2d June 1825.' *Battles, sieges and campaigns*: 'Roleia 17th August 1808... Vimiera 21 August 1808... Corunna 17 Jany. 1809... Ter Vere 29th July 1809... The Siege of Flushing August 1809... Vittoria 21st June 1813... The different Actions on the Pyrenees from 2d July to 1 August 1813... Nivelle 10th Novr. 1813... Skirmish at Cambo on or about the 18th Novr. 1813... Nive 9th Decr. 1813... Bayonne 13th Decr. 1813... Heights of Gu[ ] & over St Palais... Orthes 27th Feby. 1814... Sauratere March 1813... Toulouse 10th April 1814...

Waterloo 18th June 1815.' *Wounds received in action*: 'Slightly at Vittoria on the 21st June 1813. No grant of pay or pension has been demanded.' *Titles, honorary distinctions and medals*: 'Waterloo Medal.' *Service abroad*: 'August 1808 to January 1809, Portugal & Spain. July 1809 to Novr. 1809, Walcheren. Novr. 1812 to August 1814, Portugal, Spain, and the South of France. 19th April 1815 to 31st Octr. 1818, Belgium and France. 24th June 1824 to May 1828, Canada.' *Family*: Married Mary, 'Daughter of the Late Captn. Willm. Foster Dallon 28th Regiment', 17 Oct. 1817, Dublin. They had no children by 1830. [PRO: WO 25/799 f3]. Slightly wounded, Vittoria, 21 June 1813 (1st Battn.) [*London Gazette*]. Waterloo. MGS. Died, Oct. 1850.

+PIERREPOINT, Charles Alph., Major, Quartermaster General's Dept: Major, 26 Sept. 1811. Assistant Quartermaster General. Recorded as having been 'killed in Spain' in *1813 Army List*.

PILKINGTON, Abraham, Lt., 59th Foot: 1829 Statement of Service for Retired Officers: Aged nineteen on first appointment to the Army. Ensign, 59th Foot, 27 Feb. '1825' [ie 1805]; Lt., 59th Foot, 17 June 1807 [Army List gives 18 June]; Capt., 59th Foot, 17 June 1813; Half-pay, 25 March 1816, by reduction; Capt., 92nd Foot, 19 Oct. 1825; Half-pay, 24 Jan. 1827, 'by order of the medical Board in consequence of a Wound'. 'Being reported unfit for service by the medical Board in Dublin in December 1826, & Wound being still open Captain Pilkington from the opinion of the medical Board is apprehensive he is not fit for service.' *Where serving when wounded*: 'Storming of St Sebastian. Cambray.' *Details of pension*: One hundred pounds per annum for each wound, the first commencing 1814 'for arm', the second commencing 1825 'for Eye'.

Family: Married in St Thomas' Church, Dublin, 22 May 1816. No children. No employment. *Where generally resident during last five years*: 'Ireland'. [PRO: WO 25/771 f120]. Severely wounded, storming of San Sebastian, 31 Aug. 1813 (2nd Battn.) [*London Gazette*]. Mentioned in Graham's San Sebastian dispatch, dated Oyarzun, 1 Sept. 1813 ['Major-General Robinson ... commends highly ... Captain Pilkington, who succeeded to the command of the 59th on Captain Scott's being killed, and retained it till wounded'] [*London Gazette*]. *1818 Pension Return*, pp. 14–15. Waterloo. Died, 24 May 1843.

PIPER, John, Major, 4th Foot: Ensign, 4th Foot, 6 Feb. 1795; Lt., 4th Foot, 6 Sept., 1795; Major, 4th Foot, 16 Aug. 1810; Bvt. Lt. Col., 4th Foot, 17 Aug. 1812. Slightly wounded, during 'movements of the Army' [Retreat from Burgos: Villa Muriel], 25 Oct. 1812 [*London Gazette*]. Slightly wounded, Storming of San Sebastian, 31 Aug. 1813 (1st Battn.) [*London Gazette*]. Severely wounded, the Nive, 11 Dec. 1813 (1st Battn.) [*London Gazette*]. Pension of three hundred pounds per annum, commencing 12 Dec. 1814, 'for wounds' received in Bayonne, 1813 [*1818 Pension Return*, pp. 4–5]. *Royal Military Calendar*, vol. IV, pp. 406–9 ['In 1807 he was at Copenhagen; in the spring of 1808 at Gottenburg... From thence he went to Portugal, and marching into Spain ... commanded by Sir J. Moore... In the following year he bore a part in the expedition to the Scheldt... The malady which in its effects proved so destructive to the troops on this expedition seizing him on his return to England, he lay some time at the point of death, but by skilful treatment so far recovered as to be able to go with the 1st batt. to Portugal... During the time (three years and a half) that he remained in the Peninsula, though his health had been materially injured by the effects of the Walcheren fever, he was never absent from his regt, but saw much and very hard service, commanding the 1st batt. in many important battles. At the assault of Badajos, the command of the batt. devolved upon him early in the evening (the assault commenced at night) ... soon after he had from the scaling ladders made good his footing on the ramparts, besides having his clothes pierced in several places, he received, in the left arm, a severe contusion from a musquet ball, the force of which threw him back upon the heaps of the dead and dying... In this assault it appears, that, attended by L. Col. Harding of the 44th regt. he was the first officer who was present at the planting of the British colors in the grand square of the city... In the battle of Salamanca ... he again commanded the batt... On the retreat from Burgos ... being warmly engaged on the 25th Oct., 1812, at Ville Moriel ... received a wound in the neck ... battle of Vittoria, and was shortly after employed throughout the siege, and in the assault of St Sebastian, in which he received a wound in the leg... On the ... 11th [Dec. 1813], when in the act of cheering the men, he received a very dangerous wound in the right side of the neck, and was obliged to be carried off the field. Paralysis of the whole frame at first ensuing from the effects of the wound, and in part continuing afterwards he was (being now completely incapacitated for a long time from further service) sent to England... L.-Col. P. has the honor to wear a Cross for the siege of Badajos, battle of Salamanca, siege of St Sebastian, and battle of the Nive'].

+**PITT, William Henry, Ensign, Coldstream Guards:** Ensign, Coldstream Guards, 5 March 1812. Wounded, sortie from Bayonne, 14 April 1814 (1st Battn.) [*London Gazette*]. Died of wounds, 24 April. 1814. Return dated April 1814 [PRO: WO 25/2965]. Obituary, *The Gentleman's Magazine*, May 1814, p. 518 ['April 24... Of his wounds, before Bayonne, Ensign William Henry Pitt, of the Coldstream Guards, eldest son of Thomas P. esq. of Wimpole street.']. *Hurt*, p. 75. Portrait miniature of him by Thomas Heaphy, illustrated in *Fletcher, Wellington's Foot Guards*, p. 19. *Fletcher, Fields of Fire*, p. 164 ['Coldstream Guards cemetery, Bayonne ... those who lie here include ... Ensigns Vachell and Pitt, all of the Coldstream Guards']. *Fletcher, Gentlemen's Sons*, p. 185.

+**PITTS, Thomas J. H., 2nd Capt., Royal Engineers:** 1st Lt., Royal Engineers, 1 April 1808; 2nd Capt., Royal Engineers, 21 July 1813. Killed, 'in Action with the Enemy', 23 Feb. 1814 [*London Gazette*].

+**PLATE, Frederick, Capt., Garrison Company K.G.L.:** Capt., Garrison Company K.G.L., 21 March 1805. Died of wounds, 1 June 1811. Return dated 25 June 1811. [PRO: WO 25/2965].

PLATEL, Charles, Chevalier de, Lt., Chasseurs Britanniques: Lt., Chasseurs Britanniques, 16 June 1808. Slightly wounded, Orthes, 27 Feb. 1814 ('Charles Duplatel') [*London Gazette*].

PLUNKETT, Patrick, Ensign/Lt., 50th Foot: *1829 Statement of Service*: Born in Elphin, Ireland, 4 Dec. 1792. Aged 'sixteen years five months' on 'his first Entrance into the Army.' Ensign, 50th Foot, 18 May 1809. Lt., 50th Foot, 25 June 1812. Half Pay, 25 March 1817, 'By reduction of the supernumary Lieutenant.' Lt., Ceylon Regt., 12 June 1828. Lt., 84th Regt., 21 Aug. 1828. *Battles, sieges and campaigns*: 'Fuentes D'Onor, 5th May 1811, Ensign. Assault and Capture of Fort Napoleon near Almarez in Spain.

Vittoria, 21 June 1813, Lieut. Pyrenees, 25th July to 2nd August 1813, Lieut. Nive, 9th to 13th December 1813, Lieut.' *Distinguished conduct*: 'Commanded the Forlorn Hope at the Assault and Capture of Fort Napoleon near Almarez in Spain. Commanded the Grenadier Company of the 50th Regt. on the 25th July 1813 on the heights of Mayo on which occasion the Regiment was severely engaged with the Enemy & also at St Pierre near Bayonne and was severely wounded while leading that Company to the charge.' *Wounds received in action*: 'Received a Gun Shot wound in the breast at St Pierre near Bayonne on the 13th Decemr. 1813. The ball now lies in the muscle of the left abdomen. Received a Captns. years pay & a temporary Pension of £70 per annum made permanent from 25th June 1830.' *Service abroad*: 'August 1810 to February 1814, Peninsula and France.' *Family*: Married Frances Browne, 7 May 1816, 'in the parish of Killukan, Co. of Roscannon.' They had five children by 1830. [PRO: WO 25/801 f255]. Slightly wounded, the Nive, 13 Dec. 1813 ('Lieutenant J. W. Plunkett') (1st Battn.) [*London Gazette*]. Note: the casualty return published in the *London Gazette* identified the wrong Lt. Plunkett as having been wounded on 13 Dec. 1813: it was in fact Patrick, not John, who was wounded on that occasion. *1818 Pension Return*, pp. 14–15. MGS.

+PODE, John Spurrell, Ensign, 57th Foot: Ensign, 57th Foot, 11 Feb. 1813. Killed, the Nive, 13 Dec. 1813 (1st Battn.) [*London Gazette*].

POE, Purefoy, Ensign, 39th Foot: *1829 Statement of Service for Retired Officers*: Aged twenty-six on first appointment to the Army. Ensign, 39th Foot, 13 June 1809; Lt., 1 July 1813; Half-pay, n.d., by reduction. Served seven years on Full-pay. 'I am ready and willing to serve

His Majesty whenever he is graciously pleased to call upon me but from the nature of my wounds (a fracture of the shin bone) I am certain I would not be fit for *active* service.' Where serving when wounded: 'Penninsula'. *Details of pension*: Seventy pounds, commencing 26 July 1814. *Family*: Married in Kello Church, Co. Kilkenny, 22 April 1819. No children. No employment. *Where generally resident during last five years*: 'Rossmore Lodge, Co. of Kilkenny, Ireland'. [PRO: WO 25/771 f260]. Severely wounded, Pyrenees, 25 July 1813 (1st Battn.) [*London Gazette*]. Pension 'for wounds' received in the Pyrenees, 1813 [*1818 Pension Return*, pp. 10–11]. MGS.

POLLARD, John William, Lt., 39th Foot: Lt., 39th Foot, 20 Feb. 1806. Severely wounded, Albuera, 16 May 1811 (2nd Battn.) [*London Gazette*].

POLLOCK, Carlisle, Lt., 27th Foot: Lt., 27th Foot, 11 July 1811. Slightly wounded, storming of Badajoz, 6 April 1812 (3rd Battn.) [*London Gazette*]. Severely wounded, Pyrenees, 28 July 1813 (3rd Battn.) [*London Gazette*]. Pension of one hundred pounds per annum, commencing 29 July 1814, 'for wounds' received at Pampeluna [*1818 Pension Return*, pp. 8–9]. MGS.

POLLOCK, Samuel, Lt., 43rd Foot: *1829 Statement of Service for Retired Officers*: Aged twenty on first appointment to the Army. Ensign, 43rd Foot, 30 May 1805; Lt., 43rd Foot, 21 May 1806; Capt., 43rd Foot, 18 Feb. 1813; Half-pay, 1817, by reduction. 'Not desirous [of service], being (from the effects of a severe Wound in the foot) unfit for service'. *Where serving when wounded*: 'In the Command of a Company of the 43rd Lt. Infantry at the assault of Badajoz on the night of the 6th of April 1812'. *Details of* *pension*: Seventy pounds per annum, commencing 7 April 1813. *Family*: Married in Drogheda, 4 Feb. 1816. Seven children by 1829. *Where generally resident during last five years*: 'at Farmhill near Drogheda'. [PRO: WO 25/771 f189]. Severely wounded, storming of Badajoz, 6 April 1812 [*London Gazette*]. MGS.

PONSONBY, Hon. Frederick Cavendish, Lt. Col., 12th Light Dragoons: Lt. Col., Army, 15 March 1810. Lt. Col., 12th Light Dragoons, 11 June 1811. Mentioned in Wellington's Salamanca dispatch, commanding the 12th Light Dragoons [*London Gazette*]. Mentioned in Wellington's dispatch concerning the passage of the Douro, 7 Sept. 1812 ['The enemy retired from La Cisterniga during the night... They were closely followed by the Honourable Lieutenant-Colonel Frederick Ponsonby with a detachment of the 12th Light Dragoons through the town; but ... the enemy could not be prevented from destroying the bridge.'] [*London Gazette*]. Wounded, Monasterio, 13 Oct. 1812. Mentioned in Wellington's dis-patch of 26 Oct. 1812, concerning the action at Monasterio, 13 Oct. 1812 ["In this affair, Lieutenant-Colonel the Honourable Frederick Ponsonby, who commanded at Monasterio, was wounded but not severely, and I hope I shall soon again have the benefit of his assistance.'] [*London Gazette*]. *Kincaid, Random Shots*, pp. 99–101 [Nov. 1810: 'I was amused to see General Slade, who commanded the brigade of cavalry attached to us, order up his sumpter mule, and ... undid several packages, and presently displayed a set-out which was more than enough to tempt the cupidity of the hungry beholders ... the commanders of the twelfth and fourteenth light dragoons, (Colonels Ponsonby and Harvey,) whose olfactory nerves, at a

distance of some hundred yards, having snuffed up the tainted air, eagerly followed the scent, and came to a dead point before the general and his panniers. But although they had flushed their game they did not succeed in bagging it; for while the general gave them plenty of his own tongue, the deuce take the slice did he offer of the bullock's – and as soon as he had satisfied his appetite he very deliberately bundled up the fragments, and shouted to horse']. Born 1783, second son of Frederick, 3rd Earl of Bessborough. Was major in the 23rd Light Dragoons, assuming command of the regiment after its desperate action at Talavera; remained in Peninsula after regiment was withdrawn, as AAG, served at Busaco and Barossa, until appointed to command 12th Light Dragoons. Best known for his graphic account of his tribulations while lying wounded all night on the field of Waterloo; became major-general 1825 and died 1837. Collins, R. M., 'Colonel the Hon. Frederick Cavendish Ponsonby, 12th Light Dragoons', *Journal of the Society for Army Historical Research*, Vol. XLVI (1968).

+POOLE, Clement, Capt., 52nd Foot: Capt., 52nd Foot, 29 May 1806. Recorded as 'missing', Talavera, 27 July 1809, while serving with the 1st Batt. Detachments [*London Gazette*]. Killed, storming of Badajoz, 6 April 1812 [*London Gazette*].

POOLE, Walter Croker, Lt., 88th Foot: Lt., 88th Foot, 26 March 1812. Severely wounded, Toulouse, 10 April 1814 (1st Battn.) [*London Gazette*]. MGS.

POPHAM, Samuel Taylor, Major, 24th Foot: Major, Army, 1 Sept. 1804; Major, 24th Foot, 14 Sept. 1804. Severely wounded, Talavera, 28 July 1809 [*London Gazette*].

POPHAM, Thomas, Lt., 29th Foot: Lt., 29th Foot, 17 Feb. 1808. Severely wounded, Talavera, 27 July 1809 [*London Gazette*]. Severely wounded, Albuera, 16 May 1811 [*London Gazette*].

POPPLETON, Thomas, Capt., 53rd Foot: Capt., 53rd Foot, 13 Nov. 1806. Slightly wounded, Salamanca, 22 July 1812 (2nd Battn.) [*London Gazette*].

PORTER, James, Capt., 11th Foot: Capt., 11th Foot, 10 Aug. 1808. Severely wounded, Salamanca, 22 July 1812 (1st Battn.) [*London Gazette*]. Temporary pension of one hundred pounds per annum, commencing 23 July 1813, 'for a wound' received at Salamanca [*1818 Pension Return*, pp. 6–7].

PORTIOUS, Alexander, Lt., 61st Foot: *1829 Statement of Service for Retired Officers*: Aged twenty-three on first appointment to the Army. Ensign, 62nd Foot, 16 July 1806; Lt., 61st Foot, 23 July 1807; Capt., 60th Foot, 20 April 1815; Half-pay, 40th Foot, 24 Jan. 1816, 'at my own request in consequence of ill health'. *Where serving when wounded*: 'Twice wounded at Toulouse in France'. *Details of pension*: Seventy pounds per annum, commencing 25 Dec. 1823. *Family*: Married at Crieff, 12 Oct. 1815. One child, George Murray, born '15th Oct. 1814'. No employment. *Where generally resident during last five years*: 'near Crieff N.B.' [PRO: WO 25/771 f160]. 'Porteus' in Army List. Severely wounded, Toulouse, 10 April 1814 ('Porteous') (1st Battn.) [*London Gazette*]. MGS.

POTEN, August, Lt., 2nd Dragoons K.G.L.: Cornet, 2nd Dragoons K.G.L., 16 May 1806. Slightly wounded, in 'an Affair with the Enemy's Cavalry, in Front of the Village of Majalahonda,' 11 Aug. 1812 ('Lieutenant') [*London Gazette*]. Served in Peninsula 1812–14. Waterloo. *Beamish*, vol. II, p. 545.

POTEN, Conrad, Lt., 1st Light Dragoons/Hussars K.G.L.: Lt., 1st Light Dragoons, 14 July 1811. Slightly wounded, Toulouse, 10 April 1814 [*London Gazette*]. Served in Peninsula 1809–14. Waterloo. *Beamish*, vol. II, p. 550.

POTEN, Ernest, Lt./Capt., 1st Light Dragoons/Hussars K.G.L.: *1829 Statement of Service for Retired Officers*: Aged eighteen on first appointment to the Army. 'Since August 1803 as Recruiting Officer for the K.G.L. on the Continent'; Cornet, 1st Light Dragoons K.G.L., March 1804; Lt., 1st Light Dragoons K.G.L., 1806 [Army List gives 11 May 1806]; Capt., 1st Light Dragoons K.G.L., 12 July 1811; Half-pay, 25 April 1816, by reduction. *Where serving when wounded*: 'Fuente Ginaldo in Spain. Talavera in Spain.' *Details of pension*: One hundred pounds for the first mentioned, commencing '11th Septr. 1811' [sic], and seventy pounds for the wound received at Talavera, commencing 25 Dec. 1825. *Family*: Married in Bordenau in the Kingdom of Hannover, 17 Aug. 1816. Four children by 1829. *Where generally resident during last five years*: 'Lubeck'. [PRO: WO 25/771 f141]. Severely wounded, Talavera, 28 July 1809 [*London Gazette*]. Severely wounded, El Bodon, 25 Sept. 1811 [*London Gazette*]. Served in Peninsula 1809–11, 1813–14. Gold Medal. Waterloo. *Beamish*, vol. II, p. 549 ['severely wounded 28th July, 1809, at Talavera; severely wounded, (arm amputated) 25th September, 1811, at El-Bodon.'].

+POTTER, Leonard, Capt., 28th Foot: Capt., 28th Foot, 5 Oct. 1804. Slightly wounded, storming of Ciudad Rodrigo, 19 Jan. 1812, while serving on the Staff as Brigade-

Major [*London Gazette*]. Severely wounded, 'not dangerously', storming of Badajoz, 6 April 1812, serving on Staff as Brigade Major [*London Gazette*]. Obituary, *The Gentleman's Magazine*, June 1812, p. 595 ['April 20... At Elvas, of a wound received whilst storming the breach at Badajoz, in his 28th year, Capt. Potter, 28th reg. and Brig.-major to Maj.-gen. Hon. C. Colville.'].

POTTER, Thomas, Lt., 28th Foot; Capt., 14th Portuguese Line: *1829 Statement of Service for Retired Officers*: Aged eighteen on first appointment to the Army. Ensign, 28th Foot, 13 Nov. 1806; Lt., 28th Foot, 2 March 1809; Capt., 25 Oct. 1814, 'being then in the Portuguese Service ... which latter promotion removed me to the unattached list on full Pay until the 25th of December 1815 then placed on the Half Pay list'. 'Reduced on Half Pay with the rest of the British officers then serving in the Portuguese Service.' 'Not desirous to serve from the motive of ill health and siverity of wounds.' *Where serving when wounded*: 'At Aire in France under Lord Hill.' *Details of pension*: One hundred pounds per annum, commencing 2 March 1815. *Family*: Married in Gosport, 18 June 1818. Four children by 1829. *Where generally resident during last five years:* 'Gosport'. [PRO: WO 25/771 f186]. Slightly wounded, Pyrenees, 30 July 1813, while serving as Capt., 14th Portuguese Line [*London Gazette*]. In Portuguese Service Jan. 1812 to April 1814. *1818 Pension Return*, pp. 24–5. MGS. *Challis, Portuguese Army*, p. 58.

+POTTER, William, Capt., 23rd Foot: Capt., Army, 2 Oct. 1800; Capt., 23rd Foot, 18 June 1807. Severely wounded, ('since dead'), siege of Badajoz, 19 March 1812 [*London Gazette*]. Died of wounds, 21 March 1812. Return dated 25 April 1812. [PRO: WO 25/2965].

POUNTNEY, Henry James, Lt., 48th Foot: Ensign, 48th Foot, 31 May 1809; Lt. 16 June 1811. Slightly wounded, storming of Badajoz, 6 April 1812 [*London Gazette*]. Severely wounded, Pyrenees, 28 July 1813 (1st Battn.) [*London Gazette*]. Temporary pension of seventy pounds per annum, commencing 29 July 1814, 'for wounds' received at Pampeluna, 1813 [*1818 Pension Return*, pp. 12–13].

POVAH, John, Adjutant/Lt., 36th Foot: Adjutant, 36th Foot, 5 Oct. 1804; Lt., 36th Foot, 14 Nov. 1805. Severely wounded, Vimeiro, 21 Aug. 1808 ('Poveah') [*London Gazette*]. Not serving in 1809. 'Robert Morow, Adjutant, vice Povah' in 'Alterations while Printing', *1809 Army List*.

POWELL, Francis, Lt., 45th Foot: *1829 Statement of Service for Retired Officers*: Aged twenty-three on first appointment to the Army. Ensign, 40th Foot, 8 May 1805, 'Having influenced 99 men to volunteer & inlist into the 40th Reg. from the Bedford Militia'; Lt., 66th Foot, Feb. 1806; Lt., 45th Foot, 27 March 1806; Capt., 45th Foot, 14 May 1812; Half-pay, n.d., by reduction [Army List gives 1814]. Served ten years on Full-pay. *Where serving when wounded*: 'Badajos'. *Details of pension*: One hundred pounds, commencing 7 April 1813. Not married. *Where generally resident during last five years*: 'Bath & London'. [PRO: WO 25/771 f158]. Severely wounded, storming of Badajoz, 6 April 1812 [*London Gazette*]. *1818 Pension Return*, pp. 12–13.

POWELL, Thomas, Lt., 24th Foot: *1829 Statement of Service*: [stated to be a 'true copy completed after his death' in 1839] Born 'Derynock, Brecknockshire', 21 October 1791. Aged Sixteen years on his first Entrance into the Army. 'Ensign, 24 Infantry, Augt. 1807. Lieutenant, 29

Infantry, Feby, 1808. Lieutenant, 24 Infantry, April 1808. Captain, Glengarry Light Infantry, March 1813. Major, Canadian Chasseurs, October 1814, Corps disbanded before Confirmed. Bt. Major, May 1815, For having frequently distinguished himself in the Field. Captain, Rifle Brigade, 1816.' [Army List indicates Half-pay from 25 Nov. 1818]. His Statement suggests Captain, 57th Foot, but no date given. Between 1821–9, indicates 'At this period Employed under Govt. as Inspector Genl. of Police in Ireland.' Major, Half Pay, unattached, 1830. Major, 'Queens Royal', 29 March 1833. Lieut. Colonel, 40th, 19 Feb. 1836. Lieut. Colonel, 6th Foot, 23 Novr. 1838. Died at Karrachie on the Indus on the 23rd of March 1839 of "Cholera Morbus".' *Battles, sieges and campaigns*: 'Battle of Talavera 26 & 27 July 1809... 1810 Battle of Torres Vedras &c &c 1811. A.D.C. to Brigr. Genl. Drummond Lt Division; was present in every affair against the Enemy in his Retreat out of Portugal viz. Raderhein, Pombul, Coudexia Fasde-dros, Sabugal, Fuentes de Onoro, Guinaldi &c &c &c. 1812, attached to Major Genl. Crawford, Cuidad-de-Rodrigo – promoted to a Company in the Glengarry Lt. Infantry in March 1813. Served up to this period in the Peninsula under the Duke of Wellington. Appd. Deputy Assist. in the Qr Mr. Genls. Department for the Coast of America, under Colonel Sir Sidney Beckwith, and present at the attack of Crany Island, Hampton &c. 1814, served in Canada in the Qr Mr. Generals Department, present at the Battle of Lundys Lane near the Falls of Niagara, Storming Fort Erie, and in every affair against the Enemy under Lieut. General Sir Gordon Drummond. 1815. Canada. 1816, 17 & 18, Army of Occupation in France.' *Distinguished conduct*: 'The attack on the Enemy's Fortress, Crany Island, the attack

on Hampton, both in the Chesapeake, Conduct noticed by Sir Sidney Beckwith, vide the *London Gazette* 1813. 1814. Conducted several desultory attacks against the Enemy in Upper Canada – Conduct approved and noticed in the *London Gazette*, led the Storming Party against Fort Erie in the night and succeeded as reported in the *London Gazette*. Conducted a night attack against the Enemy, took more Prisoners than [ends in mid-sentence]' *Wounds received in action*: '1812 – Wounded at Cuidad Rodrigo, 1 Years Pay & Pension of £100 for the loss of an Eye, granted permanently, 1819. 1814, Severely Wounded at Fort Erie by a Bayonet, also a Musket Ball. 1 Years Pay.' *Service abroad*: '1809 to 1819, Portugal, Spain, Canada, France, West Indies. 1829 to Decr. 1833, East Indies. 1 Jany. 1834 to 11 Jan. 1835, East Indies. 21 Feby. 1838 to 23 Novr. 1838, East Indies.' *Family*: Married Julia Lehon, 1813, Guernsey. They had five children by 1833. [PRO: WO 25/796 f92]. See also his *1829 Statement of Service for Retired Officers* [PRO: WO 25/771 f163].

+POWER, Robert G., 1st Lt., Royal Engineers: 1st Lt., Royal Engineers, 2 Dec. 1809. Killed, Nivelle, 10 Nov. 1813 [*London Gazette*].

POWER, Thomas, Lt., 47th Foot: Lt., 47th Foot, 25 March 1808. Severely wounded, storming of San Sebastian, 31 Aug. 1813 (2nd Battn.) [*London Gazette*].

+POWER, William, Lt., 23rd Light Dragoons: Cornet, 23rd Light Dragoons, 5 Feb. 1805; Lt., 23rd Light Dragoons, 19 May 1808. Killed, Talavera, 28 July 1809 ('Powel') [*London Gazette*].

POWER, William G., Capt., Royal Artillery: 2nd Capt., Royal Artillery, 13 June 1807. Slightly wounded, siege of Ciudad Rodrigo, 19 Jan. 1812 [*London Gazette*]. Mentioned in Wellington's Ciudad Rodrigo dispatch, 20 Jan. 1812 ['The rapid execution produced by the well-directed fire kept up from our batteries, affords the best proof of the merits of the officers and men of the royal artillery... But I must particularly mention ... Captains ... Power ... of the royal artillery'] [*London Gazette*, 5 Feb. 1812]. Slightly wounded, siege of Burgos, 5–10 Oct. 1812 [*London Gazette*]. MGS.

+POWYS, Hon. Henry, Capt., 83rd Foot: Capt., 83rd Foot, 26 Jan. 1809. Severely wounded, siege of Badajoz, 26 March 1812 [*London Gazette*]. Mentioned in Wellington's dispatch, 27 March 1812 [Assault of Fort Picurina, Badajoz, 26 March: 'The attack was made by five hundred men of the 3rd division, formed into three detachments ... the centre under the Honourable Captain Powys, of the 83rd... It was first entered ... by the centre detachment of one hundred men, under the command of the Honourable Captain Powys, of the 83rd Regiment, who escaled the work at the salient angle, at a point at which the pallisades had been injured by our fire... Major-General Kempt mentions in high terms in his report the cool and persevering gallantry of the officers and troops; of which indeed the strength of the work, which they carried, affords the best proof. He particularly mentions ... Majors Shaw and Rudd, and the Honourable Captain Powys, who commanded the several detachments. These three officers were wounded, the latter on the parapet of the work, which he had been the first to mount by the ladders.'] [*London Gazette*]. Died of wounds, 4 April 1812. Return dated 25 April 1812 (2nd Battn.) [PRO: WO 25/2965]. Fifth son of Thomas, 1st Baron Lilfield. [*Burke's Peerage*].

PRATT, George, Lt., 27th Foot: *1829 Statement of Service for Retired Officers*: Aged thirty-four on first appointment to the Army. Ensign, 27th Foot, 4 Dec. 1806; Lt., 27th Foot, 9 March 1809; Half-pay, 24 June 1817, by reduction. *Where serving when wounded*: 'at Pampeluna, through the left thigh'. *Family*: Married in 'St Geo. Hanover Square, London', 21 Sept. 1795. Two children, born in 1802 and 1804. *Where generally resident during last five years:* 'Clones Ireland'. [PRO: WO 25/771 f239]. Severely wounded, Pyrenees, 28 July 1813 (3rd Battn.) [*London Gazette*].

PRATT, John, Ensign/Lt., 30th Foot: *1829 Statement of Service*: Born Feb. 1794, Castle Martyrl, Ireland. Aged seventeen on his first entrance into the Army. Ensign, 30th Foot, 25 June 1811; Lt. 25 May 1813; Half Pay 1817; Lt., 28th Foot, 1819; Capt., '97 removed to 17th Foot', 1825; Major, unattached, 3 Oct. 1826; Major, 27th Foot, 22 March 1827. *Battles, sieges and campaigns*: 'Ensign at the last siege & storming of Badajoz April 1812... Ensign at Salamanca 22 July 1812... Capture of Madrid in 1812 as an Ensign... Ensign at the Siege of Burgos, the affair of Villa Murrell on 25th or 26th Oct. and other minor affairs during the retreat from Burgos 1812. Lieut. at Quatre Bras and Waterloo 17th & 18th June 1815.' *Wounds received in action*: 'At the Siege of Badajoz in 1812 Left Leg injured. 18th June at Waterloo by a Musquet Ball in the chin & Mouth. Received for the latter one years pay.' *Titles, honorary distinctions and medals*: 'Medal for Waterloo.' *Service abroad*: '1811 to 1813, Peninsula. 1813 to 1814, Holland. 1814 to 1816, France. 1819 to 1825, Ionian Islands. Decr. 1828 to 31 Dec. 1829, West Indies.' Not married in 1830. [PRO: WO 25/790 f93]. Slightly wounded, storming of Badajoz, 6 April 1812 (2nd Battn.) [*London Gazette*].

PRATT, John D., Lt., 71st Foot: Lt., 71st Foot, 8 Aug. 1804. Severely wounded, Vimeiro, 21 Aug. 1808 [*London Gazette*].

+PRATT, Mathias, 2nd Lt./1st Lt., 95th Foot: 2nd Lt., 95th Rifles, 18 May 1805. Wounded, Vimeiro, 21 Aug. 1808 [*London Gazette*]. Severely wounded, Coa, 24 July 1810 [*London Gazette*]. *Register of officers' effects*: 1st Battn. Died, 30 July 1810. Single. He had 'No Effects'. [PRO: WO 25/2964]. *Simmons*, pp. 76, 78 [wounded, Coa, 1810], 81, 86, 87 [died of wounds: 'My poor friend Pratt was brought into the boat a corpse! We had embarked in boats upon the Mondego River and were proceeding to Coimbra. Pratt went ashore to get some milk for our breakfast... I suppose the exertion he used, the day being very hot, had assisted to remove the slough in the wound in his throat, the carotid artery being injured; he died instantly from one gush of blood. The ball had entered his jaw, taken a transverse direction, and gone out near the base of the neck. When he drank a quantity of anything, the fluid ran down his bosom, so that the gullet was also partially divided.'], p. 88. *Harris*, p. 163.

PRATT, William, Ensign, 5th Foot: Ensign, 5th Foot, 26 Sept. 1809. Severely wounded, Salamanca, 22 July 1812 (1st Battn.) [*London Gazette*].

PRECORBIN, Silvain de, Lt., Chasseurs Brittanniques: *1829 Statement of Service for Retired Officers*: 'In the year 1794, I entered as volunteer in the hussards nobles of Beon, I was then 16 years old. In 1795, I entered in the hussards nobles of Damas. In 1798 I entered in the foreign artillery as a Cadet. In 1811 I was appointed Ensign in the chasseurs britanniques. In 1812 I was promoted to the rank of a Lieutenant in the chasseurs britan-

niques. In 1814 I was placed on half pay by reduction.' [Army List gives: Ensign, Chasseurs Britanniques, 9 Oct. 1811; Lt., Chasseurs Britanniques, 4 June 1812]. *Where serving when wounded*: 'I was wounded in the retreat of Holland in the month of february; and in Spain the 31st Augt. 1812 [sic]'. 'In expectation of a Pension for wounds.' *Family*: Married in Paris, Sept. 1819, 'for the second time'. Two children from first marriage by 1816, four more from second by 1829. *Where generally resident during last five years*: 'I resided these last years at Pasry in france & have been and in England.' [PRO: WO 25/756 f18]. Severely wounded, 'in the Operations of the Army', 31 Aug. 1813 ('Lieutenant Precothoin') [*London Gazette*].

PRENDERGAST, James, Lt., 36th Foot: Lt., 36th Foot, 26 Nov. 1807. Severely wounded, Toulouse, 10 April 1814 (1st Battn.) [*London Gazette*]. MGS.

PRESCOT, Sergentson, Capt., 5th Dragoon Guards: Capt., 5th Dragoon Guards, 14 March 1800. Slightly wounded, in an 'Affair with the Enemy's Rear Guard, near Llerena', 11 April 1812 ('Major') [*London Gazette*]. Mentioned in Cotton's Llerena dispatch, 11 April 1812 ['I have great pleasure in assuring you of the good conduct of ... Major Prescott, commanding 5th dragoon guards'] [*London Gazette*].

+PRESCOTT, George, Capt., 7th Foot: Capt., Army, 27 Nov. 1806; Capt., 7th Foot, 25 Sept. 1807. Killed, Salamanca, 22 July 1812 [*London Gazette*]. Obituary, *The Gentleman's Magazine*, Sept. 1812, pp. 296-7 ['July 22. Fell nobly at the battle of Salamanca, Capt. G. Prescott, of the 7th or Royal Fusileers. Mrs P. had followed her husband's marches with the regiment from their embarkation at

Cork. When the tidings of his death reached her, in an agony of grief, she braved all dangers, and sought the body of her husband on the field of battle. Capt. P. was a meritorious officer, a tender husband, beloved by all who knew him. Mrs. P. is the daughter of Col. Skinner, late of the Newfoundland regiment, whose family have served the Crown nearly 100 years. Capt. P. served in the East Indies in the 71st reg. Some provision, it is hoped, will be made for this family.'].

PRESTON, George, Capt., 40th Foot: Capt., 40th Foot, 12 Jan. 1805. Slightly wounded, Busaco, 27 Sept. 1810, while serving as ADC to Sir B. Spencer (1st Battn.) [*London Gazette*].

+PREVOST, Henry, Lt., 7th Foot: Lt., 7th Foot, 15 Dec. 1804. Severely wounded, Albuera, 16 May 1811 (1st Battn.) [*London Gazette*]. Died of wounds, 31 May 1811. Return dated 25 June 1811 (2nd Battn.) [PRO: WO 25/2965].

+PREVOST, James, Capt., 60th Foot: Capt., Army, 2 Dec. 1806; Capt., 60th Foot, 26 Feb. 1807. Severely wounded during the repulse of a sortie from Badajoz, 10 May 1811 (5th Battn.) [*London Gazette*]. Severely wounded in 'an Affair with the Enemy near Aldea de Ponte', 27 Sept. 1811 [*London Gazette*]. Died of wounds, 20 Oct. 1811. Return dated 25 Oct. 1811. [PRO: WO 25/2965].

PREVOST, William Augustus, Lt. Col., 67th Foot: Lt.Col., Army, 1 Dec. 1804; Lt. Col., 67th Foot, 30 May 1805. Slightly wounded, Barossa, 5 March 1811 (2nd Battn.) [*London Gazette*]. Mentioned in Graham's Barossa dispatch of 6 March 1811 ['These attacks were zealously supported by ... Lieutenant-Colonel Prevost with a part of the 67th.'] [*London Gazette*]. Led the British forces in the taking of Fort St

Phillippe, Tarragona, 3–7 June 1813. Mentioned in Murray's Tarragona dispatch of 9 June 1813 ['I detached Lieutenant-Colonel Prevost's brigade ... to attack the Fort of St Philippe... The brigade of Colonel Prevost consists of the 2d 67th, and the battalion of Roll Dillon, and to these was subsequently joined the brigade of Spanish troops commanded by Colonel Lauder. The Fort has been taken, and I have the honour to enclose Colonel Prevost's report to me... This capture, in the present situation of our affairs, is of great importance... The importance of this acquisition, and the rapidity with which the fort has been taken, make it quite unnecessary for me to say how much I approve the conduct of Lieutenant-Colonel Prevost'] [*London Gazette*]. Prevost's report to Murray, concerning the taking of Fort St Phillippe, dated 'Fort San Philippe, Col de Balaguer, June 7, 1813' is in the *London Gazette*, 20 July 1813 (Signed 'Wm. Prevost, Lieut. Col., Commanding 2d Brigade 1st Division'). Gold Medal (Barrosa).

+PRÉVOT, Joseph Félix de, Capt., Chasseurs Britanniques: Capt., Chasseurs Britanniques, 3 Dec. 1803. Severely wounded, Orthes, 27 Feb. 1814 ('Felix Provost') [*London Gazette*]. Died of wounds, 6 March 1814. Return dated March 1814. [PRO: WO 25/2965].

PRICE, David, Lt., 36th Foot: *1829 Statement of Service for Retired Officers*: Aged sixteen on first appointment to the Army. Ensign, 36th Fot, 5 Dec. 1805; Lt., 36th Foot, March 1807 [Army List gives 23 April 1807]; Capt., 36th Foot, 12 Nov. 1812; Half-pay, Jan. 1815, by reduction. *Where serving when wounded*: 'Severely wounded at Salamanca. No pension'. *Family*: Married in Kingsbridge, Devon, 14 May 1817. Four children by 1829. *Title and nature of employment*: 'Adjt. Wiltshire Militia'. *Where* *generally resident during last five years*: 'Head Quarters Wilts. Militia Marlbro'. [PRO: WO 25/771 f203]. Severely wounded, Salamanca, 22 July 1812 [*London Gazette*]. MGS.

PRICE, Rice, Lt., 57th Foot: *1829 Statement of Service for Retired Officers*: Aged nineteen on first appointment to the Army. Ensign, 57th Foot, 17 March 1808; Lt., 57th Foot, 21 July 1808; Capt., 57th Foot, 27 April 1820; Half-pay, 1821, by reduction. 'Having been severely wounded in the Groin where the Ball is still lodged, am incapacitated from active service'. *Where serving when wounded*: 'Pampluna in Spain'. *Details of pension*: Seventy pounds, commencing 25 Dec. 1827. *Family*: Married in St Hilliers, Jersey, on 7 Oct. 1809. One child by 1829. No employment. *Where generally resident during last five years*: 'Glynllich, Breconshire, London, Brighton, Guernsey, Jersey'. [PRO: WO 25/771 f205]. Severely wounded, Pyrenees, 28 July 1813 (1st Battn.) [*London Gazette*]. MGS.

+PRIDHAM, James, Lt., 11th Foot: Lt., 11th Foot, 5 Oct. 1808. 'Ascertained to be a prisoner, and a leg amputated', in the siege of the Forts of St Vincente, St Cayetano, and La Merced at Salamanca, 18–24 June 1812 ('Prideman') [*London Gazette*]. Died of wounds, 5 July 1812. Return dated 25 July 1812 (1st Battn.) [PRO: WO 25/2965].

PRING, John, Capt., 27th Foot: Capt., 27th Foot, 27 April 1809. Severely wounded during the repulse of a sortie from Badajoz, 10 May 1811 (3rd Battn.) [*London Gazette*]. Temporary pension of one hundred pounds per annum, commencing 11 May 1812, 'for wounds' received at Badajoz, 1811 [*1818 Pension Return*, pp. 8–9].

PRINGLE, William Henry, Major-General: Col., 25 Oct. 1809; Major-General, 1 Jan. 1812. Severely wounded, 'in Action with the Enemy', 15 Feb. 1814 [*London Gazette*]. Mentioned in Wellington dispatch, dated 'St Jean de Luz', 20 Feb. 1814: 'On the 15th ... towards St Palais ... the 2d division ... should attack in front. Those troops made a most gallant attack upon the enemy's position, which was remarkably strong, but which was carried without very considerable loss ... the enemy ... made repeated attempts to regain the position, particularly in two attacks, which were most gallantly received and repulsed by the 39th regiment ... in Major-General Pringle''s brigade. The Major-General, and Lieutenant-Colonel Bruce, of the 39th, were unfortunately wounded'].

PRIOR, John, Capt., 39th Foot; Lt. Col., 20th Portuguese Line: Capt., Army, 12 Sept. 1805; Capt., 39th Foot, 13 July 1809; Bvt. Major, E.O.P.S., 25 Feb. 1813; 'Serv. with the Portug. Army'. In Portuguese Service Oct. 1809 to April 1814. *Challis, Portuguese Army List*, p. 58 ['Bt. Maj. E.O.P.S.; Lt. Col. 20 Line... Wd. Busaco 27 Sep. '10']. Mentioned in Skerrett's dispatch concerning the capture of Seville, 28 Aug. 1812 ['I am also much indebted to ... Lieutenant-Colonel Prior, commanding a detachment 20th Portuguese Regiment'] [*London Gazette*].

PRITCHARD, Samuel Dilman, Ensign/Lt., 52nd Foot: *1829 Statement of Service*: [completed in February 1843] 'Born in Surry England, in 1791. Aged 18 Eighteen on his first Entrance into the Army. Ensign, 52nd Regiment, 4 May 1809. Lieutenant, 52nd, 11 April 1811. Adjutant, 52nd, 1 July 1813. Captain, 52nd, 7 April 1825. Captain and Major of Brigade in Canada, 52nd, From June 1829 to Jany. 1833, when the Staff in Canada was reduced. Major, 49th Regiment, 30 Augt. 1833. Major,

71st Regt., 13 Septr. 1833. Half Pay, 26 May 1836, urgent private affairs without receiving the difference. Major, Particular Service, Full Pay, 1 Jany. 1838. Half Pay, 1 Jany. 1839, In consequence of having been appointed Major of Brigade to the Forces serving in Canada.' *Battles, sieges and campaigns*: 'Campaigns. 1810. Joined the 1st Bn. 52nd Regiment as ensign the evening after the Battle of Busaco. On retreat to the Lines of Torres Vedras the Regmt. occupying the Heights immediately above Ameda. 1811. As Lieutenant on Massena's retreat from before the same into Spain, and at the Combats of Pombal, Redinha, Cazal Nova, Foz d'Aronce, Sabugal, Defence of the Ponte de Marialva on the Azava. 1813. The Affair at an Milan. Battle of Vittoria 21st June, and pursuit of the retreating Army to Vera – when I proceeded to England to join the 2nd Bn. to which I had been appointed Adjutant. 1813 Campaign in Holland as Lieut. & Adjutant. 1814 Campaign in Flanders to April 1815 when the Staff 2nd Bn. was ordered to England, the men being given over to the 1st Battn. 1816, 1817, 1818 as Lieut. Comdg. a company with the Army of Occupation in France.' *Distinguished conduct*: 'When commanding the Sub-Division ordered to Charge the Bridge at Marialva. On the 23d April 1811 two thousand French Infantry & a squadron of Cavalry marching out of Ciudad Rodrigo, made a sudden effort to seize the Bridge of Marialva, but the Passage was bravely maintained by Captain Dobbs with only a Company of the 52nd and some Riflemen.' *Napier's History of the Peninsular War*, Vol III, Book XII, Chap V, p. 507. *Wounds received in action*: 'Returned wounded 23d April 1811, severely in the hip. Ball still lodged. Obliged to be sent to Lisbon and thence to England for recovery of health. A years pay as Lieutenant. 9th January 1814, received a double

fracture of the arm and shoulder when on the line of March from Oudenborch to Rosendael from my horse falling with me on the ice, by which I was confined three months receiving a years Pay as Lieutenant and Adjutant.' *Service abroad*: 'July 1810 to July 1811, Portugal & Spain. January 1813 to Septemr. 1813, Spain. Novemr. 1813 to April 1814, Holland. April 1814 to 1815, Flanders. Septemr. 1816 to Novemr. 1818, France. July 1822 to Novemr. 1827, North America, New Brunswick, and Novia Scotia. July 1829 to January 1833, Lower Canada. May 1838 to February 1843, Canada, where I am now serving.' *Family*: Married Emma de Montenack, 1 March 1832, Montreal, Lower Canada. They had two children by 1843. [PRO: WO 25/795 f87]. Mentioned in Wellington's dispatch, dated Villa Formosa, 1 May 1811 ['The enemy had on the 23d attacked our piquets on the Azava, but were repulsed. Captains Dobbs and Campbell, of the 52d regiment, and Lieutenant Eeles, of the 95th regiment, distinguished themselves upon this occasion, in which the allied troops defended their post against very superior numbers of the enemy. One Lieutenant (Lieutenant Pritchard) and seventeen soldiers were wounded.'] [*London Gazette*, 18 May 1811]. MGS.

PROESTLER, Frederick August von, Capt., Duke of Brunswick Oels' Corps (Infantry): Capt., Duke of Brunswick Oels' Corps (Infantry), 29 Sept. 1809. Slightly wounded, Pyrenees, 25 July 1813 [*London Gazette*].

PROTO, Joseph, Ensign, Chasseurs Britanniques: *1829 Statement of Service for Retired Officers*: Aged eighteen on first appointment to the Army. Ensign, Chasseurs Britanniques, Sept. 1810 [Army List gives 18 Oct. 1810]; Lt., Chasseurs Britanniques, [9] Oct. 1811; Half-pay, n.d. Served four years on Full-Pay. *Where serving when wounded*: 'in Spain in Fonthes d'Honore'. *Details of pension*: Seventy-pounds, commencing 5 May 1811. *Family*: Married in Rocca, Sicily, in 1827. *Where generally resident during last five years*: 'in Sicily at Melazzo'. Note added in pencil: 'This officer is not on 1/2 pay, but receives a Pension for Wounds.' [PRO: WO 25/771 f222]. Severely wounded, Fuentes de Onoro, 5 May 1811 [*London Gazette*].

PURDON, Edward, Capt., 60th Foot: *1829 Statement of Service*: 'Born in Ireland, November 1781. Aged nineteen on his first Entrance into the Army. 2 Lieut, 2 Ceylon Reg, 1 August 1800. 1st Lieutenant, 1806. Captain, 60 Foot, [27] Augt 1807. Bt. Major, 60 Foot, 12 April 1814. Major, Royal African Corp, 8 January 1824. Lieut Colonel, Royal African Corp, 17 October 1824. Lieut. Colonel, 41st Foot, 29 Janry. 1829.' With added note: 'Died 2d Decr. 1836.' *Battles, sieges and campaigns*: 'When in the 5th Batalion of the 60th Regiment – In almost all the actions fought in the Peninsula & in every action in France to the termination of Hostilities in 1814 as Captn & Bt. Major.' *Distinguished conduct*: 'I conceive it ill becomes any Officer to speak of his own merits, Best known at the Horse Guards & by my superiors.' *Wounds Received in action*: 'Received three severe wounds at Toulouse 10th April 1814, One Slight Wound at Doodawania Westn. Africa 7 April 1826, & Four other trivial flesh wounds, never noticed. I have received in consequence One Years Full pay as Captain and ever since £100 per Annum, which I presume is to continue for Life, as the Letter I have received by Order of the King has no limitation to it.' *Titles, honorary distinctions and medals*: 'None. Having only served during the whole of the Peninsula War with the Rank of Captain till I obtained

my Brevet Majority for the Battle of Toulouse in April 1814.' *Service abroad*: '1 August 1800 to latter end of 1806, Ceylon & the Continent of India. West Indies, Peninsula, France, Gibralter, America, Western Africa, East Indies. As I have not been particular in keeping an Account of Dates I shall only say that I have served upwards of 31 years on Constant service in the Four Quarters of the Globe & that I have seldom been at home except on sick leave in consequence of my wounds or the bad effects of climate.' [PRO: WO 25/793 f4]. Severely wounded, Toulouse, 10 April 1814 (5th Battn.) [*London Gazette*]. *1818 Pension Return*, pp. 16–17.

+PURVES, Patrick, Capt., 79th Foot: Capt., 79th Foot, 11 Oct. 1810. Killed, Toulouse, 10 April 1814 ('Purvis') (1st Battn.) [*London Gazette*].

+PURVIS, John, Capt., 1st Foot: Capt., Army, 27 April 1809; Capt., 1st Foot, 15 Aug. 1811. Died of wounds, France, 13 April 1814. Return dated May 1814 (3rd Battn.) [PRO: WO 25/2965].

+PYKE, Wentworth A., Lt., 7th Foot: Lt., 7th Foot, 3 Feb. 1809. Killed, storming of Badajoz, 6 April 1812 ('Pike') [*London Gazette*]. *Challis, Index*, p. 81.

+PYNE, James, Ensign, 59th Foot: Ensign, 59th Foot, 17 Oct. 1811. Slightly wounded, Vittoria, 21 June 1813 (2nd Battn.) [*London Gazette*]. Killed, storming of San Sebastian, 31 Aug. 1813 (Lieutenant) (2nd Battn.) [*London Gazette*].

+PYNE, Robert, Capt., 66th Foot: Capt., 66th Foot, 6 Dec. 1810. Severely wounded, Nivelle, 10 Nov. 1813 (2nd Battn.) [*London Gazette*]. *Hurt*, p. 80 ['D.O.W., Nivelle, Nov. 10'].

PYNN, Henry, Bvt. Major, E.O.P.S.; Lt. Col., 18th Portuguese Line: Capt., 82nd Foot; Bvt. Major, E.O.P.S., 15 Nov. 1809, 'Serving with the Portuguese Army'. Mentioned in Wellington's Fuentes de Onoro dispatch, 8 May 1811 (5 May: as Lt. Col. commanding the light companies in Col. Ashworth's Portuguese brigade) [*London Gazette*, 26 May 1811]. 'Dangerously' wounded, Pyrenees, 30 July 1813, while serving as Lt. Col., 18th Portuguese Line [*London Gazette*]. In Portuguese Service April 1809 to Aug. 1813. Gold Medal. MGS. *Challis, Portuguese Army*, p. 58.

Q

QUADE, Frederick, Ensign, 2nd Line Battn. K.G.L.: Ensign, 2nd Line Battn. K.G.L., 4 Sept. 1809. Severely wounded, siege of Burgos, 18 Oct. 1812 [*London Gazette*]. Served in Peninsula 1808-12. *Beamish*, vol. II, p. 608 [Died 'at Walsrode, in Han. 16th May 1826'].

QUEADE, William, Lt., 40th Foot; Capt., 1st Portuguese Line: Lt., 40th Foot, 3 Oct. 1805. Slightly wounded, storming of Ciudad Rodrigo, 19 Jan. 1812, while serving as Capt., 1st Portuguese Line [*London Gazette*]. In Portuguese Service May 1810 to April 1814. *Challis, Portuguese Army*, p. 58.

QUILL, Henry, Ensign, 32nd Foot: *1829 Statement of Service for Retired Officers*: Ensign, 32nd Foot, March 1809 [Army List gives 16 March], 'By Recommendation of General Ogilvie Colonel of the 32d Foot'; Lt., Half-pay, Dec. 1817, by reduction. 'The wound which has deprived me of one of my Eyes & has impaired the sight of the other (especially for the last 2 years) - the wound of the lungs from which the Ball has never been extracted has so afflicted me with serious ill health as to render me unfit or incapable of returning to the service - which you will see by a reference to the medical certificate in the late secretary of war's office. I have received an other wound in the leg, which so shattered it as narrowly to escape amputation, and for which I have never made any pecuniary claim of any kind'. *Where serving when wounded*: 'In the Trenches Before Burgos In Spain - Loss of one Eye. At Quatre Bras in Flanders June 1815 - a Severe Wound of the Lungs'. *Details of pension*: Seventy pounds, commencing 1813, for the first; seventy pounds, commencing 1816, for the latter. *Family*: Married in 'Margarets Church, Westmanister, London', 21 Aug. 1821. Two children by 1829. *Where generally resident during last five years*: 'In Jersey'. [PRO: WO 25/7711 f275]. Severely wounded, siege of Burgos, 11 Oct. 1812 [*London Gazette*]. *1818 Pension Return*, pp. 8-9. Waterloo. MGS.

R

+RADCLIFFE, Stephen, Lt., 27th Foot: Lt., 27th Foot, 13 Sept. 1808. Severely wounded, storming of Badajoz, 6 April 1812 (3rd Batt.) [*London Gazette*]. Killed, Salamanca, 18 July 1812 [*London Gazette*].

RADCLIFFE, Stephen, Ensign, 6th Foot: Ensign, 6th Foot, 20 July 1810. Slightly wounded, Pyrenees, 25 July 1813 (1st Battn.) [*London Gazette*].

RADCLIFFE, Thomas, Ensign/Lt., 27th Foot: *1829 Statement of Service for Retired Officers*: Aged 'about 16 years' on first appointment to the Army. Ensign, 27th Foot, July 1811 [Army List gives 18 July 1811]; Lt., 27th Foot, [25] Aug. 1813; Half-pay, Feb. 1817, by reduction. 'Unfit for active service'. *Where serving when wounded*: 'In the Pyrenees'. No pension. *Family*: Married in St Paul's Church, Dublin, 9 Nov. 1822. Four children by 1829. No employment. *Where generally resident during last five years*: 'Co. Roscommon and in the Co. Kildare and in Dublin'. [PRO: WO 25/772 f34]. Severely wounded, Pyrenees, 28 July 1813 (3rd Battn.) [*London Gazette*].

RADFORD, Frederick, Ensign, 52nd Foot: *1829 Statement of Service for Retired Officers*: Aged seventeen on first appointment to the Army. 'Joined the Army as a Volunteer attached to the 28th Regiment in January 1813'; Ensign, 52nd Foot, June 1813 [Army List gives 13 May 1813]; Lt., 52nd Foot, 16 June 1814; Half-pay, n.d., by reduction; Lt., 15th Foot, April 1825; Half-pay, 17th Foot, Nov. 1825, 'from my own application from the state of my private affairs'; Lt., 40th Foot, 4 July 1827; 'appointment cancelled', 4 Nov. 1827, 'by my own request from the state of my private

affairs'. *Where serving when wounded*: 'Crossing the Pyrenees'. *Family*: Married in Kensington, Middlesex, 10 May 1825. *Where generally resident during last five years*: 'England, France, & Pays Bas'. [PRO: WO 25/772 f15]. Severely wounded, the Nive, 10 Dec. 1813 (1st Battn.) [*London Gazette*].

RAINEY, Henry, Capt., 82nd Foot; Capt., 55th Foot; Major, Portuguese Staff: Capt., 82nd Foot, 13 April 1809. Slightly wounded, 'at the Siege of St Sebastian', 7-27 July 1813, while on the Portuguese General Staff as ADC to Major-General Bradford [*London Gazette*]. Severely wounded, the Nive, 11 Dec. 1813, while serving on the Portuguese General Staff as ADC to Major-General Bradford [*London Gazette*]. In Portuguese Service July 1813 to April 1814. Temporary pension of two hundred pounds per annum, commencing 11 Dec. 1814, 'for wounds' received at Bidart, 1813 [*1818 Pension Return*, pp. 14-15]. Later Major-General. MGS. *Challis, Portuguese Army*, p. 58 ['Capt. 55 Ft... Wd. San Sebastian 25 July '13'].

+RAM, Stopford, Ensign, 3rd Foot Guards: Ensign, 3rd Foot Guards, 3 April 1806. Killed, Talavera, 28 July 1809 [*London Gazette*].

+RAMADGE, Benjamin, Lt., 74th Foot: Ensign, 74th Foot, 29 Nov. 1809; Lt. 30 Oct. 1811. Slightly wounded, siege of Ciudad Rodrigo, 16 Jan. 1812 [*London Gazette*]. Killed, siege of Badajoz, 26 March 1812 [*London Gazette*].

RAMUS, Charles Louis, Capt., 5th Foot: *1829 Statement of Service for Retired Officers*: Aged twenty-one on first appointment to the Army. Ensign, 40th Foot, 1803; Lt., 50th

Foot, 1805; Capt., 5th Foot, 1809 [Army List gives 28 Sept. 1809]; Half-pay, n.d., by reduction. Served thirteen years on Full-pay. 'Rendered incapable of service, by my wounds'. *Where serving when wounded*: Monte Video. El Bodon. *Details of pension*: One hundred pounds per annum, apparently for first wound, 'last grant 1828'. *Family*: Married in Ilfracombe, North Devon, 9 May 1820. Three children by 1829. No employment. *Where generally resident during last five years*: 'Ilfracombe, Clifton, Cheltenham'. [PRO: WO 25/772 f25]. Slightly wounded, El Bodon, 25 Sept. 1811 (2nd Battn.) [*London Gazette*].

RAUTENBERG, George, Capt., 1st Light Battn. K.G.L.: Lt., 1st Light Battn. K.G.L., 12 Jan. 1806. Capt., 1st Light Battn. K.G.L., 17 March 1812. Severely wounded, Crossing the Bidassoa, 7/9 Oct. 1813 ('Rautenburg') [*London Gazette*]. Served in Peninsula 1808–14. *Beamish*, vol. II, p. 607 ['severely wounded, 7th Oct. 1813, on the Bidassoa; severely wounded 27th Feb. 1814, before Bayonne.'].

RAUTENBERG, William, Capt., 5th Line Battn. K.G.L.: Capt., 5th Line Battn. K.G.L., 15 Oct. 1812. Served in Peninsula 1808–14. *Beamish*, vol. II, p. 646 ['severely wounded, 27th Feb. 1814, before Bayonne... [Died] at Holstropp, between Lipstadt and Hanover, while on his route to the latter place, 27th Nov. 1814.'].

RAWLING, Edward, Ensign/Lt., 4th Foot: *1829 Statement of Service for Retired Officers*: Aged seventeen on first appointment to the Army. Ensign, 4th Foot, n.d. [Army List gives 6 June 1811], 'by Volunteering from the West Suffolk Militia'; Lt., 4th Foot, [19 Oct. 1813]; Half-pay, 42nd Foot, n.d., 'at my own request having considerable family affairs to settle'. Served four years on Full-pay. 'Not capable of serving from an

accident which caused a severe Ruptured Testicle'. *Where serving when wounded*: 'at Badajos and at Angulette near Bayonne'. No pension. *Family*: Married in 'St Pancras, Middlesex', Feb. 1819. Four children by 1829. No employment. Where generally resident during last five years: 'in London'. [PRO: WO 25/772 f23]. Severely wounded, storming of Badajoz, 6 April 1812 ('Rawlins') [*London Gazette*]. Slightly wounded, the Nive, 11 Dec. 1813 ('Rawlins') (1st Battn.) [*London Gazette*]. 'Rawlings' in Army List. MGS.

RAY, John Trumball, Ensign, 45th Foot: *1829 Statement of Service for Retired Officers*: Aged twenty on first appointment to the Army. 'Entered as a Volunteer 6th April at Badajos 1812'; Ensign, 45th Foot, 13 May 1812; Lt., 45th Foot, 30 March 1814; Half-pay, 25 Dec. 1814, by reduction. *Where serving when wounded*: 'At the Action of Salamanca on the 22nd July 1812'. *Details of pension*: 'Examined several times, but received the Pension of fifty Pounds, for two years only', commencing '25th December 1821, expired on 24th June 1824'. *Where generally resident during last five years*: 'Vicinity of London'. [PRO: WO 25/772 f49]. Severely wounded, Salamanca, 22 July 1812 ('Rey') (1st Battn.) [*London Gazette*].

RAY, Robert, Lt., 50th Foot; Major, 2nd Portuguese Line: *1829 Statement of Service for Retired Officers*: Aged twenty-six on first appointment to the Army. Ensign, 50th Foot, 31 July 1806; Lt., 50th Foot, Dec. 1807 [Army List gives 26 Dec. 1807]; Capt., 50th Foot, 22 Jan. 1814; 'Placed on half-pay in 1814 on the reduction of 2nd Batt. 50th Regt. But immediately replaced on full Pay unattached by remaining in the Portuguese service. Again placed on half pay 25 Decr. 1816, but not on my own request'. Bvt. Major,

4 Sept. 1817. 'Very desirous of service; But from the state of my wounds for the last 3 years, I am afraid I would not be able to manage much fatigue'. *Where serving when wounded*: 'Peninsula, 30th July 1813 when in Comd. of the 2nd Regt. Portuguese Infantry'. *Details of pension*: Two hundred and fifty pounds, commencing 31 July 1814. *Family*: Married in Elgin, 16 March 1814. Three children by 1829. *Title and nature of employment*: 'Lt. Colonel in the Portuguese Service', for which he was supposed to have been paid 'above £40 a year, but has not been paid'. *Where generally resident during last five years*: 'Elgin'. [PRO: WO 25/772 f28]. Wounded, Vimeiro, 21 Aug. 1808 ('Way') [*London Gazette*]. Slightly wounded, Pyrenees, 30 July 1813, while serving as Major, 2nd Portuguese Line [*London Gazette*]. In Portuguese Service May 1809 to April 1814. Gold Medal. *1818 Pension Return*, pp. 24–5. MGS. *Challis, Portuguese Army*, p. 58.

RAYMOND, William, Lt., 31st Foot: Lt., 31st Foot, 1 Aug. 1811. Temporary pension of seventy pounds per annum, commencing 25 Aug. 1814, 'for wounds' received in the Pyrenees, 1813 [*1818 Pension Return*, pp. 8–9].

REA, Andrew Charles, 1st Lt., Royal Marines: 1st Lt., Royal Marines, 21 Nov. 1807. Wounded, assault and capture of the Island of Santa Clara, during the siege of St Sebastian, 27 Aug. 1813 ('Lt. Raye') [*London Gazette*]. MGS.

REA, William James, Lt., 1st Foot: Lt., Army, 30 July 1807; Lt., 1st Foot, 22 June 1809. Slightly wounded, storming of Badajoz, 6 April 1812, while serving as an Acting Engineer ('Ray') [*London Gazette*]. Slightly wounded, siege of Burgos, 16 Oct. 1812, while serving as Acting Engineer ('Rae') [*London Gazette*]. Slightly wounded, Vittoria, 21 June 1813 (3rd Battn.) [*London Gazette*]. Wounded at Waterloo. *Dalton*, pp. 116, 118 ['Capt. 60th Foot 22nd June 1815. Out of said regt. before 1824.'].

+READ, Richard, Lt., 82nd Foot: Lt., 82nd Foot 18 June 1807. Wounded, 'dangerously', Rolica, 17 Aug. 1808 ('Reid') [*London Gazette*]. Died, Cadiz, 9 Nov. 1812 [PRO: WO 25/2965].

READ, Robert, Ensign, 38th Foot: Ensign, 38th Foot, 21 March 1811. Severely wounded, storming of Badajoz, 6 April 1812 ('Ried') (2nd Battn.) [*London Gazette*]. MGS.

REED, John, Capt., 68th Foot: *1829 Statement of Service*: 'Born in Winchester, 10th April 1784. Aged Fifteen on his first Entrance into the Army. Ensign, 68th Regt., 26 March 1799. Lieutenant, 68th Regt., 21 March 1800. Adjutant, 68th Regt., 26th Feby. 1805. Captain, 68th Regt., 12th May 1808. Brevet Major, 68th Regt., 27th May 1825. Major, 68th Regt., 2nd June 1825.' *Battles, sieges and campaigns*: 'Captain. 1, 3, & 5th Augt. 1809, Flushing... Moresco, 20th June 1812... Heights above Moresco, 21st June 1812. Salamanca, 22d July 1812. Fort-El-Reterio 13th Augt. 1812. Vittoria, 21st June 1813.' *Wounds received in action*: 'Wounded in the Right Shoulder at Vittoria on the 21st June 1813, Received One year's Pay as Captain.' *Service abroad*: '1st Jany. 1801 to 20th Septr. 1805, West Indies. 30th July 1809 to 25th Decr. 1809, Walcheren. 28th June 1811 to 1st March 1814, Peninsula. 3d July 1818 to 5th Septr. 1822, Canada. 25th July 1824 to 16th Octr. 1825, Canada. 22nd May 1829 to 15th Novr. 1829, Canada.' [PRO: WO 25/798 f149]. Slightly wounded, Vittoria, 21 June 1813 ('Read') (2nd Battn.) [*London Gazette*]. MGS.

REED, Samuel, Capt., 71st Foot: *1829 Statement of Service for*

Retired Officers: Aged sixteen on first appointment to the Army. Ensign, 56th Foot, 3 Feb. 1801; Lt., Half-pay, 89th Foot, 1802; Lt., 36th Foot, 1803; Capt., 6th Garrison Battn., 27 Nov. 1806; Capt., 71st Foot, 12 Nov. 1808 [Army List gives 29 Sept. 1808]; 'Capt. & Brevet Major', Half-pay, 71st Foot, 25 Oct. 1821, by reduction. 'The dates of my commissions in the 89th and 36th Regiments I am unable to give – the documents having been lost with my Baggage at Waterloo'. *Where serving when wounded*: 'Vittoria'. *Details of pension*: One hundred pounds, commencing 25 Dec. 1826. *Family*: Married in Dublin, 5 Dec. 1808. Nine children by 1829. *Where generally resident during last five years*: 'Isle of Man'. [PRO: WO 25/772 f85]. Severely wounded, Vittoria, 21 June 1813 ('Read') (1st Battn.) [*London Gazette*]. Waterloo. Died, 13 July 1842.

+REES, Abraham, Volunteer, 5th Foot: Severely wounded, Vittoria, 21 June 1813 (Volunteer) (1st Battn.) [*London Gazette*]. Died of wounds, 31 Aug. 1813. Return dated Sept. 1813 (Ensign) [*London Gazette*].

REEVES, George James, Lt. Col., 27th Foot: *1829 Statement of Service for Retired Officers*: Aged fourteen on first appointment to the Army. Ensign, 8th Foot, 9 Feb. 1791; Lt., 8th Foot, 29 June 1793; 'Lieut. & Captn.', 8th Foot, 21 Dec. 1796; Capt., 18th Foot, 20 Aug. 1801; Major, 27th Foot, 10 Oct. 1805; Bvt. Lt. Col., 27th Foot, 1 Jan. 1812; Lt. Col., 27th Foot, 4 June 1813, 'without purchase over the head of the eldest Major'; Inpecting Field Officer, Athlone District, 1815; Half-pay, 27th Foot, 25 Dec. 1816, by reduction. *Where serving when wounded*: 'Wounded when Lieut. of Grenadiers serving with Sir Charles Greys Army, at Point a Petre in Gaudeloupe on the 2nd July 1794. No pension. At Martinique in April

1794. No pension. Sp[ain] ... [in] the adva[nce] ... of Lord W[ellington's] Army' [text damaged] *Details of pension*: Three hundred pounds per annum, commencing 'about 1814'. *Family*: Married in Dublin, 10 Feb. 1803. Four children by 1829. No employment. *Where generally resident during last five years*: 'London'. [PRO: WO 25/772 f70]. Mentioned in Murray's Castalla dispatch, 14 April 1813 [12 April: 'the 2d battalion 27th regiment, commanded by Lieutenant-Colonel Reeves... On the 13th, the attack of the enemy ... was very severe ... and a most gallant charge of the 2d 27th, led by Colonel Adam and Lieutenant-Colonel Reeves, decided the fate of the day'] [*London Gazette*]. Severely wounded, 'not dangerously', Heights of Ordal, 12/13 Sept. 1813 (2nd Battn.) [*London Gazette*]. See letter of Capt. J. Waldron, 27th Foot, dated 15 Sept. 1813, published with the Tarragona dispatches in the *London Gazette*, 9 Oct. 1813 ['On the night of the 12th instant, about twelve o'clock, the enemy in great force, attacked the position of the 2d battalion 27th regiment at Ordal; and shortly after, Lieutenant-Colonel Reeves and Captain Mills [Mill] being wounded, the command of the battalion devolved upon me.']. Pension of three hundred pounds per annum, commencing 14 Sept. 1814, 'for wounds' received at Ordal [*1818 Pension Return*, pp. 8–9]. *Royal Military Calendar*, Vol. III, p. 386 [Ordal, 12 Sept. 1813: 'Colonel Adam received two wounds ... about one in the morning, and was forced to leave the field. Lieutenant-Colonel Reeves succeeded in the command: he was soon shot through the body, and also obliged to leave the field.'].

+REICHE, Johann Henry, Capt., Duke of Brunswick Oels' Corps (Infantry): Capt., Duke of Brunswick Oels' Corps Infantry, 27

Sept. 1809. Severely wounded, Heights of Villares, 20–22 June 1812 ('Reicke') [*London Gazette*]. Died of wounds, 27 June 1812. Return dated 25 July 1812 [PRO: WO 25/2965]. 'Johann Henry Keiche' in Army List.

REID, Alexander, Ensign, 50th Foot: Ensign, 50th Foot, 13 Feb. 1812. Severely wounded, Vittoria, 21 June 1813 (1st Battn.) [*London Gazette*].

REID, David, Lt., 11th Foot: *1829 Statement of Service for Retired Officers*: Aged nineteen on first appointment to the Army. Ensign, 11th Foot, Aug. 1807; Lt., 11th Foot, 1808 [Army List gives 4 Oct. 1808]; Half-pay, 54th Foot, 1818, 'on account of wounds and bad health'. *Where serving when wounded*: 'Salamanca. Toulouse'. *Details of pension*: Seventy pounds, commencing 1815. Not married. No employment. *Where generally resident during last five years*: 'Rathfritam'. [PRO: WO 25/722 f152]. Severely wounded, Salamanca, 22 July 1812 ('Read') (1st Battn.) [*London Gazette*]. Severely wounded, Toulouse, 10 April 1814 (1st Battn.) [*London Gazette*]. 'Read' in Army List.

REID, James W., Capt., 48th Foot: Capt., 48th Foot, 20 April 1810. Severely wounded, Toulouse, 10 April 1814 (1st Battn.) [*London Gazette*].

REID, William, 1st Lt., Royal Engineers: 1st Lt., Royal Engineers, 23 April 1810. Slightly wounded during the repulse of a sortie from Badajoz, 10 May 1811 [*London Gazette*]. Mentioned in Wellington's dispatch, dated Frenada, 4 Dec. 1811 ['Don Carlos D'Espagne has informed me, that he attacked the enemy on the 28th of November, on their retreat from the Sierra de Francia... Don Carlos D'Espagne mentions particularly the conduct of Lieutenant William Reid, of the royal engineers, who attended him upon this expedition, having before been employed to perform a service under his direction.']. Slightly wounded, storming of Ciudad Rodrigo, 19 Jan. 1812 [*London Gazette*]. Mentioned in Wellington's dispatch concerning the siege and capture of the forts at Salamanca, dated, Fuente la Pena, 30 June 1812 ['Major-General Clinton ... mentions in strong terms ... Lieutenant Reid, and the officers of the royal engineers'] [*London Gazette*]. Severely wounded, 'at the Siege of St Sebastian,' 7–27 July 1813 [*London Gazette*]. 2nd Capt., Royal Engineers, 20 Dec. 1814. MGS. NGS. Major-General, 1856. Died, 31 Oct. 1858. *Mullen*, p. 656.

+REILLY, Peter, 1st Lt., 95th Foot: 1st Lt., 95th Foot, 9 July 1807. Severely wounded, Coa, 24 July 1810 ('Riley') [*London Gazette*]. *Register of officers' effects*: 'Reiley, P.' 1st Battn. Died, 28 July 1810. Single. The proceeds from his effects were sent to his sister. [PRO: WO 25/2964]. *Simmons*, p. 81 [wounded, Coa], p. 82 [26 July 1810: 'Poor Reilly this morning told me it was useless tormenting himself by taking another day's journey, as he felt he could not live many hours (the ball had gone directly through the lower part of his body); he shook me by the hand and regretted our parting.'], p. 83 [died of wounds, evening of 26 July 1810].

RENNY, John, Ensign, 48th Foot: Ensign, 48th Foot, 19 May 1808. Severely wounded, Talavera, 28 July 1809 ('Kenny') (2nd Battn.) [*London Gazette*].

RENTALL, William, Capt., 52nd Foot: Lt., 52nd Foot, 17 Oct. 1805. Capt., 52nd Foot, 13 May 1812. Severely wounded, Nivelle, 10 Nov. 1813 (1st Battn.) [*London Gazette*].

RETTBERG, Leopold von, Capt., 1st Line Battn. K.G.L.: Capt., 1st Line Battn. K.G.L., 18 Aug. 1813. Served in Peninsula 1808–14. Waterloo. *Beamish*, vol. II, p. 572 ['severely wounded, 27th Feb. 1814, before Bayonne.'].

REUSS, His Serene Highness Prince Henry, Major, 2nd Light Battn. K.G.L.: Major, 2nd Light Battn. K.G.L., 23 Oct. 1812. Severely wounded, in an action near Tolosa, 24 June 1813 [*London Gazette*]. Lt. Col., 2nd Light Battn. K.G.L., 30 Dec. 1813. Served in Peninsula in 1813. Later Major-General in the Austrian service. *Beamish*, vol. II, p. 658 ['resigned 3d June 1815.'].

REYNETT, James Henry, Lt., 45th Foot: *1829 Statement of Service for Retired Officers*: Aged seventeen on first appointment to the Army. Ensign, 45th Foot, 19 Sept. 1804; Lt., 45th Foot, 4 June 1806; Capt., 45th Foot, 23 July 1812; Half-pay, 25 Dec. 1814, by reduction. *Where serving when wounded*: 'Storming of Badajos in Spain'. *Family*: Married in Steynton, Pembrokeshire, 23 Nov. 1817. *Where generally resident during last five years*: 'Milford, South Wales'. [PRO: WO 25/722 f100]. Severely wounded, storming of Badajoz, 6 April 1812 [*London Gazette*]. MGS.

REYNETT, William France, Lt., 45th Foot: *1829 Statement of Service for Retired Officers*: Aged '19 years but not certain' on first appointment to the Army. Ensign, 45th Foot, 20 July 1809; Lt., 45th Foot, 28 Feb. 1811; Half-pay, 73rd Foot, Dec. 1818, 'date not certain', 'from ill health'. *Where serving when wounded*: 'at Vittoria, 21st June 1813'. No pension. *Where generally resident during last five years*: 'Waterford, Ireland'. [PRO: WO 25/722 f95]. Severely wounded, Vittoria, 21 June 1813 ('Rennett') (1st Battn.) [*London Gazette*]. MGS.

+REYNOLDS, Bryan, Ensign, 88th Foot: Ensign, 88th Foot, 9 Jan. 1812. Severely wounded, Orthes, 27 Feb. 1814 (1st Battn.) [*London Gazette*]. Died of wounds, 1st March 1814. Return dated March 1814. [PRO: WO 25/2965].

REYNOLDS, Coyne, Lt., 39th Foot; Capt., 19th Portuguese Line: Lt., Army, 21 April 1808; Lt., 39th Foot, 26 May 1808. In Portuguese Service Nov. 1813 to April 1814. *Challis, Portuguese Army*, p. 59 ['Capt. 19 Line... Wd. Vittoria 21 June '13'].

+REYNOLDS, James, Capt., 83rd Foot: Capt., 83rd Foot, 16 July 1807. Severely wounded, 'leg amputated', Talavera, 28 July 1809 [*London Gazette*]. Died, France, 27 Dec. 1813 [PRO: WO 25/2965].

+REYNOLDS, Michael Hewetson, Ensign, 1st Foot: Ensign, 1st Foot, 23 July 1812. Severely wounded, 'at the Siege of St Sebastian,' 7–27 July 1813 (3rd Battn.) [*London Gazette*]. Died of wounds. 7 Aug. 1813 [PRO: WO 25/2965].

+RHODES, Charles S., Capt., Royal Engineers: Capt., Army, 1 July 1806; Capt., Royal Engineers, 1 May 1811. Killed, in the Storming of San Sebastian, 31 Aug. 1813 [*London Gazette*]. Obituary, *The Gentleman's Magazine*, Nov. 1813, p. 499 ['Aug. 30... At the assault of the town of St Sebastian, when gallantly leading the storming party to the breach, Capt. Rhodes, of the Royal Engineers. He was covered with wounds, having been pierced with 11 balls; the first shot, which was from a musket, struck him in the left arm, and was almost instantly succeeded by a grapeshot, which shattered the same arm to pieces; notwithstanding which he ascended the breach, and, leaping down into the midst of the enemy, received the remainder of his wounds, which terminated his existence.'].

RHODES, Robert, Ensign, 39th Foot: Ensign, 39th Foot, 16 June 1809. Severely wounded, Pyrenees, 25 July 1813 (1st Battn.) [*London Gazette*]. Temporary pension of fifty pounds per annum, commencing 26 July 1814, 'for a wound' received in the Pyrenees [*1818 Pension Return*, pp. 10–11].

RIBTON, John, 1st Lt., 95th Foot: 2nd Lt., 95th Rifles, 6 Feb. 1811; 1st Lt., 95th Foot, 25 June 1812. Slightly wounded, 'in Action with the Enemy', 20 March 1814 (3rd Battn.) [*London Gazette*]. Half-pay, 23rd Foot, 5 Feb. 1818. Temporary pension of seventy pounds per annum, commencing 9 Jan. 1816, 'for a wound' received at New Orleans, 1815 [*1818 Pension Return*, pp. 22–3]. MGS.

RICHARDS, Loftus, Lt., 71st Foot: Lt., 71st Foot, 21 April 1808. Severely wounded, Vittoria, 21 June 1813 (1st Battn.) [*London Gazette*]. Waterloo.

RICHARDSON, Edward, Lt., 50th Foot: Lt., 50th Foot, 5 May 1808. Severely wounded, 'at the Storm and Capture of Fort Napoleon, and the Enemy's other Works, in the Neighbourhood of Almarez', 19 May 1812 [*London Gazette*].

RICHARDSON, Henry, Ensign/Lt., 83rd Foot: *1829 Statement of Service for Retired Officers*: Aged nineteen on first appointment to the Army. Ensign, 83rd Foot, 20 March 1808; Lt., 83rd Foot, 30 March 1809; Lt., 13th Veteran Battn., 13 Jan. 1813, 'from ill health'. 'Never rec'd. Half Pay'. *Where serving when wounded*: 'Slightly Wounded at Talavera'. No pension. *Family*: Married in Dublin, 5 Feb. 1817. No children. No employment. *Where generally resident during last five years*: 'England and France, viz. Plymouth & St Servan'. [PRO: WO 25/772 f107].

RICHARDSON, John, Lt., 40th Foot: Lt., 40th Foot, 6 Sept. 1810. Severely wounded, Nivelle, 10 Nov. 1813 (1st Battn.) [*London Gazette*]. Waterloo. MGS.

+RICHARDSON, Samuel, Lt., 11th Foot: Lt., 11th Foot, 4 Jan. 1809. Killed, 'in the Operations of the Army', 31 Aug. 1813 (1st Battn.) [*London Gazette*].

+RIDEWOOD, Henry, Major, 52nd Foot; Lt. Col., 45th Foot: Major, 52nd Foot, 29 May 1806. Slightly wounded, Coa, 24 July 1810 [*London Gazette*]. Severely wounded, Vittoria, 21 June 1813 (1st Battn.) [*London Gazette*]. Died of wounds, 11 July 1813. Return dated July 1813. [PRO: WO 25/2965]. Obituary, *The Gentleman's Magazine*, Nov. 1813, p. 504 ['Lately... In Spain, in consequence of wounds received at the battle of Vittoria, Lieut.-col. Reldwood [sic], 45th reg.']. *Moorsom*, p. 85 [commanding three companies of the 52nd at Vimiero, 21 Aug. 1808: 'These companies succeeded perfectly in covering the retreat of the skirmishers, but suffered a greater loss than any other part of the battalion.'], p. 429 ['... was born in the 52nd, and was a Lieutenant in the regiment in 1794. Was distinguished at Vimiero; commanded the 2nd battalion at Sabugal. Saw much service with the 52nd, and was promoted to the command of the 45th Regiment, and mortally wounded at Vittoria.']. *Surtees*, p. 207 [Vittoria: 'The 45th we found posted behind a thin thorn hedge, with its commanding-officer poor Colonel Ridewood, whom I had known before, lying on its right, gasping in the agonies of death. A great many men of this regiment had fallen here.'].

+RIDGE, Henry, Major, 5th Foot: Major, 5th Foot, 25 March 1808. Mentioned in Wellington's Ciudad Rodrigo dispatch of 20 Jan. 1812

[Commanding a column under Picton at the storming of Ciudad Rodrigo: 'Major Ridge, of the 2d battalion of the 5th Regiment, having escaladed the fausse braye wall, stormed the principal breach in the body of the place... I beg particularly to draw your attention to ... Major Ridge, of the 2d battalion 5th foot'] [*London Gazette*]. Killed, storming of Badajoz, 6 April 1812 (2nd Battn.) [*London Gazette*]. Mentioned in Wellington's Badajoz dispatch, 7 April 1812 ['Lieutenant-General Picton has reported to me particularly the conduct of ... Lieutenant-Colonel Ridge of the 5th, who was unfortunately killed in the assault of the castle'] [*London Gazette*]. *Bell*, p. 25 [Storming of Badajoz: 'The brave Colonel Ridge, with a voice like thunder, called to his men to follow, raised a ladder to the wall a little further off, and met but little opposition until he got in. Another ladder was raised, and our men went pouring in, took the enemy in the flanks, and delivered a volley which very much astonished and staggered them. Here another fight commenced, and here poor Ridge fell – no man died a more glorious death in battle, although multitudes of brave men fell who deserved great military glory.'].

+**RIDGE, Thomas, Lt., Royal York Rangers; Capt., 18th Portuguese Line:** Lt., Royal York Rangers, 21 July 1808. Severely wounded, the Nive, 13 Dec. 1813, while serving as Capt., 18th Portuguese Line [*London Gazette*]. In Portuguese Service Nov. 1813 to 1814. *Challis, Portuguese Army*, p. 59 ['Died of Wounds – '14.'].

RIDGEWAY, John Allen, 2nd Lt./1st Lt., 95th Foot: *1829 Statement of Service*: Born in Pembroke, 30 Jan. 1793. Aged sixteen on first appointment to the Army. 2nd Lt., 95th Foot, 25 Jan. 1810; 1st Lt., 95th Foot, 9 May 1812; Capt., Rifle

Brigade, 24 Dec. 1829. Note added: 'H.P. 19 July 1831.' *Battles, sieges and campaigns*: 'Joined the Army under the Duke of Wellington in Spain July 1812 before the Battle of Salamanca and served in that Campaign. At the Battle of Vittoria 1813. At the Battle of Waterloo 1815. As Lieutenant.' *Distinguished conduct*: 'At the Bridge of Vera over the Bidasoa in the Pyrenees on the 31st August and morning of 1st Septr. 1813 where Two Companies of 2nd Bn. 95th Regiment nobly defended their Post against powerful attacks of the Enemy by day & night and slew numbers of them, when my Captain was killed and the Enemy had retired, I marched them to the Camp & met with the approbation of my Superiors.' *Wounds received in action*: 'Musket Shot in the right shoulder 7th October 1813 Taking of Vera heights in the Pyrenees. One year's Pay. Musket Shot left hand lost the fore finger at Waterloo 18th June 1815. Year's Pay, No Pension.' *Titles, honorary distinctions and medals*: 'Waterloo Medal.' *Service abroad*: 'May 1812 to Augt. 1814, Peninsula. March 1815 to Decr. 1815, South France and Flanders & France.' *Family*: Married Isabella Davis, 20 April 1818, St Paul's Church, Dublin. They had three children by 1830. [PRO: WO 25/804-f352]. Severely wounded, Crossing the Bidassoa, 7/9 Oct. 1813 (2nd Battn.) [*London Gazette*]. Waterloo. MGS. Died, 11 June 1856.

+**RIDOUT, George, Lt., 43rd Foot:** Lt., 43rd Foot, 2 July 1806. Severely wounded, storming of Badajoz, 6 April 1812 ('Rideout') (1st Battn.) [*London Gazette*]. Slightly wounded, Salamanca, 22 July 1812 [*London Gazette*]. Severely wounded, 'leg amputated', during operations, 15–19 Nov. 1812 ('Rideout') [*London Gazette*]. Died of wounds, 23 Nov. 1812. Return dated 25 Nov. 1812. [PRO: WO 25/2965]. *Bruce*, p. 122 [Letter of William Napier to his wife, dated Caridad Convent, Ciudad Rodrigo, 20 Nov. 1812: 'We had on the 17th marched some hours through woods when we found the French cavalry had cut us off from the other divisions, taking baggage, sick, and Sir Edward Paget. We were attacked, formed squares, and then found that their infantry were upon us; retreated... We were afterwards cannonaded severely and lost an officer wounded and some men; Rideout had his leg off.'], p. 123 [Napier to his wife, Gallegos, 1 Dec. 1812: 'Poor Rideout, who was so badly wounded, is dead. He bore the amputation with the most admirable serenity and fortitude, and two days after died of a gangrene in the *well* foot from cold. We regret him much; he was so inoffensive, so hardy, and so willing to do everybody service, that if he did not make very attached particular friends he certainly left no enemies of any kind. It was astonishing how the recollection of his unoffending manners seized upon everybody during his funeral, and people who seldom thought of him before actually wept then. I always liked him much, poor fellow!'].

RIEFKUGEL, Bernhard, Lt./Adjutant, 2nd Light Battn. K.G.L.: Lt., 2nd Light Battn. K.G.L., 18 Nov. 1811. Adjutant, 2nd Light Battn. K.G.L., 18 Nov. 1811. Slightly wounded, Nivelle, 10 Nov. 1813 ('Adjutant Bernhard Rief Kugel') [*London Gazette*]. Served in Peninsula 1808–14. Waterloo. *Beamish*, vol. II, p. 568 ['slightly wounded, 10th November 1813, at Uragne; severely wounded, 18th June 1815, at Waterloo.'].

RITTER, Lewis, Lt., 60th Foot: Lt., Army, 17 March 1804; Lt., 60th Foot, 24 March 1804. Perhaps wounded, Vimeiro, 21 Aug. 1808 ('Lewis Reith') [*London Gazette*]. Severely wounded, Talavera, 28 July 1809 [*London Gazette*].

ROBE, William, Lt. Col., Royal Artillery: Lt. Col., Royal Artillery, 13 Jan. 1807. Mentioned in Wellington's Badajoz dispatch, 7 April 1812 ['I cannot sufficiently applaud the officers and soldiers of the British and Portuguese artillery during this siege, particularly Lieutenant-Colonel Robe, who opened the breaching batteries'] [*London Gazette*]. Severely wounded, 'not dangerously', during 'movements of the Army' [Retreat from Burgos], 27 Oct. 1812 [*London Gazette*]. Gold Medal. KCB. *Webber*, p. 106 [wounded, 1 Nov. 1812: 'another skirmish took place ... in which the Artillery were engaged and a Colonel Robe received so severe a wound in his leg that he expects to lose it.' n11: 'was evacuated to England. Died of wounds at Waterloo.' This is incorrect, as it was his son, Lt. William L. Robe, who was killed. Lt. Col. Sir William Robe was not present at Waterloo.

ROBERTS, David, Capt./Major, 51st Foot: Capt., Army, 25 Sept. 1799; Capt., 51st Foot, 25 Feb. 1804. Wounded, 'in the Army lately in Spain', while serving as 'Major of Brigade' (2nd Battn.) [*March 1809 Army List*, p. 105]. Major, 51st Foot, 12 Dec. 1811; Bvt. Lt. Col., 51st Foot, 21 June 1813. Severely wounded, 'in the Operations of the Army', 31 Aug. 1813 ('Major Roberts (Lieutenant-Colonel)') [*London Gazette*]. Gold Medal. One pension of three hundred pounds per annum, commencing 25 Dec. 1811, for 'loss of an hand' at Lugo, 1809. A second pension, for two hundred pounds per annum, commencing 1 Sept. 1814, 'for wounds' in the Pyrenees, 1813 [*1818 Pension Return*, pp. 14–15]. *Porter*, p. 278 [Retreat to Corunna, 7 Jan. 1809: 'In the second encounter we took a considerable number of prisoners, and killed many of the enemy. One only of our officers was wounded, Brigade-Major Roberts, a brave veteran, whose right hand

was carried away by a shot, but not until he had gallantly buried the point which it held repeatedly in the hearts of those whose bayonets threatened him on all sides.'].
Wheeler, pp. 117–18 [March 1813: 'Colonel Mitchell has left for England on leave; we are now commanded by Major Roberts, he lost his right hand on General Moor's [sic] Retreat. I must give you an anecdote of the Major. At Lugo the regiment was engaged in a sharp skirmish with the enemy when the Major received his wound, he was retiring when one of our men observed to him "That it was Chelsea as dead as H–l." The Major wheeled round and galloped up to a French skirmisher and with his pistol shot him dead. Returning he observed to the man who had made the observation about Chelsea. "And that H–l as dead as Chelsea." He is reported to be a lion in the field. This is the first time I ever saw him, he having been employed on the staff at Bristol. I do not know what to make of him. He seems to be very fond of using the cats, and if he continues as he has begun it will not be long before evry one will get a taste.'], pp. 128–9 [June 1813: 'Major Roberts commands the regiment, and a better commander we could not have. He allows us to fill our haversacks with what we can get on the roads, often he has said to us when we have halted for a quarter of an hour's rest "Why dont you fill your haversacks." If any of the men seemed unwilling to move he would say "Be off into the field and stock yourself with field rations, you know the commessariat has none."], pp. 130–1 [June 1813: 'In the afternoon Major Roberts, as he was wont to do, came round our camp to take a peep at the camp kettles. I with some of my comrades were smoking a pipe in our tent when the Major peeped in saying very good humouredly "Well my boy have you any bread to give

away." We answered "we had no bread but if old Bob, meaning his favourite horse, wanted corn we could supply him with plenty." He smiling replied "Never mind my lads there is plenty of bread there" pointing with his stump towards Vittoria.'], pp. 134, 139 [St Steven, July 1813: 'We ascended a rocky ridge to our right. This ridge formed a natural breast work. Over this ridge, Major Roberts looked and said "There they are my lads, pepper them well." '], p. 140 ['In our front was a large field of potatoes. Several of our men, amongst whom was my comrade, was filling their haversacks. The Provost popped amongst them and seized Jack, he brought him to the quarter guard while he went in pursuit of others. In the mean time I took Jack to the rear. On passing Major Roberts's tent my comrade told him that the Provost was going to flog him for taking a few potatoes, and that he was then prisoner in the quarter guard. "Take him back" said the Major, "and when the Provost comes tell him he is in my custody and I will punish him and send the potatoes to me." Shortly after the Provost arrived and demanded his prisoner. The Serjeant followed the orders of the Major, and the Provost was obliged to go away without breeching Jack as he intended. The Major then came up and gave Jack a good lecture for being so stupid as to be caught. He ordered him to be released, saying "go to my servant and get your 'Murphys' I have only taken a few for my own dinner." '], pp. 144–5 [Near Lezaca, 31 Aug. 1813: 'He received two wounds, one in the right shoulder, the other in the stump. When he was being carried to the rear, he said "See my lads, they cannot let my stump alone. I am sorry to leave you, I hope you will stick to the rascals"; we have lost in him a good, kind, brave and generous officer.'].

493

ROBERTS, John, Lt., 71st Foot: *1829 Statement of Service for Retired Officers*: Aged 'about 21 years' on first appointment to the Army. Ensign, 71st Foot, 10 April 1808; Lt., 71st Foot, 1809 [Army List gives 12 Oct. 1809]; Capt., 71st Foot, [7 April] 1825; Half-pay, 20 June 1827. 'Not anxious for immediate employment of full pay from Family circumstances'. *Where serving when wounded*: 'Twice severely and once slightly wounded in General actions'. No pension. *Family*: Married in Cork, 1814. Three children by 1829. No employment. *Where generally resident during last five years*: 'Resident in Paris since Sept. 1827'. [PRO: WO 25/772 f247]. Recorded as 'killed', Pyrenees, 25 July 1813 (1st Battn.) [*London Gazette*]. Recorded as 'dead', *1814 Army List*. He reappears, however, in the *1815 Army List*. It seems probable, therefore, that he had been severely wounded, left for dead, and taken prisoner on 25 July 1813. Released at the war's end in 1814, he rejoined the regiment in time to participate in the Waterloo campaign, where he was again wounded. MGS. *Dalton*, pp. 179, 182 ['D. as bt.-major 16th Jan.', 1854'].

ROBERTSON, Alexander, Lt., 79th Foot: *1829 Statement of Service for Retired Officers*: Aged twenty-seven on first appointment to the Army. Ensign, '5th British Militia', Feb. 1806, 'By Grant of the Earle of Carthness'; Lt., 5th British Militia, March 1809; Ensign, 79th Foot, May 1809, 'By raising Men by Volunteering from the Militia to the 79th foot by great exertion'; Lt., 79th Foot, 4 July 1811; Half-pay, May 1816, 'from inability to perform my duty by wounds and sickness'. *Where serving when wounded*: 'Wounded five times, but, severely at Bayone in France'. No pension. *Family*: Married in 'Thurso', 29 March 1811. Six children by 1829. No employment. *Where generally*

resident during last five years*: 'At Swiney by Wick, Caithness N.B.' 'I have been in a very Bad state of health for these last three years particularly last arising principally from my Wounds. My Oldest Child Alexander has been confined to Bed for three years and two months constant and rendered a *cripple* and still confined. I have also the misfortune of my Daughter Henerette Being *Dumb* – all the above misfortunes is worthy of your Lordships consideration; and the gracious and generous assistance of His Majesty By a Grant of Pention from my Wounds or such other remuneration as His Majesty may see proper for such a Distressed famely'. [PRO: WO 25/772 f273]. Severely wounded, the Nive, 9 Dec. 1813 (1st Battn.) [*London Gazette*].

ROBERTSON, Archibald, Ensign/Lt., 94th Foot: *1829 Statement of Service*: Born in Greenock, Renfrewshire, 1 April 1787. Aged twenty-two 'on his first Entrance into the Army.' Ensign, 94th Foot, 13 April 1809, 'Without purchase, being a subaltern serving in the Renfrewshire Militia, and having volunteered with 50 men for the Line.' Lt., 94th Foot, 6 Jan. 1814, 'Without Purchase succeeded by the death of Major (Brevct Lieut. Colonel) Lloyd, near to whom Ensign Robertson stood when his brave Commanding Officer fell 10th November 1813 (at the Nivelle).' Half Pay, 25 July 1819, 'The regiment disbanded.' Lt., Ceylon Rifles, 28 Aug. 1823. Lt., 96th Foot, 29 Jan. 1824. 'In charge of the 96th Depot from 10th October 1824 to 24th June 1825 & appointed acting Paymaster to Ditto 25th June 1825.' *Battles, sieges and campaigns*: '1810 – 1. Cadiz (Fortress), defence of from 14th Feb. to 9 Sept. 2. Torres Vedras (Position), defence of from 10th Oct. 1811. 3. Redinha. 4. Cazal Nova. 5. Foz d'Arronce. 6. Sabugal. 7. Fuentes d'Onor. 8. Badajos, Siege & Blockade. 9. El

ROBINSON

Bodon. 10. Aldea de Ponte. 1812. 11. Ciudad Rodrigo, Siege & Assault. 13. Salamanca. 14. Madrid. 15. Retreat to Portugal. 1813. 16. Nivelle. [All the above as Ensign. Remainder as Lt. commanding No. 5 Company] 1814. 17. La Bastide. 18. Saureterre. 19. Orthez. 20. Vie Bigore. 21. Toulouse.' *Distinguished conduct*: 'On the evening of the 19th of January 1812, preparing to the Assault of Ciudad Rodrigo, Ensign Robertson was directed to proceed in charge of a Party of the 94th Regiment to the Ingineer Depot for Rope Ladders, Intrenching tools &c., and to receive and communicate Instructions how they were to be used in descending and clearing the Ditch. A Testimonial dated London 13th June 1825 from Major General Sir James Campbell ... certifies "that he was so selected as being an intelligent Officer – the above duty as well as all others he was employed upon, were executed by Lieut. (Ensign) Robertson to my entire satisfaction."...' *Wounds received in action*: 'Wounded on the 27th February 1814 in the left Arm, at the Battle of Orthez when Commanding a Company and received a grant of one years Pay as Captain.' *Service abroad*: '19th Jany. 1810 to 2nd June 1814, Peninsula.' *Family*: Married Dorothea Bell, 'daughter of the late George Bell Esq. of Killinure in the County of Cavan. Barrister at Law,' 2 Jan. 1818, 'Parish of Anna County Cavan, Ireland.' They had five children by 1830. [PRO: WO 25/804 f33]. Slightly wounded, Orthes, 27 Feb. 1814 [*London Gazette*]. MGS.

ROBERTSON, James, Lt., 42nd Foot: *1829 Statement of Service for Retired Officers*: Aged twenty on first appointment to the Army. Ensign, 42nd Foot, Dec. 1808; Lt., 42nd Foot, Oct 1811 [Army List gives 10 Oct.]; Adjutant, 42nd Foot, Sept. 1815; Capt., 42nd Foot, Feb. 1827; Capt., Half-pay, unattached,

'Agreeable to the General Order dated Decemr. 1826'. Served nineteen years on Full-pay. *Where serving when wounded*: 'Wounded at Toulouse, but receives no pension'. *Family*: Married in Kilkenny, 10 Jan. 1821. Three children by 1829. *Where generally resident during last five years*: 'Ayrshire, N.B.' [PRO: WO 25/772 f252]. Severely wounded, Toulouse, 10 April 1814 (1st Battn.) [*London Gazette*]. Waterloo. Died, Chatham, April 1833.

+ROBERTSON, John, Lt., 9th Foot: Lt., 9th Foot, 8 Sept. 1808. Slightly wounded, Barossa, 5 March 1811, 'Robinson' (1st Battn.) [*London Gazette*]. Severely wounded, 'since dead', 'at the Siege of St Sebastian', 7–27 July 1813, while serving as Assistant-Engineer (9th Foot) [*London Gazette*]. Died of wounds, 16 July 1813 [PRO: WO 25/2965].

ROBERTSON, John, Capt., 53rd Foot: Capt., 53rd Foot, 18 July 1805; Bvt. Lt.Col., 25 April 1808. Severely wounded, Salamanca, 22 July 1812 ('Brigadier Lieutenant-Colonel and Captain Robinson') (2nd Battn.) [*London Gazette*].

ROBERTSON, Peter, Ensign, 59th Foot: Ensign, 59th Foot, 3 Sept. 1812. Slightly wounded, storming of San Sebastian, 31 Aug. 1813 (2nd Battn.) [*London Gazette*]. Lt., 59th Foot, 11 Nov. 1813.

ROBERTSON, William Henry, Lt., 36th Foot: Lt., 36th Foot, 3 Sept. 1812. Severely wounded, Toulouse, 10 April 1814 (1st Battn.) [*London Gazette*].

ROBINSON, Andrew Delapere, Lt., 57th Foot: *1829 Statement of Service for Retired Officers*: Aged eighteen on first appointment to the Army. Ensign, 57th Foot, 18 Jan. 1810; Lt., 57th Foot, 1811; Half-pay, 25 Sept. 1816, 'from Ill Health occa-

495

sioned by a Wound, received from a Gun Shot in the Forehead'. 'That from the wound which he received, and Ill Health occasioned in consequence thereof, he is unfit for Service.' *Where serving when wounded*: 'at Pampeluna'. *Details of pension*: Seventy pounds, commencing 29 July 1814. *Family*: Married 'in the Parochial Church of Caher, in the County of Tipperary and Kingdom of Ireland', 14 Dec. 1820. No children. No employment. *Where generally resident during last five years*: 'In Caher in the County of Tipperary, Ireland'. [PRO: WO 25/772 f280]. *1818 Pension Return*, pp. 14–15.

ROBINSON, Frederick Philips, Major-General: Col., Half Pay, 91st Foot, 25 July 1810. Major-General 4 June 1813. Severely wounded, storming of San Sebastian, 31 Aug. 1813 [*London Gazette*]. Mentioned in Wellington's San Sebastian dispatch, dated Lezaca, 2 Sept. 1813 ['The loss on our side has been severe... Major-Generals Oswald and Robinson were unfortunately wounded in the breach.'] [*London Gazette*]. Mentioned in Graham's San Sebastian dispatch, dated Oyarzun, 1 Sept. 1813 ['The column of attack was formed of the second brigade of the fifth division, commanded by Major-General Robinson... Lieutenant-General Sir J. Leith expresses his great obligations to Major-Generals Hay and Robinson, (the latter was obliged to leave the field from a severe wound in the face)'. Severely wounded, the Nive, 10 Dec. 1813 [*London Gazette*]. Gold Medal. KCB. Born 1763 to a New York Loyalist family; commissioned 1777 so that at his death in 1852, as General and colonel of the 39th Foot, he was the member of the British Army with the longest service, 75 years. 'A Peninsular Brigadier: Letters of Major-General Sir F. R. Robinson, KCB, dealing with the Campaign of 1813', ed. C. T. Atkinson, *Journal of the Society for Army Historical Research*, Vol. XXXIV (1956).

ROBINSON, Henry Edward, Lt., 48th Foot: *1829 Statement of Service*: 'Born in Ireland, 3rd May 1789. Aged 17 years on his first Entrance into the Army. Ensign, 48th Foot, 28th May 1806. Lieutenant, 48th Foot, 9th Feby. 1808. Captain, 48th Foot, 26th July 1822. Major, 48th Foot, 20th Septr. 1827. Major, 30th Foot, 15th March 1831. Lieut. Colonel, 30th Foot, 1st Jany. 1834.' *Battles, sieges and campaigns*: 'Served under His Grace the Duke of Wellington, during the Peninsular War, and was present at the following Battles, Sieges &c. 1. Talavera 27th & 28th July 1809. 2. Busaco 27th Septr. 1810. 3. Torres Vedras 1810. 4. Pursuit of Massena. 5. Cuidad Rodrigo 19th Feby. 1812. 6. Badajos 6th April 1812. 7. Salamanca 22nd July 1812. Acted as Adjutant. Acted as Brigade Major from this period till after the arrival of the Army at Madrid. 8. Retreat from Madrid. 9. Vitoria 21st June 1813. 10 Pyrenees 28th July 1813.' *Wounds received in action*: 'Shot through the Left Arm at the Storming of Badajos, 6th April 1812. Severely wounded at the Battle of the Pyrenees 28th July 1813, having had Left leg severely fractured. Two years Pay. Pension of £70. Date, 28th July 1814. Permanent.' *Service Abroad*: 'March 1808 to May 1809, Gibraltar. June 1809 to Octr. 1813, Peninsula. April 1817 to Decr. 1834, New South Wales & Van Diemans Land. March 1825 to April 1829, East Indies. 20th Aug. 1834, Bermudas.' He was not married in 1830. [PRO: WO 25/794 f159]. Slightly wounded, storming of Badajoz, 6 April 1812 [*London Gazette*]. Severely wounded, Pyrenees, 28 July 1813 (1st Battn.) [*London Gazette*]. Temporary pension of seventy pounds per annum, commencing 29 July 1814, 'for wounds' received at Pampeluna, 1813 [*1818 Pension Return*, pp. 12–13]. Lt. Col., Half-pay, 10 Feb. 1843. MGS.

ROBINSON, Robert, Lt., 32nd Foot: Lt., 32nd Foot, 27 Nov. 1806. Slightly wounded, Salamanca, 22 July 1812 ('R. Robinson') (1st Battn.) [*London Gazette*].

ROBINSON, Samuel, Lt., 79th Foot: Lt., 79th Foot, 29 June 1809. Severely wounded, Fuentes de Onoro, 5 May 1811 (1st Battn.) [*London Gazette*].

RODDY, Charles, Ensign/Lt., 38th Foot: Severely wounded, storming of San Sebastian, 31 Aug. 1813 ('Ensign Roddy') (1st Battn.) [*London Gazette*]. Lt., 38th Foot, 25 Sept. 1813.

ROGERS, Adam, Lt., 87th Foot: Lt., 87th Foot, 15 March 1809. Slightly wounded, Talavera, 28 July 1809 ('Rodgers') [*London Gazette*]. MGS.

ROGERS, Henry, Capt., 6th Foot: *1829 Statement of Service*: Born 4 Dec. 1785, Woolwich. Aged sixteen on first appointment to the Army. Ensign, 85th Foot, Jan. 1800; Lt. 28 Aug. 1800; Capt., 2nd West India Regt., 12 May 1805; Capt., 4th Garrison Batt., 26 Nov. 1806; Capt., 6th Foot, 26 March 1807; Major, Army, 12 Aug. 1819; Major, 6th Foot, 20 July 1826. *Battles, sieges and campaigns*: 'Walcheren, from August to December. Vittoria, 21st June 1813. Pyrenees, 25th to 28th July. Nivelle, 10th November. Nive, 9th to 15th December. Orthes, 27th February 1814. Fort Erie in October 1814. Fort Blayer on the Garonne.' *Wounds received in action*: 'Wounded at Nivelle the 10th November 1813. Wounded at Orthes the 27th February 1814 and received 1 year's Pay as Captain.' *Service abroad*: 'November 1800 to February 1801, At Sea; February 1801 to January 1806, West Indies; January 1806 to March 1806, At Sea; 16th July 1809 to 8th August 1809, At Sea; 9th August 1809 to 9th December 1809, Walcheren; 10th December 1809 to 21 December 1809, At Sea; 12th October 1812 to 11th November 1812 1812, At Sea; 15th November 1812 to 4th May 1814, Portugal, Spain & France; 5th May 1814 to 1st July 1814, At Sea; 2nd July 1814 to 30th June 1815, Canada; 1st July 1815 to 9th August 1815, At Sea; 10th August 1815 to 30th October 1818, Holland & France; 4th July 1821 to 3rd November 1821, At Sea; 4th November 1821 to 21st March 1825, At Sea; 31st May, 1825 to 31st October 1826, Bombay; 31st December 1829 to 21st April 1830, At Sea; 22nd April 1830 to 31st December 1830, Poonah & Bombay.' Unmarried in 1830. [PRO: WO25/786 f9]. Slightly wounded, Crossing the Bidassoa, 7/9 Oct. 1813 (1st Battn.) [*London Gazette*]. Slightly wounded, Orthes, 27 Feb. 1814 (1st Battn.) [*London Gazette*]. Note: though returned as slightly wounded on 7/9 Oct. 1813, Rogers did not include this in his Statement of Service. See also his *1829 Statement of Service for Retired Officers* [PRO: WO 25/772 f217], in which he indicates that he was wounded in 'Pyrenees and Orthes'. It appears that in the former Statement he had confused the date of his first wound, believing it had occured at Nivelle (10 Nov. 1813) rather than the Crossing of the Bidassoa (7/9 Oct. 1813).

ROLSTON, Thomas, Assistant-Surgeon, 10th Foot: Assistant-Surgeon, 10th Foot, 29 Oct. 1812. Seventy pounds per annum pension, commencing 8 Aug. 1814, for 'loss of a leg' at Tarragona, 1813 [*1818 Pension Return*, pp. 6–7].

RONALD, William, Lt., 67th Foot: Lt., 67th Foot, 15 June 1809. Slightly wounded, Barossa, 5 March 1811 (2nd Battn.) [*London Gazette*].

Capt., Half-pay, 25 March 1817. MGS.

+ROOKE, John Charles, Capt. and Lt. Col., 3rd Foot Guards: Capt. and Lt. Col., 3rd Foot Guards, 26 Jan. 1809. Mentioned in Hill's Almaraz dispatch, 21 April 1812 ['I have had frequent occasions to mention to your Lordship in terms of the highest praise, the conduct of Lieutenant-Colonel Rooke, Assistant Adjutant-General. During the whole period I have had a separate command in this country, that officer has been with me, and rendered most essential service to my corps; on the present expedition he has eminently distinguished himself, and I beg leave particularly to notice his conduct.'] [*London Gazette*]. Mentioned in Wellington's Vittoria dispatch, 22 June 1813 ['Lieutenant-Colonel Rooke, of the Adjutant-General's department'] [*London Gazette*]. Severely wounded, Nivelle, 10 Oct. 1813 ('Assistant-Adjutant-General Lieutenant-Colonel C. Rooke') [*London Gazette*]. Died of wounds, 18 Dec. 1813. Return dated 25 Dec. 1813. [PRO: WO 25/2965]. Obituary, *The Gentleman's Magazine*, Feb. 1814, p. 198 ['Dec. 10. At St Jean de Luz, of wounds received on the 10th of November, Lieut.-col. Charles Rooke, captain in the 3d guards, eldest son of Lieut.-col. Rooke.'].

+ROSE, Alexander, Capt., 20th Foot: Lt., Army, 10 Feb. 1794; Lt., 20th Foot, 23 Dec. 1795; Capt. 16 June, 1800; Major, Army, 1 Jan 1812. Killed, storming of St Sebastian, 31 Aug. 1813 [*London Gazette*]. Mentioned in the *1829 Statement of Service* of Joseph Hutchison, 7th Foot: 'At the Assault of St Sebastian 31 Aug 1813 served as a Volunteer with a Detachment of the Fusiliers in the course of the Assault succeeded to the Command of the Volunteers of the Fusilier Brigade by the Death of Major Rose of the 20 Regt.' [PRO: WO 25-786 f92]

ROSS, Archibald, Capt., 91st Foot; Major/Lt. Col., 9th Portuguese Line: Capt., Army, 5 Sept. 1805; Capt., 91st Foot, 12 Sept. 1811. Slightly wounded, Salamanca, 22 July 1812, while serving as Major, 9th Portuguese Line [*London Gazette*]. Wounded, Vittoria, 21 June 1813, as Major, 9th Portuguese Line [*London Gazette*]. In Portuguese Service Feb. 1812 to Sept. 1813. Gold Medal. Pension of three hundred pounds per annum, commencing 22 June 1814, 'for a wound' received at Vittoria, while serving as Lt. Col., 9th Portuguese Line [*1818 Pension Return*, pp. 24–5]. *Challis, Portuguese Army*, p. 59.

ROSS, David, Major, 38th Foot: Capt., 38th Foot, 1 Aug. 1804; Major, Army, 1 Jan. 1805. Severely wounded, Talavera, 28 July 1809, while serving with the 1st Batt. of Detachments [*London Gazette*].

ROSS, Donald, Lt., 71st Foot: Lt., 71st Foot, 26 May 1808. Slightly wounded, 'at the Storm and Capture of Fort Napoleon, and the Enemy's other Works, in the Neighbourhood of Almaraz', 19 May 1812 [*London Gazette*].

+ROSS, George, Capt., Royal Engineers: Capt., Army, 1 March 1805; Capt., Royal Engineers, 24 June 1809. Wounded in the trenches before Badajoz, 8–15 May 1811 [*London Gazette*]. Killed, siege of Ciudad Rodrigo, 10 Jan. 1812 [*London Gazette*]. 'Killed in the trenches before Cuidad Rodrigo', 9 Jan. 1812. Return dated 25 Jan. 1812. [PRO: WO 25/2965].

ROSS, Hew Dalrymple, Capt., Royal Artillery: Capt., Royal Artillery, 24 July 1806; Lt. Col., Army, 21 June 1813. Gold Medal. Waterloo. MGS. *Dalton*, p. 220 ['Commanded the A Troop, A Brigade, R.H.A., during the Pen. War, and was dangerously wounded at the siege of Badajoz... D. lt.-gov. of Chelsea Hospital in Dec., 1868, aged 90.']. *Simmons*, pp. 58, 116, 283. *Webber*, p. 80. *Leach*, p. 131. Born 1779, died 1868; cousin of Sir James Clark Ross, the Polar explorer. Was the first artilleryman to attain the rank of field-marshal (1868).

ROSS, James, Capt., 51st Foot: Lt., 51st Foot, 21 Jan. 1804; Capt., 51st Foot, 12 Dec. 1811. Severely wounded 'in the Operations of the Army', 31 Aug. 1813 [*London Gazette*]. Waterloo. Retired in 1824. *Wheeler*, p. 144 [Wounded, 'slightly', near Lezaca, 31 Aug. 1813].

ROSS, James Kerr, Lt., 92nd Foot: Lt., 92nd Foot, 4 May 1808. Slightly wounded, Pyrenees, 25 July 1813 (1st Battn.) [*London Gazette*]. Wounded at Waterloo. MGS. *Dalton*, pp. 193, 195 ['Afterwards Maj.-Gen. J. Kerr Ross, K.H. Served through the Par. War ... where he was A.D.C. to Gen. Sir John Buchan. D. at Edinburgh, 26th April, 1872.'].

+ROSS, John, Lt. Col., Coldstream Guards: Capt. and Lt. Col., Coldstream Guards, 25 Dec. 1802. Killed, Talavera, 27 July 1809 [*London Gazette*]. Obituary, *The Gentleman's Magazine*, Aug. 1809, p. 780 ['Lieut.-colonel John Ross, who gloriously fell at the head of the Grenadier Company of the 2d (or Coldstream) Regiment of Guards in the memorable battle of Talavera in Spain, was an officer of the most promising talents, and excellent character. His death is universally lamented by all his brother officers, and by numerous friends. He was fourth son of the late Vice-admiral Sir John Lockhart-Ross, of Balnagown, bart. famed for his exploits while Captain of the Tartar frigate.'].

ROSS, John, Lt./Capt., 51st Foot: *1829 Statement of Service*: 'Born in

Cork, 30th Nov. 1788. Aged sixteen on his first Entrance into the Army. Ensign, 51st Regt., 26 March 1804. Lieutenant, 51st, 1 Novr. 1805. Captain, 51st, 15 April 1813. Major, 51st, 5 Nov. 1825.' Note added: 'Lt Col, Half Pay, unattd., 9 Decr. 1836.' *Battles, sieges and campaigns*: 'As Lieutenant: Retreat to Corunna 1808. Affair at Lugo. Battle of Corunna 1809... Siege of Flushing 1809 ... in the Peninsula, France and Belgium in 5 Campaigns in 1811, 1812, 1813, 1814 and 1815. Fuentes d'Onor 5 May 1811. Storming and Siege of Fort St Christoval June 1811. As Aide de Camp: Covering Sieges of Badajos and Ciudad Rodrigo 1812. Affair at Moresco 22 June 1812. Battle of Salamanca 22 July 1812. Capture of Reliero, Madrid 1812. Covering Siege of Burgos 1812. Retreat from Burgos 1812. Affair at San Munos 17th November 1812. As Captain: Wounded 31 August 1813 repulsing the Enemy on the Biddasoa. Battle of Nivelle and carrying the heights of Saint Pe 10th November 1813. Battle of Orthes 1814. Battle of Waterloo 1815. Capture of Cambray with other small Affairs and Skirmishes during Eight Campaigns – 8. At Bordeaux appointed by Lord Dalhousie to serve as Brigade Major.' *Wounds received in action*: 'Wounded in repulsing an attack of the Enemy when forcing the Biddasoa on the 31st August 1813. Received One Years Pay as Captain.' *Titles, honorary distinctions and medals*: 'Waterloo Medal.' *Service abroad*: '26 Mar 1804 to 24 Sept. 1807, India. July 1808 to Jany 1809, Spain. 27 June 1809 to Jany. 1810, Walcheren. 23 Jany 1811 to 27 June 1814, Peninsula, France. 23 March 1815 to 2 Jany 1816, Netherlands and France. 6 July 1819 to 15 April 1820, Heligoland. May 1821 to 7 June 1829, Ionian Islands.' [PRO: WO 25/795 f5]. Slightly wounded, 'in the Operations of the Army', 31 Aug. 1813 [*London Gazette*]. This was in the action at Salain (Heights of Lezaca) on 31 Aug., fought by the 7th Division. Severely wounded at Waterloo, and is said 'to have lost five brothers in this battle.' Later Lt. Col., St Helena Regt. Waterloo. MGS. Died at Hardway, Herts., 16 Sept. 1851. *Dalton*, pp. 164, 166. *Wheeler*, p. 144 [Wounded, 'slightly', near Lezaca, 31 Aug. 1813], pp. 202–3 [Waterloo: 'Captain John Ross' company had a very narrow escape of being made prisoners at the commencement.']. Probably this was the Capt. 'McRoss' referred to by *Wheeler*, p. 200 [Waterloo: 'Capt. McRoss' [sic] company was ordered down to reinforce the advance, who were warmly engaged... Our advance was nearly surrounded by a large body of the enemy's Lancers. Fortunately the 15th. Hussars was at hand and rendered assistance.'].

+ROSS, John, Lt., 92nd Foot; Capt., 19th Portuguese Line: Lt., 92nd Foot, 9 May 1805. Killed, Pyrenees, 31 Aug. 1813, while serving as Capt., 19th Portuguese Line ('Jaoa Ross') [*London Gazette. The Gentleman's Magazine*, Nov. 1813, p. 499 'Aug. 31... Fell at Mayo, at the head of his company, Captain John Ross, of the 19th Portuguese, and Lieutenant in the 92nd British line. He was son of the Rev. John Ross, Minister of Loggie-Eastre, co. Ross. The letter, from a brother officer of the 92d Regiment, in which he intimates this melancholy event to his Father, shews him to have been an officer of distinguished zeal, intrepidity, and experience in the service. It details, "that he very frequently distinguished himself by his gallantry in this division, so as to be thanked for it in general orders; and that he fell, after having expended the last round of ammunition, in retiring with his men for a new supply, deeply regretted by all who knew him, and more particularly by his brother officers of the 92d regiment, who all had the greatest regard for him." Thus, after ten years service,

fell, in the prime of life, an amiable youth, when rising to distinction. He had been very successful in recruiting for his regiment, afterwards saw much service, and had been promoted to a Company previous to his death being known in this Country.']. In Portuguese Service Jan. 1812 to Aug. 1813. *Challis, Portuguese Army*, p. 59.

ROSS, Robert, Major-General: Lt. Col., 20th Foot, 21 Jan. 1808; Col., Army, 25 July 1810; Major-General, 4 June 1813. Severely wounded, Orthes, 27 Feb. 1814, while serving in the General Staff [*London Gazette*]. Gold Medal. *Blakeney*, p. 51 [Retreat to Corunna: 'The foe, rendered presumptious by their easy victory gained over the defenceless stragglers, rode so close to our columns that that distinguished officer, Colonel Ross with his gallant 20th Regiment was halted and placed in an ambush, formed by the winding of the road round the slope of a hill which concealed them until nearly approached. The remainder of the reserve marched on and halted at a considerable distance. But the French were over cautious, and after a lapse of more than an hour, during which time many wounded stragglers joined the main body of the division, Colonel Ross was recalled, much disappointed by the enemy's declining to advance.'] Born 1766; on being wounded at Orthes his wife rode five days through appalling weather to be at his side to nurse him. Best known for his death, commanding the force sent to attack Baltimore in 1814; thus deprived of the honours which he would have received, the Prince Regent accorded his family the unique distinction of bearing the name 'Ross of Bladensburg', after his victory earlier in the campaign. As stated in parliament, 'his goodness of heart, coupled with a peculiar kindness and urbanity of manner, secured the regard and esteem of all who knew him. Never was an officer so universally and sincerely lamented by those under his command' [*Smythe*, p. 349]. A memoir appears in Smythe, B., *History of the XX Regiment 1688-1888* (London, 1889), pp. 340-50.

ROSS, Robert, Lt., 57th Foot: Lt., 57th Foot, 27 Dec. 1805. Severely wounded, Nivelle, 10 Nov. 1813 (1st Battn.) [*London Gazette*].

RÖSSING, Ferdinand Christian von, Lt., 1st Line Battn. K.G.L.: Lt., 1st Line Battn. K.G.L., 29 May 1809. Severely wounded, siege of Burgos, 20-26 Sept. 1812 [*London Gazette*]. Severely wounded, storming of San Sebastian, 31 Aug. 1813 ('Rossin') [*London Gazette*]. Served in Peninsula 1808-14. Waterloo. *Beamish*, vol. II, p. 572 ['severely wounded, 22d Sept. 1812, before Burgos'].

+ROSS-LEWIN, Edward, Lt., 9th Foot: Lt., 9th Foot, 3 Oct. 1811. Slightly wounded, during 'movements of the Army' [Retreat from Burgos], 25 Oct. 1812 ('Ross Lewin') [*London Gazette*]. Killed, storming of San Sebastian, 31 Aug. 1813 ('R. Lewyn') (1st Battn.) [*London Gazette*].

ROSS-LEWIN, Henry, Capt., 32nd Foot: Author of *With the 32nd in the Peninsula*. Elder brother of Thomas Ross-Lewin. Capt., 32nd Foot, 7 Sept., 1804. Slightly wounded, Salamanca, 22 July 1812 ('Captain Roslewen') (1st Battn.) [*London Gazette*]. Bvt. Major, 4 June 1814. Waterloo. *Dalton*, pp. 145, 146 ['Of Ross Hill, Kildysart, co. Clare. Son of George Ross-Lewin, of Ross Hill... Bn. 1778. Served in the Pa., and was wounded in the last charge at Salamanca. M. Anne, dau. of Wm. Burnett, of Eyrescourt, and had issue. Quitted the service before 1824. D. 27th April, 1843. Wrote his autobiography, which gives a good account of Waterloo.'].

ROSS-LEWIN, Thomas, Lt., 32nd Foot: Lt., 32nd Foot, 15 Dec. 1808. Slightly wounded, Pyrenees, 30 July 1813 ('Ross Lewyn') (1st Battn.) [*London Gazette*]. Wounded, Waterloo. MGS. Died, 1857.

ROTHARD, Adolphus John Lorenz, Lt., 5th Line Battn. K.G.L.: *1829 Statement of Service for Retired Officers*: Aged twenty three years six months on first appointment to the Army. Serjeant, 6 Oct. 1803, 2nd Light Battn. K.G.L.; 'as Sergeant Major in the 7th Line Battn. 1 year and 8 month'; Ensign, 5th Line Battn. K.G.L., 9 Sept. 1809; Lt., 5th Line Battn. K.G.L., 20 March 1812; Half-pay, 25 July 1815, 'on account of a severe wound received on the 27th February 1814 in action with the Enemy near Bajonne in France'. 'Severely wounded on the 27th February 1814 when driving in the Outposts of Bajonne in France'. *Where serving when wounded*: 'I received a years full pay as a Lieutenant as a Bounty for the Severe Wounds received on 27th February 1814 near Bajonne in France'. *Family*: Married in Luneburg, 4 Sept. 1815. Four children by 1829. *Where generally resident during last five years*: 'Luneburg'. [PRO: WO 25/772 f80]. Served in Peninsula 1808-14. *Beamish*, vol. II, p. 657.

+ROTHWELL, Thomas, Ensign, 48th Foot: Ensign, 48th Foot, 1 Feb. 1810. Killed, Albuera, 16 May 1811 (2nd Battn.) [*London Gazette*].

ROTTON, Guy, Lt., 20th Foot: Lt., 20th Foot, 30 March 1809. Severely wounded, Pyrenees, 2 Aug. 1813 [*London Gazette*].

ROUS, Thomas Bates, Ensign, 1st Foot Guards: Ensign, 1st Foot Guards, 13 Nov. 1804. Wounded, 'in the Army lately in Spain' (3rd

Battn.) [*March 1809 Army List*, p. 105]. MGS.

+ROVEREA, Alexandre de, Capt., Sicilian Regiment: Capt., Army, 3 Sept. 1806; Capt., Sicilian Regt., 11 June 1807. Severely wounded, Albuera, 16 May 1811, while serving as ADC to Major-General Cole ('Rouveria') [*London Gazette*]. At Albuera he was hit on the head by a piece of shell, and was evidently concussed as after he came round he rode about wildly until a friend took him to receive medical attention. He was killed at Sorauren, 28 July 1813. 'A Swiss Officer in Wellington's Army', G. T. Atkinson, in *Journal of the Society for Army Historical Research*, Vol. XXXV (1957).

ROYAL, John, Lt., 61st Foot: Lt., 61st Foot, 3 Oct. 1811. Two pensions, each for one hundred pounds per annum, commencing 23 July 1813, for 'loss of a leg' and 'loss of the use of an arm' at Salamanca, 1812 [*1818 Pension Return*, pp. 16–17].

ROYDS, William, Lt., 52nd Foot: Lt., 52nd Foot, 15 Feb. 1809. Slightly wounded, storming of Badajoz, 6 April 1812 [*London Gazette*]. Capt., 52nd Foot, 9 June 1814. Half-pay, 25 Feb. 1817. MGS.

+ROYLE, Job Watson, Lt., 52nd Foot: Ensign, 52nd Foot, 2 May 1810. Killed, storming of Badajoz, 6 April 1812 ('Lieut. Royal') [*London Gazette*].

ROYSE, Abraham F., Ensign, 87th Foot: Ensign, 87th Foot, 20 May 1813. Slightly wounded, Toulouse, 10 April 1814 (2nd Battn.) [*London Gazette*]. MGS.

RUDD, John, Major, 77th Foot: Capt., 77th Foot, 25 June 1803; Major, 77th Foot, 25 Jan. 1810. Severely wounded, siege of Badajoz, 26 March 1812 [*London Gazette*]. Mentioned in Wellington's dispatch, 27 March 1812 [Storming of Fort Picurina, Badajoz, 26 March 1812: 'The attack was made by five hundred men of the 3rd division, formed into three detachments ... the left under Major Rudd, of the 77th Regiment ... consisting of two hundred men... Major-General Kempt mentions in high terms in his report the cool and persevering gallantry of the officers and troops; of which indeed the strength of the work, which they carried, affords the best proof. He particularly mentions ... Majors Shaw and Rudd, and the Honourable Captain Powys, who commanded the several detachments. These three officers were wounded'] [*London Gazette*]. *Royal Military Calendar*, vol. IV, pp. 413–14 ['He was severely wounded when ascending the works, in command of the left division of the detachment, which stormed and carried La Picurina fort ... on the night of the 25th... On this occasion he obtained the brevet of L. Col.'].

RUDKIN, Mark, Lt./Capt., 50th Foot: Lt., 50th Foot, 29 Jan. 1807. Slightly wounded, Fuentes de Onoro, evening 3 May 1811 [*London Gazette*]. Recorded as 'Killed', Pyrenees, 25 July 1813 (1st Battn.) [*London Gazette*]. In fact he had been taken prisoner. Capt., half pay, 47th Foot, 5 May 1828. MGS. *Mullen*, p. 347 ['Taken prisoner, Pyrenees'].

RUDORFF, George Lewis, Capt., 1st Light Battn. K.G.L.: Capt., 1st Light Battn. K.G.L., 22 Feb. 1810. Slightly wounded, Albuera, 16 May 1811 ('Rudorf') [*London Gazette*]. Served in Peninsula 1808–14. Waterloo. *Beamish*, vol. II, p. 561 [Died '25th Dec. 1836 at Eimbeck, in Han.'].

RUMLEY, John, Lt., 30th Foot: Ensign, 30th Foot, 7 June 1809; Lt.,

30th Foot, 25 June 1811. Severely wounded, during 'movement of the Army' [Retreat from Burgos: Villa Muriel], 25 Oct. 1812 ('Lumley') [*London Gazette*]. His brother, George, also serving with the 30th Foot [Lt., 30th Foot, 6 June 1809], died in Portugal, 23 April 1811, leaving his personal effects to John. [*Register of officers' effects*: PRO: WO 25/2963]. Wounded, Waterloo. Died, 1819.

RUSE, Richard, Lt., 9th Foot: Lt., 9th Foot, 29 June 1809. Severely wounded, 'at the Siege of St Sebastian', 7–27 July 1813 (1st Battn.) [*London Gazette*]. Seventy pounds per annum pension, commencing 18 July 1814, for 'loss of an eye' at St Sebastian [*1818 Pension Return*, pp. 6–7].

RUSSELL, Hon. Francis, Lt., 7th Foot: Lt., Army, 27 June 1811; Lt., 7th Foot, 18 July 1811. Severely wounded, storming of Badajoz, 6 April 1812 [*London Gazette*]. Half-pay, 28 April 1814. ADC to the Prince of Orange at Waterloo.

RUSSELL, George William, Lord, Capt., 23rd Light Dragoons; Major, 102nd Foot: Lt., 1st Dragoons, 11 Sept. 1806; Capt., Army, 25 March 1808; Capt., 23rd Light Dragoons, 18 May 1808. Slightly wounded, Talavera, 28 July 1809 ('Lord William Russell') [*London Gazette*]. Major, 102nd Foot, 4 Feb. 1813. Lt. Col., Army, 12 April 1814. *Royal Military Calendar*, vol. V, p. 24 ['his reg. being nearly destroyed and himself wounded at the battle of Talavera... A.-d.-C. to the Duke of Wellington ... was appointed L.-Col ... on bringing home the despatches after the battle of Toulouse.']. Second son of John, 6th Duke of Bedford; born 1790; became major-general; died 1846. MGS.

RUSSELL, William, Capt., 20th Foot: *1829 Statement of Service for Retired Officers*: Aged twenty-one on first appointment to the Army. 'Ensign and Lieutenant Derby Militia in 1798 & 1799'; Ensign, 20th Foot, 10 Aug. 1799; Lt., 20th Foot, 'about the 5 October 1799'; Capt., 20th Foot, 21 Jan. 1808; Bvt. Major, 20th Foot, 3 March 1814, 'for commanding 20th Regiment at the Battle of Orthes'; Half-pay, 31st Foot, 11 Dec. 1817, 'ill health'. 'Not desirous of Service being oblidged to Retire in consequence of ill health'. *Where serving when wounded*: 'Orthes in Spain, Commanding the 20th Regiment'. No pension. *Family*: Married in Mallow, Ireland, 28 Nov. 1811. Eleven children by 1829. No employment. *Where generally resident during last five years*: 'Mallow, Ireland'. [PRO: WO 25/722 f319]. MGS.

+RUTLEDGE, William, Ensign, 60th Foot: Ensign, 60th Foot, 1 Aug. 1813. Severely wounded, the Nive, 13 Dec. 1813 (5th Battn.) [*London Gazette*]. Died of wounds, 22 Dec. 1813. Return dated 25 Dec. 1813. [PRO: WO 25/2965].

RYAN, Thomas, Lt., 50th Foot: *1829 Statement of Service*: 'Born in Ireland, 26th August 1790. Aged Fifteen on his first Entrance into the Army. Ensign, late 104th, 10th Oct. 1805. Lieutenant, 50th Reg., 28th April 1808. Captain, 50th Reg., 30 Sept. 1819. Major, 50th Reg. 13 Aug. 1830.' *Battles, sieges and campaigns*: 'Accompanied the Expedition to Walcheren in 1809... Fuentes d'Onor on the 5th May 1811.' *Distinguished conduct*: 'The Duke of Yorks satisfaction and approval of conduct at Fuentes d'Onor by his letter to the Comg. officer dated Horse Guards 3rd October 1814.' *Wounds received in action*: 'Received a severe Sabre wound in the head and several others, in action at Fuentes d'Onor 5th May 1811. Received One Years Pay as Lieutenant for wounds recd. 5th May 1811.' *Service abroad*:

'1806 to 1809, North America. 1810 to 1810, Walcheren. 1811 to 1814, Portugal, Spain, and a Prisoner in Verdun, France. 1819 to 1820, Jamaica. 1824 to 1827, Jamaica.' [PRO: WO 25/794 f340]. Reported as 'missing', Fuentes de Onoro, 5 May 1811 (1st Battn.) [*London Gazette*].

RYLANCE, Thomas, Lt., 43rd Foot: Lt., 43rd Foot, 10 Dec. 1805. Severely wounded during 'several affairs with the French Army', 18 March–7 April 1811 (1st Battn.) [*London Gazette*]. Capt., 43rd Foot, 14 May 1812.

+RYND, Goodlatt, Lt., 11th Foot: Lt., Army, 1 Nov. 1805; Lt., 11th Foot, 6 March 1806. Severely wounded, Salamanca, 22 July 1812 [*London Gazette*]. Died of wounds, 16 Aug. 1812. Return dated 25 Aug. 1812. [PRO: WO 25/2965].

+RYPKE, Augustus, Lt., 2nd Line Battn. K.G.L.: Lt., 2nd Line Battn. K.G.L., 18 Nov. 1807. Severely wounded, Salamanca, 22 July 1812 ('Repke') [*London Gazette*]. Served in Peninsula 1808–12. *Beamish*, vol. II, p. 639 [Died '30th July 1812, of the wounds he received in the battle of Salamanca, 22d of July 1812.'].

S

SACH, George, Lt., 48th Foot: Lt., 48th Foot, 31 May 1809. Reported as 'Missing', Albuera, 16 May 1811 (2nd Battn.) [*London Gazette*]. Same rank in 1814 A/L.

SAFFE, Augustus von, Lt., 1st Line Battn. K.G.L: Lt., 1st Line Battn. K.G.L., 19 Aug. 1805. Slightly wounded, Talavera, 28 July 1809 [*London Gazette*]. Served in Peninsula 1808–11. Waterloo. *Beamish*, vol. II, p. 633 ['killed in the battle of Waterloo, 18th June 1815.'].

+SAFFE, William von, Capt., 1st Line Battn. K.G.L: Capt., 1st Line Battn. K.G.L., 25 March 1807. Slightly wounded, Talavera, 28 July 1809 [*London Gazette*]. Killed, siege of Burgos, 5–10 Oct. 1812 [*London Gazette*]. Served in Peninsula 1808–12. *Beamish*, vol. II, pp. 105–6 [8 Oct. 1812: 'At two o'clock on the morning of the 8th, the garrison made another sortie with four hundred men, which, aided by darkness, and a heavy fall of rain, overthrew the advanced covering parties... The loss of the legion was considerable: – Captain von Saffe, of the first line battalion was killed'], p. 632 ['killed, 8th Oct. 1812, in the siege of the castle of Burgos.'].

+ST CLAIR, John, Lt., 5th Foot: Lt., 5th Foot, 7 July 1808. Severely wounded during 'several affairs with the French Army', 18 March–7 April 1811 (2nd Battn.) [*London Gazette*]. Died of wounds, 13 April 1811. Return dated 25 April 1811. [PRO: WO 25/2965].

ST COLOMBO, Pietro, Lt., Chasseurs Britanniques: Lt., Chasseurs Britanniques, 8 Aug. 1811. Slightly wounded, Pyrenees, 30 July 1813 ('St Columba') [*London Gazette*].

ST GEORGE, Stepney, Lt., 66th Foot: *1829 Statement of Service for Retired Officers*: Aged fourteen on first appointment to the Army. Ensign, 35th Foot, 1806; Lt., 66th Foot, Aug. 1807 [Army List gives 6 Aug.]; Half-pay, Sept. 1815, 'in consequence of ill health from wounds received in the Peninsula'; Lt., 71st Foot, March 1824; Capt., Half-pay, unattached, June 1825; Capt., 52nd Foot, Aug. 1825; Half-pay, May 1826, 'in consequence of *urgent* private affairs'. *Where serving when wounded*: 'Peninsula'. *Where generally resident during last five years*: 'Co. Galway, Ireland'. [PRO: WO 25/775 f81]. Severely wounded, 'in Action with the Enemy', 15 Feb. 1814 ('Stepney Saint George') (2nd Battn.) [*London Gazette*].

+SAINT-POL, Paul, Lt./Capt., 7th Foot: Lt., 7th Foot, 8 May 1806 (St Paul). Severely wounded, storming of Badajoz, 6 April 1812 ('St Pol') [*London Gazette*]. Obituary, *The Gentleman's Magazine*, June 1812, p. 595 'April 23... At Badajoz, after 17 days of acute suffering, from the wounds received at the head of the Royal Fusileer light company, at the storming of that fortress, in his 20th year, Capt. Paul St Pol.']. *Haythornthwaite, Die Hard*, p. 182 [Badajoz: 'Among those who fell was Captain Paul Saint-Pol of the 7th Fuzileers, "a very fine young man", who died after the amputation of a leg; he was the son of Louis Philippe, Duke of Orleans, to whom he bore a striking resemblance.']. *Table-Talk*, p. 56.

+SALISBURY, James, Lt., 62nd Foot; Capt., 21st Portuguese Line: Lt., 62nd Foot, 25 April 1806. Obituary, *The Gentleman's Magazine*, Oct. 1810, p. 398 ['Sept. 27... In the action, this day, on the Sierra de

Busaco, in Portugal, aged 23, Capt. James Salisbury, whose enterprising spirit obtained him a company in the 21st Portuguese regiment. He was the youngest son of the late Mr. S. of Hinton.']. In Portuguese Service April 1810 to Sept. 1810. *Challis, Portuguese Army*, p. 59 ['Capt. 21 Line... K/A Busaco 27 Sept. '10'].

SALVIN, Jeffery, Lt., 4th Foot: Lt., 4th Foot, 5 Feb. 1805. Slightly wounded, storming of Badajoz, 6 April 1812 [*London Gazette*]. Severely wounded, Nivelle, 10 Nov. 1813 (1st Battn.) [*London Gazette*].

+SANDERS, Henry, Ensign, 88th Foot: Severely wounded, Vittoria, 21 June 1813 (1st Battn.) [*London Gazette*]. Died of wounds, 22 June 1813. Return dated 25 June 1813. [PRO: WO 25/2965].

SANDILANDS, Patrick, Ensign/Lt. and Capt., Coldstream Guards: Ensign, Coldstream Guards, 2 May 1805. Severely wounded, 'but not dangerously', Talavera, 28 July 1809 [*London Gazette*]. Lt. and Capt., Coldstream Guards, 19 July 1810.

SANDWITH, Frederick Brown, Lt., 38th Foot: *1829 Statement of Service for Retired Officers*: Aged nineteen on first appointment to the Army. Ensign, South Mayo Militia, 21 Feb. 1801; Lt., South Mayo Militia, 1 June 1801; Ensign, 38th Foot, 8 Oct. 1806, 'Volunteer'd from the Irish Militia'; Lt., 38th Foot, 29 Aug. 1807; Capt., 31 March 1814; Half-pay, 1814, by reduction. *Where serving when wounded*: 'In Spain at St Sebastian'. *Details of pension*: 'As Lieut. on the 1st Sept. 1814 £70. Pension augmented on the 18th of June 1815 (as Capt.) to £100'. *Family*: Married in the town of Wexford, 20 Jan. 1820. Four children by 1829. No employment. *Where generally resident during last five years*: 'In the vicinity of Wexford'. [PRO: WO 25/773 f52].

Severely wounded, 'arm amputated', storming of San Sebastian, 31 Aug. 1813 (1st Battn.) [*London Gazette*]. MGS. 'Soundwith' in Army List. One hundred pounds per annum pension, commencing 1 Sept. 1814, for 'loss of an arm' at San Sebastian ('Sandwich, Frederick Browne') [*1818 Pension Return*, pp. 10–11].

SANDYS, Edwin, Lt., 6th Foot: Lt., 6th Foot, 18 May 1809. Slightly wounded, Pyrenees, 30 July 1813 (1st Battn.) [*London Gazette*].

SANDYS, Myles, Lt., 29th Foot: *1829 Statement of Service for Retired Officers*: Aged seventeen on first appointment to the Army. 'Date of 1st appointment I believe about Novr. or Decr. 1808 as Ensign in 29th Regt. foot'; Lt., 29th Foot, May 1810 [Army List gives 5 April 1810]; Lt., 11th Light Dragoons, 'July or Augst. 1815'; Half-pay, 'in the beginning of 1817', by reduction; Lt., Full-pay, 11th Light Dragoons, 'June or July in 1817'; Half-pay, 1818, 'my health not allowing my going to India with the 11th light dragoons'. *Where serving when wounded*: 'at the Battle of Albueira', no pension. *Family*: Married in Everton Church, Liverpool, 24 July 1820. No children. No employment. *Where generally resident during last five years*: 'at Ulverstone and at Sytup Hall near Ulverstone'. [PRO: WO 25/773 f44]. 'Miles Sandys' in Army List. MGS.

+SANDYS, Robert Fitzgerald, Lt./Capt., 50th Foot: Lt., 50th Foot, 12 Sept. 1805. Severely wounded, 'at the Storm and Capture of Fort Napoleon, and the Enemy's other Works, in the Neighbourhood of Almarez', 19 May 1812 [*London Gazette*]. Died 'of wounds', 18 Nov. 1812. Return dated 25 Nov. 1812 ('Sands') [PRO: WO 25/2965]. Obituary, *The Gentleman's Magazine*, Supplement 1812, Part II, p. 671 ['Nov. 18. At Ciudad Rodrigo, of fever, occasioned by excessive fatigue, Capt. R. Fitzgerald Sandes, 50th reg. fourth son of the late W. S. esq. of Sallow Glin, co. Kerry. He had served at Copenhagen, Walcheren, and with Sir J. Moore he gallantly shared in the honours of the 50th at Corunna. He had also served under the Marquis of Wellington since the commencement of the war in the Peninsula.'].

+SANKEY, Andrew, Lt., 57th Foot: Lt., 57th Foot, 26 Dec. 1805. Killed, the Nive, 13 Dec. 1813 (1st Battn.) [*London Gazette*].

SANKEY, Samuel, Capt., 9th Foot: Capt., Army, 9 July 1803; Capt., 9th Foot, 2 Aug. 1804. Wounded, Rolica, 17 Aug. 1808 [*London Gazette*]. Temporary pension of one hundred pounds per annum, commencing 25 Dec. 1811, 'for wounds' received at Rolica [*1818 Pension Return*, pp. 6–7]. MGS.

+SARSFIELD, J., Ensign, 34th Foot: Ensign, 34th Foot, 27 June 1810. Killed, Albuera, 16 May 1811 (2nd Battn.) [*London Gazette*]. Died of wounds, 17 May 1811. Return dated 25 May 1811. [PRO: WO 25/2965].

SAULX, Louis de, Capt., Chasseurs Brittaniqies: Capt., Chasseurs Britanniques, 22 Dec. 1808. Severely wounded, Pyrenees, 30 July 1813 [*London Gazette*].

+SAUNDERS, Albert Wing, Ensign, 88th Foot: Ensign, 88th Foot, 11 May 1812. Died of wounds, 27 June 1813. Return dated 25 June 1813. [PRO: WO 25/2965]. See Henry Sanders.

SAUNDERSON, Hardress, Capt., 39th Foot: *1829 Statement of Service for Retired Officers*: Aged seventeen on first appointment to the Army. Ensign, 39th Foot, 15 June 1804; Lt., 39th Foot, 18 Feb. 1806; Capt., 39th Foot, 5 May 1808;

Half-pay, 81st Foot, Jan. 1821, 'in consequence of a recommendation of the Medical Board, on account of Wounds'; Lt. and Capt., Grenadier Guards, 22 July 1824; Major, unattached, Half-pay, Jan. 1827, 'By ill Health in consequence of Wounds'. 'Desirous of service when his Health is restored, from the effects of Wounds in the Head.' *Where serving when wounded*: 'Spain'. *Details of pension*: One hundred pounds, commencing Oct. 1812. *Family*: Married in London, Feb. 1822. Four children by 1829. *Where generally resident during last five years*: 'London'. [PRO: WO 25/773 f14]. Severely wounded, Arroyo dos Molinos, 28 Oct. 1811 (2nd Battn.) [*London Gazette*]. MGS.

SAUNDERSON, William Bassett, Lt., 44th Foot: *1829 Statement of Service for Retired Officers*: Aged fifteen on first appointment to the Army. Ensign, 44th Foot, 1807; Lt., 44th Foot, 1808 [Army List gives 28 April 1808]; Capt., 72nd Foot, 1813; Half-pay, '50th Regt., 41st Regt.', 'At request of officer, Ill Health'. Served fifteen years on Full-pay. *Where serving when wounded*: 'Cadiz, Spain'. *Where generally resident during last five years*: 'Castle Saunderson, Ireland'. [PRO: WO 25/773 f13]. MGS.

+SAWATZKY, Charles, Lt., 60th Foot: Lt., 60th Foot, 25 Nov. 1805. Killed, during 'several Affairs with the French Army', 15 March 1811 (5th Battn.) [*London Gazette*].

SAWKINS, William, Lt., 50th Foot: *1829 Statement of Service for Retired Officers*: 'From the age of 13 to 22 I held a situation under Gov. at Malta & which I resigned to enter the Army. I was appointed to an Ensigncy in the 50th Regt. at the age of 23'. Ensign, 50th Foot, Dec. 1811, 'without purchase, my Father having been an old officer in the Army'; Lt., 50th Foot, Jan. 1814 [Army List gives 6 Jan.]; Half-pay, 'the latter end of 1814 or beginning of 1815'; Lt., 3rd Garrison Battn., 20 June 1815; Half-pay, 1817, by reduction. *Where serving when wounded*: 'before Toulouse'. *Details of pension*: Originally one hundred pounds per annum, commencing 11 April 1815, 'as Commanding a Compy. when wounded. Reduced to £70 in 1817'. *Family*: Married in Canterbury, Aug. 1815. One child by 1829. *Where generally resident during last five years*: 'near Bristol, Chelsea, & Lambeth'. 'Had I not been rendered unfit for the duties of a Regt. of the line by the loss of my leg I should not have remained on half pay. I have never applied to be appointed to a Veteran Battn. because I considered that my having been twice wounded, having lost a leg while in the command of a Company & having commanded a Company in several actions, together with the strong testimonials of my commanding officers, gave me a just claim to promotion, at least to a Company on the old half pay. By not entering a Veteran Battn. in 1814 I have sacrificed 5 or 600£.' [PRO: WO 25/773 f55]. Slightly wounded, Pyrenees, 30 July 1813 (1st Battn.) [*London Gazette*]. Severely wounded, Toulouse, 10 April 1814 (1st Battn.) [*London Gazette*]. Seventy pounds per annum pension, commencing 11 April 1815, for 'loss of a leg' at Toulouse [*1818 Pension Return*, pp. 14–15]. MGS.

+SCANLAN, Connell, Lt., 39th Foot: Lt., 39th Foot, 22 May 1809. Severely wounded, Pyrenees, 25 July 1813 (1st Battn.) [*London Gazette*]. Died of wounds, 31 Aug. 1813. Return dated Sept. 1813. [PRO: WO 25/2965]. *Register of Officer's Effects*: 'Wounded and taken Prisoner 25 July 1813 (since dead)'. Died 'of his Wounds'. Single. [PRO: WO 25/2963].

SCHAEFFER, Charles, Cornet, 2nd Dragoons K.G.L.: *1829 Statement of Service for Retired Officers*: Aged twenty-five on first appointment to the Army. 2nd Lt., Half-pay, Duke of Brunswick Hussars, Aug. 1809 ('a Supernummerary Officer'); Cornet, 2nd Dragoons K.G.L., Feb. 1811 [Army List gives 23 April 1811], 'the commission being lost in the Peninsula as the Officer was severely wounded and taken Prisoner near Burgos in 1812'; Lt., 2nd Dragoons K.G.L., 12 Aug. 1812; Half-pay, 24 Feb. 1816, by reduction. 'No further promotion in the British Army, but promoted titular Captain when leaving the Hanoverian Service without pension, 1818'. 'A Waterloo man'. *Where serving when wounded*: 'The officer is not in the Receipt of a Pension for his Wounds he received near Burgos in Spain for which a years pay was granted to him.' *Family*: Married 'at Riechenburg in the Kingdom of Hannover', 20 April 1820. Five children by 1829. No employment. *Where generally resident during last five years*: 'at Campen near Brunswick'. [PRO: WO 25/773 f81]. Recorded as 'Missing', during 'movements of the Army' [Retreat from Burgos], p. 23 Oct. 1812 [*London Gazette*]. Served in Peninsula in 1812. Waterloo. *Beamish*, vol. II, p. 545 ['severely wounded 23d October 1812, at Venta del Poco'].

SCHAEFFER, Henry, Lt., Duke of Brunswick Oels' Corps (Cavalry): *1829 Statement of Service for Retired Officers*: Aged twenty-nine on first appointment to Army. 'Appointed in army as a lieutenant, "Brunswick Hussars", n.d.' [Army List gives 26 Sept. 1809]; Half-pay, 1816, by reduction. *Where serving when wounded*: 'Wounded severely at Villa Franca in Spain'. *Family*: Married on 26 Sept. 1820. One child by 1829. [PRO: WO 25/773 f123]. Wounded, Heights of Ordal, 12/13 Sept. 1813 ('Schaefer') ('Brunswick Hussars') [*London Gazette*].

+SCHARNHORST, Ernest, Capt., 2nd Line Battn. K.G.L.: Capt., 2nd

Line Battn. K.G.L., 8 Feb. 1805. Severely wounded, Salamanca, 22 July 1812 [*London Gazette*]. Killed, siege of Burgos, 20–26 Sept. 1812 [*London Gazette*]. Served in Peninsula 1808–12. *Beamish*, vol. II, pp. 100–1 [Burgos, 22/23 Sept. 1812: 'a body of four hundred men, composed of about equal numbers of the guards, Scotch brigade, and King's German Legion, the latter under captain von Scharnhorst, were provided with ladders... Several gallant attempts were now made to ascend the ladders, and some individuals gained a momentary footing, but the garrison, mounting on the top of the parapet, bayonetted the foremost down, and then pouring a fire of musquetry, as well as a number of shells and combustibles among the assailants, killed the commanding officer, and caused great destruction... Captain von Scharnhorst and lieutenant Hansing of the second line battalion of the legion fell in this unfortunate attempt'], p. 632 ['severely wounded, 28th July 1809 at Talavera; severely wounded, 22d July 1812, at Salamanca. Killed 22d Sep. 1812, in the attack of the exterior line of defence of the castle of Burgos.']

SCHARNHORST, William von, 2nd Lt., Artillery K.G.L: 2nd Lt., Artillery K.G.L., 24 Nov. 1809. Slightly wounded in the siege of the Forts of St Vincente, St Cayetano, and La Merced at Salamanca, 18–24 June 1812 [*London Gazette*]. Served in Peninsula 1811–13. Waterloo. *Beamish*, vol. II, p. 536 ['slightly wounded, 20th June 1812, before the forts of Salamanca'].

+SCHARTROTH, J. Carl, Lt., Duke of Brunswick Oels' Corps (Infantry): Ensign, Duke of Brunswick Oels' Corps (Infantry), 27 Aug. 1812. Killed, Nivelle, 10 Oct. 1813 ('Lieut. George Schartorns') [*London Gazette*]. 'Lt. Schartroth' listed as 'dead', *1814 Army List*. 'J.

Carl Schartroth' in *Challis, Index*, p. 275.

SCHAUMANN, Gustavus, Lt., 1st Light Dragoons/Hussars K.G.L.: Lt., 1st Light Dragoons K.G.L., 15 Sept. 1810. Served in Peninsula 1809–14. Waterloo. *Beamish*, vol. II, p. 549 ['Slightly wounded, 1st October, 1810, at the Passage of the Mondego'].

SCHAUROTH, George von, Lt., 5th Line Battn. K.G.L.: Ensign, 5th Line Battn. K.G.L., 19 Oct. 1809; Lt. 20 March 1812. Slightly wounded, 'in the assault and capture of the exterior line of the castle of Burgos on the evening of the 4th October, 1812' [*London Gazette*]. Served in Peninsula 1810–14. Waterloo. MGS. *Beamish*, vol. II, p. 591 ['slightly wounded, 27th Feb. 1814, before Bayonne.'].

SCHLAEGER, Charles, Lt., 5th Line Battn. K.G.L.: Ensign, 5th Line Battn. K.G.L., 22 Sept. 1810; Lt., 5th Line Battn. K.G.L., 20 March 1812. Slightly wounded, siege of Burgos, 18 Oct. 1812 [*London Gazette*]. Served in Peninsula 1808–13. Waterloo. MGS. *Beamish*, vol. II, p. 592.

SCHLÜTTER, Andreas von, Lt., 1st Line Battn. K.G.L.: Lt., 1st Line Battn. K.G.L., 22 April 1805. Slightly wounded, Talavera, 28 July 1809 ('Schlutter, Sr.') [*London Gazette*]. Capt., 1st Line Battn. K.G.L., 27 Jan. 1811. Served in Peninsula 1808–12. Waterloo. *Beamish*, vol. II, p. 571.

+SCHMALHAUSEN, Edward, Ensign, 1st Light Battn. K.G.L.: Ensign, 1st Light Battn. K.G.L., 18 Jan. 1811. Slightly wounded, Albuera, 16 May 1811 ('Smalhausen') [*London Gazette*]. Died of wounds, 25 June 1811. Return dated 25 June 1811. [PRO: WO 25/2965]. Served in Peninsula in 1811. *Beamish*, vol. II, p. 640 [Died

'9th June 1811, at Elvas in Portugal, of the wounds he received in the battle of Albuera, 16th May 1811.'].

SCHMIDT, Augustus, Ensign, 2nd Line Battn. K.G.L.: Ensign, 2nd Line Battn. K.G.L., 28 Jan. 1808. Severely wounded, Talavera, 28 July 1809 [*London Gazette*]. Served in Peninsula 1808–14. *Beamish*, vol. II, p. 577 ['slightly wounded, 28th July 1809, at Talavera.'].

SCHNEIDER, Lt., Duke of Brunswick Oels' Corps (Infantry): Lt., Duke of Brunswick Oels' Corps (Infantry), 15 Oct. 1812. Severely wounded, Crossing the Bidassoa, 7/9 Oct. 1813 [*London Gazette*].

SCHÖNFELD, Charles, Count, Capt., The Duke of Brunswick Oels' Corps (Infantry): Capt., The Duke of Brunswick Oels' Corps, 29 Sept. 1809. Severely wounded while skirmishing, 9–14 Oct. 1810 [*London Gazette*]. Severely wounded, Orthes, 27 Feb. 1814 [*London Gazette*].

SCHULTZ, Carl Henry, Lt., Duke of Brunswick Oels' Corps (Infantry): *1829 Statement of Service for Retired Officers*: Aged twenty-one years old 'when promoted officer in 1812, but 18 years old when first entered His Majesty's service 1809.' '3 years, he served as a Non Commissioned officer', Duke of Brunswick Oels' Corps (Infantry), 1809; Ensign, Duke of Brunswick Oels' Corps, 25 Aug. 1812; Lt., Duke of Brunswick Oels' Corps, 18 March 1813; Half-pay, 24 Dec. 1814, by reduction. 'No higher rank obtained by the officer in the British Army while upon the Half-pay, but promoted Captain in the Brunswick Service by Commission dated 16 March 1815'. *Where serving when wounded*: 'in Spain in the battle of Salamanca, losing his left arm.' *Details of pension*: Fifty pounds per annum, commencing 23 July 1814. *Family*: Married Char-

lotte Henriette Leidloff, 'at Brunswick', 9 April 1815. Five children by 1829. No employment. *Where generally resident during last five years*: 'in the town of Brunswick in Germany.' [PRO: WO 25/773 f121].

SCHULTZE, George Lewis, Capt., 2nd Light Dragoons K.G.L.: Capt., 2nd Light Dragoons K.G.L., 25 March 1810. Slightly wounded, Arroyo dos Molinos, 28 Oct. 1811 [*London Gazette*]. Served in Peninsula 1811–12. *Beamish*, vol. II, p. 619 [Died by illness, '3d Oct. 1812, at Truxillo in Spain.'].

SCHWARZENBERG, John Daniel William Ludwig von, Lt., Duke of Brunswick Oels' Corps (Infantry): *1829 Statement of Service for Retired Officers*: Aged twenty-one on first appointment to the Army. Ensign, Duke of Brunswick Oels' Corps (Infantry), 10 Oct. 1809; Lt., Duke of Brunswick Oels' Corps (Infantry), 21 July 1811 [Army List gives 21 Feb. 1811]; Half-pay, 24 Dec. 1814, by reduction. *Where serving when wounded*: 'Serving in Spain and wounded at the assault of St Sebastian on the 25th August 1813'. *Details of pension*: Seventy pounds per annum, commencing 26 Aug. 1814. *Family*: Married in 'Cassel in Hessia', 30 July 1816. Five children by 1829. No employment. *Where generally resident during last five years*: 'always in Cassel'. Signed 'Ludwig von Schwarzenberg'. [PRO: WO 25/776 f373]. Slightly wounded, Heights of Villares, 20–22 June 1812 [*London Gazette*]. Recorded as 'Missing', during the Siege of San Sebastian, 25 Aug. 1813 ('Schwartenberg') [*London Gazette*]. 'Lud. von Schwartzenberg' in Army List. MGS.

+SCOTT, David, Ensign, 11th Foot: Ensign, 11th Foot, 18 July 1811. Killed, Salamanca, 22 July 1812 (1st Battn.) [*London Gazette*].

+**SCOTT, Francis, Capt., 59th Foot:**
Capt., 59th Foot, 2 June 1808.
Killed, storming of San Sebastian,
31 Aug. 1813 (Major) (2nd Battn.)
[*London Gazette*].

SCOTT, Francis M., Lt., 48th Foot:
Ensign, 48th Foot, 17 June 1811. Lt.,
48th Foot, 12 Aug. 1813. Severely
wounded, Nivelle, 10 Nov. 1813 (1st
Battn.) [*London Gazette*].

+**SCOTT, Henry, Lt., 6th Foot:** Lt.,
6th Foot, 5 March 1807. Killed,
Orthes, 27 Feb. 1814 (1st Battn.)
[*London Gazette*].

SCOTT, Henry, 1st Lt., 95th Foot:
*1829 Statement of Service for
Retired Officers:* Aged twenty on
first appointment to the Army. 2nd
Lt., 95th Foot, 22 Aug. 1810; 1st Lt.,
95th Foot, 11 May 1812; Half-pay,
5th Foot, 18 Feb. 1818, in consequence of 'Ill health, having
suffered much from the effects of
my wound, in the knee joints,
which is much contracted and stiff,
as also from Rheumatism'. 'Incapable of serving from the nature of
the Wound'. *Where serving when
wounded:* 'France. While commanding a Company of 95th Regiment at Battle of Nivelle 10th
November 1813.' *Details of
pension:* Seventy pounds per
annum, commencing 'year and day
from date of Wound'. *Family:*
Married in St Andrew's Church,
Dublin, 3 June 1820. Two children
by 1829. *Title and nature of employment:* 'Clerk, in office of Secretary
Commissioner Customs, Ireland:
appointed 18th May 1827... Salary
£110'. *Where generally resident
during last five years:* 'Dublin'.
[PRO: WO 25/773 f129]. Severely
wounded, Nivelle, 10 Nov. 1813 (2nd
Battn.) [*London Gazette*]. *1818
Pension Return,* pp. 22–3. MGS.
Harris, p. 185–6.

+**SCOTT, J. McKenzie, Major, 57th
Foot:** Major, Army, 25 April 1808;
Major, 57th Foot, 15 Feb. 1810.

Killed, Albuera, 16 May 1811 (1st
Battn.) [*London Gazette*].

SCOTT, Matthew, Capt., 2nd Foot:
Capt., 2nd Foot, 24 Sept. 1803.
Severely wounded, Salamanca, 22
July 1812 [*London Gazette*]. Major,
Army, 21 Sept. 1813.

**SCOTT, Samuel, Volunteer, 5th
Foot; Ensign, 52nd Foot:** *1829 Statement of Service for Retired Officers:*
Aged nineteen on first appointment
to the Army. Volunteer, 5th Foot,
June 1809; Ensign, 52nd Foot, 22
Feb. 1810; Cornet, 4th Dragoon
Guards, Nov. 1811; Lt., 4th Dragoon
Guards, 25 June 1812; Lt., 87th
Foot, 17 March 1814; Lt., 66th Foot,
1817, 'do not know the date, being
at the time in a very dangerous
state of health'; Bvt. Capt., 17 June
1824, 'in St Vincent ... in consequence of my being appointed a Bk.
Master in the West Indies, upon
which His Royal Highness was
graciously pleased to give me local
Rank as Captain in consideration of
my former services'. 'Exchanged
from 87th to 66th Regt. in the East
Indies (owing to extreme ill health)
on the latter Regt. being ordered to
St Helena; returned to England
with the 2nd Battn. 66th and was
reduced with the Battalion at
Winchester in November 1817'.
Where serving when wounded:
'Slightly wounded in the Peninsula,
but no Pension or Grant'. *Family:*
Married in St Martin's Church,
London, 23 Nov. 1813. No children.
Title and nature of employment:
'Barrack Master at NewCastle
Ireland [sic].' [West Indies]. *Where
generally resident during last five
years:* 'The entire of the last 4 years
in the West Indies, as a Barrack
Master'. [PO: WO 25/773 f114].

**SCOTT, Thomas, Ensign/Lt., 94th
Foot:** *1829 Statement of Service for
Retired Officers:* Aged 'about 19' on
first appointment to the Army.
Ensign, Edinburgh Militia, 13 Nov.
1807; Ensign, 94th Foot, 25 Aug.

1808; Lt., 94th Foot, 26 Feb. 1812 [Army List gives 28 Feb.]; Half-pay, 25 Dec. 1818, by reduction. 'Embarked at Jersey 19th Jany. 1810 and joined the army under the Command of His Grace the Duke of Wellington and remained on service untill the peace, embarked from France on the 8th July 1814 for Ireland.' 'Not desirous to serve as I don't consider myself at present fit for actual service'. *Where serving when wounded*: 'Once at Mata Gorda, Twice at Ciudad Rodrigo'. No pension. Not married. No employment. *Where generally resident during last five years*: 'at Borthwickshire by Hawick County Roxbro' N.B.' [PRO: WO 25/773 f126]. Slightly wounded, storming of Ciudad Rodrigo, 19 Jan. 1812 [*London Gazette*]. MGS.

SCOTT, William Henry, Ensign, 3rd Foot Guards: Ensign, 3rd Foot Guards, 27 Oct. 1805. Slightly wounded, Talavera, 28 July 1809 [*London Gazette*]. MGS. *Haythornthwaite, Armies of Wellington*, p. 34 ['some subalterns were given leave to complete their education before actually joining their regiment, but few cases can have been as unusual as the ensigncy in the 3rd Foot Guards awarded to William Scott, son of the major-general of the same name, who had settled in France and was consequently interned upon the resumption of war after the Peace of Amiens. Young Scott was permitted by the French to study at Weimar, during which time he was commissioned and permitted to continue his schooling; eventually he came home, joined his regiment, but was wounded and captured at Talavera and again returned to imprisonment until 1814.'].

+SEATON, James, Capt., 92nd Foot: Capt., 92nd Foot, 31 Dec. 1803. Slightly wounded, Pyrenees, 31 July 1813 ('Seton') [*London Gazette*]. Severely wounded, 'in Action with the Enemy', 15 Feb. 1814 ('Seton') (1st Battn.) [*London Gazette*]. Died of wounds, 22 March 1814. Return dated April 1814. [PRO: WO 25/2965].

SEBRIGHT, Edward, Capt. and Lt. Col., 1st Foot Guards: Lt. Col., Army, 24 April 1808; Capt. and Lt. Col., 1st Foot Guards, 10 May 1808. Severely wounded, Barossa, 5 March 1811 [*London Gazette*].

+SEDGWICK, Harry Bingley, Lt., 5th Foot: Ensign, 5th Foot, no date given for the commission, in 1808 A/L. Lt., 5th Foot, 26 Sept. 1809. Killed at the seige of Badajoz, 30 May–5 June 1811 (2nd Battn.) [*London Gazette*].

+SEGESSER, R., Lt., De Roll's Regiment: Lt., De Roll's Regiment, 18 Dec. 1808. Killed, Heights of Ordal, 12/13th Sept. 1813 ('Lieutenant Seggessar... De Rolle's Rifle Company') [*London Gazette*, 9 Oct. 1813]. 'Segeser' in revised casualty list [*London Gazette*, 23 Oct. 1813].

+SELBY, William, Lt., 3rd Dragoons: Lt., 3rd Dragoons, 7 April 1808. Killed, Salamanca, 22 July 1812 [*London Gazette*].

SERJEANT, Thomas Lloyd, Ensign, 81st Foot: Ensign, 81st Foot, 4 Feb. 1808. Wounded, 'in the Army lately in Spain' (2nd Battn.) [*March 1809 Army List*, p. 105]. *Monthly Return*, 2nd Battn., dated 25 Feb. 1809: 'Wounded, in Naval Hospl. Plymouth' [PRO: WO 17/202].

SERVAIS, Antoine, Lt., Chasseurs Britanniques: Ensign, Chasseurs Britanniques, 8 Aug. 1811; Lt., Chasseurs Britanniques, 3 June 1812. Severely wounded, Pyrenees, 30 July 1813 [*London Gazette*].

SETON, George, 7th Foot: Lt., 7th Foot, 31 May 1810. Severely wounded, Albuera, 16 May 1811 ('Seaton') (2nd Battn.) [*London*

Gazette]. Slightly wounded in 'an Affair with the Enemy near Aldea de Ponte', 27 Sept. 1811 (2nd Battn.) [*London Gazette*].

SEWARD, William, Lt., 9th Foot: *1829 Statement of Service*: Born 29 July 1792, Southampton, Hants. Aged sixteen on first appointment to the Army. Ensign, 9th Foot, 26 March 1808; Lt., 9th Foot, 26 April 1809; Capt., 9th Foot, 15 July 1819. *Battles, sieges and campaigns*: 'Campaign of 1808 under Sir A. Wellesley, Vimiera 21st August 1808 – Campaign of 1808-9 Sir John Moore. Walcheren Expedition 1809... Tarifa and neighbourhood 1810 under Major Brown 28th Regt. Barossa 5th March 1811 under Sir Thomas Graham. Expedition to Tarragona under Colonel Skeritt. Present part of Siege of Tarifa... Campaign of 1813 in Portugal and Spain... Vittoria 21st June 1813. Campaign of 1814 in France... Passage of Nive 9. 10. & 11th Decr. 1814. Bayonne April 1814.' *Wounds received in action*: 'Wounded at Barossa in Command of Light Company 2d Batt. 9th Regiment for which received One Years pay as Captain.' *Service abroad*: '19th August 1808 to 17th January 1809, Portugal and Spain. 17th July 1809 to 14th September 1809, Walcheren Expedition. 21st January 1810 to 4th January 1813, Gibralter & Mediterranean. January 1813 to 16th June 1814, Portugal Spain & France. June 1814 to July 1815, Canada. August 1815 to 30th October 1818, France. 4th April 1819 to 23rd April 1821, West Indies. January 1825 to May 1826, West Indies.' Not married in 1830. [PRO: WO 25/786 f242]. Severely wounded, Barossa, 5 March 1811 [*London Gazette*]. MGS.

+SEYMOUR, Charles, Lt., 32nd Foot: Lt., 32nd Foot, 25 Aug. 1808. Killed, Salamanca, 22 July 1812 (1st Battn.) [*London Gazette*].

SEYMOUR, Hugh, Lt. and Capt., 3rd Foot Guards: Lt. and Capt., 3rd Foot Guards, 28 March 1811. Slightly wounded, the Nive, 12 Dec. 1813 (1st Battn.) [*London Gazette*].

SHADFORTH, Thomas, Capt./ Major, 57th Foot: *1829 Statement of Service*: 'Born Newcastle upon Tyne, 1774. Aged 24 on his first Entrance into the Army. Ensign, 87 Foot, Jany or Feby 1798. Lieutenant, 47 Foot, Sept. 1798. Captain, 57th Foot, 13 May 1802. Major, 57th Foot, 20 June 1811. Lt. Colonel, Army, 12 Aug. 1819.' Note added: 'Sold out 12 April 1831.' *Battles, sieges and campaigns*: 'Albuhera, 16 May 1811.' *Wounds received in action*: 'Wounded 16 May at Albuhera, received one years pay as Captain. Pension £100 perr Annum from 16th May 1812. Increased to £200 after the Battle of Waterloo from 18 June 1815. Permanent.' *Service abroad*: '1799 to 1802, Bermuda. 1804 to 1809, Gibraltar. 1809 to 1812, Peninsula. 1813 to 1818, France. 1825 to 1829, N.S. Wales.' *Family*: Married Frances Fitt, 30 Sept. 1802, Bermuda. They had four children by 1830. [PRO: WO 25/796 f72]. Slightly wounded, Albuera, 16 May 1811 (1st Battn.) [*London Gazette*]. *1818 Pension Return*, pp. 14–15. *Royal Military Calendar*, vol. V, p. 172. MGS.

SHANNAHAN, Michael, Lt., Royal Staff Corps: Lt., Royal Staff Corps, 26 June 1806. Slightly wounded, Talavera, 28 July 1809 ('Shancham') [*London Gazette*].

SHARNHORST, Ernest, Capt., 2nd Line Battn. K.G.L.: Capt., 2nd Line Battn. K.G.L., 8 Feb. 1805. Severely wounded, Talavera, 28 July 1809 [*London Gazette*].

+SHARP, John, Lt., 48th Foot: Lt., 48th Foot, 7 March 1810. Wounded, Albuera, 16 May 1811 (2nd Battn.) [*London Gazette*]. Died, Portugal, June 1811 [PRO: WO 25/2965].

SHAW, James, Lt., 43rd Foot: Lt., 43rd Foot, 23 Jan. 1806. Slightly wounded, Coa, 24 July 1810, while serving on the Staff as ADC to Brig.-Gen. R. Crauford [*London Gazette*]. AQG at Waterloo. *Dalton*, p. 36 ['Bn. 1788... Served... at Copenhagen, and proceeded to the Pa. in 1808. Served at Corunna, and in 1809 was adjt. Was A.D.C. to Gen. Robert Craufurd during 1809 and 1810. Present at siege of Ciudad Rodrigo. Served at the siege and storming of Badajoz, at Salamanca... D... 30 May, 1865.']

+SHAWE, Charles Fielding, Capt., 6th Foot: Capt., Army, 15 Sept., 1808; Capt., 6th Foot, 3 Nov. 1808. Killed, Crossing of the Bidassoa, 7/9 Oct. 1813 [*London Gazette*].

SHAWE, Matthew, Capt., 74th Foot: Capt., 74th Foot, 30 Oct. 1804; Major, Army, 30 May 1811. Severely wounded, siege of Badajoz, 26 March 1812 [*London Gazette*]. Mentioned in Wellington's dispatch, 27 March 1812 [Assault of Fort Picurina, Badajoz, 26 March: 'The attack was made by five hundred men of the 3rd division, formed into three detachments; the right under the command of Major Shaw, of the 74th... Major-General Kempt mentions in high terms in his report the cool and persevering gallantry of the officers and troops... He particularly mentions ... Majors Shaw and Rudd, and the Honourable Captain Powys, who commanded the several detachments. These three officers were wounded'] [*London Gazette*].

SHEA, Francis, Lt., 27th Foot: *1830 Statement of Service*: Born 1789, Mullingar, Ireland. Aged sixteen on his first entrance into the Army. Ensign, 27th Foot, 20 March 1806; Lt. 1 Jan. 1807; Capt. 9 Dec. 1824. *Battles, sieges and campaigns*: 'Generally, the Battles in the South of Spain in the 2nd Batt. in 1813 under Lord Bentick.' *Service*

abroad: '9 Sept. 1808 to 1809, Portugal. 1813 to 1814, Spain. June 1814 to Dec. 1814, America. Jany. 1819 to Decr. 1823, Gibraltar. Janry 1824 to 31 Dec. 1829, W. Indies.' Not married in 1830. [PRO: WO 25/790 f103]. Severely wounded, 'not dangerously', Heights of Ordal, 12/13 Sept. 1813 (2nd Battn.) [*London Gazette*]. 'Shee' in Army List.

SHEA, Patrick, Lt., 58th Foot: Adjutant, 58th Foot, 31 Jan. 1805; Lt., 58th Foot, 28 Oct. 1806. Severely wounded, Pyrenees, 2 Aug. 1813 (2nd Battn.) [*London Gazette*].

SHEA, Robert, Lt., 48th Foot: Lt., 48th Foot, 1 Nov. 1810. Wounded, Albuera, 16 May 1811 (2nd Battn.) [*London Gazette*].

SHEARMAN, Francis, Lt., 26th Foot: Lt., 26th Foot, 10 Oct. 1805. Wounded, 'in the Army lately in Spain' (1st Battn.) [*March 1809 Army List*, p. 105].

SHEARMAN, John, Lt., 62nd Foot; Capt., Calabrian Free Corps: *1829 Statement of Service*: Aged eighteen on first appointment to the Army. Ensign, 26th Foot, Feb. 1806; Lt., 4th Garrison Battn., Nov. 1806; Lt., 62nd Foot, Nov. 1807; Capt., 60th Foot, 15 Feb. 1816; Capt., 13th Foot, March 1816; Half-pay, 7th Foot, Dec. 1821, 'at my own request ... my state of health not permitting me to accompany the 13th Regt. to India'. *Where serving when wounded*: 'Serving in Spain (under Lord Wm. Bentinck) as Captain in the Calabrian Free Corps'. *Details of pension*: One hundred pounds, commencing June 1813. Not married. No employment. *Where generally resident during last five years*: 'England, Florence & Brussels'. [PRO: WO 25/773 f169].

SHEDDON, John, Capt., 52nd Foot: Capt., 52nd Foot, 9 May 1811.

Slightly wounded, Crossing the Bidassoa, 7/9 Oct. 1813 (1st Battn.) [*London Gazette*]. Waterloo.

SHEDDON, Thomas, Ensign, 68th Foot: Ensign, 68th Foot, 18 Feb. 1813. Severely wounded, Orthes, 27 Feb. 1814 [*London Gazette*].

SHEKLETON, Robert, Surgeon, 3rd Foot: *1829 Statement of Service for Retired Officers*: Aged eighteen years nine months on first appointment to the Army. Asst. Surgeon, 66th Foot, 5 Nov. 1807; Surgeon, 3rd Foot, 9 Sept. 1813; Half-pay, 25 Dec. 1815, by reduction. *Where serving when wounded*: 'Wounded at Vieux Monguerre, South of France, 13 Dec. 1813.' No pension. *Family*: Married in Rathfarnham, County of Dublin, 27 July 1819. *Where generally resident during last five years*: Dublin. [PRO: WO 25/773 f167].

SHELTON, John, Lt., 9th Foot: Lt., 9th Foot, 26 Aug. 1807. Severely wounded, 'arm amputated', storming of San Sebastian, 31 Aug. 1813 (1st Battn.) [*London Gazette*]. One hundred pounds per annum pension, commencing 1 July 1814, for 'loss of an arm' at San Sebastian [*1818 Pension Return*, pp. 6–7].

SHELTON, John Willington, Lt., 28th Foot: Lt., 28th Foot, 22 March 1810. Slightly wounded, Albuera, 16 May 1811 (2nd Battn.) [*London Gazette*]. Four times wounded at Waterloo. MGS. Died, 19 July 1847.

SHEPHERD, John, Lt., 3rd Foot: Lt., 3rd Foot, 27 Nov. 1806. Slightly wounded, Albuera, 16 May 1811 [*London Gazette*].

+SHEPPARD, Frederick, Lt., 4th Foot: Lt., 4th Foot, 14 Dec. 1808. Severely wounded, storming of Badajoz, 6 April 1812 ('Shepperd') [*London Gazette*]. Died of wounds, 12 April 1812. Return dated 25 April 1812. [PRO: WO 25/2965].

SHEPPARD, Thomas, Lt., 9th Foot: *1829 Statement of Service for Retired Officers*: Aged seventeen on first appointment to the Army. Ensign, 9th Foot, Aug. 1807; Lt., 9th Foot, March 1808 [Army List gives 28 March]; Half-pay, 59th Foot, Oct. 1816. 'Placed on Half-Pay in consequence of being disabled from active service by my Wound received in Action which is still open, & renders me incapable of even dressing myself, in addition to a useless Limb the Neck-bone of my left thigh being completely shattered & knocked out of its socket.' *Where serving when wounded*: '9th Foot at the crossing of the Bidassoa 7 Octr. 1813, in command of a Company'. *Details of pension*: Seventy pounds, commencing 8 Oct. 1814, increased to one hundred pounds on 11 May 1816, and changed to two pensions each of seventy pounds, commencing 25 June 1817. Not married. No children. No employment. *Where generally resident during last five years*: 'Leicester ever since wounded, with the exception of about half a year at Chatham in 1815 & 1816.' [PRO: WO 25/773 f166]. Severely wounded, Crossing the Bidassoa, 7/9 Oct. 1813 ('Shepherd') (1st Battn.) [*London Gazette*]. 'Shepherd' in Army List. *1818 Pension Return*, pp. 6–7].

+SHERIDAN, Edward L., Lt., 57th Foot: Lt., 57th Foot, 9 June 1808. Slightly wounded, Albuera, 16 May 1811 [*London Gazette*]. Died of wounds, 10 June 1811. Return dated 25 June 1811. [PRO: WO 25/2965].

SHERIDAN, William, Capt. and Lt. Col., Coldstream Guards: Capt. and Lt. Col., Coldstream Guards, 25 June 1803. Wounded, 'severely but not dangerously', Talavera, 28 July 1809 [*London Gazette*].

SHEWBRIDGE, Henry, Ensign, 60th Foot: *1829 Statement of Service for Retired Officers*: Aged seventeen on first appointment to the Army. Ensign, 60th Foot, 24 Dec. 1812; Lt., 60th Foot, 24 Dec. 1814 [Army List gives 23 Dec.]; Half-pay, 24 Dec. 1818, by reduction. *Where serving when wounded*: 'Nivelle. Toulouse'. *Details of pension*: Fifty pounds, commencing 1826. *Family*: Married in Dublin, 4 June 1828. No children. No employment. *Where generally resident during last five years*: 'Portunna County Galway'. [PRO: WO 25/773 f204]. Slightly wounded, Nivelle, 10 Nov. 1813 (5th Battn.) [*London Gazette*]. Severely wounded, Toulouse, 10 April 1814 (5th Battn.) [*London Gazette*].

+**SHEWBRIDGE, Lewis, Lt., 66th Foot**: Lt., 66th Foot, 7 Feb. 1808. Slightly wounded, Talavera, 28 July 1809 [*London Gazette*]. Killed, Albuera, 16 May 1811 (2nd Battn.) [*London Gazette*].

SHIEL, Theobald, Lt., 14th Light Dragoons; Lt., 7th Foot: *1829 Statement of Service for Retired Officers*: Aged twenty-four on first appointment to the Army. Cornet, 12 Light Dragoons, 6 Feb. 1806; Lt., 60th Foot, 30 March 1808; Lt., 11th Light Dragoons, 22 June 1809; Lt., 7th Foot, 1 Oct. 1812; 'Superceded in February 1813'; Lt., 3rd Foot, 1 April 1826; Half-pay, 60th Foot, 12 July 1826. 'Not desirous [of service] now owing to impaired health and a severe wound through the Hand'. *Where serving when wounded*: 'Severely wounded in Spain.' No pension. Not married. No employment. *Where generally resident during last five years*: England and Ireland. [PRO: WO 25/773 f178]. MGS. Died, 7 Jan. 1855.

+**SHIFFNER, John Bridger, Lt. and Capt., 3rd Foot Guards**: Lt. and Capt., 3rd Foot Guards, 27 March 1811. Severely wounded, 'since dead', sortie from Bayonne, 14 April 1814 (1st Battn.) [*London Gazette*]. Died of wounds, 15 April 1814.

Return dated April 1814. [PRO: WO 25/2965]. *Hurt*, p. 75. *Fletcher, Fields of Fire*, p. 164 ['Coldstream Guards cemetery, Bayonne ... those who lie here include ... Shiffner']. *Fletcher, Gentlemen's Sons*, p. 185.

SHORE, Thomas, Ensign/Lt., 74th Foot: *1829 Statement of Service*: Born in Castleton, Derbyshire, 5 Aug. 1794. Aged eighteen on first appointment to the Army. Ensign, 74th Foot, 14 May 1812; Lt., 74th Foot, 19 May 1814; Half-pay, 25 March 1817, by reduction; Lt., 84th Foot, 25 Nov. 1828. *Battles, sieges and campaigns*: 'Vittoria, 21st June 1813, Ensign. Lara or decent from the Pyrenees, 10th Novr. 1813, Ensign. Engaged with the Company to which I was attached, on the 26th Feby. 1814, previous to crossing the G. de Pau. Orthez, 27th Feby. 1814, Ensign.' *Wounds received in action*: 'Severely on the 21st June 1813 at Vittoria. Charging through the village of Ereneas. 1 Years Pay. Severely on the 27th Feby. 1814 at Orthez. Being sent forward to dislodge a strong force of the Enemy. 1 Years Pay.' *Service abroad*: 'August 1812 to July 1814, Peninsula and France.' *Family*: Married Louisa Miles, 2 March 1815, 'In the Parish of St Mary Le Bone, County of Middx.' They had three children by 1830. [PRO: WO 25/801 f257]. See also his *1829 Statement of Service for Retired Officers*, which indicated that he had been generally resident for the previous five years at 'Brook Cottage, Enfield, Middx.' [PRO: WO 25/773 f218]. Severely wounded, Vittoria, 21 June 1813 [*London Gazette*]. Severely wounded, Orthes, 27 Feb. 1814 [*London Gazette*].

+**SHORTT, Thomas Spunner, Lt., 47th Foot**: Lt., 47th Foot, 28 March 1810. Slightly wounded, Vittoria, 21 June 1813 ("Short") (2nd Battn.) [*London Gazette*]. Killed, storming of San Sebastian, 31 Aug. 1813 ('Short') (2nd Battn.) [*London Gazette*].

SIBORN, Benjamin, Capt., 9th Foot: Capt., 9th Foot, 5 Nov. 1807. Severely wounded, the Nive, 10 Dec. 1813 (1st Battn.) [*London Gazette*]. Father of William Siborne, the historian and maker of the famous Waterloo models. *Guy*, pp. 184–5 ['acquired an ensigncy in the West Kent Militia in 1798, and exchanged into the 9th (East Norfolk) Regiment in August the next year, with which he served until his death in 1819. In the intervening period he saw a great deal of active service with the 2nd Battalion under General Sir John Moore in 1808–9, under Lord Chatham in the fever-plagued Walcheren episode of 1809; and then under Wellington's command in the Peninsula from 1810, Benjamin Siborn was gravely stricken at the battle of Nivelle (10 November 1813) [sic], receiving wounds that ultimately led to his death. In 1814 the 9th accompanied General Sir Edward Pakenham to North America, and took part in the defence of Canada returning to Europe in 1815 too late for the Battle of Waterloo. At this stage he transferred to the 1st Battalion – doubtless due to the peacetime reductions – and shared in occupation duties in France. Then the battalion was ordered to the unhealthy West Indian station, and there Siborne senior died on St Vincent on 14 July 1819, "from the after-effects of his wounds".'].

SIDLEY, Anthony Gardner, 2nd Lt., 23rd Foot: *1829 Statement of Service*: Born in Scorl, County Cork, 10 July 1796. Aged Fifteen on first appointment to the Army. 2nd Lt., 23rd Foot, 1 Aug. 1811; 1st Lt., 23rd Foot, 16 July 1812; Half-pay, 8th Foot, 18 Nov. 1818, 'in consequence of Ill Health occasioned by a wound'; Lt., 3rd Veteran Battn., 18 March 1824; Lt., 45th Foot, 26 March 1825. *Battles, sieges and campaigns*: 'Salamanca 22 July 1812... Asma 18th June 1813... Saluganna-de-Morrilla 19th June 1813...

Pyrenees 31st August 1813... Waterloo 18th June 1815... December 1825, Employed on the Irrawaddy, in Command of two companies of the 45th Regiment to open the communication between the Army and Rangoon' *Wounds received in action*: '19th June 1813 at Sabuganna de Morilla. One years Pay. 18th June 1815 at Waterloo.' *Titles, honorary distinctions and medals*: 'One Medal for Waterloo.' *Service abroad*: 'March 1812 to Decr. 1813, Peninsula. March 1815 to Novr. 1818, France. March 1825 to 31st Decr. 1829, East Indies.' *Family*: Married Anna Maria Fraser, 10th June 1817, London. They had no children by 1830. [PRO: WO 25/792 f351]. Severely wounded, 'in operations', 12–19 June 1813 ('Sedley') [*London Gazette*]. MGS.

+SILVER, John, Major, 88th Foot: Major, 88th Foot, 19 Sept. 1804. Severely wounded, 'since dead', Busaco, 27 Sept. 1810 (1st Battn.) [*London Gazette*].

SIMCOCKES, John S., Capt., 5th Foot: *1829 Statement of Service*: Born 2 April 1783, Dublin. Aged seventeen on his first entrance into the Army. Ensign, 5th Foot, 16 July 1799; Lt. 2 April 1803; Capt. 7 May 1807; Major, Army, 19 July 1821; Major, 5th Foot, Dec. 1824; Major, 20th Foot, 22 March 1827; Major, 40th Foot, 21 March 1832; 'Retired 1st May 1835.' *Battles, sieges and campaigns*: 'Sand Hills, Holland, August 1799... Buenos Ayres, July 1807... Salamanca, 22nd July 1812.' *Wounds received in action*: 'Wounded Severely at Salamanca. Received 1 year's Pay as Captain.' *Service abroad*: 'August 1799 to Novr. 1799, Holland. March 1800 to July 1802, Gibraltar. Decr. 1805 to 23 Decr. 1805, Ship wrecked & taken Prisoner. 24 Decr. 1805 to Febr. 1806, Prisoner in Holland. Sepr. 1806 to June 1807, At sea. June 1807 to Sepr. 1807, South America. May 1809 to Aug. 1810, Portugal. May

1812 to Octr. 1814, Spain & Portugal. July 1815 to Sepr. 1816, France. Aug. 1817 to Octr. 1818, France. Febr. 1819 to April 1821, West Indies. Novr. 1822 to Febr. 1824, West Indies. Novr 1824 to Febr. 1826, West Indies. 17 Febr. 1828 to 31 Decr. 1829, At Sea in the E. Indies. 17 Febr. 1828 to 28 Novr. 1834, E. Indies.' *Family*: Married Elizabeth Bamford, 2 Jan. 1815, Tamworth, Staffordshire. They had one child by 1832. [PRO: WO 25/788 f314]. Severely wounded, Salamanca, 22 July 1812 ('Simcocks') [*London Gazette*].

+SIMCOE, Francis, Lt., 27th Foot: Lt., 27th Foot, 22 Dec. 1808. Killed, storming of Badajoz, 6 April 1812 (3rd Battn.) [*London Gazette*].

SIMMONS, George, Lt., 95th Foot: Author of *A British Rifle Man: The Journals and Correspondence of Major George Simmons, Rifle Brigade, During the Peninsular War and the Campaign of Waterloo*, ed. Willoughby Verner (London, 1899). *1829 Statement of Service*: Born in Beverly, Yorkshire, 2 May 1786. Aged twenty-three 'on his first Entrance into the Army.' 2nd Lt., 95th Foot, 29 May 1809 [Army List gives 25 May]; 1st Lt., 95th Foot, 25 July 1811; Capt., Rifle Brigade, 17 April 1828. *Battles, sieges and campaigns*: 'March 19th 1810 on Picquet at barba del Puerco where the enemy attacked at Midnight and was repulsed. July 24th Battle of the Coa near Almaida. 1811 lines of Torres Vedras. In the fights of Pombal, Redinha, Casal Nova, Foz d'Aronce, Sabugal and Fuentes d'Onoro. 1812 The Siege of Ciudad Rodrigo & Badajos, and the Battles of Salamancar, the advance & retreat from Madrid. 1813 San Milan, Vittoria, Heights of Vera, & La Rhune. 1814 Battle of Orthes & Tarbes. 1815 Quartre-bras 16th June 17th and 18th at Waterloo.' *Wounds received in action*: '1810 On the 24th July at the Battle of the

Coa near Almaida, A Musket shot through the Thigh the bone injured. 1814 March the 20th A Musket ball fractured my right knee pan. 1815 June the 18th Waterloo, received a gun shot wound in my right side, the ball in its course broke two ribs passed through my liver and was afterwards cut out of my breast. A gratuity of one Year's Pay as a Second Lieut, & two Year's Pay as a First Lieut. A Subaltern's Pension granted from the 19th of June 1816 since which period my wounds have been examined three times by the Army Medical board, the Pension being consequently made permanent by the circular No. 647 War Office 21st Novr. 1829.' *Titles, honorary distinctions and medals*: 'The Waterloo Medal.' *Service abroad*: 'Embarked before I was Gazetted. 25 of May 1809 to July the 1st 1814, Portugal, Spain & France. 25th of April 1815 to 28th October 1815, Netherlands. 1st Jany. 1816 to 1st of Nov. 1818, France. 28th July 1825 to 12th July 1828, North America. 21st July 1829 to 31st Decr. 1829, North America.' [PRO: WO 25/804 f340]. Severely wounded, Coa, 24 July 1810 [*London Gazette*]. Slightly wounded, 'in Action with the Enemy', 20 March 1814 (1st Battn.) [*London Gazette*]. Wounded, Waterloo. MGS. Died in Jersey, 5 March 1858. *Du Cane*, p. 754. *Simmons*, p. 78 [Coa, 24 July 1810: 'I was shot through the thigh']. *Kincaid, Adventures*, pp. 25–6, 52 [Redinha, 12 March 1811: 'Just as Mr Simmons and myself had crossed the river, and were talking over the events of the day, not a yard asunder, there was a Portuguese soldier in the act of passing between us, when a cannon-ball plunged into his belly – his head doubled down to his feet, and he stood for a moment in that posture before he rolled over a life-less lump.'], p. 290 ['At the close of the war, when we returned to England ... George Simmons with his riddled body held together by a pair of stays, for his was no holyday waist, which naturally required such an appendage lest the burst of a sigh should snap it asunder; but one that appertained to a figure framed in nature's fittest mould to "brave the battle and the breeze!" '].

SIMMONS, Maud, Lt., 34th Foot: Ensign, 34th Foot, 13 April 1809; Lt. 14 March 1811. Slightly wounded, Pyrenees, 25 July 1813 (2nd Battn.) [*London Gazette*]. Brother of George Simmons, 95th Foot. *Simmons*, pp. 308–9 ['Pyrenees, 30th August 1813 ... it is all a lottery. Maud had escaped until the other day. He was lucky having a horse to stop the force, or the ball would have riddled him... I had a letter yesterday from Maud. He informs me that the wound he received is quite well, and he is ready for another affair'].

SINCLAIR, John, Capt., 79th Foot: Lt., 79th Foot, 14 March 1805; Capt. 4 May 1811. Slightly wounded, Fuentes de Onoro, 5 May 1811 (1st Battn.) [*London Gazette*]. Wounded, Waterloo. *Dalton*, p. 189 ['D. from his wounds'].

SINCLAIR, Temple Frederick, Lt., 44th Foot: Ensign, Army, 27 July 1809; Ensign, 44th Foot, 21 Feb. 1810; Lt., 44th Foot, 20 Feb. 1812. Severely wounded, storming of Badajoz, 6 April 1812 (2nd Battn.) [*London Gazette*]. Temporary pension of seventy pounds per annum, commencing 7 April 1813, 'for wounds' received at Badajoz [*1818 Pension Return*, pp. 12–13].

+SINGER, James, Capt., 7th Foot: Capt., 7th Foot, 14 Nov. 1805. Slightly wounded, Albuera, 16 May 1811 [*London Gazette*]. Killed, storming of Badajoz, 6 April 1812 [*London Gazette*]. *Haythornthwaite, Die Hard*, p. 186 [Badajoz: 'Next morning the staff officer quoted above [Harry Smith] found

a party of 7th Fuzileers at work, so inquired of his friends; when he mentioned Major Singer they said, "We are throwing the last shovels of earth upon his grave," the edge of which, the spot where he fell, was still marked with his blood.']. *Harry Smith*, pp. 66–7.

SINGLETON, John, Ensign/Lt., 61st Foot: *1829 Statement of Service*: 'Born in Wokingham, Berks., 5th November 1793. Aged Sixteen years, 2 Months, on his first Entrance into the Army. Ensign, 60th Regt., 11th Jany. 1810. Ensign, 61st Regt., June 1810 [Army List gives 5 April 1810]. Lieutenant, 61st Regt., 24th July 1812. Lieut., 44th Regt., Half Pay, July 1816, Exchanged to ½ pay on a/c of private affairs... Lieut., 62nd Foot, 20th April 1820. Captain, 62nd, 15th April 1824. Major, 62nd, 10th Jany. 1828.' *Battles, sieges and campaigns*: 'Present at the Siege of the Forts of Salamanca, 20th June 1812... Present at the Battle of Salamanca 22d July 1812' *Wounds received in action*: 'Slightly wounded at the Siege of the Forts of Salamanca, 20th June 1812. Twice Severely wounded at the Battle of Salamanca 22d July 1812. Received a Years pay and a permanent pension as Ensign of £50 per Annum.' *Service abroad*: '1811 to 1813, Spain and Portugal. 1822 to 1823, North America.' [PRO: WO 25/797 f2]. Severely wounded, Salamanca, 22 July 1812 [*London Gazette*]. MGS.

SITWELL, Richard Staunton, Capt., 3rd Dragoons: *1829 Statement of Service for Retired Officers*: Aged fifteen on first appointment to the Army. Cornet, 3rd Dragoons, Oct. 1802; Lt., 3rd Dragoons, 4 April 1805; Capt., 3rd Dragoons, 23 Sept. 1808; Major, 3rd Dragoons, 10 July 1823; Half-pay, unattached, 2 Aug. 1826, 'at my own request from private affairs'. *Where serving when wounded*: 'Wounded in the Peninsula'. No pension. Not married. No employment. *Where generally resident during last five years*: 'In England'. [PRO: WO 25/774 f19]. Severely wounded, in operations 12–19 June 1813 [*London Gazette*]. 'R– Hamilton Sitwell' in Army List.

SKEENE, George Harwood, Ensign/Adjutant, 48th Foot: *1829 Statement of Service for Retired Officers*: Aged seventeen 'when enlisted'. 'I had been sixteen years & 4 months in the 48th Regt. (Non-Comiss: officer & Private) subsequent to my having the honor of receiving His Majesty's Commission'. Ensign and Adjutant, 48th Foot, 11 Nov. 1813; Half-pay, 1814, 'from a severe wound, which cause'd my right thigh to be amputated'. Served only eleven months on Full-pay as a commissioned officer. 'Willing [to serve], but unable from the loss of my right leg and thigh at the battle of Toulouse on the 10th April 1814'. *Where serving when wounded*: 'Toulouse in France'. *Details of pension*: Seventy pounds, commencing 11 April 1815. *Family*: Married 'at Heigham a hamlet of Norwich', 21 June 1819. *Where generally resident during last five years*: Norwich. [PRO: WO 25/773 f213].. Severely wounded, 'right leg amputated', Toulouse, 10 April 1814 (Adjutant) (1st Battn.) [*London Gazette*]. Seventy pounds per annum pension, commencing 11 April 1815, for 'loss of a leg' at Toulouse [*1818 Pension Return*, pp. 12–13].

+SKELTON, Thomas, 1st Lt., Royal Engineers: 1st Lt., Royal Engineers, 1 Aug. 1809. Died of wounds, 15 Jan. 1812. Return dated 25 Jan. 1812. [PRO: WO 25/2965].

SKENE, Alexander, Lt., 24th Foot: *1829 Statement of Service for Retired Officers*: Aged twenty-four on first appointment to the Army. Ensign, 24th Foot, 25 Feb. 1808; Lt., 24th Foot, 24 July 1809; Capt., Royal African Corps, 11 Nov. 1813; Capt., 4th Royal Veteran Battn., 10 Nov. 1814; Capt., 7th Royal Veteran Battn., Nov. 1819. 'Disabled by the loss of a leg, but willing to serve as far as he can be useful'. *Where serving when wounded*: 'at Talavera, 28 July 1809, as Lieutenant in the 24th Foot'. *Details of pension*: One hundred pounds per annum, commencing 25 Dec. 1811, 'augmented 18 June 1815'. *Family*: Married his first wife in 'Parish of Stains', 6 April 1817. They had two children, born in 1820 and 1823. He married again in 'Old Machar', 16 June 1828. *Where generally resident during last five years*: Aberdeen. [PRO: WO 25/774 f36]. Severely wounded, Talavera, 28 July 1809 ('Ensign Skene') [*London Gazette*]. *1818 Pension Return*, pp. 6–7. 'Skeene' in Army List. MGS.

SKENE, David James, Ensign/Lt., 68th Foot: *1829 Statement of Service for Retired Officers*: Aged sixteen on first appointment to the Army. Ensign, Durham Militia, until 13 Aug. 1811; Ensign, 68th Foot, 3 Oct. 1811; Lt., 68th Foot, 30 July 1813; Half-pay, 4th Dragoon Guards, 10 Dec. 1823, 'at the request of the officer being incapable of field duty by bodily injury'. 'Is desirous of service but incapable of any field duty'. *Where serving when wounded*: 'In Spain, 21 June 1813. In Spain, 31 Aug. 1813'. *Details of pension*: Seventy pounds, commencing 1 Sept. 1814. *Where generally resident during last five years*: Durham and Brighton. [PRO: WO 25/774 f33]. Severely wounded, 'in the Operations of the Army', 31 Aug. 1813 ('Lieut. Sheene') [*London Gazette*]. Slightly wounded, Vittoria, 21 June 1813 (2nd Battn.) [*London Gazette*]. Pension 'for wounds' received at Vera, 1813 [*1818 Pension Return*, pp. 16–17].

SKERRY, John, Ensign, 36th Foot: Ensign, 36th Foot, 9 Dec. 1812.

Slightly wounded, Pyrenees, 28 July 1813 [*London Gazette*]. Slightly wounded, Nivelle, 10 Nov. 1813 (1st Battn.) [*London Gazette*].

SMELLIE, Peter, Capt., 51st Foot: Capt., 51st Foot, 21 Feb. 1811. Wounded, 9 June 1811, during the second failed attempt to storm Fort San Cristoval, Badajoz. Severely wounded, siege of Badajoz, 6–11 June 1811 [*London Gazette*]. Slightly wounded, Heights of Villares, 20–22 June 1812 [*London Gazette*]. Wounded, Salamanca, 21 June 1812. *Wheeler*, p. 65 [Wounded, Badajoz, 9 June 1811, 'Smillie'], p. 87 [Wounded, Salamanca, 21 June 1812].

SMITH, Boys Jenkin, Lt., 11th Foot: *1829 Statement of Service for Retired Officers*: Aged nineteen on first appointment to the Army. Ensign, 11th Foot, 13 Oct. 1808, 'As a Volunteer from the Queen's Co. Regt. Militia'; Lt., 11th Foot, 13 Sept. 1810; Lt., 8th Veteran Battn., 24 Feb. 1820. 'Unfit for service from wounds'. *Where serving when wounded*: 'Battle of Salamanca, Spain'. *Details of pension*: seventy pounds per annum, commencing 'believed to be 23rd July 1813, being a year and a day from the date of the Wound'. *Where generally resident during last five years*: 'in Dublin, but very frequently obliged to remove for the benifit of health consequently a considerable portion of that time spent out of it'. [PRO: WO 25/774 f62]. Severely wounded, Salamanca, 22 July 1812 (1st Battn.) [*London Gazette*]. Temporary pension of seventy pounds per annum, commencing 23 July 1813, 'for wounds' received at Salamanca ('Smith, Jenkin Boys') [*1818 Pension Return*, pp. 6–7].

SMITH, Charles Hervey, Capt., 40th Foot: *1829 Statement of Service for Retired Officers*: Aged nineteen when he joined the Militia, twenty one on first appointment to the Army. Capt., Bedford Militia, 1803; Ensign, 40th Foot, May 1805; Lt., 40th Foot, '1806 or early 1807' [Army List gives 26 Dec. 1805]; Capt., 40th Foot, [26] May 1808; Capt., 36th Foot, 1814; Half-pay, Oct. 1814, by reduction; Capt., 40th Foot, 1815; Bvt. Major, Half-pay, 1816 'at the close of the year', by reduction. 'Employed since 1814 as Major of Brigade in the Western District'. *Where serving when wounded*: 'South America and subsequently Portugal, viz. Monte Video, an alarming wound in the Head. Buonos Ayres, 3 wounds, 2 severe. Vimiera, 1 severe wound. In each instance in the 40th Foot.' *Details of pension*: Seventy pounds. 'The certificate of the Medical Board bears date August 19th 1814. The Pension was issued for 1811, and subsequently'. *Family*: Married in 'Somerley, Leicestershire', 18 April 1811. Six children 'now living'. *Where generally resident during last five years*: Plymouth. [PRO: WO 25/774 f80]. Slightly wounded, Vimeiro, 21 Aug. 1808 [*London Gazette*]. MGS.

SMITH, David Augustus, Capt., 20th Foot: Lt., 20th Foot, 3 Dec. 1806; Capt., 20th Foot, 26 Aug. 1813. Severely wounded, Orthes, 27 Feb. 1814 [*London Gazette*]. Temporary pension of one hundred pounds per annum, commencing 28 Feb. 1815, 'for wounds' received at Orthes [*1818 Pension Return*, pp. 6–7].

SMITH, Harry George Wakelyn, 1st Lt., 95th Foot: 1st Lt., 95th Foot, 15 May 1805. Present at the capture of Monte Video. Slightly wounded, Coa, 24 July 1810 ('H. C. Smith') [*London Gazette*]. Capt., 95th Foot, 28 Feb. 1812; Bvt. Major, 95th Foot, 29 Sept. 1814. Served at Bladensburg and the destruction of Washington, and battle of New Orleans. Waterloo. MGS. He died in London, 12 Oct. 1860, and is buried at Whittlesea. *Simmons*, p. 78 [wounded, Coa], pp. 88, 100,

381–3 [Appendix 1, letter written in 1846 by then General Sir Harry Smith]. *Du Cane*, pp. 753, 756 [New Orleans]. *Kincaid, Random Shots*, pp. 292–8 [Following storming of Badajoz, when Kincaid assisted the future Lady Smith: 'I was conversing with a friend the day after, at the door of his tent, when we observed two ladies coming from the city, who made directly towards us... Fourteen summers had not yet passed over her youthful countenance, which was of a delicate freshness, more English than Spanish ... to look at her was to love her – and I did love her; but I never told my love, and in the meantime another, and a more impudent fellow stepped in and won her! but yet I was happy – for in him she found such a one as her loveliness and her misfortunes claimed – a man of honour, and a husband in every way worthy of her!']. *Kincaid, Random Shots*, p. 290 ['At the close of the war, when we returned to England ... the officers commanding companies on the day of inspection, viz ... Smith with a shot in the ankle']. *The Autobiography of Sir Harry Smith*, ed. G. C. Moore Smith (London, 1910), p. 31 ['I had a ball lodged in my ankle-joint, a most painful wound']. Born 1787, became Lieut.-General Sir Harry Smith Bt., died 1860. His wife was Juana Maria de los Dolores de Leon (1798–1872), theirs being probably the most famous love-story of the age. Smith became famous for service in South Africa (victor of Boomplaate) and India (victor of Aliwal); Harrismith, Ladysmith and Aliwal North in South Africa are named after him, his devoted wife, and his victory in the 1st Sikh War. Lehmann, J. H., *Remember You Are an Englishman: A Biography of Sir Harry Smith* (London, 1977).

SMITH, John, Lt., 20th Foot: Ensign, 20th Foot, 10 April 1809; Lt.

7 Oct. 1812. Slightly wounded, Pyrenees, 25 July 1813 [*London Gazette*].

+SMITH, John, Capt., 27th Foot: Capt., 27th Foot, 11 July 1805. Killed during the repulse of a sortie from Badajoz, 10 May 1811 (3rd Battn.) [*London Gazette*].

SMITH, Michael, Lt., 40th Foot: *1829 Statement of Service for Retired Officers*: Aged twenty-three on first appointment to the Army. Ensign, 44th Foot, 29 Aug. 1811; Ensign, 40th Foot, 12 Dec. 1811; Lt., 40th Foot, 23 Aug. 1813; Half-pay, 20 April 1817, by reduction. *Where serving when wounded*: 'Near Pamplona'. *Details of pension*: Fifty pounds, commencing 28 July 1814. Not married. No employment. *Where generally resident during last five years*: 'London, until September 1826; since then Newry'. [PRO: WO 25/774 f98]. Severely wounded, Pyrenees, 28 July 1813 (1st Battn.) [*London Gazette*]. Severely wounded, Toulouse, 10 April 1814 (1st Battn.) [*London Gazette*]. *1818 Pension Return*, pp. 10–11. MGS.

+SMITH, Michael, Ensign, 44th Foot: Ensign, 44th Foot, 29 Aug. 1811. Severely wounded, during 'movements of the Army' [Retreat from Burgos: Villa Muriel], 25 Oct. 1812 [*London Gazette*]. Died of wounds, 30 Oct. 1812. Return dated 25 Nov. 1812. [PRO: WO 25/2965].

+SMITH, Molyneux, Capt., 36th Foot: Capt., 36th Foot, 25 June 1803. Obituary, *The Gentleman's Magazine*, Feb. 1813, p. 182 ['Lately... At Seville, of their wounds... Major Smith of the 36th reg.']. Died, Cuellar, 21 Aug. 1812 [PRO: WO 25/2965].

SMITH, Samuel de la Cherois, Capt., 6th Foot: *1829 Statement of Service for Retired Officers*: Aged twenty-five on first appointment to the Army. Ensign, 6th Foot, 12 Jan. 1799; Lt., 6th Foot, 25 June 1803; Capt., 6th Foot, 9 March 1809; Half-pay, 25 Feb. 1816, 'on account of Wounds'. *Where serving when wounded*: 'France. Canada'. *Details of pension*: One hundred pounds, commencing 17 Sept. 1815. *Where generally resident during last five years*: 'Lisburn Ireland'. [PRO: WO 25/774 f79]. Slightly wounded, Orthes, 27 Feb. 1814 (1st Battn.) [*London Gazette*]. 'Sam. Delacherois Smith' in Army List.

SMITH, Thomas, Lt., 14th Light Dragoons: Cornet, 14th Light Dragoons, 15 May 1806. Slightly wounded, Talavera, 28 July 1809 ('Lieut.') [*London Gazette*].

SMITH, Thomas, Lt., 5th Foot; Capt., 3rd Portuguese Line: *1829 Statement of Service*: Born in Manchester, 8 July 1786. Aged eighteen 'on his first Entrance into the Army.' Ensign, 5th Foot, 1 Dec. 1804; Lt., 5th Foot, 25 Sept. 1805; Capt., 'Portuguese Service', 25 Oct. 1814; Half-pay, Portuguese Service, 25 Dec. 1826; Capt., 97th Foot, 25 March 1824, 'on formation of the 97th Regt.' *Battles, sieges and campaigns*: 'Was present as Lieut. in the 5th Foot at the Battles of Roleia 17 Aug. 1808, Vimeria 21 Aug. 1808, in the Portuguese Service at Busaco 27th Sept. 1810, Fuentes D'Onor 5th May 1811, Ciudad Rodrigo 17th Jany. 1812, 2nd Siege and Storming of Badajoz 6th April 1812, Salamanca 21st July 1812, Vittoria 21st June 1813, where I was wounded in the left thigh. Was also present at the affair of Sabugal, Villa Moreial and Passage of the Bidassoa.' *Distinguished conduct*: 'Commanded 200 of General Spry's Brigade of Portuguese at the attack of Fort Perdeleiros, Storming of Badajoz; and Volunteered to Command a detachment of 200 men of the Portuguese Service at the attack of the village of Gamara Major Battle of Vittoria.' *Wounds*

received in action: 'Wounded in the left thigh at the Battle of Vittoria on the 21st June 1813, for which I received one years pay as Captain, and a pension of £100 per annum for six years.' *Service abroad*: 'July 1808 to Decr. 1820, Spain, Portugal and France. 11 Augt. 1825 to 9 Apr. 1831, Ceylon.' *Family*: 'Unmarried.' [PRO: WO 25/804 f88]. Severely wounded, Vittoria, 21 June 1813, while serving as Capt., 3rd Portuguese Line [*London Gazette*]. In Portuguese Service April 1809 to Nov. 1813. *Challis, Portuguese Army*, p. 59.

SMITH, Thomas, Lt., 36th Foot: Lt., 36th Foot, 2 March 1809. Severely wounded, Pyrenees, 28 July 1813 [*London Gazette*].

SMITH, Thomas Lawrence, Lt., 95th Foot: *1829 Statement of Service for Retired Officers*: Aged sixteen on first appointment to the Army. 2nd Lt., 95th Foot, March 1808; 1st Lt., 95th Foot, 7 June 1809; Half-pay, March 1819, 'in consequence of Ill Health'. *Where serving when wounded*: 'Portugal, at the Bridge of the Coa 24th June 1810'. No pension. *Family*: Married in 'Whittlesea, Cambridgeshire', 24 June 1816. 'A widower since 30th September 1827'. Five children. *Title and nature of employment*: 'Barrack Master at Galway, Ireland'. *Where generally resident during last five years*: 'On my retiring to Half Pay in March 1819, I resided in the neighbourhood of Pembroke South Wales until I was appointed Barack Master in this Country in February 1824'. Signed Galway, Ireland. [PRO: WO 25/774 f 70]. Severely wounded, Coa, 24 July 1810 [*London Gazette*]. Waterloo. MGS. Died 6 April 1877. Buried in the military cemetery, Aldershot. Brother of Harry Smith of the 95th. *Simmons*, p. 78 [wounded, Coa], pp. 81, 88, 110–11 ['Lieutenant Smith, who had a ball in his leg, and was also lame']. *Cope* ['On July 7th,

1815, the army marched into Paris, and the 2nd Batt. had the honour of being the first corps which entered, Lieut. and Adjt. Thos. Smith riding in front of the Battalion, being the first British officer who entered Paris on that famous day.'].

SMITH, William Slayter, Lt., 13th Light Dragoons: *1829 Statement of Service for Retired Officers*: Aged 'between the year of 14 & 15' on first appointment to the Army. Ensign, 2nd Garrison Battn., 25 Dec. 1806; Adjutant, 2nd Garrison Battn., 16 June 1808; Lt., 2nd Garrison Battn., 17 Nov. 1808; Lt., 13th Light Dragoons, 1 Feb. 1810; Lt., '10th Hussars', 12 Nov. 1814; Cornet and Lt., 1st Life Guards, 7 June 1819; Ensign, Half-pay, 72nd Foot, 7 Nov. 1819, 'with the expectation that rest & quietness would restore my health and constitution, both of which had been much impaired by my wounds and the Services I had undergone'. *Where serving when wounded*: 'At Campo Mayor in Portugal 25th March 1811 when serving as Lieutenant in the 13th Light Dragoons'. *Detail of pension*: Seventy pounds per annum, commencing 26 March 1812. *Family*: Married in St Mary's Church, Reading, Berkshire, 30 April 1818. No children. *Title and nature of employment*: 'Adjutant to the Yorkshire Hussar Yeomanry'. *Where generally resident during last five years*: 'Ripon, Yorkshire'. [PRO: WO 25/774 f48]. 'Badly wounded', Campo Mayor, 25 March 1811 [*London Gazette*]. *1818 Pension Return*, pp. 2–3. 'William Hayter Smith' in Army List.

SMITH, William, Ensign, 31st Foot: Severely wounded, Pyrenees, 30 July 1813 [*London Gazette*].

+SMITH, William, Major, 45th Foot: Capt., 45th Foot, 25 June 1803. Killed, Busaco, 27 Sept. 1810 ('Major') (1st Battn.)[*London Gazette*].

+SMITH, William, Lt., 77th Foot: Lt., 77th Foot, 11 June 1811. Wounded, 'dangerously', storming of Ciudad Rodrigo, 19 Jan. 1812 [*London Gazette*]. Obituary, *The Gentleman's Magazine*, March 1812, p. 298 ['Feb. 4. At Gallegos, of a wound received in the storming of Ciudad Rodrigo, on the 19th of Jan. in his 24th year, Lieut. Wm. Smith, of the 77th foot. During the short time he had served in the army, he displayed qualities which endeared him to all who knew him, as a soldier and a gentleman.'].

SMITH, William, Lt., 83rd Foot: Lt., 83rd Foot, 23 March 1809. Slightly wounded, Vittoria, 21 June 1813 (2nd Battn.).

SMYTH, Charles, Capt., 95th Foot: Major, Army, 16 June 1808; Capt., 95th Foot, 4 Oct. 1809. Severely wounded, Nivelle, 10 Nov. 1813 (1st Battn.) [*London Gazette*]. Killed, Waterloo, while Major of Brigade under Major-General Pack.

SMYTH, George B., Lt., Royal Artillery: 1st Lt., Royal Artillery, 1 June 1806. Served with A Troop R. H. A. *Webber*, pp. 68, 79–80, 82 [2 Oct. 1812: 'I was quite happy in finding Smyth had recovered his good looks and never saw him in better health. The wound of a cannon shot one would fancy was a mere trifle.'], pp. 82, 87–8, 142–3.

SNODGRASS, Kenneth, Capt., 52nd Regt; Major, 13th Portuguese Line; Lt. Col., 1st Caçadores: *1829 Statement of Service for Retired Officers*: Aged eighteen on first appointment to the Army. Ensign, 90th Foot, 22 Oct. 1803; Lt., 43rd Foot, 1804; Lt., 52nd Foot, 13 Aug. 1804; Capt., 52nd Foot, 20 Oct. 1808; Bvt. Major, 52nd Foot, 21 Sept. 1813, for 'Services in the Field'; 'Effective Major', 'Attached to Portuguese Army', 24 Oct. 1814; Bvt. Lt. Col., 'Attached Portuguese Service', 21 June 1817, for 'Services in the Field'. 'Placed on Half pay to do duty with the Portuguese Army where I remained as Colonel until the Revolution in 1820 or 1821, and am now serving as Major of Brigade since 1828'. *Where serving when wounded*: 'Orthes, France'. *Details of pension*: Two hundred pounds, commencing 'about 1821'. *Family*: Married in Renfrewshire, Scotland, 30 May 1814. Six children by 1829. *Where generally resident during last five years*: 'In Great Britain'. Statement is signed and dated 'Sydney New South Wales, 20th June 1829'. Note added: 'P.S. Since filling up the above I have received an official notification from the Right Honable the Secretary at War stating that he had been pleased to recommend me to His Majesty for the Pension of Major Commanding. The letter is dated 15th October 1828'. [PRO: WO 25/774 f129]. Mentioned in Graham's report to Wellington, concerning the taking of the convent of San Bartolome, dated 18 July 1813 [17 July: '... two hundred men of the 13th Portuguese regiment, under the command of Major Snodgrass, of that regiment'] [*London Gazette*]. Slightly wounded, 'at the Siege of St Sebastian', 7–27 July 1813, while serving as Major, 13th Portuguese Line [*London Gazette*]. Slightly wounded, the Nive, 11 Dec. 1813, while serving as Lt. Col., 1st Caçadores [*London Gazette*]. Severely wounded, Orthes, 27 Feb. 1814, as Lt. Col., 1st Caçadores [*London Gazette*]. In Portuguese Service Nov. 1812 to April 1814. Gold Medal. MGS. *Challis, Portuguese Army*, p. 59. *Simmons*, p. 164. In his Statement of Service, he apparently only gave details of the wound that subsequently resulted in a pension.

SODEN, R. Conyngham, Ensign, 31st Foot: Ensign, 31st Foot, 25 Nov. 1808. Slightly wounded, Talavera, 27 July 1809 ('Sorden') [*London Gazette*].

SOMERSALL, Anthony William, Capt., 87th Foot: Capt., Army, 7 April 1808; Capt., 87th Foot, 7 July 1808. Slightly wounded, Talavera, 27 July 1809 (2nd Battn.) [*London Gazette*]. Severely wounded, Barossa, 5 March 1811 [*London Gazette*].

SOMERSET, Lord Fitzroy James Henry, Capt., 43rd Foot: Youngest son of Henry, 5th Duke of Beaufort. Lt., 4th Dragoons, 30 May 1805; Capt., Army, 5 May 1808; Capt., 43rd Foot, 18 Aug. 1808. Slightly wounded, Busaco, 27 Sept. 1810, while serving as ADC to Lord Wellington [*London Gazette*]. Lt. Col., Army, 27 April 1812. Mentioned in Wellington's Vittoria dispatch, 22 June 1813 ['I am likewise indebted much to ... Lord Fitzroy Somerset ... and the officers of my personal staff'] [*London Gazette*]. Capt. and Lt. Col., 1st Foot Guards, 25 July 1814. Waterloo. MGS. Born 1788; died, Crimea, 28 June 1855. *Dalton*, p. 9 ['Was Wellington's ADC and "right hand" throughout the campaign in Spain and Portugal. Lost his right arm at Waterloo, from a shot fired from the top of La Haye Sainte farmhouse after its capture by the French. Created Baron Raglan a month after Wellington's death. F.-M. and C.-in-C. of the British army of the Crimea in Nov., 1854. D. in the Crimea during the siege of Sebastopol, at a farmhouse overlooking the plains of Balaklava']. *Mullen*, p. 16 [Incorrectly states 'ADC to FM Lord Raglan']. Sweetman, J., *Raglan: from the Peninsula to the Crimea* (London, 1993).

SORLIE, Sholto, Lt., 68th Foot: Lt., Army, 25 April 1806; Lt., 68th Foot, 25 Dec. 1806. Slightly wounded, Vittoria, 21 June 1813 ('Sorly') (2nd Battn.) [*London Gazette*].

SPEIRS, Alexander, Lt., 39th Foot: Lt., 39th Foot, 25 Oct. 1810. Slightly wounded, Vittoria, 21 June 1813 ('Spiers') (1st Battn.) [*London Gazette*]. MGS. 'Alexander J. Spiers (or Spears)' in *Challis, Index*, p. 124.

SPENCER, Lord Charles, Lt., 52nd Foot; 1st Lt., 95th Foot: Lt., Army, 9 Sept. 1813. 1st Lt., 95th Rifles, 9 Dec. 1813. Severely wounded, the Nive, 13 Dec. 1813, while serving as ADC to Lt.-Gen. Sir W. Stewart ('52d Foot') [*London Gazette*].

SPOTTISWOODE, George, Capt., 71st Foot: *1829 Statement of Service for Retired Officers*: Aged nineteen years ten months on first appointment to the Army. Ensign, 52nd Foot, 5 Jan. 1804; Lt., 52nd Foot, 15 Aug. 1804; Capt., 71st Foot, 19 June 1806; Major, 71st Foot, 31 March 1814; Half-pay, 25 March 1816, by reduction. 'Still incapable of Active Service in consequence of wounds'. *Where serving when wounded*: 'Assault of Badajos'. *Details of pension*: One hundred pounds, commencing 6 April 1813, augmented to two hundred pounds, 18 June 1815, Not married. No employment. *Where generally resident during last five years*: 'Phoenix Park, Dublin'. [PRO: WO 25/774 f158]. Severely wounded, storming of Badajoz, 6 April 1812, while serving on the Staff as ADC to Major-General Colville [*London Gazette*]. *1818 Pension Return*, pp. 16–17.

SPRING, William Collis, Major, 57th Foot: Major, 57th Foot, 1 Sept. 1804. Slightly wounded, Albuera, 16 May 1811 (1st Battn.) [*London Gazette*].

STABLES, Henry, Capt., 1st Foot Guards: Lt. and Capt., 1st Foot Guards, 26 May 1808. Severely wounded, Barossa, 5 March 1811 [*London Gazette*].

STACK, George Fitzgerald, Lt., 24th Foot: *1829 Statement of*

Service: Born 1789, Ballyconry, Kerry, Ireland. Aged sixteen on his first entrance into the Army. Ensign, 38th Foot, 13 June 1805; Lt., 8th Garrison Battalion, 4 Dec. 1806; Lt., 24th Foot, 20 Feb. 1808; Capt., 1st Garrison Batt., 25 May 1815; Capt., 54th Foot, 10 Aug. 1815; Half Pay 14 Jan. 1819; Capt., 24th Foot, 22 July 1824; Major, 24th Foot, 26 Oct. 1835. 'Retired on Full Pay 7th Jan. 1841.' *Battles, sieges and campaigns*: 'Talavera, 27 & 28 July 1809; Busaco, 1810; Espinelle, 1811; Foys D'Aronce, 1811; Skirmishes during the Retreat of the French Army from Santerem, 1811; Seige of Cuidad Rodrigo, 1811; Repulse of the Sortie at Cuidad Rodrigo on 14 January 1811; Battle of Salamanca, 1812; Different Skirmishes on the advance to Madrid, 1812; Surrender of the Reteiro, 1812; Taking of the Hills and Hornwork before Burgos, 1812; Seige of Burgos, 1812; Storming of the Breaches at Burgos on 4 October 1812; Different Skirmishes with the Rear Guard and covering party at the Bridge over the Carrion on the Retreat from Burgos, 1812; Battle of Orthes, 1814.' *Distinguished conduct*: 'During the Retreat of the French Army from Santerem 1811, Occasionally employed as a mounted officer, Reconnoitreing carrying order &c &c. Acted as Adjutant for a considerable time & occasionally acted as Brigade Major. Ordered Home as Acting Adjutant with the 2d Battlion 24 Regt. in 1813 and returned same year to the Peninsula with a Detachment of 4 officers & 100 men under his command to join the 3d Provisional Battalion.' *Wounds received in action*: 'Slightly wounded (but not in the Returns), Talavera, the Regt. lost in killed & wounded 355 men supporting the Guards with the 48th Regt. Severe Contusion, Received a Captains years pay for Commanding the Grenadier

Company at the Storming of the Breaches of Burgos on 4 October 1812. Orthes 27 Feby. 1814, Severely wounded by a Ball which shattered the left elbow joint, the Ball could not be extracted. Orthes, 6th April, left arm amputated twice, Exfoliation of the Bone from the Shoulder Joint for the space of two years. Received a pension of £100 per annum. Constitution much impaired at that time.' *Titles, honorary distinctions and medals*: 'For Services in the Peninsula appointed Knight of the 3rd Class of the Hanoverian Guelphic Order.' *Service abroad*: '2nd March 1809 to 20 Feby. 1813, Peninsula. 2nd Dec. 1813 to 26 July 1814, Peninsula and France; 1 October 1815 to 28 Decr. 1815, Paris, Bois-de-Boulogne and Ville de Bois. 30 July 1829 to 31 Oct. 1835, Canada; 28 Jan 1839 to 7 Jan 1841, Canada.' [PRO: WO 25/789 f256]. Severely wounded, Orthes, 27 Feb. 1814 (2nd Battn.) [*London Gazette*]. MGS. *1818 Pension Return*, pp. 6–7.

STACK, Richard, Volunteer, 14th Foot: *1829 Statement of Service*: Born Tralee, Ireland, 10th June 1787. 'Aged Twenty One on his first Entrance into the Army. Volunteer, 14th Foot, Augt. 1808. Ensign, 14th Foot, 24th Jany. 1809. Lieutenant, 3rd March 1811. Captain, 45th Foot, 12th Novemr. 1827.' Note added: 'Bvt. Maj., 6 Dec. '29. Major, 15 June 1830. Died in London 31 Oct. 1840.' *Battles, sieges and campaigns*: 'Ensign 14th Foot Campaign in Spain and Battle of Corunna 16th January 1809... Three Actions at sea in November 1809, [under command of] Major Hinlock. Capture of the Isle of France 1st December 1810... Actions of 10th and 22nd and Storming Fort Cornwallis 26th August 1811... Capture of the defences of the Pirates of Sambas on the Island Borneo July 1813... Capture of the Fort of

Flatrass February 1817... In the Mahratta Campaigns 1817 and 1818... Storm of Bhurtpore 18th Jany. 1826.' *Distinguished conduct*: 'Selected to Command the Amboynese Corps at Samerang in the Island of Java in 1812 by General Gillespie.' *Wounds received in action*: 'At Corunna 16th January 1809. At the Storm of Fort Corwallis 26th August 1811. At Bhurtpore 18th Jany. 1826. One years Pay Granted. No Pension. Received £100 from the India Government for Gallant conduct in the actions in the Bay of Bengal in November 1809.' *Service abroad*: 'Augt. 1808 to Jany. 1809, Spain. June 1809 to 31 Decr. 1829, East Indies.' Note added: 'East Indies to 8 July 1837.' *Family*: Married Sarah Rice, 28 March 1814, in Berhampore, East Indies. They had four children prior to 1827. Following the death of Sarah, he remarried, this time to Caroline Frigg, 24 March 1834, St Marylebone, London.' [PRO: WO 25/793 f334].

+STAFFORD, John B., Ensign, 87th Foot: Ensign, 87th Foot, 17 Sept. 1812. Slightly wounded, Vittoria, 21 June 1813 (2nd Battn.) [*London Gazette*]. *Register of officers' effects*: Died, 10 April 1814, Bilboa. Single. Effects totalled £29. 18s. 5d. [PRO: WO 25/2964].

STAINFORTH, John, Capt., 57th Foot: *1829 Statement of Service for Retired Officers*: Aged seventeen on first appointment to the Army. Ensign, 57th Foot, 24 March 1803; Lt., 57th Foot, n.d. 'do not recollect & have no documents to refer to, it was in 1804 or 1805' [Army List gives 23 July 1803]; Capt., 57th Foot, 19 Feb. 1807; Half-pay, 11 July 1816, 'at my own request from private motives'. *Where serving when wounded:* 'Wounded Battle of Albuera, also in the Pyrenees'. *Family*: Married in York, 15 July 1822. Two children by 1829. *Where generally resident during last five*

STAINFORTH

years: York. [PRO: WO 25/775 f17]. Slightly wounded, Albuera, 16 May 1811 (1st Battn.) [*London Gazette*]. MGS.

+STAINFORTH, William George, Capt., 23rd Foot: Capt., 23rd Foot, 15 May 1806. Slightly wounded, Albuera, 16 May 1811 (1st Battn.) [*London Gazette*]. Severely wounded, storming of Badajoz, 6 April 1812 [*London Gazette*]. Killed, Pyrenees, 28 July 1813 (1st Battn.) [*London Gazette*].

STAINTON, Joseph, Ensign, 94th Foot: *1829 Statement of Service*: Born in Keswick, Cumberland, 20 May 1794. Aged sixteen on 'his first Entrance into the Army.' Ensign, 94th Foot, 24 Jan. 1811. Lt., York Chasseurs, 8 Nov. 1813. Capt., Half Pay, York Chasseurs, 2 Dec. 1819. Capt., 37th Foot, 29 March 1821. Half Pay, Sicilian Regt., 3 Sept. 1825. Capt., 95th Foot, 8 June 1826. *Battles, sieges and campaigns*: 'Fuentes d'Onor 3d & 5th May 1811, Ensign... Badajos May & June 1811, Ensign... El Bodon, 25th Septr. 1811, Ensign... Salamanca, 22d July 1812... Vittoria 21st June 1813...Capture of Guadaloupe 9th Augt. 1815, Lieut.' *Distinguished conduct*: 'Dispatch of the Action of Vittoria. Led the advance of the York Chassrs. at the attack of Guadaloupe 9th August 1815.' *Wounds received in action*: 'Wounded severely by Cannon Shot in the Right Shoulder 21st June 1813 at Vittoria, being in Command of the Grenadier Company received One years pay as Lieutenant. Permanent Pension of £50 per annum.' *Service abroad*: 'Feby. 1811 to Octr. 1813, Peninsula. Nov. 1814 to Octr. 1819, West Indies. Mar. 1821 to July 1825, Canada.' [PRO: WO 25/803 f299]. Severely wounded, Vittoria, 21 June 1813 [*London Gazette*].

+STANDLEY, William, Ensign, 44th Foot: Ensign, 44th Foot, 9 Aug.

1810. Killed, Salamanca, 22 July 1812 (2nd Battn.) [*London Gazette*].

+STANHOPE, Hon. Charles Banks, Major, 50th Foot: Capt., Army, 18 Feb. 1804; Capt., 52nd Foot, 9 June 1804; Major, 50th Foot, 21 April 1808. Killed, 'in the Army lately in Spain' (1st Battn.) [*March 1809 Army List*, p. 105]. *Blakeney*, p. 121 [Corunna: 'the 50th Regiment, who were formed on the left of the village, commanded by Major Napier, and seconded by Major Stanhope, made a most desperate charge through the village [Elvina]; but Napier's impetuosity carrying him forward through some stone walls beyond the village, he was desperately wounded, and fell into the hands of the enemy; and Major Stanhope was killed. The general [Sir John Moore] cheered the regiment during this charge, crying out, "Bravo, 50th, and my two brave majors!" ']. Lengthy obituary, *The Gentleman's Magazine*, March 1809, pp. 283–4 ['It was a source of extreme mortification to Major Stanhope that he returned from Sicily and Sweden, without being able to justify, by his conduct, the expectations which his friends had naturally formed of his character. In Spain he was no longer aide-de-camp to the General under whom he served, and whom he loved with a filial affection; but was appointed, with Major [Charles] Napier, his particular friend, to the command of the fiftieth regiment. Never were men more attached to Officers than the soldiers of this regiment to their noble-minded and heroic Majors... The body of Major Napier was not found [in fact he had been taken prisoner]; but that of Major Stanhope was carried to his tent till the battle was won. His younger brother, Captain James Stanhope, who had shared in the dangers of the day as aide-de camp to General Moore, paid the last tribute of respect and sincere affection to the

528

remains of the Major. The fatal bullet had passed through the heart of the deceased; and so instantaneous must have been the death of Major Stanhope, that a sense of pain had not torn from his countenance that smile which the bravery of his soldiers and the applause of his commander had excited.'] Born 1785, the second son of Charles, 3rd Earl Stanhope, and half-brother of the famous Lady Hester Stanhope. Brother of James Hamilton Stanhope of the 1st Foot Guards. [*Burke's Peerage*].

STANHOPE, Charles George, Lt., 29th Foot: *1829 Statement of Service for Retired Officers*: Aged seventeen years eight months on first appointment to the Army. Ensign, 29th Foot, 29 Jan. 1807; Lt., 29th Foot, 3 March 1808; Capt., 4th Garrison Battn., 6 Oct. 1814; Capt., 14th Foot, 3 Nov. 1814; Capt., 29th Foot, 2 March 1815; Half-pay, 25 Oct. 1821, 'retired ... suffering at the time from the Effects of my wound'. 'In consequence of the aforesaid wound I do not think myself fit for actual service'. *Where serving when wounded*: 'Talavera in Spain & a prisoner there & in France in consequence for nearly 5 years'. *Details of pension*: 'None for the suffering under the cure of my wound for ten months. I never afterwards felt any bad effect from it for nearly ten years when a severe varicose affection took place causing much pain & soreness in the limb with occasional severe swellings and lameness & on applying for a pension so long afterwards the answer was my case did not come under the order for granting a Pension'. *Family*: Married in 'Parish of Urney Tyrone, North of Ireland', 6 Nov. 1820. One child by 1829. *Where generally resident during last five years*: 'at Urney Park near Strabane in Ireland'. [PRO: WO 25/775 f13]. Severely wounded, Talavera, 28 July 1809 [*London Gazette*]. Born

1789, youngest son of Rear-Admiral John Stanhope; became captain, died 1833; his son George Philip became 8th Earl of Chesterfield. [*Burke's Peerage*].

STANHOPE, Hon. James Hamilton, Lt. and Capt., 1st Foot Guards: Born 7 Sept. 1788. Lt. and Capt. 14 Jan. 1808. Slightly wounded, siege of Ciudad Rodrigo, 14 Jan. 1812, while serving as ADC to Lt.-Gen. Graham [*London Gazette*]. Severely wounded, 'at the Siege of St Sebastian,' 7-27 July 1813, while serving on the Staff as Assistant-Quarter-Master-General ('Major the Honourable J. Stanhope') [*London Gazette*]. Lt. Col., Army, 17 March 1814; Capt. and Lt. Col., 1st Foot Guards, 25 July 1814. Waterloo. Born 1788, third son of Charles, 3rd Earl Stanhope, brother of Charles Banks Stanhope of the 50th Foot. MGS. Died, 5 March 1825. [*Burke's Peerage*].

STANHOPE, Hon. Lincoln Edwin Robert, Major, 16th Light Dragoons: Major, 16th Light Dragoons, 11 June 1807. Slightly wounded in the shoulder, in action with the advanced post of the French army at Albergaria Nova, 10 May 1809 [*London Gazette*]. Born 1781, the second son of Charles, 3rd Earl of Harrington; became major-general; died 1840. [*Burke's Peerage*].

STANNUS, Robert, Lt., 29th Foot: Ensign, 29th Foot, 24 Jan. 1805; Lt., 29th Foot, 5 Feb. 1808. Wounded, Rolica, 17 Aug. 1808 [*London Gazette*]. Severely wounded, Talavera, 28 July 1809 ('Stanns') [*London Gazette*]. Severely wounded, Albuera, 16 May 1811 [*London Gazette*]. Capt., 29th Foot, 1 July 1813. Temporary pension of seventy pounds per annum, commencing 17 May 1812, 'for wounds' received at Talavera and Albuera [*1818 Pension Return*, pp. 8-9]. MGS. *Mullen*, p. 248 ['Wounded and taken prisoner at Roleia. Later Maj. Ret Nov 1827.'].

STANWAY, Frank, Lt., Royal Engineers: 1st Lt., Royal Engineers, 18 Nov. 1807. Slightly wounded, Talavera, 28 July 1809 [*London Gazette*]. Mentioned in Wellington's dispatch, 27 March 1812 [Storming of Fort Picurina, Badajoz, 26 March 1812: 'Major-General Kempt ... particularly mentions ... Lieutenant ... Stanway, of the Royal Engineers, who conducted the several detachments to the points of attack'] [*London Gazette*]. 2nd. Capt., Royal Engineers, 21 July 1813. Waterloo. Died, Limerick, 9 Dec. 1832. *Rice Jones*, pp. 7, 11 ['Lisbon, April 5, 1809... Lt. Stanway, a very young officer of ours'], pp. 29–31 ['Abrantes, June 17th, 1809... On the 10th instant the French endeavoured to force the Bridge of Alcantara, a town in Spain about 50 or 60 miles off, upon the river Tagus; our people blew up the bridge by a mine which Lt. Stanway of our Corps had prepared, and which, luckily for him succeeded'], pp. 30–1, 37 ['Friday, 28th July [1809]... Stanway was slightly wounded in the belly'], p. 38 ['Lt. Stanway was struck by a ball which spent itself in passing thro' his horse'].

+STAPLETON, Henry, Lt., 68th Foot: Ensign, 68th Foot, 28 July 1808; Lt., 68th Foot, 9 Nov. 1809. Severely wounded, 'in Action with the Enemy', 23 Feb. 1814, 'since dead' ('Stapylton') [*London Gazette*]. Died of wounds, 26 Feb. 1814. Return dated March 1814. [PRO: WO 25/2965]. *Register of officers' effects*: 'Stapylton'. Died of wounds, Agarve, France, 25 Feb. 1814. Single. Effects totalled £19. 15s. 6d. [PRO: WO 25/2964]. *Hurt*, p. 80 ['Lt. Hy. Stapylton, D.O.W., Gave D'Oloron, Feb. 23 [1814]']. Mentioned in the obituary of James U. M. Leith, *The Aberdeen Journal*, Wednesday 30 March 1814 ['... on the 23d ult ... in front of Perion-

hasse ... [Leith] received the fatal shot ... allowing him only time to say to Lieutenant Stapleton, who was following him: "Lead on, Stapleton, I am no more;" and who in emulating his noble example, is but too likely to share his fate, having received a wound immediately after, which I much fear will prove mortal.'].

+STARKENFELS, La Roche de, Capt., 1st Line Battn. K.G.L.: Capt., 1st Line Battn. K.G.L., 5 Nov. 1803. Mentioned in Wellington's Ciudad Rodrigo dispatch, 20 Jan. 1812 ['In my dispatch of the 15th, I reported to your Lordship the attack of the Convent of Santa Cruz... The first-mentioned enterprise was performed by Captain Laroche de Stackenfels, of the 1st Line Battalion King's German Legion'] [*London Gazette*, 5 Feb. 1812]. Wounded, 'dangerously', siege of Burgos, 18 Oct. 1812 ('Capt. Laroche') [*London Gazette*]. Died of wounds, 31 Oct. 1812. Return dated 25 Nov. 1812. [PRO: WO 25/2965]. *Beamish*, vol. II, p. 637 [Died 'at Arevalo in Spain, 31st Oct. 1812, of the wounds he received before the castle of Burgos, 18th October 1812.']. Gold Medal.

+STAVELEY, Francis., Lt., 4th Foot: Lt., 4th Foot, 22 Oct. 1804 [Army List gives 'T. Staveley']. Killed, storming of Badajoz, 6 April 1812 ('Stavely') (1st Battn.) [*London Gazette*].

STAVELEY, John, Lt., 4th Foot: Lt., 4th Foot, 9 March 1809. Slightly wounded, the Nive, 11 Dec. 1813 ('Stavely') (1st Battn.) [*London Gazette*].

STAVELY, William, Lt., Royal Staff Corps: *1829 Statement of Service for Retired Officers*: Aged fourteen on first appointment to the Army. 'Lt., 2nd Battn. Caithness Legion, June 1798; Ensign, 1st Battn. Caithness Legion, 1799; Lt., Caithness

Volunteers, 1803; Capt., Caithness Volunteers; Ensign, Royal Staff Corps, 14 June 1804; Lt., Royal Staff Corps, 1808 [Army List gives 21 April 1808]; Capt., Royal African Corps, 1813; Deputy Assistant Quarter Master General, 1813, "Peninsula, France"; D.A.Q.M.G., 1814, Canada; Bvt. Major, 1814; Capt., Royal Staff Corps, 12 Jan. 1815; Bvt. Lt. Col., 18 June 1825; Capt., Half-pay, unattached, 29 Sept. 1825; D.Q.M.G., Half-pay, 29 Sept. 1825, "Mauritius" '. *Where serving when wounded*: 'Spain, France'. No pension. *Family*: 'Married in Boulogne sur Mer, re-married at Hythe in Kent, 23 Jan. 1817'. *Title and nature of employment*: 'Director of Roads & Bridges at Mauritius'. *Where generally resident during last five years*: Mauritius. [PRO: WO 25/775 f161]. Slightly wounded, storming of Ciudad Rodrigo, 19 Jan. 1812 [*London Gazette*] Waterloo. Major-General, 9 Nov. 1846. CB. MGS. Died, March 1854.

STAWELL, James, Capt., 53rd Foot: Capt., Army, 18 June 1800; Capt., 53rd Foot, 28 Aug. 1806. Slightly wounded, Talavera, 28 July 1809 ('Stowell') (2nd Battn.) [*London Gazette*].

STEEL, William R., Lt./Adjutant, 48th Foot: Lt., 48th Foot, 16 June 1808. Adjutant, 48th Foot, 16 Feb. 1809. Slightly wounded, Albuera, 16 May 1811 ('Steele') [*London Gazette*]. MGS.

STEELE, Alexander, Lt., 43rd Foot: *1829 Statement of Service for Retired Officers*: Aged eighteen on joining the militia, nineteen on first appointment to the Army. Ensign, 1st West York Militia, n.d.; Lt., 1st West York Militia, n.d.; Ensign, 43rd Foot, 1809 [Army List gives 14 Dec.]; Lt., 43rd Foot, n.d. [Army List gives 7 Nov. 1811]; Half-pay, 28th Foot, n.d. [1822]. Served fourteen years on Full-pay. *Where*

serving when wounded: 'Peninsula.' *Details of pension*: 'None. Wounded three times once so seriously that I shall never have the same use of my leg'. *Family*: Married in Dublin, 13 Jan. 1823. Recorded that 'My Wife has three children'. *Title and nature of employment*: 'Barrack Master of Belfast'. *Where generally resident during last five years*: Belfast. [PRO: WO 25/775 f97]. Slightly wounded, Nivelle, 10 Nov. 1813 (1st Battn.) [*London Gazette*]. Severely wounded, in a skirmish near Bayonne involving advancement of outposts of the Light Division, 23 Nov. 1813 (1st Battn.) [*London Gazette*].

+STEELE, Denton, Lt., 66th Foot: Lt., 66th Foot, 21 Sept. 1808. Severely wounded, Talavera, 28 July 1809 ('Steel') (2nd Battn.) [*London Gazette*]. Obituary, *The Gentleman's Magazine*, Oct. 1809, p. 984 ['Sept... Lieutenants Steel and Humbly, of the 66th Foot. These officers were returned severely wounded in the battle of Talavera.']. Mentioned in his father's (Capt. John Steele, 88th Foot) *1829 Statement of Service for Retired Officers*: 'my first marriage, by which I had Six children, three sons, & three Daughters, the Sons all in the service, the eldest died in the East Indies from Climate, the second fell at the Battle of Talavera Lt. in the 66th Regt.' [PRO: WO 25/775 f117].

STEELE, James, Lt., 27th Foot: Lt., 27th Foot, 11 Feb. 1806. Recorded as 'missing', Heights of Ordal, 12/13th Sept. 1813 (2nd Battn.) [*London Gazette*]. Recorded as 'wounded and prisoner', Heights of Ordon, 12/13 Sept. 1813, in revised list [*London Gazette*].

STEIGER, Rodolphe, Lt., Watteville's Regt.; Capt., 23rd Portuguese Line: *1829 Statement of Service for Retired Officers*: Aged sixteen years five months on first appointment to the Army. Ensign, 2nd Light Battn. K.G.L., May 1806; Lt., de Watteville's Regt., 9 July 1807; Capt., 23rd Portuguese Line, 21 Jan. 1813; Capt., 'in the British Army & to serve with the Portuguese Army', 25 Oct. 1815; Half-pay, 25 March 1816, 'at my own request from ill health in consequence of wounds received in action'. *Where serving when wounded*: 'In the Peninsula with the Army of Field Marshal the Duke of Wellington as Captain in the 23rd Portug. Infy.' *Details of pension*: One hundred pounds per annum, commencing 19 Dec. 1819. *Family*: Married in 'Serriere near Neuchatel', 25 Sept. 1815. Five children by 1829. *Title and nature of employment*: 'Prefect of Interlaken Canton de Berne in Switzerland'. *Where generally resident during last five years*: 'Interlaken'. [PRO: WO 25/775 f45]. Slightly wounded, Pyrenees, 25–28 July 1813, as Capt., 23rd Portuguese Line [*London Gazette*]. In Portuguese Service Jan. 1813 to April 1814. MGS. *Challis, Portuguese Army*, p. 59.

STEPHENS, Henry William, Capt., 66th Foot: *1829 Statement of Service for Retired Officers*: Aged twenty-two on first appointment to the Army. 'Having previously served 5 years in the Wexford Militia, & was holding the rank of Captain Lieut. in that corps, when, on application to H.R.H. The Duke of York, was appointed to an Ensigncy in the line'. Ensign, 63rd Foot, Aug. 1804; Lt., 53rd Foot, June 1805; Lt., 45th Foot, July 1805; Adjutant, 45th Foot, Oct. 1806; Capt., 66th Foot, 26 Feb. 1807; Capt., 6th Foot, 16 Nov. 1815; Half-pay, 24 Feb. 1816, by reduction. 'General ill health, & the nature of my wound, which rendered riding on horseback painful and dangerous, prevented me from applying to be reinstated on full pay at the time of the reduction of my Battalion. The same difficulties still existing, I do not feel

that I am equal to any further service at present.' *Where serving when wounded*: 'Was very severely wounded at Talavera while, as second in command of the Battn., doing duty as Field officer by order of M. Genl. (now Genl. Lord) Hill, issued immediately after the passage of the Douro, & being taken prisoner was detained in France until the end of the war.' *Details of pension*: One hundred pounds, commencing 1811. *Family*: Married in 'Hitcham, Bucks.', 30 July 1821. One child by 1829. *Where generally resident during last five years*: 'Bishops Teignton near Chudleigh, Devon'. [PRO: WO 25/775 f103]. MGS.

+STEPHENS, Maurice, Lt., 51st Foot: Lt., 51st Foot, 7 Dec. 1809. Killed, Nivelle, 10 Nov. 1813 [*London Gazette*].

STEPHENS, Thomas, Lt., 11th Foot: *1829 Statement of Service*: 'Born in the County of the City of Dublin, May 13th 1787. Aged 19 years on his first Entrance into the Army. Ensign, 7th Garrn. Battn., 18th Novr. 1806. Ensign, 5th Foot, 1807, Removed by memorials. Lieutenant, 11th Foot, [18] August 1808. Captain, 11th Foot, 23rd Decr. 1813. Half Pay, 25th March 1815, by reduction of 2d Battn. in Gibraltar. Captain, 49th Foot, 4th Decr. 1817.' *Battles, sieges and campaigns*: 'Expeditn. to Walcheren, July 1809... Siege of Flushing. Peninsula & France... 1810. March. Arrived. Sept 27th, Battle of Busaco. 1811. April. Siege of Almeida. May 3d & 5th Battle of Fuentes. 1812. June. Storming Forts at Salamanca. July 22d Battle of Salamanca. Octr. Siege of Burgos. 25th Action of Cabecon. 1813. May 21 Battle of Vittoria. Siege of Pampelona. July Battles of Pyrenees. Novr. 10th Battle of Nivelle. Decr. 12th Battle of Nive. 1814. Feby. 27th Battle of Ortes. April 10th Battle of Toulouse. *Many* minor affairs not worth particularizing.' *Wounds received in action*: 'Returned severely wounded (being shot through the thigh) at the Battle of Salamanca on the 22d July 1812. Received one years pay as Captain being in Command of a Company when wounded.' *Service abroad*: July 1809 to the return of Expedition from Walcheren, Walchern. March 1810 to the return of the Army after peace of Toulouse, Peninsula and France. Augt. 1814 to April 1815, Gibraltar. December 1824 to December 1828, Cape of Good Hope. December 1828 to Present time, India.' Note added: '12 Decr. 28 to 5 April 40, India. 6 April 40 to 29 July 42, at sea & Expedition in China.' *Family*: Married Ellen Shewin, '15 Nov. 1831' [sic], in Dublin. According to the Statement, the couple had one daughter, born 25 Oct. 1819. Presumably the date of marriage is incorrect, as Stephens was stationed in India at that time, so it is unlikely he could be married in Dublin. [PRO: WO 25/794 f252]. Severely wounded, Salamanca, 22 July 1812 ('Stevens') [*London Gazette*].

STEPHENS, William, Capt., 3rd Foot: Capt., Army, 30 Nov. 1806; Capt., 3rd Foot, 19 Nov. 1807. Severely wounded and taken prisoner, Albuera, 16 May 1811 ('Stevens') [*London Gazette*].

STEPHENS, W. H., Capt., 66th Foot: Capt., 66th Foot, 26 Feb. 1807. One hundred pounds per annum pension, commencing 25 Dec. 1811, 'for wounds' received at Talavera, 1809 [*1818 Pension Return*, pp. 16–17]. MGS.

STEPHENSON, Arthur J., Lt., 83rd Foot: Lt., Army, 23 March 1807; Lt., 85th Foot, 16 Nov. 1809; Lt., 83rd Foot, 25 Jan. 1813. Slightly wounded, Orthes, 27 Feb. 1814 ('A. Stevenson') (2nd Battn.) [*London Gazette*].

STEPHENSON, John, Lt., 43rd Foot: *1829 Statement of Service*: Born Dec. 1788, London. Aged nineteen years and five months on his first entrance into the Army. Ensign, 43rd Foot, May 1808; Lt. 25 May 1809; Lt., 6th Dragoon Guards, 28 Feb. 1812; Capt. 27 July 1815; Major 29 Jan. 1824. *Battles, sieges and campaigns*: 'Vimieria 21st August 1808. Corunna January 1809.' *Wounds received in action*: 'Severely wounded at Cabeza Negra 24th July 1810, under General Sir Robt. Crawford.' *Service abroad*: 'July 1808 to Jany. 1809, Peninsula. March 1809 to Decr. 1810, Peninsula.' *Family*: Married Catherine Isabella Hay, Oct. 1813, Philipstown near Dundalk. They had one child prior to her death. He married his second wife, Ann Burrell, Sept. 1820, Newcastle Upon Tyne, and had a further three children prior to 1830. [PRO: WO 25/781 f164]. Severely wounded, Coa, 24 July 1810 ('Stevenson') [*London Gazette*]. MGS.

STERLING, George, Lt., 9th Foot: Lt., 9th Foot, 19 Oct. 1808. Severely wounded, Crossing the Bidassoa, 7/9 Oct. 1813 (1st Battn.) [*London Gazette*]. MGS.

+STERNE, John H., Lt., 60th Foot: Lt., 60th Foot, 17 Feb. 1810. Killed, storming of Badajoz, 6 April 1812 [*London Gazette*].

+STERNFELD, George von, Capt., Duke of Brunswick Oels' Corps (Infantry): Capt., Duke of Brunswick Oels' Corps, Infantry, 25 Sept. 1809. Killed, during 'movements of the Army' [Retreat from Burgos: Villa Muriel], 25 Oct. 1812 ('Sternfeldt') [*London Gazette*].

STEWART, Alexander, Lt., 42nd Foot: Lt., 42nd Foot, 27 Dec. 1810. Severely wounded, Toulouse, 10 April 1814 (1st Battn.) [*London Gazette*]. Temporary pension of seventy pounds per annum, commencing 11 April 1814, 'for a wound' received at Toulouse [*1818 Pension Return*, pp. 12–13].

STEWART, Archibald, Lt., 95th Foot: 1st Lt., 95th Foot, 2 Oct. 1809. Slightly wounded, storming of Badajoz, 6 April 1812 (3rd Battn.) [*London Gazette*]. Waterloo. *Simmons*, p. 232 [storming of Badajoz].

STEWART, Charles, Lt., 71st Foot: *1829 Statement of Service*: 'Born Callert, Inverness, 24th March 1788. Ensign, 71st Regt., 24th March 1808. Lieutenant, 71st Regt., 29th Decr. 1808. Captain, 71st Foot, 27th July 1820.' *Battles, sieges and campaigns*: 'Tobral October 1810... Fuentes d'Onor 3d 4th & 5th May 1811... Arroya de Molino... Almaraz 19th May 1812... Waterloo 18th June 1815.' *Wounds received in action*: 'Slightly wounded at Fuentes d'Onor, received no Pay or Pension.' *Titles, honorary distinctions and medals*: 'Waterloo Medal.' *Service abroad*: 28 Sept. 1810 to 12 June 1813, Spain & Portugal. 15th April 1815 to 31 Octr. 1818, Netherlands & France. 24th June 1824 to 20th June 1830, Canada.' [PRO: WO 25/799 f13]. Waterloo. MGS. Died, 24 Dec. 1851.

STEWART, Duncan, Lt., 42nd Foot: Lt., 42nd Foot, 1 Jan. 1807. Severely wounded, Orthes, 27 Feb. 1814 (1st Battn.) [*London Gazette*]. Wounded, Waterloo. MGS.

+STEWART, George, Capt., 42nd Foot: Capt., 42nd Foot, 3 March 1808. Killed, the Nive, 9 Dec. 1813 (1st Battn.) [*London Gazette*]. Obituary, *The Gentleman's Magazine*, Feb. 1814, p. 198 ['Dec. 9. In action with the Enemy at Bayonne, in his 26th year, Capt. G. Stewart, 42d reg.; an excellent officer, and a most sincere and valuable friend.']. *Anton*, pp. 88–9 [near Ustritz, 9 Dec. 1813: 'Towards the close of the day, the enemy retired upon a farm-house situated on a commanding eminence, having some of the adjoining fields enclosed by low dry-stone walls and quickset hedges, behind which they appeared in considerable force, supported by some artillery. In dislodging these troops, Captain George Stewart and Lieutenant James Stewart, both of the light company, were killed on the spot'].

STEWART, George, Lt., 61st Foot: Lt., 61st Foot, 15 Dec. 1813. Severely wounded, Toulouse, 10 April 1814 (1st Battn.) [*London Gazette*].

STEWART, George Charles, Lt., 88th Foot: Ensign, 88th Foot, 9 May 1811. Severely wounded, Orthes, 27 Feb. 1814 ('Lieutenant C. G. Stewart') [*London Gazette*]. Lt., 88th Foot, 20 April 1814.

STEWART, Gilbert, Lt., 61st Foot: Lt., 61st Foot, 6 Nov. 1806. Slightly wounded, siege of Burgos, 20–26 Sept. 1812, while serving as Acting Engineer [*London Gazette*]. One pension for one hundred pounds per annum, commencing 23 Sept. 1813, for 'loss of an eye' at Burgos; another, also for one hundred pounds per annum, commencing 23 Sept. 1813, 'for other wounds' at Burgos [*1818 Pension Return*, pp. 16–17].

STEWART, James, Capt., 1st Foot: Capt., 1st Foot, 3 Feb. 1810. Slightly wounded, 'in the assault and capture of the exterior line of the castle of Burgos on the evening of the 4th October, 1812', while serving as Acting Engineer [*London Gazette*]. Slightly wounded, 'at the Siege of St Sebastian,' 7–27 July 1813 (3rd Battn.) [*London Gazette*]. MGS.

STEWART, James, Lt., 11th Foot: Lt., 11th Foot, 18 Feb. 1811. Slightly wounded, Salamanca, 22 July 1812 (1st Battn.) [*London Gazette*].

+STEWART, James, Lt., 42nd Foot: Lt., 42nd Foot, 21 June 1810. Slightly wounded, storming of Fort St Michael, 19 Sept. 1812 (1st Battn.) [*London Gazette*]. Killed, the Nive, 9 Dec. 1813 (1st Battn.) [*London Gazette*]. *Anton*, pp. 88–9 [see George Stewart].

STEWART, James, Ensign, 45th Foot: Ensign, 45th Foot, 18 Oct. 1810. Slightly wounded, storming of Badajoz, 6 April 1812 [*London Gazette*].

STEWART, James, Capt., 82nd Foot: Capt., 82nd Foot, 9 Aug. 1810. Slightly wounded, Barossa, 5 March 1811 (2nd Battn.) [*London Gazette*].

STEWART, James, Lt., 88th Foot: *1829 Statement of Service for Retired Officers*: Aged twenty-one on first appointment to the Army. Ensign, 69th Foot, 12 Jan. 1809; Lt., 88th Foot, 23 Nov. 1809; Half-pay, 'June or July 1819', 'at my own request, not from private motives but from ill health, arising solely from severe Wounds'. *Where serving when wounded*: 'At Badajoz 6th April 1812 at the Escalade with the Flank Compaies 88th Foot on which occasion I had my left arm shattered, it is now nine inches shorter than the right one. & at Orthes by a musket ball through the thick of the left thigh.' *Details of pension*: 'It is my intention to forward my claims for Pension to the Right Honorable the Secretary at War, having recently received Certificates from Surgeon Johnstone 88th regiment from Corfu'. *Family*: Married in Glasgow, 26 June 1818. No children. *Where generally resident during last five years*: 'At Tyrone, Newport ... Mayo'. [PRO: WO 25/773 f153].

+STEWART, James, Lt./Adjutant, 95th Foot: 1st Lt., 95th Foot, 6 May 1805; Adjt. 27 June 1805. Mentioned in Wellington's dispatch for Barba del Puerco, 19 March 1810 ['The Adjutant Lieutenant Stewart distinguished himself.'] [*London Gazette*]. Killed, Freixeda/Frexeda, 28 March 1811. Reported killed during 'several affairs with the French Army', 18 March–7 April 1811, in Wellington's dispatch, 9 April 1811 ['Brigade-Major Stewart (Lieutenant)'] [*London Gazette*]. *Simmons*, p. 160 [killed, Freixeda, 28 March 1811: 'we had to regret the loss of a gallant fellow in Brigade-Major Stewart, who was killed on incautiously entering the town, some French soldiers firing at him quite close, from a window. I was requested to examine his wound by Colonel Beckwith, and report how he came by his death, as his head was deeply cut in the forehead and it was feared by some that when wounded he had been deliberately murdered. I gave my opinion that from a musket ball having entered his left breast, and passed through his heart as he rode forward, he had instantly fallen upon his head.']. *Leach*, p. 204–5 ['From Celerico, Massena bent his steps towards Guarda; and in following him, the advanced guard came up with, in the end of March, part of the French rear-guard near Freixadas. Colonel Beckwith directed an attack on them by a party of the 95th Rifleman, who soon drove them from a windmill where they were at work, and through the village. On this occasion our battalion sustained a loss by the death of its adjutant, Mr. Stewart. It is perhaps not too much to say, that no man in any corps ever filled the situation of adjutant better than he did, and very few half so well. He was open-hearted, manly, friendly, and independent, a most gallant and zealous officer, and much devoted to his own corps. He neither cringed to, nor worshipped any man, but did his duty manfully, and with impartiality, – two qualities inestimable in adjutants. By the soldiers he was idolised, and very justly. When his duties as adjutant did not interfere, he was amongst the first to enter into any frolic and fun; and a more jovial soul never existed.']. *Kincaid, Adventures*, pp. 29–30 [10 Nov. 1810: '... it was late in the day before we ... advanced in pursuit. In passing by the edge of a mill-pond, after dark, our adjutant and his horse tumbled in, and, as the latter had no tail to hold on by, they were both nearly drowned.'], pp. 64–5 [Frexedas, 30 March 1811 [sic]: 'We had no difficulty in tracing the enemy, by the wrecks of houses and the butchered peasantry, and overtook their rearguard, this day, busy grinding corn, in some windmills, near the village of Frexedas. As their situation offered a fair opportunity for us to reap the fruits of their labours, we immediately attacked and drove them from it, and, after securing what we wanted, we withdrew gain, across the valley... The only person we had hit in this affair was our adjutant, Mr. Stewart, who was shot through the head from a window. He was a gallant soldier, and deeply lamented. We placed his body in a chest, and buried it in front of Colonel Beckwith's quarters.']. *Brett-James, Random Shots*, pp. 151–3 [Frexedas, 28 March 1811: '[He] was a public loss, for he was a shrewd, active, and intelligent officer; a gallant soldier, and a safe, jovial, and honourable companion. I was not one of the party engaged on that occasion, but with many of my brother officers, watched their proceedings with my spy-glass from the church-yard of Alverca. Our rejoicings on the flight of the enemy were quickly turned into mourning by observing in the procession of our returning victorious party, the gallant adjutant's well-known bay horse with a dead body laid across the saddle. We at first indulged in the hope that he had given it to the use of some more humble comrade; but long ere they reached the

village we became satisfied that the horse was the bearer of the inanimate remains of his unfortunate master, who but an hour before had left us in all the vigour of health, hope, and manhood. At dawn of day on the following morning the officers composing the advanced guard, dragoons, artillery, and riflemen, were seen voluntarily assembled in front of Sir Sidney Beckwith''s quarters, and the body, placed in a wooden chest, was brought out and buried there amid the deep but silent grief of the spectators.'].

STEWART, John, Assistant Surgeon, 42nd Foot: *1829 Statement of Service for Retired Officers*: Aged twenty-one on first appointment to the Army. Assistant Surgeon, 38th Foot, 4 May 1809; Assistant Surgeon, 42nd Foot, 20 July 1809; Half-pay, n.d. [1818], by reduction. Served nineteen and a half years on full pay. 'Being ruptured not desirous of service'. *Where serving when wounded*: 'Battle of Tholouse'. *Details of pension*: Fifty pounds per annum, commencing 11 April 1815, increased to seventy pounds per annum on 25 Sept. 1816. *Family*: Married in Stirling, 29 Dec. 1818. Five children by 1829. *Where generally resident during last five years*: Perth. [PRO: WO 25/775 f114]. Waterloo. Died, Perth, 2 Jan. 1837.

+STEWART, John, Major, 95th Foot: Major, 95th Foot, 10 Dec. 1807. Severely wounded, Cazal Nova, 14 March 1811 (1st Battn.) [*London Gazette*]. Died of wounds, 16 March 1811. Return dated 25 March 1811. [PRO: WO 25/2965]. *Simmons*, pp. 140, 142, 143 [wounded, Cazal Nova: 'a fine gallant fellow, who commanded the attack ... Major Stewart, as many others have done, asked me if he was mortally wounded. I told him he was. He thanked me, and died the day following.'], pp. 154–5. *Leach*, p. 203

[March 1811: 'During the operations of the last few days, our corps had to regret the loss of many of its members. Amongst the number must not be omitted the name of Major Stewart, who commanded one wing of our 1st battalion, as the head of which he fell, whilst gallantly leading it to the attack. By his death the regiment was deprived of an officer who thoroughly understood the command of light troops, and was quite at home at outpost duty. He had a quick and accurate eye in taking advantage of ground, was devoted to the particular nature of our service, and his mind soared far above the uninteresting minutiae of barrack-yard drill – the exact distance from button to button on the soldier's jacket, the widst of his leather stock, and other matters of the kind, which in too many regiments are considered of vital importance.']. *Kincaid, Random Shots*, p. 137 [Casal Nova, 14 March 1811: 'Our general of division was on leave of absence in England during this important period, and it was our curse in the interim to fall into the hands successively of two or three of the worthiest and best men, but whose only claims to distinction as officers was their sheet of parchment. The consequence was ... on the occasion referred to we were the whole day battering our brains out against stone walls at a great sacrifice of life, whereas, had we waited with common prudence ... the whole of the loss would have been on the other side, but as it was, I am afraid that although we carried our point we were the greatest sufferers. Our battalion had to lament the loss of two very valuable officers on that occasion, Major Stewart and Lieutenant Strode.'].

STEWART, Ralph Smyth, Lt., 45th Foot: *1829 Statement of Service for Retired Officers*: Aged seventeen on first appointment to the Army.

Ensign, 45th Foot, 2 March 1812; Lt., 45th Foot, 1 April 1813; Half-pay, 11 Feb. 1814, by reduction. 'I was wounded through the Chest in such a manner as to raise one of my shoulders half an inch higher than the other, and subsequently the flesh has wasted off my arm which is now fixed to the side. Could not wear uniform without inducing severe inflammation in the parts wounded, and it is for these reasons I am not desirous of service'. *Where serving when wounded*: 'Orthez, South of France'. *Details of pension*: Seventy pounds per annum, commencing 28 Feb. 1815. *Title and nature of employment*: 'Barrack Master in charge of the public buildings and Barrack stores at Tobago. Also private Secretary to the Governor, but the situation has been recently done away with'. *Where generally resident during last five years*: 'University of Edinburgh and Tobago'. [PRO: WO 25/775 f178]. Severely wounded, Orthes, 27 Feb. 1814 (1st Battn.) [*London Gazette*]. *1818 Pension Return*, pp. 12–13.

STEWART, Robert, Lt., 91st Foot: *1829 Statement of Service for Retired Officers*: Aged seventeen on first appointment to the Army. Ensign, 91st Foot, 31 Aug. 1805; Lt., 91st Foot, 16 April 1808 [Army List gives 12 May 1808]; Capt., 91st Foot, 27 April 1820; Half-pay, n.d. [1826]. Served twenty-one years on Full-pay. *Where serving when wounded*: 'With the Army under the Duke of Wellington, Spain'. *Details of pension*: Seventy pounds, commencing 1820. *Family*: Married in Edinburgh, 27 Sept. 1825. One child by 1829. No employment. [PRO: WO 25/775 f76]. Slightly wounded, Pyrenees, 28 July 1813 (1st Battn.) [*London Gazette*]. MGS.

STEWART, Roger, Lt., 42nd Foot: Lt., 42nd Foot, 11 July 1811. Severely wounded, Toulouse, 10 April 1814

(1st Battn.) [*London Gazette*]. Waterloo. Died, 1833, while serving in the Royal African Corps.

STEWART, W., Lt., 88th Foot: Severely wounded, storming of Badajoz, 6 April 1812 (1st Battn.) [*London Gazette*].

STEWART, Hon. William, Major-General: Colonel 2 April 1801; Major-General 25 April 1808; Colonel commanding 95th Foot, 31 Aug. 1809. Slightly wounded, Albuera, 16 May 1811 [*London Gazette*]. Severely wounded, Pyrenees, 25 July 1813 [*London Gazette*]. *Sherer*, [After Albuera, at Almendralejo: 'We found three hundred French soldiers, all wounded, who had been left in a convent, and recommended to our protection... The Hon. William Stewart, our division general, paid great attention to such of the enemy as were left in Almendralojoz, he almost daily visited their hospitals, and satisfied himself, by personal inquiries, whether they were properly taken care of. I have more than once been present at these visits, and the gratitude of these poor fellows was strongly pictured on their countenances, and in every thing they said.']. Gold Medal. Born 1774, fourth son of John, 7th Earl of Galloway; instrumental (with Coote Manningham) in the formation of the Experimental Rifle Corps, later 95th, which he commanded at Ferrol and Copenhagen. Became lieutenant-general, died 1827. Very popular with the men under his command, he rejoiced in the nickname 'Auld Grog Willie' from his issuance of extra rations of rum.

STEWART, William, Capt., 30th Foot: Capt., 30th Foot, 21 Feb. 1811. Severely wounded, Pyrenees, 25 July 1813, while serving as on Staff as Brigade-Major [*London Gazette*]. Temporary pension of one hundred pounds per annum, commencing 26 July 1814, 'for wounds' received at Pampeluna, 1813 [*1818 Pension Return*, pp. 8-9]. MGS.

+STEWART, William, Ensign, 50th Foot: Ensign, 50th Foot, 17 March 1808. Killed, 'in the Army lately in Spain' (1st Battn.) [*March 1809 Army List*, p. 105]. *Regimental Muster*, 1st Battn., 25 Dec. 1808– 24 March 1809: 'Dead at Corunna 24 Feb.' [PRO: WO 12/6113].

STIBBERT, Thomas, Capt. and Lt. Col., Coldstream Guards: Ensign, 1st Foot, 12 May 1790. Ensign, Coldstream Guards, 23 Jan. 1793. Lt. and Capt., Coldstream Guards, 5 Nov. 1794; Capt. and Lt. Col., Coldstream Guards, 25 June 1803. Wounded, 'severely but not dangerously', Talavera, 28 July 1809 [*London Gazette*].

STILWELL, John, 2nd Lt., 95th Foot: 2nd Lt., 95th Foot, 12 Oct. 1809; 1st Lt., 95th Foot, 26 Sept. 1811. Slightly wounded, in a skirmish near Bayonne involving advancement of outposts of the Light Division ('Lieutenant John Sitwell') (1st Battn.) [*London Gazette*]. Killed at Waterloo. Supposed to be the illegitimate son of the Duke of York. *Du Cane*, p. 755 [Vittoria: 'an officer named Stillwell [sic], said to have been a natural son of the Duke of York, who went in the regiment by the name of Scamp, seeing a carriage abandoned, jumped in to see what it might contain, when an officer of rank rode up and asked what he was doing there. "I'm looking for papers, sir," said Scamp. "Go back to your regiment at once, sir," which order was, of course, obeyed; but Scamp went back again very soon; when the staff officer had gone away, and found some plunder.'], p. 757 [Waterloo].

+STOKES, James M., 1st Lt., 95th Foot: 2nd Lt., 95th Foot, 20 April

1809; 1st Lt., 95th Foot, 2 May 1811. Killed, storming of Badajoz, 6 April 1812 [*London Gazette*]. *Simmons*, p. 135 ['Lieutenant Stokes, a friend of mine'], p. 226 [Storming of Fort Picurina, 26 March 1812: 'A storming party was ordered a little after dark, and part of our working party, under Lieutenant Stokes, was ordered to carry the ladders to mount the walls. He was, after placing the ladders, the first in the place.'], p. 232 [Killed].

STOLTE, William, Lt./Capt., 2nd Light Battn. K.G.L.: *1829 Statement of Service for Retired Officers*: Aged thirty-five on first appointment to the Army. Lt., 2nd Light Battn. K.G.L., 21 April 1805; Capt., 2nd Light Battn. K.G.L., 24 April 1811; Half-pay, 25 Feb. 1816, by reduction. *Where serving when wounded*: 'In King's German Legion in the Battle of Buzaco & Badajoz (Peninsula)'. No pension. *Family*: Married in Lingen, Hanover, 6 Aug. 1819. Five children by 1829. No employment. *Where generally resident during last five years*: Emden. [PRO: WO 25/775 f92]. Severely wounded, Busaco, 27 Sept. 1810 (2nd Line Battn.) [*London Gazette*]. Served in Peninsula 1808–14. Waterloo. *Beamish*, vol. II, p. 567 ['severely wounded, 27th Sept. 1810, at Busaco.'].

STOPFORD, Hon. Edward, Major-General: Col., 3rd Foot Guards, 25 April 1808; Major-General 4 June 1811. Slightly wounded, sortie from Bayonne, 14 April 1814 [*London Gazette*]. Report of Colville to Wellington, Baucaut, 14 April 1814: 'Major-General Stopford is wounded, not, I hope, severely' [*London Gazette*, 27 April 1814]. *Gronow*, p. 22 [commanding 3rd Foot Guards, Bayonne: 'the gallant Colonel Stopford']. Born 1766, second son of James, 2nd Earl of Courtown; became Lieutenant-General Sir Edward; died 1837. [*Burke's Peerage*].

STOPFORD, James, Capt., 60th Foot: Capt., Army, 17 Feb. 1808. Capt., 99th Foot, 31 March 1808; Capt., 60th Foot, 9 April 1812. Severely wounded, Nivelle, 10 Nov. 1813 (5th Battn.) [*London Gazette*]. Major, 60th Foot, 10 Feb. 1814.

+STOPFORD, Roger, Lt., 68th Foot: Lt., 68th Foot, 21 June 1810. Killed, Nivelle, 10 Nov. 1813 [*London Gazette*]. *Register of officers' effects*: Single. Effects totalled £14. 13s. 4d. [PRO: WO 25/2964].

STOREY, Robert, Ensign, 9th Foot: *1829 Statement of Service for Retired Officers*: Aged nineteen on first appointment to the Army. Ensign, 9th Foot, 15 April 1813, 'By raising Volunteers from the 2nd Somerset Militia'; Lt., 9th Foot, 9 Feb. 1815; Half-pay, 24 Feb. 1816, by reduction; Paymaster, 15th Hussars, 5 Aug. 1819; Half-pay, 62nd Foot, 'from private motives of the officers own request'. *Where serving when wounded*: 'Nr Bayonne in the Actions of the 9th 10th & 11th Decr. 1813 (severely)'. No pension. *Family*: Married in 'Littlebourne nr. Canterbury', 28 March 1826. No employment. *Where generally resident during last five years*: 'In Shaftsbury since being placed on Half Pay'. [PRO: WO 25/775 f126]. Severely wounded, the Nive, 11 Dec. 1813 ('Story') (1st Battn.) [*London Gazette*].

STOYTE, John, Ensign/Lt., 1st Foot: *1829 Statement of Service*: Born 29 Nov. 1795, Carlow, Ireland. Aged sixteen on his first appointment to the Army. Ensign, 1st Foot, 21 March 1811; Lt., 1st Foot, 4 July 1813; Half-pay, 25 June 1817; Full-pay, 1st Foot, 18 Feb. 1818; Capt., 1st Foot, 27 Jan. 1825; Capt., 24 Foot, 19 May 1825. *Battles, sieges and campaigns*: 'Badajoz, Storming, 6 April 1812... In front of Salamanca 18 July 1812 – carried Colours as Ensign, Passage of Guarena. Battle of Salamanca 22d

July 1812, Carried Colours as Ensign... Assault on Bergen-op-Zoom 8 March 1814, Commanded Light Company... Quatre Bras & Waterloo, 16 & 18 June 1815.' Shipwrecked in 1830. *Wounds received in action*: 'Lost one finger and wounded through the Left Hand and in the Breast while carrying the Colours – Standard shot away – 1 years pay as Ensign at Battle of Salamanca 22d July 1812. Wounded through Right Hand and taken prisoner at Bergen-op-Zoom 8th March 1814. Received one years pay as Lieutenant and pension of £70 per annum commencing in 1815, Permanent.' *Titles, honorary distinctions and medals*: 'Waterloo Medal.' *Service abroad*: '18 April 1811 to 18 Jany. 1813, Peninsula. 1 July 1813 to May 1814, Swedish Pomerania, Germany & Holland. May 1815 to June 1817, Belgium & France. 28 May 1818 to 8 Decr. 1821, India.' *Family*: Married Elizabeth Flood, 11 April 1829. No children by 1830. [PRO: WO 25/789 f258; WO 76/231 f25]. Severely wounded, Salamanca, 22 July 1812 [*London Gazette*]. Wounded, Waterloo. MGS. Died, Bath, 13 Dec. 1854.

STRANGE, Alexander, Lt., 42nd Foot: Ensign, 42nd Foot, 2 Feb. 1809; Lt., Army, 10 Oct. 1811; Lt., 42nd Foot, 18 Dec. 1811. Severely wounded, 'right arm amputated', Toulouse, 10 April 1814 (1st Battn.) [*London Gazette*]. Pension of seventy pounds per annum, commencing 11 April 1815, for 'loss of an arm' at Toulouse [*1818 Pension Return*, pp. 12–13]. Son of Alexander Strange, Paymaster, 13th Light Dragoons. In his father's 1829 Statement of Service, it is noted that this son died 'of Wounds received at the battle of Thoulouse.' [PRO: WO 25/784 f130]. Nevertheless, Alexander Strange continues to be shown as a lieutenant in the 42nd Foot in the Army Lists up to and including that of 1823. The *1824 Army List* notes

'Strange 42F' as having died. From his father's comments it seems likely that he suffered for almost ten years from the effects of the wound he received at Toulouse.

+STRAWBENZIE, George van, Lt., 40th Foot: Lt., 40th Foot, 16 July 1807. Severely wounded during the repulse of a sortie from Badajoz, 10 May 1811 (1st Battn.) [*London Gazette*]. Died of wounds, 8 Jne 1811. Return dated 25 June 1811. [PRO: WO 25/2965].

STREATFIELD, Thomas, Lt. and Capt., 1st Foot Guards: Lt. and Capt., 1st Foot Guards, 23 Nov. 1809. Slightly wounded, the Nive, 12 Dec. 1813 ('Stretfield') (3rd Battn.) [*London Gazette*]. Wounded, Waterloo. Died, Penshurst, 26 Sept. 1852.

+STREET, Alfred, Lt., 40th Foot: Lt., 40th Foot, 10 Feb. 1807. Slightly wounded during the repulse of a sortie from Badajoz, 10 May 1811 [*London Gazette*]. Severely wounded, storming of Badajoz, 6 April 1812 (1st Battn.) [*London Gazette*]. Died of wounds, 9 April 1812. Return dated 25 April 1812. [PRO: WO 25/2965].

STRETTON, William Lynam, Ensign/Lt., 68th Foot: *1829 Statement of Service*: 'Born at Nottingham, 14th May 1793. Aged Nineteen on his first Entrance into the Army. Ensign, 68th Foot, 11th June 1812. Lieutenant, 68th Foot, 6th Jany. 1814. Lieutenant, Half Pay, Octr. 1819, Reduction of Supernumerary Lieutenant. Lieutenant, 68th Foot, 3rd Feby. 1820. Captain, Half Pay, Unattached, 13 Augt. 1825. Captain, 64th Foot, 29th Decr. 1825.' *Battles, sieges and campaigns*: 'Peninsula 1812, and 1813, Ensign 68th Regiment. At the Battle of Vittoria in Spain 21st June 1813.' *Wounds received in action*: 'Two Gun Shot Wounds at the Battle of Vittoria in 1813. One still lodged in the Groin. Temporary Pension of £50 from June 1814.' *Service abroad*: '1812 to 1813, Peninsula. 1818 to 1819, Canada. 1823 to 1825, Canada. 1826 to 1827, Gibraltar.' [PRO: WO 25/797 f254]. Severely wounded, Vittoria, 21 June 1813 (Ensign) (2nd Battn.) [*London Gazette*]. *1818 Pension Return*, pp. 16–17. MGS. *Mullen*, p. 410 ['From Nottingham Militia ... Lt Col 64th Foot'].

+STRODE, John P., 1st Lt., 95th Foot: Joined the 95th with John Kincaid, from the North York Militia, March 1809. Lt., Army, 17 April 1806; 1st Lt., 95th Foot, 30 March 1809. Wounded, during 'several Affairs with the French Army', 14 March 1811 (Cazal Nova) [*London Gazette*]. Died of wounds, 3 April 1811. Return dated 25 April 1811. [PRO: WO 25/2965]. *Simmons*, pp. 113–14, 143 [wounded, Cazal Nova], p. 143 ['Lieutenant Strode died of his wound some little time after at Coimbra.'], pp. 154–5 ['Strode when he fell called to me to take his rifle, exclaiming, "This, Simmons, may be of service." ']. *Kincaid, Random Shots*, pp. 15–16 [March 1809, joining Rifles from the North York Militia: 'On the breaking up of our encampment at Chatham we marched to Deal, where one of the periodical volunteerings from the militia, (to fill up the ranks of the line,) took place... On those occasions any subaltern who could persuade a given number of men to follow him, received a commission in whatever regiment of the line he wished, provided there was a vacancy for himself and followers. I therefore chose ... the old ninety-fifth, now the Rifle Brigade. – "Hurrah for the first in the field and the last out of it, the bloody fighting ninety-fifth," was the cry of my followers while beating up for more recruits – and as glory was their object, a fighting and a bloody corps the gallant fellows found it, for out of the many who followed Captain Strode and

me to it, there were but two sergeants and myself, after the sixth campaign, alive to tell the tale.'], p. 137 [Casal Nova, 14 March 1811: 'Our general of division was on leave of absence in England during this important period, and it was our curse in the interim to fall into the hands successively of two or three of the worthiest and best of men, but whose only claims to distinction as officers was their sheet of parchment. The consequence was, that ... on the occasion referred to we were the whole day battering our brains out against stone walls at a great sacrifice of life, whereas, had we waited with common prudence until the proper period ... the whole of the loss of life would have been on the other side, but as it was, I am afraid that although we carried our point we were the greatest sufferers. Our battalion had to lament the loss of two very valuable officers on that occasion, Major Stewart and Lieutenant Strode.'].

STRODE, Thomas Lear, Capt., 43rd Foot: Capt., 43rd Foot, 25 Dec. 1807. Slightly wounded, storming of Badajoz, 6 April 1812 ('Stroud') [*London Gazette*].

STROUD, Thomas, Lt., 48th Foot: Lt., 48th Foot, 26 Aug. 1807. Slightly wounded, storming of Badajoz, 6 April 1812 ('Stroud') [*London Gazette*]. Slightly wounded, Salamanca, 22 July 1812 ('Stroud') [*London Gazette*].

STUART, Capt., 66th Foot: Severely wounded, Talavera, 28 July 1809 (2nd Batt.) [*London Gazette*].

STUART, Alexander, Lt., 42nd Foot: *1829 Statement of Service for Retired Officers*: Aged twenty-three on first appointment to the Army. 'Ensign in North or Gordon Fencibles in 1799. Then a Lieutent. in Alve Company of Volunteers & afterwards Lieut. in Inverness shire

Militia'; Ensign, 42nd Foot, 26 May 1808; Lt., 42nd Foot, 25 Dec. 1810; Half-pay, 10 April 1817. 'Unfit for Service from a Wound'. *Where serving when wounded*: 'Toulouse'. *Details of pension*: Seventy pounds per annum, commencing 'in the year 1815'. Not married. No employment. *Where generally resident during last five years*: 'Knock near Grantown N.B.' [PRO: WO 25/775 f152].

+STUART, John, Lt. Col., 9th Foot: Lt. Col., Army, 13 Dec. 1803; Lt. Col., 9th Foot, 29 May 1806. Severely wounded, Rolica, 17 Aug. 1808 [*London Gazette*]. Obituary, *The Gentleman's Magazine*, Nov. 1808, p. 964 ['in the general engagement of the 21st of August, at Vimiera [sic] ... fell ... Col. Stuart, of the 9th, a natural son of the late Lord Blantyre.']. *Leach*, p. 47 ['Battle of Roleia... The Honourable Colonel Lake of the 29th, and Colonel Stewart of the 9th, fell at the head of their regiments.']. Large statue and memorial in Canterbury Cathedral, showing Stuart holding his head, supported by a figure of Britannia ['Sacred to the Memory of Lieut. Colonel JOHN STUART, who fell at the Head of the 9th Regiment of Infantry in the 32nd Year of his Age, at the Battle of Roleia, on the 17th of August, 1808, while the British Arms were successfully supporting the cause of Portugal against the usurpation of France. He was lost to his Country at a period of Life when his Attainments and natural Endowments might have secured to her Benefit the most important Advantages but it is the private Loss that the Officers of his Regiment would Chiefly deplore, in paying this Tribute of Veneration to his beloved Memory. He Lives revered in the Recollection of all who ever knew him, but they are anxious to transmit to later Ages some Memorial of a distinguished Example of worth and Excellence.'].

STUART, Samuel, Lt., 59th Foot: *1829 Statement of Service for Retired Officers*: Aged eighteen on first appointment to the Army. 2nd Lt., Royal Marines, 17 Dec. 1804; Ensign, 83rd Foot, 21 Feb. 1807; Lt., 8th Garrison Battn., 31 Dec. 1807; Lt., 59th Foot, 21 Feb. 1810; Half-pay, 86th Foot, 15 June 1815, 'from wounds received in action'. 'Not desirous of service, being wounded and married'. *Where serving when wounded*: 'Near Bayonne with 59th Regt. 9 Decr. 1813'. *Details of pension*: Seventy pounds, commencing 10 Dec. 1814. *Family*: Married in 'Parish Church of Billy in the Diocese of Connor', 2 Oct. 1827. No children by 1829. No employment. *Where generally resident during last five years*: 'Bushmills, Co. Antrim'. [PRO: WO 25/775 f31]. Slightly wounded, storming of San Sebastian, 31 Aug. 1813 ('Stewart') (2nd Battn.) [*London Gazette*]. Severely wounded, the Nive, 9 Dec. 1813 ('Stewart') (2nd Battn.) [*London Gazette*]. 'Stewart' in Army List.

STUART, William, Lt., 3rd Dragoon Guards: Lt., 3rd Dragoon Guards, 16 July 1812. Severely wounded, Vittoria, 21 June 1813 ('Lieutenant W. Stewart') [*London Gazette*]. MGS.

+STUBBS, George, Capt., 61st Foot: Capt., Army, 3 Oct. 1805; Capt., 61st Foot, 25 Oct. 1805. Killed, Salamanca, 22 July 1812 (1st Battn.) [*London Gazette*].

+STURGEON, Henry, Major, Royal Staff Corps: Born 1781. Major, Royal Staff Corps attached to the Quarter-Master General's Department, 1 June 1809. Mentioned in Wellington's Ciudad Rodrigo dispatch, dated 20 Jan. 1812 ['I have likewise particularly to report to your Lordship the conduct of Major Sturgeon, of the royal staff corps. He constructed and placed for us the bridge over the Agueda, without which the enterprise could not have been attempted; and he afterwards materially assisted Lieutenant-General Graham and myself, in our reconnoissance of the place, on which the plan of the attack was founded; and he finally conducted the 2d battalion 5th Regiment, as well as the 2d Caçadores, to their points of attack.'] [*London Gazette*, 5 Feb. 1812]. Mentioned in Wellington's Salamanca dispatch, 24 July 1812 ['I am particularly indebted to ... the officers of ... the staff corps, for the assistance I received from them, particularly ... Lieutenant-Colonel Sturgeon'] [London Gazette]. Killed, 'in Action with the Enemy', 19 March 1814, while serving on the General Staff as AQMG [*London Gazette*]. *Register of officers' effects*: Bvt. Lt. Col. Killed in action, 19 March 1814, 'Vic Bigiarre'. Single. [PRO: WO 25/2964]. Obituary, *The Gentleman's Magazine*, April 1814, p. 416 ['March 19... During the march of the British army upon Vic, Col. Sturgeon. This place is surrounded for nearly two miles by vineyards; amongst which this gallant officer having unguardedly advanced, a shot from a concealed Enemy terminated his existence. Col. S. had distinguished himself on many occasions, and his loss is greatly lamented.']. *Rous*, p. 102 [18 March 1814: 'Unluckily for us, our Post Master is a clever fellow, and amuses himself with constructing bridges instead of attending to his office. The consequence is that our letters come in a bullock car from San Sebastian, and take six days to perform a journey which mules would do in one.'], p. 102n1 ['This was Lieutenant Colonel Richard Sturgeon (1781–1814), of the Royal Staff Corps. Sturgeon had constructed the temporary bridge at Alcantra and the bridge of boats over the Adour. In April 1813 he had been placed in charge of the Post Office but incurred Wellington's

wrath when the service became disorganised following the Battle of Orthes. Either through remorse or because his pride had been hurt, he deliberately got himself killed at the outposts at Vic-en-Bigorre on March 19th 1814.']. S. G. P. Ward, *Wellington's Headquarters* (London, 1957), p. 191. J. Haswell, *The First Respectable Spy; The Life and Times of Colquhoun Grant, Wellington's Head of Intelligence* (London, 1969), p. 208. Mentioned in the *1829 Statement of Service* of Mark Johnson, Paymaster, 3rd Dragoons ['By the Instructions and Orders from Col. Sturgeon effected a communication, with a Party of the 3rd Kings Own Dragoons, from Genl. Ponsonby's Brigade passing at first thro a part of the Rear Guard of the Enemy and proceeding thro' the files of the advance of our Army, to His Grace the Duke of Wellington, from whom he received orders to proceed to Genl. Lord Hill's division then marching on Vic Bigorre in France and conducted it to that Town. Colonel Sturgeon having another Party from the Regt. was killed in the evening of that Day.'] [PRO: WO 25/782 f157].

SUCKLING, Horace, Ensign/Lt., 1st Foot: *1829 Statement of Service*: Born in Bradford, Wiltshire, 28 Aug. 1791. Aged nineteen 'on his first Entrance into the Army.' Ensign, 1st Foot, 22 Nov. 1810. Lt., 1st Foot, [28] Feb. 1812. Capt., 1st Foot, 21 Oct. 1824. Capt., 90th Foot, 13 Jan. 1825. *Battles, sieges and campaigns*: 'Badajos, Seige, April 1812, Ens. Domo, Retreat, July 1812, Lieut. Salamanca, Battle, July 1812. Palentia & Duanas, Retreat from Burgos, Oct. 1812. Vittoria, Battle, June 1813. St Sebastian, Seige, Aug. 1813. Campaigns of 1811, 1812 and 1813... Campaigns of 1816, 1817, & 1818 in the Army of the Decan under General Sir Thos. Hislop.' *Wounds received in action*: 'Wound through the Right Hip and

SUCKLING

Right Hand at the Storming of St
Sebastian on 31st August 1813. 1
Year's Pay received on account of
wounds.' *Service abroad*: 'June 1811
to Nov. 1813, Peninsula. Decr. 1815
to 24 June 1820, New South Wales &
India. 4 Jany. 1827 to 5 Decr. 1829,
Mediteranean.' *Family*: Married
Miss Mary Marrow, 8 June 1823, in
Dublin. They had two children by
1830. [PRO: WO 25/802 f319].
Slightly wounded, storming of San
Sebastian, 31 Aug. 1813 (3rd Battn.)
[*London Gazette*].

**+SULLIVAN, Sir Henry, Lt. and
Capt./Capt. and Lt. Col., Coldstream Guards:** Capt., Army, 30
Oct. 1801; Lt. and Capt., Coldstream Guards, 2 Dec. 1803. Killed,
sortie from Bayonne, 14 April 1814
(1st Battn.) [*London Gazette*].
Fletcher, Fields of Fire, p. 164
['Coldstream Guards cemetery,
Bayonne... The cemetery, which lies
literally in the corner of a field, was
the site of the Coldstream Guards'
camp and those who lie here
include Lt. Col. Sir Henry Sullivan,
Lt. Col. W. G. Collier, Captains
Crofton and Burroughs, and
Ensigns Vachell and Pitt, all of the
Coldstream Guards, Ensign Vane of
the 1st Foot Guards, and Captains
White and Shiffner, and Lieutenant
Holbourne, all of the 3rd Foot
Guards. Lieutenant Hamilton of
the 60th Regiment is also buried
here.']. Obituary, *The Gentleman's
Magazine*, May 1814, p. 517 ['At
Bayonne... Sir H. Sullivan, bart.
M.P. for the city of Lincoln.'].

**SUMMERFIELD, Thomas, Capt.,
83rd Foot:** *1829 Statement of
Service*: Born in Whiton Aston,
Stafford, Aug. 1775. Aged 18 on his
first Entrance into the Army. Quartermaster, 83rd Foot, Sept. 1796.
Ensign, 83rd Foot, 4 Dec. 1798. Lt.,
83rd Foot, 20 Feb. 1800. Capt., 83rd
Foot, 19 Sept. 1804. Bt. Major., 83rd
Foot, 4 June 1814. Major, 83rd Foot,
21 Dec. 1820. *Battles, sieges and
campaigns*: 'Memorandum. Entered

the 83d Regiment on its formation
in 1793, as a Volunteer, from 55th
Regt. under Colonel Commandant
William Filch, and was present with
him, against the Maroons, when he
lost his life in the Cockpits, & also
with Major Godley when he was
engaged with the Maroons; on each
occasion the loss was very severe.'
'At Oporto, as Captain... At
Talavera, as Captain... At Talavera,
as Captain Commanding the Regiment, after the death of Lt. Colonel
Gordon...' *Distinguished conduct*:
'Was selected by His Excellency,
General Lord Charles Somerset, to
proceed to the Interior of Africa,
with five companies of the 83rd
Regiment (afterwards augmented
to Eight) and two Troops of the 21
Lt. Dragoons, in consequence of a
partial revolt of the Boors and
Hottentots, joined by a party of
Caffrees, which Revolt ended by a
mutual understanding betwixt
them and the Government. For this
Service, His Excellency was pleased
to express his entire approbation
in General Orders, dated 3rd
December 1816, accompanied by
an Address from the inhabitants of
the Interior of Africa.' *Wounds
received in action*: 'Wounded in
the Neck, 28th July, 1809, in the
Action of Talavera, and taken Pris-
oner. Received One year's pay as
Major for the above mentioned
wound.' *Service abroad*: 'Septr.
1796 to 22 August 1802, W. Indies.
6th April 1809 to 24th July 1814,
Portugal, Spain and France. 10th
March 1816 to 1 October 1817,
Cape of Gd. Hope. 3rd December
1817 to 6 March 1827, Ceylon.'
Family: Married Margaret
Duncan, 1791, Edinburgh. They
had five children by 1830. [PRO:
WO 25/801 f148]. 'Somerfield' in
Army List. Slightly wounded,
Talavera, 28 July 1809 [*London
Gazette*].

**SUNHARRY, Frederick de, Lt.,
Chasseurs Britanniques:** Lt., Chasseurs Britanniques, 19 Feb. 1811.

Severely wounded, Pyrenees, 30 July 1813 [*London Gazette*].

SUTHERLAND, Andrew, Lt./Capt., 11th Foot: *1829 Statement of Service for Retired Officers*: Aged nineteen on first appointment to the Army. Lt., Sutherland Fencibles, 7 May 1779; Lt., Sutherland Fencibles, 7 March 1793; Ensign, 11th Foot, 7 April 1804; Lt., 11th Foot, 27 June 1805; Capt., 11th Foot, 13 May 1813; Capt., Royal Veteran Battn., 23 Sept. 1813; Capt., 5th Royal Veteran Battn., 1 Nov. 1819. 'Put on the retired list, as unfit for service'. *Where serving when wounded*: 'Spain'. No pension. *Family*: Married in Edinburgh, 23 April 1792. *Where generally resident during last five years*: 'Stonehouse, Plymouth'. [PRO: WO 25/775 f199]. MGS.

SUTHERLAND, John, Lt., 3rd Foot; Capt., 6th Portuguese Line: *1829 Statement of Service for Retired Officers*: Aged twenty on first appointment to the Army. Ensign, 'in the Cap Regt. of Infty', 29 June 1806 [Army List gives as 'A Regiment at the Cape of Good Hope']; Lt., 3rd Foot, 31 Aug. 1809; Capt., 6th Portuguese Line, 11 July 1812; Bvt. Capt., 'in the British Army', 25 Oct. 1814; Capt., 3rd Foot, 29 April 1820; Half-pay, 1821, by reduction, 'at this my feelings was so much hurt at the very idea of Half-pay ... that I unadvisedly [sold] my company... Immediately after ... purchased a Ensigncy on half or full pay with a view of endeavouring to obtain my Rank again'; Ensign, Half-pay, 26th Foot, 24 Oct. 1821. 'Not desirous of service in my present rank having served so long a Captain in the Campaigns under the present Commander in Chief'. *Where serving when wounded*: 'Action in which took place in front of Pamplona on the 30th July 1813. And again on the 13th Decbr. in that which was fought close to Bayonne in the same year'. *Family*:

Married in 'Thurso, Caithness-Shire', 14 Aug. 1823. *Where generally resident during last five years*: 'near Wick Caithness-Shire'. [PRO: WO 25/775 f210]. Severely wounded, the Pyrenees, 30 July 1813, as Capt., 6th Portuguese Regt. [*London Gazette*]. Slightly wounded, the Nive, 13 Dec. 1813, as Capt., 6th Portuguese Regt. [*London Gazette*]. In Portuguese Service July 1812 to April 1814. MGS. *Challis, Portuguese Army*, p. 59.

SUTHERLAND, John, Lt., 4th Foot: Lt., 4th Foot, 21 Sept. 1813. Slightly wounded, the Nive, 11 Dec. 1813 (1st Battn.) [*London Gazette*]. Recorded as 'Killed in Action' [New Orleans] prior to March 1815, in the *1815 Army List* ('Alterations and Additions while Printing').

SUTHERLAND, Robert, Ensign, 67th Foot: Ensign, 67th Foot, 7 Sept. 1809. Severely wounded, Barossa, 5 March 1811 (2nd Battn.) [*London Gazette*]. MGS.

SUTHRILL, T., Volunteer, 1st Foot: Severely wounded, in operations, 12–19 June 1813 [*London Gazette*]. Not in *Challis, Index*.

SWABEY, William, Lt., Royal Artillery: 1st Lt., Royal Artillery, 13 Aug. 1807. Severely wounded, Vittoria, 21 June 1813 ('Swaby') [*London Gazette*]. MGS. Author of *Diary of Campaigns in the Peninsula for the Years 1811, 12 and 13*, ed. F. A. Whinyates (London, 1895). *Swabey*, p. 8 [Introduction by Whinyates: 'A summary of the principal events of his life has been kindly sent me by his son, the Rev. Maurice Swabey, and is as follows:– William Swabey was born in Doctors Commons, London, on the 13th of June, 1789. He was the third and youngest son of Maurice Swabey, of Langley Marish, Bucks, ... His early education was received at the Westminster School and the Royal Military Academy at Woolwich. On the

1st of July, 1806, at the age of 16 years, he received a commission in the Royal Regiment of Artillery, and, in 1807, was present with Captain Cockburn's No. 7 Company, 1st Battalion, in the land force which co-operated with Admiral Lord Gambier at the bombardment of Copenhagen. He was ordered in July, 1811, to the Peninsula, with "E" Troop, R.H.A., and served in it during a considerable portion of the war. He was severely wounded at the battle of Vittoria and invalided home, but rejoined the army before the close of the war. He was present at the battle of Toulouse, and, marching through France to Calais, returned home in 1814 with the troop, which the following year he accompanied to Belgium and was with in the retreat from Quatre Bras, and at the battle of Waterloo. He received the Peninsular and Waterloo medals. Shortly after promotion to the rank of 2nd Captain, he retired, in March, 1825, from the service and settled down in Buckinghamshire, where he became J.P. and D.L., and captain of a troop of Bucks Yeomanry Cavalry. In 1840, he emigrated with nearly all his family to Prince Edward's Island, of which his friend, Sir Charles Fitzroy (an old Waterloo officer), was then Lieut.-Governor. Captain Swabey continued in the colony till 1861... Captain Swabey married, in 1820, Marianne, third daughter of Edward Hobson, of Somerly, Hants, and Hope Hall, Lancashire, Esquire, and had a family of eleven children. He died on the 6th of February, 1872, having, towards the close of his life, resided for some years at Wavenden House, Bucks, a county endeared to him by family ties and early associations.'], pp. 201–2 [Vittoria, 21 June 1813: 'We came into action twice in the centre of the enemy's columns, but always, such was the nature of the country, on low ground. At the last place my favorite horse, poor Telemachus, was shot, Sutton being on him, and we had hardly got through the second village when in the act of leading my guns off the road to an eminence where we were to come into action, I received a ball in my knee... The moment I found I was hit I turned my horse round and quietly walked to the village where I met Sutton actually in tears at the loss of the horse, which he said was like losing his best companion. I laughed at him, and told him the state I was in, but still he kept prating about the horse; he helped me off and I got into the first hovel I could find. I found there the doctor with two or three of our men likewise wounded. As soon as they were dressed he came to me, and on examination we found the ball had to all appearances gone directly in between my knee-cap and the top of the leg bone, taking in the cloth of my overalls and drawers, and the piece in the wound not being entirely separated from the cloth outside, I vainly thought I could pull the ball out with it. In this I failed.'], pp. 209–10 ['16th July.– My leg having been for some time stationary, I consulted a mr. Gunning, a surgeon of known eminence sent here for the purpose to assist in obscure cases, who on probing my knee pronounced very decidedly that, though he could not find it, the ball was there, and he said he felt cloth or some foreign body in the wound... 17th July.– When the tormenter came, whose arrival I anticipated, I had had time to think with dread of his knife... He had changed his mind about cutting, which I did not disapprove of, and had recourse to another scheme for extending my wound, of which I know not the technical term; but it consists in soaking sponge in melted wax, then forcibly compressing it and leaving it to dry. It is then cut into pegs, which are then inserted into the sinus of the wound, and the wax melting the sponge expands and forcibly opens it, to the no small annoyance of the patient, who is obliged to keep his bed and does not fail to curse the invention... 20 July.- A thorough opening being now made, no less than two wiseacres gave my knee a thorough probing and examination, but nothing could be found, so that between their opinion and Gunning's I know not what to think; however, as they all now agree that the ball is in my knee they look on my recovery as distant, and recommended my going to England which at length I have consented to... It is unlucky to be obliged to go to England because here is the place where I must lay the foundation of future fortunes.'], p. 217 [Conclusion, by Whinyates: 'The bullet which he received in his leg at Vitoria could never be extracted, and was a source of much inconvenience in after life... He was well read, an accomplished linguist, and possessed of the dignity, courtesy, and refined manners of a past generation – qualities which the rush and hurry of modern life have well nigh driven out of existence. Finally he was a good, active and keen soldier – one of those who by zeal, energy, and a high sense of duty and discipline have contributed so largely to the prestige of the arm to which he belonged.']. *Webber*, p. 60.

+SWANN, William Henry, Lt. and Capt., 3rd Foot Guards: Ensign, 3rd Foot Guards, 17 Jan. 1804; Lt. and Capt., 3rd Foot Guards, 22 June 1809. Killed, Barossa, 5 March 1811 [*London Gazette*]. Obituary, *The Gentleman's Magazine*, April 1811, p. 396 ['March 5. At the battle of Barrosa... in his 24th year, Lieut. swann, only son of Henry S. esq. M.P. of Ufford-hall, near Stamford.'].

+SWANSON, John, Capt., 42nd Foot: Capt., 42nd Foot, 14 Dec. 1809. Killed, Toulouse, 10 April 1814 (1st Battn.) [*London Gazette*].

SWEENEY, James, Ensign, 50th Foot: Ensign, 50th Foot, 23 Oct. 1813. Slightly wounded, Orthes, 27 Feb. 1814 (1st Battn.) [*London Gazette*]. Severely wounded, 'in Action with the Enemy', 20 March 1814 ('Sweeny') (1st Battn.) [*London Gazette*].

SWEENY, Samuel, Lt., 28th Foot: Lt., 28th Foot, 22 Nov. 1810. Severely wounded, Vittoria, 21 June 1813 (1st Battn.) [*London Gazette*].

SWETENHAM, Clement, Capt., 16th Light Dragoons: Capt., 16th Light Dragoons, 15 Aug. 1805. Wounded slightly, Heights of Grijon, 11 May 1809 ('Sweatman') [*London Gazette*]. Waterloo. MGS. Died, 17 Nov. 1852.

SWINBURNE, Joseph, N.C.O./Ensign/Adjutant/Lt., 83rd Foot: *1829 Statement of Service*: Born in Solihull, Warwick, 19 Sept. 1785. Aged '17 years, 280 Days' on first appointment to the Army. 'Memo. Ballotted into the 9th Battalion, Army of Reserve, on the 25th June 1803, and joined the 83rd Regiment as Serjeant on the 25th June 1805'; Ensign, 83rd Foot, 16 Aug. 1809; Adjutant, 83rd Foot, 6 July 1811; Lt., 83rd Foot, 4 June 1812; Capt., 83rd Foot, 6 Oct. 1825. *Battles, sieges and campaigns*: 'Oporto, 12 May 1809, Serjt. Major. Talavera, 27 July 1809, Serjt. Major. Busaco, Oct. 1810, then Ensign. Following the Retreat of Marshal Massena, from Santerhion where the Regiment was engaged most days skirmishing with the Enemy, particularly at Pombal, Leyria, Condeixa, Fleur-de-lis, Guarda, and Sabugal in February 1811. First sieges of Badajos, June 1811, then Ensign. Elboden, 16th Septr. 1811, then Ensign & Adjutant. Second siege of Badajos, April 1812, then Ensn. & Adjt. Salamanca, July 1812, Lieutenant & Adjutant. Vittoria, June 1813... Pyrenees, Augt. 1813... Nivelle, 10th Novr. 1813... Salvaterre, Feby. 1814... Orthes, Feby. 1814... Vigmagore, Mar. 1814... Toulouse, Apl. 1814...' *Wounds received in action*: 'Wounded in the Right Elbow & Right Foot at Talavera. Wounded in the Neck at Orthes, did not receive any pay or pension in consequence.' *Service abroad*: '16th August 1809 to 24th July 1814, Portugal, Spain & France. 16th Novr. 1817 to 16th April 1829, Ceylon.' *Family*: Married Alice Quin, 22 Feb. 1808, Nenagh. They had seven children by 1830. [PRO: WO 25/801 f160]. Slightly wounded, Orthes, 27 Feb. 1813 (2nd Battn.) [*London Gazette*]. MGS.

SYDSERFF, John Buchan, Ensign/Lt., 82nd Foot: Ensign, 82nd Foot, 24 Oct. 1811. Severely wounded, Nivelle, 10 Nov. 1813 ('Lieutenant') (1st Battn.) [*London Gazette*]. Lt., 82nd Foot, 6 Jan. 1814.

+SYMPHER, Frederick, 1st Capt., K.G.L. Artillery: 1st Capt., K.G.L.

Artillery, 19 Sept. 1810. Killed, Orthes, 27 Feb. 1814 ('Captain Frederick Lympher (Major)') [*London Gazette*]. Served in Peninsula 1810–14. *Beamish*, vol. II, p. 612.

SYNGE, Charles, Lt., 10th Light Dragoons; Capt., Portuguese Staff: Lt., 10th Light Dragoons, 8 Feb. 1810. Severely wounded, Salamanca, 22 July 1812, while serving on Portuguese Staff as ADC to Brigadier-General Pack [*London Gazette*]. ADC to General Parkes at Nive, Orthes and Toulouse. Capt., 20th Dragoons, 12 Nov. 1814. In Portuguese Service July 1811 to Aug. 1813. Pension of one hundred pounds per annum, commencing 23 July 1813, 'for a wound' received at Salamanca [*1818 Pension Return*, pp. 2–3]. MGS. *Brotherton*, pp. 31–2. *Challis, Portuguese Army*, p. 59.

T

+TAGGART, Charles, Lt., 43rd Foot: Lt., 43rd Foot, 22 May 1806. Killed, storming of Badajoz, 6 April 1812 [*London Gazette*].

TALBOT, John, Ensign, Coldstream Guards: Ensign, Coldstream Guards, 17 Nov. 1808; Lt. and Capt. 26 Nov. 1812. Slightly wounded, Barossa, 5 March 1811 [*London Gazette*]. *London Evening Standard*, 11 June 1993 [The Guards Club (in London) 'having been founded in 1810 by a subaltern in the Coldstreams called Jack Talbot, of whom it was said that "if he were tapped for blood, pure claret would come out" and who died, an empty sherry bottle beside him, at the age of 27.'].

+TALBOT, Neil, Lt. Col., 14th Light Dragoons: Capt., Army, 10 July 1794; Capt., 14th Light Dragoons, 19 Oct. 1796; Lt. Col. 22 Aug. 1805. His death is noted in Wellington's dispatch from Alverca of 11 July 1810 ['There was an affair between our picquets and those of the enemy this morning, in which the enemy lost two officers and thirty-one men, and twenty-nine horses prisoners. We had the misfortune to lose Lieutenant-Colonel Talbot, and eight men of the 14th Light Dragoons killed, and twenty-three men wounded.'] *London Gazette*. Obituary, *The Gentleman's Magazine*, Aug. 1810, p. 189 ['10 [July]... On the Plains of Almeida, at the head of eight squadrons of the 14th and 15th Light Dragoons, whilst gallantly charging the French cavalry, supported by 300 of their infantry. Lieut.-col. Talbot. The French fired, and killed two subalterns of the 16th, and about ten privates; both the fore legs of Col. T.'s horse were broken; the animal plunged forward and fell, and the Colonel fell over his head on the bayonets of the Enemy, who instantly dispatched him. He was born at Malahyde, near Dublin, and was the brother to R. W. Talbot, esq. M.P. for the county of Dublin.']. In Portuguese Service May 1809 to July 1810. *Challis, Portuguese Army*, p. 59. *Simmons*, p. 73 [killed, Villa de Cieruos, 11 July 1810: '... the infantry, amounting to sixty or seventy men, were in the flat below... The French infantry were attacked by Colonel Talbot, though it was pretty evident that they would have had to surrender without firing a shot had he waited. He charged with a squadron of the 14th and fell dead amongst them, as also his quartermaster; thirty men were killed and wounded and twenty horses...']. *Brotherton*, pp. 22–4 [killed, Sexmiro, 11 July 1810: 'At the village of Sexmiro we encountered a square of French infantry. It was lying down, concealed in some high-standing corn, and only rose when my squadron came within pistol-shot of it, and was beautifully steady. We charged it most gallantly, but they fired a deadly volley into us, and half my men fell killed or wounded. Colonel Talbot, who commanded the Regiment, had put himself at the head of the squadron along with me. Poor fellow, he fell pierced by eight balls, literally on the enemy's bayonets... I went out with a flag of truce to fetch his body ... and we buried him on the glacis of Fort Conception. A few days afterwards the premeditated explosion of this fort took place, when his body was blown into the air... He was a delightful fellow, a friend (whose loss) I most deeply regretted, but singular and eccentric, particularly in his dress. He was dressed, the day he was killed, in nankeen pantaloons.']. *Leach*, p.

549

141 ['Colonel Talbot, at the head of the 14th Light Dragoons, rode gallantly at and charged the little phalanx with great impetuosity, but without being able to break it, No troops on earth could have conducted themselves with greater gallantry than the old and often-tried 14th Light Dragoons; and in so determined a manner did this distinguished corps make their charge, that Colonel Talbot, whose body I saw a few minutes after he was killed, bore the marks not only of bullets but of bayonets: and it is equally true, that he and many of his brave followers who actually reached the square, met their death by the bayonets of this invincible little body of Frenchmen'], p. 143. *Perrett*, p. 17 [Talavera, 28 July 1809: 'Colonel Hawker, who was among the wounded, was awarded a gold medal. He returned home shortly after the battle and command passed to Lt-Colonel Neil Talbot, a popular officer whom Brotherton describes as "a delightful fellow, but singular and eccentric, particularly in his dress".'], p. 18 ['a resolute individualist to the last'].

TALBOT, William, Lt., 27th Foot: *1829 Statement of Service for Retired Officers*: Aged sixteen on first appointment to the Army. Ensign, 48th Foot, 27 May 1806; Lt., 27th Foot, 7 Feb. 1808; Capt., 27th Foot, 7 April 1825; Half-pay, unattached, 18 Jan. 1827, 'from ill health'. *Where serving when wounded*: 'Spain, Ordail'. Not married. *Where generally resident during last five years*: 'Three years in the West Indies and two between England & Ireland'. [PRO: WO 25/776 f8]. Severely wounded, 'not dangerously', Heights of Ordal, 12/13th Sept. 1813 (2nd Battn.) [*London Gazette*]. Waterloo.

TAPP, Hammond A., 1st Lt., Royal Engineers: 1st Lt., Royal Engineers, 1 March 1810. Severely wounded,

'at the Siege of St Sebastian,' 7–27 July 1813 [*London Gazette*].

TAPPE, Charles, Cornet, 1st Dragoons K.G.L.; Lt., 1st Light Dragoons K.G.L.: *1829 Statement of Service for Retired Officers*: Aged twenty-seven on first appointment to the Army. 'From 1805 to 1811 was Private, Sergeant &c'; Cornet, 1st Dragoons K.G.L., 1811; Lt., 1st Light Dragoons K.G.L., 24 Sept. 1812, 'The Regiment changed from Heavy Dragoons to Light Dragoons'; Half-pay, 1815, 'From ill-health and was severely wounded'. *Where serving when wounded*: 'Salamanca'. *Details of pension*: Fifty pounds, commencing 23 July 1812, increased to seventy pounds on 25 Dec. 1819. *Family*: Married in 'Salzhausen, Kingdom Hannover', 23 Oct. 1817. Three children by 1829. *Where generally resident during last five years*: 'Salzhausen'. [PRO: WO 25/776 f35]. Severely wounded, in an Affair with the Enemy's Rear-Guard near La Serna, 23 July 1812 [*London Gazette*]. Served in Peninsula in 1812. *Beamish*, vol. II, p. 623 ['placed upon half-pay, 25th April 1815. [Resident] at Salzhausen, amt. Winsen on the Lube, in Han.'].

TARLETON, George Matcham, Lt., 6th Foot: *1829 Statement of Service for Retired Officers*: Aged seventeen on first appointment to the Army. Ensign, 6th Foot, 6 Feb. 1806; Lt., 6th Foot, 16 April 1807; Half-pay, 3rd Garrison Battn., 13 June 1821, 'at my request from ill Health'. 'Ill health and suffering from a severe wound not equal to active service but capable of Garrison situation'. *Where serving when wounded*: 'Severely wounded on the Hights of Echelar Pyrenees'. *Family*: Married in 'New Marledorm Church London', 15 May 1819. Five children by 1829. *Where generally resident during last five years*: 'Two years and a half in Boulogne, previous in England'. [PRO: WO

25/776 f16]. Severely wounded, Pyrenees, 2 Aug. 1813 (1st Battn.) [*London Gazette*]. MGS.

TARLETON, Henry, Capt., 7th Foot: Capt., Army, 18 Aug. 1808; Capt., 7th Foot, 7 June 1810. Slightly wounded, Albuera, 16 May 1811 ('Parleton') (2nd Battn.) [*London Gazette*]. Recorded as 'missing', Pyrenees, 28 July 1813 [*London Gazette*]. *Cooper*, p. 95 [Battle of Pampeluna, 28 July 1813: 'Hardly had I served out the ammunition and thrown on my knapsack, before a swarm of the enemy suddenly rushed over the brow of the hill, and swept our much reduced company down the craggy steep behind. Some of them seized the captain of the 9th company, and attempted to pull off his epaulets, but he resented this by a blow of his left fist. However, he was led off a prisoner.'].

TAYLOR, Anselin E., Lt., 9th Foot; Lt., 12th Light Dragoons: Lt., 9th Foot, 27 April 1809. Wounded, 'dangerously', Barossa, 5 March 1811 [*London Gazette*]. Lt., 12th Light Dragoons, 1 Aug. 1811. Wounded, during 'movements of the Army' [Retreat from Burgos], 23 Oct. 1812 [*London Gazette*]. *Blakeney*, pp. 146–7 [Gibraltar, April 1810: ['The first person who addressed me on landing was Lieutenant Taylor, 9th Regiment (afterwards shot through the body at Barossa), demanding, without any prelude whatever, if Captain Godwin of his regiment was wounded.'].

TAYLOR, Arthur Sanders, Lt., 94th Foot: Lt., Army, 16 April 1807; Lt., 94th Foot, 11 Oct. 1810. Wounded, 'dangerously', storming of Ciudad Rodrigo, 19 Jan. 1812 [*London Gazette*]. Pension of one hundred pounds per annum, commencing 20 Jan. 1813, 'for wounds' received at Ciudad Rodrigo [*1818 Pension Return*, pp. 20–1].

+TAYLOR, Charles D., Lt. Col., 20th Light Dragoons: Capt., 7th Light Dragoons, 16 Sept. 1795; Lt. Col., 20th Light Dragoons, 24 Feb. 1803. Killed, Vimeiro, 21 Aug. 1808 [*London Gazette*]. Obituary, *The Gentleman's Magazine*, Nov. 1808, p. 963 ['Lieut.-col. Charles Taylor, of the 20th Dragoons, fell in the flower of his age, at 36, in the general engagement of the 21st of August, at Vimiera. "He was killed", to use the words of a brother officer, "at the head of his regiment, in one of the most determined charges, I believe, ever made. In his death our Army has lost one of its most active and intelligent Officers." According to another private account, the Enemy having been driven back after a fiece attack and desperate conflict, he led the regiment through the French lines of Infantry, with little loss; and charging their cavalry, who retreated, he encouraged his men, who followed him, through a vineyard; where the enemy's cavalry and voltigeurs taking advantage of the situation to rally, he received a ball through his body, which produced instantaneous death. He had already had his horse wounded in the early part of the day, as he was reconnoitring the French lines; and he declared, with a noble enthusiasm, that "he was determined for honour for himself and his regiment on that day.".... Col. Taylor had not more than 200 men with him. He was buried that evening on the spot by an officer's party, who went on purpose to pick up all wounded, and bury all killed, officers. Col. Taylor's bravery has attracted the praise of an enemy; and that enemy a French General. It is said that "General Kellerman gives an account, that he was close to Colonel Taylor when he was killed. He speaks of him as a very brave man; he says that none but a truly brave man would have advanced as he did; and not having infantry to support him, the French cavalry surrounded him, and he lost his life in cutting his way through them. Kellerman had possession of his horse; but he handsomely gave it up to the regiment, in admiration of the owner of it." – Col. Taylor was the only child of Dr. Taylor, an eminent physician at Reading in Berkshire... Col. T. was brought up at Westminster school; whence he obtained a studentship of Christchurch, Oxford... Thence he obtained a cornetcy, in 1793, in the 7th Dragoons, in which regiment he rose to a Majority; and thence was promoted about six years ago, to the Lieut.-colonlcy of the 20th. He had served with his former regiment in Holland in the late war, and only returned from Sicily in the summer of 1807... Col. Taylor has left three infant children, two sons and a daughter, by Elizabeth, eldest daughter of John Baker, esq. M.P. for Canterbury, whom he married in the spring of 1803.']. *Leach*, p. 52 [Vimeiro: 'The French column ... was assailed in its retreat by the 20th Light Dragoons, who dashed gallantly in amongst the fugitives, and, in the ardour of the moment, following them to a distance from any support, encountered a very superior body of French cavalry, which obliged the 20th to fall back with some loss. Lieutenant-colonel Taylor fell, whilst gallantly leading on his regiment in this charge.']. Memorial tablet to his son in Canterbury Cathedral ['To the Memory of Brigadier General CHARLES CYRIL TAYLOR C.B., son of LIEUT. COLN. CHARLES D. TAYLOR, born 29th March A.D. 1804, died 10th February A.D. 1846. The father fell at Vimeira, the first triumph of the British Arms in the War of the Peninsula. The son at Sobron, the crowning victory of the British Arms in India...'].

+**TAYLOR, James, Capt., 38th Foot:** Capt., 38th Foot, 22 April 1807. Killed, Salamanca, 22 July 1812 [*London Gazette*].

TAYLOR, James, Capt., 48th Foot: Capt., 48th Foot, 4 June 1807. Mentioned in Graham's report to Wellington concerning the taking of the convent of San Bartolome, dated 18 July 1813 ['P.S. I omitted to mention, that Major-General Hay mentions his great obligations to Captain Taylor, of the 48th regiment, his Brigade-Major.'] [*London Gazette*].

TAYLOR, John, Lt., 9th Foot: *1829 Statement of Service*: Born 6 Feb. 1789, Wexford. Aged sixteen on his first Entrance into the Army. Ensign, 99th Foot, 28 Feb. 1805; Lt. 1 Oct. 1807; Capt. 2 Oct. 1817; Major 1 April 1824; Lt. Col. 22 March 1827. *Battles, sieges and campaigns*: 'Campaign of 1808 under Sir A. Wellesley Battle of Vimeira Campaign of 1809 at Oporto and North of Portugal. Campaign of 1810 Battle of Busaco. Campaign of 1811 in Portugal. Campaign of 1812 in Spain and Portugal, Battle of Salamanca, and retreat from Burgos and Combat at Villa Murial, Campaign of 1814, Sortie at Bayonne.' *Wounds received in action*: 'Wounded at the Battle of Vimeira. Wounded on the 25 October 1812 at Villa Murial for which received a Years Pay as Captain.' *Service abroad*: 'June 1806 to March 1808, Bermuda. August 1808 to February 1813, Portugal & Spain. October 1813 to June 1814, Spain & Portugal. July 1814 to June 1815, America. July 1815 to October 1818, France, April 1820 to January 1827, West Indies.' *Family*: Married Sophia Barton, 9th April 1828, Eccles, Lancashire. They had two children by 1830. [PRO: WO 25/786 f236]. Severely wounded, during 'movements of the Army' [Retreat from Burgos: Villa Muriel], 25 Oct. 1812 [*London Gazette*].

TAYLOR, John, Lt. Col., 88th Foot: Lt. Col., Army, 28 Feb. 1805; Lt. Col., 88th Foot, 18 May 1809. Severely wounded, Orthes, 27 Feb. 1814

('Lieutenant-Colonel John Taylor (Colonel)') (1st Battn.) [*London Gazette*]. *Colville*, p. 170 [Letter from John Keane to Sir Charles Colville, 17 March 1814: 'Taylor was wounded in the neck but is up again.'].

TAYLOR, John, Ensign, 91st Foot: *1829 Statement of Service for Retired Officers*: Aged eighteen on first appointment to the Army. 'Militia Service 2½ years'; Ensign, 91st Foot, 30 July 1812; Lt., 91st Foot, July 1814; Half-pay, 25 Dec. 1815, by reduction; Lt., 90th Foot, 20 March 1817; Half-pay, Dec. 1818, by reduction. 'Ensign in the 91st Regiment without purchase in consequence of a memorial to the late Duke of York stating that I had obtained 33 volunteers from the 21st Militia Regt. to the 91st of the Line by my personal influence and giving the men *additional Bounty*, when 35 or 36 was all the Regt. had to furnish, the other 3 men went to the Guards'. 'Very desirous of service if the state of my wound admits'. *Where serving when wounded*: 'Peninsula Army under the Duke of Wellington. Wounded in the Action of Orthez'. *Details of pension*: 'Fifty pounds, commencing 28 Feb. 1815'. *Family*: Married in 'Girthon Parish, Stewartry of Kirkcudbright', 30 April 1822. Four children by 1829. *Where generally resident during last five years*: 'Stranraer N.B.' [PRO: WO 25/776 f28]. Severely wounded, Orthes, 27 Feb. 1814 (1st Battn.) [*London Gazette*]. MGS.

TAYLOR, John, 2nd Capt., Royal Artillery: 2nd Capt., Royal Artillery, 1 June 1806. Slightly wounded, Talavera, 28 July 1809 [*London Gazette*].

+TAYLOR, John D., Lt., 51st Foot: Ensign, 51st Foot, 12 Dec. 1811; Lt., 51st Foot, 16 Sept. 1813. Killed, Nivelle, 10 Nov. 1813 ('Lieutenant John D. Taylor') [*London Gazette*].

TAYLOR, Thomas John, Ensign, 36th Foot: *1829 Statement of Service*: Born in Dublin, Ireland, 14 Sept. 1793. 'Aged eighteen years six months on first appointment to the Army. Ensign, 36th Foot, 12 March 1812; Lt., 36th Foot, 7 Sept. 1814; Half-pay, 25 Dec. 1814, by reduction; Lt., 36th Foot, 26 Octr. 1815; Half-pay, 25 March 1817, by reduction; Lt., 78th Foot, 25 May 1820.' *Battles, sieges and campaigns*: 'Investment & Blockade of Pampeluna. Battles in the Pyrenees 28th, 29th and 30th of July 1813. Blockade of Bayonne, Battle of Orthes 27 Feby. 1814, the Affair of Tarbes March 1814, Battle of Toulouse 10 of April 1814, as Ensign in the 36th Foot.' *Wounds received in action*: 'Severely Wounded at the Battle of Toulouse. Received One year's Pay.' *Service abroad*: '2d Feby. 1813 to July 1814, Portugal, Spain and France. 23 April 1826 to 31 Decr. 1829, Ceylon.' [PRO: WO25/800 f177]. Severely wounded, Toulouse, 10 April 1814 (1st Battn.) [*London Gazette*]. Army List gives as 'Thomas M.' or 'Thomas Medlicott Taylor'. MGS.

+TAYLOR, William, Lt./Adjutant, 27th Foot: Ensign and Adjutant, 27th Foot, 25 April 1807; Lt., 27th Foot, 22 Nov. 1809. Killed, Heights of Ordal, 12/13 Sept. 1813, while serving as Adjutant (2nd Battn.) [*London Gazette*]. *Register of officers' effects*: Killed, 13 Sept. 1813, 'Pass of Ordall'. Married. His effects were sent to his widow. [PRO: WO 25/2963].

TAYLOR, William, Capt., 38th Foot: Capt., 38th Foot, 7 Sept. 1804. Severely wounded, the Nive, 9 Dec. 1813 (1st Battn.) [*London Gazette*]. Temporary pension of one hundred pounds per annum, commencing 10 Dec. 1814, 'for wounds' received at Bayonne, 1813 [*1818 Pension Return*, pp. 10–11].

TAYLOR, William Vere, Lt./Capt., 28th Foot: Lt., 28th Foot, 28 Jan.

1805. Capt., 28th Foot, 29 Oct. 1811. Severely wounded, the Nive, 9 Dec. 1813 (1st Battn.) [*London Gazette*]. Pension of one hundred pounds per annum, commencing 10 Dec. 1814, 'for wounds' received at the Nive [*1818 Pension Return*, pp. 8–9]. *Blakeney*, p. 104 [Retreat to Corunna].

TEALE, George, Capt., 11th Foot: Capt., 11th Foot, 16 Oct. 1806. Slightly wounded in the siege of the Forts of St Vincente, St Cayetano, and La Merced at Salamanca, 18–24 June 1812 [*London Gazette*].

TELFORD, Robert, Capt., 20th Foot: Capt., 20th Foot, 17 Oct. 1811. Severely wounded, Orthes, 27 Oct. 1814 ('Tilford') [*London Gazette*]. Temporary pension of one hundred pounds per annum, commencing 28 Feb. 1815, 'for wounds' received at Orthes [*1818 Pension Return*, pp. 6–7].

TEMPLE, William Henry, Lt., 52nd Foot; Capt., 6th Caçadores: Lt., 52nd Foot, 26 Feb. 1807. Severely wounded, the Nive, 9 Dec. 1813, while serving as Capt. 6th Caçadores [*London Gazette*]. Slightly wounded, Pyrenees, 30 July 1813, while serving as Capt., 6th Caçadores [*London Gazette*]. In Portuguese Service March 1811 to April 1814. Temporary pension of one hundred pounds per annum, commencing 10 Dec. 1814, 'for a wound' received at the Nive [*1818 Pension Return*, pp. 14–15]. MGS. *Challis, Portuguese Army*, p. 60.

TENCH, Henry, Lt., 61st Foot: *1829 Statement of Service for Retired Officers*: Aged twenty-three on first appointment to the Army. Ensign, 61st Foot, 9 July 1803; Lt., 61st Foot, 'do not recollect the date' [Army List gives 15 Dec. 1804]; Capt., 61st Foot, 12 July 1812; Half-pay, 10th Foot, May 1815, 'as well as I can recollect', by reduction. 'I had been on the half pay of the 61st Regiment for a short time after returning from France where I had been a Prisoner of War for nearly 4 years'. 'Am too old to commence the army again having been so long in a torpid state I would be worse than a conscript and my constitution is very far from being to my likeing'. *Where serving when wounded*: 'Tellavera'. No pension. Not married. 'Never have been employed in a civil capacity'. *Where generally resident during last five years*: 'In Wexford, there 12 years, never left it for more than a few days at a time'. [PRO: WO 25/776 f52]. Slightly wounded, Talavera, 28 July 1809 [*London Gazette*].

TETLOW, William, Lt., 3rd Foot: Lt., 3rd Foot, 5 April 1807. Slightly wounded, Albuera, 16 May 1811 [*London Gazette*]

TEUTO, Bernhard, Cornet/Lt, 1st Light Dragoons K.G.L: Slightly wounded, Talavera, 28 July 1809 ('Cornet Teuts') [*London Gazette*]. Lt., 1st Light Dragoons K.G.L., 12 Dec. 1810. Severely wounded, Salamanca, 22 July 1812 ('Fueto') [*London Gazette*]. *Beamish*, vol. II, pp. 549–50. Died at Bredenbeck near Hanover, 10 March 1820.

+TEW, William, Lt./Capt., 74th Foot: Lt., 74th Foot, 5 Nov. 1807. Severely wounded, storming of Ciudad Rodrigo, 19 Jan. 1812 ('Feu') [*London Gazette*]. Slightly wounded, Pyrenees, 30 July 1813 (1st Battn.) [*London Gazette*]. Capt., 74th Foot, 26 Aug. 1813. Severely wounded, Toulouse, 10 April 1814 (1st Battn.) [*London Gazette*]. Died of wounds, 16 April 1814. Return dated April 1814. [PRO: WO 25/2965]. Hurt, p. 80.

THACKWELL, Joseph, Capt., 15th Light Dragoons: *1829 Statement of Service*: In his 1829 Statement of Service, he notes that his date of birth was 'Not known, never having been Registered, but supposed from oral testimony to be the 2nd Feby. 1784.' He was born in the Parish of Berrow, County of Worcester, and was believed to have been aged sixteen years and three months on his first appointment to the Army. Cornet, 15th Light Dragoons, 23 April 1800; Lt., 15th Light Dragoons, 13 June 1801; Half-pay, 25 June 1802; Lt., 15th Light Dragoons, 20 April 1804; Capt., 15th Light Dragoons, 9 April 1807; Major, 15th Light Dragoons, 18 June 1815; Bvt. Lt. Col., 15th Light Dragoons, 21 June 1817; Lt. Col., 15th Hussars, 15 June 1820. *Battles, sieges and campaigns*: 'Served as a Captain in the Campaigns in Gallicia & Leon under Lt. Genl. Sir John Moore. I was in several skirmishes & at the Battle of Corunna tho not engaged. As Captain in the Peninsula and France in the campaigns of 1813 and 1814. In the Battle of Vittoria June 21 1813. In the Battle of the Pyrenees in front of Pamplona July 27, 28, 29 & 30th. Commanded a squadron of the 10th and one of the 15th Hussars at the Blockade of Pampluna from 18th Oct. to the 31st when it surrendered. In the Battle of Orthes Feby. 27th 1814. In the affair of Tarbes March 20th. In the Battle of Toulouse Apl. 10th. And in many affairs of advanced Guards and outposts &c... Campaign in the Netherlands & France 1815 ... as Captain in Battle of Waterloo June 18th 1815.' *Distinguished conduct*: 'At the passage of the Ezla May 31st 1813 commanded the squadron which formed the advanced Guard, & was opposed by the 16th French Dragoons. In the Battle of Vittoria June 21st 1813. At the Affair of Grenada March 1st 1814 with the 13th French Chasseurs when in command of the advanced Guard. Noticed in General Orders & was recommended by L. General Lord Combermere, M. General Lord Edward Somerset, & Sir Colquhoun Grant for the Brevet of Major. At Waterloo June 18th 1815.'

Wounds received in action: 'A contusion on the right shoulder at Vittoria June 21st 1813. Wounded severely at Waterloo in charging a square of Infantry. Left arm amputated close to the shoulder. For this a years pay as Major was granted and a permanent pension of £30 per annum. A severe wound from a brick bat on the head in suppressing a riot at Birmingham on the 28th of April 1816.' *Titles, honorary distinctions and medals*: 'A medal in common with others, for the Battle of Waterloo.' *Service abroad*: 'Embarked 27th Oct. 1808 to Landed in England Jany. 27th 1809, Spain, in Gallicia & Leon. Embarked Jany. 15th 1813 to Landed in England July 17th 1814, Portugal, Spain & France. Embarked May 9th 1815 to Landed in England May 15th 1816, The Netherlands and France.' *Family*: Married Maria Audriah Roche, 9 July 1825, Parish of Aghada, near Cloque, Cork. They had two children by 1830. [PRO: WO 25/784 f194]. Colonel, 3rd Light Dragoons, 10 Jan. 1837. Died at Aghada Hall, co. Cork, 8 April 1859. Waterloo. MGS. *Dalton*, pp. 83–4 ['During the Par. war he boldly attacked and forced back at Granada 200 French dgns. with 50 men of his regt., making several prisoners, for which he was recommended for a bt. majority. At Waterloo, when charging with his regt., Thackwell was wounded in the fore-arm of his left arm, "but he instantly seized the bridle with his right hand, in which was his sword, and still dashed on at the head of his regt., the command of which had devolved upon him. Another shot took effect on same arm, but he immediately seized the bridle with his teeth." At the close of the day his left arm was amputated close to the shoulder.']

THATCHER, Sackville, Ensign/Lt., 48th Foot: *1829 Statement of Service*: Born 1795, Halpenden,

Wiltshire. Aged fifteen on his first entrance into the Army. Ensign, 48th Foot, 1 Nov. 1810; Lt. 26 Aug. 1813; Half Pay 1814; Lt., 103rd Foot, 19 Jan. 1815; Half Pay 25 March 1817; Lt., 37th Foot, Oct. 1825; Lt., 29th Foot, 9 April 1826. *Battles, sieges and campaigns*: 'At the Battle of Fuento Guinaldo, and the Siege of Cuidad Rodrigo the 19th January 1812 and that of Badajoz the 6th of April 1812. At the Battles of Salamanca, Vittoria, Pampeluna, Pyrenees, Lara, Nivelle, Nive, Orthes, & Toulouse.' *Wounds received in action*: 'Wounded at Salamanca, Badajoz, & Lara. Received for Wounds, Two Years Pay, One as Ensign and the other as Lieutenant.' *Service abroad*: 'August 1811 to 1814, Portugal & Spain. September 1815 to 13th June 1817, North America. 25th September 1826 to 31st December 1829, Mauritius.' Not married in 1830. [PRO: WO 25/790 f273]. Slightly wounded, storming of Badajoz, 6 April 1812 [*London Gazette*]. Slightly wounded, Salamanca, 22 July 1812 [*London Gazette*]. Slightly wounded, Nivelle, 10 Nov. 1813 ('Zachariah Thatcher') (1st Battn.) [*London Gazette*]. Army List gives as 'Zaccheus Thatcher'.

+THELLUSSON, Hon. George, Lt., 11th Light Dragoons: Cornet, 11th Light Dragoons, 12 Sept. 1811. Killed, Vittoria, 21 June 1813, ('Lieutenant the Honourable G. Thelluson, attached to the 16th Light Dragoons') [*London Gazette*]. *Register of officers' effects*: Lieutenant. Single. 'The amount of Effects not sent to this Regt. he being attached to 16th Dragoons'. [PRO: WO 25/2963]. Born 1791, second son of Peter, 1st Baron Rendlesham. [*Burke's Peerage*].

THIELE, Friderick Carl, Lt., Duke of Brunswick Oels' Corps (Infantry): Lt., Duke of Brunswick Oels' Corps, 27 Sept. 1809. Slightly wounded, Crossing the Bidassoa, 7/9 Oct. 1813 ('Theide') [*London Gazette*]. Slightly wounded, Orthes, 27 Feb. 1814 ('Lieutenant Charles Thiete') [*London Gazette*]. 'Friderick Carl Theile' in *Challis, Index*, p. 275.

+THIELE, Henry, 2nd Lt., K.G.L. Artillery: 2nd Lt., K.G.L. Artillery, 21 April 1807. Severely wounded, Albuera, 16 May 1811 [*London Gazette*]. Slightly wounded, siege of Badajoz, 31 March–2 April 1812 [*London Gazette*]. Killed, 'blown up', 'at the Storm and Capture of Fort Napoleon, and the Enemy's other Works, in the Neighbourhood of Almaraz', 19 May 1812 [*London Gazette*]. Mentioned in Hill's Almaraz dispatch, 21 May 1812 ['Lieutenant Thiele, of the Royal German Artillery, was blown up; and we have to regret in him a most gallant officer; he had particularly distinguished himself in the assault.'] [*London Gazette*]. Served in Peninsula 1809–12. *Beamish*, vol. II, p. 613 ['slightly wounded, 1st April 1812, before Badajos; killed by the explosion of a Tower, in Fort Ragusa, near Puente d'Almaraz in Spain, 19th May 1812.'].

+THOMAS, Edward Price, Ensign, 3rd Foot: Ensign, 3rd Foot, 4 Jan. 1810. Killed, Albuera, 16 May 1811 [*London Gazette*]. *Haythornthwaite, Die Hard*, p. 148 [Albuera: 'A most furious fight developed around the Buff's Colours. The Regimental Colour was carried by 16-year-old Ensign Edward Thomas; as the cavalry swept over the battalion, he held up the flag and tried to rally his company after its officer commanding, Captain William Stevens, was wounded. Thomas called out, "Rally on me, men, I will be your pivot"; and when summoned to yield his precious burden he replied "Only with my life!" He was cut down and the Colour was taken. After the battle his body was buried by a sergeant and a private, the only survivors of the 63 men who had formed his company.'].

+THOMPSON, Alexander, Lt., 10th Foot: Lt., Army, 11 June 1807; Lt., 10th Foot, 19 Nov. 1807. Killed, Castalla, 12 April 1813 [*London Gazette*]. *Register of officers' effects*: Single. 'Effects Remitted by Major Bayer either to Agent or friends, amount not known. Effects left in Sicily sold for £7. 15s. & Remitted to Regl. Agent. £29. 5s. Paid to liquidate in part his debts.' [PRO: WO 25/2963].

+THOMPSON, Alexis, Lt., 27th Foot: Lt., Army, 12 June 1799; Lt., 27th Foot, 12 March 1807. Severely wounded, storming of Badajoz, 6 April 1812 (3rd Battn.) [*London Gazette*]. Obituary, *The Gentleman's Magazine*, Nov. 1812, p. 493 ['Sept. 16. At Salamanca, Lieut. A. Thompson, 27th Foot.'].

THOMPSON, Benjamin, Ensign, 48th Foot: Ensign, 48th Foot, 11 July 1811. Slightly wounded, storming of Badajoz, 6 April 1812 ('Thomson') [*London Gazette*]. Severely wounded, Nivelle, 10 Nov. 1813 (1st Battn.) [*London Gazette*]. MGS.

+THOMPSON, Charles William, Lt. and Capt., 1st Foot Guards: Capt., Army, 28 feb. 1812; Lt. and Capt., 1st Foot Guards, 24 Sept. 1812. Killed, the Nive, 12 Dec. 1813 ('Lieutenant Charles Thompson (Captain)') (1st Battn.) [*London Gazette*].

THOMPSON, George, Capt., Royal Artillery: Capt., Royal Artillery, 20 July 1804. Slightly wounded, Fuentes de Onoro, 5 May 1811 ('Royal Foot Artillery') [*London Gazette*]. Mentioned in Murray's Castalla dispatch, 14 April 1813 ['The different brigades of guns, under Captain Lacy, Thomson [sic],

and Gilmour ... were extremely useful, and most gallantly served'] [*London Gazette*].

THOMPSON, James Doyne, Lt., 87th Foot: *1829 Statement of Service for Retired Officers*: Aged twenty-one on first appointment to the Army. Ensign, City of Dublin Militia, 16 Nov. 1806; Ensign, 87th Foot, 27 Oct. 1807, 'by volunteering'; Lt., 87th Foot, 20 Oct. 1808; Capt., 87th Foot, 7 Sept. 1815; Half-pay, 1 Feb. 1817, by reduction. *Where serving when wounded*: 'Wounded at Orthes in France'. No pension. *Family*: Married in 'Rapho County Donegal, Ireland', 29 Dec. 1825. One child by 1829. No employment. *Where generally resident during last five years*: 'Rathmelton & Raphor Co. Donegal, Ireland'. [PRO: WO 25/776 f122]. Severely wounded, Orthes, 27 Feb. 1814 (2nd Battn.) [*London Gazette*].

THOMPSON, John, Ensign, 79th Foot: Ensign, 79th Foot, 31 Oct. 1811. Slightly wounded, Nivelle, 10 Nov. 1813 (1st Battn.) [*London Gazette*]. Lt., 79th Foot, 18 Nov. 1813. Waterloo.

+THOMPSON, Joseph, Capt., 88th Foot: Capt., 88th Foot, 4 Aug. 1804. Killed in the trenches before Badajoz, March/April 1812 ['We were very soon obliged to creep on all fours as we advanced, for there were sharpshooters on the lookout who popped at every head that appeared and who, as it seems, were good marksmen, for they had killed many of our men in this way. Under the care of my friend Thompson, we returned in safety; but what was my horror when less than two hours after this, an officer of the 88th came to me with the information that our poor friend Thompson had been shot through the head while engaged with a friend in the same manner as he had but so lately been with me. An officer of another regiment had called upon him immediately after his return from the trenches with me, and had also expressed a wish to see the state of the trenches; Thompson offered to accompany him, and they proceeded but a short way, when Thompson, in bravado, stood up, looking directly at the spot from whence the shot came every now and then, believing he was out of reach, when he was struck on the head by a bullet, and fell dead.'] [*Fletcher*, p. 27, quoting Sir James McGrigor, *The Autobiography of Sir James McGrigor, Bt., Late Director General of the Army Medical Department* (1861)].

THOMPSON, Thomas, Lt., 26th Foot: Lt., 26th Foot, 19 Feb. 1806. Wounded, 'in the Army lately in Spain' (1st Battn.) [*March 1809 Army List*, p. 105].

THOMSON, Alexander, Capt., 74th Foot: *1829 Statement of Service for Retired Officers*: Aged eighteen on first appointment to the Army. Ensign, 74th Foot, 23 Sept. 1803; Lt., 74th Foot, 29 Feb. 1804; Capt., 74th Foot, 14 May 1807; Bvt. Major, 74th Foot, 9 April 1812, 'for my services at the Siege of Ciudad Rodrigo'; Bvt. Lt. Col., 74th Foot, 21 Sept. 1813, 'for my services at the Siege of St Sebastian in Spain, on which occasion I received also the esteemed Badge of Honor granted by His Majesty the Prince Regent a Medal'; Half-pay, 98th Foot, 1 April 1819, 'at my own request to enable me to settle family affairs then pending in the Court of Chancery in Ireland'. *Where serving when wounded*: 'At the Storming of Badajos was wounded. At the Siege of the Forts of Salamanca was wounded. At the Battle of Salamanca was wounded'. *Family*: Married in 'Thomas's Church, Dublin', 20 July 1826. One child by 1829. *Where generally resident during last five years*: 'Newport near Swords County of Dublin'. [PRO: WO 25/776 f99]. Mentioned

in Wellington's Ciudad Rodrigo dispatch, 20 Jan. 1812 ['It is but justice also the the 3d division to report, that the men who performed the sap belonged to the 45th, 74th, and 88th Regiments, under the command of ... Captain Thompson, of the 74th ... and they distinguished themselves not less in the storm of the place, than they had in the performance of their laborious duty during the siege.'] [*London Gazette*, 5 Feb. 1812]. Slightly wounded, storming of Badajoz, 6 April 1812 [*London Gazette*]. Slightly wounded while serving as acting engineer, in the siege of the Forts of St Vincente, St Cayetano, and La Merced at Salamanca, 18–24 June 1812 ('Brevet Major') [*London Gazette*]. Mentioned in Wellington's dispatch concerning the siege and capture of the forts at Salamanca, dated Fuente la Pena, 30 June 1812 ['Major-General Clinton ... mentions in strongest terms ... Major Thompson of the 74th Regiment, who acted as an engineer during these operations.'] [*London Gazette*]. Severely wounded, Salamanca, 22 July 1812 ('Captain and Brevet Major Thompson') [*London Gazette*]. Gold Medal. MGS.

THOMSON, Alexander, 1st Lt., Royal Engineers: 1st Lt., Royal Engineers, 24 June 1809. Severely wounded, storming of Ciudad Rodrigo,19 Jan. 1812 [*London Gazette*]. 2nd Capt., Royal Engineers 21 July 1813. Wounded, Cambray, June 1815. Waterloo. Died Edinburgh, 20 June 1830.

THOMSON, James, Capt., 6th Foot: *1829 Statement of Service for Retired Officers*: Aged seventeen years six months on first appointment to the Army. Cornet, Fife Fencible Cavalry, 30 Dec. 1794; Lt. and Adjutant, Fife Fencible Cavalry, 8 May 1795; 'Capt. Lieut.', Fife Fencible Cavalry, 20 Feb. 1797; Capt., Fife Fencible Cavalry, 21 Nov.

1799; Ensign, 59th Foot, 1 Sept. 1804; Lt., 6th Foot, 27 June 1805; Capt., 6th Foot, 22 Oct. 1807; Bvt. Major, 6th Foot, 19 July 1821; Major, 6th Foot, 15 May 1827; Half-pay, 1826. *Where serving when wounded*: 'Orthes'. *Details of pension*: One hundred pounds, commencing 25 June 1815. *Where generally resident during last five years*: 'Isle of Wight in Command of the Regl. Depot. With my Regt. in Bombay & in France since my return from India as half pay Major'. [PRO: WO 25/776 f79]. Severely wounded, Orthes, 27 Feb. 1814 ('Thompson') (1st Battn.) [*London Gazette*].

THOREAU, John, Lt., 40th Foot: Lt., 40th Foot, 28 May 1807 ('Thorau'). Severely wounded during the repulse of a sortie from Badajoz, 10 May 1811 ('Thoreau') (1st Battn.) [*London Gazette*]. Slightly wounded, Pyrenees, 26 July 1813 ('Thoreau') (1st Battn.) [*London Gazette*]. Waterloo.

THORN, Nathaniel, Capt., 3rd Foot: Capt., 3rd Foot, 4 Jan. 1810. Mentioned in Hill's Almaraz dispatch, 21 April 1812 ['Lieutenant-Colonel Offeney, my Assistant Quarter-Master-General, of whose valuable aid I have been deprived during the latter part of this expedition... Captain Thorn, Deputy Assistant Quarter-Master-General, succeeded to his duties; and I am indebted to him for his assistance'] [*London Gazette*]. Slightly wounded, the Nive, 13 Dec. 1813, while serving as Deputy Assistant-Quarter-Master General [*London Gazette*]. Major, Army, 3 March 1814. MGS. *Mullen*, p. 16 ['Thorne... Served with 3rd Foot and Staff in America. At battle of Plattsburg.'].

+THORNE, George, Lt., 4th Foot: Lt., 4th Foot, 9 Jan. 1805. Killed, Vittoria, 21 June 1813 ('Thorn') (1st Battn.) [*London Gazette*]. Obituary, *The Gentleman's Magazine*, July 1813, p. 91 ['June 21. Killed in the moment of victory, at the ever-memorable battle of Vittoria, Lieut. George Thorne, of the 4th or King's Own Infantry. He was a fine, handsome, open-hearted young man; and had it pleased God to have spared his life, would, no doubt, have continued, as he lived, an honour to his profession. He had seen much service; was at the attack on Copenhagen in 1807; in Sir John Moore's expedition and retreat to and from Corunna in 1809; at the storming and capture of Badajoz in 1812, in which he was slightly wounded by a spent ball (but did not return himself as so); in several other affairs in the Peninsula; and finally at Vittoria, where he closed his short but glorious career of ten years hard service, at the early age of 26. He was killed just 109 years after the death of his great uncle, a Lieutenant in the same regiment, who lost his life (when very young) at the attack and capture of Gibraltar in 1704, the regiment then acting as Marines on board the fleet commanded by Sir George Rooke. Ever since the raising of the 4th, or King's Own, in 1680 ... there has been, with the exception of a very few years, one of this ancient and respectable family always in the regiment.'].

+THORNHILL, Badham, Lt., 9th Foot: Lt., 9th Foot, 17 Dec. 1807. Killed, Siege of St Sebastian, 7–27 July 1813, while serving as Adjutant (1st Battn.) [*London Gazette*]. Obituary, *The Gentleman's Magazine*, Nov. 1813, p. 504 ['Lately... Before St Sebastian, Adj. and Lieut. Thornhill, of Devonshire cottage, near Bath.'].

THORNHILL, William, Major, 7th Light Dragoons: Second son of Bache Thornhill of Stanton-in-Peak, near Bakewell. Capt., Army, 5 May 1804; Capt., 7th Light Dragoons, 12 June 1806; Major, 7th

Light Dragoons, 8 April 1813. Severely wounded, Orthes, 27 Feb. 1814 [*London Gazette*]. Wounded, Waterloo. MGS. Died at Wimborne, 9 Dec. 1850.

THORNTON, Henry C., Major/Lt.Col., 40th Foot: Major, 40th Foot, 2 Aug. 1804; Bvt. Lt. Col., 40th Foot, 4 June 1811. Slightly wounded during the repulse of a sortie from Badajoz, 10 May 1811 [*London Gazette*]. Lt. Col, 40th Foot, 13 June 1811. Severely wounded, Nivelle, 10 Nov. 1813 (1st Battn.) [*London Gazette*]. Gold Medal. MGS. *Lawrence*, pp. 170–1, 191.

THORNTON, John, Lt., 94th Foot: *1829 Statement of Service for Retired Officers*: Aged seventeen on first appointment to the Army. Ensign, 94th Foot, 27 Aug. 1807; Lt., 94th Foot, 2 Aug. 1810; Half-pay, 42nd Foot, 3 Aug. 1817, 'rendered unfit for service from a severe wound, & obliged to retire'. 'Unfit for service'. *Where serving when wounded*: 'Battle of Nivelle in France, 10th Novr. 1813'. *Details of pension*: Seventy pounds per annum, commencing 10 Dec. 1814. Not married. No employment. *Where generally resident during last five years:* 'Straiton Cottage, Liberton, Edinburgh'. [PRO: WO 25/776 f123]. Severely wounded, Nivelle, 10 Nov. 1813 [*London Gazette*]. Pension 'for wounds' received at Sara, 1813 *1818 Pension Return*, pp. 20–1. MGS.

THORNTON, William Henry, Lt., 32nd Foot; 12th Portuguese Line: *1829 Statement of Service for Retired Officers*: Aged twenty-three on first appointment to the Army. Ensign, 32nd Foot, 28 Aug. 1804; Lt., 32nd Foot, 23 Oct. 1806; Capt., 'in the Army & to Serve with the Portuguese Army', 25 Oct. 1814; Half-pay, 25 Dec. 1816, by reduction. 'Remained as Major in the Portuguese Army until the Revolu-

tion of 1820'. 'Totally unfit for all Military Duty (as a Captain of Infantry) from the loss of the use of the Right Leg by a Wound; and a Ball Remaining Lodged in the Knee. But capable of Serving as a Major of Infantry or in the Cavalry should my Services be Required'. *Where serving when wounded*: 'At the battle of Pampeluna otherwise the Pyrenees on the 28th July 1813 while Serving with the 12th Portuguese Infantry'. *Details of pension*: One hundred pounds, commencing 29 July 1814. *Family*: Married in Lisbon, 29 Jan. 1818. Five children by 1829. *Title and nature of employment*: 'Barrack Master at Carlew Ireland, and Major on Half Pay of the Portuguese Army'. *Where generally resident during last five years*: 'Barrack Master in Ireland'. [PRO: WO 25/776 f143]. Severely wounded, Pyrenees, 25–28 July 1813, while serving as Capt., 12th Portuguese Line [*London Gazette*]. In Portuguese Service Aug. 1809 to April 1814. *1818 Pension Return*, pp. 24–5. MGS. *Challis, Portuguese Army*, p. 60.

THORPE, Samuel, 1st Lt., 23rd Foot; Capt., 39th Foot: *1829 Statement of Service for Retired Officers*: Aged sixteen on first appointment to the Army. Cadet, Royal Military College; Ensign, 14th Foot, 2 April 1807; Lt., 14th Foot, 16 Jan. 1808 [Army List gives 14 Jan.]; [Army List gives: 1st Lt., 23rd Foot, 5 May 1808]; Capt., 23rd Foot, 12 April 1812 [Army List gives 16 April]; [Capt., 39th Foot, 30 July 1812]; Half-pay, 8th Foot, Sept. 1820, 'From the effects of wounds in the Peninsula'. 'Is desirous of Service, having reestablished his health by a residence of two years in the South of France'. *Where serving when wounded*: 'Albuera, Spain, with R. W. Fuzileers. Toulouse, France, with 39th Regt.' No pension. *Family*: Married in 'Castlebar', 14 Feb. 1820. *Where generally resident during* *last five years*: 'Boyd's Hill, Aldenham, Herts.' [PRO: WO 25/776 f82]. Slightly wounded, Albuera, 16 May 1811 (1st Battn. 23 Foot) [*London Gazette*]. Severely wounded, Toulouse, 10 April 1814 ('Thomas Thorpe') (1st Battn. 39th Foot) [*London Gazette*]. MGS.

THURSTON, Charles Thomas, Ensign, 51st Foot: *1829 Statement of Service for Retired Officers*: Aged twenty-two on first appointment to the Army. 'Served 5 years as a Subaltern in the Militia Previously to Volunteering into the 51st Regt.'; Ensign, 51st Foot, 4 June 1812; Lt., 51st Foot, 22 Nov. 1813 [Army List gives 6 Jan. 1814]; Half-pay, 36th Foot, n.d. [1814], 'at my own request from impaired health'. Served two years on Full-pay. *Where serving when wounded*: 'Severely at Lazaca in the Pyrenees 31 August 1813'. No pension. *Family*: Married in 'St Georges, Dublin', Sept. 1814. *Where generally resident during last five years*: 'Dublin & Bromley, Kent'. [PRO: WO 25/776 f136]. Severely wounded, 'in the Operations of the Army', 31 Aug. 1813 ('Ensign') [*London Gazette*]. MGS. *Wheeler*, p. 144 [Wounded, near Lezaca, 31 Aug. 1813].

THWAITES, George Saunders, Capt., 48th Foot: Capt., Army, 2 July 1803; Capt., 48th Foot, 7 March 1805. Slightly wounded, Salamanca, 22 July 1812 [*London Gazette*]. Severely wounded, Pyrenees, 26 July 1813 (1st Battn.) [*London Gazette*]. MGS. *Mullen*, p. 337 ['Egypt in 10th Foot. Later 57th Foot. HP 6/2/17'].

TIENSCH, Godfried, Ensign, 2nd Line Battn. K.G.L.: Ensign, 2nd Line Battn. K.G.L., 27 Nov. 1807. Slightly wounded, Talavera, 28 July 1809 ('Tinch') [*London Gazette*]. Lt., 2nd Line Battn. K.G.L., 17 March 1812. Served in Peninsula 1808–14. Waterloo. *Beamish*, vol. II, p. 577.

TINCOMBE, Francis, Ensign, 30th Foot: Ensign, 30th Foot, 4 June 1812. Slightly wounded, during 'movements of the Army' [Retreat from Burgos: Villa Muriel], 25 Oct. 1812 [*London Gazette*]. Lt., 30th Foot, 8 Sept. 1814. Waterloo.

TITTLE, John Moore, Lt., 38th Foot: *1829 Statement of Service for Retired Officers*: Aged sixteen on first appointment to the Army. Ensign, 38th Foot, 7 July 1808; Lt., 38th Foot, 1 Nov. 1810; Half-pay, Royal African Corps, 12 April 1821. *Where serving when wounded*: 'St Sebastian, Spain'. *Details of pension*: Seventy pounds, 'granted 1814, discontinued Dec. 1817. Granted again 25th December 1826'. *Family*: Married in the Cape of Good Hope, 11 March 1820. Four children by 1829. *Where generally resident during last five years*: 'Farmhill, Coleraine, Ireland'. [PRO: WO 25/776 f160]. Severely wounded, storming of San Sebastian, 31 Aug. 1813 (1st Battn.) [*London Gazette*]. MGS.

TOBIN, John, Assistant Surgeon, 50th Foot: *1829 Statement of Service for Retired Officers*: Aged twenty-four on first appointment to the Army. Hospital Mate, 1809; Assistant Surgeon, 50th Foot, 1811 [Army List gives 19 Dec. 1811]; Half-pay, 9th Lancers, n.d., due to 'ill health'. Served nine years on Full-pay. *Where serving when wounded*: 'Spain'. *Details of pension*: Seventy pounds per annum, commencing 1813. *Family*: Married in Chelsea, 1816. Three children by 1829. No employment. *Where generally resident during last five years*: 'Brussels'. [PRO: WO 25/776 f163]. 'William Toben' in *1813 Army List*; 'John Tobin' thereafter. MGS.

TODD, Alexander, Capt., Royal Staff Corps: Capt., Royal Staff Corps, 21 April 1808. Slightly wounded, Talavera, 28 July 1809 [*London Gazette*]. *Simmons*, p. 137.

+**TODD, Andrew, Capt., 38th Foot:** Capt., 38th Foot, 25 Oct. 1810. Killed, during 'movements of the Army' [Retreat from Burgos: Villa Muriel], 25 Oct. 1812 (1st Battn.) [*London Gazette*]. Obituary, *The Gentleman's Magazine*, Feb. 1813, p. 182 ['Lately... In withdrawing from the siege of Burgos, Capt. A. Todd.'].

TODD, George, Capt., 29th Foot: Capt., 29th Foot, 24 July 1803. Recorded as 'Missing', Rolica, 17 Aug. 1808 ('Tod') [*London Gazette*]. Slightly wounded, Albuera, 16 May 1811 [*London Gazette*]. Pension of one hundred pounds per annum, commencing 17 May 1812, 'for wounds' received at Albuera ('Tod') [*1818 Pension Return*, pp. 8–9].

TOMKINSON, William, Lt., 16th Light Dragoons: *1829 Statement of Service for Retired Officers*: Aged seventeen on first appointment to the Army. Cornet, 16th Light Dragoons, 16 Dec. 1807; Lt., 16th Light Dragoons, 'Autumn of 1808' [Army List gives 6 Oct. 1808]; Capt., 60th Foot, 'Spring of 1812' [12 March 1812]; Capt., 16th Light Dragoons, 'about three months after last promotion' [3 June 1812]; Bvt. Major, 16th Light Dragoons, 21 Jan. 1819; Half-pay, 24th Light Dragoons, 1821. *Where serving when wounded*: 'Received a years pay for wounds received at Oporto in 1809'. Not married, 'a single man living with my sisters'. *Where generally resident during last five years*: 'Nantwich, Cheshire'. [PRO: WO 25/776 f178]. Author of *The Diary of a Cavalry Officer*, edited by his son James. Severely wounded, Heights of Grijon, 11 May 1809 [*London Gazette*]. Waterloo. Born 18 Jan. 1790, 4th son of Henry Tomkinson, of Dorfold. MGS. Died in 1872.

TOMLINSON, Richard, Lt., 28th Foot: Lt., 28th Foot, 3 April 1806. Slightly wounded, Pyrenees, 25 July 1813 (1st Battn.) [*London Gazette*].

TOMPSON, Joseph, Ensign/Lt., 20th Foot: Ensign, 20th Foot, 11 June 1812. Slightly wounded, Pyrenees, 25 July 1813 [*London Gazette*]. Lt., 20th Foot, 10 Feb. 1814.

TOOLE, Archer, Ensign/Lt., 61st Foot: *1829 Statement of Service*: Born 'Garranish, Co. Wexford', 5 Sept. 1793. Aged fifteen on first appointment to the Army. Ensign, 61st Foot, 11 May 1809; Lt, 61st Foot, 30 Jan. 1812; Adjutant, 61st Foot, 9 Oct. 1819; Paymaster, 61st Foot, 1 May 1828. *Battles, sieges and campaigns*: 'Busaco 27th Sepr. 1810. Fuentes de Honor 5 May 1811. Fort Salamanca 21 June '12. Battle of Salamanca 22 July '12. Pyrenees 28th, 29th, 30th, 31st July 1813. Nivelle 10th Novr. 1813.' *Wounds received in action*: 'Severely in the left Arm at the Battle of Salamanca. Severely in the right leg at the Battle of Nivelle. One years pay as Lieut. for the wound in the arm. One years pay as Captain for the wound in the Leg having Commanded the Co. during the Battle.' *Service abroad*: '1 Feby. 1810 to 27 March 1814, Peninsula. 21 Decr. 1816 to 27 May 1822, Jamaica. 30 June 1829 to 31 Decr. 1829, Ceylon.' Not married in 1830. [PRO: WO 25/797 f67]. Severely wounded, Salamanca, 22 July 1812 [*London Gazette*]. Severely wounded, Nivelle, 10 Nov. 1813 ('Arthur Toole') (1st Battn.) [*London Gazette*]. MGS.

TOOLE, William, Lt., 40th Foot: *1829 Statement of Service for Retired Officers*: Aged sixteen on first appointment to the Army. Ensign, 40th Foot, 5 Dec. 1805; Lt., 40th Foot, 7 Feb. 1807 [Army List gives 25 Aug. 1807]; Capt., 40th Foot, 9 Nov. 1814 [Army List gives 19 April 1817]; Half-pay, 19 April 1817, by reduction. 'Afraid he is unable to serve in consequence of the still bad effects of his wounds'. *Where serving when wounded*:

'Badajoz'. *Details of pension*: Seventy pounds, commencing 7 April 1813, increased to one hundred pounds on 25 Dec. 1822. *Where generally resident during last five years*: 'Wexford'. [PRO: WO 25/776 f187]. Severely wounded, storming of Badajoz, 6 April 1812 (1st Battn.) [*London Gazette*]. MGS.

TOOLE, William Henry, Capt., 32nd Foot: *1829 Statement of Service for Retired Officers*: Aged seventeen on first appointment to the Army. Ensign, Minorca Regt., May 1799; Ensign, 58th Foot, 23 May 1799; Lt., 58th Foot, 25 Sept. 1799; Capt., 32nd Foot, 7 Sept. 1804; Bvt. Major, 4 June 1814; Capt., 4th Royal Veteran Battn., 16 May 1816, 'Retired full Pay'. 'Totally disabled from wounds'. *Where serving when wounded*: 'Alexandria in Egypt, 21st March 1801. Salamanca Spain, 22nd June 1812. Pyrenees Spain, 30th July 1813. Quatre Bras, 16th June 1815'. *Details of pension*: One hundred pounds, commencing 31 July 1814. One hundred and fifty pounds, commencing 25 June 1828. *Family*: Married in Falmouth, Cornwall, 16 July 1805. Five children by 1829. *Where generally resident during last five years*: Edinburgh. [PRO: WO 25/776 f172]. Slightly wounded, Salamanca, 22 July 1812 (1st Battn.) [*London Gazette*]. Severely wounded, Pyrenees, 30 July 1813 (1st Battn.) [*London Gazette*]. Temporary pension of one hundred pounds per annum, commencing 31 July 1814, 'for wounds' received at Pampeluna, 1813 [*1818 Pension Return*, pp. 8–9]. Waterloo. Died 17 Aug., 1831.

+TOPP, Richard, Ensign, 94th Foot: Ensign, 94th Foot, 11 June 1812. Killed, 'in Action with the Enemy', 24 Feb. 1814 [*London Gazette*].

TOPP, Robert, Ensign/Adjutant, 24th Foot: Ensign and Adjutant, 24th Foot, 18 May 1809. Slightly wounded, Talavera, 28 July 1809 [*London Gazette*].

TORRENS, Robert, Ensign, 57th Foot: Ensign, 57th Foot, 12 Jan. 1809. Slightly wounded, Albuera, 16 May 1811 [*London Gazette*]. In Portuguese Service April 1812 to Aug. 1813. *Challis, Portuguese Army*, p. 60 ['Capt. 4 Line'].

TORRIANO, William, Ensign/Lt., 71st Foot: Ensign, 71st Foot, 16 Oct. 1809; Lt. 12 Dec. 1811. Severely wounded, Vittoria, 21 June 1813 (1st Battn.) [*London Gazette*]. Slightly wounded, the Nive, 13 Dec. 1813 (1st Battn.) [*London Gazette*]. Waterloo. MGS. *Dalton*, pp. 180, 183 ['... joined the 1st Batt. 71st in 1811 and proceeded to Portugal. Promoted lieut. into 2nd Batt. at home, but remained with 1st Batt. in the field until the return of the army from France. Was present at Arroyos des Molinos, Almaraz, with covering army before Badajoz; severely wounded at Vittoria and taken prisoner, but shortly after retaken at Nive; Bayonne (twice wounded); Orthes, and Toulouse, besides many minor affairs. ... D. at Budleigh Salterton, Devonshire, 1862.'].

+TOURNEFORT, Joseph B. de, Capt., Chasseurs Britanniques: Capt., Chasseurs Britanniques, 7 Sept. 1809. Slightly wounded, Fuentes de Onoro, 5 May 1811 [*London Gazette*]. Killed, Pyrenees, 30 July 1813 [*London Gazette*].

TOWERS, William R., Ensign, 3rd Foot Guards: Ensign, 3rd Foot Guards, 31 Oct. 1805. Slightly wounded, Talavera, 28 July 1809 [*London Gazette*]. Later 6th Garrison Battn. MGS.

TOWNSEND, John, Lt./Capt., 14th Light Dragoons: *1829 Statement of Service*: Born 11 June 1789, Castle Townsend, County Cork. Cornet, 14th Light Dragoons, 24 Jan. 1805;

Lt. 8 March 1806 ('Obtained by Recruiting for the Service'); Capt. 6 June 1811; Major, Army, 21 Jan. 1819; Major, 14th Light Dragoons, 13 Sept. 1821; Lt. Col. 16 April 1829; Colonel 23 Nov. 1841. 'Died at Castle Townsend Co. Cork, 22nd April 1845.' *Battles, sieges and campaigns*: 'Lieutenant when first engaged in the different affairs of the 10th, 11th, and in crossing the Duoro on the 12th May 1809. In the Engagements of the 27th & 28th July 1809 at Talavera... In an Affair with the Enemy's Advanced Posts on the 11th July 1810 in front of Cuidad Rodrigo under the command of Lieut. Colonel Talbot, who was killed. Engaged with the Enemy the 24th July at the passage of the Coa... In several skirmishes of the Rear Guard from Almeida, to the Lines of Torres Vedras... in 1810. In the several affairs on the Enemy's retreat from Santurem to the frontiers of Spain from the 6th March to the 4th April 1811; In the Engagements of the 3rd & 5th May 1811 at Fuentes d'Onor; Captain in an affair with the Enemy's Lancers, on the 25th September 1811; Employed on Duty at the siege of Badajos, 1812... In an Affair with the Enemy's Cavalry on the 11th April 1812, at Usagre and Slerena... In an Affair on the 16th June 1812, in front of Salamanca; In an Affair with the Enemy's cavalry on the 18th July 1812, near Castillos. At the Battle of Salamanca on the 22nd July 1812; In an Affair with the Enemy's Rear Guard near Pameranda on the 23rd July 1812. From the 24th Octr to the 20th November 1812 in the several skirmishes from Madrid to near Cuidad Rodrigo; In the several Affairs & skirmishes from the 26th May near Salamanca to the Battle of Vittoria on the 21st June 1813, at the taking of a Gun from the Enemy near Pampeluna under the command of Major Brotherton; In the several engagements & skirmishes from the entrance of the British Army into France on the

10th November 1813 to the Battle of Orthes on the 27th February 1814 and until taken prisoner near the City of Pau in France on the 8th March 1814 and remained as such until the termination of the Peninsula War... Embarked for America in October 1814, was present at the Attack on New Orleans on the 8th Jany. 1815 under the command of Major General Pakenham who was killed. Returned to England on the 23rd May 1815.' *Wounds received in action*: 'Slightly wounded on the 5th May 1811 at Fuentes d'Onor.' *Titles, honorary distinctions and medals*: 'Promoted to the Rank of Brevet Major for Meritorious Services during the Peninsula War.' *Service abroad*: '22nd Dec. 1808 to 14th July 1814, Portugal, Spain, & France. 24th Oct. 1814 to 16th May 1815, America.' He had not been married by 1830. [PRO: WO 25/784 f143]. Recorded as 'missing', 'in Action with the Enemy', 7 March 1814 [*London Gazette*].

TOWNSHEND, Hon. Horatio George Powis, Capt. and Lt. Col., 1st Foot Guards: Capt. and Lt. Col., 1st Foot Guards, 26 Oct. 1809. Severely wounded, and 'missing', sortie from Bayonne, 14 April 1814 (3rd Battn.) [*London Gazette*]. Wounded, Waterloo. Died, unmarried, 24 May 1843. *Dalton*, pp. 97, 100. *Gronow*, pp. 11–12 ['Among the many officers of the Guards who were taken prisoner in the unfortunate sortie from Bayonne, was the Hon. H. Townshend, commonly called Bull Townshend. He was celebrated as a bon vivant, and in consequence of his too great indulgence in the pleasures of the table, had become very unwieldy, and could not move quick enough to please his nimble captors, so he received many prods in the back from a sharp bayonet. After repeated threats, however, he was dismissed with what our American friends would be pleased to designate "a severe booting." ']

TREEVE, Richard, 1st Lt., 23rd Foot: *1829 Statement of Service for Retired Officers:* Aged twenty-four on first appointment to the Army. 2nd Lt., 23rd Foot, 18 July 1805, 'without Purchase, from the Wiltshire Militia in which I had served about four years and Volunteered for the Line'; 1st Lt., 23rd Foot, 29 May 1806; Capt., 23rd Foot, 1 Oct. 1812; Half-pay, 24 Oct. 1814, by reduction; 'Major of Brigade to the Forces at the Island of Jersey', 25 Sept. 1814 to 24 March 1822, 'when discontinued in consequence of the District being reduced'; 'Inspector of Strangers', Jersey, 19 June 1824; Barrack Master, Jersey, 23 Aug. 1825. *Where serving when wounded:* 'Albuera'. *Details of pension:* Seventy pounds, commencing 17 May 1812, increased to one hundred pounds on 18 June 1815. *Family:* Married in 'St Gluvias by the Borough of Penryn, County of Cornwall', 12 Aug. 1813. Seven children by 1829. *Title and nature of employment:* 'Serving as Barrack Master in the Island of Jersey from the 23rd August 1825'. *Where generally resident during last five years:* 'In St Savioux Parish, Island of Jersey'. [PRO: WO 25/776 f221]. Slightly wounded, Albuera, 16 May 1811 (1st Battn.) [*London Gazette*]. *1818 Pension Return*, pp. 6–7. MGS.

TRENCH, Hon. Richard Le Poer, Lt. Col., 74th Foot: Ensign, 27th Foot, 30 Oct. 1799; Lt., 67th Foot, 9 Dec. 1800; Capt., 93rd Foot, 25 May 1803; Major, 96th Foot, 25 Oct. 1806; Bvt. Lt. Col. and Insp. Field-Officer of Militia in Canada, 28 Jan. 1808; Lt. Col., 74th Foot, 21 Sept. 1809. Mentioned in Wellington's Fuentes de Onoro dispatch, 8 May 1811 [5 May: 'the piquets of the 3d division, under the command of the Honourable Lieutenant-Colonel Trench.'] [*London Gazette*, 26 May 1811]. Slightly wounded, storming of Badajoz, 6 April 1812 ('the Honourable Power French') [*London Gazette*]. Mentioned in

Wellington's Badajoz dispatch, 7 April 1812 ['Lieutenant-General Picton has reported to me particularly the conduct of ... Lieutenant-Colonels Trench and Manners of the 74th Regiment'] [*London Gazette*]. Slightly wounded, Pyrenees, 30 Aug. 1813 [*London Gazette*]. Colonel, Army, 4 June 1814. *Royal Military Calendar*, vol. IV, pp. 191–2 ['... he was present at the battles of Busaco and Fuentes D'Onor; siege of Badajos; battles of Salamanca, Vittoria, Pyrenees, Nivelle, and Toulouse, for which occasions he has the honor of wearing a cross and four clasps. He is a Knight Commander of the Order of the Bath, and of the Tower and Sword of Portugal. [Vide also the Duke of Wellington's Despatches, Vol. I. pp. 181, 189, 207 and 230.]'].

TREVOR, John Evans, Lt., 45th Foot: Lt., 45th Foot, 18 Oct. 1810. Severely wounded, Toulouse, 10 April 1814 (1st Battn.) [*London Gazette*].

TRIMBLE, Matthew, Ensign, 11th Foot: Ensign, 11th Foot, 16 July 1812. Severely wounded, Nivelle, 10 Nov. 1813 (1st Battn.) [*London Gazette*]. Pension of fifty pounds per annum, commencing 11 Nov. 1814, 'for wounds' received at Nivelle [*1818 Pension Return*, pp. 6–7].

TRYON, Charles, Lt., 88th Foot: Lt., 88th Foot, 4 April 1805. Severely wounded, Salamanca, 22 July 1812, while serving on Staff as Deputy Assistant Adjutant-General [*London Gazette*].

TUCKER, Thomas Edwardes, Lt., 23rd Foot: 1st Lt., 23rd Foot, 22 Sept. 1808. Severely wounded, storming of Badajoz, 6 April 1812 [*London Gazette*]. Temporary pension of one hundred pounds per annum, commencing 7 April 1813, 'for wounds' received at Badajoz

[*1818 Pension Return*, pp. 6–7].
MGS.

TUGGINER, Edward de, Ensign, De Roll's Regt.: *1829 Statement of Service for Retired Officers*: Aged twenty on first appointment to the Army. Ensign, Roll's Regt., 20 Sept. 1810; Lt., Roll's Regt., 29 Sept. 1813; Half-pay, 25 Oct. 1816, by reduction. *Where serving when wounded*: 'In Spain.' *Details of pension*: 'Grant of a years Pay as Ensign. No Pension. By Warrant of the Secretary of War 30th August 1817.' *Family*: Married in Soleure, Switzerland, 30 March 1818. Four children by 1829. *Title and nature of civil employment*: 'Membre du Tribunal du Canton de Soleure... Directeur de la Police de Soleure...' *Where generally resident during last five years*: 'at Soleure.' [PRO: WO 25/756 f52].

+TULLOCH, William, Capt., 36th Foot: Capt., 36th Foot, 10 Sept. 1803. Killed, Salamanca, 22 July 1812 ('Tullok') [*London Gazette*].

TULLOH, Alexander, Capt., Royal Artillery; Major/Lt. Col., Portuguese Artillery: 2nd Capt., Royal Artillery, 19 July 1804; Capt., Royal Artillery, 8 May 1811. Wounded, storming of Badajoz, 6 April 1812, while serving as a Major in the Portuguese Army ('Tulloch') [*London Gazette*]. Lt. Col., Royal Artillery, 27 April 1812. Mentioned in Lt.-Gen. Hamilton's dispatch of 11 Nov. 1812, concerning the Affair at Alba de Tormes, 10–11 Nov. 1812 ['Lieutenant-Colonel Tulloh has made so good an arrangement of his two brigades of guns, that ... I consider my flanks secure.'] [*London Gazette*]. Severely wounded, the Nive, 13 Dec. 1813, while Lt. Col., Portuguese Artillery [*London Gazette*]. In Portuguese Service Sept. 1811 to April 1814. Gold Medal. *Webber*, p. 88 [n39: 'He was ... Sir Rowland Hill's CRA.'], pp. 127–8 [arrested for court martial, 15 Dec. 1812], p. 153 [1

June 1813: 'Colonel Tulloh's two Brigades of Portuguese Artillery']. *Royal Military Calendar*, vol. IV, pp. 418–20 ['...Whilst on leave of absence in France, during the short peace of Amiens, he was made a prisoner of war ... and detained as a hostage ... until the year 1810; when in Nov. he escaped from the citadel of Verdun, and after three months travelling in the night ... he succeeded, with some naval officers, in seizing a vessel in the river Meuse, and arrived in England in March, 1811.']. *Challis, Portuguese Army*, p. 60 ['Lt.Col. 3 Arty.'].

TUNSTALL, William, Lt., 36th Foot: *1829 Statement of Service for Retired Officers*: Aged seventeen on first appointment to the Army. Ensign, 36th Foot, 11 May 1809, 'by volunteering from the Royal Cardigan Militia'; Lt., 36th Foot, 21 Jan. 1812; Half-pay, 1 May 1819, at officer's own request, 'in consequence of ill health arising from the effects of my wound'. *Where serving when wounded*: 'at the Battle of the Nivelle'. *Details of pension*: Seventy pounds per annum, commencing 'twelve Months after I rec'd my wound', increased to one hundred pounds on 25 Dec. 1822, 'relative to the state of my left eye'. Not married. *Where generally resident during last five years*: 'Ascott near Shrewsbury'. 'Shortly after my first appointment to the 36th Regt. I was ordered to repair to the Isle of Wight to join the Corps of Embodied Detachments which were then forming under the Command of the Honble. Basil Cochrane. I afterwards Embarked with that Corps at Cowes on the 15th July 1809 and served with it at the taking of the Island of Walcheren, & was present at the Sieges of Flushing, Tervere, &c &c. I beg leave to add, that I became a severe sufferer from the Fever of that Island and from the effects of which I believe I have to attribute a great deal of subsequent ill health, even up to the present period. On the 20th January 1811, having become effective in the 1st Battalion of my Regt. I embarked with it at Portsmouth on Board His Majesty's Ship Victory, destined for Portugal, where I served with it during the Campaigns of 1811, & 1812. Was present at the Investment of Almeida, was in action with the Enemy at the Pass of the Agueda, at Barba del Puerco, & was also at the siege of Burgos, &c. Towards the end of 1812, having been long subject to relapses of the Walcheren Fever, I was under the necessity of appearing before a Medical Board, which granted me leave of absence to England, for the recovery of my health. I accordingly set sail from Portugal on the 1st January 1813. On the 8th October 1813, I again Embarked at Portsmouth with a Detachment of my Regt. to join the Army, then Encamped on the Pyrenees. I reach'd the Head Quarters of the Regt. at the Maya Pass on the 8th Novr. and was present on the 10th of the same month at the Battle of Nivelle, where I had the misfortune to be severely wounded by a musket shot in the Face. The Ball having entered close under the Left Eye, making its exit near the right Temple. In consequence of which, I was totally deprived of the sight of my right Eye, & the vision of the left has been materially affected by it, & what I have most to regret is, it has ever since been very susceptible to attacks of Inflamation. Owing to the nature of the wound a Medical Board granted me leave of absence to England & I sail'd from Passages on the 12th Jany. 1814. In Jany. 1815, I was sufficiently recovered to join my Regt. at Barracks in Ireland. In the beginning of July following, I embarked with the Regt. at the Cove of Cork, destined to join the Army under the Duke of Wellington. We landed at Ostend & march'd to Paris, where we join'd Headquarters. In the end of Decr. of

the same year I embark'd with the Regt. at Calais for England. On the 1st Jany. 1816 we march'd into Portsmouth where I continued to do duty in the Garrison until 29th July 1817 when I again Embarked with my Regt. for the Island of Malta, where I remained doing Garrison duty for the space of 10 months, at which time I obtained leave of absence to return to England. During my stay in Malta I was at different times subject to attacks of Inflamation in my Left Eye, caused, as I was given to understand in great measure by the heat of the Climate. Under these circumstances, together with the strong recommendation of the Surgeon of the Regt. not to remain on the station that placed my sight in such iminent danger, I memorialed to His late Royal Highness the Commander in Chief to be allowed to go upon half pay, which request he was pleased to grant me.' [PRO: WO 25/776 f240]. Severely wounded, Nivelle, 10 Nov. 1813 (1st Battn.) [*London Gazette*]. Seventy pounds per annum pension, commencing 11 Nov. 1814, for 'loss of an eye' at St Pe, 1813 [*1818 Pension Return*, pp. 10–11]. MGS.

+TURING, William, Capt., 18th Light Dragoons: Capt., Army, 15 Jan. 1807; Capt., 18th Light Dragoons, 5 March 1807. Killed, Vittoria, 21 June 1813 [*London Gazette*].

+TURNBULL, Middleton, Lt., 11th Foot: Lt., 11th Foot, 4 March 1806. Severely wounded in the siege of the Forts of St Vincente, St Cayetano, and La Merced at Salamanca, 18–24 June 1812 (1st Battn.) [*London Gazette*]. Died of wounds, 26 June 1812. Return dated 25 July 1812. [PRO: WO 25/2965].

TURNER, Charles, Lt. Col., Royal West India Rangers; Portuguese Service: Lt. Col., Royal West India Rangers, 18 April 1807. Severely wounded, during the repulse of a sortie from Badajoz, 10 May 1811 [*London Gazette*]. Three hundred pounds per annum pension, commencing 10 May 1812, for 'loss of an arm' at Badajoz, 1811 [*1818 Pension Return*, pp. 8–9]. Bvt. Col., Royal West India Rangers, 4 June 1814. In Portuguese Service April 1811 to Nov. 1813. *Challis, Portuguese Army*, p. 60 ['Col. 17 Line... Wd. 1st Sge. Badajos 8 May '11'].

TURNER, Charles Barker, Capt., 11th Foot: *1829 Statement of Service*: Born 23 July 1788, Nottinghamshire. Aged eighteen on first appointment to the Army. Ensign, 11th Foot, 10 Sept. 1806; Lt., 11th Foot, 10 March 1807; Capt., 11th Foot, 12 Oct. 1812; Major, 11th Foot, 26 March 1826; Major, unattached, 9 Nov. 1830; 'Appointed Insectg. Field Officer of Militia New Brunswick.' *Battles, sieges and campaigns*: 'Battle of Busaco 28th Sept. 1810, as Lieutenant of Lt. Company, and Adjt. of Light Battalion 4th Division. Battle of Fuentes de Onor 5th May 1811. Siege of Badajos June 1811. Siege and Storming of Ciudad Rodrigo Jany 1812, as Capt. of 2d Portuguese Caçadores. Battle of Salamanca 22d July 1812, as A.D.C. to Col. Collis, Commanding Portuguese Brigade 7th Division, Siege of Burgos in October 1812, as Captain 2d Caçadores. Investment of Pamplona July 1813. Battles of the Pyrenees 28th 29th & 30th July 1813. Battle & Passage of the Nivelle 10th Novr 1813, as Captin Comg. Lt. Company of the 11th Regiment, besides being engaged in 28 Affairs and skirmishes in different parts of Portugal & France. Served the Campaigns of 1809, 1810, 1811, 1812, and 1813. Was present during the whole of the Retreat of the Army to the Lines of Torres Vedras, and the whole of the Retreat from Burgos to Portugal in 1812.' *Distinguished conduct*: 'The 2d Caçadores thanked in Division orders by the Earl of Dalhousie for their conduct in the Defence of the Bridge of Vallodolid on the Retreat from Burgos in which I bore a part. Commanded and brought three Companies of the 11th Regt. out of Action at the Battle of the Pyrenees on the 28th July 1813, after the mortal Wounds of Captain Wrenn who was in Command. Led the Attack of the 6th Division at the Battle and Passage of the Nivelle 10th Novr. 1813, and brought the Light Companies of the Brigade out of Action after the Death of Captain Furnace 61st Regiment.' *Wounds received in action*: 'Shot in the shoulder on the Evening of the 10th Novr. 1813, whilst pressing the Rear Guard of the Enemy after the Action:– Ball extracted nine days after from under the Blade Bone of the shoulder, sent to England for my recovery and got a Grant of one year's Pay for it. Lost the lower and thin part of the Blade Bone of my shoulder from it, and I suffer very considerable pain & inconvenience from it in Cold or damp Weather, and Cannot bear my Arm suspended for any time without much pain. No Pension.' *Titles, honorary distinctions and medals*: 'Received a Medal from the Portuguese Government for my Services whilst employed in their Army.' *Service abroad*: '24th Decr 1807 to Sept 1809, Madeira. 2d Aug. 1809 to January 1814, Portugal, Spain and France. March 1816 to January 1821, Gibraltar. January 1827 to March 1828, Portugal. March 1828 to 31st Decr. 1829, Corfu. 1st Jany. 1830 to 1st June 1830, Corfu.' *Family*: Married Isabella Dillon, 2 April 1823, St. Mary's Church, Dublin. She died during childbirth with their first child, 1 Sept. 1825. Turner married Eliza Hassard, 18 Oct. 1828, Palace of St Michael and St George, Corfu, 18 Oct. 1828. They had one child by 1830. [PRO: WO 25/787 f3]. Severely wounded, Nivelle, 10 Nov. 1813 (1st Battn.) [*London Gazette*]. In

Portuguese Service Nov. 1810 to Dec. 1812. *Challis, Portuguese Army*, p. 60. MGS.

TURNER, William, Lt., 50th Foot: *1829 Statement of Service*: 'Born in the City of Dublin, June 1793. Aged Fourteen on his first Entrance into the Army. Ensign, 50th Foot, 9th April 1807. Lieutenant, 50th, 26th Aug. 1808. Captain, 50th, 4th Novr. 1819.' *Battles, sieges and campaigns*: 'Roliea 17th Aug. 1808. Vimiera 21 Augt. 1808. Corunna 16 Jany. 1809. Siege of Flushing Island of Walcheren July 1809. Fuentes De Honor 3 & 5 May 1811. Arroyo Del Molino 28 Octr. 1811. Almaraz 19th May 1812. Albadetarnos 1812. Beighar February 1813. Vittoria 21 June 1813.' *Wounds received in action*: 'Loss of Right Arm at Vittoria 21st June 1813. One Years Pay. £70 a Year Permanent.' *Service abroad*: 'Novr. 1807 to Nov. 1813, Portugal, Spain & Holland. 8th March 1819 to 24th Decr. 1825, Jamaica.' [PRO: WO 25/794 f342]. Severely wounded, Vittoria, 21 June 1813 (1st Battn.) [*London Gazette*]. Pension for 'loss of an hand' at Vittoria [*1818 Pension Return*, pp. 14–15].

TURNPENNY, J. F., Capt., 48th Foot: Lt., 48th Foot, 26 Oct. 1804; Capt. 11 July 1811. Slightly wounded in 'an Affair with the Enemy near Aldea de Ponte', 27 Sept. 1811 [*London Gazette*]. Slightly wounded, storming of Badajoz, 6 April 1812 [*London Gazette*].

TURTON, Richard, Capt., 40th Foot: Capt., 40th Foot, 10 Feb. 1808. Slightly wounded, Toulouse, 10 April 1814 (1st Battn.) [*London Gazette*]. Brother of William Turton.

+TURTON, William, Lt., 40th Foot: Lt., 40th Foot, 8 Dec. 1808. Severely wounded, storming of Badajoz, 6 April 1812 (1st Battn.) [*London Gazette*]. Slightly wounded, Salamanca, 22 July 1812 [*London Gazette*]. Severely wounded, 'since dead', storming of San Sebastian, 31 Aug. 1813 ('Detachment 40th Foot') [*London Gazette*]. Died of wounds, 31 Aug. 1813. Return dated Sept. 1813. [PRO: WO 25/2965]. Obituary, *The Gentleman's Magazine*, Supplement 1813, Part II, p. 699 ['Sept. 2. In Spain, of wounds received at the storming of St Sebastian's, in his 22d year, Lieut. Wm. Turton, of the 40th regiment, son of Wm. Turton, esq. late Captain of the same regiment, and nephew of Sir Thomas Turton, bart.... Very early in the contest, he joined his regiment in the Peninsula, and was actively engaged in all the various sieges and battles of the last three or four years. At the storming of Badajos, his regiment was amongst the most forward in entering the breach, where he received a severe wound, being shot through the body. This separated him from his regiment for some months; but, before he was returned fit for duty, having received intelligence that the Army was advancing into Spain, he left the Sick depot, and joined his gallant companions in time to share the glories and dangers of the battle of Salamanca, at which he was again wounded, although slightly. At the glorious battle of Vittoria, his regiment conspicuously shone amongst the foremost... After the battle, the calm which succeeded ... ill suited the ardent mind of this young soldier. On the resolution being taken to storm the Fort of St Sebastian, he volunteered his services (although not with the besieging army) on that dangerous and forlorn hope. To his honour, and as a proof of the respect borne him by his comrades in arms, sixty men sprang from the ranks, to share the glory and danger of their young Hero; and most of them alas! like him, have fallen victims to their patriotic ardour and courage.– The feelings of his Parents on a loss so irreparable can be easily conceived; nor is that agony diminished by the never-ceasing anxiety they feel for their only remaining Child, an Officer in the same regiment [Richard Turton], who, sharing in merit with his deceased brother, justly divided the affection of his Parents. May the blessings of peace shortly relieve their anxiety, and restore to them their only solace and last hope!'].

TWEEDDALE, George, Marquess of, Lt. and Capt., 1st Foot Guards; Major, 44th Foot: Capt., Army, 14 May 1807; Lt. and Capt., 1st Foot Guards, 21 April 1808. Slightly wounded, Busaco, 27 Sept. 1810, while serving on the Staff as DAQMG ('Tweddle') [*London Gazette*]. Capt., 15th Light Dragoons, 25 July 1811. Slightly wounded, Vittoria, 21 June 1813, while serving as AQMG on General Staff ('Major... 44th Regiment') [*London Gazette*]. Lt. Col., Army, 21 June 1813; Lt. Col., 100th Foot, 20 Jan. 1814. Family name was Hay. George Hay succeeded his father George, 7th Marquess, in 1804, following the latter's death in captivity at Verdun (the 7th Marquess' wife, 8th Marquess' mother, also died while a prisoner at Verdun); George, 8th Marquess, was born 1787, became a field marshal, died 1876. His brother was Lord James Hay, Colville's ADC at Waterloo.

TWEEDIE, James, Lt., 94th Foot: *1829 Statement of Service for Retired Officers*: Aged thirty-five on first appointment to the Army. Ensign, 94th Foot, 18 March 1808, 'Volunteer from the Renfrewshire Militia'; Lt., 94th Foot, 27 Feb. 1812; Half-pay, 28 Nov. 1816, 'being unable for military duty'. *Where serving when wounded*: 'Leading a party of 125 men to the successfull assault of Fort Picurina in front of Badajos on the evening 25 of March 1812,

under the immediate command of General Sir James Kempt'. *Details of pension*: Seventy pounds, commencing 26 March 1813. *Family*: Married in Edinburgh, July 1795. Five children, the last born in 1801. No employment. *Where generally resident during last five years*: 'Edinburgh & Ayr North Britain'. [PRO: WO 25/776 f264]. Slightly wounded, Nivelle, 10 Nov. 1813 [*London Gazette*].

TWIGG, James, Lt., 62nd Foot: *1829 Statement of Service for Retired Officers*: Aged nineteen years seven months twenty-three days on first appointment to the Army. Ensign, 62nd Foot, 28 Feb. 1805; Lt., 1 May 1806; Capt., 15 Oct. 1818; Half-pay, 5 Sept. 1819, by reduction. *Where serving when wounded*: 'Wounded slightly in the shoulder at Palimira under command of Major Darley but did not allow my name to be returned among the wounded'. *Family*: Married in Newry, 31 Jan. 1821. *Where generally resident during last five years*: Newry. [PRO: WO 25/776 f267].

TWIGG, John, Lt., 3rd Foot: Lt., 3rd Foot, 24 Aug. 1813. Severely wounded, the Nive, 13 Dec. 1813 (1st Battn.) [*London Gazette*]. MGS.

TWIGG, Thomas G., Ensign, 38th Foot: Ensign, 38th Foot, 25 Jan. 1810. Slightly wounded, 'in the assault and capture of the exterior line of the castle of Burgos on the evening of the 4th October, 1812' [*London Gazette*]. Lt., 38th Foot, 8 Sept. 1812.

TYLER, John, Ensign/Lt., 45th Foot; Capt., 93rd Foot: *1829 Statement of Service*: Born in London, 31 Aug. 1791. Aged sixteen 'on his first Entrance into the Army.' Ensign, 45th Foot, 23 Feb. 1808. Lt., 45th Foot, [28] Dec. 1809. Capt., 93rd Foot, 14 Feb. 1814. 'Appointed Brevet Major 18th June 1815.' Half

Pay, 53rd Foot, 1819, 'in consequence of Private affairs.' Capt., 97th Foot, 27 April 1827. Major, 97th Foot, 18 Decr. 1829. *Battles, sieges and campaigns*: 'Was present as Ensign in the 45th Regt. at the Battles of Roleia, Vimeria, Oporto and Talavera. Was present as Lieutenant in the 45th Regt. at the Battle of Busaco, was sent to Lisbon after this Battle in consequence of being severely wounded through the shoulder, returned and joined my Regiment in the Lines of Torres Vedras before the commencement of the Retreat of the French Army, and was with my Regiment following up the Enemy's retreat. Immediately after this appointed A.D. Camp to Lieut. General Sir Thos. Picton. Was present at the Battle of Fuentes D'Onor, and at the first siege of Badajos from June 6th to June 14th 1811. Was also present at the affair of Elbadon, Aldea-de-Ponte, Siege and Capture of Ciudad Rodrigo, Siege and Capture of Badajos on 6th April 1812, Battles of Vittoria and Pyrenees. Entrance into France Nov. 10th 1813. Was present as Captain in the 93rd Regt. at the Battles of Orthes, Toulouse, Quatre-Bras and Waterloo, where I received my Brevet Rank as Major on the 18th June 1815. After the Death of Sir Thomas Picton was appointed on the Field as A.D.C. to Lt. Genl. Sir Jas. Kempt (then Major General in the Command of the Division) and remained as his A.D.C. during the whole time with the Army of occupation in France. The various affairs in which the 3rd Division was Engaged under Sir Thos. Picton, and which are not General Actions I was also present with.' *Wounds received in action*: 'Wounded in the left shoulder at the Battle of Busaco on the 27 Septr. 1810, for which I received one years pay as Lieutenant.' *Titles, honorary distinctions and medals*: 'Received a Medal for the Battle of Waterloo.' *Service abroad*: '1st Augt. 1808 to April 1814, Spain, Portugal and France. 11th June 1815 to Nov. 1818, France & Holland.' *Family*: Married Sophia Cholmondelly Probyn, 9 Dec. 1826, Marylebone, London. They had no children by 1830. [PRO: WO 25/804 f84]. Severely wounded, Busaco, 27 Sept. 1810 (1st Battn.) [*London Gazette*].

U

+UNIACKE, John, Capt., 95th Foot: 1st Lt., 95th Foot, 9 May 1805; Capt., 1 May 1811. Severely wounded, Fuentes de Onoro, evening 3 May 1811 (3rd Battn.) [*London Gazette*]. Severely wounded, storming of Ciudad Rodrigo, 19 Jan. 1812 (3rd Battn.) [*London Gazette*]. Died of wounds, 27 Jan. 1812. Return dated 25 Feb. 1812. [PRO: WO 25/2965]. *Simmons*, pp. 75, 222 [Ciudad Rodrigo: 'A circumstance which probably saved me from being blown up with a friend of mine, Lieutenant Uniacke, was, when we got into the ditch together he observed, "this is the way." In the bustle I said, "Impossible. Here are the ladders. I shall go up them," fancying my Portuguese friend had placed them right, so that ultimately the ladders served me. Poor Uniacke got round the corner just in time enough to get scorched from head to foot in a frightful manner, and died a few hours after in great agony.']. *Leach*, p. 249 [Ciudad Rodrigo: 'Whilst the 3d Division was engaged at the large breach, one of the enemy's expence magazines exploded with a terrible crash, which blew up a great number of both parties... Captain Uniacke, of our battalion, who had been sent, before the storm commenced, to keep up the communication between the two divisions along the glacis, and to endeavour to keep down the fire of the French infantry from behind the ramparts, was blown up, with many men of his company. He was a remarkably fine young man, and greatly regretted.']. *Kincaid, Random Shots*, pp. 23–4 ['In one of the actions in which our regiment was engaged, in covering the retreat to Corunna, a superior body of the enemy burst upon the post of a young officer of the name of Uniacke, compelling him to give way in disorder, and in the short scramble which followed, he very narrowly escaped being caught by the French officer who had led the advance, – a short stout fellow, with a cocked hat, and a pair of huge jack-boots. Uniacke was one of the most active men in the army, and being speedily joined by his supporting body, which turned the tables upon his adversary, he resolved to give his friend a sweat in return for the one he had got, and started after him, with little doubt, from his appearance and equipment, that he would have him by the neck before he had got many yards further; but, to his no small mortification, the stout gentleman plied his seven-league boots so cleverly that Uniacke was unable to gain an inch upon him.'].

UNRUH, Wilelm von, Capt., Duke of Brunswick Oels' Corps (Infantry): Lt., Duke of Brunswick Oels' Corps, 25 Sept. 1809; Capt., Duke of Brunswick Oels' Corps, 26 Nov. 1812. Severely wounded, Nivelle, 10 Nov. 1813 ('Lieutenant Wm. Unruh') [*London Gazette*].

+UNTHANK, William Samuel, Lt., 44th Foot: Lt., 44th Foot, 20 Sept. 1810. Killed, storming of Badajoz, 6 April 1812 [*London Gazette*].

+URQUHART, Charles, Capt., 45th Foot: Lt., Army, 28 April 1804; Lt., 45th Foot, 7 Aug. 1804. Killed, Busaco, 27 Sept. 1810 (1st Battn.) [*London Gazette*].

URQUHART, Donald, Capt., 84th Foot: Capt., 84th Foot, 21 May 1808. Severely wounded, the Nive, 9 Dec. 1813 (2nd Battn.) [*London Gazette*].

URQUHART, William, Lt., 42nd Foot: *1829 Statement of Service for*

Retired Officers: Aged eighteen on first appointment to the Army. Ensign, 42nd Foot, 12 Feb. 1812; Lt., 42nd Foot, 5 Jan. 1814; Half-pay, 1814, by reduction. 'Not desirous [to serve] from bad health'. *Where serving when wounded*: 'Toulouse, France'. *Where generally resident during last five years*: 'Bordeaux France & Aberdeenshire N.B.' [PRO: WO 25/776 f390]. Severely wounded, Toulouse, 10 April 1814 (1st Battn.) [*London Gazette*].

+**USLAR, Frederick von, Capt., 2nd Dragoons K.G.L.**: Lt., 2nd Dragoons K.G.L., 11 May 1806. Killed, in an Affair with the Enemy's Rear-Guard near La Serna, 23 July 1812 ('Captain Usslar') [*London Gazette*]. Served in Peninsula 1812. *Beamish*, vol. II, p. 614 ['killed in the combat of Garcia Hernandez, 23 July 1812.'].

USLAR, Fredrich von, Capt., 1st Dragoons K.G.L.: *1829 Statement of Service for Retired Officers*: Aged twenty-four years three months on first appointment to the Army. Lt., 1st Dragoons K.G.L., 9 Feb. 1804; 'Captain and Brigade Major', 'Heavy Brigade of the King's German Legion, Staff of Ireland', 3 Jan. 1809; Capt., 1st Dragoons K.G.L., 1810 [Army List gives 24 Nov. 1809]; Half-pay, 24 Feb. 1816, by reduction. *Where serving when wounded*: 'In a Cavalry engagement at Las Mosao on the 11th of August 1812'. *Family*: 'Married Baroness Helena Lueneburg', in 'Wathlingen Principality Lueneburg', 2 Nov. 1817. They had four children by 1829. *Where generally resident during last five years*: 'Osnabrueck in the Kingdom of Hannover'. [PRO: WO 25/776 f393]. Slightly wounded, in 'an Affair with the Enemy's Cavalry, in Front of the Village of Majalahonda', 11 Aug. 1812 [*London Gazette*]. Served in Peninsula 1812–14. Gold Medal. Waterloo. *Beamish*, vol. II, p. 540 ['Frederick von Uslar ... slightly wounded, 11th Aug. 1812, at Majalahonda.'].

V

+VACHELL, Frederick, Ensign, Coldstream Guards: Ensign, Army, 27 Dec. 1810; Ensign, Coldstream Guards, 19 Sept. 1811. Severely wounded, sortie from Bayonne, 14 April 1814 (1st Battn.) [*London Gazette*]. Died of wounds, 13 May 1814. Return dated May 1814. [PRO: WO 25/2965]. *Hurt*, p. 75. *Fletcher, Fields of Fire*, p. 164 ['Coldstream Guards cemetery, Bayonne... Ensigns Vachell and Pitt'].

+VANCE, Richard, Ensign, 29th Foot: Ensign, 29th Foot, 26 Oct. 1810. Killed, Albuera, 16 May 1811 [*London Gazette*]. *Haythornthwaite, Die Hard*, p. 153 [Albuera: 'one of their [the 29th Foot] colour-bearers, Ensign Edward Furnace ... was hit again and killed. His replacement, Ensign Richard Vance, observing the regiment dying around him, tore the Colour from its pike lest it fall into French hands. After the battle he was found dead, with the flag concealed in the breast of his coat.'].

+VANDELEUR, Frederick, Capt., 87th Foot: Capt., 87th Foot, 8 Sept. 1808. Severely wounded, Vittoria, 21 June 1813 (2nd Battn.) [*London Gazette*]. Died of wounds, 6 July 1813. Return dated July 1813. [PRO: WO 25/2965]. Obituary, *The Gentleman's Magazine*, Nov. 1813, p. 504 ['Lately... Of wounds received in the battle of Vittoria ... Captain Vandeleur... of the 87th.'].

VANDELEUR, John Ormsby, Major-General: Born 1763. Served under Lord Lake in India. Commanded a cavalry brigade in the Peninsula. Major-General, 4 June 1811. Slightly wounded, storming of Ciudad Rodrigo, 19 Jan. 1812 [*London Gazette*]. Mentioned in Wellington's Ciudad Rodrigo

dispatch of 20 Jan. 1812 ['Major-General Vandeleur was likewise wounded in the same manner [leading troops during the storming], but not so severely [as Craufurd], and he was able to continue in the field.'] [*London Gazette, 5 Feb. 1812*]. Gold Medal. Waterloo. Died, 1 Nov. 1849. *Leach*, p. 249 [storming of Ciudad Rodrigo: 'General Vandeleur, who commanded a brigade of the Light Division, was also severely wounded.']. From Sept. 1811 to June 1813 he commanded a brigade of the Light Division. Knighted in 1815; rose to the rank of general. His injury at Ciudad Rodrigo was in the shoulder. George Napier wrote that he 'is a fine, honourable, kind-hearted, gallant soldier, and an excellent man. No man can or ought to be more respected than he is' [*Passages in the Early Military Life of General Sir George T. Napier*, ed. Gen. W. C. E. Napier (London, 1884) p. 218].

VANDELEUR, John, Ensign, 71st Foot: Ensign, 71st Foot, 9 July 1809. Severely wounded, Fuentes de Onoro, 5 May 1811 (1st Batt.) [*London Gazette*]. Lt., 12th Light Dragoons, 10 July 1811. *Hay*, p. 72 [following Salamanca]. Waterloo. MGS.

VANDER MEULEN, Charles Jewett, Ensign/Lt., 48th Foot: *1829 Statement of Service*: 'Born in St Albans, Hertfordshire, 3rd January 1794. Aged Sixteen on his first Entrance into the Army. Ensign, 48th, From 26th November 1807 to August 10th 1809. Lieutenant, 48th, From 10th August 1809 to November 25th 1823. Captain, 48th, From 25th November 1823 to December 31st 1829.' *Battles, sieges and campaigns*: 'Present in the Campaigns of 1809, 1810, 1811, part of 1812, 1813, 1814 in the Peninsula and France under the Command of His Grace the Duke of Wellington. Present with my Regiment at the Battle of Talavera, Busaco, Albuera, Vittoria, Pyrenees, Nivelle, Orthes, and Toulouse – besides various minor engagements and skirmishes with the Light Company to which I was always appointed.' *Distinguished conduct*: 'Always with my Regiment when employed abroad except disabled by wounds received in action and have received the approbation of my respective Commanding Officers viz. Lieutenant Colonel Donelan, Major Middlemore, Lieutenant Colonel Sir James Wilson, Colonel Sir William Hutchinson, Colonel Erskine, Lieutenant Colonel Taylor, and Lieutenant Colonel Bell now in command of the Regiment.' *Wounds received in action*: 'Severely wounded at Talavera with the 1st Battalion on the 28th July 1809. Severely wounded at Albuera on the 16th May 1811 and sent to England for recovery. Severely wounded at the battle of the Pyrenees on the 28th July 1813. Received a years Pay for each wound one as Ensign one as Lieutenant, and the last as Captain in consequence of having the command of a company.' *Service abroad*: 'September 1808 to May 1809, Gibraltar. May 1809 to August 1811, Peninsula. September 1812 to August 1814, Peninsula and France. March 1817 to March 1824, New South Wales. March 1824 to December 1829, India.' *Family*: Married Margaret Edwards, step daughter of Lieutenant and Adjutant Wild 48th Regiment, 18 May 1818, 'Seydny,' New South Wales. They had no children by 1830. [PRO: WO 25/794 f161]. Listed under 'Alterations while Printing' in 1808 Army List ['48 F... Charles Vandermedlan, Ensign']. Severely wounded, Talavera, 28 July 1809 (2nd Battn.) [*London Gazette*]. Lt., 48th Foot, 10 Aug. 1809. Severely

wounded, Albuera, 16 May 1811 ('Vander Meulen') (2nd Battn.) [*London Gazette*]. Severely wounded, Pyrenees, 28 July 1813 (Vandermeulen) (1st Battn.) MGS.

+VANE, Walter, Ensign, 1st Foot Guards: Ensign, 1st Foot Guards, 11 Sept. 1811. Severely wounded, sortie from Bayonne, 14 April 1814 (3rd Battn.) [*London Gazette*]. Died of wounds, 20 April 1814. Return dated April 1814. [PRO: WO 25/2965]. *Hurt*, p. 75. *Fletcher, Fields of Fire*, p. 164 ['Coldstream Guards cemetery, Bayonne ... those who lie here include ... Ensign Vane of the 1st Foot Guards"].

VARDY, Edward, Lt., 24th Foot: Lt., Army, 29 Nov. 1806; Lt., 24th Foot, 21 April 1808. Slightly wounded, Talavera, 28 July 1809 [*London Gazette*]. Capt., 11th Foot, 4 June 1813.

VAUGHAN, Edward, Ensign/Lt., 47th Foot: *1829 Statement of Service*: Born in Cardiganshire, 11 Dec. 1792. Aged seventeen 'on his first Entrance into the Army.' Ensign, 47th Foot, 19 Oct. 1809. Lt., 47th Foot, 24 Sept. 1812. Half Pay, Nov. 1814, 'Reduction of 2nd Battalion.' Lt., 77th Foot, Jan. 1815. Capt., Royal African Corps, 15 Sept. 1815. Half Pay, July 1819, 'Reduction of Corps.' Capt., 98th Foot, 24 March 1824. Major, 98th Foot, 22 March 1827. *Battles, sieges and campaigns*: 'Defence of Cadiz from October 1810 to September 1812. Defence of Tariffa Decr. 1811. Entry into France and Engagements 10th November and on the 9th, 10th, 11th & 12th Decr. 1814. Nive & Nivelle and Bayonne.' *Wounds received in action*: 'Severely wounded at the Puente De Largo at Aranguiz in defence of the Bridge Octr. 1812.' *Service abroad*: 'March 1810 to May 1810, Gibraltar. May 1810 to January 1813, Peninsula. July 1813 to August 1814, Peninsula and South France. August 1816 to

July 1817, Senegal & Sierra Leona. July 1817 to May 1819, Cape Good Hope. Decr. 1824 to February 1827, Cape Good Hope. April 1828 to Decr. 1830, Cape Good Hope.' [PRO: WO 25/804 f159].

VAVASOUR, John, Lt., 83rd Foot: Ensign, 83rd Foot, 25 July 1811; Lt., 83rd Foot, 16 Dec. 1813. Slightly wounded, storming of Badajoz, 6 April 1812 (2nd Battn.) [*London Gazette*].

+VEITCH, James, Lt., 57th Foot: Lt., 57th Foot, 25 May 1809. Slightly wounded, Albuera, 16 May 1811 [*London Gazette*]. Died, Spain, 1813 [PRO: WO 25/2965]. *Haythornthwaite, Die Hard,* p. 152 [Albuera: 'The very Colours were riddled, the Regimental Colour receiving 21 bullet-holes and the King's Colour seventeen and a broken staff; Ensign James Jackson, who carried the latter, was wounded in three places and handed it to Ensign James Veitch; when Jackson returned from having his wounds dressed he found that Veitch, though himself wounded, refused to give up the precious burden.'].

+VENABLES, Joseph, Capt., 83rd Foot: Lt., 83rd Foot, 20 March 1805; Capt. 13 June 1811. Slightly wounded, Vittoria, 21 June 1813 (2nd Battn.) [*London Gazette*]. Died, France, 24 March 1814 [PRO: WO 25/2965].

VEREKER, Henry T., Lt., 83rd Foot: Lt., 83rd Foot, 29 Sept. 1808. Severely wounded, Fuentes de Onoro, 5 May 1811 (2nd Battn.) [*London Gazette*]. Lt., Half-pay, 62nd Foot, 7 March 1822. MGS.

+VERSALLE, Capt., 1st Light Batt. K.G.L: Killed, Talavera, 28 July 1809 [*London Gazette*].

+VEVERS, Charles Nicholas, Ensign/Lt., 59th Foot: Ensign, 59th Foot, 29 Nov. 1810. Killed, storming

of San Sebastian, 31 Aug. 1813 (Lieutenant) (2nd Battn.) [*London Gazette*].

VICKERS, Gentle, 2nd Lt., 95th Foot: 2nd Lt., 95th Foot, 4 Oct. 1810. Severely wounded, Crossing the Bidassoa, 7/9 Oct. 1813 (3rd Battn.) [*London Gazette*]. Waterloo. Died, South America, 1823.

VIGORS, Nicholas Aylward, Ensign, 1st Foot Guards: Ensign, 1st Foot Guards, 7 Dec. 1809. Severely wounded, Barossa, 5 March 1811 [*London Gazette*]. Recorded amongst 'officers who have resigned and retired' in *1812 Army List*.

VINCENT, Edward, Lt., 48th Foot: *1829 Statement of Service for Retired Officers:* Aged twenty on first appointment to the Army. Ensign, 48th Foot, 12 Dec. 1805; Lt., 48th Foot, 4 Feb. 1808; Half-pay, 24 June 1823, 'at his request from private motives'. *Where serving when wounded:* 'Salamanca'. *Details of pension:* Seventy pounds per annum, commencing 23 July 1813. *Family:* Married in 'Maynooth in the County of Kildare, Ireland', 17 Jan. 1817. One child by 1829. No employment. *Where generally resident during last five years:* 'partly in Dublin but generally in Cork where he now lives'. [PRO: WO 25/776 f310]. Slightly wounded, Albuera, 16 May 1811 [*London Gazette*]. Severely wounded, Salamanca, 22 July 1812 [*London Gazette*]. *1818 Pension Return,* pp. 12–13.

VIVIAN, Richard Hussey, Lt. Col., 7th Light Dragoons: Lt. Col., Army, 28 Sept., 1804; Lt. Col., 7th Light Dragoons, 1 Dec. 1804; Col., Army, 20 Feb. 1812. Severely wounded, 'in Action with the Enemy', 8 April 1814 ('Colonel Hussey Vivian') [*London Gazette*]. ADC to His Royal Highness the Prince Regent, *1814 Army List.* Gold Medal.

Waterloo. *Dalton*, pp. 6, 28 ['Richard Hussey Vivian, eldest son of John Vivian, of Truro, Cornwall ... was born 28th July, 1775, and entered the army as ensign in the 20th Foot, in July, 1793... On 1st Dec., 1804, was appointed a lt.-col. in 7th Lt. Dns. Served with his regt. in the retreat from Corunna. In 1813 commanded the 7th Dns. in the Pa., and in Nov. of same year was appointed to the command of a cavalry brigade, and was present at the battle of the Nive. Was sev. wnded. in the advance upon Toulouse... When the 18th Hussars were approaching two squares of the Old Guard at Waterloo, Gen. Vivian rose up to the regt. with the brief address: "Eighteenth, you will follow me." The 18th responded, in expressive language, that they were ready to follow the general *anywhere*. The charge was made on the cavalry and guns, and was eminently successful. G.C.B. and G.C.H. Was created a baronet 1828, and a baron in the peerage of England, 1841. Col.-in-Chf. 12th Dns. Master-Gen. of the Ordnance, 1835-41. Was twice married, and left issue by both wives. D., 20th Aug., 1842.']. *Hart's 1840 Army List* [Ens. 31 July 1793; Lt. 20 Oct. 1793; Capt. 7 May 1794. Served in Flanders and Holland, under the Duke of York, from June 1794 until the return of the British army in 1795. Present in the sortie from Nimeguen, and was left with a picquet of the 28th Foot, in conjunction with other picquets, to hold it after the retreat of the army. Present in the affair at Geldermalsen, in which his regt. (the 28th) suffered severely, and in other skirmishes. Also present in all the different battles which took place during the expedition to the Helder, excepting on the landing. Major 9 March 1803; Lt. Col. 28 Sept. 1804. Commanded the 7th Hussars in the campaign under Sir John Moore, in 1808-9. Col. 20 Feb. 1812. Commanded a brigade of cavalry in the Peninsula, from Sept.

1813, until the return of the army; including the battles of Orthes, Nive, and Toulouse. Severely wounded in carrying the bridge of Croix d'Orade, near Toulouse. Gold Medal with one clasp for Sahagun and Benevente, and Orthes. Maj.-Gen. 4 June 1814. Served at Waterloo. Lt.-Gen. 22 July 1830; Col., 1st Dragoons, 20 Jan. 1837]. His father was John Vivian, vice-warden of the Stannaries. His memorial at St Mary's, Truro, noted that 'His nobleness of character, his charity, benevolence, and integrity endeared him to all who knew him. The widow and orphan never appealed in vain; and the deserving soldier always found him a friend' (quoted in Mackenzie, R. H., 'Lieut. General Richard Hussey, First Lord Vivian', in *Cavalry Journal* X (1920), p. 25. Vivian C., *Lord Vivian: a Memoir* (London, 1897).

VÖLGER, William, Lt., 7th Line Battn. K.G.L.: Lt., 1st Line Battn. K.G.L., 10 Jan. 1806. Slightly wounded, Talavera, 28 July 1809 ('1st Line Battn ... Volgee') [*London Gazette*]. Served in Peninsula 1808-11. *Beamish*, vol. II, p. 598.

+VOSS, Augustus von, Lt., 1st Dragoons K.G.L.: Lt., 1st Dragoons K.G.L., 3 Jan. 1809. Killed, in an Affair with the Enemy's Rear-Guard near La Serna, 23 July 1812 [*London Gazette*]. Served in Peninsula in 1812. *Beamish*, vol. II, p. 615 ['killed in the combat of Garcia Hernandez, 23d July 1812.']. *Kincaid, Random Shots*, p. 338 ['The day after the battle of Salamanca a brigade of heavy German dragoons, under the late Baron Bock, made one of the most brilliant charges in history ... broke through the squares, and took the whole of the infantry – the enemy's cavalry and artillery having fled.'].

+VOSS, Frederick von, Capt., 2nd Light Dragoons K.G.L: Capt., 2nd

Light Dragoons K.G.L., 20 Jan. 1806. Severely wounded, 'since dead', Barossa, 5 March 1811 [*London Gazette*]. Died of wounds, 5 March 1811. Return dated 25 March 1811. [PRO: WO 25/2965]. Served in Peninsula 1810–11.

Beamish, vol. II, p. 616. Mentioned in Frederick Grahn's Statement of Service: 'Fought the Battle of Barrossa 5th March, where I lost my Capt. Voss, killed in a charge upon the 1st Regt. of french Dragoons.' [PRO: WO 25/760 f111].

W

WACKERHAGEN, George, Capt., 2nd Light Battn. K.G.L.: *1829 Statement of Service for Retired Officers*: Aged twenty on first appointment to the Army. Lt., 2nd Light Battn. K.G.L., 6 Jan. 1806; Capt., 2nd Light Battn. K.G.L., 24 Dec. 1811; Half-pay, n.d., 'By Wounds'. 'His Majesty as King of Hannover, was pleased to give me the Commission of Brevet Major. Having been in the Hannoverian Service before I entered in the Kings German Legion'. Served nine years five months on Full-pay. *Where serving when wounded*: 'Before Bayonne in France'. *Details of pension*: One hundred pounds, commencing 15 April 1815. *Family*: Married in 'Reden, a noblemans seat in the Diocese of Pattensen, near Hannover', 18 July 1815. Three children by 1829. *Where generally resident during last five years*: 'At Pattensen near Hannover'. [PRO: WO 25/777 f112]. Recorded as 'missing', sortie from Bayonne, 14 April 1814 [*London Gazette*]. Served in Peninsula 1808–14. *Beamish*, vol. II, p. 656 ['placed upon half-pay 25th May 1815.'].

WACKHOLTZ, Friederich Ludwig, Capt., Duke of Brunswick Oels' Corps (Infantry): Capt., Duke of Brunswick Oels' Corps, 29 Sept. 1809. Slightly wounded, Crossing the Bidassoa, 7/9 Oct. 1813 ('Wackholz') [*London Gazette*].

WADE, Thomas Francis, Capt., 42nd Foot: Capt., 42nd Foot, 13 July 1809. Severely wounded, Albuera, 16 May 1811, while serving as ADC to Major-General Cole [*London Gazette*].

WAHRENDORFF, Augustus, Lt., 1st Light Battn. K.G.L.: *1829 Statement of Service for Retired Officers*: Aged sixteen on first appointment to the Army. Ensign, 1st Light Battn. K.G.L., 17 July 1809; Lt., 1st Light Battn. K.G.L., 16 April 1811; Capt., 1st Light Battn. K.G.L., 4 July 1816; Half-pay, 25 Feb. 1816, by reduction. *Where serving when wounded*: 'in the Peninsula'. *Details of pension*: Seventy pounds, commencing 7 Oct. 1813. *Family*: Married in the 'City of Hanover', 29 May 1817. Five children by 1829. No employment. *Where generally resident during last five years*: 'Celle in the Kingdom of Hanover'. [PRO: WO 25/777 f113]. Slightly wounded, in an action near Tolosa, 24 June 1813 [*London Gazette*]. Severely wunded, Crossing the Bidassoa, 7/9 Oct. 1813 ('Wahrendorf') [*London Gazette*]. Served in Peninsula 1811–14. Waterloo. *Beamish*, vol. II, p. 562 ['severely wounded, 24th June 1813, at Villafranca; severely wounded, 7th Oct. 1813, on the Bidassoa; slightly wounded, 18th June 1815, at Waterloo.'].

WAINMAN, William, Lt., 14th Light Dragoons: Lt., 14th Light Dragoons, 1 Dec. 1808. Slightly wounded, Talavera, 28 July 1809 [*London Gazette*]. Capt. 13 Feb. 1812. MGS. *Brotherton*, p. 23.

WALDRON, Charles, Lt., 5th Foot; Capt., 11th Portuguese Line: *1829 Statement of Service for Retired Officers*: Aged nineteen on first appointment to the Army. Ensign, 54th Foot, Dec. 1799, 'Volunteered from Roscommon Militia'; Lt., 54th Foot, Dec. 1800; Half-pay, 24 June, 1802, 'Reduced with 2nd Battn., Gibraltar 24th June 1802'; Lt., 5th Foot, 2 April 1807; Capt., 37th Foot, 2 July 1813; Half-pay, 9th Foot, 22 March 1818. 'Had served in the Portuguese Service as Captain four years and a Half (4th Division) 11th Regt. Portuguese Infantry'. *Where serving when wounded*: 'Rodinha,

Badajos'. No pension. *Family*: Married in Bristol, 12 Jan. 1808. Nine children by 1829. *Where generally resident during last five years*: 'Jersey & France'. [PRO: WO 25/777 f23]. Wounded, during 'several Affairs with the French' [action near Redinha], 12 March 1811, while serving as a Capt. in 11th Portuguese Regt. [*London Gazette*]. In Portuguese Service April 1810 to Sept. 1813. *Challis, Portuguese Army*, p. 60.

WALKER, Colin, Ensign, 42nd Foot: Ensign, 42nd Foot, 15 Oct. 1812. Severely wounded, Toulouse, 10 April 1814 ('Collin Walker') (1st Battn.) [*London Gazette*].

+WALKER, George, Ensign, 66th Foot: Ensign, 66th Foot, 11 May 1809. Severely wounded, Albuera, 16 May 1811 (2nd Battn.) [*London Gazette*]. Died of wounds, 17 May 1811. Return dated 25 May 1811. [PRO: WO 25/2965].

+WALKER, George Henry, Lt., 59th Foot: Lt., 59th Foot, 6 April 1809. Severely wounded, 'since dead', Vittoria, 21 June 1813 (2nd Battn.) [*London Gazette*].

WALKER, George Townsend, Lt. Col., 50th Foot; Major-General: Lt. Col., 50th Foot, 6 Sept. 1798; Major-General, 4 June 1811. Severely wounded, storming of Badajoz, 6 April 1812 [*London Gazette*]. Mentioned in Wellington's Badajoz dispatch, 7 April 1812 ['The gallantry and conduct of Major-General Walker, who was also wounded, and that of the officers and troops under his command, were highly conspicuous.']. Slightly wounded, Orthes, 27 Feb. 1814, while serving on the General Staff [*London Gazette*]. Pension of three hundred and fifty pounds, commencing 7 April 1813, 'for wounds' received at Badajoz [*1818 Pension Return*, pp. 24–5]. *Surtees*, p. 151 [Badajoz: 'General Walker also, who commanded a part of the 5th division, bravely forced an entrance into the town at the opposite side, overcoming every one of the numerous barriers and obstacles which presented themselves; and where he himself, in the act, I believe, of mounting the rampart, received a most desperate wound. It was said, but I know not how truly, that when he fell, the French soldier who wounded him was about to repeat the blow, which in all probability would have deprived him of life, but that the General, whether intentionally or not it is not said, made the masonic sign, which was understood by one of the Frenchmen, and that he instantly interfered in his behalf and stopped the blow. They say the General some time after found out that his brave deliverer had been sent to Scotland with his fellow-prisoners, and that he had him searched for and handsomely rewarded, and, I believe, procured him his liberty.'].

WALKER, Harry, 1st Lt., 23rd Foot: *1829 Statement of Service for Retired Officers*: Aged twenty-four on first appointment to the Army. Cornet, Royal Waggon Train, 16 Jan. 1804; Lt., Royal Waggon Train, 28 Aug. 1804; Half-pay, 24 Dec. 1806, by reduction; Lt., Nova Scotia Fencibles, 19 Feb. 1807; Lt., 23rd Foot, 21 Sept. 1808 [Army List gives 1st Lt., 20 Sept.]; Capt., 67th Foot, 22 July 1813; Capt., 2nd Royal Veteran Battn., 29 Aug. 1815; Capt., Royal Veteran Battn., 'Novr. or Decr.' 1819. 'Ready & willing to serve ... as far as my bodily health will permit, suffering at certain periods from a severe wound in the right thigh'. *Where serving when wounded*: 'Storming of Badajoz, 6th Apl. 1812'. *Family*: Married in 'St Johns Newfoundland', 7 Sept. 1809. No children. *Where generally resident during last five years*: 'St Hilliers, Island of Jersey'. [PRO: WO 25/777 f46]. Severely wounded, storming of Badajoz, 6 April 1812 [*London Gazette*].

+WALKER, James Perriman, Lt., 20th Foot: Lt., 20th Foot, 23 Nov. 1809. Slightly wounded, Pyrenees, 25 July 1813 [*London Gazette*]. Died of wounds, 18 Oct. 1813. Return dated Oct. 1813. [PRO: WO 25/2965].

WALKER, James, Capt., 42nd Foot: Capt., 42nd Foot, 28 Sept. 1804. Slightly wounded, Orthes, 27 Feb. 1814 (1st Battn.) [*London Gazette*]. Slightly wounded, Toulouse, 10 April 1814 (1st Battn.) [*London Gazette*].

WALKER, Leslie, Capt., 71st Foot: Capt., 71st Foot, 28 Aug. 1804. Severely wounded, Pyrenees, 30 July 1813 (1st Battn.) [*London Gazette*]. Capt., 71st Foot, 2 Sept. 1813. Waterloo.

+WALKER, Richard, Capt., 23rd Foot: Capt., 23rd Foot, 26 Nov. 1807. Killed, Pyrenees, 28 July 1813 (1st Battn.) [*London Gazette*].

+WALKER, Samuel, Lt. and Capt., 3rd Foot Guards: Lt. and Capt., 3rd Foot Guards, 11 Oct. 1799. Killed, Talavera, 28 July 1809 [*London Gazette*]. Obituary, *The Gentleman's Magazine*, Aug. 1809, p. 780 ['Captain Walker, of the 3d Dragoon Guards [sic], and Captain Beckett, Brigade-Major in the Coldstream Guards, killed in the battle of Talavera, were both natives of Leeds. The former was the fourth son of William Walker, esq. of Killingbeck-hall, and the latter was one of the sons of John Beckett, esq. of Meanwood, an Alderman of Leeds.'].

WALKER, William, Capt., 5th Dragoon Guards: Capt., 5th Dragoon Guards, 8 Aug. 1811. Severely wounded, in 'an Affair with the Enemy's Rear Guard, near Llerena', 11 April 1812 ('Lieutenant') [*London Gazette*].

WALKER, William, Lt., 11th Foot: *1829 Statement of Service for Retired Officers*: Aged thirty on first appointment to the Army. Lt., Fifeshire Militia, 'volunteered with upwards of sixty men & appointed Ensign'; Ensign, 90th Foot, 7 Aug. 1807; Lt., 11th Foot, 14 Sept. 1808; Capt., 11th Foot, 30 Dec. 1819; Half-pay, Aug. 1820, 'in consequence of wounds & bad health'. *Where serving when wounded*: 'Commanding a Company at the Battle of Salamanca, 22d July 1812'. *Details of pension*: Seventy pounds, commencing 22 July 1813. *Where generally resident during last five years*: 'Pathhead and Dysart Fifeshire'. [PRO: WO 25/777 f60]. Severely wounded, Salamanca, 22 July 1812 (1st Battn.) [*London Gazette*]. MGS.

WALLACE, Alexander, Lt. Col., 88th Foot: Lt. Col., Army, 28 Aug. 1804; Lt. Col., 88th Foot, 6 Feb. 1805. Mentioned in Wellington's Fuentes de Onoro dispatch, 8 May 1811 [5 May: 'The troops in Fuentes de Honour were besides supported, when pressed by the enemy, by the ... 88th regiment, under Lieutenant-Colonel Wallace, belonging to Colonel Mackinnon's brigade; and on one of these occasions the 88th, with the 71st and 79th, under the command of Colonel Mackinnon, charged the enemy, and drove them through the Village; and Colonel Mackinnon has reported particularly the conduct of Lieutenant-Colonel Wallace'] [*London Gazette*, 26 May 1811]. Mentioned in Wellington's Salamanca dispatch, 24 July 1812 ['Lieutenant-Colonel Wallace, of the 88th, commanding a brigade in the 3rd division'] [*London Gazette*]. Col., Army, 4 June 1813. Gold Medal. *Haythornthwaite, The Armies of Wellington*, p. 98 ['Alexander Wallace made a ... speech to his 88th, warning them that if ever they had to form square, they should expect to be in "a damned ugly way, and have plenty of noise about you"; and "by God, if you are once broken, you'll be running here and there like a parcel of frightened pullets!" '], p. 203 [Quoting his speech to the 88th before Busaco: 'Now, Connaught Rangers, mind what you are going to do; pay attention to what I have so often told you, and when I bring you face to face with those French rascals, drive them down the hill – don't give the false touch, but push home to the muzzle! I have nothing more to say, and if I had it would be of no use, for in a minute or two there'll be such an infernal noise about your ears that you won't be able to hear yourselves.'], pp. 247–8. *Grattan, United Services Journal,* II, 1831, pp. 33, 181.

WALLACE, Charles, Ensign/Lt., 40th Foot: *1829 Statement of Service for Retired Officers:* Aged seventeen on first appointment to the Army. Ensign, 40th Foot, April 1812 [Army List gives 23 April]; Lt., 40th Foot, 24 Aug. 1813; Half-pay, Feb. 1817, by reduction. *Where serving when wounded:* 'Peninsula'. *Family:* Married in Dublin, 4 July 1827. One child by 1829. *Where generally resident during last five years:* 'Lime Park fort Ireland'. [PRO: WO 25/777 f102].

WALLACE, Hugh Ritchie, Lt., 7th Foot: *1829 Statement of Service for Retired Officers:* Aged seventeen on first appointment to the Army. Ensign, 1st Foot, n.d., 'was an Ensign 4 months'; Lt, 7th Foot, Nov. 1809 [Army List gives 16 Nov.]; Half-pay, n.d., 'at my own request ... seeing no prospect of Promotion after serving during the whole Peninsula War'. Served nine years on Full-pay. *Where serving when wounded:* 'Twice severely wounded'. No pension. No employment. *Where generally resident during last five years:* 'in France England Scotland & Jamaica, presently'. 'Served with the Royal Fusiliers in all the principal actions in Portugal, Spain, America & France'. [PRO: WO 25/777 f6]. Lt., 7th Foot, 16 Nov. 1809. Slightly wounded in 'an Affair

with the Enemy near Aldea de Ponte', 27 Sept. 1811 [*London Gazette*]. Slightly wounded, Salamanca, 22 July 1812 [*London Gazette*]. MGS.

+WALLACE, William, Lt. Col., 20th Foot: Lt. Col., 20th Foot, 7 May 1807. Slightly wounded, Pyrenees, 25 July 1813 [*London Gazette*]. Died of wounds, 29 July 1813. Return dated Aug. 1813. [PRO: WO 25/2965].

WALLER, Edward, Ensign, 87th Foot: Ensign, 87th Foot, 24 May 1810. Slightly wounded, Tarifa, 31 Dec. 1811 (2nd Battn.) [*London Gazette*].

WALLER, Robert, Capt., 103rd Foot: Capt., Army, 3 May 1800; Capt., 103rd Foot, 21 Jan. 1808; Severely wounded, Albuera, 16 May 1811, while serving as DAQMG [*London Gazette*]. Bvt. Major, 103rd Foot, 20 June 1811; Bvt. Lt. Col., 103rd Foot, 26 Aug. 1813; Major on the Staff, as permanent AQMG, 10 Nov. 1814. Gold Medal. Pension of three hundred pounds per annum, commencing 16 May 1812, 'for wounds' received at Albuera, while serving as 'Chief of the Quarter Master Genls. Staff' [*1818 Pension Return*, pp. 24–5]. *Royal Military Calendar,* vol. IV, p. 489. *Webber,* p. 62.

WALLEY, William, 1st Lt., 23rd Foot: 1st Lt., 23rd Foot, 10 Dec. 1807. Severely wounded, storming of Badajoz, 6 April 1812 ('Whaley') [*London Gazette*]. Waterloo. Capt., 23rd Foot, 19 July 1815; Half-pay, 14th Foot, 6 April 1820.

WALPOLE, Volunteer, 88th Foot: Severely wounded, Orthes, 27 Feb. 1814 (1st Battn.) [*London Gazette*]. Ensign, 84th Foot, 20 Jan. 1814. *Challis, Index,* p. 204 ['to 84 Ft'].

WALPOLE, Hon. John, Lt. and Capt., Coldstream Guards: Ensign,

Coldstream Guards, 18 Feb. 1804; Lt. and Capt., Coldstream Guards, 23 June 1808. Severely wounded, siege of Burgos, 18 Oct. 1812 [*London Gazette*]. Capt. and Lt. Col., Coldstream Guards, 25 July 1814. Pension of one hundred pounds per annum, commencing 19 Oct. 1813, 'for a wound' received at Burgos [*1818 Pension Return*, pp. 2–3]. MGS. *Royal Military Calendar*, vol. V, p. 73. Born 1878, fourth son of Horatio, 2nd Earl of Orford; died 1859. [*Burke's Peerage*].

WALSH, Charles, Ensign, 3rd Foot: Ensign, 3rd Foot, 3 Jan. 1810, Severely wounded, Albuera, 16 May 1811, while serving as one of the senior Ensigns [*London Gazette*]. Lt., 3rd Foot, 19 June 1811. In the *1811 Army List* in the Bodleian Library, Oxford, is written the notation: 'Died Oct. 30/46, at Lorrha, Co. Tipperary. Stated in obituary to have saved the colours of the Buffs at Albuhera, May 16/11. See Mil. [-]ron, Nov. 1811, page 7.' *Haythornthwaite, Die Hard*, p. 148 [Albuera: 'The King's Colour was borne by Ensign Charles Walsh; its pike was broken by a roundshot, Walsh was wounded and about to be taken prisoner when Lieutenant Matthew Latham seized the Colour from him. Latham was immediately surrounded by French cavalry, one of whom dealt him a dreadful, disfiguring blow across the face; but he continued to defend himself with his sword until another massive sabre-blow severed his left arm. Dropping his sword, Latham seized what remained of the colour-pike with his right arm and continued to struggle until he was ridden down, trampled and speared by lancers endeavouring to capture the flag. With the last of his strength he tore the fabric from the pike and concealed it in the breast of his coat.'], p. 160 ['After the battle, both the Buffs' lost Colours were recovered ... astonishingly Matthew

Latham was found still alive, with the King's Colour in his coat. Originally, Charles Walsh was credited with saving this invaluable treasure, and was praised for it in the House of Commons; but when Walsh escaped from the French he confirmed the truth. Latham was accordingly promoted to captain (in February 1813) and presented by his regiment with a gold medal worth £100 which portrayed his act of heroism, and which he was permitted to wear in uniform. The Prince Regent defrayed the expenses of a leading surgeon who repaired Latham's facial injury, and on his retirement in 1820 he received a pension of £170 per annum.'].

+WALSH, Edward, Capt., 3rd Foot: Capt., 3rd Foot, 17 Aug. 1809. Killed, Pyrenees (2nd Sorauren), 30 July 1813 [*London Gazette*].

WALSH, James, Capt., 91st Foot: Capt., 91st Foot, 28 Aug. 1804. Reported as missing, Talavera, 27 July 1809, while serving with 1st Battn. Detachments [*London Gazette*]. Slightly wounded, Toulouse, 10 April 1814 (1st Battn.) [*London Gazette*]. Bvt. Major, 91st Foot, 12 April 1814. Waterloo. Major, 91st Foot, 3 April 1818; Bvt. Lt. Col., 91st Foot, 21 Jan. 1819. *Royal Military Calendar*, vol. V., p. 153.

WALSH, Lawence De Courcy, Lt., 34th Foot: Lt., 34th Foot, 8 June 1809. Wounded, Albuera, 16 May 1811 (3rd Battn.) [*London Gazette*].

WALSH, Theodore, Ensign, 38th Foot: Ensign, 38th Foot, 22 April 1813. Temporary pension of fifty pounds per annum, commencing 26 July 1814, 'for wounds' received at San Sebastian, 1813 [*1818 Pension Return*, pp. 10–11]. MGS.

+WALTON, Richard, Lt., 24th Foot: Lt., 24th Foot, 14 Feb. 1808. Severely wounded, 'since dead', siege of Burgos, 20–26 Sept. 1812 (2nd Battn.) [*London Gazette*].

WALTON, Robert, Capt., 39th Foot: *1829 Statement of Service*: Born 22 Dec. 1784, Edinburgh. Aged sixteen on first appointment to the Army. Ensign, 39th Foot, 3 Dec. 1800; Lt. 19 March 1801; Capt. 18 June 1809; Half Pay 21 March 1816. Paymaster, 9th Foot, 29 July 1819. *Battles, sieges and campaigns*: 'Sicily 1810 Sir John Stewart. Peninsula 1812. Vittoria 21st June 1813. Nivelle 10 November 1813. Nive 10th December 1813. Bayonne 13th December 1813. Orthes 27th February 1814. Toulouse 10th April 1814... Platsburgh US America 1815.' *Wounds received in action*: '21st June 1813 Vittoria 1 Years Pay and a Temporary Pension of £100 per Annum from 22d June 1814 to 24th June 1817.' *Service abroad*: '21st June 1801 to 24th April 1803, South America and West Indies. 19th April 1805 to 1st May 1816, Malta Sicily Peninsula Canada France. 16th September 1819 to 19th January 1827, West Indies.' *Family*: Married Constantina Josepha Bryan, 25 Fen. 1808, Malta. They had four children by 1830. [PRO: WO 25/786 f298]. Severely wounded, Vittoria, 21 June 1813 (1st Battn.) [*London Gazette*].

WARD, Adam, 1st Lt., Royal Artillery: 1st Lt., Royal Artillery, 9 Sept. 1810. Severely wounded, 'right leg amputated', 'in Action with the Enemy', 19 March 1814 ('Lieutenant Ward') [*London Gazette*]. Waterloo. Died, Dublin, 28 Feb. 1827.

WARD, John R., Capt., 27th Foot; Major, 7th Caçadores: Capt., 27th Foot, 12 June 1806; Bvt. Lt. Col., 27th Foot, 1 Jan. 1812. Severely wounded, storming of Badajoz, 6 April 1812 ('Captain Ward (Lieutenant-Colonel)') (3rd Battn. 27th Foot) [*London Gazette*]. Major, 36th Foot, 26 Nov. 1812. Gold

Medal. MGS. *Royal Military Calendar*, vol. IV, p. 386 ['was attached to the Portuguese Army: commanded the 7th Caçadores at the battle of Salamanca, siege of Badajos, and the battle of the Pyrenees']. *Challis, Portuguese Army*, p. 60 ['Maj. 7 Cacad ... P/S Feb. to Dec. '12']. It appears that he was attached to the 7th Caçadores at the time he received his wound, though was returned with his British regiment.

WARDE, John, Lt., 4th Foot: Lt., 4th Foot, 31 Oct. 1810. Severely wounded, Vittoria, 21 June 1813 ('Ward') [*London Gazette*].

+WARDLAW, John, Lt., 52nd Foot; Capt., 4th Caçadores: Lt., 52nd Foot, 2 Nov. 1809. Killed, Salamanca, 22 July 1812, while serving as Capt., 4th Caçadores [*London Gazette*]. In Portuguese Service March 1811 to July 1812. *Challis, Portuguese Army*, p. 60.

WARING, J. Thurloe Scott, Ensign, 28th Foot: Ensign, 28th Foot, 17 Sept. 1812. Severely wounded, the Nive, 13 Dec. 1813 (1st Battn.) [*London Gazette*]. Capt., 28th Foot, 31 March 1814. Half Pay, on reduction of the regiment, 1814.

WARNMAN, William, Lt., 14th Light Dragoons: *1829 Statement of Service for Retired Officers*: Aged eighteen on first appointment to the Army. Cornet, 14th Light Dragoons, 25 Sept. 1806; Lt., 16th Foot, 10 Nov. 1808; Lt., 14th Light Dragoons, 1 Dec. 1808; Capt., 14th Light Dragoons, 13 Feb. 1812; Half-pay, 25 March 1816, by reduction. *Where serving when wounded*: 'Wounded as Lieut. in 14th Lt. Dr. at the battle of Talavera but never received any pension'. *Family*: Married in Yorkshire, 7 April 1828. No children. No employment. *Where generally resident during last five years*: 'Heddingley, Leeds'. [PRO: WO 25/777 f79].

WARREN, Richard Burke, Lt., 84th Foot: *1829 Statement of Service*: Born Triarn, Ireland, 1 Nov. 1792. Aged sixteen 'on his first Entrance into the Army.' Ensign, 84th Foot, 17 May 1808. Lt., 84th Foot, 12 Sept. 1809. Half Pay, 24 June 1818. Lt., 54th Foot, 5 July 1824. Half Pay, 24th Foot, 24 July [illegible]. Lt., 96th Foot, 17 July 1828. Note added: 'Capt unattached 26 [illegible] '30.' *Battles, sieges and campaigns*: 'Walcheren, 1809. Terveer, Flushing... Ensn. & Lt. Peninsular. Nive 9th Decr. 1813, Lt.' *Wounds received in action*: 'Left Collar Bone broken, & Ball still lodged in the cavity of the chest, at the Battle of the Nive 9th Decr. 1813. [Pension] dated the [illegible] Decr. 1814, Permanent.' *Service abroad*: '1809, Walcheren. 15 Augt. 1813 to 29th Jany. 1814, Peninsular.' [PRO: WO25/804 49]. [Note: much of the above statement was illegible]. Severely wounded, the Nive, 9 Dec. 1813 (2nd Battn.) [*London Gazette*].

+WARRINGTON, J., Ensign, 27th Foot: Ensign, 27th Foot, 11 July 1811. Severely wounded, 'since dead', storming of Badajoz, 6 April 1812 (3rd Battn.) [*London Gazette*]. Died of wounds, 8 April 1812. Return dated 25 April 1812. [PRO: WO 25/2965].

WARTON, Thomas William, Ensign, 48th Foot: Ensign, Army, 3 May 1810; Ensign, 48th Foot, 12 June 1811. Slightly wounded, Salamanca, 22 July 1812 [*London Gazette*].

WATERS, John, Bvt. Lt. Col., E.O.P.S.: Capt., Army, 24 Sept. 1803; Capt., 1st Foot, 28 Feb. 1805; Major, Army, 16 Feb. 1809 (Spain and Portugal – Not holding Regimental Commission); Bvt. Lt. Col., E.O.P.S., 30 May 1811, 'Spain and Portugal – Not holding Regimental Commission'. Recorded as 'missing' during 'several affairs with the French Army', 18 March–7 April 1811, while serving with the 1st Portuguese Line ('late 1st Foot') [*London Gazette*]. Signed the casualty returns after Salamanca, 22 July 1812, as 'Lieut.-Col. and A.A.G.' Mentioned in Wellington's Salamanca dispatch, 24 July 1812 ['I am particularly indebted to ... Lieutenant-Colonel Waters, at present at the head of the Adjutant-General's department at headquarters']. Slightly wounded, Pyrenees, 28 July 1813 ('Lieut.-Col. Waters, A.A.G.') [*London Gazette*]. Gold Medal. AAG at Waterloo. Died, 21 Nov. 1842. *Challis, Portuguese Army*, p. 60 ['P.W. Sabugal 3 May '11, but escaped; Wd. Pyrenees']. Gold Cross. *Gronow*, pp. 14–18 ['the well-known and highly popular Quartermaster-General Sir John Waters, who was born at Margam, a Welsh village in Glamorganshire. He was one of those extraordinary persons that seem created by kind nature for particular purposes; and without using the word in an offensive way, he was the most admirable spy that was ever attached to an army... He could assume the character of Spaniards of every degree and station, so as to deceive the most acute of those whom he delighted to imitae... But what rendered him more efficient than all was his wonderful power of observation and accurate description, which made the information he gave so reliable and valuable to the Duke of Wellington. Nothing escaped him... His acquaintance with the Spanish language was marvellous... Nor was he incapable of passing off, when occasion required, for a Frenchman; but as he spoke the language with a strong German accent, he called himself an Alsatian... Great was the disappointment when it was ascertained beyond a doubt that just after leaving the camp he had been taken prisoner, before he had time to exchange his uniform. Such, however, was the case: a troop of dragoons had intercepted him, and carried him off... The following morning, being again mounted, he overheard a conversation between his guards, who deliberately agreed to rob him, and to shoot him at a mill where they were to stop, and to report to their officer that they had been compelled to fire at him in consequence of his attempt to escape. Shortly before they arrived at the mill, for fear that they might meet with some one who would insist on having a portion of the spoil, the dragoons took from their prisoner his watch and his purse, which he surrendered with a good grace. On their arrival at the mill they dismounted, and in order to give some appearance of truth to their story, they went into the house, leaving their prisoner outside, in the hope that he would make some attempt to escape. In an instant Waters threw his cloak upon a neighbouring olive bush, and mounted his cocked hat on the top. Some empty flour sacks lay upon the ground, and a horse laden with well-filled flour sacks stood at the door. Sir John contrived to enter one of the empty sacks and throw himself across the horse. When the soldiers came out to the house they fired their carbines at the supposed prisoner, and galloped off at the utmost speed. A short time after the miller came out and mounted his steed; the general contrived to rid himself of the encumbrance of the sack, and sat up, riding behind the man, who, suddenly turning round, saw a ghost, as he believed, for the flour that still remained in the sack had completely whitened his fellow-traveller and given him a most unearthly appearance ... a push from the white spectre brought the unfortunate man to the ground, when away rode the gallant quarter-master... On reaching the English camp, where Lord Wellington was anxiously deploring his fate, a sudden shout from the soldiers made his lordship turn round, when a figure, resembling the statue in "Don Juan," galloped up to him. The duke, affectionately shaking him by the hand, said – "Waters, you never yet deceived me; and though you have come in a most questionable shape, I must congratulate you and myself." ']

WATKINS, Edmund, Ensign/Lt., 9th Foot: *1829 Statement of Service*: Born 3 August 1789, Whitchurch, Herefordshire. Aged nineteen on his first Entrance into the Army. Ensign, 9th Foot, 13 April 1809; Lt. 13 Aug. 1812; Capt. 1 April 1824; Major 22 March 1827. *Battles, sieges and campaigns*: Ensign at the Siege of Tarifa which commenced on the 20th Decr 1811, and the Enemy retired from the Town on the 5th June 1812, the British Troops under the command of Colonel Skeritt 47th Regiment. Spain and France from Octr. 1813 to March 1814 at Lieut. present at Nivelle and Nive.' *Wounds received in action*: 'Wounded on the 10th Decr. 1813 at the passage of the Nive in France, One Years Pay granted at Lieut. and at the expiration of the year a Pension of £70 pr. Annum which has been made permanent.' *Service abroad*: '17th July 1809 to 15th September 1809, Walcheren Expedition. 15 January 1810 to 19 June 1811, Gibraltar. 19 June 1811 to 26 July 1811, Expedition under Col. Skeritt, Taragona Minorca. July 1811 to 5 December 1811, Gibraltar. 3rd December 1811 to February 1812, Tarifa. February 1812 to March 1812, Gibraltar. April 1812 to May 1812, Ceuta. 20 May 1812 to 17 June 1813, Gibraltar. 23rd October 1813 to March 1814, Spain and France. 13 August 1815 to 1 November 1815, France. December 1819 to May 1823, West Indies. April 1825 to 3 February 1827, West Indies.' *Family*: Married Elizabeth Lechmere, 16 Jan. 1828, Cheltenham. No children by 1830. [PRO:

WO 25/786 f238]. Severely wounded, the Nive, 10 Dec. 1813 ('Edward Watkins') (1st Battn.) [*London Gazette*].

WATKINS, William Newell, Capt., 48th Foot: Capt., 48th Foot, 8 March 1810. Severely wounded, Albuera, 16 May 1811 (2nd Battn.) [*London Gazette*]. MGS.

WATSON, Charles, Lt., 83rd Foot: Lt., 83rd Foot, 14 Aug. 1809. Slightly wounded, Nivelle, 10 Nov. 1813 (2nd Battn.) [*London Gazette*].

+WATSON, Henry Robert, Ensign/Adjutant/Lt. and Capt., 3rd Foot Guards: Ensign, 3rd Foot Guards, 25 Dec. 1807. Slightly wounded, Barossa, 5 March 1811 [*London Gazette*]. Adjutant, 3rd Foot Guards, 5 March 1812; Lt. and Capt., 3rd Foot Guards, 9 Oct. 1812. Killed, the Nive, 12 Dec. 1813 ('Captain Henry Robert Watson, Adjutant') (1st Battn.) [*London Gazette*]. *Brett-James*, p. 72 ['During a third such auction [of a deceased officer's possessions], this time at St Jean de Luz, of Captain Henry Watson of the 3rd Foot Guards, Judge-Advocate General Larpent bought a very tolerable saddle with holsters, half worn, for eighteen dollars. He bid 10s for a curry-comb and brush, "bad, but of English make, and in England worth about 3s or 4s – it went for a guinea!" He was also outbid for a Suffolk Punch horse, though he went as high as 200 dollars.'].

WATSON, Henry, Bvt. Major, E.O.P.S.; Lt. Col., 1st Portuguese Dragoons: *1829 Statement of Service for Retired Officers*: Aged thirteen on first appointment to the Army. Cornet, 3rd Dragoons, May 1795; Lt., 3rd Dragoons, 1796; Capt., 3rd Dragoons, 1803; Capt., 48th Foot, 1808; Bvt. Major, unattached, 1810, 'by promotion into the Portuguese Service' [Army List gives: Bvt. Major, E.O.P.S., 18 Jan.

1810, 'Serving with the Portuguese Army']; Bvt. Lt. Col., unattached, 1812 [Army List gives: Lt. Col., E.O.P.S., 28 July 1814]; Half-pay, 1814, 'yet employed in Command of Portuguese Cavalry till the year 1820, at which time he was withdrawn in consequence of the Portuguese Revolution'. 'While unattached commanded the 1st Portuguese Cavalry'. *Where serving when wounded*: 'Salamanca'. *Details of pension*: Three hundred pounds, commencing 1812. *Family*: Married on 20 Dec. 1821. No children. No employment. *Where generally resident during last five years*: 'England'. [PRO: WO 25/777 f61]. Wounded, Salamanca, 22 July 1812, while serving as Lt. Col., 1st Portuguese Dragoons [*London Gazette*]. In Portuguese Service Sept. 1809 to Oct. 1812. Gold Medal. *1818 Pension Return*, pp. 24–5. MGS. *Challis, Portuguese Army*, p. 60.

+WATSON, James, Lt., 42nd Foot: Ensign, 42nd Foot, 28 May 1812. Severely wounded, Toulouse, 10 April 1814 ('Lieutenant') (1st Battn.) [*London Gazette*]. Died of wounds, 11 April 1814. Return dated April 1814. [PRO: WO 25/2965]. *Anton*, pp. 125, 136 [Toulouse: 'The company in which I was doing duty lost four officers... Watson mortally wounded'].

+WATSON, Lawrence, Ensign, 59th Foot: Killed, storming of San Sebastian, 31 Aug. 1813 ('Watsen') (2nd Battn.) [*London Gazette*].

WATSON, William, Ensign, 50th Foot: Ensign, 50th Foot, 15 Oct. 1807. Wounded, 'in the Army lately in Spain' (1st Battn.) [*March 1809 Army List*, p. 105].

WATSON, William, Ensign/Lt., 94th Foot: *1829 Statement of Service*: Born 24 May 1784, P. Tongue, Sutherlandshire. Aged twenty-four years and 128 days on his first entrance into the Army. Ensign, 94th Foot, 29 Sept. 1808; Lt. 23 Sept. 1813; Half Pay 25 Feb. 1819; Lt., 20th Foot, 27 Nov. 1821; Capt., 57th Foot, 4 July 1834; 'Died in Passage to England 31 July 1835.' *Battles, sieges and campaigns*: 'Defence of Cadiz under Lord Lyndock, 1810. Bussaco, Sept. 1810. Alrobaca, Octr. 1810. Torres Vedras, 1810. Rio Mayor, 6th March 1811. Redinha, 13th March 1811. Conduca, 14th March 1811. Foss de Yeuss, 15th March 1811. Subgal, 3rd April 1811. Fuentes de Honor, 3rd & 5th May 1811. Badajos, June 1811. Albedon & Pastor, Sept. 1811. Ciudad Rodrigo, February 1812. Badajo, April 1812. Vittoria, June 1813. Pyrenees, July 1813. St Sebastian, August 1813. Neville, 10th Novr. 1813. Nive, 31st Decr. 1813. Gaur de la Long, 3 Feby. 1814. Othes, 27th Feby. 1814. Tarbes, March 1814. Toulouse, 10th April 1814.' *Wounds received in action*: 'Wounded 31st Augst. 1813, Storm San Sebastian. Received one years pay as Ensign. Pension £50 per annum, permanent from 25 Decr. 1823.' *Service abroad*: '26th Septr. 1809 to 28th Augt. 1814, Spain, Portugal, France. 3rd Jany. 1823 to 24th Augt. 1824, East Indies (from embarkation until arrival in England). 19 March 1830 to 31 Aug. 1835, E. Indies.' *Family*: Married Isabella, daughter of the late Leaser Coldough Esq., New Cross County Wexford, 24 May 1820, Dublin. They had no children by 1830. [PRO: WO 25/788 f338].

+WATTS, Michael, Ensign, Coldstream Guards: Ensign, Coldstream Guards, 20 Oct. 1808. Killed, Barossa, 5 March 1811 [*London Gazette*].

+WAUCHOPE, Andrew, Lt. Col., 20th Foot: Lt. Col., 20th Foot, 8 June 1809. Severely wounded, Pyrenees, 2 Aug. 1813 [*London Gazette*]. 1st Battn. Died of wounds, 15 Sept.

1813. Return dated Sept. 1813. [PRO: WO 25/2965]. Obituary, *The Gentleman's Magazine*, Oct. 1813, p. 403 ['Sept. 15... At Passages, of a wound received on the 2d of August, Lieut.-col. Wauchope, 20th foot, eldest son of Andrew W. esq. of Niddrie.'].

WAUGH, Robert Andrew, Capt., 48th Foot: Capt., 48th Foot, 15 Feb. 1810. Slightly wounded, Albuera, 16 May 1811 (2nd Battn.) [*London Gazette*].

WAY, Gregory Holman Bromley, Major, 29th Foot: : Aged nineteen on first appointment to the Army. Ensign, 26th Foot, 24 Aug. 1797; Lt., 35th Foot, 3 Nov. 1799; Capt., 35th Foot, 13 Aug. 1802; Half-pay, 1802, by reduction; Capt., 5th Foot, 20 Jan. 1803; Major, 29th Foot, 25 Feb. 1808; Bvt. Lt. Col., 29th Foot, 30 May 1811, 'By special recommendation after the Battle of Albuiera in Spain'; Lt. Col., 29th Foot, 4 July 1811; Half-pay, 24 Oct. 1814, 'In consequence of Wounds & fractured limb in action'; Bvt. Col., 3rd Veteran Battn., 24 Nov. 1822; Half-pay, 24 April 1825, by reduction. 'Desirous [of service] if the situation should be compatible with state of general health much injured in consequence of wounds, & a disabled arm, fractured by a musket Ball through the shoulder with only the swing motion remaining & particular use of the left hand.' *Where serving when wounded*: 'Peninsula. Battle of Albuiera in Spain'. *Details of pension*: Two hundred pounds per annum, commencing 1811. *Family*: Married in 'St George's, London', 15 May 1815. No employment. *Where generally resident during last five years*: 'England'. [PRO: WO 25/777 f41]. Wounded, Rolica, 17 Aug. 1808 [*London Gazette*]. Slightly wounded, Albuera, 16 May 1811 [*London Gazette*]. Pension 'for wounds' received at Albuera [*1818 Pension Return*, pp. 8–9].

WEBB, John Wynne, Lt., 79th Foot; Capt., 16th Portuguese Line: *1829 Statement of Service for Retired Officers*: Aged twenty-one on first appointment to the Army. 'York Light Inf. Volunteers'; Ensign, 79th Foot, 15 March 1808; Lt., 79th Foot, 1811 [Army List gives 20 July 1810]; 'Appointed to a company in the 16th Portuguese Infantry in January 1812 & cotinued with that army until wounded at Salamanca, 22 July 1812'; Capt., 79th Foot, 23 Sept. 1813; Capt., 3rd Royal Veteran Battn., 23 Aug. 1813, 'disbanded 24 June 1816'; Capt., 7th Royal Veteran Battn., 15 Nov. 1819, 'disbanded in March 1821'. 'Never on half pay'. *Where serving when wounded:* 'Peninsula. Fuentes d'Onor 5 May 1811. Salamanca 22 July 1812.' 'Right thigh bone broken in two places by separate balls and also a contusion in the side. Four months confined to bed, and two years upon crutches'. *Details of pension:* One hundred pounds per annum, commencing 'believed to have been in August 1813'. *Family*: Married in 'Saint Martin's, London', 18 Oct. 1815, 'but now a widower'. Two children, born in 1820 and 1821. No employment. *Where generally resident during last five years:* 'Bath & Weymouth'. [PRO: WO 25/777 f137]. Severely wounded, Fuentes de Onoro, 5 May 1811 (1st Battn. 79th Foot) [*London Gazette*]. Severely wounded, Salamanca, 22 July 1812, while serving as Capt., 16th Portuguese Line [*London Gazette*]. In Portuguese Service Jan. 1812 to Feb. 1813. Pension 'for wounds' received at Salamanca [*1818 Pension Return*, pp. 18–19]. MGS. *Challis, Portuguese Army*, p. 60.

WEBSTER, Henry, Capt., 9th Light Dragoons: Lt., 9th Light Dragoons, 13 June 1811. Slightly wounded, Vittoria, 13 June 1813, while serving as Extra ADC to Major-General Brisbane [*London Gazette*]. Extra ADC to the Prince of Orange at Waterloo.

+WEIR, John Laing, Major, 59th Foot: Lt. Col., Army, 15 May 1806; Major, 59th Foot, 19 May 1808. Severely wounded, Vittoria, 21 June 1813 ('Major Weir (Lieutenant-Colonel)') (2nd Battn.) [*London Gazette*]. Died of wounds, 4 July 1813. Return dated July 1813. [PRO: WO 25/2965]. Obituary, *The Gentleman's Magazine*, Nov. 1813, p. 504 ['Lately... Of wounds received at the battle of Vittoria, Lieut.-col. John Laing Weir, major of the 59th foot, fourth son of the late R. Laing, esq. of Stronzie, co. Orkney. His remains were interred in the garden of a convent at Vittoria, by the side of his commanding officer, the late Lieut.-col. Fane, of the same regiment.'].

WEIR, William, Lt., 27th Foot: Lt., 27th Foot, 17 Oct. 1811. Slightly wounded, storming of Badajoz, 6 April 1812 (3rd Battn.) [*London Gazette*]. Wounded, Vittoria, 21 June 1813 (3rd Battn.) [*London Gazette*]. MGS.

WELLS, Joseph, Major, 43rd Regt: Capt., 43rd Foot, 8 Feb. 1804; Major, 43rd Foot, 10 Oct. 1811. Severely wounded, storming of Badajoz, 6 April 1812 (1st Battn.) [*London Gazette*]. Gold Medal. Lt. Col., 43rd Foot, 4 Aug. 1814. MGS. Died 4 Feb. 1853. *Simmons*, pp. 77–8.

WELSH, Jonas, Lt. 5th Foot: Lt., 5th Foot, 22 Sept. 1805. Wounded, 'very slightly', Vittoria, 21 June 1813 ('Welch') (1st Battn.) [*London Gazette*]. MGS.

+WELSTEAD, Benjamin, Lt., 82nd Foot: Lt., 82nd Foot, 9 Aug. 1810. Killed, 'in the Operations of the Army', 31 Aug. 1813 ('Welsted') (1st Battn.) [*London Gazette*].

+WEMYSS, Charles J., Lt./Capt., 7th Foot: Lt., 7th Foot, 27 March 1806. Slightly wounded, Albuera, 16 May 1811 (1st Battn.) [*London Gazette*]. Capt., 7th Foot, 18 July

1813. Severely wounded, Pyrenees, 28 July 1813 (1st Battn.) [*London Gazette*]. Died of wounds, 3 Aug. 1813. Return dated Aug. 1813. [PRO: WO 25/2965]. Obituary, *The Gentleman's Magazine*, Sept. 1813, p. 298 ['July 28... Of a wound received in Spain, Capt. Wemyss, 7th Foot, or Royal Fuzileers, second son of Major W. of the Portsmouth division of Royal Marines.']. *Cooper*, pp. 97–8 [Following the Battle of Pampeluna, 28 July 1813: 'Looking about, I saw a surgeon that formerly belonged our regiment. I told him my case, and was directed to go to a large house close by and take charge of a captain and a lieutenant who were both mortally wounded. "They are your own officers, and both will die," said he. "See that their servants do not rob them." I went accordingly. The captain was wounded in the left side, and so was the lieutenant, but the shot had gone quite through the lieutenant's body. Lieutenant Frazer [sic] died on the second or third day after the battle; Captain Wemyss on the fourth or fifth. There was something very affecting in the case of the captain's death. He had a brother who was an aid-de-camp in General Hill's division, and who had been wounded some days before in a skirmish. He hearing that his brother was mortally wounded, rode off in search of him; but for some days fruitlessly. At last he ascertained where his brother was lying, and hastened to the place. A short time before he came to the door, the dying captain asked his servant if he could read. He said he could. "Then," said the captain, "take that Prayer Book, and read to me." The servant did so. Soon after, there was a loud knocking at the street door, and then a well known voice in the stairs. The dying man sprang from his bed, flew to the door, and fell dead into his brother's arms. His parents lived on Southsea Common in 1815, to whom I took a letter from our colonel, but did not make myself known. A coffin was made of some old furniture, and the captain was buried in a garden beside the lieutenant.'].

WEMYSS, Thomas, Capt., 50th Foot: *1829 Statement of Service for Retired Officers*: Aged seventeen on first appointment to the Army. Ensign, 65th Foot, 9 June 1803; Lt., 19th Foot, 1 March 1804; Capt., 6th Garrison Battn., 30 Nov. 1806; Capt., 50th Foot, 12 Nov. 1807; Bvt. Major, 50th Foot, 21 June 1813; Bvt. Lt. Col., 21 Jan. 1819; Major, 50th Foot, 4 Nov. 1819; Half-pay, 99th Foot, 10 Feb. 1820, 'by request on account of Private affairs'. *Where serving when wounded*: 'In the Peninsula, once severely, three or four times slight'. No pension. *Family*: Married in Reading, Berkshire, 6 May 1819. Six children born by 1829, though two had died. No employment. *Where generally resident during last five years*: 'Wick, Worcestershire & Aberystwyth, Cardiganshire'. [PRO: WO 25/777 f136]. Mentioned in Hill's Almaraz dispatch, 21 May 1812 ['I cannot too strongly express how much I am satisfied with the conduct of Major-General Howard... He was ably assisted by his Staff, Brigade-Major Wemyss, of the 50th'] [*London Gazette*]. Severely wounded, Pyrenees, 31 July 1813 ('Brigade-Major Wemyss') [*London Gazette*]. Brother of Charles Wemyss of the 7th Foot.

WENCKSTERN, Frederick von, Lt., 2nd Line Battn. K.G.L.: *1829 Statement of Service for Retired Officers*: Aged eighteen on first appointment to the Army. Ensign, 2nd Line Battn. K.G.L., 'April or May 1804 ... lost my Commission on board the Sallisbury Transport by ship wreck on the 11th Decemb. 1804'; Lt., 2nd Line Battn. K.G.L., 27 Jan. 1806; Capt., 2nd Line Battn. K.G.L., 17 Aug. 1813; Half-pay, n.d., by reduction. Served eleven years eight months on Full-pay. *Where serving when wounded*: 'Was wounded by a musket-ball in the right leg on the 28th of July 1809 in the battle of Talavera in Spain, when I served 6 years, and having passed the 17th January 1815 at Brussell in the Netherlands a Medical Board, received Two years pay (118£). The ball hurt the shin-bone and makes me suffer at present very much, the wound being, since two years, burnt out again'. *Family*: Married in 'Mecklenburg', 13 Dec. 1816. Nine children by 1829. *Where generally serving for last five years*: 'at Neu-Strelitz in Mecklenburg'. [PRO: WO 25/777 f174]. Severely wounded, Talavera, 28 July 1809 ('Winkstern') [*London Gazette*]. Waterloo. Half-pay 24 Feb. 1816. MGS. *Beamish*, vol. II, p. 576.

+**WERGE, John, Capt., 38th Foot:** Capt., Army, 1 July 1802; Capt., 38th Foot, 26 Dec. 1805. Killed, storming of San Sebastian, 31 Aug. 1813 ('Major') [*London Gazette*].

+**WERSEBE, Christian von, Capt., 1st Line Battn. K.G.L.:** Lt., 1st Line Battn. K.G.L., 12 Feb. 1804. Served in Peninsula 1808–9. *Beamish*, vol. II, p. 632 ['captain Christian von Wersabe ... killed in the battle of Talavera de la Reyna in Spain, 28th July 1809.']. 'Christ. *Baron* Wersabe' in Army List.

WESSELL, Frederick, Lt., 2nd Line Battn. K.G.L.: Lt., 2nd Line Battn. K.G.L., 10 Aug. 1807. Severely wounded, Talavera, 28 July 1809 [*London Gazette*]. Served in Peninsula 1808–10. *Beamish*, vol. II, p. 648 [Died 'in London 15th March 1814.'].

WEST, Charles Augustus, Lt. and Capt., 3rd Foot Guards: Lt. and Capt., 3rd Foot Guards, 25 Aug. 1809. Slightly wounded, sortie from Bayonne, 14 April 1814 (1st Battn.) [*London Gazette*]. Capt. and Lt. Col., 3rd Foot Guards, 25 July 1814.

Wounded, Waterloo. MGS. Died, 1872.

WESTCOTT, George J., Capt., 77th Foot: Capt., 77th Foot, 5 Aug. 1807. Severely wounded, Orthes, 27 Feb. 1814 [*London Gazette*]. MGS. *Mullen*, p. 17 ['Bde Maj 4th Div'].

WESTERN, Charles Maximilian Thomas, Lt., 29th Foot; Capt., 8th Caçadores: Lt., 29th Foot, 25 May 1809. Severely wounded, during 'movements of the Army' [Retreat from Burgos: Villa Muriel], 25 Oct. 1812, while serving as Capt., 8th Caçadores [*London Gazette*]. In Portuguese Service Dec. 1808 to Dec. 1809 and Sept. 1810 to April 1814. Gold Medal. Pension of one hundred pounds per annum, commencing 26 Oct. 1813, 'for a wound' received at Carrion, 1812 [*1818 Pension Return*, pp. 26–7]. *Challis, Portuguese Army*, p. 60 ['Maj. 14 Line ... promoted Major for distinguished service 22 Oct. '12'].

+**WESTLEY, William, Lt., 95th Foot:** 1st Lt., 95th Foot, 3 Nov. 1809. Killed, Fuentes de Onoro, 5 May 1811 ('Westby') (3rd Battn.) [*London Gazette*].

WESTMACOTT, John, Lt., Royal Staff Corps: Lt., Royal Staff Corps, 31 May 1809. Severely wounded at the siege of Badajoz, 6–11 June 1811 [*London Gazette*].

WESTROPP, Lionel John, Capt., 58th Foot: *1829 Statement of Service for Retired Officers*: Aged sixteen on first appointment to the Army. Ensign, 58th Foot, 9 July 1803; Lt., 58th Foot, Feb. 1806; Capt., 58th Foot, 5 March 1807; Half-pay, 95th Foot, Nov. 1819, 'in consequence of ill health on returning from the West Indies in 1819'. *Where serving when wounded*: 'Calabria 1806. Pyrenees 1813. Canada 1814'. *Details of pension*: Seventy pounds, commencing 1820. *Family*: Married in

Cork, 17 April 1819. Five children by 1829. No employment. *Where generally resident during last five years*: 'Cork'. [PRO: WO 25/777 f143]. Slightly wounded, Pyrenees, 2 Aug. 1813 (2nd Battn.) [*London Gazette*]. MGS.

+WESTROPP, Ralph, Lt., 51st Foot: Lt., Army, 29 May 1805; Lt., 51st Foot, 17 Aug. 1809. Killed, at the siege of Badajoz, 6–11 June 1811 [*London Gazette*]. Died of his wounds, 10 June 1811. Return dated 25 June 1811. [PRO: WO 25/2965]. *Wheeler*, p. 62 [Second assault on Fort San Cristoval, Badajoz, 9 June: 'After some time the fire slackened, as if the enemy were tired of slaughter, when an officer Lieutenant Westropp came running from the western angle of the fort calling out to retire – the enemy were entering the trench by the salley port. We then began to leave the trench. Poor Mr. Westropp was assisting a wounded man in getting out, when he was shot dead just as he had effected his purpose.'], pp. 64–5.

WEYLAND, Richard, Lt., 16th Light Dragoons: Lt., Army, 17 Dec. 1806; Lt., 16th Light Dragoons, 26 March 1807. Severely wounded, Fuentes de Onoro, 5 May 1811 [*London Gazette*]. Capt., Army, 18 July 1811; Capt., 16th Light Dragoons, 5 Sept. 1811. Wounded, Waterloo. MGS. Born, 25 March 1780; died, Oct. 1864. *Cocks*, p. 103 [Fuentes d'Onoro: wounded], p. 108 ['run through the body'].

+WHEATLEY, John, Ensign, 38th Foot: Ensign, 38th Foot, 13 April 1809. Severely wounded, Salamanca, 22 July 1812 (1st Battn.) [*London Gazette*]. Killed, storming of San Sebastian, 31 Aug. 1813 (1st Battn.) [*London Gazette*].

WHICHCOTE, George, Ensign, 52nd Foot: *1829 Statement of Service for Retired Officers*: Aged sixteen on first appointment to the Army. 'I joined the 52nd the latter end of 1810 as a Volunteer'; Ensign, 52nd Foot, Jan. 1811 [Army List gives 10 Jan.]; Lt., 52nd Foot, [8 July] 1812; Capt., 3rd Foot, 22 Jan. 1818; Half-pay, 1821, by reduction; Capt., 4th Dragoon Guards, 1821; Major, unattached, 1825. 'Having served in the most Brilliant part of the Peninsula War, and having devoted the best part of my life to the Service, I certainly cannot resign that active life without feelings of regret, and shall therefore be glad of Employment. I have served in the following Engagements in the 52nd: Sabugal, Fuentes D'Onor, Siege & storming of Rederigo, Siege & storming of Badajoz, Salamanca, Vittoria, Vera, Nivelle, Nive, Orthes, Toulouse, Waterloo. I was twice slightly wounded but received no Pension, nor was I returned'. *Where serving when wounded*: 'Badajoz & Waterloo. Slightly wounded twice. No Pension'. Not married. No employment. *Where generally resident during last five years*: 'at Glaston Uppingham Rutland'. [PRO: WO 25/777 f215]. MGS. Quite a well-known individual by virtue of longevity, one of the longest-lived Waterloo (and certainly Peninsular) veterans. Born 1794, son of Sir Thomas Whichcote Bt.; became General 1871; died 1891. Was supposedly the first member of the British Army to enter Toulouse. Educated at Rugby, where he was the fag of the actor Macready. Photograph and brief biographical details in Gaskell, K. Kynaston, *Catalogue of Waterloo Medals in the Collection of Henry Gaskell* (London, 1905).

WHITAKER, Richard, Ensign, 82nd Foot: Ensign, 82nd Foot, 28 Nov. 1811. Severely wounded, Nivelle, 10 Nov. 1813 ('Lieutenant') (1st Battn.) [*London Gazette*].

+WHITE, Benjamin, Lt., 45th Foot: Lt., 45th Foot, 7 Jan. 1808. Killed at the siege of Badajoz, 31 March–2 April 1812 [*London Gazette*].

+WHITE, Charles Lawrence, Lt. and Capt., 3rd Foot Guards: Lt. and Capt., 3rd Foot Guards, 8 Sept. 1808. Severely wounded, Salamanca, 22 July 1812 (1st Battn.) [*London Gazette*]. Severely wounded, 'since dead', sortie from Bayonne, 14 April 1814 (1st Battn.) [*London Gazette*]. Died of wounds, 15 April 1814. Return dated April 1814. [PRO: WO 25/2965]. *Hurt*, p. 75 ['D.O.W., Bayonne, Apl. 15.']. *Fletcher, Fields of Fire*, p. 164 ['Coldstream Guards cemetery, Bayonne ... those who lie here include ... Captains White and Shiffner, and Lieutenant Holbourne, all of the 3rd Foot Guards.']. *Fletcher, Gentlemen's Sons*, p. 185.

+WHITE, Daniel, Lt. Col., 29th Foot: Lt. Col., Army, 1 Jan. 1805; Lt. Col., 29th Foot, 2 Sept. 1808. Severely wounded, Albuera, 16 May 1811 [*London Gazette*]. Died of wounds, 8 June 1811. Return dated 25 June 1811. [PRO: WO 25/2965]. Obituary, *The Gentleman's Magazine*, July 1811, p. 88 ['June 3. At Eylas, of the wounds he received in the battle of Albuera, while leading the gallant 29th regiment into action, Lieut.-col. White. His remains were interred near those of the late Lieut.-gen. Hoghton.'].

WHITE, Henry, Adjutant/Lt., 74th Foot: *1829 Statement of Service for Retired Officers*: Aged only ten on first appointment to the Army. 'Inlisted in 1st foot Guards 11 March 1791'; Ensign and Adjutant, 74th Foot, 5 April 1810; Lt. and Adjutant, 74th Foot, 29 April 1812; Lt., 7th Veteran Battn., 28 Dec. 1815, 'Recommended by Lt. General the Hon. Sir A. Hope from 74th Foot to enable me to hold the Town-Majorship of Hull in consideration of arduous Service in the Field during the whole of the late Wars'. 'Now serving as Town Major of Portsmouth to which I exchanged from Hull 2nd Oct. 1823'. *Where serving when wounded*: 'Spain, Portugal &c.' *Details of pension*: 'Seventy pounds per annum, commencing 25 June 1814'. *Family*: Married in 'White Chapel Church London', 16 June 1803. Six children by 1829. *Where generally resident during last five years*: 'Portsmouth'. [PRO: WO 25/777 f202]. Slightly wounded, Fuentes de Onoro, 5 May 1811 [*London Gazette*]. Severely wounded, Vittoria, 21 June 1813 (Adjutant) [*London Gazette*]. Pension 'for wounds' received at Vittoria, 1813 [*1818 Pension Return*, pp. 18–19]. MGS.

+WHITE, Michael, Lt, 27th Foot: Lt., 27th Foot, 30 Aug. 1810. Killed, storming of Badajoz, 6 April 1812 ('Whyte') (3rd Battn.) [*London Gazette*].

+WHITE, Robert, Ensign, 50th Foot: Ensign, 50th Foot, 1 Oct. 1812. Severely wounded, Pyrenees, 25 July 1813 (1st Battn.) [*London Gazette*]. Died of wounds, 25 July 1813. Return dated Oct. 1813 (2nd Battn.). [PRO: WO 25/2965].

+WHITE, William, Capt., 13th Light Dragoons: Capt., 13th Light Dragoons, 18 Feb. 1804. Mentioned in Wellington's dispatch of 29 Aug. 1810, for a skirmish near Fraxedas, 22 Aug. 1810 ['A patrole ... belonging to [the French second] corps fell in with a squadron of dragoons consisting of one troop of the 13th British, and one troop of the 4th Portuguese ... under the command of Captain White of the 13th, and the whole of them were taken with the exception of the Captain and one man who, I since understand, have been killed. I enclose the copy of Brigadier-General Fane's report of Lieutenant-General Hill of this affair, which it appears was highly creditable to Captain White and the allied troops engaged.'] [*London Gazette*]. Severely wounded, 'since dead', Salamanca, 22 July 1812, while serving on the Staff as DAQMG [*London Gazette*]. Died of wounds, 2 July 1812 [sic]. Return dated 25 July 1812. [PRO: WO 25/2965]. *Rice Jones*, p. 66 [Concerning the skirmish of Aug. 1810: 'This dashing little affair, in which the hitherto-despised Portuguese cavalry gave a specimen of their mettle, is less known than it deserves to be. Capt. Warre, on the staff of Marshal Beresford, wrote to a friend, under date, Aug. 29, – "Capt. White of the 13th Light Dragoons speaks very highly of the gallantry and good conduct of Cornet Raymundo Oliveira and the troop of the 4th cavalry who charged along with his own troop, and tumbled the mounseers over in a minute (near Castello Branco). they attacked 60 French Cavalry, and without loss of man or horse, took 50 men. 7 corporals, 3 sergeants, 2 officers; others were killed by the peasantry; not one went back to tell the tale." ']

+**WHITE, William, Lt., 38th Foot; Capt., 12th Portuguese Line:** Lt., 38th Foot, 18 June 1807. Severely wounded, siege of Burgos, 15 Oct. 1812, while serving as Capt., 12th Portuguese Line [*London Gazette*]. Obituary, *The Gentleman's Magazine*, Jan. 1813, p. 83 ['Nov. 20. At Almeida, of a wound at the siege of Burgos, in his 25th year, Capt. W. White, 12th Portuguese reg. eldest son of J. W. esq. of Rock Castle, Ireland. He was wounded in an act of the most laudable kindness: having ordered a soldier to take one of his comrades, who had been wounded, from where he lay, several refusing, he shewed them that he never required a command of his to be obeyed that would expose them more to the Enemy than he was himself: he went to the assistance of his wounded fellow-soldier, and whilst stooping down, received that

fatal shot, which deprived his parents of a most excellent son, England of a hero, and his acquaintance of an inestimable friend.']. In Portuguese Service Aug. 1809 to Nov. 1812. *Challis, Portuguese Army*, p. 60 ['Died of wounds 20 Nov. '12'].

WHITE, William Grove, Major, 48th Foot: Major, 48th Foot, 25 Nov. 1809. Severely wounded, Pyrenees, 28 July 1813 (1st Battn.) [*London Gazette*].

WHITE, William, Ensign, 61st Foot: Ensign, 61st Foot, 14 Aug. 1809. Severely wounded, Salamanca, 22 July 1812 ('Whyte') [*London Gazette*]. Lt., 61st Foot, 24 July 1812. Severely wounded, Toulouse, 10 April 1814 (1st Battn.) [*London Gazette*]. Temporary pension of seventy pounds per annum, commencing 11 April 1815, 'for wounds' received at Toulouse [*1818 Pension Return*, pp. 16–17].

+**WHITELAW, William, Ensign/Lt., 88th Foot:** Lt., 88th Foot, 9 July 1809. Severely wounded, Talavera, 28 July 1809 ('Ensign') [*London Gazette*]. Severely wounded, storming of Badajoz, 6 April 1812 [*London Gazette*]. Died of wounds, 8 June 1812. Return dated 25 June 1812. [PRO: WO 25/2965]. Obituary, *The Gentleman's Magazine*, June 1812, p. 596 ['May 7... At Estremoz, Portugal, of a wound received in his leg at the storming of Badajoz, to the escalade of which he led on a detachment of his own regiment, which composed a part of the Forlorn Hope, Lieut. W. Whitelaw, 88th foot, son of Rev. W. W. of Dublin. He was also wounded in the action of Talavera.'].

WHITLEY, James, Lt., 9th Foot: Lt., 9th Foot, 17 Dec. 1806. Recorded as 'Missing', during 'movements of the Army' [Retreat from Burgos: Villa Muriel], 25 Oct. 1812 (1st Battn.) [*London Gazette*]. Capt., 9th Foot, 17 June 1813. MGS.

WHITNEY, Benjamin, Ensign, 44th Foot: *1829 Statement of Service*: Born 22 Sept. 1795, Waterford, Ireland. Aged Eighteen on his first entrance into the Army. Ensign, 44th Foot, 25 Feb. 1813; Lt. 20 Nov. 1817; Capt. 28 April 1825; Capt., 14th Foot, 16 Sept. 1826. *Battles, sieges and campaigns*: 'In the Campaigns in Spain & Portugal in 1813... In the Campaigns in the Island of Tholan in Holland & in Flanders in 1814. Was at the Battle and Capture of Merxin 2d & at the Seige of Antwerp & attack on the French Fleet on the 2d. 3d. & 4th of February and at the Storm of Bergen-op-Zoom on the night of the 8th & Morning of the 9th March 1814... In the Campaigns in Flanders and France in 1815. Was at the Battle of Qr. Bras and Watterloo the 16th. 17th. & 18th June 1815... Was in the Campaign in Arakan (Ava) in 1824 & 1825. Was at the Battle on the Padway Mountain the 26th at the Storming of Matratty on the 27th and at the Seige and Capture of Arakan on the 29th. 30th & 31st March 1st April 1825.' *Wounds received in action*: 'Wounded on crossing the Mondego in Spain, but not returned. Severely Wounded & Prisoner at Bergen op Zoom. Severely Wounded at Quatre Bras. Wounded at Waterloo. Received a years Pay for my wound at Waterloo.' *Titles, honorary distinctions and medals*: 'Waterloo Medal.' *Service abroad*: 'Dates not known. Spain and Portugal, The Isle of Tholan, Holland, Flanders, France, Bengal, Arakan, Ava, Bengal.' Unmarried in 1830. [PRO: WO 25/787 f269].

+WHITNEY, John, Lt., 2nd Light Battn. K.G.L.: Lt., 2nd Light Battn. K.G.L., 15 Oct. 1810. Killed, Albuera, 16 May 1811 [*London Gazette*]. Served in Peninsula in 1811. *Beamish*, vol. II, p. 635.

+WHITTING, William, Capt., 74th Foot: Capt., Army, 22 Dec. 1804; Capt., 74th Foot, 29 Aug. 1805. Killed, Pyrenees, 30 July 1813 [*London Gazette*].

WHITTINGHAM, Samuel Ford, Capt., 13th Light Dragoons; Lt. Col., Army; General, Spanish Army: Capt., Army, 14 Feb. 1805; Capt., 13th Light Dragoons, 13 June 1805. Slightly wounded, Talavera, 28 July 1809, while serving on the Staff as Deputy Assistant Quarter Master General [*London Gazette*]. Lt. Col., Army ('Serv. with the Portug. Army' [sic]), 30 May 1811. Mentioned in an 'Extract of a Letter from Lieutenant-General Sir J. Murray to General the Marquess of Wellington, dated Castalla, March 23, 1813' ['Since I had last the honour of addressing your Lordship, there have been several trifling affairs with the enemy. General Whittingham has forced him to retire beyond the Puerto de Albayda, with a very considerable loss. In this affair, which General Whittingham conducted with great judgement, and in which the Spanish troops behaved with great gallantry and order, the General was slightly wounded, as were an officer and seven men.'] [*London Gazette*]. Later contracted his first names into 'Samford'. *Memoir of Lieut. Gen. Sir Samuel Ford Whittingham*, ed. Maj. Gen. Ferdinand Whittingham (London, 1868).

WHITTLE, John, Lt., 88th Foot: Lt., 88th Foot, 28 Aug. 1804. Severely wounded, Talavera, 28 July 1809 [*London Gazette*].

+WHYTE, Thomas, Capt., 27th Foot: Capt., Army, 9 June 1803; Capt., 27th Foot, 2 Aug. 1804. Killed, Pyrenees, 28 July 1813 (3rd Battn.) [*London Gazette*].

+WIDDRINGTON, George John Tinling, Capt., 34th Foot; Major, 83rd Foot: Capt., Army, 29 Oct. 1802; Capt., 34th Foot, 9 May 1805.

Wounded, Albuera, 16 May 1811 (3rd Battn.) [*London Gazette*]. Major, 83rd Foot, 1 Aug. 1811. Severely wounded, Vittoria, 21 June 1813 ('Widderington') (2nd Battn.) [*London Gazette*]. Obituary, *The Gentleman's Magazine*, Nov. 1813, p. 504 ['Lately ... of wounds received in the battle of Vittoria, Major Widdrington, of the 83rd.']. Died 'of wounds', 30 June 1813 [PRO: WO 25/2965].

WIDENHAM, Joseph A., Volunteer, 40th Foot: Slightly wounded, storming of Badajoz, 6 April 1812 ('Volunteer') [*London Gazette*]. Ensign, 40th Foot, 14 May 1812; Lt., 40th Foot, 24 Feb. 1814. MGS.

WIEBOLD, David Charles Cornelius, Cornet, 2nd Light Dragoons K.G.L.: *1829 Statement of Service for Retired Officers*: Aged twenty-eight on first appointment to the Army. Cornet, 2nd Light Dragoons K.G.L., 20 May 1811 [Army List gives 10 May], 'from Gentleman Cadet'; Lt., 2nd Light Dragoons K.G.L., 29 Aug. 1812; Half-pay, Feb. 1816, by reduction. *Where serving when wounded*: 'Slightly wounded at the taking of Seville in Spain, 28 August 1812'. *Where generally resident during last five years*: 'Baden-Baden, Great Duchy of Baden, Germany'. [PRO: WO 25/778 f137]. Mentioned in Skerrett's dispatch concerning the capture of Seville, 28 Aug. 1812 ['I must ... mention the detachment of the King's German Legion, commanded by Cornet Wiebolt'] [*London Gazette*].

WIERING, Frederick, Capt., 2nd Light Dragoons/Hussars K.G.L.: Capt., 2nd Light Dragoons K.G.L., 21 Dec. 1804. Served in Peninsula in 1811. *Beamish*, vol. II, p. 618 ['slightly wounded, 23d June 1811, at Quinta de Gremezia. [Died by illness] 19th July 1811, at the hospital of Zabucca de Vide in Portugal.'].

+WILDE, Brigade Major: Mentioned in Wellington's Fuentes de Onoro dispatch, 8 May 1811 [5 May: 'the 88th, with the 71st and 79th, under the command of Colonel Mackinnon, charged the enemy, and drove them through the Village; and Colonel Mackinnon has reported particularly the conduct of ... Brigade-Major Wilde'] [*London Gazette*, 26 May 1811]. Killed, siege of Badajoz, 26 March 1812 [*London Gazette*]. Mentioned in Wellington's dispatch, 27 March 1812 [Storming of Fort Picurina, Badajoz, 26 March 1812: 'Major-General Kempt ... particularly mentions ... Brigade-Major Wilde, who was unfortunately killed by a cannon-shot after the work was in our possession'] [*London Gazette*]. Not in the 71st, 79th or 88th Foot.

WILDE, Benjamin, Lt./Adjutant, 29th Foot: Lt., 29th Foot, 8 June 1809; Adjutant, 29th Foot, 18 Jan. 1810. Severely wounded, Albuera, 16 May 1811 ('Wild') [*London Gazette*].

WILDING, Ernest, Lt., 1st Line Battn. K.G.L.: Lt., 1st Line Battn. K.G.L., 22 May 1811. Served in Peninsula 1811–14. *Beamish*, vol. II, p. 572 ['severely wounded, 27th Feb. 1814, before Bayonne.'].

WILDMAN, Edward, Lt., 4th Dragoons: *1829 Statement of Service*: Born 23 March 1790, London. Aged sixteen years and two months on his first entrance into the Army. Ensign, 13th Foot, 2 May 1806; Lt. 6 May 1807; Lt., 4th Dragoons, 29 Oct. 1807; Capt., 60th Foot, Decr. 1814; Capt., 7th Light Dragoons, Feb. 1815; Half Pay 25 March 1816; Capt., 20th Light Dragoons, 4 Sept. 1817; Major, 6th Dragoon Guards, 24 Sept. 1818; Lt. Col. 25 Sept. 1823. *Battles, sieges and campaigns*: 'Battle of Talavera 1809. Busaco 27th Septr. 1810. Redinha 1811. Albuhera. Retreat from Salamanca to Portugal 1812. Vittoria 21st June

1813. Battle of Pyrenees in front of Pampalona. Torbes. Toulouse. Waterloo.' *Wounds received in action*: 'Albuhera: received two severe Wounds in Head & Arm & made Prisoner, escaped and was sent home for recovery. Received One Year's Pay.' *Service abroad*: 'April 1809 to Septr. 1811, Peninsula. July 1812 to Septr. 1814, Peninsula & France. Feby. 1815 to Jany. 1816, Belgium & France.' *Family*: Married Antonia Mahona Oakes, daughter of Lieut. General Sir Hildebrand Oakes, 18 June 1818, St George's Church, Hanover Square, London. They had five children by 1830. [PRO: WO 25/781 f162]. Recorded as 'slightly' wounded, Albuera, 16 May 1811 [*London Gazette*]. Died 1846. Portrait illustrated and described in *Journal of the Society for Army Historical Research*, Vol. XVII (1938).

WILKINSON, John Frederick, Lt., 28th Foot: Ensign, 28th Foot, 26 June 1806; Lt. 8 Sept. 1808. Severely wounded, Barossa, 5 March 1811 (1st Battn.) [*London Gazette*]. Temporary pension of seventy pounds per annum, commencing 5 March 1812, 'for wounds' received at Barossa [*1818 Pension Return*, pp. 8–9]. Wounded, Waterloo.

WILKINSON, William, Capt., 59th Foot: *1829 Statement of Service for Retired Officers*: Aged twenty-three on first appointment to the Army. Ensign, 15th Foot, Dec. 1799; Lt., 15th Foot, 4 March 1801; Half-pay, [1802], 'by Reduction at the Peace of Amiens'; Lt., 59th Foot, 1804; Capt., 59th Foot, 1 Sept. 1808; Half-pay, 1817, 'occasioned by suffering from Wound in the East Indies in 1817, and received the difference to enable him to pay the Passage of his Wife and family to Europe'. *Where serving when wounded*: 'on the Peninsula at the Battle of the Nive'. *Details of pension*: One hundred pounds per annum, commencing 1818. *Family*: Married in 'St Paul,

Covent Garden', 24 Aug. 1815. Five children by 1829. *Where generally resident during last five years*: 'Barnes Terrace, Surrey and St Omer, France'. [PRO: WO 25/778 f 85]. Severely wounded, the Nive, 10 Dec. 1813 (2nd Battn.) [*London Gazette*].

WILL, Andrew, Lt., 92nd Foot: Lt., 92nd Foot, 18 Feb. 1808. Severely wounded, 'in an Affair at Alba de Tormes', 10–11 Nov. 1812 [*London Gazette*]. Waterloo. Died of yellow fever, Jamaica, 7 Oct. 1819.

WILLCOCKS, Robert H., Ensign/ Lt., 38th Foot: *1829 Statement of Service*: Born in Dublin, 10 Oct. 1794. Aged Seventeen on his first Entrance into the Army. Ensign, 38th Foot, 11 Sept. 1811 [Army List gives 12 Sept.]. Lt., 38th Foot, 26 Aug. 1813. Half Pay, 25 March 1817, 'Reduction of the additional Lieut.' 'Lt., 38th Foot, May 1817. Capt., 38th Foot, 21 July 1825. Capt., 81st Foot, 22 Oct. 1825.' Note added: 'The Cape Corps having been raised in Octr. 1819 at Grahamstown I was appointed by Lord Chas. Somerset to a company in it. I joined it on 25th October 1819, & did Duty with it as Captain until Novr. 1820.' *Battles, sieges and campaigns*: 'Salamanca, Burgos, Vittoria, Nive, Investment to Capture of St Sebastian, Bayonne.' *Wounds received in action*: 'Salamanca 22nd July 1812, In Hand & Leg. Nive 9th Decr. 1813, in the Right Arm. Years Pay as Captain.' *Service abroad*: 'May 1812 to Novr. 1814, Peninsula. May 1815 to Octr. 1816, France. April 1818 to Decr. 1821, Cape Good Hope. 14th July 1826 to 14th Novr. 1829, North America. 15th Novr. 1829 to 31st Decr. 1829, Bermuda.' Not married in 1830. [PRO: WO 25/801 f9]. Slightly wounded, Salamanca 22 July 1812 ('Wilcocks') (1st Battn.) [*London Gazette*]. Slightly wounded, the Nive, 9 Dec. 1813 ('Wilcocks') (1st Battn.) [*London Gazette*]. MGS.

WILLIAMS

WILLIAMS, Edmund Keynton, Capt., 81st Foot; Lt. Col., 4th Caçadores: *1829 Statement of Service*: 'Born Marthern, Monmouthshire, 21 October 1781. Aged Seventeen years & Nine Months on his first Entrance into the Army. Ensign, 4 King's Own, July 1799. Lieutenant, 4 King's Own, 18 April 1800. Lieutenant, 81 Foot, 9 July 1803. Captain, 25 Sept. 1807. Bv. Major, 10 Sept. 1812. Bv. Lt. Colonel, 21 June 1813. Regt. Major, 4 King's Own, 21 March 1822. Lt. Colonel, 41 Foot, 9 Aug. 1827. Colonel, 22 July 1830.' *Battles, sieges and campaigns*: '2nd & 6th October 1799 as Ensign under the Duke of York. Maida 4 July 1807... Taking the Island of Ischia, Bay of Naples, as Lieutenant under General Lumley. Battle of Busaco Sept. 1811 as Major. Badajos in 1811... Salamanca 22nd July 1812... Burgos October 1812... Vittoria 21 June 1813... Tolosa July 1813 as L Colonel under Sir T Graham. St Sebastian 1st 2nd & 3rd assaults... Crossing the Bidassoa Sept 1813 in advance of the Guards 1st Division under Sir J Hope. Neville October 1813... Nive November 1813... Crossing the Adour Decr 1813. Siege of Bayonne Decr 1813.' *Distinguished conduct*: 'Battle of Busaco – Noticed in Genl Orders. Salamanca – Noticed in General Orders. Burgos – Noticed in G Orders. Vittoria – Noticed in Genl. Orders. Tolosa – Noticed in Genl Orders.' *Wounds received in action*: '6 October 1799 Wounded Slightly. Busaco, Wounded Slightly. Salamanca, Wounded twice Once Severely, received One Years Full pay as Lieutenant Colonel. St Sebastian, Wounded Slightly 2nd Assault. Siege of Bayonne, Wounded Slightly.' *Titles, honorary distinctions and medals*: 'Busaco, Medal. Salamanca, Medal. Vittoria, Medal. St Sebastian, Cross. Neville, Medal. Nive, Medal.' *Service abroad*: 'Septr 1799 to January 1800, Holland. July 1805 to January 1820, 4 years & 4 months Sicily, 10 yrs 2 months Portugal. Sept 1822 to August 1825, West Indies. February 1828 to 31 December 1829, East Indies.' *Family*: Married Caroline Hawke, Dec. 1814, in Plymouth. They had two children by 1829. [PRO: WO 25/793 f2]. Severely wounded, Salamanca, 22 July 1812, as Lt. Col., 4th Caçadores [*London Gazette*]. Mentioned in Wellington's dispatch concerning the capture of Fort St Michael, Burgos, 19 Sept. 1812 ['As soon as it was dark the same troops ... attacked and carried by assault the hornwork which the enemy had occupied in strength. In this operation ... Major Williams of the 4th Caçadores. .. distinguished themselves'] [*London Gazette*]. Mentioned in Sir Thomas Graham's dispatch concerning the action near Tolosa, 24–25 June 1813 ['The next morning (the 25th)... The enemy was driven from the summit of an important hill, lying between the Pampeluna and Vittoria roads, by a very skilful attack of Lieutenant-Colonel Williams, with two companies of the Grenadiers of the 1st regiment, and three of the 4th Caçadores'] [*London Gazette*]. Slightly wounded, 'at the Siege of St Sebastian', 7–27 July 1813, as Lt. Col. in 4th Caçadores [*London Gazette*]. In Portuguese Service March 1810 to Nov. 1811 and Feb. 1812 to Jan. 1814. Gold Medal. MGS. *Challis, Portuguese Army*, p. 60.

WILLIAMS, James, Lt., 11th Foot: *1829 Statement of Service for Retired Officers*: Aged nineteen on first appointment to the Army. Ensign, 11th Foot, 9 April 1807; Lt., 11th Foot, 10 Aug. 1808; Capt., 11th Foot, 14 Sept. 1813; Half-pay, 25 Feb. 1816, 'at my own request being incapable of doing Regimental Duty in consequence of ill health, from the severe injury I received from a wound at the Battle of Salamanca with the loss of the use of my left Arm & hand'. 'Having lost the use of my left arm I do not feel myself competent for active

service'.

service'. *Where serving when wounded*: 'at Salamanca'. *Details of pension*: One hundred pounds per annum, commencing 22 July 1813. *Family*: Married twice: the first time at 'Barnstaple', 7 May 1814. They had one child, born in 1823. Married the second time, also at Barnstaple, 1 Jan. 1828. *Where generally resident during last five years*: 'at Bichington near Barnstaple'. [PRO: WO 25/778 f68]. Severely wounded, Salamanca, 22 July 1812 (1st Battn.) [*London Gazette*]. *1818 Pension Return*, pp. 6–7. MGS.

WILLIAMS, John, Lt., 2nd Foot: Lt., 2nd Foot, 17 March 1807. Slightly wounded, Salamanca, 22 July 1812 [*London Gazette*].

WILLIAMS, John, Ensign, 50th Foot: Ensign, 50th Foot, 9 May 1811. Severely wounded, Vittoria, 21 June 1813 (1st Battn.) [*London Gazette*].

+WILLIAMS, John, Ensign, 74th Foot: Ensign, 74th Foot, 12 Oct. 1809. Killed, Busaco, 27 Sept. 1810 [*London Gazette*].

+WILLIAMS, John A., Capt., Royal Engineers: 2nd Capt., Royal Engineers, 24 June 1809. Severely wounded, storming of Badajoz, 6 April 1812 [*London Gazette*]. Killed, siege of Burgos, 20–26 Sept. 1812 [*London Gazette*]. Webber, p. 83 [Burgos, Sept. 1812: 'Two attempts to enter have already been made and failed with the loss of 45 officers and 700 men, killed and wounded; amongst the former Captain Williams of the Engineers, one of my contemporaries at the Academy.'].

+WILLIAMS, Trevor, Lt., 39th Foot: Ensign, 39th Foot, 23 May 1809. Killed, 25 July 1813 ('Lieut.') (1st Battn.) [*London Gazette*].

+WILLIAMS, William, Cornet, 11th Light Dragoons: Cornet, 11th Light

Dragoons, 11 July 1811. Severely wounded, Salamanca, 18 July 1812 [*London Gazette*]. *Register of officers' effects*: Died of wounds, 18 July 1812, Spain. Married. 'His son received his Effects he being with at his Decease'. [PRO: WO 25/2963]. Return dated 25 Aug. 1812. [PRO: WO 25/2965].

WILLIAMS, William, Ensign, 5th Foot: Ensign, 5th Foot, 16 Aug. 1809. Severely wounded during 'several affairs with the French Army', 18 March–7 April 1811 (2nd Battn.) [*London Gazette*]. Two pensions, each for seventy pounds, commencing 4 April 1812, 'for wounds more than equal to loss of limb' at Sabugal, 1811 [*1818 Pension Return*, pp. 4–5].

WILLIAMS, William, Major, 81st Foot; Lt. Col., 60th Foot: Major, Army, 24 June 1802; Major, 81st Foot, 26 Oct. 1804. Wounded, 'in the Army lately in Spain' (2nd Battn.) [*March 1809 Army List*, p. 105]. Lt. Col., 60th Foot, 15 Nov. 1809. Slightly wounded, Busaco, 27 Sept. 1810 (5th Battn.) [*London Gazette*]. Severely wounded, Fuentes de Onoro, evening 3 May 1811 (5th Battn.) [*London Gazette*]. Mentioned in Wellington's Fuentes de Onoro dispatch of 8 May 1811 ['Shortly after the enemy had formed on the ground on the right of the Duas Casa, on the afternoon of the 3d, they attacked with a large force the Village of Fuentes de Honor, which was defended in a most gallant manner by Lieutenant-Colonel Williams, of the 5th battalion 60th regiment, in command of the light infantry battalions belonging to Major-General Picton's division... Lieutenant-Colonel Williams was unfortunately wounded, but I hope not dangerously, and the command devolved upon Lieutenant-Colonel Cameron, of the 79th regiment... I particularly request your Lordship's attention to the conduct of Lieutenant-Colonel Williams'] [*Lon-*

don Gazette, 26 May 1811]. Slightly wounded, storming of Badajoz, 6 April 1812 (5th Battn.) [*London Gazette*]. Mentioned in Wellington's Badajoz dispatch, 7 April 1812 ['Lieutenant-General Picton has reported to me particularly the conduct of Lieutenant-Colonel Williams of the 60th'] [*London Gazette*]. Slightly wounded, Salamanca, 22 July 1812 [*London Gazette*]. Mentioned in Wellington's Salamanca dispatch, 24 July 1812 [*London Gazette*]. Gold Cross with 1 clasp (Corunna, Fuentes d'Onor, Ciudad Rodrigo, Badajoz, Salamanca), first as Major 81st Foot, remainder as Lt. Col., 5th Battn. 60th Foot. K.C.B. Later Col. 13th Foot. *Leach*, p. 212 [Fuentes de Onoro].

+**WILLIAMSON, Donald, Capt., 42nd Foot:** Capt., 42nd Foot, 18 Feb. 1804. Slightly wounded, storming and capture of Fort St Michael, Burgos, 19 Sept. 1812 (1st Battn.) [*London Gazette*]. Severely wounded, siege of Burgos, 20–26 Sept. 1812 (1st Battn.) [*London Gazette*]. Died of wounds, 2 Oct. 1812. Return dated 25 Oct. 1812. [PRO: WO 25/2965]. Obituary, *The Gentleman's Magazine*, Nov. 1812, p. 494 ['Oct. 2... At Burgos, in consequence of wounds received at the siege of the castle of Burgos, Capt. Donald Williamson, 42d reg foot, eldest son of Lieut.-col. W. of Banniskirk, inspecting field-officer of volunteers for the Northern district. A few days before his death, by the recommendation of Marquis Wellington, the Prince Regent conferred upon him the brevet rank of major. He did not survive long enough to be informed of this gratifying proof of the estimation in which his conduct and services were held. The Colonel's only other son, Capt. W. of the 94th, fell at the head of the grenadiers of that regiment, in the storming of Ciudad Rodrigo, on the 20th of January last.'].

+**WILLIAMSON, James, Capt., 94th Foot:** Capt., Army, 8 June 1809; Capt., 94th Foot, 18 Jan. 1810. Killed in the storming of Ciudad Rodrigo, 19 Jan. 1812 [*London Gazette*]. Brother of Donald Williamson of the 42nd.

WILLIAMSON, John, Capt., 4th Foot: Capt., 4th Foot, 6 Aug. 1804. Wounded, 'in the Army lately in Spain' (1st Battn.) [*March 1809 Army List*, p. 105]. Severely wounded, storming of Badajoz, 6 April 1812 [*London Gazette*]. Severely wounded, Vittoria, 21 June 1813 (1st Battn.) [*London Gazette*]. Severely wounded, Storming of San Sebastian, 31 Aug. 1813 (1st Battn.) [*London Gazette*]. Mentioned in Graham's San Sebastian dispatch, dated Oyarzun, 1 Sept. 1813 ['Lieutenant-General Sir J. Leith ... recommends to your Lordship's notice ... Captain Williamson ... of that regiment [4th foot] ... [who] was severely wounded in the command of the 4th, following the forlorn hope in the best style, and remaining long after his wound.'] [*London Gazette*]. Pension of two hundred pounds per annum, commencing 7 April 1813, 'for wounds' received at Badajoz [*1818 Pension Return*, pp. 4–5].

+**WILLSHIRE, John, Capt., 38th Foot:** Lt., 38th Foot, 28 May 1807. Severely wounded, in the siege of San Sebastian, 8 Aug. 1813 ('Captain John Willshire') (1st Battn.) [*London Gazette*]. Died of wounds, 7 Sept. 1813. Return dated Sept. 1813 ('Wilshire') (2nd Battn.) [PRO: WO 25/2965].

WILLSHIRE, Thomas, Capt., 38th Foot: *1829 Statement of Service*: Born 24 Aug. 1779, Halifax, North America. Aged fifteen 'on his first Entrance into the Army.' Ensign, 38th Foot, 24 June 1795; Lt., 5 Sept. 1795; Capt. 28 Aug. 1804; Bvt. Major, 31 Aug. 1813; Bvt. Lt. Col., 4 Dec. 1815; Major, 46th Foot., 10 Sept.

1823; Lt. Col., 2nd Foot, 30 Aug. 1827; Col. by Bvt. in India, 5 June 1829; Bvt. Col. 10 Jan. 1837; Maj. Gen. by Bvt. in India, 10 Jan. 1837. Retired on Half Pay, 27 Nov. 1841. *Battles, sieges and campaigns*: Roleia; Vimeira; retreat to and battle of Corunna; Walcheren (Capt., Light Company); Salamanca (ditto); 'retreat from Burgos, & action at Villa Marilla (Capt. commanding Brigade Light Company)'; Vittoria (Capt., Light Company); 'First assault & failure, St Sebastian 25 July 1812 (light company). Second Assault & capture, St Sebastian, 31 Aug. 1812 (Capt. light company). Crossing the Bidassoa (Bt. Major commanding Brigade of light company).' Nivelle. Nive. 'Repulsed with 300 men the attack of near 10,000 Kaffires upon the open village of Graham Town on the Frontier of the Cape of Good Hope 22 April 1819... Capture of Kittoor ... in the East Indies Dec. 1824... Assault and capture of Ghuznee, 23 July 1839... Maj. Gen. commanding 2nd Infantry Division, Army of the Indies, storming & capture of Tulah, 13 Nov. 1839.' *Wounds received in action*: 'Twice wounded in the Battle of Salamanca.' *Titles, honorary distinctions and medals*: 'Obtained the Brevet Rank of Major in Sept. 1813, Storming of St Sebastian. Obtained the Brevet Rank of Lt. Colonel for Commanding a Brigade of Light Companies when a Brevet Major in the actions of the Bidasoa, 7 Oct. 1813, Nivelle, 10 Nov. 1813, Nive 9, 10 & 11 Dec. 1813; which services were overlooked 'till brought to the notice of His Grace the Duke of Wellington when at Paris 4 Dec. 1815 (by the present Major Genl. Sir Charles Greville who in 1813 Commanded the Brigade to which the Light Companies I commanded belonged) when I was immediately noted by His Grace for the Rank of Lt. Colonel, but most unfortunately my Rank bears date only for *that day*, the 4 Decr 1815, which being so

long subsequent to the services for which it was granted must of course make them appear unconnected and in consequence I never have in any sense enjoyed the intended benifit of the Rank conferred on me, for to this moment there are even many Military Men who are ignorant I obtained the Rank of Lieut. Colonel for services in 1813... Was appointed Companion of the most Honble. Military Order of the Bath 19 July 1838 on the coronation of Her Majesty Queen Victoria. Was appointed Knight Comr of the same order 11th Decr 1839 for services when comg the Bombay Troops of the Army of the Indus and Baronet of the United Kingdom on the 13 June 1840.' Received the thanks of both Houses of Parliament in Feb. 1840. *Service abroad*: 'Aug. 1797–Aug. 1800 – West Indies; June 1807–June 1808 – South America and Cape of Good Hope; July 1808–Jan 1809 – Peninsula; July 1809 – Walcheren; June 1812–May 1814 – Peninsula; June 1815–Dec. 1815 – France; June 1818–March 1822 – Cape of Good Hope; May 1822–Dec. 1829 – Bengal, Madras & Bombay; 1 Jan. 1830–30 No. 1838 – East Indies; 1 Dec. 1838–20 Feb. 1840 – Scinde & Affghanistan; 21 Feb 1840–30 Sept. 1840 – East Indies.' [PRO: WO 25/785 f152]. Slightly wounded, Salamanca, 22 July 1812 ('Wilshire') [*London Gazette*]. MGS.

WILMOT, Edward, Capt., Royal Artillery: 2nd Capt., Army, 12 Sept. 1803; 2nd Capt., Royal Artillery, 19 July 1804. *Blakeney*, pp. 22–4 [Advance with Moore, Oct. 1808: 'On the route, through Guarda, one battery of artillery accompanied us, whom Captain Wilmot commanded. They consisted of six light six-pounders; and even these had the greatest difficulty in getting through the pass of Villavelha. The first gun conveyed across had two drag ropes attached, and to resist its rapidity while being trailed

WILMOT

downhill these ropes were held by as many soldiers as the short and frequent turning of this zigzag descent would permit; yet their resistance was scarcely sufficient to preserve the guns from rolling over the precipice. This in a great measure arose from Captain Wilmot having opposed locking any of the wheels, alleging that by so doing the carriages would suffer materially, and consequently become unserviceable much sooner. Trailing the guns down in this manner was excessively laborious to the soldiers... I can attest that there was not one soldier of the 28th Light Company who had heels to his shoes after the drag. They were a good deal shaken and much dissatisfied'], p. 29 ['we returned to the stream to aid the artillery, and hauled the guns safely across, notwithstanding the depth and rapidity of the current, now literally a torrent. Under the circumstances this duty was excessively fatiguing and harassing; but the indefatigable zeal and anxiety which Captain Wilmot showed during the whole of the march to bring his guns and horses perfect into action, induced every individual willingly to come forward and put his shoulder to the wheel.'].

WILSON, Ensign, 43rd Foot: Wounded, Vimeiro, 21 Aug. 1808 [*London Gazette*].

WILSON, George David, Capt., 4th Foot: Lt., 4th Foot, 7 Aug. 1799. Served with the 4th Foot on the expedition to the Helder in 1799. Capt., 4th Foot, 7 Aug. 1804. Siege of Copenhagen in 1807. Wounded in the retreat from Corunna. Served in the Walcheren expedition, 1809. Severely wounded, storming of Badajoz, 6 April 1812 [*London Gazette*]. Wounded at Badajoz while leading the advance of the storming party of the 5th Division to the escalade of the St Vicante bastion, for which he received a

Gold Medal. ADC to Gen. Sir W. Pringle in 1812. Major, Army, 21 Sept. 1813. Wounded, Waterloo. Half-pay, 21 March 1822. MGS. Died at Romford, Essex, 11 Jan. 1863. *Dalton*, pp. 120, 121 ['His proper name was "George Davis Willson." '].

WILSON, James, Capt./Major, 48th Foot: *1829 Statement of Service for Retired Officers*: Aged eighteen on first appointment to the Army. Ensign, 27th Foot, 12 Dec. 1798; Lt., 27th Foot, 27 Aug. 1799; Capt., 27th Foot, May 1801; Half-pay, 1802, by reduction; Capt., 48th Foot, July 1803 [Army List gives 9 July]; Major, 48th Foot, 20 June 1811; Bvt. Lt. Col., 48th Foot, 19 April 1812; Half-pay, 25 Sept. 1814, by reduction. 'Unable to serve from continual sufferings from severe wounds recd. in the Peninsula.' *Where serving when wounded*: 'Albuera. Badajos. Vittoria. Pampeluna. Toulouse'. *Details of pension*: Three hundred pounds, commencing 1814. *Family*: Married in Winchester, Hants., 24 March 1805. No children. *Where generally resident during last five years*: 'Burnett nr. Bath, Somerset'. [PRO: WO 25/778 f35]. Slightly wounded, Albuera, 16 May 1811 [*London Gazette*]. Major, 48th Foot, 20 June 1811. Slightly wounded, storming of Badajoz, 6 April 1812 [*London Gazette*]. Severely wounded, Pyrenees, 26 July 1813 ['Major Wilson (Lieut. Col.)'] [*London Gazette*]. *1818 Pension Return*, pp. 12–13.

WILSON, John, Major, 97th Foot; Brigadier, Portuguese Service: Capt., Queen's German Regt. of Foot, 18 Jan. 1799; Major, 97th Foot, 27 May 1802. Wounded, Vimeiro, 21 Aug. 1808 [*London Gazette*]. Lt. Col., Royal York Rangers, 22 Dec. 1808. In Portuguese Service Jan. 1809 to April 1814. Gold Medal. Lt.-General, 28 June 1838. MGS. *Challis, Portuguese Army*, p. 60 ['Brigadier... Wd. near Bayonne 18 Nov. '13'].

+**WILSON, John N., Lt., 50th Foot:** Lt., 50th Foot, 14 Nov. 1805. Wounded, Vimeiro, 21 Aug. 1808 [*London Gazette*]. *Monthly Return*, 1st Battn., dated 1 Sept. 1808: 'Wounded (on board), 21 Aug. 1808' [PRO: WO 17/164]. *Monthly Return*, 1st Battn., dated 1 Oct. 1808: 'Oporto' [PRO: WO 17/164]. Killed, 'in the Army lately in Spain' (1st Battn.) [*March 1809 Army List*, p. 105]. *Regimental Pay List*, 1st Battn., 25 Dec. 1808–24 March 1809: 'Dead 16 Jany.' [PRO: WO 12/6113].

WILSON, John, Ensign, 31st Foot: Ensign, 31st Foot, 31 Aug. 1809. Severely wounded, Albuera, 16 May 1811 ('Willson') (2nd Battn.) [*London Gazette*].

WILSON, Thomas, Capt., 28th Foot: *1829 Statement of Service for Retired Officers*: Aged eighteen on first appointment to the Army. Ensign, 28th Foot, 23 Oct. 1800; Lt., 28th Foot, 7 Jan. 1801; Half-pay, June 1802; returned to Full-pay, 28th Foot, 27 Aug. 1802; Capt., 28th Foot, 14 Nov. 1805; Bvt. Major, 28th Foot, 12 Aug. 1819; Half-pay, 60th Foot, 9 May 1821, 'at own request from private motives & at the same time unequal to the Service from Wound'. 'Not equal to Service on acct. of wounds'. *Where serving when wounded*: 'Shot through the upper part of both thighs & the lower part of the Body at the Battle of Vittoria'. *Details of pension*: One hundred pounds per annum, commencing 24 June 1814. *Family*: Married in Long Melford, Suffolk, 20 April 1815. Two children by 1829. *Where generally resident during last five years*: 'Alverstoke & Titchfield Co. Hants'. [PRO: WO 25/778 f48]. Served in Egypt. Severely wounded, Vittoria, 21 June 1813 (1st Battn.) [*London Gazette*]. *1818 Pension Return*, pp. 8–9. MGS.

WILSON, Thomas P., Capt., 59th Foot: Capt., 59th Foot, 2 Jan. 1806. Wounded, 'in the Army lately in Spain' (2nd Battn.) [*March 1809 Army List*, p. 105]. MGS.

WINCHESTER, Robert, Lt., 92nd Foot: *1829 Statement of Service*: Born in Aberdeenshire, Scotland, 5 Oct. 1785. Aged nineteen 'on his first Entrance into the Army.' Ensign, 92nd Foot, 18 Sept. 1805. Lt., 92nd Foot, 6 Feb. 1808. Capt., 92nd Foot, 19 July 1815. Major, 92nd Foot, 16 Aug. 1825. Note added: 'Bvt. Lt. Col., 92nd Foot, 28 June 1838. Retired from the service 1 November 1842 on Full Pay.' *Battles, sieges and campaigns*: 'Present at the Seige of Copenhagen on the 7th Septr. 1807 as Ensign... Expedition to Walcheren August 1809 as Lieut... Campaign in Portugal in 1810 at Lt... Lines of Torres Vedras 1810. Arroya del Monlinos 28 Octr. 1811. Lieut. Almaraz, 19 May 1812, Lieut. Alva de Tormes, 11, 12, 13 Nov. 1812. Vittoria 21 June 1813. Puerta de Maya 4 & 8 July 1813... Pyrenees, 25th 30th & 31st July 1813. Ronces Valles 7 Novr. 1813. Nivelle 10 Novr. 1813. Cambo 12 Novr. 1813. Nive 9th & 13th Decr. 1813. Hellette 14 Feby. 1814. Garris 15th Feby. 1814. Ariverette 17th Feby. 1814. Orthes 27 Feby. 1814. Airs 2d March 1814. Tarbes 20th March 1814. Quatre Bras 16 June 1815. Waterloo 18 June 1815.' *Distinguished conduct*: 'Distinguished at the pass of Maya on the 25th July 1813 in Command of the Lt. Company, which covering the left flank of the 50th Regiment and received the thanks of Sir William Stewart who commanded the 2d Division of the Army. Not noticed in General Orders. Distinguished himself, while in Command of the Light Company in the Campaign of 1814 in the South of France and received the approbation of Sir William Stewart who commanded the 2d Division of the Army. Not noticed in General Orders. Gallant Conduct noticed By Lieut. Colonel McDonald commanding the 92nd Highlanders while under his immediate

Command at Quatre Bras and Waterloo.' *Wounds received in action*: "Wounded in the right arm on the 25th July 1813 at the Pyrenees. Wounded in the left Testicle on the 13th Decr. 1813 at the Battles of the Nive and received one years pay. Wounded in the left hand at Quatre Bras 16th June 1815. On the 18th June 1815 at Waterloo wounded in the right arm (fractured) and received one years pay as Captn.' *Titles, honorary distinctions and medals*: '1. Medal for the Battle of Waterloo.' Note added: '2. Was appd. by H.R.H. King William 4th on 17 Jany. 1834 a Knight of the Rl. Hanoverian Guelphic Order on acct. of services perfd. during the late war.' *Service abroad*: '16 Augt. 1807 to 12 Nov. 1807, Expedition to Copenhagen. 1st Augt. 1809 to 3 Septr. 1809, Expedition to Walcheren. 8th Oct. 1810 to 29th July 1814, Portugal, Spain and France. 11 May 1815 to 20 Jany. 1816, Netherlands & France. 4 June 1819 to 20th Augt. 1820, Jamaica. 26th July 1825 to 21 May 1827, Jamaica.' Note added: '23 May 1839 to 3 April 1841, Malta. 4 April 1841 to 9 March 1842, West Indies.' *Family*: Married Rachael Cumming Walsh, 2 Jan. 1827, St Andrews, Jamaica. They had no children by 1830. [PRO: WO 25/803 f76]. Slightly wounded, Pyrenees, 25 July 1813 (1st Battn.) [*London Gazette*]. Severely wounded, the Nive, 13 Dec. 1813 (1st Battn.) [*London Gazette*]. Waterloo. *Dalton*, pp. 193, 195 ['Afterwards Lt.-Col. Robert Winchester, K.H. Retd. as bt.-col. Nov., 1842. Served in the Pa. and was wounded both at Quatre Bras and Waterloo. Son of Charles Winchester, of Aberdeen. D. 23rd July, 1846, at Edinburgh.'].

WINCKLER, Augustus, Ensign/Lt., 5th Line Battn. K.G.L.: Ensign, 5th Line Battn. K.G.L., 1 Aug. 1810. Recorded as having been killed, siege of Burgos, 5–10 Oct. 1812 ('Lieutenant') [*London Gazette*].

This was not accurate, though it appears likely that he had been severely wounded as he apparently did not return to campaign service until early 1814. See *Beamish, King's German Legion*, vol. II, p. 592. Joined as NCO, 1–4 Aug. 1810. Served in the Peninsula campaigns of 1811 and 1812, and the South of France in 1814. Waterloo. Half-pay at Holzminden, duchy of Brunswick.

WINGATE, John, 2nd Lt., 23rd Foot: 2nd Lt., 23rd Foot, 6 Nov. 1811. Severely wounded, storming of Badajoz, 6 April 1812 ('Winyates') [*London Gazette*].

WINSER, William, Capt., 27th Foot: Capt., 27th Foot, 9 July 1811. Severely wounded, Heights of Ordal, 12/13 Sept. 1813 (2nd Battn.) [*London Gazette*]. Temporary pension of one hundred pounds per annum, commencing 14 Sept. 1814, 'for wounds' received at Ordal [*1818 Pension Return*, pp. 8–9]. MGS.

WINTERBOTTOM, John, Adjutant/Lt., 52nd Foot: *1829 Statement of Service*: 'Born in Saddleworth, Yorkshire, 1st November 1781. Aged Eighteen on his first Entrance into the Army. Private, 52nd Foot, 17 October 1799 to March 1801. Corporal, 52nd, April 1801 to November 1803. Sergeant, 52nd, December 1803 to 10th June 1805. Sergeant Major, 52nd, 11th June 1805 to 23rd Novr. 1808. Ensign & Adjutant, 52nd, 24th November 1808 to 27th February 1810. Lieut. & Adjutant, 52nd, 25th February 1810 to 30th May 1821. Paymaster, 52nd, 31st May 1821 to 31st Decr. 1829. NB. On the 4th July 1816, he was under the necessity of resigning the Adjutancy, in consequence of a severe wound received in the head in the Battle of Waterloo, until his health should be reestablished, when he again on the 23rd Septr. 1819, at the desire of Major Genl. Sir John Colborne, then in the

Command of the 52nd Lt. Infantry, returned to his former situation of Adjutant, in which duty he continued until the 17th of May 1821; he then retired to half Pay for 14 days to enable him to succeed to his present situation of Paymaster, seeing no prospect of promotion.' *Battles, sieges and campaigns*: 'Private. Ferroll, 26th Augt. 1800... Sergeant Major. Kroge near Copenhagen and siege of Copenhagen, 26 Augt. 1807... Vimiera, 21 Augt. 1808... Ensign & Adjutant. Campaign of 1808 and the early part of 1809 on the retreat to Corunna. Battle of Corunna, 16th Jany. 1809. Affair on the River Coa, 24 July 1810. Lt. & Adjt. Battle of Busaco, 27 Sept. 1810. Affair at Pombal, 11th March 1811. Affair at Redinha, 12 March 1811. Siege & Storming of Badajoz, from 17 March to 6 April 1812. Battle of Salamanca, 22d July 1812. Affair at San Munoz, 17th June 1813. Battle of Vittoria, 21 June 1813. Affair at Bridge near Vera, 30th Aug. 1813. Heights of Vera, 7th Oct. 1813. Passage of the Neville, 10 Nov. 1813. Affair with Picquets near Arbonne, 20th Novr. 1813. Passage of the Nive, 9th, 10th, & 11th Decr. 1813. Battle of Orthes, 27th Febr. 1814. Affair at Tarbes, 20th March 1814. Battle of Toulouse 10 April 1814. Battle of Waterloo, 18 June 1815.' *Distinguished conduct*: [this section apparently written by M. Gen. J. Colborne, in his handwriting] 'From the unremitted exertions of Lt. Winterbottom in performing the active duties of Adjutant to the 52d Infantry, during the ten years he was under my command, it is difficult to point out every instance of his good conduct and useful services. I must however state that I had opportunities of observing his distinguished conduct at the Assault of Ciudad Rodrigo, the attack of the heights of Vera, the passage of the Nive, the Battle of Orthes, and at Waterloo. J. Colborne M Genl.' *Wounds received in action*: 'Severely in the left hip

with a Cannon Shot on the 12th March 1811. Slightly in the head in the Assault of Badajoz on the 6th April 1812. Slightly in the Groin at San Munoz on the 17th November 1812. Severely in the head in the Battle of Waterloo on the 18th June 1815.' Was granted a Lieutenants pension from 25 December 1821, which was made permanent per War Office letter dated 8th November 1826. Received One Years Pay as Adjutant for the wound received in Action on the 12th of March 1811, and One Years Pay of the same rank for the wound received in the Battle of Waterloo on the 18th June 1815.' *Titles, honorary distinctions and medals*: 'A Medal for the Battle of Waterloo.' *Service abroad*: '25 June 1800 to 24 June 1801, Ferrol & Cadiz (Spain). 23d July 1807 to 6th November 1807, Copenhagen. 16th July 1808 to 14th February 1809, Portugal & Spain. 25 May 1809 to 28th June 1814, Portugal, Spain & France. 4th January 1815 to 26th November 1818, Netherlands & France. 9th June 1823 to 31st December 1829, New Brunswick and Nova Scotia.' *Family*: Married 'the widow of the late Captain Jenkins of the 4th Royal Veterans Battalion', 13 Nov. 1824, Fredericton, New Brunswick. They had one son born by 1830. [PRO: WO 25/795 f145]. [See also another copy of his *1829 Statement of Service*, misfiled in PRO: WO 25/778 f19, and 'Memorandum', misfiled in PRO: WO 25/778 f18 encl.]. Previous to enlisting in the 52nd, in 1799, worked as a cloth weaver. Wounded, during 'several Affairs with the French Army', 12 March 1811 [*London Gazette*]. Slightly wounded, storming of Badajoz, 6 April 1812 (Adjt.) [*London Gazette*]. Wounded, Waterloo. Died of yellow fever at St Anne's, Barbados, 26 Nov. 1838. *Haythornthwaite, Armies*, p. 28 ['John Winterbottom of the 52nd ... rose from the rank of private in 1799 to ensign in 1808 and lieutenant in

1810, and was never absent from the regiment from his enlistment to his death from yellow fever in Barbados in 1838, save for his period of recuperation from wounds received at Redinha, Badajoz and Waterloo. Upon his death 130 officers who had served with him entered a subscription to raise an impressive memorial in the parish church of his native Saddleworth, to commemorate "his extraordinary talents as an officer, and his acknowledged worth as a man"; it still exists, topped by a sculpted shako, sash, sword and belt.'].

WISCH, Hieronimus von der, Lt., 1st Light Dragoons K.G.L: Lt., 1st Light Dragoons K.G.L., 17 Sept. 1810. Slightly wounded, Salamanca, 18 July 1812 [*London Gazette*]. Served in Peninsula 1809–14. Waterloo. *Beamish*, vol. II, p. 549 ['slightly wounded, 18th July 1812, at Canizal'].

WITTE, John Frederick Charles von, Lt., 5th Line Battn. K.G.L.: *1829 Statement of Service for Retired Officers*: Aged nineteen on his first appointment to the Army. Ensign, 5th Line Battn. K.G.L., 11 Dec. 1809; Lt., 5th Line Battn. K.G.L., 20 March 1812; Half-pay, 25 Feb. 1816, by reduction. *Where serving when wounded*: 'South of France and at Waterloo.' *Details of pension*: Seventy pounds, commencing 25 Dec. 1819. *Family*: Married at Tournay in Flanders, 11 Jan. 1815. Five children by 1829. *Where generally resident during last five years*: 'City of Hanover.' [PRO: WO 25/755 f148]. Severely wounded, Nivelle, 10 Nov. 1813 ('Charles Wille') [*London Gazette*]. Served in Peninsula 1808–14. Waterloo. *Beamish*, vol. II, p. 591 ['Charles von Witte'].

WITTE, Lewis von, Ensign, 1st Line Battn. K.G.L: Ensign, 1st Line Battn. K.G.L., 12 March 1811 ('de Witte'). Slightly wounded, siege of

Ciudad Rodrigo, 14 Jan. 1812 ('Ensign Whitte') [*London Gazette*]. Served in Peninsula 1808–13. Lt., 2nd Hussars K.G.L., 8 Oct. 1814. *Beamish*, vol. II, p. 554 [Died 'at Nienburg, 21st June, 1823.'].

WITZENDORF, Hartwig von, Lt./Adjutant, 1st Dragoons K.G.L.: Lt., 1st Dragoons K.G.L., 28 Aug. 1810; Adjutant, 1st Dragoons K.G.L., 28 Aug. 1810. Severely wounded, in 'an Affair with the Enemy's Cavalry, in Front of the Village of Majalahonda,' 11 Aug. 1812 [*London Gazette*]. Served in Peninsula 1812–14. *Beamish*, vol. II, p. 540.

+WITZENDORFF, Adolphus von, Lt., 2nd Light Battn. K.G.L.: Lt., 2nd Light Battn. K.G.L., 8 May 1811. Died of wounds, 23 March 1814. Return dated March 1814. [PRO: WO 25/2965]. *Beamish*, vol. II, p. 639 [Died '19th March 1814, of the wounds he received in action before Bayonne on the 27th Feb. 1814.'].

WOLFE, Edward, Lt./Capt., 28th Foot: Lt., 28th Foot, 9 Jan. 1806. Severely wounded, Vittoria, 21 June 1813 ('Wolf') [*London Gazette*]. Capt., 28th Foot, 9 Sept. 1813. Severely wounded, the Nive, 13 Dec. 1813 (1st Battn.) [*London Gazette*]. MGS.

WOLFE, John, Lt., 61st Foot: *1829 Statement of Service*: 'Born Haughton Castle, Northumberlandshire, 12th May 1787. Aged 20 ½ years on his first Entrance into the Army. Ensign, 61st Regt., 25 Decr. 1807. Lieut., 61st, 22 June 1809. Captain, 61st, 24 Oct. 1821. Half Pay, May 1822, by reduction of 2 Companies. Captain, 61st, Full Pay, 10 July 1823. Major, 61st, 10 Augt. 1826.' *Battles, sieges and campaigns*: 'Talavera 27 & 28th July 1809... Forts of Salamanca June 1812. Battle of Salamanca 22

July 1812. Forts of Burgos in October 1812. Battle of the Pyrenees 28th & 30th July 1813. Battle of the Nive 1813. Orthes 27th February 1814. Toulouse 10th April 1814.' *Wounds received in action*: 'Battle of Salamanca 22nd July 1812, slightly wounded. Battle of Pyrenees 30th July severely wounded. Battle of Toulouse severely wounded 10 April 1814. One years pay as Captain received in 1814, having had the command of a company at the Battle of the Pyrenees, and the Grenadier Company at Toulouse.' *Service abroad*: 'October 1808 to June 1809, Gibralter. July 1809 to Decemr. 1809, Spain & Portugal. October 1811 to July 1814, Portugal, Spain & France. 14 October 1816 to 27 May 1822, Jamaica. 30 June 1828 to 31 Decr. 1829, Ceylon.' Not married in 1830. [PRO: WO 25/797 f5]. Slightly wounded, Salamanca, 22 July 1812 [*London Gazette*]. Severely wounded, Pyrenees, 30 July 1813 (1st Battn.) [*London Gazette*]. Severely wounded, Toulouse, 10 April 1814 (1st Battn.) [*London Gazette*].

WOLFF, John Anthony, Capt., 60th Foot: *1829 Statement of Service for Retired Officers*: Aged thirty-four on first appointment to the Army. Ensign, 'Isle of Wight Riflemen', 1 Aug. 1796; Lt., Isle of Wight Riflemen, 1 March 1797; 'in the year 1797 this Regiment became incorporated in the Army to form the 5th Battalion of the 60th Regiment as Riflemen, we received new commissions'; Lt., 60th Foot, 30 Dec. 1797; Capt., 60th Foot, 5 June 1806; Half-pay, n.d., 'Upon my humble request for Reason of ill-health ... in consequence of my badly state of health from my severe Wounds'. Served eighteen years on Full-pay. 'At present as I am nearly 67 years of age, I am certainly unfit for any Service'. *Where serving when wounded*: 'Serving in the 5th Battailion of the 60th Regiment and wounded by a shot through the Body at the Batle of Talavera de la Reina on the 28th of July 1809, and in consequence was made a prisoner at France'. *Details of pension*: One hundred pounds per annum. 'After Exchange of prisoners in the year 1814 arriving at London I was examined by the Army Medical Department and received my pension from the 4th of November 1814; but His Majesty graciously pleased, that the said pension should commence from the 25th of December 1811'. Not married. No employment. *Where generally resident during last five years*: 'at Hamburg'. [PRO: WO 25/778 f149]. Severely wounded, Talavera, 27 July 1809 ('Wolf') [*London Gazette*]. *1818 Pension Return*, pp. 14–15.

WOLFRADT, Frideric Henry, Capt., Duke of Brunswick Oels' Corps (Infantry): Capt., Duke of Brunswick Oels' Corps, 16 Aug. 1810. Severely wounded, Crossing the Bidassoa, 7/9 Oct. 1813 [*London Gazette*].

WOLLRABE, Hermann, Lt., 1st Light Battn. K.G.L.: Ensign, 1st Light Battn. K.G.L., 26 March 1811; Lt., 1st Light Battn. K.G.L., 20 March 1812. Severely wounded, in an action near Tolosa, 24 June 1813 [*London Gazette*]. Severely wounded, sortie from Bayonne, 14 April 1814 ('Wollrabe') [*London Gazette*]. 'Herman Wolrabe' in Army List. Served in Peninsula 1812–14. Waterloo. *Beamish*, vol. II, p. 657 ['severely wounded, 18th June 1815, at Waterloo ... placed on half-pay, 25th Oct. 1815. [Died] at Pomrau near Klotze, in Han. 14th Feb. 1820.'].

WOOD, Charles, Lt., 52nd Foot: Lt., 52nd Foot, 7 March 1810. Slightly wounded, Busaco, 27 Sept. 1810 (1st Battn.) [*London Gazette*]. Capt., 10th Light Dragoons, 12 Nov. 1814; Bvt. Major, 10th Light Dragoons, 16 March

1815. Waterloo. Half-pay, 5 April 1821. MGS. *Green*, p. 131 ['28th [Jan. 1813]. This morning the colonel sent for me saying he was going to send me to the head quarters of the army [at Freynada], to be servant to a captain, who had just been transferred from the 52nd regiment to ours [68th]: his name was Captain Charles Wood, Deputy Assistant Adjutant General... My master dined with Lord Wellington about twice a week.'], pp. 132-3, 134 ['Indeed, my master neglected me very much; but I excuse him, for he was young and inexperienced.'], pp. 135-6, 137 ['About the 10th of April [1813], orders came for my master to leave Portugal, and to join our army in Russia, in the capacity of aid-decamp to General Stewart. My master was brother to Colonel Wood, of the royal east Middlesex militia, and nephew to the late Marquis of Londonderry.'], pp. 138-43. *Brett-James*, pp. 201-2 ['That January [1813], once more round the village of Freineda, foxes were plentiful, but they escaped all too easily into holes among the rocks by the Coa. Faced with this problem, Captain Charles Wood of the 52nd, a Deputy Assistant Adjutant-General, who was in charge of the sixteen couple of foxhounds which straggled about and ran badly for want of a huntsman, used to ride out and stop the holes overnight, give a loud "halloo!" and then gallop sharply away. Despite his efforts, in the course of one month, hunting usually three times a week, the hounds killed one fox only, and that was "mobbed".']. *Moorsom*, p. 434 ['Entered the 52nd in 1809. Served with the regiment in Spain and Portugal, and was wounded at Busaco. In 1813 he exchanged to Cavalry, and subsequently served in Flanders, and was present at the battle of Waterloo. Colonel Wood has received the Prussian Order of Merit.']. *Dalton*, pp. 68, 70.

WOOD, George, Lt., 82nd Foot: Lt., 82nd Foot, 17 Dec. 1807. Severely wounded, Pyrenees, 30 July 1813 (1st Battn.) [*London Gazette*].

+WOOD, H. F., Capt., 48th Foot: Lt., 48th Foot, 9 July 1803; Capt., 48th Foot, 31 May 1809. Slightly wounded, Talavera, 28 July 1809 [*London Gazette*]. Slightly wounded, Albuera, 16 May 1811 [*London Gazette*]. Severely wounded, Pyrenees, 28 July 1813 (1st Battn.) [*London Gazette*]. Died of wounds, 28 July 1813. Return dated Aug. 1813. [PRO: WO 25/2965]. Obituary, *The Gentleman's Magazine*, Nov. 1813, p. 504 ['Lately... In Spain, Capt. Wood, 48th reg. having been before three times severely wounded at the head of his company; in the late actions in the Pyrenees he received a mortal wound.'].

WOOD, James Charles, Capt., 58th Foot: *1829 Statement of Service for Retired Officers*: Aged sixteen years three months five days on first appointment to the Army. Ensign, 15th Foot, 9 Dec. 1800; Half-pay, 24 June 1802, by reduction; Lt., 58th Foot, 9 July 1803; Capt., 58th Foot, 15 Nov. 1809; Half-pay, 24 Feb. 1816, by reduction. *Where serving when wounded*: 'Severely wounded at Ortes in France, the Ball not yet extracted'. *Family*: Married in Sligo, 21 Nov. 1817. Two children by 1829. *Where generally resident during last five years*: 'Generally in Sligo, occasionly in Dublin'. [PRO: WO 25/778 f162]. Severely wounded, Orthes, 27 Feb. 1814 (2nd Battn.) [*London Gazette*].

+WOOD, John, Major, 32nd Foot: Major, 32nd Foot, 2 Aug. 1804; Bvt. Lt. Col., 32nd Foot, 4 June 1811. Severely wounded, Pyrenees, 28 July 1813 (1st Battn.) [*London Gazette*]. Died of wounds, 31 July 1813. Return dated Aug. 1813. [PRO: WO 25/2965].

WOOD, Nesbitt, Ensign, 58th Foot: Severely wounded, Orthes, 27 Feb. 1814 (2nd Battn.) [*London Gazette*].

WOOD, Robert Henry, Capt. 40th Foot: Capt., 40th Foot, 20 Feb. 1806. Wounded in the trenches before Badajoz, 8–15 May 1811 (1st Battn.) [*London Gazette*]. In Portuguese Service June 1811 to July 1812. *Challis, Portuguese Army*, p. 60 ['Maj. 12 Cacad.'].

WOOD, Thomas, Capt., Coldstream Guards: Lt. and Capt., Coldstream Guards, 27 March 1806. Slightly wounded, Talavera, 28 July 1809 [*London Gazette*].

WOODFORD, Alexander George, Capt. and Lt. Col., Coldstream Guards: Lt., Army, 11 Dec. 1799; Lt. and Capt., Coldstream Guards, 20 Dec. 1799; Capt. and Lt. Col., Coldstream Guards, 8 March 1810. Mentioned in Wellington's Salamanca dispatch, 24 July 1812 ['I must also mention Lieutenant-Colonel Woodford, commanding the light battalion of the brigade of guards, who, supported by two companies of the fusileers, under the command of Captain Crowder, maintained the village of Arapiles against all the efforts of the enemy, previous to the attack upon their position by our troops.'] [*London Gazette*]. Col., Army, 4 June 1814; Second Major, Coldstream Guards, 25 July 1814. Commanded the (2nd Battn.) Coldstream Guards at Waterloo. Waterloo Medal. *Dalton*, pp. 107–8 ['Afterwards F.-M. Sir Alexander Woodford, G.C.B. and G.C.M.G. Elder brother of Col. John G. Woodford (see Staff). On the death of Sir Ralph Woodford, Bart., Governor of Trinidad, Alexander Woodford became the head of this ancient family... [He defended] the farm of Hougomont in the early part of the afternoon of Waterloo Day against the repeated and vigorous attacks of the French. C.B. for Waterloo. Had previously served in the Pa. and received the gold cross and one clasp. Was also K.M.T., and K. St G. of Russia. Filled high commands in the Ionian Islands and elsewhere. Col.-in-Chf. 40th Foot, 1842. Transferred to the Scots Fusilier Guards 15th Dec., 1861. D. 26th Aug., 1870.']. *Blakeney*, p. 130 [Walcheren expedition: 'Lieutenant-Colonel Woodford, with his light company of the Coldstream Guards... I more than once in later days met Colonel Woodford in London, and remember not only his polished address and courteous manner, but also his prompt recognition and ready kindness.'].

WOODFORD, John George, Lt. and Capt., 1st Foot Guards: Lt. and Capt., 1st Foot Guards, 13 Nov. 1804; Capt. and Lt. Col., 1st Foot Guards, 1 July 1813. Gold Medal. Temporary Pension of one hundred pounds per annum, commencing 25 Dec. 1811, 'for wounds' received at Corunna, 1809 ('Woodforde') [*1818 Pension Return*, pp. 2–3]. MGS. Waterloo. *Royal Military Calendar*, vol. IV, p. 480 ['Woodforde... Served in Spain and Portugal as an Assist.-Quar.-Mast.-Gen.']. Younger brother of Alexander Woodford of the Coldstream Guards. Crosthwaite, J. F., *Brief Memoir of Maj. Gen. Sir John George Woodford* (London and Keswick, 1881).

WOODGATE, John, Lt., 52nd Foot: Lt., 52nd Foot, 11 Feb. 1808. Severely wounded, Heights of Grijon, 11 May 1809, while serving with the 1st batt. detachments [*London Gazette*]. Severely wounded 'in carrying a Redoubt before Ciudad Rodrigo', 9 Jan. 1812 [*London Gazette*]. Capt., Army, 20 Feb. 1812; Capt., 20th Light Dragoons, 11 June 1812. MGS.

WOODGATE, William, Major, 60th Foot: Major, 60th Foot, 13 Aug. 1807. Slightly wounded, Fuentes de Onoro, 5 May 1811 (5th Battn.)

[*London Gazette*]. Mentioned in Wellington's Fuentes de Orono dispatch, 8 May 1811 (5 May: commanding the light infantry battalions of the 3rd Division) [*London Gazette*, 26 May 1811]. Bvt. Lt. Col., 60th Foot, 30 May 1811. Gold Medal. MGS. *Royal Military Calendar*, vol. IV, p. 343.

+WOODHAM, John, Capt., 9th Foot: Capt., 9th Foot, 17 Oct. 1811. Killed, 'at the Siege of St Sebastian,' 7–27 July 1813 (1st Battn.) [*London Gazette*].

WOODS, Richard, Lt., 3rd Foot: *1829 Statement of Service for Retired Officers*: Aged twenty on first appointment to the Army. Ensign, 7th Garrison Battn., 2 Dec. 1806; Ensign, 3rd Foot, Aug. 1807; Lt., 3rd Foot, 28 Nov. 1809; Capt., 5th West India Regt., 13 Aug. 1812; Capt., 2nd Royal Veteran Battn., 15 Oct. 1812; 'Placed on the Retired List', 2nd Royal Veteran Battn., 25 Jan. 1815; Capt., 8th Royal Veteran Battn., 25 May 1815; 'Placed on the Retired List', 25 June 1816, by reduction. 'Is unfit for Military Service having lost his right leg & part of the thigh at the Battle of Albuera on the 16th May 1811'. *Where serving when wounded*: 'In the Peninsula' [Albuera]. *Details of pension*: Seventy pounds per annum, commencing 16 May 1812, increased to one hundred pounds on 18 June 1816. *Family*: Married in 'Rathfarnham Co. Dublin', 3 Dec. 1812. Seven children by 1829. No employment. *Where generally resident during last five years*: 'Parsonstown, King's County'. [PRO: WO 25/778 f169]. Severely wounded, Albuera, 16 May 1811 [*London Gazette*]. *1818 Pension Return*, pp. 4–5. MGS.

WOODS, William, Lt., 3rd Foot: Lt., 3rd Foot, 31 Jan. 1811. Severely wounded, the Nive, 13 Dec. 1813 (1st Battn.) [*London Gazette*]. Slightly wounded, Aire, 2 March 1814 (1st Battn.) [*London Gazette*].

WOODS, William, Lt., 48th Foot: *1829 Statement of Service for Retired Officers*: Aged twenty-one years six months on first appointment to the Army. Ensign, 48th Foot, 7 April 1808; Lt., 48th Foot, 28 Dec. 1809; Lt., 4th Dragoon Guards, 24 March 1812; Half-pay, 6th Dragoons, 15 Feb. 1816, 'from private motives'. 'On account of my numerous family & being now in my forty third year I am not desirous of serving'. *Where serving when wounded*: 'Albuera'. 'No Pension but received one Yrs. Pay as Lieutenant'. *Family*: Married in 'Parish of St Andrews, Newcastle upon Tyne', 11 Feb. 1815. Six children by 1829. *Title and nature of employment*: 'I hold no civil office but am Adjutant in the Northumberland & Newcastle Yeomanry Cavalry'. *Where generally resident during last five years*: 'Newcastle upon Tyne'. [PRO: WO 25/778 f163]. Reported as 'Missing', Albuera, 16 May 1811 ('Wood') (2nd Battn.) [*London Gazette*]. MGS.

+WOODYEAR, Lumley, 1st Lt., Royal Artillery: 1st Lt., Royal Artillery, 1 Feb. 1808. Slightly wounded, Vittoria, 21 June 1813, while serving on the General Staff ('Captain Woodyer') [*London Gazette*]. Died of wounds, 2 Sept. 1813. Return dated Sept. 1813. [PRO: WO 25/2965].

+WOOLCOMBE, Philip J., 1st Lt., Royal Artillery: 1st Lt., Royal Artillery, 20 July 1804. 'Dangerously wounded, since dead', Barossa, 5 March 1811 [*London Gazette*]. Died of wounds, 5 March 1811. Return dated 25 March 1811 ('Woollcombe') [PRO: WO 25/2965].

WOOLLCOMBE, Robert, 1st Lt., Royal Artillery: 1st Lt., Royal Artillery, 18 June 1807. Slightly wounded, Fuentes de Onoro, 5 May 1811 [*London Gazette*]. MGS. Born 1788, died 1849. 'The Diary of Lieutenant Robert Woollcombe, R.A.,

1812–13', ed. S. C. P. Ward, in *Journal of the Society for Army Historical Research*, Vol. LII (1974).

WORSLEY, Thomas Taylor, 2nd Lt./1st Lt., 95th Rifles: 2nd Lt., 95th Rifles, 14 Feb. 1811. Severely wounded, storming of Badajoz, 6 April 1812 (3rd Battn.) [*London Gazette*]. 1st Lt., 95th Rifles, 2 Oct. 1812. Wounded, Waterloo. Half-pay, 11 Feb. 1816. MGS. Died 25 Oct. 1851. *Kincaid, Random Shots*, p. 173 ['at the storming of Badajos, in April, 1812, one of our officers (Lieutenant Worsley) got a musket-ball in the right ear, which came out at the back of the neck, and, though after a painful illness, he recovered, yet his head got a twist, and he was compelled to wear it, looking over the right shoulder. At the battle of Waterloo, in 1815, (having been upwards of three years with his neck awry,) he received a shot in the left ear, which came out within half an inch of his former wound in the back of his neck, and it set his head straight again! This is an anecdote which I should scarcely have dared to relate were it not that, independent of my personal knowledge of the facts, the hero of it still lives to speak for himself, residing on his property, in Nottinghamshire, alike honoured and respected as a civilian, as he was loved and esteemed as a gentleman and a gallant soldier.'].

WRAY, Hugh Boyd, Ensign/Lt., 40th Foot: *1829 Statement of Service for Retired Officers*: Aged seventeen on first appointment to the Army. Ensign, 40th Foot, Jan. 1811 [Army List gives 23 Jan.]; Lt., 40th Foot, 10 Sept. 1812; Half-pay, 1817, by reduction. Served at Waterloo. *Where serving when wounded*: 'Was twice slightly wounded but rec. no pension.' *Family*: Married in Queen's County, 10 May 1823. One child, born in 1824. *Title and nature of employment*: 'Chief Constable & Pay Clerk of Police in the Queens

County.' *Where generally resident during last five years*: 'Queens Co.' [PRO: WO 25/767 f95].

+WRAY, Thomas Fawcett, Lt., 7th Foot: Lt., 7th Foot, 13 April 1809. Severely wounded, Albuera, 16 May 1811 (2nd Battn.) [*London Gazette*]. Killed, storming of Badajoz, 6 April 1812 [*London Gazette*].

WRAY, William G., Surgeon, 27th Foot: Assistant Surgeon, 27th Foot, 20 Nov. 1805; Surgeon, 27th Foot, 6 Aug. 1812. Slightly wounded, Pyrenees, 28 July 1813 (Surgeon) (3rd Battn.) [*London Gazette*].

+WREN, Robert, Capt., 11th Foot: Capt., 11th Foot, 7 Dec. 1809. Mentioned in Skerrett's dispatch from Tarifa, 24 Dec 1811 ['On the 21st, Captain Wren, of the 11th, destroyed, with his company, a small piquet of the enemy.'] [*London Gazette*]. Severely wounded, Pyrenees, 28 July 1813 ('Wrenn') (1st Battn.) [*London Gazette*]. Died of wounds, 15 Aug. 1813. Return dated Aug. 1813. [PRO: WO 25/2965].

WRIGHT, John, Ensign, 61st Foot: Ensign, 61st Foot, 16 Nov. 1812. Severely wounded, Toulouse, 10 April 1814 (1st Battn.) [*London Gazette*].

WRIGHT, Peter, 1st Lt., Royal Engineers: 1st Lt., Royal Engineers, 25 March 1811. Slightly wounded, siege of Badajoz, 20 March 1812 [*London Gazette*]. Mentioned in Hill's Almaraz dispatch, 21 May 1812 ['Lieutenant Wright, of the Royal Engineers, has also rendered me very essential service; he is a most intelligent, gallant, and meritorious officer'] [*London Gazette*]. Slightly wounded, Vittoria, 21 June 1813 [*London Gazette*].

WRIGHT, Samuel, Lt., 3rd Foot: Lt., 3rd Foot, 13 Aug. 1807. Slightly wounded, Albuera, 16 May 1811 [*London Gazette*]. Slightly wounded, the Nive, 13 Dec. 1813 (1st Battn.) [*London Gazette*]. MGS.

WRIGHT, Thomas, Lt., 48th Foot: Lt., 48th Foot, 5 Feb. 1808. Slightly wounded, Albuera, 16 May 1811 [*London Gazette*].

+WRIXEN, Jonathan, Ensign, 20th Foot: Ensign, 20th Foot, 18 June 1812. Killed, Pyrenees, 2 Aug. 1813 (1st Battn.) [*London Gazette*].

+WURMB, Adolphus William von, Major, 2nd Line Battn. K.G.L.: Major, 2nd Line Battn., 18 Feb. 1809. Slightly wounded, Busaco, 27 Sept. 1810 [*London Gazette*]. Killed, siege of Burgos, 19 Oct. 1812 [*London Gazette*]. Served in Peninsula 1808–12. Gold Medal. *Beamish*, vol. II, pp. 108–9 [Assault of Burgos: 'The Germans were divided into two principal bodies, consisting of two hundred men, under the immediate command of major Wurmb... Wurmb's bold soldiers were not to be deterred, and attacking the third line with desperate valour, three officers and several men actually gained the summit! Their triumph was however, short ... after all their officers had been either killed or wounded, they were forced back through the breach... The gallant Wurmb, a distinguished officer, fell in this assault'], p. 631 ['killed in storming the interior line of defence of the castle of Burgos in Spain, 18th Oct. 1812.'].

+WYATT, Henry, 1st Lt., Royal Artillery: 1st Lt., Royal Artillery, 1 Feb. 1808. Killed, Talavera, 28 July 1809 [*London Gazette*].

WYATT, Herbert, Ensign/Lt., 83rd Foot: *1829 Statement of Service for Retired Officers:* Aged seventeen on first appointment to the Army. Ensign, 83rd Foot, 28 March 1811; Lt., 83rd Foot, 17 June 1813; Lt., 2nd

Life Guards, 15 Oct. 1816; Half-pay, 1st Foot, 28 Sept. 1818, 'in consequence ill effects of Wound recd. at Nivelle'. *Where serving when wounded:* 'at Nivelle, Spain'. *Details of pension:* Seventy pounds, commencing 25 June 1815. Not married. No employment. *Where generally resident during last five years:* 'London'. [PRO: WO 25/778 f224]. Severely wounded, Nivelle, 10 Nov. 1813 (2nd Battn.) [*London Gazette*]. *1818 Pension Return*, pp. 18–19. MGS.

+WYATT, John, Capt., 34th Foot: Capt., Army, 11 Sept. 1806; Capt., 34th Foot, 17 Sept. 1807. Wounded, Albuera, 16 May 1811 (3rd Battn.) [*London Gazette*]. Killed, Pyrenees, 25 July 1813. *Bell*, pp. 16, 83 [25 July 1813: 'On Sunday morning, the 25th, at dawn of day, the pickets and outposts were suddenly attacked. The signal-gun was fired, when we got away up hill as fast as we could... The enemy had full possession of the ground. Some 10,000 men were there... It was death to go on against such a host; but it was the order, and on we went to destruction ... we had no chance... The Captain of Grenadiers (Wyatt), a very fine handsome man, being next in advance, was shot through the head. He never spoke again.']. Note: not included in the casualty returns for actions in the Pyrenees published in the *London Gazette*, which lists Lt. and Adjutant John Day as the sole death in the 34th Foot on the 25th July. Bell, is, however, clear about both the identity of the individual and his fate, and clearly distinguishes between Wyatt and Day. See John Day. *Sherer*, p. 258 [Aretesque, Pass of Maya, 25 July 1813: 'Among other brave victims, our captain of grenadiers nobly fell, covered with wounds'].

WYCK, Charles von, Lt., 2nd Line Battn. K.G.L.: Ensign, 2nd Line

Battn. K.G.L., 27 Jan. 1806; Lt., 2nd Line Battn. K.G.L., 18 Aug. 1808. Severely wounded, Talavera, 28 July 1809 ('Week') [*London Gazette*]. 'Charles, *Baron* Wick' in Army List. Served in Peninsula 1808–12. *Beamish*, vol. II, p. 648 [Died from illness or accident 'at Lucinde in Portugal, 17th April 1813.']

WYLDE, John Newman, Lt., 5th Foot: *1829 Statement of Service for Retired Officers*: Aged twenty-four on first appointment to the Army. Ensign, 5th Foot, 24 Jan. 1807; Lt., Sept. 1808 [Army List gives 15 Sept.]; Capt., 56th Foot, 9 Nov. 1813; Half-pay, 6 Sept. 1817, by reduction. *Where serving when wounded*: 'In Spain at Ciudad Rodrigo'. *Details of pension*: Seventy pounds, commencing 1816 ('I believe'). *Family*: Married in Burrington near Bristol, Somerset, 29 June 1819. *Where generally resident during last five years*: 'In Somerset and Devonshire'. [PRO: WO 25/778 f215]. Severely wounded, storming of Ciudad Rodrigo, 19 Jan. 1812 ('Wilde') [*London Gazette*]. *1818 Pension Return*, pp. 4–5.

WYLDE, Ralph, Capt., 89th Foot; Major, 14th Portuguese Line: Capt., Army, 8 Dec. 1806; Capt., 89th Foot, 28 Feb. 1811. In Portuguese Service Aug. 1811 to Nov. 1813. 'Wilde' in Army List. *Challis, Portuguese Army*, p. 60 ['Maj. 14 Line... Wd. Salamanca 22 July '12'].

WYLLY, Alexander Campbell, Capt., 7th Foot: Lt., 7th Foot, 11 July 1805; Capt., 7th Foot, 19 June 1811. Severely wounded in 'an Affair with the Enemy near Aldea de Ponte', 27 Sept. 1811 ('Willey') [*London Gazette*]. AAG at Waterloo. *Dalton*, p. 31 ['served in Spain and Portugal as A.D.C. to Sir Edward Pakenham; also in the American campaign in similar capacity... D. in Malta, 10th Nov., 1827.']

+WYNCH, James, Lt. Col., 4th Foot: Lt. Col., 4th Foot, 15 Nov. 1799. Wounded, 'in the Army lately in Spain' (1st Battn.) [*March 1809 Army List*, p. 105]. Obituary, *The Gentleman's Magazine*, Feb. 1811, p. 88 ['Jan. 6. At Lisbon, of a typhus fever, sincerely lamented by all who knew him, Col. James Lynch, of the 4th reg. or King's Own, who was promoted to the command of a brigade, and placed on the staff a short time before his decease. This gallant officer had long distinguished himself by his uniform exertions and bravery; and had served successively in every expedition of importance during the war. At the Helder he was severely wounded, and at the battle of Corunna was shot through the body; from which latter wound he never entirely recovered.']. *Blakeney*, p. 116 [Battle of Corunna: 'Sir John Moore ... then rode up to the right of Baird's line, and told Colonel Wench [sic], of the 4th Regiment, that his throwing back the right of his regiment was just what he wished.']. *Simmons*, pp. 115, 136 [8 Feb. 1809: 'Colonel Drummond took command of the 2nd Brigade of the Light Division vice Winch [sic] deceased.'].

WYNEKEN, Christian William Augustus John Ernest, Capt., 1st Light Battn. K.G.L.: *1829 Statement of Service for Retired Officers*: Aged twenty on first appointment to the Army. Ensign, 1st Light Battn. K.G.L., 20 Dec. 1803; Lt., 1st Light Battn. K.G.L., 21 March 1805; Capt., 1st Light Battn. K.G.L., 17 Dec. 1811; Half-pay, n.d. [1816], by reduction. Served twelve years one month on Full-pay, plus an additional two years for Waterloo. *Where serving when wounded*: '25th of June 1813 at Taluza in Spain, slightly. 14th of April 1814 at Bayonne, slightly. 18th June 1815 Waterloo, slightly'. No pension. *Family*: Married in 'Rethem Parish near Hanover', 27 July 1817. Three children by 1829. *Title and nature of employment*: 'Major in the Rifle Guards, Hanoverian Service'. *Where generally resident during last five years*: 'Hanover'. [PRO: WO 25/778 f212]. Slightly wounded, in an action near Tolosa, 25 June 1813 ('Wynecken') [*London Gazette*]. Slightly wounded, sortie from Bayonne, 14 April 1814 ('Winecke') [*London Gazette*]. 'Wyneke' in Army List. Served in Peninsula 1808–14. Waterloo. *Beamish*, vol. II, p. 562.

WYNEKEN, Ernest Claus Henry, Lt., 2nd Line Battn. K.G.L.: Lt., 2nd Line Battn. K.G.L., 25 Jan. 1806. Severely wounded, siege of Burgos, 5–10 Oct. 1812 ('Wynecke') [*London Gazette*]. 'Claus Wyneke' in Army List. Served in Peninsula 1808–13. Waterloo. *Beamish*, vol. II, p. 576 ['severely wounded, 8th Oct. 1812, before Burgos... [Died] in Hanover, 18th Oct. 1818, captain Han. grenadier guards.'].

WYNEKEN, Frederick Heinrich Christoph Wilhelm, Capt., 2nd Light Battn. K.G.L.: *1829 Statement of Service for Retired Officers*: Aged twenty-one on first appointment to the Army. Ensign, 2nd Light Battn. K.G.L., Nov. 1803; Lt., 2nd Light Battn. K.G.L., 1 Oct. 1805; Capt., 2nd Light Battn. K.G.L., 8 July 1811; Capt., 1st Foreign Veteran Battn. K.G.L., 17 Aug. 1815; Half-pay, 25 April 1816, 'by Reduction and ill-health'. *Where serving when wounded*: 'three wounds received near Salamanca 22nd June 1812. Wounds 27th February 1814. Wound 14th April 1814 near Bayonne'. *Details of pension*: Two hundred pounds, commencing 15 April 1815. *Family*: Married on 9 Dec. 1815.

Three children by 1829. *Where generally resident during last five years*: 'at Lelle, Kingdom of Hannover & Gr. Britton'. [PRO: WO 25/778 f220]. Severely wounded, Heights of Villares, 20–22 June 1812 ('Winecke') [*London Gazette*]. Slightly wounded, the Nive, 9 Dec. 1813 ('F. Wynecken') [*London Gazette*]. Severely wounded, sortie from Bayonne, 14 April 1814 ('Winecken') [*London Gazette*]. Served in Peninsula 1808–14. MGS. *Beamish*, vol. II, p. 607.

WYNNE, Abraham William, Lt., 60th Foot: *1829 Statement of Service for Retired Officers*: Aged nineteen on first appointment to the Army. Ensign, 60th Foot, April 1807; Lt., 60th Foot, July 1809 [Army List gives 3 Oct. 1809]; Capt., 60th Foot, July 1817; Half-pay, n.d., by reduction. 'The state of his health at present prevents him of immediate employment'. *Where serving when wounded*: 'Portugal'. *Details of pension*: Seventy pounds, commencing Dec. 1813. Not married. No employment. *Where generally resident during last five years*: 'England'. Signed in 'Cheltenham January 14th 1829'. [PRO: WO 25/778 f218]. Slightly wounded, during 'several Affairs with the French Army', 14 March 1811 (5th Battn.) [*London Gazette*]. Slightly wounded, Fuentes de Onoro, 5 May 1811 [*London Gazette*]. Pension 'for a wound' received at Fuentes de Onoro [*1818 Pension Return*, pp. 14–15]. MGS. 'William Wynne' in Army List.

WYNNE, Henry, Capt., 23rd Foot: Capt., 23rd Foot, 29 Sept. 1808. Severely wounded, Orthes, 27 Feb. 1814 (1st Battn.) [*London Gazette*].

Y–Z

YATES, William Wingfield, Capt., 47th Foot: Capt., 47th Foot, 1 Aug. 1811. Severely wounded, Vittoria, 21 June 1813 (2nd Battn.) [*London Gazette*]. MGS.

YORKE, Charles, Lt./Capt., 52nd Foot: Lt., Army, 18 Feb. 1808; Lt., 52nd Foot, 25 Feb. 1808. Slightly wounded, storming of Badajoz, 6 April 1812 ('York') [*London Gazette*]. Slightly wounded, Nivelle, 10 Nov. 1813 ('York') (1st Battn.) [*London Gazette*]. Capt., 52nd Foot, 24 Dec. 1813. Severely wounded, Orthes, 27 Feb. 1814 ('York') (1st Battn.) [*London Gazette*]. Waterloo. MGS. *Dalton*, pp. 6, 27, 169 [Maj.-Gen. 11 Nov. 1851. Staff, Cape of Good Hope, 1853. Succeeded Sir W. Gomm as Constable of the Tower of London. Field Marshal Sir Charles Yorke, G.C.B., Col.-in-Chief of the Rifle Brigade, died in London, 20 Nov. 1879, aged 90.]. *Moorsom*, p. 279 ['On the 9th of June of this year [1825], Captain Charles Yorke left the regiment, on promotion to an unattached Majority. Few officers had seen so much service with so little promotion up to this period as Captain Yorke. He entered the 52nd in 1807, and was present at the battles of Vimiero, Fuentes d'Onor, Salamanca, Vittoria, the Pyrenees, the Nivelle (where he was wounded), the Nive, and Orthes (where he was again wounded), besides several smaller affairs during the same period. He served at the sieges of Ciudad Rodrigo and Badajoz, at the latter of which he was wounded. He also served at Waterloo, on the Staff. He subsequently served in the Caffre campaigns of 1850 to 1853, as second in command to Sir George Cathcart, and is now [1859] Military Secretary to the Commander-in-Chief at the Horse-Guards. Lieut.-

General Sir Charles Yorke is a K.C.B., and has received the war medal with ten clasps.'].

ZERSEN, Bernhard Frederick Augustus von, Capt., 1st Line Battn. K.G.L.: Capt., 1st Line Battn. K.G.L., 7 Nov. 1803. Severely wounded, Talavera, 28 July 1809, while serving as ADC to General Langworth ('Zerssen') [*London Gazette*]. Served in Peninsula 1808–10. *Beamish*, vol. II, p. 652 ['retired on an allowance of 3s. per day, 11th Aug. 1810. [Died] in Italy in 1810.'].

ZOLLIKOFER, William H. von, Lt./Adjutant, The Duke of Brunswick Oels' Corps (Infantry): Lt. and Adjutant, Duke of Brunswick Oels' Corps (Infantry), 25 Sept. 1809. Slightly wounded, Fuentes de Onoro, 5 May 1811 ('Zolikofer') [*London Gazette*].

ZUHLCKE, George Henry, Lt., 60th Foot: *1829 Statement of Service for Retired Officers*: Aged twenty-three on first appointment to the Army. Ensign, 60th Foot, 25 Dec. 1797; Lt., 60th Foot, 6 Aug. 1800; Capt., 60th Foot, 10 Jan. 1810; Major, Portuguese Service, 2 June 1814; Major, Half-pay, Portuguese Service, 25 Dec. 1816, 'by the general reduction of the Officers serving in Portugal'. *Where serving when wounded*: 'at the Battle of Talavera'. *Details of pension*: Seventy pounds, commencing July 1810. *Family*: Married twice: the first time in 'Sidney Island of Cape Breton', 8 Feb. 1804; the second in Edinburgh, 5 July 1825. One child, born to the first marriage in June 1805. Not employed. 'I beg leave to observe, that I have been promoted to the Rank of Lieut. Colonel in His Majesty's Army the 4 Septbr. 1817' [ie Portuguese Service]. *Where*

ZUHLCKE

generally resident during last five years: 'London and Germany'. [PRO: WO 25/779 f39]. Severely wounded, Talavera, 28 July 1809 ('Zulke') (5th Battn.) [*London Gazette*]. In Portuguese Service Oct. 1810 to April 1814. Gold Medal. Seventy pounds per annum pension, commencing 25 Dec. 1811, 'for a wound' received at Talavera ('Zuhlcke') [*1818 Pension Return*, pp. 16–17]. 'Zulke' in Army List.

Challis, Portuguese Army, p. 60 ['Zulke']. *Royal Military Calendar*, vol. V, pp. 147–8 ['in the battle of Talavera, where he received a severe wound, and was taken prisoner... The 26th April [1810] ... effected his escape from the enemy. In July following, arriving in Lisbon, applied to the Duke of Wellington to be placed in the Portuguese service, and the 22d Oct. was appointed Maj. in the 2d batt. of Caçadores.'].

APPENDIX
NON-COMBAT CASUALTIES
COMMISSIONED OFFICERS WHO DIED OF DISEASE, EXHAUSTION, NATURAL CAUSES AND ACCIDENT IN THE PENINSULA

Note: This is not a defintive list. It is taken primarily from War Office and regimental records in the PRO and gives place and date of death, with cause, if indicated in records. Spelling as in original manuscripts. This list includes only those officers not already included in the main text.

* indicates obituary in *The Gentleman's Magazine*.

Adamson, George, Lt., 30th Foot: 'naturally', Lisbon, 19 Jan. 1812.
Allen, James, Ensign, 11th Foot: 'of sickness', Santander, 18 Sept. 1813.
Anderson, George, Ensign, 26th Foot: Peninsula, 27 Dec. 1811.
Annesley, James, Capt., 38th Foot: 'of disease', Peza de Regoa, 6 Feb. 1813.
Annesly, William, Lt., 3rd Foot: Placentia, Spain, 9 April 1813.
Anstruther, General: 'of an inflammation of the lungs', Corunna, Jan. 1809.*
Armstrong, Lt., 4th Dragoons: Portugal, 2 Oct. 1811.
Armstrong, Robert, Ensign, 50th Foot: Lisbon, 20 Nov. 1810.
Assiotti, George, Deputy Commissary-General: Gijon, Spain, 27 Nov. 1808.
Augspurg, Charles A., Ensign, 2nd Light Bn. K.G.L.: shipwrecked on passage to England, Feb. 1809.

Baird, J., Lt., 36th Foot: Abrantes, 10 Oct. or 15 Oct. 1812.
Barbaz, James L., Lt., 60th Foot: Peninsula, 12 Sept. 1813.
Barr, Mathew, Asst. Surgeon, 68th Foot: France, 1814.
Barton, Royster B., Capt., 82nd Foot: Peninsula, 7 Dec. 1813.
Baxter, William, Capt., 57th Foot: Portugal, 20 Aug. 1810.
Beacham, Richard, Surgeon, Medical Dept.: Portugal, 20 Nov. 1811.
Beale, George, Lt., 57th Foot: Portalegre, 11 Sept. or 13 Sept. 1811.*
Bell, Surgeon, Medical Dept.: Peninsula, 16 Sept. 1812.
Belson, Henry, Lt., 50th Foot/Major, Port. 50th Regt.: Oct. 1812.
Bennett, Asst. Surgeon, 94th Foot: Portugal, 27 Aug. 1811.
Berger, Christ., Asst. Surgeon, 60th Foot: France, 23 March 1814.
Bernard, Francis, Lt., 9th Light Dragoons: Alter de Chuon, Portugal, 24 Jan. 1813.*
Bevan, C., Lt. Col., 4th Foot: Portalegre, 8 July or 12 July 1811.*
Bevan, Edward, Lt., 1st Foot: Santarem, 23 Feb. 1813.
Black, Andrew, Lt., 2nd Foot: Peninsula, 29 Aug. 1812.
Blackwell, Thomas, Lt., 36th Foot: Portugal, 25 Aug. 1811.
Bock, Otto George von, Major-General, K.G.L.: shipwrecked on passage to England, 21 Jan. or 17 March 1814.
Boursignott, Richard, Ensign, 3rd Foot: Cortizada, Portugal, 17 Sept. 1810.
Brandis, Frederick von, Capt., 5th Line Bn. K.G.L.: Attalaya, Portugal, 23 June 1809.
Broad, Richard, Major, 47th Foot: Truxillo, 31 Oct. 1812.
Brock, William, Asst. Surgeon, 27th Foot: Lisbon, 5 Oct. 1811.
Brockman, Henry L.D., Lt., 43rd Foot: 'of a typhus fever, owing to excessive fatigue', Elvas, Portugal, 22 Aug. 1809.*

Burke, J. E., Ensign, 30th Foot: 'naturally', Portugal, 24 March 1812.
Burton, Cecil H., Capt., 34th Foot: France, 1814.
Butler, Robert, Lt., 1st Foot: Portugal, 1 Jan. 1811.

Cabbell, G., Physician to the Forces: 'of a putrid fever caught in the zealous discharge of his duty', Coimbra, 11 Jan. 1813.*
Campbell, Alexander, Capt., 9th Foot: 'natural death', Lisbon, 8 Dec. 1810.
Campbell, William H., Lt. Col., 31st Foot/Brig.-General, Portuguese Army: 'of an inflammatory fever', Trocifal, 2 Jan. 1811.*
Campbell, William, Lt., 88th Foot: Cambo, France, 13 Dec. 1813.
Carp, John, Capt., 53rd Foot: France, 6 March 1814.
Carr, Robert, Lt., 44th Foot: Coimbra, c. Dec. 1813.
Carrol, John, Capt., 82nd Foot: Peninsula, 19 Jan. 1814.
Carter, John V., Ensign, 30th Foot: sun-stroke, Ciudad Rodrigo, 23 July 1812.*
Carthew, R., Capt., Royal Artillery: 'through excessive fatigue', on passage from Spain, Jan. 1809.*
Chard, Samuel, Veterinary Surgeon, 13th Light Dragoons: Peninsula, 15 Oct. 1812.
Charlton, John, Lt., Royal Waggon Train: France, 23 March 1814.
Chawner, Anthony, Ensign, 9th Foot: France, 22 March 1814.
Christie, David, Asst. Surgeon, Medical Dept.: France, 30 March 1814.
Church, James, 2nd Lt., 95th Foot: France, 10 Dec. 1813.
Clarke, John, Surgeon, 27th Foot: Lisbon, 13 Aug. 1811.
Clifford, Thomas, Lt., 58th Foot: Lisbon, 6 Aug. 1812.
Clindinning, Ensign, 11th Foot: Portugal, 1811.
Clutterbuck, George, Capt., 1st Foot Guards: following a 'long and painful illness ... occasioned by the rupture of a blood-vessel, after the great fatigue he underwent at the Battle of Barrosa', Warkworth, England, 19 March 1813.*
Coates, Baker, Lt., 52nd Foot: Spain, 9 Sept. 1812.
Colborne, J. B., Lt., 2nd Light Bn. K.G.L.: 'in consequence of excessive fatigue in Spain and Portugal, whence he had lately returned', Lymington, England, 8 May 1813.*
Colman, Francis-John, Brig.-General: 'from fever and debility, brought on by exertions', Portugal, 12 Dec. 1811.*
Couche, William A., Capt., 82nd Foot: Peninsula, 23 Sept. 1813.
Craufurd, James-Catlin, Brig.-General: Abrantes, Portugal, 25 Sept. 1810.*
Craufurd, John, Ensign, 30th Foot: Portugal, 8/9 Jan. 1811.
Crawford, Edward, Capt., 66th Foot: Peninsula, 15 Oct. 1812.
Crawford, J. H., Lt., 26th Foot: while Prisoner of War, n.d.
Croker, Richard, Lt., 5th Foot: of fever, Ferrarin, 31 Dec. 1812.
Crosbie, William, Capt., 1st Dragoons: Albergaria, 26 Sept. 1811.
Cullimore, John, Lt., 58th Foot/Capt., 15th Port. Regt.: 20 Oct. 1810.
Cullon, Walter, Ensign, 43rd Foot: Portugal, 1811.
Curby, Thomas, Asst. Surgeon, Medical Dept.: Peninsula, 10 Jan. 1813.

Dalling, E., Major, Coldstream Guards: 'of fever, brought on by fatigue', Portugal, July/Aug. 1811.
Dankarts, John, D.A.C.G.: Peninsula, 24 Sept. 1812.
Darby, Frederick J., Capt., 10th Light Dragoons: 'of a fever, occasioned by excessive fatigue', Corunna, 2 Jan. 1809.*
Darley, Edward, Capt., 39th Foot: Villa Nueva, 20 May 1813.
Davies, George, Asst. Surgeon, 11th Foot: Spain, 1813.
Dean, Surgeon, Medical Dept.: 'of fever, caught in the hospital', Elvas, Portugal, 28 Dec. 1809.*

Deane, Lt., 38th Foot: Portugal, 6 July 1811.
De Bree, Charles C., Lt., 60th Foot: Peninsula, late 1812.
De Salve, Peter, Capt., K.G.L. Staff: Lisbon, 6 May 1810.
Dickens, Thomas, Lt., Royal Waggon Train: Peninsula, 31 Aug. 1812.
Dickinson, Alexander, Lt., 42nd Foot: 'murdered', Aldea de Serra, Portugal, 22 March 1813.
Dinar, Lt., Brunswick Oels': murdered, Spain, 1 May 1813.
Downs, Roger, Lt., 48th Foot: of sickness, Celorico, 4 Oct. 1811.
Drummond, Archibald, Lt. Col., 3rd Foot: on passage from Lisbon, 22 July 1810.*

Elers, Hungerford R., Major, 43rd Foot: Celorico, 29 Aug. 1811.*
Elliott, Lt., 83rd Foot: Portugal, 23 April 1811.
Engel, Edward A., Capt., 7th Line Bn. K.G.L.: Lisbon, 11 Feb. 1811.
Enright, John, Surgeon, 94th Foot: Ariscoun, Spain, 23 Sept. 1813.*
Erskine, William, Major-General: threw himself out of a window, 'in a fit of delirium', Lisbon, 13 Feb. 1813.*
Evans, John B., Capt., 1st Foot Guards: near Bayonne, 20 May 1814.*

Farquharson, John, Lt., 47th Foot: shot in the back by a Spanish sentry following a scuffle, Cadiz, Feb. 1812.*
Ferguson, Charles J., Lt., 3rd Foot: 'of sickness', Lisbon, 11 March 1811.
Fidlor, David, Ensign, 43rd Foot: Madrid, 8 Sept. 1812.
Fidlor, James, Ensign, 43rd Foot: 'of fever brought on by fatigue', Madrid, 15 Dec. 1812.*
Foley, M., Ensign, 48th Foot: 'of sickness', Madrid, 5 Oct. or 15 Oct. 1812.
Forbes, Henry, Ensign, 68th Foot: Portugal, 6 Aug. 1811.
Forth, Jephson G., Capt., 26th Foot: Horsham, Sussex, 'of a typhus fever, brought on by excessive fatigue in the late campaign', 1809.*
Friesland, Otto, Capt., 2nd Dragoons K.G.L.: Madrid, 24 Aug. 1812.
Frost, Thomas, Lt., 4th Dragoon Guards: Peninsula, 19 Nov. 1812.

Gilchrist, Robert, Surgeon, 11th Light Dragoons: Portugal, 25 Jan. 1813.*
Giles, John, Ensign, 11th Foot: Lisbon, 13 Feb. 1811.
Gilfillan, James, Ensign, 1st Foot: Lisbon, 2 March 1811.
Gore, Saunders, Capt., 94th Foot: Peninsula, 5 Jan. 1814.
Grant, Donald, Lt., 42nd Foot: Maya, Spain, 6 Sept. 1813.
Griffiths, Thomas W., Lt., 3rd Dragoons: El Badon, 17 Nov. 1812.*
Grubbe, William H., Lt., Royal Horse Guards: Spain, 23 Sept. 1813.
Gunn, Gordon, Ensign, 50th Foot: Peninsula, 14 Oct. 1812.

Haggerty, James, Lt., 5th Foot: 'fever', Ferrarin, 31 Dec. 1812.
Hall, Thomas, Lt., 16th Light Dragoons: Peninsula, 26 Sept. 1813.
Halletts, R. S., Lt., 52nd Foot: 'an ague caught at Ciudad Rodrigo', 5 Aug. 1812.*
Hamilton, Robert, Asst. Surgeon, 51st Foot: 'shot by accident', Llerena, 26 March 1812.
Handley, Benjamin, Lt., 9th Light Dragoons: drowned boarding a transport, Lisbon, 17 April 1813.*
Harkness, Thomas, Lt., 79th Foot: Peninsula, 21 Nov. 1812.
Harrop, James, Lt., 28th Foot/Capt., 16th Port. Regt.: Lisbon, June 1810.
Hay, Alexander, Ensign, 50th Foot: 'a burning sun ...[caused] inflammatory fever', Portalegre, 15 Sept. 1811.*
Heatly, John, Lt., 83rd Foot: Peninsula, 7 Nov. 1812.
Heiliger, Augustus, staff officer: 'died at sea off Corunna', Jan. 1809.

Heimbruch, George von, Lt., 2nd Light Bn. K.G.L.: shipwrecked on passage to England, Feb. 1809.

Henderson, John, Asst. Surgeon, 91st Foot: Peninsula, 25 Sept. 1813.

Hertel, Capt., Brunswick Oels': Portugal, 19 Jan. 1811.

Hesledon, Edward, Ensign, 45th Foot: on passage to England, 10 Feb. 1814.

Heylinger, Augustus, Capt., 15th Light Dragoons: on passage from Corunna, Jan. 1809.*

Hill, John, Lt., 92nd Foot: Peninsula, 23 Oct. 1812.

Hilton, Thomas, Capt., Royal Waggon Train: Peninsula, 2 Sept. 1812.

Hincks, George P., Lt., 83rd Foot: Salamanca, 28 Aug. 1812.*

Hoblyn, Capt., 40th Foot: during the retreat to Portugal, Aug/Sept. 1809.*

Hodenberg, Charles von, Capt., 1st Dragoons K.G.L.: shipwrecked on passage to England, 21 Jan. 1814.

Holmes, Samuel, Lt., 4th Dragoons: Peninsula, 25 Aug. 1812.

Hoye, Thomas, Asst. Surgeon, Royal Waggon Train: Peninsula, 29 Aug. 1812.

Huddleston, Charles A., Lt., 28th Foot: Coimbra, 13 Dec. 1812.

Hugo, Frederick von, Capt., 5th Line Bn. K.G.L.: San Christoval, Spain, 6 Sept. 1812.

Hulse, Major-General: Peninsula, 7 Sept. 1812.

Hulton, George, Capt., 1st Dragoons: Tauste, Spain, 26 Feb. 1814.*

Hurtzig, Henry P., Major, 2nd Light Bn. K.G.L.: St Jean de Luz, France, 11 March 1814.

Ingles, John, Asst. Surgeon, 84th Foot: Peninsula, 7 Dec. 1813.

Innes, John, Major, 94th Foot: 'dysentery contracted in Cadiz', Portsmouth, 'he had but landed a few hours', 27 Aug. 1810.*

Ireland, D., Ensign, 87th Foot: Peninsula, 12 Nov. 1812.

Irwin, Thomas, Asst. Surgeon, 30th Foot: Portugal, 2 Feb. 1811.

Issendorf, George von, Capt., 1st Dragoons K.G.L.: Lisbon, 13 Feb. 1813.

Jackson, Henry, Lt., 52nd Foot: Lisbon, 22 July 1810.

Jeffreys, Edward, Lt., 3rd Dragoon Guards: Portugal, 5 Sept. 1811.

Jervoise, Richard P., Major, 1st Dragoons: Portugal, 17 Sept. 1811.

Johnson, George P., Capt., 81st Foot: 'of fever', Portugal, March/April 1812.*

Johnstone, W., Lt., Royal Artillery: 'drowned crossing the Tagus', 15 June 1811.

Johnstone, William, Cornet, Royal Waggon Train: Celorico, Portugal, 3 Oct. 1811.

Keappock, Bartholomew, Lt., 95th Foot: Portugal, 8 Aug. 1811.

Keffenbrinck, Lt., Brunswick Oels': Portugal, 4 July 1811.

Keith, Capt., 23rd Foot: Portugal, 29 Aug. 1811.

Kelly, F., Ensign, 30th Foot: 'of fatigue', near Celorico, 2 Dec. 1812.

King, George, Asst. Surgeon, 74th Foot: Jan. 1813.

Kirby, William, Volunteer: 'fatigue and liver disease', Lisbon, Feb. 1809.*

Kirkpatrick, William, Ensign, 62nd Foot: 10 Dec. 1813.

Klingsöhr, George H., Col., 5th Line Bn. K.G.L.: Oyarzun, Spain, 4 Aug. 1813.

Knatchbull, Wyndham, Ensign, 1st Foot Guards: on passage to England, 'the day the ship arrived in Spithead', 14 Oct. 1813.*

Koch, Charles, Capt., 2nd Hussars K.G.L.: Belem, Portugal, 12 Dec. 1811.

Korfes, Lt. Col., Brunswick Oels': Portugal, 30 Dec. 1810.

Kretchmer, F., Brunswick Oels': 18 Feb. 1813.

Lambert, Edward, Ensign, 1st Foot Guards: Cadiz, 1812.
Lambert, Thomas, Lt., 82nd Foot: Peninsula, 18 Aug. 1812.
Leacroft, Frederick, Ensign, 27th Foot: Peninsula, 30 Dec. 1812.
Leah, George, Lt., Royal Artillery: Corunna campaign, Jan. 1809.*
Leatham, William F., Capt., 4th Dragoon Guards: 'of a violent fever, brought on by fatigue and exertion', Elvas, 2 Aug. 1812.*
Lecky, James, Capt., 28th Foot: Portugal, 3 Feb. 1811.
Lefebure, George, Capt., Royal Artillery: Peninsula, 22 Oct. 1812.
Lehmann, Alexander, Lt., 5th Line Bn. K.G.L.: Salamanca, 25 Sept. 1812.
Leicester, Frederick, Capt., Staff Corps: Peninsula, 16 Oct. 1812.
Le Maistre, Frederick H., Capt., Chasseurs Britanniques: Cadiz, 19 Aug. 1811.
Lenny, John C., Asst. Surgeon, Royal Artillery: Spain, 1813.*
Lernon, Desiré, Lt., Chasseurs Britanniques: Peninsula, 4 Feb. 1813.
Lewis, Tubal, Capt., 77th Foot: Peninsula, 29 Nov. 1811.
Lindener, Lewis, Ensign, 2nd Line Bn. K.G.L.: 'drowned while bathing', Talavera, 14 July 1809.
Livingston, F., Capt., 90th Foot: Lisbon, 11 Oct. 1812.*
Lloyd, Thomas, Surgeon, 84th Foot: Peninsula, 14 Jan. 1814.
Loesecke, Lewis von, Lt., 5th Line Bn. K.G.L.: Belem, Portugal, 29 Dec. 1808.
Lueder, Frederick, Major, 2nd Dragoons K.G.L.: Estremoz, Portugal, 16 April 1812.

McCall, John, Asst. Surgeon, 42nd Foot: 'fever and ague', Medina del Campo, 6 Aug. 1812.
McCally, R., Lt., 45th Foot: Lisbon, 17 April 1812.
McGlashan, Neil, Capt., 42nd Foot: Lisbon, 9 July 1811.
McGregor, Ensign, 88th Foot: Portugal, 1811.
McGregor, John, Asst. Surgeon, 77th Foot: Peninsula, 23 Jan. 1814.
McIver, John, Lt., 61st Foot: Peninsula, 31 Dec. 1813.
Macken, Ensign, 83rd Foot: Peninsula, 12 Jan. 1813.
Mackintosh, Staff Surgeon, Medical Dept.: Peninsula, 10 April 1813.
McLachlan, Duncan, Lt., 77th Foot: Portugal, 30 Aug. 1811.
McLeod, Donald, Lt., 45th Foot: Salamanca, 28 Aug. 1812.
McMillan, Ensign, 63rd Foot, attached Adjutant General's Dept.: Portugal, 4 Aug. 1811.
Mahon, Peter, Lt., 11th Foot: Villa Franche near Bayonne, 24 Feb. 1814.
Major, John, Lt., 1st Foot: Portugal, 2 Sept. 1810.
Malone, Robert H., Capt., 82nd Foot: Peninsula, 30 Oct. 1813.
Marlow, Thomas, Capt., 39th Foot: Peninsula, 15 Oct. 1812.
Marsden, John, Capt., 11th Foot: Coimbra, 4 Aug. 1810.
Marshall, George, Lt., 92nd Foot: Peninsula, 27 Aug. 1812.
Martin, G., Lt., Royal Artillery: Portugal, 30 Aug. 1811.
Massey John, Lt., 3rd Dragoons: Peninsula, 2 Oct. 1812.
Mathews, Asst. Surgeon, 32nd Foot: Passages, 7 Dec. 1813.
Mathews, Edward, Lt., 9th Foot: Peninsula, 21 Sept. 1812.
Maxwell, John, Lt., 24th Foot: Portugal, 1811.
Mayne, Charles, Lt., 43rd Foot: 'from fatigue', Portugal, 22 Jan. 1813.
Meadows, Philip, Capt., Royal Artillery: Portugal, 4 Sept. 1811.
Millar, George, Ensign, 31st Foot: Peninsula, 31 Aug. 1812.
Miller, General, Portuguese Service: 'excessive hardships and anxiety', right bank of the Douro, c. Feb. 1811.*
Milton, William, Ensign, 32nd Foot: Coimbra, 3 Oct. 1811.
Mitchelson, George, Surgeon, 44th Foot: Lisbon, 25 Dec. 1810.

APPENDIX

Mitton, William, Ensign, 32nd Foot: Coimbra, 3 Oct. 1811.
Moeller, Frederick, Lt., 5th Line Bn. K.G.L.: Gouveia, Portugal, 14 Aug. 1810.
Mooney, John, Asst. Surgeon, 34th Foot: 'fever', Zafra, 25 July 1812.
Moore, H., 2nd Lt., 95th Foot: Portugal, 22 Nov. 1811.
More, Henry J., 2nd Lt., 95th Foot: Portugal, 22 Nov. 1811.
Morgan, David, Asst. Surgeon, 50th Foot: 'of disease', Coria, Spain, 31 Dec. 1812.
Morse, William, Lt., 1st Foot: Portugal, 1811.
Murphy, William, Lt., 43rd Foot/Lt., 8th Port. Regt.: 7 Oct. 1813.
Murray, William H., Lt., 1st Foot: 'drowned while bathing in the Tagus', Portugal, 7 July 1811.*
Myler, William, D.A.C.G., Commissary Dept.: Peninsula, 5 Jan. 1814.

Neville, Hon. Henry, Capt., 14th Light Dragoons: 'of a fever, occasioned by excessive fatigue', Santa Cruz, Spain, 30 July 1809.
Nevin, Thomas, Lt., 74th Foot: Peninsula, 16 Sept. 1812.
Newlay, Thomas F., senior surgeon of the Army in the Peninsula: of fever contracted 'in the discharge of his professional duties' in Cadiz, on passage to England, 14 April 1811.*
Nixon, Bromley, Capt., 37th Foot: France, 1814.
Nunn, Henry, Ensign, 24th Foot: Peninsula, 16 Sept. 1812.

Oakley, Asst. Surgeon, 2nd Foot: Peninsula, 26 Dec. 1812.
O'Brian, Morgan, Lt., 7th Foot: Lisbon, 28 Sept. 1811.
Offeney, Otto W., Lt. Col., 7th Line Bn. K.G.L., A.Q.M.G.: of 'illness', Belem, Portugal, 15 Aug. 1812.*
O'Grady, Lt., 11th Light Dragoons: 'of a fever', Portugal, 11 Oct. 1811.*
Ompteda, Augustus von, Brig. Major, K.G.L. Staff: Elvas, Portugal, 21 April 1811.
Otto, Henry, Lt., Garrison Co. K.G.L.: Belem, Portugal, 6 Dec. 1809.

Palmer, Joseph, Lt., 27th Foot/Lt., 21st Port. Regt.: Nov. 1813.
Patrick, Robert W., Major, E.O.P.S./Lt. Col., 12th Port. Regt.: Lamego, 10 May 1810.
Penefather, K., Lt., 68th Foot: 'of disease', Bilboa, 8 Jan. 1814.
Percy, Hon. Francis J., Capt., 23rd Foot: Cuellar, Spain, 23 Aug. 1812.*
Phelan, William, Capt., 47th Foot: Peninsula, 18 March 1813.
Plate, Frederick, Capt., Garrison Co. K.G.L.: Coimbra, Portugal, 27 May 1811.
Plenderleath, Staff Surgeon, Medical Staff: 'of a typhus fever', Coimbra, 18 July 1811.*
Pratt, M., Capt., 95th Foot: Portugal, 11 Sept. 1811.
Precht, Frederick, Veterinary Surgeon, 1st Hussars K.G.L.: Belem, Portugal, 15 Dec. 1810.
Price, Veterinary Surgeon, Royal Artillery Drivers: Cadiz, 5 Nov. 1812.

Racster, Thomas S., Lt., 36th Foot/Capt., 17th Port. Regt.: 1813.
Radonitz, Leopold, Capt., Brunswick Oels': Peninsula, 14 Oct. 1812.
Reed, John, Surgeon, 36th Foot: Portugal, 28 Feb. 1813.
Reinbold, Charles von, Lt. Col., 5th Line Bn. K.G.L.: Sacarom near Lisbon, 1 March 1809.
Reynolds, William, Surgeon, 45th Foot: Momento de Beira, 3 Feb. 1813.*
Richardson, Ensign, 94th Foot: Portugal, 3 March 1811.
Riddle, William, Ensign, 2nd Light Bn. K.G.L.: shipwrecked on passage to England, Feb. 1809.

Roberts, George, Ensign, 28th Foot: Spain, 25 Dec. 1813.
Robertson, Ernest von, Capt., 2nd Light Bn. K.G.L.: Belem, Portugal, 28 Nov. 1811.
Robertson, William, Adjutant, 95th Foot: Peninsula, 28 Jan. 1813.
Roester, Thomas S., Lt., 36th Foot: Peninsula, 15 Nov. 1812.
Rose, Hamilton, Major, 42nd Foot: Lisbon, 5 Sept. 1811.
Ross, Andrew, Major-General, 70th Foot: Carthagena, 26 Sept. 1812.*
Ross, David, Lt. Col., 57th Foot: Elvas, 24 Dec. 1809.
Ross, Thomas C., Lt., 2nd Foot/Capt., 11th Caçadores: 26 May 1813.
Rozea, Asst. Surgeon, 16th Light Dragoons: Portugal, 24 Oct. 1811.
Rumley, George, Lt., 30th Foot: Portugal, 23 April 1811.
Russell, Andrew H., Capt., 28th Foot: Portugal, 28 Aug. 1811.

Salmon, Thomas, Capt., 7th Foot: Portugal, 31 Jan. 1811.
Sander, William, Asst. Surgeon, 7th Line Bn. K.G.L.: Lisbon, 6 Oct. 1810.
Scatcherd, I. N., Ensign, 9th Foot: Portugal, 18 Oct. 1811.
Scott, William, 1st Lt., 95th Foot: Campo Maior, 4 Dec. 1809.
Seacroft, Frederick, Ensign, 27th Foot: 'fever', Celorico, 30 Dec. 1812.
Shanley, Francis, Capt., 51st Foot: Lisbon, 23 March 1811.
Sherston, Capt., R.Vet. Battn.: Spain, 29 June 1813.
Sidney, Philip, Ensign, 43rd Foot: Coimbra, 11 Dec. 1811.
Sloane, Crawford, Ensign, 58th Foot: Portugal, 24 June 1811.
Smail, George, Ensign, 34th Foot: 'assassinated by persons unknown', Lisbon, Jan. 1810.
Small, William, Lt., 83rd Foot: Peninsula, 5 Oct. 1812.
Smith, Joshua, Lt., 88th Foot: 'natural death', Salamanca, 5 Oct. 1812.
Smyth, J., Lt., Royal Waggon Train: Peninsula, 18 Feb. 1813.
Soden, Mossom, Capt., 68th Foot: 'of disease', Elvas, 24 April 1812.
Sontag, Lt., Brunswick Oels': Peninsula, 18 April 1813.
Sparks, Frederick, Major, 51st Foot: Castello Branco, 13 Nov. 1811.
Squire, John, Lt. Col., Royal Engineers: 'of fever, occasioned by excessive exertion during the siege of Badajoz', Truxillo, Spain, 19 May 1812.*
Stewart, Charles, Lt. Col., 50th Foot: 'disease', Coria, Spain, 11 Dec. 1812.
Stewart, Richard, Major-General: 'in consequence of a fall from a balcony, whose banister had been removed', Lisbon, Oct. 1810.
Stisser, William, Lt., 5th Line Bn. K.G.L.: Talavera la Real, Spain, 14 Sept. 1809.
St. Martin, Lewis, Lt., 1st Foot/Capt., 9th Port. Line: Coimbra, 7 Oct. 1811.
Strutt, Henry G., Major, 3rd Dragoon Guards: 'of the fever', Spain, 3 Oct. 1809.*
Styles, Sir Thomas, Ensign, 1st Foot Guards: Peninsula, 8 Nov. 1813.
Symes, Michael, Lt. Col., 76th Foot: 'in consequence of extraordinary fatigue and exertions in the Spanish campaign', on passage to England, 22 Jan. 1809.*

Taylor, John, Lt., 24th Foot: Peninsula, 1 Nov. 1812.
Thurnley, Thomas, Lt., 30th Foot: Portugal, 23 April 1811.
Tiddeman, Thomas E., Capt., 38th Foot: France, n.d.
Travers, St. John, Capt., 9th Foot/Major, 19th Port. Reg.: 3 Oct. 1811.
Tully, Patrick W., Lt., 82nd Foot: Salamanca, 6 Aug. 1812.
Vallance, Hugh, Lt., 42nd Foot: St Jean de Luz, 1 March 1814.
Vandeleur, Richard, Major, 88th Foot: 'after a few days illness', Campo Maior, Portugal, 17 Oct. 1809.*
Vaughan, James, Lt., 76th Foot: Portsmouth, 'recently returned from Spain', 5 Jan. 1809.*

Venables, John, Capt., 83rd Foot: France, 24 March 1814.
Volger, Otto Henry, Major, 2nd Dragoons K.G.L.: Santarem, Portugal, 19 Sept. 1812.

Wade, William, Lt. Col., 6th Foot: Peninsula, 26 Feb. 1813.
Wakefield, Edward, Capt., 76th Foot: Peninsula, 23 Jan. 1814.
Watson, Samuel, Capt., Royal Waggon Train: 16 Oct. 1812.
Welch, G., M.D., Medical Staff: 'suddenly, while eating his breakfast in a coffee-house', Belem, Portugal, April 1811.*
Whalley, Francis, Lt., 12th Light Dragoons: Peninsula, 26 May 1812.
Wheatley, William, Major-General, 1st Foot Guards: 'of a typhus fever', at the Palace of Escurial, near Madrid, 1 Sept. 1812.
Whitaker, A.D.A.C.G.: 22 Dec. 1812.
White, John, Capt., 27th Foot/Major, 6th Caçadores: Torres Vedras, 10 or 18 March 1811.
Whitford, John, Lt., 48th Foot: Portugal, 28 Sept. 1811.
Wilcken, Gideon, Lt., 7th Line Bn. K.G.L.: Talavera la Real, Spain, 5 Oct. 1809.
Williams, Thomas, Lt., 1st Foot: Lisbon, 22 Sept. 1811.
Willis, Henry, Lt., 13th Light Dragoons: 30 Oct. 1813.
Wilson, Asst. Surgeon, 1st Foot: Coimbra, 25 June 1811.
Wilson, George, Lt. Col., 39th Foot: 'of a remittent fever', Moralejo, 5 Jan. 1813.*
Wilson, Richard, Ensign, 51st Foot: Salamanca, 28 Oct. 1812.
Wingate, Robert F., Capt., 74th Foot: 20 Oct. 1812.
Wingfield, Hon. J., Ensign, Coldstream Guards: Coimbra, Portugal, 4 May or 14 May 1811.*
Wood, John, Capt., 4th Foot: 'of fever', Portugal, 10 Jan. 1811.*
Wright, Staff Surgeon: Cadiz, 19 Oct. 1812.
Wynn, Watkin, 1st Lt., 23rd Foot: 'of sickness', Estremoz, 1 Aug. 1811.

BIBLIOGRAPHY

MANUSCRIPT SOURCES

Public Record Office, Kew, London:

a) WO 25/749 to 779 – Services of Retired Officers on Full and Half Pay. Returns to the circular letter of 22 Oct. 1828.
b) WO 25/780 to 805 – Services of Officers on Full Pay, 1829.
c) WO 25/806 to 807 – Returns of Officers' Services, 1829–31.
d) WO 25/808 to 823 – Services of Retired Officers (rendered under the WO Memorandum of 31 Aug. 1847).
e) WO 25/2963 to 2964 – Register of Officers' Effects, 1810–15 (by Regt).
f) WO 25/2965 – Register of Deceased Officers, 1811–14.
g) WO 17 – Monthly Returns by Regt.
h) WO 76 – Records concerning Officers' service (by Regt).
i) *Lionel S. Challis, 'The Peninsula Roll Call'* (1948 typescript index).
j) WO 12 – Regimental Musters.

PUBLISHED CONTEMPORARY SOURCES

The Dispatches of Field Marshal the Duke of Wellington during his Campaigns in India, Denmark, Portugal, Spain, the Low Countries and France, from 1799 to 1818. Compiled by Lieutenant Colonel Gurwood (London, 1837–39).
The Gentleman's Magazine, 1808–14.
HART, H.G., *The New Army List*, various dates.
A List of all the Officers of the Army and Royal Marines on Full and Half Pay, various dates.
The London Gazette (1808–15).
Return of the Names of the Officers in the Army who receive Pensions for the loss of Limbs, or for Wounds (London, 1818).
The Royal Military Calendar, or Army Service and Commission Book, 4 vols., (3rd Edition, London, 1820).
The Waterloo Medal Roll, Compiled From the Muster Rolls (London, 1992).

PUBLISHED MEMOIRS AND AUTOBIOGRAPHIES

[Anonymous] 'Table-Talk of an Old Campaigner', by 'A Constant Reader', *United Service Journal*, 1834, III.
AITCHISON, John, *An Ensign in the Peninsular War: The Letters of John Aitchison*, ed. W. F. K. Thompson (London, 1994).
ANTON, James, *Retrospect of a Military Life* (Edinburgh, 1841).
BELL, Sir George, *Soldier's Glory; Being 'Rough Notes of an Old Soldier'*, ed. Brian Stuart (Tunbridge Wells, 1991).
BLAKENEY, Robert, *A Boy in the Peninsular War; The Services, Adventures and Experiences of Robert Blakeney, Subaltern in the 28th Regiment*, ed. Julian Sturgis (London, 1899. Reprinted London, 1989).
BRAGGE, William, *Peninsular Portrait, 1811-1814; The Letters of Captain William Bragge, Third (King's Own) Dragoons*, ed. S. A. C. Cassels (London, 1963).

BROTHERTON, Thomas, *A Hawk at War: The Peninsular War Reminiscences of General Sir Thomas Brotherton, CB*, ed. Bryan Perrett (Chippenham, 1986).

BUNBURY, Henry Edward, *Narrative of Some Passages in the Great War with France* (London, 1927).

COCKS, Hon. Edward Charles, *Intelligence Officer in the Peninsula; Letters and Diaries of Major the Hon. Edward Charles Cocks, 1786–1812*, ed. Julia V. Page (Tunbridge Wells, 1986).

COOPER, John Spencer, *Rough Notes of Seven Campaigns, in Portugal, Spain, France and America, During the Years 1809–1815* (Carlisle, 1869).

COSTELLO, Edward, *The Peninsular and Waterloo Campaigns* (London, 1967).

DICKSON, Alexander, *The Dickson Manuscripts* (Woolwich, 1908).

DONALDSON, Joseph, *The Eventful Life of a Soldier* (London, 1863).

DU CANE, Edmund F., 'The Peninsula and Waterloo: Memories of an Old Rifleman', *Cornhill Magazine* (December, 1897). [Stories told by John Molloy, 95th Rifles].

GLEIG, George Robert, *The Subaltern* (London, 1845).

GORDON, Alexander, *The Journal of a Cavalry Officer in the Corunna Campaign* (London, 1913).

GRATTAN, William, *Adventures with the Connaught Rangers, 1809–1814* (London, 1847. Reprinted London, 1989).

GREEN, John, *The Vicissitudes of a Soldier's Life, or a Series of Occurrences from 1806 to 1815* (Louth, 1827. Reprinted Wakefield, 1973).

GRONOW, Rees Howell, *The Reminiscences and Recollections of Captain Gronow, 1810–1860*, 2 vols. (London, 1900).

HARRIS, Benjamin ['John'], *Recollections of Rifleman Harris*, ed. Henry Curling (London, 1929. Reprinted many times).

HAWKER, Peter, *Journal of a Regimental Officer* (London, 1810. Reprinted London, 1981).

HAY, William, *Reminiscences 1808–1815 Under Wellington* (London, 1901. Reprinted Cambridge, 1995).

HENNELL, George, *A Gentleman Volunteer: The Letters of George Hennell from the Peninsular War, 1812–13*, ed. Michael Glover (London, 1979).

JONES, Rice, *An Engineer Officer Under Wellington in the Pyrenees*, ed. H. V. Shore (CRE Journal, London 1912–13. Reprinted Cambridge, 1986).

KINCAID, John, *Adventures in the Rifle Brigade, in the Peninsula, France, and the Netherlands* (London, 1830. Reprinted many times, most recently Staplehurst, 1998).

——, *Random Shots from a Rifleman* (London, 1835).

LAWRENCE, William, *The Autobiography of Sergeant William Lawrence, A Hero of the Peninsular and Waterloo Campaigns*, ed. George Nugent Bankes (London, 1886).

LEACH, Lieut.-Colonel J., *Rough Sketches of the Life of an Old Soldier* (London, 1831).

LONG, Robert Ballard, *Peninsular Cavalry General, 1811–1813*, ed. J.H. McGuffie (London, 1951).

MILLS, John, *For King and Country; The Letters and Diaries of John Mills, Coldstream Guards, 1811–1814*, ed. Ian Fletcher (Staplehurst, 1995).

OMPTEDA, Christian, *Memoirs of Baron Ompteda* (London, 1892).

PEARSON, Andrew, *The Soldier Who Walked Away: Autobiography of Andrew Pearson, A Peninsular War Veteran*, ed. Arthur H. Haley (Liverpool, n.d.).

PORTER, Robert Ker ('An Officer'), *Letters from Portugal and Spain,*

*Written During the March of the British Troops Under Sir John Moore...
By An Officer* (London, 1809).

ROUS, John Edward Cornwallis, *A Guards Officer in the Peninsula*, ed. Ian Fletcher (Tunbridge Wells, 1992).

SHERER, Moyle, *Recollections of the Peninsula* (Philadelphia, 1824, from 2nd London ed. Reprinted Staplehurst, 1997).

SIMMONS, George, *A British Rifle Man: The Journals and Correspondence of Major George Simmons, Rifle Brigade, During the Peninsular War and the Campaign of Waterloo*, ed. Willoughby Verner (London, 1899. Reprinted London, 1986).

SMITH, Harry, *The Autobiography of Lieutenant General Sir Harry Smith*, ed. G. C. Moore Smith (London, 1901).

SURTEES, William, *Twenty-Five Years in the Rifle Brigade* (London, 1833. Reprinted London, 1996).

SWABEY, William, *Diary of Campaigns in the Peninsula for the Years 1811, 12 and 13*, ed. F. A. Whinyates (London, 1895).

WEBBER, William, *With the Guns in the Peninsula: The Peninsular War Journal of Captain William Webber, Royal Artillery*, ed. Richard Henry Wollocombe (London, 1991).

WHEELER, William, *The Letters of Private Wheeler*, ed. B. H. Liddell Hart (London, 1952).

WOOD, George, *The Subaltern Officer: A Narrative by Captain George Wood, of the Line* (London, 1826. Reprinted Cambridge, 1994).

PUBLISHED SECONDARY SOURCES

ANNAND, Major A. McK., 'Brigadier-General C. R. Cureton, CB, ADC', *Journal Society of Army Historical Research*, Vol. XLVII (1964), pp. 157–161.

BEAMISH, North Ludlow, *History of the King's German Legion* (London, 1832–37).

BRETT-JAMES, Antony, *Life in Wellington's Army* (London, 1972; 1994 edition).

BRUCE, H. A., ed., *Life of General Sir William Napier, KCB*, 2 vols. (London, 1861).

CHALLIS, Lionel S., 'British Officers Serving in the Portuguese Army, 1809–1814,' *Journal of the Society for Army Historical Research*, Vol. XXVII (1949) pp. 50–60.

COLVILLE, John, *The Portrait of a General: A Chronicle of the Napoleonic Wars* (Salisbury, 1980).

COPE, Sir William H., *The History of the Rifle Brigade (The Prince Consort's Own) Formerly the 95th* (London, 1877).

DALTON, Charles, *The Waterloo Roll Call* (2nd. Edition, London, 1904. Reprinted London, 1971)

FLETCHER, Ian, *In Hell Before Daylight: The Siege and Storming of the Fortress of Badajoz, 16 March to 6 April 1812* (New York, 1984).

——, *Wellington's Regiments: The Men and their Battles* (Staplehurst, 1994).

——, *Fields of Fire: Battlefields of the Peninsular War* (New York, 1994).

——, *Wellington's Foot Guards* (London, 1994).

FLETCHER, Ian, and Poulter, Ron, *Gentlemen's Sons: The Guards in the Peninsula and at Waterloo, 1808–1815* (Tunbridge Wells, 1992).

FORTESCUE, Sir John, *History of the British Army* (London, 1910–30).

FOSTER, K. O. N., *The Military General Service Medal, 1793–1814* (1947).

GUY, Alan J., ed., *The Road to Waterloo: The British Army and the Struggle Against Revolutionary and Napoleonic France, 1793–1815* (London, 1990).

HAYTHORNTHWAITE, Philip J., *British Infantry of the Napoleonic Wars* (London, 1987).

———, *British Cavalryman, 1792–1815* (London 1994).

———, *The Armies of Wellington* (London, 1994).

———, *The Napoleonic Source Book* (London, 1990).

———, *Die Hard! Dramatic Actions from the Napoleonic Wars*, (London, 1996).

HURT, Philip A., *The Guards' Cemeteries, St. Etienne, Bayonne* (2nd ed., London, 1887).

MOORSOM, William Searth, *Historical Record of the Fifty-Second Regiment (Oxfordshire Light Infantry) from the Year 1755 to the Year 1858* (London, 1860).

MULLEN, A. L. T., *The Military General Service Roll 1793–1814* (London, 1990).

NAPIER, Sir William, *History of the War in the Peninsula* (London, 1876. Reprinted London, 1993).

OMAN, Sir Charles, *History of the Peninsular War* (Oxford, 1902–30. Reprinted London, 1995–97).

PERRETT, Bryan, *The Hawks; A Short History of the 14th/20th King's Hussars* (Chippenham, 1984).

PETERKIN, A., and JOHNSTON, William, *Commissioned Officers in the Medical Services of the British Army, 1660–1960*, 2 vols. (London, 1968).

SPEECKAERT, Georges Patrick, and Baecker, Isabelle, *Les 135 Vestiges et Monuments Commemoratifs des Combats de 1815 en Belgique* (Waterloo, 1990).

INDEX

OF CASUALTIES BY REGIMENT

INDEX OF CASUALTIES BY REGIMENT

Crowder, J.
+Cuthbert, R.
+Despard, W.
Devey, H.
+Erck, G.
Fowler, R.
+Fraser, J.
Garrett, R.
George, J.
Gibbons, F.
Hamerton, W.
Hannam, P.
Hartley, T.
Hay, J.
Healy, J.
Henry, G.
Holden, J.
Hutchison, J.
+Irwin, E.
Johnson, R.
Johnston, R.
Johnston, S.
+Jones, H.
King, J.
Kirwan, R.
+Knowles, R.
Lester, T.
Loggan, G.
Lorentz, C.
Magennis, R.
Mair, J.
Meagher, T.
Morgan, E.
Moses, T.
+Moultrie, T.
Mullins, T.
Muter, R.
+Myers, W.
Nantes, R.
Nunn, J.
Orr, J.
Orr, M.
Page, W.
Penrice, E.
+Prescott, G.
+Prevost, H.
+Pike, W.
Russell, F.
+Saint-Pol, P.
Seton, G.
Shiel, T.
+Singer, J.
Tarleton, H.
Wallace, H.
+Wemyss, C.
+Wray, T.
Wylly, A.

9th Foot:
Ackland, J.
+Bolton, G.
Brookes, R.
Cameron, H.
Cameron, J.
Campbell, C.
+Chadwick, J.
Cockburn, W.
+Craufurd, H.

Curzon, W.
Dale, R.
Dallas, R.
Dumaresq, H.
Ferrars, T.
Fiddes, T.
Ford, J.
+Fraser, E.
Godwin, H.
Gomm, W.
Holmes, D.
Jervoise, I.
+Kenny, C.
Kenny, E.
+Le Mesurier, P.
Lindsay, G.
Macadam, W.
Molle, G.
+Morrant, R.
Nash, H.
Nicholls, S.
Ogle, J.
Perry, F.
+Robertson, J.
+Ross-Lewin, E.
Ruse, R.
Sankey, S.
Seward, W.
Shelton, J.
Sheppard, T.
Siborn, B.
Sterling, G.
Storey, R.
+Stuart, J.
Taylor, A.
Taylor, J.
+Thornhill, B.
Watkins, E.
Whitley, J.
+Woodham, J.

10th Foot:
Rolston, T.
+Thompson, A.

11th Foot:
Christian, J.
Cuyler, G.
Daniell, R.
Daniell, W.
Dolphin, J.
+Donavan, D.
+Dunkley, W.
Ffennell, J.
Gethin, R.
+Gualey, F.
Hamilton, J.
McDowall, J.
+McGeachy, A.
McGregor, W.
Moore, W.
Mowlds, J.
Porter, J.
+Pridham, J.
Reid, D.
Richardson, S.
+Rynd, G.
+Scott, D.

Smith, B.
Stephens, T.
Stewart, J.
Sutherland, A.
Teale, G.
Trimble, M.
+Turnbull, M.
Turner, C.
Walker, W.
Williams, J.
+Wren, R.

14th Foot:
Stack, R.

20th Foot:
Bainbrigge, J.
+Bent, J.
+Brooke, G.
+Buist, R.
Champagne, F.
Connor, C.
Crokat, W.
Fitzgerald, F.
Godfrey, E.
Hogg, J.
Jackson, E.
Lewis, R.
Lutyens, E.
+Mackenzie, M.
+Murray, J.
Murray, J.
Oakley, R.
Obins, H.
+Rose, A.
Rotton, G.
Russell, W.
Smith, D.
Smith, J.
Telford, R.
Tompson, J.
+Walker, J.
+Wallace, W.
+Wauchope, A.
Wrixen, J.

21st Foot:
Adam, F.

23rd Foot:
+Bassett, J.
Booker, G.
Brice, A.
Browne, G.
Browne, T.
Cane, J.
Castle, R.
Clyde, J.
+Collins, G.
Dalmer, T.
Ellis, H.
Enoch, J.
Fryer, C.
Griffiths, W.
+Hall, H.
Harris, I.
Harrison, J.
Hawtyn, J.

Holmes, R.
Hurford, W.
Johnson, H.
Jolliffe, C.
Leaky, J.
+Ledwith, H.
Lillie, T.
Llewelyn, E.
Macdonald, C.
+Macdonald, J.
Maclellan.
+Maw, J.
Montague, F.
Nevill, J.
+Offley, F.
O'Flaherty, F.
Payne.
Pearson, T.
+Potter, W.
Sidley, A.
+Stainforth, W.
Thorpe, S.
Treeve, R.
Tucker, T.
Walker, H.
+Walker, R.
Walley, W.
Wingate, J.
Wynne, H.

24th Foot:
Anderson, J.
Barckhausen, A.
Brickell, J.
Collis, J.
Coote, T.
+Drummond, G.
Easter, J.
+Evans, J.
Fleming, H.
Grant, F.
Ingram, J.
+Ireland, E.
Jesseman, A.
Johnson, A.
Kelly, W.
Le Mesurier, W.
Lepper, J.
Marsh, R.
Meacham, J.
Popham, S.
Powell, T.
Skene, A.
Stack, G.
Topp, R.
Vardy, E.
+Walton, R.

26th Foot:
Campbell, C.
+Chevers, L.
Maxwell, W.
Messiter, H.
+Nunn, J.
Shearman, F.
Thompson, T.

INDEX OF CASUALTIES BY REGIMENT

635

637